Management:
The New
Workplace

Richard L. Daft
Vanderbilt University

Dorothy Marcic
Vanderbilt University

THOMSON

SOUTH-WESTERN

To our daughters Roxanne, Solange and Elizabeth,
who have taught us the importance of good management in everyday life
In memory of Heidi Grebacher (1944–2005) whose love through many years was a solace and joy

Management: The New Workplace
Richard L. Daft and Dorothy Marcic

VP/Editorial Director:
Jack W. Calhoun

VP/Editor-in-Chief:
Dave Shaut

Sr. Acquisitions Editor:
Joe Sabatino

Sr. Developmental Editor:
Emma F. Guttler

Sr. Marketing Manager:
Rob Bloom

Sr. Marketing Communications Manager:
Jim Overly

Sr. Production Project Manager:
Emily S. Gross

Manager of Technology, Editorial:
Vicky True

Technology Project Editor:
Kristen Meere

Web Coordinator:
Karen Schaffer

Manufacturing Coordinator:
Doug Wilke

Production House:
GEX Publishing Services

Printer:
Transcontinental

Art Director:
Tippy McIntosh

Internal and Cover Designer:
Tippy McIntosh

Cover Images:
© Getty Images

Photography Manager:
Deanna Ettinger

Photo Researcher:
Charlotte Goldman

Library of Congress Control Number:
2005932185

For more information about our products, contact us at:

Thomson Learning Academic Resource Center

1-800-423-0563

Thomson Higher Education
5191 Natorp Boulevard
Mason, OH 45040
USA

Preface

The New Workplace

We are entering a new era, one unlike any before, and the major difference can be summed up in a word: change. The tremendous forces behind such change include the intensity of increased globalization; the movement of people around the world with its accompanying multi-culturalism; and, perhaps most of all, the explosion of the information age. *Management*: *The New Workplace*, was developed to help students grasp these changes and cope with the emerging world economies, and it has particular relevance to those who are interested in understanding the value and dynamics of small and medium-sized organizations. Unlike traditional management texts, this book does not rely on abstract theories and examples from corporations that are applicable only to top managers of billion-dollar companies. Rather, our vision is to appeal to students on a practical level and to provide insight and meaningful information for them to succeed in their futures of "working for a living." To this end, *Management: The New Workplace* contains several distinctive elements:

Current Management Thinking

The vision for the international edition of *Management*: *The New Workplace* is to explore the new management ideas in a way that is interesting and valuable to students, while retaining the best of traditional management thinking. To achieve this vision, the most recent management concepts and research are included as well as the contemporary application of management ideas in organizations. The combination of established scholarship, new ideas, and real-life applications gives students a taste of the energy, challenge, and adventure inherent in the dynamic field of management. Examples were selected for their relevance and appeal to students interested in real management issues and how problems are being addressed in local companies. These management concepts are especially applicable to readers with interest in small business management and entrepreneurship.

Reinforcement of Management Concepts

Case applications, boxed items, key terms, exhibits, photo captions, and end of chapter materials are heavily oriented toward middle management and explore supervisory issues being dealt with in smaller companies. *Management: The New Workplace*, focuses on vivid illustrations of real organizations that affect people at every level, whatever the size of the company. In our view, this is the most interesting, up to date, and practical way to reinforce our vision of the book, and it is an effective way to help students identify with and fully comprehend the changing state of current management situations. The textual and graphic portions of the textbook help students grasp the abstract and sometimes distant world of management.

Full Technology Coverage

In recognition of the role of technology in today's world, each chapter of the text integrates coverage of the Internet and emerging technology into the various topics covered in the chapter. In addition, most chapters contain a *Digital, Inc.* box that features a technologically savvy company or highlights a trend that is impacting today's organizations.

Focus on the Future

The world of work is changing rapidly. In response, the field of management is undergoing a revolution. The result is "Managing in Turbulent Times," the theme of this edition of *Management: The New Workplace*. Demands on today's managers go well beyond the techniques and ideas traditionally taught in management courses. The traditional world of work assumed the purpose of management was to control and limit people, enforce rules and regulations, seek stability and efficiency, design a top-down hierarchy to direct people, and achieve bottom-line results. The new workplace and emerging management paradigm recognizes that managers need different skills to engage workers' hearts and minds as well as take advantage of their physical labor. The new workplace asks that managers focus on leading change, on harnessing people's creativity and enthusiasm, on finding shared vision and values, and on sharing information and power. Teamwork, collaboration, participation, and learning are guiding principles that help managers and employees maneuver the difficult terrain of the complex business environment. Managers focus on developing, not controlling, people to adapt to new technologies and extraordinary environmental shifts and, thus, achieve total corporate effectiveness.

The new workplace and the traditional paradigm are guiding management actions. The vision for the international edition of *Management: The New Workplace* is to explore the new management ideas in a way that is interesting and valuable to students, while retaining the best of traditional management thinking. To achieve this vision, the most recent management concepts and research as well as the contemporary application of management ideas in organizations are included. The combination of established scholarship, new ideas, and real-life applications gives students a taste of the energy, challenge, and adventure inherent in the dynamic field of management. The textual portion of this book has been enhanced through the engaging, easy-to-understand writing style and the many in-text examples and boxed items that make the concepts come alive for students. In addition to the easy-to-understand book's writing style, many practical examples and profiles are of real people involved in real business dilemmas. The graphic component has been enhanced with several new exhibits and a new set of photo essays that illustrate specific management concepts.

Management: The New Workplace provides a book of utmost quality that captures the excitement of organizational management, creating in students respect for the changing field of management and confidence that they can understand and master it.

New and Improved Topic Coverage and Organization

The chapter sequence in *Management: The New Workplace* is organized around the management functions of planning, organizing, leading, and controlling. These four functions encompass management research and characteristics of the manager's job. The international edition of *Management: The New Workplace* focuses on the future of management education by identifying and describing emerging elements and examples of the new workplace and the changing management paradigm.

Part One

Part One introduces the world of management, including the nature of management, issues surrounding the new workplace, the learning organization, and historical perspectives on management.

- **Chapter 1** introduces the new workplace and defines the changing management paradigm. The chapter explores the growing importance of leadership and new management competencies needed to thrive in the business world. It discusses the forces affecting organizations and managers, including a segment on managing during crises and unexpected events, both of which are important skills in the volatile workplace. Additionally, it contains a significantly expanded discussion of the behavioral sciences approach. This chapter contains a new section on managing the technology-driven workplace, introducing the concepts of e-business (B2B, B2C, and C2C), intranets and extranets, enterprise resource planning, and knowledge management. There is continued coverage of the historical development of management and organizations.

Part Two

Part Two examines the environments of management and organizations. This section includes material on the business environment and corporate culture, the global environment, ethics and social responsibility, the natural environment, and the environment of entrepreneurship and small business management.

- **Chapter 2** includes a section on culture. The four types of culture (adaptability culture, achievement culture, bureaucratic culture, and clan culture) are explored in terms of their relationship to the external environment. A complete section of this chapter is devoted to trends such as virtual teams and telecommuting that put demands on managers creating strong adaptive cultures.

- **Chapter 3** includes an updated and enlarged discussion of GATT and WTO.

- **Chapter 4** presents an updated and expanded exploration of environmental responsibility and how today's organizations are meeting their responsibilities in this area. This chapter includes a new section on ethical leadership, including a new discussion of ethical issues associated with information technology.

Part Three

Part Three presents three chapters on planning, including organizational goal setting and planning, strategy formulation and implementation, and the decision-making process.

- **Chapter 5** incorporates a new section on crisis management planning and considers the impact of the Internet and e-business on strategy.

- **Chapter 6** includes a discussion of new decision approaches for the new workplace, encompassing the more active involvement required of everyone in the organization as a result. The chapter contains a new section on the Internet and e-business, including e-business strategies, a discussion of e-marketplaces, using ERP and CRM to improve business operations, and knowledge management. It explores trends in information technology, such as the wireless Internet and instant messaging, and how they affect organizations and managers.

Part Four

Part Four focuses on organizing processes. These chapters describe dimensions of structural design, the design alternatives managers can use to achieve strategic objectives, structural designs for promoting innovation and change, the design and use of the human resource function, and the ways managing diverse employees are significant to the organizing function.

- **Chapter 7** has an expanded and updated discussion of the network organization, and includes a new section on virtual organizations. Additionally, this chapter discusses how digital technology affects structure. This chapter contains expanded coverage of innovations such as network and virtual organizations, comparing and contrasting the characteristics of traditional organizations with those of the emerging workplace.

- **Chapter 8** has been thoroughly revised and updated to reflect the various aspects of change and development as exhibited in the workplace.

- **Chapter 9** looks at how human resource management is changing due to globalization, information technology, and the need to build human capital. It also explores leveraging the power of diversity for the organization's benefit.

Part Five

Part Five describes the controlling function of management, including basic principles of total quality management, the design of control systems, information technology, and techniques for control of operations management.

- **Chapter 10** presents information on Six Sigma quality control measurements and market value-added financial control measurements. It includes information on global and virtual teams.

Part Six

Part Six is devoted to leadership. This section begins with a chapter on organizational behavior, providing a foundation for understanding people in organizations. This paves the way for subsequent discussion of leadership, motivating employees, communication, and team management.

- **Chapter 11** includes a section on multicultural teams and employee network groups as ways to build and support a diverse workforce, leveraging the power of diversity for the benefit of the organization. The chapter places emphasis on the challenges faced by minorities and includes a discussion of the potential benefits and difficulties of emotional connections in the workplace.

- **Chapter 12** presents a new section on emotional intelligence and a discussion of employees' and organizations' responses to stress management in organizations.

- **Chapter 13** includes a discussion about leadership for the workplace, including Level 5 leadership, male versus female methods of leading, virtual leadership, and servant leadership. It has a brief new discussion of visionary leadership.

- **Chapter 14** contains an added discussion of the Q12: a Gallup Organization survey of the factors that influence employee motivation.

- **Chapter 15** has a section on feedback and learning as important components of the communication process.

Appendices

The appendices include a continuing case and the answers to select end-of-chapter Manager's Workbook exercises.

Distinguishing Features

One major goal of this book is to offer better ways of using the textbook medium to convey management knowledge to the reader. To this end, the book includes several special features:

Chapter Outline and Objectives. Each chapter begins with a clear statement of its learning objectives and an outline of its contents. These devices provide an overview of what is to come and can be used by students to guide their study and test their understanding and retention of important points.

Manager's Challenge and Solution. The text portion of each chapter begins with a real-life problem faced by an organization manager. The problem pertains to the topic of the chapter and will heighten students' interest in chapter concepts. The questions posed in the Manager's Challenge are resolved in the Manager's Solution at the end of the chapter, where chapter concepts guiding the management's actions are highlighted.

Boxed Features. *Management: The New Workplace*, contains a unique set of pedagogy addressing topics straight from the field of management of special interest to students, thus heightening their interest in the subject matter and providing an auxiliary view of management issues typically unavailable in textbooks. These features may describe a contemporary topic or problem relevant to chapter content, or they may contain a diagnostic questionnaire or a special example of how managers handle a problem: **Best Practice boxes** feature companies that make ethical decision regarding their business practices and their employees' well-being; **Digital, Inc. boxes** focuses on technology as used by companies to achieve their business goals; **Focus On… boxes** cover company practices as they relate to issues of diversity, cooperation, and entrepreneurship.

Take Action. New to this edition, the Take Action marginal box appears several times in each chapter to reinforce the application of management principles into the learner's personal best practices.

Contemporary Examples. Every chapter of the text contains a large number of written examples of management incidents. They are placed at strategic points in the chapter and are designed to demonstrate the application of concepts to specific companies. These in-text examples—indicated by an icon in the margin—include well-known entrepreneurs and companies, such as eBay, Verizon, and Toyota, and put students in touch with the real world of organizations so they can appreciate the value of management concepts.

Business Blooper. New to this edition, this boxed feature addresses what happens when good business practices go bad. Like individuals, businesses learn from their mistakes and are as prone to lapses in judgment. In the end, what matters is the response to the mistake. This box describes incidents involving Donald Trump, Wal-Mart, and many other individuals and companies.

Concept Connection Photo Essays. A key feature of the book is the use of photographs accompanied by detailed photo essay captions that enhance learning. Each caption highlights and illustrates one or more specific concepts from the text to reinforce student understanding of the concepts. Though the photos are beautiful to look at, they convey the vividness, immediacy, and concreteness of management events in the business world.

Exhibits. Many aspects of management are research based, and some concepts tend to be abstract and theoretical. To enhance students' awareness and understanding of these concepts, many exhibits have been included throughout the book. These exhibits consolidate key points, indicate relationships among variables, and visually illustrate concepts. They make effective use of color to enhance their imagery and appeal.

Glossaries. Learning the management vocabulary is essential to understanding contemporary management. This process is facilitated in three ways. First, key concepts are boldfaced and defined where they first appear in the text. Second, brief definitions are set out in the margins for easy review and follow-up. Third, a glossary summarizing key terms and definitions appears at the end of the book for handy reference.

Manager's Solution and Discussion Questions. Each chapter closes with a summary of key points that students should retain. The discussion questions are a complementary learning tool enabling students to check their understanding of key issues, to think beyond basic concepts, and to determine areas requiring further study. The summary and discussion questions help students discriminate between main and supporting points and provide mechanisms for self-teaching.

Manager's Workbook and Manager's Workshop. End-of-chapter exercises provide self-assessments for students and an opportunity to experience management issues in a personal way. These exercises take the form of questionnaires, scenarios, and activities; many provide an opportunity for students to work in teams. Answers to some Manager's Workbook exercises can be found in Appendix B.

Cases for Critical Analysis. At the end of each chapter is a substantive case that provides an opportunity for student analysis and class discussion. Many of these cases are about companies whose names students will recognize; others are based on real management events with the identities of companies and managers disguised. These cases allow students to sharpen their diagnostic skills for management problem solving.

Continuing Case. Found in Appendix A, the Continuing Case is a running discussion of management topics as experienced by one company as they relate to the material discussed in that part. Focusing on one company, Ford, allows students to follow the managers' and the organization's problems and solutions in a long-term way.

Supplemental Materials: Leading by Example

The international edition's ancillary package, another market innovation from Daft and Marcic, is loaded with powerful resources for instructors. Completely integrated with the text, this comprehensive package continues to lead the market with its innovative and real-world management application.

Instructor Resources include the following:

- **Instructor's Manual** Designed to provide support for instructors new to the course, as well as innovative materials for experienced instructors, the Instructor's Manual includes Chapter Outlines, annotated learning objectives, Lecture Notes, and sample Lecture Outlines. Additionally, the Instructor's Manual includes answers and teaching notes to end-of-chapter materials, including the continuing case. The Instructor's Manual is available for download on the instructor's web site at http://aise.swlearning.com.

- **Test Bank** Scrutinized for accuracy, the Test Bank (available at http://aise.swlearning.com) includes more than 2,000 true/false, multiple choice, short answer, and essay questions. Each question has been rated for level of difficulty and is designated as factual or application so instructors can provide a balanced set of questions for student exams.

To help you meet **AACSB** standards in your course, a number of questions are labeled from a list of management-specific knowledge and skills areas provided by the AACSB's guidelines.

- **PowerPoint Lecture Presentation** Available online at http://aise.swlearning.com, the PowerPoint Lecture Presentation enables instructors to customize their own multimedia classroom presentation. Containing approximately 350 slides, the package includes figures and tables from the text, and outside materials to supplement chapter concepts. Material is organized by chapter and can be modified or expanded for individual classroom use. PowerPoints are printable to create customized transparency masters.

Acknowledgements

It was a gratifying experience to work with the team of dedicated professionals at South-Western who were committed to the vision of producing the best management text ever. We are grateful to Joe Sabatino, Senior Acquisitions Editor, whose enthusiasm, creative ideas, assistance, and vision kept this book's spirit alive. Rob Bloom, Senior Marketing Manager, provided keen market knowledge and innovative ideas for instructional support. Emma Guttler, Senior Developmental Editor, provided superb project coordination and offered excellent ideas and suggestions to help the team meet a demanding and sometimes arduous schedule. Emily Gross, Senior Production Project Manager, cheerfully and expertly guided us through the production process.

Here at Vanderbilt, I want to extend special appreciation to my assistant, Barbara Haselton. Barbara provided excellent support and assistance on a variety of projects that gave me time to write. I want to acknowledge an intellectual debt to my colleagues, Bruce Barry, Ray Friedman, Neta Moye, Rich Oliver, David Owens, and Bart Victor. Thanks also to Dean Jim Bradford, who has supported my writing projects and developed a positive scholarly culture in the school. *r.l.d.*

Working on this book has been so gratifying and fun. I want to thank my assistant, Stephanie Capps, who was there whenever I needed her. Bill Geisler was always there supplying new ideas and his wife, Diti gave spiritual sustenance. My good friend and colleague, Jennie Carter Thomas, of Belmont University, was a breath of fresh air and a wonderful companion. Other friends and colleagues who gave their support include Peter L. Loewy, Phil Hinton, Adrienne Corn, Loree Gold, Peter Vaill, Mary Watson, Joe Seltzer, Joe Garcia, Nan Allison, Amy Lynch, Holly Tashien, Leslie Asplund, Ron Browning, Shidan Majidi, plus my agent John Willig, and my manager Andy Barton.

How can one do such a project without family love and support. My sister, Janet Mittelsteadt is a true friend; my cousins: Marilyn Nowak is a bright light, Michael Shoemaker is the genealogist who has helped me find my own roots, and Katherine Runde is so precious; my Aunt Babe is forever a link to the past. There is no way to imagine my life without my three beautiful daughters: Roxanne, Solange, and Elizabeth, who have taught me more than all my degrees combined. And finally, my husband and partner, Dick Daft, whose collaboration on this book indicates one aspect of our unity and connection. *d.m.*

Thanks to Jane Woodside for her detailed research and meticulous writing of the Part Openers. As part of her research and to guarantee content, Jane involved writer/director/producer Leslie B. Hill and actor Pat Cronin. Thanks to Leslie B. Hill for providing valuable background on the movie director's role, and thanks to Pat Cronin who reviewed the Part Openers to insure accuracy.

Other people who made major contributions to the textbook are the management experts who provided advice, reviews, answers to our questions, and suggestions for changes, insertions, and clarification. We thank these colleagues for their valuable feedback and suggestions: David Adams, Manhattanville College; Hal Babson, Columbus State Community College; Kristin Backhaus, SUNY – New Paltz; Jan Beyer, University of Texas; Katharine Bohley, University of Indianapolis; Bonnie Chavez, Santa Barbara Community College; Sally Dresdow, University of Wisconsin, Green Bay; Diane Duca, Central Washington University; Janice Edwards, College of the Rockies; John Edwards, Southern Illinois University – Carbondale; Mary Beth Klinger, College of Southern Maryland; Martin Lecker, Rockland Community College; Susan Leshnower – Midland College; Don Lisnerski, University of North Carolina – Ashville; Joseph Martelli, University of Findlay; Rachel Mather, Adelphi University; Susan Smith Nash, University of Oklahoma; Stephen Peters, Walla Walla Community College; Brian Porter, Hope College; Gerald Ramsey, Indiana University Southeast; Amit Shah, Frostburg State University; Jessica Simmons, University of Texas; H. Daniel Stage, Loyola Marymount; Kent Zimmerman, James Madison University.

About the Authors

Richard L. Daft, Ph.D., is the Brownlee O. Currey, Jr. Professor of Management in the Owen Graduate School of Management at Vanderbilt University. Professor Daft specializes in the study of organization theory and leadership and enjoys applying these ideas in his role as Associate Dean. Dr. Daft is a Fellow of the Academy of Management and has served on the editorial boards of *Academy of Management Journal*, *Administrative Science Quarterly*, and *Journal of Management Education*. He was the Associate Editor-in-Chief of *Organization Science* and served for three years as associate editor of *Administrative Science Quarterly*.

Professor Daft has authored or co-authored 12 books including *Organization Theory and Design* (South-Western College Publishing, 2007), *The Leadership Experience* (South-Western College Publishing, 2005) and *What to Study: Generating and Developing Research Questions* (Sage, 1982). He also published *Fusion Leadership: Unlocking the Subtle Forces That Change People and Organizations* (Berrett-Koehler, 2000, with Robert Lengel). He has alsoauthored dozens of scholarly articles, papers, and chapters. His work has been published in *Administrative Science Quarterly*, *Academy of Management Journal*, *Academy of Management Review*, *Strategic Management Journal*, *Journal of Management*, *Accounting Organizations and Society*, *Management Science*, *MIS Quarterly*, *California Management Review*, and *Organizational Behavior Teaching Review*.

Dr. Daft is also an active teacher and consultant. He has taught management, leadership, organizational change, organizational theory, and organizational behavior. He has been involved in management development and consulting for many companies and government organizations including the American Banking Association, Bell Canada, National Transportation Research Board, Nortel, TVA, Pratt & Whitney, State Farm Insurance, Tenneco, the United States Air Force, the U.S. Army, J. C. Bradford & Co., Central Parking System, Entergy Sales and Service, Bristol-Meyers Squibb, First American National Bank, and the Vanderbilt University Medical Center.

Dorothy Marcic, Ed.D and M.P.H, is a faculty member at Vanderbilt University. Dr. Marcic is a former Fulbright Scholar at the University of Economics in Prague and the Czech Management Center, where she taught courses and did research in leadership, organizational behavior, and cross-cultural management. She teaches courses at the Monterrey Institute of International Studies and the University of Economics, in Prague, and has taught courses or given presentations at the Helsinki School of Economics, Slovenia Management Center, College of Trade in Bulgaria, City University of Slovakia, Landegg Institute in Switzerland, the Swedish Management Association, Technion University in Israel, and the London School of Economics. Other international work includes projects at the Autonomous University in Guadalajara, Mexico, and a training program for the World Health Organization in Guatemala. She has served on the boards of the Organizational Teaching Society, the Health Administration Section of the American Public Health Association, and the Journal of Applied Business Research.

Dr. Marcic has authored 12 books, including *Organizational Behavior: Experiences and Cases* (South-Western Publishing, 6th Edition, 2001), *Management International* (West Publishing, 1984), *Women and Men in Organizations* (George Washington University, 1984), and *Managing with the Wisdom of Love: Uncovering Virtue in People and Organizations* (Jossey-Bass, 1997), which was rated one of the top ten business books of 1997 by *Management General*. In addition, she has had dozens of articles printed in such publications as *Journal of Management Development, International Quarterly of Community Health Education, Psychological Reports*, and *Executive Development*. She has recently been exploring how to use the arts in the teaching of leadership and has a new book, *RESPECT: Women and Popular Music* (Texere, 2002), the basis for the musical theater production, Respect: A Musical Journey of Women.

Professor Marcic has conducted hundreds of seminars on various business topics and consulted for executives at AT&T Bell Labs; the Governor and Cabinet of North Dakota; the US Air Force; Slovak Management Association; Eurotel; Czech Ministry of Finance; the Cattaraugus Center; USAA Insurance; State Farm Insurance; and the Salt River-Pima Indian Tribe in Arizona.

Brief Contents

Contents

Best Practices
Rolling Stones, Inc. 266
Business Blooper
Total Care
Technologies 271
Digital, Inc.
Tightening the Reins at Oracle 263
Focus on Collaboration
Delta Forces 262
Imagination Ltd. 267
Focus on Skills
Kate Spade 259
How to Delegate 260

Best Practices
PayMaxx 297
Business Blooper
War for Talent 299
Digital, Inc.
Nestlé: Making "E-business the Way We Do Business" 309
Focus on Innovation
W.L. Gore 299
Focus on Skills
Cartoon Network's Late Night 294
New Line Cinema 305

Best Practices
Eastern Mountain Sports (EMS) 337
Business Blooper
Tasty Flavors Sno Biz 361
Digital, Inc.
Living on BlackPlanet.com 356

xix

Management:
The New Workplace

Introduction to Management

Making movies: It is an art, a business, a team effort, and, always, a high-stakes gamble. There, standing in the middle of it all, is the director, managing what often feels like an unmanageable process. Though producing a film involves hundreds of people, when those box office receipts roll in over that closely scrutinized first weekend, responsibility for the movie's success or failure rests squarely on the director's shoulders.

Every movie tells a story, and the director must determine the story's essence. For example, Peter Jackson, the *Lord of the Rings* director, recalled "cracking the code" to J.R.R. Tolkien's massive trilogy when he realized that the plot, in its simplest form, was the story of Frodo carrying the ring to Mordor and then destroying it. That simple yet potent concept served as his touchstone during the years Jackson supervised all the many elements that go into films—screenplays, actors, costumes, sets and special effects, lighting, camera work, scores and soundtracks, and the editing of millions of feet of footage into a final product. Alfred Hitchcock, the director who gave us *Psycho* among other masterpieces, once pointed out, "I didn't walk into this business without proper knowledge of it. I've been a technician; I've been an editor; I've been an art director; I've been a writer. I have a feeling for all these people." Like Hitchcock, directors must have at least a working knowledge of the increasingly sophisticated techniques crews employ. Without that knowledge, directors cannot determine what is realistic to achieve and then effectively communicate with the professionals who work for them. But at the same time, directors need not to get so caught up in the details that they lose sight of "the big picture."

The best directors come to the set with considerable people skills. They need all of their understanding of human nature as they, for instance, supervise casting, elicit the best possible performances from actors, or mediate differences of opinion. Even the most controlling of directors must know how to collaborate since film is fundamentally a collaborative enterprise. They must be open to suggestions, decide which ones make sense, and then reject the rest without discouraging and alienating the people who offered them. It all works best when everyone feels the movie is theirs, and the story they are telling is one that needs to be told.

Finally, directors can never forget they answer to investors: the group of individuals, a studio, or both. They have put up the millions of dollars it takes to make a film today because they believe (and it usually is a matter of faith) they will make a return on their investment. So, they expect the director to finish on time and to live within the budget. Investors, being businessmen first and foremost, expect the director will make the often inefficient and sometimes chaotic creative process as efficient and orderly as possible.

What a movie director is, when all is said and done, is a high-profile middle manager charged with turning dreams into a facsimile of reality and then making them pay for themselves.

CHAPTER

1

The Changing Paradigm of Management & Foundations of Learning Organizations

LEARNING OBJECTIVES

After studying this chapter, you should be able to do the following:

1 **Explain the difference between efficiency and effectiveness and their importance for organizational performance.**

2 **Define ten roles that managers perform in organizations.**

3 **Discuss the management competencies needed to deal with today's turbulent environment, including issues such as diversity, globalization, rapid change, and the skills needed for crisis management.**

4 **Describe the learning organization and the changes in structure, empowerment, and information sharing managers make to support it.**

5 **Understand how historical forces influence the practice of management.**

6 **Identify and explain major developments in the history of management thought.**

7 **Describe the major components of the classical and humanistic management perspectives.**

8 **Discuss the scientific management perspective and its current use in organizations.**

9 **Define the role contingency plays in organizations.**

10 **Explain the major concepts of total quality management.**

Manager's Challenge

CEO Michael Dell saw his company slip from its premier position in 2001 and he knew he had to do something. He had been only 19 when he took $1,000 and started Dell Computers (Dell) from his University of Texas dorm room. He built the company based on the belief he could provide low-cost, made-to-order computers and sell them directly to consumers, thus cutting overhead costs related to inventory and sales commissions to outside sellers. The company took off, but in 1991, Dell made a tactical error that could have doomed the company. He decided to sell some computers at retailers such as CompUSA, Staples, and Sam's Club. The company realized the mistake before it was too late. Since then, Dell has not wavered from its model. But new troubles loomed. In 2001, the personal computer (PC) market collapsed and sales were so sluggish that Dell was forced to lay off 1,700 employees, the first job elimination in its 16-year history. CEO Dell met with President Kevin Rollins privately that fall to make plans for Dell's comeback. Based on sales figures, they felt Dell's performance in the marketplace would improve, but their own performance was something else. Employee interviews showed Dell was seen as emotionally detached and too impersonal, while Rollins was seen as antagonistic and autocratic. No one felt loyalty to the leaders. Anger and resentment was building since the first mass firing. Half of the employees said they would quit if they found another job. Dell and Rollins realized they could not move the company back to its stellar performance without a motivated workforce and knew a mass staff exodus would doom them.[1]

If you were Michael Dell, what would you do to ensure your company's comeback?

Dell Computer's difficulties might seem exceptional, but Michael Dell is not the only CEO who has had to deal with uncertainty and change on an almost daily basis. Consider the strife and confusion in the music industry, where traditional recording labels and music stores are battling with online services such as Kazaa and Grokster that let people download and share music for free. The once-hot Tower Records declared bankruptcy due to the steep decline in music sales through traditional stores. Music industry lawsuits against the file-sharing services and threats of legal action against consumers have not slowed the transition to online music.[2]

Managers in all organizations are continually dealing with uncertainty and unexpected events, whether they are something as small as the loss of a key employee or something as large and dramatic as a plant explosion. Moreover, the frequency and intensity of crises have increased over the past couple of decades, with a sharp increase in the rate of intentional acts such as product tampering, workplace violence, or terrorism.[3]

Solid management skills and actions are the key to helping any organization weather a crisis and remain healthy, inspired, and productive.

The nature of management is to cope with diverse and far-reaching challenges. Managers have to keep pace with advancing technology, find ways to incorporate the Internet and e-business into their strategies and business models, and remain competitive in the face of increasingly tough global competition, uncertain environments, cutbacks in personnel and resources, and massive worldwide economic, political, and social shifts. The growing diversity of the workforce creates other dynamics: How can managers maintain a strong corporate culture while supporting diversity, balancing work and family concerns, and coping with conflicting demands of all employees wanting a fair shot at power and responsibility? New ways of working, such as virtual teams and telecommuting, put additional demands on today's managers.

To navigate the turbulence of today's world, managers need to shift their mindsets. The field of management is undergoing a revolution that asks managers to do more with less, to engage whole employees, to see change rather than stability as the nature of things, and to create vision and cultural values that allow people to create a collaborative workplace. This new management approach is different from a traditional mindset that emphasizes tight top-down control, employee separation and specialization, and management by impersonal measurements and analysis. When people are struggling and fear for their jobs, as they were at Dell Computers after the layoffs, an impersonal, highly analytical approach could destroy the company faster than anything else.

Making a difference as a manager today and tomorrow requires integrating solid, tried-and-true management skills with new approaches that emphasize the human touch, enhance flexibility, and involve employees' hearts and minds as well as their bodies. Successful departments and organizations do not happen but are managed to be that way. Managers in every organization today face major challenges and have the opportunity to make a difference. For example, Lorraine Monroe made a difference at Harlem's Frederick Douglass Academy when she transformed it from one of the worst to one of the best schools in New York City. Stephen Quesnelle, head of quality programs at Mitel Corporation in Ottawa, Canada, made a difference when he organized "sacred cow hunts" to encourage employees to track down and do away with outdated policies and procedures holding the company back. Today, signs of energy, change, and renewal are everywhere at Mitel.[4]

These managers are common. Every day, managers solve difficult problems, turn organizations around, and achieve astonishing performances. To be successful, every organization needs skilled managers.

This textbook introduces and explains management processes and the changing ways of thinking about and perceiving the world, processes and ways that are becoming increasingly critical for managers of today and tomorrow. By reviewing the actions of

Take ACTION

Become a better manager of yourself: meet assignment deadlines, balance needs of different courses, and manage a positive relationship with your professors.

successful and less successful managers, you will learn the fundamentals of management. By the end of this chapter, you will recognize some of the skills that managers use to keep organizations on track. By the end of this book, you will understand fundamental management skills for planning, organizing, leading, and controlling a department or an entire organization. In the remainder of this chapter, we will define management and look at the ways in which roles and activities are changing for today's managers. The final section of the chapter talks about a new kind of workplace that has evolved as a result of changes in technology, globalization, and other forces and examines how managers can meet the challenges of this new environment and manage unexpected events.

The Definition of Management

What do managers, such as Michael Dell, Stephen Quesnelle, and Lorraine Monroe, have in common? They get things done through their organizations. Managers create the conditions and environment that enable organizations to survive and thrive beyond the tenure of any specific supervisor or manager. Consider Elvis Presley Enterprises, Inc. Elvis died nearly 30 years ago, but managers have created and managed a successful organization with offices in Memphis, Tennessee, and Los Angeles, California, that continues, employing more than 300 people and bringing in millions of dollars in sales and admission fees to Graceland. The organization's charitable arm supports a transitional housing program in Memphis, provides scholarships in the creative arts, and provides funding for many programs in the arts, education, and children's services.[5]

A key aspect of managing is recognizing the role and importance of others. Good managers know that the only way they can accomplish anything is through the organization's people. Early twentieth-century management scholar Mary Parker Follett defined management as "the art of getting things done through people."[6]

More recently, management theorist Peter Drucker stated that the job of managers is to give direction to their organizations, provide leadership, and decide how to use organizational resources to accomplish goals.[7]

Getting things done through people and other resources and providing leadership and direction are what managers do. These activities apply to top executives, such as Michael Dell, and to the leader of a security team, a supervisor of an accounting department, and a director of sales and marketing. Moreover, management is often considered universal because it uses organizational resources to accomplish goals and attain high performance in all profit and not-for-profit organizations. Thus, our definition of management is as follows:

> *Management is the effective and efficient attainment of organizational goals through planning, organizing, leading, and controlling organizational resources.*

Two important ideas are in this definition: (1) the four functions of planning, organizing, leading, and controlling and (2) the attainment of organizational goals in an effective and efficient manner. Managers use a multitude of skills to perform these functions. Management's conceptual, human, and technical skills are discussed later in the chapter. Exhibit 1.1 illustrates the process of how managers use resources to attain organizational goals. Though some management theorists identify additional management functions, such as staffing, communicating, or decision

Take *ACTION*
As a leader, expect the best from people and you are more likely to get it.

management
The effective and efficient attainment of organizational goals through planning, organizing, leading, and controlling organizational resources.

Courtesy of Ronald G. Greenwood

CONCEPT CONNECTION

*Mary Parker Follett (1868–1933) Follett was a major contributor to the **administrative principles** approach to management. Her emphasis on worker participation and shared goals among managers was embraced by many businesspeople of the day and has been recently "rediscovered" by corporate America.*

Management Functions

Planning
Select goals and
ways to attain them

Resources
- Human
- Financial
- Raw materials
- Technological
- Information

Controlling
Monitor activities
and make corrections

Organizing
Assign
responsibility for task
accomplishment

Leading
Use influence to
motivate employees

Performance
- Attain goals
- Products
- Services
- Efficiency
- Effectiveness

EXHIBIT 1.1

*The Process of
Management*

making, those additional functions will be discussed as subsets of the four primary functions in Exhibit 1.1. Chapters of this book are devoted to the multiple activities and skills associated with each function, as well as to the environment, global competitiveness, and ethics, which influence how managers perform these functions.

Organizational Performance

Take ACTION

Always remember how
important the organi-
zation or group is to
get things done.

The other part of our definition of management is the efficient and effective attainment of organizational goals. Management is important because organizations are important. In an industrialized society where complex technologies dominate, organizations bring together knowledge, people, and raw materials to perform tasks no individual could do alone. Without organizations, how could technology be provided that enables us to share information around the world in an instant, electricity be produced from huge dams and nuclear power plants, and thousands of DVDs be made available for our entertainment? Organizations pervade our society. Most college students will work in an organization, such as Sun Microsystems, Toronto General Hospital, Cinergy, or Hollywood Video. College students may be members of several organizations, such as a university, junior college, YMCA, church, fraternity, or sorority. College students deal with organizations every day: to renew a driver's license, be treated in a hospital emergency room, buy food from a supermarket, eat in a restaurant, or buy new clothes. Managers are responsible for these organizations and for seeing that resources are used wisely to attain organizational goals.

organization

A goal-directed and deliberately structured
social entity.

Our formal definition of an **organization** is a goal-directed and deliberately structured social entity. *Goal-directed* means designed to achieve some outcome, such as make a profit (Old Navy, Verizon Communications), win pay increases for members (AFL-CIO), meet spiritual needs (Methodist church), or provide social satisfaction (college sorority). *Deliberately structured* means that tasks are divided and responsibility for their performance is assigned to organization members. *Social entity* means being made up of two or more people. These definitions apply to all organizations, including profit and not-for-profit. Small, offbeat, and not-for-profit organizations are more numerous than large, visible corporations and are just as important to society.

Based on our definition of management, the manager's responsibility is to coordinate resources effectively and efficiently to accomplish the organization's goals. **Organizational effectiveness** is the degree to which the organization achieves a *stated goal* or succeeds in accomplishing what it tries to do. Organizational effectiveness means providing a product or service that customers value. **Organizational efficiency** refers to the amount of resources used to achieve an organizational goal. It is based on how much raw material, money, and people are necessary for producing a given output volume. Efficiency can be calculated as the amount of resources used to produce a product or service.

Efficiency and effectiveness can rank high in the same organization. For example, during the tough economy of the early 2000s, companies like Eaton Corporation, which makes hydraulic and electrical devices, struggled to wring as much production as they could from scaled-back factories and a reduced workforce. Managers initiated process improvements, outsourced some work to companies that could do it more cheaply, streamlined ordering and shipping procedures, and shifted work to the most efficient assembly lines. At Eaton, these adjustments enabled the company to cut costs, hold the line on prices, and meet its quality and output goals.[8]

Sometimes, however, managers' efforts to improve efficiency can hurt organizational effectiveness. This is especially true in relation to severe cost cutting. At Delta Airlines, former CEO Ronald Allen dramatically increased cost efficiency by cutting spending on personnel, food, cleaning, and maintenance. Allen believed the moves were needed to rescue the company from a financial tailspin, but Delta fell to last place among major carriers in on-time performance, the morale of employees sank, and customer complaints about dirty planes and long lines at ticket counters increased by more than 75 percent.[9]

Current CEO Gerald Grinstein came in with a goal to maintain the efficiencies instituted by Allen and to improve organizational effectiveness.

The ultimate responsibility of managers is to achieve high **performance**, which is the attainment of organizational goals by efficiently and effectively using resources.

Management Skills

A manager's job is complex and multidimensional and, as we shall see throughout this book, requires a range of skills. Though some management theorists propose a long list of skills, the necessary skills for managing a department or an organization can be summarized in three categories: conceptual, human, and technical.[10] As illustrated in Exhibit 1.2, the application of these skills changes as managers move up in the organization. Though the degree of each skill necessary at different levels of an organization may vary, all managers must possess skills in each of these important areas to perform effectively. Joe Torre demonstrated proficiency in human and technical skills in his management of the New York Yankees, as shown on the following page.

organizational effectiveness

The degree to which the organization achieves a stated goal.

organizational efficiency

Refers to the amount of resources used to achieve an organizational goal. Efficiency is the use of minimal resources—raw materials, money, and people—to produce a desired volume of output.

Take **ACTION**

As a leader, create more value in the product or service than went in to its production.

performance

The attainment of organizational goals by efficiently and effectively using resources.

EXHIBIT 1.2

Relationship of Conceptual, Human, and Technical Skills to Management Level

Management Level
Top Managers

Middle Managers

First-Line Managers

Nonmanagers (Individual Contributors)

| Conceptual Skills | Human Skills | Technical Skills |

| **Joe Torre** | Joe Torre was fired three times in his 15-year management career before signing on as manager of the New York Yankees. After an 18-year World Series drought, in his first year he guided the Yankees to six World Series during his nine years and he is the first Yankees manager to lead them to nine straight post-season appearances. Though Torre is the first to point out that the team's success depends on a combination of factors, his management approach plays a big role. |

Torre believes his years of dedication, learning, and growing as a manager finally paid off. One of the biggest lessons he learned is that success and winning differ. Success, says Torre, is "playing—or working—to the best of your ability." His philosophy is that people should strive every day to fulfill their potential as individuals and as team members, and to help them do this requires a management approach that puts the needs and feelings of people first. Torre's approach is based on knowing his team members as individuals and treating everyone with fairness, respect, and trust, the three elements he considers essential for productive work relationships. Torre does not give a lot of big motivational speeches. Instead, he relies on one-to-one communication. He watches, listens, and tries to understand the needs, motivations, and problems of each person, recognizing that what is going on in the players' lives off the field affects their performance. When Torre needs to sort out a problem with a player, he does it privately. He never uses fear, manipulation, or public humiliation to motivate or control players.

In addition, Torre understands that every player sometimes hits a slump, and he does not treat players differently because they are playing poorly. "I've worked for organizations in the past that are real quick to jump off the bandwagon when things aren't going well…," says pitcher Mike Stanton. "With Joe, you don't really have to look over your shoulder because you'll lose confidence in yourself a long time before Joe loses confidence in you." Torre sticks by his players, and he absorbs the flak from upper management without passing it on to the team. He does not burden players with a lot of strict rules, preferring to treat them as responsible adults who are all working toward a shared goal.

Torre's emphasis on people and relationships has created a high-performance workplace where mistakes and failure are routinely accepted. It is the kind of workplace most organizations need in today's volatile environment. They can achieve it, Torre says, by handling their jobs based on the values of "respect, trust, integrity, and commitment to our work and the people we work with."[11]

Management Types

Managers use conceptual, human, and technical skills to perform the four management functions of planning, organizing, leading, and controlling in all organizations whether they are large or small, manufacturing or service, profit or nonprofit, traditional or Internet-based. But managers' jobs differ. Managers are responsible for different departments, work at different levels in the hierarchy, and meet different requirements for achieving high performance. Kevin Kurtz is a middle manager at Lucasfilm, where he works with employees to develop marketing campaigns for some of the entertainment company's hottest films.[12] Domenic Antonellis is CEO of the New England Confectionary Co. (NECCO), the company that makes those tiny pastel candy hearts stamped with phrases such as "Be Mine" and "Kiss Me."[13] Both are managers and must contribute to planning, organizing, leading, and controlling their organizations but in different amounts and ways.

When Skills Fail

During turbulent times, managers have to stay on their toes and use all their skills and competencies to benefit the organization and its stakeholders, i.e., employees, customers, investors, and the community. In recent years, numerous, highly publicized examples have shown what happens when managers fail effectively and ethically to apply their skills to meet the demands of an uncertain, rapidly changing world. The profusion of company failures is alarming. Companies like Enron Corp., Tyco, and WorldCom were flying high in the 1990s but came crashing down under the weight of financial scandals. Others, such as Rubbermaid, Kmart, and Xerox are struggling because of years of management missteps.

Other critical management missteps include the following: poor communication skills and failure to listen; treating people only as instruments to be used; suppressing dissenting viewpoints; and the inability to build a management team characterized by mutual trust and respect.[14]

The financial scandals of the early twenty-first century, from Enron to mutual fund mismanagement, shows what can happen when, for instance, top managers pay more attention to money and Wall Street than they do to their employees and customers. As another example, consider what happened at *The New York Times* when it became publicly known that Jayson Blair, a rising young reporter, had fabricated and plagiarized many of his stories. Only then did top executives acknowledge the pervasive unhappiness that existed in the newsroom. Executive Editor Howell Raines, who had created an environment that favored certain editors and reporters and made others afraid to offer dissenting viewpoints or tell their managers the truth, resigned under pressure following the scandal. *The Times* continues to regain its footing and reclaim its honorable image.[15] Adapting to turbulent conditions requires a tolerance of ambiguity.

Take **ACTION**

To be a better manager, learn to listen and treat people with respect.

Take a moment to fill out the instrument below to see your own tolerance for ambiguity.

Tolerance for Ambiguity Scale

Read each of the following statements. Rate each of them in terms of the extent to which you agree with the statement using the following scale:

Completely Disagree		Neither Agree nor Disagree				Completely Agree
1	2	3	4	5	6	7

Place the number that best describes your degree of agreement in the blank to the left of each statement.

1. An expert who does not come up with a definite answer probably does not know much.

2. I would like to live in a foreign country for a while.

3. The sooner everyone acquires similar values and ideals the better.

4. A good teacher makes you wonder about your way of looking at things.

5. I like parties where I know most of the people more than ones where all or most of the people are complete strangers.

6. Teachers or supervisors who hand out vague assignments give a chance for one to show initiative and originality.

7. A person who leads an even, regular life, in which few surprises or unexpected happenings arise, has a lot to be grateful for.

8. Many of our most important decisions are based upon insufficient information.

9. All problems can be solved.

10. People who fit their lives to a schedule probably miss most of the joy of living.

11. A good job is one where what is to be done and how it is to be done are clear.

12. It is more fun to tackle a complicated problem than to solve a simple one.

13. In the long run, it is possible to get more done by tackling small, simple problems rather than large and complicated ones.

14. Often, the most interesting and stimulating people are those who do not mind being different and original.

15. What we are used to is always preferable to what is unfamiliar.

Scoring:

For odd-numbered questions, add the total points.

For even-numbered questions, use reverse scoring (7 minus the score), and add the total points.

Your score is the total of the even-numbered and odd-numbered questions.

This survey asks 15 questions about personal and work situations with ambiguity. You were asked to rate each situation on a scale of 1 to 7. A tolerant person would score 15 and an intolerant person 105. Scores ranging from 20 to 80 have been reported, with a mean of 45. Company managers had an average score of about 45, and nonprofit managers had an average score of about 43 though scores in both groups varied widely.

Typically, people who tolerate ambiguity (low score) will be comfortable in organizations characterized by rapid change, unclear authority, empowerment, and movement toward a learning organization. People with low tolerance for ambiguity (high score) are comfortable in more stable, well-defined situations. However, individuals can grow in the opposite direction of their score if they so choose.

SOURCE: Paul C. Nutt, The Tolerance for Ambiguity and Decision Making, The Ohio State University College of Business Working Paper Series, WP880291, March 1988. Adapted from Stanley Budner, Intolerance of ambiguity as a personality variable, *Journal of Personality*, 30:1 (March 1962), table 1, 34. Copyright Duke University Press, 1962.

Manager Activities

One of the most interesting findings about managerial activities is how busy managers are and how hectic the average workday can be. At Google, project manager Minnie Ingersoll never looks at her calendar more than five minutes in advance because her schedule is so frantic and things change so quickly. On a typical day, Ingersoll might have four meetings and a conference call before grabbing a quick lunch and catching up with work on her laptop. Managers at Google use scooters to zip back and forth to meetings in different buildings.[16] Some top managers are even busier. Office Depot CEO Bruce Nelson typically works 14-hour days, visits stores in several different states each week, and is continuously tracking operations at 947 stores in eight time zones.[17]

Adventures in Multitasking. Managerial activity is characterized by variety, fragmentation, and brevity.[18] The manager's involvements are so widespread and voluminous that little time remains for quiet reflection. The average time spent on any one activity is fewer than nine minutes. Managers shift gears quickly. Significant crises are interspersed with trivial events in no predictable sequence. One example of two typical hours for general manager, Janet Howard, follows. Note the frequent interruptions and the brevity and variety of tasks.

7:30 A.M.	Janet arrives at work and begins to plan her day.
7:37 A.M.	A subordinate, Morgan Cook, stops in Janet's office to discuss a dinner party the previous night and to review the cost-benefit analysis for a proposed enterprise resource planning (ERP) system.
7:45 A.M.	Janet's secretary, Pat, motions for Janet to pick up the telephone. "Janet, they had serious water damage at the downtown office last night. A pipe broke, causing about $50,000 damage. Everything will be back in shape in three days. Thought you should know."
8:00 A.M.	Pat brings in the mail. She asks instructions for formatting a report Janet gave her yesterday.
8:14 A.M.	Janet gets a phone call from the accounting manager, who is returning a call from the day before. They talk about an accounting problem.
8:25 A.M.	A Mr. Nance is ushered in. Mr. Nance complains that a sales manager mistreats his employees and something must be done. Janet rearranges her schedule to investigate this claim.
9:00 A.M.	Janet returns to the mail. One letter is from an irate customer. Janet types out a helpful, restrained reply. Pat brings in phone messages.
9:15 A.M.	Janet receives an urgent phone call from Larry Baldwin. They discuss lost business, unhappy subordinates, and a potential promotion.[19]

Life on Speed Dial. The manager performs a great deal of work at an unrelenting pace.[20] Managers' work is fast-paced and requires great energy. The managers observed by Henry Mintzberg processed 36 pieces of mail each day, attended eight meetings, and took a tour through the building or plant. Technology such as e-mail, instant messaging, cell phones, and laptops have intensified the pace. Managers commonly receive hundreds of e-mail messages a day. As soon as a manager's daily calendar is set, unexpected disturbances erupt. New meetings are required. During time away from the office, executives catch up on work-related reading, paperwork, and e-mails.

At O'Hare International Airport, an unofficial count one Friday found operations manager Hugh Murphy interacting with about 45 airport employees. In addition, he listened to complaints from local residents about airport noise, met with disgruntled executives of a French firm who built the airport's new $128 million people-mover system, attempted to soothe a Hispanic city alderman who complained that Mexicana Airlines passengers were being singled out by overzealous tow-truck operators, toured the airport's fire station, and visited the construction site for the new $20 million tower, and all that was before the events of September 11, 2001, which changed airport operations and made them more complex. Hugh Murphy's unrelenting pace is typical for managers.[21] Management can be rewarding, but it can be frustrating and stressful, as discussed in the Focus on Leadership box on page 14.

Take **ACTION**

Students often long to be done with school and enter the "real world" of work. A few years later, they are pining for the days when their classes were done at noon and they had time to hang out.

FOCUS ON LEADERSHIP

Do You Want to Be a Manager?

The first training course aspiring managers at Federal Express (FedEx) take is called "Is Management for Me?" Becoming a manager is considered by most people to be a positive, forward-looking career move. Indeed, life as a manager has many appealing aspects. However, it has many challenges, and not every person will be happy and fulfilled in a management position. Here are some of the issues would-be managers should consider before deciding they want to pursue management careers:

The increased workload. Managers typically work 70-hour to 80-hour weeks, and some work longer. A manager's job always starts before a shift and ends hours after the shift is over. Matt Scott, a software engineer promoted to management at Fore Systems, Inc., found himself frustrated by the increased paperwork and crowded meeting schedule.

The unrelenting sense of obligation. A manager's work is never done. Nancy Carreon, an associate partner for an architectural firm, sometimes wakes up in the middle of the night thinking about something she needs to do, so she gets up and does it. George Pollard, a senior human resources official at FedEx, says, "Managers are always on the clock. We're representatives of [the company] even when we're not at work."

The headache of responsibility for other people. Many people get into management because they like the idea of having power, but the reality is that many managers feel overwhelmed by the responsibility of supervising and disciplining others. Laura Kelso, who thrives on the fast pace and responsibility of being a manager, says that the first time she had to fire someone, she agonized for weeks over how to do it. New managers are often astonished at the amount of time it takes to handle "people

problems." Kelly Cannell, who quit her job as a manager, puts it this way: "What's the big deal [about managing people]? The big deal is that people are human.... To be a good manager, you have to mentor them, listen to their problems, counsel them, and at the end of the day you still have your own work on your plate.... Don't take the responsibility lightly, because no matter what you think, managing people is not easy."

Being caught in the middle. For many people, this is the most difficult aspect of management. Except for those in the top echelons, managers find themselves acting as a backstop, caught between upper management and the workforce. A computer software designer explains why she wanted out of management: "I didn't feel comfortable touting the company line in organizational policies and technical decisions I disagreed with. It was very hard asking folks to do things I wouldn't do myself, like put in gobs of overtime or travel at the drop of a hat." Even when managers disagree with the decisions of top executives, they are responsible for implementing them.

For some people, the frustrations of management are not worth it. For others, management is a fulfilling and satisfying career choice and the emotional rewards can be great. One key to being happy as a manager may be carefully evaluating whether you can answer yes to the question, "Do I want to be a manager?"

SOURCES: Heath Row, "Is Management for Me? That is the Question." *Fast Company* (February–March 1998): 50–52; Timothy D. Schellhardt, "Want to Be a Manager? Many People Say No, Calling Job Miserable," *The Wall Street Journal* (April 4, 1997): A1, A4; Matt Murray, "A Software Engineer Becomes a Manager, with Many Regrets," *The Wall Street Journal* (May 14, 1997): A1, A14; Hal Lancaster, "Managing Your Career: Nancy Carreon Works Long, Hard Weeks. Does She Need To?" *The Wall Street Journal* (May 13, 1997): B1; and Matt Murray, "Managing Your Career—The Midcareer Crisis: Am I in This Business to Become a Manager?" *The Wall Street Journal* (July 25, 2000): B1.

Manager Roles

role
A set of expectations for a manager's behavior.

Mintzberg's observations and subsequent research indicate that diverse manager activities can be organized into ten roles.[22] A **role** is a set of expectations for a manager's behavior. Exhibit 1.3 provides examples of each of the roles. These roles are divided into three conceptual categories: informational (managing by information), interpersonal (managing through people), and decisional (managing through action). Each role represents activities that managers undertake to ultimately accomplish the functions of planning, organizing, leading, and controlling. Though managers must separate their job components to understand their different roles and activities, the real job of management cannot be practiced as a set of independent parts; all the roles interact in the real world of management. As Mintzberg says, "The manager who only communicates or only conceives never gets anything done, while the manager who only 'does' ends up doing it all alone."[23]

Take **ACTION**

Do not make the mistake of always "doing" as a manager because you need to plan and think.

EXHIBIT 1.3

Ten Manager Roles

Category	Role	Activity
Informational	**Monitor**	Seek and receive information; scan periodicals and reports; maintain personal contacts.
	Disseminator	Forward information to other organization members; send memos and reports; make phone calls.
	Spokesperson	Transmit information to outsiders through speeches, reports, memos.
Interpersonal	**Figurehead**	Perform ceremonial and symbolic duties such as greeting visitors, signing legal documents.
	Leader	Direct and motivate subordinates; train, counsel, and communicate with subordinates.
	Liaison	Maintain information links both inside and outside organization; use mail, phone calls, meetings.
Decisional	**Entrepreneur**	Initiate improvement projects; identify new ideas; delegate idea responsibility to others.
	Disturbance handler	Take corrective action during disputes or crises; resolve conflicts among subordi-nates; adapt to environmental crises.
	Resource allocator	Decide who gets resources; schedule, budget, set priorities.
	Negotiator	Represent department during negotiation of union contracts, sales, purchases, budgets; represent departmental interests.

SOURCES: Adapted from Henry Mintzberg, *The Nature of Managerial Work* (New York: Harper & Row, 1973), 92–93; and Henry Mintzberg, "Managerial Work: Analysis from Observation," *Management Science* 18 (1971), B97–B110.

Managing in Small Businesses and Nonprofit Organizations

Small businesses are growing in importance. Hundreds of small businesses are opened every month by people who have found themselves squeezed out of the corporation due to downsizing, who voluntarily leave the corporate world to be their own bosses, or who seek a slower pace and a healthier balance between work and family life. Many small businesses are opened by women or minorities who find limited opportunities for advancement in large corporations. In addition, the Internet has opened new avenues for small-business formation. The huge wave of dot-com start-ups in the late 1990s was driven by dreams of wealth and by the desire of people to get out of big corporations and start something new and exciting.

Today's environment for small businesses is highly complicated. Advances in technology, globalization, government regulations, and increasing customer demands require that even the smallest of businesses have solid management expertise. However, small companies sometimes have difficulty developing the managerial dexterity needed to survive in a turbulent environment. One survey on trends and future developments in small businesses found that nearly half of respondents saw inadequate management skills as a threat to their companies, as compared to less than 25 percent of larger organizations.[24]

Managers in small businesses tend to emphasize roles different from those of managers in large corporations. Managers in small companies often see their most important roles as spokespersons because they must promote the small, growing company to the outside world. The entrepreneur role is important in small businesses because managers have to be creative and help their organizations develop new ideas to remain competitive. Small-business managers tend to rate lower on the leader and information processing roles, compared with their counterparts in large corporations. One CEO of a medium-sized company who has retained the entrepreneurial drive is David Neeleman of JetBlue, described in the Best Practices box below.

Nonprofit organizations (nonprofits) represent a major application of management talent. The American Red Cross, the Girl Scouts, Good Samaritan Ministries, Berea College, Parkland Memorial Hospital, the Boston Public Library, and the Nashville Symphony require excellent management. The functions of planning, organizing, leading, and controlling apply to nonprofits as they do to business organizations, and managers in nonprofit organizations use similar skills and perform similar activities. The primary difference is that managers in businesses direct their activities toward earning money for the company, but managers in nonprofits direct their efforts toward generating social impact. The unique characteristics and needs of nonprofit organizations created by this distinction present unique challenges for managers.[25]

BEST PRACTICES

JetBlue

When was the last time you were on a plane being served coffee and biscotti by the airline's CEO? And while you are filing out, he is on all fours, picking up garbage off the floor. That is not in the job description of most executives. But JetBlue's David Neeleman—who's worth $215 million—finds serving customers inflight snacks is the best way to stay in communication with them, and he hops a flight once a week. He found out customers would rather have TVs than meals and prefer leather seats to fabric.

JetBlue is only one of two sizable airlines making money, when the industry as a whole is losing $7 billion this year. "Our profit margins are 17.5 percent," he boasts to customers. "Southwest's was 3.9 percent." Barely more than 5 years old, JetBlue started from scratch, is not unionized, and spends only 25 percent of revenues on labor, compared to Southwest's 33 percent. JetBlue capitalized on a slump in the airline industry, hiring personnel who had been laid off, like 45-year-old pilot Gary Correia, who made $80,000 at US Airways before he lost his job. Now at JetBlue, he makes $65,000, plus an additional 15 percent of that on profit sharing and gets stock options. He flies 80 hours a month and then helps flight attendants—and the occasional CEO—clean cabins after flights. A unionized pilot does not walk into the cabin except to the rest room. Flight attendants earn $20–30 per hour, and reservation-takers make $8.25 per hour and work from home, thus saving the company overhead.

Like Southwest, they have one type of plane, which saves on maintenance costs. Not only did Neeleman pioneer e-tickets, but he developed a "paperless" cockpit system to eliminate messy and time-consuming paper. All his careful planning and sleek innovations have made JetBlue second in cents per passenger mile: Southwest is 6.33, Jet is 6.43 and US Airways is 12.45 cents.

Neeleman started JetBlue after being fired from Southwest following the acquisition of his previous airline, Morris Air. He had too many ideas, was too wired to sit still in endless meetings, and felt handcuffed by too many rules. He was known for selling $299 Hawaii round-trip seats on Morris charter planes by hawking them at shopping malls.

A few years later, he had JetBlue in the sky, but not before he interviewed many current and previous airline executives, as well as studying their successes and failures. During the past year, the airline industry has seen some of its bleakest times, with several bankruptcies and Chapter 11 filings. JetBlue's profits fell, but it is still only one of two airlines with any profit.

For Neeleman, customer contact once a week is not enough. He wants constant information on what is happening. He is paged on his Blackberry if any flight is late by more than one minute. His wife knows not to complain because he wears his Blackberry to bed every night.

SOURCES: Melanie Wells, "Lord of the Skies," *Forbes* (Oct. 14, 2002): 130–138; Arlyn Tobias Gajilan, "The Amazing JetBlue," *FSB* (May 2003): 51; "UAL Posts Wider Loss, JetBlue's Profits Tumble," *The Wall Street Journal* (Jan. 28, 2005): A3.

Financial resources for nonprofit organizations typically come from government appropriations, grants, and donations rather than from the sale of products or services to customers. In businesses, managers focus on improving the organization's products and services to increase sales revenues. In nonprofits, however, services are typically provided to nonpaying clients, and a major problem for many organizations is securing a steady stream of funds to continue operating. Nonprofit managers, committed to serving clients with limited resources, must keep organizational costs as low as possible.[26] Donors generally want their money to go directly to helping clients rather than for overhead costs. If nonprofit managers cannot demonstrate efficient use of resources, they might have a hard time securing additional donations or government appropriations.

In addition, since nonprofit organizations do not have a conventional bottom line, managers may struggle with the question of what constitutes results and effectiveness. Whereas it is easy to measure dollars and cents, nonprofit managers have to measure intangibles such as "improve public health" or "make a difference in the lives of the disenfranchised." Gauging the performance of employees and managers is more difficult when the goal is providing a public service rather than increasing sales and profits. Managers in nonprofit organizations must market their services to attract clients and the volunteers and donors on whom they depend. An added complication is that volunteers and donors cannot be supervised and controlled in the same way a business manager deals with employees.

The roles defined by Mintzberg apply to nonprofit managers, but these roles may differ somewhat. We might expect managers in nonprofit organizations to place more emphasis on the roles of spokesperson (to sell the organization to donors and the public), leader (to build a mission-driven community of employees and volunteers), and resource allocator (to distribute government resources or grant funds that are often assigned from the top down).

Managers in all organizations—large corporations, small businesses, and nonprofit organizations—integrate and adjust the management functions and roles to meet new challenges within their own circumstances and to keep their organizations healthy. One way in which many organizations are meeting new challenges is through increased Internet usage. Some government agencies are using the Internet to cut bureaucracy, improve efficiency, and save money, as described in this chapter's Digital, Inc. box.

Management and the New Workplace

Over the past decade or so, the central theme being discussed in management has been the pervasiveness of dramatic change. Rapid environmental shifts are causing fundamental transformations that have a dramatic impact on the manager's job. These transformations are reflected in the transition to a new workplace, as illustrated in Exhibit 1.4.

The primary characteristic of the new workplace is that it is centered around bits rather than atoms, i.e., information and ideas rather than machines and physical assets. Low-cost computing power means ideas, documents, movies, music, and all sorts of other data can be zapped around the world at the speed of light. The digitization of business has radically altered the nature of work, employees, and the workplace.[27] The old workplace is characterized by routine, specialized tasks and standardized control procedures. Employees typically perform their jobs in one specific company facility, such as an automobile factory located in Detroit or an insurance agency located in Des Moines. The organization is coordinated and controlled through the vertical hierarchy, with decision-making authority residing with upper-level managers.

Take **ACTION**

As a nonprofit manager, balance the mission with efficient use of resources.

DIGITAL, INC.

Click Here for Lower Taxes

Government agencies are often thought of as plodding, inefficient bureaucracies that waste the public's time as well as money. But new ideas are changing that perception, as some government agencies apply Internet technology to save taxpayers money and make their lives easier.

The U.S. Internal Revenue Service (IRS) (*http://www.irs.gov*) provides one of the best examples in the government or corporate world of a Web site that is central to the organization's mission. Distributing tax forms has always been an expensive logistical nightmare for the IRS. Hordes of form pullers, envelope stuffers, label addressers, and so forth are needed to process the millions of mail-in requests for various tax publications and forms. The cost of handling a single request is around three dollars. The IRS recognized the problem and made the distribution of tax forms a major focus when it opened its Web site in the mid-1990s. Today, more than 100 million tax forms are downloaded directly from the site, with each request costing the IRS (and the taxpayers) only a fraction of a penny. E-filing of tax returns saves additional time and expense for taxpayers and the IRS. State governments in the United States are tapping into the power of the Web by allowing people to renew drivers licenses, file for unemployment benefits, pay quarterly taxes, apply for various permits, find suitable nursing homes, and access a range of other services electronically.

The United States is by no means alone in moving to the Internet. In a study of global e-government success, the consulting and technology services firm Accenture identified Canada as a leader in tailoring government services that meet the needs of citizens as "customers." The Canadian federal government site (*http://canada.gc.ca*) was the sixth most popular Internet site in the country in 2003. In Spain, the government is developing the first Internet ID card. Spanish citizens can insert the card into a reader attached to their home computers and order passports and other government services. Russia launched a $2.4 billion, 8-year-long *e-Russia* project in May 2003 to stimulate internal cooperation between departments and to make more government information available to the public. Finally, the United Kingdom has a goal of having all public services available online by 2005.

The transition to the Internet is a welcome one for citizens around the world. A market research study of e-government services in 32 countries found that the number of Internet-using adults who have accessed government services online grew to 40 percent in 2003 and continues to increase. The Internet is helping to shatter the image of government workers as paper shufflers and replace it with one of people providing valuable public services.

SOURCES: Heather Walmsley, "State of e-Nation: Everyone in UK Will Have Online Access to Government Services by 2005—But Only If We Take Up Those Ideas Successfully Implemented Overseas," *Internet Magazine* (February 2004): 44+; Les Gomes, "Fix It and They Will Come; E-commerce Isn't Dead, Just Broken," *The Wall Street Journal* (February 12, 2001): R4; and "E-Governance A Hit in Metros, Says Survey," *Asia Africa Intelligence Wire* (December 9, 2003).

In the new workplace, by contrast, work is flows freely and flexibly. The shift is most obvious in e-commerce and high-tech organizations, which have to respond to changing markets and competition quickly. However, other organizations, such as McKinsey & Company, CNA Life, and Nokia, are incorporating mechanisms to enhance speed and flexibility. Empowered employees are expected to seize opportunities and solve problems as they emerge. Structures are flatter, and decision-making authority is pushed down to lower levels.[28] The workplace is organized around networks rather than rigid hierarchies, and work is often virtual, with managers having to supervise and coordinate people who never come to work in the traditional sense. Thanks to modern information and communications technology, employees can perform their jobs from home or another remote location, at any time of the day or night. Flexible hours, telecommuting, and virtual teams are increasingly popular ways of working that require new skills from managers. Using virtual teams allows organizations to use the best people for a particular job, no matter where they are located, thus enabling a fast response to competitive pressures. When IBM needs to staff a project, for example, it gives a list of skills needed to the human resources department, which provides a pool of qualified people. The team leader assembles the best combination of people for the project, which can mean pulling people from different locations. IBM

EXHIBIT 1.4

The Transition to a New Workplace

Characteristics	The New Workplace	The Old Workplace
Resources	Bits—information	Atoms—physical assets
Work	Flexible, virtual	Structured, localized
Workers	Empowered employees, free agents	Dependable employees
Forces on Organizations		
Technology	Digital, e-business	Mechanical
Markets	Global, including Internet	Local, domestic
Workforce	Diverse	Homogenous
Values	Change, speed	Stability, efficiency
Events	Turbulent, more frequent crises	Calm, predictable
Management Competencies		
Leadership	Dispersed, empowering	
Focus	Connection to customers, employees	Autocratic Profits
Doing Work	By teams	
Relationships	Collaboration	By individuals
Design	Experimentation, learning organization	Conflict, competition Efficient performance

estimates that about a third of its employees participate in virtual teams.[29] Teams in today's organizations may include outside contractors, suppliers, customers, competitors, and interim managers who are not affiliated with a specific organization but work on a project-by-project basis. The valued worker is one who learns quickly, shares knowledge, and is comfortable with risk, change, and ambiguity, as illustrated in the Focus on Skills box.

Take ACTION

As a team leader, develop an acute ability to recognize talent in others and to create a sense of collaboration among people in different fields and often different locations.

FOCUS ON SKILLS

At Tech Target, Freedom to Leave Makes Employees Stay

Many companies proclaim to be more interested in employees' performance than in their attendance, but few prove it as loudly as Tech Target, an interactive media company based in Needham, Massachusetts. For the 210 people who work there, no guidelines dictate work schedules, personal leave, sick days, or vacation time. Amazingly, employees have the freedom to come and go as they please. Sounds like a formula for disaster, right?

Contrary to what many people would think, Tech Target's open-leave policy makes people more, not less, committed, responsible, and productive. Founder and CEO Greg Strakosch believes the open-leave policy is a competitive weapon, and he attributes increases in revenue largely to effects of the policy. For open-leave to work, managers have to reorient their approach. At Tech Target, supervisors set quarterly goals and

timetables, and employees are given the freedom and independence to achieve them. Managers pay attention to results, not to time, and they learn to trust people to be aboveboard when it comes to managing their own activities. Tech Target's employees appreciate open-leave for different reasons. For example, those with young children believe the policy eliminates the guilt and worry that accompanies being a good parent and employee, thus enabling them to be better at both.

Far from being lax, Tech Target sets high standards for performance and shows little tolerance for sloppy, lazy, or careless work habits. As Strakosch says, "We don't carry people who underachieve." Tech Target has a stringent hiring process because it wants to hire people with the right attitudes to function in the "loose yet tight" environment. For those who make the grade, it is a great arrangement. Where else could you take the afternoon off for a bike ride?

SOURCE: Patrick J. Sauer, "Open-Door Management," *INC.* (June 2003): 44.

Forces on Organizations

The most striking change now affecting organizations and management is technology. Consider that computing power has roughly doubled every 18 months over the past 30 years while the cost has been declining by half or more every 18 months.[30] In addition, the Internet, which was little more than a curiosity to many managers a decade ago, has transformed the way business is done. Many organizations use digital networking technologies to tie together employees and company partners in far-flung operations. Companies are becoming interconnected, and managers have to learn how to coordinate relationships with other organizations, as shown below.

Halo Video Game

It used to be that movie studios made movies. Now software companies want to get in the business. Microsoft and its agent, Creative Artists Agency (CAA) approached Hollywood studios about collaborating on a Xbox video game "Halo" based movie. Managers at both Microsoft and the studios were working with people in a different industry and negotiations did not go as first thought. The auction Microsoft expected never materialized. Perhaps it was the $10 million dollar upfront cost the software company demanded. Or to have final creative control. Maybe it was the 60 first-class plane tickets for Microsoft people and friends to attend the movie's opening. Based on these factors, within one day of reading the script five of seven studios dropped out. The remaining two, Universal Pictures and Twentieth Century Fox, moaned at the price. Finally, Microsoft and CAA hammered out a deal, though not final. Many in the industry saw it all as hubris on the part of both Microsoft and CAA, both not known for humility. Even if "Halo" is one of the most popular video franchises, ever, it still irked Hollywood that Microsoft demanded creative control, without investing one dime of its own in the project. Universal and Fox agreed to a deal with less financial restrictions—$5 million upfront, but acknowledge things may still fall apart over creative control. As a veteran movie exec said, "The one thing about Hollywood is that it is very hard to bully anyone when you are asking for that kind of price."[31]

The Internet and other new technologies are also tied closely to globalization. Global interconnections bring many opportunities to organizations, but they bring many threats, raise new risks, and accelerate complexity and competitiveness as well. Think about the trend toward outsourcing company activities to low-cost providers in other countries. U.S. companies have been sending manufacturing work to other countries for years to cut costs. Now, high-level knowledge work from U.S. organizations is being outsourced to countries such as India, Malaysia, and South Africa. India's Wipro Ltd., for example, writes software, performs consulting work, integrates back-office solutions, performs systems integration, and handles technical support for some of the biggest corporations in the United States, and they do it for 40 percent less than comparable U.S. companies can do the work.[32] Diversity of the population and the workforce in the United States is another fact of life for all organizations. The general U.S. population, and thus the workforce, is growing more ethnically and racially diverse. In addition, generational diversity is a powerful force in today's workplace, with employees of all ages working together on teams and projects in a way rarely seen in the past.

In the face of these transformations, organizations are learning to value change and speed over stability and efficiency. The fundamental paradigm during much of the twentieth century was a belief that things can be stable. In contrast, the new paradigm recognizes change and chaos as the natural order of things.[33] Events in today's world are turbulent and unpredictable, with small and large crises occurring on a more frequent basis. Rock star David Bowie has staked the newest phase of his career on that turbulence, as described on the following page.

Take **ACTION**

Practice adapting yourself to changes and new ways of thinking. Rather than arguing, ask questions of others.

When David Bowie was a huge rock star in the '70s, complete with flaming groupies, or a reformed punk artist in the '80s, he was never slated to become the smartest entrepreneur in the rock business. Of course, back then he was abusing drugs, which did not leave him much brainpower for the kinds of deals he is working now. Currently he is so clean he will not even take Advil because, as he says, "I have such an addictive personality." With his newly clear intelligence and his own ability to be ahead of the times, he has secured continued success.

Influenced by the IPO craze, he raised $55 million by becoming the first big music star to take his music catalog/song royalties public, through 1997's Bowie Bonds. Later, he started the high-tech company Ultrastar and his own Internet Service Provider (ISP) that happens to be his fan club (www.davidbowie.com). In 2004, Ultrastar created strategic alliances with several other companies, such as Circuit City's digital music club MusicNow. Recently, starting his own record label called Iso, he has a short-term distribution agreement with Sony as he gets the label up and running.

His keen sense of music's business environment makes him uneasy about the future. Not certain he even wants to be on a label in a few years, he thinks it will not work anymore by labels and distribution. "The absolute transformation of everything we ever thought about music will take place within ten years, and nothing is going to be able to stop it.... I'm truly confident that copyright, for instance, will no longer exist in ten years, and authorship and intellectual property is in for such a smashing." He believes he has to take advantage of these last years of the music business as it has been. "You'd better be prepared for doing a lot of touring because that's the only unique situation that's going to be left." Even with all the changes he expects, he is still looking forward to it. "It's terribly exciting," he says.[34]

New Management Competencies

In the face of these transitions, managers have to rethink their approach to organizing, directing, and motivating employees. Today's best managers give up their command-and-control mindset to embrace ambiguity and create organizations that are fast, flexible, adaptable, and relationship-oriented. The Digital, Inc. box describes the benefits one company has gained from a new approach to management. In many of today's best companies, leadership is dispersed throughout the organization, and managers empower others to gain the benefit of their ideas and creativity. Moreover, managers often supervise employees who are scattered in various locations, requiring a new approach to leadership that focuses more on coaching and providing direction and support than on giving orders and ensuring that they are followed.

©AP/Wide World Photos

CONCEPT CONNECTION

One of the hottest television shows of recent years is Donald Trump's The Apprentice, where contestants vie for a $250,000-a-year job as president of one of Trump's companies. On one hand, it seems like an exercise in backstabbing. However, on the other hand, it's a search for a leader with **new management competencies**—one who knows how to be a team player and build collaborative relationships to help the organization benefit from everyone's creativity and skills. In the photo, Trump chats with hopeful contestants for the hit show.

Success in the new workplace depends on the strength and quality of collaborative relationships. Rather than a single-minded focus on profits, today's managers recognize the critical importance of staying connected to employees and customers. The Internet has given increased knowledge and power to consumers, so organizations have to remain flexible and adaptable to respond quickly to changing demands or competition. New ways of working emphasize collaboration across functions and hierarchical levels as well as with other companies. Team-building skills are crucial. Instead of managing a department of employees, many managers act as team leaders of continually shifting, temporary projects. At SEI Investments, all work is distributed among 140 teams. Some are permanent, such as those that serve major customers or focus on specific markets, but many are designed to work on short-term projects or problems. Computer linkups, called pythons, drop from the ceiling. As people change assignments, they unplug their pythons, move their desks and chairs to a new location, plug into a new python, and get to work on the next project.[35]

An important management challenge in the new workplace is to build a learning organization by creating an organizational climate that values experimentation and risk taking, applies current technology, tolerates mistakes and failure, and rewards nontraditional thinking and the sharing of knowledge. Everyone in the organization participates in identifying and solving problems, enabling the organization to experiment, improve, and increase its capability. The role of managers is not to make decisions but to create learning capability, where everyone is free to experiment and learn what works best. Sometimes, the best learning comes through failure, as shown in the Business Blooper box.

Turbulent Times: Managing Crises and Unexpected Events

Take *ACTION*

Whenever you make a mistake or something does not work, get in the habit of asking yourself what could you have done differently to improve it.

Many managers may dream of working in an organization and a world where life seems relatively calm, orderly, and predictable, but their reality is one of increasing turbulence and disorder. Today's managers and organizations face various levels of crisis every day, everything from the loss of computer data, charges of racial discrimination, a factory fire, to workplace violence. However, these organizational crises have been compounded by crises on a more global level. Consider a few of the major events that have affected U.S. companies within the last few years:

1. The bursting of the dot-com bubble, which led to the failure of thousands of companies and the rapid decline of technology stocks

2. The massacre at Columbine High School, which prompted schools all over the country to form crisis teams to deal with school violence

3. The crash of high-flying Enron due to a complex series of unethical and illegal accounting gimmicks, and the subsequent investigations of numerous other corporations for similar financial shenanigans

---

BUSINESS BLOOPER

Excite.com

At 32, Joe Kraus has had more excitement than most, starting the search engine Excite.com with others in a garage after graduating from college. Worth upward of $500 a nano-sencond, Kraus watched it collapse quickly. He cashed out his stake, so he is not broke financially. After spending years building Excite.com, he was emotionally devastated when it fell apart. Mature beyond his years, Kraus understands what went wrong, including his own part. One problem: After the merger with @Home, the cable company dissolved in infighting. Strategic errors occurred, such as the $780 million cash acquisition of an online greeting card company. It seemed a reasonable price then until everything was devalued. Excite.com did not realize—as Google did—that businesses would pay to be part of a search engine. Kraus was "fried" after the experience. He backpacked around the world, came home, got married, had a son and has now re-emerged into the business world, co-founder of Jotspot, an application wiki—Web pages that anyone can write to or edit. Hopefully, he is smarter and wiser after the exciting lessons he learned.

SOURCES: Jennifer Reingold, "What We Learned in the New Economy," *Fast Company* (March 2004): 57–66; Jon Schwartz, "Hitting the Dot-comeback Trail," *USA Today* (Nov. 3, 2004): B3.

4. Terrorist attacks in New York City and Washington, D.C., that destroyed the World Trade Center, seriously damaged the Pentagon, killed thousands of people, and interrupted business around the world

5. Anthrax and ricin scares that altered companies' advertising and marketing plans as they weighed the public's perceptions of the U.S. mail

6. The uncertainty and confusion associated with reconstruction efforts following the war in Iraq, and continuing terrorist threats against the United States and its allies.

These and other events have brought the uncertainty and turbulence of today's world to the forefront of everyone's mind, and crisis management has become a critical skill for every manager.

Dealing with the unexpected has always been part of the manager's job, but our world has become so fast, interconnected, and complex that unexpected events happen more frequently and often with greater and more painful consequences. All of the new management skills and competencies we have discussed are important to managers in such an environment. In addition, crisis management places further demands on today's managers. Some of the most recent thinking on crisis management suggests the importance of five leadership skills:[36]

1. Stay calm.

2. Be visible.

3. Put people before business.

4. Tell the truth.

5. Know when to get back to business.

Stay Calm. Leaders' emotions are contagious, so leaders have to stay calm, focused, and optimistic about the future. Perhaps the most important part of a manager's job in a crisis situation is to absorb people's fears and uncertainties. Leaders have to suppress their own fears, doubts, and pain to encourage others. Though they acknowledge the difficulties, they must remain rock-steady and hopeful, which gives comfort, inspiration, and hope to others.

Be Visible. When people's worlds have become ambiguous and frightening, they need to feel someone is in control. The Monday following the September 11, 2001, terrorist attacks, Michael Dolan, the CEO of Young & Rubicam Advertising shook hands with every employee as he or she entered the headquarters. Crisis is a time when leadership cannot be delegated. When Russian President Vladimir Putin continued his holiday after the sinking of the submarine Kursk in August 2000, his reputation diminished worldwide.[37]

Put People Before Business. The companies that weather a crisis best, whether the crisis is large or small, are those in which managers make people and human feelings their top priority. As Ray O'Rourke, managing director for global corporate affairs at Morgan Stanley, said following September 11, "...even though we are a financial services company, we didn't have a financial crisis on our hands; we had a human crisis. After that point, everything was focused on our people."[38]

Tell the Truth. Managers should get as much information from as many diverse sources as they can, do their best to determine the facts, and then be open and straightforward about what is going on. Following the collapse of Enron and charges of unethical and possibly illegal activities, top managers at Enron compounded the crisis by

Take *ACTION*

Do Not Cover Up the Truth. People often find out and then you look worse for not fessing up.

destroying documents, refusing to be straightforward with employees and the media, and stonewalling investigators by pleading the Fifth Amendment. Managers at Arthur Andersen, Enron's accounting firm, reportedly mishandled the crisis by destroying documents and pleading the Fifth Amendment.

Know When to Get Back to Business. Though managers should first deal with the physical and emotional needs of people, they need to get back to business as soon as possible. The company has to keep going, and there is a natural human tendency to want to rebuild and move forward. Business rejuvenation is a sign of hope and an inspiration to employees. Moments of crisis present excellent opportunities for looking forward and using the emotional energy that has emerged to build a better company.

This is a challenging time to be entering the management field. Throughout this book, you will learn much more about the new workplace, the new and dynamic roles managers are playing in the twenty-first century, and how you can be an effective manager in a complex, changing world.

The Learning Organization

One of the toughest challenges for managers today is to get people focused on adaptive change to meet the demands of a turbulent and rapidly changing environment. Many problems have no ready-made solutions and require people throughout the company to think in new ways and learn new values and attitudes.[39] This requires a new approach to management and a new kind of organization. Managers began thinking about the concept of the learning organization after the publication of Peter Senge's book, *The Fifth Discipline: The Art and Practice of Learning Organizations.*[40] Senge described the kind of changes managers needed to undergo to help their organizations adapt to an increasingly chaotic world. These ideas gradually evolved to describe characteristics of the organization. No single view existed of what the learning organization looks like. The learning organization is an attitude or philosophy about what an organization can become.

The **learning organization** can be defined as one in which everyone is engaged in identifying and solving problems, enabling the organization to experiment, change, and improve continuously, thus increasing its capacity to grow, learn, and achieve its purpose. The essential idea is problem solving, in contrast to the traditional organization designed for efficiency. In the learning organization, all employees look for problems, such as understanding special customer needs. Employees solve problems, which means putting things together in unique ways to meet a customer's needs.

To develop a learning organization, managers make changes in all the subsystems of the organization. Three important adjustments to promote continuous learning are shifting to a team-based structure, employee empowerment, and information sharing. These three characteristics are illustrated in Exhibit 1.5 and each is described.

learning organization

Can be defined as one in which everyone is engaged in identifying and solving problems, enabling the organization to experiment, change, and improve continuously, thus increasing its capacity to grow, learn, and achieve its purpose.

EXHIBIT 1.5

Elements of a Learning Organization

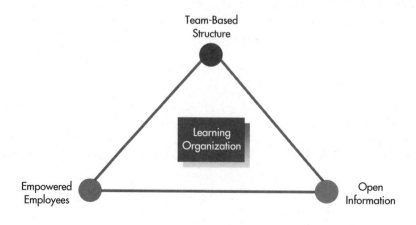

Team-Based Structure

Learning Organization

Empowered Employees

Open Information

Team-Based Structure. An important value in a learning organization is collaboration and communication across departmental and hierarchical boundaries. Self-directed teams are the basic building blocks of the structure. These teams are made up of employees with different skills who share or rotate jobs to produce an entire product or service. Traditional management tasks are pushed down to lower levels of the organization, with teams often taking responsibility for training, safety, scheduling, and decisions about work methods, pay and reward systems, and coordination with other teams. Although team leadership is critical, in learning organizations the traditional boss is practically eliminated. People on the team are given the skills, information, tools, motivation, and authority to make decisions central to the team's performance and to respond creatively and flexibly to new challenges or opportunities.

Employee Empowerment. Empowerment means unleashing the power and creativity of employees by giving them the freedom, resources, information, and skills to make decisions and perform effectively. Traditional management tries to limit employees, but empowerment expands their behavior. Empowerment may be reflected in self-directed work teams, quality circles, job enrichment, and employee participation groups as well as through decision-making authority, training, and information so people can perform jobs without close supervision.

In learning organizations, people are a manager's primary source of strength, not a cost to be minimized. Companies that adopt this perspective believe in providing competitive wages and good working conditions, as well as investing time and money in training programs and opportunities for personal and professional development. In addition, they often provide a sense of employee ownership by sharing gains in productivity and profits.[41]

Information Sharing. A learning organization is flooded with information. To identify needs and solve problems, people have to be aware of what is going on. They must understand the whole organization as well as their part in it. Formal data about budgets, profits, and departmental expenses must be available to everyone. "If you really want to respect individuals," says Solectron Corp.'s Winston Chen, "you've got to let them know how they're doing and let them know soon enough so they can do something about it."[42] Managers know that providing too much information is better than providing too little. In addition, managers encourage people throughout the organization to share information. For example, at Viant Inc., which helps companies build and maintain Web-based businesses, people are rewarded for their willingness to absorb and share knowledge. Rather than encouraging consultants to hoard specialized knowledge, CEO Bob Gett says, "We value you more for how much information you've given to the guy next to you."[43]

Managing the Technology-Driven Workplace

The shift to the learning organization goes hand-in-hand with the current transition to a technology-driven workplace. The physical world that Frederick Winslow Taylor and other proponents of scientific management measured determines less of what is valued in organizations and society. Our lives and organizations have been engulfed by information technology (IT). Ideas, information, and relationships are becoming more important than production machinery, physical products, and structured jobs.[44] Many employees perform much of their work on computers and may work in virtual teams, connected electronically to colleagues around the world. Even in factories that produce physical goods, machines have taken over much of the routine and uniform work, freeing workers to use more of their minds and abilities. Managers and employees in today's companies focus on opportunities rather than efficiencies, which requires they be flexible, creative, and unconstrained by rigid rules and structured tasks.

Take **ACTION**
To foster learning, share information, and talk often to people in other units.

The Shifting World of E-Business. Today, much business takes place by digital processes over a computer network rather than in physical space. **E-business** refers to the work an organization does by using electronic linkages (including the Internet) with customers, partners, suppliers, employees, or other key constituents. For example, organizations that use the Internet or other electronic linkages to communicate with employees or customers are engaged in e-business.

E-commerce specifically refers to business exchanges or transactions that occur electronically. E-commerce replaces or enhances the exchange of money and products with the exchange of data and information from one computer to another. Three types of e-commerce—*business-to-consumer*, *business-to-business*, and *consumer-to-consumer*—are illustrated in Exhibit 1.6.

Companies such as Gateway, Amazon.com, 1-800-Flowers, Expedia.com, and Progressive are engaged in business-to-consumer (B2C) e-commerce because they sell products and services to consumers over the Internet. Even though this is probably the most visible expression of e-commerce to the public, the fastest growing area of e-commerce is business-to-business (B2B) e-commerce, which refers to electronic transactions between organizations. Today, much B2B e-commerce takes place over the Internet.[45] Large organizations such as Wal-Mart, General Electric, Carrier Corp., General Motors, and Ford Motor Company buy and sell billions of dollars worth of goods and services a year via public or private Internet linkages.[46] For example, General Motors sells about 300,000 previously owned vehicles a year online through SmartAuction. Ford purchases a large portion of the steel it uses to build cars through e-Steel.[47]

Some companies have taken e-commerce to high levels to achieve amazing performance. Dell Computers pioneered the use of end-to-end digital supply-chain networks to keep in touch with customers, take orders, buy components from suppliers, coordinate with manufacturing partners, and ship customized products directly to consumers. This trend is affecting every industry, prompting a group of consultants at a Harvard University conference to conclude that businesses today must "Dell or be

e-business

Refers to the work an organization does by using electronic linkages (including the Internet) with customers, partners, suppliers, employees, or other key constituents.

e-commerce

Specifically refers to business exchanges or transactions that occur electronically. E-commerce replaces or enhances the exchange of money and products with the exchange of data and information from one computer to another.

EXHIBIT 1.6

Three Types of E-commerce

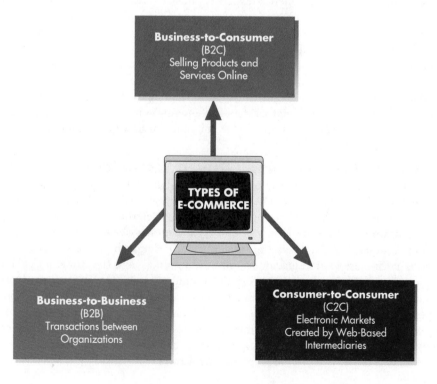

Delled."[48] These advances mean managers need to be technologically savvy and become responsible for managing a web of relationships that reaches far beyond the boundaries of the physical organization, building flexible e-links among a company and its employees, suppliers, partners, and customers.[49]

The third area of e-commerce, consumer-to-consumer (C2C), is made possible when an Internet-based business acts as an intermediary between and among consumers. One of the best-known examples of C2C e-commerce is Web-based auctions such as those made possible by eBay. Internet auctions have created a large electronic marketplace where consumers can buy and sell directly with one another, often handling practically the entire transaction via the Web. In 2003, an estimated 30 million people bought and sold more than $20 billion in merchandise over eBay.[50] Another growing area of C2C commerce is peer-to-peer file-sharing networks. Companies such as Kazaa and Gnutella provide the technology for swapping music files, video clips, software, and other files. Online music sharing, in particular, has zoomed in popularity, and though music companies and record retailers are currently engaged in a heated battle with file-sharing services, these companies are likely here to stay.[51]

Technology in the Workplace.   New electronic technologies shape the organization and how it is managed. A century ago, Taylor described the kind of worker needed in the iron industry: "Now one of the first requirements for a man who is fit to handle pig iron as a regular occupation is that he shall be so stupid and so phlegmatic that he more nearly resembles in his mental makeup the ox than any other type."[52] The philosophy of scientific management was that managers structured and controlled jobs so carefully that thinking on the part of employees was not required; indeed, it was usually discouraged. How different things are today. Many organizations depend on employees' minds more than their physical bodies. In companies where the power of an idea determines success, managers' primary goal is to tap into the creativity and knowledge of every employee.

Technology provides the architecture that supports and reinforces this new workplace. For example, one approach to information management is enterprise resource planning (ERP) systems, which weave together all of a company's major business functions, such as order processing, product design, purchasing, inventory, manufacturing, distribution, human resources, receipts of payments, and the forecasts of future demand.[53] ERP supports a companywide management system in which everyone, from the CEO down to a machine operator on the factory floor, has instant access to critical information. People can see the big picture and act quickly, based on timely information. Thus, ERP supports management attempts to harness and leverage organizational knowledge.

Peter Drucker coined the term *knowledge work* more than 40 years ago,[54] but it is only in recent years that managers have genuinely recognized knowledge as an important organizational resource that should be managed just as they manage cash flow or raw materials. **Knowledge management** refers to the systematic efforts to find, organize, and make available a company's intellectual capital and to foster a culture of continuous learning and knowledge sharing so a company's activities build on what is known.[55] IT plays an important role by enabling the storage and dissemination of data and information across the organization, but technology is only one part of a larger management system.[56] A complete knowledge management system includes the technology for capturing and storing knowledge for easy access and the new management values that support risk taking, learning, and collaboration. Rather than seeing employees as production factors and looking for ways to use human and material resources for greatest efficiency, today's most successful managers cherish people for their ability to think, create, share knowledge, and build relationships.

Take **ACTION**

Consider how often you buy something at Amazon.com or other online merchants and that ten years ago little was sold via the Web.

Take **ACTION**

Think of knowledge as a product, something you can perfect and make valuable to a customer.

knowledge management

Refers to the systematic efforts to find, organize, and make available a company's intellectual capital and to foster a culture of continuous learning and knowledge sharing so a company's activities build on what is known.

Management and Organization

A historical perspective on management provides a context or environment in which to interpret current opportunities and problems. However, studying history does not mean arranging events in chronological order; it means developing an understanding of the impact of societal forces on organizations. Studying history is a way to achieve strategic thinking, see the big picture, and improve conceptual skills. We will start by examining how social, political, and economic forces have influenced organizations and management practice.[57]

Social forces refer to those aspects of a culture that guide and influence relationships among people. What do people value? What do people need? What are people's behavior standards? These forces shape what is known as the social contract, which refers to the unwritten, common rules and perceptions about relationships among people and between employees and management.

A significant social force today is the changing attitudes, ideas, and values of Generation X and Generation Y employees. Generation X workers, in their thirties, have had a profound impact on the workplace, and Generation Y may have a greater one. These young workers, the most educated generation in the history of the United States, grew up technologically adept and globally conscious. Some trends sparked by Generation X and Y workers are completely reshaping the social contract.[58] Career life cycles are getting shorter, with workers typically changing jobs every few years and changing careers several times during their lifetime. Some consultants predict that the traditional 20-year career-building cycle will transform into a 20-month skills-building process.[59] Young workers expect access to cutting-edge technology, opportunities to learn and further their careers and personal goals, and the power to make substantive decisions and changes in the workplace. Finally, there is a growing focus on work/life balance, reflected in trends such as telecommuting, flextime, shared jobs, and organization-sponsored sabbaticals.

Political forces refer to the influence of political and legal institutions on people and organizations. Political forces include basic assumptions underlying the political system, such as the desirability of self-government, property rights, contract rights, the definition of justice, and the determination of innocence or guilt of a crime. The spread of capitalism throughout the world has dramatically altered the business landscape. The dominance of the free market system and growing interdependencies among the world's countries require organizations to operate differently and managers to think in new ways. At the same time, strong anti-American sentiments in many parts of the world create challenges for U.S. companies and managers. Another potent political force is the empowerment of citizens throughout the world. Power is being diffused within and among countries as never before.[60] People are demanding empowerment, participation, and responsibility in all areas of their lives, including their work.

Economic forces pertain to the availability, production, and distribution of resources in a society. Governments, military agencies, churches, schools, and business organizations in every society require resources to achieve their goals, and economic forces influence the allocation of scarce resources. The economy of the United States and other developed countries is shifting dramatically, with the sources of wealth, the fundamentals of distribution, and the nature of economic decision making undergoing significant changes.[61] The emerging new economy is based largely on ideas, information, and knowledge rather than material resources. Supply chains and distribution of resources have been revolutionized by digital technology. Surplus inventories, which once could trigger recessions, are declining or completely disappearing. Shifts in the economic landscape are similar to those of many decades ago.

Another economic trend is the booming importance of small and mid-sized businesses, including start-ups, which early in the twenty-first century grew at three times

---

social forces

Refer to those aspects of a culture that guide and influence relationships among people. What do people value? What do people need? What are people's behavior standards?

Take **ACTION**

Make an effort to create balance in your life between work and family. You will be happier for it.

---

political forces

Refer to the influence of political and legal institutions on people and organizations. Political forces include basic assumptions underlying the political system, such as the desirability of self-government, property rights, contract rights, the definition of justice, and the determination of innocence or guilt of a crime.

---

economic forces

Pertain to the availability, production, and distribution of resources in a society.

the rate of the national economy. "I call it 'the invisible economy,' yet it is *the* economy," says David Birch of Cognetics Inc., a Cambridge, Massachusetts, firm that tracks business formation.[62]

A massive shift in the economy has upheavals, of course. In the early 2000s, years of seemingly endless growth ground to a halt as stock prices fell, particularly for dot-com and technology companies. Numerous Internet-based companies went out of business, and organizations throughout the United States and Canada began laying off hundreds of thousands of workers. However, this economic downturn may be a stimulus for greater technological innovation and small-business vitality.

Management practices and perspectives vary in response to these social, political, and economic forces in the larger society. During difficult times, managers have looked for ideas to help them cope with environmental turbulence and keep their organizations vital. A survey by Bain & Company, for example, found a dramatic increase in 2002 in the various management ideas and techniques used by managers in the surveyed companies. With a tough economy and rocky stock market, lingering anxieties over war and terrorism, and the public suspicion and skepticism resulting from corporate scandals, executives have been searching for any management tool that could help them get the most out of limited resources.[63] This search for guidance is reflected in a proliferation of books, scholarly articles, and conferences dedicated to examining management fashions and trends.[64]

Exhibit 1.7 illustrates the evolution of significant management perspectives over time, each of which will be examined in the remainder of this chapter. The timeline reflects the dominant time period for each approach, but elements of each are still used in today's organizations.

Classical Perspective

The practice of management can be traced to 3000 B.C. to the first government organizations developed by the Sumerians and Egyptians, but the formal study of management is relatively recent.[65] The early study of management as we know it today began with what is now called the *classical perspective*.

The classical perspective on management emerged during the nineteenth and early twentieth centuries. The factory system that began to appear in the 1800s posed challenges that earlier organizations had not encountered. Problems arose in tooling the

EXHIBIT 1.7

*Management
Perspectives
over Time*

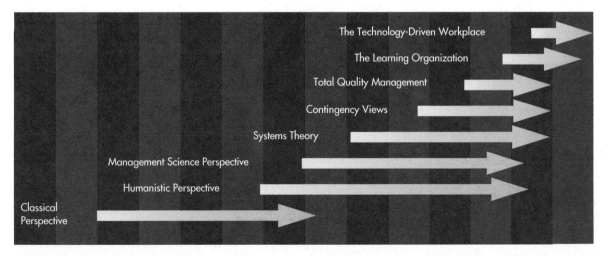

plants, organizing managerial structure, training employees (many of them non-English-speaking immigrants), scheduling complex manufacturing operations, and dealing with increased labor dissatisfaction and resulting strikes.

These problems and the development of large, complex organizations demanded a new approach to coordination and control, and a "new subspecies of economic man—the salaried manager"[66]—was born. Between 1880 and 1920, the number of professional managers in the United States grew from 161,000 to more than a million.[67] These professional managers began developing and testing solutions to the mounting challenges of organizing, coordinating, and controlling large numbers of people and increasing worker productivity. Thus began the evolution of modern management with the classical perspective.

In this section, we will examine the classical perspective, with its emphasis on efficiency and organization, as well as other perspectives that emerged to address new concerns, such as employee needs and the role of the environment. Elements of each perspective are still used in organization design, although they have been adapted and revised to meet changing needs.

scientific management

Postulates that decisions about organizations and job design should be based on precise, scientific study of individual situations.

Efficiency is Everything.   Pioneered by Frederick Winslow Taylor, **scientific management** postulates that decisions about organizations and job design should be based on precise, scientific study of individual situations.[68] To use this approach, managers develop precise, standardized procedures for doing each job, select workers with appropriate abilities, train workers in the standard procedures, plan work, and provide wage incentives to increase output. Taylor's approach is illustrated by the unloading of iron from railcars and reloading finished steel for the Bethlehem Steel plant in 1898. Taylor calculated that with correct movements, tools, and sequencing, each man was capable of loading 47.5 tons per day instead of the typical 12.5 tons. He also worked out an incentive system that paid each man $1.85 per day for meeting the new standard, an increase from the previous rate of $1.15. Productivity at Bethlehem Steel shot up overnight. These insights established organizational assumptions that the role of management is to maintain stability and efficiency, with top managers doing the thinking and workers doing what they are told.

© Bettman/CORBIS

CONCEPT CONNECTION

Frederick Taylor's **scientific management** *techniques were expanded by automaker Henry Ford, who replaced workers with machines for heavy lifting and moving. One of the first applications of the moving assembly line was the Magneto assembly operations at Ford's Highland Park plant in 1913. Magnets moved from one worker to another, reducing production time by one half. The same principle was applied to total-car assembly, improving efficiency and reducing worker-hours required to product a Model-T Ford to less than two. Under this system, a Ford rolled off the assembly line every 10 seconds.*

How to Get Organized.   Another subfield of the classical perspective took a broader look at the organization. Whereas scientific management focused primarily on the technical core—on work performed on the shop floor—administrative principles looked at the design and functioning of the organization as a whole. For example, Henri Fayol proposed 66 principles of management, such as "each subordinate receives orders from only one superior" (unity of command) and "similar activities in an organization should be grouped together under one manager" (unity of direction). These principles formed the foundation for modern management practice and organization design.

The scientific management and administrative principles approaches were powerful and gave organizations fundamental new ideas for establishing high productivity and increasing prosperity. In particular, administrative principles contributed to the development of bureaucratic organizations, (Exhibit 1.8), which emphasized designing and managing organizations on an impersonal, rational basis through such elements as clearly defined authority and responsibility, formal recordkeeping, and uniform application of standard rules. Though the term *bureaucracy* has taken on negative connotations in today's organizations, bureaucratic characteristics worked well for the needs of the Industrial Age.

Bureaucracy has taken on a negative meaning in today's organizations and is associated with endless rules and red tape. We have all been frustrated by waiting in lines or following seemingly silly procedures. However, rules and other bureaucratic procedures provide a standardized way of dealing with employees. Everyone gets equal treatment, and everyone knows the rules. This has enabled many organizations to become extremely efficient.

One problem with the classical perspective, however, is that it failed to consider the social context and human needs. Many parts of this book relate research about the human needs of organizations. Exhibit 1.9 illustrates a number of management innovations that have become popular over the past 50 years. Note the trend of new management concepts from the behavioral sciences, increasing about 1970 and then again from 1980 to the present. The rapid pace of change and the increased pressure of global competition have spurred even greater interest in improved behavioral approaches to management.

What About People? Early work on industrial psychology and human relations received little attention because of the prominence of scientific management. However, a major breakthrough occurred with a series of experiments at a Chicago electric company, which came to be known as the *Hawthorne Studies*. Interpretations of these studies concluded that positive treatment of employees improved their motivation and productivity. The publication of these findings led to a revolution in worker treatment and laid the groundwork for subsequent work examining treatment of workers, leadership, motivation, and human resource management. From a historical perspective, whether the studies were academically sound is less important than that they stimulated an increased interest in looking at employees as more than extensions of production machinery. The interpretation that employees' output increased when managers treated them positively started a revolution in worker treatment for improving organizational productivity. Despite flawed methodology or inaccurate conclusions, the findings provided the impetus

Take **ACTION**

Think of ways you can make your work more efficient, by where you place your computer and books, or when you rest.

Take **ACTION**

You may hear bureaucracy used as a derogatory term, but it was a social innovation. Previously, decisions were made on the whim of the manager, and people were more likely exploited.

Take **ACTION**

Get away from seeing an organization as a machine and treat workers as human beings.

Elements of Bureaucracy

1 Labor is divided with clear definitions of authority and responsibility that are legitimized as official duties.

2 Positions are organized in a hierarchy of authority, with each position under the authority of a higher one.

3 All personnel are selected and promoted based on technical qualifications, which are assessed by examination or according to training and experience.

4 Administrative acts and decisions are recorded in writing. Recordkeeping provides organizational memory and continuity over time.

5 Management is separate from the ownership of the organization.

6 Managers are subject to rules and procedures that will ensure reliable, predictable behavior. Rules are impersonal and uniformly applied to all employees.

EXHIBIT 1.8

Characteristics of Weberian Bureaucracy

SOURCE: Adapted from Max Weber, *The Theory of Social and Economic Organizations*, ed. and trans. A.M. Henderson and Talcott Parsons (New York: Free Press, 1947), 328–337.

EXHIBIT 1.9

*Theory X and
Theory Y*

Assumptions of Theory X

- The average human being has an inherent dislike of work and will avoid it if possible.
- Because of the human characteristic of dislike for work, most people must be coerced, controlled, directed, or threatened with punishment to get them to put forth adequate effort toward the achievement of organizational objectives.
- The average human being prefers to be directed, wishes to avoid responsibility, has relatively little ambition, wants security above all.

Assumptions of Theory Y

- The expenditure of physical and mental effort in work is as natural as play or rest. The average human being does not inherently dislike work.
- External control and the threat of punishment are not the only means for bringing about effort toward organizational objectives. A person will exercise self-direction and self-control in the service of objectives to which he or she is committed.
- The average human being learns, under proper conditions, not only to accept but to seek responsibility.
- The capacity to exercise a relatively high degree of imagination, ingenuity, and creativity in the solution of organizational problems is widely, not narrowly, distributed in the population.
- Under the conditions of modern industrial life, the intellectual potentialities of the average human being are only partially utilized.

SOURCE: Douglas McGregor, *The Human Side of Enterprise* (New York: McGraw-Hill, 1960), 33–48.

for the human relations movement. IBM was one of the earliest proponents of a human relations approach, as described in the Focus on Collaboration box. This approach shaped management theory and practice for well over a quarter of a century, and the belief that human relations is the best approach for increasing productivity persists today.

Abraham Maslow (1908–1970), a practicing psychologist, observed that his patients' problems usually stemmed from an inability to satisfy their needs. Thus, he generalized his work and suggested a hierarchy of needs. Maslow's hierarchy started with physiological needs and progressed to safety, belongingness, esteem, and, finally, self-actualization needs. Chapter 11 discusses his ideas in more detail.

CONCEPT CONNECTION

In situations such as that shown here, studies were carried out at the Hawthorn plant of Western Electric plant to evaluate worker productivity. Professors Mayo and Roethlisberger evaluated conditions such as rest breaks and workday length, physical health, amounts of sleep and diet. Gradually the researchers began to realize they had created a change in supervisory style and **human relations***, which they believed was the true cause of the increased productivity.*

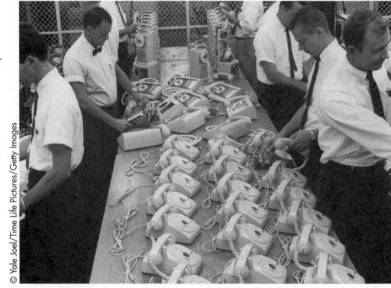

© Yale Joel/Time Life Pictures/Getty Images

FOCUS ON COLLABORATION

Watson Opens the Door at IBM and Finds Happier Employees

During the early 1900s, managers in most manufacturing companies were focused on reducing jobs to repetitive, standardized tasks, following the scientific management approach advocated by Taylor and others. However, the ideals that Thomas Watson, Sr. planted at IBM were based on a different approach, and they helped transform the company into a corporate giant.

In 1914, Watson joined a failing conglomerate that primarily made scales, coffee grinders, cheese slicers, and time clocks. The Computing-Tabulating-Recording component of the conglomerate grew quickly and soon overtook the other businesses. The name was changed to International Business Machines (IBM) in 1924. Rather than put the production system first, as Taylor advised, Watson vowed to make people the cornerstone of his corporate culture. He abolished piecework, spruced up factories, paid above-average wages, and borrowed money to fund in-house education programs. Foremost among his innovations was an open-door policy that encouraged any employee to take a complaint directly to himself. He almost guaranteed lifetime employment (even during the Great Depression) so workers would feel free to speak their minds. In the early years of Watson's tenure with IBM, when the company did not have funds for generous benefit plans, Watson sponsored company picnics, complete with bands, to build spirit and keep workers motivated. As the company prospered, he passed the good times on. A group life insurance plan was launched in 1934, with survivor benefits and paid vacations added afterward.

The human relations approach to management was continued by Thomas Watson, Jr., who took over as CEO in 1956 and pushed the company into computers. Leading IBM through one of the longest and most spectacular periods of growth in business history, the younger Watson was known as a hard charger and a tough boss. However, he maintained his father's emphasis on treating employees fairly. IBM became famous for putting all employees on salary and for its generous compensation and benefit plans, as well as the continued guarantee of lifetime employment. Watson liberally distributed stock options to his executives, but stopped taking them as early as 1957, saying, "We didn't want to look like pigs." Many factors were involved in IBM's successful history. However, the early emphasis on treating employees well helped put the company on the map. Watson's belief that a focus on people and meeting the needs of employees was the key to increased productivity and performance was ahead of its time.

SOURCES: "IBM: The Open Door," from Matthew Boyle, "How the Workplace Was Won," *Fortune* (January 22, 2001): 139; and Thomas A. Stewart, Alex Taylor III, Peter Petre, and Brent Schlender, "The Businessman of the Century," *Fortune* (November 22, 1999): 108–128.

Douglas McGregor (1906–1964) had become frustrated with the early simplistic human relations notions while president of Antioch College in Ohio. He challenged the classical perspective and the early human relations assumptions about human behavior. Based on his experiences as a manager and consultant, his training as a psychologist, and the work of Maslow, McGregor formulated his Theory X and Theory Y, which are explained in Exhibit 1.10.[69] McGregor believed that the classical perspective was based on Theory X assumptions about workers. He felt that a modified version of Theory X fit early human relations ideas. In other words, human relations ideas did not go far enough. McGregor proposed Theory Y as a more realistic view of workers for guiding management thinking.

Theory X and Theory Y

Assumptions of Theory X.

- The average human being has an inherent dislike of work and will avoid it if possible.

- Because of the human characteristic of dislike for work, most people must be coerced, controlled, directed, or threatened with punishment to get them to put forth adequate effort toward the achievement of organizational objectives.

- The average human being prefers to be directed, wishes to avoid responsibility, has relatively little ambition, and wants security above all.

EXHIBIT 1.10

Ebbs and Flows of Management Innovations, 1950–2000

SOURCE: Adapted from Fig 1.3, Richard Tanner Pascale, *Managing on the Edge* (New York: Touchstone/Simon & Schuster, 1990), 20. Copyright © 1990 by Richard Pascale.

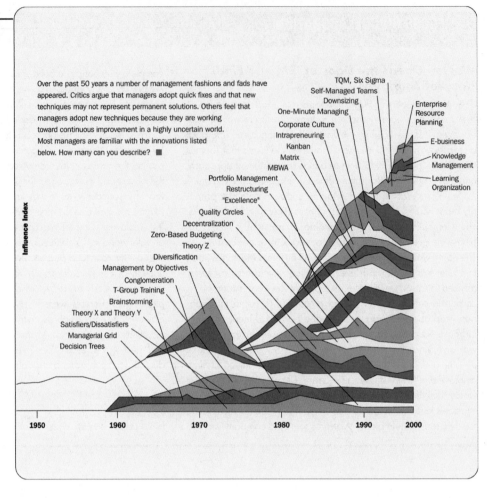

Assumptions of Theory Y.

- The expenditure of physical and mental effort in work is as natural as play or rest. The average human being does not inherently dislike work.

- External control and the threat of punishment are not the only means for bringing about effort toward organizational objectives. A person will exercise self-direction and self-control in the service of objectives to which he or she is committed.

- The average human being learns, under proper conditions, to accept and seek responsibility.

- The capacity to exercise a relatively high degree of imagination, ingenuity, and creativity in the solution of organizational problems is widely, not narrowly, distributed in the population.

- Under the conditions of modern industrial life, the average human being's intellectual potentialities are only partially utilized.[70]

The point of Theory Y is that organizations can take advantage of the imagination and intellect of all their employees. Employees will exercise self-control and will contribute to organizational goals when given the opportunity. A few companies still use Theory X management, but many are trying Theory Y techniques.

These human relations and behavioral approaches added important contributions to the study of management and organizations. Behavioral approaches can help us understand how people work and how systems develop, such as the use of paper in different eras for organizations, as described in the Focus on Skills box.

However, the hierarchical system and bureaucratic approaches that developed during the Industrial Revolution remained the primary approach to organization design and functioning well into the 1980s. In general, this approach worked for most organizations until the past few decades. However, during the 1980s, it began to lead to problems. Increased competition, especially on a global scale, changed the playing field.[71] North American companies had to find a better way.

The 1980s produced new corporate cultures that valued leanness, flexibility, rapid customer response, employee motivation, customer care, and quality products.

FOCUS ON SKILLS

What Happened to Paperless?

The next time you take a plane somewhere think of this: As the plane takes off, the flight info (type of plane, requested altitude, destination, radar ID) is printed on a stiff paper called a flight strip. As the plane flies up and down, though different air sectors, changes speeds, and so on, the air traffic controller jots down notes and moves that paper around on his desk. This is all done while watching a large radar console, talking to the 25 different planes the controller is in charge of, and jotting notes down on those other 24 flight strips. Air traffic control depends on technology and the good, old-fashioned paper and pencil. In this day of high-tech breakthroughs, why must airplane handling be done like breakfast orders at the all-night diner?

Several years ago Apple Computer Inc. studied paper on desks and found they have great meaning. People can wax eloquent about each pile and how important it is. The team found that piles represent active and ongoing thinking, that knowledge workers use desk space to organize thoughts they have not quite figured out yet what to do with or how to categorize, which is why they have not filed those papers away. Messy desks might be a sign of complex work and thinking.

Large organizations where complex reports are developed find that paper works better than electronic documents. With paper, professionals at the International Monetary Fund (IMF) bring each sheet and lay it out in front of the group. Pieces are passed around and are annotated and reassembled, tasks more cumbersome done on computers.

How did we get to this situation, anyway? The paper proliferation began at the end of the nineteenth century with the advent of large corporations and scientific management.

Coping with new complexities of the industrial economy meant weekly sales reports, company newsletters, and an office manual. One innovation was the typewriter, which made creating documents quickly possible, especially when carbon paper arrived soon after. A secretary in a railroad company, for example, could type ten copies of the railroad schedule and send them to stations on the rail line. It was efficiency and control.

What to do with all this paper? They were stored in cumbersome cases or pigeonholes in secretaries desks. Along came Melvil Dewey, whose life was devoted to cataloging information. He is mostly remembered for founding the Dewey decimal system for organizing library books, but he also developed the vertical file, a place where all that paper could be filed and found, putting those railroad schedules, for example, under "S."

Modern knowledge work is characterized by the pile rather than the file. People who pressure others to keep their desks clean are harking back to the nineteenth-century value of paper being best put away. Who needs files anyway, when computers are more efficient information storers? Even if you want them, you might be out of luck. Many organizations, including the federal courts across the country, are mandating paperless work.

So, the issue for modern workers is not to use less paper but to keep less paper. If the purpose of paper nowadays is to promote creative thinking, then once that thinking is expressed, the paper has served its purpose and is ready for the round file, i.e., the trash bin.

SOURCES: Malcom Gladwell, "The Social Life of Paper," *The New Yorker* (March 25, 2002): 92–96; Abigail Sellen and Richard Harper, *The Myth of the Paperless Office* (Cambridge, MA: MIT Press, 2003); Alicia Caldwell, "Courthouse Faces Hurdles on the way to Paperless Office, *Denver Post* (Dec. 26, 2004): C6.

Over the past two decades, organizations have undergone more profound and far-reaching changes. The Internet and other advances in IT, globalization, rapid social and economic changes, and other challenges from the environment call for new management perspectives and more flexible approaches to organization design.

Do Not Forget the Environment. Many problems occur when all organizations are treated as similar, which was the case with scientific management and administrative principles approaches that attempted to design all organizations alike. The structures and systems that work in a conglomerate's retail division will not be appropriate for the manufacturing division. The organization charts and financial procedures best for anentrepreneurial Internet firm like eBay or MaMaMedia will not work for a large food processing plant.

contingency

This means that one thing depends on other things, and for organizations to be effective, there must be a "goodness of fit" between their structure and the conditions in their external environment.

Contingency means that one thing depends on other things, and for organizations to be effective, there must be a "goodness of fit" between their structure and the conditions in their external environment.[72] What works in one setting may not work in another setting. There is no one best way. Contingency theory means "it depends." For example, some organizations experience a certain environment, use a routine technology, and desire efficiency. In this situation, a management approach that uses bureaucratic control procedures, a hierarchical structure, and formal communication would be appropriate. Likewise, free-flowing management processes work best in an uncertain environment with a nonroutine technology. The correct management approach is contingent on the organization's situation.

Take **ACTION**

Try doing equally well in all courses and you might see why the contingency theory works.

Today, almost all organizations operate in highly uncertain environments. Thus, we are involved in a significant transition, in which concepts of organizations and management are changing as dramatically as they were changed with the dawning of the Industrial Revolution.

Total Quality Management (TQM)

The quality movement in Japan emerged partly as a result of American influence after World War II. The ideas of W. Edwards Deming, known as the "father of the quality movement," were initially scoffed at in America, but the Japanese embraced his theories and modified them to help rebuild their industries into world powers.[73] Japanese companies achieved a significant departure from the American model by gradually shifting from an inspection-oriented approach to quality control toward an approach emphasizing employee involvement in the prevention of quality problems.[74]

total quality management (TQM)

A concept that focuses on managing the total organization to deliver quality to customers. Four significant elements of TQM are employee involvement, focus on the customer, benchmarking, and continuous improvement.

During the 1980s and into the 1990s, **total quality management (TQM)**, which focuses on managing the total organization to deliver customer quality, was at the forefront in helping managers deal with global competition. The approach infuses quality values throughout every activity within a company, with front-line workers intimately involved in the process. Four significant elements of quality management are employee involvement, focus on the customer, benchmarking (noting where they are now and working toward higher quality), and continuous improvement.

Take **ACTION**

Benchmark your papers and assignments so you can become a better student.

Employee involvement means that TQM requires companywide participation in quality control. All employees are focused on the customer; TQM companies find out what customers want and try to meet their needs and expectations. Benchmarking refers to a process whereby companies find out how others do something better than they do and then imitate or improve on it. Continuous improvement is the implementation of small, incremental improvements in all organizational areas on an ongoing basis. TQM is not a quick fix, but companies, such as Motorola, Procter & Gamble, and DuPont have achieved astonishing results in efficiency, quality, and customer satisfaction through TQM.[75] TQM is still an important part of today's organizations, and many companies pursue challenging quality goals to demonstrate their commitment to improving quality.

For example, *Six Sigma* is a highly ambitious quality standard popularized by Motorola that specifies a goal of no more than 3.4 defects per million parts. Numerous companies, including DuPont, Texas Instruments, GE, and Nokia, pursue Six Sigma quality standards. Quality goals and initiatives will be discussed further in Chapter 10.

Manager's Solution

This chapter introduced a number of important concepts and described the changing nature of management. High performance requires the efficient and effective use of organizational resources through the four management functions of planning, organizing, leading, and controlling. To perform the four functions, managers need three skills: conceptual, human, and technical.

Two characteristics of managerial work were explained in the chapter: managerial activities involving variety, fragmentation, and brevity and managers performing much work at an unrelenting pace. Managers are expected to perform activities associated with ten roles: the informational roles of monitor, disseminator, and spokesperson; the interpersonal roles of figurehead, leader, and liaison; and the decisional roles of entrepreneur, disturbance handler, resource allocator, and negotiator.

These management characteristics apply to small businesses, entrepreneurial start-ups, and nonprofit organizations as they do in large corporations. In addition, they are being applied in a new workplace and a rapidly changing world. In the new workplace, work flows freely and flexibly to encourage speed and adaptation, and empowered employees are expected to seize opportunities and solve problems. The workplace is organized around networks rather than vertical hierarchies, and work is often virtual. These changing characteristics have resulted from forces such as advances in technology and e-business, globalization, increased diversity, and a growing emphasis on change and speed over stability and efficiency. Managers need new skills and competencies in this environment. Leadership is dispersed and empowering. Customer relationships are critical, and most work is done by teams that work directly with customers. In the new workplace, managers focus on building relationships, which may include customers, partners, and suppliers. In addition, they strive to build learning capability throughout the organization. An emerging need is for leadership during crises and unexpected events. Managers in crisis situations should stay calm, be visible, put people before business, tell the truth, and know when to get back to business. Human skills become critical during times of turbulence and crisis.

This chapter examined the historical background leading up to new approaches to managing learning organizations and the digital workplace. An understanding of the evolution of management helps current and future managers understand where we are and continue to progress toward better management.

The three major perspectives on management that have evolved since the late 1800s are the classical perspective, the humanistic perspective, and the management science perspective. Recent extensions include the contingency view and TQM. The most recent thinking about organizations has been brought about by today's turbulent times and the shift to a new workplace.

Many managers are redesigning their companies toward the learning organization, which fully engages all employees in identifying and solving problems. The learning organization is characterized by a team-based structure, empowered employees, and open information. The learning organization represents a substantial departure from the traditional management hierarchy.

The shift to a learning organization goes hand-in-hand with today's transition to a technology-driven workplace. Ideas, information, and relationships are becoming more important than production machinery and physical assets, which requires new approaches to management. E-business is burgeoning as more economic activity takes place over digital computer networks rather than in physical space. Two specific management tools that support the digital workplace are ERP and knowledge management. Both require managers to think in new ways about the role of employees in the organization. Managers value employees for their ability to think, build relationships, and share knowledge, which is different from the scientific management perspective.

An excellent example of a leader during turbulent times is Michael Dell, CEO of Dell Computers, described in the chapter opening. Dell is off the critical list for now, but Michael Dell knows it can happen again if the company does not remain vigilant.

How Dell and Kevin Rollins handled the negative feedback says a lot about the company's style. While many CEOs would have shrugged off the stinging information, blaming selfish employees, Dell and Rollins met with the top 20 managers and dealt with the gripes, each offering their own frank and honest self-critique. Dell admitted to being shy and his pulling away sometimes could be seen as aloof and condescending. The company did not stop there but went out to all the company managers, several thousand people, and showed them the videotape of that intense meeting with top management. Dell and Rollins got desk-top props to remind them of needed behavior changes: Dell's plastic bulldozer helped him remember not to ram ideas through without consulting others, and Rollin's Curious George doll cautioned him to listen to team members before making a decision. Did the strategy work? Dell's stock is now valued at 40, more than Microsoft, GE, or Wal-Mart. Listening was only the first part. They had to institute changes on order-taking, logistics, and information management. But without listening, some of those changes would never have surfaced as ideas. Michael Dell has learned that sustained success cannot come without the top leaders facing themselves and to change, often with great pain. And when success does come, it is greeted with a few seconds of praise and five hours of analysis on what could have been done better.[76]

Discussion Questions

1. Assume you are a research engineer at a petrochemical company, collaborating with a marketing manager on a major product modification. You notice that every memo you receive from her has been copied to senior management. At every company function, she spends time talking to the big shots. You are also aware that sometimes when you are slaving away over the project, she is playing golf with senior managers. What is your evaluation of her behavior?

2. What do you think the text means by a management revolution? Do you expect to be a leader or follower in this revolution? Explain.

3. What similarities do you see among the four management functions of planning, organizing, leading, and controlling? Do you think these functions are related; that is, is a manager who performs well in one function likely to perform well in the others?

4. What is the difference between efficiency and effectiveness? Which is more important for performance? Can an organization succeed in both simultaneously?

5. What changes in management functions and skills occur as one is promoted from a nonmanagement to a management position? How can managers acquire the new skills?

6. If managerial work is characterized by variety, fragmentation, and brevity, how do managers perform basic management functions such as planning, which would seem to require reflection and analysis?

7. A college professor told her students, "The purpose of a management course is to teach students about management, not to teach them to be managers." Do you agree or disagree with this statement? Discuss.

8. Describe the characteristics of the new management paradigm. How do these characteristics compare to those of an organization in which you have worked? Would you like to work or manage in a learning organization? Discuss.

9. How could the teaching of management change to better prepare future managers to deal with workforce diversity? With empowerment? Do you think diversity and empowerment will have a substantial impact on organizations in the future? Explain.

10. A management professor once said that for successful management, studying the present was most important, studying the past was next, and studying the future was least important. Do you agree? Why?

11. Which of the six characteristics of learning organizations do you find most appealing? Which would be hardest for you to adopt?

12. Some experts believe that leadership is more important than ever in a learning organization. Do you agree? Explain.

13. What is the behavioral sciences approach? How does it differ from earlier approaches to management?

14. Why can an event such as the Hawthorne studies be a major turning point in the history of management even if the idea is later shown to be in error? Discuss.

15. Do you think management theory will ever be as precise as theories in the fields of physics, chemistry, or experimental psychology? Why or why not?

Manager's Workbook

Management Aptitude Questionnaire
Rate each of the following questions according to this scale:

5. I always am like this.
4. I often am like this.
3. I sometimes am like this.
2. I rarely am like this.
1. I never am like this.

1. When I have a number of tasks or homework to do, I set priorities and organize the work around the deadlines.   C   1   2   3   4   5

2. Most people would describe me as a good listener.   H   1   2   3   4   5

3. When I am deciding on a particular course of action for myself (such as hobbies to pursue, languages to study, which job to take, special projects to be involved in), I typically consider the long-term (3 years or more) implications of what I would choose to do.   C   1   2   3   4   5

4. I prefer technical or quantitative courses rather than those involving literature, psychology, or sociology.   T   1   2   3   4   5

5. When I have a serious disagreement with someone, I hang in there and talk it out until it is completely resolved.   H   1   2   3   4   5

6. When I have a project or assignment, I really get into the details rather than the "big picture" issues.*   C   1   2   3   4   5

7. I would rather sit in front of my computer than spend a lot of time with people.   T   1   2   3   4   5

8. I try to include others in activities or when there are discussions.   H   1   2   3   4   5

9. When I take a course, I relate what I am learning to other courses I have taken or concepts I have learned elsewhere.   C   1   2   3   4   5

10. When somebody makes a mistake, I want to correct the person and let her or him know the proper answer or approach.*   H   1   2   3   4   5

11. I think it is better to be efficient with my time when talking with someone, rather than worry about the other person's needs, so that I can get on with my real work.   T   1   2   3   4   5

12. I know my long-term vision for career, family, and other activities and have thought it over carefully. C
    1   2   3   4   5

13. When solving problems, I would much rather analyze some data or statistics than meet with a group of people. T   1   2   3   4   5

14. When I am working on a group project and someone doesn't pull a full share of the load, I am more likely to complain to my friends rather than confront the slacker.* H   1   2   3   4   5

15. Talking about ideas or concepts can get me really enthused and excited. C   1   2   3   4   5

16. The type of management course for which this book is used is really a waste of time. T   1   2   3   4   5

17. I think it is better to be polite and not to hurt people's feelings.* H   1   2   3   4   5

18. Data or things interest me more than people. T
    1   2   3   4   5

Scoring Key

Add the total points for the following sections. Note that starred * items are reverse scored, as such:

1. I always am like this.
2. I often am like this.
3. I sometimes am like this.
4. I rarely am like this.
5. I never am like this.

1, 3, 6, 9, 12, 15 Conceptual skills total score _____

2, 5, 8, 10, 14, 17 Human skills total score _____

4, 7, 11, 13, 16, 18 Technical skills total score _____

The above skills are three abilities needed to be a good manager. Ideally, a manager should be strong (though not necessarily equal) in all three. Anyone noticeably weaker in any of the skills should take courses and read to build up that skill. For further background on the three skills, please refer to the model on p. 9.

*reverse scoring item

Manager's Workshop

The Worst Manager

1. By yourself, think of two managers you have had—the best and the worst. Write down a few sentences to describe each.

The best manager I ever had was . . .

The worst manager I ever had was . . .

2. Divide into groups of five to seven members. Share your experiences. Each group should choose a couple of examples to share with the whole group. Complete the table below as a group.

	Management principle followed or broken	Skills evident or missing	Lessons to be learned	Advice you would give managers
The best managers				
The worst managers				

1. What are the common problems managers have?

2. Prepare a list of "words of wisdom" you would give as a presentation to a group of managers. What are some basic principles they should use to be effective?

Management in Practice: Ethical Dilemma

The Supervisor

Karen Lowry, manager of a social service agency in a mid-sized city in Illinois, loved to see her employees learn and grow to their full potential. When a rare opening for a supervising clerk occurred, Karen quickly decided to give Charlotte Hines a shot at the job. Charlotte had been with the agency for 17 years and had shown herself to be a true leader. Charlotte worked hard at being a good supervisor, just as she had always worked hard at being a top-notch clerk. She paid attention to the human aspects of employee problems and introduced modern management techniques that strengthened the entire agency.

However, the Civil Service Board decided that a promotional exam should be given to find a permanent placement for the supervising clerk position. For the sake of fairness, the exam was an open competition—anyone, even a new employee, could sign up and take it. The board wanted the candidate with the highest score to get the job but allowed Karen, as manager of the agency, to have the final say.

Since she had accepted the provisional opening and proven herself on the job, Charlotte was upset that the entire clerical force was deemed qualified to take the test. When the results came back, she was devastated. Charlotte placed twelfth in the field of candidates, while one of her newly hired clerks placed first. The Civil Service Board, impressed by the new clerk's high score, is urging Karen to give her the permanent supervisory job. Karen wonders if it's fair to base her decision only on the test results.

What Do You Do?

1. Ignore the test. Charlotte has proven herself and deserves the job.
2. Give the job to the candidate with the highest score. You don't need to make enemies on the Civil Service Board, and, after all, it is an objective way to select a permanent placement.
3. Devise a more comprehensive set of selection criteria—including test results as well as supervisory experience, ability to motivate employees, and knowledge of agency procedures—that can be explained and justified to the board and to employees.

SOURCE: Based on Betty Harrigan, "Career Advice," *Working Woman*, July 1986, pp. 22–24.

Case for Critical Analysis

Electra-Quik

Barbara Russell, a manufacturing vice president, walked into the monthly companywide meeting with a light step and a hopefulness she hadn't felt in a long time. The company's new, dynamic CEO was going to announce a new era of empowerment at Electra-Quik, an 80-year-old publicly held company that had once been a leading manufacturer and retailer of electrical products and supplies. In recent years, the company experienced a host of problems: market share was declining in the face of increased foreign and domestic competition; new product ideas were few and far between; departments such as manufacturing and sales barely spoke to one another; morale was at an all-time low, and many employees were actively seeking other jobs. Everyone needed a dose of hope.

Martin Griffin, who had been hired to revive the failing company, briskly opened the meeting with a challenge: "As we face increasing competition, we need new ideas, new energy, new spirit to make this company great. And the source for this change is you—each one of you." He then went on to explain that under the new empowerment campaign, employees would be getting more information about how the company was run and would be able to work with their fellow employees in new and creative ways. Martin proclaimed a new era of trust and cooperation at Electra-Quik. Barbara felt the excitement stirring within her; but as she looked around the room, she saw many of the other employees, including her friend Harry, rolling their eyes. "Just another pile of corporate crap," Harry said later. "One minute they try downsizing, the next reengineering. Then they dabble in restructuring. Now Martin wants to push empowerment. Garbage like empowerment isn't a substitute for hard work and a little faith in the people who have been with this company for years. We made it great once, and we can do it again. Just get out of our way." Harry had been a manufacturing engineer with Electra-Quik for more than

20 years. Barbara knew he was extremely loyal to the company, but he—and a lot of others like him—were going to be an obstacle to the empowerment efforts.

Top management assigned selected managers to several problem-solving teams to come up with ideas for implementing the empowerment campaign. Barbara loved her assignment as team leader of the manufacturing team, working on ideas to improve how retail stores got the merchandise they needed when they needed it. The team thrived, and trust blossomed among the members. They even spent nights and weekends working to complete their report. They were proud of the ideas they had come up with, which they believed were innovative but easily achievable: permit a manager to follow a product from design through sales to customers; allow salespeople to refund up to $500 worth of merchandise on the spot; make information available to salespeople about future products; and swap sales and manufacturing personnel for short periods to let them get to know one another's jobs.

When the team presented their report to department heads, Martin Griffin was enthusiastic. But shortly into the meeting he had to excuse himself because of a late-breaking deal with a major hardware store chain. With Martin absent, the department heads rapidly formed a wall of resistance. The director of human resources complained that the ideas for personnel changes would destroy the carefully crafted job categories that had just been completed. The finance department argued that allowing salespeople to make $500 refunds would create a gold mine for unethical customers and salespeople. The legal department warned that providing information to salespeople about future products would invite industrial spying.

The team members were stunned. As Barbara mulled over the latest turn of events, she considered her options: keep her mouth shut; take a chance and confront Martin about her sincerity in making empowerment work; push slowly for reform and work for gradual support from the other teams; or look for another job and leave a company she really cared about. Barbara realized there would be no easy choices and no easy answers.

Questions

1. How might top management have done a better job changing Electra-Quik into a learning organization? What might they do now to get the empowerment process back on track?
2. Can you think of ways Barbara could have avoided the problems her team faced in the meeting with department heads?
3. If you were Barbara Russell, what would you do now? Why?

SOURCE: Based on Lawrence R. Rothstein, "The Empowerment Effort That Came Undone," *Harvard Business Review* (January-February 1995), 20–31.

The Environment

of Management

After nearly a century in the film-making business, Hollywood can call on all its accumulated experience, add in some modern market research techniques for good measure, but still cannot reliably predict whether a movie will break records, break even, or fail dismally. Stephen Spielberg, a director of such blockbuster hits as *Jaws*, *E.T.*, and *Jurassic Park*, observed that if you create something no one's ever seen before, "counting on 10 or 20 million people, individuals, to go into the theater to make or break that film—that's a gamble."[1] Even in relatively stable times, filmmakers need to know how to live with uncertainty.

But these are not relatively stable times in the film business. Back in the mid-1980s, about the time Spielberg was musing about the slim odds of drawing enough people to a cinema so a film breaks even, movie theaters were the major revenue source for feature films. That is no longer true. Recently, domestic income from videotape and digital video disk (DVD) sales and rentals runs more than two and a half times that of box office revenues. In addition, cable and pay-per-view television have emerged as important basic markets for Hollywood releases, increasing demand for films in the process. Then, beginning in the late 1970s with George Lucas's *Star Wars* movies, the sales of spin-off products—lots of little plastic toys, T-shirts, and video games, for example—became significant. If money is to be made on a film, it is often sales from all these non-theatrical sources that put a project into the black.

Some would argue that these recent changes in the industry will pale in comparison with a digital revolution they see waiting in the wings. Already filmmakers can assemble a fully digital cinema system from cameras, editing machines, and projectors that are becoming ever more sophisticated. Movies that exist as computer files rather than on film can be transmitted with increasing ease over the Internet, a fact that has resulted in the industry's beginning to be plagued by illegal downloads similar to those that have concerned the music business for several years. If at some point theaters convert to digital projection systems, transmitting movies over the Internet or by satellite could drastically alter the current, expensive distribution system, which ships film prints to individual theaters.

Most directors already use digital editing machines, and many have dazzled audiences with sophisticated, computer-generated special effects. But what impact will digital technology have on producing a feature film? That is a matter of debate. George Lucas, of *Star Wars* fame, is a leading proponent of digital cinema. In 1997, he predicted, "Digital technology is the same revolution as adding sound to pictures, and the same revolution as adding color to pictures. Nothing more and nothing less."[2] Others are not so sure Hollywood directors will abandon film, a technology that is familiar, has served the industry well for decades, and still produces a superior image. So the question remains: Will directors choose to change their ways? Will they shoot with digital cameras as well? And what will their decision mean for the industry as a whole?

CHAPTER 2

The Environment and Corporate Culture

LEARNING OBJECTIVES

After studying this chapter, you should be able to do the following:

1. **Describe the general and task environments and the dimensions of each.**

2. **Explain the strategies managers use to help organizations adapt to an uncertain or turbulent environment.**

3. **Define corporate culture and give organizational examples.**

4. **Explain organizational symbols, stories, heroes, slogans, and ceremonies and their relationship to corporate culture.**

5. **Describe how corporate culture relates to the environment.**

6. **Define a cultural leader and explain the tools a cultural leader uses to create a high-performance culture.**

Kathleen Wehner was content to be the helpmate of her husband, owner of New Jersey's airplane parts reseller Cirrus Aviation. She helped out at the office and cared for their four sons. It was natural because the world of aviation was a small one, an old boys' network used to handshakes and spoken-word contracts. Then her husband died of brain cancer and Kathleen assumed her sons would take over the company. But their lives were on different courses and they were not interested. Still almost paralyzed from grief and knowing nothing about airplanes, Kathleen Wehner became president of Cirrus Aviation. She forced herself out into the world, networked, asked a lot of questions, and read technical books.

Just when she had learned the business enough to keep it afloat, terrorists struck the World Trade Center. Her business nosedived; no one was flying, so the spare parts in her warehouse started getting rusty. Then she realized the company only had two weeks of operating capital.[3]

If you were Kathleen Wehner, what would you do? Would you sell the company, realizing the environment had changed so much that there was not much hope? Or would you salvage the company? How?

In aviation and high-tech industries, environmental conditions are volatile. You read in Chapter 1 about the problems Dell Computers faced because managers missed cues from the environment. Cirrus Aviation has been struggling to keep up with changes in the economy and the industry. Even in seemingly low-tech industries, shifts in the environment can wreak havoc on an organization. Dixon Ticonderoga Company makes pencils and once had a large share of the U.S. market. Today, though, more than 50 percent of the pencils sold in the United States come from overseas, compared to only 16 percent a decade ago. As another example, the Gerber Products Company has faced challenges from Greenpeace and other activist groups over the use of genetically altered grains.[4]

Government actions and red tape can affect an organization's environment and create problems. Scandals in the mutual fund industry have prompted the U.S. Securities and Exchange Commission (SEC) to propose a ban on special incentive payments to brokerage firms. The beef and dairy industries in the United States were hurt by increased rules and restrictions following the discovery of mad cow disease in Washington state. However, the organic and natural beef industry experienced an upturn as consumers grew more cautious about where their meat comes from and how it is produced. Consider thousands of public schools that use a common land snail called *Helix aspera* as a major unit in their science curricula. The U.S. Department of Agriculture's (USDA) unexpected ban on the interstate transport of the snails threw school science programs into disarray around the nation.[5]

The environment surprises many managers and leaves them unable to adapt their companies to new competition, shifting consumer interests, or new technologies. The study of management traditionally has focused on factors within the organization—a closed systems view—such as leading, motivating, and controlling employees. The classical, behavioral, and management science schools described in Chapter 1 focused on internal aspects of organizations over which managers have direct control. These views are accurate but incomplete. Globalization and worldwide societal turbulence affect companies in new ways. Even for those companies that operate solely on the domestic stage, events with the greatest impact typically originate in the external environment. To be effective, managers must monitor and respond to the environment, which is an open systems view.

This chapter explores components of the external environment and how they affect the organization. We will examine the corporate cultures, which is a major part of the organization's internal environment. Corporate culture is shaped by the external environment and is an important part of the context within which managers do their jobs.

The External Environment

The tremendous and far-reaching changes occurring in today's world can be understood by defining and examining components of the external environment. The external **organizational environment** includes all elements existing outside the boundary of the organization that have the potential to affect the organization.[6] The environment includes competitors, resources, technology, and economic conditions that influence the organization. It does not include those events so far removed from the organization that their impact is not perceived.

The organization's external environment can be further conceptualized as having two layers: general and task environments, as illustrated in Exhibit 2.1.[7]

The **general environment** is the outer layer that is widely dispersed and affects organizations indirectly. It includes social, demographic, and economic factors that influence all organizations about equally. Increases in the inflation rate or the percentage of dual-career couples in the workforce are part of the organization's general

---

Take **ACTION**

As a manager, read and follow news to keep up on coming changes.

---

organizational environment

All elements existing outside the organization's boundaries that have the potential to affect the organization.

---

general environment

The layer of the external environment that affects the organization indirectly.

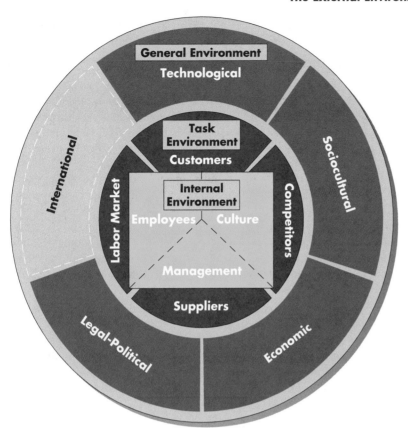

environment. These events do not directly change daily operations, but they do affect all organizations eventually. One impact of the environment is that as parents become more educated and affluent, they have higher demands for educational toys, a situation one company is exploiting, as shown in the example below.

LeapFrog

Talk about asking for trouble. The U.S. toy industry is dominated by giants: Mattel, Hasbro, Fisher Price, Little Tikes, etc. With so many failed start-ups in recent years (anyone remember Purple Moon?), it would be foolish for a new company to introduce a toy that would compete with the big guys, would it not? Not only that, educational toys do not usually make money. Luckily, Mike Wood and Jim Marggraff at LeapFrog did not know that. When high-paid law partner Wood got frustrated looking for materials to teach his three-year-old to read, he started building an electronic toy that would help children make sounds that corresponded to letters of the alphabet. Clumsy prototype in hand, he got an order for 40,000 units from Toys "R" Us. That was enough for him to bid the law firm goodbye, raise $800,000 from friends and family, and start his own company, LeapFrog. After a series of follow-up toys, Wood took $40 million for a majority stake in his company to Knowledge Universe, owned by Michael Milken (former junk bond king of the 1980s) and others.

That is when Jim Marggraff entered the picture. He had left a lucrative job at Cisco Systems to launch his innovative globe that had an interactive pen-like pointer. Marggraff's pointer together with Wood's unit ultimately became LeapPad, a paper book placed on top of a pad that looks like an Etch-a-Sketch. When a child touches the pen to the paper, the book "talks" that word.

Still, they had all those big toy companies to worry about. Few companies lived to tell about it. In a market dominated by GameBoy, Pokemon and Playstation, the odds were against LeapFrog. Still, its $49.99 LeapPad became the bestselling plaything in 2000, outdoing even the red-hot Razor scooter. Good things kept happening. Revenues have been over $400 million. With Wal-Mart and Toys "R" Us the biggest customers, LeapFrog wants to increase sales to schools.

This year, Leapfrog has introduced a talking-pen computer that has character recognition software. The $99 Fly allows teens and tweens to draw a piano and then play it, or translate words from English to Spanish. Its design includes elements of a calculator, notepad, and alarm clock. With this new product, LeapFrog is growing with its customers, allowing them to keep buying their products as they get older. Now they can Fly.[8]

task environment

The layer of the external environment that directly influences the organization's operations and performance.

The **task environment** is closer to the organization and includes the sectors that conduct daily transactions with the organization and directly influence its basic operations and performance. It is generally considered to include competitors, suppliers, and customers.

The organization has an **internal environment**, which includes the elements within the organization's boundaries. The internal environment is composed of current employees, management, and corporate culture, which defines employee behavior in the internal environment and how well the organization will adapt to the external environment.

internal environment

The environment that includes the elements within the organization's boundaries.

Exhibit 2.1 illustrates the relationship among the general, task, and internal environments. As an open system, the organization draws resources from the external environment and releases goods and services back to it. We will discuss the two layers of the external environment in more detail. Then, we will discuss corporate culture, the key element in the internal environment. Other aspects of the internal environment, such as structure and technology, will be covered in Parts Four and Five of this book.

General Environment

The general environment represents the outer layer of the environment. These dimensions influence the organization over time but often are not involved in daily transactions with it. The general environment includes international, technological, sociocultural, economic, and legal–political dimensions.

international dimension

The portion of the external environment that represents events originating in foreign countries as well as opportunities for U.S. companies in other countries.

International Dimension.   The **international dimension** of the external environment represents events originating in foreign countries as well as opportunities for U.S. companies in other countries. In Exhibit 2.1, the international dimension represents a context that influences all other aspects of the external environment. The international environment provides new competitors, customers, and suppliers and shapes social, technological, and economic trends.

Today, every company has to compete on a global basis. High-quality, low-priced automobiles from Japan and Korea have permanently changed the American automobile industry. Toyota recently overtook Ford to become the world's second largest automaker, and managers plan to take the company to number one by 2010.[9] Foreign companies such as Toyota, Sony, and Nokia have made huge jumps in recent years on *Fortune* magazine's list of the World's Most Admired Companies. Nokia is the world's top maker of cell phones, and Korea's Samsung Corp. is rapidly closing in on U.S.-based Motorola for the number two spot.[10] For many U.S. companies, such as Starbucks and Wal-Mart, domestic markets have become saturated and their only potential for growth lies overseas. Even e-commerce organizations are making international expansion a priority. The United States' share of worldwide e-commerce is falling as foreign companies set up their own e-commerce ventures.[11] When operating globally, managers have to consider legal, political, sociocultural, and economic factors in their home countries and in other countries. For example, a drop in the U.S. dollar's foreign exchange rate lowers the price of U.S. products overseas, increasing export competitiveness. Many companies have had to cut prices to remain competitive in the new global economy.

The global environment represents a changing and uneven playing field compared with the domestic environment. Managers who are used to thinking only about the domestic environment must learn new rules to cope with goods, services, and ideas circulating around the globe. Chapter 3 describes how today's businesses are operating in an increasingly borderless world and examines how managing in a global environment differs from the management of domestic operations. Perhaps the hardest lesson for U.S. managers to learn is that they do not always know best. U.S. decision makers know little about issues and competition in foreign countries. In addition, one recent study found that only 28 percent of surveyed U.S. executives think multicultural experience is important.[12] U.S. arrogance is a shortcut to failure. To counter this, Pall Corporation keeps a team of Ph.D.s traveling around the world gathering current information on markets and issues.[13]

Technological Dimension. The **technological dimension** includes scientific and technological advancements in a specific industry and in society at large. In recent years, this dimension has created massive changes for organizations in all industries. Twenty years ago, many organizations did not use desktop computers. Today, computer networks, Internet access, videoconferencing capabilities, cell phones, personal digital assistants (PDAs), fax machines, and laptops are practically taken for granted as the minimum tools for doing business. Technological advancements that make the Internet accessible to nearly everyone have changed the nature of competition and of organizations' relationships to customers. Many companies are adopting sophisticated e-business methods that use private networks or the Internet to handle practically all their operations. Communications and computing devices are shrinking and becoming more powerful and affordable. One estimate is that 70 percent of the adult U.S. population owned a mobile phone in late 2003, and the use of advanced features such as photo messaging is growing.[14] Exploiting the growing use of cell phones is shown on the following page and in the Digital, Inc. box.

Take **ACTION**

How many languages do you speak? How many friends do you have from other countries? How prepared would you be to work overseas if your job required it?

technological dimension

The dimension of the general environment that includes scientific and technological advancements in the industry and society at large.

Take **ACTION**

Your generation is more technologically savvy, and greater technological innovations will come. Make it your business to stay on top of the new technologies no matter what age you are.

Photo courtesy of PPL Corporation

CONCEPT CONNECTION

PPL Corporation controls about 12,000 megawatts of generating capacity in the United States and sells energy in key U.S. markets. The company utilizes advances in the **technological dimension** of its environment to understand the complexities of today's ever-changing energy market. In the photo, members of PPL's risk management office, which reports directly to CEO William Hecht, analyze data to improve decision making, while controlling risk. Such high-tech analysis is essential to keeping the company competitive in the electricity market.

DIGITAL, INC.

Ringtones

Remember the old days when you used to buy $13 CDs in stores and play them on stereo sets? Now you can hear songs on video game soundtracks, on iPods and your cell phone. Rapper 50 Cent squeezed in studio time to record a voice tone and voice ring back, which cell phone users paid $2 to download onto their phones. Then the single "Candy Shop" was adapted for a ringtone. Music moguls know that having breakout artists adapt their songs to cell phones is good not only for exposure, but it also supplies an important revenue source. They see cell phones as an important as MP3 players, CDs, iPods, and music videos. In fact, many music corporations see so much possibility they are creating mobile-business divisions. "With 180 million handsets in the U.S., how could we not be bullish on the mobile market, especially now that downloads to phones are possible?" says Sony BMG's Thomas Hesse, president of its global digital business.

Even with all their successes, music managers still face an uphill battle with illegal song swapping online, which has caused a decrease in album sales in recent years. To get an idea of the problem, consider that 750 million songs are illegally downloaded each month, while the successful and legal iTunes has downloaded only 300 million songs in the two years it has been operating.

Though digital music now makes up about 2 percent of global sales, executives expect it to reach 25 percent, including subscriptions and ringtone sales. As the quality of ringtones keeps increasing, so will the demand. Some teens even swap out ringtones three to four times a week, which is good news for the industry. "Ringtones are all about personalization. They are self-expression. "You buy a ringtone for a different reason than you buy a download of a song," says Rio Caraeff, vice president of Universal Mobile Music. What about using Joss Stone's *You Had Me* for someone who recently got dumped? Or giving Sinatra's *New York, New York* to a Manhattan cousin?

The music business is where the movie business was 20 years ago. Movie attendance was down and the business had to find other revenue streams, releasing movies to VHS movies, premium cable and later DVDs. In both industries, new technologies allow companies to wring more profits out of old catalogs. In music, profit margins for CDs are around 12 percent, while digital music earns about 18 percent.

If there was any doubt about the importance of ringtones to the music industry, the industry-standard, *Billboard*, recently added a regular weekly chart: the 20 Hot Ringtones worldwide. Now there's something to chirp about.

SOURCE: Tom Lowry, Ringtones: Music to Music Moguls' Ears, *Business Week*, April 25, 2005, p. 68.

InPhonic

David Steinberg left college with a degree in economics, average grades, and a path to fill his father's desired career path: going to law school. A dyslexic who changes words from "anecdotally" to "anitdotally," he got a job clipping newspaper items and came across an ad to sell life insurance door-to-door. Steinberg told his father about the job, who flipped at the thought of his son putting off law school for a year, So, Steinberg beseeched his stepfather, Irv Siegel, who realized the importance of the young man learning to sell. During his 18 months hawking insurance, he was promoted to manager and made a ton of money. Just when he thought he had found his niche in life, he found a bright yellow coupon for a free cell phone and immediately drove to the store, asking how they could possibly make any money. The saleswoman told him she got paid $300 for each phone activation and the phones cost her $150. Steinberg immediately saw the business opportunity. "Wow, you make $150 each time you give away one of these for free?" He turned to his friend as they walked out and said, "I'm in the wrong business."

His step-father would not loan him money to start a business, believing he needed to work with an experienced professional who would mentor him in the business. But Steinberg was too impatient and started the business anyway. Without any money for a store and unable to get a carrier to sign him as a dealer, he began in his basement, subcontracting with a another dealer with whom the step-father vouched for his creditworthiness.

With five friends from his insurance company, he went door-to-door and soon was selling upward of $300,000 a month, more than the dealer they represented. Siegel co-signed a loan so that Steinberg could open a store front for Cellular One. He was only 23 years old. Six years later, he had built it up to 58 locations. Growing so fast, they needed some high-powered management. Enter old friend Brad LaTour, who wanted to start his own business. At lunch, Steinberg convinced him otherwise with these words: "If you take this job, I will make you a success." He wrote those words down on a napkin and signed it.

The business is humming along, but it takes a lot of work. Steinberg's wife says she would be happier if he worked a normal 40-hour week and made only a "nice income."[15]

Other technological advances will affect organizations and managers. The decoding of the human genome could lead to revolutionary medical advances. Cloning technology and stem cell research are raising scientific and ethical concerns. High-tech composites, embedded with sensors that enable them to think for themselves, are being used to earthquake-proof bridges and highways as well as build better airplanes and railcars.[16] Advances in nanotechnology, which refers to seeing and manipulating matter at the molecular and atomic level, will enable scientists to create amazing electronic, structural, biological, and medicinal materials.[17] Examples in use include "smart gels" that mold to human needs on cue, self-repairing optical coatings, and cleansers that repair a surface at the molecular level while cleaning it. Technological advances in television have brought satellite and digital TV, flatscreens, and TiVo. Likewise, changes have come in ancillary companies, such as Nielsen Media Research, desribed below.

Nielsen Media Research

As long as there were only a few main TV channels, Nielsen Media Research's business model worked. It measured a sample of 5,000 national household to determine TV ratings. Its sample can fairly accurately determine how many millions of sets are watching, say, "Friends" or "NYPD Blue." But being accurate on how many households are tuned in to "Toad Patrol" on the Toon channel is more of a challenge. Nielsen cannot always provide meaningful numbers on the myriad of small cable channels since not enough of those families are in Nielsen's sample.

To keep up with the ever-fragmenting digital age, Nielsen plans to increase the number of households to 10,000. Families are recruited by "membership representatives" who bear candy and fruit as they approach people to be part of the sample. Payment rates go from $50–$300 per year, depending on demographics. Black and Hispanics usually receive more as they are harder to recruit.

Because so many TVs are going digital, Nielsen has to pay $70 million to change its technology. And it is joining forces with Arbitron to measure the so-called "away from home" viewers, which include college dorm students, treadmill walkers at gyms, hotel travelers, etc. In addition, it has partnered with the first video game advertising network, Massive Incorporated, to provide accountability and measurement, which will be used for ad rates.

Nielsen has a history of not pleasing everyone. No perfect system has been developed that measures everything accurately, but Nielsen is trying, spending big bucks, rather than sitting back and watching its profits grow. David Poltrack of CBS says, "They have a plan for measuring the future and are keeping on top of things." Now if it could make sure better shows are on TV, that would be perfect.[18]

Sociocultural Dimension.   The **sociocultural dimension** of the general environment represents the demographic characteristics as well as the norms, customs, and values of the general population. Important sociocultural characteristics are geographical distribution, population density, age, and education levels. Today's demographic profiles are the foundation

© Meredith Heuer

CONCEPT CONNECTION

American consumers' growing taste for international foods reflects a change in the **sociocultural dimension** *of the environment. Interest in Italian cuisine, for example, has been growing rapidly. Gourmet pasta maker Monterey Pasta is one of the fastest-growing companies in the United States and in 2004 announced new low-carb products and its seventh consecutive profitable year.*

sociocultural dimension

The dimension of the general environment representing the demographic characteristics, norms, customs, and values of the population within which the organization operates.

of tomorrow's workforce and consumers. Forecasters see increased globalization of consumer markets and the labor supply, with increasing diversity within organizations and consumer markets.[19] Consider the following key demographic trends in the United States:

1. The United States is experiencing the largest influx of immigrants in more than a century. By 2050, non-Hispanic whites will make up only about half of the population, down from 74 percent in 1995 and 69 percent in 2004. Hispanics are expected to make up about a quarter of the U.S. population.[20]

2. The huge post-World War II baby boom generation is aging and losing its interest in high-cost goods. Meanwhile, their sons and daughters, sometimes called Generation Y, rival the baby boomers in size and will soon rival them in buying power.

3. The fastest-growing type of living arrangement is single-father households, which rose 62 percent in 10 years, even though two-parent and single-mother households are more numerous.[21]

4. In an unprecedented demographic shift, married couple households have slipped from 80 percent in the 1950s to just over 50 percent in 2003. Couples with kids total 25 percent, with the number projected to drop to 20 percent by 2010. By that year, it is expected that 30 percent of homes will be inhabited by someone who lives alone.[22]

The sociocultural dimension includes societal norms and values. Currently, the low-carb craze has replaced the low-fat concerns of previous years. From pre-teens to grandparents, people are piling on the bacon and eggs, pork chops and cheese sticks and avoiding carbohydrates like the plague. A market research firm in Chicago estimated that more than 10 million people are following a low-carb regimen. The trend got hot fast and some analysts predict it will cool as quickly, but restaurants are altering their menus and supermarkets are devoting shelf space to a growing array of low-carb products.[23] Even the Girl Scouts are affected. In the 2004 Girl Scout cookie season, sales were down an average of 10 percent nationwide. More on this trend is described in the Focus on Skills box.

Other sociocultural trends affect organizations. A groundswell of interest in spirituality and personal development in the United States since the mid-1990s has led to a proliferation of books and other materials related to religion and spiritual growth.[24] Handgun manufacturers have been tugged back and forth as public acceptance and support of guns in the home fell in the wake of tragic school shootings and then surged following the September 11, 2001, terrorist attacks.

economic dimension

The dimension of the general environment representing the overall economic health of the country or region in which the organization operates.

Economic Dimension.   The **economic dimension** represents the general economic health of the country or region in which the organization operates. Consumer purchasing power, the unemployment rate, and interest rates are part of an organization's economic environment. Because organizations are operating in a global environment, the economic dimension has become exceedingly complex and creates enormous uncertainty for managers. The economies of countries have become more closely tied together. For example, an early 2000s economic recession and the decline of consumer confidence in the United States have affected economies and organizations around the world. Similarly, economic problems in Asia and Europe have had a tremendous impact on U.S. companies and the stock market.

Low-Carb Craze

Thirty years ago, Dr. Atkins published his first low-carb diet book and was considered a quack by many. Now his low-carb lifestyle has taken over American thinking on eating and changed business for the food and restaurant industry. Because more than 10 million people are following some form of low-carb diet (including the Zone or South Beach diets), nearly every part of the food industry has introduced low-carb products.

Should companies form a partnership with Atkins or South Beach and gain instant recognition, or go it alone, have more options and fewer licensing fees. T.G.I. Friday's has nine "Atkin's-approved" items on its menu. The Atkins company manufactures 129 grocery items and it is looking for more restaurants to work with. Other chains—PF Chang's, Ruby Tuesday, and KFC—are bringing out their own versions of low-carb. Panera Bread is developing several low-carb breads. Hardees and Carl's Junior have come out with lettuce-wrap, bunless hamburgers. CEO of both chains, Andy Puzder, explains the strategy: "When you partner with these guys, it becomes a very complex and expensive process. We'd rather keep prices down and keep control of our product."

How much money to invest into this new craze? Is it sustainable? Those are real concerns of a company. One fourth of all new products are low-carb-based, but will this be another phase or will it stick? Some chains report that 19 percent of customers are on low-carb regimes. T.G.I. Friday's spokesperson says, "If this is a fad, it's the biggest fad I've ever seen."

SOURCES: Julie Dunn, "Restaurant Chains, Too, Watch Their Carbs," *The New York Times* (Jan. 4. 2004): 19; Matthew Boyle, "Atkins World," *Fortune* (Jan. 12, 2004): 94–104.

One significant recent trend in the economic environment is the frequency of mergers and acquisitions. Citibank and Travelers merged to form Citigroup, IBM purchased PricewaterhouseCoopers Consulting, and Cingular is acquiring AT&T Wireless. In the toy industry, the three largest toy makers—Hasbro, Mattel, and Tyco—gobbled up at least a dozen smaller competitors within a few years. At the same time, however, there is a tremendous vitality in the small-business sector.

Legal-Political Dimension.   The **legal-political dimension** includes government regulations at the local, state, and federal levels, as well as political activities designed to influence company behavior. The U.S. political system encourages capitalism, and the government tries not to overregulate business. However, government laws do specify rules of the game. The federal government influences organizations through the Occupational Safety and Health Administration (OSHA), U.S. Environmental Protection Agency (EPA), fair trade practices, libel statutes allowing lawsuits against business, consumer protection legislation, product safety requirements, import and export restrictions, and information and labeling requirements. The Federal Communications Commission (FCC), which regulates broadcast television to limit potentially offensive material, has been striving to extend its regulatory authority to the cable networks. Incidents such as Bono's use of a four-letter word at the 2003 Golden Globe Awards and the outrage over Janet Jackson's "wardrobe malfunction" at the 2004 Super Bowl have triggered increased attention to what is shown on television.[25] Many organizations have to contend with government and legal issues in other countries. For example, the European Union (EU) has recently adopted new environmental and consumer protection rules that are costing American companies hundreds of millions of dollars a year. Companies like Hewlett-Packard (HP), Ford Motor Company, and General Electric (GE) have to pick up the bill for recycling the products they sell in the EU.[26]

Managers must recognize various **pressure groups** that work within the legal-political framework to influence companies to behave in socially responsible ways. Automobile manufacturers, toy makers, and airlines have been targeted by Ralph Nader's Center for Responsive Law. Tobacco companies are feeling the far-reaching power of antismoking groups. Middle-aged activists who once protested the Vietnam War have gone to battle to keep Wal-Mart from "destroying the quality of small-town

---

Take ACTION

A steady stream of immigrants, often people of color, will keep coming into North America, making it more diverse. Try to learn more about them.

legal-political dimension

The dimension of the general environment that includes federal, state, and local government regulations and political activities designed to influence company behavior.

pressure group

An interest group that works within the legal-political framework to influence companies to behave in socially responsible ways.

life." Some groups have attacked the giant retailer on environmental issues, which likely will be one of the strongest pressure points in coming years.[27] Two of the hottest current issues for pressure groups that are also related to environmental concerns are biotechnology and world trade. Environmental and human rights protesters have disrupted World Trade Organization (WTO), World Bank, and the International Monetary Fund (IMF) meetings to protest a system of worldwide integration that has food, goods, people, and capital moving freely across borders. This current international issue will be discussed in more detail in Chapter 3.

In short, the world we live in is changing as you read this. To get a sense of how great those changes have been, complete the instrument below. What do these themes say about the world you are moving into?

Take a moment to complete the exercise below to help you understand changes occurring in your environment.

Changing Environment Assessment
Find a family member, friend, or other associate, who is at least 20 years older than you are. Fill out the left column in table below, interviewing this person to find out what the world was like when he or she was your age. Later, fill out the right-hand column to indicate your current world.

	Name of person interviewed:	You
Discuss town where you lived: size, appearance, population, types of jobs for people, educational opportunities, etc.		
How did you get around, types of transportation? Did you have a car? What kind?		
What kind of house did you live in?		
How did you communicate with people: family, friends, business colleagues?		
What kind of work did you do?		
Where did you travel to?		
What did you expect out of life?		
What stressors did you have? Things that made you feel under a lot of stress?		
What was a dream you were never able to realize? Why?		

Task Environment
As described earlier, the task environment includes those sectors that have a direct working relationship with the organization, among them customers, competitors, suppliers, and the labor market.

Customers. Those people and organizations in the environment who acquire goods or services from the organization are **customers**. As recipients of the organization's output, customers are important because they determine the organization's success. Patients are the customers of hospitals, students the customers of schools, and travelers the customers of airlines. Toy companies have to stay in close touch with the whims of young customers and their parents. Mattel is hoping that by snapping up rights to make toys tied to Yu-Gi-Oh!, a popular Japanese monster-themed show, and SpongeBob SquarePants, it can create products that will fly off the shelves rather than sit in warehouses. Mattel is also bringing out a toy that can pick up digital signals from the new Warner Bros. *Batman* cartoon shows running on cable networks, meaning a toy Batmobile will zoom across the floor at the exact moment the cartoon car shows up on the television screen.[28]

A big concern for managers today is that the Internet has given increased power to customers who can directly impact the organization. For example, gripe sites such as *http://walmartsucks.org*, where customers and sales associates cyber-vent about the nation's largest retailer, and *http://untied.com*, where United Airlines employees and disgruntled fliers rail against the air carrier, can quickly damage a company's reputation and sales. "In this new information environment," says Kyle Shannon, CEO of e-commerce consultancy Agency.com, "you've got to assume everyone knows everything."[29]

Competitors. Other organizations in the same industry or type of business that provide goods or services to the same set of customers are referred to as **competitors**. Each industry is characterized by specific competitive issues. The recording industry differs from the steel industry and the pharmaceutical industry.

Competitive wars are being waged worldwide in all industries. Coca-Cola and PepsiCo continue to battle it out for the soft-drink market. United Parcel Service (UPS) and Federal Express (FedEx) are fighting the overnight delivery wars. Home Depot and Lowe's are brawling in the retail home improvement market, trying to out-do one another in terms of price, service, and selection.[30] The example below describes how retailer Target has achieved a competitive edge with strategic use of the Internet. In the travel and tourism industry, Internet companies like Expedia.com and Hotels.com have hurt the hotel chains. These chains are fighting back by undercutting the brokers' prices on the hotels' own Web sites. In addition, five of the largest chains have banded together to create Travelweb.com, which is aimed directly at the online brokers.[31]

customers

People and organizations in the environment who acquire goods or services from the organization.

Take **ACTION**

Have you ever been flamed? Has someone passed along a secret e-mail of yours to someone else or to 100 other people? Imagine the power thousands of angry consumers have toward one company.

competitors

Other organizations in the same industry or business that provide goods or services to the same set of customers.

Target

Target has fewer than half the number of retail stores as Wal-Mart, but on the Internet, the smaller retailer gets almost as much business as the giant. Managers at Target have succeeded online better than those of any other mass retailer.

Target.com sells items that are too big to stock in retail stores, such as Little Tikes kiddie furniture. In addition, Target test-markets new products on the Web before committing to shelf space for them in the stores. One example is the $200 Graco jogging stroller, which debuted on Target.com in the spring of 2002. When it rapidly became the best-selling stroller online, Target managers added it to the product lineup for bricks-and-mortar stores.

The biggest success for Target.com, however, has been the "Web as gift-shop" approach. The site has sold thousands of "Student Survival Kits," such as the Movie Night package that contains a bucket of popcorn, candy, soda, and a blank VCR tape and has sold as many "Cold Comfort" get-well boxes containing medicine along with a cuddly teddy bear. The site's bridal and baby registries are hot destinations, and these areas account for about 22 percent of the site's total sales.

Target.com is helping to get more customers into the retail stores. One technique is to use the Target Visa smart card, which contains a microchip, as a repository of customer information, helping Target keep in closer touch with customer needs. Customers can download personalized coupons from the Web site onto their smart cards. But they can only can use the coupons at their nearest Target store.[32]

Suppliers.   The raw materials the organization uses to produce its output are provided by **suppliers.** A steel mill requires iron ore, machines, and financial resources. A small, private university may utilize hundreds of suppliers for paper, pencils, cafeteria food, computers, trucks, fuel, electricity, and textbooks. Companies from toolmakers to construction firms and auto manufacturers were hurt recently by an unanticipated jump in the price of steel. As they were starting to see an upturn in their business, the cost of raw materials from suppliers jumped 30 percent in a two-month period.[33] Many companies are using fewer suppliers and building good relationships with them so they will receive high-quality parts at lower prices. The relationship between manufacturers and suppliers has traditionally been an adversarial one, but many companies are finding cooperation is the key to saving money, maintaining quality, and speeding products to market.

Labor Market.   The **labor market** represents people in the environment who can be hired to work for the organization. Every organization needs a supply of trained, qualified personnel. Unions, employee associations, and the availability of certain classes of employees can influence the organization's labor market. Labor market forces affecting organizations now include (1) the growing need for computer-literate information technology (IT) workers; (2) the necessity for continuous investment in human resources through recruitment, education, and training to meet the competitive demands of the borderless world; and (3) the effects of international trading blocs, automation, outsourcing, and shifting facility location upon labor dislocations, creating unused labor pools in some areas and labor shortages in others.

Changes in these various sectors of the environment can create tremendous challenges, especially for organizations operating in complex, rapidly changing industries. Nortel Networks, a Canadian company with multiple U.S. offices, is an example of an organization operating in a complex environment.

The external environment for Nortel Networks (formerly Northern Telecom) is illustrated in Exhibit 2.2.

The Canadian-based company began in 1895 as a manufacturer of telephones and has reinvented itself many times to keep up with changes in the environment. Since the late 1990s, the company has been undergoing another re-invention, transforming itself into a major player in wireless technology and equipment for connecting businesses and individuals to the Internet. When John Roth took over as CEO in 1997, the company was about to be run over by rivals, such as Cisco Systems, focused on Internet gear. Roth knew he needed to do something bold to respond to changes in the technological environment. A name change to Nortel Networks symbolized and reinforced the company's new goal of providing unified network solutions to customers worldwide.

One response to the competitive environment was to spend billions to acquire data and voice networking companies, including Bay Networks (which makes Internet and data equipment), Cambrian Systems (a hot maker of optical technology), Periphonics (maker of voice-response systems), and Clarify (customer management software). These companies brought Nortel top-notch technology to help the company, as Roth put it, "move at Net speed." Nortel began snatching customers away from rivals Cisco and Lucent Technologies. In addition, even during rough economic times, Nortel kept spending nearly 20 percent of its revenues on research and development to keep pace with changing technology.

Internationally, Nortel has made impressive inroads in Taiwan, China, Brazil, Mexico, Colombia, Japan, and Sweden, among other countries. It has won customers by recognizing the continuing need for traditional equipment and offering hybrid gear that combines old telephone technology with new Internet features, allowing companies to transition from the old to the new. Bold new technologies for Nortel include optical systems that move voice and data at the speed of light and third-generation wireless networks (3G), which zap data and video from phone to phone. Nortel is considered a leader in wireless gear and recently won contracts from Verizon

---

suppliers

People and organizations who provide the raw materials the organization uses to produce its output.

labor market

The people available for hire by the organization.

EXHIBIT 2.2

The External Environment of Nortel Networks

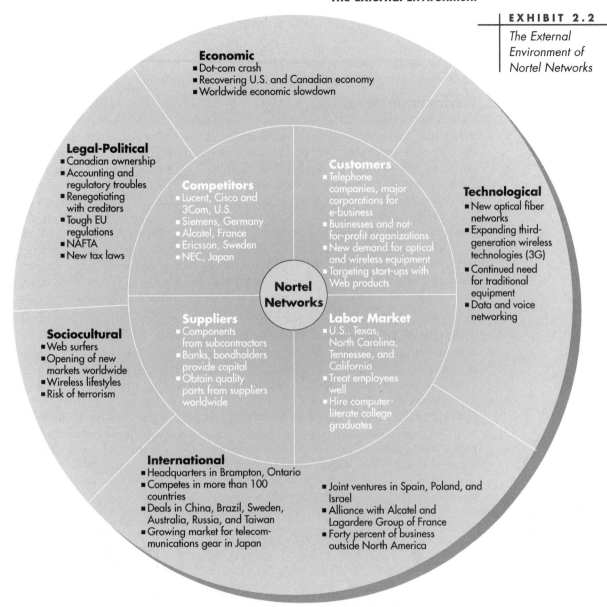

SOURCES: W. C. Symonds, J. B. Levine, N. Gross, and P. Coy, "High-Tech Star: Northern Telecom Is Challenging Even AT&T," *BusinessWeek*, July 27, 1992, 54–58; I. Austen, "Hooked on the Net," *Canadian Business*, June 26–July 10, 1998, 95–103; J. Weber with A. Reinhardt and P. Burrows, "Racing Ahead at Nortel," *BusinessWeek*, November 8, 1999, 93–99; "Nortel's Waffling Continues: First Job Cuts, Then Product Lines, and Now the CEO," *Telephony*, May 21, 2001, 12; and M. Heinzl, "Nortel's Profits of 499 Million Exceeds Forecast," *The Wall Street Journal*, January 30, 2004, B4.

Communications and Orange SA, a unit of France Telecom, to supply equipment that sends phone calls as packets of digital data like that used over the Internet.

Companies moving in a Net speed environment risk a hard landing, and during the economic slump of the early 2000s, Nortel's business was devastated. The company cut two thirds of its workforce and closed dozens of plants and offices. In late 2002, Nortel's stock was trading for less than a dollar. Two years later, though, positive changes in the telecom industry and the economic environment had Nortel back on an uphill swing. The stock rebounded with news of the Verizon deal and current CEO Frank Dunn's announcement of a fourth-quarter 2003 profit of $499 million. Nortel was once again recognized as an industry leader.[34]

The Organization–Environment Relationship

Why do organizations care so much about factors in the external environment? The reason is that the environment creates uncertainty for organization managers, and they must respond by designing the organization to adapt to the environment.

Environmental Uncertainty

Organizations must manage environmental uncertainty to be effective. *Uncertainty* means that managers do not have sufficient information about environmental factors to understand and predict environmental needs and changes.[35] As indicated in Exhibit 2.3, environmental characteristics that influence uncertainty are the number of factors that affect the organization and the extent to which those factors change. A large multinational, like Nortel Networks, has thousands of factors in the external environment creating uncertainty for managers. When external factors change rapidly, the organization experiences high uncertainty. Examples are telecommunications and aerospace firms, computer and electronics companies, and e-commerce organizations that sell products and services over the Internet. Companies have to make an effort to adapt to the rapid changes in the environment. When an organization deals with a few external factors and these factors are relatively stable, such as for soft drink bottlers or food processors, managers experience low uncertainty and can devote less attention to external issues.

Adapting to the Environment

If an organization faces increased uncertainty with respect to competition, customers, suppliers, or government regulation, managers can use several strategies to adapt to these changes, including boundary-spanning roles, interorganizational partnerships, and mergers or joint ventures.

People in departments such as marketing and purchasing span the boundary to work with customers and suppliers, face-to-face and through market research. Some organizations are staying in touch with customers through the Internet, such as by monitoring gripe sites, communicating with customers on company Web sites, and contracting with market research firms such as Look-Look that use the Web to monitor rapidly changing marketplace trends.[36]

EXHIBIT 2.3

The External Environment and Uncertainty

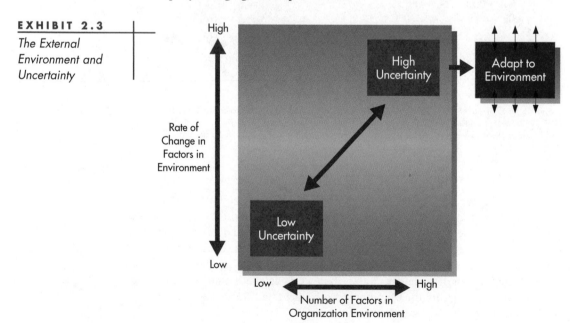

A growing area in boundary spanning is competitive intelligence (CI), which refers to activities to get as much information as possible about one's rivals. Managers need good information about their competitors, customers, and other elements of the environment to make good decisions. In today's turbulent environment, the most successful companies involve everyone in boundary-spanning activities. People at the grass-roots level, for instance, are often able to see and interpret significant changes sooner than managers who are more removed from the daily work.[37] However, top executives need to stay in tune with the environment. Tom Stemberg, CEO of Staples, visits a competitor's store once a week and shares what he learns with others on the management team.[38]

Managers have shifted from an adversarial orientation to a partnership orientation, as summarized in Exhibit 2.4. The new paradigm is based on trust and the ability of partners to work out equitable solutions to conflicts so everyone profits from the relationship. Managers work to reduce costs and add value to both sides rather than getting all the benefits for their own company. The new model is characterized by a high level of information sharing, including e-business linkages for automatic ordering, payments, and other transactions. In addition, much person-to-person interaction provides corrective feedback and solve problems. People from other companies may be onsite or participate in virtual teams to enable close coordination. Partners are frequently involved in one another's product design and production, and they are committed for the long term. Business partners commonly help one another, even outside of what is specified in the contract.[39] The Best Practices box further examines the new partnership orientation and offers some guidelines for building successful partnerships.

The Internal Environment: Corporate Culture

The internal environment within which managers work includes corporate culture, production technology, organization structure, and physical facilities. Of these, corporate culture has surfaced as important to competitive advantage. The internal culture must fit the needs of the external environment and company strategy. When this fit occurs, committed employees create a high-performance organization that is tough to beat.[40]

The concept of culture has been of growing concern to managers since the 1980s, as turbulence in the external environment has grown, often requiring new values and

From Adversarial Orientation ⟶	To Partnership Orientation
• Suspicion, competition, arm's length	• Trust, value added to both sides
• Price, efficiency, own profits	• Equity, fair dealing, everyone profits
• Information and feedback limited	• E-business links to share information and conduct digital transactions
• Lawsuits to resolve conflict	• Close coordination; virtual teams and people onsite
• Minimal involvement and up-front investment	• Involvement in partner's product design and production
• Short-term contracts	• Long-term contracts
• Contracts limit the relationship	• Business assistance goes beyond the contract

EXHIBIT 2.4

The Shift to a Partnership Paradigm

BEST PRACTICES

The New Golden Rule: Cooperate

News flash: Companies around the world are sleeping with the enemy. A decade ago, many managers would have considered it heresy to collaborate with competitors, but today they are finding that collaboration is necessary to compete in a rapidly changing environment. Worldwide, research and development budgets are shrinking as technological complexity grows by leaps and bounds. Collaboration in product development is sweeping every field from autos to aircraft to biotechnology.

Suppliers are a part of this new collaborative business model. Speed is essential in today's economy, which requires a seamless integration between a company and its suppliers. Volkswagen, Europe's biggest automaker, has stretched the supplier relationship to new limits at its revolutionary plant in Brazil. Twelve international suppliers work directly in Volkswagen's factory, making their own components and then fastening them together into finished trucks and buses. Though few have stretched the supplier relationship as far as VW, other auto companies, including Ford Motor Company, DaimlerChrysler, and General Motors, are experimenting with this modular approach, in which suppliers provide premade chunks of a vehicle that can be quickly assembled into a finished car or truck by a handful of workers. Manufacturers win with lower costs, suppliers gain in higher volume, and transaction costs go down for everyone. In the quest for speed and efficiency, collaboration is a trend that is likely to go further in coming years.

Here are a few tips from the experts about what makes a collaborative relationship successful:

- Enter the relationship with a spirit of true partnership. An arm's-length, semiadversarial, untrusting, "dump-them-tomorrow-if-we-get-a-better-deal" mindset guarantees failure. Successful partnerships are based on openness, trust, and long-term commitment.

- When choosing partners, pay attention to culture and values. Too often, managers perform due diligence on matters such as markets, products, and technologies but overlook the "softer" side of partnerships. Incompatibility of culture and values can doom a partnership faster than anything else.

- Clarify what each partner is expected to give and to get from the relationship. This includes defining who will lead the project, the decision-making process, review and oversight responsibilities, and who has final authority regarding any negotiations, contract approvals.

- Put together the right team, including top management. Top management support and active involvement is crucial for the success of the partnership. In addition, team members should represent all functions, levels, and areas of expertise. The most successful alliance managers are those with open minds, strong relationship skills, and a desire for learning.

- Put it in writing. An open, trusting relationship does not mean there should not be a legal contract and clear, written guidelines for how the partnership will conduct business. A legal contract prevents misunderstandings and provides continuity through changes in personnel and management. However, experts warn that you can kill a partnership by turning to the contract at the first hint of any conflict. Partners should learn to resolve disagreements in a collaborative, no-blame manner.

SOURCES: Based on information in Lynn A. Isabella, "Managing an alliance is nothing like business as usual," *Organizational Dynamics 15*, no. 1 (2002): 47–59; Oren Harari, "The logistics of success," *Management Review* (June 1999): 24–26; Gail Dutton, "The new consortiums," *Management Review* (January 1999): 46–50; Lee Berton, "Shall we dance?" *CFO* (January 1998): 28–35; David Woodruff with Ian Katz and Keith Naughton, "VW's factory of the future," *BusinessWeek* (October 7, 1996): 52–56; and Philip Siekman, "Building 'em better in Brazil," *Fortune* (September 6, 1999): 246(c)–246(v).

culture

The set of key values, beliefs, understandings, and norms that members of an organization share.

attitudes. Organizational culture has been defined and studied in many ways. For the purposes of this chapter, we define **culture** as the set of key values, beliefs, understandings, and norms shared by members of an organization.[41] The concept of culture helps managers understand the hidden, complex aspects of organizational life. Culture is a pattern of shared values and assumptions about how things are done within the organization. This pattern is learned by members as they cope with external and internal problems and taught to new members as the correct way to perceive, think, and feel.

Culture can be analyzed at three levels, as illustrated in Exhibit 2.5, with each level becoming less obvious.[42] At the surface level are visible artifacts, which include such things as manner of dress, patterns of behavior, physical symbols, organizational ceremonies, and office layout. Visible artifacts are all the things one can see, hear, and observe by watching members of the organization. At a deeper level are the expressed

BUSINESS BLOOPER

Carly Fiorina at HP

Carly Fiorina was the much-trumpeted CEO of Hewlett-Packard, the first woman appointed as CEO of a Fortune 100 company. Coming from high visibility as CEO of Lucent Technologies, she was charged with changing and updating HP, one of the first high-tech companies, a firm that many were saying was too stodgy to compete in tumultuous times. Fiorina's style was big and sought attention. She held big forums with huge video screens hung high, showing her image—with a Tony Robbins headset microphone. Her forums kept her from roaming the halls connecting with employees. She tried to force a centralized style on a decentralized structure, a marketing culture on a deeply entrenched engineering culture. Finally, after five and a half years, Carly Fiorina was asked to resign in early February 2005, the result of HP's culture rejecting her style.

SOURCE: Claudia H. Deutsch, "Carl Fiorina? He'd Probably Be Out of Work, Too," *The New York Times* (Feb. 13, 2005): 5.

values and beliefs, which are not observable but can be discerned from how people explain and justify what they do.

These are values that members of the organization hold at a conscious level. They can be interpreted from the stories, language, and symbols organization members use to represent them. Some values become so deeply embedded in a culture that members are no longer consciously aware of them. These basic, underlying assumptions and beliefs are the essence of culture and subconsciously guide behavior and decisions. In some organizations, a basic assumption might be that people are essentially lazy and will shirk their duties whenever possible; thus, employees are closely supervised and given little freedom, and colleagues are frequently suspicious of one another. More enlightened organizations operate on the basic assumption that people want to do a good job; in these organizations, employees are given more freedom and responsibility, and colleagues trust one another and work cooperatively. Xerox nearly went bankrupt when it hired an outside CEO who did not know the culture. Luckily, the company promoted an insider who is now helping Xerox get back on its feet.

> **Take *ACTION***
>
> To understand culture, ask yourself what is the culture of most of your courses? Is it serious, playful, angry? Does the culture require you to behave in a certain way to your instructors? To other students?

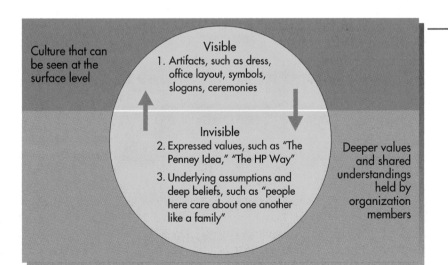

EXHIBIT 2.5

Levels of Corporate Culture

Xerox

Xerox used to be the Gold Standard in copying. But by the time Anne Mulcahy took over as CEO, the company was in a state of total chaos. She followed G. Richard Thoman, an outsider brought in to shore up the company, who only made matters worse partly because he did not know the culture. As a 27-year veteran of the company, Mulcahy knew the company, the culture, the people. Still, she faced one crisis after another. "You didn't get promoted," Warren Buffett told Mulcahy. "You went to war." Xerox suffered seven straight quarters of steep losses. In Xerox's core copier business, Japanese competitors such as Canon and Ricoh were devouring market share. Top managers at Xerox had ignored the digital revolution going on around them, so the company was slow to develop new products that could fill the gaps in the declining copy machine business. The stock was free falling, thousands of employees had lost their jobs, and morale was in the pits. Many of the best managers were jumping ship for brighter prospects. In addition, even the most loyal of Xerox's customers had grown alienated by a flawed sales restructuring that tied billing procedures up in knots. Mulcahy—who had considered quitting work to spend more time with her sons—never expected to be thrown into this mess, but love for the company and her fellow employees compelled her to take on the challenge.

Though Xerox's woes are far from over, Mulcahy has gotten the company off the critical list. Because she has spent 27 years at the company, she knows how it ticks, she has relationships with many employees, and she tells the truth. "Part of her DNA is to tell you the good, the bad, and the ugly," says one colleague. Mulcahy is fiercely concerned about people. Even during the darkest days, she refused to consider bankruptcy, preferring instead to focus everyone on rebuilding for the future. Her willingness to work with subordinates on the front lines has expanded her credibility and enabled her to energize people who were previously demoralized and hopeless. Despite the company's financial distress, she rejected a plan to abolish raises, and she implemented symbolic gestures of appreciation, like giving employees their birthdays off. She hid her own fears and insecurities to motivate people with a vision of what Xerox could be if everyone pulled together. Mulcahy definitely believes in being visible. She met face-to-face with customers to smooth ruffled feathers and with creditors to renegotiate credit agreements and assure them the company would pay its enormous debts. When she had to make the tough decision to close the struggling personal computer division and lay off employees, she personally walked the halls to tell people she was sorry and let them vent their anger. "She was leading by example," says one creditor. "Everybody at Xerox knew she was working hard, and that she was working hard for them." Employees rallied around her, and startling improvements occurred in performance. Costs were reduced significantly, and all the company's divisions returned to profitability. Though it remains to be seen whether Mulcahy can make Xerox great again, she is masterfully leading it through the greatest crisis in its 100-year history.[43]

The fundamental values that characterize an organization's culture can be understood through the visible manifestations of symbols, stories, heroes, slogans, and ceremonies.

Symbols

symbol

An object, act, or event that conveys meaning to others.

A **symbol** is an object, act, or event that conveys meaning to others. Symbols can be considered a rich, non-verbal language that vibrantly conveys the organization's important values concerning how people relate to one another and interact with the environment.[44] For example, managers at a New York-based start-up that provides Internet solutions to local television broadcasters wanted a way to symbolize the company's unofficial mantra of "drilling down to solve problems." They bought a dented old drill for $2 and dubbed it The Team Drill. Each month, the drill is presented to a different employee in recognition of exceptional work, and the employee personalizes the drill in some way before passing it on to the next winner.[45] Rick Sapio found the simple practice of closing his company's books each day was a symbolic act that kept them from going broke, as shown on the following page.

Building up a new business does not take as much discipline when the economy is thriving. Ask Rick Sapio. When he started his Dallas-based Mutuals.com to provide direct sales mutual fund advisory services, as well as account management, for a flat fee, he found it easy to raise money. It all started when Sapio was watching TV one day listening to the founder of Flowers.com, and Rick wondered why Charles Schwab never thought of that. Before you can say "dial 1-800," Sapio had a new phone number: 1-800.MUTUALS. Not long after, he dropped everything, quit his engineering job, and decided to fulfill a long-time dream of starting a financial company. So, he moved from Hacksensack, New Jersey, in a U-Haul to Dallas, Texas. That is when he started to look for investors.

He raised $14 million during those years. Raising so much money was not necessarily a good thing because he got used to spending high. Even though revenues were going up at 114 percent a year, Mutuals.com was consistently in debt. Maybe it was from that extra office Sapio wanted in lower Manhattan. Or the company-sponsored gym membership, expensive parking space, or membership dues to professional organizations. Not to mention Sapio paid himself generously because was he not worth it? Then there were the $400,000 television advertising bills, which brought few customers. Employees spent freely, too. And why not? They were bringing in plenty of money from accounts and investors. None of this was a problem until the stock market crashed. Investments dwindled. Sapio's company was headed on a downward spiral and the future was not rosy.

But Rick Sapio realized changing conditions required different approaches in strategy and in financial focus. He learned an important lesson in business: Profits equal revenues minus expenses. In the stock market boom years, he worried more about revenues and less about expenses. Now, he no longer had that luxury. The first thing he did was look carefully at all expenses. He started a practice where the books are closed every day, to get a real-time view of the company's true revenue and expenses. Every day at 4:37 PM, after the stock market closes, he huddles with his managers and they look at all the expenses to see if any are out of whack, looking for ways to reduce costs in areas getting bloated. If employees overspend without approval, they pay out of their own pockets. Sapio closed the Manhattan office; it was just too costly. The company quit paying for his gym and parking. Sapio slashed his own salary by $20,000 and asked employees to take some pay as stock options, which resulted in savings of $70,000. They agreed to stop TV ads and focus on print and Internet ads, saving $1 million. Finally, Sapio realized he needed to change his business model to suit the changing times. The company went from direct sales to selling through large institutional investors. Reports had shown that 85 percent of revenues came from 35 percent of customers, so they fired 65 percent of the customers and saved 90 percent of their expenses. Sapio learned that by reducing expenses, profits will be maximized and that becomes its own marketing tool. His results: In 2005, Mutuals.com funds were ranked in the top 1 percent.[46]

Steelcase Corp. built a new, pyramid-shaped corporate development center to symbolize new cultural values of collaboration, teamwork, and innovation. Whereas designers, engineers, and marketers had previously been located in different buildings, they are now all housed in the pyramid. The six-floor building features an open atrium from ground floor to ceiling, with a giant pendulum to remind people of constant change. Open areas and thought stations with white boards encourage brainstorming and the exchange of ideas.[47]

Stories

A **story** is a narrative based on true events that is repeated frequently and shared among organizational employees. Stories are told to new employees to keep the organization's primary values alive. One of Nordstrom's primary means of emphasizing the importance of customer service is through corporate storytelling. An example is the story about a sales representative who took back a customer's 2-year-old blouse with no

story

A narrative based on true events that is repeated frequently and shared among organizational employees.

questions asked.[48] A frequently told story at UPS concerns an employee who, without authorization, ordered an extra Boeing 737 to ensure timely delivery of a load of Christmas packages that had been left behind in the holiday rush. As the story goes, rather than punishing the worker, UPS rewarded his initiative. By telling this story, UPS workers communicate that the company stands behind its commitment to worker autonomy and customer service.[49]

Heroes

hero

A figure who exemplifies the deeds, character, and attributes of a strong corporate culture.

A **hero** is a figure who exemplifies the deeds, character, and attributes of a strong culture. Heroes are role models for employees to follow. Sometimes heroes are real, such as the female security supervisor who once challenged IBM's chairman because he was not carrying the appropriate clearance identification to enter a security area.[50] Other times they are symbolic, such as the mythical sales representative at Robinson Jewelers who delivered a wedding ring directly to the church because the ring had been ordered late. The deeds of heroes are out of the ordinary, but not so far out as to be unattainable by other employees. Heroes show how to do the right thing in the organization. Companies with strong cultures take advantage of achievements to define heroes who uphold key values.

At 3M Corp., top managers keep alive the heroes who developed projects that were killed by top management. One hero was a vice president who was fired earlier in his career for persisting with a new product even after his boss had told him, "That's a stupid idea. Stop!" After the worker was fired, he would not leave. He stayed in an unused office, working without a salary on the new product idea. He was rehired, the idea succeeded, and he was promoted to vice president. The lesson of this hero as a major element in 3M's culture is to persist at what you believe in.[51]

Slogans

slogan

A phrase or sentence that succinctly expresses a key corporate value.

A **slogan** is a phrase or sentence that succinctly expresses a key corporate value. Many companies use a slogan or saying to convey special meaning to employees. H. Ross Perot of Electronic Data Systems established the philosophy of hiring the best people he could find and noted how difficult it was to find them. His motto was, "Eagles don't flock. You gather them one at a time." Averitt Express uses the slogan, "Our driving force is people" on its trucks to express its commitment to treating employees and customers well. Cultural values can be discerned in written public statements, such as corporate mission statements or other formal statements that express the organization's core values. The mission statement for Hallmark Cards, for example, emphasizes values of excellence, ethical and moral conduct in all relationships, business innovation, and corporate social responsibility.[52]

Take ACTION

What are the slogans on your campus? List as many as you can. What does that tell you about what the culture values?

Ceremonies

ceremony

A planned activity that makes up a special event and is conducted for the benefit of an audience.

A **ceremony** is a planned activity that makes up a special event and is conducted for the benefit of an audience. Managers hold ceremonies to provide dramatic examples of company values. Ceremonies are special occasions that reinforce valued accomplishments, create a bond among people by allowing them to share an important event, and anoint and celebrate heroes.[53]

The value of a ceremony can be illustrated by the presentation of a major award. Mary Kay Cosmetics Company holds elaborate awards ceremonies, presenting gold and diamond pins, furs, and luxury cars to high-achieving sales consultants. The setting is typically an auditorium, in front of a large, cheering audience, and everyone dresses in glamorous evening clothes. The most successful consultants are introduced by film clips, like the kind used to present award nominees in the entertainment industry. These ceremonies recognize and celebrate high-performing employees and emphasize the rewards for performance.[54] A company can bestow an award secretly by mailing it to the employee's home or, if a check, by depositing it in a bank. But such procedures would not make the bestowal of rewards a significant organizational event and would be less meaningful to the employee.

In summary, organizational culture represents the values, norms, understandings, and basic assumptions that employees share, and these values are signified by symbols, stories, heroes, slogans, and ceremonies. Managers help define important symbols, stories, and heroes to shape the culture.

Environment and Culture

A big influence on internal corporate culture is the external environment. Cultures can vary across organizations; however, organizations within the same industry often reveal similar cultural characteristics because they are operating in similar environments.[55] The internal culture should embody what it takes to succeed in the environment. If the external environment requires extraordinary customer service, the culture should encourage good service; if it calls for careful technical decision making, cultural values should reinforce managerial decision making.

Adaptive Cultures

Research at Harvard University on 207 U.S. firms illustrated the critical relationship between corporate culture and the external environment. The study found that a strong corporate culture alone did not ensure business success unless the culture encouraged healthy adaptation to the external environment. As illustrated in Exhibit 2.6, adaptive corporate cultures have different values and behavior from unadaptive corporate cultures. In adaptive cultures, managers are concerned about customers and those internal people and processes that bring about useful change. In the unadaptive corporate cultures, managers are concerned about themselves, and their values tend to discourage risk taking and change. Thus, a strong culture alone is not enough because an unhealthy culture may encourage the organization to march resolutely in the wrong direction. Healthy cultures help companies adapt to the environment.[56] In a time of airline bankruptcies, JetBlue keeps profitable by having an adaptive culture and by being responsive to customers and employees, as shown on the following page.

	Adaptive Corporate Cultures	Unadaptive Corporate Cultures
Visible Behavior	Managers pay close attention to all their constituencies, especially customers, and initiate change when needed to serve their legitimate interests even if it entails taking some risks.	Managers tend to behave somewhat insularly, politically, and bureaucratically. As a result, they do not change their strategies quickly to adjust to or take advantage of changes in their business environments.
Expressed Values	Managers care deeply about customers, stockholders, and employees. They strongly value people and processes that can create useful change, e.g., leadership initiatives up and down the management hierarchy.	Managers care mainly about themselves, their immediate work group, or some product (or technology) associated with that work group. They value the orderly and risk-reducing management process much more highly than leadership initiatives.

EXHIBIT 2.6

Environmentally Adaptive versus Unadaptive Corporate Cultures

JetBlue

When JetBlue CEO David Neeleman serves inflight snacks, he is not only impacting the customers, but he is shaping the company's culture. Employees see him working the crowds on the plane or in the airports, they watch him working overtime and know he is not sitting at his desk counting stock options. They hear him announce new plans and they enthusiastically share the word. The CEO is not some distant figure whom they only know from his photo in the inflight magazine. He is on the front lines with them and they know he means it when he says they are all on the same team together because they regularly see him working, doing the same tasks they do.

As a result, JetBlue is one of only two sizable airlines making profits (the other is Southwest) with an astounding level of respect, trust, and goodwill. Toward the end of the flight, attendants announce that JetBlue keeps down costs and reduces turnaround time by having everyone clean up the cabin, asking for customers to hand in trash. Sure, this happens on lots of flights. But on JetBlue, everyone pitches in with great fervor and they all become part of the clean-up team, including David Neeleman.[57]

Types of Cultures

adaptability culture

A culture characterized by values that support the company's ability to interpret and translate signals from the environment into new behavior responses.

In considering what cultural values are important for the organization, managers consider the external environment as well as the company's strategy and goals. Studies have suggested that the right fit between culture, strategy, and the environment is associated with four categories or types of culture, as illustrated in Exhibit 2.7. These categories are based on two dimensions: the extent to which the external environment requires flexibility or stability and the extent to which a company's strategic focus is internal or external. The four categories associated with these differences are adaptability, achievement, involvement, and consistency.[58]

The **adaptability culture** emerges in an environment that requires fast response and high-risk decision making. Managers encourage values that support the company's

EXHIBIT 2.7

Four Types of Corporate Cultures

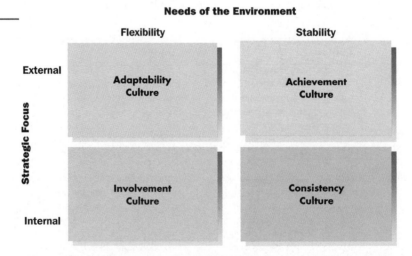

SOURCES: Based on D. R. Denison and A. K. Mishra, "Toward a Theory of Organizational Culture and Effectiveness," *Organization Science* 6, no. 2 (March–April 1995): 204–223; R. Hooijberg and F. Petrock, "On Cultural Change: Using the Competing Values Framework to Help Leaders Execute a Transformational Strategy," *Human Resource Management* 32, no.1 (1993): 29–50; and R.E. Quinn, *Beyond Rational Management: Mastering the Paradoxes and Competing Demands of High Performance* (San Francisco: Jossey-Bass, 1988).

ability to detect, interpret, and translate signals rapidly from the environment into new behavior responses. Employees have autonomy to make decisions and act freely to meet needs, and responsiveness to customers is highly valued. Managers actively create change by encouraging and rewarding creativity, experimentation, and risk taking. Another good example of an adaptability culture is Nokia.

Nokia has been the world's leading maker of cell phone handsets since 1998. One reason is that innovation and adaptability are built into the corporate culture. Nokia's top goal is to keep churning out new products because what is hot in this industry one day is stone cold a few months later.

Nokia managers encourage "uninhibited dabbling," whereby people feel free to try crazy ideas and never shirk from making mistakes. To spur creativity and fresh thinking, people are rotated to different jobs and divisions, e.g., a lawyer might be shifted to running a division or a network engineer moved to handset design. The company keeps divisions and teams small and gives them the power to implement their ideas. Friendly internal competitions celebrate individual creativity, such as photo contests where employees take pictures of their vacation homes or favorite pets with Nokia camera phones.

Nokia faces challenges as the mobile phone market matures, and market share has been dropping as consumers turn to less expensive, mid-range cell phone models from Samsung Corp. and Motorola. The history of Nokia indicates that it is not afraid to take a dramatic turn if the environment demands it: In its lifetime, Nokia has gone from manufacturing paper to making rubber boots, then raincoats, hunting rifles, and consumer electronics, before concentrating on cellular phones.[59]

Most companies in the electronics industry, as well as those involved in e-commerce, cosmetics, and fashion, use an adaptability culture because they must move quickly to respond to rapid changes in the environment.

The **achievement culture** is suited to organizations that are concerned with serving specific customers in the external environment but without the intense need for flexibility and rapid change. This results-oriented culture values competitiveness, aggressiveness, personal initiative, and willingness to work long and hard to achieve results. An emphasis on winning and achieving specific ambitious goals is the glue that holds the organization together.[60] Siebel Systems, which sells complex software systems, has thrived on an achievement culture. Professionalism and aggressiveness are core values. Employees are forbidden to eat at their desks or to decorate with more than one or two personal photographs. People who succeed at Siebel are focused, competitive, and driven to win. Those who perform and meet stringent goals are handsomely rewarded; those who do not are fired.[61]

The **involvement culture** has an internal focus on the involvement and participation of employees to meet changing needs from the environment. This culture places high value on meeting the needs of employees, and the organization may be characterized by a caring, family-like atmosphere. Managers emphasize values such as cooperation, consideration of employees and customers, and avoidance of status differences. One company that illustrates an involvement culture is J. M. Smucker & Co., which in 2004 became the first manufacturer to earn the top spot on *Fortune* magazine's list of "The 100 Best Companies to Work For." Co-CEOs Tim and Richard Smucker, known to employees as "the boys," have continued their father's emphasis on treating people well. Their code of conduct for managers is to listen with full attention, always look for the good in others, have a sense of humor, and say "thank you" for a job well done. Plant supervisors sometimes hold barbeques to celebrate reaching goals; managers routinely thank employees for their service with gift certificates and lunches. "At first I was skeptical," said Brian Kinsey, director of operations. "But this family feel is for real." Thanks to Smucker's involvement culture, turnover is low and employee satisfaction high, helping the company consistently meet productivity, quality, and customer service goals in a changing marketplace.[62] One company to achieve success with an involvement culture is SAS Institute, based in Cary, North Carolina.

achievement culture

A results-oriented culture that values competitiveness, personal initiative, and achievement.

involvement culture

A culture that places high value on meeting the needs of employees and values cooperation and equality.

Take *ACTION*

Are your courses more adaptability, achievement, or involvement cultures? What about your student clubs or where you live?

| **SAS Institute** | The SAS Institute gives out free M&Ms to employees every Wednesday, a holdover from the time when the company was smaller and free candy was an easy way to show how much the company cared about its employees. After 27 years of revenue growth, the $1.3 billion company has 10,000 employees and an annual budget of $45,000 for M&Ms. |

SAS, which stands for statistical analysis software, writes software that makes it possible to gather and understand data, producing products that set the industry standard in the world of knowledge management. It is a competitive field with high stakes, but the atmosphere at SAS headquarters in Cary, North Carolina, is relaxed, almost serene. Jim Goodnight, co-founder of SAS, created a caring corporate culture where employees are respected and given the freedom and information they need to perform at the top of their abilities.

The most important value is taking care of employees and making sure they have whatever they need to be satisfied and productive. Employees are encouraged to lead a balanced life rather than to work long hours and express a hard-charging, competitive spirit. The company adopted a seven-hour workday to give employees more personal time. SAS offers amazing benefits, including two Montessori day-care centers, a 36,000-square-foot fitness center, unlimited sick days, an on-site health clinic, elder care advice and referrals, and live music in the cafeteria, where employees may eat with their families. Other key values at SAS are equality, fairness, and cooperation.

SAS's culture places a high value on people and human relationships. Managers at the company trust employees to do their jobs to the best of their ability, and then they expect them to go home and enjoy their friends and families. As one employee put it, "Because you're treated well, you treat the company well."[63]

Thanks to SAS's clan culture, employees care about one another and about the company, a focus that has helped SAS adapt to stiff competition and changing markets. In recent years, while other high-tech companies were laying off, SAS kept hiring. That is why they consume 22 tons of M&Ms each year.[64]

consistency culture

A culture that values and rewards a methodical, rational, orderly way of doing things.

The final category of culture, the **consistency culture**, has an internal focus and a consistency orientation for a stable environment. Following the rules and being thrifty are valued, and the culture supports and rewards a methodical, rational, orderly way of doing things. In today's changing world, few companies operate in a stable environment, and most managers are shifting toward more flexible cultures in tune with changes in the environment.

One thriving new company, Pacific Edge Software, has successfully implemented elements of a consistency culture, ensuring that all its projects are on time and on budget.

BUSINESS BLOOPER

Kryptonite

When bloggers outed Kryptonite U-shaped bicycle locks, with videos showing them easily opened with a 50 cent Bic pen, the company at first denied any problems, saying the locks still provide "an effective deterrent to theft." It did concede, however, that it was developing a newer, pen-resistant strain of locks. "The world just got tougher and so did our locks," it said. But consumers, bloggers, and bike magazines would not let up until the company agreed to a lock exchange. To the company's credit, it took only a week for it to come around, but during that seven days, a lot of jokes were made at Kryptonite's expense. It's a bird, it's a plane, it's a....

SOURCES: "Business 2.0 Magazine Unveils 101 Dumbest Moments in Business of 2004;" *Business Wire* (Jan 31, 2005): 1; Nathan Leaf, "Kryptonite lock has Achilles heel," *Wisconsin State Journal* (Sept. 14, 2004): A1.

The husband-and-wife team of Lisa Hjorten and Scott Fuller implanted a culture of order, discipline, and control from the moment they founded the company. The emphasis on order and focus means employees can generally go home by 6:00 P.M. rather than working all night to finish an important project. Hjorten insists that the company's culture is not rigid or uptight, just careful. Though sometimes being careful means being slow, so far Pacific Edge has managed to keep pace with the demands of the external environment.[65]

Each of these four categories of culture can be successful. In addition, organizations usually have values that fall into more than one category. The relative emphasis on various cultural values depends on the needs of the environment and the organization's focus. Managers are responsible for instilling the cultural values the organization needs to be successful in its environment.

Shaping Corporate Culture for Innovative Response

Research conducted by a Stanford University professor indicates that the one factor that increases a company's value the most is people and how they are treated.[66] In addition, a business magazine survey found that CEOs cite organizational culture as their most important mechanism for attracting, motivating, and retaining talented employees, a capability they consider the single best predictor of overall organizational excellence.[67] Corporate culture plays a key role in creating an organizational climate that enables learning and innovative responses to threats from the external environment, challenging new opportunities, or organizational crises. However, managers cannot focus all their attention on values; they need a commitment to consistent business performance.

Managing the High-Performance Culture

Companies that succeed in a turbulent world are those that pay attention to cultural values and to business performance. Cultural values can energize and motivate employees by appealing to higher ideals and unifying people around shared goals. Values boost performance by shaping and guiding employee behavior, so everyone's actions are aligned with strategic priorities.[68] Exhibit 2.8 illustrates four organizational outcomes based on the relative attention managers pay to cultural values and business performance.[69] A company in Quadrant A pays little attention to values or business results and is unlikely to survive for long. Managers in Quadrant B organizations are highly focused on creating a strong culture, but they do not tie organizational values directly to goals and desired business results. A strong, cohesive culture can be positive for a company, especially in terms of employee morale and satisfaction. However, if the culture is not connected to business performance, it is not likely to benefit the organization during hard times. For example, Levi Strauss has always focused on values, even tying part of managers' pay to how well they toe the values line. The problem is that top executives lost sight of the business performance side of the issue; that is, they stopped thinking about what it took to make blue jeans profitably.[70] Another danger of having a strong culture with less emphasis on results is shown in the Focus on Skills box.

Quadrant C represents organizations that focus primarily on bottom-line results and pay little attention to organizational values. This may be profitable in the short run, but the success is difficult to sustain over the long term because the "glue" that holds the organization together—that is, shared values—is missing. Think about the numerous get-rich-quick goals of dot-com entrepreneurs. Thousands of companies sprang up in the 1990s that were aimed primarily at fast growth and quick profits, with little effort to build a solid organization based on long-term mission and values. When the crash came, these companies failed. Those that survived were typically companies that had instilled cultural values that helped them weather the storm. Giants eBay and

Take **ACTION**

Is this desirable? Quadrant C courses where students have cut-throat competition on grades, where the teacher does not care about the people, only how well they do on assignments and tests.

EXHIBIT 2.8

Combining Culture and Performance

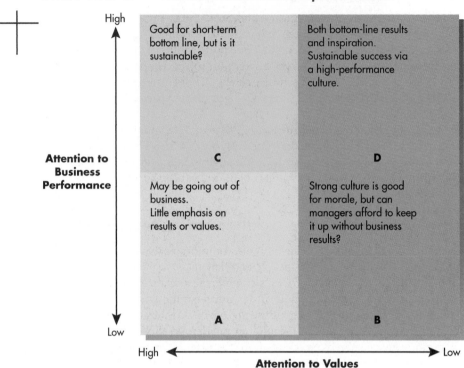

C Good for short-term bottom line, but is it sustainable?	**D** Both bottom-line results and inspiration. Sustainable success via a high-performance culture.
A May be going out of business. Little emphasis on results or values.	**B** Strong culture is good for morale, but can managers afford to keep it up without business results?

Attention to Business Performance (High / Low)

High ← **Attention to Values** → Low

SOURCE: Adapted from Jeff Rosenthal and Mary Ann Masarech, "High-Performance Cultures: How Values Can Drive Business Results," *Journal of Organizational Excellence* (Spring 2003), 3–18.

Amazon.com have paid careful attention to organizational values, as have smaller e-commerce companies such as Canada's Mediagrif Interactive Technologies, an online business-to-business (B2B) brokerages that allows businesses to meet online and trade their goods.[71]

FOCUS ON SKILLS

Passive-aggressive companies

During your next ten jobs, three will be for passive-aggressive companies. Those are the places where everyone is polite, if strained, in meetings and hallways. No one disagrees with the boss, who is pleasant to workers, until annual review when he nails them to the wall. Employees are seething inside and go by the dictum: Get hurt, get mad, get even. Retaliation becomes missed deadlines, sloppy work, and confused orders. Meetings become one-way communication from boss to workers, who sit quietly and then go back to their offices and do business as usual, hoping the new proposed plans will just blow over.

Passive-aggressive companies hurt employees by creating a noxious work environment, where productivity suffers. Changing such a culture is a long, slow process. Because the culture is built on pretends, fibs, and make-believe, it is difficult to get people to speak the truth. They have seen people fired for less.

In passive-aggressive cultures, everyone is friendly, but when things go wrong, fingers start pointing at other people, other departments. Without looking at themselves and determining what they could have done differently, people will not learn, will not grow. Writer Stephen Covey says that many companies remind him of 6-year-olds playing soccer. Lots of energy and everyone wants to win, but no one knows what to do.

One antidote to passive-aggressive cultures is to have meetings and set "outrageous goals," beyond anyone's reach. The idea is to stretch people's minds and get them working on projects without getting blamed at the end when goals are not met. Such activities can help groups to become more responsible, so they act their age at work, rather than the age of their kids.

SOURCE: Del Jones, "When You're Smiling, Are You Seething Inside?" *USA Today* (April 12, 2004), B1.

Finally, companies in Quadrant D emphasize culture and consistent business performance as drivers of organizational success. Managers in these organizations align values with the company's daily operations, e.g., hiring practices, performance management, budgeting, criteria for promotions and rewards. Quadrant D represents the high-performance culture, a culture that (1) is based on a solid organizational mission or purpose, (2) embodies shared adaptive values that guide decisions and business practices, and (3) encourages individual employee ownership of bottom-line results and the organization's cultural backbone.[72] An example from Nordstrom, which has strong values of outstanding customer service, provides an illustration. A sales associate had shown a woman nine pairs of shoes, but the store did not have the right combination of style, size, and color the woman wanted. As she was leaving, another sales associate approached her and offered to see if he could find the shoes at another store. He informed her that he had located them at a competitor's store (Macy's) and would have the shoes shipped directly to her home. Nordstrom's would pick up the overnight shipping charge. Later, this associate reprimanded his peer for failing to try harder. "You really let us down," he said.[73] Nordstrom is a Quadrant D organization, where employees are strongly committed to the cultural values that drive the organization's success and are willing to challenge one another when they fail to honor them.

One of the most important things managers do is create and influence organizational culture to meet strategic goals, because culture has a significant impact on performance. In *Corporate Culture and Performance*, John P. Kotter and James L. Heskett provided evidence that companies that intentionally managed cultural values outperformed similar companies that did not. Jim Collins found culture to be a key factor in his studies of successful companies compared to ones that have not done so well.[74] Caterpillar Inc. developed its Cultural Assessment Process (CAP) to measure and manage culture's contributions to organizational effectiveness. The process gave top executives hard data documenting millions of dollars in savings attributed directly to cultural factors.[75]

Cultural Leadership

One way managers shape cultural norms and values to build a high-performance culture is through *cultural leadership*. Managers must overcommunicate to ensure that employees understand the new culture values, and they signal these values in actions as well as words.

A **cultural leader** defines and uses signals and symbols to influence corporate culture. Cultural leaders influence culture in two key areas:

1. *The cultural leader articulates a vision for the organizational culture that employees can believe in.* This means the leader defines and communicates central values that employees believe in and will rally around. Values are tied to a clear and compelling mission or core purpose

2. *The cultural leader heeds the daily activities that reinforce the cultural vision.* The leader ensures work procedures and reward systems match and reinforce the values. Actions speak louder than words, so cultural leaders "walk their talk."[76]

Leaders can create a culture that brings people together by ensuring that people have a voice in what the important values should be. Managers at United Stationers built a new, adaptive culture from the ground up by asking all 6,000 globally dispersed employees to help define the values that would be the building blocks of the culture.[77] Other companies, though, have found small teams and focus groups that include people from all functions and levels of the company to be more effective than trying to include everyone. Tony Wild, CEO of the pharmaceutical company MedPoint, put together a team of trusted managers and surveyed key employees who exemplified the qualities managers wanted to see embodied in the culture.[78] Lennar Corporation's CEO uses song to transmit the company's values and culture, as shown in the example on the following page.

Take **ACTION**

Have you had a course where the students work hard because they respect the teacher, who is a smart and approachable person with high standards? Did you like it?

cultural leader
A manager who uses signals and symbols to influence corporate culture.

Lennar Corporation

Not many CEO's lead corporate meetings reading Dr. Seuss books. Or call themselves "Dr. Seuss" and pen company songs, such as "Scratchings from the Little Red Hen." Meet 43-year-old Stuart Miller, CEO of Lennar Corporation, a fast-growing company that has recently become the number two home builder in the United States and was named as one of three publicly traded stocks that had an unusually high return on investment (ROI).

What may seem like peculiar practices have helped the upstart company maintain its unity and strength as it went through explosive growth in recent years. Begun by Miller's father in 1954 with a $10,000 investment, Lennar acquired so many companies, the rate of growth was dizzying. Still, something worked. Even during an economic downturn last year, profits soared by 32 percent.

Outsiders may not know much about the Little Red Hen, but the company song is printed on little cards and distributed to all workers, who often recite lines to one another at meetings and gatherings.

Chief Financial Officer Bruce Gross thought the Little Red Hen was too weird and tried to talk executives out of reciting it in front of a banker's meeting, worried it would hurt the credibility of the company. But the bankers loved it.

Lennar made some smart strategic decisions. Several years ago, subdivision home builders offered with customized floor plans. Wanting to be more efficient, Lennar cut down on the number of options available in tiles, appliances and moldings despite warnings against this strategy. But its practice paid off, helping it to trim costs, only adding to its attractiveness to its mid-price and low-price home shoppers.

Some people think the wacky culture means no discipline. On the contrary. Units are held to high standards and every month all 50 division heads sends a one-page report to Miller on their status in meeting financial goals.

At a recent seminar for 150 employees, the company had a hotel decorated in a jungle theme and simulated the "Survivor" show under a banner that read "In search of RONA" (return on net assets), where participants were grilled on financial goals, as well as taught responses to tough media questions and how to handle crisis situations.

It is a company "Yertle, the Turtle" would be proud of.[79]

CONCEPT CONNECTION

Eileen Fisher's award-winning company makes simple, comfortable clothing for women following the firm's mission to support collaboration, individual growth, and social consciousness.

Managers widely communicate the cultural values through words and actions. Values statements that are not reinforced by management behavior are meaningless or even harmful for employees and the organization. Consider Enron Corp., whose values statement included things like communication, respect, and integrity. Managers' actions at the corporation clearly belied those stated values.[80] For values to guide the organization, managers have to model them every day. "I have the values in my office in a prominent place where I can see them from my desk, and I try to use them as a guidepost for all my decisions," says Christopher Rice, president and CEO of BlessingWhite, an international training and consulting firm. "I have a group of employees who know (the values) cold and they tell me every time I violate one. This is good behavior!"[81] At MTW Corp., managers work with every new employee to create an "expectations agreement," an evolving document that ensures that actions and work procedures that reinforce the company's cultural values will be adhered to by managers and workers.[82] Top executives at Weirton Steel act as cultural leaders by participating in every team training session to symbolize their commitment to a team-based culture, which is a significant commitment in an 8,000-employee organization.[83] Cultural leaders uphold their commitment to values during difficult times or crises. Xilinx, a Silicon Valley semiconductor manufacturer, is based on a culture of respect and has adhered to a strict no-layoffs policy throughout the technology downturn by negotiating with workers to take pay cuts. Significantly, top leaders were the hardest hit, with the

FOCUS ON COLLABORATION

Eileen Fisher

Simple, elegant, and natural. That describes not only Eileen Fisher's clothing designs but the way the $143 million, 400-employee, company is run. It began when graphics designer Fisher got overwhelmed getting dressed every morning for work. Why could women's clothes not be attractive and as simple and un-changing as men's? She bought a $350 terry cloth remnant in 1984, stitched up four garments, and took them to a trade show and got $3,000 in orders, and $40,000 the following month. Eileen Fisher Inc. (EF) was born.

EF designs are simple and elegant, made from natural, organic fabrics of cotton, wool, or silk. Each piece can be mixed and matched with other pieces, much like a Lego system, so it simplifies a wardrobe. Fisher herself says she was inspired by her parochial school uniforms, which made getting dressed in the morning so easy. The goal is to help customers achieve a simple and joyful life.

The company, too, has developed a culture that matches. "We call it simple, comfortable clothing," says Fisher, "and a simple, comfortable environment." Everything about the firm—from headquarters to distribution center—mirrors Fisher's mission to support collaboration, individual growth, and social consciousness. Each year, employees share in about 10 percent of profits. Fisher offers each employee $1,000 for education and another $1,000 for self-care: activities such as yoga, massage, and voice lessons. After ten years of employment, each person gets $5,000 toward a trip.

And then there is the free clothes. Each worker receives between $500–$2,500 of EF clothes each year. This focus on wellness helps create an energized and creative workforce. Does it pay off? While turnover in the retail industry is 50 percent, in EF stores, it is only 19 percent, saving the company $325,000 per year in recruiting costs.

A few years ago, Eileen Fisher moved her company to Irvington, New York, where everyone could get to work without a car. Right on a river, the location gives a sense of calm to workers. Her values call for the development of the "natural woman" for customers and the same kind of natural person philosophy for employees. "It's not about money," she said. "It's about people, friends, family and community and how people treat each other. There has to be natural growth. It can't be something you force."

Eileen Fisher is designing her strategy to reinforce the culture. Goals include creating wellness in the business development process, nurturing relationships with customers and employees, helping people to tell the truth to one another. "You must love the product and the people," says Fisher.

SOURCES: Claudia Z. Carlin, "Eileen Fisher Simplifies," *Westchester Magazine* (May 2002): 44–45+; Merri Rosenberg, "A Designer Who Lives Like her Clients," *The New York Times* (Sept. 10, 2000): 8; Ellyn Spragins, "The Best Boss: The Nurturer," *Fortune Small Business* (October 2003), 44; "Go for the green," *PR Newswire* (Feb. 11, 2005): 1.

CEO cutting his salary by 20 percent.[84] Maintaining consistency with the cultural values helps organizations weather the storm and come out stronger on the other side. Eileen Fisher is one CEO who lives her values in the workplace, as described in the Focus on Collaboration box.

Creating and maintaining a high-performance culture is not easy in today's turbulent environment and changing workplace, but through their words—and particularly their actions—cultural leaders let everyone in the organization know what really counts.

Manager's Solution

This chapter has discussed several important ideas about internal and external organizational environments. Events in the external environment are considered important influences on organizational behavior and performance. The external environment consists of two layers: the task environment and the general environment. The task environment includes customers, competitors, suppliers, and the labor market. The general environment includes technological, sociocultural, economic, legal-political, and international dimensions. Management techniques for helping the organization adapt to the environment include boundary-spanning roles, interorganizational partnerships, and mergers and joint ventures.

A major internal element for helping organizations adapt to the environment is culture. Corporate culture is a major element of the internal organizational environment and includes the key values, beliefs, understandings, and norms that organization members share. Organizational activities that illustrate corporate culture include symbols, stories, heroes, slogans, and ceremonies. For the organization to be effective, corporate culture should be aligned with organizational strategy and the needs of the external environment.

Four types of culture are adaptability, achievement, involvement, and consistency. Strong cultures are effective when they enable an organization to meet strategic goals and adapt to changes in the external environment. Culture is important because it can have a significant impact on organizational performance. Managers emphasize values and business results to create a high-performance culture, enabling the organization to achieve consistent business performance through the actions of motivated employees who are aligned with the mission and goals of the company. Managers create and sustain adaptive high-performance cultures through cultural leadership. They define and articulate important values tied to a clear and compelling mission, and they widely communicate and uphold the values through their words and particularly their actions. Work procedures, budgeting, decision making, reward systems, and other daily activities are aligned with the cultural values.

In the opening challenge, Kathleen Wehner became president of Cirrus Aviation after her husband's death. After 9/11 the business almost went bankrupt because no one was flying and, therefore, buying their space parts. With only two weeks of operating capital left, Wehner decided to keep the company going, to make adjustments, to remake the business. Her sons and general manager Carmine Carviello helped as she shifted Cirrus's target market from large-engine airplanes toward small-engine and prop planes. She learned to research, finding out how to import plane engines from South America. She got the bank to give her a new line of credit and updated the company in regards to FAA regulations. She opened a plane repair shop in Arizona. Sales are up, last year at $4 million. Her family and friends, as well as the old boy aviation world (of which she is now a part) think she is quite remarkable. Not ready to stop her learning, Wehner says, "I'm a work in progress."[85]

Discussion Questions

1. Some scientists predict major changes in the earth's climate, including a temperature rise of 8°F over the next 60 years. Should any companies be paying attention to this long-range environmental trend? Explain.

2. Would the task environment for a bank contain the same elements as that for a government welfare agency? Discuss.

3. What forces influence organizational uncertainty? Would such forces typically originate in the task environment or the general environment?

4. *In Search of Excellence,* by Peters and Waterman, argued that customers were the most important element in the external environment. Are there company situations for which this may not be true?

5. Caterpillar Corporation was thriving until the mid-1980s, when low oil prices, high interest rates, a worldwide recession, a soaring U.S. dollar, and Japanese competition stunned the giant equipment builder. Discuss the type of response Caterpillar's management might take.

6. Define corporate culture and explain its importance for managers.

7. Why are symbols important to a corporate culture? Do stories, heroes, slogans, and ceremonies also have symbolic value? Discuss.

8. Describe the cultural values of a company for which you have worked. Did those values fit the needs of the external environment? Of employees?

9. What type of environmental situation is associated with a baseball team culture? How does this culture differ from the academy culture?

10. Do you think a corporate culture with strong values is better for organizational effectiveness than a culture with weak values? Are there times when a strong culture might reduce effectiveness? Discuss.

Manager's Workbook

What Is a Strong Corporate Culture?

Think about an organization with which you are familiar, such as your school or a company for which you have worked. Answer the questions below based on whether you agree that they describe the organization.

Disagree Strongly			Agree Strongly	
1	2	3	4	5

1. Virtually all managers and most employees can describe the company's values, purpose, and customer importance. 1 2 3 4 5

2. There is clarity among organization members about how their jobs contribute to organizational goals. 1 2 3 4 5

3. It is very seldom that a manager will act in a way contrary to the company's espoused values. 1 2 3 4 5

4. Warmth and support of other employees is a valued norm, even across departments. 1 2 3 4 5

5. The company and its managers value what's best for the company over the long term more than short-term results. 1 2 3 4 5

6. Leaders make it a point to develop and mentor others. 1 2 3 4 5

7. Recruiting is taken very seriously, with multiple interviews in an effort to find traits that fit the culture. 1 2 3 4 5

8. Recruits are given negative as well as positive information about the company so they can freely choose whether to join. 1 2 3 4 5

9. Employees are expected to acquire real knowledge and mastery—not political alliances—before they can be promoted. 1 2 3 4 5

10. Company values emphasize what the company must do well to succeed in a changing environment. 1 2 3 4 5

11. Conformity to company mission and values is more important than conformity to procedures and dress. 1 2 3 4 5

12. You have heard stories about the company's leaders or "heroes" who helped make the company great. 1 2 3 4 5

13. Ceremonies and special events are used to recognize and reward individuals who contribute to the company in significant ways. 1 2 3 4 5

Total Score

Compute your score. If your total score is 52 or above, your organization has a strong culture, similar to a Procter & Gamble or Hewlett-Packard. A score from 26 to 51 suggests a culture of medium strength, which is positive for the organization, such as for American Airlines, Coca-Cola, and Citibank. A score of 25 or below indicates a weak culture, which is probably not helping the company adapt to the external environment or meet the needs of organization members. Discuss the pros and cons of a strong culture. Does a strong culture mean everyone has to be alike?

SOURCE: Adapted from Richard Pascale, "The Paradox of 'Corporate Culture': Reconciling Ourselves to Socialization," *California Management Review* 27 (2) (1985); and David A. Kolb, Joyce S. Osland, and Irwin M. Rubin, *Organizational Behavior: An Experiential Approach,* 6th ed. (Englewood Cliffs, N.J.: Prentice-Hall, 1995), pp. 346–347.

Manager's Workshop

Scavenger Hunt: Looking for the University's Culture

1. Divide into groups of four to seven members. These may be ad hoc or ongoing groups.

2. You are asked to find examples of the university's culture. Use 4″ × 6″ notecards. Put one symbol on each card, with the category listed at the top in capital letters. During a future class session, you will be asked to give a five-minute presentation of your findings to the class. You must find all four items from the required list and any four items from the elective list (except if you choose the cartoon option, then you need only two from the elective list).

3. Do NOT steal anything, and do not buy any item. Your group is limited to $7.00 to make copies or take photos.

What is needed for scavenger hunt?

Required list of symbols

1. Mission of university (teaching, research, service)

2. Customer/clients (students, researchers, business, community, country)

3. Locational information (e.g., city, county, state, U.S. or world map indicates local or cosmopolitan orientation)

4. Constituents (students, faculty, administrators, support staff, athletic teams, taxpayers, board of trustees)

Elective list (choose any four)

1. Leadership (representation, roles, administration or faculty or student)

2. The future of the university (short-term or long-term)

3. Inappropriate elements on campus (anything that is a mismatch between item and university culture)

4. Rules and policies (organizational policies on Americans With Disabilities Act, sexual harrassment, etc.)

5. Pranks or jokes (may be funny or hurtful masked as funny)

6. List of unique language to university and the meanings of words

7. Cartoons hung on faculty doors and bulletin boards. If you do this one, find enough of them to make comparisons between faculty levels and departments or schools. Are there different types of cartoons, for example, in the business school versus liberal arts? This one counts as three electives, since it is more time-consuming and requires more planning.

8. The value of a college education (technical skills, employability, increased income, life-long learning, intellectual heritage)

SOURCE: Adapted from Lizabeth A. Barclay and Kenneth M. York, "The Scavenger Hunt: Symbols of Organizational Culture," *Journal of Management Education*, Vol. 20 (1), Feb. 1996, pp. 125–128; Susan Rueschoff, "Scavenger Hunt," in Dorothy Marcic, *Instructor's Manual to Accompany Organizational Behavior: Experiences and Cases*, West Publishing, 1995; and Anand Narasimhan, Vanderbilt University.

Management in Practice: Ethical Dilemma

Watching Out for Larry

It was the end of the fourth quarter, and Holly Vasquez was completing the profitability statement for her division's regional manager. She was disturbed to see that, for the first time during her tenure as a sales manager for Wallog Computers, her group was not in the top 10 percent of the region. She had watched sales slip during the past year but hoped the fourth quarter might save their numbers. The company was under pressure from stockholders to increase sales. Vasquez was afraid that Wallog would be cutting staff and altering the "people culture" that had kept her there for the past 10 years.

As she entered the individual results in the spreadsheet, she saw her main problem: Larry Norris. After 27 years with the company, Norris had more career sales than anyone in the region, but, for the past three years, he had not even met his quota. Unlike some of her newer salespeople, Norris was uninformed on new products, and his old-style selling techniques didn't seem to be working. Vasquez had suggested he consult with the "new guys" on technical information and new sales techniques, but Norris was stubborn.

Vasquez knew she had the performance information to move him out of his position, but there was nowhere for him to go at Wallog. At 56, he was too young for retirement but too old to find a job elsewhere at his current salary. Not only was Larry Norris a friend, but also he was well liked in her department, and Vasquez wondered what effect his replacement would have on morale. She didn't want to fire him, but she couldn't risk her team's standing or her own reputation by protecting him anymore.

What do you do?

1. Fire Larry Norris and give him two-weeks' notice, a generous severance package, and all the help you can provide him in his job hunt.
2. Give him an ultimatum to meet his sales quota or else, and let him find the way. It is his responsibility to stay current and meet his quota.
3. Assign him to study the new products and the sales techniques of the top salespeople—then hope he improves and the others don't slip.

Case for Critical Analysis

Society of Equals

Ted Shelby doesn't make very many mistakes, but . . .

"Hey Stanley," says Ted Shelby, leaning in through the door, "you got a minute? I've just restructured my office. Come on and take a look. I've been implementing some great new concepts!"

Stanley is always interested in Ted Shelby's new ideas, for if there is anyone Stanley wants to do as well as, it is Edward W. Shelby IV. Stanley follows Ted back to his office and stops, nonplussed.

Restructured is right! Gone are Ted's size B (Junior Executive) walnut veneer desk and furniture, and his telephone table. In fact, the room is practically empty save for a large, round, stark white cafeteria table and the half-dozen padded vinyl swivel chairs that surround it.

"Isn't it a beauty! As far as I know, I'm the first executive in the plant to innovate this. The shape is the crucial factor here—no front or rear, no status problems. We can all sit there and communicate more effectively."

We? Communicate? Effectively? Well, it seems that Ted has been attending a series of Executive Development Seminars given by Dr. Faust. The theme of the seminars was (you guessed it) "participative management." Edward W. Shelby IV has always liked to think of himself as a truly democratic person.

"You see, Stanley," says Ted, managing his best sincere/intense attitude, "the main thing wrong with current mainstream management practice is that the principal communication channel is down-the-line oriented. We on the top send our messages down to you people, but we neglect the feedback potential. But just because we have more status and responsibility doesn't mean that we are necessarily" (Stanley duly noted the word, "necessarily") "better than the people below us. So, as I see the situation, what is needed is a two-way communication network: down-the-line and up-the-line."

"That's what the cafeteria table is for?" Stanley says.

"Yes!" says Ted. "We management people don't have all the answers, and I don't know why I never realized it before that seminar. Why . . . let's take an extreme example . . . the folks who run those machines out there. I'll bet that any one of them knows a thing or two that I've never thought of. So I've transformed my office into a full-feedback communication net."

"That certainly is an innovation around here," says Stanley.

A few days later Stanley passed by Ted Shelby's office and was surprised that Ted's desk, furniture, and telephone table were back where they used to be.

Stanley, curious about the unrestructuring, went to Bonnie for enlightenment. "What happened," he asked, "to Shelby's round table?"

"That table we were supposed to sit around and input things?" she said. "All I know is, about two days after he had it put in, Mr. Drake came walking through here. He looked in that office, and then he sort of stopped and went back—and he looked in there for a long time. Then he came over to me, and you know how his face sort of gets red when he's really mad? Well, this time he was so mad that his face was absolutely white. And when he talked to me, I don't think he actually opened his mouth; and I could barely hear him, he was talking so low. And he said, 'Have that removed. Now. Have Mr. Shelby's furniture put back in his office. Have Mr. Shelby see me.'"

My, my. You would think Ted would have known better, wouldn't you? But then, by now you should have a pretty firm idea of just why it is those offices are set up as they are.

Questions

1. How would you characterize the culture in this company? What are the dominant values?

2. Why did Ted Shelby's change experiment fail? To what extent did Ted use the appropriate change tools to increase employee communication and participation?

3. What would you recommend Ted do to change his relationship with subordinates? Is it possible for a manager to change cultural values if the rest of the organization, especially top management, does not agree?

SOURCE: R. Richard Ritti and G. Ray Funkhouser, *The Ropes to Skip & The Ropes to Know*, 3d. ed. (New York: Wiley, 1987), pp. 176–177. Reprinted by permission of John Wiley & Sons, Inc.

CHAPTER

3

Managing in a Global Environment

LEARNING OBJECTIVES

After studying this chapter, you should be able to do the following:

1 **Describe the emerging borderless world.**

2 **Define international management and explain how it differs from the management of domestic business operations.**

3 **Indicate how dissimilarities in the economic, sociocultural, and legal-political environments throughout the world can affect business operations.**

4 **Describe market entry strategies that businesses use to develop foreign markets.**

5 **Describe the characteristics of a multinational corporation.**

6 **Explain the challenges of managing in a global environment.**

Manager's Challenge

Having conquered the U.S. retail market with its cheerful environment and everyday low prices, Wal-Mart is on a mission to do the same in the rest of the world. Wal-Mart, the world's largest company, opened its first foreign store in Mexico in 1991 and by early 2004 had more than 1,300 overseas units. It has become the biggest retailer in the United States, Mexico, and Canada, and has a growing presence in Asia, Europe, and South America. Every week, more than 100 million shoppers visit a Wal-Mart store somewhere in the world. Yet international expansion has not come without some costly blunders. Consider the situation in Germany, Europe's biggest consumer market. Germany had well-established discounters when Wal-Mart entered the market by purchasing 95 stores from two small German chains. To fend off the stiff local competition, Wal-Mart managers rushed to cut prices before their computerized inventory monitoring systems were in place, wreaking havoc with operations. Costs in Germany are high, and tough union rules and labor laws made it difficult to cut wages to compensate. Laws and regulations created other problems. Under strict fair competition rules, for example, local rivals won an injunction prohibiting Wal-Mart from selling products below purchase cost. Stringent zoning laws make it difficult to build new stores, and the time frame for remodeling existing stores stretches to years because of rules and red tape. Moreover, the renovations cost five times what managers could expect in the United States. The biggest hurdle for Wal-Mart in Germany, though, may be a clash of shopping cultures. Germans do not favor shopping in huge "everything under one roof" stores, and are willing to shop around for exactly what they want. German customers say they do not care if the cashier is smiling as long as they can find what they want and the price is right. Doing things "the Wal-Mart way" has alienated some customers, employees, and local suppliers. Six years after entering the German market, Wal-Mart had closed two stores and was losing an estimated $100 million annually. One retail analyst in Frankfurt described Wal-Mart's German operation as "a fiasco."[1]

If you were in charge of Wal-Mart Germany, how would you explain the difficulties duplicating its U.S. success in Germany? What recommendations would you have for Wal-Mart managers as they continue their quest to conquer the German retail market?

Wal-Mart has deep pockets and can afford to lose money while it builds its international business. However, the organization is facing enormous challenges in Germany, South America, and Japan, where the company's way of doing business is clashing with cultural values. Other large, successful U.S. businesses, including Federal Express (FedEx) and Nike, have found that "the rest of the world is not the United States of America," as one FedEx competitor put it. All of these companies recognize that international expansion is necessary despite the risks. Companies such as McDonald's, IBM, Coca-Cola, Kellogg, Texas Instruments, and Gillette rely on international business for a substantial portion of their sales and profits. Internet-based companies headquartered in the United States, such as Amazon.com, Yahoo, eBay, and America Online (AOL), are rapidly expanding internationally and finding that, even on the Web, going global is fraught with difficulties. These and other online companies have encountered problems ranging from cultural blunders to violations of foreign laws. All organizations face special problems in tailoring their products and business management to the unique needs of foreign countries. If they succeed, the whole world will be their marketplace.

How important is international business to the study of management? If you are not thinking international, you are not thinking business management. It is that serious. As you read this page, ideas, takeover plans, capital investments, business strategies, products, and services are traveling around the planet by telephone, computer, fax, and overnight mail. Isolation from global events is impossible. The future of our businesses and our societies will be determined by global rather than local relationships.[2]

Rapid advances in technology and communications have made the international dimension an important part of the external environment discussed in Chapter 2. Companies can locate different parts of the organization wherever it makes the most business sense: top leadership in one place, technical brainpower and production in other locales. Virtual connections enable close, rapid coordination and communication among people working in different parts of the world, so keeping all operations in one place has become unnecessary. Samsung Corp., the Korean electronics giant, moved its semiconductor-making facilities to the Silicon Valley to be closer to the best scientific brains in the industry. Canada's Nortel Networks selected a location in southwest England as its world manufacturing center for a new fixed-access radio product. Siemens of Germany has moved its electronic ultrasound division to the United States, and the U.S. company DuPont shifted its electronic operations headquarters to Japan.[3]

If you think you are isolated from global influence, think again. Even if you do not budge from your hometown, your company may be purchased tomorrow by the English, Japanese, or Germans. People in the United States working for Ben & Jerry's Ice Cream, RCA, Dr. Pepper, Greyhound Bus Lines, and the Bic Pen Company work for foreign bosses.

All this means that the environment for companies is becoming extremely complex and extremely competitive. Less-developed countries (LDCs) are challenging mature countries in a number of industries. India has become a major player in software development, for example. China manufactures many of the world's computers and cellular phones and is rapidly staking a claim in the business of chip making. As many as 19 advanced new semiconductor plants were in or nearing operation by 2004.[4]

This chapter introduces basic concepts about the global environment and international management. First, we consider the difficulty managers have operating in an increasingly borderless world. We will address challenges—economic, legal-political, and sociocultural—facing companies within the global business environment. Then we will discuss multinational corporations and touch upon the various strategies and techniques needed for entering and succeeding in foreign markets.

©DIBYANGSHU SARKAR/AFP/Getty Images

A Borderless World

Why do companies such as Wal-Mart, FedEx, and AOL want to pursue a global strategy despite failures and losses? They recognize that business is becoming a unified, global field as trade barriers fall, communication becomes faster and cheaper, and consumer tastes in everything from clothing to cellular phones converge. Thomas Middelhoff of Germany's Bertelsmann AG, which purchased U.S. publisher Random House, put it this way: "There are no German and American companies. There are only successful and unsuccessful companies."[5]

Companies that think globally have a competitive edge. Consider Gayle Warwick Linens, whose luxury linens are woven in Europe, embroidered in Vietnam, and sold primarily in Britain and the United States. A French company handles logistics. Gayle Warwick and her one employee in London spend their time managing a web of global relationships.[6]

In addition, domestic markets are saturated for many companies. The only potential for significant growth lies overseas. Kimberly-Clark and Procter & Gamble, which spent years slugging it out in the flat U.S. diaper market, are targeting new markets such as China, India, Israel, Russia, and Brazil. The demand for steel in China, India, and Brazil together is expected to grow 10 percent annually in the coming years, three times the U.S. rate, providing opportunities for companies such as Nucor and North Star Steel.[7] For online companies, too, going global is a key to growth as a growing percentage of Internet users are outside the United States. Western Europe and Japan account for a huge share of the world's e-commerce revenue.[8]

The reality of today's borderless companies means consumers can no longer tell from which country they are buying. U.S.-based Ford Motor Company owns Sweden's Volvo, while Chrysler, still considered an American brand, is owned by Germany's DaimlerChrysler and builds its PT Cruiser in Mexico. Toyota is a Japanese company, but it has manufactured more than 10 million vehicles in North American factories.

Corporations can participate in the international arena on various levels. The process of globalization typically passes through four distinct stages, as illustrated in Exhibit 3.1.

Take **ACTION**

To understand globalization better: Take out several items of clothing and look at the labels (or alternately, get in a group and have everyone read the label on the top back of the shirt). Look for "Made in..." How many countries are there?

	1. Domestic	2. International	3. Multinational	4. Global
Strategic Orientation	Domestically oriented	Export-oriented, multidomestic	Multinational	Global
Stage of Development	Initial foreign involvement	Competitive positioning	Explosion of international operations	Global
Cultural Sensitivity	Of little importance	Very important	Somewhat important	Critically important
Manager Assumptions	"One best way"	"Many good ways"	"The least-cost way"	"Many good ways"

EXHIBIT 3.1

Four Stages of Globalization

SOURCE: Based on Nancy J. Adler, *International Dimensions of Organizational Behavior*, 4th ed. (Cincinnati, Ohio: South-Western, 2002), 8–9.

For many years, Mattel has been making toys based on the premise that kids in different countries have different interests and want different playthings. Mattel would produce many toys and other gear in various styles. The Barbie dolls sold in Japan, for example, had Asian features, black hair, and Japanese-inspired clothing.

Through research and focus groups, however, Mattel managers learned that blonde-haired, blue-eyes Barbies sold as well in Tokyo or Madrid as they did in Kansas City, USA. The worldwide expansion of cable and satellite television has combined with movies and the Internet to create global kids, who share similar values and interests because they are exposed to the same cultural icons. The shift began with the global deluge of toys, games, and gadgets associated with the release of the first *Harry Potter* movie, because J.K. Rowling's book series already had a global audience. Mattel managers started thinking about the possibilities for global launches of other toys. Movement of people around the world, as immigrants to a new country, can create now business opportunities, as shown below.

Tortasperu

By using computers and cakes, Edwin San Roman and his wife, Maria del Carmen Vucetich, came up with an idea to service a waiting market: Peruvian expatriates around the world, particularly in the United States. For example, Pedro in Los Angeles could visit the Tortas Peru Web site (*http://www.tortasperu.com.pe*) and order a home-baked cake, as a way of showing his love to his Peruvian family. Finding women to bake the cakes was no problem. Through Vucetich's network, she found women all over the country, most of whom needed to earn extra money but found it difficult to work outside the home. Orders would be sent to the women from the Web site via e-mail. Though few people in Peru have computers, the country is well-covered with Internet cafes, where women can access their own e-mail accounts. These women would make the cake to order and personally deliver it to the customer's Peruvian loved one. Average cost: $20. Because a large percentage of the customers were Peruvians living in the United States, payment was made by having them send a check to an American address. However, it took several days for the check to clear and sometimes the cake arrived too late for the special event. Customers were losing interest. Yet, other means of payment were uncommon in Peru. Roman and Vucetich realized if they did not find some other solution that would meet customers needs and be implementable in Peru, their short-lived business would crumble.

Roman was asked to speak at a virtual seminar on tourism in Peru. One of the other speakers was using a credit card system that was workable in Peru, so Roman and his wife signed up for that service. They still take personal checks sent to the U.S. address, or they do bank transfers. With a way to collect money, Tortas Peru expanded to seven Peruvian cities and promises to deliver a cake to any of those cities within 72 hours of the order. They take a digital picture of the cake being delivered and send it back to the customer in the United States. Tortas Peru is such a successful business model that when it entered the 2001 Stockholm Challenge with 62 other contenders for the New Economy Award, it was the only winner. More importantly, it provides a service to Peruvian expatriates and provides much needed income to Peruvian housewives who do not have to leave their homes or their cake pans.[9]

Today, the number of global or stateless corporations is increasing and the awareness of national borders is decreasing, as reflected by the frequency of foreign participation at the management level. Rising managers are expected to know a second or third language and to have international experience. The need for global managers is intense. The need for global managers with cross-cultural sensitivity is intense, as discussed in the Focus on Skills box. Corporations around the world want the brightest and best candidates for global management, and young managers who want their careers to move forward recognize the importance of global experience. According to Harvard Business School professor Christopher Bartlett, author of *Managing Across Borders*, people should get global exposure when they are young to start building skills and networks that will grow throughout their careers.[10] Consider the makeup of today's global companies. Nestlé (Switzerland) personifies the stateless corporation with 98 percent of sales and 96 percent of employees outside the home country. Nestlé's CEO is Austrian-born Peter Brabeck-Letmathe, and half of the company's general managers are not Swiss. The CEO puts strong faith in regional managers who are native to the region and know the local culture. With 8,000 brands, Nestlé is the largest food company in the world.[11]

The International Business Environment

International management is the management of business operations conducted in more than one country. The fundamental tasks of business management, including the financing, production, and distribution of products and services, do not change substantially when a firm is transacting business across international borders. The basic management functions of planning, organizing, leading, and controlling are the same whether a company operates domestically or internationally. However, managers will experience greater difficulties and risks when performing these management functions on an international scale, as in these examples:

- When U.S. chicken entrepreneur Frank Purdue translated a successful advertising slogan into Spanish, "It takes a tough man to make a tender chicken" came out as "It takes a virile man to make a chicken affectionate."[12]

- It took McDonald's more than a year to figure out that Hindus in India do not eat beef. The company's sales took off only after McDonald's started making burgers sold in India out of lamb.[13]

- In Africa, the labels on bottles show pictures of what is inside so illiterate shoppers can know what they are buying. When a baby food company showed a picture of an infant on its label, the product did not sell well.[14]

- United Airlines discovered that colors can doom a product. The airline handed out white carnations when it started flying from Hong Kong, only to discover that to many Asians such flowers represent death and bad luck.[15]

Some of these examples might seem humorous, but there is nothing funny about them to managers operating in a competitive global environment. Companies seeking to expand their international presence on the Internet can encounter cross-cultural problems, as discussed in the Digital, Inc. box. What should managers of emerging global companies look for to avoid obvious international mistakes? When they are comparing one country with another, the economic, legal-political, and

Take ACTION

Take advantage of any opportunity you can to do international internships or school trips over breaks or summers. The working world will value those with international experience.

international management

The management of business operations conducted in more than one country.

FOCUS ON SKILLS

Cross-cultural communication

American managers are often at a disadvantage when doing business overseas. Part of this is the lack of foreign language skills, as well as inexperience in dealing with other cultures and less-than-ideal living conditions. Consequently, many mistakes are made, mistakes which could easily be avoided.

The manager's attitude is perhaps the most important factor in success. Those who go abroad with a sense of "wonder" about the new culture are better off than those with a judgmental view of "If it is different, then my culture must be better." Seeing differences as new and interesting is more productive than being critical. One way is to begin to appreciate rather than evaluate cultural differences. Such evaluations lead to an "us versus them" approach, which sits badly with the locals.

Though every culture has its own way of communicating, here are some basic principles to follow in international business relations:

1. Always show respect and listen carefully. Do not be in a hurry to finish the "business." Many other cultures values the social component of these interactions.

2. Gain an appreciation for the differences between Geert Hofstede's "masculine" and feminine" cultures. American masculine business behaviors include high achievement and the aquisition of material goods and efficiency, but other, more feminine, cultures value relationships, leisure time with family, and developing a sense of community. Do not mistake this more feminine approach with lack of motivation. Similarly, cultures that value "being and inner spiritual development" rather than compulsively "doing," are not necessarily inferior.

3. Understand that your way may not be the best. This can come across as arrogance and rubs salt in deep wounds in some lesser-developed countries.

4. Emphasize points of agreement.

5. When there are disagreements, check on the perceived definitions of words. Often, a huge or subtle shade of meaning may be causing the problem. Both of you may be saying the same thing.

6. Save face and "give" face as well, for this can be a way of showing honor to others.

7. Do not go alone. Take someone who knows the culture or language better than you. If you are discussing in English and the others "know" your language, you might be surprised how much they miss. Often, taking an excellent translator along is a good investment.

8. Do not assume the other country sees leadership in the same way as you do. In many other cultures, "empowerment" seems more like anarchy and the result of an ineffectual manager.

9. Do not lose your temper.

10. Do not embarrass anyone in front of others. Even if you meant it as a "joke," it likely will not be taken that way.

11. Avoid clique-building and interact with the locals as much as possible. Often, Americans tend to hang together in packs or tribes, which is unwelcoming to the locals.

12. Most Asian countries are high-context cultures that are based on a complicated system of relationships and moral codes (some of which might not seem "moral" to you). The United States is low context, meaning people are more direct and they rely on legal codes.

13. Leave the common American task-oriented, fast-paced style at home. Effective transfer of skills to other cultures requires a patient non-judgmentalism. Hasty criticisms of the foreigner's ideas only serve to shut that person down and close the door to meaningful interactions.

14. Understand the pace of other countries because some, such as Israel, are faster-paced and people there get impatient with Americans' small talk.

15. Be sensitive to the difference between the North American low-context culture, where employees are encouraged to be self-reliant, and high-context cultures (much of Asia, Africa, South America), where workers expect warmly supportive relationships with their American supervisors and co-workers.

16. If you travel to the increasingly visited out-of-the-way locations, learn to tolerate unpredictiability and go without what you may consider basic amenities. Avoid complaining to business clients about poor phone service, lack of hot water (or any, for that matter), erratic availability of electricity, or unsavory food. You are a guest and should act with the grace that goes along with that role.

SOURCES: Peter Cowley and Barbara E. Hanna, "Cross-Cultural Skills – Crossing the Disciplinary Divide," *Language & Culture* (Jan. 2005): 1–17; Pui-Wing Tam, "Culture course," *The Wall Street Journal* (May 25, 2004): B1, B12;; Lalita Khosla, "You Say Tomato," *Forbes* (May 21, 2001): 36; Geert Hofstede, "Motivation, leadership and organization: Do American theories apply abroad?" *Organizational Dynamics* (Summer 1980): 42–63.

© Tom Stoddard/Getty Images

CONCEPT CONNECTION

*Exxon Mobile operates in an **international business environment** with a presence in more than 200 countries and territories. Here, 40 ft sections of pipeline will carry oil from land-locked oil fields of Chad through the jungles of Cameroon to the Gulf of Guinea. The 660 mile Exxon Mobil pipeline cost $3.5 billion and will carry 225,000 barrels of oil a day to a marine terminal for export. It is a constant challenge to managers to protect the safety and health of employees while producing oil, energy and chemical products.*

sociocultural sectors present the greatest difficulties. Key factors to understand in the international environment are summarized in Exhibit 3.2. Negotiating deals can be troublesome without understanding the other culture, as explained in the Focus on Skills box.

The Economic Environment

The economic environment represents the economic conditions in the country where the international organization operates. This part of the environment includes such factors as economic development, infrastructure, resource and product markets, and exchange rates, each of which is discussed in the following sections. In addition, factors such as inflation, interest rates, and economic growth are part of the international economic environment. One area that often differs among countries is how services are rendered, as shown in the Business Blooper box.

Economic Development

Economic development differs widely among the countries and regions of the world. Countries can be categorized as developing or developed. Developing countries are referred to as less-developed countries (LDCs). The criterion traditionally used to classify countries as developed or developing is per capita income, which is the income

BUSINESS BLOOPER

Aeroflot

A passenger on Russia's Aeroflot airline got tired of the sloppy service he was receiving from two flight attendants, who had sampled from the liquor tray and were way over the legal limit. After more frustration dealing with the drunk attendants, he asked if there was a sober employee who would be able to serve him. Their response may indicate a need for customer service training. The two intoxicated crew members beat him up.

SOURCE: Adam Horowitz, Mark Athitakis, Mark Lasswell and Owen Thomas, "101 Dumbest Moments in Business," *Business 2.0* (Jan./Feb. 2005): 103–112.

EXHIBIT 3.2

Key Factors in the International Environment

DIGITAL, INC.

Virtual Reality: Negotiating the Cross-Cultural Web

With worldwide acceptance of the Internet blossoming, going global has the green light. But technological and cultural issues are so tightly interwoven that there are a multitude of new ways to offend or alienate customers in other nations. For instance, certain gestures, colors, and phrases do not translate well or are considered offensive. A thumb's up sign means approval or encouragement to Americans and many Europeans, but the gesture is considered an obscenity in Greece. Purple is a sign of royalty in some parts of the world, but in others it is associated with death. Credit cards are the backbone of e-commerce in the United States, but they are still a rarity in many countries, causing all sorts of payment problems. And consumers in Germany view credit as a crutch for people who cannot control their finances.

Managers should consider that many online shoppers want to buy from sites that cater to their native language: Research has found that Japanese managers are much more likely to conduct an online transaction when addressed in Japanese. Unfortunately, though 6 percent of the world's people speak English as a first language, a majority of e-commerce sites are written in English. In the early 2000s, fewer than half of U.S. companies had attempted to pattern their Web sites to the culture or language of foreign users. Some companies are taking the lead in overcoming global challenges on the Internet. The Walt

Disney Internet Group has almost 24 Web sites tailored to individual countries, and foreign users account for 42 percent of the audience for the group's sites. The National Basketball Association (NBA) has nine versions of NBA.com aimed at foreign markets, including Brazil, China, and Taiwan. The National Football League (NFL) is way ahead of most businesses in creating Web sites that serve foreign audiences in their native languages. The NFL's new Chinese site features commentary by Chad Lewis, a Philadelphia Eagles tight end who speaks Mandarin as a result of missionary work he did in Taiwan.

Businesses have been slow to build foreign language Web sites because they require significant investment with no guarantee of returns. However, overseas markets are experiencing tremendous Internet growth. In mid-2003, for example, China had 68 million Internet users, which represented a 15 percent increase in six months. The virtual reality for managers is that they have to shape their Web sites if they want to reach this growing international market.

SOURCES: Bob Tedeschi, "American Web Sites Speak the Language of Overseas Users," *The New York Times* (January 12, 2004), accessed at http://www.nytimes.com/2004/01/12/business/12ecom.html; Steve Ulfelder, "All the Web's a Stage," CIO (October 1, 2000): 133–142; Daniel Pearl, "Lost in the Translation," *The Wall Street Journal* (February 12, 2001): R12, R14; and Adam Lincoln, "Lost in Translation," *eCFO* (Spring, 2001): 38–43.

R&H Design

Manufacturing clothing is a lot more complicated than it used to be. Just ask Russ Berens, founder and CEO of casual apparel company R&H Design (R&H). He spent his whole adult life building the company to $20 million revenues and 200 employees in California. A few years ago, troubles started. Other manufacturers were moving offshore and sold garments for $20 less than R&H could produce them. After laying off employees in 2003, Berens saw two choices: get out of the business, or move offshore. He opted for the second in China.

Trouble is, Berens had never been to China and did not care to go. He is the true Californian, who, at age 65, says "dude" a lot. Most companies hire a trading company to work overseas, but Berens was worried about quality loss. So, he went himself, with Tim Runyon an entrepreneuer/logistics specialist. They found a suitable factory, had some test garments run and tested the factory's productivity levels, even sending a Chinese colleague to the factory at night to make sure they were told the whole truth.

A big challenge was in deal-making. Americans are used to being direct, but the Chinese are not. Berens learned to follow their lead. He discovered that an effective strategy is often long silences or walking out of the room. Runyon found that instead of raising his voice, it worked better to decline a lunch invitation or leave a competitor's business card out in plain view. Because of these tactics, they negotiated a better deal.

Berens makes clothing in China at about 50 percent of the previous cost. His goal: By next year, half the clothes will be manufactured abroad. But he wants to keep the California plant open though scaled back. It has not been easy. Berens and Runyon have been criticized for sending jobs overseas. A golf buddy called them names for 17 holes. And neither of them feels good about what they had to do, but they agree this was necessary to save the company. Still, it is a rocky road they are on. "I'm not going to sit here and say how great going China is," says Berens, "But we'll do what we have to so that we'll survive."

SOURCE: Carlye Adler, "Little Trouble in Big China," *Fortune FSB* (March 2004): 56–61.

---

generated by the nation's production of goods and services divided by total population. The developing countries have low per capita incomes. LDCs are generally located in Asia, Africa, and South America. Developed countries are generally located in North America, Europe, and Japan.

Most international business firms are headquartered in the wealthier, economically advanced countries. However, smart companies are investing heavily in Asia, Eastern Europe, and Latin America.[16] For example, the number of Internet users and the rate of e-commerce in Latin America is rapidly growing.[17] Computer companies have launched online stores for Latin American customers to buy computers over the Internet. AOL sees Latin America as crucial to expanding its global presence even though Universo Online International (UOL), based in Brazil, got a tremendous head start over AOL.[18] These companies face risks and challenges, but they stand to reap huge benefits in the future. Dr. Greg Allgood needed persevence to bring his product to developing nations, as shown in the Best Practices box.

Infrastructure

A country's physical facilities that support economic activities make up its **infrastructure**, which includes transportation facilities such as airports, highways, and railroads; energy-producing facilities such as utilities, power plants; and communication facilities such as telephone lines and radio stations. Companies operating in LDCs must contend with lower levels of technology and perplexing logistical, distribution, and communication problems. Undeveloped infrastructures represent opportunities for some firms, such as United Technologies Corporation, based in Hartford, Connecticut, whose businesses include jet engines, air conditioning and heating systems, and elevators. As countries such as China, Russia, and Vietnam open their markets, new buildings need elevators and air and heating systems; opening remote regions for commerce requires more jet engines and helicopters.[19] Cellular telephone companies have found tremendous opportunities in LDCs, where land lines remain limited. In Latin America, for example, the number of mobile phone lines skyrocketed from 100,000 in 1990 to

Take ACTION

If you can go to a developing country and get outside of the foreigners complex to see how average people live, you will be astounded at how people manage to survive on so little.

infrastructure

A country's physical facilities that support economic activities.

BEST PRACTICES

P&G's Pur

As part of his job at Procter & Gamble (P&G), toxicologist Dr. Greg Allgood sometimes has to chug water that only 20 minutes before was brown with clumps of dirt. It is part of the demonstration he gives on his company's product, Pur, a water purification powder. P&G had spent four years and $10 million on research and development but could not get anyone in developing countries interested. At 10 cents a packet, it was relatively expensive; the mixing and straining of it and waiting 20 minutes seemed too complicated. The company was ready to write off the project. Allgood had to worry about what to do with the millions of packets sitting in a Manila warehouse.

Then came a tsunami in December 2004, and his cell phone would not stop ringing. One relief organization after another called him for the product. At first, P&G charged 3.5 cents per packet and then donated them when it realized the enormity of the damage. P&G even added another shift to its factory to meet its promise of shipping 28 million packets.

Dr. Allgood's first trip to Sri Lanka was typical. It was a country where Pur was unknown and he spent days driving from one village to another, demonstrating how the product works. He took his bucket to a well that had been covered in 5 feet of water after the first wave. The well water was contaminated with debris and dirt, and he showed the villagers how to fill the bucket, pour in Pur, and stir for five minutes. Clumps of dirt appeared but later fell to the bottom. The villagers commented as Allgood poured water into another bucket, straining it through a cloth, and then waited for 20 minutes. No one wanted to drink the water, so Allgood guzzled some and asked them to do the same.

People were interested in the product if only they still had buckets left after the tsunami. One or two rupees seemed reasonable to them, but not eight rupees, which equals less than two cents. The company has three pricing structures: retail of nine cents, nonprofits for eight cents, and selling it at cost— 3.5 cents—to relief organizations.

Getting a new product introduced after a disaster can be difficult. Relief workers, pressed for time, use the product quickly, leaving locals confused after they leave. P&G abandoned selling the product in Iraq after a nonprofit worker was kidnapped. That was when they realized gathering people together for demonstrations was not a good idea.

Armed with a list of the 40 countries with the highest infant mortality rate caused by impure water, Allgood is embarking on a 20-year strategy, introducing Pur into two new developing countries per year. Would it not be nice if his plan succeeds?

SOURCE: Sarah Ellison and Eric Bellman, "Clean Water, No Profit," *The Wall Street Journal* (Feb. 23, 2005): B1, B2.

---

38 million by 1999, and estimates are that the number will jump to 170 million by 2008.[20] Helping countries develop their infrastructure often falls on the shoulders of international agencies such as the World Bank, which discovered the Web as a major asset, as described in the example below.

World Bank

Computers and networks are changing lives for poor people around the world. For example, like so many other developing countries, Pakistan has crumbling roads. With even worse finances, it asked the World Bank for help in rating a cheap paving method. Several years ago, it would have taken bank experts nine months to research the problem. Using the Internet, it was solved in one day. After it posted a query on its Web site, the bank got a reply from one of its employees in Argentina, who had written a book on the subject.

The Web is helping the World Bank to be a leader in knowledge management, unleashing the human expertise in its ranks worldwide. Its site acts like a giant chat room, with topics and data relating to concepts like health care, education, or urban planning as it forges expert communities across borders. A recent project linked experts from ten Latin American cities, with competences in solid waste, municipal engineering, and transport. "Knowledge sharing will allow us to really have an impact on poverty," says Robert Chavez, a World Bank urban planner. The bank and other development agencies funded these projects: Vijay Bhatkar developed computer software that allows illiterates to use computers with only icons. Five hundred telehouses in rural Hungary serve 1 million people, allowing them access to the Internet, Web site design, and construction for local businesses. In Mali and India, farmers are helped with solar-powered computers, e-mail, and e-kiosks to give them information on market prices, soil erosion, and other ways to increase their profits.

Instead of shuffling money from richer nations to poorer ones and hoping the needy are helped, this new way of doing business fundamentally changes the agency's operations. Timely know-how can be given, helping funds to be used more wisely. It creates a "different vision," says knowledge management director Stephen Denning. If the new economy keeps moving ahead, Third World countries might have a healthier road to economic recovery.[21]

Resource and Product Markets

When operating in another country, company managers must evaluate the market demand for their products. If market demand is high, managers may choose to export products to that country. To develop plants, however, resource markets for providing needed raw materials and labor must be available. For example, the greatest challenge for McDonald's, which sells Big Macs on every continent except Antarctica, is to obtain supplies of everything from potatoes to hamburger buns to plastic straws. At McDonald's in Cracow, the burgers come from a Polish plant, partly owned by Chicago-based OSI Industries; the onions come from Fresno, California; the buns come from a production and distribution center near Moscow; and the potatoes come from a plant in Aldrup, Germany. McDonald's contracts with local suppliers when possible. In Thailand, McDonald's helped farmers cultivate Idaho russet potatoes of sufficient quality to produce their golden french fries.[22]

Exchange Rates

Exchange rate is the rate at which one country's currency is exchanged for another country's. Volatility in exchange rates has become a major concern for companies doing business internationally.[23] Changes in the exchange rate can have major implications for the profitability of international operations that exchange millions of dollars into other currencies every day.[24] For example, assume that the U.S. dollar is exchanged for 0.8 euros. If the dollar increases in value to 0.9 euros, U.S. goods will be more expensive in France because it will take more euros to buy a dollar's worth of U.S. goods. It will be more difficult to export U.S. goods to France, and profits will be slim. If the dollar drops to a value of 0.7 euros, however, U.S. goods will be cheaper in France and can be exported at a profit.

The Legal-Political Environment

Businesses must deal with unfamiliar political systems when they go international, as well as with more government supervision and regulation. Government officials and the general public often view foreign companies as outsiders or even intruders and are suspicious of their impact on economic independence and political sovereignty. Some of the major legal-political concerns affecting international business are political risk, political instability, and laws and regulations.

Political Risk and Political Instability

A company's **political risk** is defined as its risk of loss of assets, earning power, or managerial control due to politically based events or actions by host governments.[25] Political risk includes government takeovers of property and acts of violence directed

---

Take ACTION

When you travel overseas, never buy foreign money on the streets. In many places, this is illegal and you can end in jail or with counterfeit money. Use regular banks, legal money changers or ATMs.

political risk

A company's risk of loss of assets, earning power, or managerial control due to politically based events or actions by host governments.

against a firm's properties or employees. In Mexico, business executives and their families are a prime target for gangs of kidnappers, many of which are reportedly led by state and local police. The daughter of the local head of a Japanese tire company, for example, was kidnaped in 2000 and the company paid a $1 million ransom. Estimates are that big companies in Mexico typically spend between 5 and 15 percent of their annual budgets on security.[26] Companies operating in other countries also formulate special plans and programs to guard against unexpected losses. Executives at Tricon, which owns KFC and Pizza Hut restaurants, monitor events through an international security service to stay on top of potential hot spots.[27] Some companies buy political risk insurance, and political risk analysis has emerged as a critical component of environmental assessment for multinational organizations.[28] To reduce uncertainty, organizations sometimes rely on the *Index of Economic Freedom*, which ranks countries according to the impact political intervention has on business decisions, and the *Corruption Perception Index*, which assesses 91 countries according to the level of perceived corruption in government and public administration.[29]

Though most companies would prefer to do business in stable countries, some of the greatest growth opportunities lie in areas characterized by instability. The greatest threat of violence is in countries experiencing political, ethnic, or religious upheaval. In China, for example, political winds have shifted rapidly and often dangerously. Yet it is the largest potential market in the world for the goods and services of developed countries.

Laws and Regulations

Government laws and regulations differ from country to country and make doing business a challenge for international firms. Host governments have a myriad of laws concerning libel statutes, consumer protection, information and labeling, employment and safety, and wages. International companies must learn these rules and regulations and must abide by them. In addition, the Internet has increased the impact of foreign laws on U.S. companies because it expands the potential for doing business on a global basis. Sometimes dealing with other countries, laws can be unexpectedly helpful, as Iqbal S. Quadir found in Bangladesh, described in the example below.

GrameenPhone	Twelve years ago, when Iqbal S. Quadir tried to get investors for a mobile phone network in Bangladesh, he got lots of rejection, such as the New York cell phone executive who said, "We're not the Red Cross." That is precisely the kind of thinking that keeps countries poor, says Harvard lecturer Quadir, because companies do not see enough of the profit possibilities in underdeveloped areas.

Proving the naysayers wrong, Quadir's GrameenPhone posted profits of $27 million last year, after eight years in operation. It has doubled the number of phones in the past year, now up to 2 million, with 63 percent market share. No one thought that possible. Not even business mogul-turned philanthropist Bill Gates, who has said there is no market for such electronic devices in poor and remote areas. Certainly the government did not think it would take off either. They did not charge Quadir an upfront licensing fee, as they held the common belief that cell phones would be a marginal business only for the rich. But Quadir managed to pull together a group of private individuals with some government loans as well.

One of Quadir's early investors was Bangldesh's Grameen Bank, world famous for its microloans to small businesses in poor countries. Grameen Bank follows a similar model. It offers normal cellular service to urban customers and has another tier, Village Phone. That is where women in areas with no phone service get small loans to buy a phone and air time, turning around and selling time on their phones to people in their village. GrameenPhone boasts 575,000 subscribers in more than 12,000 villages, more than the national telecom.

©Caroline Penn/CORBIS

Quadir is now on the board of many organzations, including DigitalDivide.com, devoted to this system of public and private funding to aid entrepreneurs in poor countries. His next venture might prove more challenging: Setting up a cell phone company in Afghanistan, a country with no visible banking or telecommunications. Undaunted, he pushes forth. "I've done it before."[30]

The Sociocultural Environment

A nation's culture includes the shared knowledge, beliefs, and values, as well as the common modes of behavior and ways of thinking, among members of a society. Cultural factors can be more perplexing than political and economic factors when working or living in a foreign country. Cultural clashes can come in unusual ways, as described in the example below.

Miss Pakistani Earth

Neelam Nourani won the Miss Pakistani Earth competition a couple of years ago without wearing a bathing suit, so as not to offend Muslim sensibilities about revealing women's bodies. Judges were told to speculate whether the contestants had "nice healthy bodies" underneath their roomy trouser and tunic costumes. Now Nourani will have to buy a swimsuit to compete in the international Miss Earth contest.

Along with other concerns in Muslim countries, there has been some pressure to "develop." Along with fast food, beauty contests have become a measure of westernization that some countries shun, including Malaysia and Indonesia, which have the world's largest Muslim population. Others adapt it to the Muslim way. That was

Muhammed Usman's idea in 1994 when he saw rival India take the Miss World and Miss Universe crowns. Both countries have nuclear weapons, reasoned Usman. "Why not beauty queens?" So, he hooked up with the Miss Earth contest, which has a "green theme," and have "beauties for a cause."

Using family and friends as investors, Usman held the first contest in 2002, where 73 people showed up to watch the 18 contestants sing and dance or recite Urdu poetry. Britney Spears fan Nourani used a disco Pakistani song for her energetic performance. Other contests were held in 2003 and 2004.

Winner Nourani had to hire bodyguards on her promotional tour to protect herself from Islamic extremists. "In Pakistan, if you take part in beauty contests," she says, you are considered a scandalous woman. Afghani Zohra Yusof Daoud would like to see that changed. Living in California and an activist for women's rights, she was the 1972 Miss Afghanistan. She wants the world to see that Afghani women are more than faceless burka-wearers. But it would have to "incorporate Muslim values," she notes, and she is not sure how that could be done.

Having spent some of her formative years in the United States, Nourani has a western frankness that made her an outcast amongst the contestants. "We are Allah's creation," she says. "We have a right to represent womanhood."[31]

Social Values

Culture is intangible, pervasive, and difficult for outsiders to learn. One way managers can comprehend local cultures and deal with them effectively is to understand differences in social values.

Hofstede's Value Dimensions. Research done by Geert Hofstede on 116,000 IBM employees in 40 countries identified four dimensions of national value systems that influence organizational and employee working relationships.[32] Examples of how countries rate on the four dimensions are shown in Exhibit 3.3.

1. Power distance. High **power distance** means that people accept inequality in power among institutions, organizations, and people. Low power distance means that people expect equality in power. Countries that value high power distance are Malaysia, the Philippines, and Panama. Countries that value low power distance are Denmark, Austria, and Israel.

2. Uncertainty avoidance. High **uncertainty avoidance** means that members of a society feel uncomfortable with uncertainty and ambiguity and, thus, support beliefs that promise certainty and conformity. Low uncertainty avoidance means that people have high tolerance for the unstructured, unclear, and unpredictable. High uncertainty avoidance countries include Greece, Portugal, and Uruguay. Countries with low uncertainty avoidance values are Singapore and Jamaica.

3. Individualism and collectivism. **Individualism** reflects a value for a loosely knit social framework in which individuals are expected to take care of themselves. **Collectivism** means a preference for a tightly knit social framework in which individuals look after one another and organizations protect their members' interests. Countries with individualist values include the United States, Canada, Great Britain, and Australia. Countries with collectivist values are Guatemala, Ecuador, and China.

4. Masculinity/femininity. **Masculinity** stands for preference for achievement, heroism, assertiveness, work centrality (with resultant high stress), and material success. **Femininity** reflects the values of relationships, cooperation, group decision making, and quality of life. Societies with strong masculine values are Japan,

power distance
The degree to which people accept inequality in power among institutions, organizations, and people.

uncertainty avoidance
A value characterized by people's intolerance for uncertainty and ambiguity and resulting support for beliefs that promise certainty and conformity.

individualism
A preference for a loosely knit social framework in which individuals are expected to take care of themselves.

collectivism
A preference for a tightly knit social framework in which individuals look after one another and organizations protect their members' interests.

masculinity
A cultural preference for achievement, heroism, assertiveness, work centrality, and material success.

femininity
A cultural preference for relationships, cooperation, group decision making, and quality of life.

Country	Power Distance[a]	Uncertainty Avoidance[b]	Individualism[c]	Masculinity[d]
Australia	7	7	2	5
Costa Rica	8 (tie)	2 (tie)	10	9
France	3	2 (tie)	4	7
West Germany	8 (tie)	5	5	3
India	2	9	6	6
Japan	5	1	7	1
Mexico	1	4	8	2
Sweden	10	10	3	10
Thailand	4	6	9	8
United States	6	8	1	4

[a] 1=highest power distance
   10=lowest power distance
   1=highest uncertainty avoidance
[b] 10=lowest uncertainty avoidance

[c] 1=highest individualism
   10=highest collectivisim
[d] 1=highest masculinity
   10=highest femininity

EXHIBIT 3.3

Rank Orderings of Ten Countries along Four Dimensions of National Value System

SOURCE: From Dorothy Marcic, *Organizational Behavior and Cases,* 4th ed. (St. Paul, Minn.: West, 1995). Based on Geert Hofstede, *Culture's Consequences* (London: Sage Publications, 1984); and *Cultures and Organizations: Software of the Mind* (New York: McGraw-Hill, 1991).

Austria, Mexico, and Germany. Countries with feminine values are Sweden, Norway, Denmark, and France. Both men and women subscribe to the dominant value in masculine and feminine cultures.

Hofstede and his colleagues later identified a fifth dimension, long-term orientation versus short-term orientation. The **long-term orientation**, found in China and other Asian countries, includes a greater concern for the future and highly values thrift and perseverance. A **short-term orientation**, found in Russia and West Africa, is more concerned with the past and the present and places a high value on tradition and meeting social obligations.[33] Researchers have continued to explore and expand on Hofstede's findings. For example, in the last 25 years, more than 1,400 articles and numerous books have been published on individualism and collectivism alone.[34]

Globe Project Value Dimensions. Recent research by the GLOBE Project extends Hofstede's assessment and offers a broader understanding for today's managers. The Global Leadership and Organizational Behavior Effectiveness (GLOBE) project used data collected from 18,000 managers in 62 countries to identify nine dimensions that explain cultural differences, including those identified by Hofstede.[35]

1. Assertiveness. A high value on assertiveness means a society encourages toughness, assertiveness, and competitiveness. Low assertiveness means that people value tenderness and concern for others over being competitive.

2. Future orientation. Similar to Hofstede's time orientation, this refers to the extent to which a society encourages and rewards planning for the future over short-term results and quick gratification.

3. Uncertainty avoidance. As with Hofstede's study, this is the degree to which members of a society feel uncomfortable with uncertainty and ambiguity.

4. Gender differentiation. This dimension refers to the extent to which a society maximizes gender role differences. In countries with low gender differentiation, such as Denmark, women typically have a higher status and stronger role in decision making. Countries with high gender differentiation accord men higher social, political, and economic status.

long-term orientation

A greater concern for the future and high value on thrift and perseverance.

short-term orientation

A concern with the past and present and a high value on meeting social obligations.

Take ACTION

To understand, consider: Americans are much more individualistic than Eastern countries. In those places, the person's identity is closely tied to their extended family and many obligations result, coupled with deep ties of love.

Take **ACTION**

Remember: People from some Eastern countries have more obligations with their families, while Americans have fewer family obligations but more workplace obligations. It all evens out.

5. Power distance. This dimension is the same as Hofstede's and refers to the degree to which people expect and accept equality or inequality in relationships and institutions.

6. Societal collectivism. This term is defined as the degree to which practices in institutions such as schools, businesses, and other social organizations encourage a tightly knit collectivist society, in which people are an important part of a group, or a highly individualistic society.

7. Individual collectivism. Rather than looking at how societal organizations favor individualism versus collectivism, this dimension looks at the degree to which individuals take pride in being members of a family, close circle of friends, team, or organization.

8. Performance orientation. A society with a high performance orientation places high emphasis on performance and rewards people for performance improvements and excellence. A low performance orientation means people pay less attention to performance and more attention to loyalty, belonging, and background.

9. Humane orientation. The final dimension refers to the degree to which a society encourages and rewards people for being fair, altruistic, generous, and caring. A country high on humane orientation places high value on helping others and being kind. A country low on this orientation expects people to take care of themselves. Self-enhancement and gratification is of high importance.

Exhibit 3.4 gives examples of how some countries rank on several of the GLOBE dimensions. These dimensions give managers an added tool for identifying and managing cultural differences. While Hofstede's dimensions remain valid, the GLOBE research provides a more comprehensive view of cultural similarities and differences.

Social values have great influence on organizational functioning and management styles. Consider the difficulty that managers have had implementing self-directed work teams in Mexico. As shown in Exhibit 3.3, Mexico is characterized by high power distance and a relatively low tolerance for uncertainty, characteristics that often conflict

EXHIBIT 3.4

Examples of Country Rankings on Selected GLOBE Value Dimensions

Dimension	Low	Medium	High
Assertiveness	Sweden Switzerland Japan	Egypt Iceland France	Spain United States Germany (former East)
Future Orientation	Russia Italy Kuwait	Slovenia Australia India	Denmark Canada Singapore
Gender Differentiation	Sweden Denmark Poland	Italy Brazil Netherlands	South Korea Egypt China
Performance Orientation	Russia Greece Venezuela	Israel England Japan	United States Taiwan Hong Kong
Humane Orientation	Germany France Singapore	New Zealand Sweden United States	Indonesia Egypt Iceland

SOURCE: Mansour Javidan and Robert J. House, "Cultural Acumen for the Global Manager: Lessons from Project GLOBE," *Organizational Dynamics* 29, no. 4 (2001), 289–305.

with the American concept of teamwork, which emphasizes shared power and authority, with team members working on various problems without formal guidelines, rules, and structure. Many workers in Mexico, as well as in France and Mediterranean countries, expect organizations to be hierarchical. In Russia, people are good at working in groups and like competing as a team rather than on an individual basis. Organizations in Germany and other central European countries typically strive to be impersonal, well-oiled machines. Effective management styles differ in each country, depending on cultural characteristics.[36]

Take a moment to complete the statements below to help you understand how behaviors in culture follow from values and beliefs.

AS..IF Instrument

Complete the thoughts below. Use as many sentences are you need to get your point across.

What would a society be like IF it believed implicitly:

1. in reincarnation and karma.

2. that all other people are infidels.

3. that all events in the world are determined by Fate.

4. in the passive approach to life as preferable to an action orientation.

5. that certain ethnic or racial groups are intellectually inferior and emotionally immature.

6. that old people were to be revered, honored, and deferred to in all instances.

7. that aesthetic values are of supreme importance and should be used to determine every major issue in life.

8. that rights of groups are more important than those of the individual.

9. that women are superior.

Developed by Christopher Taylor, University of Arizona.

Other Cultural Characteristics

Other cultural characteristics that influence international organizations are language, religion, attitudes, social organization, and education. Some countries, such as India, are characterized by linguistic pluralism, meaning that several languages exist there. Other countries rely heavily on spoken versus written language. Religion includes sacred objects, philosophical attitudes toward life, taboos, and rituals. Attitudes toward achievement, work, and people can affect organizational productivity. For example, a recent study found that the prevalent American attitude that treats employees as a resource to be used (an instrumental attitude toward people) can impede business success in countries where people are valued as an end in themselves rather than as a

ethnocentrism

A cultural attitude marked by the tendency to regard one's own culture as superior to others.

means to an end (a humanistic attitude). U.S. companies sometimes use instrumental human resource policies that conflict with local humanistic values.[37]

Ethnocentrism, which refers to a natural tendency of people to regard their own culture as superior and to downgrade or dismiss other cultural values, can be found in all countries. Strong ethnocentric attitudes within a country make it difficult for foreign firms to operate there. Other factors include social organization, such as status systems, kinship and families, social institutions, and opportunities for social mobility. Education influences the literacy level, the availability of qualified employees, and the predominance of primary or secondary degrees.

American managers are regularly accused of an ethnocentric attitude that assumes the American way is the best way. At an executive training seminar at IMD, a business school in Lausanne, Switzerland, managers from Europe expressed a mixture of admiration and disdain for U.S. managers. "They admire the financial results," says J. Peter Killing, an IMD professor, "but when they meet managers from the United States they see that even these educated, affluent Americans do not speak any language besides English, do not know how or when to eat and drink properly, and do not know anything about European history, let alone geography."[38] Take the quiz in the Focus on Skills box to see how much you know about cross-cultural communication and etiquette.

As business grows increasingly global, U.S. managers are learning that cultural differences cannot be ignored if international operations are to succeed. For example, Coca-Cola withdrew its two-liter bottle from the Spanish market after discovering that compartments of Spanish refrigerators were too small for it. Wal-Mart goofed by stocking footballs in Brazil, a country where soccer rules.[39] Companies can improve their success by paying attention to culture. Consider how addressing cultural differences helped McDonald's thrive in France even as the corporation's U.S. business stalled.

In January 2003, McDonald's posted its first ever quarterly loss (for October–December 2002) and announced the closing of 175 outlets worldwide. Yet, during that same time period, a new McDonald's restaurant was opening in France every six days.

Take **ACTION**

Notice your own tendencies toward ethnocentrism. When you see people from another culture dressing, eating, or interacting differently, are you immediately critical or do you curiously wonder why the behave so? If you traveled to a Buddhist or Hindu country, would you insist on ostentatiously celebrating Christmas or some other religious holiday?

⟨FOCUS ON SKILLS⟩

How Well Do You Play the Culture Game?

How good are you at understanding cross-cultural differences in communication and etiquette? For fun, see how many of the following questions you can answer correctly. The answers appear at the end.

1. You want to do business with a Greek company, but the representative insists on examining every detail of your proposal for several hours. This time-consuming detail means that the Greek representative

    a. does not trust the accuracy of your proposal

    b. is being polite and does not want to go ahead with the deal

    c. is signaling you to consider a more reasonable offer but does not want to ask directly

    d. is uncomfortable with detailed proposals and would prefer a simple handshake

    e. is showing good manners and respect to you and your proposal

2. Male guests in many Latin American countries often give their visitors an *abrazzo* when greeting them. An *abrazzo* is

    a. a light kiss on the nose

    b. a special gift, usually wine or food

(continued)

FOCUS ON SKILLS CONTINUED

c. clapping hands in the air as the visitor approaches

d. a strong embrace, or kiss with hand on shoulder

e. a firm two-handed handshake, lasting almost one minute

3. Japanese clients visit you at your office for a major meeting. Where should the top Japanese official be seated?

a. closest to the door

b. as close to the middle of the room as is possible

c. anywhere in the room; seating location is not important to Japanese businesspeople

d. somewhere away from the door with a piece of artwork behind him or her

e. always beside rather than facing the host

4. One of the most universal gestures is

a. a pat on the back (congratulations)

b. a smile (happiness or politeness)

c. scratching your chin (thinking)

d. closing your eyes (boredom)

e. arm up, shaking back and forth (waving)

5. While visiting a German client, you give a compliment about the client's beautiful pen set. What will probably happen?

a. the client will insist very strongly that you take it

b. the client will tell you where to buy such a pen set at a good price

c. the client will accept the compliment and get on with business

d. the client will probably get upset that you are not paying attention to the business at hand

e. the client will totally ignore the comment

6. Managers from which country are least likely to tolerate someone being five minutes late for an appointment?

a. United States

b. Australia

c. Brazil

d. Sweden

e. Saudi Arabia

7. In which of the following countries are office arrangements NOT usually an indicator of the person's status?

a. United Kingdom

b. Germany

c. Saudi Arabia

d. China

e. United States

8. In many Asian cultures, a direct order such as "Get me the Amex report" is most likely to be given by

a. senior management to most subordinates

b. a junior employee to a peer

c. senior management only to very junior employees

d. junior employees to outsiders

e. none of the above

9. In the United States, scratching one's head usually means that the person is confused or skeptical. In Russia, it means

a. "You're crazy!"

b. "I am listening carefully."

c. "I want to get to know you better."

d. "I'm confused or skeptical."

e. None of the above

10. A polite way to give your business card to a Japanese business person is

a. casually, after several hours of getting to know the person

b. when first meeting, presenting your card with both hands

c. at the end of the first meeting

d. casually during the meeting, with the information down to show humility

e. never because it is considered rude in Japan to give business cards

SOURCES: Steven L. McShane and Mary Ann Von Glinow, *Organizational Behavior: Emerging Realities for the Workplace Revolution*, 3d ed. (New York: McGraw-Hill/Irwin, 2004); "Cross-Cultural Communication Game" developed by Steven L. McShane, based on material in R. Axtell, *Gestures: The Do's and Taboos of Body Language Around the World* (New York: Wiley, 1991); R. Mead, *Cross-Cultural Management Communication* (Chichester, UK: Wiley, 1990), chapter 7; and J.V. Thill and C. L. Bovée, *Excellence in Business Communication* (New York: McGraw-Hill, 1995), chapter 17.

Managers who responded to cultural and social differences rather than transferring the American fast food concept wholesale have McDonald's French subsidiary booming. Consumers in France were initially resentful of the U.S.-based chain, and one anti-globalization activist was hailed as a national hero for razing a partially built restaurant. Denis Hennequin, the French subsidiary's CEO, responded by running a series of edgy advertisements depicting fat, ignorant Americans who could not understand why McDonald's France used locally produced food that was not genetically modified. Hennequin believed a sense of humor was the best way to address the French opposition to bio-engineered food and their distrust of all things American.

Hennequin has followed a clever strategy for giving McDonald's France its own identity and boosting the chain's attractiveness to customers. Rather than building red and yellow boxes, leaders are adapting restaurant designs to fit with the local architecture and remodeling existing outlets to include features such as hardwood floors, wood-beam ceilings, comfortable armchairs, and music videos. Rather than streamlining the menu, they have added items such as espresso, brioche, and more upscale sandwiches, including a hot ham and cheese sandwich dubbed the Croque McDo. The upscale styling does not come cheaply, but the Gallic twists have helped sales soar. Unlike in the United States, where customers want quick service and cheap, tasty eats, the French want higher quality food and a friendly atmosphere that encourages them to linger. The average McDonald's customer in France spends $9 per visit, compared to an average of $4 per visit in the United States.[40]

Recognizing and managing cultural differences can help organizations like McDonald's be more competitive and successful. However, differences in cultural and social values can create significant barriers to successful communication and collaboration for all companies operating internationally.

<aside>
Take **ACTION**

To learn other cultures: Start watching more foreign movies, noticing how people interact, what values are important to the characters, and what outcomes are desired.
</aside>

International Trade Alliances

One of the most visible changes in the international business environment in recent years has been the development of regional trading alliances and international trade agreements. These developments are significantly shaping global trade.

GATT and the World Trade Organization (WTO)

The General Agreement on Tariffs and Trade (GATT), signed by 23 nations in 1947, started as a set of rules to ensure nondiscrimination, clear procedures, dispute negotiation, and the participation of lesser-developed countries in international trade. GATT and its successor, the World Trade Organization (WTO), primarily use tariff concessions as a tool to increase trade. Member countries agree to limit the level of tariffs they will impose on imports from other members. The **most favored nation clause** calls for each member country to grant to every other member country the most favorable treatment it accords to any country with respect to imports and exports.[41]

The goal of the WTO is to guide and sometimes urge the nations of the world toward free trade and open markets.[42]

<aside>
most favored nation clause

A term describing a GATT clause that calls for member countries to grant other member countries the most favorable treatment they accord any country concerning imports and exports.
</aside>

European Union (EU)

Formed in 1957 to improve economic and social conditions among its members, the European Economic Community, now called the European Union (EU), has grown to the 25-nation alliance illustrated in Exhibit 3.5. The biggest expansion came in 2004, when the EU welcomed ten new members from southern and eastern Europe: Cyprus, the Czech Republic, Estonia, Hungary, Latvia, Lithuania, Malta, Poland, Slovakia, and Slovenia. In addition, Bulgaria, Romania, and Turkey have opened membership negotiations. A treaty signed in early 2003 formalized new rules and policies to ensure that the EU can continue to function efficiently with 25 or more members.[43]

EXHIBIT 3.5

The Nations of the European Union

Legend:
- European Union Countries
- Joined EU in 2004
- In negotiations to join

Another significant aspect to countries operating globally is the EU's monetary revolution and the introduction of the **euro**. In January 2002, the euro, a single European currency, replaced national currencies in 12 member countries and unified a huge marketplace, creating a competitive economy second only to the United States.[44] Belgium, Germany, Greece, France, Spain, Italy, Ireland, the Netherlands, Austria, Finland, Portugal, and Luxembourg traded their deutschemarks, francs, lira, and other currencies to adopt the euro, a currency with a single exchange rate. The United Kingdom (UK) has thus far refused to accept the euro, in part because of a sense of nationalism, but many believe that the United Kingdom and new EU members will adopt the currency.

euro

A single European currency that replaced the currencies of 12 European nations.

North American Free Trade Agreement (NAFTA)

The North American Free Trade Agreement, which went into effect on January 1, 1994, merged the United States, Canada, and Mexico into a megamarket with more than 421 million consumers. The agreement breaks down tariffs and trade restrictions on most agricultural and manufactured products over a 15-year period. The treaty built on the 1989 U.S.-Canada agreement and was intended to spur growth and investment, increase exports, and expand jobs in all three nations.[45]

In the past decade, U.S. trade with Mexico increased more than threefold, and trade with Canada rose dramatically.[46] NAFTA has spurred the entry of small businesses into the global arena. On the tenth anniversary of the agreement in January 2004, opinions over the benefits of NAFTA appeared to be as divided as they were when talks began, with some people calling it a spectacular success and others referring to it as a dismal failure.[47] Although NAFTA has not lived up to its grand expectations, experts stress that it has increased trade, investment, and income and continues to enable companies in all three countries to compete more effectively with rival Asian and European firms.[48]

The Globalization Backlash

As the world becomes increasingly interconnected, a backlash over globalization is occurring. Perhaps the first highly visible antiglobalization protest occurred at the meeting of the WTO in Seattle, Washington, in the fall of 1999, where business and political leaders were caught off guard by the strong sentiments. Since then, protesters have converged on the International Monetary Fund (IMF) and the World Bank. These three organizations are sometimes referred to as *The Iron Triangle* of globalization.

A primary concern is the loss of jobs as companies export work to countries with lower wages.[49] Consider, for example, that a 26-year-old engineer in Bangalore, India, designs next-generation mobile phone chips at a Texas Instruments research center for a salary of $10,000 a year. Boeing has used aeronautical specialists in Russia to design luggage bins and wing parts for planes. They make around $650 a month, compared to a counterpart in the United States making $6,000. IBM has plans to shift thousands of high-paying programming jobs to cheap-labor sites in China, India, and Brazil.[50] The transfer of jobs such as making shoes, clothing, and toys began two decades ago. Today, services and knowledge work are rapidly moving to developing countries. Outsourcing of white-collar jobs to India has exploded, with a 60 percent jump in 2003 compared to the year before. An analyst at Forrester Research Inc. predicts that at least 3.3 million, mostly white-collar, jobs and $136 billion in wages will shift from the United States to low-wage countries by 2015.[51]

Activists charge that globalization hurts people who lose their jobs in the United States, contributes to worldwide environmental destruction, and locks poor people in developing nations into a web of poverty and suffering.[52] Political leaders have struggled to assure the public of the advantages of globalization and free trade,[53] with President George Bush recently admonishing those who oppose globalization as "no friends to the poor." Business leaders, meanwhile, insist that the economic benefits flow back to the U.S. economy in the form of lower prices, expanded markets, and increased profits that can fund innovation.[54] Yet the antiglobalization fervor is getting hotter and is not likely to dissipate soon. Managers who once saw antiglobalists as a fringe group are starting to pay attention to the growing concerns. In the end, it is not whether globalization is good or bad, but how business and government can work together to ensure that the advantages of a global world are fully and fairly shared.

Getting Started Internationally

Small and medium-sized companies have a couple of ways to become involved internationally. One is to seek cheaper sources of supply offshore, which is called outsourcing. Another is to develop markets for finished products outside their home countries, which may include exporting, licensing, and direct investing. These are called **market entry strategies** because they represent alternative ways to sell products and services in foreign markets. Most firms begin with exporting and work up to direct investment. Exhibit 3.6 shows the strategies companies can use to enter foreign markets.

market entry strategies

An organizational strategy for entering a foreign market.

Outsourcing

Global outsourcing, sometimes called global sourcing, means engaging in the international division of labor so that manufacturing can be done in countries with the cheapest sources of labor and supplies. A company may take away a contract from a domestic supplier and place it with a company in the Far East 8,000 miles away. Many manufacturers in Asia and Latin America are wired to the Internet to help them compete in an e-business world, such as the example shown on the following page.

global outsourcing

Engaging in the international division of labor so as to obtain the cheapest sources of labor and supplies regardless of country; also called global sourcing.

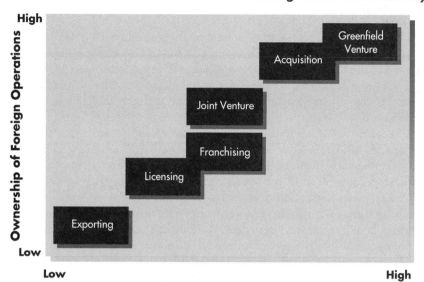

EXHIBIT 3.6

*Strategies for
Entering International
Markets*

**Real-Time
Garments**

If you buy a shirt at Guess or the Limited, chances are it was outsourced through Li & Fung Limited in Hong Kong. Run by Harvard graduates and Hong Kong natives William and Victor Fung, Li & Fung has no machines, no factories, no fabrics. The Fungs only deal in information. And work with 7,500 suppliers in 38 countries, taking orders from companies such as Abercrombie & Fitch, Disney, Levi Strauss, and American Eagle Outfitters. "There are no secrets to manufacturing," says Managing Director William. "A shirt is a shirt." Instead, they build on proprietary information, such as how to make that shirt faster or more efficiently.

When an order comes in, the Fungs use personalized Web sites to fine-tune the specifications with the customer. Taking that information and feeding it into their own Intranet, they are able to find the best supplier of raw materials and the best factories to make assembly. An order for pants from an American brand ended up this way: fabric woven in China because it could do dark green dyes; fasteners from Hong Kong and Korea for durability; everything then shipped to Guatemala for sewing. "For simple things like pants with four seams, Guatemala is great," says division manager Ada Liu. With is proximity to the United States, it takes only a few days for delivery. If production problems occur in Guatemala, Li & Fung can tap into its extensive database to find another place. As the order progresses, customers can make last-minute changes on their Web site.

As recently as eight years ago, when the company was run by phone and fax, Li & Fung would get an order to 50,000 cargo pants and have it delivered five months later instead of the few weeks it takes today. Now, with customers online making adjustments to color or cutting right before those are done, there are fewer mistakes or unhappy customers. Because this new system has increased productivity, profits have risen 21 percent to HK$502 million.

Until a few years ago, stores changed their clothes four times a year for each season. In this new economy, some of them rotate their clothes every week. It makes the name of the store, Express, take on a new meaning.[55]

Exporting

With exporting, the corporation maintains its production facilities within the home nation and transfers its products for sale in foreign countries.[56] Exporting enables a country to market its products in other countries at modest resource cost and with limited risk. Exporting does entail numerous problems based on physical distances, government regulations, foreign currencies, and cultural differences, but it is less expensive than committing the firm's own capital to building plants in host countries.

The size and volume of international business are so large that they are hard to comprehend. The revenue of General Electric (GE) is comparable to the gross national income (GNI) of South Africa. The GNI (formerly referred to as gross national product, or GNP) of Toyota is comparable to the size of Iran's GNI, and that of Philip Morris to the GNI of Malaysia.[57]

As discussed earlier in this chapter, a large volume of international business is being carried out in a seemingly borderless world by large international businesses that can be thought of as global corporations, stateless corporations, or transnational corporations. In the business world, these large international firms typically are called multinational corporations (MNCs), which have been the subject of enormous attention. MNCs can move a wealth of assets from country to country and influence national economies, politics, and cultures.

Though there is no precise definition, an MNC typically receives more than 25 percent of its total sales revenues from operations outside the parent's home country.

Managing in a Global Environment

Managing in a foreign country is particularly challenging. Managers working in foreign countries often face tremendous personal difficulties. In addition, they must be sensitive to cultural subtleties and understand that the ways to provide proper leadership, decision making, motivation, and control vary in different cultures. A clue to the complexity of working internationally comes from a study of the factors that contribute to global manager failures. Based on extensive interviews with global managers, researchers found that personal traits, the specific cultural context, or management mistakes made by the organization could all contribute to failure in an international assignment.[58]

Personal Challenges for Global Managers

When managing in a foreign country, the need for personal learning and growth is critical. Managers will be most successful in foreign assignments if they are culturally flexible and can easily adapt to new situations and ways of doing things. A tendency to be ethnocentric—to believe that your own country's cultural values and ways of doing things are superior—is a natural human condition. One study found that the best global managers come from countries where people have grown up learning how to understand, empathize, and work with others who are different from themselves. For example, Singaporeans consistently hear English and Chinese spoken side by side. The Dutch have to learn English, German, and French, as well as Dutch, to interact and trade with their economically dominant neighbors. English Canadians must be well-versed in American culture and politics and must consider the views and ideas of French Canadians, who, in turn, must learn to think like North Americans and as a member of a global French community, Canadians, and Quebecois.[59] People who have grown up without this kind of diversity typically have more difficulties with foreign assignments, but managers from any country can learn to break down their prejudices and appreciate other viewpoints. Though they may never come to understand the local culture like a native, they can be sensitive to cultural differences and understand that other ways of thinking and doing are valid.

Take **ACTION**

How many of your friends are a different color than you, come from other countries, practice other religions, or are from a different socio-economic class? How prepared are you to work cross-culturally?

Most managers in foreign assignments face a period of homesickness, loneliness, and culture shock from being suddenly immersed in a culture with different languages, foods, values, beliefs, and ways of doing things. **Culture shock** refers to the frustration and anxiety that result from constantly being subjected to strange and unfamiliar cues about what to do and how to do it. Even simple, daily events can become sources of stress.[60] In addition, managers in foreign countries may have to cope with political issues, government corruption, threats of violence, and other contextual factors without the kind of support systems they would have in their home country.[61]

Preparing managers to work in foreign cultures is essential. Some companies give future managers exposure to foreign cultures early in their careers, when people are typically more open and adaptable. American Express Company's Travel-Related Services unit gives American business school students summer jobs in which they work outside the United States for up to ten weeks. Colgate-Palmolive selects 15 recent graduates each year and then provides up to 24 months of training prior to multiple overseas job stints.[62]

culture shock
Feelings of confusion, disorientation, and anxiety that result from being immersed in a foreign culture.

Managing Cross-Culturally

Which two of the following three items go together: a panda, a banana, and a monkey? If you said a monkey and a banana, you answered like a majority of Asians; if you said a panda and a monkey, you answered like a majority of people in Western Europe and the United States. Where Westerners see distinct categories (animals), Asians see relationships (monkeys eat bananas).[63] Though this is not a definitive test, it serves to illustrate an important fact for managers. There are cultural differences in how people think and see the world, and these differences affect working relationships. To be effective on an international level, managers need to interpret the culture of the country and organization in which they are working and develop the sensitivity required to avoid making costly cultural blunders.[64]

"Americans tend to think everyone's the same," says Steven Jones of East-West Business Strategies in San Francisco. "It's a dangerous assumption."[65] One way managers prepare for foreign assignments is to understand how the country differs in terms of the Hofstede and GLOBE projects discussed earlier in this chapter. These values influence how a manager should interact with subordinates and colleagues in the new assignment. For example, the United States scores high on individualism, and a U.S. manager working in a country such as Japan, which scores high on collectivism, will have to modify his or her approach to leading and controlling in order to be successful. The following examples illustrate how cultural differences can be significant for expatriate managers.

Take **ACTION**
Remember: When you return from an extended time abroad, you experience reverse culture shock, which means adapting back to your own culture. It is often more difficult than going abroad.

Leading. In relationship-oriented societies that rank high on collectivism, such as those in Asia, the Arab world, and Latin America, leaders should use a warm, personalized approach with employees. One of the greatest difficulties U.S. leaders have had doing business in China, for example, is failing to recognize that to the Chinese any relationship is a personal relationship.[66] Managers are expected to have periodic social visits with workers, inquiring about morale and health. Leaders should be especially careful about criticizing others. To Asians, Africans, Arabs, and Latin Americans, the loss of self-respect brings dishonor to themselves and their families. One researcher tells of a Dutch doctor managing a company clinic who had what he considered a "frank discussion" with a Chinese subordinate. The subordinate, who perceived the doctor as a father figure, took the criticism as a "savage indictment" and committed suicide.[67] Though this is an extreme example, the principle of saving face is highly important in some cultures.

Take **ACTION**

Do not get frustrated with people in high power distance countries if they do not take initiative or want to make decisions. Just realize their culture is different, and they do not have to be like you.

Decision Making. In the United States, mid-level managers may discuss a problem and give the boss a recommendation. On the other hand, managers in Iran, a country that reflects South Asian cultural values, expect the boss to make a decision and issue specific instructions.[68] In Mexico, employees often do not understand participatory decision making. Mexico ranks extremely high on power distance, and many workers expect managers to exercise their power in making decisions and issuing orders. American managers working in Mexico have been advised to explain a decision rarely, lest workers perceive this as a sign of weakness.[69] In contrast, managers in many Arab and African nations are expected to use consultative decision making in the extreme.

Motivating. Motivation must fit the incentives within the culture. A recent study confirmed that intrinsic factors such as challenge, recognition, and the work are less effective in countries that value high power distance. It may be that workers in these cultures perceive manager recognition and support as manipulative and, therefore, demotivating.[70] In places like the United States and the United Kingdom, by contrast, intrinsic factors can be highly motivating. The British outpost of global giant Microsoft incorporates intrinsic factors to keep people inspired and engaged, as described in the Focus on Collaboration box.

In Japan, which values collectivism, employees are motivated to satisfy the company. A financial bonus for star performance would be humiliating to employees from Japan, China, or Ecuador. An American executive in Japan offered a holiday trip to the top salesperson, but employees were not interested. After he realized that Japanese are motivated in groups, he changed the reward to a trip for everyone if together they achieved the sales target. They did. Managers in Latin America, Africa, and the Middle

FOCUS ON COLLABORATION

At Microsoft UK, Work-Life Balance Pays Off

How does a company where people work long, hard hours win an award for work-life balance? It seems a paradox, but employees voted Microsoft UK the best company to work for in the UK partly because of its attention to work-life balance issues.

Steve Harvey, Microsoft UK's director of people and culture, says employees choose to work long and hard because they love technology. However, they have the flexibility to work when and where they need to. If employees want to work Sunday and go golfing on Monday, they are empowered to do so. People have laptops and broadband Internet access at home so they can work flexibly. As long as employees get their work done, no one questions them. This trust and openness is a cornerstone of Microsoft UK's culture, and a big part of the reason 89 percent of employees surveyed by the *Sunday Times* said they "love working there." Microsoft UK incorporates other benefits, such as subsidized gym memberships, free private health care for life partners and families, and wellness clinics that help employees have better, more well-rounded lives.

Harvey says people who do not fit into Microsoft's technology-loving culture become isolated and leave. But the company is committed to finding and keeping the best and the brightest, which is why two of Harvey's staff members work on

an initiative called *great company*. The theme runs through Harvey's entire people and culture strategy. The goal is to make sure employees understand what Microsoft stands for, where it is going, and what its long-term strategies mean at the grassroots level. Another component is an extraordinary openness and honesty. Every new employee is told, "If you see something and think it's stupid, tell me and we'll get rid of it. And what you've seen in best practice elsewhere, share it." Employees respond because they know it is not just talk; managers live up to the promise. When the company tried to take away fuel cards and get people to charge fuel to their Amex cards, negative feedback was so strong that the policy was scrapped within half an hour.

Microsoft's attention to people and culture pays off. The attrition rate of hard-to-find technical employees is at 2 percent. An astounding 93 percent of employees say they "feel proud to work for the company." Moreover, they strongly believe the company they work for "makes a positive difference to the world." With that kind of commitment, employees will keep Microsoft humming for a long time.

SOURCE: Joy Persaud, "Keep the Faithful," People Management (June 2003): 37–38.

East improve motivation by showing respect for employees as individuals with needs and interests outside of work.[71]

Controlling. When things go wrong, managers in foreign countries often are unable to get rid of employees who do not work out. Consider the following research finding: When asked what to do about an employee whose work had been subpar for a year after 15 years of exemplary performance, 75 percent of Americans and Canadians said fire her; only 20 percent of Singaporeans and Koreans chose that solution.[72] In Europe, Mexico, and Indonesia, as well, to hire and fire based on performance seems unnaturally brutal. In addition, workers in some countries are protected by strong labor laws and union rules.

In foreign cultures, managers should not control the wrong things. A Sears manager in Hong Kong insisted that employees come to work on time instead of 15 minutes late. The employees did as they were told, but they also left on time instead of working into the evening as they had previously. A lot of work was left unfinished. So, the manager told the employees to go back to their old ways. His attempt at control had a negative effect.

Manager's Solution

This chapter has emphasized the growing importance of an international perspective on management. Successful companies are expanding their business overseas and are competing with foreign companies on their home turf. Major alternatives for serving foreign markets are exporting, licensing, franchising, and direct investing through joint ventures or wholly owned subsidiaries. Business in the global arena involves special risks and difficulties because of complicated economic, legal-political, and sociocultural forces. Moreover, the global environment changes rapidly as illustrated by the emergence of the WTO, the EU, the NAFTA, and other emerging trade alliances. The expansion of free-trade policies has sparked a globalization backlash among people who are fearful of losing their jobs and economic security, as well as those who believe economic globalization hurts poor people worldwide.

Much of the growth in international business has been carried out by large businesses called MNCs. These large companies exist in an almost borderless world, encouraging the free flow of ideas, products, manufacturing, and marketing among countries to achieve the greatest efficiencies. Managers in MNCs as well as those in smaller companies doing business internationally face many challenges. Managers often experience culture shock when transferred to foreign countries. They must learn to be sensitive to cultural differences and tailor their management style to the culture. Social and cultural values differ across cultures, and these influence appropriate patterns of leadership, decision making, motivation, and managerial control.

International markets provide many opportunities but are fraught with difficulty, as Wal-Mart, described at the beginning of this chapter, discovered. The company first began expanding internationally nearly 15 years ago and has learned a great deal about doing business in foreign countries. However, its success in some markets led it to underestimate the potential difficulties it would face when entering Germany. Managers are having to step back and reevaluate the competition, the cultural clashes, and the regulatory hurdles they face. They believe the company's troubles there can be overcome with time and experience. The German situation may have taught Wal-Mart executives to take a more cautious approach as the company moves into Japan. In that country, where Wal-Mart faces tremendous cultural, societal, and organizational obstacles, managers see a slow, step-by-step process as the best route toward eventual success. Wal-Mart chose to work with a local partner, Seiyu, whose name still remains on stores. The American giant is staying in the shadows for now, focusing on getting all its systems in place and training local managers. It goofed in Germany by rushing to overhaul stores and lower prices before basic operational systems were ready. The Japanese managers are helping Wal-Mart understand and respond to local needs, and the subtle, patient approach is enabling executives to learn through trial and error.[73] For a large, rich company like Wal-Mart, managers can afford to lose money internationally as the price of learning. Smaller organizations have to be more cautious and well-prepared when entering the global marketplace. As a means of learning across borders, here is a poem that addresses cultural differences.

An Asian View of Cultural Differences

We live in time. You live in space.

We are always at rest. You are always on the move.

We are passive. You are aggressive.

We like to contemplate. You like to act.

We accept the world as it is. You try to change the world according to your blueprint.

We live in peace with nature. You try to impose your will in her.

Religion is our first love. Technology is your passion.

We delight to think about the meaning of life. You delight in physics.

We believe in freedom of silence. You believe in freedom of speech.

We lapse into meditation. You strive for articulation.

We marry first, then love. You love first, then marry.

Our marriage is the beginning of a love affair. Your marriage is the happy end of a romance.

It is an indissoluble bond. It is a contract.

Our love is mute. Your love is vocal.

We try to conceal it from the world. You delight in showing it to others.

Self-denial is the secret to our survival. Self-assertiveness is the key to your success.

We are taught from the cradle to want less and less. You are urged every day to want more and more.

We glorify austerity and renunciation. You emphasize gracious living and enjoyment.

In the sunset years of life we renounce the world and prepare for the hereafter. You retire to enjoy the fruits of your labor.[74]

Discussion Questions

1. Why do you think international businesses traditionally prefer to operate in industrialized countries? Discuss.

2. What considerations in recent years have led international businesses to expand their activities into less-developed countries?

3. What policies or actions would you recommend to an entrepreneurial business wanting to do business in Europe?

4. What steps could a company take to avoid making product design and marketing mistakes when introducing new products into a foreign country?

5. What does it mean to say that the world is becoming "borderless"? That large companies are "stateless"?

6. What might managers do to avoid making mistakes concerning control and decision making when operating in a foreign culture?

7. What is meant by the cultural values of individualism and masculinity/femininity? How might these values affect organization design and management processes?

8. How do you think trade alliances such as NAFTA and the EU may affect you as a future manager?

Manager's Workbook

State of the World Test

How aware are you of the rest of the planet? If you will be working internationally, the better you know about the world, the more successful you are likely to be.

1. Six countries contain one-half the total population of the world. What are the six countries?

    1.   4.
    2.   5.
    3.   6.

2. Another nineteen countries account for 25 percent of the world's people. What are those countries?

    1.   11.
    2.   12.
    3.   13.
    4.   14.
    5.   15.
    6.   16.
    7.   17.
    8.   18.
    9.   19.
    10.

3. The ten most commonly spoken first languages are:

    1.   6.
    2.   7.
    3.   8.
    4.   9.
    5.   10.

4. How many languages are there in the world that have at least one million speakers?

    a. 73
    b. 123
    c. 223

5. How many nations were there in 1992?

    a. 288
    b. 188
    c. 88

6. Which nation is home to the largest number of commercial banks?

7. Which nation is home to the most transnational corporations?

8. Between 1970 and 1986, global agricultural (plant and livestock) production

    a. declined substantially.
    b. declined slightly.
    c. remained about the same.
    d. increased slightly.
    e. increased substantially.

9. Between 1970 and 1985, the number of people in the world suffering from malnutrition

    a. declined.
    b. remained about the same.
    c. increased.

10. Let one dot represent all the firepower used in World War II: This would be the equivalent of 200 Hiroshima-sized A-bombs. How many dots would you need to represent the firepower held in the combined U.S. and the former USSR before it dissolved?

   a. 60
   b. 600
   c. 6,000
   d. 60,000

11. Between 1960 and 1987, the world spent approximately $10 trillion on health care. How much did the world spend on military?

   a. $7 trillion
   b. $10 trillion
   c. $17 trillion
   d. $25 trillion

12. According to the United Nations, what percentage of the world's work (paid and unpaid) is done by women?

   a. 1/3
   b. 1/2
   c. 2/3
   d. 3/4

13. According to the United Nations, what percentage of the world's income is earned by women?

   a. 1/10
   b. 3/10
   c. 5/10
   d. 7/10

14. The nations of Africa, Asia, Latin America, and the Middle East, often referred to as the Third World, contain about 78 percent of the world's population. What percentage of the world's monetary income do they possess?

   a. 10 percent
   b. 20 percent
   c. 30 percent
   d. 40 percent

15. Americans constitute approximately 5 percent of the world's population. What percentage of the world's resources do Americans consume?

   a. 15 percent
   b. 25 percent
   c. 35 percent
   d. 45 percent

Note to Student: See Appendix B to check your responses.

SOURCE: United Nations Web site, 1999; Jan Drum, Steve Hughes, and George Otere, "State-of-the-World Test," in *Global Winners*, Yarmouth, Maine: Intercultural Press, 1994, pp. 9–12.

Manager's Workshop

Global Economy Scavenger Hunt

In order to get a perspective on the pervasiveness of the global economy, you will be asked to find a number of things and bring them back to class.

1. Divide into teams of four to six members.
2. Each team is to bring items to a future class from the list below.
3. On the day in class, each team will give a short, two-minute presentation on the items that were the most difficult to find or the most interesting.
4. How many countries did your team get items from? How many for the entire class?

List for scavenger hunt:

1. Locate brochures of Annual Reports of four multinational corporations.
2. Gather evidence from three local businesses to show that they do business internationally.
3. Locate a retail store that sells only products listing them as "Made in America."
4. Find 10 toys or games that originate in other countries.
5. Find five toys or games that have components from one country and were assembled in another—or show how they were otherwise developed in more than one country.
6. List food items from 25 different countries.
7. List articles of clothing from 15 different countries.
8. List books sold in your town from authors of 12 different countries. Where were the books published? Who translated them?
9. List 12 films in the past five years that starred someone from another country.
10. List five films in the past five years that had multinational crews and locations. Include at least one that was co-produced by two or more countries.
11. Gather descriptions of interviews from five foreigners (not from your team or the class), in which they were asked to list six things they like about the United States and six things they don't like.
12. Create a list of eight places where a language other than English is displayed (on a bulletin board, poster, etc.).
13. Find two maps of the world drawn before 1900.
14. List five items in your town that were manufactured in another country and were not being made in that country six years ago.

SOURCE: Adapted from Jan Drum, Steve Hughes, and George Otere, "Global Scavenger Hunt," in *Global Winners*, Yarmouth, Maine: Intercultural Press, 1994, pp. 21–23.

Management in Practice: Ethical Dilemma

Quality or Closing

On the way home from the launch party celebrating Plaxcor Metals' entrance into the international arena, Donald Fields should have been smiling. He was part of the team that had closed the deal to sell component parts to Asian Business Machine, after his company had spent millions trying to break into this lucrative market. There were several more deals riding on the successful outcome of the first international venture.

The expansion into new markets was critical to Plaxcor's survival. As President Leslie Hanson had put it, "If we aren't global within five years, we may as well close up shop." Fields was tense because of news he learned tonight: intense bidding for the first sale and several last-minute changes requested by the customer had forced Plaxcor to heavily modify its production process. The production manager had confided that "the product is a mess but still better than most of the competition." He went on to assure him that, although well below normal standards, the variability would "probably not cause any problems" and could be worked out after a few more orders.

Fields had spent the last few months selling Plaxcor on its quality reputation. He knew they could probably get by with the first runs and meet the opening deadline. He was afraid that telling the customer of the potential problems or extending the deadline would risk not only this deal but pending projects as well. But he knew if problems arose with the products, Plaxcor's future in the Asian market would be bleak. Donald Fields wasn't sure Plaxcor could afford to gamble its entrance in the international market on a substandard product.

What Do You Do?

1. Ask the customer for an extension of the deadline and bring the products up to standard.
2. Gamble on the first runs and hope the products don't fail.
3. Inform the customer of the problem and let the customer make the decision.

Case for Critical Analysis

Unocal Corporation

Unocal Corporation seems an unlikely candidate for a high-risk global rampage. Consumers everywhere recognize the ubiquitous 76 logo of this quintessential California oil company. They know it as the nation's 11th largest petroleum retailer, with a prestigious downtown headquarters and important role as a Los Angeles civic booster. Casting aside its reputation as a conservative company with tightly defined domestic markets and focused petroleum interests in California, Unocal has rapidly transformed itself into an international company with major investments in some of the world's least-developed economies. It has also become a prominent topic among political activists, human-rights groups, and President Clinton's foreign policy team. Some observers say that Unocal will become a casualty of its high-risk policies.

Immediately after becoming chairman of Unocal in 1995, Roger Beach began to sell off domestic retail assets and eliminate exploration and refining activities in the United States. Resources shifted to unlikely places where few other major oil producers had risked operations—places such as Myanmar (more commonly known as Burma), Turkmenistan, Uzbekistan, and the strife-ridden Balkans. Beach turned up the heat on company investments in Indonesian oil fields, launched full-service energy subsidiaries through government alliances in Thailand, broadened holdings in Malaysia, and began negotiations for an integrated refining/ retailing enterprise in Pakistan. Nearly 40 percent of Unocal's exploration and extraction budget was thrown into these emerging markets, much of it pinpointed for very high risk locations in the former Soviet republics and the Persian subcontinent.

Why take these risks? Beach answers that Unocal was unable to compete head-to-head with the oil industry giants for capital markets and decided to create an extremely attractive strategic package of full-service energy production in countries grasping to develop infrastructure. "What every government likes about Unocal's strategy is one-stop shopping; one group able to take the whole project from development to the marketing end," Beach said. "We have become partners in their development and as important to them as they are to us." The Unocal strategy defies normal industry trends based on distributing huge capital investments to tie up oil reserves and mineral rights, then cutting deals for operations. Instead, Unocal comes in the front door with packaged energy services ranging from turning the first spade of dirt on exploration to delivering power to the end user, and that proposal includes oil, gas, or electric power generation.

Beach sees far less risk than industry analysts perceive in the emerging markets. The dangers of war, political upheaval, and currency fluctuations are clear and present, yet the company says it has hedged against these threats by diversifying investments. By 2000, it intends to have reached its goal of establishing nearly 80 percent of its exploration and production capabilities in these underdeveloped areas, and by the end of 1996, it had almost totally abandoned domestic exploration, having sold off nearly $3 billion in assets and oil-field holdings in California. However, according to Beach, success will depend on creating a globally managed company capable of understanding and participating in foreign-market environments. Consequently, in 1996, he initiated a major transformation in Unocal's management systems, beginning by relocating its headquarters from its stately downtown offices to a small, highly efficient suite near the Los Angeles International Airport. Mid-level managers were either repositioned in regional offices, such as Singapore, Istanbul, or Jakarta, or they left the company. The executive core, which had been distinctly Los Angeles in character, gained a multicultural character, representing Eastern European and Asian group alliances. Subsidiaries in Jakarta, Thailand, and Burma took on local names and corporate identities, shedding their American profiles, and Unocal's many foreign alliances have made it part of the communities in which it operates.

In Thailand, Unocal has worked on the country's privatization plan to convert its Petroleum Authority of Thailand (PTT) operations into privately owned and operated international oil services. Unocal and the PTT have begun to build pipelines in the Gulf of Thailand linking Unocal's hydrocarbon fields in the nation's rugged peninsula, and a joint venture in Malaysia has begun to open regional energy markets from Burma to the Philippines. Surface evaluations have hailed this consortium as a master stroke of strategy; however, related activities have exposed Unocal to strong criticism. Unocal became the largest single U.S. investor in Burma as part of the expansion, but Burma's military government has languished in political and economic isolation as a result of U.S. legislation aimed at boycotting the country for its unacceptable human-rights practices. Political activists in more than a dozen U.S. states have won passage of legislation barring imports from Burma and outlawing private investments there by U.S. firms. Municipal governments in five states have passed boycott laws as well, and Unocal, together with PepsiCo and several other American companies operating in Burma, have become major targets for international pressure groups. PepsiCo bowed to the pressure and recently moved out of Burma, but Unocal has flatly refused to budge.

The company's insistence on remaining in Burma, however, is not a vote in support of the country's human-rights record. Indeed, Unocal would find it difficult to withdraw, because it has formed an equity agreement with the giant French petrochemical company Total, which also has substantial pipeline investments with Unocal in the Persian Gulf and southern Asia. Unocal's contracts with Total make it a de facto partner of the French government. Moreover, Unocal has invested in public and private interests in Burma that spread to five other major Southeast Asian states. But a Unocal representative cites the importance of the company's role in helping the nation's development. "To withdraw and isolate Burma would have no effect. Questionable human-rights leadership and political practices would continue and perhaps proliferate," she said. "On the other hand, our strength and the fact that we can provide meaningful jobs and ethical international business encourages changes for the good. Even if every American firm vacated, firms from other nations would welcome the chance to develop Burma without American competition."

That position doesn't relieve the political or financial risk to Unocal. Ethics and U.S. policies aside, Burma lacks a strong track record for keeping its promises. As a closed military state, self-isolated for ideological reasons since the end of World War II, it has few friends anywhere in the world. For years, it was linked to the Soviet Union for aid and military support, and Burma backed insurgent forces in several neighboring civil conflicts. These situations did not endear the government to potential regional economic allies. However, the country is strategically positioned within the Southeast Asian theater, and it has attracted consideration, with much controversy, for membership in ASEAN.

Unocal holds a rather exposed position in the country, as it does in Uzbekistan, Turkmenistan, and the Balkans. An American company without the legal or political support of its home government can expect little help should the host government decide to freeze its assets, bar currency repatriation, or resort to outright expropriation. Meanwhile, Unocal has tied up several billion dollars in the region while maintaining no safety net at home. Indeed, it faces potentially costly threats from home, and if the company is pushed to the wall by legislation, the chairman says, he will take Unocal out of U.S. control.

Questions

1. What market entry strategies has Unocal used, based on the activities described in the case? Would you classify Unocal as a multinational corporation (MNC)? Why or why not?

2. Identify and discuss the various types of risks faced by Unocal in emerging markets (consider the economic, legal-political, and sociocultural environment). Which risks seem most threatening to the company?

3. What do you think of the Unocal representative's statement that "to withdraw and isolate Burma would have no effect" regarding that country's poor human-rights record? Do you believe U.S. companies should stay in such countries in the hope of improving the ethical climate? Discuss.

SOURCE: David H. Holt, "Unocal Corporation," from *International Management: Text and Cases*, pp. 143–145, Copyright 1998 by Harcourt, Inc., reprinted by permission of the publisher.

CHAPTER 4

Managerial Ethics and Corporate Social Responsibility

CHAPTER OUTLINE

LEARNING OBJECTIVES

After studying this chapter, you should be able to do the following:

1 **Define ethics and explain how ethical behavior relates to behavior governed by law and free choice.**

2 **Explain the utilitarian, individualism, moral rights, and justice approaches for evaluating ethical behavior.**

3 **Describe how individual and organizational factors shape ethical decision making.**

4 **Define corporate social responsibility and how to evaluate it along economic, legal, ethical, and discretionary criteria.**

5 **Describe four organizational approaches to environmental responsibility, and explain the philosophy of sustainability.**

6 **Discuss how ethical organizations are created through ethical leadership and organizational structures and systems.**

7 **Identify important stakeholders for an organization and discuss how managers balance the interests of various stakeholders.**

Timberland is known for great shirts and solid climbing boots. The company has had a good financial history with decent revenues and profits. But CEO Jeffrey Swartz wanted something more. In the early 1990s, he began transforming Timberland into a company known as much for philanthropy as it is for its boots. It began when the community projects-oriented nonprofit City Year asked for boots for its workers. Swartz convinced other Timberland executives to answer the call, over time providing free boots and uniforms for about 10,000 people. Visiting some of the community projects, Swartz was deeply moved by what volunteers were accomplishing. "I saw what real power was that day," Swartz recalls. "I didn't realize how hungry I was for that kind of purpose." Timberland began shutting down operations one day each year so the company's thousands of employees could get paid to take part in various company-sponsored philanthropic projects, such as building homeless shelters or cleaning up playgrounds. The company started giving employees 16 hours of paid leave annually to volunteer at charities of their choosing. But the emphasis on social responsibility does not come cheap.

The all-day event alone costs about $2 million a year in lost sales, project expenses, and wages for employees. When Timberland's profits were soaring, that seemed fine, but then the company hit a rough patch. It reported its first operating loss since going public, laid off some employees, and shipped some work overseas to cut costs.

So, when one of the company's bankers implied that the focus on philanthropy was hurting the company and its stakeholders, Swartz found himself in a quandary. One of Timberland's bankers bluntly told Swartz that the company needed to "cut this civic stuff out and get back to business." Swartz began wondering if the banker was right. Maybe managers were failing the organization and its stakeholders by plowing too many resources into philanthropic activities.[1]

If you were in this position, would you cut out the charity work and focus everything on returning Timberland to profitability? If charity begins at home, is Timberland being ethical by spending money for philanthropic activities at the same time it is shipping jobs overseas and laying off workers?

The situation at Timberland illustrates how difficult ethical issues can be and symbolizes the growing importance of discussing ethics and social responsibility. Managers often face situations where it is difficult to determine what is right. Thus, ethics has always been a concern for managers. However, in recent years, widespread moral lapses and corporate financial scandals have brought the topic to the forefront. Corporations are rushing to adopt codes of ethics, strengthen ethical and legal safeguards, and develop socially responsible policies. Every decade sees its share of corporate, political, and social villains, but the pervasiveness of ethical lapses in the early 2000s was astounding. It began with Enron Corp., America's seventh-largest corporation in mid-2000. The mighty company was destroyed by a combination of deceit, arrogance, shady financial dealings, and inappropriate accounting practices that inflated earnings and hid debt. Soon, the names of other revered companies became synonymous with greed, dishonesty, and financial chicanery: Arthur Andersen, Adelphia, WorldCom, Tyco, HealthSouth. A poll taken in fall 2002 found that 79 percent of respondents believed questionable business practices were widespread. Fewer than one third said they thought most CEOs were honest.[2] Moreover, more than 20 percent of U.S. employees surveyed reported having first-hand knowledge of managers making false or misleading promises to customers, discriminating in hiring or promotions, and violating employees' rights.[3]

However, the positive news to report is that actor Paul Newman and his friend A. E. Hotchner started a company, Newman's Own, that makes salad dressings, spaghetti sauce, and other foods and gives all the profits to charity. Boston's Bain & Company set up the nonprofit Bridgespan Group that gives charitable organizations world-class consulting advice at steep discounts. And Computer Associates each year pairs 75 employee volunteers with 75 employees from major customers to build playgrounds in needy areas.[4] A number of companies have begun tying managers' pay to ethical factors such as how well they treat employees or how effectively they live up to the stated corporate values.

This chapter expands on the ideas about environment, corporate culture, and the international environment discussed in Chapters 2 and 3. We will focus on the topic of ethical values, which builds on the idea of corporate culture. Then, we will examine corporate relationships to the external environment as reflected in social responsibility. Ethics and social responsibility are hot topics in corporate America. This chapter discusses fundamental approaches that help managers think through ethical issues. Understanding ethical approaches helps managers build a solid foundation on which to base future decision making.

What Is Managerial Ethics?

ethics

The code of moral principles and values that govern the behaviors of a person or group with respect to what is right or wrong.

Ethics is difficult to define in a precise way. In a general sense, **ethics** is the code of moral principles and values that governs the behaviors of a person or group with respect to what is right or wrong. Ethics sets standards as to what is good or bad in conduct and decision making.[5] Ethics deals with internal values that are a part of corporate culture and shapes decisions concerning social responsibility with respect to the external environment. An ethical issue is present in a situation when the actions of a person or organization may harm or benefit others.[6]

Ethics can be more clearly understood when compared with behaviors governed by laws and by free choice. Exhibit 4.1 illustrates that human behavior falls into three categories. The first is codified law, in which values and standards are written into the legal system and enforceable in the courts. In this area, lawmakers have ruled that people and corporations must behave in a certain way, such as obtaining licenses for cars or paying corporate taxes. The courts alleged that Enron Corp. executives broke the

EXHIBIT 4.1

Three Domains of Human Action

law, for example, by manipulating financial results, such as using off-balance sheet partnerships to create income and hide debt improperly.[7] The domain of free choice is at the opposite end of the scale and pertains to behavior about which the law has no say and for which an individual or organization enjoys complete freedom. A manager's choice of where to eat lunch or a music company's choice of the number of CDs to release are examples of free choice.

Between these domains lies the area of ethics. This domain has no specific laws, yet it does have standards of conduct based on shared principles and values about moral conduct that guide an individual or company. Executives at Enron Corp., for example, did not break any specific laws by encouraging employees to buy more shares of stock even when they believed the company was in financial trouble and the price of the shares was likely to decline. However, this behavior was a clear violation of the executives' ethical responsibilities to employees.[8] These managers were acting based on their own interests rather than their duties to employees and other stakeholders. In the domain of free choice, obedience is strictly to oneself. In the domain of codified law, obedience is to laws prescribed by the legal system. In the domain of ethical behavior, obedience is to unenforceable norms and standards about which the individual or company is aware. An ethically acceptable decision is legally and morally acceptable to the larger community.

Many companies and individuals get into trouble with the simplified view that choices are governed by law or free choice. It leads people to assume mistakenly that if it is not illegal, it must be ethical as if there were no third domain.[9] A better option is to recognize the domain of ethics and accept moral values as a powerful force for good that can regulate behaviors inside and outside corporations. As principles of ethics and social responsibility are more widely recognized, companies can use codes of ethics and their corporate cultures to govern behavior, thereby eliminating the need for additional laws and avoiding the problems of unfettered choice. Sometimes deregulation of an industry has removed laws and increased unethical behaviors where companies did not have socially responsible cultures, as in the case of radio promoters, described below:

Radio Promoters

Nashville's RCA Label Group has terminated the use of independent radio promoters who serve as liaisons between radio stations and its country music labels. These independent promoters are third parties hired by the record companies to work with radio stations, hoping to persuade them to play the record company's songs. The practice of hiring promoters was a reaction to the payola scandals 50 years ago, when disk jockeys took money to play certain songs. Outlawed by U.S. Congress in 1960, payment for airplay was forbidden unless financial transactions were aired publicly.

In recent years, though, a new and quasi-legal kind of payola has emerged, partly as a result of the 1996 deregulation of radio that was supposed to let the capitalist system determine rules. The problem is, deregulation has worked poorly in the area of payola. To skirt the law, payment is not made directly to disk jockeys for particular songs. Instead, promoters—or middlemen—pay radio owners large fees as high as $1 million to have exclusive first access to that station's playlist for a period of time. Then record companies and artists pay the promoters to make sure their music gets on the radio.

Critics charge this system has led to a homogenization of the air waves and artists complain they are hurt if they do not go with the program. One promoter allegedly retaliated against Britney Spears and other artists who refused to use their concert promotion services.

Another result of deregulation has been the consolidation of the radio industry. Under the regulated system, there was a limit to the number of stations anyone could own. Now, that limit is gone. Whereas there were 5,133 owners of radio stations in 1966, in 2002 there were primarily four radio station groups: Clear Channel, Chancellor, Infinity, and Capstart, which control access to 63 percent of 41 million listeners. This consolidation has increased the power of the promoters and encouraged the new payola system.

Profit pressure from radio stations and record companies has "pushed the economics and ethics of radio promotion beyond the point where labels can police themselves," says music industry executive Tim Dubois, of Universal South label. "We need a new set of rules," he says. "We have to know where the line is drawn, and it has to be brighter than it is now." RCA is doing its best to define those lines by being the first major label to distance itself from independent promoters, a group being investigated by New York Attorney General Eliot Spitzer, who is scrutinizing how music gets promoted and how airplay is determined.[10]

Because ethical standards are not codified, disagreements and dilemmas about proper behavior often occur. Ethics is always about making decisions, and some issues are difficult to resolve. An **ethical dilemma** arises in a situation concerning right or wrong when values are in conflict.[11] Right and wrong cannot be clearly identified.

The individual who must make an ethical choice in an organization is the moral agent.[12] Consider the dilemmas facing a moral agent in the following situations:

ethical dilemma

A situation that arises when all alternative choices or behaviors have been deemed undesirable because of potentially negative consequences, making it difficult to distinguish right from wrong.

- A top employee at your small company tells you he needs some time off because he has AIDS. You know the employee needs the job as well as the health insurance benefits. Providing health insurance has already stretched the company's budget, and this will send premiums through the roof. You know the federal courts have upheld the right of an employer to modify health plans by putting a cap on AIDS benefits. Should you investigate whether this is a legal possibility for your company?

- As a sales manager for a major pharmaceuticals company, you have been asked to promote a new drug that costs $2,500 per dose. You have read the reports saying the drug is only 1 percent more effective than an alternative drug that costs less than one-fourth as much. Can you in good conscience aggressively promote the $2,500-per-dose drug? If you do not, could lives be lost that might have been saved with that 1 percent increase in effectiveness?

- Your company is hoping to build a new overseas manufacturing plant. You could save about $5 million by not installing standard pollution control equipment that is required in the United States. The plant will employ many local workers in a poor country where jobs are scarce. Your research shows that pollutants from the factory could potentially damage the local fishing industry. Yet building the factory with the pollution control equipment will likely make the plant too expensive to build.[13]

- You are the accounting manager of a division that is $15,000 below profit targets. Approximately $20,000 of office supplies were delivered on December 21. The accounting rule is to pay expenses when incurred. The division general manager asks you not to record the invoice until February.

- You have been collaborating with a fellow manager on an important project. One afternoon, you walk into his office a bit earlier than scheduled and see sexually explicit images on his computer monitor. The company has a zero-tolerance sexual harassment policy, as well as strict guidelines regarding personal use of the Internet. However, your colleague was in his own office and not bothering anyone else.[14]

Managers must deal with these dilemmas that fall squarely in the domain of ethics. Now turn to approaches to ethical decision making that provide criteria for understanding and resolving these difficult issues.

Criteria for Ethical Decision Making

Most ethical dilemmas involve a conflict between the needs of the part and the whole: the individual versus the organization or the organization versus society as a whole. For example, should a company install mandatory alcohol and drug testing for employees, which might benefit the organization as a whole but reduce the individual freedom of employees? Should products that fail to meet tough FDA standards be exported to other countries where government standards are lower, benefiting the company but being potentially harmful to world citizens? Sometimes ethical decisions entail a conflict between two groups. For example, should the potential for local health problems resulting from a company's effluents take precedence over the jobs it creates as the town's leading employer? What about baseball, where some players evidently benefit from steroid use? Though the substance is banned, there has yet to be an all-out effort to stop the practice, indicating some moral ambivalence about the practice.

| **Steroid Storm** |

After New York Yankee Jason Giambi was accused of steroids use and almost confessed, the practice is still believed to be common yet undiscussed. "At least half the guys are using steroids," said National League Most Valued Player Ken Caminiti, who was the first high-profile player to admit to a long-whispered practice. That estimate had been earlier affirmed by Arizona Diamondbacks pitcher Curt Schilling, who added, "Is that a problem? It depends on what you consider a problem. It certainly has tainted records; there's no doubt about that." Congressional hearings on the matter have caused some stars to fall. The former St. Louis Cardinals' Mark McGwire was so evasive on whether he used steroids that a lot of people are disappointed in the man who got an unprecedented 70-homer season. A Missouri congressman even wants McGwire's name taken off a highway.

One person has confessed: Jose Canseco said he used steroids and named others. He said baseball managers and owners knew about the common steroid use. What gets forgotten is how steroids only benefit the players who cheat as opposed to smaller ball-parks or a lower mound, which benefit all players equally.

Unlike basketball, football and hockey, major league baseball does no drug testing. But with so many record-breaking players, many assumed steroids were being used freely. It increases the incidence of heart and liver damage and strokes. NFL star Lyle Alzado went public in 1992 about his brain cancer being caused by long-time steroid use.

So why take the risks? Steroid use increases muscle mass and can lead to better performance and hence high contract dollars. Replying to concerns, Schilling said, "If you can get an advantage somewhere, even if it involves crossing an ethical line, people will do it. Home runs are money."

Caminiti said that the practice was so prevalent, players who did not do it put themselves at a disadvantage. One of the biggest hurdles in the way of drug testing has been the baseball players themselves, through their union. The tide may be turning, though. Diamondback first baseman Mark Grace says that players are finally getting fed up with inflated statistics and record-breaking. "I personally would love to see it banned."[15]

Managers faced with these kinds of tough ethical choices often benefit from a normative strategy—one based on norms and values—to guide their decision making. Normative ethics uses several approaches to describe values for guiding ethical decision making. Four of these that are relevant to managers are the utilitarian approach, individualism approach, moral rights approach, and justice approach.[16]

Utilitarian Approach

utilitarian approach
The ethical concept that moral behaviors produce the greatest good for the greatest number.

The **utilitarian approach**, espoused by the nineteenth-century philosophers Jeremy Bentham and John Stuart Mill, holds that moral behavior produces the greatest good for the greatest number. Under this approach, a decision maker is expected to consider the effect of each decision alternative on all parties and select the one that optimizes the satisfaction for the greatest number of people. Because actual computations can be complex, simplifying them is considered appropriate. For example, an economic frame of reference could be used by calculating dollar costs and dollar benefits. A decision could be made that considers only the people who are directly affected by the decision, not those who are indirectly affected. The utilitarian ethic is cited as the basis for the recent trend among companies to police employee personal habits such as alcohol and tobacco consumption on the job, and in some cases after hours because such behavior affects the entire workplace. Similarly, many companies argue that monitoring how employees spend their time on the Internet is necessary to maintain the company's ethical climate and workplace productivity. If employees are viewing pornographic sites, visiting racist chat rooms, or spending hours shopping or day trading online, the entire organization will suffer.[17]

Take **ACTION**

Make decisions that benefit others, not just yourself.

The utilitarian ethic was the basis for the state of Oregon's decision to extend Medicaid to 400,000 previously ineligible recipients by refusing to pay for high-cost, high-risk procedures such as liver transplants and bone marrow transplants. Though a few people needing these procedures have died because the state would not pay, many people have benefitted from medical services they would otherwise have had to go without.[18] Critics claim that the Oregon decision does not fully take into account the concept of justice toward the unfortunate victims of life-threatening diseases.[19] The justice approach will be discussed later in this section.

Individualism Approach

individualism approach
The ethical concept that acts are moral when they promote the individual's best long-term interests, which ultimately leads to the greater good.

The **individualism approach** contends that acts are moral when they promote the individual's best long-term interests. Individual self-direction is paramount, and external forces that restrict self-direction should be severely limited.[20] Individuals calculate the best long-term advantage to themselves as a measure of a decision's goodness. The action that is intended to produce a greater ratio of good to bad for the individual compared with other alternatives is the right one to perform. In theory, with everyone pursuing self-direction, the greater good is ultimately served because people learn to accommodate each other in their own long-term interest. Individualism is believed to lead to honesty and integrity because that works best in the long run. Lying and cheating for immediate self-interest causes business associates to lie and cheat in return. Thus, individualism ultimately leads to behavior toward others that fits standards of behavior people want toward themselves.[21] One value of understanding this approach is to recognize short-term variations if they are proposed. People might argue for short-term self-interest based on individualism, but that misses the point. Because individualism is easily misinterpreted to support immediate self-gain, it is unpopular in today's highly organized and group-oriented society. Dozens of disgraced top executives from WorldCom, Enron Corp., Tyco, and other companies demonstrate the flaws of the individualism approach. This approach is closest to the domain of free choice described in Exhibit 4.1.

Moral Rights Approach

The **moral rights approach** asserts that human beings have fundamental rights and liberties that cannot be taken away by an individual's decision. Thus, an ethically correct decision is one that best maintains the rights of those people affected by it.

Six moral rights should be considered during decision making:

1. *The right of free consent.* Individuals are to be treated only as they knowingly and freely consent to be treated.

2. *The right to privacy.* Individuals can choose to do as they please away from work and have control of information about their private life.

3. *The right of freedom of conscience.* Individuals may refrain from carrying out any order that violates their moral or religious norms.

4. *The right of free speech.* Individuals may criticize truthfully the ethics or legality of actions of others.

5. *The right to due process.* Individuals have a right to an impartial hearing and fair treatment.

6. *The right to life and safety.* Individuals have a right to live without endangerment or violation of their health and safety.

To make ethical decisions, managers need to avoid interfering with the fundamental rights of others. For example, a decision to eavesdrop on employees violates the right to privacy. Sexual harassment is unethical because it violates the right to freedom of conscience. The right of free speech would support whistle-blowers who call attention to illegal or inappropriate actions within a company.

Justice Approach

The **justice approach** holds that moral decisions must be based on standards of equity, fairness, and impartiality. Three types of justice are of concern to managers: distributive justice, procedural justice, and compensatory justice. **Distributive justice** requires that different treatment of people not be based on arbitrary characteristics. Individuals who are similar in respects relevant to a decision should be treated similarly. Thus, men and women should not receive different salaries if they are performing the same job. However, people who differ in a substantive way, such as job skills or responsibilities, can be treated differently in proportion to the differences in skills or responsibility among them. This difference should have a clear relationship to organizational goals and tasks.

Procedural justice requires that rules be administered fairly. Rules should be clearly stated and be consistently and impartially enforced. **Compensatory justice** argues that individuals should be compensated for the cost of their injuries by the responsible party. Moreover, individuals should not be held responsible for matters over which they have no control.

The justice approach is closest to the thinking underlying the domain of codified law in Exhibit 4.1 because it assumes that justice is applied through rules and regulations. This theory does not require complex calculations such as those demanded by a utilitarian approach, and it does not justify self-interest as the individualism approach does. Managers are expected to define attributes on which different treatment of employees is acceptable. Questions such as how minority workers should be compensated for past discrimination are difficult. However, this approach does justify as ethical behavior efforts to correct past wrongs, play fair under the rules, and insist on job-relevant differences as the basis for different levels of pay or promotion opportunities. Most of the laws guiding human resource management (Chapter 9) are based on the justice approach.

---

moral rights approach

The ethical concept that moral decisions are those that best maintain the rights of those people affected by them.

Take ACTION

Take time to make decisions so you treat others fairly, with justice.

justice approach

The ethical concept that moral decisions must be based on standards of equity, fairness, and impartiality.

distributive justice

The concept that different treatment of people should not be based on arbitrary characteristics. In the case of substantive differences, people should be treated differently in proportion to the differences among them.

procedural justice

The concept that rules should be clearly stated and consistently and impartially enforced.

compensatory justice

The concept that individuals should be compensated for the cost of their injuries by the responsible party and that individuals should not be held responsible for matters over which they have no control.

Understanding these various approaches is only a first step; managers still have to consider how to apply them. The approaches offer general principles that managers can recognize as useful in making ethical decisions. The Focus on Ethics box lists some further guidelines that can help managers make ethical decisions.

Factors Affecting Ethical Choices

When managers are accused of lying, cheating, or stealing, the blame is usually placed on the individual or on the company situation. Most people believe that individuals make ethical choices because of individual integrity, which is true, but it is not the whole story. Ethical or unethical business practices usually reflect the values, attitudes, beliefs, and behavior patterns of the organizational culture; thus, ethics is as much an organizational as a personal issue.[22] Examine how the manager and the organization shape ethical decision making.[23]

The Manager

Managers bring specific personality and behavioral traits to the job. Personal needs, family influence, and religious background all shape a manager's value system. Specific personality characteristics, such as ego strength, self-confidence, and a strong sense of independence, may enable managers to make ethical decisions.

One important personal trait is the stage of moral development.[24] A simplified version of one model of personal moral development is shown in Exhibit 4.2. At the preconventional level, individuals are concerned with external rewards and punishments

FOCUS ON ETHICS

Guidelines for Ethical Decision Making

If a *60 Minutes* crew were waiting on your doorstep one morning, would you feel comfortable justifying your actions to the camera? One young manager, when confronted with ethical dilemmas, gives them the *60 Minutes* test. Others say they use such criteria as whether they would be proud to tell their parents or grandparents about their decisions, or whether they could sleep well at night and face themselves in the mirror in the morning. Managers often rely on their own personal integrity in making ethical decisions. But knowing what to do is not always easy. As a future manager, you will almost surely face ethical dilemmas one day. The following guidelines will not tell you exactly what to do, but taken in the context of the text discussion, they will help you evaluate the situation more clearly by examining your own values and those of your organization. The answers to these questions will force you to think about the social and ethical consequences of your behavior.

1. Is the problem/dilemma what it appears to be? If you are not sure, find out.

2. Is the action you are considering legal? Ethical? If you are not sure, find out.

3. Do you understand the position of those who oppose the action you are considering? Is it reasonable?

4. Whom does the action benefit? Harm? How much? How long?

5. Would you be willing to allow everyone to do what you are considering doing?

6. Have you sought the opinion of others who are knowledgeable and objective regarding the subject?

7. Would your action be embarrassing to you if it were made known to your family, friends, coworkers, or superiors?

8. Even if you are sure the decision is reasonable and that you could defend it to others, does your gut instinct tell you it is the wrong thing to do?

There are no correct answers to these questions in an absolute sense. Yet, if you determine that an action is potentially harmful to someone or would be embarrassing to you, or if you do not know the ethical or legal consequences, these guidelines will clarify whether the action is socially responsible.

SOURCES: Anthony M. Pagano and Jo Ann Verdin, *The External Environment of Business* (New York: Wiley, 1988): Chapter 5; Joseph L. Badaracco, Jr. and Allen P. Webb, "Business Ethics: A View from the Trenches," *California Management Review* 37:2 (Winter 1995): 8–28; and Sherry Baker, "Ethical Judgment," *Executive Excellence* (March 1992): 7–8.

© Michael Lewis

*Julius Walls, Jr., chief executive of Greyston Bakery, demonstrates the **postconventional level of moral development**. Greyston makes gourmet brownies, cakes, and tarts. Walls hires employees off the street, first come, first served, because he thinks everyone deserves a chance at a job. He also helps workers with problems whether or not they're job related. Greyston serves the poor by feeding the rich. Much of its $4 million in annual sales are generated by selling bits of brownies to Ben & Jerry's for its chocolate fudge brownie ice cream and frozen yogurt, and the company donates all profits to the needy.*

and obey authority to avoid detrimental personal consequences. In an organizational context, this level may be associated with managers who use an autocratic or coercive leadership style, with employees oriented toward dependable accomplishment of specific tasks. At level two, called the conventional level, people learn to conform to the expectations of good behavior as defined by colleagues, family, friends, and society. Meeting social and interpersonal obligations is important. Work group collaboration is the preferred manner for accomplishment of organizational goals, and managers use a leadership style that encourages interpersonal relationships and cooperation. At the postconventional, or principled level, individuals are guided by an internal set of values and standards and may disobey rules or laws that violate these principles. Internal values become more important than the expectations of significant others. For example, when the *USS Indianapolis* sank after being torpedoed during World War II, one Navy

EXHIBIT 4.2

Three Levels of Personal Moral Development

Level 3: Postconventional

Follows self-chosen principles of justice and right. Aware that people hold different values and seeks creative solutions to ethical dilemmas. Balances concern for individual with concern for common good.

Level 2: Conventional

Lives up to expectations of others. Fulfills duties and obligations of social system. Upholds laws.

Level 1: Preconventional

Follows rules to avoid punishment. Acts in own interest. Obedience for its own sake.

Leadership Style:	Autocratic/coercive	Guiding/encouraging, team oriented	Transforming, or servant leadership
Employee Behavior:	Task accomplishment	Work group collaboration	Empowered employees, full participation

SOURCES: Based on L. Kohlberg, "Moral Stages and Moralization: The Cognitive-Developmental Approach," in *Moral Development and Behavior: Theory, Research, and Social Issues*, ed. T. Lickona (New York: Holt, Rinehart, and Winston, 1976), 31–53; and Jill W. Graham, "Leadership, Moral Development and Citizenship Behavior," *Business Ethics Quarterly* 5, no. 1 (January 1995), 43–54.

Take **ACTION**

Listen to your conscience and take moral actions; independently investigage where the truth lies and what is the right thing to do.

pilot disobeyed orders and risked his life to save men who were being picked off by sharks. The pilot was operating from the highest level of moral development in attempting the rescue despite a direct order from superiors. When managers operate from this highest level of development, they use transformative or servant leadership, focusing on the needs of followers and encouraging others to think for themselves and to engage in higher levels of moral reasoning. Employees are empowered and given opportunities for constructive participation in governance of the organization.

The great majority of managers operate at level two. A few have not advanced beyond level one. Only about 20 percent of American adults reach the third level of moral development. People at level three are able to act in an independent, ethical manner regardless of expectations from others inside or outside the organization. Managers at level three of moral development will make ethical decisions whatever the organizational consequences for them. What level of moral development do you think Shepard Fairey is at? He experiences cognitive dissonance between his street image and his contracts with huge corporations, as shown in the Focus on Leadership box.

One interesting study indicates that most researchers have failed to account for the different ways in which women view social reality and develop psychologically and have, thus, consistently classified women as being stuck at lower levels of development. Researcher Carol Gilligan has suggested that the moral domain be enlarged to include responsibility and care in relationships. Women may, in general, perceive moral complexities more astutely than men and make moral decisions based not on a set of absolute rights and wrongs but on principles of not causing harm to others.[25]

FOCUS ON LEADERSHIP

Studio Number One

Shepard Fairey likes to think of himself as a rebel, a maverick. The 34-year-old is one of his generation's most notorious and prolific street artists. He recently split with his long-time creative partner and started his own marketing design firm, Studio Number One (see *http://www.subliminalprojects.com*). He gets invited to speak at conferences and travels to Japan with his wife to visit a shop that sells clothing with his images. He works with huge business firms who hope Fairey can connect them to a much-desired demographic.

But Fairey cannot stay away from bad-boy stuff. He and his friends went to New York's Chinatown one night and went "bombing," as they call it. Finding a blank billboard, Fairey managed to get to the roof of the building with an 8-foot rolled poster and some paste. He got the image on, but someone called the police and he was arrested for criminal mischief and trespassing, spending 48 hours in jail, his ninth bust. Even with that rapsheet, he gets courted by mainstream firms. His previous company BLK/MRKT has worked with Mountain Dew, Levi Strauss, Sunkist, Dr. Pepper, and Universal Pictures. After he posted bail, he had work to do, including designs for Express Jeans and Obey Giant clothing, based on his continuing Obey Giant images. These companies love him because they have trouble reaching the elusive demographic of young males, who are difficult to target, watch little television, and are cynical toward normal advertisements. When young people take Fairey's posters or stickers and put them on their own bulletin boards, the advertisers know the campaign worked. But how can you achieve this kind of success. Fairey says its instinct, like Louis Armstrong's response when he was asked to define jazz: "If you have to ask, you'll never know."

Often clients are vague with Fairey. Make it cool, they say. Make it urban. He retorts: "Urban like hip-hop, like black? Or urban like disaffected suburban white graffiti kids?" Then they get more specific.

Fairey's former company BLK/MRKT took in $1 million per year and it will not be long before Studio Number One follows suit. He hates ads that insult the customer, that are unintelligent.

How can Fairey remain true to his street image when he is raking in the dough from the fat multinational corporations (MNCs)? He is not alone. Many entrepreneurs struggle with issues of integrity, the conflict between what they want to do and what the market is going to pay them to do. "Sometimes I feel like a double agent," he says. He wants to do work that is fun, with clients that can be hip, and he does have his boundaries: no tobacco companies. If he could redo the advertising world so all marketing materials were smart, creative, and art-like, well, that would be great. He says, "It sounds pretty utopian to me."

SOURCE: Rob Walker, "The Buzz Guru," *Inc. Magazine* (March 2004): 105–109.

One reason higher levels of ethical conduct are increasingly important is the impact of globalization. Globalization has made ethical issues even more complicated for today's managers.[26] American managers working in foreign countries need sensitivity and an openness to other systems, as well as the fortitude to resolve difficult issues. For example, though tolerance for bribery is waning, a recent survey revealed disturbing results. Transparency International, an international organization that monitors corruption, publishes an annual report ranking countries according to how many bribes are offered by their international businesses. Exhibit 4.3 shows results of the organization's most recent available report. International businesses based in countries like Russia, China, Taiwan, and South Korea were found to be using bribes "on an exceptional and intolerable scale." However, multinational firms in the United States, Japan, France, and Spain revealed a relatively high propensity to pay bribes overseas.[27]

The Organization

Rarely can ethical or unethical corporate actions be attributed solely to the personal values of a single manager. The values adopted within the organization are highly important, especially when we understand that most people are at the level two of moral development, which means they believe their duty is to fulfill obligations and expectations of others. Consider, for example, accounting managers at WorldCom, which disintegrated in an $11 billion fraud scandal.

WorldCom

WorldCom started out as a small long-distance company and rapidly became a dazzling star during the late 1990s Wall Street telecom boom. Just as rapidly, it all came crashing down as one executive after another was hauled away on conspiracy and securities fraud charges.

For Betty Vinson and Troy Normand, the first signs of serious trouble came in mid-2000. With the telecom industry in a slump, top executives were scrambling to meet Wall Street's expectations for the quarter. Vinson and Normand's boss, Buford Yates, called the two into his office and broke the news. CEO Bernard Ebbers and Chief Financial Officer Scott Sullivan had asked that they make some highly questionable accounting adjustments—to the tune of $828 million—that would reduce expenses and boost the company's earnings for the quarter. Though the managers were initially shocked by the request and resisted, they agreed to go along. Despite the misgivings they and Yates all felt, the accountants continued to make increasingly irregular adjustments over the course of six quarters, hoping that each one would be the last.

Top executives persuaded these managers, who were all known as hardworking, dedicated employees, that their gimmicks would help pull WorldCom out of its troubles

EXHIBIT 4.3

The Transparency International Bribe Payers Index 2002

SOURCE: Transparency International, http://www.transparency.org.

Rank		Score	Rank		Score
1	Australia	8.5	12	France	5.5
2	Sweden	8.4	13	United States	5.3
2 (tie)	Switzerland	8.4	13 (tie)	Japan	5.3
4	Austria	8.2	15	Malaysia	4.3
5	Canada	8.1	15 (tie)	Hong Kong	4.3
6	Netherlands	7.8	17	Italy	4.1
6 (tie)	Belgium	7.8	18	South Korea	3.9
8	United Kingdom	6.9	19	Taiwan	3.8
9	Singapore	6.3	20	People's Republic of China	3.5
9 (tie)	Germany	6.3	21	Russia	3.2
11	Spain	5.8			

A score of 10 represents zero propensity to pay bribes, while a score of 0 reflects very high levels of bribery.

and get everything back to normal. A colleague of Vinson's says she felt that she needed to go along with her bosses' requests despite her own concerns. To assuage her guilt, the colleague says, Vinson rationalized that CFO Sullivan had been hailed as one of the country's top chief financial officers. Therefore, if he thought the transfers and other gimmicks were all right, she was not one to question it.

When WorldCom's problems exploded into public view, Yates, Normand, and Vinson found themselves in the middle of the largest fraud case in corporate history. All three pled guilty to conspiracy and securities fraud, which will likely result in jail time.[28]

Vinson, Normand, and Yates were not unscrupulous people. All three had misgivings about what they were doing, but they continued to go along with their superiors' requests. All ethical decisions are made within the context of our interactions with other people, and the social networks within an organization play an important role in guiding other people's actions. For most of us, doing something we know is wrong becomes easier when everyone else is doing it. In organizations, the norms and values of the team, department, or organization as a whole have a profound influence on ethical behavior. Perhaps HealthSouth's lapses in ethics, as shown in the Business Blooper, contributed to its legal problems.

Research has verified that these values strongly influence employee actions and decision making.[29] In particular, corporate culture, as described in Chapter 2, lets employees know what beliefs and behaviors the company supports and those it will not tolerate. If unethical behavior is tolerated or even encouraged, it becomes routine. For example, an investigation of thefts and kickbacks in the oil business found that the cause was the historical acceptance of thefts and kickbacks. Employees were socialized into those values and adopted them as appropriate. In many companies, employees believe that if they do not go along, their jobs will be in jeopardy or they will not fit in.[30]

Below is a questionnaire about ethical work environments. Fill it out to determine your level of ethical awareness.

Ethical Work Climates

Answer the following questions by circling the number that best describes an organization for which you have worked.

Disagree				Agree
1	2	3	4	5

1. What is the best for everyone in the company is the major consideration here.

1 2 3 4 5

BUSINESS BLOOPER

HealthSouth

Stars such as Faith Hill, Reba McEntire, and KC and the Sunshine Band performed at the annual mega-event (known as "The Prom") for HealthSouth managers, seven years in a row. Each meeting ran around $3 million, most costs passed on to Medicare. This was only one of the many reasons the Justice Department accused the company of accounting fraud two years ago, settling recently with HealthSouth, which had to pay $325 million to the U.S. government. Those free-flowing parties/meetings did not help. When the Commodores were featured at "The Prom" two years ago, they should have sang, "I'm Easy."

SOURCE: Michael Tomberlin, "Medicare Paid for Big Stars," *Birmingham News* (Feb. 13, 2005): 1D, 3D.

2. Our major concern is always what is best for the other person.

1   2   3   4   5

3. People are expected to comply with the law and professional standards over and above other considerations.

1   2   3   4   5

4. In this company, the first consideration is whether a decision violates any law.

1   2   3   4   5

5. Following the company's rules and procedures is important here.

1   2   3   4   5

6. People in this company strictly obey the company policies.

1   2   3   4   5

7. In this company, people are mostly out for themselves.

1   2   3   4   5

8. People are expected to do anything to further the company's interests regardless of the consequences.

1   2   3   4   5

9. In this company, people are guided by their own personal ethics.

1   2   3   4   5

10. People in this company decide for themselves what is right and wrong.

1   2   3   4   5

Scoring

Subtract each of your scores for questions 7 and 8 from the number 6. Then, add up your adjusted scores for all ten questions:_____. These questions measure the dimensions of an organization's ethical climate. Questions 1 and 2 measure caring for people, questions 3 and 4 measure lawfulness, questions 5 and 6 measure rules adherence, questions 7 and 8 measure emphasis on financial and company perform-ance, and questions 9 and 10 measure individual independence. A total score above 40 indicates a positive ethical climate. A score from 30 to 40 indicates above-average ethical climate. A score from 20 to 30 indicates a below-average ethical climate, and a score below 20 indicates a poor ethical climate.

Go back over the questions and think about changes that you could have made to improve the ethical climate in the organization. Discuss with other students what you could do as a manager to improve ethics in future companies you work for.

SOURCE: Based on Bart Victor and John B. Cullen, "The Organizational Bases of Ethical Work Climates," *Administrative Science Quarterly* 33 (1988): 101–125.

Culture can be examined to see the kinds of ethical signals given to employees. Exhibit 4.4 indicates questions to ask to understand the cultural system. High ethical standards can be affirmed and communicated through public awards and ceremonies. Heroes provide role models that can either support or refute ethical decision making. Culture is not the only aspect of an organization that influences ethics, but it is a major force because it defines company values. Other aspects of the organization, such as explicit rules and poli-cies, the reward system, the extent to which the company cares for its people, the selec-tion system, emphasis on legal and professional standards, and leadership and decision processes, can have an impact on ethical values and manager decision making.[31]

EXHIBIT 4.4

Questions for Analyzing a Company's Cultural Impact on Ethics

SOURCE: Linda Klebe Treviño, "A Cultural Perspective on Changing and Developing Organizational Ethics," in *Research in Organizational Change and Development*, ed. R. Woodman and W. Pasmore (Greenwich, Conn.: JAI Press, 1990), 4.

1. Identify the organization's heroes. What values do they represent? Given an ambiguous ethical dilemma, what decision would they make and why?

2. What are some important organizational rituals? How do they encourage or discourage ethical behavior? Who gets the awards; people of integrity or individuals who use unethical methods to attain success?

3. What are the ethical messages sent to new entrants into the organization—must they obey authority at all costs, or is questioning authority acceptable or even desirable?

4. Does analysis of organizational stories and myths reveal individuals who stand up for what's right, or is conformity the valued characteristic? Do people get fired or promoted in these stories?

5. Does language exist for discussing ethical concerns? Is this language routinely incorporated and encouraged in business decision making?

6. What informal socialization processes exist, and what norms for ethical/unethical behavior do they promote?

What Is Social Responsibility?

Now turn to the issue of social responsibility. In one sense, the concept of corporate social responsibility, like ethics, is easy to understand: It means distinguishing right from wrong and doing the right thing. It means being a good corporate citizen. The formal definition of **social responsibility** is management's obligation to make choices and take actions that will contribute to the welfare and interests of society as well as the organization.[32]

As straightforward as this definition seems, social responsibility can be a difficult concept to grasp because different people have different beliefs as to which actions improve society's welfare.[33] To make matters worse, social responsibility covers a range of issues, many of which are ambiguous with respect to right or wrong. For example, if a bank deposits the money from a trust fund into a low-interest account for 90 days, from which it makes a substantial profit, is it being a responsible corporate citizen? How about two companies engaging in intense competition? Is it socially responsible for the stronger corporation to drive the weaker one into bankruptcy or a forced merger? Or consider companies such as Chiquita, Kmart, or Global Crossing, all of which declared bankruptcy—which is perfectly legal—to avoid mounting financial obligations to suppliers, labor unions, or competitors. These examples contain moral, legal, and economic considerations that make socially responsible behavior hard to define. A company's environmental impact must also be considered.

social responsibility

The obligation of organization management to make decisions and take actions that will enhance the welfare and interests of society as well as the organization.

Organizational Stakeholders

One reason for the difficulty understanding social responsibility is that managers must confront the question, "Responsibility to whom?" Recall from Chapter 2 that the organization's environment consists of several sectors in the task and general environment. From a social responsibility perspective, enlightened organizations view the internal and external environment as various stakeholders.

A **stakeholder** is any person or group within or outside the organization that has a stake in the organization's performance. Each stakeholder has a different criterion of responsiveness because it, he, or she has a different interest in the organization.[34] For example, Wal-Mart uses aggressive bargaining tactics with suppliers so that it can provide low prices for customers. Some stakeholders see this as responsible corporate behavior because it benefits customers and forces suppliers to be more efficient. Others, however, argue that the aggressive tactics are unethical and socially irresponsible because they force U.S. manufacturers to lay off workers, close factories, and outsource from low-wage countries. For instance, Wal-Mart now purchases nearly 10 percent of all Chinese imports to the United States. One supplier said clothing is being sold so cheaply at Wal-Mart that many U.S. companies could not compete even if they paid their employees nothing.[35]

stakeholder

Any person or group within or outside the organization that has a stake in the organization's performance.

The organization's performance affects stakeholders, but stakeholders can have a tremendous effect on the organization's performance and success. Consider the case of Monsanto, a leading competitor in the life sciences industry.

Monsanto

Over the past decade or so, Monsanto has been transformed from a chemical firm into a biotechnology company. The organization has a vast array of stakeholders from around the wolrd, including customers, investors, suppliers, partners, health and agriculture organizations, regulatory agencies, research institutes, and governments.

Monsanto has experienced some big problems in recent years because of its failure to satisfy various stakeholder groups. For example, the company's genetic seed business has been the target of controversy and protest. European consumers rebelled against a perceived imposition of unlabeled, genetically modified food ingredients. Research institutes and other organizations took offense at what they perceived as Monsanto's arrogant approach to the new business. Activist groups accused the company of creating "Frankenstein foods." Partly as a result of these public sentiments, Monsanto has had trouble getting regulatory approval for its genetically modified organisms, including seeds for wheat, corn, soy, and other crops. Investor confidence in the company waned, too, and the stock took a downhill slide.

The leadership has promised an ongoing dialogue between Monsanto managers and various stakeholder constituencies. If it cannot effectively manage critical stakeholder relationships, Monsanto is not likely to survive as a business.[36]

Exhibit 4.5 illustrates important stakeholders for Monsanto. Most organizations are similarly influenced by various stakeholder groups. Investors and shareholders, employees, customers, and suppliers are considered primary stakeholders, without whom the organization cannot survive. Investors, shareholders, and suppliers' interests are served by managerial

EXHIBIT 4.5

Major Stakeholders Relevant to Monsanto Company

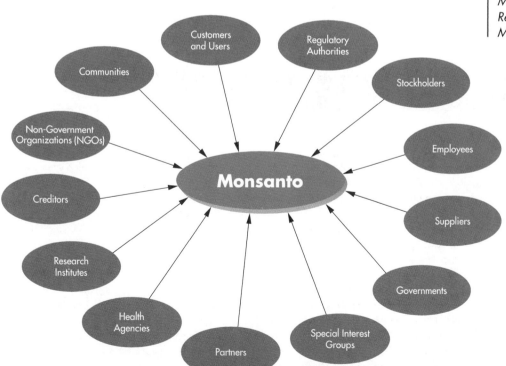

SOURCES: Based on information in D. Wheeler, B. Colbert, and R. E. Freeman, "Focusing on Value: Reconciling Corporate Social Responsibility, Sustainability, and a Stakeholder Approach in a Networked World," *Journal of General Management* 28, no. 3 (Spring 2003). 1–28; and J. E. Post, L. E. Preston, and S. Sachs, "Managing the Extended Enterprise: The New Stakeholder View," *California Management Review* 45, no. 1 (Fall 2002), 6–28.

efficiency, that is, use of resources to achieve profits. Employees expect work satisfaction, pay, and good supervision. Customers are concerned with decisions about the quality, safety, and availability of goods and services. When any primary stakeholder group becomes seriously dissatisfied, the organization's viability is threatened.[37] A unique approach to stakeholders is taken by PeaceWorks, as described in the Focus on Leadership box.

Other important stakeholders are the government and the community. Most corporations exist only under the proper charter and licenses and operate within the limits of safety laws, environmental protection requirements, antitrust regulations, and other laws and regulations in the government sector. The community includes local government, the natural and physical environments, and the quality of life provided for residents. Special interest groups (SIGs), still another stakeholder, may include trade associations, political action committees, professional associations, and consumerists. Social activists have discovered the power of the Internet for organizing stakeholders and pressuring corporations to honor their ethical, human rights, and environmental responsibilities. One organization, the As You Sow foundation (AYS), uses the Internet to mobilize investors and shareholders to push for social reforms, as described in the Digital, Inc. box.

Socially responsible organizations consider the effects of their actions on all stakeholder groups and may invest in a number of philanthropic causes that benefit stakeholders. Bristol-Myers Squibb Company, for example, provides funding for health clinics in areas of Texas, California, and Florida to hire promotoras de salud, or peer health educators, to help fight Type 2 diabetes in the Hispanic population. Typically, Hispanic women who themselves have diabetes, the promotoras de salud are trained to work full time as accessible community resources. By answering questions, assuring compliance with medications, and providing nutritional advice, they help patients control their disease and provide needed support for overworked and stressed nurses who do not have the time or Spanish language skills to address all the concerns of their many patients.[38]

Today, SIGs continue to be one of the largest stakeholder concerns that companies face. Environmental responsibility has become a primary issue as business and the public acknowledge the damage that has been done to our natural environment.

FOCUS ON LEADERSHIP

PeaceWorks

Daniel Lubetzky is solving the world's problems, on a microlevel anyway, through condiments and coconut milk. The recent Stanford Law grad was in Tel Aviv 10 years ago when he ate something so mouth-watering he wanted more: sun-dried tomato spread. After he bought the store out, he tracked down the manufacturer, Israeli Yoel Benesh, who had gone out of business. Lubetzky made Benesh a business proposition: If he would get the sun-dried tomatoes from Turkey rather than Italy, olives and oil from Palestine, and jars from Egypt instead of Portugal, Lubetzky would take care of marketing the product in the United States. Lubetzky figured the condiments would benefit Israelis and Arabs as they would be forced to trade together, weaving a profitable web of commerce between them.

With $10,000 of his savings and some from his parents, he launched PeaceWorks and introduced its first product: Moshe and Ali Spratés. Later, it began marketing a women-owned line from Indonesia which brings together Muslims, Buddhists, and Christians; plus a Sri Lankan coconut milk that brings collaboration between the warring Tamils and Sinhalese. Lubetzky says his company is "not only for-profit"—meaning it not only makes money but serves a social cause. In addition, it donates a portion of profits to its foundation, which promotes forums between Palestinians and Israelis to resolve conflicts.

PeaceWorks sells its products in 5,000 U.S. stores and grosses $10 million. But it is not all rosy. Violence in the Middle East has not stopped. Still, the Mexican-born, 36-year-old son of a Holocaust survivor takes comfort in small victories. "At the company, micro, personal level, this works," he says. Which means the Arabs and Israelis who work together or the 1,000 Muslims, Jews, and Christians he employs. "I never think this is a waste of time. There are times when I wonder if it will ultimately help change the situation. But I can't live my life accepting defeat."

SOURCES: Elaine Pofelt, "Food for Peace," *FSB*, (Jan. 2005): 100–104; Jessica Steinberg, "One Heart at a Time," *Fast Company* (Nov. 2004): 49.

DIGITAL, INC.

Using the Web to Promote Social Responsibility

The Internet has become a crucial weapon in the fight to make corporations more socially responsible. For example, social activists have long used shareholder pressure as an important means of promoting their goals. Now, with the ability to rapidly spread information on the Web, nonprofit organizations such as the As You Sow foundation (AYS) can quickly rally shareholders and mount campaigns against corporate practices they consider irresponsible.

AYS is a not-for-profit organization with a mission to promote corporate responsibility and "hold corporations accountable for complying with consumer, workplace, and environmental laws." It does so by engaging in dialogue with corporations concerning social responsibility issues and by organizing shareholder campaigns when companies balk at voluntary efforts. AYS works closely with other activist organizations such as the Interfaith Center on Corporate Responsibility (ICCR), a group of Protestant, Catholic, and Jewish institutional investors that pioneered shareholder

activism in the 1970s, and the Shareholder Action Network, an information, networking, and resource center that AYS helped to found. One shareholder campaign resulted in Home Depot agreeing to phase out the sale of old-growth timber, for example.

AYS is currently involved in dialogues with companies like Wal-Mart, Nike, McDonald's, and the Walt Disney Company concerning labor and human rights abuses in contract supplier plants. A current shareholder campaign against genetically altered foods, targeting companies such as DuPont, Hershey, Kellogg, and Sysco, has become the fastest growing shareholder movement in history. Project director Tracey Rembert explains the value of using the Internet for social activism: "It used to be you'd call 20 people you know on the telephone and ask them to write a letter.... Now you can bring together many more people with just one e-mail. You can accomplish in one year what it might have taken ten years of pickets and protests in the streets to accomplish."

SOURCE: Mark Schapiro, "All Over the Board," *grok* (February–March 2001): 110–112; and *http://www.asyousow.org* accessed on February 27, 2004.

The Ethic of Sustainability and the Natural Environment

When the first Earth Day celebration was held in 1970, most managers considered environmentalists to be an extremist fringe group and felt little need to respond to environmental concerns.[39] Today, environmental issues are a hot topic among business leaders, and managers and organizations in all industries are jumping on the environmental bandwagon.

One model uses the phrase *shades of green* to evaluate a company's commitment to environmental responsibility.[40] The various shades, which represent a company's approach to addressing environmental concerns, are illustrated in Exhibit 4.6. With a legal approach, the organization does what is necessary to satisfy legal requirements. In general, managers and the company show little concern for environmental issues. For example, Willamette Industries of Portland, Oregon, agreed to install $7.4 million worth of pollution control equipment in its 13 factories to comply with U.S. Environmental Protection Agency (EPA) requirements. The move came only after Willamette was fined a whopping $11.2 million for violating emissions standards.[41] The next shade, the market approach, represents a growing awareness of and sensitivity to environmental concerns, primarily to satisfy customers. A company might provide environmentally friendly products because customers want them, for instance, not necessarily because of strong management commitment to the environment. Judy Wicks provides environmentally friendly products, and she uses green energy for her restaurant, as described in the Best Practices box.

© AP/Wide World Photos

CONCEPT CONNECTION

Recently, Roxanne Quimby sold 80 percent of her company, Burt's Bees, a leading natural personal care brand, to a private-equity firm for more than $175 million. She plans to donate half the proceeds to a land trust to establish a national park in northern Maine, demonstrating her commitment to the **natural environment** *and the ethic of* **sustainability**.

EXHIBIT 4.6

*The Shades of
Corporate Green*

Activist
Approach
Actively conserve
the environment

Stakeholder Approach
Address multiple
stakeholder concerns

Market Approach
Respond to customers

Legal Approach
Satisfy legal requirements regarding
environmental conservation

SOURCE: Based on R.E. Freeman, J. Pierce, and R. Dodd, *Shades of Green: Ethics and the Environment* (New York: Oxford University Press, 1995).

Take ACTION

Do your part to recycle at work and at home.

A further step is to respond to multiple demands from the environment. The stakeholder approach means that companies attempt to answer the environmental concerns of various stakeholder groups, such as customers, the local community, business partners, and special interest groups. Ontario Power Generation, Shell, and Alcan Aluminum are among the large companies that are partnering with Environmental Defense to reduce greenhouse gases.[42] The move comes in response to growing concerns among customers, communities where the companies operate, and environmental groups, as well as a recognition that emissions will probably be regulated by government actions.

BEST PRACTICES

White Dog Enterprises

Judy Wicks got into the restaurant business by accident. Having just left her first husband (with whom she founded Urban Outfitters), she was driving her car in Philadelphia when she ran a light and rammed into another car. Broke and jobless, she poured out her heart to a bystander on the street who happened to own a nearby restaurant and needed a waitress. Wicks stayed there for 13 years, getting promoted to manager at La Terrasse. Toward the end, she was running a muffin shop out of her house down the street. When the expected offer to be co-owner of the restaurant did not materialize, she finished serving breakfast one day, quit La Terrasse, and expanded White Dog Café's menu, a practice she continues to this day.

Wick's efforts to make the world a better place include being the first Pennsylvania business run on electricity generated from wind power. Believing in building up the local economy, she gets her meats and vegetables come from local organic farms, and she helps them with small loans to buy supplies. She loves debates, even with the green business world, where she often proclaims, "Businesses should not grow bigger." Seeing business as a way of life, rather than merely a means for profit, she compares her feelings for White Dog Enterprises the same way farmers feel about their land. "My business," she says, "is really a way of expressing my love of life."

SOURCE: Jess McCuan, "Entrepreneurs We Love: Judy Wicks," *Inc. Magazine* (April 2004): 142.

Finally, at the highest level of green, organizations take an activist approach to environmental issues by actively searching for ways to conserve the Earth's resources. A growing number of companies around the world are embracing a revolutionary idea called sustainability or sustainable development. **Sustainability** refers to economic development that generates wealth and meets the needs of the current generation while saving the environment so future generations can meet their needs as well.[43] With a philosophy of sustainability, managers weave environmental and social concerns into every strategic decision, revise policies and procedures to support sustainability efforts, and measure their progress toward sustainability goals.

U.S. organizations as diverse as DuPont, McDonald's, and United Parcel Service (UPS) are grappling with issues related to sustainability. McDonald's, for example, buys some of its energy from renewable sources, has stopped buying poultry treated with antibiotics, and offers incentives to suppliers that support sustainable practices.[44] UPS released its first Corporate Sustainability Report in 2002, outlining how the company balances economic concerns with social responsibility and environmental stewardship.[45] The UPS fleet, for instance, includes around 2,000 alternative fuel vehicles, which emit 35 percent less pollution than standard diesel engines. The company is investing $600 million on new package flow technologies that optimize how UPS delivers packages to improve service and reduce miles driven.[46] DuPont has developed biodegradable materials for plasticware, a stretchable fabric called Sorona that is made partially from corn, and a housing insulation wrap that saves far more energy than is required to produce it. The company's new mission is to manage a collection of businesses that can go on forever without depleting any natural resources.[47]

Despite these impressive advances, few U.S. firms have fully embraced the principles of sustainability, as reflected in a resistance to adopting ISO 14001 standards.[48] ISO 14001 is an international environmental management system that aims to boost the sustainability agenda. To become ISO 14001-compliant, firms develop policies, procedures, and systems that reduce the organization's impact on the natural environment. Sustainability argues that organizations can find innovative ways to create wealth at the same time they are preserving natural resources. ZipCar, for example, rents cars by the hour, 24 hours a day, with no paperwork. By reducing private car usage, ZipCar contributes to reduced emissions and reduced load on the nation's transit infrastructure.[49]

Evaluating Corporate Social Performance

A model for evaluating total corporate social responsibility is presented in Exhibit 4.7. The model indicates that total corporate social responsibility can be subdivided into four primary criteria: economic, legal, ethical, and discretionary responsibilities.[50] These four criteria fit together to form the whole of a company's social responsiveness. Managers and organizations are typically involved in several issues simultaneously, and a company's ethical and discretionary responsibilities are increasingly considered as important as economic and legal issues Social responsibility has become an important topic on the corporate agenda in the light of corporate scandals, concerns about globalization, and a growing mistrust of business.[51]

Note the similarity between the categories in Exhibit 4.7 and those in Exhibit 4.1. In both cases, ethical issues are located between the areas of legal and freely discretionary responsibilities. Exhibit 4.7 has an economic category because profits are a major reason for corporations' existence.

sustainability
Economic development that meets the needs of the current population while preserving the environment for the needs of future generations.

© AP/Wide World Photos

CONCEPT CONNECTION

For businesses, the first criterion of corporate social responsibility is **economic responsibility**. Recently, companies such as Enron, Lucent, and Nortel have failed to carry out their economic responsibility, especially when the value of the company stock plummeted. Not only did Enron employees such as those in the photo lose their jobs, but some lose most of their 401(k) retirement plans. One 61-year-old administrative assistant, who had dutifully placed 15 percent of her salary into a 401(k) plan, invested the entire amount in the company's rapidly climbing stock. She amassed close to $500,000, only to be forced out of work with a 401(k) worth only $22,000 when Enron collapsed.

Total Corporate Social Responsibility

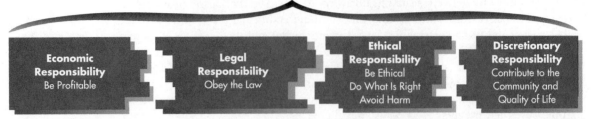

| Economic Responsibility Be Profitable | Legal Responsibility Obey the Law | Ethical Responsibility Be Ethical Do What Is Right Avoid Harm | Discretionary Responsibility Contribute to the Community and Quality of Life |

SOURCE: Based on Archie B. Carroll, "A Three-Dimensional Conceptual Model of Corporate Performance," *Academy of Management Review* 4 (1979), 499; and "The Pyramid of Corporate Social Responsibility: Toward the Moral Management of Corporate Stakeholders," *Business Horizons* 34 (July–August 1991), 42.

EXHIBIT 4.7
Criteria of Corporate Social Performance

Economic Responsibilities

The first criterion of social responsibility is economic responsibility. The business institution is, above all, the basic economic unit of society. Its responsibility is to produce the goods and services that society wants and to maximize profits for its owners and shareholders. Economic responsibility, carried to the extreme, is called the profit-maximizing view, advocated by Nobel economist Milton Friedman. This view argues that the corporation should be operated on a profit-oriented basis, with its sole mission to increase its profits so long as it stays within the rules of the game.[52]

The purely profit-maximizing view is no longer considered an adequate criterion of performance in Canada, the United States, and Europe. This approach means that economic gain is the only social responsibility but, in tody's world, can lead companies into trouble.

Legal Responsibilities

All modern societies lay down ground rules, laws, and regulations that businesses are expected to follow. Legal responsibility defines what society deems as important with respect to appropriate corporate behavior.[53] Businesses are expected to fulfill their economic goals within the legal framework. Legal requirements are imposed by local town councils, state legislators, and federal regulatory agencies.

Organizations that knowingly break the law are poor performers in this category. Intentionally manufacturing defective goods or billing a client for work not done is illegal. Tenet Healthcare paid $54 million to settle a federal lawsuit charging that one of its hospitals was cheating Medicare by performing unnecessary cardiac procedures.[54] Managers at numerous other companies have learned that organizations ultimately pay for ignoring their legal responsibilities. An example of the punishment given to one company that broke the law is described in the press release shown in Exhibit 4.8.

Ethical Responsibilities

Ethical responsibility includes behaviors that are not necessarily codified into law and may not serve the corporation's direct economic interests. As described earlier in this chapter, to be ethical, organization decision makers should act with equity, fairness, and impartiality, respect the rights of individuals, and provide different treatment of individuals only when relevant to the organization's goals and tasks.[55] Unethical behavior occurs when decisions enable an individual or company to gain at the expense of other people or society as a whole. For example, at *The New York Times,* there are indications that managers suspected star reporter Jayson Blair was fabricating research on top news stories, but they ignored the signals partly to protect the paper's reputation and because they were concerned about questioning a rising young African-American reporter. Their head-in-the-sand approach ultimately backfired when the deception became known and the paper published a lengthy story admitting how Blair had systematically fabricated or plagiarized as many as three dozen stories.[56]

EXHIBIT 4.8

One Company's Punishment for Breaking the Law

⊕EPA United States
Environmental Protection Agency

Headquarters Press Release
Washington, DC

Date Published:	07/12/2001
Title:	WASHINGTON STATE/ALASKA COMPANY SENTENCED IN ASBESTOS CASE

FOR RELEASE: THURSDAY, JULY 12, 2001
WASHINGTON STATE/ALASKA COMPANY SENTENCED IN ASBESTOS CASE

Luke C. Hester 202-564-7818 / hester.luke@epa.gov

On June 27, Great Pacific Seafood, a Washington State corporation operating in Alaska, and its General Manager, Roger D. Stiles, were sentenced for violations of the Clean Air Act. Great Pacific Seafood was sentenced to serve five years probation, pay a $75,000 fine, pay $7,000 in restitution, publish a public apology statement in the local newspaper and adopt an environmental management program. Stiles was sentenced to pay a $5,000 fine, perform 120 hours of community service, and serve two to three years probation. Great Pacific Seafood and Stiles pleaded guilty to having five of its employees directly or indirectly exposed to asbestos fibers without the proper training, equipment or protective clothing. The hazardous nature of abatement was never disclosed to two of the employees. Failure to follow asbestos work practices can expose workers to the inhalation of airborne asbestos fibers which can cause lung cancer, a lung disease known as "asbestosis" and mesothelioma, a cancer of the chest and abdominal cavities. This case was investigated by the EPA Criminal Investigation Division, the FBI and the Alaska State Occupational Safety and Health Administration. Technical assistance was provided by the EPA Office of Air Quality. The case was prosecuted by the U.S. Attorney's Office in Anchorage.

R-105 ###

Discretionary Responsibilities

Discretionary responsibility is purely voluntary and is guided by a company's desire to make social contributions not mandated by economics, law, or ethics. Discretionary activities include generous philanthropic contributions that offer no payback to the company and are not expected. An example of discretionary behavior occurred when General Mills spent $2.5 million and donated thousands of hours of employee time to help rid a neighborhood of crime and drugs. Known as the *Hawthorne Huddle,* General Mills executives worked with law enforcement, politicians, community leaders, and residents to clean up the Minneapolis, Minnesota, neighborhood. Today, Hawthorne homicides have dropped 32 percent and robberies 52 percent. Crack houses have been bulldozed to make way for a new elementary school, and low-income families are buying and repairing homes with General Mills' grants. The company has been a leader in fulfilling discretionary responsibilities since the late 1800s, when it built an orphanage that continues today as a child guidance center.[57] Discretionary responsibility is the highest criterion of social responsibility because it goes beyond societal expectations to contribute to the community's welfare.

Managing Company Ethics and Social Responsibility

Many managers are concerned with improving the ethical climate and social responsiveness of their companies. As one expert on the topic of ethics said, "Management is

discretionary responsibility

Organizational responsibility that is voluntary and guided by the organization's desire to make social contributions not mandated by economics, law, or ethics.

Take ACTION

Remember that your company needs to make a profit, be a good citizen, and follow the law, as well as being moral.

CONCEPT CONNECTION

In 2004, The Home Depot demonstrated its commitment to **discretionary responsibility** by celebrating its 25th anniversary with its first ever Week of Service. During the week, 34,500 associates donated more than 260,000 volunteer hours to complete over 1,600 service projects in partnership with national nonprofit organizations, Hands on Network and KaBOOM! Based on its inaugural success, the Week of Service will now be an annual celebration of volunteerism.

Courtesy of The Home Depot.

responsible for creating and sustaining conditions in which people are likely to behave themselves."[58] Managers must take active steps to ensure that the company stays on an ethical footing. As we discussed earlier in this chapter, ethical business practices depend on individual managers and the organization's values, policies, and practices. Exhibit 4.9 illustrates the three pillars that support an ethical organization.[59]

Ethical Individuals

Managers who are essentially ethical individuals make up the first pillar. These individuals possess honesty and integrity, which is reflected in their behavior and decisions. People inside and outside the organization trust them because they can be relied

EXHIBIT 4.9

The Three Pillars of an Ethical Organization

The Ethical Organization

Ethical Individuals
- Integrity
- Honesty
- Inspire Trust
- Treat People Right
- Play Fair
- High Level of Moral Development

Ethical Leadership
- Role Modeling
- Uphold Ethical Values in Organization
- Communicate About Ethics and Values
- Reward Ethical Behavior
- Swift Discipline of Unethical Behavior

Organizations Structures and Systems
- Corporate Culture
- Code of Ethics
- Ethics Committee
- Chief Ethics Officer
- Ethics Training
- Whistle-Blowing Mechanisms

SOURCE: Adapted from Linda Klebe Treviño, Laura Pincus Hartman, and Michael Brown, "Moral Person and Moral Manager," *California Management Review* 42, No. 4 (Summer 2000, 128–142.

on to follow the standards of fairness, treat people properly, and be ethical in their dealings with others. Ethical individuals strive for a high level of moral development, as discussed earlier in the chapter. Patrick Kuhse knows the dangers of not being ethical, as described in the Focus on Skills box.

However, being a moral person and making ethical decisions is not enough. Ethical managers must encourage the moral development of others.[60] They find ways to focus the entire organization's attention on ethical values and create an organizational environment that encourages, guides, and supports the ethical behavior of all employees. Two additional pillars are needed to provide a strong foundation for an ethical organization: ethical leadership and organizational structures and systems.

Ethical Leadership

In a study of ethics policy and practice in successful, ethical companies, no point emerged more clearly than the crucial role of leadership.[61] Employees are acutely aware of their bosses' ethical lapses, and the company grapevine quickly communicates situations in which top managers choose an expedient action over an ethical one.[62] The primary way in which leaders set the tone for an organization's ethics is through their own behavior. In addition, leaders make a commitment to ethical values and help others throughout the organization embody and reflect those values.[63]

If people do not hear about values from top leadership, they get the idea that ethical values are not important in the organization. Peter Holt, CEO of the Holt Companies, sees himself as the company's chief ethics officer. Ethical values are woven into the organizational culture, and Holt continually works to renew the values and signal his total commitment to them. Most importantly, he visits each of the firm's locations twice a year to meet with employees, answer questions, and talk about the importance of each employee upholding Holt's core values every day in every action. Holt's evaluation and reward systems are tied to how well managers and employees live the values in their everyday actions.[64] Using performance reviews and rewards effectively is a powerful way for managers to signal that ethics counts. Consistently rewarding ethical behavior and disciplining unethical conduct at all levels of the company is a critical component of providing ethical leadership.[65]

Take **ACTION**

As a leader, others look to you as a role model for ethical behavior.

FOCUS ON SKILLS

Patrick Kuhse

After spending four years in the federal penitentiary, Patrick Kuhse wants to warn college students that lapses in ethical behavior can be dangerous. His quest for money and a feeling of invincibility—common for young people, he says—were part of the reason he bribed a public official while working at a financial planning company. To avoid prosecution, he fled to Costa Rica but soon realized he did not want to live as an outlaw and turned himself in to the American Embassy.

Now he gives talks at universities whenever he can. Maybe he can help prevent others from making the same mistakes. You do a little here, cut a little there, he says, and soon you see the world differently. Whether it is music sharing or plagiarizing, students make ethical decisions that shape their future mindsets. Unethical behavior looks increasingly correct.

Sometimes you get a job, sign an ethics statement, and then your boss takes you into another room and says, "Now this is the way we really do this here." That's why Kuhse thinks college students need to learn the old adage: Money is not everything.

Kuhse advises to surround yourself with mentors, people of integrity whom you trust, such as your parents, siblings, spouse. Then listen to them. "I was relatively OK," he says, "until I stopped listening to my mom and my wife."

SOURCE: Zachary Mesenbourg, "Speaker Challenges Students Ethics," *The Post-Standard* (April 23, 2004): C6.

Organizational Structures and Systems

The third pillar of ethical organizations is the set of tools that managers use to shape values and promote ethical behavior throughout the organization. Three of these tools are a code of ethics, ethical structures, and mechanisms for supporting whistle-blowers.

code of ethics

A formal statement of the organization's values regarding ethics and social issues.

Code of Ethics. A code of ethics is a formal statement of the company's values concerning ethics and social issues; it communicates to employees what the company stands for. A code of ethics tends to exist in two types: principle-based statements and policy-based statements. Principle-based statements are designed to affect corporate culture; they define fundamental values and contain general language about company responsibilities, quality of products, and treatment of employees. General statements of principle are often called corporate credos. One good example is Johnson & Johnson's "The Credo."[66] Another view of such a code comes from Wolf von Bergstedt, as shown in the Focus on Ethics box.

Policy-based statements generally outline the procedures to be used in specific ethical situations. These situations include marketing practice, conflicts of interest, observance of laws, proprietary information, political gifts, and equal opportunities. Examples of policy-based statements are Boeing's "Business Conduct Guidelines," Chemical Bank's "Code of Ethics," GTE's "Code of Business Ethics" and "Anti-Trust and Conflict of Interest Guidelines," and Norton's "Norton Policy on Business Ethics."[67]

A code of ethics states the values or behaviors that are expected and those that will not be tolerated, backed up by management's action. A survey of *Fortune* 1,000 companies found that 98 percent address issues of ethics and business conduct in formal corporate documents, and 78 percent of those widely distribute a separate code of ethics.[68] When top management supports and enforces these codes, including rewards for compliance and discipline for violation, ethics codes can uplift a company's ethical climate.[69] The code of ethics for *The Milwaukee Journal Sentinel* gives employees some guidelines for dealing with ethical questions.

Take ACTION

Prepare your own code of ethics for how you want to do business, be a student, and live your life.

FOCUS ON ETHICS

Code of Ethics

Wolf von Bergstedt thinks we need a new set of world commandments because we live in a technological age with factories and MNCs, which have massive wealth. Von Bergstedt calls them "Universal Laws." Here they are:

1. No planet damage

2. No body damage

3. No lying

4. No stealing

5. No abandonment

6. No enslavement

7. No rape

8. No murder

9. No death wars

Imagine if all companies followed these Universal Laws. Number 1 would restrain pollution and number 2 would require factories and workplaces to be safe. Take a look at number 3. It does not say that you cannot lie about others; it just says no lying. That includes you. Therefore, managers and executives would have to tell the truth about what they did, could not cover up wrongdoing, and could not inflate revenues to increase stock prices. Number 4 means they could not embezzle money or use company funds for personal use (like former Tyco CEO Dennis Koslowski who spent $5,000 of Tyco money for his home shower curtain). The only other two that are directly related to business are number 5, about mass layoffs with no safety net, and number 6, which covers sweat shops exploiting workers in developing countries.

Here is a code of ethics easy to read, easy to print on a little card, and easy to remember. Without the "NOs" it is only 12 words. Words to live by. Words for business.

SOURCE: Wolf von Bergstedt, "Code of Ethics," *The Tennessean* (March 4, 2005): 11A.

In recent years, a spotlight has been cast on newspaper publishers and other media outlets in the wake of charges of plagiarism and other ethical violations. As a result, many companies are putting renewed emphasis on journalistic standards of integrity.

Executives at Journal Communications, the parent company of *The Milwaukee Journal Sentinel*, hope the company's clear and comprehensive code of ethics will reinforce the public's trust as well as prevent ethical misconduct. This excerpt from the opening sections of the code outlines some broad provisions for what the company stands for:

"Journal Communications and its subsidiaries operate in a complex and changing society. The actions of the company's employees, officers, and directors clearly affect other members of that society. Therefore, every employee has an obligation to conduct the day-to-day business of the company in conformity with the highest ethical standards and in accordance with the various laws and regulations that govern modern business operations....

Journal Communications' ethical standards embrace not only the letter of the law, but also the spirit of the law. To that end, we must apply plain old-fashioned honesty and decency to every aspect of our job. We must never sacrifice ethics for expedience. Broadly put, we should treat others fairly and with respect.

If faced with an ethical question, we should ask:

- Is this action legal?

- Does it comply with company policies and/or good business conduct?

- Is it something I would not want my supervisors, fellow employees, subordinates or family to know about?

- Is it something I would not want the general public to know about?

We must not condone illegal or unethical behavior...by failing to report it, regardless of an employee's level of authority.... The company will protect us if we bring unethical activity to its attention."

Journal Communications' code of ethics includes statements concerning respect for people, respect for the company, conflicts of interest, unfair competition, relationships with customers, suppliers, and news sources, confidential information, and accepting gifts and favors.[70]

By giving people some guidelines for confronting ethical questions and promising protection from recriminations for people who report wrongdoing, Journal Communications' code of ethics gives all employees the responsibility and the right to maintain the organization's ethical climate.

Ethical Structures. Ethical structures represent the various systems, positions, and programs a company can undertake to implement ethical behavior. An **ethics committee** is a group of executives appointed to oversee company ethics. The committee provides rulings on questionable ethical issues. The ethics committee assumes responsibility for disciplining wrongdoers, which is essential if the organization is to directly influence employee behavior. For example, Motorola has an Ethics Compliance Committee charged with interpreting, clarifying, and communicating the company's code of ethics and with adjudicating suspected code violations. Many companies, such as Sears Roebuck, Northrop Grumman, and Columbia/HCA Healthcare, have set up ethics offices with a full-time staff to ensure that ethical standards are an integral part of company operations. These offices are headed by a **chief ethics officer**, a company executive who oversees all aspects of ethics and legal compliance, including establishing and broadly communicating standards, ethics training, dealing with exceptions or problems, and advising senior

ethics committee
A group of executives assigned to oversee the organization's ethics by ruling on questionable issues and disciplining violators.

chief ethics officer
A company executive who oversees ethics and legal compliance.

managers in the ethical and compliance aspects of decisions.[71] The title of chief ethics officer was almost unheard of a decade ago, but the demand for these ethics specialists has grown because of highly publicized ethical and legal problems faced by companies in recent years. The Ethics Officer Association, a trade group, reports that membership has soared to more than 955 companies, up from only 12 in 1992.[72] Most ethics offices work as counseling centers to help employees resolve difficult ethical issues. A toll-free confidential hotline allows employees to report questionable behavior as well as seek guidance concerning ethical dilemmas.

ethics training

Training programs to help employees deal with ethical questions and values.

Ethics training programs also help employees deal with ethical questions and translate the values stated in a code of ethics into everyday behavior.[73] Training programs are an important supplement to a written code of ethics. Boeing and Verizon Communications require all employees to go through ethics training each year; at Boeing, senior managers get at least five hours annually. At McMurray Publishing Company in Phoenix, Arizona, all employees attend a weekly meeting on workplace ethics, where they discuss how to handle ethical dilemmas and how to resolve conflicting values.[74]

A strong ethics program is important, but it is no guarantee against lapses, as shown in the Business Blooper box. Krispy Kreme Donut's problems do not stop with donuts. It has recently admitted to grossly overinflating its earnings.

Enron Corp. boasted of a well-developed ethics program, but managers failed to live up to it. Enron's problems sent a warning to other managers and organizations. Having an impressive ethics program is not enough. The ethics program must be merged with daily operations, encouraging ethical decisions to be made throughout the company.

whistle-blowing

The disclosure by an employee of illegal, immoral, or illegitimate practices by the organization.

Whistle-Blowing. Employee disclosure of illegal, immoral, or illegitimate practices on the employer's part is called **whistle-blowing**.[75] No organization can rely exclusively on codes of conduct and ethical structures to prevent all unethical behavior. Holding organizations accountable depends to some degree on individuals who are willing to blow the whistle if they detect illegal, dangerous, or unethical activities. Whistle-blowers often report wrongdoing to outsiders, such as regulatory agencies, senators, or newspaper reporters. One HealthSouth bookkeeper tried to blow the whistle by posting his concerns on a Yahoo! Inc. forum, but no one took the tip seriously.[76] Some firms have instituted innovative programs and confidential hotlines to encourage and support internal whistle-blowing. For this to be an effective ethical safeguard, however, companies must view whistle-blowing as a benefit to the company and make dedicated efforts to protect whistle-blowers.[77]

Take ACTION

Change the name from whistle-blower to conscience-seeker and see how the behavior changes its meaning.

When no effective protective measures exist, whistle-blowers suffer. Though whistle-blowing has become widespread in recent years, it is still risky for employees, who can lose their jobs, be ostracized by coworkers, or be transferred to lower-level positions. When Colleen Rowley of the Federal Bureau of Investigation (FBI) wrote a 13-page memo to FBI director Robert Mueller about agency failures and lapses that may have contributed to the September 11, 2001, terrorist attacks, she was well aware of the risks. "Due to the frankness with which I have expressed myself...," Rowley wrote, "I hope

BUSINESS BLOOPER

Krispy Kreme Donuts

Evidently not aware that the National Institutes of Health and other agencies have warned of rising childhood obesity, Palm County, Florida's Krispy Kreme Donuts started a school program that awards a free donut to students for every A on their report cards. This shows a surprising lack of awareness regarding social consciousness of their customer base. Maybe from eating too much sugar.

SOURCE: Adam Horowitz, Mark Athitakis, Mark Lasswell, and Owen Thomas, "101 Dumbest Moments in Business," *Business 2.0* (Jan/Feb. 2005): 103–110.

my continued employment with the FBI is not somehow placed in jeopardy." Fearing recriminations and suspecting that the FBI would suppress her allegations, Rowley also sent a copy of the memo to the Senate Intelligence Committee.[78]

Laws protect government and private whistle-blowers from recrimination. However, many managers still look upon whistle-blowers as disgruntled employees who are not good team players. To maintain high ethical standards, organizations need people who are willing to point out wrongdoing. Managers can be trained to view whistle-blowing as a benefit rather than a threat, and systems can be created to protect employees who report illegal or unethical activities.

Ethical Challenges in Turbulent Times

The problem of lax ethical standards in business is nothing new, but in recent years it seems to have escalated. In addition, public reaction has been swift and unforgiving. Any ethical misstep can cost a company its reputation and hurt its profitability and performance. Consider Martha Stewart. Within months after she was charged with insider trading, her company's market capitalization plummeted $400 million. After a jury found her guilty in early 2004, some were concerned about whether the company could even survive. Companies like Nike and Gap have been hurt by accusations of exploitative labor practices in Third World factories. Oil companies have been targeted for allegedly abusing the environment and contributing to a host of social ills in developing nations, and pharmaceutical firms have been accused of hurting the world's poor by pricing drugs out of their reach. Some have been accused of withholding information about their products. Organizational stakeholders including employees, shareholders, governments, and the general community are taking a keen interest in how companies conduct their business. Online dating companies have ethical issues regarding who they let use their services, as shown below.

Take ACTION

Honesty is always the best policy even if it is late and it means fessing up.

Dating in Bytes

Looking for a date? There are more than 850 sites on-line to find that perfect mate. Do not worry about having to wade through hundreds of inappropriate people. You can go find someone who is simpatico with your values, your ethnic group, or your religion: BigChurch.com for Christians, SeniorFriendFinder.com for seniors, AsiaFriendFinder, Amigos.com, JewishFriendFinder, etc.

After breaking up with his girlfriend, Wei-Li Tjong needed an ego boost and a way to meet new women. On a whim, he went to one site and posted his Johnny Depp look-a-like picture with a description of him as "passionate and sexy." He got 12 responses that day. Within a few months, he had dated 70 women, most for after-dinner drinks of low commitment. He says about one third of the women went home with him. Maybe that is why customers are more willing to open their wallets for online dating services. The geographic reach is large, the results are immediate.

Some of the companies are large, subsidiaries of larger companies. For example, Match.com is owned by Ticketmaster and brings in about $60 million yearly revenues for its parent company.

Issues these companies face are ethical and strategic. Do they allow married people to post ads? Yahoo! Inc., says yes, if they are truthful about their status, as they do not want to be "paternalistic." Since almost one third of visitors to some sites are married, this is an important question. Some sites, such as Match.com, screen the application before they will post an ad, hoping to keep it to "singles only." Important decisions involve how far to take this dating service. Matchmaker.com has periodic events where people can meet each other and is considering offering customers help with flowers, restaurants, etc.

People still keep signing up. Personal ads are more acceptable to the younger crowd, who see it as an opportunity to meet lots of potential dates. Older folks are not as likely to fork over the cash, and they tend to see personal ads as a last resort for losers. Even with the twenty-somethings, there are problems. Mr. Tjong found out people are not always truthful. One woman had gained "significant" weight since her photo. Others did not always live up to their descriptions. And, not surprisingly, the rate of second dates is quite low.

For Mr. Tjong, it took 70 dates to fall in love. Some might find that more exhausting than fun.[79]

One reason for the proliferation of ethical lapses is the turbulence of our times. Things are moving so fast that managers who are not firmly grounded in ethical values can find themselves making poor choices because they do not have the time to weigh the situation carefully and exercise considered judgment. When organizations operate in highly competitive industries, rapidly changing markets, and complex cultural and social environments, a strong corporate culture that emphasizes ethical behavior becomes more important because it guides people to do the right thing in the face of confusion and change.[80]

The combination of a turbulent domestic environment, the globalization of business, and increasing public scrutiny has convinced many managers to pay close attention to ethics and social responsibility as a business issue.[81] New global standards are emerging that raise the public's expectations about corporate responsibility to environmental and social ills. For example, in 1999, the United Nations General Assembly completed a Global Compact that outlines global ethical principles in the areas of human rights, labor standards, and the environment.[82] At the same time, varied stakeholders are pushing new reporting initiatives connected to the sustainability movement that emphasize the triple bottom line of economic, social, and environmental performance. Today's international environment includes a great deal of piracy of CDs, DVDs, and other goods. As a defense, some companies are trying to match the price of the pirates to win back customers.

Pirating DVD Movies	If you cannot beat 'em, join 'em. Or so it seems for Warner Brothers and NBC Universal movies, both of which have gotten badly beaten by rampant piracy in Russia, China, and Mexico. Even though DVDs in those countries only cost about $3, it remains a huge gap for the people to pay when they can buy a pirated copy for only $1. Warner Brothers and NBC Universal decided to give consumers a cheap and legal alternative to the illegitimate copies. They have started selling high-quality DVDs for around $2 in China and Mexico, and will soon start one in Russia. Encouraged by the success Apple Computer had against Internet piracy by pricing its iPod songs at 99 cents, the movie studios hope to woo back international customers by slashing prices of CDs and DVDs that are legally manufactured. "There's a value in legitimacy," says Bob Wright, CEO of NBC Universal. But still, the companies are pushing for greater law enforcement abroad, as well.

Their plan may not work since the CDs and DVDs will still cost more than pirated copies. The movie studios will release more than 125 movies in each country next year, hoping to outdo the pirates. Some think it is a fool's errand and the only solution is higher-priced copies with added features that cannot be copied. EMI just released Mexican band Intocable's enhanced album, including a double CD, video, and photo album. Sales were 40,000 in the first three weeks. The signs are good.[83]

Economic Performance

The relationship of a corporation's ethics and social responsibility to its financial performance concerns managers and management scholars and has generated a lively debate.[84] One concern of managers is if good citizenship will hurt performance; after all, ethics programs cost money. A number of studies have been undertaken to determine if heightened ethical and social responsiveness increases or decreases financial performance. Studies have provided varying results but generally have found that small positive relationship exists between social responsibility and financial performance.[85] For example, a recent study of the financial performance of large U.S. corporations considered "best corporate citizens" found that they have superior reputations and superior financial performance.[86] Similarly, Governance Metrics International, an independent corporate governance ratings agency in New York, found that the stocks of companies that run on more selfless principles perform better than those run in a self-serving manner. Top-ranked companies such as Pfizer, Johnson Controls, and Sunoco outperformed lower-ranking companies in measures such as return on assets, return on investment, and return on capital.[87] Though results from these studies are not proof, they do provide an indication that use of resources for ethics and social responsibility does not hurt companies.[88]

Companies are making an effort to measure the nonfinancial factors that create value. Researchers have found, for example, that people prefer to work for companies that demonstrate a high level of ethics and social responsibility, so these organizations can attract and retain high-quality employees.[89] Customers pay attention too. A study by Walker Research indicates that, price and quality being equal, two thirds of customers say they would switch brands to do business with a company that is ethical and socially responsible.[90] Enlightened companies realize that integrity and trust are essential elements in sustaining successful and profitable business relationships with an increasingly connected web of employees, customers, suppliers, and partners. Though doing the right thing might not always be profitable in the short run, it develops a level of trust that money cannot buy and will ultimately benefit the company. Many companies are becoming more socially responsible because they believe it provides a competitive advantage.[91]

Social Entrepreneurship

Some organizations are taking social responsibility to the extreme, building whole companies that combine good business with good citizenship. Maria Otero is CEO of ACCIÓN International, a leader in the microfinance industry. ACCIÓN partners with existing banks to give microloans that are used to start tiny businesses in poor countries. For example, a Bolivian woman used a $100 loan to start a bread-making business using the mud oven in her one-room home. Six years later, she borrowed $2,800 to expand to five mud ovens and a backyard storefront.[92] Or consider Mitch Tobol. Tobol runs a full-service marketing agency in Port Washington, New York, that serves clients such as Weight Watchers International and Long Island Savings Bank. However, he and a friend also started an organization called Sparks, a sort of social club for learning disabled teens and adults.[93] The Sparks program serves 20 members, taking them to sporting events, dinners, and the theater, giving them opportunities to build strong social bonds and do the kinds of things most have never had a chance to do.

A new breed of entrepreneur has emerged—the **social entrepreneur**. Social entrepreneurs are leaders who are committed to good business and changing the world for the better. Social entrepreneurs have a primary goal of improving society rather than maximizing profits, but they demand high performance standards and accountability for results. One writer referred to the breed as a cross between Richard Branson (high-powered CEO of Virgin Airlines) and Mother Teresa.[94] Social entrepreneurship is not new, but the phenomenon has blossomed over the past 15 years, and the organizations being created defy the traditional boundaries between business and welfare.[95] For example, David Green, founder of Project-Impact, helped start a factory in India that makes inexpensive plastic lenses used in cataract surgery. The factory provides lenses, some at no cost, for 200,000 poor Indians a year. It also makes money—30 percent profit margins in 2003—and has captured 10 percent of the global market for intraocular lenses. Green has expanded his approach to other parts of the world, as well as the United States, and is adding hearing aids to the product mix.[96] The organizations created

social entrepreneur

Entrepreneurial leaders who are committed to good business and changing the world for the better.

by social entrepreneurs may or may not make a profit, but the bottom line for these companies is always social betterment rather than economic return.

Not every organization wants to become this closely involved in solving the world's social problems. However, companies that make an unwavering commitment to maintaining high standards of ethics and social responsibility will lead the way toward a brighter future for business and society.

Manager's Solution

Ethics and social responsibility are hot topics for today's managers. The ethical domain of behavior pertains to values of right and wrong. Ethical decisions and behavior are typically guided by a value system. Four value-based approaches that serve as criteria for ethical decision making are utilitarian, individualism, moral rights, and justice. For an individual manager, the ability to make correct ethical choices will depend on individual and organizational characteristics. An important individual characteristic is the level of moral development. Corporate culture is an organizational characteristic that influences ethical behavior. Strong ethical cultures become more important in turbulent environments because they help people make the right choices in the face of confusion and rapid change.

Corporate social responsibility concerns a company's values toward society. How can organizations be good corporate citizens? The model for evaluating social performance uses four criteria: economic, legal, ethical, and discretionary. Evaluating corporate social behavior often requires assessing its impact on organizational stakeholders. One issue of growing concern is environmental responsibility. Organizations may take a legal, market, stakeholder, or activist approach to addressing environmental concerns. Sustainability is a growing movement that emphasizes economic development that meets the needs of today while preserving resources for the future.

Ethical organizations are supported by three pillars: ethical individuals, ethical leadership, and organizational structures and systems, including a code of ethics, ethics committees, chief ethics officers, training programs, and mechanisms to protect whistle-blowers. Ethical and socially responsible companies perform as well as—and often better than—those that are not socially responsible. Social entrepreneurship is burgeoning as new leaders create innovative organizations that blur the boundaries between business and welfare. These organizations may or may not make a profit, but the overriding goal is to improve society.

Our management challenge at the beginning of the chapter illustrates how difficult issues of ethics and social responsibility can be. Timberland decided to continue its commitment to social causes. In fact, later the same year that Swartz was faced with this dilemma, the company doubled the number of hours it underwrote for employees to do community service. That number has now increased to a full 40-hour week, plus the company offers paid sabbaticals for people to work six months full time in community nonprofits. This commitment to discretionary responsibility has contributed to exceptional loyalty among many employees because people feel good about the work they do. One vice president says she has turned down lucrative offers from other companies because at Timberland she does not feel as if she has to check her values at the door. Timberland consistently ranks in *Fortune* magazine's survey of the 100 Best Companies to Work For, and more than 50 percent of Timberland's employees say the focus on community service is the main reason they work there. However, some people felt that Timberland should have cut out the charity activities to focus on meeting its economic responsibilities when the company hit difficult times. In addition, some felt that the company was failing to meet its ethical responsibilities by spending money on community service when it was laying people off and shipping jobs overseas. Some employees bluntly asked, "Doesn't charity begin at home?" Swartz said he believed, however, that cutting out community service would damage morale and lower commitment without solving the financial problems. Fortunately, Timberland rebounded from its difficulties and continued to grow. However, managers will continue to face challenges concerning how to best meet their responsibilities to all stakeholders.[97]

Discussion Questions

1. Dr. Martin Luther King, Jr., said, "As long as there is poverty in the world, I can never be rich. . . . As long as diseases are rampant, I can never be healthy. . . . I can never be what I ought to be until you are what you ought to be." Discuss this quote with respect to the material in this chapter. Would this be true for corporations, too?

2. Environmentalists are trying to pass laws for oil spills that would remove all liability limits for the oil companies. This would punish corporations financially. Is this the best way to influence companies to be socially responsible?

3. Compare and contrast the utilitarian approach with the moral-rights approach to ethical decision making. Which do you believe is the best for managers to follow? Why?

4. Imagine yourself in a situation of being encouraged to inflate your expense account. Do you think your choice would be most affected by your individual moral development or by the cultural values of the company for which you worked? Explain.

5. Is it socially responsible for organizations to undertake political activity or join with others in a trade association to influence the government? Discuss.

6. The criteria of corporate social responsibility suggest that economic responsibilities are of the greatest magnitude, followed by legal, ethical, and discretionary responsibilities. How do these four types of responsibility relate to corporate responses to social demands? Discuss.

7. From where do managers derive ethical values? What can managers do to help define ethical standards for the corporation?

8. Have you ever experienced an ethical dilemma? Evaluate the dilemma with respect to its impact on other people.

9. Lincoln Electric considers customers and employees to be more important stakeholders than shareholders. Is it appropriate for management to define some stakeholders as more important than others? Should all stakeholders be considered equal?

10. Do you think a code of ethics combined with an ethics committee would be more effective than leadership for implementing ethical behavior? Discuss.

Manager's Workbook

The spread of technology into the workplace has raised a variety of new ethical questions, and many old ones still linger. Compare your answers with those of other Americans surveyed.

Office Technology

1. Is it wrong to use company e-mail for personal reasons?
   Yes   No

2. Is it wrong to use office equipment to help your children or spouse do schoolwork?
   Yes   No

3. Is it wrong to play computer games on office equipment during the workday?
   Yes   No

4. Is it wrong to use office equipment to do Internet shopping?
   Yes   No

5. Is it unethical to blame an error you made on a technological glitch?
   Yes   No

6. Is it unethical to visit pornographic Web sites using office equipment?
   Yes   No

Gifts and Entertainment

7. What's the value at which a gift from a supplier or client becomes troubling?
   $25 $50 $100

8. Is a $50 gift to a boss unacceptable?

   Yes   No

9. Is a $50 gift *from* the boss unacceptable?

   Yes   No

10. Of gifts from suppliers: Is it OK to take a $200 pair of football tickets?

    Yes   No

11. Is it OK to take a $120 pair of theater tickets?

    Yes   No

12. Is it OK to take a $100 holiday food basket?

    Yes   No

13. Is it OK to take a $25 gift certificate?

    Yes   No

14. Can you accept a $75 prize won at a raffle at a supplier's conference?

    Yes   No

Truth and Lies

15. Due to on-the-job pressure, have you ever abused or lied about sick days?

    Yes   No

16. Due to on-the-job pressure, have you ever taken credit for someone else's work or idea?

    Yes   No

Note to Student: See Appendix B to check your responses.

SOURCES: Ethics Officer Association, Belmont, Mass.; Ethical Leadership Group, Wilmette, Ill.; surveys sampled a cross-section of workers at large companies and nationwide; "The Wall Street Journal Workplace-Ethics Quiz," *The Wall Street Journal*; Oct. 21, 1999, pp. B1, B4.

Manager's Workshop

Ethics Investigation

Divide into groups of four to six members and choose a real ethical dilemma that members of some organization faced. Some examples include the Nestlé infant formula controversy, HB Fuller and glue-sniffing in Honduras, Kathy Lee Gifford and sweatshops, Silkwood, Nuremburg Trials, Valdez oil spill, CIA involvement in crack, Iran-Contra, trial behavior in the O.J. Simpson case, Whitewater, West Point honor code, sexual harassment cases in the Army or Navy, admission of women to the Virginia military academy, CEO salaries, Shell Oil in Nigeria, corporate downsizing, questionable political contributions, deception to consumers, Tobacco industry and teenage smokers, managed health care, globalization as a new kind of imperialism, politicians "bought" by PAC's and special interest groups, the NRA and national policy, violence in schools, and the like.

Your instructor will assign you one of the following two options, either A or B:

A. Debate

1. Prepare both sides of a debate on the "ethical" versus nonethical behaviors the company, person, or institution might have chosen. Back up your arguments with ethical theories and sound reasoning.

2. Your instructor will assign you to either write up the whole debate, or present both sides to the rest of the class.

B. Investigation

1. Consider that you have been hired as a consultant to a major ethics think tank. Conduct a thorough research on the subject and collect articles, which may include interviews, eyewitness reports, news magazines, editorials, and such. Try to find any movie or video clips that may be relevant, as well.

2. Write up a case study/report, keeping in mind the time frame and the historical context of this situation. Explicitly identify ethical issues and conflicts as they occur. Remember, the think tank is very concerned with these issues and wants you to particularly highlight them. Refer back to ethical concepts in the chapter and see which are relevant. In your case study, include what happened. What did the major "actors" do? How did they handle the dilemmas? Finally, describe how you would "rewrite the script" to make the behaviors more ethical. How would that change the outcome?

3. Develop an ethical "code of behavior" based on the events in your dilemma.

4. (optional) Be prepared to hand out copies of your case study and code of behavior to the rest of the class. Conduct a discussion. You may be asked to show the video clips, as well.

SOURCE: Copyright 1999 Dorothy Marcic; adapted from Karen L. Vinton and Melody M. Zajdel, "The Ethics Packet Assignment," *The Organizational Behavior Teaching Review*, Vol. 12 (2), pp. 108–110.

Management in Practice: Ethical Dilemma

Baby-Friendly Hospitals

Jason Rutledge sat in his office and wondered what to recommend in his report. As assistant administrator of 180-bed Babcock Memorial Hospital, he was charged with evaluating a proposal by a U.S. Committee for UNICEF group to become a "Baby-Friendly Hospital." Many U.S. hospitals tend to encourage bottle feeding through a combination of giving away free formula supplied by pharmaceutical companies, as well as employing underskilled staff, and this committee was appealing to hospitals to reverse the trend.

Their arguments were compelling. Breastfed babies cry less, and they are healthier, with reduced risk for ear infections, juvenile diabetes, allergies, dental caries, and Sudden Infant Death Syndrome. Every year, 200,000 U.S. children are hospitalized for diarrhea, most of which are bottle-fed babies. By six months, only 20 percent of mothers breastfeed. Though low-income mothers are 40 percent less likely to breastfeed as middle-income women, they feel a heavier burden with the $1,000 yearly cost of formula. Costs to HMOs and other insurers for basic health care are about 70 percent more for bottle-fed babies than those breastfed.

Still, Babcock Memorial was not an insurer nor even a parent. Jason's responsibilities were to help the hospital continue to trim unnecessary costs. Any help they could get was usually appreciated. Currently, formula companies were paying the hospital about $14,000 a year for formula, bottles, nipples, and feeders. If Babcock became a baby-friendly hospital, it would mean they would have to stop taking these "freebies" from the formula companies and would seriously start to encourage breastfeeding.

It was up to Jason to recommend either accepting the proposal or passing on it, and he realized what a difficult choice it was.

Questions:

1. Which of the normative approaches to ethical decision making is most relevant for Jason to use?
2. Give examples of the four decisions Jason would make using each of the four possible responses to social demands.
3. If you were Jason, what would you recommend?

SOURCES: Margaret Kyenkya-Isabirye, "UNICEF Launches Baby-Friendly Hospital Initiative," *Maternal and Child Nursing*, Vol. 17, 1992, pp. 177–179; "Baby-Friendly Expert Work Group in the United States: Blowing the Whistle," *Birth*, Vol. 22, June 1995, pp. 59–62; various hospital sources.

Case for Critical Analysis

Colt 45 and the Ad Hoc Group Against Crime

The Ad Hoc Group Against Crime, a Kansas City organization, recently accepted a contribution from Colt 45—the group will get a 25-cent donation for every case of Colt 45 malt liquor sold through participating vendors. In accepting the money, Ad Hoc opened itself to an ethical dilemma that has hounded minority interest groups for decades. Violent crime hits many minority communities hard, and numerous studies have linked crime to alcohol consumption. Studies have also shown that although African Americans have higher rates of abstinence than whites, they still have higher death rates tied to alcohol abuse.

Ad Hoc's president, Alvin Brooks, says the group doesn't see this as encouraging sales of Colt 45. "We are saying to the alcohol companies: 'If you are taking something away from the community, you are going to have to give something back.'" Brooks also notes that Ad Hoc is not in a financial position to turn away viable fund-raising opportunities. Other minority interest groups have long accepted alcohol and tobacco funds for the same reason, and over the years a loyalty has developed—a loyalty that the alcohol and tobacco companies began actively courting decades ago. Studies have shown that billboards advertising tobacco products are placed in black communities four to five times more often than in predominantly white communities and that the number of liquor outlets in proportion to the population is much higher in inner-city neighborhoods.

A spokesperson for Colt 45 said the fund-raiser is simply a way for retailers to show their support for the community. In general, large alcohol and tobacco companies are reluctant to discuss their funding of minority causes. A Philip Morris representative, commenting that the contributions are important in keeping communities economically able to buy products, said, "Their vibrancy is our vibrancy."

Questions

1. Are companies such as Colt 45 and Philip Morris acting in an ethical and socially responsible way? What criteria of social responsibility are these companies following?
2. Is the Ad Hoc Group Against Crime being socially responsible by accepting this money? Should this group take a symbolic stand against alcohol?
3. Can you think of more socially responsible ways Colt 45 might contribute to minority communities?

SOURCE: Based on Mary Sanchez, "When Charity Taps 'Vice' for Money," *The Tennessean*, August 6, 1995, p. 2D.

PART

3

Planning

It is the first day of shooting. Actors in costume arrive on the set fresh from make-up sessions. Technicians have set up huge lights, crew members are in position behind cameras, while others prepare to hoist boom microphones. They are ready for the director to call out "action" for the first time.

It has taken months of what is called "pre-production" to get to this day. This phase is when all the planning that goes into a film takes place. The director goes through the script, often with the cinematographer, translating the words on the page into visual images. Casting directors help find actors, and those actors may spend time in rehearsals. Art directors come up with an overall look for the production, the art department members are busy designing sets, costumes, and special effects, and scouts find suitable locations for outside shoots. Assistant directors prepare a detailed shooting schedule, and producers draw up the final budget. All through pre-production, the director is involved in all of the countless decisions that need to be made.

At some point—the earlier, the better—directors formulate a vision that guides these choices. They arrive at that vision, as Peter Jackson did for *Lord of the Rings*, by answering the question, "What is this story about?" For example, Clint Eastwood knew that *Million Dollar Baby* was "a love story between a surrogate father and his surrogate daughter." Sophia Coppola, director of *Lost in Translation*, explained that the tale of a middle-aged actor and a young bride striking up a brief friendship while in Tokyo was about disconnected people searching for connection. "It's about moments in life that are great but don't last...but you always have the memory, and they have an effect on you."

Directors usually do not arrive at this vision all by themselves. They collaborate. After a careful reading of the script, they consult with their boss, the film's producer, the person who originated the project and obtained the financing. And they thrash ideas out at meetings with key members of their creative team. Once directors have a firm grasp of the story's essence, they communicate that vision to the cast and crew so everyone understands what the goal is. Roger Deakins, cinematographer for *O Brother Where Art Thou?*, reports that the Coen brothers succeed at conveying their ideas effectively. "Everyone is so in sync," he reports. "We all are as a crew by the time we get to the first day of shooting."

The director's vision needs to be solid, but not set in concrete. It needs be solid enough to keep the project from wandering astray but flexible enough that it leaves room for further collaboration and allows for everyone's understanding of the meaning of the story they are telling to deepen as filming progresses. Figuring out how to walk a tightrope between a vision that is sufficiently clear-cut and one that is too rigid does not guarantee a film's success. But if a director cannot achieve this balance, the project is probably doomed to failure.

CHAPTER

5

Organizational Goal Setting and Planning

LEARNING OBJECTIVES

After studying this chapter, you should be able to do the following:

1. Define goals and plans and explain the relationship between them.

2. Explain the concept of organizational mission and how it influences goal setting and planning.

3. Describe the goals an organization should have and why they resemble a hierarchy.

4. Define the characteristics of effective goals.

5. Describe the four essential steps in the management by objectives (MBO) process.

6. Explain the difference between single-use plans and standing plans.

7. Describe and explain the importance of the three stages of crisis management planning.

8. Discuss how planning in a turbulent environment differs from traditional approaches to planning.

9. Define the components of strategic management.

10. Describe the strategic planning process and strengths, weaknesses, opportunities, and threats (SWOT) analysis.

11. Describe business-level strategies, including Michael E. Porter's competitive forces and strategies and partnership strategies.

12. Explain the major considerations in formulating functional strategies.

13. Discuss the organizational dimensions used for implementing strategy.

Manager's Challenge

The Nintendo Entertainment System was the hottest toy on the market in the mid-1980s, and the company ruled the video game industry for years. But a series of strategic blunders has left the formerly influential Nintendo tagging along as number three behind Sony's PlayStation, which owns a whopping 65 percent of the U.S. market for videogame systems, and Microsoft's Xbox, at 20 percent market share and growing. Back when Nintendo was king, the majority of video console players were younger than 18, but the opposite has become true, and the average player is 29. Though Sony and Microsoft have catered to older customers with cutting-edge games, Nintendo has continued to provide mostly kiddie content. In addition, Sony and Microsoft game consoles are morphing into all-in-one home entertainment systems. Meanwhile, Nintendo has stuck to its more-of-the-same strategy, arguing that people who buy and play video games enjoy the familiar and are not interested in new gimmicks. Perhaps Nintendo's biggest strategic error, though, has been its failure to see partnership as a key to competitive advantage. Sony's PlayStation was originally built to merge Sony's hardware with Nintendo's software, but Nintendo pulled the plug on the joint project because managers did not want to help a potential competitor. Nintendo's relationships with game developers has been adversarial, whereas Sony and Microsoft have forged close partnerships with outside game designers to keep their all-important game libraries fresh and exciting. In one decade, Nintendo's share of the U.S. video console market shriveled from 90 percent to about 15 percent. As sales continue to slip, Nintendo's new CEO and president Satoru Iwata faces some serious strategic decisions.[1]

If you were the CEO of Nintendo, would you continue to focus exclusively on games or compete head on with Sony and Microsoft in the battle for broader home entertainment? What strategies might you adopt to help Nintendo regain a competitive edge in the console industry?

The story of Nintendo's decline and the rise of Sony's PlayStation illustrates the importance of strategic planning. Managers at Sony formulated and implemented strategies that have made PlayStation the player to beat in the video console business, while Nintendo managers failed to respond to increased competition and changing customer expectations. Satoru Iwata is analyzing the situation and considering strategies that can ignite growth and revive the declining company.

One of the primary responsibilities of managers is to decide where the organization should go in the future and how to get it there. But how do managers plan for the future in a constantly changing environment? As we discussed in Chapter 2, most organizations are facing turbulence and growing uncertainty. The economic, political, and social turmoil of recent years has left many managers wondering how to cope and has sparked a renewed interest in organizational planning, particularly planning for unexpected problems and events.

In some organizations, typically small ones, planning is informal. In others, managers follow a well-defined planning framework. The company establishes a basic mission and develops formal goals and strategic plans for carrying it out. Companies such as Royal Dutch/Shell, IBM, and United Way undertake a strategic planning exercise each year by reviewing their missions, goals, and plans to meet environmental changes or the expectations of important stakeholders such as the community, owners, or stockholders. Many of these companies develop contingency plans for unexpected circumstances and disaster recovery plans for what the organization would do in the event of a major disaster such as a hurricane, earthquake, or terrorist attack.

Of the four management functions—planning, organizing, leading, and controlling—described in Chapter 1, planning is considered the most fundamental. Everything else stems from planning. Yet planning is the most controversial management function. Planning cannot read an uncertain future. Planning cannot tame a turbulent environment. A statement by General Colin Powell, former U.S. Secretary of State, offers a warning for managers: "No battle plan survives contact with the enemy."[2]

In this chapter, we will explore the process of planning and consider how managers develop effective plans that can grow and change to meet new conditions. Special attention is given to goal setting, for that is where planning starts. Then, we discuss the various types of plans that managers use to help the organization achieve those goals, with special attention paid to crisis management planning. Finally, we will examine new approaches to planning that emphasize the involvement of employees, customers, partners, and other stakeholders in strategic thinking and execution. Chapter 5 will look at strategic planning and examine a number of strategic options managers can use in a competitive environment. In Chapter 6, we will look at management decision making. Proper decision-making techniques are crucial to selecting the organization's goals, plans, and strategic options.

Take *ACTION*

Practice planning every day. Make a list of your goals for the day and for the week, and it will become second nature.

Overview of Goals and Plans

goal

A desired future state that the organization attempts to realize.

Goals and plans have become general concepts in our society. A **goal** is a desired future state that the organization attempts to realize.[3] Goals are important because organizations exist for a purpose and goals define and state that purpose. A **plan** is a blueprint for goal achievement and specifies the necessary resource allocations, schedules, tasks, and other actions. Goals specify future ends; plans specify today's means. The word **planning** usually incorporates both ideas; it means determining the organization's goals and defining the means for achieving them.[4]

plan

A blueprint specifying the resource allocations, schedules, and other actions necessary for attaining goals.

Exhibit 5.1 illustrates the levels of goals and plans in an organization. The planning process starts with a formal mission that defines the basic purpose of the organization, especially for external audiences. The mission is the basis for the strategic (company)

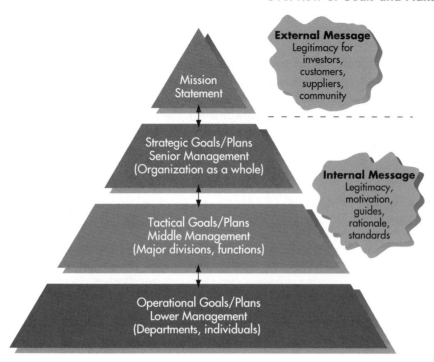

EXHIBIT 5.1
Levels of Goals/ Plans and Their Importance

level of goals and plans, which in turn shapes the tactical (divisional) level and the operational (departmental) level.[5] Top managers are typically responsible for establishing strategic goals and plans that reflect a commitment to both organizational efficiency and effectiveness as described in Chapter 1. Tactical goals and plans are the responsibility of middle managers, such as the heads of major divisions or functional units. A division manager will formulate tactical plans that focus on the major actions the division must take to fulfill its part in the strategic plan set by top management. The U.S. Army uses sofware to implement a tactical plan as described below.

planning
The act of determining the organization's goals and the means for achieving them.

United States Joint Forces Command

Collateral damage—when innocent civilians or friendly troops are killed—is one of the most heartbreaking results of any war. Needless to say, no battle commander wants to injure or kill innocent civilians or friendly troops. Now, technology may provide a way to reduce the likelihood.

A new software application, called Joint Time Sensitive Targeting Manager (JTSTM), was used in Iraq for the first time in live operations. With this system, ground, air, and maritime commanders logged onto the JTSTM network can all see a common picture of the battlefield. Using chat rooms, e-mail, and instant messaging, battle planners collaboratively figure out the situation and assess options. "The software was specifically designed to force commanders to look at a target before it can be executed," said Lt. Col. Mark Werth, head of the joint fires initiative at the U.S. Joint Forces Command. Many people can see the same picture, maximizing the chance that someone can pinpoint a risky mission, such as whether the target is too close to friendly forces or civilians.

Typically, in battle situations, the Air Force might be chasing a target on the ground without the Army or special operations forces having any notion about what is occurring. With JTSTM, every group is aware of what every other group of services is doing. The program provides a seamless, horizontal knowledge base that improves fire mission coordination. The joint fires initiative is evolving to apply to any targeting mission, not just those that pop up on short notice. JTSTM is one of the software applications developed under the Automated Deep Operations Coordination System (ADOCS), funded by the U.S. Department of Defense. ADOCS taps into various databases, such as the Global Command and Control System (location of friendly forces), and the Joint Targeting Toolkit (restricted target list and no-strike target list) to provide users with one-stop shopping for assessing and coordinating tactical battle plans.

The process of using this sophisticated technology was first tested in a war fighting experiment in 2002, and its use in real-life operations in Iraq was far from smooth. However, the U.S. Joint Forces Command believes the technology will be a key factor in improving coordination and avoiding friendly fire in future conflicts. The initiative will continue to evolve and is expected to be integrated into military service programs by 2006.[6]

Operational plans identify the specific procedures or processes needed at lower levels of the organization, such as individual departments and employees. Front-line managers and supervisors develop operational plans that focus on specific tasks and processes and meet tactical and strategic goals. Planning at each level supports the other levels.

Take a moment to complete the form below, which looks at your personal goals regarding this management course.

Goal Setting

Consider goals for yourself regarding doing well in this course. What do you need to do to get a good grade? Goals should be according to the "Criteria for Effective Goals" in the chapter on page 166. In addition, you need a system to monitor your progress, such as the table below, which shows the types of goals you may choose to select for yourself.

Goals	Class weeks			
	First week (from now)	Second week	Third week	Fourth week
1. 100% attendance				
2. Class notes				
3. Read assigned chapters				
4. Outline chapters				
5. Define vocabulary words				
6. Answer end-of-chapter questions				
7. Complete "Workbook" assignments				
8. Class participation				
9.				
10.				

copyright 1996 by Dorothy Marcic.

SOURCE: Nancy C. Morey, "Applying Goal Setting in the Classroom," *The Organizational Behavior Teaching Review,* 11:4 (1986–87): 53–59.

Purposes of Goals and Plans

The complexity of today's environment and uncertainty about the future overwhelm many managers and cause them to focus on operational issues and short-term results rather than long-term goals and plans. However, planning generally positively affects a company's performance.[7] In addition to improving financial and operational performance, developing explicit goals and plans at each level illustrated in Exhibit 5.1 is important because of the external and internal messages they send. These messages go to external and internal audiences and provide important benefits for the organization:[8]

- *Legitimacy.* An organization's mission describes what the organization stands for and its reason for existence. It symbolizes legitimacy to external audiences such as investors, customers, and suppliers. The mission helps them and the local community look on the company in a favorable light and, hence, accept its existence. A strong mission has an impact on employees, enabling them to become committed to the organization because they can identify with its overall purpose and reason for existence. One of the traits often cited by employees in *Fortune* magazine's list of the "100 Best Companies to Work For in America" is a sense of purpose and meaning.[9] For example, at Medtronic, a medical products company, employees are inspired by the mission to "alleviate pain, restore health, and extend life."[10]

- *Source of motivation and commitment.* Goals and plans facilitate employees' identification with the organization and help motivate them by reducing uncertainty and clarifying what they should accomplish. Ji Baek created her mission of having character in her nail salons to help motivate her employees, as described in below.

> **Rescue Beauty Salons**
>
> Ji Baek studied to be a classical musician, something of which her Korean-born parents could be proud. When tendonitis forced her career change, her parents were not pleased. "When I told my mom I was going to open a nail salon, she fainted," says Baek. "I am Korean, so it was just so stereotypical."
>
> From the beginning, she wanted to distinguish her first salon, opened in 1988. She had gone to beauty school, not to be a nail technician, but to learn the skill so she could run the business. "For me, business is very exciting. I work seven days a week, nonstop, but I love what I do." She decided to offer what she would want as a client. At the time, nail salons were dirty and dingy, or they were the high-end day spas. Baek created a salon in between, something new.
>
> Each of her three salons has a different look, an unusual character. "Character is an advantage you can have when you run a small business," she says. It helped them break through the nail salon stereotype. When her mother came to the salon for the first time, she understood why her daughter was doing this. And she approved.[11]

At Boeing, the manufacturing department has a goal of moving a plane, once the wings and landing gear are attached, along the assembly line and out the door in five days. Managers are revising processes and procedures, mechanics are coming up with innovative machine adjustments, and assembly line workers are trying new techniques to meet this ambitious goal.[12] Lack of a clear goal can damage employee motivation and commitment because people do not understand what they are working toward. A goal provides the "why" of an organization's or subunit's existence, and a plan tells the "how." A plan lets employees know what actions to undertake to achieve the goal.

Take *ACTION*
Your goals will motivate you, so keep it up!

- *Resource allocation.* Goals help managers decide where they need to allocate resources, such as employees, money, and equipment. For example, DuPont has a goal of generating 25 percent of revenues from renewable resources by 2010 (up from 14 percent in 2003). This goal lets managers know they need to use resources to develop renewable and biodegradable materials, acquire businesses that produce products with renewable resources, and buy equipment that reduces waste, emissions, and energy usage. As another example, the Federal Bureau of Investigation (FBI) has pulled more than 600 agents off their regular beats and reassigned them to terrorist-related cases due to new goals of fighting domestic terrorism. The FBI is allocating resources to rebuild an archaic computer network, open foreign offices, and form terrorism task forces.[13]

- *Guides to action.* Goals and plans provide a sense of direction. They focus attention on specific targets and direct employee efforts toward important outcomes. Hartford Technology Services Co., for example, set goals to establish a customer profile database, survey customer satisfaction, and secure service agreements with ten new customers.[14]

- *Rationale for decisions.* Through goal setting and planning, managers learn what the organization wants to accomplish. They can make decisions to ensure that internal policies, roles, performance, structure, products, and expenditures will be made in accordance with desired outcomes. Decisions throughout the organization will be in alignment with the plan.

- *Standard of performance.* Because goals define desired outcomes for the organization, they serve as performance criteria. They provide a standard of assessment. If an organization wishes to grow by 15 percent, and actual growth is 17 percent, managers will have exceeded their prescribed standard.

The following example illustrates how goals and plans serve these important purposes.

| **Chevrolet** | Chevrolet may have ruled the roads back in the 1960s and 1970s, but in recent years its sales have lagged. In late 2003, General Motors managers announced that the company will launch 10 new Chevrolet vehicles over 20 months to reach its goal of boosting U.S. sales to 3 million vehicles a year, a level Chevy has not achieved since 1979. That is a 15 percent increase over 2003 levels, an ambitious target that requires everyone in the company to focus on the goal.

Employees throughout the company are striving to meet lower-level targets that will help the company achieve its overall objective. Dealers, too, are motivated by the stretch goals laid out in a plan called "Road to 3 Million." Managers are pumping resources into design and engineering, advertising, and dealer incentives. Dealers can win trips and other prizes if they hit their targets. A new, edgy multimillion-dollar ad campaign, taglined, "An American Revolution," focuses on the cars and trucks but gives potential customers a feeling of freedom and "attitude." Managers and employees are looking for alternative ways to reach new markets. Every decision at Chevrolet is made with the goal of selling 3 million vehicles a year in mind.

Managers will use the goal as a standard of performance. Some doubt that Chevrolet can reach the target during the first year, but managers will evaluate how well the company performed and revise plans to help meet the goal of selling 3 million vehicles a year.[15]

Chevrolet and General Motors managers recognize the importance of a clear goal and carefully thought out plans to help achieve it. The overall planning process prevents managers from thinking merely in terms of daily activities. When organizations drift away from goals and plans, they can get into trouble.

Goals in Organizations

Setting goals starts with top managers. The overall planning process begins with a mission statement and strategic goals for the organization as a whole.

Organizational Mission

At the top of the goal hierarchy is the **mission**, the organization's reason for existence. The mission describes the organization's values, aspirations, and reason for being. A well-defined mission is the basis for development of all subsequent goals and plans. Without a clear mission, goals and plans may be developed haphazardly and may not take the organization in the direction it needs to go.

The formal **mission statement** is a broadly stated definition of purpose that distinguishes the organization from others of a similar type. A well-designed mission statement can enhance employee motivation and organizational performance.[16] The content of a mission statement often focuses on the market and customers and identifies desired fields of endeavor. Some mission statements describe company characteristics such as corporate values, product quality, location of facilities, and attitude toward employees. Mission statements often reveal the company's philosophy as well as purpose. One example is the mission statement for Bristol-Myers Squibb Company, presented in Exhibit 5.2. Such short, straightforward mission statements describe basic business activities and purposes, as well as the values that guide the company. Another example of this type of mission statement is that of State Farm Insurance:

"State Farm's mission is to help people manage the risks of everyday life, recover from the unexpected, and realize their dreams.

We are people who make it our business to be like a good neighbor; who built a premier company by selling and keeping promises through out marketing partnership; who bring diverse talents and experiences to our work of serving the State Farm customer.

Our success is built on a foundation of shared values—quality service and relationships, mutual trust, integrity, and financial strength."[17]

Because of mission statements such as those of Bristol-Myers Squibb and State Farm, employees as well as customers, suppliers, and stockholders know the company's stated purpose and values. Mission can come from a deeper sense of values and social responsibility, as it did for Jacqueline Danforth and described in the Focus on Ethics box.

mission

The organization's reason for existence.

mission statement

A broadly stated definition of the organization's basic business scope and operations that distinguishes it from similar types of organizations.

Take **ACTION**

Decide on your personal mission, that is, what is your purpose in life?

The Bristol-Myers Squibb Pledge

Our company's mission is to extend and enhance human life by providing the highest-quality pharmaceutical and related health care products.

We pledge—to our patients and customers, to our employees and partners, to our shareholders and neighbors, and to the world we serve— to act on our belief that the priceless ingredient of every product is the honor and integrity of its maker.

 Bristol-Myers Squibb Company

EXHIBIT 5.2

Mission Statement for Bristol-Myers Squibb

FOCUS ON ETHICS

New Horizons

As a teenager, Jacqueline Danforth was out of control. Drinking, taking drugs, sneaking out at night to party at New York's famous Studio 54, even running away. She knew her adopted parents loved her, but their high-powered lifestyle did not fit with a girl who wanted to be on a farm milking cows. That her mother was celebrity newswoman Barbara Walters did not help because she had to worry if people liked her for herself. By the time Danforth was 14, Walters knew something had to be done, so she took Danforth, kicking and screaming, to a rugged emotional growth boarding school in Idaho, where she stayed for three years. "It saved my life," Danforth now says.

In 2001, inspired to help other troubled teens, Danforth started her own company, New Horizons, the Maine-based wilderness program where girls ages 12–18 spend nine weeks camping out with trained therapists and wilderness guides, learning about themselves and gaining self-esteem and self-control. Its mission is to inspire adolescent females—using the combined resources of the natural environment, caring, knowledgeable professionals, and the power of self-discovery—to enhance their individual mental, physical, social, and spiritual well-being.

Danforth spent months getting licenses and insurance, building a Web site, developing curriculum, buying land, hiring staff, flying around the country to educational conferences to get the word out to teachers who could refer girls to New Horizons.

You would think Danforth would call on her mom for seed money, but the daughter wanted to do it on her own and found her own group of investors. So determined was she to do it alone, that "she didn't want my accountants or lawyer," says Walters. The tuition of $2,800 per week covers all staff salaries, food, medical staff, even high-quality all-weather gear for the girls. Danforth will not yet pay herself a salary.

While some other wilderness programs operate like boot camp, with yelling and severe punishment, New Horizons has strict boundaries but operates on the philosophy that "these girls are good at heart," says Danforth.

Most of the girls arrive in Bangor, Maine, angry and scared but within a few weeks are changing. "It's not like you just work on your own problems," reports a girl who drunkenly crashed her mother's car enroute to a drug rehab program.

Danforth knows there are many struggles ahead as the organization develops. But it is worth it. "Now I have a mission in life, "she says. "My mother is a hard act to follow" because she has impacted so many people. Even though Danforth may not reach that many people, she is content with her goals. "I do want to feel that I'm giving back."

SOURCE: Jacqueline Danforth, personal communication, (March 2005); Beth Johnson, "Finding Her Own Path," *Good Housekeeping* (April 2002): 102–106.

Goals and Plans

strategic goals

Broad statements of where the organization wants to be in the future; pertaining to the organization as a whole rather than to specific divisions or departments.

Broad statements describing where the organization wants to be in the future are called **strategic goals.** They pertain to the organization as a whole rather than to specific divisions or departments. Strategic goals are often called official goals because they are the stated intentions of what the organization wants to achieve. For example, five years after he started Physician Sales and Service (PSS), Pat Kelly set a strategic goal for PSS to become the first national physician supply chain, a goal he soon reached. Now, Kelly wants the company to become a global distributor of medical products.[18] Another example of a strategic goal is for the new chief executive of the New York Stock Exchange to restore the credibility of the exchange with government regulators and the public.

strategic plans

The action steps by which an organization intends to attain strategic goals.

Strategic plans define the action steps by which the company intends to attain strategic goals. The strategic plan is the blueprint that defines the organizational activities and resource allocations—in the form of cash, personnel, space, and facilities—required for meeting these targets. Strategic planning tends to define organizational action steps from two to five years in the future. The purpose of strategic plans is to turn organizational goals into realities within that time period.

Take ACTION

From your mission statement, determine how you will achieve it—that is your strategy.

As an example, a small company wanted to improve its market share from 15 percent to 20 percent over the next three years. This strategic goal was pursued through the following strategic plans: allocate resources for the development of new, competitive products with high growth potential, improve production methods to achieve higher output at lower costs, and conduct research to develop alternative uses for current products and services.[19]

© AP/Wide World Photos

The results that major divisions and departments within the organization intend to achieve are defined as **tactical goals**. These goals apply to middle management and describe what major subunits must do so the organization will achieve its overall goals.

Tactical plans are designed to help execute major strategic plans and to accomplish a specific part of the company's strategy.[20] Tactical plans typically have a shorter time horizon than strategic plans of over the next year or so. The word *tactical* originally comes from the military. In a business or nonprofit organization, tactical plans define what major departments and organizational subunits will do to implement the organization's strategic plan. For example, the overall strategic plan of a large florist might involve becoming the number one telephone and Internet-based purveyor of flowers, which requires high-volume sales during peak seasons such as Valentine's Day and Mother's Day. Human resource managers will develop tactical plans to ensure that the company has the dedicated order takers and customer service representatives it needs during these critical periods. Tactical plans might include cross-training employees so they can switch to different jobs as departmental needs change, allowing order takers to transfer to jobs at headquarters during off-peak times to prevent burnout, and using regular order takers to train and supervise temporary workers during peak seasons.[21] These actions help top managers implement their overall strategic plan. Normally, it is the middle manager's job to take the broad strategic plan and identify specific tactical plans.

The results expected from departments, work groups, and individuals are the **operational goals**. They are precise and measurable. "Process 150 sales applications each week," "achieve 90 percent of deliveries on time," "reduce overtime by 10 percent next month," and "develop two new elective courses in accounting" are examples of operational goals. At the Internal Revenue Service (IRS), one operational goal is to give accurate responses to 85 percent of taxpayer questions.[22]

Operational plans are developed at the lower levels of the organization to specify action steps toward achieving operational goals and to support tactical plans. The operational plan is the department manager's tool for daily and weekly operations. Goals are stated in quantitative terms, and the department plan describes how goals will be achieved. Operational planning specifies plans for supervisors, department managers, and individual employees.

Schedules are an important component of operational planning. Schedules define precise time frames for the completion of each operational goal required for the organization's tactical and strategic goals. Operational planning must be coordinated with the budget because resources must be allocated for desired activities. For example,

tactical goals

Goals that define the outcomes that major divisions and departments must achieve for the organization to reach its overall goals.

tactical plans

Plans designed to help execute major strategic plans and to accomplish a specific part of the company's strategy.

operational goals

Specific, measurable results expected from departments, work groups, and individuals within the organization.

operational plans

Plans developed at the organization's lower levels that specify action steps toward achieving operational goals and that support tactical planning activities.

Apogee Enterprises, a window and glass fabricator with 150 small divisions, is fanatical about operational planning and budgeting. Committees are set up to review and challenge budgets, profit plans, and proposed expenditures. Assigning the dollars makes the operational plan work for everything from hiring new salespeople to increasing travel expenses.

Hierarchy of Goals

Effectively designed organizational goals fit into a hierarchy; that is, the achievement of goals at low levels permits the attainment of high-level goals.

Criteria for Effective Goals

To ensure goal-setting benefits for the organization, certain characteristics and guidelines should be adopted. The characteristics of goals and the goal-setting process are listed in Exhibit 5.3. These characteristics pertain to organizational goals at the strategic, tactical, and operational levels:

Take ACTION

Make your goals measurable, so you can know when you achieve them.

- *Specific and measurable.* When possible, goals should be expressed in quantitative terms, such as increasing profits by 2 percent, decreasing scrap by 1 percent, or increasing average teacher effectiveness ratings from 3.5 to 3.7. A team at Sealed Air Corporation, a manufacturer of packaging materials, was motivated by a goal to reduce the average time needed to change machine settings by two hours.[23] Not all goals can be expressed in numerical terms, but vague goals have little motivating power for employees. By necessity, goals are qualitative as well as quantitative, especially at the top of the organization. The important point is that the goals be precisely defined and allow for measurable progress.

- *Cover key result areas.* Goals cannot be set for every aspect of employee behavior or organizational performance; if they were, their sheer number would render them meaningless. Instead, managers should identify a few key result areas, perhaps up to four or five for any organizational department or job. Key result areas are those activities that contribute most to company performance.[24] Most companies use a balanced approach to goal setting. For example, Northern States Power Co. tracks measurements in four key areas: financial performance, customer service and satisfaction, internal processes, and innovation and learning.[25]

- *Challenging but realistic.* Goals should be challenging but not unreasonably difficult. One new manager discovered that his staff would have to work 100-hour weeks to accomplish everything expected of them. When goals are unrealistic, they set employees up for failure and lead to decreasing employee morale.[26] However, if goals are too easy, employees may not feel motivated. Stretch goals are ambitious but realistic goals that challenge employees to meet high standards. One example comes from 3M Corp., where top managers set a goal that 30 percent of sales must come from products introduced in the past four years; the old standard was 25 percent. Setting ambitious goals helps to keep 3M churning out innovative new products—more than 500 in one recent year alone—and has entrenched the company as a leader in some of today's most dynamic markets.[27] The key to effective stretch goals is ensuring that goals are set within the existing resource base, not beyond departments' time, equipment, or financial resources.

EXHIBIT 5.3

Characteristics of Effective Goal Setting

Goal Characteristics
- Specific and measurable
- Covered key result areas
- Challenging but realistic
- Defined time period
- Linked to rewards

• *Defined time period.* Goals should specify the time period over which they will be achieved. A time period is a deadline stating the date on which goal attainment will be measured. A goal of implementing a new customer relationship management system, for instance, might have a March 15, 2006, deadline. If a strategic goal involves a two-to-three-year time horizon, specific dates for achieving parts of it can be set up. For example, strategic sales goals could be established on a three-year time horizon, with a $100 million target in year one, a $129 million target in year two, and a $165 million target in year three.

- *Linked to rewards.* The ultimate impact of goals depends on the extent to which salary increases, promotions, and awards are based on goal achievement. People who attain goals should be rewarded. Rewards give meaning and significance to goals and help commit employees to achieving goals. Failure to attain goals is often due to factors outside employees' control. For example, failure to achieve a financial goal may be associated with a drop in market demand due to industry recession; thus, an employee could not be expected to reach it. A reward might still be appropriate if the employee partially achieved goals under difficult circumstances.[28]

Planning Types

Managers use strategic, tactical, and operational goals to direct employees and resources toward achieving specific outcomes that enable the organization to perform efficiently and effectively. Managers use a number of planning approaches. Among the most popular are management by objectives (MBO), single-use plans, standing plans, and contingency plans.

Management by Objectives

Management by objectives (MBO) is a method whereby managers and employees define goals for every department, project, and person and use them to monitor subsequent performance.[29] A model of the essential steps of the MBO process is presented in Exhibit 5.4. Four major activities must occur for MBO to be successful:[30]

1. Set goals. This is the most difficult step in MBO. Setting goals involves employees at all levels and looks beyond daily activities to answer the question, "What are we trying to accomplish?" A good goal should be concrete and realistic, provide a specific target and time frame, and assign responsibility. Goals may be quantitative or qualitative. Quantitative goals are described in numerical terms, such as "Salesperson Jones will obtain 16 new accounts in December." Qualitative goals use statements such as "Marketing will reduce complaints by improving customer service next year." Goals should be jointly derived. Mutual agreement between employee and supervisor creates the strongest commitment to achieving goals. In the case of teams, all team members may participate in setting goals.

management by objectives (MBO)

A method of management whereby managers and employees define goals for every department, project, and person and use them to monitor subsequent performance.

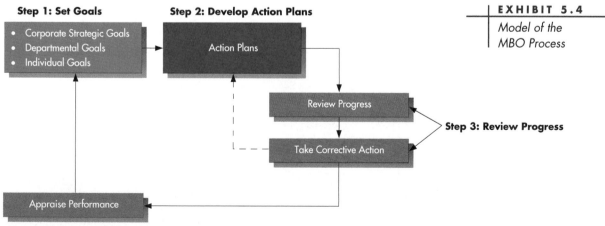

EXHIBIT 5.4

Model of the MBO Process

2. Develop action plans. An action plan defines the course of action needed to achieve the stated goals. Action plans are made for individuals and departments.

3. Review progress. A periodic progress review is important to ensure that action plans are working. These reviews can occur informally between managers and subordinates, where the organization may wish to conduct three-month, six-month, or nine-month reviews during the year. This periodic checkup allows managers and employees to see whether they are on target or whether corrective action is necessary. Managers and employees should not be locked into predefined behavior and must be willing to take whatever steps are necessary to produce meaningful results. The point of MBO is to achieve goals. The action plan can be changed whenever goals are not being met.

4. Appraise overall performance. The final step in MBO is to evaluate whether annual goals have been achieved for individuals and departments. Success or failure to achieve goals can become part of the performance appraisal system and the designation of salary increases and other rewards. The appraisal of departmental and overall corporate performance shapes goals for the next year. The MBO cycle repeats itself on an annual basis.

Many companies, including Intel, Tenneco, Black & Decker, and DuPont, have adopted MBO, and most managers think MBO is an effective management tool.[31] Managers believe they are better oriented toward goal achievement when MBO is used. In recent years, the U.S. Congress has required that federal agencies use an MBO system to focus government employees on achieving specific outcomes, rather than focusing only on activities and work processes.[32] Like any system, MBO achieves benefits when used properly but results in problems when used improperly. Benefits and problems are summarized in Exhibit 5.5.

The benefits of the MBO process can be many. Corporate goals are more achievable when they focus manager and employee efforts. Using a performance measurement system, such as MBO, helps employees see how their jobs and performance contribute to the business, giving them a sense of ownership and commitment.[33] Performance is improved when employees are committed to attaining the goal, are motivated because they help decide what is expected, and are free to be resourceful. Goals at lower levels are aligned with and enable the attainment of goals at top management levels.

Problems with MBO occur when the company faces rapid change. The environment and internal activities must have some stability for performance to be measured and compared against goals. When new goals must be set every few months, there is no time for action plans and appraisal to take effect. Poor employer-employee relations can reduce effectiveness because there is an element of distrust between managers and

Take **ACTION**

Periodically review your goals to see how you are doing and if you need to adjust them.

EXHIBIT 5.5

MBO Benefits and Problems

Benefits of MBO	Problems with MBO
1. Manager and employee efforts are focused on activities that will lead to goal attainment.	**1.** Constant change prevents MBO from taking hold.
2. Performance can be improved at all company levels.	**2.** An environment of poor employer–employee relations reduces MBO effectiveness.
3. Employees are motivated.	**3.** Strategic goals may be displaced by operational goals.
4. Departmental and individual goals are aligned with company goals.	**4.** Mechanistic organizations and values that discourage participation can harm the MBO process.
	5. Too much paperwork saps MBO energy.

workers. Sometimes goal "displacement" occurs if employees focus exclusively on their operational goals to the detriment of other teams or departments. Overemphasis on operational goals can harm the attainment of overall goals. Another problem arises in mechanistic organizations characterized by rigidly defined tasks and rules that may not be compatible with MBO's emphasis on mutual determination of goals by employee and supervisor. In addition, when participation is discouraged, employees will lack the training and values to set goals jointly with employers. Finally, if MBO becomes a process of filling out annual paperwork rather than energizing employees to achieve goals, it becomes an empty exercise. Once the paperwork is completed, employees forget about the goals, perhaps even resenting the paperwork in the first place.

Single-Use and Standing Plans

Single-use plans are developed to achieve a set of goals unlikely to be repeated in the future. **Standing plans** are ongoing plans that are used to provide guidance for tasks performed repeatedly within the organization. Exhibit 5.6 outlines the major types of single-use and standing plans. Single-use plans typically include programs and projects. The primary standing plans are organizational policies, rules, and procedures. Standing plans generally pertain to such matters as employee illness, absences, smoking, discipline, hiring, and dismissal. Many companies are discovering a need to develop standing plans regarding the use of e-mail, as discussed in the Digital, Inc. box.

single-use plans
Plans developed to achieve a set of goals unlikely to be repeated in the future.

standing plans
Ongoing plans used to provide guidance for tasks performed repeatedly within the organization.

Single-Use Plans

Program

- Plans for attaining a one-time organizational goal

- Major undertaking that may take several years to complete

- Large in scope; may be associated with several projects

Examples: Building a new headquarters
Converting all paper files to digital

Project

- Also a set of plans for attaining a onetime goal

- Smaller in scope and complexity than a program; shorter time horizon

- Often one part of a larger program

Examples: Renovating the office
Setting up a company intranet

Standing Plans

Policy

- Broad in scope—a general guide to action

- Based on organization's overall goals/strategic plan

- Defines boundaries within which to make decisions

Examples: Drug-free workplace policies
Sexual harassment policies

Rule

- Narrow in scope

- Describes how a specific action is to be performed

- May apply to specific setting

Example: No-smoking rule in areas of plant where hazardous materials are stored

Procedure

- Sometimes called a standard operating procedure

- Defines a precise series of steps to attain certain goals

Examples: Procedures for issuing refunds
Procedures for handling employee grievances

EXHIBIT 5.6

Major Types of Single-Use and Standing Plans

DIGITAL, INC.

Regulating E-mail in the Workplace

Top executives around the globe are discovering that casual e-mail messages can come back to haunt them—in court. The American Management Association (AMA) surveyed 1,100 companies and found that 14 percent of them had been ordered to disclose e-mail messages. In 2002, eight brokerage firms were fined $8 million for not keeping and producing e-mail in accordance with SEC guidelines. Some companies have had to pay millions to settle sexual harassment lawsuits arising from inappropriate e-mail.

As with any powerful tool, e-mail has the potential to be hazardous, backfiring not only on the employee but on the organization as well. One study found that "potentially dangerous or nonproductive" messages account for fully 31 percent of all company e-mail. Experts say a formal written policy is the best way for companies to protect themselves, and they offer some tips for managers on developing effective policies governing the use of e-mail.

- *Make clear that all e-mail and its contents are the property of the company.* Many experts recommend warning employees that the company reserves the right to read any messages transmitted over its system. "Employees need to understand that a company can access employees' e-mail at any time without advance notice or consent," says lawyer Pam Reeves. This helps to discourage frivolous e-mails or those that might be considered crude and offensive.

- *Tie the policy to the company's sexual harassment policy or other policies governing employee behavior on the job.* In almost all sexual harassment cases, judges have ruled that the use of e-mail was considered part of the workplace environment.

- *Establish clear guidelines on matters such as the use of e-mail for jokes and other non-work-related communications, the sending of confidential messages, and how to handle junk e-mail.* At Prudential Insurance, for example, employees are prohibited from using company e-mail to share jokes, photographs, or any kind of nonbusiness information.

- *Establish guidelines for deleting or retaining messages.* Retention periods of 30 to 90 days for routine messages is typical. Most organizations also set up a centralized archive for retaining essential e-mail messages.

- *Consider having policies pop up on users' screens when they log on.* It is especially important to remind employees that e-mail belongs to the employer and may be monitored.

Even deleted e-mails can usually be tracked down by a computer-forensics expert. An effective policy is the best step companies can take to manage the potential risks of e-mail abuse.

SOURCES: "E-mail: The DNA of Office Crimes," *Electric Perspectives* 28, no. 5 (September–October 2003), 4; Marcia Stepanek with Steve Hamm, "When the Devil Is in the E-mails," *BusinessWeek* (June 8, 1998), 72–74; Joseph McCafferty, "The Phantom Menace," *CFO* (June 1999), 89–91; and "Many Company Internet and Email Policies Are Worth Revising," *The Kiplinger Letter* (February 21, 2003), 1.

Contingency Plans

When organizations are operating in a highly uncertain environment or dealing with lengthy time horizons, sometimes planning can seem like a waste of time. In fact, strict plans may even hinder rather than help an organization's performance in the face of rapid technological, social, economic, or other environmental change. In these cases, managers can develop multiple future alternatives to help them form more flexible plans. **Contingency plans** define company responses to be taken in the case of emergencies, setbacks, or unexpected conditions. To develop contingency plans, managers identify important factors in the environment, such as possible economic downturns, declining markets, increases in cost of supplies, new technological developments, or safety accidents. Managers then forecast a range of alternative responses to the most likely high-impact contingencies, focusing on the worst case.[34] For example, if sales fall 20 percent and prices drop 8 percent, what will the company do? Managers can develop contingency plans that might include layoffs, emergency budgets, new sales efforts, or new markets. As another example, top managers at Duke Energy Corp., which invested heavily in building new power plants to meet increasing demand, developed contingency plans for what the company would do if

contingency plans
Plans that define company responses to specific situations, such as emergencies, setbacks, or unexpected conditions.

Take **ACTION**
If things do not work out as expected, try something different.

© Benjamin Lowy/CORBIS

CONCEPT CONNECTION

*A desert flare marks the area where geologists discovered Libya's rich Zilten oilfield in the 1950s. At their peak in 1970, Libyan oil fields operated by Occidental Petroleum were producing 660,000 barrels a day, more than the company's total oil production in 2003. Today, with economic sanctions against Libya lifted by the U.S. government, big oil companies like Occidental, Chevron Texaco, and Exxon Mobil are again ready to do business with Libya's National Oil Corporation. Yet, the current environment of terrorist threats and general uncertainty means managers have to be prepared for whatever might happen. They are busy developing **contingency plans** to define how their companies will respond in case of unexpected setbacks associated with renewed Libyan operations. Companies are willing to take the risks because the potential rewards are huge.*

U.S. economic growth slowed to 1 percent a year, leaving the company with too much capacity amid weakening prices.[35] As another example, Tim Armitage and his colleagues were able to have a successful start-up because they spent nine months doing contingency planning, before they opened for business as shown in the Focus on Skills box.

Planning in a Turbulent Environment

Today, contingency planning has taken on a whole new urgency. As Leah Modigliani, a portfolio strategist at Morgan Stanley put it, "On September 10 [2001], our worst case was a global recession."[36] For U.S. firms, in particular, the events of September 11, 2001, marked a turning point, when the turbulence and uncertainty of today's world became clear. Since then, managers have renewed their emphasis on bracing for unexpected—even unimaginable—events. Two recent extensions of contingency planning are building scenarios and crisis management planning.

FOCUS ON SKILLS

Pitch

Tim Armitage left his comfy corporate job last year and started a sales consulting business with two partners. They soon realized they had a lot to learn. Lining up clients was the easy part, but it was all the clerical work and building infrastructure that surprised them. "I had to buy desks," he said, "and figure out how to put them together." He hung Ikea shelves, figured out how to replace copier toner. Before, he used to be able to call another office to fix these problems. Now there is no other office. No one else to perform the mundane tasks they were taught to delegate. Consultants do not require a corporate infrastructure to do what they love, but they find out how much the infrastructure did for them once they leave.

Clients started rolling in, based solely in the reputations of the three founders. But there were problems. When their new Flash-based Web site went up, they send out e-mails to 1,000 potential clients, only to have many angry executives from people whose computer's couldn't handle the technology. Quickly, they developed a parallel site.

Luckily for them, they had spent nine months planning on how to build the infrastructure. They developed their client base, plotted strategy, figured out how to become profitable. And they learned an important lesson: "You can't help clients if the phones don't work."

SOURCE: Suzanne McGee, "Brains for Hire," *Inc. Magazine* (April 2004): 61–63.

Building Scenarios

scenario building

Looking at trends and discontinuities and imagining possible alternative futures to build a framework within which unexpected future events can be managed.

One way managers cope with greater uncertainty is with a forecasting technique known as scenario building. **Scenario building** involves looking at current trends and discontinuities and visualizing future possibilities. Rather than looking only at history and thinking about what has been, managers think about what could be. Managers cannot predict the future, but they can rehearse a framework within which future events can be managed.[37] With scenario building, a broad base of managers mentally rehearse different scenarios based on anticipating varied changes that could impact the organization. Scenarios are like stories that offer alternative vivid pictures of what the future will look like and how managers will respond. Typically, two to five scenarios are developed for each set of factors, ranging from the most optimistic to the most pessimistic view.[38] Scenario building forces managers to mentally rehearse what they would do if their best-laid plans collapse.

Royal Dutch/Shell has been using scenario building to help managers navigate the turbulence and uncertainty of the oil industry. One scenario Shell managers rehearsed in 1970, for example, focused on an imagined accident in Saudi Arabia that severed an oil pipeline, which in turn decreased supply. The market reacted by increasing oil prices, which allowed the Organization of Petroleum Exporting Countries (OPEC) nations to pump less oil and make more money. This story caused managers to reexamine the standard assumptions about oil price and supply and imagine what would happen and how they would respond if OPEC increased prices. By rehearsing this scenario, Shell's managers were much more prepared than the competition when OPEC announced its first oil embargo in October 1973. This speedy response to a massive shift in the environment enabled Shell to move within two years from being the world's eighth largest oil company to being number two.[39]

Take **ACTION**

When planning, think through all the steps you need to take and all the possible outcomes that might happen. Then consider how you would react to the various outcomes.

Crisis Management Planning

Managers cannot always anticipate future events and build scenarios to cope with them. In addition, some unexpected events are so sudden and devastating that they require immediate response. Consider events such as the November 12, 2001, crash of American Airlines Flight 587 in a New York neighborhood devastated by terrorist attacks, the 1993 deaths due to *E. Coli* bacteria from Jack-in-the-Box hamburgers, or the 2003 crash of the Columbia space shuttle. Companies face many smaller crises that call for rapid response, such as the conviction of Martha Stewart, chairman of Martha Stewart Living Omnimedia, on charges of insider trading, allegations of tainted Coca-Cola in Belgium, or charges that Tyson Foods hired illegal immigrants to work in its processing plants. Crises have become integral features of our organizations.[40] For managers to respond appropriately, they need thought-out and coordinated plans. Though crises may vary, a good crisis management plan (CMP) can be used to respond to any disaster at any time of the day or night. In addition, crisis management planning reduces the incidence of trouble, much like putting a good lock on a door reduces burglaries.[41]

Exhibit 5.7 outlines the three stages of crisis management.[42] The prevention stage involves activities managers undertake to prevent crises from occurring and to detect warning signs of potential crises. The preparation stage includes all the detailed planning to handle a crises when it occurs. Containment focuses on the organization's response to an actual crisis and any follow-up concerns. The Europa Hotel had its own crises to take care of, as shown on the following page.

EXHIBIT 5.7

Three Stages of Crisis Management

SOURCE: Based on information in W. Timothy Coombs, *Ongoing Crisis Communication: Planning, Managing, and Responding* (Thousand Oaks, Calif.: Sage Publications, 1999).

Prevention
- Build relationships.
- Detect signals from environment.

Preparation
- Designate crisis management team and spokesperson.
- Create detailed crisis management plan.
- Set up effective communications system.

Containment
- Rapid response: Activate the crisis management plan.
- Get the awful truth out.
- Meet safety and emotional needs.
- Return to business.

Europa Hotel

When the 12-story Europa Hotel first opened on Belfast's Grand Victoria Street in 1971, it was a symbol of hope and glamor for a town sorely in need of both. The Europa was the first hotel in Northern Ireland to offer bathrooms en suite and a popular top-floor nightclub. But within a month, the Europa had been bombed by the Irish Republican Army, who saw its act as a powerful strike against British capitalism. Twenty more explosions followed over the next four years, leading hotel management to erect security barriers and institute policies requiring that all guests be frisked and their luggage searched. The tourist trade disappeared, leaving only business customers and journalists who came to cover the Northern Ireland conflict from the perfect vantage point. Business gradually increased over the years, but the Europa remained a high-profile terrorist target. The hotel has been bombed at least 30 times, making it second only to the Holiday Inn, in Sarajevo, for the enviable title of "world's most bombed hotel." And yet, the Europa has survived and remains an important Belfast landmark. In fact, John Toner, current general manager of the four-star hotel, believes the Europa has become a stronger, more robust business because of the adversity its managers have faced. During each crisis, hotel managers followed thought-out plans for ensuring the safety of guests and employees, securing the building, and getting back to business as quickly as possible. Says Toner, "security is in the bones of the people who work here."[43]

The Europa, like most major hotels, has long had clear procedures for evacuation and dealing with disasters, and the hotel has a good record of getting people out quickly. Amazingly, no one has ever been killed by a bomb at the Europa. Because the Europa has had so much experience dealing with crises, managers and employees have become ever alert to even the smallest signals that something is amiss, so they have been able to take quick action and prevent greater damage or loss of life. The Europa is highly skilled at handling the containment stage of crisis. After one bomb ripped a huge hole in the side of the hotel and injured 13 people, everyone was back to work as usual by lunchtime. Toner uses every crisis as a way to learn more, be better prepared, and make the company better and stronger. He believes the tendency to look for ways to cut costs and lay people off immediately following a crisis is dangerous. "I don't look for cost savings. I don't look at the bottom line; it'll look after itself," he says. Instead, Toner focuses on taking care of employees and guests and finding ways to make the business better. Because of that attention, hotel staff and guests have remained resolutely loyal to the Europa.[44]

© ROBYN BECK/AFP/Getty Images

CONCEPT CONNECTION

*Why would the U.S. Department of Agriculture want to scan a cow's eye? Because it is part of the **prevention stage** of their **Crisis Management Plan (CMP)** for dealing with Mad Cow or Foot-and Mouth-Disease. The pattern of veins in each cow's retina is unique, and Optibrand Ltd. of Fort Collins, Colorado, has invented a device that farmers can use to scan their cows' retinas. This allows tracking of the animal through every step of the beef production process and helps the USDA meet its CMP goal of tracing the source of any disease—within two days of an outbreak. Since radio frequency identification tags, as in the photo, are subject to damage and tampering, retinal scanning coupled with implantable computer chips may provide the fastest and most reliable form of prevention and containment of these diseases.*

Take **ACTION**

Prevent crises through frequent communication, building trust, and careful planning.

Prevention. Though unexpected events and disasters will happen, managers should do everything they can to prevent crises. A critical part of the prevention stage is building trusting relationships with key stakeholders such as employees, customers, suppliers, governments, unions, and the community. By developing favorable relationships, managers can prevent crises from happening and can respond more effectively to those that cannot be avoided. For example, organizations that have open, trusting relationships with employees and unions may avoid crippling labor strikes.

Good communication helps managers identify problems early so they do not turn into major issues. Nike had early warning from distributors in the Middle East that its flame logo on a basketball shoe looked like the word Allah in Arabic script and would be considered offensive to Muslims. Though the company made some minor changes, managers failed to take the warning seriously. Nike had to recall nearly 40,000 pairs of the shoes and issue an apology to Muslims.[45] Similarly, Coca-Cola suffered a major crisis in Europe because it failed to respond to reports of "foul-smelling" Coke in Belgium. Former CEO Douglas Daft observed that every problem the company has faced in recent years "can be traced to a singular cause: We neglected our relationships."[46]

Preparation. Three steps in the preparation stage are designating a crisis management team and spokesperson, creating a detailed CMP, and setting up an effective communications system. Some companies are setting up crisis management offices, with high-level leaders who report directly to the CEO.[47] Though these offices are in charge of crisis management, people throughout the company must be involved. The crisis management team, for example, is a cross-functional group of people who are designated to swing into action if a crisis occurs. They are closely involved in creating the CMP, and they will be called upon to implement the plan if a disaster hits. The U.S. Office of Personnel Management in Washington, D.C., has nearly 200 people assigned and trained to take immediate action if a disaster occurs, including eight employees assigned to each of ten floors to handle an evacuation.[48] The organization should designate a spokesperson who will be the voice of the company during the crisis.[49] The spokesperson in many cases is the organization's top leader. However, organizations typically assign more than one spokesperson so someone else will be prepared if the top leader is unavailable.

The CMP is a detailed, written plan that specifies the steps to be taken, and by whom, if a crisis occurs. The CMP should include plans for dealing with various types of crises, such as natural disasters like fires or earthquakes, normal accidents like economic crises or industrial accidents, and abnormal events such as product tampering or acts of terrorism.[50] The plan should include details for ensuring the well-being of employees and customers, procedures for the backup and recovery of computer systems and the protection of proprietary information, details on where people should go if they need to be evacuated, plans for alternative work sites if needed, and guidelines for handling media and other outside communications. Morgan Stanley Dean Witter, the World Trade Center's largest tenant with 3,700 employees, adopted a crisis management plan for abnormal events after bomb threats during the Persian Gulf War in 1991. Top managers credit its detailed evacuation procedures for saving the lives of all but six employees during the September 11, 2001, attack. "Everybody knew about the...plan," said a spokesman. "We met constantly to talk about it."[51] A key point is that a crisis management plan should be a living, changing document that is regularly reviewed, practiced, and updated as needed.

A major part of the CMP is a communications plan that designates a crisis command center and sets up a complete communications and messaging system. The command center serves as a place for the crisis management team to meet, gather data and monitor incoming information, and disseminate information to the media, employees, and the public. All employees should have multiple ways to get in touch with the organization and report their whereabouts and status after a disaster.

Containment. Some crises are inevitable no matter how well prepared an organization is. When crisis hits, a rapid response is crucial. The team should be able to immediately implement the crisis management plan, so training and practice are important. In addition, the organization should "get the awful truth out" to employees and the public as soon as possible.[52] This is the stage where it becomes critical for the organization to speak with one voice so people do not get conflicting stories about what is going on and what the organization is doing about it. Consider what happened when doctors at Duke University Hospital made one of the worst mistakes in medical history—transplanting the wrong heart and lungs into 17-year-old Jessica Santillan, who died later. Though the story was out, it took nine days for Duke leaders to admit the hospital's mistake. By that time, rumors and misinformation were rampant, further damaging the hospital's reputation and prolonging its recovery from the crisis.[53]

After ensuring people's physical safety in a crisis, the next focus should be on responding to the emotional needs of employees, customers, and the public. Giving facts and statistics to downplay the disaster always backfires because it does not meet people's emotional need to feel that someone cares about them and what the disaster has meant to their lives. After a crisis as devastating as the 2001 terrorist attacks or the Columbine school shootings, companies may provide counseling and other services to help people cope.

> **Take ACTION**
> In a physical crisis, first make sure everyone is safe.

Organizations strive to give people a sense of security and hope by getting back to business quickly. Companies that cannot get up and running within ten days after any major crisis are not likely to stay in business.[54] People want to feel they are going to have a job and be able to take care of their families. Taking steps to protect people from danger during future disasters is important at this stage. In this sense, crisis management planning comes full circle because managers use the crisis to bolster their prevention abilities and be better prepared in the future. A crisis is an important time for companies to strengthen their stakeholder relationships. By being open and honest about the crisis and putting people first, organizations build stronger bonds with employees, customers and other stakeholders and gain a reputation as a trustworthy company.

Planning for High Performance.

The purpose of planning and goal setting is to help the organization achieve high performance. Overall organizational performance depends on achieving outcomes identified by the planning process. In a complex and competitive business environment, traditional planning, done by a select few, no longer works. Strategic thinking and execution become the expectation of every employee. For an example of a company that is finding hidden sources of ideas and innovation by involving all its workers in planning, consider Springfield Remanufacturing Corporation (SRC), described on the following page.

SRC Holdings Corporation

Jack Stack and 12 other former International Harvester managers started Springfield Remanufacturing Corporation (SRC) on a shoestring in 1983. The company still exists, but has become part of SRC Holdings Corporation, a group of 22 semiautonomous companies located in the Springfield, Missouri, area. Stack, CEO of SRC Holdings, has built this successful corporation by tapping into people's universal desire to win. Stack's philosophy is that "the best, most efficient, most profitable way to operate a business is to give everybody a voice in how the company is run and a stake in the financial outcome, good or bad."

SRC involves everyone in the planning process and uses a bonus system based on hitting the plan's targets. Top managers meet with middle managers, supervisors, and front-line employees throughout their divisions to develop and sell their long-range plans. If a manager's plan is beyond the plant's capacity, the workers feel free to suggest workable alternatives. By the time managers present their plans to the top brass, everyone in the various divisions has had a say and has developed a sense of ownership in the plan.

All SRC businesses make their operating and financial performance numbers freely available so employees can compare performance to the plan. People "huddle" at least weekly around mural-sized charts in the employee cafeteria to talk about the numbers and what needs to be done to meet the targets. Employees take the company's success personally because they all own shares in the company through employee stock ownership plans (ESOPs). SRC has invested heavily in financial education for all workers so that everyone understands what is at stake and what is to be gained. "What we're doing," Stack says, "is showing people how to get through life without fear. Once people understand what it takes to be a businessperson, not just a cog in the system but someone on the brighter side of capitalism, then their lives can change forever."[55]

The process of planning is changing to be more in tune with a rapidly changing environment. Traditionally, strategy and planning have been the domain of top managers. Today, though, managers involve people throughout the organization, which can spur higher performance because people understand the goals and plans and buy into them. We will now examine traditional, top-down approaches to planning and then examine some of the newer approaches that emphasize bottom-up planning and the involvement of stakeholders in the planning process.

Start with a Strong Mission and Vision. Planning for high performance requires flexibility. Employees may have to adapt plans to meet new needs and respond to changes in the environment. During times of turbulence or uncertainty, a powerful sense of purpose (mission) and direction for the future (vision) becomes more important. Without a strong mission and vision to guide employee thinking and behavior, the resources of a fast-moving company, such as some of today's high-tech businesses, can quickly become uncoordinated, with employees pursuing radically different plans and activities. A compelling mission and vision can increase employee commitment and motivation, which are critical to helping organizations compete in a changing environment.[56]

Set Stretch Goals for Excellence. Stretch goals are ambitious goals that are so clear, compelling, and imaginative that they fire up employees and engender excellence. As we discussed earlier in the chapter, an important criterion for effective goals is that they be challenging yet realistic. In today's workplace, stretch goals are important because things are moving so quickly. A company that focuses on gradual, incremental improvements in products, processes, or systems will get left behind.

Take **ACTION**

Develop ambitious goals to get people enthused.

Managers can use stretch goals to compel employees to think in new ways that can lead to bold, innovative breakthroughs. Motorola used stretch goals to achieve Six Sigma quality, as described in Chapter 1, which has now become the standard for numerous companies. Managers first set a goal of a tenfold increase in quality over a two-year period. After this goal was met, they set a new stretch goal of a hundredfold improvement over a four-year period.[57]

Create a Culture that Encourages Learning. Today's best managers create a culture that celebrates diversity, encourages initiative, and supports continuous experimentation and learning. Managers advocate individual lifelong learning, and they invest in education and training to keep people's minds and skills sharp.[58] An important value in these organizations is questioning the status quo. Tomorrow's opportunities might come from different directions than the basis of today's success. For example, soft drink makers missed out on huge opportunities for new drinks such as flavored waters, sports drinks, and New Age beverages because they were focused on continuing the status quo rather than experimenting with new products.[59] Managers sometimes have to change plans quickly, which requires a mindset that embraces ambiguity, risk taking, making mistakes, and learning.

Embrace Event-Driven Planning. In changing environments, managers have to be in tune with what is happening now, rather than focusing only on long-range goals and plans. Long-range strategic planning is not abandoned, but it is accompanied by event-driven planning, which responds to the current reality of what the environment and the marketplace demands.[60] Exhibit 5.8 compares calendar-driven planning to event-driven planning. **Event-driven planning** is a continuous, sequential process rather than a staid planning document. It is evolutionary and interactive, taking advantage of unforeseen events to shift the company as needed to improve performance. Event-driven planning allows for flexibility to adapt to market forces or other shifts in the environment, rather than being tied to a plan that no longer works. For example, Redix International, a software development firm, has a long-term plan for items it wants to incorporate into the software. However, the plan is modified at least four or five times a year. The shifts in direction are based on weekly discussions President and CEO Randall King has with key Redix managers, where they examine what demands from clients indicate about where the marketplace is going.[61]

> **event-driven planning**
>
> This is a continuous, sequential process rather than a staid planning document. It is evolutionary and interactive, taking advantage of unforeseen events to shift the company as needed to improve performance.

Use Temporary Task Forces. A **planning task force** is a temporary group of managers and employees who take responsibility for developing a strategic plan. Many of today's companies use interdepartmental task forces to help establish goals and make plans for achieving them. The task force often includes outside stakeholders as well, such as customers, suppliers, strategic partners, investors, or members of the general community. Today's companies are focused on satisfying the needs and interests of all stakeholder groups, so they bring these stakeholders into the planning and goal-setting process.[62] LendLease, an Australian real estate and financial services company, involves numerous stakeholders, including community advocates and potential customers, in the planning process for every new project it undertakes.[63]

> **planning task force**
>
> A group of managers and employees who develop a strategic plan.

Planning Still Starts and Stops at the Top. Top managers create a mission and vision that is worthy of employees' best efforts and provides a framework for planning

Calendar-Driven Planning	Activity
Is based on time	Is based on events—small and large
Produces a document	Produces a sequential process
Is declared	Is evolutionary and interactive
Focuses on goals	Focuses on process
Creates obstacles to change once set	Allows for continuous change
Creates strategy implementers	Creates organizationwide strategists

EXHIBIT 5.8

Comparing Two Planning Styles

SOURCE: Chuck Martin, "How to Plan for the Short Term," book excerpt from Chuck Martin, *Managing for the Short Term* (New York: Doubleday, 2002), in *CIO* (September 15, 2002), 90–97.

and goal setting. Though planning is decentralized, top managers must show support and commitment to the planning process. Top managers must accept responsibility when planning and goal setting are ineffective, rather than blaming the failure on lower-level managers or employees.

Thinking Strategically

strategic management

The set of decisions and actions used to formulate and implement strategies that will provide a competitively superior fit between the organization and its environment so as to achieve organizational goals.

The first part of this chapter provided an overview of the types of goals and plans that organizations use. In this section, we will explore strategic management, which is considered one specific type of planning. Strategic planning in for-profit business organizations typically pertains to competitive actions in the marketplace. In not-for-profit organizations such as the Red Cross, strategic planning pertains to events in the external environment. The final responsibility for strategy rests with top managers and the chief executive. For an organization to succeed, the CEO must be actively involved in making the tough choices and trade-offs that define and support strategy.[64] However, senior executives at such companies as General Electric, 3M Corp., and Johnson & Johnson want middle-level and low-level managers to think strategically. Some companies are finding ways to get front-line workers involved in strategic thinking and planning. Strategic thinking means to take the long-term view and to see the big picture, including the organization and the competitive environment, and to consider how they fit together. Understanding the strategy concept, the levels of strategy, and strategy formulation versus implementation is an important start toward strategic thinking.

© Cat Gwynn/Getty Images

CONCEPT CONNECTION

*Rivalry between hotels in Las Vegas is fierce! To compete, Mirage Hotel opened Cravings, a new $12 million buffet restaurant. Gone are the low-priced steam-warmed vats of lasagna; dinner is now $20.50 per person. Food is cooked fresh at individual stations, served up on small, stylish plates, and can be made to order. This restaurant transformation, designed by renowned designer Adam Tihany, is a part of the Mirage's **grand strategy of growth**. In the photo are chefs at the Cravings sweets station. The success of Mirage's plan to attract new customers was reflected recently by comments from two patrons, who drove over an hour to dine at Cravings: "I've eaten in so many buffets but I've never seen anything as beautiful as this."*

What Is Strategic Management?

Strategic management is the set of decisions and actions used to formulate and implement strategies that will provide a competitively superior fit between the organization and its environment so as to achieve organizational goals.[65] Managers ask questions such as, "What changes and trends are occurring in the competitive environment? Who are our customers? What products or services should we offer? How can we offer those products and services most efficiently?" Answers to these questions help managers make choices about how to position their organizations in the environment with respect to rival companies.[66] Superior organizational performance is not a matter of luck. It is determined by the choices that managers make. Top executives use strategic management to define an overall direction for the organization, which is the firm's grand strategy. Sometimes that grand strategy is one of growth, as is eBay's, described in the Focus on Skills box.

Purpose of Strategy

Within the overall grand strategy of an organization, executives define an explicit **strategy**, which is the plan of action that describes resource allocation and activities for dealing with the environment, achieving a competitive advantage, and attaining the organization's goals. **Competitive advantage** refers to what sets the organization apart from others and provides it with a distinctive edge for meeting customer needs in the marketplace. The essence of formulating strategy is choosing how the organization will be different.[67] As shown in the Business Blooper box, Hollywood needs to think more about its movies being different from one another.

eBay: Building on Success

At a time when almost every Internet and technology company was handing out pink slips, the scene was quite different within the walls of San Jose, California-based, eBay. In fact, the online auction company kept adding to its workforce during the downturn. eBay, which began as a site for selling collectibles and attic trash, is pursuing a growth strategy, successfully molding itself into a new kind of enterprise: a whole online community where 30 million people buy and sell more than $20 billion in merchandise, everything from computers to cosmetics. More used cars sell on eBay than the number one U.S. auto dealer. The company has its own police force to patrol listings for fraud, an educational system that holds classes around the country to teach people how to buy and sell on the site, and something like its own bank. Problems are starting to loom though.

There are several elements to CEO Meg Whitman's strategic plan for growth. First, to branch out from its auction format, the company purchased Half.com, a site where new and used items can be listed at a fixed price. Then it added the "Buy It Now" feature, which allows users to acquire an item immediately, omitting the time-consuming auction process altogether. At least 35 percent of all items listed by sellers on eBay now offer that option, which accelerates the site's trading rate. To get its online car market going, eBay bought a collector-car auction company, Kruse International, and partnered with AutoTrader.com to list its classifieds. The company acquired payment processor PayPal, which enables people to make electronic payments to sellers who do not have a merchant credit card account. eBay is on a global expansion binge, acquiring trading sites in Canada, Britain, Germany, Korea, and China since 2000.

Another growth strategy has been to allow businesses such as JCPenney, IBM, and Sears Roebuck to set up virtual storefronts. eBay expected to attract around 2,000 businesses, but nearly ten times that number wanted a piece of the action, recognizing the inexpensive potential for reaching millions of consumers. The most recent element of eBay's growth plan is selling information. Companies such as PGA of America and Intuit use eBay data to show the market value of items or help taxpayers estimate the value of charitable donations on their IRS forms. With auctions closing every minute on eBay's site, the company can provide real-time market information. Though managers do not expect this new part of the business to be an instant moneymaker, selling data will likely become an important part of eBay's business in future years.

As one manager of a struggling dot-com said, "eBay is what all of us wanted our Internet businesses to be." As eBay continues its astounding growth, no one seems to know just how far it can go. "We don't actually control this," Whitman admits. "We have a unique partner—millions of people." But wait a minute: Those partners are getting upset with the rate increases eBay has recently put on them. For some, it means paying eBay another $150 a month, with no increase in sales volume. They are so mad, they are boycotting, looking for other sites. It remains to be seen if eBay will still rule.

SOURCES: Verne Kopytoff, "Sellers Rebelling Against Higher eBay Fees," *Chicago Sun-Times* (Feb. 19, 2005): 44; Robert D. Hof, "The eBay Economy," *BusinessWeek* (August 25, 2003): 124+; Nick Wingfield, "At eBay, Even Sales Prices Are For Sale," *The Wall Street Journal* (December 8, 2003): B1, B7; and Miguel Helft, "What Makes eBay Unstoppable?" *The Industry Standard* (August 6–13, 2001): 32–37.

Managers make decisions about whether the company will perform different activities or will execute similar activities differently than competitors do. Strategy necessarily changes to fit environmental conditions, but to remain competitive, companies develop strategies that focus on core competencies, develop synergy, and create value for customers.

Core Competence. A company's **core competence** is something the organization does especially well in comparison to its competitors. A core competence represents a competitive advantage because the company acquires expertise that competitors do not have. A core competence may be in the area of superior research and development (R&D), expert technological know-how, process efficiency, or exceptional customer service.[68] At Amgen, a pharmaceutical company, strategy focuses on the company's core competence of high-quality scientific research. Rather than starting with a specific disease and working backward, Amgen takes brilliant science and finds unique uses for it.[69] Home Depot thrives because of a strategy focused on superior customer service. Managers stress to all employees that listening to customers and helping them solve

strategy

The plan of action that describes resource allocation and activities for dealing with the environment, achieving a competitive advantage, and attaining the organization's goals.

competitive advantage

What sets the organization apart from others and provides it with a distinctive edge for meeting customer needs in the marketplace.

BUSINESS BLOOPER

Hollywood Ratings

Hollywood's strategy to make lots of R-rated films does not translate to higher revenues. Studies show that the biggest grossing and most profitable movies are the G-rated ones, earning about 150 percent of the profits of R movies. And yet, of all the films done each year, only about 3 percent are G, 22 percent are P or PG and 55 percent are R. But do not despair because it looks as if more G-rated movies are on the way. Hail to Harry Potter and Bambi.

SOURCE: David Germain, "A boom year for G films," *The Record* (July 5, 2002): 8; Robert A. Sirico, "Watch Your Bottom Line, Hollywood," *Forbes* (April 19, 1999): 169.

their do-it-yourself worries takes precedence over making a sale.[70] In each case, leaders identified what their company does well and built strategy around it. Dell Computers has succeeded with its core competencies of speed and cost efficiency.

Dell

Dell Computers is constantly changing, adapting, and finding new ways to master its environment, but one thing has not changed since the days Michael Dell first began building computers in his dorm room: the focus on speed and low cost. A major factor in Dell's success is that it has retained a clear image of what it does best. The company spent years developing a core competence in low cost and speedy delivery by squeezing time lags and inefficiencies out of the manufacturing and assembly process and then extending the same brutal standards to the supply chain. Good relationships with a few key suppliers and precise coordination mean that Dell can sometimes receive parts in minutes rather than days.

Consider how the system works at the Topfer Manufacturing Center, the newest of Dell's seven plants. Inside the cavernous factory, located near Dell's headquarters in Round Rock, Texas, parts storage takes up about the space of an average bedroom. The factory is a blur of activity. Boxes of microchips and electronic components skitter by on double-decker conveyor belts. Assembly workers use an integrated computer system that practically hands them the right part—whether it be any of a dozen different microprocessors or a combination of software—at the right time. The system cuts costs and saves time by decreasing the number of worker touches per machine. On a typical day, 25,000 finished computers head off toward happy customers. Dell's system offers completely transparent information about sales, orders, shipments, and other data to employees, customers, and suppliers. Precise coordination, aided by sophisticated supply chain software, means Dell can keep just two hours' worth of parts inventory and replenish only what it needs throughout the day. The just-in-time system works so smoothly that nearly 85 percent of orders are built, customized, and shipped within eight hours.

Dell's fixation with speed and thrift is being challenged as the company moves into new areas of business, such as storage systems, networking gear, and information services. However, founder and chairman Michael Dell believes the core competencies that made Dell a star in PCs and servers can make the company a winner as it seizes new opportunities. To anyone who doubts that Dell can compete in new markets, he says, "Bring them on. We're coming right at them."[71]

core competence

Something the organization does especially well in comparison to its competitors. A core competence represents a competitive advantage because the company acquires expertise that competitors do not have.

Synergy. When organizational parts interact to produce a joint effect that is greater than the sum of the parts acting alone, **synergy** occurs. The organization may attain a special advantage with respect to cost, market power, technology, or management skill. When properly managed, synergy can create additional value with existing resources, providing a big boost to the bottom line.[72] Federal Express (FedEx) hopes to achieve synergy with its recent acquisition of Kinko's Inc. Kinko's document delivery and office services complement FedEx's package delivery and give FedEx a greater presence among small and mid-sized businesses, a market it has long coveted. By providing full-service counters in Kinko's stores, FedEx has the potential to double its locations over the next few years, particularly overseas, where Kinko's has centers in eight countries.[73]

Synergy can be obtained by good relations with suppliers, as at Dell Computer, or by strong alliances among companies. Sweden's appliance giant Electrolux partnered with Ericsson, the Swedish telecommunications giant, in a joint venture called *e2 Home* to create a new way to make and sell appliances. Together, Electrolux and Ericsson are offering products such as the Screenfridge, a refrigerator with Internet connections that enables users to check traffic conditions, order take-out, or buy groceries, and an experimental pay-per-use washing machine. Neither company could have offered these revolutionary products on its own. "The technology was there, the appliances were there, but we needed a way to connect those two elements—to add value for consumers," said Per Grunewald, e2 Home's president.[74] Israel-based Power Paper has created a thriving company by staying with its core competence and by building strategic relationships that bring synergy as described in the Focus on Innovation box.

Value Creation.   Delivering value to the customer is at the heart of strategy. Value can be defined as the combination of benefits received and costs paid by the customer. Managers help their companies create value by devising strategies that exploit core competencies and attain synergy. The cable company Charter Communications is attempting to provide better value to customers to counter charges of excessive prices and to compete with the growing clout of satellite television companies. New cable value packages offer a combination of basic cable, digital premium channels, and high-speed Internet for a reduced cost. Laura Alber, president of Pottery Barn, uses the company's thick bath towels to illustrate the value Pottery Barn delivers to customers: "For us, this represents a combination of design, quality, and price," Alber says. "If this were $60, you'd still like it. But at $24, you go, 'This is incredible.'"[75] To meet its needs, the band, The String Cheese Incident (SCI), wanted to deliver value to their fans, and it found that the core competence of managing its own destiny helped them do just that as described in the Focus on Collaboration box.

synergy
When organizational parts interact to produce a joint effect that is greater than the sum of the parts acting alone.

FOCUS ON INNOVATION

Power Paper

One day soon you will be wearing one-millimeter-thick batteries on your clothes, or using them as anti-aging skin patches; that is, if Israeli entrepreneurs Zvi Nitzan and Baruch Levanon have anything to say about it. They left their companies in 1997, used up all their savings, and cashed in retirement accounts to start the company with the first patent they had: environmentally friendly batteries, printed onto organic materials such as paper.

To most people, it must have seemed like science fiction, but not to them. They were convinced the true revolution in chips and electronics was 20 years down the pike, and they were going to be part of it. Realizing they were on to something big, they developed two parts to their strategy. One was to get major funding, so the company could grow to its potential, and the second was to stay focused. Though the company now submits two patent applications per week, they must stick to the knitting. This means sticking to R&D and not get sidetracked with manufacturing. Instead, they partner with big companies, creating strategic relationships. But they keep their patents secret, much as Coca-Cola does. So far, they have signed contracts with Hallmark Cards, which makes musical greeting cards, and Hasbro, whose Thin-Tronix stickers play 12 seconds of music when touched. Their biggest customers, though, are in the pharmaceutical area, bringing in 80 percent of their $5 million per-year revenue, with such products as a battery incorporated onto a skin patch, where electrical circuits bring moisturizer to the face over a period of eight hours. CEO Shalom Daskal believes they are part of the coming revolution. "In this market," he says, "we could be a kind of Israeli Nokia."

SOURCES: Oded Hermoni and Tzuri Dar, "Perhaps an Israeli Nokia at Last," *Ha'aretz* (March 23, 2004); "12 Hot Start-ups: Power Paper," *Business2.0* (Jan/Feb. 2004): 94.

The String Cheese Incident (SCI)

Most bands focus primarily on their music, the creativity, the soul. Not SCI. The Boulder, Colorado-based, jazzy band improvises its music, but not its business. The five-member band has developed a loyal following during the past 11 years of non-stop touring. During a time when the music business was cutting back and piracy was eating into album sales, SCI built a $15 million-dollar business that employs 45 people.

The secret: exploiting the Internet, including selling downloads of live concerts. "Our goal from the beginning," says bass player Keith Moseley, "was to control our own destiny and to maintain artistic control." Interestingly, the band was that way from the start, always seeing itself as a serious business opportunity. Taking advantage of all the people the members came in contact with on the road, they grilled successful musicians about how they managed their careers, from tour operations to record deals. And they were not impressed with the answers because they saw the music business model was falling apart. Band manager Jeremy Stein says, "We wanted a new model for ourselves."

Looking to the one great business-model band, The Grateful Dead, which built brand loyalty by catering to its die-hard fans with low ticket prices and permission to tape concerts. SCI wanted to do that with one advantage: the Internet. Live shows bring in 50 percent of their revenue and they now sell a major portion of their tickets online (after settling a lawsuit against Ticketmaster). Customers can save 10 percent by booking through SCI rather than Ticketmaster. Then they set up their own travel agency, which helps fans plan trips to their concerts, as well as concerts of 20 other bands. It is all about putting themselves in their fans' shoes and making the whole experience easier.

Benefiting most from the Internet is online album sales, which account for 20 percent of its CD sales, and it is a much more profitable deal than selling in retail stores. Last year, the band started selling downloads of its concerts for $10 each on its Web site (*http://www.livecheese.com*). Though piracy is a threat, they are going to carry on offering the cheap downloads. "We're going to continue to make music available, even if that means giving it away," says Moseley. "The more people are exposed to our music, the better it is for the band."

SOURCE: David Kushner, "String Theory," *FSB* (Jan. 2005): 95–96.

The Strategic Management Process

The overall strategic management process is illustrated in Exhibit 5.9. It begins when executives evaluate their current position with respect to mission, goals, and strategies. Then, they scan the organization's internal and external environments and identify strategic factors that might require change. Internal or external events might indicate a need to redefine the mission or goals or to formulate a new strategy at the corporate, business, or functional level. The final stage in the strategic management process is implementation of the new strategy.

Strategy Formulation versus Implementation

Strategy formulation includes the planning and decision making that lead to the establishment of the firm's goals and the development of a specific strategic plan.[76] **Strategy formulation** may include assessing the external environment and internal problems and integrating the results into goals and strategy. This is in contrast to **strategy implementation**, which is the use of managerial and organizational tools to direct resources toward accomplishing strategic results.[77] Strategy implementation is the administration and execution of the strategic plan. Managers may use persuasion, new equipment, changes in organization structure, or a revised reward system to ensure that employees and resources are used to make formulated strategy a reality.

strategy formulation

May include assessing the external environment and internal problems and integrating the results into goals and strategy.

strategy implementation

The use of managerial and organizational tools to direct resources toward accomplishing strategic results.

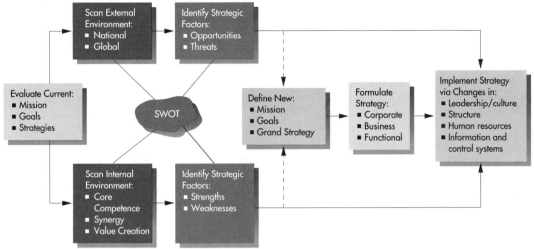

EXHIBIT 5.9
The Strategic
Management Process

Situation Analysis

Formulating strategy often begins with an assessment of the internal and external factors that will affect the organization's competitive situation. **Situation analysis** typically includes a search for strengths, weaknesses, opportunities, and threats (SWOT) that affect organizational performance. Situation analysis is important to all companies but is crucial to those considering globalization because of the diverse environments in which they operate. External information about opportunities and threats may be obtained from various sources, including customers, government reports, professional journals, suppliers, bankers, friends in other organizations, consultants, or association meetings. Many firms hire special scanning organizations to provide them with newspaper clippings, Internet research, and analyses of relevant domestic and global trends. In addition, many companies are hiring competitive intelligence professionals to scope out competitors as we discussed in Chapter 2.

Executives acquire information about internal strengths and weaknesses from various reports, including budgets, financial ratios, profit and loss statements, and surveys of employee attitudes and satisfaction. Managers spend 80 percent of their time giving and receiving information. Through frequent face-to-face discussions and meetings with people at all hierarchical levels, executives build an understanding of the company's internal strengths and weaknesses. Brown Johnson used situational analysis to help her redesign children's programming at Nickelodeon as described in the Best Practices Box.

Internal Strengths and Weaknesses. *Strengths* are positive internal characteristics that the organization can exploit to achieve its strategic performance goals. *Weaknesses* are internal characteristics that might inhibit or restrict the organization's performance. Some examples of what executives evaluate to interpret organizational strengths and weaknesses are given in Exhibit 5.10. The information sought typically pertains to specific functions such as marketing, finance, production, and R&D. Internal analysis also examines overall organization structure, management competence and quality, and human resource characteristics. Based on their understanding of these areas, managers can determine their strengths or weaknesses vis-à-vis other companies.

situation analysis
Typically includes a search for strengths, weaknesses, opportunities, and threats (SWOT) that affect organizational performance.

Take ACTION
When considering a strategy, look carefully at its SWOT. Do not just jump into a course of action.

BEST PRACTICES

Nickelodeon

"**S**esame Street" and "Mister Rogers Neighborhood" used to dominate children's television. That was before Brown Johnson came to Nickelodeon 18 years ago and took on the preschool market. Cartoon network exec Alice Cahn says that Brown was the first commercial challenge to public television for preschoolers. "They looked very smartly at the market," she said. As a young girl, Johnson was only allowed to watch one hour of TV a week, but now she sees attitudes have changed. "Like it or not, parents are not [feeling] guilty at all about calling the TV set a baby sitter for them. It allows them to make dinner or get dressed or take a shower. So, whatever is on, you better make it good. You'd better make it the very best it can be."

Brown's innovation of "the pause" set her apart from the beginning. Many of her shows have a well-placed pause in the program, long enough to allow children to solve puzzles or problems along with the characters. This pause allows the child viewers to feel part of the story, not merely passive viewers.

Always trying something new, Johnson had looked at children's TV and found many shows patronizing, telling kids what to do. Even "Sesame Street." Those shows started with education, whereas Johnson started thinking about the child. She gathered child development specialists, educators, storytellers, puppeteers and poets to find out what children wanted on TV. As a result, she started to move children's TV toward longer narratives and away from the short, staccato form initiated by "Sesame Street." "People were making TV for kids that was lots of short pieces strung together like beads on a string," said Johnson, who thought, "We can tell a story that's longer because otherwise we're all going to have ADD."

Has the strategy worked? Nickelodeon's parent Viacom's cable divisions increased revenue 17 percent last year, to $6.6 billion. Nickelodeon alone brought in $100 million from cable operators, consumer products, and advertising. It takes about two years and millions of dollars to create new shows, which then cost between $20,000 to $600,000 per episode.

Still pushing limits, Johnson's newest show is "Lazy Town," shot on location about an Icelandic acrobatic champion named Magnus Scheving, a health-conscious superhero who encourages children to eat carrots and drink water, rather than follow junk-food-loving Robbie Rotten. Maybe Magnus will be an antidote to the Supersize food culture.

SOURCE: Tania Ralli, The Mother of "Blue" and "Dora" Takes a Step up at Nickelodeon," *The New York Times* (Feb. 28, 2005): C1, C6.

© ATEF HASSAN/Reuters/CORBIS

CONCEPT CONNECTION

*The effects of this oil fire in Iraq are being felt thousands of miles away—in the executive suites at companies such as United Airlines, the number 2 air carrier in the United States. Uncertainty about oil supplies is a significant **external threat** to the nation's airlines. Other threats United faces as it struggles to recover from bankruptcy are customers' continuing fear of terrorism and stiff competition from low-cost carriers like Jet Blue.*

External   Opportunities   and   Threats. *Opportunities* are characteristics of the external environment that have the potential to help the organization achieve or exceed its strategic goals. *Threats* are characteristics of the external environment that may prevent the organization from achieving its strategic goals. Executives evaluate the external environment with information about the nine sectors described in Chapter 2. The task environment sectors are the most relevant to strategic behavior and include the behavior of competitors, customers, suppliers, and the labor supply. The general environment contains those sectors that have an indirect influence on the organization but, nevertheless, must be understood and incorporated into strategic behavior. The general environment includes technological developments, the economy, legal-political and international events, and sociocultural changes. Additional areas that might reveal opportunities or threats include pressure groups, interest groups, creditors, natural resources, and potentially competitive industries.

The *Milwaukee Journal Sentinel* used SWOT analysis to formulate a strategy to compete with new rivals in a low-growth metropolitan area hard hit by the manufacturing recession.[78] Careful SWOT analysis forced managers to recognize that the newspaper needed to develop a strategy that enabled it to run efficient operations as well as find ways to distinguish the paper from any other source of news and information in Milwaukee. As a result, the *Journal Sentinel* has become a stronger, more flexible organization and the paper and its associated Web sites are clearly the region's leading source

EXHIBIT 5.10

Checklist for Analyzing Organizational Strengths and Weakness

Management and Organization

Management quality
Staff quality
Degree of centralization
Organization charts
Planning, information, control systems

Marketing

Distribution channels
Market share
Advertising efficiency
Customer satisfaction
Product quality
Service reputation
Sales force turnover

Human Resources

Employee experience, education
Union status
Turnover, absenteeism
Work satisfaction
Grievances

Finance

Profit margin
Debt-equity ratio
Inventory ratio
Return on investment
Credit rating

Production

Plant location
Machinery obsolescence
Purchasing system
Quality control
Productivity/efficiency

Research and Development

Basic applied research
Laboratory capabilities
Research programs
New-product innovations
Technology innovations

of news and information. Quality, reader satisfaction, and profitability all improved as a result of the new strategy.

Kraft Foods provides another example of how situation analysis can be used to help executives formulate the correct strategy as described below.

Kraft Foods

Kraft Foods has some of the most recognizable brand names in the grocery store, but the giant food company has been facing some difficult challenges in recent years. To get things back on track, managers are evaluating the company by looking at their SWOT.

Kraft's greatest strengths are its powerful brands, its positive reputation, its track record as an innovator, and a well-funded R&D budget. Its biggest weaknesses include the loss of top management talent in recent years, a sluggish response to environmental changes, and declining market share and profits.

Kraft managers recognize *opportunities* in the environment, as well. Trends show that Americans are looking for more snack foods and comfort foods, which presents a golden opportunity for Kraft, whose name for many Americans is almost synonymous with comfort food. But, several major threats have been building for a couple of years. The first is that cheaper, private-label brands are successfully stealing market share from Kraft's core brands such as Kraft Singles cheese slices, Maxwell House coffee, Oscar Mayer cold cuts, and Ritz Crackers. At the same time, other major food companies have been quicker to respond to growing consumer demands for less fattening, more healthful food choices. PepsiCo began cutting trans-fats from Doritos, Tostitos, and Cheetos and saw sales increase by 28 percent. A third threat to Kraft is that more people are eating ready-made lunches rather than consuming home-prepared lunch foods such as sandwiches made of cheese and cold cuts.

What does SWOT analysis suggest for Kraft's future strategy? Kraft managers will capitalize on the company's strengths by investing research dollars to develop healthier snack and pre-packaged lunch foods, such as lower-fat versions of its popular "Lunchables." To bolster core brands, Kraft has pumped an additional $200 million into its multi-billion-dollar marketing and advertising budget. Managers are exploring new vending opportunities for giant Kraft-branded machines that churn out ready-made food at movie theaters, shopping malls, and other public venues.[79]

Formulating Business-Level Strategy

Now we turn to strategy formulation within the strategic business unit, in which the concern is how to compete. The same three generic strategies—growth, stability, and retrenchment—apply at the business level, but they are accomplished through competitive actions rather than the acquisition or divestment of business divisions. One model for formulating strategy is Michael E. Porter's competitive strategies, which provide a framework for business unit competitive action.

Porter's Competitive Forces and Strategies

Michael E. Porter studied a number of business organizations and proposed that business-level strategies are the result of five competitive forces in the company's environment.[80] More recently, Porter has examined the impact of the Internet on business-level strategy.[81] New Web-based technology is influencing industries in positive and negative ways, and understanding this impact is essential for managers to analyze their competitive environments and design appropriate strategic actions.

Five Competitive Forces.   Exhibit 5.11 illustrates the five competitive forces that exist in a company's environment and indicates some ways Internet technology is affecting each area. These forces help determine a company's position vis-à-vis competitors in the industry environment.

1. Potential new entrants. Capital requirements and economies of scale are examples of two potential barriers to entry that can keep out new competitors. It is far more

EXHIBIT 5.11

*The Five Forces
Affecting Industry
Competition*

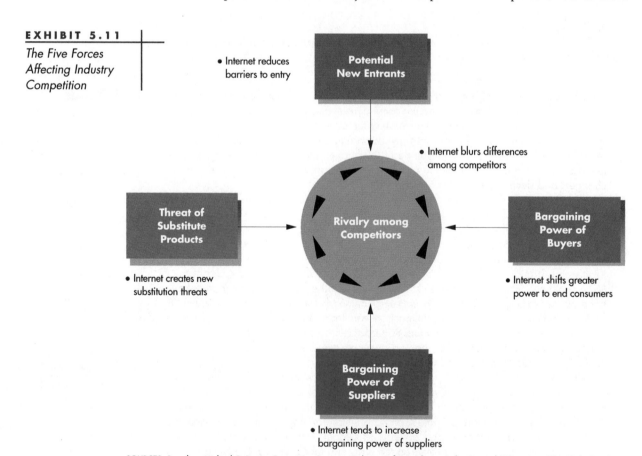

SOURCES: Based on Michael E. Porter, Competitive Strategy: Techniques for Analyzing Industries and Competitors (New York: Free Press, 1980); and Michael E. Porter, "Strategy and the Internet," Harvard Business Review (March, 2001), 63–78.

costly to enter the automobile industry, for instance, than to start a specialized mail order business. In general, Internet technology has helped new companies to enter an industry by curtailing the need for such organizational elements as an established sales force, physical assets such as buildings and machinery, or access to existing supplier and sales channels.

2. Bargaining power of buyers. Informed customers become empowered customers. The Internet provides easy access to a wide array of information about products, services, and competitors, thereby greatly increasing the bargaining power of end consumers. For example, a customer shopping for a car can gather extensive information about various options, such as wholesale prices for new cars or average value for used vehicles, detailed specifications, repair records, and whether a used car has ever been involved in an accident.

3. Bargaining power of suppliers. The concentration of suppliers and the availability of substitute suppliers are significant factors in determining supplier power. The sole supplier of engines to a manufacturer of small airplanes will have great power, for example. The impact of the Internet in this area can be positive and negative. That is, procurement over the Web tends to give a company greater power over suppliers, but the Web gives suppliers access to more customers, as well as the ability to reach end users. Overall, the Internet tends to raise suppliers' bargaining power.

4. Threat of substitute products. The power of alternatives and substitutes for a company's product may be affected by changes in cost or in trends such as increased health consciousness that will deflect buyer loyalty. Companies in the sugar industry suffered from the growth of sugar substitutes, and manufacturers of aerosol spray cans lost business as environmentally conscious consumers chose other products. The Internet has created a greater threat of new substitutes by enabling new approaches to meeting customer needs. For example, traditional travel agencies have been hurt by the offering of low-cost airline tickets over the Internet.

5. Rivalry among competitors. As illustrated in Exhibit 5.11, rivalry among competitors is influenced by the preceding four forces, as well as by cost and product differentiation. With the leveling force of the Internet and information technology, many companies are having trouble finding ways to distinguish themselves from their competitors, so rivalry has intensified.

Porter referred to the "advertising slugfest" when describing the scrambling and jockeying for position that often occurs among fierce rivals within an industry. Famous examples include the competitive rivalry between PepsiCo and Coca-Cola, between UPS and FedEx, and between Home Depot and Lowe's. The rivalry between Gillette and Schick (Schick being the number two maker of razors) may soon be just as heated. Though Gillette is still way ahead, the introduction of the Schick Quattro and a massive advertising campaign helped Schick's sales grow 149 percent in 2004, while Gillette's razor sales slipped.[82] IBM and Oracle Corp. are involved in a fight for the number one spot in the $50 billion corporate software market. IBM rented a billboard near Oracle's headquarters proclaiming a "search for intelligent software." A few days later, Oracle fired the next shot with a competing billboard retorting, "Then you've come to the right place."[83]

Competitive Strategies. In finding its competitive edge within these five forces, Porter suggests that a company can adopt one of three strategies: differentiation, cost leadership, and focus. Companies can use the Internet to support and strengthen the strategic approach they choose. The organizational characteristics typically associated with each strategy are summarized in Exhibit 5.12.

differentiation

An attempt to distinguish the firm's products or services from others in the industry. The organization may use advertising, distinctive product features, exceptional service, or new technology to achieve a product perceived as unique.

1. **Differentiation** involves an attempt to distinguish the firm's products or services from others in the industry. The organization may use advertising, distinctive product features, exceptional service, or new technology to achieve a product perceived as unique. The differentiation strategy can be profitable because customers are loyal and will pay high prices for the product. Examples of products that have benefited from a differentiation strategy include Mercedes-Benz automobiles, Maytag appliances, and Tommy Hilfiger clothing, all of which are perceived as distinctive in their markets. Service companies can use a differentiation strategy. For example, Washington Mutual Inc. has grown rapidly in the consumer banking industry by using a differentiation strategy. When the company moved into Chicago, it opened 28 branches on a single day, flooded the market with quirky advertising, and sent out employees with pizza delivery people, offering prospective customers "free pizza from the home of free banking."[84] The Harleysville Group uses its corporate culture to differentiate itself in the insurance industry as described below.

Harleysville Group

The Harleysville Group is not your average, run-of-the-mill insurance company, and employees as well as customers know it. At Harleysville, managers strive to provide their employees with an appealing atmosphere and plenty of perks. The goal is to create a work environment that makes people want to stay. The managers must be doing things right, because the Harleysville Group boasts a 95 percent retention rate over the past several years. That translates into experienced, knowledgeable employees who can provide top-quality service. Customers who have grown tired of working with companies where the staff is constantly changing can appreciate the difference that comes from working with people who are happy and knowledgeable.

Harleysville does plenty to keep employees happy. Besides an impressive vacation plan, extensive medical benefits, a cafeteria that serves freshly made food, and snack carts that go about the building selling coffee and pastries, the company provides on-site ATMs and a clothes-cleaning service that includes pickup and delivery. A massage therapist comes in once a week, and employees pay $10 for a 15-minute session, which is often below the market rate. The CEO pays for a 15-minute session each week and often gives it away to an employee as a way to say thanks for some extra effort. Two other, highly important perks are the company's project bonuses and matching 401(k) investments. The company often hands out checks for $1,500 or $2,000 to reward people for excellent work on a team project. For the 401(k) plan, Harleysville will match an employee's contribution anywhere from 25 percent to 100 percent, depending on company performance. In the last four years, the

CONCEPT CONNECTION

The MINI's trademarked term "Whiptastic Handling" is one of the ways the company distinguishes itself in the automobile industry. MINI, a division of BMW of North America, is thriving with its **differentiation** strategy. The company trademarked the Whiptastic name to emphasize that driving a MINI Cooper is unlike anything else. Customers seem to agree; sales are zooming.

© China Photos/Getty Images

Strategy	Organizational Characteristics
Differentiation	Acts in a flexible, loosely knit way, with strong coordination among departments
	Strong capability in basic research
	Creative flair, thinks "out of the box"
	Strong marketing abilities
	Rewards employee innovation
	Corporate reputation for quality or technological leadership
Cost Leadership	Strong central authority; tight cost controls
	Maintains standard operating procedures
	Easy-to-use manufacturing technologies
	Highly efficient procurement and distribution systems
	Close supervision; finite employee empowerment
	Frequent, detailed control reports
Focus	May use combination of above policies directed at particular strategic target
	Values and rewards flexibility and customer intimacy
	Measures cost of providing service and maintaining customer loyalty
	Pushes empowerment to employees with customer contact

EXHIBIT 5.12

Organizational Characteristics of Porter's Competitive Strategies

SOURCE: Based on Michael E. Porter, *Competitive Strategy: Techniques for Analyzing Industries and Competitors* (New York: The Free Press, 1980); Michael Treacy and Fred Wiersema, "How Market Leaders Keep Their Edge," *Fortune*, February 6, 1995, 88–89; and Michael A. Hitt, R. Duane Ireland, and Robert E. Hoskisson, *Strategic Management* (St. Paul, Minn.: West, 1995), 100–113.

company has matched contributions on a one-to-one ratio. For example, if an employee put in $5,000, the company would add that amount.

Other perks are aimed at increasing employees' knowledge and career skills. Techno-savvy workers are critical to the Harleysville Group, so the company spends more than $600,000 every year in technical training for the IS department alone. And that does not include the corporate funding for employees who are taking college courses and working toward higher degrees. To make it easier, the company brings community college professors to the company campus so employees can take some courses without having to travel at the end of their work day.

Harleysville refuses to pay high salaries, but the extensive benefits and the people-friendly work environment help the company stand out in the insurance industry. Inevitably, some employees do leave, but it usually is not for a $5,000 raise, notes CEO Wayne Ratz. "It's more for an extravagant opportunity or for a lifestyle change."[83]

Companies that pursue a differentiation strategy typically need strong marketing abilities, a creative flair, and a reputation for leadership.[86] A differentiation strategy can reduce rivalry with competitors if buyers are loyal to a company's brand. Successful differentiation can reduce the bargaining power of large buyers because other products are less attractive, and this helps the firm fight off threats of substitute products. In addition, differentiation erects entry barriers in the form of customer loyalty that a new entrant into the market would have difficulty overcoming. Consider the example of eBay, described earlier in the chapter. Rather than cutting prices when Amazon.com and other rivals entered the online auction business, eBay focused on building a distinctive community, offering customers services and experiences they could not get on other sites. Customers stayed loyal to eBay rather than switch to low-cost rivals.

2. With a **cost leadership strategy**, the organization aggressively seeks efficient facilities, pursues cost reductions, and uses tight cost controls to produce products more efficiently than competitors. A low-cost position means that the company can undercut competitors' prices and still offer comparable quality and earn a reasonable profit. Comfort Inn and Motel 6 are low-priced alternatives to Holiday Inn and Ramada Inn. Enterprise Rent-a-Car is a low-priced alternative to Hertz.

cost leadership strategy

Aggressively seeking efficient facilities, pursues cost reductions, and uses tight cost controls to produce products more efficiently than competitors.

Take *ACTION*

To succeed, try to really differentiate your product, or else have competitive prices.

Being a low-cost producer provides a successful strategy to defend against the five competitive forces in Exhibit 5.11. For example, the most efficient, low-cost company is in the best position to succeed in a price war while still making a profit. Low-cost leader Dell Computers declared a brutal price war just as the PC industry entered its worst slump ever. The result? Dell racked up $361 million in profits while the rest of the industry reported losses of $1.1 billion. Likewise, the low-cost producer is protected from powerful customers and suppliers because customers cannot find lower prices elsewhere, and other buyers would have less slack for price negotiation with suppliers. If substitute products or potential new entrants occur, the low-cost producer is better positioned than higher-cost rivals to prevent loss of market share. The low price acts as a barrier against new entrants and substitute products.[87]

focus strategy

Concentrating on a specific regional market or buyer group. The company will use a differentiation or low-cost approach, but only for a narrow target market.

3. *Focus.* With a **focus strategy**, the organization concentrates on a specific regional market or buyer group. The company will use a differentiation or low-cost approach, but only for a narrow target market. Low-cost leader Southwest Airlines, for example, was founded in 1971 to serve only three cities—Dallas, Houston, and San Antonio—and did not fly outside of Texas for the first eight years of its history. Managers aimed for controlled growth, gradually moving into new geographic areas where Southwest could provide short-haul service from city to city. By using a focus strategy, Southwest was able to grow rapidly and expand to other markets. It is now second only to Delta Airlines in domestic passenger share though it continues to operate primarily as a short-haul carrier.[88] Edward Jones Investments, a St. Louis-based brokerage house, uses a focused differentiation strategy, building its business in rural and small-town America and providing clients with conservative, long-term investment advice. According to management consultant Peter Drucker, the safety-first orientation means Edward Jones delivers a product "that no Wall Street house has ever sold before: peace of mind."[89]

Managers consider which strategy will provide their company with its competitive advantage. Gibson Guitar Corp., famous in the music world for its innovative, high-quality products, found that switching to a low-cost strategy to compete against Japanese rivals such as Yamaha and Ibanez hurt the company. When managers realized people wanted Gibson products because of their reputation, not their price, they went back to a differentiation strategy and invested in new technology and marketing.[90] In his studies, Porter found that some businesses did not consciously adopt one of these three strategies and were stuck with no strategic advantage. Without a strategic advantage, businesses earned below-average profits compared with those that used differentiation, cost leadership, or focus strategies. Similarly, a recent five-year study of management practices in hundreds of businesses, referred to as the *Evergreen Project,* found that a clear strategic direction was a key factor that distinguished winners from losers.[91]

In addition, because the Internet is having such a profound impact on the competitive environment in all industries, it is more important than ever that companies distinguish themselves through careful strategic positioning in the marketplace.[92] The Internet tends to erode cost leadership and differentiation advantages by providing new tools for managing costs and giving consumers greater access to comparison shopping. However, managers can find ways to incorporate the Internet into their strategic approaches in a way that provides unique value to customers in an efficient way. Sears Roebuck, for example, uses the Web to showcase its line of Kenmore appliances, building the brand's reputation by providing detailed information in an inexpensive way. [93]

Partnership Strategies

So far, we have been discussing strategies that are based on how to compete with other companies. An alternative approach to strategy emphasizes collaboration. In some situations, companies can achieve competitive advantage by cooperating with other firms rather than competing. Partnership strategies are becoming increasingly popular as firms in all industries join with other organizations to promote innovation, expand markets, and pursue joint goals. Partnering was once a strategy adopted primarily by small firms that needed greater marketing muscle or international access. Today, however, it has become a way of life for most large and small companies. The question is no longer whether to collaborate, but rather where, how much, and with whom.[94] Competition and cooperation often exist at the same time. Time Warner Cable, for instance, abruptly dropped Disney's ABC network in several major cities because of a dispute over fees for the Disney Channel. The companies engaged in all-out war that included front-page headlines and intervention of the Federal Communications Commission (FCC). This conflict, however, masked a simple fact: The two companies could not live without each other. Disney and Time Warner are wedded to one another in separate business deals around the world. Disney's ABC network, for example, is a major buyer of shows produced by Warner Brothers, while Time Warner's WB network carries Disney-produced programs. The two organizations will never let competition in one area upset their larger cooperation on a global scale.[95] As an additional example, consider producer Michael London who was careful about whom he partners with on movies as described in the Focus on Skills box.

The Internet is driving and supporting the move toward partnership thinking. The rapid and smooth ability to conduct transactions, communicate information, exchange ideas, and collaborate on complex projects via the Internet means that companies such as Citigroup, Dow Chemical, and Herman Miller have been able to enter new businesses by partnering in unimaginable business areas.[96] Many companies, including Target, Circuit City, Land's End, and Golfsmith International, are gaining a stronger online presence by partnering with Amazon.com. Amazon.com maintains the site and processes orders, while the retailers fill the orders from their own warehouses. The arrangement gives Amazon.com a new source of revenue and frees the retailers to focus on their bricks-and-mortar business while gaining new customers online.[97]

Mutual dependencies and partnerships have become a fact of life, but the degree of collaboration varies. Organizations can choose to build cooperative relationships in many ways, such as through preferred suppliers, strategic business partnering, joint ventures, or mergers and acquisitions. Exhibit 5.13 illustrates these major types of strategic business relationships according to the degree of collaboration involved. With preferred supplier relationships, a company such as Wal-Mart, for example, develops a special relationship with a key supplier such as Procter & Gamble that eliminates

---

FOCUS ON SKILLS

Do Not Bend Sideways

Michael London produced *House of Sand and Fog*, *Thirteen*, and *Sideways*. Because producers are like contractors who hire electricians, plumbers and carpenters, they need to know a little about a lot of things. So, he looks for people with the requisite skills and for those who share values and vision and care about similar things. And a crucial element is balancing needs of financing with creative vision.

When working on *Sideways*, London got offers from big studios, but he turned them down because he was afraid they would throw so much money at the project, and if it did not make money right away, they would become nervous. Fox Searchlight, though, knew it was not as much about

aggressive marketing as it was about being agile, clever and patient.

They had a lot of battles over casting. The three leads, Paul Giamatti, Thomas Hayden Church, and Virginia Madsen, were not considered likely candidates. But the director saw them as perfect for the roles. London had to give the bad news to agents, studio execs, and investors who wanted other choices. "In this business," he said, "There are so many moments when you're tempted to make compromises or take on projects that don't mean much to you." His learned his lesson: Follow your instincts and do not bend to others' notions.

SOURCE: Michael London, "Refusing to Bend Sideways," *Fast Company* (March 2005): 41.

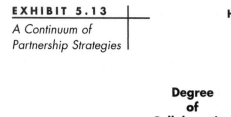

EXHIBIT 5.13

A Continuum of Partnership Strategies

SOURCE: Adapted from Roberta Maynard, "Striking the Right Match," *Nation's Business* (May 1996), 18–28.

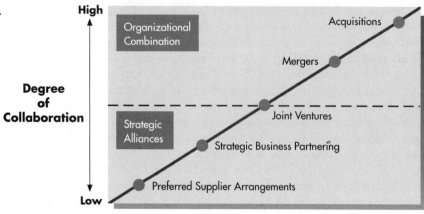

middlemen by sharing complete information and reducing the costs of salespeople and distributors. Preferred supplier arrangements provide long-term security for both organizations, but the level of collaboration is low. Strategic business partnering requires a higher level of collaboration. Five of the largest hotel chains—Marriott International, Hilton Hotels Corp., Six Continents, Hyatt Corp., and Starwood Hotels and Resorts Worldwide Inc.—have partnered to create their own Web site, Travelweb.com, to combat the growing power of middlemen such as Expedia.com and Hotels.com. According to one senior vice president, the hotels felt a need to "take back our room product, and...sell it the way we want to sell it and maximize our revenues." At the same time, some chains are building more beneficial partnerships with the third-party brokers.[98]

A still higher degree of collaboration is reflected in joint ventures, which are separate entities created with two or more active firms as sponsors. For example, MTV Networks was originally created as a joint venture of Warner Communications and American Express Company in the late 1970s. In a joint venture, organizations share the risks and costs associated with the new venture. It is estimated that the rate of joint venture formation between U.S. and international companies has been growing by 27 percent annually since 1985.[99]

Mergers and acquisitions represent the ultimate step in collaborative relationships. U.S. business has been in the midst of a tremendous merger and acquisition boom. IBM acquired PricewaterhouseCoopers Consulting, the U.S. pharmaceuticals company Upjohn merged with Sweden's Pharmacia, Cingular acquired AT&T Wireless, Comcast Corp. bought AT&T's Broadband division, Norwest merged with Wells Fargo, and Yahoo! Inc. is buying France's comparison shopping service Kelkoo SA.

Using these various partnership strategies, today's companies embrace competition and cooperation. Few companies can go it alone under a constant onslaught of international competition, changing technology, and new regulations. Consider how Motorola's approach to strategy has changed in today's turbulent environment.

Motorola

Motorola's $8 billion business in semiconductor products shriveled to less than $5 billion in less than a year when a combination of new competition, new technologies, and shifting market conditions totally transformed the industry. Revenues dropped 37 percent overnight. Rather than taking a standard response by cutting costs, laying off workers, and tinkering with operational details, Motorola managers decided to take a new approach to strategy.

Motorola has always been highly competitive and determined to go it alone, but the new environment demanded a strategy that relies more on partnership. Every few years, engineers figure out how to build bigger silicon wafers that will yield more chips, lowering the per-chip cost. Managers realized that to build a new factory capable of producing the current 12-inch wafer would cost at least $2.5 billion, and it would have to operate at near-maximum capacity to justify the investment. Motorola's output was too small to make that approach feasible. At the same time, big-wafer factories that have sprung up in China, Singapore, and Taiwan enjoy tremendous advantages because of lower labor costs and government support. These factories produce chips for anyone with a design, lowering the traditional barriers to entry for small semiconductor makers.

Faced with these facts, Motorola changed the strategy for how it does business. Only a few years ago, Motorola felt that it had to own all its manufacturing facilities and hoard its technology. The new strategy is: "If we don't have to own it, let's not own it. And if we do have to own it, let's reduce the risk by sharing it." By 2003, Motorola's 18 wafer-making facilities had been reduced to eight. Thirty percent of its chip revenue came from products made, tested, or assembled by contractors such as Taiwan Semiconductor Manufacturing. The company is collaborating in a joint venture with Philips and STMicroelectronics on new semiconductor designs and processes.

Another strategic shift is that Motorola no longer keeps all its own technology secret for use only in the company's own cell phones. Today, Motorola licenses its technology to partners around the world. As of 2003, ten phone makers had taken advantage of the new partnerships. Motorola executives know they are enabling smaller competitors to get into the business faster, but they know that if they do not do it, someone else will. They believe that in the current business environment, collaboration is the only strategy to help the organization survive and thrive.[100]

Motorola managers realized the company could no longer compete in the way it always had. Faced with a radically new environment, they created a new approach to strategy that emphasizes partnership and sharing rather than independence and proprietary technology. Today, most businesses choose a combination of competitive and partnership strategies that add to their overall sustainable advantage.[101]

Strategy Implementation and Control

The final step in the strategic management process is implementation or how strategy is put into action. Some people argue that strategy implementation is the most difficult and important part of strategic management.[102] No matter how creative the formulated strategy, the organization will not benefit if the strategy is not skillfully implemented. In today's competitive environment, there is an increasing recognition of the need for more dynamic approaches to implementing strategies.[103] Strategy is not a static, analytical process; it requires vision, intuition, and employee participation. Many organizations are abandoning central planning departments, and strategy is becoming an everyday part of the job for workers at all levels. Strategy implementation involves using several tools—parts of the firm that can be adjusted to put strategy into action—as illustrated in Exhibit 5.14. Once a new strategy is selected, it is implemented through changes in leadership, structure, information and control systems, and human resources.[104] For strategy to be implemented, all aspects of the organization need to be in congruence with the strategy. Implementation involves regularly making difficult decisions about doing things in a way that supports rather than undermines the organization's chosen strategy. Remaining chapters of this book examine in detail topics such as leadership, organizational structure, information and control systems, and human resource management.

Leadership

The primary key to strategy implementation is leadership. Leadership is the ability to influence people to adopt the new behaviors needed for strategy implementation. An important part of implementing strategy is building consensus. People throughout the organization must believe in the new strategy and have a strong commitment to achieving

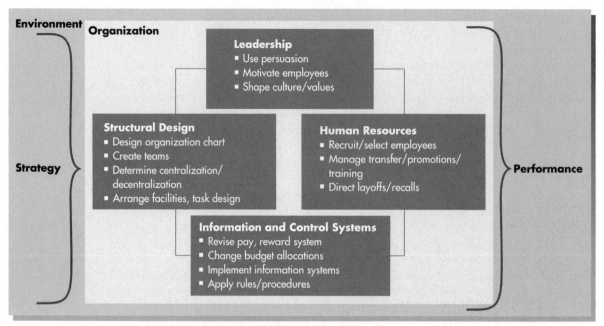

SOURCE: Adapted from Jay R. Galbraith and Robert K. Kazanjian, *Strategy Implementation: Structure, Systems, and Process,* 2d ed. (St. Paul, Minn.: West, 1986), 115. Used with permission.

EXHIBIT 5.14

Tools for Putting Strategy into Action

Take *ACTION*

Use consensus and persuasion to build support for your strategy.

the vision and goals. Leadership means using persuasion, motivating employees, and shaping culture and values to support the new strategy. Managers can make speeches to employees, build coalitions of people who support the new strategic direction, and persuade middle managers to go along with their vision for the company. At IBM, for example, CEO Sam Palmisano is using leadership to get people throughout the organization aligned with the new e-business on demand strategy. He dismantled the executive committee that previously presided over strategic initiatives and replaced it with committees made up of people from all over the company who have a voice in strategy formulation and implementation. He is investing tons of money to teach managers at all levels how to lead rather than control their staff. And he is talking to people all over the company, appealing to their sense of pride and getting them fired up about making IBM great once more by uniting behind the on-demand vision.[105] With a clear sense of direction and a shared purpose, employees feel motivated, challenged, and empowered to pursue new strategic goals. Another way leaders build consensus and commitment is through broad participation. When people participate in strategy formulation, implementation is easier because managers and employees understand the reasons for the new strategy and feel more committed to it.

Human Resources

The organization's human resources are its employees. The human resource function recruits, selects, trains, transfers, promotes, and lays off employees to achieve strategic goals. For example, training employees can help them understand the purpose and importance of a strategy or help them develop the skills and behaviors. New strategies involve change, which naturally generates some resistance. Sometimes employees may have to be let go and replaced. One newspaper shifted its strategy from an evening to a morning paper to compete with a large newspaper from a nearby city. The new strategy required a change from working days to working from 1 P.M. to about midnight or so, fostering resentment and resistance among department heads. To implement it, 80 percent of the department heads had to be let go because they refused to cooperate. New people were recruited and placed in those positions, and the morning newspaper strategy was a resounding success.[106]

Implementation During Turbulent Times

The challenges of implementing strategy have escalated with the increased complexity and turbulence in today's business environment. Many managers feel confident that they have found the right strategy to provide a competitive advantage, but they are less optimistic about their ability to implement it. Three issues that are particularly critical for implementing strategy during turbulent times are adopting a global mindset, paying attention to corporate culture, and embracing the Internet and other information technologies.

Global Mindset. To implement strategies on a global scale, managers need to adopt a global mindset and be aware of implementation issues. Flexibility and openness emerge as mandatory leadership skills. Structural issues are more complex, as managers struggle to find the right mix to achieve the desired level of global integration and local responsiveness, as discussed earlier. Information, control, and reward systems have to fit the values and incentives within the local cultures. Finally, the recruitment, training, transfer, promotion, and layoff of international human resources create an array of problems not confronted in North America. To be effective internationally, managers have to apply a global perspective to strategy implementation. For example, one well-respected multinational corporation (MNC) formed a task force of U.S. employees to review and revise workforce policies in connection with a new strategy. Employees from different levels and functional areas met for months and sent out employee surveys to all U.S.-based facilities to get wider input. The final draft was reviewed and approved by top executives. They were surprised when the streamlined workforce manual, which reduced the number of policies from 120 to 10 core ones, was met with resistance and hostility by the overseas units. Managers lack of a global mindset had led them to assume incorrectly that the international units would accept whatever was handed down from the U.S. headquarters. Another MNC that used a worldwide task force for a similar process had much greater success with implementation.[107]

Corporate Culture. In addition to a global mindset, managers have to create and maintain a cohesive corporate culture that supports strategy. Culture is the link between strategy and performance outcomes, and different culture styles are better suited to different strategic directions.[108] Recall our discussion of different types of culture and the high-performance culture from Chapter 2. A study of the world's most admired companies, as reported annually in *Fortune* magazine, found that managers in these organizations pay close attention to culture and to the values that contribute to strategic success.[109] Managers want to develop a culture that is oriented toward performance, encourages the behaviors and attitudes needed to meet the company's strategic goals, and holds everyone responsible for success.[110] One big problem Boeing has had in recent years is a shift in cultural values that has hampered the company from implementing its strategy. CEO Philip Condit, who resigned abruptly under complaints of mismanagement and allegations of improper conduct, failed to pay attention to the culture Boeing needed to retain its position as a technology leader. As the culture grew weaker under Condit's leadership, Boeing fell behind in technology and efficiency, enabling European rival Airbus to take the lead, delivering more new planes than Boeing for the first time in 2003.[111]

Internet and Information Technology. A final concern for managers implementing strategy during turbulent times is to incorporate the Internet and other information technology. Dell Computers pioneered the use of an online system to let customers configure computers to their exact specifications and submit the order over the Web, saving the cost of salespeople. Many firms use online mass customization to decrease costs, enhance their product mix, and build their brand reputation.[112] Another company that successfully uses the Internet to implement strategy is retailer Target, which uses its Web site (Target.com) to sell items not available in stores, keep in touch with customer needs, and target customers with coupons that lure them into retail stores.[113] Target's Web strategy was discussed in more detail in Chapter 2's Focus on Leadership box.

Manager's Solution

This chapter focused on organizational planning. Organizational planning involves defining goals and developing a plan with which to achieve them. An organization exists for a single, overriding purpose, which is its mission: the basis for strategic goals and plans. Goals within the organization are defined in a hierarchical fashion, beginning with strategic goals followed by tactical and operational goals. Plans are defined similarly, with strategic, tactical, and operational plans used to achieve the goals. Other goal concepts include characteristics of effective goals and goal-setting behavior.

Several types of plans were described, including strategic, tactical, operational, single-use, standing, and contingency plans, as well as management by objectives. Two extensions of contingency planning are scenario building and crisis management planning. Scenarios are alternative vivid pictures of what the future might be like. They provide a framework for managers to cope with unexpected or unpredictable events. Crisis management planning involves the stages of prevention, preparation, and containment.

This chapter described important concepts of strategic management. Strategic management begins with an evaluation of the organization's current mission, goals, and strategy. This evaluation is followed by situation analysis (called SWOT analysis), which examines strengths and weaknesses within the organization as well as opportunities and threats in the external environment. Situation analysis leads to the formulation of explicit strategies, which indicate how the company intends to achieve a competitive advantage. Managers formulate strategies that focus on core competencies, develop synergy, and create value.

Even the most creative strategies have no value if they cannot be translated into action. Implementation is the most important and difficult part of strategy. Managers implement strategy by aligning all parts of the organization to be in congruence with the new strategy. Four areas that managers focus on for strategy implementation are leadership, structural design, information and control systems, and human resources. Three additional issues for managers in today's turbulent and complex environment are adopting a global mindset, paying attention to corporate culture, and embracing use of the Internet and information technology.

Returning to the opening problem at Nintendo, CEO and president Satoru Iwata is still evaluating strengths, weaknesses, opportunities, and threats to see how Nintendo should position itself for the future. In the short term, a functional level strategy of enhanced advertising and price cuts helped Nintendo increase its sales during the critical holiday sales period. Sony and Xbox took a big hit from Nintendo's price cuts by failing to do enough marketing. In addition, Nintendo plans to bring out its next generation console ahead of Sony's and Microsoft's, giving the company a competitive edge. For the long range, Iwata is sticking to a focused differentiation strategy rather than competing as an all-in-one entertainment company. His strategy calls for focusing all the company's energies on building great games, but his new mantra is "5-year-olds to 95-year-olds." To build a wider customer base, Iwata is investing heavily in internal game development, building a new R&D facility, and adding 50 new developers to design entertainment for all ages. He is working hard to mend fences with third-party game publishers and partner with them on game design, something unheard of in Nintendo's past. The new inclination toward partnership may be carried further if Iwata decides his company cannot survive on games alone. He has hinted that he would not mind making Nintendo's technology available for incorporating into other kinds of hardware, perhaps building a joint venture with a major electronics power such as Panasonic, which already sells a device that combines a DVD player with a Nintendo GameCube. Some observers believe such a move is the best approach for the ailing company, but Iwata still believes that if Nintendo builds great games, it can thrive as a niche player in the entertainment industry. There is also a possibility that the all-in-one strategies of Sony and Microsoft will backfire, leading to higher prices that consumers are not willing to pay.[114]

Discussion Questions

1. If you were either Attorney General or head of INS (Immigration and Naturalization Service), what type of planning would you have used to help respond in the Elían Gonzales case?

2. Write a brief mission statement for a local business. Try to capture the purpose and values of a small organization in a written statement.

3. What strategies could the college or university at which you are taking this management course adopt to compete for students in the marketplace? Would these strategies depend on the school's goals?

4. If you were a top manager of a small real estate sales agency, how would you use MBO? Give examples of goals you might set for managers and sales agents.

5. A new business venture has to develop a comprehensive business plan to borrow money to get started. Companies such as Federal Express, Nike, and Rolm Corporation say they did not follow the original plan very closely. Does that mean that developing the plan was a waste of time for these eventually successful companies?

6. A famous management theorist proposed that the time horizons for all strategic plans are becoming shorter because of the rapid changes in the external environments of organizations. Do you agree? Would the planning time horizon for IBM or Ford Motor Company be shorter than it was 20 years ago?

7. What are the characteristics of effective goals? Is it better to have no goals at all or goals that do not meet these criteria?

8. Assume Southern University decides to raise its admission standards and initiate a business fair to which local townspeople will be invited. What types of plans would it use to carry out these two activities?

9. Assume you are the general manager of a local hotel and have formulated a strategy of renting banquet facilities to corporations for big events. At a monthly management meeting, your sales manager informs the head of food operations that a big reception in one week will require converting a large hall from a meeting room to a banquet facility in only 60 minutes—a difficult, but doable operation that will require precise planning and extra help. The food operations manager is furious about not being informed earlier. What is wrong here?

10. Perform a situation (SWOT) analysis for the university you attend. Do you think university administrators consider these factors when devising their strategy?

11. What is meant by the core competence and synergy components of strategy? Give examples.

12. Using Porter's competitive strategies, how would you describe the strategies of Wal-Mart, Bloomingdale's, and Kmart? Do any of these companies also use cooperative strategies? Discuss.

Manager's Workbook

Goal Setting

Consider goals for yourself regarding doing well in this course. What do you need to do in order to get a good grade? Goals should be according to the "Criteria for Effective Goals" in the chapter on pp. 166–167. In addition, you need a system to monitor your progress, such as the following table, which shows the types of goals you may choose to select for yourself.

GOALS		CLASS WEEKS		
	First week (from now)	Second week	Third week	Fourth week
1. 100 percent attendance				
2. Class notes				
3. Read assigned chapters				
4. Outline chapters				
5. Define vocabulary words				
6. Answer end of chapter questions				
7. Complete "Workbook" assignments				
8. Class participation				
9.				
10.				

Your instructor may ask you to turn in your monitor sheets at the end of the course.

1. According to goal-setting theory, using and monitoring goals is supposed to help performance. Did you do better as a result of your goals?

2. What did you learn from this that could help you in other classes?

Copyright 1996 by Dorothy Marcic. SOURCE: Nancy C. Morey, "Applying goal setting in the classroom," *The Organizational Behavior Teaching Review*, Vol. 11 (4), 1986–87, pp. 53–59.

Manager's Workshop

Outcome Designed Problem Solving

A. Think of a problem you are currently trying to solve. Consider either your work or personal life. Answer the following questions to yourself and then in groups of four to six members (have an even number of people in each group):

1. What's the reason this is a problem?

2. What caused the problem?

3. Who or what can be blamed?

4. What are the blocks keeping me from solving this problem?

5. What is the likelihood that I can solve the problem?

B. Now consider the same problem, but do as the instructions indicate below.

Divide your group into teams of two. With your partner, take turns being the manager and the employee with the problem. The manager asks the employee the following questions:

1. What would you rather have than this problem? Come up with a desired outcome.

2. How will you know when you have reached your desired outcome? List examples of what you would see, measure, hear, etc.

3. What advantage would this outcome be for you? What could you lose? Is it worth the risk?

4. Explain what the first step would be to work toward your outcome. Now, as a class, discuss the differences in the two different problem-solving approaches.

Bob Bostrom reports that when groups do the problem-based discussions, they become deenergized and even depressed. But when groups engage in the outcome-based discussions, enthusiasm and positive attitudes prevail, increasing the likelihood of an enduring solution being achieved.

Management in Practice: Ethical Dilemma

Repair or Replace?

After only a few months in sales at ComputerSource, a full-service computer business, Sam Nolan realized there were serious problems in the software department. Most of the complaints from customers were related to the incorrect selection or installation of the software needed to meet their needs. He discussed the problem with his sales manager, who was part owner and partner with the head of service for ComputerSource. They both were aware of the problem, but they were facing an industrywide shortage of qualified software engineers.

Nolan received an urgent call from Katherine Perry, operations manager for Ross & Lindsey, a fast-growing financial management firm that was becoming one of his best accounts. She was calling to report that they were having daily network problems that were interfering with her staff's productivity and morale. She needed an immediate solution to the problem. Like many firms, Ross & Lindsey had a hodgepodge of computer equipment and software on their network. They had bought from a series of vendors, with a patchwork approach to problems.

Nolan realized it would take an expert software engineer days or weeks of work to fix all the bugs in their existing system, which ComputerSource could not afford. A costlier alternative was to recommend a system upgrade, replacing the older hardware and loading a newer software version on the entire network. Perry had already confided that she had pushed her bosses as far as they wanted to go on computer expenditures this year, but Nolan knew she was desperate. He didn't want to risk losing her business, but he didn't trust the software engineers to fix the problems. He was also pretty sure Perry would face the same dilemma at any computer retailer in town.

What Do You Do?

1. Gamble on the service department to fix their existing system, within the limits of their budget and their frustration. If it doesn't work, it is their problem.
2. Recommend a system upgrade to correct the problem, even though it will cost the clients more than they want to pay and may jeopardize future sales.
3. Confide in the clients about your perception of the problem, give them the chance to make an informed choice, and risk having them take their business elsewhere.

Case for Critical Analysis

Starbucks Coffee

Beginning with nine Seattle stores in 1987, Starbucks CEO Howard Schultz has exported the company's chic cafes throughout the country. Service is anything but fast, and the price of a cup of coffee could make the Dunkin' Donuts crowd faint, but each week almost two million Americans hit Starbucks to sip skinny lattes or no-whip mochas.

Despite a slowdown in sales from established stores, Starbucks is pursuing rapid expansion. It made its first acquisition in 1994, buying The Coffee Connection Inc., a 23-store Boston rival. With more than 400 stores in place, Schultz plans to open 200 more within a year and has announced plans to team up with foreign partners to open stores in Asia and Europe. In addition, Starbucks has entered into a venture with PepsiCo to develop a new bottled coffee drink. Schultz's strategies are risky, but some analysts think Starbucks has the flexibility and management strength to succeed.

Many managers at Starbucks have years of experience from such companies as Burger King, Taco Bell, Wendy's, and Blockbuster. Schultz believes a CEO should "hire people smarter than you are and get out of their way." Equally crucial to the success of Starbucks are the "baristas" who prepare coffee drinks. Starbucks recruits its workers from colleges and community groups and gives them 24 hours of training in coffee making and lore—a key to creating the company's hip image and quality service. To maintain quality control, Starbucks roasts all its coffee in-house. The company also has turned down lucrative alternatives such as franchising and supermarket distribution.

A computer network links the expanding Starbucks empire, and Schultz hired a top information-technology specialist from McDonald's to design a point-of-sale system to enable managers to track sales. Every night, computers from all 400-plus stores send information to headquarters in Seattle so that executives can spot regional buying trends.

For Schultz, a man who has already changed America's coffee-drinking habits, the risks Starbucks is taking are just another challenge.

Questions

1. Which of Porter's competitive strategies is Starbucks using?

2. Discuss how Schultz is using leadership, structure, information and control systems, and human resources to implement strategy at Starbucks.

3. What challenges may Schultz face in trying to expand Starbucks internationally?

SOURCES: Dori Jones Yang, "The Starbucks Enterprise Shifts into Warp Speed," *Business Week*, October 24, 1994, p. 76; and Michael Treacy, "You Need a Value Discipline—But Which One?" *Fortune*, April 17, 1995, p. 195.

CHAPTER 6

Managerial Decision Making and Information Technology

CHAPTER OUTLINE

LEARNING OBJECTIVES

After studying this chapter, you should be able to do the following:

1. **Explain why decision making is an important component of good management.**

2. **Explain the difference between programmed and nonprogrammed decisions and the decision characteristics of risk, uncertainty, and ambiguity.**

3. **Describe the classical, administrative, and political models of decision making and their applications.**

4. **Identify the six steps used in managerial decision making.**

5. **Explain four personal decision styles used by managers.**

6. **Discuss the advantages and disadvantages of participative decision making.**

7. **Identify techniques for improving decision making in today's turbulent environment.**

8. **Describe the importance of information technology (IT) for organizations and the attributes of quality information.**

Robert Michael MacDonald and Robert Garff were partners in the Bountiful (Utah) Mazda franchise for six years before they sold the dealership to the Utah Auto Collection. But when the Auto Collection broke apart in January 2002, MacDonald decided he wanted his old dealership back. Now, he could not be happier than he is running the Bountiful Mazda franchise in partnership with his brother and wife. But the car-selling business has changed a lot since 1998. Today, Web-savvy buyers are causing dealers a lot of headaches. More than half of all customers have been bargain hunting online before they ever step foot on the car lot. They show up carrying their quotes like a shield against high sales prices. Salespeople dread to see them coming because they realize the customer has the upper hand, equipped with information on dealer invoice value, average retail price, and other data. These customers are frustrated by annoying and time-consuming questions about budget and transportation needs, where the sales staff tries to gauge how likely they are to buy and how much they are willing to pay. All these customers want is to test drive the vehicle and seal the deal at the price they want. MacDonald knows that Mazda is offering seed money and financing for a revamp of its dealerships. He wonders if there is a way to include information technology (IT) to please and profit from the new breed of Web-savvy customer.[1]

If you were Michael MacDonald and Mazda, what advice would you give them about turning the Internet's power to their advantage? How can IT be used to increase dealership effectiveness and improve customer relationships?

Almost every company has problems with information systems, and we will discuss this later in the chapter. Mazda's customer relations issues are common, and other companies are enduring similar challenges. After suffering through a 15-year slide, sales of Tupperware shot up in the early 2000s, helped along by management decisions to set up booths in shopping malls and push sales over the Internet in addition to the traditional Tupperware parties. The icon of 1950s suburban America looked poised to keep growing, winning over a whole new generation to its unique food storage products and kitchen gadgets. Overseas, in places such as China, Indonesia, and India, sales were booming. Managers knew, though, that Tupperware was facing some stiff competition from companies that were coming out with products that promised to do the same job at lower prices. To fight back, it decided to supplement home parties—the source of 90 percent of Tupperware's U.S. revenues—by placing Tupperware products in Target stores and recruiting volunteer salespeople to demonstrate the merchandise. It seemed to solve the vexing problem of how to sell products face-to-face in an age when people have little time and patience for a home sales pitch. But the decision turned out to be a disaster. Some Target stores and shoppers did not know how to deal with the influx of Tupperware salespeople, who ended up feeling slighted. Many salespeople stopped volunteering for store duty. Others—some with great sales records—quit Tupperware entirely. Interest in home parties dwindled, decreasing sales and cutting down on opportunities for recruiting new salespeople. Tupperware's sales in North America fell to a three-year low and profits plummeted 47 percent.[2]

At Tupperware, feedback and evaluation revealed that the decision to sell Tupperware in Target stores was a failure, so a new decision cycle has begun. Problem recognition was easy: Sales and profits have been on a downhill slide. In diagnosing the causes, managers determined that the shift in how the company does business has left salespeople feeling slighted. Their earnings have decreased because of dwindling parties and recruiting opportunities, further damaging morale and motivation. Some of the highest performers have left. In addition, the image of Tupperware as stuck in the 1950s has not helped lure modern women who could help the company rebound. Managers have considered alternatives and are implementing three of their choices. One decision was to update the product line to stay ahead of new competitors, such as adding a new Chef Series line of stainless steel pans and knives. Managers are reinventing the Tupperware party, making it a more sophisticated social event where guests can drink wine and sample easy-to-make dishes prepared with Tupperware gadgets and served straight out of Tupperware pans and bowls. The company plans to implement a new compensation structure that will enable Tupperware salespeople to earn more, which managers hope will lure back some of their lost salespeople as well as appeal to new ones. Managers will gather information to see how well these new decisions are implemented and if they are successful. So far, limited feedback indicates that the updated "Taste of Tupperware" party is effective. When people try various gadgets, they tend to buy more. The new format is now ready to roll out across the United States with celebrity chefs doing demonstrations in various venues.[3]

The story of Tupperware illustrates how difficult decision making can be. Top executives at Tupperware have made many good decisions over the years, helping the company maintain its clout despite changing times. When the company hit a tough spot in the 1980s, for example, it regained its footing by creating "Rush Hour" and "Office" parties to reach increasingly busy women. The decision to sell through mall kiosks and the Internet has paid off. However, the rapid push into retail stores was a failure, and Tupperware pulled its products from Target shelves within a year. Managers now face some difficult decisions that will affect the future of their business. Every organization grows, prospers, or fails as a result of decisions by its managers.

Managers often are referred to as decision makers. Though many of their important decisions are strategic, managers make decisions about every other aspect of an organization, including structure, control systems, responses to the environment, and human resources. Managers scout for problems, decide how to solve them, and monitor the consequences to see if additional decisions are required. Good decision making is a vital part of good management because decisions determine how the organization solves its problems, allocates resources, and accomplishes its goals.

The business world is full of evidence of good and bad decisions. For example, Nokia became a $10 billion leader in the cell phone industry because managers at the company decided to sell off unrelated businesses such as paper, tires, and aluminum and concentrate the company's resources on electronics.[4] Cadillac managers ditched stuffy golf and yachting sponsorships and instead tied in with Hollywood movies such as *The Matrix: Reloaded* and *Bad Boys II*. The decision boosted sales by 43 percent, and the brand was on track in late 2003 toward a level of sales not seen since 1994.[5] On the other hand, Boeing's decision to step up airplane production at the same time the factory was switching to a new automated manufacturing system was a fiasco. The massive assembly lines nearly broke down and the plant had to stop two lines so workers could catch up, costing the company $2.6 billion. Or, consider the decision of Timex managers to replace the classic tag line, "It takes a licking and keeps on ticking," with the bland "Life is ticking." The desire to modernize their company's image led Timex managers to ditch one of the most recognizable advertising slogans in the world in favor of a lame and depressing new one.[6] Decision making is difficult. It must be done amid ever-changing factors, unclear information, and conflicting points of view.

Chapter 5 described strategic planning. This chapter explores the decision process that underlies strategic planning. Plans and strategies are arrived at through decision making; the better the decision making, the better the strategic planning. First, we will examine decision characteristics. Then, we will look at decision-making models and the steps executives should take when making important decisions. We will examine participative decision making and discuss techniques for improving decision making in today's organizations. Later in the chapter, we will explore the management of IT and e-business. We begin by developing a basic understanding of IT and the types of information systems frequently used in organizations. Finally, the chapter will look at the growing use of the Internet and e-business, including a discussion of fundamental e-business strategies, business-to-business marketplaces, use of IT in business operations, and the importance of knowledge management.

Types of Decisions and Problems

A **decision** is a choice made from available alternatives. For example, an accounting manager's selection among Colin, Tasha, and Jennifer for the position of junior auditor is a decision. Many people assume that making a choice is the major part of decision making, but it is only a part.

Decision making is the process of identifying problems and opportunities and then resolving them. Decision making involves effort before and after the actual choice. Thus, the decision to select Colin, Tasha, or Jennifer requires the accounting manager to ascertain if a new junior auditor is needed, determine the availability of potential job candidates, interview candidates to acquire necessary information, select one candidate, and follow up with the socialization of the new employee into the organization to ensure the decision's success.

decision
A choice made from available alternatives.

decision making
The process of identifying problems and opportunities and then resolving them.

Programmed and Nonprogrammed Decisions

programmed decisions

Decisions made in response to a situation that has occurred often enough to enable decision rules to be developed and applied in the future.

Management decisions typically fall into one of two categories: programmed and nonprogrammed. **Programmed decisions** involve situations that have occurred often enough to enable decision rules to be developed and applied in the future.[7] Programmed decisions are made in response to recurring organizational problems. The decision to reorder paper and other office supplies when inventories drop to a certain level is a programmed decision. Other programmed decisions concern the types of skills required to fill certain jobs, the reorder point for manufacturing inventory, exception reporting for expenditures 10 percent or more over budget, and selection of freight routes for product deliveries. Once managers formulate decision rules, subordinates and others can make the decision, freeing managers for other tasks.

nonprogrammed decisions

Decisions made in response to a unique situation, are poorly defined and largely unstructured, and have important consequences for the organization.

Nonprogrammed decisions are made in response to unique, poorly defined, and largely unstructured situations that have important consequences for the organization. Many nonprogrammed decisions involve strategic planning, because uncertainty is great and decisions are complex. Decisions to build a new factory, develop a new product or service, enter a new geographical market, or relocate headquarters to another city are all nonprogrammed decisions. One good example of a nonprogrammed decision is NBC Entertainment's search for a new sitcom. With *Friends* ending its ten-season run and *Frasier* running out of steam, president Jeffrey Zucker and other managers know the network desperately needs a new hit. But the process of finding a hit sitcom is complex, not subject to rational analysis and decision rules. The stakes are high in terms of money and the network's image.[8] Another example of a nonprogrammed decision was when Ronald Zarella, president of General Motors North American operations, shelved plans to introduce a new design for the company's best-selling car, the Chevrolet Cavalier. He delayed building new factories and invested the millions of dollars saved in getting innovative new models of trucks and sport utility vehicles on the market quickly. Zarrella and his top executives had to analyze complex problems, evaluate alternatives, and make a decision about the best way to reverse GM's declining market share.[9]

Atkins Nutritionals was up against big threats and executives had to figure out a way to solve the problems, using nonprogrammed decision making as shown in the Focus on Skills box.

Take ACTION

If you have a decision to make that is repeated periodically, determine the average time between decisions and then enter a "to do" reminder in your calendar or PDA.

Certainty, Risk, Uncertainty, and Ambiguity

One primary difference between programmed and nonprogrammed decisions relates to the degree of certainty or uncertainty that managers deal with in making the decision. In a perfect world, managers would have all the information necessary for making decisions. In reality, however, some things are unknowable; thus, some decisions will fail to solve the problem or attain the desired outcome. Managers obtain information about decision alternatives that will reduce decision uncertainty. Every decision situation can be organized on a scale according to the availability of information and the possibility of failure. The four positions on the scale are certainty, risk, uncertainty, and ambiguity, as illustrated in Exhibit 6.1. Whereas programmed decisions can be made in situations involving certainty, many situations that managers deal with every day involve some degree of uncertainty and require nonprogrammed decision making.

certainty

All the information the decision maker needs is fully available.

Certainty. Certainty means that all the information the decision maker needs is available.[10] Managers have information on operating conditions, resource costs, or constraints, and information on each course of action and possible outcome. For example, if a company considers a $10,000 investment in new equipment that it knows will yield $4,000 in

FOCUS ON SKILLS

Atkins Nutritionals

Plopping down a Snickers bar at a management meeting, Atkins Nutritionals' executive Scott Kabak issued a challenge, letting the others know what they were up against.

When *Dr. Atkins' Diet Revolution* had first came out, the book did all right, but health professionals saw it as worse than snake oil. Atkins was called a quack and people were warned against the diet. Plus the country was in the low-fat phase. Reissued in 1992, the paperback sold more than 15 million copies. People were ready for it. But Atkins and his company were not. They had no low-carb replacements for food, selling mostly vitamins. The business was mostly "an interesting hobby" for Atkins. In the late 1990s, they started producing bake mixes and shakes and a macadamia-not bar, but they were all flavor-challenged. Other companies jumped on the band wagon. Carbolite started making candy bars and convinced grocery stores to stock them next to Snickers, and the bars were a runaway hit.

Finally Atkins brought in new management to run the company. That is when Kabak issued his Snickers challenge. Other problems loomed. Nutritionists still warned of kidney damage, bad breath, and other awful consequences.

The new managers faced an important decision: how to counteract all the bad publicity? CEO Paul Wolff created a group called Atkins Health and Medical Information Services (AHMIS), which started reaching not only consumers, but "influencers," such as physicians, government officials, and reporters. The AHMIS developed a newsletter with information about the latest research in low-carb eating and expanded the Web site to more than 7,000 pages. In the past year, the site went from 125,000 unique visitors a month to more than 2.4 million. The new message is about the diet being a "nutritional approach," it is not about eating lots of cholesterol-laden meat but is about cutting back on refined carbohydrates. Vegetarians can go Atkins. It is not for diets but rather for people who want "to reach 85 gracefully and with dignity."

Not all the Web sites in the world could have done what happened with the 2002 *New York Times Magazine* article, "What If It's All Been a Big Fat Lie?" It said the higher-fat Atkins diet was healthier than low-fat, which might even be responsible for the obesity epidemic. Who knows, though, how much the new Atkins message helped to get the *The New York Times* interested in the story? While it was pushing bread to candy into shelves, the article sped it all up, with the company now providing 95 products.

Will all this make people thinner? Only time will tell. And if there was some agreement on what a carb was, that would be even better. Their bars might say 21 carbs, but only two are "net carbs." What does that mean, anyway?

SOURCE: Susan Orenstein, "Dr. Atkins is Getting Fat," *Business 2.0* (April 2003): 73–78.

cost savings per year over the next five years, managers can calculate a before-tax rate of return of about 40 percent. If managers compare this investment with one that will yield only $3,000 per year in cost savings, they can confidently select the 40 percent return. However, few decisions are certain in the real world. Most contain risk and/or uncertainty.

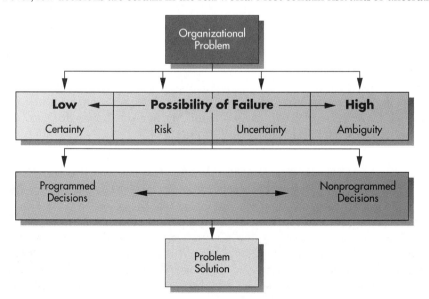

EXHIBIT 6.1

Conditions That Affect the Possibility of Decision Failure

risk

A decision has clear goals and good information is available, but the future outcomes associated with each alternative are subject to chance.

Risk. Risk means that a decision has clear goals and that good information is available, but the future outcomes associated with each alternative are subject to chance. However, enough information is available to allow the probability of a successful outcome for each alternative to be estimated.[11] Statistical analysis could calculate the probabilities of success or failure. The measure of risk captures the possibility that future events will render the alternative unsuccessful. For example, to make restaurant location decisions, McDonald's can analyze potential customer demographics, traffic patterns, supply logistics, and the local competition to come up with reasonably good forecasts of how successful a restaurant will be in each possible location.[12] General Electric Aircraft Engines (GEAE) took a risk on the development of regional jet engines, the engines that power smaller planes with seating for up to 100 and ranges of up to 1,500 miles. Based on trends in the environment, GEAE's managers predicted that use of regional jets would grow, so they invested more than $1 billion in new engine technology at a time when no one else was paying attention to the regional jet market. The decision paid off as full-service carriers have declined and smaller regional and low-fare airlines have grown. Between 1993 and 2003, the number of regional jets in service increased from 85 to 1,300, and the number is expected to grow. GEAE finds itself in an enviable position with a near lock on one of the few growing market segments in commercial aviation.[13]

uncertainty

Managers know which goals they wish to achieve, but information about alternatives and future events is incomplete.

Uncertainty. Uncertainty means managers know which goals they wish to achieve, but information about alternatives and future events is incomplete. Managers do not have enough information to be clear about alternatives or to estimate their risk. Factors that may affect a decision, such as price, production costs, volume, or future interest rates, are difficult to analyze and predict. Managers may have to make assumptions from which to forge the decision even though it will be wrong if the assumptions are incorrect. Managers may have to come up with creative approaches to alternatives and use personal judgment to determine which alternative is best.

John Reed, the interim chairman and CEO of the New York Stock Exchange (NYSE), faced tremendous uncertainty as he struggled to restore credibility and morale following the forced resignation of Chairman Richard Grasso in late 2003. With so many constituents and diverse interests, just defining the issues was a challenge. Decisions included what kinds of corporate governance reforms to recommend, how to conduct a probe into alleged illegal trading activity of NYSE specialist firms, and whether to alter the open outcry/auction model, where every trade passes through at least one live trader on the NYSE floor.[14] Decisions such as these have no clear solutions and require that managers rely on creativity, judgment, intuition, and experience to craft a response.

Many decisions made under uncertainty do not produce the desired results, but managers face uncertainty every day. They find creative ways to cope with uncertainty in order to make more effective decisions. Judy Henderson-Townsend faced uncertainty in her new business venture.

Mannequin Madness

Going to a garage sale changed Judi Henderson-Townsend's life. A journalism grad who was worked in pharmaceutical sales, she felt confined by corporate rigidity and believed she could run a company as well as some of the people she worked for. A few weeks after she finished a course on starting a small business, she was trying to buy a mannequin for a yard sculpture. The seller was a former window dresser who rented mannequins. Because he was closing shop and moving out of town, Henderson-Townsend impulsively paid $2,500 for all 50 mannequins. Standing all her mannequins in her basement, she decided to start her own business: Mannequin Madness (http://www.mannequinmadness.com). She has done so well that her inventory takes up the huge basement, the garage, and a storage facility.

Henderson-Townsend buys out-of-style department store mannequins and then sells or rents them to photographers, brides, clothing stores, and theater groups. Often, men will get a female torso to pose at a frat house or on a bar. (Asians are in high demand.) Some companies, unable to provide a live security guard, will dress a mannequin and hunch it over a desk in a lit office. Her snap decision a few years ago has brought rewards. With two employees, she brought in $150,000 in revenue last year, up from $100,000 in 2003. Most of her business (70 percent) comes from sales, the rest from rentals. Her customers come equally from her Web site, eBay, and repeat customers.

A big surprise for her has been the demand for body parts. Jewelers want a hand, for example, and leg lamps are popular.[15]

Ambiguity.   Ambiguity is by far the most difficult decision situation. Ambiguity means the goals to be achieved or the problem to be solved is unclear, alternatives are difficult to define, and information about outcomes is unavailable.[16] Ambiguity is what students would feel if an instructor created student groups, told each group to complete a project, but gave the groups no topic, direction, or guidelines. Ambiguity has been called a wicked decision problem. Managers have a difficult time coming to grips with the issues. Wicked problems are associated with manager conflicts over goals and decision alternatives, rapidly changing circumstances, fuzzy information, and unclear linkages among decision elements.[17] Sometimes managers will come up with a "solution" only to realize that they had not clearly defined the problem.[18] A recent example of a wicked decision problem was when managers at Ford Motor Company and Firestone confronted the problem of tires used on the Ford Explorer coming apart on the road, causing deadly blowouts and rollovers. Just defining the problem and whether the tire or the Explorer design was at fault was the first hurdle. Information was fuzzy and changing, and managers were arguing how to handle the problem. Neither side has dealt with this decision situation effectively, and the reputations of both companies have suffered as a result. Fortunately, most decisions are not characterized by ambiguity. When they are, managers must conjure up goals and develop reasonable scenarios for decision alternatives in the absence of information.

ambiguity
The goals to be achieved or the problem to be solved is unclear, alternatives are difficult to define, and information about outcomes is unavailable.

Take *ACTION*
When faced with a difficult and ambiguous decision, develop a "Worst Case Scenario" for each of the possible choices to help you determine which course of action you want.

Decision-Making Models

The approach managers use to make decisions usually falls into one of three types: the classical model, administrative model, or political model. The choice of model depends on the manager's personal preference, if the decision is programmed or nonprogrammed, and the extent to which the decision is characterized by risk, uncertainty, or ambiguity.

Classical Model

The **classical model** of decision making is based on economic assumptions. This model has arisen within the management literature because managers are expected to make decisions that are economically sensible and in the organization's best economic interests. The four assumptions underlying this model are as follows:

1. The decision maker operates to accomplish known and agreed upon goals. Problems are precisely formulated and defined.

2. The decision maker strives for conditions of certainty, gathering complete information. All alternatives and the potential results of each are calculated.

3. Criteria for evaluating alternatives are known. The decision maker selects the alternative that will maximize the economic return to the organization.

classical model
A decision-making model based on the assumption that managers should make logical decisions that will be in the organization's best economic interests.

4. The decision maker is rational and uses logic to assign values, order preferences, evaluate alternatives, and make the decision that will maximize the attainment of organizational goals.

normative

An approach that defines how a decision maker should make decisions and provides guidelines for reaching an ideal outcome for the organization.

The classical model of decision making is considered to be **normative**, which means it defines how a decision maker should make decisions. It does not describe how managers make decisions so much as it provides guidelines on how to reach an ideal outcome for the organization. The value of the classical model has been its ability to help decision makers be more rational. Many managers rely solely on intuition and personal preferences for making decisions.[19] For example, during this era of rising medical costs, decisions in hospitals and medical centers about who gets scarce resources such as expensive procedures and drugs are usually made on an ad hoc basis. Administrators at the University of Texas Medical Branch, however, are using the classical model to provide some clear guidelines and rules that can be consistently applied. A committee of administrators, doctors, and mid-level staffers codified a top-to-bottom system for allocating medical services. Patients without insurance must pay up front to see a doctor. Strict rules bar expensive drugs being given to patients who cannot pay for them. Screeners see patients as soon as they come in and follow clear, rational procedures for determining who is eligible for what services. A special fund can pay for drugs that are off limits to poor patients, but approval has to come from the chief medical director, who often uses cost-benefit analysis to make his or her decisions. The hospital's rationing system is controversial. However, top managers argue that it helps the institution impartially care for the poor at the same time it adheres to rational budget restrictions needed to keep the institution financially solid.[20]

In many respects, the classical model represents an "ideal" model of decision making that is often unattainable by real people in real organizations. It is most valuable when applied to programmed decisions and to decisions characterized by certainty or risk because relevant information is available and probabilities can be calculated. For example, new analytical software programs automate many programmed decisions, such as freezing the account of a customer who has failed to make payments.[21] GE Energy Rentals uses a system that captures financial and organizational information about customers to help managers evaluate risks and make credit decisions. The system has enabled the division to reduce costs, increase processing time, and improve cash flow. In the retail industry, software programs analyze current and historical sales data to help companies such as Home Depot and Gap decide when, where, and how much to mark down prices.[22] This chapter's Digital, Inc. box describes how Southwest Airlines uses quantitative models to help keep costs low and retain its position as the low-cost leader. The growth of quantitative decision techniques that use computers has expanded the use of the classical approach. Quantitative techniques include such things as decision trees, payoff matrices, break-even analysis, linear programming, forecasting, and operations research models. The NBC television network uses a computer-based system to create optimum advertising schedules.

For television viewers, news and entertainment is the primary function of the NBC network. But for NBC managers, one of the biggest concerns is optimizing the advertising schedule. Each year, managers have to develop a detailed advertising plan and a schedule that meets advertisers' desires in terms of cost, target audience, program mix, and other factors. At the same time, the schedule has to get the most revenues for the available amount of inventory (advertising slots).

Creating an advertising plan and schedule can be complex, with numerous decision constraints and variables, such as product conflict restraints, airtime availability restraints, client requirements, or management restrictions. NBC offices use a

DIGITAL, INC.

Southwest Uses Technology to Keep a Hawk's Eye on Costs

The airline industry has been in the worst slump in history and the three largest carriers lost a total of $5.8 billion in 2003. But Southwest Airlines is going strong, despite the industry downturn, rising fuel prices, difficult union negotiations, and a crop of new low-fare competitors. Southwest's 2003 profits totaled $442 million, more than all the other U.S. airlines combined. Southwest's wacky, people-oriented culture has often been cited as a key factor in the company's success. But managers point out that keeping a hawk's eye on costs is as much a part of the culture as the silliness and fun.

One way managers keep a lid on costs is by applying technology to support decision making. Consider the use of a new breed of simulation software to help make decisions about the airline's freight operations. BiosGroup, a joint venture between Santa Fe Institute biologist Stuart Kauffman and the consulting firm Cap Gemini Ernst & Young, uses adaptive, agent-based computer modeling to help companies such as Southwest and Procter & Gamble solve complex business problems. For the Southwest project, the computer simulation model represented individual baggage handlers and other employees. The model was created to see how thousands of individual daily decisions and interactions determined the behavior of the airline's overall freight operation.

A BiosGroup team spent many hours interviewing all the employees whose jobs related to freight handling. Then, they programmed the computer to simulate the people in the freight house who accepted a customer's package, those who figured out which flight the package should go on, those on the ramp who were loading the planes, and so forth. When the computer ran a simulation of a week's worth of freight operations, various aspects of operations were measured, such as how many times employees had to load and unload cargo or how often freight had to be stored overnight. The simulation indicated that, rather than unloading cargo from incoming flights and putting it on the next direct flight to its destination, Southwest would be better off to let the freight take the long way around. Paradoxically, this approach turned out to get the freight to its destination faster and saved the time and cost of unloading and reloading.

Southwest managers lost no time in implementing the decision to change the freight handling system. By applying technology to find a more efficient way of doing things, Southwest is saving an estimated $10 million over five years. Now that is one way to become the most profitable airline in the country.

SOURCES: Mitchell Waldrop, "Chaos, Inc.," *Red Herring* (January 2003): 38–40; and Andy Serwer, "Southwest Airlines: The Hottest Thing in the Sky," *Fortune* (March 8, 2004): 86–106.

---

computerized system that quickly and efficiently makes optimal use of advertising slots. When an advertiser makes a request, planners enter all the information into the system, including the budgeted amount the customer is willing to pay for a total package of commercials, the number of people the advertiser wants to reach, the targeted demographic characteristics, how the budget is to be distributed over four quarters of the year, the number of weeks in the program year, the unit lengths of commercials, the specific shows the advertiser is interested in, and so forth. Management ranks the shows and weeks of the year by their importance, and these data are entered into the system, with the availability of advertising slots during each week and other constraints. The system formulates an advertising plan that uses the least amount of premium inventory subject to meeting client requirements.

By using the classical approach, NBC generates optimal plans that meet the advertiser's needs while at the same time saving millions of dollars of premium inventory, which can be used to lure new advertisers who will pay high fees to advertise on the hottest shows.[23]

Administrative Model

The **administrative model** of decision making describes how managers make decisions in difficult situations, such as those characterized by nonprogrammed decisions, uncertainty, and ambiguity. Many management decisions are not sufficiently programmable to lend themselves to any degree of quantification. Managers are unable to make economically rational decisions even if they want to.[24]

administrative model

A decision-making model that describes how managers make decisions in situations characterized by nonprogrammed decisions, uncertainty, and ambiguity.

bounded rationality

The concept that people have the time and cognitive ability to process a limited amount of information on which to base decisions.

satisficing

To choose the first solution alternative that satisfies minimal decision criteria regardless of whether better solutions are presumed to exist.

Take **ACTION**

Remember that "Perfection is the enemy of greatness." Do not become paralyzed in decision making by seeking unrealistically great outcomes.

Bounded Rationality and Satisficing.   The administrative model of decision making is based on the work of Herbert A. Simon. Simon proposed two concepts that were instrumental in shaping the administrative model: bounded rationality and satisficing. **Bounded rationality** means that people have limits, or boundaries, on how rational they can be. The organization is complex, and managers have the time and ability to process only a limited amount of information with which to make decisions.[25] Because managers lack the time or cognitive ability to process complete information about complex decisions, they must satisfice. **Satisficing** means that decision makers choose the first solution alternative that satisfies minimal decision criteria. Rather than pursuing all alternatives to identify the single solution that will maximize economic returns, managers will opt for the first solution that appears to solve the problem even if better solutions are presumed to exist. The decision maker cannot justify the time and expense of obtaining complete information.[26]

An example of bounded rationality and satisficing occurs when a junior executive on a business trip spills coffee on her blouse before an important meeting. She will run to a nearby clothing store and buy the first satisfactory replacement she finds. Having neither the time nor the opportunity to explore all the blouses in town, she satisfices by choosing a blouse that will solve the immediate problem. In a similar fashion, managers generate alternatives for complex problems only until they find one they believe will work. For example, several years ago, then-Disney chairman Ray Watson and chief operating officer Ron Miller attempted to thwart takeover attempts, but they had limited options. They satisficed with a quick decision to acquire Arivda Realty and Gibson Court Company. The acquisition of these companies had the potential to solve the problem at hand; thus, they looked no further for possibly better alternatives.[27]

The administrative model relies on assumptions different from those of the classical model and focuses on organizational factors that influence individual decisions. It is more realistic than the classical model for complex, nonprogrammed decisions. According to the administrative model:

1. Decision goals are often vague, conflicting, and lack consensus among managers. Managers often are unaware of problems or opportunities that exist in the organization.

2. Rational procedures are not always used, and when they are, they are confined to a simplistic view of the problem that misses the complexity of real organizational events.

3. Managers' searches for alternatives are limited because of human, information, and resource constraints.

4. Most managers settle for a satisficing rather than a maximizing solution. This is partly because they have limited information and because they have vague criteria for what constitutes a maximizing solution.

descriptive

An approach that describes how managers make decisions rather than how they should.

The administrative model is considered to be **descriptive**, meaning it describes how managers make decisions in complex situations rather than dictating how they should make decisions according to a theoretical ideal. The administrative model recognizes the human and environmental limitations that affect the degree to which managers can pursue a rational decision-making process. For example, interviews with CEOs in high-tech industries found that they strived to use some rational process in making decisions, but the way they decided things was through a complex interaction with other managers, subordinates, environmental factors, and organizational events.[28]

intuition

The immediate comprehension of a decision situation based on past experience but without conscious thought.

Intuition.   Another aspect of administrative decision making is intuition. **Intuition** represents a quick apprehension of a decision situation based on past experience but without conscious thought.[29] Intuitive decision making is not arbitrary or irrational because it is based on years of practice and hands-on experience that enable managers to identify solutions without going through painstaking computations. In today's fast, turbulent business environment, intuition plays an increasingly important role in decision making. A study of 60 business professionals from various industries, for example, found that nearly half said they relied on intuition often in making decisions in the workplace, while another 30 percent reported using intuition sometimes.[30]

Cognitive psychologist Gary Klein has studied how people make good decisions using their intuition under time pressure and uncertainty.[31] Klein has found that intuition begins with recognition. When people build a depth of experience and knowledge in a particular area, the right decision often comes quickly and effortlessly with a recognition of information largely forgotten by the conscious mind. For example, firefighters make decisions by recognizing what is typical or abnormal about a fire, based on their experience as shown in the Focus on Skills box.

Similarly, in the business world, managers are continuously perceiving and processing information that they may not consciously be aware of, and their base of knowledge and experience helps them make decisions that may be characterized by uncertainty and ambiguity. Research by a growing number of psychologists and neuroscientists has affirmed the power of our unconscious minds in making decisions. Studies of intuition indicate that the unconscious mind has cognitive abilities that sometimes surpass those of the conscious mind.[32]

The entertainment industry provides many good examples of intuition because of the complex and uncertain nature of picking hit shows. For example, when Sherry Lansing of Paramount Pictures decided to do the movie *Forrest Gump*, few people expected it to be successful. "It was a film about a guy on a bench," Lansing said.

FOCUS ON SKILLS

Wildland Firefighters

If you ever fall from a highway overpass onto the metal struts of a sign, just hope you get rescue workers who practice good decision making on the spot. In such a case, the wrong kind of rescue gear, even a seemingly good position for the victim, can spell disaster. Traditional thinking argues that the rescue worker should carefully consider the many options available. Unfortunately, these situations do not allow for the luxury of decision analysis. According to cognitive psychologist Gary Klein, only novices need to be burdened by the practice of evaluating every possible course of action. Experienced workers know the various consequences so well they intuitively make the right choice.

Klein's best decision makers are wildland firefighters, who work in western United States, as well as Australia and New Zealand, and are constantly putting out scorching fires. Thereby, they build a rich reservoir of experience to draw upon. Obsessive about learning from experience, they are always doing an after-action review to see what could have been done better. As for leadership, the top people started at the bottom, so they know what it means to be in the midst of a killer fire. One fire commander claimed he had ESP. During a raging house fire, he ordered the hose team into the house, but the fire blazed on, baffling the commander with its persistence. Then, his so-called "sixth sense" kicked in, and he suddenly ordered everyone out of the house. Just as they vacated, the house collapsed. Rather than ESP, Klein says the commander's experience made him see that the fire was not matching his expectations. The fire was burning through the floor, so the sound was more quiet than usual and it was hotter than normal, indicating other, more treacherous conditions.

What can companies learn from this? Decision making in times of uncertainty, risk, and time pressure requires experience, which allows the person to look for clues or patterns to help guide the course of action. It is the ability to size up a situation quickly. Novices need the decision-making models, but real experience is the best teacher.

SOURCE: Stephen Turner, "Intuition at Work: Why Developing Your Gut Instincts Will Make You Better at What You Do," *Library Journal* (Feb. 1, 2003): 99; Bill Breen, "What's Your Intuition," *Fast Company* (Sept 2000): 290–300.

"It was one of the riskiest films ever made." But Lansing's intuition told her Tom Hanks sitting on a bench and explaining how "life is like a box of chocolates" would work, and the film reaped $329 million at the box office. Another example comes from the Fox television network, where prime time ratings were dismal until Steven Chao came up with *America's Most Wanted* and *Cops*. Initially, everyone hated the idea of these raw, crime-oriented shows, but Chao and his boss Barry Diller stuck with their gut feelings and pushed the projects.[33]

Political Model

The third model of decision making is useful for making nonprogrammed decisions when conditions are uncertain, information is limited, and there is disagreement among managers about what goals to pursue or what course of action to take. Most organizational decisions involve many managers who are pursuing different goals, and they have to talk with one another to share information and reach an agreement. Managers often engage in coalition building for making complex organizational decisions. A **coalition** is an informal alliance among managers who support a specific goal. Coalition building is the process of forming alliances among managers. In other words, a manager who supports a specific alternative, such as increasing the corporation's growth by acquiring another company, talks informally to other executives and wants to persuade them to support the decision. When the outcomes are unpredictable, managers gain support through discussion, negotiation, and bargaining. Without a coalition, a powerful individual or group could derail the decision-making process. Coalition building gives several managers an opportunity to contribute to decision making, enhancing their commitment to the alternative that will be adopted.[34]

The political model closely resembles the real environment in which most managers and decision makers operate. Decisions are complex and involve many people, information is often ambiguous, and disagreement and conflict over problems and solutions are normal. There are four basic assumptions of the political model:

1. Organizations are made up of groups with diverse interests, goals, and values. Managers disagree about problem priorities and may not understand or share the goals and interests of other managers.

2. Information is ambiguous and incomplete. The attempt to be rational is limited by the complexity of many problems as well as personal and organizational constraints.

3. Managers do not have the time, resources, or mental capacity to identify all dimensions of the problem and process all relevant information. Managers talk to each other and exchange viewpoints to gather information and reduce ambiguity.

4. Managers engage in the push and pull of debate to decide goals and discuss alternatives. Decisions are the result of bargaining and discussion among coalition members.

To support a U.S.-led campaign against terrorism and a war in Iraq, President George W. Bush tried to take a lesson from his father, who was known as a consummate coalition builder. The elder Bush always sought a broad-based coalition at the start of any important decision process, such as the 1990 Persian Gulf War. The younger president has been criticized for pushing his own priorities and opinions too aggressively and is engaging in stronger coalition building for making decisions

coalition

An informal alliance among managers who support a specific goal.

Take ACTION

Practice collaborating and developing alliances because good ideas are not enough: You will need to build coalitions.

concerning overseas campaigns. The inability of leaders to build coalitions often hampers managers to get their decisions implemented. Hershell Ezrin resigned as CEO of Canada's Speedy Muffler King because he was unable to build a coalition of managers who supported his decisions for change at the troubled company. Many senior-level executives resented Ezrin's appointment and refused to go along with his ideas for reviving the company.[35] Sometimes the leadership in a company does not make the best decisions, but then new executives come in and correct past errors, as happened with Paramount's movie catalog.

Paramount DVDs

Viacom was waiting for a rainy day to turn its Paramount movie catalog into DVDs. Now it is a thunderstorm and new leadership says it is time to cash in. Other studios have turned many of their movies—and lots of TV shows—into DVD sales. One example is "O.C.: The Complete Season 1" which rushed out only months after it aired. Paramount has yet to exploit many of its movies or TV series, "Happy Days," "The Brady Bunch," "Beverly Hills 90210," and "Melrose Place." All of this means money for Paramount. A recent TV show, "Charmed," for example, will likely bring $60 million in sales with $15 million of that from profits.

If this new strategy works, Paramount's contribution to Viacom's bottom line could increase, welcome news in a time of financial disaster. Paramount has released less than half of its DVD collection, compared to Time Warner, and it has 95 percent of its TV library yet unused. Worldwide DVD revenue is expected to be $3 billion for Viacom.

This new revenue is not free, however. Going back to put old TV shows on DVD means negotiating fees with actors and producers and securing music clearance. Just for season 1 of "Happy Days," music licensing cost $1 million. No doubt those songwriters are having lots of happy days these days.[36]

The key dimensions of the classical, administrative, and political models are listed in Exhibit 6.2. Recent research into decision-making procedures has found rational, classical procedures to be associated with high performance for organizations in stable environments. However, administrative and political decision-making procedures and intuition have been associated with high performance in unstable environments in which decisions must be made rapidly and under more difficult conditions.[37]

EXHIBIT 6.2

Characteristics of Classical, Administrative, and Political Decision-Making Models

Classical Model	Administrative Model	Political Model
Clear-cut problem and goals	Vague problem and goals	Pluralistic; conflicting goals
Condition of certainty	Condition of uncertainty	Condition of uncertainty/ambiguity
Full information about alternatives and their outcomes	Limited information about alternatives and their outcomes	Inconsistent viewpoints; ambiguous information
Rational choice by individual for maximizing outcomes	Satisficing choice for resolving problem using intuition	Bargaining and discussion among coalition members

Decision-Making Steps

Whether a decision is programmed or nonprogrammed and regardless of managers' choice of the classical, administrative, or political model of decision making, six steps typically are associated with effective decision processes. These are summarized in Exhibit 6.3.

Recognition of Decision Requirement

problem

A situation in which organizational accomplishments have failed to meet established goals.

opportunity

A situation in which managers see potential organizational accomplishments that exceed current goals.

Managers confront a decision requirement in the form of a problem or an opportunity. A **problem** occurs when organizational accomplishment is less than established goals. Some aspect of performance is unsatisfactory. An **opportunity** exists when managers see potential accomplishment that exceeds specified current goals. Managers see the possibility of enhancing performance beyond current levels. Oprah Winfrey's agent saw opportunities for her that she never dreamed of as described in the Best Practices box.

Awareness of a problem or opportunity is the first step in the decision sequence and requires surveillance of the internal and external environment for issues that merit executive attention.[38] This resembles the military concept of gathering intelligence. Managers scan the world around them to determine whether the organization is satisfactorily progressing toward its goals. Some information comes from periodic financial reports, performance reports, and other sources that are designed to discover problems before they become too serious.

EXHIBIT 6.3

Six Steps in the Managerial Decision-Making Process

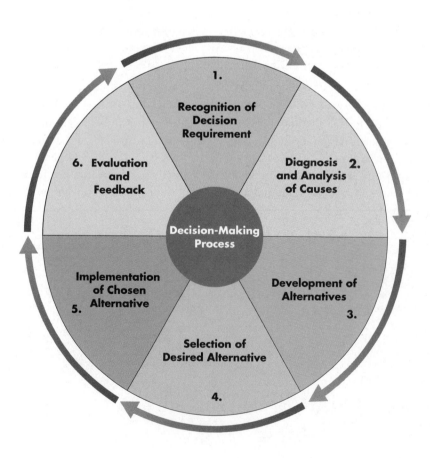

BEST PRACTICES

Oprah, Inc.

With her Oprah Brand designed around the mantra, "You are responsible for your own life," it might seem strange that Oprah Winfrey describes her decision making as "leaps of faith" and that she embraces an instinctual management style. That is part of the story. The other part of the picture is about her business manager, Jeff Jacobs, who is president of Oprah's company, Harpo, Inc. He was a young entertainment lawyer when the T-shirt and flip-flop wearing Oprah asked for help in 1984 with a new contract. With an instinct for business potential, Jacobs convinced her to invest in herself rather than remaining an actor-for-hire where most entertainers are.

While Oprah develops her themes and images, Jacobs works behind the scenes, keeping the business running and making tough decisions. For every gut instinct Oprah has, its backed up with Jacobs' realistic business experience and knowing when to "multipurpose the content," for example. That means Dr. Phil appears on Oprah, writes a column in Harpo's *O Magazine*, which will be spun off on his own Harpo-produced TV show. Still,

Oprah has a strong sense of her mission, and her decisions follow her purpose and values. Sometimes, her wishes clash with business concerns. She has the *O Magazine* table of contents on page two rather than the more common 22. Advertisers prefer for people to page wade through their glossy ads before finding the table of contents. But Oprah would not have it. "Let's put the readers first," she commanded.

Oprah tries to live her message: to be strong, courageous, and a good role model. She has yet to make the decision to give up control of her Brand—Oprah—unlike Martha Stewart who sold her name rights to the now Chapter 11ed K-Mart and took her company public. Oprah feels strongly about maintaining her self in the process. "If I lost control of the business, I'd lost myself or at least the ability to be myself. Owning is a way to be myself." She regrets her decision, based on financial gain, to sell rights to Oprah reruns. "It's not a commodity. It's my soul. It's who I am."

SOURCE: Patricia Sellers, "The Business of Being Oprah," *Fortune* (April 1, 2002): 50–64.

For example, sharply declining sales figures in the Oldsmobile and Buick divisions of General Motors signaled a problem that needed to be addressed. Managers could see that Oldsmobile and Buick had been on a downhill slide for years as the loyal buyers of these brands were aging and the cars failed to appeal to younger buyers.[39] Recognition of the problem led managers to focus on decisions about the fate of these two divisions in their overall efforts to lead GM out of the downturn. Managers take advantage of informal sources. They talk to other managers, gather opinions on how things are going, and seek advice on which problems should be tackled or which opportunities embraced.[40]

Recognizing decision requirements is difficult because it often means integrating bits and pieces of information in novel ways.

BUSINESS BLOOPER

Nokia N-Gage

Nokia launched N-Gage in October 2003. Executives called it "the biggest innovation in gaming since the joystick." Though the market was not necessarily calling out for a phone that plays games, there were about 131 million gamers in the United States alone. Nokia bet it could unload 6 million combo phones within two years. Why wouldn't customers grab a Bluetoothed Web-browsing MP3 player that happened to be a cell phone and a platform for gaming? Because gamers do not

seem to like the thing. They say it has a small screen, slow frames, and only eight games available. *GameSpy* editor Dave Kosak says the N-Gage has no credibility at all. Nokia disagrees. Though the company has shipped many units, it just is not selling. Nokia's mistake was market the product before it had lined up third-party software support. Hardware purchase is driven by content. And they forgot that basic b-school principle.

SOURCE: Matthew Maier, "It's Two, Two, Two Flops in One," *Business 2.0* (Feb. 2004): 64–66.

Diagnosis and Analysis of Causes

diagnosis

The step in the decision-making process in which managers analyze underlying causal factors associated with the decision situation.

Once a problem or opportunity has come to a manager's attention, the understanding of the situation should be refined. **Diagnosis** is the step in the decision-making process in which managers analyze underlying causal factors associated with the decision situation. Managers make a mistake if they jump right into generating alternatives without first exploring the cause of the problem more deeply.

C. Kepner and B. Tregoe, who have conducted extensive studies of manager decision making, recommend that managers ask a series of questions to specify underlying causes, including the following:

- What is the state of disequilibrium affecting us?
- When did it occur?
- Where did it occur?
- How did it occur?
- To whom did it occur?
- What is the urgency of the problem?
- What is the interconnectedness of events?
- What result came from which activity?[41]

Take ACTION

Train your mind to analyze problems: In your own situation, practice diagnosing your own problems.

Such questions clarify what happened and why. Managers at McDonald's are struggling to diagnose the underlying factors in the company's recent troubles. The problem is an urgent one, as the stock price fell 60 percent in three years, sales and profits are declining, and quality and service lag behind those of rival fast food restaurants. Managers are examining the multitude of problems facing the fast food giant, tracing the pattern of the decline, and looking at the interconnectedness of issues such as changing eating habits, a struggling economy, increased competition, poor headquarters planning, weak control systems, and a decline in training and evaluation for franchisees.[42]

Development of Alternatives

Once the problem or opportunity has been recognized and analyzed, decision makers consider taking action. The next stage is to generate possible alternative solutions that will respond to the needs of the situation and correct the underlying causes. One study found that limiting the search for alternatives is a primary cause of decision failure in organizations.[43]

For a programmed decision, feasible alternatives are easily identifable and usually available within the organization's rules and procedures. Nonprogrammed decisions, however, require developing new courses of action that will meet the company's needs. For decisions made under conditions of high uncertainty, managers may develop only one or two custom solutions that will satisfice for handling the problem.

Take ACTION

Always have several options to solve problems, so you can choose among them.

Decision alternatives can be thought of as the tools for reducing the difference between the organization's current and desired performance. At McDonald's, executives are considering alternatives such as using mystery shoppers and unannounced inspections to improve quality and service, motivating demoralized franchisees to get them to invest in new equipment and programs, taking R&D out of the test kitchen and encouraging franchisees to help come up with successful new menu items, and closing some stores to avoid cannibalizing its own sales.[44]

Selection of Desired Alternative

Once feasible alternatives have been developed, one must be selected. The decision choice is the selection of the most promising of alternative courses of action. The best alternative is one in which the solution best fits the organization's overall goals and values and achieves the desired results using the fewest resources.[45] The manager selects the choice

© Don Murray/Getty Images

CONCEPT CONNECTION

Jon Bon Jovi is a rock star and entrepreneur, who co-owns the Philadelphia Soul, an expansion team of the Arena Football League (AFL). Bon Jovi and his partner, businessman Craig Spencer, spotted an **opportunity** *to capitalize on Bon Jovi's personality and fame, as well as his savvy marketing skills, by acquiring the franchise. Bon Jovi personally made decisions such as naming the team the Soul (because "anybody can have soul," he says) and creating a mascot (the Soul Man), and he is actively involved in decisions regarding everything from advertising budgets to where to place the autograph tables after a game. Today, the Soul leads the AFL in ticket sales, advertising sales, and merchandising revenue.*

with the least amount of risk and uncertainty. Because some risk is inherent for most non-programmed decisions, managers gauge prospects for success. Under conditions of uncertainty, they might have to rely on their intuition and experience to estimate if a given course of action will succeed. Basing choices on overall goals and values can effectively guide selection of alternatives. For example, stockbroker Edward Jones was hit hard by the gloomy stock market and the declining economy in late 2001. To make decisions about how to cope, managers relied on the company's values and goals of treating employees right and building long-term relationships. Not a single employee was laid off (the company has not laid off an employee in 34 years), and though bonuses were reduced, the company issued them a week early to help employees hurt by the trading decline. Edward Jones' values-based decision making helped win the company the number one spot two years in a row on *Fortune* magazine's list of best companies to work for.[46]

Making choices depends on managers' personality factors and willingness to accept risk and uncertainty. For example, **risk propensity** is the willingness to undertake risk with the opportunity of gaining an increased payoff. The level of risk a manager is willing to accept will influence the analysis of cost and benefits to be derived from any decision. Consider the situations in Exhibit 6.4. In each situation, which alternative would you choose? A person with a low risk propensity would tend to take assured moderate returns by going for a tie score, building a domestic plant, or pursuing a career as a physician. A risk taker would go for the victory, build a plant in a foreign country, or embark on an acting career. The Focus on Skills box describes biases to avoid when selecting the desired alternative.

risk propensity

The willingness to undertake risk with the opportunity of gaining an increased payoff.

For each of the following decisions, which alternative would you choose?	**EXHIBIT 6.4**
1. In the final seconds of a game with the college's traditional rival, the coach of a college football team may choose a play that has a 95 percent chance of producing a tie score or one with a 30 percent chance of leading to victory or to sure defeat if it fails.	*Decision Alternatives with Different Levels of Risk*
2. The president of a Canadian company must decide whether to build a new plant within Canada that has a 90 percent chance of producing a modest return on investment or to build it in a foreign country with an unstable political history. The latter alternative has a 40 percent chance of failing, but the returns would be enormous if it succeeded.	
3. A college senior with considerable acting talent must choose a career. She has the opportunity to go on to medical school and become a physician, a career in which she is 80 percent likely to succeed. She would rather be an actress but realizes that the opportunity for success is only 20 percent.	

FOCUS ON SKILLS

Decision Biases to Avoid

At a time when decision making is so important, many managers do not know how to make a good choice among alternatives. They might rely on computer analyses or personal intuition without realizing that their own cognitive biases affect their judgment. Many errors in judgment originate in the human mind's limited capacity and in the natural biases most managers display during decision making. Awareness of the six biases below can help managers make more enlightened choices:

1. Being influenced by initial impressions: When considering decisions, the mind often gives disproportionate weight to the first information it receives. These initial impressions, statistics, or estimates act as an anchor to our subsequent thoughts and judgments. Anchors can be as simple as a random comment by a colleague or a statistic read in a newspaper. Past events and trends act as anchors. For example, in business, managers frequently look at the previous year's sales when estimating sales for the coming year. Giving too much weight to the past can lead to poor forecasts and misguided decisions.

2. Justifying past decisions: Many people fall into the trap of making choices that justify their past decisions, even if those decisions seem invalid. For example, managers may invest tremendous time and energy into improving the performance of a problem employee whom they realize should never have been hired in the first place. Another example is when a manager continues to pour money into a failing project, hoping to turn things around. People do not like to make mistakes, so they continue to make flawed decisions in an effort to correct the past.

3. Seeing what you want to see: People frequently look for information that supports their existing instinct or point of view and avoid information that contradicts it. This bias affects where managers look for information and how they interpret the information they find. People tend to give too much weight to supporting information and too little to information that conflicts with their established viewpoints. Managers must be honest with themselves about their motives and to examine all the evidence with equal rigor. Having a devil's advocate to argue against a decision can avoid this decision trap.

4. Perpetuating the status quo: Managers may base decisions on what has worked in the past and fail to explore new options, dig for additional information, or investigate new technologies. For example, DuPont clung to its cash cow,

nylon, despite growing evidence in the scientific community that a new product, polyester, was superior for tire cords. Celanese, a relatively small competitor, blew DuPont out of the water by exploiting this new evidence, quickly capturing 75 percent of the tire market.

5. Being influenced by problem framing: The decision response of a manager can be influenced by the mere wording of a problem. For example, consider a manager faced with a decision about salvaging the cargo of three barges that sank off the coast of Alaska. If managers are given the option of approving (A) a plan that has a 100 percent chance of saving the cargo of one of the three barges, worth $200,000, or (B) a plan that has a one third chance of saving the cargo of all three barges, worth $600,000 and a two thirds chance of saving nothing, most managers choose option A. The same problem with a negative frame would give managers a choice of selecting (C) a plan that has a 100 percent chance of losing two of the three cargoes, worth $400,000, or (D) a plan that has a two thirds chance of losing all three cargoes but a one-third chance of losing no cargo. With this framing, most managers choose option D. Because both problems are identical, the decision choice depends strictly on how the problem is framed.

6. Overconfidence: Most people overestimate their ability to predict uncertain outcomes. Before making a decision, managers have unrealistic expectations of their ability to understand the risk and to make the right choice. Overconfidence is greatest when answering questions of moderate to extreme difficulty. For example, when people are asked to define quantities about which they have little direct knowledge ("What was Wal-Mart's 2003 revenue?" "What was the market value of Microsoft as of March 14, 2004?"), they overestimate their accuracy. Evidence of overconfidence is illustrated in cases in which subjects were so certain of an answer that they assigned odds of 1,000 to 1 of being correct but were correct only about 85 percent of the time. When uncertainty is high, managers may unrealistically expect that they can successfully predict outcomes and, hence, select the wrong alternative.

SOURCES: Based on John Hammond, Ralph L. Keeney, and Howard Raiffa, "The Hidden Traps in Decision Making," *Harvard Business Review* (September–October 1998): 47–58; Oren Harari, "The Thomas Lawson Syndrome," *Management Review* (February 1994): 58–61; Dan Ariely, "Q&A: Why Good CIOs Make Bad Decisions," *CIO* (May 1, 2003): 83–87; Leigh Buchanan, "How To Take Risks In a Time of Anxiety," *Inc.* (May 2003): 76–81; and Max H. Bazerman, *Judgment in Managerial Decision Making*, 5th ed. (New York: John Wiley & Sons, 2002).

implementation

The step in the decision-making process that involves using managerial, administrative, and persuasive abilities to translate the chosen alternative into action.

Implementation of Chosen Alternative

The **implementation** stage involves the use of managerial, administrative, and persuasive abilities to ensure the chosen alternative is carried out. This is similar to the idea of strategic implementation described in Chapter 5. The ultimate success of the chosen alternative depends on if it can be translated into action.[47] Sometimes an alternative never becomes reality because managers lack the resources or energy needed to make things happen. Implementation may require discussion with people affected by the decision. Communication, motivation, and leadership skills must be used to see that the decision is carried out. When employees see that managers follow up on their decisions by tracking implementation success, they are more committed to positive action.[48]

At General Motors, CEO Rick Wagoner has hired new top executives, including Bob Lutz, former product development chief at Chrysler, who share his vision and can help implement his decisions for livening up GM's product portfolio. For example, as vice president for product development, Lutz is personally ensuring designers and engineers pay attention to all the small details that determine a new model's appeal: everything from how the stereo knob feels when you turn it to the width of the gaps where the car hood meets the headlights. By communicating with people on the front lines Lutz is helping to implement small decisions every day aimed at helping to revamp the passenger car product line and revive the image of GM's brands.[49]

If managers lack the ability or desire to implement decisions, the chosen alternative cannot be carried out to benefit the organization.

Evaluation and Feedback

In the evaluation stage of the decision process, decision makers gather information that tells them how well the decision was implemented and if it achieved its goals. For example, Tandy executives evaluated their decision to open computer centers for businesses and feedback revealed poor sales performance. Feedback indicated that implementation was unsuccessful, and computer centers were closed so Tandy could focus on its successful Radio Shack retail stores.

Feedback is important because decision making is a continuous process. Decision making is not completed when an executive or board of directors votes yes or no. Feedback provides decision makers with information that can precipitate a new decision cycle. The decision may fail, thus generating a new analysis of the problem, an evaluation of alternatives, and a selection of a new alternative. Many problems are solved by trying several alternatives in sequence, each providing modest improvement. Feedback is the part of monitoring that assesses whether a new decision needs to be made.

To illustrate the overall decision-making process, including evaluation and feedback, we can look at the decision to introduce a new deodorant at Tom's of Maine.

> Tom's of Maine, known for its all-natural personal hygiene products, saw an opportunity to expand its line with a new natural deodorant. However, the opportunity became a problem when the deodorant worked only half of the time with half of the customers who used it, and its all-recyclable plastic dials were prone to breakage.
>
> The problem of the failed deodorant led founder Tom Chappell and other managers to analyze and diagnose what went wrong. They determined the company's product development process had run amok. The same group of merry product developers was responsible from conception to launch of the product. They were so attached to the product that they failed to test it properly or consider potential problems becoming, instead, "a mutual admiration society." Managers considered several alternatives for solving the problem. The decision to admit publicly the problem and recall the deodorant was an easy one for Chappell, who runs his company on principles of fairness and honesty. The company apologized to its customers, and it listened to their complaints and suggestions. Chappell helped answer calls and letters. Though the recall cost the company $400,000 and led to a stream of negative publicity, the company improved its relationships with customers.
>
> Evaluation and feedback also led Tom's of Maine to set up *acorn groups*, from which it hopes mighty oaks of successful products will grow. Acorn groups are cross-departmental teams that will shepherd new products from beginning to end. The cross-functional teams are

Take _ACTION_

When you make a decision, develop the mental discipline to carry it out.

Take _ACTION_

If something you try fails, do an after-action review to evaluate what went wrong and what you would do differently next time.

Tom's of Maine

a mechanism for catching problems and new opportunities that would ordinarily be missed. They pass on their ideas and findings to senior managers and the product development team.

Tom's was able to turn a problem into an opportunity, thanks to evaluation and feedback. The disaster helped the company solidify relationships with customers, and it led to a formal mechanism for learning and sharing ideas, something the company did not have before.[50]

Tom's of Maine's decision illustrates all the decision steps, and the process ended in success. Strategic decisions always contain some risk, but feedback and follow-up decisions can get companies back on track. By learning from their decision mistakes, managers and companies can turn problems into opportunities.

Personal Decision Framework

Imagine you were a manager at Tom's of Maine, General Motors, a local movie theater, or the public library. How would you go about making important decisions that might shape the future of your department or company? So far we have discussed a number of factors that affect how managers make decisions. For example, decisions may be programmed or nonprogrammed, situations are characterized by various levels of uncertainty, and managers may use the classical, administrative, or political model of decision making. In addition, the decision-making process has six recognized steps.

However, not all managers go about making decisions in the same way. In fact, there are significant differences in the ways individual managers may approach problems and make decisions concerning them. These differences can be explained by the concept of personal **decision styles**. Exhibit 6.5 illustrates the role of personal style (in a personal decision framework) in the decision-making process. Personal decision style refers to differences among people with respect to how they perceive problems and make decisions. Research has identified four major decision styles: directive, analytical, conceptual, and behavioral.[51]

decision styles

Differences among people with respect to how they perceive problems and make decisions.

1. The *directive style* is used by people who prefer simple, clear solutions to problems. Managers who use this style often make decisions quickly because they do not like to deal with a lot of information and may consider only one or two alternatives. People who prefer the directive style generally are efficient and rational and prefer to rely on existing rules or procedures for making decisions.

2. Managers with an *analytical style* like to consider complex solutions based on as much data as they can gather. These individuals carefully consider alternatives and often base their decisions on objective, rational data from management control systems and other sources. They search for the best possible decision based on the information available.

EXHIBIT 6.5
Personal Decision Framework

3. People who tend toward a *conceptual style* like to consider a broad amount of information. However, they are more socially oriented than those with an analytical

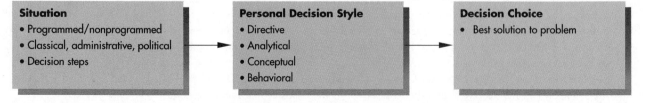

Situation	Personal Decision Style	Decision Choice
• Programmed/nonprogrammed • Classical, administrative, political • Decision steps	• Directive • Analytical • Conceptual • Behavioral	• Best solution to problem

style and like to talk to others about the problem and possible alternatives for solving it. Managers using a conceptual style consider many broad alternatives, rely on information from people and systems, and like to solve problems creatively.

4. The *behavioral style* is often the style adopted by managers having a deep concern for others as individuals. Managers using this style like to talk to people one-on-one and understand their feelings about the problem and the effect of a given decision upon them. People with a behavioral style usually are concerned with the personal development of others and may make decisions that help others achieve their goals.

Most managers have a dominant decision style. For example, Jeff Zucker at NBC Entertainment uses a primarily conceptual style, which makes him well suited to the industry. He consults with dozens of programmers about possible new shows and likes to consider many broad alternatives before making decisions.[52] However, managers frequently use several different styles or a combination of styles in making the varied decisions they confront daily. A manager might use a directive style for deciding on which printing company to use for new business cards, yet shift to a more conceptual style when handling an interdepartmental conflict. The most effective managers are able to shift among styles as needed to meet the situation. Being aware of one's dominant decision style can help a manager avoid making critical mistakes when his or her usual style may be inappropriate to the problem at hand.

Increasing Participation in Decision Making

Managers do make some decisions as individuals, but decision makers are more often part of a group. Indeed, major decisions in the business world are rarely made entirely by an individual. Effective decision making often depends on whether managers involve the right people in the right ways in helping to solve problems. One model that provides guidance for practicing managers was originally developed by Victor Vroom and Arthur Jago.[53]

The Vroom-Jago Model

The **Vroom-Jago model** helps a manager gauge the appropriate amount of participation by subordinates in making a specific decision. The model has three major components: leader participation styles, a set of diagnostic questions with which to analyze a decision situation, and a series of decision rules.

Leader Participation Styles. The model employs five levels of subordinate participation in decision making, ranging from highly autocratic (leader decides alone) to highly democratic (leader delegates to group), as illustrated in Exhibit 6.6.[54] The exhibit shows five decision styles, starting with the leader making the decision alone (Decide); presenting the problem to subordinates individually for their suggestions and then making the decision (Consult Individually); presenting the problem to subordinates as a group, collectively obtaining their ideas and suggestions, then making the decision (Consult Group); sharing the problem with subordinates as a group and acting as a facilitator to help the group arrive at a decision (Facilitate); or delegating the problem and permitting the group to make the decision within prescribed limits (Delegate).

Vroom-Jago model

A model designed to help managers gauge the amount of subordinate participation in decision making.

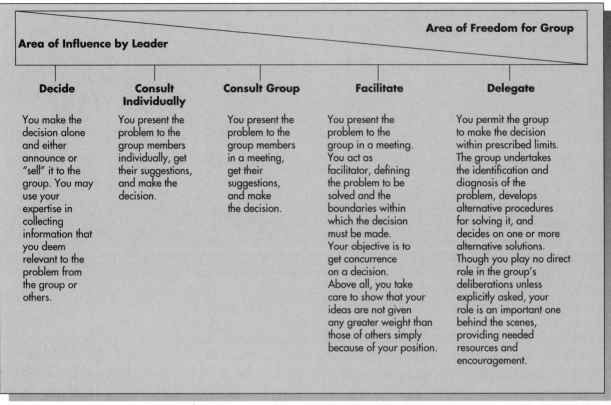

EXHIBIT 6.6

Five Leader Participation Styles

SOURCE: Victor H. Vroom, "Leadership and the Decision Making Process," *Organizational Dynamics* 28, 4 (Spring 2000), 82–94. This is Vroom's adaptation of Tannenbaum and Schmidt's Taxonomy. Used with permission.

Diagnostic Questions. How does a manager decide which of the five decision styles to use? The appropriate degree of decision participation depends on a number of situational factors, such as the required level of decision quality, the level of leader or subordinate expertise, and the importance of having subordinates commit to the decision. Leaders can analyze the appropriate degree of participation by answering seven diagnostic questions.

1. Decision significance: How significant is this decision for the project or organization? If the quality of the decision is important to the success of the project or organization, the leader has to be involved.

2. Importance of commitment: How important is subordinate commitment to carrying out the decision? If implementation requires a high level of commitment to the decision, leaders should involve subordinates in the decision process.

3. Leader expertise: What is the level of the leader's expertise in relation to the problem? If the leader does not have a high amount of information, knowledge, or expertise, the leader should involve subordinates to obtain it.

4. Likelihood of commitment: If the leader were to make the decision alone, would subordinates have high or low commitment to the decision? If subordinates typically go along with whatever the leader decides, their involvement in the decision-making process will be less important.

5. Group support for goals: What is the degree of subordinate support for the team's or organization's objectives at stake in this decision? If subordinates have low support for the goals of the organization, the leader should not allow the group to make the decision alone.

6. Group expertise: What is the level of group members' knowledge and expertise in relation to the problem? If subordinates have a high level of expertise in relation to the problem, more responsibility for the decision can be delegated to them.

7. Team competence: How skilled and committed are group members to working together as a team to solve problems? When subordinates have high skills and high desire to work together cooperatively to solve problems, more responsibility for decision making can be delegated to them.

These questions seem detailed, but considering these seven situational factors can narrow the options and point to the appropriate level of group participation in decision making.

Selecting a Decision Style. The decision matrix in Exhibit 6.7 allows a manager to adopt a participation style by answering the diagnostic questions in sequence. The manager enters the matrix at the left-hand side, at Problem Statement, and considers the seven situational questions in sequence from left to right, answering high (H) or low (L) to each

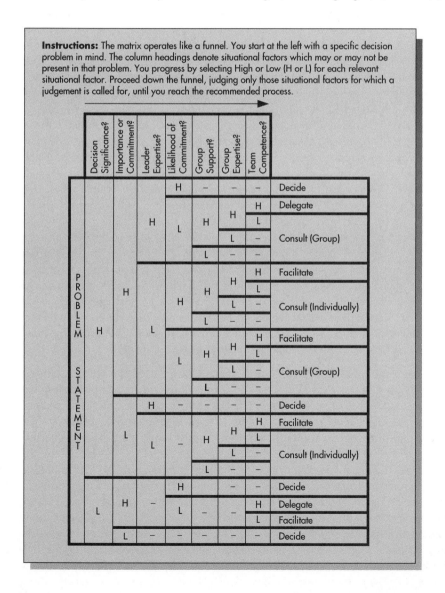

Instructions: The matrix operates like a funnel. You start at the left with a specific decision problem in mind. The column headings denote situational factors which may or may not be present in that problem. You progress by selecting High or Low (H or L) for each relevant situational factor. Proceed down the funnel, judging only those situational factors for which a judgement is called for, until you reach the recommended process.

SOURCE: Victor H. Vroom, "Leadership and the Decision Making Process," *Organizational Dynamics* 28, no. 4 (Spring 2000), 82–94.

EXHIBIT 6.7

Vroom-Jago Decision Model for Determining an Appropriate Decision-Making Style—Group Problems

one and avoiding crossing any horizontal lines. The first question would be: *How significant is this decision for the project or organization?* If the answer is High, the leader proceeds to importance of commitment: *How important is subordinate commitment to carrying out the decision?* An answer of High leads to a question about leader expertise: *What is the level of the leader's expertise in relation to the problem?* If the leader's knowledge and expertise is High, the leader next considers likelihood of commitment: *If the leader were to make the decision alone, how likely is it that subordinates would be committed to the decision?* If there is a high likelihood that subordinates would be committed, the decision matrix leads directly to the Decide style of decision making, in which the leader makes the decision alone and presents it to the group.

The Vroom-Jago model has been criticized as being imperfect,[55] but it is useful to managers and the body of supportive research is growing.[56] Managers can use the model to make timely, high-quality decisions. Consider the application of the model to the following problem at Madison Manufacturing.

Madison Manufacturing

When Madison Manufacturing won a coveted contract from a large auto manufacturer to produce an engine to power their flagship sports car, Dave Robbins was thrilled to be selected as project manager. This project has dramatically enhanced the reputation of Madison, and Robbins and his team of engineers have taken great pride in their work. However, their enthusiasm was dashed by a recent report of serious engine problems in cars delivered to customers. Taking quick action, the auto manufacturer suspended sales of the sports car, halted current production, and notified owners of the current model not to drive the car. Everyone involved knows this is a disaster. Unless the engine problem is solved quickly, Madison Manufacturing could be exposed to extended litigation. In addition, Madison's valued relationship with one of the world's largest auto manufacturers would likely be lost forever.

As the project manager, Robbins has spent two weeks in the field inspecting the seized engines and the auto plant where they were installed. Based on this extensive research, Robbins has some good ideas about what is causing the problem, but he knows his team members may have stronger expertise for solving it. In addition, while he has been traveling in the field, other team members have been evaluating the operations and practices in Madison's plant where the engine is manufactured. Therefore, Robbins chooses to get the team together and discuss the problem before making his final decision. The group meets for several hours, discussing the problem in detail and sharing their varied perspectives, including the information Robbins and team members have gathered. Following the group session, Robbins makes his decision, which will be presented at the team meeting the following morning, after which testing and correction of the engine problem will begin.[57]

The Vroom-Jago model in Exhibit 6.7 shows that Robbins used the correct decision style. Moving from left to right in Exhibit 6.7, the questions and answers are as follows: *How significant is the decision?* Definitely high. The company's future might be at stake. *How important is subordinate commitment to the decision?* Also high. The team members must support and implement Robbins' solution. *What is the level of Robbins' information and expertise?* Probably low. Though he has spent several weeks researching the seized engines, other team members have additional information and expertise that needs to be considered. *If Robbins makes the decision on his own, would team members have high or low commitment to it?* The answer to this question is probably low. Though team members respect Robbins, they take pride in their work as a team and know Robbins does not have complete information. This leads to the question, *What is the degree of subordinate support for the team's or organization's objectives at stake in this decision?* Definitely high. This leads to the question, *What is the level of group members' knowledge and expertise in relation to the problem?* The answer to this question is low, which leads to the Consult Group decision style, as described earlier in Exhibit 6.6. Thus, Robbins used the style that would be recommended by the Vroom-Jago model.

In many situations, several decision styles might be equally acceptable. However, smart managers are encouraging greater employee participation in solving problems whenever possible. The use of new knowledge management technologies allows for accessing the ideas and knowledge of a much broader group of people, inside and outside the organization.[58] Broad participation often leads to better decisions. Involving others in decision making contributes to individual and organizational learning, which is critical for rapid decision making in today's turbulent environment.

New Decision Approaches for Turbulent Times

The ability to make fast, widely supported, high-quality decisions on a frequent basis is a critical skill in today's fast-moving organizations.[59] In many industries, the rate of competitive and technological change is so extreme that opportunities are fleeting, clear and complete information is seldom available, and the cost of a slow decision means lost business or even company failure. Does this mean managers in today's workplace should make the majority of decisions on their own? No. The rapid pace of today's business environment calls for the opposite, that is, for people throughout the organization to be involved in decision making and have the information, skills, and freedom they need to respond immediately to problems and questions. Managers at Atlas Container discovered the power of involving everyone in decision making as described below.

Atlas Container

How do you take a nickel-and-dime, down-and-dirty business like box manufacturing and turn it into a fast-growing, exciting place to work? Paul and Peter Centenari did it by having their employees decide on almost everything, including how the company would spend its money.

The Centenaris were young, starry-eyed Harvard Business School graduates when they began looking for a low-tech business that could use some new life. They found it at Atlas Container, but their early days were rough. What they bought as a profitable, debt-free little company was on the verge of bankruptcy. The brothers thought of selling out, but then they had another idea: Let us set some ambitious goals and build a big company by acquiring competitors and keep swiping market share from the stodgy manufacturers who rule this low-margin industry. To do that, the Centenaris needed a fresh approach, one that involved everyone in the company. To do that meant opening the books so people had access to the information they needed, providing plenty of training and education opportunities, letting people participate in the decisions that would affect their jobs, and giving employees a stake in the business.

Today, Atlas is definitely a different kind of box manufacturer. For one thing, there is a big room called the Learning Center where employees can take company-sponsored classes or pursue self-directed learning. Managers hold regular employee meetings where they review sales, costs, profits, and other data about the business. Employees, not hoards of supervisors, make decisions about how to run the plant. Employees at Atlas have voted on such matters as disciplinary policies, whether to keep managers in their jobs, and which supplier to use for a new component for the corrugating machine. The Centenaris honored the employees' choice for the new $1 million piece of equipment, though they both preferred another vendor. Installing and learning to operate the new equipment was accomplished in three days, when it might easily have taken a week. The employees saw it as "their" machine, so they had a lot invested in making the process run smoothly.

In addition, when everyone is involved in making tough decisions, everyone is paying attention to details. "It isn't just about being nice," Paul Centenari says. "The open books and democracy are ways to shape a company that can do things that its competitors can't." Despite the hot, dirty work, Atlas plants practically hum with the energy and enthusiasm of employees who feel like an important part of the business.[60]

In today's fast-moving businesses, people often have to act first and analyze later.[61] Top managers do not have the time to evaluate options for every decision, conduct research, develop alternatives, and tell people what to do and how to do it. When speed matters, a slow decision may be as ineffective as the wrong decision, and companies can learn to make decisions fast. Effective decision making under turbulent conditions relies on the following guidelines.

Start with Brainstorming.   One of the best-known techniques for rapidly generating creative alternatives is **brainstorming**. Brainstorming uses a face-to-face interactive group to suggest a wide range of alternatives for decision making. The keys to effective brainstorming are that people can build on one another's ideas; all ideas are acceptable, no matter how crazy they seem; and criticism and evaluation are not allowed. The goal is to generate as many ideas as possible. Brainstorming has been found to be highly effective for generating a wide range of alternate solutions to a problem, but it does have some drawbacks. For one thing, people in a group often want to conform to what others are saying, a problem sometimes referred to as groupthink. Others may be concerned about pleasing the boss or impressing colleagues. In addition, many creative people have social inhibitions that limit their participation in a group session or make it difficult to come up with ideas in a group setting. In fact, one study found that when four people are asked to "brainstorm" individually, they typically come up with twice as many ideas as a group of four brainstorming together.

One recent approach, electronic brainstorming, takes advantage of the group approach while overcoming some disadvantages. **Electronic brainstorming**, sometimes called brainwriting, brings people together in an interactive group over a computer network.[62] One member writes an idea, another reads it and adds other ideas, and so on. Recent studies show that electronic brainstorming generates about 40 percent more ideas than individuals brainstorming alone, and 25 to 200 percent more ideas than regular brainstorming groups, depending on group size.[63] Why? Because the process is anonymous, the sky is the limit in terms of what people feel free to say. People can write down their ideas immediately, avoiding the possibility that a good idea might slip away while the person is waiting for a chance to speak in a face-to-face

---

brainstorming

A technique that uses a face-to-face group to suggest a broad range of alternatives spontaneously for decision making.

Take *ACTION*

When brainstorming, remember not to judge the ideas, as that dimishes the output.

electronic brainstorming

Bringing people together in an interactive group over a computer network to suggest alternatives; sometimes called brainwriting.

CONCEPT CONNECTION

At design firm IDEO, one of today's most innovative companies, people follow a five-step process for "creating experiences, not just products" for companies like Intel, Nestlé, Lufthansa, and Samsung. One important step is **brainstorming**, where people come up with as many ideas as possible for meeting client needs. Brainstorming sessions at IDEO have been described as "managed chaos," where as many as 100 ideas are generated in a one-hour session. Managers encourage wild ideas and rapid-fire thinking, and there are strict rules against interrupting colleagues or showing disrespect and judgment of others' ideas.

© Mark Richards/Photo Edit

group. Social inhibitions and concerns are avoided, which typically allows for a broader range of participation. Another advantage is that electronic brainstorming can potentially be done with groups made up of employees from around the world, further increasing the diversity of alternatives.

Learn, Do not Punish.   Decisions made under conditions of uncertainty and time pressure produce many errors, but smart managers are willing to take the risk in the spirit of trial and error. If a chosen decision alternative fails, the organization can learn from it and try another alternative that better fits the situation. Each failure provides new information and learning. People throughout the organization are encouraged to engage in experimentation, which means taking risks and learning from their mistakes. Good managers know that every time a person makes a decision, whether it turns out to have positive or negative consequences, it helps the employee learn and be a better decision maker the next time around. By making mistakes, people gain valuable experience and knowledge to perform more effectively in the future.

When people are afraid to make mistakes, the company is stuck. For example, when Robert Crandall led American Airlines, he built a culture in which any problem that caused a flight delay was followed by finding someone to blame. People became so scared of making a mistake that whenever something went wrong, no one was willing to jump in and try to fix the problem. In contrast, Southwest Airlines uses what it calls team delay, which means a flight delay is everyone's problem. This puts the emphasis on fixing the problem rather than on finding an individual to blame.[64] In a turbulent environment, managers do not use mistakes and failure to create a climate of fear. Instead, they encourage people to take risks and move ahead with the decision process, despite the potential for errors.

Know When to Bail.   Though managers encourage risk taking and learning from mistakes, they are not hesitant to pull the plug on something that is not working. Research has found that organizations often continue to invest time and money in a solution despite strong evidence that it is inappropriate. This tendency is referred to as **escalating commitment**. Managers might block or distort negative information because they do not want to be responsible for a bad decision or they might refuse to accept that their solution is wrong. In today's successful companies, people do not get so attached to their own ideas that they are unwilling to recognize when to move on. According to Stanford University professor Robert Sutton, the key to successful creative decision making is to "fail early, fail often, and pull the plug early."[65]

Practice the Five Whys.   One way to encourage good decision making under high uncertainty is to get people to think more broadly and deeply about problems rather than going with a superficial understanding and a first response. However, this does not mean people have to spend hours analyzing a problem and gathering research. One simple procedure adopted by a number of leading companies is known as the five whys.[66] For every problem, employees learn to ask "Why?" not just once, but five times. The first *why* generally produces a superficial explanation for the problem, and each subsequent *why* probes deeper into the causes of the problem and potential solutions. The point of the five whys is to improve how people think about problems and generate alternatives for solving them.

Engage in Rigorous Debate.   An important key to better decision making under conditions of uncertainty is to encourage a rigorous debate of the issue at hand.[67] Good managers recognize that constructive conflict based on divergent points of view can bring a problem into focus, clarify people's ideas, stimulate creative thinking, create a broader understanding of issues and alternatives, and improve decision quality.[68] Chuck Knight, the former CEO of Emerson Electric, always sparked heated debates during strategic planning meetings. Knight believed rigorous debate gave people a

Take **ACTION**

If someone makes a mistake, use it as a chance to learn and not to criticize.

escalating commitment

Continuing to invest time and resources in a failing decision.

clearer picture of the competitive landscape and forced managers to look at all sides of an issue, helping them reach better decisions.[69]

There are several ways to stimulate rigorous debate. One way is by ensuring the group is diverse in terms of age and gender, functional area of expertise, hierarchical level, and experience with the business. Some groups assign a **devil's advocate**, who has the role of challenging the assumptions and assertions made by the group.[70] The devil's advocate may force the group to rethink its approach to the problem and avoid reaching premature conclusions. Jeffrey McKeever, CEO of MicroAge, often plays the devil's advocate, changing his position in the middle of a debate to ensure other executives do not just go along with his opinions.[71] Another approach is to have group members develop as many alternatives as they can as quickly as they can.[72] This allows the team to work with multiple alternatives and encourages people to advocate ideas they might not prefer to encourage debate. Another way to encourage constructive conflict is to use a technique called **point-counterpoint**, which breaks a decision-making group into two subgroups and assigns them different, often competing responsibilities.[73] The groups then develop and exchange proposals and discuss and debate the various options until they arrive at a common set of understandings and recommendations.

Decision making in today's high-speed, complex environment is one of the most important—and most challenging—responsibilities for managers. By using brainstorming, learning from mistakes rather than assigning blame, knowing when to bail, practicing the five whys, and engaging in rigorous debate, managers can improve the quality and effectiveness of their organizational decisions.

devil's advocate

A decision-making technique in which an individual is assigned the role of challenging the assumptions and assertions made by the group to prevent premature consensus.

point-counterpoint

A decision-making technique in which people are assigned to express competing points of view.

Wal-Mart's IT

Almost every company uses some form of information technology. Indeed, the strategic use of information technology is one of the defining aspects of organizational success in today's world. A classic example is the success of Wal-Mart, which can be traced partly to the extensive use of IT to manage every aspect of the business. Managers use information systems that rely on a massive data warehouse to make decisions about what to stock, how to price and promote it, and when to reorder or discontinue items. Handheld scanners enable managers to keep close tabs on inventory and monitor sales at the end of each workday, and orders for new merchandise are sent by computer to headquarters, where they are automatically organized and sent to regional distribution centers, which have electronic linkages with key suppliers for reordering. A recent innovation is using tiny chips with identification numbers on shipments of products, which enables close tracking of inventory all through the supply chain. As the merchandise moves from the warehouse to stores and off the shelves, electronic readers automatically track its progress and send the data to a network, where everyone can track the movement of goods. Back at headquarters, top Wal-Mart executives analyze buying patterns and other information, enabling them to spot problems or opportunities and convey the information to stores.[74] Many other companies, in industries from manufacturing to entertainment, are using IT to get closer to customers, enter new markets, and streamline business processes.

IT and e-business have changed the way people and organizations work and, thus, present new challenges for managers. Despite the dot-com collapse of the early 2000s, the Internet continues to disrupt and transform traditional ways of doing business.[75] E-business still has a bright and bold future as it makes good on the promise of helping companies cut costs, increase efficiency, speed up innovation, and improve productivity. This chapter will explore the management of IT and e-business. We begin by developing a basic understanding of IT and the types of information systems frequently used in organizations. Then, the chapter will look at the growing use of the Internet and e-business, including a discussion of fundamental e-business strategies, business-to-business marketplaces, use of information technology in business operations, and the importance of knowledge management. The next section will discuss the management implications of using new information technology. Finally, we will briefly examine some recent information technology trends.

Information Technology

An organization's **information technology** (IT) consists of the hardware, software, telecommunications, database management, and other technologies it uses to store data and make them available in the form of information for organizational decision making.

By providing managers with more information, more quickly than ever before, modern IT improves efficiency and effectiveness at each stage of the strategic decision-making process. Whether through computer-aided manufacturing, information sharing with customers, or international inventory control, IT aids operational processes and decision making. Consider the pharmaceutical giant Eli Lilly, which set up an online scientific forum called InnoCentive. The forum is open to anyone and is available in multiple languages. Lilly posts thorny research problems and offers cash awards to anyone who can solve them, thus increasing its knowledge and speeding innovation without expanding its R&D budget. At General Motors, CEO Rick Wagoner and other top managers keep tabs on GM operations around the world and around the clock by logging on to the corporate network from secure Wi-Fi connections at home. This timely information helps GM executives make better decisions "in a world where everything is moving faster."[76]

Data versus Information

The ability to generate more information with technology presents a serious challenge to information technicians, managers, and other users of information. They must sort through overwhelming amounts of data to identify only that information necessary for a particular purpose. **Data** are raw facts and figures that by themselves may be useless. To be useful, data must be processed into finished **information**, that is, data converted into a meaningful and useful context for specific users. An increasing challenge for managers is being able to identify and access useful information. For example, American Greetings Corporation, which sells greeting cards, might gather data about demographics in various parts of the country. These data are then translated into information; for example, stores in Florida require an enormous assortment of greeting cards directed at grandson, granddaughter, niece, and nephew, and stores in some other parts of the country might need a larger percentage of slightly irreverent, youth-oriented products.[77]

The magnitude of the job of transforming data into useful information is reflected in organizations' introduction of the chief information officer (CIO) position. CIOs are responsible for managing organizational databases and implementing new information technology. As they make decisions involving the adoption and management of new technologies, CIOs integrate old and new technology to support organizational decision making, operations, and communication. Effective CIOs manage the technology infrastructure and focus on information design, so managers have high-quality information to improve decision making, solve problems, and boost performance.[78] Ideally, the CIO combines a knowledge of technology with the ability to help managers identify their information needs and how the organization can use its IT capabilities to support competitive strategy. An important part of the CIO's job is establishing systems that shape disjointed data into clear, meaningful, and useful information.

information technology (IT)
Consists of the hardware, software, telecommunications, database management, and other technologies it uses to store data and make them available in the form of information for organizational decision making.

data
Raw facts and figures that by themselves may be useless.

information
Data converted into a meaningful and useful context for specific users.

Take **ACTION**

When giving your boss a report, make sure it is not merely data but has useful information the boss can act upon.

Characteristics of Useful Information

Organizations depend on high-quality information to develop strategic plans, identify problems, and interact with other organizations. High-quality information has characteristics that make it useful for these tasks. The high-quality information characteristics fall into three broad categories, as illustrated in Exhibit 6.8.[79]

1. *Time.* Information should be available and provided when needed, timely, and related to the appropriate time period (past, present, or future).

2. *Content.* Useful information is error free, suited to the user's needs, complete, concise, relevant (that is, it excludes unnecessary data), and an accurate measure of performance.

3. *Form.* The information should be provided in a form that is easy for the user to understand and that meets the user's needs for the level of detail. The presentation should be ordered and use the combination of words, numbers, and diagrams most helpful to the user. Information should be presented in a useful medium (e.g., printed documents, video display, sound).

Types of Information Systems

Most managers appreciate the value of making information readily available in some kind of formal, computer-based information system. Such a system combines hardware, software, and human resources to support organizational information and communication needs. One way to distinguish among the many types of information systems is to focus on the functions they perform and the people they serve in an organization. Two broad categories of information systems widely used today are shown in Exhibit 6.9. **Operations information systems** support information-processing needs of a business's daily operations and low-level operations management functions. Management information systems typically support the strategic decision-making needs of higher-level managers.

operations information sytems

These support information-processing needs of a business's daily operations and low-level operations management functions.

EXHIBIT 6.8

Characteristics of High-Quality Information

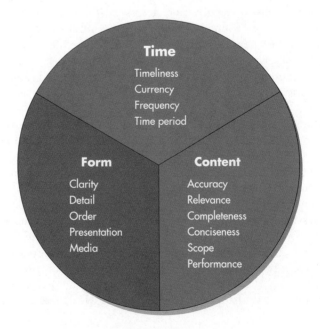

SOURCE: Adapted from James A. O'Brien, *Introduction to Information Systems*, 8th ed. (Burr Ridge, IL: Irwin, 1997), 284–285.

EXHIBIT 6.9
Types of Information Systems

Operations Information Systems
- Transaction-processing systems
- Process control systems
- Office automation systems

Management Information Systems
- Information-reporting systems
- Decision support systems
- Executive information systems
- Groupware

Operations and Management Information Systems

Types of operations information systems include transaction processing systems, process control systems, and office automation systems. Each of these supports daily operations and decisions that typically are made by nonmanagement employees or lower-level managers.

A **transaction processing system (TPS)** records and processes data resulting from business operations. It includes information systems that record sales to customers, purchases from suppliers, inventory changes, and wages to employees. A TPS collects data from these transactions and stores them in a database. Employees use the database to produce reports and other information, such as customer statements and employee paychecks. Most of an organization's reports are generated from these databases. Transaction processing systems identify, collect, and organize the fundamental information from which an organization operates.

Though a transaction processing system keeps track of the size, type, and financial consequences of the organization's transactions, companies also need information about the quantity and quality of their production activities. Therefore, they may use process control systems to monitor and control ongoing physical processes. For example, petroleum refineries, pulp and paper mills, food manufacturing plants, and electric power plants use **process control systems** with special sensing devices that monitor and record physical phenomena such as temperature or pressure changes. The system relays the measurements or sensor-detected data to a computer for processing; and employees and operations managers can check the data to look for problems requiring action.

Office automation systems combine modern hardware and software such as word processors, desktop publishers, e-mail, and teleconferencing to handle the tasks of publishing and distributing information. Office automation systems are used to transform manual accounting procedures to electronic media. Companies such as Wal-Mart, Chevron, and American Airlines send thousands of electronic payments a month to suppliers, eliminating the need for writing and mailing checks. Merrill Lynch uses electronic office automation to manage consultants' travel and entertainment expenses, cutting the time it takes to process a report and issue reimbursement from six weeks to four days and slashing the average cost of processing a report from $25 to only a few dollars. [80] These systems enable businesses to streamline office tasks, reduce errors, and improve customer service. In this way, office automation systems support the other kinds of information systems.

Operations information systems aid organizational decision makers in many ways and across various settings. For example, Enterprise Rent-a-Car's Computer Assisted Rental System (Ecars) provides front-line employees with timely information that enables them to provide exceptional service to each customer. The computer-based system helps Enterprise keep track of the 1.4 million transactions the company logs every hour. If a customer visits a branch office and requests a certain kind of car, the

transaction processing system (TPS)

Records and processes data resulting from business operations.

Take *ACTION*

As a manager, find ways to get more information that can help you measure how well the organization is doing.

process control systems

These special sensing devices monitor and record physical phenomena such as temperature or pressure changes.

office automation systems

These combine modern hardware and software such as word processors, desktop publishers, e-mail, and teleconferencing to handle the tasks of publishing and distributing information.

agent can immediately determine if one is available anywhere in the city. Insurance companies such as Geico can link their claims systems directly to Enterprise's automated rental system, book a reservation, and send payments electronically, eliminating the need for paper invoices and checks.[81]

Similarly, when Tim Doreck learned to use an information system, his business improved.

Monterrey Express Diving Charters

When Tim Doreck relied on his answering machine, he lost business. Not long ago, 12 people wanted to hire his dive boat that day. By the time he called them back, they had another boat. His loss: $1,000.

That was a lesson he will not forget. Now, Doreck's Monterrey Express Diving Charters uses the Web-based reservation system Time-Trade, letting customers book their own charters. After they log on, they can see what is available and reserve it, receiving an immediate online confirmation plus an e-mail. Is it worth the $49.95 he pays a month as a sole proprietor? Doreck says his phone and cellular bills have been cut dramatically, he spends 70 percent less time sending e-mails to inquiring customers, and his business is up 30 percent. Customers seem to like the online booking. "They are more inclined to book trips further ahead," he notes, " and they're more inclined to book when they just think of it."[82]

Management Information Systems

Until the 1960s, information systems were used primarily for transaction processing, accounting, and recordkeeping. Then, the introduction of computers using silicon chip circuitry allowed for more processing power per dollar. As computer manufacturers promoted these systems and managers began visualizing ways in which the computers could help them make important decisions, management information systems were born. A **management information system (MIS)** is a computer-based system that provides information and support for effective managerial decision making. The basic elements of a management information system are illustrated in Exhibit 6.10. The MIS is supported by the organization's operations information systems and by organizational databases (and frequently databases of external data as well). An MIS typically includes reporting systems, decision support systems, executive information systems, and groupware, each of which will be explained in this section.

---

management information system (MIS)

This is a computer-based system that provides information and support for effective managerial decision making.

EXHIBIT 6.10

Basic Elements of Management Information Systems

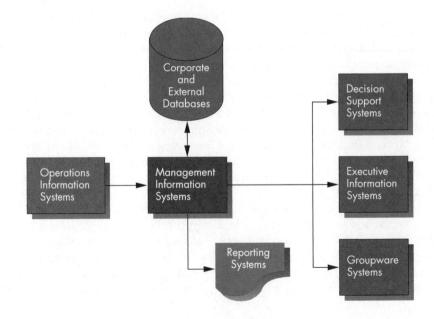

SOURCE: Adapted from Ralph M. Stair and George W. Reynolds, *Principles of Information Systems: A Managerial Approach*, 4th ed. (Cambridge, Mass.: Course Technology, 1999), 391.

An MIS typically supports strategic decision-making needs of mid-level and top management. However, as technology becomes more widely accessible, more employees are wired into networks, and organizations push decision making downward in the hierarchy, these kinds of systems are seeing use at all levels of the organization.

Take a moment to complete this experiential exercise to assess your MIS style

Personal Inventory to determine your MIS style

In the following 14 statements, circle the number that indicates how much you agree that each statement is characteristic of you. The statements refer to how you use information and make decisions.

Strongly Disagree   Strongly Agree

  1   2   3   4   5

1. I like to wait until all relevant information is examined before deciding something.

   1   2   3   4   5

2. I prefer information that can be interpreted in several ways and leads to different but acceptable solutions.

   1   2   3   4   5

3. I like to keep gathering data until an excellent solution emerges.

   1   2   3   4   5

4. To make decisions, I often use information that means different things to different people.

   1   2   3   4   5

5. I want just enough data to make a decision quickly.

   1   2   3   4   5

6. I act on logical analysis of the situation rather than on my "gut feelings" about the best alternative.

   1   2   3   4   5

7. I seek information sources or people that will provide me with many ideas and details.

   1   2   3   4   5

8. I try to generate more than one satisfactory solution for the problem faced.

   1   2   3   4   5

9. When reading something, I confine my thoughts to what is written rather than search for additional understanding.

   1   2   3   4   5

10. When working on a project, I narrow, not broaden, the scope so it is clearly defined.

    1   2   3   4   5

11. I typically acquire all possible information before making a final decision.

1   2   3   4   5

12. I like to work on something I have done before rather than take on a complicated problem.

1   2   3   4   5

13. I prefer clear, precise data.

1   2   3   4   5

14. When working on a project, I like to explore various options rather than maintain a narrow focus

1   2   3   4   5

Scoring and Interpretation

Your information-processing style determines the extent to which you will benefit from computer-based information systems. First, subtract each of your scores for statements 5, 6, 9, 10, 12, and 13 from the number 6 and indicate the adjusted score next to each statement. Use the adjusted scores to calculate your totals as follows:

The odd-numbered statements pertain to the "amount of information" you like to use. Your total score for odd-numbered statements: _____. A score of 28 or more suggests you prefer a large amount of information. A score of 14 or less indicates you like a small amount.

The even-numbered statements pertain to the "focus of information" you prefer. Your total score for even-numbered statements: _____. A score of 28 or more suggests you are comfortable with ambiguous, multifocused information, while a score of 14 or less suggests you like clear, unifocused data.

If you are a person who likes a large amount of information and clear, focused data, you will tend to make effective use of MISs. You could be expected to benefit greatly from an EIS or MIS in your company. If you are a person who prefers a small amount of information and data that are multifocused, you would probably not get the information you need to make decisions through formal information systems. You probably will not utilize an EIS or MIS to a great extent, preferring instead to get decision data from other convenient sources, including face-to-face discussions.

SOURCES: This questionnaire is adapted from Richard L. Daft and Norman B. Macintosh, "A Tentative Exploration into the Amount and Equivocality of Information Processing in Organizational Work Units," *Administrative Science Quarterly* 26 (1981): 207–224; and Dorothy Marcic, *Organizational Behavior: Experiences and Cases*, 4th ed. (St. Paul, Minn.: West, 1995).

The Internet and E-Business

Internet

A global collection of computer networks linked together for the exchange of data and information.

World Wide Web (WWW or Web)

A set of central servers for accessing information on the Internet.

In recent years, most organizations have incorporated the Internet as part of their information technology strategy.[83] The **Internet** is a global collection of computer networks linked together for the exchange of data and information. The **World Wide Web (WWW or Web)** is a set of central servers for accessing information on the Internet. Originally developed for use by the U.S. military, the Internet and the Web have become household words and an important part of our personal and work lives. Businesses and nonprofit organizations realized the potential of the Internet for expanding their operations globally, improving business processes, reaching new customers, and making the most of their resources. E-business began to boom. **E-business** can be defined as any business that takes place by digital processes over a computer network rather than in physical space. Most commonly today, it refers to electronic linkages over the Internet with customers, partners, suppliers, employees or other key constituents. **E-commerce** is a more limited term that refers specifically to business exchanges or transactions that occur electronically.

Some organizations are set up as e-businesses that are run completely over the Internet, such as eBay, Amazon.com, Expedia, and Yahoo!. These companies would not exist without the Internet. However, most established organizations, including General Electric, the City of Madison, Wisconsin, Target, and the U.S. Postal Service, extensively use the Internet, and we will focus on these types of organizations in the remainder of this section. The goal of e-business for established organizations is to digitalize as much of the business as possible to make the organization more efficient and effective. Companies are using the Internet and the Web for everything from filing expense reports and calculating daily sales to connecting directly with suppliers for the exchange of information and ordering of parts.[84]

Exhibit 6.11 illustrates the key components of e-business for two organizations, a manufacturing company and a retail chain. First, each organization uses an **Intranet**, an internal communications system that uses the technology and standards of the Internet but is accessible only to people within the company. The next component is a system that allows the separate companies to share data and information. Two options are

© Jonathan Blair/CORBIS

e-business

This can be defined as any business that takes place by digital processes over a computer network rather than in physical space.

e-commerce

This is a more limited term that refers specifically to business exchanges or transactions that occur electronically.

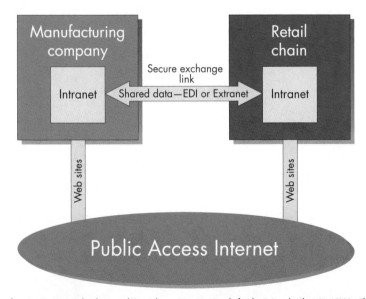

EXHIBIT 6.11

The Key Components of E-Business for Two Traditional Organizations

SOURCE: Based on Jim Turcotte, Bob Silveri, and Tom Jobson, "Are You Ready for the E-Supply Chain?" *APICS—The Performance Advantage* (August 1998), 56–59.

Intranet

An internal communications system that uses the technology and standards of the Internet but is accessible only to people within the company.

Take **ACTION**

As a manager, think of new ways your company can use the Internet.

an electronic data interchange network or an extranet. **Electronic data interchange (EDI)** networks link the computer systems of buyers and sellers to allow the transmission of structured data primarily for ordering, distribution, and payables and receivables.[85] An **Extranet** is an external communications system that uses the Internet and is shared by two or more organizations. With an Extranet, each organization moves certain data outside of its private Intranet but makes the data available only to the other companies sharing the Extranet. The final piece of the overall system is the Internet, which is accessible to the general public. Organizations make some information available to the public through their Web sites, which may include products or services offered for sale. For example, at the Web site of Herman Miller, the first office furniture maker to design and sell a line of products over the Internet, dealers and consumers can place orders for furniture online and check order status or make changes with a few mouse clicks.

E-Business Strategies and E-Marketplaces

The first step toward a successful e-business is for managers to determine why they need such a business to begin with.[86] Failure to align the e-business initiative with corporate strategy can lead to e-business failure. Two basic strategic approaches for traditional organizations setting up an Internet operation are illustrated in Exhibit 6.12. Some companies embrace e-business to expand into new markets and reach new customers. Others use e-business as a route to increased productivity and cost efficiency. As shown in the exhibit, these strategies are implemented by setting up an in-house Internet division or by partnering with other organizations to handle online activities.

Market Expansion.   An Internet division allows a company to establish direct links to customers and expand into new markets. The organization can provide access around the clock to a worldwide market and, thus, reach new customers. Eddie Bauer estimates that more than half of the customers making purchases on its electronic storefront are new to the site, supporting the idea that e-business helps reach new customers and markets.[87]

An e-business division also enables customization of offerings at significantly lower costs than traditional distribution channels, helping a company differentiate its products and services. The market expansion strategy is competitively sustainable because

electronic data interchange (EDI)

These networks link the computer systems of buyers and sellers to allow the transmission of structured data primarily for ordering, distribution, and payables and receivables.

extranet

This is an external communications system that uses the Internet and is shared by two or more organizations.

EXHIBIT 6.12
Strategies for Engaging Clicks with Bricks

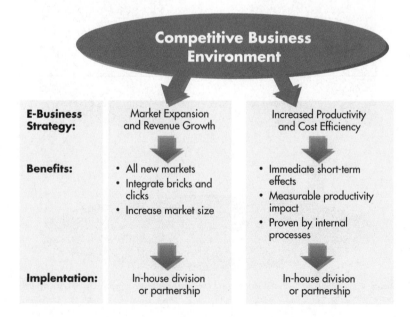

E-Business Strategy:	Market Expansion and Revenue Growth	Increased Productivity and Cost Efficiency
Benefits:	• All new markets • Integrate bricks and clicks • Increase market size	• Immediate short-term effects • Measurable productivity impact • Proven by internal processes
Implentation:	In-house division or partnership	In-house division or partnership

the e-business division works in conjunction with the established bricks-and-mortar company. One example is National Public Radio (NPR), which simulcasts pictures on its Web site connected to radio shows such as *Morning Edition*, serving to increase listener traffic to the show. Consider how REI, an outdoor equipment retailer, uses its online business for market expansion.

REI

> When REI wanted to boost its in-store sales, it turned to its Web site to do it. Customers who order online can have the item shipped free to the nearest REI retail outlet, where they pick it up and save the shipping cost.
>
> Managers soon discovered that one out of every three people who buy something online will spend about $90 more when they come to pick up the item. People are swayed to spend more when they enter the store and see the colorful displays of bikes, climbing gear, and outdoor clothing. Another successful approach has been REI's gift registry. People can set up a gift list and friends or relatives can purchase requested items either online or at any retail channel. Once a person sets up a gift registry, REI sends notices to a designated list of recipients. The gift registry has been an effective way of expanding sales to people who do not traditionally shop at REI, and some have become new regular customers.
>
> By integrating their online products and services with their traditional retail operations, REI has increased its sales and expanded its market reach.[88]

Customer Relationship Management

In addition to better internal information management and information sharing with suppliers and other organizations, companies are using e-business solutions to build stronger customer relationships. One approach is **customer relationship management (CRM)** systems that help companies track customers' interactions with the firm and allow employees to call up a customer's past sales and service records, outstanding orders, or unresolved problems.[89] CRM stores all the customer information in a database that small-town store owners would keep in their heads: the names of all their customers, what they bought, what problems they have had with their purchases, and so forth. CRM helps to coordinate sales, marketing, and customer service departments so all are smoothly working together to best serve customer needs. For example, when a customer places an order, the salesperson enters the order and the CRM software updates the database. Whenever the customer calls with a question or problem, CRM automatically brings up the customer's record so the customer service or technical support representative has all pertinent information at hand and is able to provide personalized service, make additional sales pitches based on the customer's purchasing history, and update the database with information related to the call. Data from Web site customer contacts is automatically entered into the database. Marketing can use the detailed customer information to implement tailored marketing programs. Organizations use CRM to cut costs while improving service. Morgan Stanley uses CRM to calculate each customer's profitability and assign service levels since the company does not have the staff and resources to give every customer the red carpet treatment. Stanely LoFrumento, executive director for CRM, says the program has paid for itself in reduced costs and more targeted cross-selling efforts.[90]

Increasingly, what distinguishes an organization from its competitors are its knowledge resources, such as product ideas and the ability to identify and find solutions to customers' problems. Exhibit 6.13 lists examples of how CRM and other IT can shorten the distance between customers and the organization, contributing to organizational success through customer loyalty, superior service, better information gathering, and organizational learning.

customer relationship management (CRM)

This system helps companies track customers' interactions with the firm and allows employees to call up a customer's past sales and service records, outstanding orders, or unresolved problems.

Take ACTION

As a manager, keep finding ways to help your customers interact with you online in simpler and more elegant ways.

EXHIBIT 6.13

Competitive Advantages Gained from Customer Relationship Management (CRM) Systems

Competitive Advantage	Example
• Increase in customer loyalty	Full information about customer profile and previous requests or preferences is instantly available to sales and servicerepresentatives when a customer calls.
• Superior service	Customer representatives can provide personalized service offer new products and services based on customer's purchasing history.
• Superior information gathering and knowledge sharing	The system is updated each time a customer contacts the organization, whether the contact is in person, by phone, or via the Web. Sales, marketing, service support, and technical support have access to shared database.
• Organizational learning	Managers can analyze patterns to solve problems and anticipate new ones.

knowledge management

This comprises the efforts to gather knowledge systematically, make it available throughout the organization, and foster a culture of learning.

Knowledge Management

The Internet plays a key role in the recent emphasis managers are putting on **knowledge management**, the efforts to gather knowledge systematically, make it available throughout the organization, and foster a culture of learning. Some researchers believe that intellectual capital will soon be the primary way in which businesses measure their value.[91] Therefore, managers see knowledge as an important resource to manage, just as they manage cash flow, raw materials, and other resources. An effective knowledge management system may incorporate various technologies, supported by leadership that values learning, an organizational structure that supports communication and information sharing, and processes for managing change.[92] Two specific technologies that facilitate knowledge management are business intelligence software and corporate Intranets or networks. The use of new business intelligence software helps organizations make sense out of huge amounts of data. These programs combine related pieces of information to create knowledge. Knowledge that can be codified, written down, and contained in databases is referred to as explicit knowledge. However, much organizational knowledge is unstructured and resides in people's heads. This tacit knowledge cannot be captured in a database, making it difficult to formalize and transmit. Intranets and knowledge-sharing networks can support the spread of tacit knowledge.

Management Implications of Information Technology

IT and e-business can enable managers to be better connected with employees, the environment, and each other. In general, IT has positive implications for the practice of management though it can present problems. Some specific implications of IT for managers include improved employee effectiveness, increased efficiency, empowered employees, information overload, and enhanced collaboration.

Improved Employee Effectiveness

IT can provide employees with all kinds of information about their customers, competitors, markets, and service, as well as enable them to share information or insights with colleagues. In addition, time and geographic boundaries are dissolving. A management team can work throughout the day on a project in Switzerland and, while they are sleeping, a team in the United States can continue where the Swiss team left off. Employees all over the world have instant access to databases at any time of the day or night and the ability to share information via an Intranet. Advanced IT allows managers and employees to work whenever and wherever they are most needed and most productive.

In general, IT enables managers to design jobs to provide employees with more intellectual engagement and more challenging work. IT's availability does not guarantee increased job performance, but when implemented and used appropriately, it can have a dramatic influence on employee effectiveness. Siemens is developing a high-speed global Intranet that will enable its 450,000 employees around the world to share knowledge and collaborate on projects to provide better solutions for customers. One example that has occurred is when employees in the information and communications division collaborated with the medical division to develop products for the healthcare market.[93]

Increased Efficiency

New IT offers significant promise for speeding work processes, cutting costs, and increasing efficiency. For example, at IBM, automating customer service helped reduce the number of call center employees and saved $750 million in one year alone. Companies like IBM are moving all aspects of purchasing to the Web, helping slash costs and wring deeper discounts from suppliers.

Sweeping away administrative paperwork and automating mundane tasks is another advantage of new technology. At EZRider, a Massachusetts-based retailer of snowboards, whenever a salesperson keys in a purchase, the company's computer system records the amount of the sale; at the end of the pay period, the system automatically computes the salesperson's commission in a matter of seconds.[94]

Empowered Employees

IT is profoundly affecting the way organizations are structured. Through implementing IT, organizations change the locus of knowledge by providing information to people who would not otherwise receive it. Lower-level employees are increasingly challenged with more information and are expected to make decisions previously made by supervisors. Nurses, bellhops, truck drivers, utility repair workers, and warehouse staffers all need easy access to information to do their jobs well in today's fast-paced environment.[95]

These changes support the objectives of knowledge management by enabling decisions to be made by the employees who are in the best position to implement the decisions and see their effects. For example, the U.S. Army is beginning to use new IT that pushes information about battlefield conditions, the latest intelligence on the enemy, and so forth, down the line to the lower troops. Armed with better data and trained to see patterns in the barrage of information, lieutenants in the field will be making more of the tough decisions once made by commanders.[96]

Information Overload

One problem associated with advances in technology is that the company can become a quagmire of information, with employees so overwhelmed by the sheer volume that they are unable to sort out the valuable from the useless.[97]

In many cases, the ability to produce data and information is outstripping employees' ability to process it. One British psychologist claims to have identified a new mental disorder caused by too much information; he has termed it Information Fatigue Syndrome.[98] IT is a primary culprit in contributing to this new "disease." However, managers have the ability to alleviate the problem and improve information quality. The first step is to ensure that

IT suppliers and CIOs work closely with employees to identify the kinds of questions they must answer and the data and information they need. Specialists are often enamored with the volume of data a system can produce and overlook the need to provide small amounts of quality information in a timely and useful manner for decision making. Top executives should be actively involved in setting limits by focusing the organization on key strategies and on the critical questions that must be answered to pursue those strategies.[99]

Enhanced Collaboration

IT enhances collaboration within the organization and with customers, suppliers, and partners. The Internet, corporate networks, knowledge management systems, and collaborative work systems can connect employees around the world for the sharing and exchange of information and ideas. An interesting example is Petfinder.com, an online organization that was set up by a young couple in New Jersey to increase collaboration among animal shelters, humane societies, and pet rescue groups, and to connect more adoptable pets with potential adopters. Through enhanced collaboration, Petfinder.com has facilitated the placement of millions of animals that once might have faced euthanasia in shelters.[100] In businesses, one of the most effective uses of IT for collaboration has been in the area of product development as described below. Extranets are increasingly important for linking companies with contract manufacturers and outsourcers, supporting the development of the virtual network organization, which will be discussed in Chapter 7.

| **General Motors** | It used to take General Motors at least 12 weeks to complete a full mock-up of a new car design. Today, it takes two. The complete design cycle time has been cut from 44 months to just 18 months. Have managers hired smarter, more creative, more efficient employees? No, they have applied IT to help the smart, creative, and efficient employees they had do their work faster and better. |

By using collaborative product development technologies, GM employees around the world can collaborate with one another and with external auto parts suppliers in real time to share product design information. Prior to 1999, GM had no way to coordinate its complex auto designs across 14 engineering sites scattered around the world, plus the dozens of worldwide partners that design subsystems for GM. Then, managers implemented a collaboration system from EDS that lets more than 16,000 employees collaborate and keep track of parts and subassemblies. The system serves as a central clearinghouse for all design data. When changes are finalized, the system automatically updates the master design.

Now GM is kicking collaboration up another notch. By the end of 2004, employees in Asia, Europe, Latin America, and the United States were scheduled to begin working together in virtual reality studios. The computer-linked studios allow design engineers and managers to view three-dimensional, full-sized representations of vehicle designs. Designers in different parts of the world can simultaneously view the same images, down to the level of surface details, and review and revise projects together.

Perhaps the biggest advantage of the enhanced collaboration is the time and the money GM saves by cutting product development time. The company has slashed about $1 billion from product development and engineering costs, and improved accuracy resulting from virtual reality collaboration is expected to save millions more each year. However, an equally important advantage is that employees around the world can have input into every new design and have the time and tools to think more creatively.[101]

The emphasis on using IT rather than personal travel for collaboration has increased in response to reduced travel budgets, concern over incidents such as international terrorism, and world health epidemics such as the SARS virus.[102] As we discussed in

Chapters 1 and 5, a company's normal business operations may be disrupted by crises or unexpected events, and IT plays a key role in helping to maintain essential channels of communication. The Centers for Disease Control, in Atlanta, for example, sponsors PulseNet, an information network that uses collaborative information technology to help federal and state agencies stay up to date regarding food-borne disease outbreaks.[103]

Information Technology Trends in the New Workplace

IT continues to evolve, and new concepts and applications are emerging every day. Some recent trends in IT that are having the greatest impact are wireless applications, peer-to-peer technology, new communication tools such as blogs and wikis, and international expansion.

Wireless Internet

A promising technology is Internet's Wireless Fidelity, or Wi-Fi. Early estimates of the growth of Wi-Fi proved to be grossly exaggerated, but Wi-Fi advocates continue to suggest that the technology will change the way we work and play on the Web.[104] Going wireless means employees can gain access to bits of data and information over handheld devices when and where they need it. With 21 million or so workers on the move on any given day, wireless technologies are becoming critical for helping people be more efficient and effective outside of the office. At Starbucks, 600 district managers access Wi-Fi in Starbucks stores, enabling them to spend more time in the field and less at headquarters. A representative of enterprise software maker J. D. Edwards says two-thirds of his clients are interested in wireless versions of the company's sales-force automation software. That means salespeople can stay where they are most needed, on the road drumming up new business and keeping old business satisfied.[105] Celanese Chemical's remote sales force can access real-time company information from the company's ERP system via wireless devices. One saleswoman obtained an instant confirmation on availability of a product and promise immediate shipment, helping her close a lucrative sale. "If the system saves just one order," says William Schmitt, a senior IT executive at Celanese, "it will practically pay for itself."[106]

Peer-to-Peer File Sharing

Napster and other music-sharing services have gotten into trouble for enabling the illegal sharing and distribution of copyrighted music. However, the technology behind Napster is finding various uses in legitimate business. Software can enable one person to locate and download files, such as songs, directly from another person's personal computer. This cutting-edge technology, called **peer-to-peer (P2P) file sharing**, allows personal computers (PCs) to communicate directly with one another over the Internet, bypassing central databases, servers, control points, and Web pages.[107] P2P software lets any individual's computer "talk" directly to another PC without an intermediary, enhancing the opportunities for information sharing and collaboration. PCs have enormous storage capacity, and P2P technology improves efficiency by allowing for the sharing of PC files directly between two PCs, eliminating the need for setting up and managing huge central storage systems. GlaxoSmithKline uses P2P technology to let its employees and researchers outside the company share their drug test data digitally and work collaboratively on new projects. Law firm Baker & McKenzie uses it to allow major clients to tap directly into its attorney's files stored on computers worldwide. For example, clients closing a merger can monitor the progress of the deal without attorneys having to keep files in one place or send lengthy electronic documents, improving organizational speed and efficiency.[108]

peer-to-peer (P2P) file sharing

This allows personal computers (PCs) to communicate directly with one another over the Internet, bypassing central databases, servers, control points, and Web pages.

Blogs and Wikis

A recent approach being embraced by corporate America is writing Web logs, or blogs. A **blog** is a running Web log that allows an individual to post opinions and ideas on anything from products to management.[109] Internal blogs can serve as superb horizontal and bottom-up communication tools, enabling people to get a better picture of what is going on all around the organization. Blogs contribute to collaboration and knowledge sharing as well. When IBM initiated blogging, within three months, 500 people in more than 30 countries were using it to discuss software development and other business projects. The simplicity and informality of blogs make them an easy and comfortable medium for people to communicate and share ideas. Unlike many knowledge management tools, blog software is simple to use and fits well with employees' regular daily communications. Some companies extend the approach to external blogs, which provide a way to communicate with customers, market products, and monitor public opinion about the organization. An extension of blogs is an emerging collaboration tool referred to as wikis.[110] Unlike blogs, which allow individuals to broadcast their views to an online audience, wikis are free-form, allowing visitors to edit what they find on the site or add content to it. Wikis have not yet caught on in the corporate world, but technology watchers expect this to be a growing approach to communication, collaboration, and knowledge sharing.

Manager's Solution

This chapter made several important points about the process of organizational decision making. The study of decision making is important because it describes how managers make successful strategic and operational decisions. Managers must confront many types of decisions, including programmed and nonprogrammed, and these decisions differ according to the amount of risk, uncertainty, and ambiguity in the environment.

Three decision-making approaches were described: the classical model, the administrative model, and the political model. The classical model explains how managers should make decisions so as to maximize economic efficiency. The administrative model describes how managers make nonprogrammed, uncertain decisions with skills that include intuition. The political model relates to making nonprogrammed decisions when conditions are uncertain, information is limited and ambiguous, and there is conflict among managers about what goals to pursue or what course of action to take. Managers have to engage in discussion and coalition building to reach agreement for decisions.

Decision making should involve six basic steps: problem recognition, diagnosis of causes, development of alternatives, choice of an alternative, implementation of the alternative, and feedback and evaluation.

Another factor affecting decision making is the manager's personal decision style. The four major decision styles are directive, analytical, conceptual, and behavioral. The chapter explained the Vroom-Jago model, which managers can use to determine when a decision calls for group participation. Involving others in decision making contributes to individual and organizational learning, which is critical during turbulent times and in high-tech industries. Decisions often have to be made quickly and with limited information. Managers can use the following guidelines: start with brainstorming; learn, do not punish; know when to bail; practice the five whys; and engage in rigorous debate. These techniques improve the quality and effectiveness of decision making in today's turbulent business environment.

IT and e-business are changing the way people and organizations work. Organizations are evolving into information cultures in which managers and employees can share information and knowledge across boundaries of time and geography. In addition, customers, partners, and suppliers are brought into the information network.

Modern IT gathers huge amounts of data and transforms them into useful information for decision makers. The systems that use this technology should be designed to generate information with appropriate time, content, and form attributes. Many organizations hire a CIO to help manage decisions regarding technology infrastructure and information design.

Information systems combine hardware, software, and human resources to organize information and make it readily available. Operations information systems, including transaction processing systems, process control systems, and office automation systems, support daily business operations and the needs of low-level managers. Management information systems, including information reporting systems, decision support systems, and executive information systems, typically support the decision-making needs of middle-level and upper-level managers. Collaborative work systems allow groups of managers or employees to share information, collaborate electronically, and have access to computer-based support data for group decision making and problem solving.

Most organizations have incorporated the Internet and e-business as part of their IT strategy. Traditional organizations use an online division primarily for market expansion or to increase productivity and reduce costs. Two primary ways e-business strategies are implemented are through an in-house dot-com division or by partnering with other organizations for the Internet business. Companies are benefitting from participation in electronic marketplaces, where many different sellers offer products and services to many different buyers through an online hub.

Recall the opening case of Bountiful Mazda, which was looking for a way to use new Internet technology to increase effectiveness. Owner Michael MacDonald decided to participate in a Mazda-supported makeover of its dealership (the company kicks in around $350,000 and plans to overhaul 200 dealerships by 2008). A big part of the makeover is to invite customers to do their price research on new and used cars right inside the dealership. Bountiful has become a Wi-Fi hotspot, where customers and employees can use their own wireless devices to check prices and specifications. Several computer kiosks are scattered around the dealership. Unlike some dealers that keep their onsite PCs locked down to the maker's own Web site, Bountiful encourages users to browse anywhere they want and even catch up on e-mail or personal business. A separate Internet café near the showroom is off-limits to sales staff members unless they are invited inside by a customer to discuss terms or draw up paperwork. Gone are the high-pressure sales pitches and the "closing booths," where customers are often pressed into paying higher prices. Bountiful has a fleet of washed, waxed, and polished vehicles gassed up and ready to take for a spin the minute a customer walks on the lot. Talk comes later, with customer and salesperson armed with on-the-spot information from the Web. The new, friendlier approach and open information via the Internet has translated into some big results. Customers tend to let their guard down in this open atmosphere, enabling the salesperson to upsell, cross-sell, and accessorize. A customer who feels he or she is getting the lowest price on the car is often more willing to tack on a $2,800 warranty package or a $2,000 in-dash global positioning system (GPS). Overall, the Bountiful store and Mazda's five other revamped showrooms are seeing 32 percent jumps in annual sales and generating twice the profit of older dealerships.[111]

Discussion Questions

1. You are a busy partner in a legal firm, and an experienced secretary complains of continued headaches, drowsiness, dry throat, and occasional spells of fatigue and flu. She tells you she believes air quality in the building is bad and would like something done. How would you respond?

2. Why is decision making considered a fundamental part of management effectiveness?

3. Explain the difference between risk and ambiguity. How might decision making differ for each situation?

4. Analyze three decisions you made over the past six months. Which of these were programmed and which were nonprogrammed?

5. Why are many decisions made by groups rather than by individuals?

6. The Vroom-Jago model describes five decision styles. How should a manager go about choosing which style to use?

7. What are the major differences between the administrative and political models of decision making?

8. What is meant by bounded rationality and satisficing? Why don't managers strive to find the economically best solution for many organizational decisions?

9. What techniques could you use to improve your own creativity and effectiveness in decision making?

10. Which of the six steps in the decision-making process do you think is most likely to be ignored by a manager? Explain.

11. Why is it important for managers to understand the difference between data and information?

12. Choose a business. In what ways would the role of a CIO be important?

13. What types of information technology do you use as a student on a regular basis? How might your life be different if you did not have this technology available to you?

14. How might the organizers of the upcoming Olympics use an extranet to get all the elements of the event up and running on schedule?

15. Choose a worldwide retail or restaurant chain. How might groupware be useful?

16. Do you think that a geographic information system would be beneficial to a smaller, specialty-type company? Why or why not?

Manager's Workbook

What Is Your MIS Style?

Following are 14 statements. Circle the number that indicates how much you agree that each statement is a characteristic you possess. The questions refer to how you use information and make decisions.

	Disagree Strongly				Agree Strongly
1. I like to wait until all relevant information is examined before deciding something.	1	2	3	4	5
2. I prefer information that can be interpreted in several ways and leads to different but acceptable solutions.	1	2	3	4	5
3. I like to keep gathering data until an excellent solution emerges.	1	2	3	4	5
4. To make decisions, I often use information that means different things to different people.	1	2	3	4	5
5. I want just enough data to make a decision quickly.	1	2	3	4	5
6. I act on logical analysis of the situation rather than on my "gut feelings" about the best alternative.	1	2	3	4	5
7. I seek information sources or people that will provide me with many ideas and details.	1	2	3	4	5
8. I try to generate more than one satisfactory solution for the problem faced.	1	2	3	4	5
9. When reading something, I confine my thoughts to what is written rather than search for additional understanding.	1	2	3	4	5
10. When working on a project, I try to narrow, not broaden, the scope so it is clearly defined.	1	2	3	4	5
11. I typically acquire all possible information before making a final decision.	1	2	3	4	5
12. I like to work on something I've done before rather than take on a complicated problem.	1	2	3	4	5
13. I prefer clear, precise data.	1	2	3	4	5
14. When working on a project, I like to explore various options rather than maintain a narrow focus.	1	2	3	4	5

Total Score _____

Your information-processing style determines the extent to which you will benefit from computer-based information systems.

The odd-numbered questions pertain to the "amount of information" you like to use. A score of 28 or more suggests you prefer a large amount. A score of 14 or less indicates you like a small amount of information.

The even-numbered questions pertain to the "focus of information" you prefer. A score of 28 or more suggests you are comfortable with ambiguous, multifocused information, while a score of 14 or less suggests you like clear, unifocused data.

If you are a person who likes a large amount of information and clear, focused data, you will tend to make effective use of management information systems. You could be expected to benefit greatly from an EIS or MIS in your company. If you are a person who prefers a small amount of data and data that are multifocused, you would probably not get the information you need to make decisions through formal information systems. You probably won't utilize EIS or MIS to a great extent, preferring instead to get decision data from other convenient sources, including face-to-face discussions.

SOURCES: This questionnaire is adapted from Richard L. Daft and Norman B. Macintosh, "A Tentative Exploration into the Amount and Equivocality of Information Processing in Organizational Work Units," *Administrative Science Quarterly*, 26 (1981), pp. 207–224; and Dorothy Marcic, *Organizational Behavior: Experiences and Cases*, 4th ed. (St. Paul, Minn.: West, 1995).

Manager's Workshop

Decision Styles

Think of some recent decisions that have influenced your life. Choose two significant decisions that you made and two that other people made. Then fill out the following table. Use Exhibit 6.1 on decision conditions to choose which condition it was (column B). Decide how bounded rationality worked (column C), and use the information on decision biases to fill in column D. In groups of three to six members, discuss your results. What did you learn about how you make decisions? How can you improve your decision-making style?

Column A	B	C	D	E
Your decisions	Decision condition relevant	Bounded rationality: Was there satisficing?	Which decision biases were working?	Outcomes— recommendations for improvement?
1.				
2.				
Decisions by others				
1.				
2.				

SOURCE: © Dorothy Marcic. Adapted from "Action Assignment" in Jennifer M. Howard and Lawrence M. Miller, *Team Management*, Miller Consulting Group, 1994, p. 205.

Manager's Workshop

Listed below are some situations that require a decision. In groups of three to six members, discuss which of the decision-making models (as discussed in the chapter) would be most relevant for each problem. Do not come up with the actual decision, but rather talk about which model is the best for that situation. Often we jump too quickly to solutions and spend too little time in the process of how to arrive at the best outcome.

Situation	Different variables	Which decision-making model is best?
1. Whether to quit your job	a. You are main breadwinner, have three school-aged children, you are in a difficult field; a new job—if you found it—would mean a move, unless you changed fields.	
	b. You are single and in a field where good jobs are plentiful.	
	c. You are married with no children, spouse with good job, and maybe you could find a decent job without moving.	
1. Whether to start a business	a You have an inheritance of $50,000 and several ideas, but have not done reality check yet.	
	b. You have no money in bank and your family counts on your income, but you hate working for other people and you have some hot ideas.	
	c. You have a solid idea, a family friend who told you two years ago he would back you in a business, and a spouse who works and earns almost enough for expenses.	

© Dorothy Marcic.

Discussion Questions:

1. Do you often analyze the process of decision making before actually making the decision?

2. How can it be helpful to attend to the process?

3. What will you do next time you have an important decision to make?

Management in Practice: Ethical Dilemma

The Unhealthy Hospital

When Bruce Reid was hired as Blake Memorial Hospital's new CEO, the mandate had been clear: Improve the quality of care, and set the financial house in order.

As Reid struggled to finalize his budget for approval at next week's board meeting, his attention kept returning to one issue—the future of six off-site clinics. The clinics had been set up six years earlier to provide primary health care to the community's poorer neighborhoods. Although they provided a valuable service, they also diverted funds away from Blake's in-house services, many of which were underfunded. Cutting hospital personnel and freezing salaries could affect Blake's quality of care, which was already slipping. Eliminating the clinics, on the other hand, would save $256,000 without compromising Blake's internal operations.

However, there would be political consequences. Clara Bryant, the recently appointed commissioner of health services, repeatedly argued that the clinics were an essential service for the poor. Closing the clinics could jeopardize Blake's access to city funds. Dr. Susan Russell, the hospital's director of clinics, was equally vocal about Blake's responsibility to the community, although Dr. Winston Lee, chief of surgery, argued forcefully for closing the off-site clinics and having shuttle buses bring patients to the hospital weekly. Dr. Russell argued for an entirely new way of delivering health care—"A hospital is not a building," she said, "it's a service. And wherever the service is needed, that is where the hospital should be." In Blake's case, that meant funding more clinics. Russell wanted to create a network of neighborhood-based centers for all the surrounding poor and middle-income neighborhoods. Besides improving health care, the network would act as an inpatient referral system for hospital services. Reid considered the proposal: If a clinic network could tap the paying public and generate more in-patient business, it might be worth looking into. Blake's rival hospital, located on the affluent side of town, certainly wasn't doing anything that creative.

What Do You Do?

1. Close the clinics and save a quick $256,000, then move on to tackle the greater problems that threaten Blake's long-term future.

2. Gradually abandon the neighborhood altogether and open free-standing clinics in more affluent suburbs, at the same time opening a minihospital in the poor neighborhood for critical care.

3. Tighten internal efficiency to deal with immediate financial problems. Keep the clinics open for now, bring Clara Bryant into the decision-making process, and begin working with community groups to explore unmet health-care needs and develop innovative options for meeting them.

SOURCE: Based on Anthony R. Kovner, "The Case of the Unhealthy Hospital," *Harvard Business Review,* September–October 1991, pp. 12–25.

Case for Critical Analysis

Greyhound Lines Inc.

Everyone agreed that Greyhound Lines had problems. The company was operating on paper-thin margins and could not afford to dispatch nearly empty vehicles or have buses and drivers on call to meet surges in demand. In the terminals, employees could be observed making fun of passengers, ignoring them, and handling their baggage haphazardly. To reduce operating costs and improve customer service, Greyhound's top executives put together a reorganization plan that called for massive cuts in personnel, routes, and services, along with the computerization of everything from passenger reservations to fleet scheduling.

However, middle managers disagreed with the plan. Many felt that huge workforce reductions would only exacerbate the company's real problem regarding customer services. Managers in computer programming urged a delay in introducing the computerized reservations system, called Trips, to work out bugs in the highly complex software. The human resources department pointed out that terminal workers often had less than a high school education and would need extensive training before they could be expected to use the system effectively. Terminal managers warned that many of Greyhound's low-income passengers didn't have credit cards or even telephones to use Trips. Despite the disagreements, executives rolled out the new system, emphasizing that the data they had studied showed that Trips would improve customer service, make ticket buying more convenient, and allow customers to reserve space on specific trips. A nightmare resulted. The time Greyhound operators spent responding to phone calls dramatically increased.

Many callers couldn't even get through because of problems in the new switching mechanism. Most passengers arrived to buy their tickets and get on the bus just like they always had, but the computers were so swamped that it sometimes took 45 seconds to respond to a single keystroke and five minutes to print a ticket. The system crashed so often that agents frequently had to hand write tickets. Customers stood in long lines, were separated from their luggage, missed connections, and were left to sleep in terminals overnight. Discourtesy to customers increased as a downsized workforce struggled to cope with a system they were ill-trained to operate. Ridership plunged sharply, and regional rivals continued to pick off Greyhound's dissatisfied customers.

Questions

1. Was the decision facing Greyhound executives programmed or nonprogrammed?

2. Do you think they should have used the classical, administrative, or political model to make their decision? Which do you believe they used? Discuss.

3. Analyze the Greyhound case in terms of the six steps in the managerial decision-making process. Do you think top executives paid adequate attention to all six steps? If you were a Greyhound executive, what would you do now and why?

SOURCE: Robert Tomsho, "How Greyhound Lines Re-Engineered Itself Right Into a Deep Hole," *The Wall Street Journal*, October 30, 1994, p. A1.

PART

4

Organizing

*S*tephen Spielberg once described what it was like to cast a movie: "You reached into a crowded world and pulled a man, a woman or a child from thin air and plugged them into your vision."

With basic job responsibilities for everyone (including the director) usually shaped by union rules, film crews are typically organized into functional departments—camera, art, and sound, for example. Department heads report to the director; the director, in turn, reports to a producer, who oversees the entire enterprise. Though the director often has some input, the producer hires the crew's key personnel. However, casting is the director's responsibility, and it is an important one. "Sometimes, the best thing I can do is cast the movie well," says Spielberg.

How a director casts a movie can determine its artistic success or failure. Recruiting begins with the director generally picturing the actors he or she thinks would be right for a role. For instance, writer Buck Henry remembers that in the mid-1960s, when they were casting *The Graduate*, they envisioned Southern California types: "All blond, all healthy—surfboards is what we called them. We wanted a family of surfboards."

If a director would like to attract a major star, he or she often sends the script to the actor or actress, hoping the star will be intrigued enough to meet and discuss possible participation in the project. For most roles, though, the director supervises the drafting of casting notices, the film industry's want ads. With outside casting agencies often doing the legwork, directors send notices to publications and, increasingly, post them on the Internet. The notice gives a synopsis and other basic facts about the project and lists the roles they are casting. Usually, they supply the character's name and gender, give an age range, and then briefly describe important physical characteristics or personality traits, such as the character is plump or rail-thin, two-faced or sincere. Likely candidates audition, which often includes a screen test where they perform in front of a camera. Sometimes during the audition process, directors discover—as *The Graduate*'s Mike Nichols did when he cast the dark-haired Dustin Hoffman as the anti-hero, Benjamin—that the right person is different from the one they had imagined.

Casting decisions can have major implications for a project's bottom line. Until the 1950s and 1960s, studios controlled a film's costs because they employed the actors as well as writers, directors, and film crews. When the studios' system collapsed, they no longer had actors on their payroll, and power shifted to stars and the agents who negotiated deals for them. Today a top film actor can command $20 million a picture, a salary that sometimes accounts for as much as one-third of a project's budget. Though studios want costs contained, they sometimes withhold financing unless producers and directors hire "bankable" stars like Julia Roberts or Tom Cruise in the (sometimes vain) hope they will pull audiences into theaters.

All a director needs to do, then, is find a cast of available, skilled, enthusiastic actors who are affordable but still well-known enough to attract an audience. It is a tall order.

CHAPTER

7

Structure and Fundamentals of Organizing

LEARNING OBJECTIVES

After studying this chapter, you should be able to do the following:

1   **Discuss the fundamental characteristics of organizing, including such concepts as work specialization, chain of command, span of management, and centralization versus decentralization.**

2   **Describe functional and divisional approaches to structure.**

3   **Explain the matrix approach to structure and its application to domestic and international organizations.**

4   **Describe the contemporary team and virtual network structures and why they are being adopted by organizations.**

5   **Explain why organizations need coordination across departments and hierarchical levels, and describe mechanisms for achieving coordination.**

6   **Identify how structure can be used to achieve an organization's strategic goals.**

7   **Illustrate how organization structure can be designed to fit environmental uncertainty.**

8   **Define production technology (manufacturing, service, and digital) and explain how it influences organization structure.**

Manager's Challenge

Creating a hit TV show is no easy matter. Just ask "Everwood" head writer Greg Berlanti, known as "show runner." He is the head writer of the hip and heartwarming show, he supervises the production team, cast and crew, and he is the liaison with the executives at the studio and network. He is responsible for 22 shows a year, each with 52-page scripts—one every eight days. It is like producing ten movies a year. Berlanti is a rising star for his creative ability and for his management skills. He has got to keep people happy above and below him, all the while balancing ominous deadlines with several projects. Studio and network bosses make last-minute demands on scripts, stars, plot scenarios, and budgets, requiring Berlanti to learn horse-trading, or negotiating for some things while sacrificing others. Now it is time to develop the season finale plot, which needs to be more intricate than usual, one that finishes up some storylines and creates a cliffhanger. Most shows are penned by one of the seven writers, a structure different from other shows, where writers research and talk but the head writer does the script. Berlanti is struggling with the demands from the network and studio, as well as his own high standards. How do you channel all the creative energy of the group to come up with the best script possible?[1]

If you were Berlanti, how would you structure the work to get an excellent season finale script?

The problem confronting "Everwood" is one of structural design. Greg Berlanti wants to use elements of structure to define authority and responsibility for writers, producers, studio and network, and improve coordination so "Everwood" can create a final script that will keep fans happy and want them to tune in for next season. Every firm wrestles with the problem of how to organize. Reorganization is often necessary to reflect a new strategy, changing market conditions, or innovative technology. In recent years, many companies, including American Express, Apple, IBM, Microsoft, and Ford Motor Company, have realigned departmental groupings, chains of command, and horizontal coordination mechanisms to attain new strategic goals. Structure is a powerful tool for reaching strategic goals, and a strategy's success often is determined by its fit with organization structure.

Many companies have found a need to make structural changes compatible with use of the Internet for e-business, which requires stronger horizontal coordination. For example, Brady Corporation, a Milwaukee-based manufacturer of identification and safety products, is reorganizing to increase cross-functional collaboration in connection with the rollout of a new system that links customers, distributors, and suppliers over the Internet.[2] Hewlett-Packard consolidated its 83 independently run units into four major divisions to increase internal collaboration and enhance flexibility.[3] Some companies operate as network organizations, limiting themselves to a few core activities and letting outside specialists handle the rest. Each of these organizations is using fundamental concepts of organizing. **Organizing** is the deployment of organizational resources to achieve strategic goals. The deployment of resources is reflected in the organization's division of labor into specific departments and jobs, formal lines of authority, and mechanisms for coordinating diverse organization tasks.

Organizing is important because it follows from strategy, the topic of Part 3. Strategy defines what to do, and organizing defines how to do it. Organization structure is a tool that managers use to harness resources for getting things done. Part 4 explains the various organizing principles and concepts used by managers. This chapter covers fundamental concepts that apply to all organizations and departments, including organizing the vertical structure and using mechanisms for horizontal coordination. The chapter examines how managers tailor the various elements of structural design to the organization's situation. Chapter 8 discusses how organizations can be structured to facilitate innovation and change. Chapter 9 considers how to utilize human resources to the best advantage within the organization's structure.

Organizing the Vertical Structure

The organizing process leads to the creation of organization structure, which defines how tasks are divided and resources deployed. **Organization structure** is defined as (1) the set of formal tasks assigned to individuals and departments; (2) formal reporting relationships, including lines of authority, decision responsibility, number of hierarchical levels, and span of managers' control; and (3) the design of systems to ensure effective coordination of employees across departments.[4]

The set of formal tasks and formal reporting relationships provides a framework for vertical control of the organization. The characteristics of vertical structure are portrayed in the **organization chart**, which is the visual representation of an organization's structure.

A sample organization chart for a soda bottling plant is illustrated in Exhibit 7.1. The plant has four major departments: accounting, human resources, production, and marketing. The organization chart delineates the chain of command, indicates departmental tasks and how they fit together, and provides order and logic for the organization. Every employee has an appointed task, line of authority, and decision responsibility.

organizing

The deployment of organizational resources to achieve strategic goals.

organization structure

The framework in which the organization defines how tasks are divided, resources are deployed, and departments are coordinated.

organization chart

The visual representation of an organization's structure.

The following sections discuss several important features of vertical structure in detail.

Work Specialization

Organizations perform many tasks. A fundamental principle is that work can be performed more efficiently if employees are allowed to specialize.[5] **Work specialization**, sometimes called division of labor, is the degree to which organizational tasks are subdivided into separate jobs. Work specialization in Exhibit 7.1 is illustrated by the separation of production tasks into bottling, quality control, and maintenance. Employees within each department perform only the tasks relevant to their specialized function. When work specialization is extensive, employees specialize in a single task. Jobs tend to be small, but they can be performed efficiently. Work specialization is readily visible on an automobile assembly line where each employee performs the same task repeatedly. It would be inefficient to have a single employee build the entire automobile or perform a large number of unrelated jobs.

Despite the apparent advantages of specialization, many organizations are moving away from this principle. With too much specialization, employees are isolated and do only a single, boring job. Many companies are enlarging jobs to provide greater challenges or assigning teams so employees can rotate among the several jobs performed by the team. One company that has followed work specialization, though, is Kate Spade, as described in the Focus on Skills box.

Chain of Command

The **chain of command** is an unbroken line of authority that links all persons in an organization and shows who reports to whom. It is associated with two underlying principles. Unity of command means that each employee is held accountable to only one supervisor. The scalar principle refers to a clearly defined line of authority in the organization that includes all employees. Authority and responsibility for different tasks should be distinct. All persons in the organization should know to whom they report as well as the successive management levels all the way to the top. In Exhibit 7.1, the payroll clerk reports to the chief accountant, who in turn reports to the vice president, who in turn reports to the company president.

Authority, Responsibility, and Delegation.   The chain of command illustrates the authority structure of the organization. **Authority** is the formal and legitimate right of a manager to make decisions, issue orders, and allocate resources to achieve organizationally desired outcomes. Authority is distinguished by three characteristics:[6]

1. *Authority is vested in organizational positions, not people.* Managers have authority because of the positions they hold, and other people in the same positions would have the same authority.

2. *Authority is accepted by subordinates.* Though authority flows from the top down through the organization's hierarchy, subordinates comply because they believe

© Chris McPherson

CONCEPT CONNECTION

Successful artist Shepard Fairey has proven himself to be an effective manager too. Fairey runs his own marketing design firm, Studio Number One, a studio to design unique graphics and logos used in untraditional advertising campaigns, and on labels for clothing, soft drinks, and other products. Fairey manages a creative team of seven full-time employees and a handful of part-timers and interns. Even in a small organization such as this, **organizing** *is a critical part of good management. Fairey has to be sure people are assigned and coordinated to do all the various jobs necessary to satisfy clients such as Express, Levi's, and Dr. Pepper/Seven Up. The right* **organization structure** *enables Studio Number One to be "fast, deadline-sensitive, and responsive."*

work specialization
The degree to which organizational tasks are subdivided into individual jobs; also called division of labor.

EXHIBIT 7.1

Organization Chart for a Soda Bottling Plant

President

Vice President Accounting

Director Human Resources

Vice President Production

Director Marketing

Information Center

Financial Analyst

Chief Accountant

Benefits Administrator

Industrial Relations Manager

Maintenance Supervisor

Quality Control Manager

Bottling Plant Super- intendent

Mountain Region Sales

Midstate Sales

Western Sales

Accounts Payable

Payroll Clerk

Bottling Supervisors

chain of command

An unbroken line of authority that links all individuals in the organization and specifies who reports to whom.

Take **ACTION**

Make an organization chart of the place you work so you can understand reporting relationships.

authority

The formal and legitimate right of a manager to make decisions, issue orders, and allocate resources to achieve organizationally desired outcomes.

Take **ACTION**

As a manager, look for ways to group tasks by similar skills and assign competent people to each job.

responsibility

The duty to perform the task or activity an employee has been assigned.

accountability

That the people with authority and responsibility are subject to reporting and justifying task outcomes to those above them in the chain of command.

that managers have a legitimate right to issue orders. The acceptance theory of authority argues that a manager has authority only if subordinates choose to accept his or her commands. If subordinates refuse to obey because the order is outside their zone of acceptance, a manager's authority disappears.[7]

3. *Authority flows down the vertical hierarchy.* Positions at the top of the hierarchy are vested with more formal authority than are positions at the bottom.

Responsibility is the flip side of the authority coin. **Responsibility** is the duty to perform the task or activity an employee has been assigned. Typically, managers are assigned authority commensurate with responsibility. When managers have responsibility for task outcomes but little authority, the job is possible but difficult. They rely on persuasion and luck. When managers have authority exceeding responsibility, they may become tyrants, using authority toward frivolous outcomes.[8]

Accountability is the mechanism through which authority and responsibility are brought into alignment. **Accountability** means people with authority and responsibility are subject to reporting and justifying task outcomes to those above them in the chain of command.[9] For organizations to function well, everyone needs to know what they are accountable for and accept the responsibility and authority for performing it. Accountability can be built into the organization structure. For example, at Whirlpool, incentive programs tailored to different hierarchical levels provide strict accountability. Performance of all managers is monitored, and bonus payments are tied to successful outcomes.

Another concept related to authority is delegation.[10] **Delegation** is the process managers use to transfer authority and responsibility to positions below them in the hierarchy. Most organizations today encourage managers to delegate authority to the lowest

Kate Spade

Kate Spade never thought she would be a designer. She wanted to work in publishing. After college at Arizona State University (where she met her future husband, Andy), she went to New York and got a job as an editorial assistant at *Mademoiselle* for $14,500 per year. Soon, Andy followed and they got a tiny apartment in SoHo. Andy moved up the career ladder in advertising agencies. Kate was so successful that by 28 she was senior fashion editor for accessories, but she didn't want to keep doing the same thing. She told Andy, "I just want something that will keep me busy." A temporary thing. He suggested she launch a line of accessories. She was flabbergasted and did not know where to start, but Andy kept prodding her. It was the process they would continue for ten years: Andy with a bold vision and Kate as the more conservative who executes his idea with great style and attention to detail. Their deal was he would work to pay rent and provide startup capital, and she would get the business going.

Starting with a purse was, she says, "kind of random." As a fashion stylist, she had looked for unusual accessories that were not there. Purses were all blacks and browns back in 1993. With no fashion training, Kate was scared to take on

design, but Andy kept urging her on. She made a prototype out of construction paper and found a sewer to make a sample: a simple burlap square. After a few more samples, they went to the Accessories Circuit show in New York and signed up the three hottest retailers: Fred Segal, Barneys, and Charivari. Refusing outside money, Andy kept working at the ad agency until they started making enough money for him to work full time at the company.

Structuring the workload was a challenge. Andy loved the creative role, but he took on the CEO role though he had little experience or interest in the operational side.

By 1999, Neiman Marcus and Saks adopted the lines for their stores, making revenues soar. Further, Neiman bought a 56 percent share for $34 million. Andy and Kate Spade built a business that is worth $175 million. Splitting the task responsibilities was smart. Though Andy didn't want to be CEO, he turned out to have the right aptitude. Now that Kate is pregnant, they are both reassessing their priorities. First on the board: hire a new CEO and give Kate and Andy some breathing space. And space for Baby Spade.

SOURCE: Linda Tischler, "Power Couple," *Fast Company*, (March 2005): 44–51.

---

possible level to provide maximum flexibility to meet customer needs and adapt to the environment. However, many managers find delegation difficult. For example, Microsoft's Chief Financial Officer John Conners nearly resigned because of CEO Steven Ballmer's inability to delegate. By taking it upon himself to make financial decisions, Ballmer undermined the role of Conners and his team. Ballmer is learning to cede some control and delegate more so people can do their jobs more effectively.[11] Techniques for effective delegation are discussed in the Focus on Skills box.

delegation
The process managers use to transfer authority and responsibility to positions below them in the hierarchy.

Line and Staff Authority.   An important distinction in many organizations is between line authority and staff authority, reflecting whether managers work in line or staff departments in the organization's structure. Line departments perform tasks that reflect the organization's primary goal and mission. In a software company, line departments make and sell the product. In an Internet-based company, line departments would be those that develop and manage online offerings and sales. Staff departments include all those that provide specialized skills in support of line departments. Staff departments have an advisory relationship with line departments and typically include marketing, labor relations, research, accounting, and human resources.

Line authority means that people in management positions have formal authority to direct and control immediate subordinates. **Staff authority** is narrower and includes the right to advise, recommend, and counsel in the staff specialists' area of expertise. Staff authority is a communication relationship; staff specialists advise managers in technical areas. For example, the finance department of a manufacturing firm would have staff

Take **ACTION**
Practice delegating. If you find it difficult, ask yourself why you have the wrong people, they are not trained properly, or else you just do not trust them.

line authority
A form of authority in which individuals in management positions have the formal power to direct and control immediate subordinates.

FOCUS ON SKILLS

How to Delegate

The attempt by top management to decentralize decision making often gets bogged down because middle managers are unable to delegate. Managers may cling tightly to their decision-making and task responsibilities. Failure to delegate occurs for a number of reasons: Managers are most comfortable making familiar decisions, they feel they will lose personal status by delegating tasks, they believe they can do a better job themselves, or they have an aversion to risk. They will not take a chance on delegating because performance responsibility ultimately rests with them.

Yet decentralization offers an organization many advantages. Decisions are made at the right level, lower-level employees are motivated, and employees have the opportunity to develop decision-making skills. Overcoming barriers to delegation to gain these advantages is a major challenge. The following approach can help each manager delegate more effectively:

1. *Delegate the whole task.* A manager should delegate an entire task to one person rather than dividing it among several people. This gives the individual complete responsibility and increases his or her initiative while giving the manager some control over the results.

2. *Select the right person.* Not all employees have the same capabilities and degree of motivation. Managers must match talent to task if delegation is to be effective. They should identify subordinates who have made independent decisions in the past and have shown a desire for more responsibility.

3. *Ensure that authority equals responsibility.* Merely assigning a task is ineffective delegation. Managers often load subordinates with increased responsibility but do not extend their decision-making range. In addition to having responsibility for completing a task, the worker must be given the authority to make decisions about how best to do the job.

4. *Give thorough instruction.* Successful delegation includes information on what, when, why, where, who, and how. The subordinate must understand the task and the expected results. It is a good idea to write all provisions discussed, including required resources and when and how the results will be reported.

5. *Maintain feedback.* Feedback means keeping open lines of communication with the subordinate to answer questions and provide advice but without exerting too much control. Open lines of communication make it easier to trust subordinates. Feedback keeps the subordinate on the right track.

6. *Evaluate and reward performance.* Once the task is complete, the manager should evaluate results and not methods. When results do not meet expectations, the manager must assess the consequences. When they do meet expectations, the manager should reward employees for a job well done with praise, financial rewards when appropriate, and delegation of future assignments.

Are You a Positive Delegator?

Positive delegation is the way an organization implements decentralization. Do you help or hinder the decentralization process? If you answer yes to more than three of the following questions, you may have a problem delegating the following:

- I tend to be a perfectionist.
- My boss expects me to know all the details of my job.
- I don't have the time to explain how to accomplish a task.
- I often end up doing tasks myself.
- My subordinates typically are not as committed as I am.
- I get upset when other people do not do the task right.
- I enjoy doing the details of my job to the best of my ability.
- I like to be in control of task outcomes.

SOURCES: Thomas R. Horton "Delegation and Team Building: No Solo Acts Please," *Management Review* (September 1992): 58–61; Andrew E. Schwartz, "The Why, What, and to Whom of Delegation," *Management Solutions* (June 1987): 31–38; "Delegation," *Small Business Report* (June 1986): 38–43; and Russell Wild, "Clone Yourself," *Working Woman* (May 2000): 79–80.

---

staff authority

A form of authority granted to staff specialists in their area of expertise.

span of management

The number of employees reporting to a supervisor; also called span of control.

authority to coordinate with line departments about which accounting forms to use to facilitate equipment purchases and standardize payroll services.

Span of Management

The **span of management** is the number of employees reporting to a supervisor. Sometimes called the span of control, this characteristic of structure determines how closely a supervisor can monitor subordinates. Traditional views of organization design recommended a span of management of about seven subordinates per manager. However, many lean organizations today have spans of management of 30, 40, and more. For example, at Consolidated Diesel's team-based engine assembly plant, the span of management is 100.[12] Research over the past 40 or so years shows that span of management varies widely and that several factors influence the span.[13] Generally, when supervisors must be closely involved with subordinates, the span should be small; when supervisors need little involvement with subordinates, it can be large. The following factors are associated with less supervisor involvement and, thus, larger spans of control:

1. Work performed by subordinates is stable and routine.

2. Subordinates perform similar work tasks.

3. Subordinates are concentrated in a single location.

4. Subordinates are highly trained and need little direction in performing tasks.

5. Rules and procedures defining task activities are available.

6. Support systems and personnel are available for the manager.

7. Little time is required in nonsupervisory activities such as coordination with other departments or planning.

8. Managers' personal preferences and styles favor a large span.

The average span of control used in an organization determines whether the structure is tall or flat. A **tall structure** has an overall narrow span and more hierarchical levels. A **flat structure** has a wide span, is horizontally dispersed, and has fewer hierarchical levels.

The trend in recent years has been toward wider spans of control as a way to facilitate delegation.[14] For example, a study of 300 large U.S. corporations found that the average number of division heads reporting directly to the CEO tripled between the years of 1986 and 1999.[15] Exhibit 7.2 illustrates how an international metals company was reorganized. The multilevel set of managers shown in panel *a* was replaced with ten operating managers and nine staff specialists reporting directly to the CEO, as shown in panel *b*. The CEO welcomed this wide span of 19 management subordinates because it fit his style, his management team was top quality and needed little supervision, and they were all located on the same floor of an office building.

tall structure

A management structure characterized by an overall narrow span of management and a relatively large number of hierarchical levels.

flat structure

A management structure characterized by an overall broad span of control and relatively few hierarchical levels.

EXHIBIT 7.2

Reorganization to Increase Span of Management for President of an International Metals Company

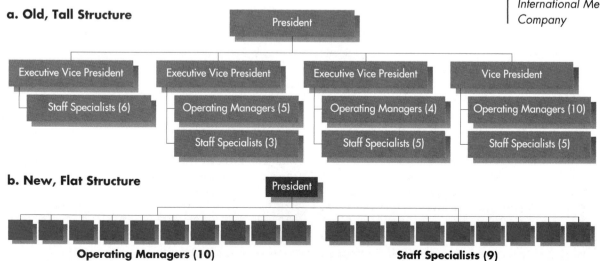

a. Old, Tall Structure

President

Executive Vice President — Staff Specialists (6)

Executive Vice President — Operating Managers (5) — Staff Specialists (3)

Executive Vice President — Operating Managers (4) — Staff Specialists (5)

Vice President — Operating Managers (10) — Staff Specialists (5)

b. New, Flat Structure

President

Operating Managers (10)   Staff Specialists (9)

Centralization and Decentralization

Centralization and decentralization pertain to the hierarchical level at which decisions are made. **Centralization** means that decision authority is located near the top of the organization. With **decentralization**, decision authority is pushed down to lower organization levels. Organizations may have to experiment to find the correct hierarchical level at which to make decisions.

centralization

The location of decision authority near top organizational levels.

decentralization

The location of decision authority near lower organizational levels.

In the United States and Canada, the trend over the past 30 years has been toward greater decentralization of organizations. Decentralization is believed to relieve the burden on top managers, make greater use of employees' skills and abilities, ensure decisions are made close to the action by well-informed people, and permit more rapid response to external changes.

However, this trend does not mean that every organization should decentralize all decisions. Managers should diagnose the organizational situation and select the decision-making level that will best meet the organization's needs. Factors that typically influence centralization versus decentralization are as follows:

Take ACTION

As a manager, determine which areas you can decentralize and which should be centralized.

1. *Greater change and uncertainty in the environment are usually associated with decentralization.* A good example of how decentralization can help cope with rapid change and uncertainty occurred following the September 11, 2001, attacks in the United States. UPS trucks, which carry 7 percent of the country's gross domestic product on any given day, were able to keep running on time in New York, thanks largely to a decentralized management system that gives local managers authority to make key decisions.[16] The changing environment relating to defense has caused the U.S. Army to go through major restructuring and decentralization in recent years, as described in the Focus on Collaboration box.

2. *The amount of centralization or decentralization should fit the firm's strategy.* For example, Johnson & Johnson gives almost complete authority to its 180 operating companies to develop and market their own products. Decentralization fits the corporate strategy of empowerment that gets each division close to customers so it can speedily adapt to its needs.[17] Taking the opposite approach, Larry Ellison at Oracle is using technology to centralize operations, cut costs, and get everyone focused, as described in the Digital, Inc. box.

FOCUS ON COLLABORATION

Delta Forces

Part of the job interview is a 20-hour, 50-mile march, carrying a 70-pound load. The exercise "revealed clearly those candidates who had character, real determination, self-discipline and self-sacrifice, and those who did not," said Delta Forces founder Army Col. Charles Beckwith, former Vietnam Green Beret. Created in 1977 to rescue hostages, one of its first missions was the 1980 botched rescue of the 53 Iran hostages, where the hostages were not saved, and eight U.S. soldiers were killed.

Realizing the unit was not functioning correctly, the Army restructured Delta Forces, which has since had successful operations in Grenada, in Panama capturing dictator Noriega, in the Gulf War destroying scud missile launchers, and most recently in Iraq. In fact, it has been so successful that the Army's training of Iraqi forces is based on the Delta Forces model.

Unlike the regular army, with its hierarchical structure and authority, Delta Forces are much more team-based and composed of small units. Recruiting is selective for endurance, for language skills, and the ability to adapt or blend in to another culture. To reduce hierarchy, they call each other primarily by nicknames, rather than the normal military titles, and plans are not made high above but instead by the non-commissioned officers in the unit.

Though the job requires tough behavior, it is not just brawn they are looking for, which is why the 50-mile march is such an important selection criterion. "A lot of really physically strong guys try out for Delta," Beckwith said," "but the guys who make an impression are the ones that don't give up, even after they've attained the minimum requirement."

SOURCE: Linda Robinson, A Few Good Men; U.S. Special Operations Forces Are Turning Iraqi Soldiers into Well-trained Commandos, *US News & World Report* (Feb. 14, 2005): 26; Delta Forces' Secret Wielders of Death, *VFW: Veterans of Foreign Wars Magazine* (March 2002): 16–18; "Covert U.S. Military Units Att..." *The Washington Post* (April 28, 2002): A3.

DIGITAL, INC.

Tightening the Reins at Oracle

Much has been written about the power of the Internet to give employees more information and greater freedom. But Larry Ellison, CEO of Oracle Corporation, knows the global network offers a major opportunity for strengthening top management command and control. By requiring employees to do their work via the Internet, Ellison can track, analyze, and control the behavior of each unit, manager, and employee on a global basis.

Oracle got into trouble some years ago because sales managers were cutting back-room deals or hammering out private, individualized compensation agreements with salespeople in different countries. Today all the terms, including sales contracts and commissions, are dictated from the top and are spelled out in a global database. In addition, all deals must be reported into the database, where they can easily be tracked by Ellison back at headquarters. "I love running the business now," Ellison says. "I love getting involved in every detail...." Clearly, Larry Ellison loves being in control, but he has solid business reasons for centralizing information and decision making. Several years ago, Oracle realized its future rested on building a complete suite of Internet applications that could work together on a global basis, and Ellison knew the first step would be to roll out the global system inside Oracle, or as Ellison put it, to "eat our own dog food."

He first had to dismantle the separate fiefdoms that had developed inside Oracle. Each country manager had separate e-mail, human resources, and financial reporting systems, which were supported by more than 40 data centers scattered around the world. "Not only did we have 70 separate accounting systems in 70 different countries, but all of those countries hired IT departments to change them in different ways," Ellison marvels. Naturally, managers balked when the CEO decreed that there would now be only two data centers (one at headquarters and a backup center in Colorado Springs) and a single global database for each major function. To break down resistance, Ellison started by globalizing e-mail, allowing managers to see how much easier, more effective, and cheaper it was to do business. Then, he gradually rolled out other global Internet-based applications.

Some managers remain unhappy about the tighter grip Ellison has over global operations, but the CEO believes it is needed to manage a sprawling, global company. "Executives. We sit up here...and think very hard on something, tell people to do something," Ellison says. "But as these orders go out through many layers of bureaucracy, they change and change and change." Ellison believes using the Internet to centralize control and manage more "scientifically" is the best way to take Oracle to the next level.

SOURCE: G. Christian Hill, "Dog Eats Dog Food. And Damn If It Ain't Tasty," *ECompany News* (November 2000): 168–178.

3. *In times of crisis or risk of company failure, authority may be centralized at the top.* When Honda could not get agreement among divisions about new car models, President Nobuhiko Kawamoto made the decision himself.[18]

Departmentalization

Another fundamental characteristic of organization structure is **departmentalization**, which is the basis for grouping positions into departments and departments into the total organization. Managers make choices about how to use the chain of command to group people together to perform their work. Five approaches to structural design reflect different uses of the chain of command in departmentalization, as illustrated in Exhibit 7.3. The functional, divisional, and matrix approaches rely on the chain of command to define departmental groupings and reporting relationships along the hierarchy. Two contemporary approaches are the use of teams and networks, which have emerged to meet changing organizational needs in a turbulent global environment.

The basic difference among structures illustrated in Exhibit 7.3 is the way in which employees are departmentalized and to whom they report.[19] Some of the structural approaches is described in detail in the following sections.

departmentalization
The basis on which individuals are grouped into departments and departments into the total organization.

EXHIBIT 7.3

*Five Approaches to
Structural Design*

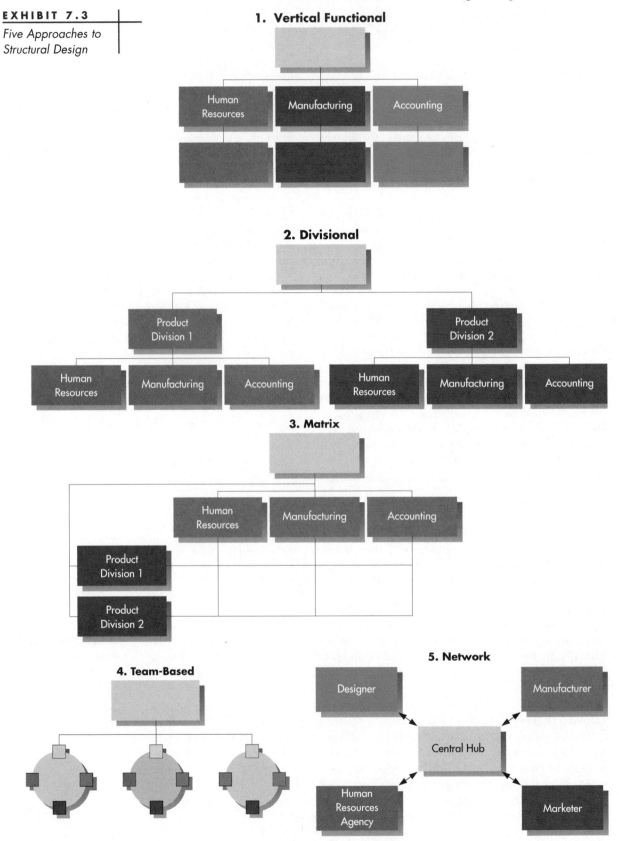

1. Vertical Functional

2. Divisional

3. Matrix

4. Team-Based

5. Network

Take a moment to complete the table below, an exercise to help you understand organizations and their departments.

Family Business

You are the parent of ten children and have used your inheritance to acquire a medium-sized pharmaceutical company. Last year's sales were down 18 percent from the previous year, and the last three years have been losers. You want to clean house of current managers over the next 10 years and bring your children into the business. Being a loving parent, you agree to send your children to college to educate each of them in one functional specialty. The ten children are five sets of twins one year apart. The first set will begin college this fall, followed by the remaining sets over the next four years. The big decision is which specialty each child should study. You want to have the most important functions taken over by your children as soon as possible, so you will ask the older children to study the most important areas.

Your task right now is to rank the functions to which your children will be assigned in order of priority and develop reasons for your ranking.

The ten functions follow:

1. Distribution

2. Manufacturing

3. Market Research

4. New-Product Development

5. Human Resources

6. Product Promotion

7. Quality Assurance

8. Sales

9. Legal and Governmental Affairs

10. Office of the Controller

Analyze your reasons for how functional priority relates to the company's environmental/strategic needs. Now rank the functions as part of a group. Discuss the problem until group members agree on a single ranking. How does the group's reasoning and ranking differ from your original thinking?

Team Approach

What It Is.   Probably the most widespread trend in departmentalization in recent years has been the implementation of team concepts. The vertical chain of command is a powerful means of control, but passing all decisions up the hierarchy takes too long and keeps responsibility at the top. The team approach gives managers a way to delegate authority, push responsibility to lower levels, and be more flexible and responsive in the competitive global environment. Chapter 15 will discuss teams in detail. The Rolling Stones use the team-design approach for their business model, which is one reason they are one of the world's most enduring organizations.

BEST PRACTICES

Rolling Stones, Inc.

The Rolling Stones jump like crazy guys on stage, but they are the most successful music business group. Since their rebirth in 1989, their revenues from tours, records, merchandise, and song rights have exceeded $1.5 billion. That's more than Bruce Springsteen, U2, Michael Jackson, or Britney Spears. After four decades of trial and error, they have learned how to maximize their assets. They are now a large business: global taxpayers, with budgets, P&L statements, lawyers, accountants, bankers, and computer technology issues. What separates them from any other band is that the Rolling Stones know what they are doing.

Some of their income is steady, but most is not. Revenue streams from touring are torrential when the band is on the road, and nothing when they are not. Record sales go up and down depending on if a new album is released. Music rights are the most predictable. To harness these assets, to make them interlock, the Stones have set up a unique business structure. The top four partners are like the owners/principals in a blue-chip law firm or consulting practice. Overall management of the finances goes to Prince Rupert zu Lowenstein, the Stone's chief business advisor for three decades. Beyond that, the work falls to teams assigned specific parts of the business. Tour director Michael Cohl and business manager Joe Rascoff supervise a group of "companies" called Promotour, Promopub, Promotone, and Musidor, each with its own responsibilities. During tours, the whole company employs more than 350 people, but other times it is only a few dozen.

When they started out, no one was making any money in rock & roll. They went from gig to gig and maybe there would be lights, maybe the sound would work. Gradually, a touring industry has developed with traveling sound, stage, and lights. Mick Jagger was instrumental in professionalizing this part of the business, often negotiating himself with promoters in various cities. But once the group brought in Canadian rock promoter Michael Cohl, the Stones learned to exploit all the financial potential. It started with the 1989 Steel Wheels Tour that Cohl organized himself, promising $40 million for 40 shows, unbelievable back then. He did this by cross-promoting, selling bus tours, sky boxes, TV/movie and merchandising deals, getting corporate sponsors like Tommy Hillfiger. And he worked with the band to turn the stage into a theater, the first time anyone did this. By the end, Steel Wheels made $250 million. In recent years, they are learning that doing smaller venues with fewer stadiums saves money. With stadiums, they had to have three stages and three crews. Now they have one stage and one crew. Less costs, more profits.

They have come a long way since the 1960s, when they signed deals that made them no money even if they were a hot group. Now they look hard and sober at cost structures, revenue streams, and loss reduction. At their age, no one knows how much longer they can tour. The music rights business can keep going on forever, but their bodies will not hold out for stage antics much longer. When that day arrives, it will be the end of one of the most successful enterprises in a crazy business.

SOURCE: Andy Serwer, "Rolling Stones, Inc.," *Fortune* (Sept. 30, 2002): 59–72; "The Rolling Stones Rock and Roll Circus Big Top Show on the Big Screen at Regal Entertainment Group Theatres," *Business Wire* (Sept. 20, 2004): 1.

---

cross-functional teams

A group of employees from various functional departments that meet as a team to resolve mutual problems.

Take ACTION

When developing teams, try having people learn one another's jobs, as it gives you more flexibility and keeps the workers more interested in their work.

How It Works.   There are two ways to think about using teams in organizations. **Cross-functional teams** consist of employees from various functional departments who are responsible to meet as a team and resolve mutual problems. Team members typically report to their functional departments, but they also report to the team, one member of whom may be the leader. Cross-functional teams are used to provide needed horizontal coordination to complement an existing divisional or functional structure. A frequent use of cross-functional teams is for changing projects, such as new product or service innovation. A cross-functional team of mechanics, flight attendants, reservations agents, ramp workers, luggage attendants, and aircraft cleaners, for example, collaborated to plan and design a new low-fare airline for US Airways.[20]

The second approach is to use **permanent teams**, groups of employees who are brought together similar to a formal department. Each team brings together employees from all functional areas focused on a specific task or project, such as parts supply and logistics for an automobile plant. Emphasis is on horizontal communication and information sharing because representatives from all functions are coordinating their work and skills to complete a specific organizational task. Authority is pushed down to lower levels, and front-line employees are often given the freedom to make decisions and take action on their own. Team members may share or rotate team leadership. With a team-based structure, the entire organization is made up of horizontal teams that coordinate their work and work directly with customers to accomplish the organization's goals. Imagination Ltd., Britain's largest design firm, is based entirely on teamwork. Imagination puts together a diverse team at the beginning of each new project it undertakes, whether it be creating the lighting for Disney cruise ships or redesigning the packaging for Ericsson's cell phone products. The team then works closely with the client throughout the project.[21] Imagination Ltd. has managed to make every project a smooth, seamless experience by building a culture that supports teamwork, as described in the following Focus on Collaboration box.

Virtual Network Approach

What It Is.   The most recent approach to departmentalization extends the idea of horizontal coordination and collaboration beyond the boundaries of the organization. In various industries, vertically integrated, hierarchical organizations are giving way to loosely interconnected groups of companies with permeable boundaries.[22] Outsourcing, which means farming out certain activities, such as manufacturing or credit processing, has become a significant trend. In addition, partnerships, alliances, and other complex collaborative forms are a leading approach to accomplishing strategic goals. In the music industry, firms such as Vivendi Universal and Sony have formed networks of alliances with Internet Service Providers, digital retailers, software firms, and other companies to bring music to customers in new ways.[23] Some organizations take this networking approach to the extreme to create a new kind of structure. The **virtual network structure** means that the firm subcontracts most of its major functions to separate companies and coordinates their activities from a small headquarters organization.[24]

permanent teams

A group of participants from several functions who are permanently assigned to solve ongoing problems of common interest.

team-based structure

Structure in which the entire organization is made up of horizontal teams that coordinate their activities and work directly with customers to accomplish the organization's goals.

virtual network structure

An organization structure that disaggregates major functions to separate companies that are brokered by a small headquarters organization.

FOCUS ON COLLABORATION

Imagination Ltd.

The essence of teamwork is that people contribute selflessly, putting the good of the whole above their own individual interests. It does not always work that way, but Imagination Ltd. seems to have found the secret ingredient to seamless teamwork. According to Adrian Caddy, Imagination's creative director: "The culture at Imagination is this: You can articulate your ideas without fear."

Imagination Ltd. has created a company made up of teams of designers, architects, lighting experts, writers, theater people, film directors, and artists, in addition to IT specialists, marketing experts, and other functional specialties. By having employees with a wide range of skills, the company can assemble a diverse team to provide each client with a new approach to its design problems. Imagination is deliberately nonhierarchical; only four people have formal titles, and on most project teams, no one is in charge. Teams meet weekly, and everyone participates in every meeting from the beginning, so there is no perception that any particular talent is primary or secondary. IT specialists, production people, and client-contact personnel are as much a part of the team as the creative types. In addition,

each person is expected to come up with ideas outside his or her area of expertise. The philosophy is that people at Imagination must be willing to make all kinds of suggestions and to take all kinds of suggestions. So many ideas get batted around, revised, and adapted at the weekly meetings that no one can claim ownership of a particular element of the project. The team works closely with the client as a source of ideas and inspiration.

Talent and respect make the system work. Imagination hires its employees carefully, based on the quality of their work and on their open-mindedness and curiosity about the world beyond their functional area of expertise. Then, the company makes sure everyone's work is so closely integrated that people gain an understanding and respect for what others do. "The integrated approach breeds respect for one another," says writer Chris White. "When you work alone, or in isolation within your discipline, you can get an overblown sense of your own importance to a project."

SOURCE: Charles Fishman, "Total Teamwork: Imagination Ltd.," *Fast Company* (April 2000): 156–168.

How It Works.   The organization may be viewed as a central hub surrounded by a network of outside specialists, as illustrated in Exhibit 7.4 showing a network approach to departmentalization. Rather than being housed under one roof, services such as accounting, design, manufacturing, and distribution are outsourced to separate organizations that are connected electronically to the central office.[25] Networked computer systems, collaborative software, and the Internet enable organizations to exchange data and information so rapidly and smoothly that a loosely connected network of suppliers, manufacturers, assemblers, and distributors can look and act like one seamless company.

The idea behind networks is that a company can concentrate on what it does best and contract out other activities to companies with distinctive competence in those specific areas. This enables a company to do more with less.[26] The Birmingham, England-based company, Strida, provides an excellent example of the virtual network approach.

Strida

How do two people run an entire company that sells thousands of high-tech folding bicycles all over the world? Steedman Bass and Bill Bennet do it with a virtual network approach that outsources design, manufacturing, customer service, logistics, accounting, and almost everything else to other organizations.

Bass, an avid cyclist, got into the bicycle business when he and his partner Bennet bought the struggling British company Strida, which was having trouble making enough quality bicycles to meet minimum orders. The partners soon realized why Strida was struggling. The design for the folding bicycle was a clever engineering idea, but it was a manufacturing nightmare. Bass and Bennet immediately turned over production engineering and new product development to an American bicycle designer, with intentions of building the bikes at the Birmingham factory. However, a large order from Italy sent them looking for other options. They transferred all manufacturing to Ming Cycle Company of Taiwan, which builds the bikes with parts sourced from parts manufacturers in Taiwan and mainland China.

Finally, the last piece of the puzzle was to contract with a company in Birmingham that would take over everything else, from marketing to distribution. Bass and Bennet concentrate their energies on managing the partnerships that make the network function smoothly.[27]

modular approach

A manufacturing company uses outside suppliers to provide large components of the product, which are then assembled into a final product by a few workers.

With a network structure such as that used at Strida, it is difficult to answer the question, "Where is the organization?" in traditional terms. The different organizational parts may be spread all over the world. They are drawn together contractually and coordinated electronically, creating a new form of organization. Much like building blocks, parts of the network can be added or taken away to meet changing needs.[28]

A similar approach to networking is called the **modular approach**, in which a manufacturing company uses outside suppliers to provide entire chunks of a product, which are

EXHIBIT 7.4
Network Approach to Departmentalization

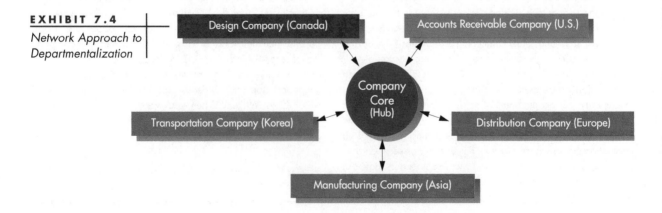

assembled into a final product by a handful of workers. The Canadian firm Bombardier's new Continental business jet is made up of about a dozen huge modular components from all over the world: the engines from the United States; the nose and cockpit from Canada; the mid-fuselage from Northern Ireland; the tail from Taiwan; the wings from Japan; and so forth.[29] Automobile plants, including General Motors (GM), Ford Motor Company, Volkswagen, and DaimlerChrysler, are leaders in using the modular approach. GM has a modular factory in Brazil and is building several more. The modular approach hands off responsibility for engineering and production of entire sections of an automobile, such as the chassis or interior, to outside suppliers. Suppliers design a module, making some of the parts themselves and subcontracting others. These modules are delivered right to the assembly line, where a handful of employees bolt them together into a finished vehicle.[30]

Advantages and Disadvantages of Each Structure

Each of these approaches to departmentalization—functional, divisional, matrix, team, and network—has strengths and weaknesses. The major advantages and disadvantages of each are listed in Exhibit 7.5.

Structural Approach	Advantages	Disadvantages
Functional	Efficient use of resources; economies of scale in-depth skill specialization and development Top manager direction and control	Poor communications across functional departments Slow response to external change, lagging innovation Decision concentrated at top of hierarchy, creating delay
Divisional	Fast response, flexibility in unstable environment Fosters concern for customer needs Excellent coordination across functional departments	Duplication of recourses across divisions Less technical depth and specialization Poor coordination across divisions
Matrix	More efficient use of recourses than single hierarchy Flexibility, adapt ability to changing environment Interdisciplinary cooperation, expertise available to all divisions	Frustration and confusion from dual chain of command High conflict between two sides of the matrix Many meetings, more discussion than action
Team	Reduced barriers among departments, increased compromise Shorter response time, quicker decisions Better morale, enthusiasm from employee involvement	Dual loyalties and conflict Time and resources spent on meetings Unplanned decentralization
Virtual Network	Can draw on expertise worldwide Highly flexible and responsive Reduced overhead costs	Lack of control, weak boundaries, greater demands on managers Employee loyalty weakened

EXHIBIT 7.5

Structural Advantages and Disadvantages

Team Approach.   The team concept breaks down barriers across departments and improves cooperation. Team members know one another's problems and compromise rather than blindly pursue their own goals. The team concept enables the organization to adapt to customer requests and environmental changes quickly and speeds decision making because decisions need not go to the top of the hierarchy for approval. Another big advantage is the morale boost. Employees are enthusiastic about their involvement in bigger projects rather than narrow departmental tasks. But the team approach has disadvantages as well. Employees may be enthusiastic about team participation, but they may experience conflicts and dual loyalties. A cross-functional team may make different demands on members than do their department managers, and members who participate in more than one team must resolve these conflicts. A large amount of time is devoted to meetings, thus increasing coordination time. Unless the organization truly needs teams to coordinate complex projects and adapt to the environment, it will lose production efficiency with them. Finally, the team approach may cause too much decentralization. Senior department managers who traditionally made decisions might feel left out when a team moves ahead on its own. Team members often do not see the big picture of the corporation and may make decisions that are good for their group but bad for the organization.

Virtual Network Approach.   The biggest advantages to a virtual network approach are flexibility and competitiveness on a global scale. A network organization can draw on resources and expertise worldwide to achieve the best quality and price and can sell its products and services worldwide. Flexibility comes from the ability to hire whatever services are needed and to change a few months later without constraints from owning plant, equipment, and facilities. The organization can continually redefine itself to fit new product and market opportunities. Finally, this structure is perhaps the leanest of all organization forms because little supervision is required. Large teams of staff specialists and administrators are unnecessary. A network organization may have only two or three levels of hierarchy, compared with ten or more in traditional organizations.[31] One of the major disadvantages is lack of hands-on control. Managers do not have all operations under one roof and must rely on contracts, coordination, negotiation, and electronic linkages to hold things together. Each partner in the network necessarily acts in its own self-interest. The weak and ambiguous boundaries create higher uncertainty and greater demands on managers for defining shared goals, coordinating activities, managing relationships, and keeping people focused and motivated.[32] Finally, in this type of organization, employee loyalty can weaken. Employees might feel they can be replaced by contract services. A cohesive corporate culture is less likely to develop, and turnover tends to be higher because emotional commitment between organization and employee is weak.

Organizing for Horizontal Coordination

One reason for the growing use of teams and networks is that many companies are recognizing the limits of traditional vertical organization structures in today's shifting environment. In general, the trend is toward breaking down barriers between departments, and many companies are moving toward horizontal structures based on work processes rather than departmental functions.[33] Regardless of the type of structure, every organization needs mechanisms for horizontal integration and coordination. An organization's structure is incomplete without designing the horizontal as well as the vertical dimensions of structure.[34]

The Need for Coordination

As organizations grow and evolve, two things happen. First, new positions and departments are added to deal with factors in the external environment or with new strategic

BUSINESS BLOOPER

Total Care Technologies

Starting with nothing and building up a $10 million software company is no mean feat, especially for a former police officer and new entrepreneur. That's exactly what Al Hildebrandt did with his Canadian company (headquartered in British Columbia) Total Care Technologies. But then they forgot to coordinate one part of the organization with the other. They got so involved with Australia hospital installations of their staff-scheduling software that they forgot about sales. On top of that, they neglected signs that the Y2K bug fear had reduced software sales worldwide. By the time they realized what was happening, even a $2 million loan wasn't enough to save them from receivership.

SOURCE: Rick Spence, Avoiding seven deadly sins: One thing entrepreneurs have in common, they tend to share the same business mistakes. Toronto Star, Oct. 16, 2003, P. H02.

needs. For example, many organizations have established Information Technology (IT) departments to cope with the proliferation of new information systems or chief knowledge officers (CIOs) to find ways to leverage organizational knowledge in today's information-based economy. As companies add positions and departments to meet changing needs, they grow more complex, with hundreds of positions and departments performing diverse activities.

Second, senior managers have to find a way to tie all of these departments together. The formal chain of command and the supervision it provides is effective, but it is not enough. The organization needs systems to process information and enable communication among people in different departments and at different levels. **Coordination** refers to the quality of collaboration across departments. Without coordination, a company's left hand will not act in concert with the right hand, causing problems and conflicts. Coordination is required regardless of whether the organization has a functional, divisional, or team structure. Employees identify with their immediate department or team, taking its interest to heart, and may not want to compromise with other units for the good of the organization as a whole.

Without a major effort at coordination, an organization may be like Chrysler Corporation in the 1980s when Lee Iacocca took over:

> *What I found at Chrysler were 35 vice presidents, each with his own turf.... I couldn't believe, for example, that the guy running engineering departments wasn't in constant touch with his counterpart in manufacturing. But that's how it was. Everybody worked independently. I took one look at that system and I almost threw up. That's when I knew I was in really deep trouble.*
>
> *I'd call in a guy from engineering, and he'd stand there dumbfounded when I'd explain to him that we had a design problem or some other hitch in the engineering-manufacturing relationship. He might have the ability to invent a brilliant piece of engineering that would save us a lot of money. He might come up with a terrific new design. There was only one problem: He didn't know that the manufacturing people couldn't build it. Why? Because he had never talked to them about it. Nobody at Chrysler seemed to understand that interaction among the different functions in a company is absolutely critical. People in engineering and manufacturing almost have to be sleeping together. These guys weren't even flirting!*[35]

If one thing changed at Chrysler (now DaimlerChrysler) in the years before Iacocca retired, it was improved coordination. Cooperation among engineering, marketing, and manufacturing enabled the rapid design and production of the Chrysler PT Cruiser, for example.

Take **ACTION**

Remember that the more departments you have, the more time you need to devote to the various departments talking to one another.

coordination

The quality of collaboration across departments.

The problem of coordination is amplified in the international arena because organizational units are differentiated by goals and work activities, by geographical distance, time differences, and cultural values, and perhaps by language as well. How can managers ensure that domestic and global coordination will take place in their company? Coordination is the outcome of information and cooperation. Managers can design systems and structures to promote horizontal coordination. For example, to support its global strategy, Whirlpool is decentralizing its operations, giving more authority and responsibility to teams of designers and engineers in developing countries like Brazil, and establishing outsourcing relationships with manufacturers in China and India.[36] Exhibit 7.6 illustrates the evolution of organizational structures, with a growing emphasis on horizontal coordination. Though the vertical functional structure is effective in stable environments, it does not provide the horizontal coordination needed in times of rapid change. Innovations such as cross-functional teams, task forces, and project managers work within the vertical structure but provide a means to increase horizontal communication and cooperation. The next stage involves reengineering to structure the organization into teams working on horizontal processes. The vertical hierarchy is flattened, with perhaps only a few senior executives in traditional support functions such as finance and human resources.

Task Forces, Teams, and Project Management

A **task force** is a temporary team or committee designed to solve a short-term problem involving several departments.[37] Task force members represent their departments and share information that enables coordination. For example, the Shawmut National Corporation created two task forces in human resources to consolidate all employment services into a single area. The task force looked at job banks, referral programs, employment procedures, and applicant tracking systems; found ways to perform these functions for all Shawmut's divisions in one human resource department; and then disbanded.[38] In addition to creating task forces, companies also set up cross-functional teams, as described earlier. A cross-functional team furthers horizontal coordination because participants from several departments meet regularly to solve ongoing problems of common interest.[39] This is similar to a task force except that it works with continuing rather than temporary problems and might exist for several years. Team members think in terms of working together for the good of the whole rather than for their own department.

Companies use project managers to increase coordination between functional departments. A **project manager** is a person who is responsible for coordinating the activities of several departments for the completion of a specific project.[40] Project managers are critical because many organizations must constantly reinvent themselves, creating flexible structures and working on projects with an ever-changing assortment of people and organizations.[41] Project managers might work on several different projects at one time and might have to move in and out of new projects at a moment's notice.

The distinctive feature of the project manager position is the person is not a member of one of the departments being coordinated. Project managers are located outside of the departments and have responsibility for coordinating several departments to achieve

task force

A temporary team or committee formed to solve a specific short-term problem involving several departments.

project manager

A person responsible for coordinating the activities of several departments on a full-time basis for the completion of a specific project.

EXHIBIT 7.6

Evolution of Organizational Structures

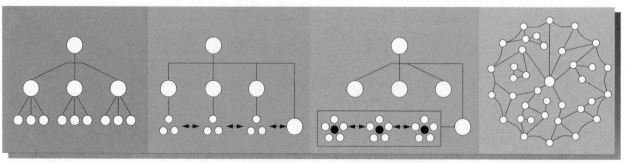

| Traditional Vertical Structure | Teams and Project Managers for Horizontal Coordination | Reengineering to Horizontal Processes | New Workplace Learning Organization |

Reprinted by permission of PepsiCo.

desired project outcomes. For example, General Mills, Procter & Gamble, and General Foods all use product managers to coordinate their product lines. A manager is assigned to each line, such as Cheerios, Bisquick, and Hamburger Helper. Product managers set budget goals, marketing targets, and strategies and obtain the cooperation from advertising, production, and sales personnel needed for implementing product strategy.

In some organizations, project managers are included on the organization chart, as illustrated in Exhibit 7.7. The project manager is drawn to one side of the chart to indicate authority over the project but not over the people assigned to it. Dashed lines to the project manager indicate responsibility for coordination and communication with assigned team members, but department managers retain line authority over functional employees.

Project managers might have titles such as product manager, integrator, program manager, or process owner. Project managers need excellent people skills.

They use expertise and persuasion to achieve coordination among various departments, and their jobs involve getting people together, listening, building trust, confronting problems, and resolving conflicts and disputes in the best interest of the project and the organization. Consider the role of Hugh Hoffman at American Standard Companies.

Take ACTION

When you are doing a class group assignment and you are the leader, use project management skills with the other students and the instructor.

EXHIBIT 7.7

Example of Project Manager Relationship to Other Departments

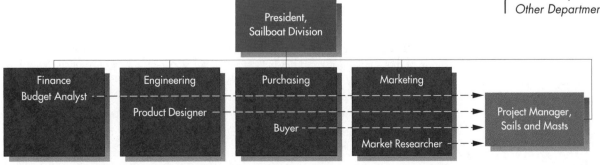

American Standard	Hugh J. Hoffman began working at American Standard Companies as a ceramic engineer in 1970. Today, he works as a full-time project manager in the company's chinaware business, which makes toilets and bidets. Hoffman, whose official title is Process Owner, Chinaware Order Fulfillment, coordinates all the activities that ensure that American Standard's factories turn out the products customers order and deliver them on time. Hoffman's job requires that he think about everything that happens between the time an order comes in and the time it gets paid for, including design, manufacturing, painting, sales, shipping and receiving, and numerous other tasks. Project managers such as Hoffman have to act as if they are running their own business, setting goals and developing strategies for achieving them. It is often difficult because Hoffman works outside the boundaries and authority structure of traditional departments. His years of experience and good people skills help him motivate others and coordinate the work of many departments and geographically dispersed factories. "I move behind the scenes," Hoffman says. "I understand the workings of the company and know how to get things done."[42]

Using project managers has helped American Standard do things faster, better, and more cheaply than competitors. Many organizations move to a stronger horizontal approach such as the use of permanent teams, project managers, or process owners after going through a redesign procedure called reengineering.

Reengineering

reengineering

The radical redesign of business processes to achieve dramatic improvements in cost, quality, service, and speed.

Reengineering, sometimes called business process reengineering, is the radical redesign of business processes to achieve dramatic improvements in cost, quality, service, and speed.[43] Because the focus of reengineering is on process rather than function, reengineering generally leads to a shift away from a strong vertical structure to one emphasizing stronger horizontal coordination and greater flexibility in responding to changes in the environment.

Reengineering changes the way managers think about how work is done in their organizations. Rather than focusing on narrow jobs structured into distinct, functional departments, they emphasize core processes that cut horizontally across the company and involve teams of employees working to provide value directly to customers.[44] A

process

An organized group of related tasks and activities that work together to transform inputs into outputs and create value.

process is an organized group of related tasks and activities that work together to transform inputs into outputs and create value. Common examples of processes include new product development, order fulfillment, and customer service.[45]

Reengineering frequently involves a shift to a horizontal team-based structure, as described earlier in this chapter. All the people who work on a particular process have easy access to one another so they can easily communicate and coordinate their efforts, share knowledge, and provide value directly to customers.[46] For example, reengineering at Texas Instruments led to the formation of product development teams that became the fundamental organizational unit. Each team is made up of people drawn from engineering, marketing, and other departments, and takes full responsibility for a product from conception through launch.[47]

Reengineering can squeeze out the dead space and time lags in work flows as illustrated by reengineering of the travel system at the U.S. Department of Defense.

U.S. Department of Defense (DoD)	The Pentagon can act quickly to move thousands of tons of humanitarian aid material or hundreds of thousands of troops, but until recently, sending employees on routine travel has been a different story. Before Pentagon travelers could even board a bus, they had to secure numerous approvals and fill out reams of paperwork. Coming home wasn't any easier: The average traveler spent six hours preparing vouchers for reimbursement following a trip.
	The DoD set up a task force to reengineer the cumbersome travel system, aiming to make it cheaper, more efficient, and more customer friendly. The reengineered system

reduces the steps in the pre-travel process from 13 to four, as shown in Exhibit 7.8. Travel budgets and authority to approve travel requests and vouchers, which have traditionally rested in the budget channels of the various service commands, were transferred to local supervisors. Travelers make all their arrangements through a commercial travel office, which prepares a "should-cost" estimate for each trip. This document is all a traveler needs before, during, and after a trip: With a supervisor's signature, it becomes a travel authorization; during travel, it serves as an itinerary; after amendments to reflect variations from plans, it becomes an expense report. Other travel expenses and needed cash or travelers' checks can be charged to a government-issued travel card, with payment made directly to the travel card company through electronic funds transfer.[48]

As illustrated by this example, reengineering can lead to stunning results, but like all business ideas, it has its drawbacks. Defining the organization's key business processes can be mind-boggling. AT&T's Network Systems division started with a list of 130 processes and then began working to pare them down to 13 core ones.[49] Organizations often have difficulty realigning power relationships and management processes to support work redesign and, thus, do not reap the intended benefits of reengineering. According to some estimates, 70 percent of reengineering efforts fail to reach their intended goals.[50] Because reengineering is expensive, time consuming, and usually painful, it seems best suited to companies facing serious competitive threats.

Factors Shaping Structure

Despite the trend toward horizontal design, vertical hierarchies continue to thrive because they often provide important benefits for organizations.[51] How do managers know whether to design a structure that emphasizes the formal, vertical hierarchy or one with an emphasis on horizontal communication and collaboration? The answer lies in the contingency factors that influence organization structure. Research on organization design shows that structure depends on various contingencies, as defined in Chapter 1. The right structure is designed to "fit" the contingency factors of strategy,

EXHIBIT 7.8

Reengineering the Travel System—U.S. Department of Defense

Steps in the Pre-Travel Process—Old System

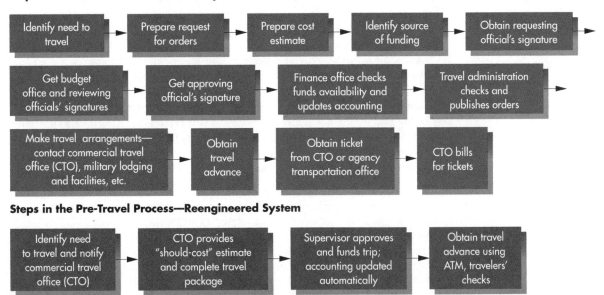

Steps in the Pre-Travel Process—Reengineered System

SOURCE: Richard Koonce, "Reengineering the Travel Game," *Government Executive* (May 1995), 28–34, 69–70.

EXHIBIT 7.9

Contingency Factors that Influence Organization Structure

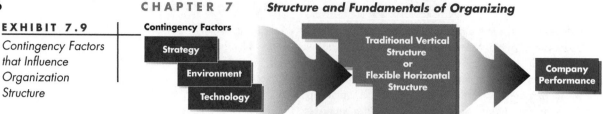

environment, and production technology, as illustrated in Exhibit 7.9. These three areas are changing dramatically for most organizations, creating a need for stronger horizontal coordination.

Structure Follows Strategy

In Chapter 5 we discussed several strategies that business firms can adopt. Two strategies proposed by Porter are differentiation and cost leadership.[52] With a differentiation strategy, the organization attempts to develop innovative products unique to the market, which is MTV International's strategy as described below.

MTV

MTV was there first internationally in many countries: India in 1991, Russia in 1993. As a result, it has been ahead of the competition for 24-hour music channels in nearly every market. In some of the markets, it has adopted the strategy of taking on local partners. And if strategy determines structure, MTV has found it needs to be more decentralized in these situations, giving up control so that 70 percent of programming is local content. The idea that MTV brings homogenized American pop (think Britney Spears and Usher) around the world is not supported by the evidence. Nor does it give viewers in other countries credit for choosing what they watch. India's MTV has lots of color, humor, and street culture; China emphasizes family values; Indonesia's large Muslim population helped bring a call to prayer five times a day on its MTV; Brazil's is sexy: Italy's is full of food shows; and MTV Japan is full of wireless techie shows.

Sometimes local programming choices cause problems, such as the nude wrestling program that cropped up in Taiwan (MTV Central pulled it off the air), or the early programmers in India who thought Bollywood music (from India's vast movie industry) was uncool. After viewers left en masse, local programmers got the message and reinstated Bollywood music. Since then, its ratings have soared 700 percent.

Following this strategy can be time consuming. MTV Networks International president Bill Roedy spent an entire evening listening to Chinese opera, and participating in endless karaoke sessions, as he tried to cultivate relationships in China. It worked because MTV Mandarin is seen in 60 million homes and last year over 10,000 Chinese teens competed to become the next MTV Mandarin veejay. Some of the local programming could only happen in that country. Take Italy's *MTV Kitchen*, where singers and songwriters chat while cooking. The one in Brazil, *Rockgol*, is a soccer championship pitting Brazilian musicians with recording industry executives. It would be like having Lenny Kravitz and Michael Jackson on a football team against Tommy Mottola and David Geffen.[53]

With a cost leadership strategy, the organization strives for internal efficiency. The strategies of cost leadership versus differentiation typically require different structural approaches, so managers pick congruent strategies and structures.

Exhibit 7.10 shows a simplified continuum that illustrates how structural approaches are associated with strategic goals. The pure functional structure is appropriate for achieving internal efficiency goals. The vertical functional structure uses task specialization and a strict chain of command to gain efficient use of scarce resources, but it does not enable the organization to be flexible or innovative. In contrast, horizontal teams are appropriate when the primary goal is innovation and flexibility. Each team is small, is able to be responsive, and has the people and resources necessary for

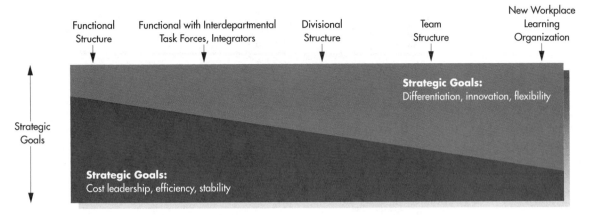

EXHIBIT 7.10

Relationship of Strategic Goals to Structural Approach

performing its task. The flexible horizontal structure enables organizations to differentiate themselves and respond quickly to the demands of a shifting environment but at the expense of efficient resource use. Changing strategies shape structure in government organizations. Under financial pressure to cut costs and political pressure to keep customers happy, Departments of Motor Vehicles (DMV) are farming out DMV business whenever possible by building strong partnerships with other companies. For example, in many states, auto dealers register new cars on site when they are sold.[54]

Exhibit 7.10 also illustrates how other forms of structure represent intermediate steps on the organization's path to efficiency or innovation. The functional structure with cross-functional teams and project managers provides greater coordination and flexibility than the pure functional structure. The divisional structure promotes differentiation because each division can focus on specific products and customers though divisions tend to be larger and less flexible than small teams. Exhibit 7.11 does not include all possible structures, but it illustrates how structures can be used to facilitate the strategic goals of cost leadership or differentiation.

Structure Reflects the Environment

In Chapter 2, we discussed the nature of environmental uncertainty. Environmental uncertainty means that decision makers have difficulty acquiring good information and predicting external changes. Uncertainty occurs when the external environment is rapidly changing and complex. An uncertain environment causes three things to happen within an organization.

1. *Increased differences occur among departments.* In an uncertain environment, each major department—marketing, manufacturing, research and development—focuses on the task and environmental sectors for which it is responsible and, hence, distinguishes itself from the others with respect to goals, task orientation, and time horizon.[55] Departments work autonomously. These factors create barriers among departments.

Take **ACTION**

As a manager, if your strategy changes, you need to revisit the structure to make sure it is appropriate.

EXHIBIT 7.11

Relationship between Environment and Structure

STRUCTURE

	Vertical	Horizontal
Uncertain (Unstable)	Incorrect Fit: Vertical structure in uncertain environment Structure too tight	Correct Fit: Horizontal structure in uncertain environment
Certain (Stable)	Correct Fit: Vertical structure in certain environment	Incorrect Fit: Horizontal structure in certain environment Structure too loose

ENVIRONMENT

CONCEPT CONNECTION

Since China joined the World Trade Organization, companies such as Angang Iron and Steel have experienced greater **environmental uncertainty** that comes from participating in the global economy. Angang, one of the largest and most prestigious metal-bending companies in China, is **restructuring** to become more flexible with a trimmed, more efficient workforce. Angang has cut 30,000 people from its workforce of 165,000 at steel plants such as the one shown in the photo.

© GOH CHAI HIN/ AFP/Getty Images

2. *The organization needs increased coordination to keep departments working together.* Additional differences require more emphasis on horizontal coordination to link departments and overcome differences in departmental goals and orientations. The Salvation Army finds its needs for coordination increase during some disasters, as described below.

| Salvation Army |

You might not think the Rolling Stones and the Salvation Army have much in common, but a study cites them as among the world's most enduring organizations.

The Salvation Army is a frugal organization. Nobody makes much money, and accounting practices demand strict accountability for every penny spent. So, imagine the possible panic that could occur when they step in to help with an emergency and commit to spending $250,000 without even knowing where they money will come from. Without a flexible structure, the organization would find itself schizophrenic or else with one side—strict financial controls or generous donations—winning out. The Salvation Army has figured out how to have it both ways by having several organizations in one. Its daily financial accountability reputation allows it to raise emergency funds quickly.

At the same time, it needs to organize for emergencies using the Incident Command Model used by government and relief agencies. The model is a highly structured, command-and-control formula that allows anyone to know who is in charge of what. But other circumstances require a more entrepreneurial approach and The Army has the flexibility to allow that. During the 1997 upper Midwest floods, for example, Major Dahlberg (they go by military titles) brought in real estate specialist-Salvation Army people, who were given general guidelines and then allowed to go off on their own to acquire properties and find rental units. There was not time for supervisors to sign off on every transaction, so the specialists were given authority to make deals on the spot, under the agreed-upon format. Other Army people focused on networking, working the horizontal relationships to enhance their service. During that time, Wal-Mart helped them assess logistical needs and then sent in 26 experienced warehouse staff to help them organize the distribution of clothing, food, and household items. As a result, they reduced the wait time in the distribution centers to 45 minutes, down from 2.5 hours.

The Salvation Army has a flexible structure that allows various units to adapt to the work being done, or environmental conditions. Some workers are almost independent contractors, who clean houses and prepare food; office workers have much more control and supervision. The structure is driven by the mission of that unit, as well. A risk is developing too many "hero" types who love to save people during disasters. But those are not the ones likely to spend their time in staff development, organization design or planning. Without those, however, disasters will be just that: disasters. So, through years of experience, the Salvation Army has learned how to replace people who crave the adrenaline and excitement more than a desire to serve. Such a model allows that organizational flexibility to remain. It is about good management.[56]

3. *The organization must adapt to change.* The organization must maintain a flexible, responsive posture toward the environment. Changes in products and technology require cooperation among departments, which means additional emphasis on coordination through the use of teams, project managers, and horizontal information processing.[57] Though he is only a company of one person, Adam Smith has found that to adapt to environmental change, he had to expand horizontally, working with more suppliers to increase his inventory and please customers.

Fog City News

Adam Smith has become a snob. A chocolate snob. Whereas he used to be happy with M&Ms or Snickers, now he prefers the "flavor profile" of imported chocolate, with an average price of four dollars. "I've discovered a wonderful world of complexity," declares the owner of San Francisco chocolate retailer, Fog City News.

After running giant newsstand Fog City News (with 3,000 magazines, including 700 foreign) for two years at a modest profit, his friends urged him to start selling Canadian chocolate, including Smarties. They were such a hit that he started carrying other foreign chocolates and now carries 225 bars from 15 countries. Sales last year were $500,000, up 20 percent from the previous year. Some bars cost as much as $13.95, but they tell the customer it is for a chocolate bar.

Smith wants his customers to be as savvy about cocoa beans (he prefers to call them cacao beans) as Starbuck's patrons are about coffee beans. People will soon want to know whether their bar has single-bean chocolates versus blends.[58]

The terms *mechanistic* and *organic* can be used to explain structural responses to the external environment.[59] When the environment is stable, the organization uses a mechanistic system. It typically has a rigid, vertical, centralized structure, with most decisions made at the top. The organization is highly specialized and characterized by rules, procedures and a clear hierarchy of authority. In rapidly changing environments, however, the organization tends to be looser, free-flowing, and adaptive, using an organic system. The structure is more horizontal, and decision-making authority is decentralized. People at lower levels have more responsibility and authority for solving problems, enabling the organization to be more fluid and adaptable to changes in the environment.[60]

The contingency relationship between environmental uncertainty and structural approach is illustrated in Exhibit 7.11. When the external environment is more stable, the organization can succeed with a mechanistic structure that emphasizes vertical control. There is little need for change, flexibility, or intense coordination. The structure can emphasize specialization, centralized decision making, and wide spans of control. When environmental uncertainty is high, a flexible organic structure that emphasizes lateral relationships such as teams and horizontal projects is appropriate. Vertical structure characteristics, such as specialization and centralization, should be downplayed. In an uncertain environment, the organization figures things out as it goes along, departments must cooperate, and decisions should be decentralized to the teams and task forces working on specific problems. The flight deck of the *USS Dwight D. Eisenhower*, a nuclear-powered aircraft carrier, provides an excellent example of the relationship between structure and the environment.

USS Dwight D Eisenhower	On an aircraft carrier, such as the *USS Dwight D. Eisenhower*, thousands of disastrous accidents are waiting to happen. Launching or landing a plane from the oil-slicked deck of a nuclear-powered carrier is a tricky, finely balanced procedure. A sudden wind shift, a mechanical breakdown, or the slightest miscommunication can spell disaster. Yet, surprisingly, flight deck operations generally run as smooth as silk, and accidents are rare. The reason has a lot to do with organizational structure.

At first glance, a nuclear aircraft carrier is structured in a rigid, hierarchical way: The captain issues orders to commanders, who direct lieutenants, who pass orders on to ensigns, and on down the hierarchy. There is a strict chain of command, and people are expected to follow orders promptly and without question. Manuals detail standard operating procedures for everything. But an interesting thing happens in times of high demand, such as the launching and recovery of planes during real or simulated wartime. In this different environment, the hierarchy dissolves and a loosely organized, collaborative structure in which sailors and officers work together as colleagues takes its place. People discuss and negotiate the best procedure to use, and everyone typically follows the lead of whoever has the most experience and knowledge in a particular area, no matter the person's rank or job title. During this time, no one is thinking about job descriptions, authority, or chain of command; they are thinking about getting the job done safely. With planes landing every 60 seconds, there is no time to send messages up the chain of command and wait for decisions to come down from the top. Anyone who notices a problem is expected to respond quickly, and each member of the crew has the power—and the obligation—to shut down flight operations immediately if the circumstances warrant it.[61]

Researchers have studied this ability to glide smoothly from a rigid, hierarchical structure to a loosely structured, horizontal one on aircraft carriers and in organizations that have to respond to environmental changes, for example, air traffic controllers or workers at nuclear power plants. The hierarchical side helps keep discipline and ensure adherence to rules that have been developed and tested over many years to cope with expected and well-understood problems and situations. However, during times of complexity and high uncertainty, the most effective structure is one that loosens the lines of command and enables people to work across departmental and hierarchical lines to anticipate and avoid problems.[62]

Not all organizations have to be as responsive to the environment as the *USS Dwight D. Eisenhower*, but using the correct structure for the environment is important for businesses. When managers use the wrong structure for the environment, reduced performance results. A rigid, vertical structure in an uncertain environment prevents the organization from adapting to change. Likewise, a loose, horizontal structure in a stable environment is inefficient. Too many resources are devoted to meetings and discussions when employees could be more productive focusing on specialized tasks.

Structure Fits the Technology

Technology includes the knowledge, tools, techniques, and activities used to transform organizational inputs into outputs.[63] Technology includes machinery, employee skills, and work procedures. A useful way to think about technology is as production activities.

The production activities may be to produce steel castings, television programs, or computer software. Technologies vary between manufacturing and service organizations. In addition, new digital technology has an impact on structure.

Woodward's Manufacturing Technology. The most influential research into the relationship between manufacturing technology and organization structure was conducted by Joan Woodward, a British industrial sociologist.[64] She gathered data from 100 British firms to determine whether basic structural characteristics, such as administrative overhead, span of control, and centralization were different across firms. She found that manufacturing firms could be categorized according to three basic types of production technology:

1. *Small-batch and unit production.* **Small-batch production** firms produce goods in batches of one or a few products designed to customer specification. Each customer orders a unique product. This technology is used to make large, one-of-a-kind products, such as computer-controlled machines. Small-batch manufacturing is close to traditional skilled craftwork because human beings are a large part of the process. Examples of items produced through small-batch manufacturing include custom clothing, special-order machine tools, space capsules, satellites, and submarines.

2. *Large-batch and mass production.* **Mass production** technology is distinguished by standardized production runs. A large volume of products is produced, and all customers receive the same product. Standard products go into inventory for sale as customers need them. This technology makes greater use of machines than does small-batch production. Machines are designed to do most of the physical work, and employees complement the machinery. Examples of mass production are automobile assembly lines and the large-batch techniques used to produce tobacco products and textiles.

3. *Continuous process production.* In **continuous process production**, the entire work flow is mechanized. This is the most sophisticated and complex form of production technology. Because the process runs continuously, there is no starting and stopping. Human operators are not part of production because machinery does the work. Human operators read dials, fix machines that break down, and manage the production process. Examples of continuous process technologies are chemical plants, distilleries, petroleum refineries, and nuclear power plants.

The difference among the three manufacturing technologies is called **technical complexity**. Technical complexity is the degree to which machinery is involved in the production to the exclusion of people. With a complex technology, employees are hardly needed except to monitor the machines.

The structural characteristics associated with each type of manufacturing technology are illustrated in Exhibit 7.12. Centralization is high for mass production technology and low for continuous process. Unlike small-batch and continuous process, standardized mass-production machinery requires centralized decision making and well-defined rules and procedures. The administrative ratio and the percentage of indirect labor required increase with technological complexity. Because the production process is non-routine, closer supervision is needed. More indirect labor in the form of maintenance people is required because of the machinery's complexity; thus, the indirect/direct labor ratio is high. Span of control for first-line supervisors is greatest for mass production. On an assembly line, jobs are so routine that a supervisor can handle an average of 48 employees. The number of employees per supervisor in small-batch and continuous process production is lower because closer supervision is needed. Overall, small-batch and continuous process firms have somewhat loose, flexible structures (organic), and mass production firms have tight vertical structures (mechanistic).

small-batch production

A type of technology that involves the production of goods in batches of one or a few products designed to customer specification.

mass production

A type of technology characterized by the production of a large volume of products with the same specifications.

continuous process production

A type of technology involving mechanization of the entire work flow and nonstop production.

technical complexity

The degree to which complex machinery is involved in the production process to the exclusion of people.

Take **ACTION**

As a manager, always consider technical complexity when deciding on what structure to use.

EXHIBIT 7.12

Relationship between Manufacturing Technology and Organization Structure

SOURCE: Based on Joan Woodward, *Industrial Organizations: Theory and Practice* (London: Oxford University Press, 1965).

	Manufacturing Technology		
	Small Batch	**Mass Production**	**Continuous Process**
Technical Complexity of Production Technology	Low	Medium	High
Organization structure:			
Formalization	Low	High	Low
Centralization	Low	High	Low
Top administrator ratio	Low	Medium	High
Indirect/direct labor ratio	1/9	1/4	1/1
Supervisor span of control	23	48	15
Communication:			
Written (vertical)	Low	High	Low
Verbal (horizontal)	High	Low	High
Overall structure	Flexible	Rigid	Flexible

The important conclusion about manufacturing technology was described by Woodward as follows: "Different technologies impose different kinds of demands on individuals and organizations, and these demands have to be met through an appropriate structure."[65] Woodward found that the relationship between structure and technology was directly related to company performance. Low-performing firms tended to deviate from the preferred structural form, often adopting a structure appropriate for another type of technology. High-performing organizations had characteristics similar to those listed in Exhibit 7.12.

Service Technology. Service organizations are increasingly important in North America. For the past two decades, more people have been employed in service organizations than in manufacturing organizations. Examples of service organizations include consulting companies, law firms, brokerage houses, airlines, hotels, advertising firms, amusement parks, and educational organizations. In addition, service technology characterizes many departments in large corporations, even manufacturing firms. In a manufacturing company such as Ford Motor Company, the legal, human resources, finance, and market research departments all provide service. Thus, the structure and design of these departments reflect their own service technology rather than the manufacturing plant's technology. **Service technology** can be defined as follows:

service technology

Technology characterized by intangible outputs and direct contact between employees and customers.

1. *Intangible output.* The output of a service firm is intangible. Services are perishable and, unlike physical products, cannot be stored in inventory. The service is consumed immediately or lost forever. Manufactured products are produced at one point in time and can be stored until sold at another time.

2. *Direct contact with customers.* Employees and customers interact directly to provide and purchase the service. Production and consumption are simultaneous. Service firm employees have direct contact with customers. In a manufacturing firm, technical employees are separated from customers, and hence, no direct interactions occur.[66]

One distinct feature of service technology that directly influences structure is the need for employees to be close to the customer.[67] Structural characteristics are similar to those for continuous manufacturing technology, shown in Exhibit 7.12. Service firms tend to be flexible, informal, and decentralized. Horizontal communication is high because employees must share information and resources to serve customers and solve problems. Services also are dispersed; hence, each unit is often small and located geographically close to customers. For example, banks, hotels, fast food franchises, and doctors' offices disperse their facilities into regional and local offices to provide faster and better service to customers.

Some services can be broken into explicit steps so employees can follow set rules and procedures. For example, McDonald's has standard procedures for serving customers, and Marriott has standard procedures for cleaning hotel rooms. When services can be standardized, a tight centralized structure can be effective, but service firms in general tend to be more organic, flexible, and decentralized.

Digital Technology.   Digital technology is characterized by use of the Internet and other digital processes to conduct or support business online. E-commerce organizations such as Amazon.com, which sells books and other products to consumers over the Internet; eBay, an online auction site; Google, an Internet search engine; and Priceline.com, which allows consumers to name their own prices and then negotiate electronically with its partner organizations on behalf of the consumer, are all examples of firms based on digital technology. In addition, large companies such as General Electric (GE), Dell Computers, and Ford Motor Company are involved in business-to-business (B2B) commerce, using digital technology to conduct transactions with suppliers and partners.

Like service firms, organizations based on digital technology tend to be flexible and decentralized. Horizontal communication and collaboration are typically high, and these companies frequently may be involved in virtual network arrangements. Digital technology is driving the move toward horizontal forms that link customers, suppliers, and partners into the organizational network, with everyone working together as if they were one organization. People may use electronic connections to link themselves together into teams. For example, an employee may send an e-mail to people within and outside the organization who can help with a particular customer problem and form a virtual team to develop a solution.[68] In other words, digital technology encourages boundarylessness, where information and work activities flow freely among various organizational participants. Centralization is low, and employees are empowered to work in teams to meet changing needs. Verbal and electronic communication is high, up and down as well as across the organization because timely information is essential. In the digital world, advantage comes from seeing first and moving fastest, which requires extraordinary openness and flexibility.[69]

digital technology
Technology characterized by use of the Internet and other digital processes to conduct or support business operations.

Manager's Solution

This chapter introduced a number of important organizing concepts. Fundamental characteristics of organization structure include work specialization, chain of command, authority and responsibility, span of management, centralization, and decentralization. These dimensions represent the vertical hierarchy and define how authority and responsibility are distributed.

Another major concept is departmentalization, which describes how organization employees are grouped. Three traditional approaches are functional, divisional, and matrix; contemporary approaches are team and virtual network structures. The functional approach groups employees by common skills and tasks. The opposite structure is divisional, which groups people by organizational output such that each division has a mix of functional skills and tasks. The matrix structure uses two chains of command simultaneously, and some employees have two bosses. The team approach uses permanent teams and cross-functional teams to achieve better coordination and employee commitment than is possible with a pure functional structure. The network approach means that a firm concentrates on what it does best and subcontracts other functions to separate organizations that are connected to the headquarters electronically. Each organization form has advantages and disadvantages and can be used by managers to meet the needs of the competitive situation. In addition, managers adjust elements of the vertical structure, such as the degree of centralization or decentralization, to meet changing needs.

As organizations grow, they add new departments, functions, and hierarchical levels. A major problem for management is how to tie the organization together. Horizontal coordination mechanisms provide coordination across departments and include reengineering, task forces, project managers, and horizontal teams.

Contingency factors of strategy, environment, and production technology influence the correct structural approach. When a firm's strategy is to differentiate its products or services, an organic flexible structure using teams, decentralization, and empowered employees is appropriate. A mechanistic structure is appropriate for a low-cost strategy. Similarly, the structure needs to be looser and more flexible when environmental uncertainty is high. For manufacturing firms, small batch, continuous process, and flexible manufacturing technologies tend to be structured loosely, whereas a tighter vertical structure is appropriate for mass production. Service technologies are people oriented, and firms are located geographically close to dispersed customers. In general, services have more flexible, horizontal structures, with decentralized decision making. Similarly, organizations based on new digital technology are typically horizontally structured and highly decentralized.

Recall Greg Berlanti, the "Everwood" head writer in the opening case. He was besieged with problems from above and below and had to organize the writers to do the season finale script. Rather than do their usual manner of one writer, or as other shows did with all the writers talking but the head writer doing the penning, Berlanti assigned the season finale to his three strongest writers. One would be responsible for the opening voiceover, another did the teen dialogue, and the third did the scenes with Dr. Brown's mentor and Ephram. After ten days, the writers turned in their parts, Berlanti gave feedback, and they went for another round of rewrites, all the while working on earlier episodes. But Berlanti realized one of the scenes—with hiking—was too sweet, as the network had warned him. With only 48 hours before filming, he assembled the writers' notes, got the writers on conference calls, and decided to have the kids go to a graduation party. Then Berlanti wove it all together into one coherent script. While doing it, though, he had to keep using the writers as an ersatz audience to test out scenes with them. It was an intense collaboration, but they got it done and on time.[70]

Discussion Questions

1. Sonny Holt, manager of Electronics Assembly, asked Hector Cruz, his senior technician, to handle things in the department while Sonny worked on the budget. Sonny needed peace and quiet for at least a week to complete his figures. After 10 days, Sonny discovered that Hector had hired a senior secretary, not realizing that Sonny had promised interviews to two other people. Evaluate Sonny's approach to delegation.

2. Many experts note that organizations have been making greater use of teams in recent years. What factors might account for this trend?

3. Contrast centralization with span of management. Would you expect these characteristics to affect each other in organizations? Why?

4. An organizational consultant was heard to say, "Some aspect of functional structure appears in every organization." Do you agree? Explain.

5. The divisional structure is often considered almost the opposite of a functional structure. Do you agree? Briefly explain the major differences in these two approaches to departmentalization.

6. What is the network approach to structure? Is the use of authority and responsibility different compared with other forms of departmentalization? Explain.

7. Why are divisional structures frequently used in large corporations?

8. Carnival Cruise Lines provides pleasure cruises to the masses. Carnival has several ships and works on high volume/low price rather than offering luxury cruises. What would you predict about the organization structure of a Carnival Cruise ship?

9. Why is structure different depending on whether a firm's strategy is low cost or differentiation?

10. The chapter suggested that structure should be designed to fit strategy. Some theorists argue that strategy should be designed to fit the organization's structure. With which theory do you agree? Explain.

11. What is the difference between a task force and a project manager? Which would be more effective in achieving coordination?

12. Discuss why an organization in an uncertain environment requires more horizontal relationships than one in a certain environment.

13. Why are empowered employees, open information, and cultural values of minimal boundaries and equality important in a learning organization as opposed to a traditional, vertical organization?

14. What is the difference between manufacturing and service technology? How would you classify a university, a local discount store, a nursery school? How would you expect the structure of a service organization to differ from that of a manufacturing organization?

15. Flexible manufacturing systems combine elements of both small batch and mass production. What effect might this new form of technology have on organization structure? Explain.

Manager's Workbook

Loose versus Tight Organization Structure

Interview an employee at your university, such as a department head or secretary. Have the employee rate the following thirteen statements about his or her job and organizational conditions.

		Disagree Strongly				Agree Strongly
1.	Your work would be considered routine.	1	2	3	4	5
2.	There is a clearly known way to do the major tasks you encounter.	1	2	3	4	5
3.	Your work has high variety and frequent exceptions.	1	2	3	4	5
4.	Communications from above consist of information and advice rather than instructions and directions.	1	2	3	4	5
5.	You have the support of peers and your supervisor to do your job well.	1	2	3	4	5
6.	You seldom exchange ideas or information with people doing other kinds of jobs.	1	2	3	4	5
7.	Decisions relevant to your work are made above you and passed down.	1	2	3	4	5
8.	People at your level frequently have to figure out for themselves what their jobs are for the day.	1	2	3	4	5

	Disagree Strongly				Agree Strongly
9. Lines of authority are clear and precisely defined.	1	2	3	4	5
10. Leadership tends to be democratic rather than autocratic in style.	1	2	3	4	5
11. Job descriptions are written and up-to-date for each job.	1	2	3	4	5
12. People understand each other's jobs and often do different tasks.	1	2	3	4	5
13. A manual of policies and procedures is available to use when a problem arises.	1	2	3	4	5

Total Score _____

A score of 52 or above suggests that the employee is working in a "loosely structured" organization. The score reflects a flexible structure that is often associated with uncertain environments and small-batch technology. People working in this structure feel empowered. Many organizations today are moving in the direction of flexible structures and empowerment.

A score of 26 or below suggests a "tight structure." This structure utilizes traditional control and functional specialization, which often occurs in a certain environment, a stable organization, and routine or mass-production technology. People in this structure may feel controlled and constrained.

Discuss the pros and cons of loose versus tight structure. Does the structure of the employee you interviewed fit the nature of the organization's environment, strategic goals, and technology? How might you redesign the structure to make the work organization more effective?

Manager's Workshop

You and Organization Structure

In order to better understand the importance of organization structure in your life, do the following assignment in groups of four to six people.

Select one of the following situations to organize:
a. the registration process at your university or college
b. a new fast-food franchise
c. a sports rental in an ocean resort area, such as jetski, etc.
d. a bakery

Background

Organization is a way of gaining some power against an unreliable environment. The environment provides the organization with inputs, which include raw materials, human resources, and financial resources. There is a service or product to produce that involves technology. The output goes to clients, a group that must be nurtured. The complexities of the environment and the technology determine the complexity of the organization.

Planning your organization:

1. Write down the mission or purpose of the organization in a few sentences.

2. What are the specific things to be done to accomplish the mission?

3. Based on the specifics in problem 2, develop an organization chart. Each position in the chart will perform a specific task or is responsible for a certain outcome.

4. Add duties to each job position in the chart. These will be the job descriptions.

5. How can you make sure people in each position will work together?

6. What level of skill and abilities is required at each position and level in order to hire the right people?

7. Make a list of the decisions that would have to be made as you developed your organization.

8. Who is responsible for customer satisfaction? How will you know if the needs of customers are met?

9. How will information flow within the organization?

SOURCE: Adapted by Dorothy Marcic from "Organizing," in Donald D. White and H. William Vroman, *Action in Organizations*, 2nd ed. Boston: Allyn and Bacon, p. 154.

Management in Practice: Ethical Dilemma

Caught in the Middle

Tom Harrington loved his new job as an assistant high-quality control officer for Rockingham Toys. After six months of unemployment, he was anxious to make a good impression on his boss, Frank Golopolus. One of the responsibilities of his boss was ensuring that new product lines met federal safety guidelines. Rockingham had made several manufacturing changes over the past year. Golopolus and the rest of the high-quality control team had been working 60-hour weeks to troubleshoot the new production process.

While sorting incoming mail during the past weeks, Harrington had become aware of numerous changes in product safety guidelines that he knew would impact the new Rockingham toys. Golopolus was taking no action to implement new guidelines, and he didn't seem to understand or care about them. Harrington, who avoided the questions he received from the floor to cover for his boss, was beginning to wonder if Rockingham would have time to make changes with the Christmas season rapidly approaching.

Harrington knew it was not his job to order the changes, and he didn't want to alienate Golopolus by interfering, but he was beginning to worry what might happen if he didn't act. Rockingham had a fine product safety reputation and was rarely challenged on matters of quality. He felt loyalty to Golopolus for giving him a job, but he worried Golopolus was in over his head.

What Do You Do?

1. Prepare a memo to Golopolus, summarizing the new safety guidelines that affect the Rockingham product line and recommending implementation.

2. Mind your own business. You do not have authority to monitor the federal regulations. Besides, you've been unemployed and need this job.

3. Send copies of the reports anonymously to the operations manager, who is Golopolus's boss.

SOURCE: Based on Doug Wallace, "The Man Who Knew Too Much," *What Would You Do? Business Ethics*, vol. II (March–April 1993), pp. 7–8.

Case for Critical Analysis

Tucker Company

In 1978, the Tucker Company underwent an extensive reorganization that divided the company into three major divisions. These new divisions represented Tucker's three principal product lines. Mr. Harnett, Tucker's president, explained the basis for the new organization in a memo to the board of directors as follows:

The diversity of our products requires that we reorganize along our major product lines. Toward this end I have established three new divisions: commercial jet engines, military jet engines, and utility turbines. Each division will be headed by a new vice president who will report directly to me. I believe that this new approach will enhance our performance through the commitment of individual managers. It should also help us to identify unprofitable areas where the special attention of management may be required.

For the most part, each division will be able to operate independently. That is, each will have its own engineering, manufacturing, accounting departments, etc. In some cases, however, it will be necessary for a division to utilize the services of other divisions or departments. This is necessary because the complete servicing with individual divisional staffs would result in unjustifiable additional staffing and facilities.

The old companywide laboratory was one such service department. Functionally, it continued to support all of the major divisions. Administratively, however, the manager of the laboratory reported to the manager of manufacturing in the military jet engine division.

From the time the new organization was initiated until February 1988, when the laboratory manager Mr. Garfield retired, there was little evidence of interdepartmental or interdivisional conflict. His replacement, Mr. Hodge, unlike Mr. Garfield, was always eager to gain the attention of management. Many of Hodge's peers perceived him as an empire builder who was interested in his own advancement rather than the company's well-being. After about six months in the new position, Hodge became involved in several interdepartmental conflicts over work that was being conducted in his laboratory.

Historically, the engineering departments had used the laboratory as a testing facility to determine the properties of materials selected by the design engineers. Hodge felt that the laboratory should be more involved in the selection of these materials and in the design of experiments and subsequent evaluations of the experimental data. Hodge discussed this with Mr. Franklin of the engineering department of the utility turbine division. Franklin offered to consult with Hodge but stated that the final responsibility for the selection of materials was charged to his department.

In the months that followed, Hodge and Franklin had several disagreements over the implementation of the results. Franklin told Hodge that, because of his position at the testing lab, he was unable to appreciate the detailed design considerations that affected the final decision on materials selection. Hodge claimed that Franklin lacked the materials expertise that he, as a metallurgist, had.

Franklin also noted that the handling of his requests, which had been prompt under Garfield's management, was taking longer and longer under Hodge's management. Hodge explained that military jet engine divisional problems had to be assigned first priority because of his administrative reporting structure. He also said that if he were more involved in Franklin's problems, he could perhaps appreciate when a true sense of urgency existed and could revise priorities.

The tensions between Franklin and Hodge reached a peak when one of Franklin's critical projects failed to receive the scheduling that he considered necessary. Franklin phoned Hodge to discuss the need for a schedule change. Hodge suggested that they have a meeting to review the need for the work. Franklin then told Hodge that this was not a matter of his concern and that his function was merely to perform the tests as requested. He further stated that he was not satisfied with the low-priority rating that his division's work received. Hodge reminded Franklin that when Hodge had suggested a means for resolving this problem, Franklin was not receptive. At this point, Franklin lost his temper and hung up on Hodge.

Questions

1. Sketch out a simple organization chart showing Tucker Company's three divisions, including the location of the laboratory. Why would the laboratory be located in the military jet engine division?

2. Analyze the conflict between Mr. Hodge and Mr. Franklin. Do you think the conflict is based on personalities or on the way in which the organization is structured?

3. Sketch out a new organization chart showing how you would restructure Tucker Company so that the laboratory would provide equal services to all divisions. What advantages and disadvantages do you see in the new structure compared to the previous one?

SOURCE: Reprinted with permission of Macmillan Publishing Company from "The Laboratory," *Organizational Behavior: Readings and Cases*, 2d ed., pp. 385–387, by L. Katz, prepared under the supervision of Theodore T. Herbert. Copyright 1981 by Theodore T. Herbert.

CHAPTER

8

Innovation and Change

LEARNING OBJECTIVES

After studying this chapter, you should be able to do the following:

1 **Define organizational change and explain the forces for change.**

2 **Describe the sequence of four change activities that must be performed for change to be successful.**

3 **Explain the techniques managers can use to facilitate the initiation of change in organizations, including idea champions, new-venture teams, idea incubators, and open innovation.**

4 **Define sources of resistance to change.**

5 **Explain force-field analysis and other implementation tactics that can overcome resistance to change.**

6 **Discuss the differences among technology, product, structure, and culture/people changes.**

7 **Explain the change processes—bottom up, top down, horizontal—associated with each type of change.**

8 **Define organizational development and large-group interventions.**

Manager's Challenge

When Harvard Business School (HBS) student Andrew Ive realized his dorm room had no fire escape, he bought one and it splintered under his weight. He got fellow HBS student Aldo DiBelardino, who had an engineering background, to design a spiffy and safe ladder, while Ive polished the X-It Products business plan. Within three years, X-It had an innovative product: a lightweight ladder that could collapse to a shoebox size. After showing the product for a couple of years at Chicago's National Hardware Show to such giants as Wal-Mart and Lowe's, it was selling to the Southwest market of Home Depot, as well as through Amway and Kmart. They were even approached by market leader British Kidde Safety to buy out X-It. But at the upcoming trade show, Ive noticed a ladder almost exactly like theirs being sold at the Kidde booth. Ive screamed foul, but Kidde said X-It's patent was only pending. X-It filed suit, a case that took two years to win and cost $3 million in legal fees, at the same time the company's revenues slumped 31 percent to $248,000. The company was deteriorating financially, and the two founders had opposite ideas on how to save the company. Ive wanted to add to infrastructure with extensive customer service, a new and more convenient office. DiBelardino, on the other hand, saw cost-cutting as the only salvation. At a meeting with the investors, they decided to take DiBelardino's proposal, which meant the exit of Ive.[1]

If you were DiBelardino, what would you do now to keep X-It from collapsing?

Ive, DeBelardino, and X-It are not alone. Every organization sometimes faces the need to change quickly and dramatically to survive in a changing environment. Sometimes, changes are brought about by forces outside the organization, such as when a powerful retailer such as Wal-Mart demands annual price cuts or when a key supplier goes out of business. In China, many companies are feeling pressure from the government to increase wages to help workers cope with rising food costs. At the same time, the costs of steel and other raw materials are skyrocketing.[2] These outside forces compel managers to look for greater efficiencies in operations and other changes to keep their organizations profitable. Other times managers within the company want to initiate major changes, such as introducing a paperless accounting system, forming employee-participation teams, or instituting new training systems, but they do not know how to make the change successful. Organizations must embrace many types of change. Businesses must develop improved production technologies, create new products desired in the marketplace, implement new administrative systems, and upgrade employees' skills. Companies such as BMW, 3M, and Dell Computers implement all of these changes and more.

How important is organizational change? Consider this: The parents of today's college students grew up without digital cameras, e-mail, laptop computers, DVDs, Web-access cell phones, and online shopping. Companies that produce the new products and services have prospered, but many companies caught with outdated products and technologies have failed. Today's successful companies are constantly coming up with new products and services. For example, Johnson & Johnson Pharmaceuticals uses biosimulation software from Entelos that compiles everything that is known about a disease, such as diabetes or asthma, and runs extensive virtual tests of new drug candidates. With a new drug failure rate of 50 percent even at the last stage of clinical trials, the process helps scientists cut the time and expense of early testing and focus on the most promising prospects. Engineers at automakers such as DaimlerChrysler, General Motors (GM), and Toyota are perfecting fuel cell power systems that could make today's internal combustion engine as obsolete as the steam locomotive.[3] Computer companies are working on developing computers smart enough to configure themselves, balance huge workloads, and know how to anticipate and fix problems before they happen.[4] Organizations that change successfully remain profitable and admired.

organizational change

The adoption of a new idea or behavior by an organization.

Organizational change is defined as the adoption of a new idea or behavior by an organization.[5] In this chapter, we will look at how organizations can be designed to respond to the environment through internal change and development. First, we will examine the basic forces for organizational change. Then, we will examine how managers facilitate two change requirements: initiation and implementation. Finally, we will discuss the four major types of change—technology, new product, structure, and culture/people—and how the organization can be designed to facilitate each.

Turbulent Times and the Changing Workplace

Today's organizations continuously need to adapt to new situations if they are to survive and prosper. As we discussed in Chapter 1, one of the most dramatic elements of change is the shift to a technology-driven workplace in which ideas, information, and relationships are becoming important. Many changes are being driven by advances in information technology and the Internet. New trends such as e-business, supply chain integration, and knowledge management require profound changes in the organization. In the previous chapter, we talked about new horizontal forms of organization that are a response to environmental turbulence and uncertainty. These new structural mechanisms break down boundaries within the organization, as well as with other companies, to promote collaboration for learning and change.

Managers make many other organizational changes, such as changes in work procedures, administrative policies, technology, products, or corporate culture. Today's successful organizations simultaneously embrace two types of planned change: *incremental change*, which refers to organizational efforts to improve basic operational and work processes in different parts of the company; and *transformational change*, which involves redesigning and renewing the entire organization.[6] Change, particularly transformational change, does not happen easily. However, managers can learn to anticipate and facilitate change to help their organizations keep pace with the rapid changes in the external environment.

©Shelly Harrison

CONCEPT CONNECTION

After years of wowing investors with stories of laboratory developments rather than predictable earnings, many biotechnology firms are undergoing **transformational change** *to redesign and renew their entire organizations and show concrete evidence of growth. For example, Millennium Pharmaceuticals Inc., in the photo, is buying CORTherapeutics to get its experienced sales force and an established anticlotting drug. To compete with huge pharmaceutical companies such as Pfizer, biotech companies need to expand their product lines and make changes in systems, structures, and culture to promote growth.*

Model of Planned Organizational Change

Change can be managed. By observing external trends, patterns, and needs, managers use planned change to help the organization adapt to external problems and opportunities.[7] When organizations are caught flat-footed, failing to anticipate or respond to new needs, management is at fault.

An overall model for planned change is presented in Exhibit 8.1. Four events comprise the change sequence: (1) internal and external forces for change exist; (2) organization managers monitor these forces and become aware of a need for change; (3) the perceived need triggers the initiation of change; and (4) the change is then implemented. How each of these activities is handled depends on the organization and managers' styles.

We will now discuss the specific activities associated with the first two events— forces for change and the perceived need for the organization to respond and change.

Forces for Change

Forces for organizational change exist in the external environment and within the organization.

Environmental Forces. As described in Chapters 2 and 3, external forces originate in all environmental sectors, including customers, competitors, technology, economic forces, and the international arena. The Focus on Skills box shows that competition is a formidable force in bringing innovation into an industry.

Take **ACTION**

As a manager, anticipate change and help prepare employees.

EXHIBIT 8.1

Model of Change
Sequence of Events

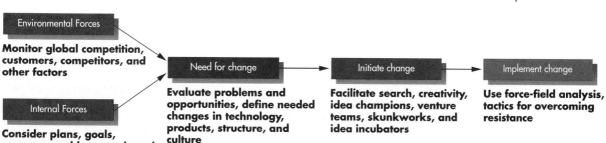

Cartoon Network's Late Night

With many homes having more than 400 TV channels to choose from, cable stations must struggle constantly to remain competitive. As a result, after the Powderpuff girls are in bed, Cartoon Network has courted another viewer: adult males who have never outgrown their love of animation. If "Adult Swim" seems to late-night unwitting channel-surfers as incoherent craziness, there is a method in the madness. The channel has turned over the show to non-professionals, who are not locked into the "rules" of animation and are pushing the boundaries of what animation can do. The animators, and most viewers, are from the same demographic: young, male, and addicted to any kind of media. One such show is "Robot Chicken," a stop-motion action hero satire.

It began with 1994's first original series, "Space Ghost, Coast to Coast," a talk show with recycled bits from Hanna-Barbara's "Space Ghost." It morphed into a show with unlikely 10-minute bits of Space Ghost sneaking up behind an ant. Emboldened by the show's success, network executives sought out more young adult fare and started "Aqua Teen Hunger Force," about three fastfood products—a beef patty, a milkshake, and a cartoon of fries—which live together in New Jersey. Done on a tight budget, animators used Apple's Final Cut Pro and Adobe's After Effects. The creators did not have the $2 million weekly budget of "The Simpsons" and preferred it that way. "If we knew we could write anything and just pay to get it done, it wouldn't be as much fun. It's more fun to say, 'Let's have this action,' and then try to figure out how to do that for $5."

"Adult Swim: Uncle Tom Goes to the Mayor" creators Eric Wareheim and Tim Heidecker are using a new technique in their shows. Rather than hand-drawn characters, they use photos of themselves reproduced to look like low-resolution photocopies, and then these images are animated against storyboard style backgrounds. The biggest challenge for the creators is explaining to their parents, aunts, and uncles what is so funny about their show.

SOURCE: Dave Itzkoff, "Destroying Television, Toon by Toon," *The New York Times* (March 13, 2005): 34–36.

Further, changes in technology and the health-care needs of customers caused Medtronic to shift how it views medical devices, from providing therapy to monitoring a patient's health condition. The company's cardioverter difibrillators, for example, can send information to a secure server, allowing medical personnel to review the patient's condition in real time and see if any problems exist.[8] Yellow Freight changed how it did business when a combination of poor economic conditions and shifting customer demands led to a loss of $30 million. Yellow now bills itself as customers' one-stop source for a broad range of transportation needs. The company uses a sophisticated integrated information system to accelerate order processing, manage customer relationships, monitor thousands of trucks and shipping orders, and facilitate rapid loading and unloading of trailers.[9]

Internal Forces. Internal forces for change arise from internal activities and decisions. If top managers select a goal of rapid company growth, internal actions will have to be changed to meet that growth. New departments or technologies will be created and additional people hired to pursue growth opportunities. Demands by employees, labor unions, and production inefficiencies all can generate a force to which management must respond with change. To support growth goals at Procter & Gamble (P&G), CEO A. G. Lafley has acquired the beauty care companies Clairol and Wella, revised manufacturing systems, switched some suppliers, and put greater emphasis on partnerships, such as a joint venture with Clorox to develop Glad Press 'n Seal food wrap.[10]

Take a moment to complete the inventory to see how open to change your company is.

Is Your Company Open to Change?

An effective way to assess the openness to change and the creative climate of an organization for which you have worked is to fill out the following questionnaire. Answer each question based on your work experience in that firm. Discuss the results with members of your group, and talk about whether changing the firm along the dimensions in the questions would make it more open to change.

Instructions: Answer each of the following questions using the five-point scale (Note: *There is no rating of 4*):

0 We never do this

1 We rarely do this

2 We sometimes do this

3 We frequently do this

5 We always do this

1. We are encouraged to seek help anywhere inside or outside the organization with new ideas for our work unit. 0 1 2 3 5

2. Assistance is provided to develop ideas into proposals for management review. 0 1 2 3 5

3. Our performance reviews encourage risky, creative efforts, ideas, and actions. 0 1 2 3 5

4. We are encouraged to fill our minds with new information by attending professional meetings and trade fairs, visiting customers, and so on. 0 1 2 3 5

5. Our meetings are designed to allow people to free-wheel, brainstorm, and generate ideas. 0 1 2 3 5

6. All members contribute ideas during meetings. 0 1 2 3 5

7. During meetings, there is much spontaneity and humor. 0 1 2 3 5

8. We discuss how company structure and our actions help or spoil creativity within our work unit. 0 1 2 3 5

9. During meetings, the chair is rotated among members. 0 1 2 3 5

10. Everyone in the work unit receives training in creativity techniques and maintaining a creative climate. 0 1 2 3 5

Scoring and Interpretation

Add your total score for all ten questions: _____

To measure how effectively your organization fosters openness to change and creativity, use the following scale:

Highly effective: 35–50
Moderately effective: 20–34
Moderately ineffective: 10–19
Ineffective: 0–9

SOURCE: Adapted from Edward Glassman, *Creativity Handbook: Idea Triggers and Sparks that Work* (Chapel Hill, N.C.: LCS Press, 1990). Used by permission. (919/967-2015)

Need for Change

As indicated in Exhibit 8.1, external or internal forces translate into a perceived need for change within the organization. Many people are unwilling to change unless they perceive a problem or a crisis. For example, many U.S. companies changed how they conduct business as a result of the terrorist attacks of September 11, 2001. Top managers at E Commerce Group, a company that processes payments by phone and online, had been trying to find ways to promote teamwork and collaboration, but they kept running into resistance. However, after the hijacked planes struck the World Trade Center across the street from E Commerce's offices, employees immediately began pitching in to help one another any way they could. "This crisis broke down the barriers," said Marc Mehl, co-founder and chief operating officer. The crisis enabled people to perceive the value of helping one another.[11]

In many cases, no crisis prompts change. Most problems are subtle, so managers have to recognize them and make others aware of the need for change.[12] One way managers sense a need for change is with a **performance gap**—a disparity between existing and desired performance levels. They try to create a sense of urgency so others in the organization will recognize and understand the need for change. For example, the chief component-purchasing manager at Nokia noticed that order numbers for some of the computer chips it purchased from Philips Electronics were not adding up, and he discovered that a fire at Philips' Albuquerque, New Mexico, plant had delayed production. The manager moved quickly to alert top managers, engineers, and others throughout the company that Nokia could be caught short of chips unless it took action. Within weeks, a crisis team had redesigned chips, found new suppliers, and restored the chip supply line. In contrast, managers at Ericsson, a competitor that purchased chips from Philips, had the same information but failed to recognize or create a sense of crisis for change, which left the company millions of chips short of what it needed to produce a key product.[13]

performance gap
A disparity between existing and desired performance levels.

Recall from Chapter 5 the discussion of strengths, weaknesses, opportunities, and threats (SWOT) analysis. Managers are responsible for monitoring threats and opportunities in the external environment as well as strengths and weaknesses within the organization to determine whether a need for change exists. Farsheed Ferdowsi runs his company with the knowledge that continuous change is the best model, as shown in the Best Practices box.

Managers in every company must be alert to problems and opportunities because the perceived need for change is what sets the stage for subsequent actions that create a new product or technology. Big problems are easy to spot. Sensitive monitoring systems are needed to detect gradual changes that can fool managers into thinking their company is doing fine. An organization may be in greater danger when the environment changes slowly because managers may fail to trigger an organizational response. Failing to use planned change to meet small needs can place the organization in hot water, as illustrated in the following passage:

> *When frogs are placed in a boiling pail of water, they jump out—they do not want to boil to death. However, when frogs are placed in a cold pail of water, and the pail is placed on a stove with the heat turned very low, over time the frogs will boil to death.*[14]

Initiating Change

After the need for change has been perceived and communicated, change must be initiated. This is a critical phase of change management, the stage where the ideas that solve perceived needs are developed. Responses that an organization can make are to search for or create a change to adopt.

BEST PRACTICES

PayMaxx

Farsheed Ferdowsi is used to winning business awards for his smart start-up. And no wonder. All you have to do is turn on your computer, log into the PayMaxx Web site, enter employee information, and bam—payroll checks (with deductions) come printing out. No software, no complicated tutorials. PayMaxx generally deals with smaller companies, even ones of 1–10 employees, wanting to outsource their payroll and taxes. Because of his engineering background, he started the company systematically, with a focus on the prize: becoming one of the top five companies in that industry. He never had a doubt his destiny was to own his own business. The first one was in 1979 with $1,900 in capital and a $50,000 equipment loan— signed by his brother. He never got any outside capital until 1996. That was two years after he started PayMaxx, which has a number of business units within it.

In 1998, he saw the Internet could be the best vehicle to offer payroll and tax-filing services to under-100-employee companies.

Thus was born PowerPayroll.com, which now has 2,000 customers and $4 million revenue, constituting one third of PayMaxx's total income. He keeps trying new ideas, offshoots of PayMaxx. If the new venutre takes off within a reasonable time, fine. It stays. If not, he lets it go and tries something else. You can say he has developed a learning organization that is constantly churning innovations. His model sees every new venture as having life cycles of birth, growth, maturity, age, and death. If the new unit does not grow after birth, he drops it. But he also knows that each unit will ultimately mature and decline. That's why he needs new innovations in the pipeline. The company keeps growing. The secret is lots of new ideas and not being attached to any one of them. He is a true entrepreneur.

SOURCES: Farsheed Ferdowsi, "PayMaxx: An Entrepreneur's Journey," unpublished manuscript (2005); "PayMaxx Inks Deal With Transactional," *PR Newswire* (Dec. 7, 2004): 1; Candy McCampbell, "Hall of Famers Share Secrets," *The Tennessean* (Sept. 2001): 1.

Search

Search is the process of learning about current developments inside or outside the organization and can be used to meet the perceived need for change. Search typically uncovers existing knowledge that can be applied or adopted within the organization. Managers talk to friends and colleagues, read professional reports, or hire consultants to learn about ideas used elsewhere.

Many needs, however, cannot be resolved through existing knowledge but require that the organization develop a new response. Initiating a new response means that managers must design the organization so as to facilitate creativity of individuals and departments, encourage innovative people to initiate new ideas, or create structural elements such as new-venture departments, skunkworks, and idea incubators.

Creativity

Creativity is the generation of novel ideas that might meet perceived needs or respond to opportunities for the organization. Creativity is the essential first step in innovation, which is vital to long-term organizational success.[15] People noted for their creativity include Edwin Land, who invented the Polaroid camera; Frederick Smith, who came up with the idea for Federal Express's overnight delivery service during an undergraduate class at Yale; and Swiss engineer George de Mestral, who created Velcro after noticing the tiny hooks on the burrs caught on his wool socks. Each of these people saw unique and creative opportunities in a familiar situation.

Each of us has the capacity to be creative. Characteristics of highly creative people are illustrated in the left-hand column of Exhibit 8.2. Creative people are often known for originality, open-mindedness, curiosity, a focused approach to problem solving, persistence, a relaxed and playful attitude, and receptivity to new ideas.[16]

Creativity can be designed into organizations. Companies or departments within companies can be organized to be creative and initiate changes. Most companies want more highly creative employees and often seek to hire creative individuals. However, the individual is only part of the story, and everyone has some potential for creativity.

search

The process of learning about current developments inside or outside the organization that can be used to meet a perceived need for change.

Take **ACTION**

Remember to keep networking within the organization, as it will help you bring about needed changes.

creativity

The generation of novel ideas that might meet perceived needs or offer opportunities for the organization.

Take **ACTION**

As a manager, learn to appreciate employees creativity, or off-the-wallness.

SOURCES: Based on Gary A. Steiner, ed., *The Creative Organization* (Chicago: University of Chicago Press, 1965), 16–18; Rosabeth Moss Kanter, "The Middle Manager as Innovator," *Harvard Business Review* (July–August 1982), 104–105; James Brian Quinn, "Managing Innovation: Controlled Chaos," *Harvard Business Review* (May–June 1985), 73–84; and Robert I. Sutton, "The Weird Rules of Creativity," *Harvard Business Review* (September 2001), 94–103.

EXHIBIT 8.2

Characteristics of Creative People and Organizations

The Creative Individual	The Creative Organization or Department

1. Conceptual fluency
   Open-mindedness
	1. Open channels of communication
	   Contact with outside sources
	   Overlapping territories
	   Suggestion systems, brainstorming, group techniques

2. Originality	2. Assigning nonspecialists to problems
	   Eccentricity allowed
	   Hiring people who make you uncomfortable

3. Less authority
   Independence
   Self-confidence
	3. Decentralization, loosely defined positions, loose control
	   Acceptance of mistakes
	   People encouraged to defy their bosses

4. Playfulness
   Undisciplined exploration
   Curiosity
	4. Freedom to choose and pursue problems
	   Not a tight ship, playful culture, doing the impractical
	   Freedom to discuss ideas, long-time horizon

5. Persistence
   Commitment
   Focused approach
	5. Resources allocated to creative personnel and projects without immediate payoff
	   Reward system encourages innovation
	   Absolution of peripheral responsibilities

Managers are responsible for creating a work environment that allows creativity to flourish.[17] The characteristics of creative organizations correspond to those of individuals, as illustrated in the right-hand column of Exhibit 8.2. Creative organizations are loosely structured. People find themselves in a situation of ambiguity, assignments are vague, territories overlap, tasks are poorly defined, and much work is done through teams.[18] Creative organizations have an internal culture of playfulness, freedom, challenge, and grass-roots participation.[19] They harness all potential sources of new ideas from within. Many participative management programs are born out of the desire to enhance creativity for initiating changes. People are not stuck in the rhythm of routine jobs.

At IDEO, the design company that came up with the idea for stand-up toothpaste tubes, Apple Computer's first mouse, and the Palm V, the mantra is "If at first the idea does not sound absurd, then there is no hope for it." Managers help stimulate creativity by getting people to empathize with potential users of a product through a process of learn, look, ask, and try.[20] To keep creativity alive at Nokia, managers sponsor friendly internal competitions, such as a photography contest where workers take pictures of their pets or summer homes with Nokia camera phones. The photographs are shown on a slide projector in the company cafeteria as a way to further stimulate new ideas.[21] At W.L. Gore, the maker of Gore-Tex fabrics, Glide dental floss, Elixir guitar strings, and numerous other innovative products, leaders let people choose the projects they will work on, ensuring that employees (called associates) feel a passion for the work. In addition, research associates get to spend 10 percent of their work hours as dabble time, where they can explore developing their own ideas, as shown in the Focus on Innovation box.[22]

The most creative companies embrace risk and encourage employees to experiment and make mistakes. One manager at Intel used to throw a dinner party every month for the "failure of the month," to show people that failure was an inevitable and accepted part of risk-taking.[23] Jim Read, president of the Read Corporation, says, "When my employees make mistakes trying to improve something, I give them a round of applause. No mistakes mean no new products. If they ever become afraid to make one, my company is doomed."[24] Employees perceived as superiorly competent or creative can be overvalued, as this chapter's Business Blooper demonstrates.

W.L. Gore

According to *Fast Company*, the most innovative company, pound-for-pound, in America is W.L. Gore, maker of Gore-Tex. This is because it has new and unique product lines, and it looks at divergent ways of doing business, improving its business processes. It all goes back a few decades ago when Wilbert (Bill) L. Gore left DuPont and started his own company. He soon saw that the best communication happened in the car pool because that was the one place where there was no hierarchy. His second realization: During a crisis, people throw out the rules and come together quickly to solve problems, making breakthroughs. Why wait for a crisis? So he got rid of most titles, most hierarchy, insisted on lots of one-on-one communication, allowing anyone to talk to anyone else, without fear of violating chain of command. Even though the company is large,

with 6,300 employees and $1.6 billion revenues, he keeps the size of workgroups no more than 150 or 200 tops, so everyone will get to know everyone else.

Gore took the no-hierarchy to heart in his personal life, too. He and his wife stayed in the same simple house they were in when the company started, even though their wealth had become considerable. When traveling, Gore always went coach. Keeping the company privately held has allowed it to let certain products develop with a lot of patience, something a bottom-line company might not do. Now that Gore is gone, the company is still thriving, but it faces challenges to keep up the pace of innovation that its founder had.

SOURCE: Alan Deutschman, "The Fabric of Creativity," *Fast Company* (Dec. 2004): 54.

Idea Champions and New-Venture Teams

If creative conditions are successful, new ideas will be generated that must be carried forward for acceptance and implementation. This is where idea champions come in. The formal definition of an **idea champion** is a person who sees the need for and champions productive change within the organization. For example, Wendy Black of Best Western International championed the idea of coordinating the corporate mailings to the company's 2,800 hoteliers into a single packet every two weeks. Some hotels were receiving three special mailings a day from different departments. Her idea saved $600,000 a year in postage alone.[25]

Often a new idea is rejected by management. Champions are committed to a new product or idea despite rejection by others. At Kyocera Wireless, lead engineer Gary Koerper was a champion for the Smartphone, a device that combines a high-end mobile phone with a Palm digital assistant. When he could not get his company's testing department to validate the new product, he had an outside firm do the testing for him—at a cost of about $30,000—without approval from Kyocera management. Once the Smartphone was approved and went into production, demand was so great the company could barely keep up.[26]

idea champion
A person who sees the need for and champions productive change within the organization.

Take **ACTION**
Change does not occur by itself. Personal energy and effort are required to promote a new idea.

War for Talent

Several years ago, one of the top management consulting firms did an exhaustive study of U.S. companies and found that the best leaders were obsessed with finding the best and brightest talent. Dubbed the War for Talent, this concept justified the high salaries paid to top-tier graduates. This particular consulting company had a big client—totalling $10 million/year at the end—who followed the Gospel of Talent and hired lots of expensive and smart people. That would be Enron, whose talent pool could not help them out of fiscal problems and indictments of executives. But the War for Talent turned out

to be little more than indulging "A "employees or at least those perceived as being in the "A" group. The larger failing, said Malcolm Gladwell, was the erroneous belief that the intelligence of the system is the sum of intelligences of its members. They did not see the importance of systems. "They were there looking for people who had the talent to think outside the box. It never occurred to them that, if everyone had to think outside the box, maybe it was the box that needed fixing."

SOURCES: Danielle Sacks, "The Accidental Guru," *Fast Company* (January 2005): 65; Malcolm Gladwell, "The Talent Myth," *The New Yorker* (July 22, 2002): 28.

Championing an idea requires roles in organizations, as illustrated in Exhibit 8.3. Sometimes a single person may play two or more of these roles, but successful innovation in most companies involves an interplay of different people, each adopting one role. The inventor develops a new idea and understands its technical value but has neither the ability nor the interest to promote it for acceptance within the organization. The champion believes in the idea, confronts the organizational realities of costs and benefits, and gains the political and financial support needed to bring it to reality. The sponsor is a high-level manager who approves the idea, protects the idea, and removes major organizational barriers to acceptance. The critic counterbalances the zeal of the champion by challenging the concept and providing a reality test with hard-nosed criteria. The critic prevents people in the other roles from adopting a bad idea.[27]

Managers can directly influence whether champions will flourish. When Texas Instruments (TI) studied 50 of its new product introductions, a surprising fact emerged: Without exception, every new product that had failed had lacked a zealous champion. In contrast, most of the new products that succeeded had a champion. TI's managers made an immediate decision: No new product would be approved unless someone championed it. Researchers have found that new ideas that succeed are generally those that are backed by someone who believes in the idea wholeheartedly and is determined to convince others of its value.[28]

new-venture team
A unit separate from the mainstream of the organization that is responsible for developing and initiating innovations.

Another way to facilitate corporate innovation is through a **new-venture team**. A new-venture team is a unit separate from the rest of the organization and is responsible for developing and initiating a major innovation.[29] New-venture teams give free rein to members' creativity because their separate facilities and location free them from organizational rules and procedures. These teams typically are small, loosely structured, and flexible, reflecting the characteristics of creative organizations described in Exhibit 8.2. 3M recently launched a corporate-wide initiative called 3M Acceleration, which is designed to support venture teams and accelerate product innovation and commercialization. A person with a good idea, such as Steve Saxe, who came up with the idea for a portable digital whiteboard, can recruit people from around the company to work on the new-venture team. The organization provides the space, funding, and freedom the team needs to fast-track the idea into a marketable product.[30]

skunkworks
A separate, small, informal, highly autonomous, and often secretive group that focuses on breakthrough ideas for the business.

One variation of a new-venture team is called a **skunkworks**.[31] A skunkworks is a separate, small, informal, highly autonomous, and often secretive group that focuses on breakthrough ideas for the business. The original skunkworks, which still exists, was created by Lockheed Martin more than 50 years ago. The essence of a skunkworks is that highly talented people are given the time and freedom to let creativity rein.[32] The laser printer was invented by a Xerox researcher who was transferred to a skunkworks,

EXHIBIT 8.3
Four Roles in Organizational Change

Inventor	**Champion**	**Sponsor**	**Critic**
Develops and understands technical aspects of idea	Believes in idea	High-level manager who removes organizational barriers	Provides reality test
Does not know how to win support for the idea or make a business of it	Visualizes benefits	Approves and protects idea within organization	Looks for shortcomings
	Confronts organizational realities of cost, benefits		Defines hard-nosed criteria that idea must pass
	Obtains financial and political support		
	Overcomes obstacles		

SOURCES: Based on Harold L. Angle and Andrew H. Van de Ven, "Suggestions for Managing the Innovation Journey," in *Research in the Management of Innovation: The Minnesota Studies*, ed. A.H. Van de Ven, H.L. Angle, and Marshall Scott Poole (Cambridge, Mass.: Ballinger/Harper & Row, 1989); and Jay R. Galbraith, "Designing the Innovating Organization," *Organizational Dynamics* (Winter 1982), 5–25.

the Xerox Palo Alto Research Center (PARC), after his ideas about using lasers were stifled within the company for being "too impractical and expensive."[33]

A related idea is the **new-venture fund**, which provides resources from which individuals and groups can draw to develop new ideas, products, or businesses. Intel, for example, has been highly successful with Intel Capital, which provides new-venture funds to employees and outside organizations to develop promising ideas. An Intel employee came up with the idea for liquid crystal on silicon, a technology that lowers the cost of big-screen TV projection. "We took an individual who had an idea, gave him money to pursue it, and turned it into a business," said Intel CEO Craig Barrett.[34]

Another popular way to facilitate the development of new in-house ideas is the **idea incubator**. An idea incubator is run entirely in-house but provides a safe harbor where ideas from employees throughout the organization can be developed without interference from company bureaucracy or politics.[35] One value of an internal incubator is that an employee with a good idea has somewhere to go with it, rather than having to shop the idea all over the company and hope someone pays attention. Companies as diverse as Boeing, Adobe Systems, Ball Aerospace, United Parcel Service, and Ziff Davis are using incubators to produce products and services related to the company's core business.[36]

Open Innovation

Lack of innovation is widely recognized as one of the biggest problems facing today's businesses. Thus, many companies are undergoing a transformation in the way they find and use new ideas.[37] Traditionally, most businesses have generated their own in-house ideas and then developed, manufactured, marketed, and distributed them, a closed innovation approach. Today, though, forward-looking companies are embracing open innovation. **Open innovation** means extending the search for and commercialization of new ideas beyond the organization's boundaries and perhaps beyond the industry's boundaries.[38] For example, P&G hits such as the Crest Spin Brush and the heartburn medicine Prilosec were created by other organizations and bought by P&G. The technology that helps P&G's Swiffer products pick up so much dust and debris came from a competitor in Japan. P&G's CEO A. G. Lafley has set a goal to get 50 percent of the company's innovation from outside the organization, up from about 35 percent in 2004.[39] Service companies are turning to open innovation as well. Home Depot and Allstate are collaborating on an innovative project whereby insurance adjusters encourage contractors to buy materials from Home Depot, where prices are low. The arrangement reduces costs for Allstate and drives significant new business to Home Depot.[40]

In line with the new way of thinking we discussed in Chapter 1, that sees partnership and collaboration as more important than independence and competition, the boundaries between an organization and its environment are becoming porous so ideas flow back and forth among different companies that engage in partnerships, joint ventures, licensing agreements, and other alliances. Sometimes customers are brought into the innovation loop as well, so their experiences spark innovations in products or services.[41]

Implementing Change

Creative culture, idea champions, new-venture teams, idea incubators, and open-innovation are ways to facilitate the initiation and development of new ideas. The final step to be managed in the change process is implementation. A new, creative idea will not benefit the organization until it is placed and being fully used. One frustration for managers is that employees often seem to resist change for no apparent reason. To manage the implementation process, managers should be aware of the reasons people resist change and use techniques to enlist employee cooperation.

new-venture fund
A fund providing resources from which individuals and groups can draw to develop new ideas, products, or businesses.

idea incubator
An in-house program that provides a safe harbor where ideas from employees throughout the organization can be developed without interference from company bureaucracy or politics.

open innovation
Extending the search for and commercialization of new ideas beyond the organization's boundaries and perhaps beyond the industry's boundaries.

Take *ACTION*
Know your employees, so you can help them embrace change.

Resistance to Change

Idea champions often discover that other employees are unenthusiastic about their new ideas. Members of a new-venture group may be surprised when managers in the regular organization do not support or approve their innovations. Managers and employees not involved in an innovation often seem to prefer the status quo. Employees appear to resist change for several reasons, and understanding them helps managers implement change more effectively.

Self-Interest.   Employees typically resist a change they believe will take away something of value. A proposed change in job design, structure, or technology may lead to a real or perceived loss of power, prestige, pay, or company benefits. The fear of personal loss is perhaps the biggest obstacle to organizational change.[42] When Federal Express (FedEx) expanded into ground transportation to be more competitive with UPS, managers were aware that FedEx Express air service employees might feel threatened. Similarly, the recent acquisition of Kinko's requires FedEx managers to recognize that the self-interest of Kinko's employees might trigger resistance.[43]

Lack of Understanding and Trust.   Employees often distrust the intentions behind a change or do not understand the intended purpose of a change. If previous working relationships with an idea champion have been negative, resistance may occur. One manager had a habit of initiating a change in the financial reporting system about every 12 months, losing interest, and then not following through. After the third time, employees no longer went along with the change because they did not trust the manager's intention to follow through to their benefit.

Uncertainty.   Uncertainty is the lack of information about future events. It represents a fear of the unknown. Uncertainty is especially threatening for employees who have a low tolerance for change and fear anything out of the ordinary. They do not know how a change will affect them and worry about whether they will be able to meet the demands of a new procedure or technology.[44] For example, union leaders at General Motors' Steering Gear Division in Saginaw, Michigan, resisted the introduction of employee participation programs. They were uncertain about how the program would affect their status and, thus, initially opposed it.

Different Assessments and Goals.   Another reason for resistance to change is that people who will be affected by an innovation may assess the situation differently from an idea champion or new-venture group. Critics frequently voice legitimate disagreements over the proposed benefits of a change. Managers in each department pursue different goals, and an innovation may detract from performance and goal achievement for some departments. For example, if marketing gets the new product it wants for its customers, the cost of manufacturing may increase, and the manufacturing superintendent will resist. Resistance may call attention to problems with the innovation. At a consumer products company in Racine, Wisconsin, middle managers resisted the introduction of a new employee program that turned out to be a bad idea. The managers believed that the program would do more harm than good.[45]

These reasons for resistance are legitimate in the eyes of employees affected by the change. The best procedure for managers is not to ignore resistance but to diagnose the reasons and design strategies to gain acceptance by users.[46] Strategies for overcoming resistance to change typically involve two approaches: the analysis of resistance through the force-field technique and the use of selective implementation tactics to overcome resistance.

Force-Field Analysis

Force-field analysis grew from the work of Kurt Lewin, who proposed that change was a result of the competition between driving and restraining forces.[47] Driving forces can be thought of as problems or opportunities that provide motivation for change within the organization. Restraining forces are the various barriers to change, such as a lack of resources, resistance from middle managers, or inadequate employee skills. When a change is introduced, management should analyze both forces that drive change (problems and opportunities) as well as the forces that resist it (barriers to change). By selectively removing forces that restrain change, the driving forces will be strong enough to enable implementation, as illustrated by the move from A to B in Exhibit 8.4. As barriers are reduced or removed, behavior will shift to incorporate the desired changes.

Just-in-time (JIT) inventory control systems schedule materials to arrive at a company as they are needed on the production line. In an Ohio manufacturing company, management's analysis showed that the driving forces (opportunities) associated with the implementation of JIT were (1) large cost savings from reduced inventories, (2) savings from needing fewer workers to handle the inventory, and (3) a quicker, more competitive market response for the company. Restraining forces (barriers) discovered by managers were (1) a freight system that was too slow to deliver inventory on time, (2) a facility layout that emphasized inventory maintenance over new deliveries, (3) inappropriate worker skills for handling rapid inventory deployment, and (4) union resistance to job loss. The driving forces were insufficient to overcome the restraining forces.

To shift the behavior to JIT, managers attacked the barriers. An analysis of the freight system showed that delivery by truck provided the flexibility and quickness needed to schedule inventory arrival at a specific time each day. The problem with facility layout was met by adding four new loading docks. Inappropriate worker skills were attacked with a training program to instruct workers in JIT methods and in assembling products with uninspected parts. Union resistance was overcome by agreeing to reassign workers no longer needed for maintaining inventory to jobs in another plant. With the restraining forces reduced, the driving forces were sufficient to allow the JIT system to be implemented.

Implementation Tactics

The other approach to managing implementation is to adopt specific tactics to overcome employee resistance. For example, resistance to change may be overcome by educating employees or inviting them to participate in implementing the change. Researchers have studied various methods for dealing with resistance to change. The following five tactics, summarized in Exhibit 8.5, have proven successful.[48]

> **force-field analysis**
> The process of determining which forces drive and which resist a proposed change.

> Take **ACTION**
> Practice doing force-field analysis on one of your own problems.

> **EXHIBIT 8.4**
> *Using Force-Field Analysis to Change from Traditional to Just-in-Time Inventory System*

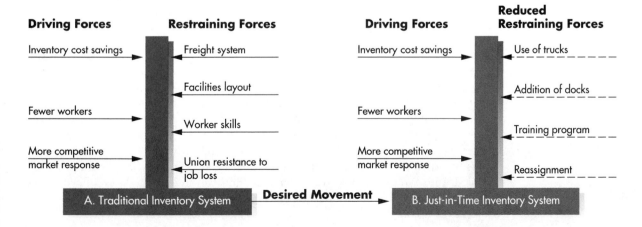

EXHIBIT 8.5

*Tactics for
Overcoming
Resistance to Change*

SOURCE: Based on J.P. Kotter and L.A. Schlesinger, "Choosing Strategies for Change," *Harvard Business Review 57* (March–April 1979), 106–114.

Approach	When to Use
Communication, education	• Change is technical • Users need accurate information and analysis to understand change
Participation	• Users need to feel involved • Design requires information from others • Users have power to resist
Negotiation	• Group has power over implementation • Group will lose out in the change
Coercion	• A crisis exists • Initiators clearly have power • Other implementation techniques have failed
Top management support	• Change involves multiple departments or reallocation of resources • Users doubt legitimacy of change

Communication and Education.   Communication and education are used when solid information about the change is needed by users and others who may resist implementation. Education is especially important when the change involves new technical knowledge or users are unfamiliar with the idea. Canadian Airlines International spent a year and a half preparing and training employees before changing its entire reservations, airport, cargo, and financial systems as part of a new "Service Quality" strategy. Smooth implementation resulted from this intensive training and communications effort, which involved 50,000 tasks, 12,000 people, and 26 classrooms around the world.[49] Managers should remember that implementing change requires speaking to people's hearts (touching their feelings) as well as to their minds (communicating facts). Emotion is a key component in persuading and influencing others. People are much more likely to change their behavior when they understand the rational reasons for doing so and see a picture of change that influences their feelings.[50]

Take ACTION

During change, remember to give adequate training to employees.

Participation.   Participation involves users and potential resisters in designing the change. This time-consuming approach pays off because users understand and become committed to the change. Participation helps managers determine potential problems and understand the differences in perceptions of change among employees.[51] When GM tried to implement a new management appraisal system for supervisors in its Adrian, Michigan, plant, it met with immediate resistance. Rebuffed by the lack of cooperation, top managers proceeded more slowly, involving supervisors in the design of the new appraisal system. Through participation in system design, managers understood what the new approach was all about and dropped their resistance to it.

Negotiation.   Negotiation is a more formal means of achieving cooperation. Negotiation uses formal bargaining to win acceptance and approval of a desired change. For example, if the marketing department fears losing power if a new management structure is implemented, top managers may negotiate with marketing to reach a resolution. Companies that have strong unions frequently must formally negotiate change with the unions. The change may become part of the union contract reflecting the agreement of both parties. For example, when GM changed the way it runs Saturn, a part of implementation involved negotiating new labor rules with the United Auto Workers union local. Meredith Finn had to learn high-level negotiation skills to do her job as shown in the Focus on Skills box.

New Line Cinema

Meredith Finn never went to film school and did not even think she might ever work in film. But here she is, negotiating purchases of movies for New Line Cinema. She has to have confidence in her abilities to do her work well. She knows she is passionate and opinionated and feels others should challenge her assumptions; otherwise, they are not doing their work.

Her job has two highs. First, it has the speed and competitiveness of how much money was dealt to purchase a film to distribute to theaters. Then when she goes to a screening, she gets an adrenaline rush, and by the time it is finished, she loves the movie, wants the movie, and wants New Line to distribute the movie. When she and her two associates saw *Sea Inside*, the three of them (who normally heatedly debate every movie) cried during the morning screening. By afternoon they put in their first bid and had a deal by 3 a.m. The talks during negotiations get heated and competitive, but Finn has learned the vital skill of remaining calm. Her instincts are often good, too. She was rallying for *American Splendor* when others were not. At times like that, she has to negotiate and persuade the rest of the team, saying, "This is right for us, I think this director's going to pop, or I think this movie is going to resonate, and this is why." Finn believes that to risk on a film, you have to be willing to identify with its success or failure. But, at the same time, detachment is important. Negative intensity can make a deal go sour. "Losing a movie over hurt feelings is a huge mistake."

SOURCE: Meredith Finn, "The Confidence Inside," *Fast Company* (March 2005): 40.

Coercion. Coercion means that managers use formal power to force employees to change. Resisters are told to accept the change or lose rewards or their jobs. In most cases, this approach should be avoided because employees feel like victims, are angry at change managers, and may sabotage the changes. However, coercion may be necessary in crisis situations when a rapid response is urgent. For example, a number of top managers at Coca-Cola were reassigned or forced out after they refused to go along with a new CEO's changes for revitalizing the sluggish corporation.[52]

Top Management Support. The visible support of top management helps overcome resistance to change. To all employees, top management support symbolizes the change is important for the organization. Top management support is especially important when a change involves multiple departments or when resources are being reallocated among departments. Fred Smith, founder of FedEx, got personally involved in communicating about the addition of ground shipping services. By giving speeches on the corporate television network, going on road trips, and communicating via e-mail and newsletter, Smith signaled that the change was an important step for the company's future success. Without top management support, changes can get bogged down in squabbling among departments. Moreover, when change agents fail to enlist the support of top executives, these leaders can inadvertently undercut the change project by issuing contradictory orders.

The following example illustrates how smart implementation techniques can smooth the change process. Remploy, the United Kingdom's top employer of disabled people, owns 82 manufacturing sites making a diverse range of products, including car headrests, school furniture, and protective clothing for military and civil use. Top managers set some audacious growth goals—to increase staff from 12,500 to 25,000 and triple output within four years, but they knew meeting the goals would require massive changes in how work was done. To ensure success, Remploy used a team of internal consultants to identify the weakest link in a production process, fix it, and then move on to whatever emerged as the next weakest link.

The entire change process was at first frightening and confusing to Remploy's workers, 90 percent of whom have some sort of disability. However, by communicating with employees, providing training, and closely involving them in the change process, the implementation occurred smoothly. For example, at Remploy's Stirling site, top executives ensured that factory manager Margaret Harrison understood the program and could communicate its importance to the plant workers. Harrison and the consultants trained people on the factory floor to look for ways to improve day-to-day work processes. "The more we involved the shopfloor people, the more they bought into it, because they were part of the decision-making process," Harrison said. As people saw their ideas implemented, they proposed more solutions. One worker, for example, suggested sticking colored tape on the machinists' tables to ensure absolute accuracy while accelerating the process. Another group repositioned a huge overhanging machine so shopfloor workers could see one another, communicate more easily, and pitch in to overcome any workflow slowdowns.

Communication and participation have been the keys to smooth implementation of significant changes at Remploy's factories. These changes have helped Remploy achieve a 5 percent increase in its profit margin and the first growth in business in more than a decade. "If you think, 'I can do this a different way,' you approach the team leaders and tell them," machinist Helen Galloway said. "It's all teamwork. Change is frightening but, because we all have a say, we feel more confident making those changes."[53]

Types of Planned Change

Now that we have explored how the initiation and implementation of change can be carried out, let us look at the different types of change that occur in organizations. We will address two issues: what parts of the organization can be changed and how managers can apply the initiation and implementation ideas to each type of change.

The types of organizational change are strategy, technology, products, structure, and culture/people, as illustrated in Exhibit 8.6. Organizations may innovate in one or more areas, depending on internal and external forces for change. In the rapidly changing toy and fashion industries, for example, manufacturers have to introduce new products frequently. In a mature, competitive industry, production technology changes are adopted to improve efficiency. The arrows connecting the types of change in Exhibit 8.6 show that a change in one part may affect other parts of the organization: A new product may require changes in technology, and a new technology may require new people skills or a new structure. When Boston-based New Balance installed sophisticated new technology as a way to make its U.S. athletic shoe factories more efficient, managers found that the structure had to be decentralized, employees had to be cross-trained to perform different jobs, and a more participative culture was needed. Today, New Balance, with five U.S. factories, is the industry's only company with domestic manufacturing facilities.[54] The new technology is one change that gave New Balance an edge and prevented U.S. factory shutdowns. However, related changes were required for the new technology to increase efficiency.

EXHIBIT 8.6

Types of Organizational Change

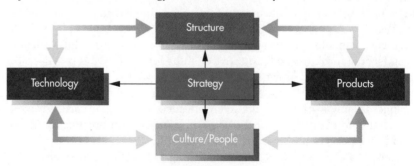

SOURCE: Based on Harold J. Leavitt, "Applied Organizational Change in Industry: Structural, Technical, and Human Approaches," in *New Perspectives in Organization Research*, ed. W. W. Cooper, H. J. Leavitt, and M. W. Shelly II (New York: Wiley, 1964), 55–74.

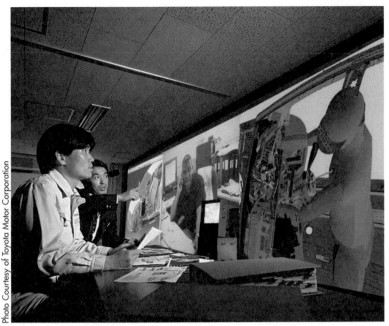

Photo Courtesy of Toyota Motor Corporation

Technology Changes

A **technology change** is related to the organization's production process, i.e., how the organization does its work. Technology changes are designed to make the production of a product or service more efficient. The adoption of automatic mail-sorting machines by the U.S. Postal Service is an example of a technology change, as is the adoption by supermarkets of computer-based, self-service checkout systems. These are examples of technology change in service organizations. Manufacturing organizations adopt many technology changes. For example, at Dana Corporation's Elizabethtown, Kentucky, plant, a new system for automatically loading steel sheets into a forming press was a technology change that saved the auto parts manufacturer $250,000 a year.[55] The changes made in work processes and procedures at the Remploy factories described in the previous section are another example of technology change.

How can managers encourage technology change? The general rule is that technology change is bottom up.[56] The bottom-up approach means that ideas are initiated at lower organization levels and channeled upward for approval. Lower-level technical experts act as idea champions and invent and champion technological improvements. Employees at lower levels understand the technology and have the expertise needed to propose changes. A top-down approach to technology change usually does not work.[57] Top managers are not close to the production process, and they lack expertise in technological developments. The spark for a creative new idea comes from people close to the technology. Bottom up does not mean much if you are the lone entrepreneur. John Bloor saw a change in the environment—customers once again interested in Triumph motorcycles, but soon realized he needed new technology for his company to succeed, as described in the example below.

technology change
A change that pertains to the organization's production process.

Triumph Motorcycles

When John Bloor was looking for an abandoned factory to buy, he instead bought an abandoned motorcycle company. With England's motorcycle manufacturing going belly-up in the early 1980s, Bloor took on a big challenge with his $200,000 purchase price of the company. Japan's Suzuki and Honda, plus the United State's Harley-Davidson, were ruling the globe. But Bloor was betting on his own ingenuity and the nostalgic power of the Triumph brand, which had been a premier brand in the 1950s and 1960s, even having Marlon Brando riding one in *The Wild Ones.*

Realizing technology was key to success, he first hired three former Triumph employees, who had helped develop new models. Next, he hopped on a plane to Japan and managed to visit the Kawasaki, Yamaha, and Suzuki plants. They did not think he was a threat, so why not let him in? These visits made him realize he and his associates had to start from scratch with new models and new factory processes. When he opened the new factory in 1991, he had state of the art equipment from Japan and tapped nearby brainpower of engineers who build race cars. Their decision to keep a three-cylinder engine from the original lineup has given the company a distinctive calling card and part of the company's rebirth, with 2001 sales of $245 million.

A former home-builder, Bloor did not exactly know what he was getting into, how complex the design and manufacturing would be. "You need to multiply by two or three whatever money you think you will need," he says. And hope you do not hit a lot of speed bumps in the process.[58]

Further thinking has refined these ideas with respect to proposing an innovation versus implementing the innovation.[59] A loose structure and employee freedom are great for creating and initiating ideas; however, these same conditions often make implementing a change difficult because employees are less likely to comply. Companies often resolve this problem with an ambidextrous approach, which means incorporating structures and processes appropriate for innovation creation and implementation. They encourage flexibility and freedom to innovate with creative departments, new venture teams, skunkworks, and so forth, as described earlier, but they use a more rigid, centralized, and standardized approach for implementing innovations. Honda, for example, uses teams of young staff members who are not entrenched in the "old way of doing things" to explore new ideas. The teams are given the authority to do whatever is needed to develop new technologies even if it means breaking rules that are important in the larger manufacturing facility for implementing the new ideas.[60]

New Product Changes

product change

A change in the organization's product or service output.

A **product change** is a change in the organization's product or service output. New product innovations have major implications for an organization because they often are an outcome of a new strategy and may define a new market.[61] In addition, product life cycles are getting shorter, so companies need to invent continuously with innovative ideas for new products and services that meet needs in the marketplace. Product innovation is the primary way in which many organizations adapt to changes in markets, technologies, and competition.[62] Examples of new products include Apple Computer's iPod portable music player, Glad Press 'n Seal food wrap, and Toyota's Scion xB vehicle.

Product development is a risky, high-stakes game. Some experts estimate that 80 percent of new products fail upon introduction and another 10 percent disappear within five years. Despite the high failure rate, and that successfully launching a new product costs $50 million or more, approximately 25,000 new products appeared in one recent year, including 5,000 new toys.[63] Many of those products will never generate an economic return.[64] Consider such flops as Procter & Gamble's Fit Produce wash, Gerber's "Singles," a line of meals for adults, or the Segway $4,000 Human Transporter scooter, a motorized two-wheeler you ride standing up. Companies that successfully develop new products usually have the following characteristics:

1. People in marketing have a good understanding of customer needs.

2. Technical specialists are aware of recent technological developments and make effective use of new technology.

Take ACTION

As a manager, allow openness for creativity, but more discipline for implementation.

3. Members from key departments—research, manufacturing, and marketing—cooperate in the development of the new product.[65]

These findings mean that the ideas for new products typically originate at the lower levels of the organization as they do for technology changes. The difference is that new product ideas flow horizontally among departments. Product innovation requires expertise from several departments simultaneously. A new product failure is often the result of failed cooperation.[66]

Structural Changes

Structural changes involve the hierarchy of authority, goals, structural characteristics, administrative procedures, and management systems.[67] Almost any change in how the organization is managed falls under the category of structural change. For example, in response to changes in the kind of threats and duties the U.S. military faces in the twenty-first century, Army leaders are considering major structural changes. Their plan includes options such as altering how officers are trained; shifting resources away from high-intensity combat units to areas such as military police, engineers, and civil affairs officers; revamping the Army's intelligence systems; upgrading communications and information technology; and changing how units are organized.[68]

Other examples of structural or administrative change include shifting to a team-based structure, implementing policies regarding e-mail and Internet use, revising payroll systems, and centralizing information and accounting systems. At Nestlé USA, CEO Joe Weller has initiated a number of structural changes, as described in the Digital, Inc. box.

structural changes
Any change in the way in which the organization is designed and managed.

DIGITAL, INC.

Nestlé: Making "E-business the Way We Do Business"

Leaders at Nestlé USA are turning to the Internet to change everything about how the giant company operates, from buying raw materials to processing purchase orders, to marketing the company's 2,000 or so products, such as Nestlé Crunch bars, Toll House cookie dough, and Lean Cuisine frozen dinners. The size and past success of the company make some people reluctant to change (the "if it ain't broke, don't fix it" mindset), but top managers are determined to implement administrative and structural changes to help reach Chairman and CEO Joe Weller's goal to "make e-business the way we do business."

Change at Nestlé USA, the largest subsidiary of the world's largest food company, began at the top, on the twenty-first floor of the company's glass-and-steel headquarters office building in Glendale, California. Top managers rolled up their Oriental rugs and moved their offices down several floors to work more closely with people in the trenches, turning the former executive suites into meeting rooms and temporary office space for telecommuters and virtual workers. Weller implemented a number of top-down changes designed to make the company a leaner, faster organization. One was the "No meetings after 10 a.m. on Friday" rule. Weller believed people were spending so much time in meetings that they did not have time to think about strategy and long-term goals. Another was his "Blueprint for Success"

document, a two-sided sheet of paper that serves as a mission statement as well as a guide for turning Nestlé into a fast-moving, entrepreneurial company.

But the biggest change is the Internet strategy. Instead of creating a separate e-business division, top leaders decided to make e-business an integral part of every division and department in the company. Each operating division was assigned an "e-business catalyst" who helps managers develop business-to-consumer (B2C) and business-to-business (B2B) functions. The company's overall B2C strategy is focused on creating sites that help and inform consumers rather than push Nestlé's brands. A VeryBestBaking.com site offers recipes and cooking tips; VeryBestPets.com gives advice on grooming, health care, and nutrition for dogs and cats. The goal is that the sites will increase the percentage of consumers who have a "bonded relationship" to Nestlé products. As for B2B, the company recently launched NestléEZOrder, which will eliminate many of the 100,000 phone and fax orders the company gets each year and the high transaction costs that go along with them.

Nestlé's USA's top managers still face challenges getting buy-in for all these structural changes from employees, but they believe with careful implementation the changes will take root and become the everyday way the company does business.

SOURCE: Bill Breen, "Change is Sweet," *Fast Company* (June 2001): 168–177.

The top-down process does not mean coercion is the best implementation tactic. Implementation tactics include education, participation, and negotiation with employees. Unless there is an emergency, managers should not force structural change on employees. They may hit a resistance wall, and the change will fail. Consider the recent sweeping overhaul of the Internal Revenue Service (IRS), when the agency replaced its geographically based structure with four customer-oriented operating divisions, rewrote personnel policies and job descriptions, cut several layers of management, and totally revised rules for hiring, training, evaluating, and rewarding employees. Charles Mader, a leading member of the management team in charge of the overhaul, took great pains to talk with lower-level managers and employees to explain what was happening, get their input, and enlist their participation in the changes. One of Mader's most important challenges was working with the National Treasury Employees Union and helping to move the agency and union toward a less adversarial, more collaborative relationship.[69]

Top-down change means that initiation of the idea occurs at upper levels and is implemented downward. It does not mean that lower-level employees are not educated about the change or allowed to participate in it.

Culture/People Changes

Changes in structure, technologies, products, or services do not happen on their own, and changes in any of these areas require changes in people as well. For example, putting together a horizontal, cross-functional team for new product development does not ensure a collaborative process unless it is accompanied by significant changes in the attitudes and beliefs of employees and managers. Employees have to adopt new, collaborative ways of thinking and acting, and managers have to be willing to give up control and empower teams to make decisions and take action.[70]

culture/people change

A change in employees' values, norms, attitudes, beliefs, and behavior.

A **culture/people change** refers to a change in employees' values, norms, attitudes, beliefs, and behavior. Changes in culture and people pertain to how employees think; these are changes in mindset. Culture change pertains to the organization as a whole, such as when the IRS shifted its basic mindset from an organization focused on collection and compliance to one dedicated to informing, educating, and serving customers (taxpayers).[71] People change pertains to a few employees, such as when a handful of middle managers is sent to a training course to improve their leadership skills. Two specific tools for changing people and culture are training and development programs and organizational development (OD).

Training and Development

Training is one of the most frequently used approaches to changing people's mindset. A company might offer training programs to large blocks of employees on subjects such as teamwork, diversity, emotional intelligence, quality circles, communication skills, or participative management. Training and development programs aimed at changing individual behavior and interpersonal skills have become a big business for consultants, universities, and training firms.

Some companies particularly emphasize training and development for managers, with the idea that the behavior and attitudes of managers will influence people throughout the organization and lead to culture change. A number of Silicon Valley companies, including Intel, Advanced Micro Devices (AMD), and Sun Microsystems, regularly send managers to the Growth and Leadership Center (GLC), where they learn to use emotional intelligence to build better relationships. Nick Kepler, director of technology development at AMD, was surprised to learn how his emotionless approach to work was intimidating people and destroying the rapport needed to shift to a culture based on collaborative teamwork.[72] Some people involved with training and motivational speaking are not always what they want you to think. Neil Mullarkey is doing his best to raise people's consciousness about this issue.

He calls himself "Tom Peters of the Britney Spears generation" and he goes by the name L. Vaughan Spencer—call him L-Vo—but his real name is Neil Mullarkey, a guy with a goatee and ponytail who is not trying to sell you his brand of cheese or fish. He's a British comedian (you might remember him as the quartermaster clerk in *Austin Powers* who returns a pump to the spy), who dresses up as a dubious motivational speaker. It all started with a comedy troupe he began with Mike Meyers in 1985, where they tried to bring out the creative side of executives, including those at P&G, Publicis, and the Body Shop. As Mullarkey did research on the topic, he discovered "how much guruness and charlatanism there is," he says. This motivated him to parody the self-help speakers and he created L. Vaughan Spencer, a egotistical guru who teaches letterology (like numerology but with letters), Tong Shui—or being at one with your hair shafts—and the metrosexual secret to business success: "If you have the right moisturizer, then you're guaranteed success." He has been so successful, he now gets serious gigs, except that he never gets serious in this line of work. He batters the audience with insults, revealing himself to be the loser because he needs to take others down to make himself feel better. His message: "Don't trust these people. Trust yourself."[73]

Organization Development

Organization development (OD) is a planned, systematic process of change that uses behavioral science knowledge and techniques to improve an organization's health and effectiveness through its ability to adapt to the environment, improve internal relationships, and increase learning and problem-solving capabilities.[74] OD focuses on the human and social aspects of the organization, works to change attitudes and relationships among employees, and strengthens the organization's capacity for adaptation and renewal.[75] OD can help managers address at least three types of current problems:[76]

organization development (OD)

The application of behavioral science techniques to improve an organization's health and effectiveness through its ability to cope with environmental changes, improve internal relationships, and increase learning and problem-solving capabilities.

1. *Mergers/acquisitions.* The disappointing financial results of many mergers and acquisitions are caused by the failure of executives to determine whether the administrative style and corporate culture of the two companies fit. Executives may concentrate on potential synergies in technology, products, marketing, and control systems but fail to recognize that two firms may have widely different values, beliefs, and practices. These differences create stress and anxiety for employees, and these negative emotions affect future performance. Cultural differences should be evaluated during the acquisition process, and OD experts can be used to smooth the integration of two firms.

2. *Organizational decline/revitalization.* Organizations undergoing a period of decline and revitalization experience various problems, including a low level of trust, lack of innovation, high turnover, and high levels of conflict and stress. The period of transition requires opposite behaviors, including confronting stress, creating open communication, and fostering creative innovation to emerge with high levels of productivity. OD techniques can contribute greatly to cultural revitalization by managing conflicts, fostering commitment, and facilitating communication.

3. *Conflict management.* Conflict can occur at any time and place within a healthy organization. For example, a product team for the introduction of a new software package was formed at a computer company. Made up of strong-willed individuals, the team made little progress because members disagreed on project goals. At a

Take *ACTION*

As a manager, use OD to assess organization health and then prescribe and implement an intervention strategy.

manufacturing firm, salespeople promised delivery dates to customers that were in conflict with shop supervisor priorities for assembling customer orders. In a publishing company, two managers disliked each other intensely. They argued at meetings, lobbied politically against each other, and hurt the achievement of both departments. Organization development efforts can help solve these kinds of conflicts, as well as conflicts that are related to growing diversity and the global nature of today's organizations.

OD can be used to solve problems just described and many others. However, to be valuable to companies and employees, OD practitioners go beyond looking at ways to solve specific problems. Instead, they become involved in broader issues that contribute to improving organizational life, such as encouraging a sense of community, pushing for an organizational climate of openness and trust, and ensuring the company provides employees with opportunities for personal growth and development.[77] Specialized techniques have been developed to help meet OD goals.

OD Activities.   A number of OD activities have emerged in recent years. Three of the most popular and effective are as follows:

1. *Team-building activities.* **Team building** enhances the cohesiveness and success of organizational groups and teams. For example, a series of OD exercises can be used with members of cross-departmental teams to help them learn to act and function as a team. An OD expert can work with team members to increase their communication skills, facilitate their ability to confront one another, and accept their common goals.

2. *Survey-feedback activities.* **Survey feedback** begins with a questionnaire distributed to employees on values, climate, participation, leadership, and group cohesion within their organization. After the survey is completed, an OD consultant meets with groups of employees to provide feedback about their responses and the problems identified. Employees are engaged in problem solving based on the data.

3. *Large-group interventions.* In recent years, there has been a growing interest in applications of OD techniques to large-group settings, which are more attuned to bringing about fundamental organizational change in today's complex, changing world.[78] The **large-group intervention** approach brings together participants from all parts of the organization—often including key stakeholders from outside the organization as well—to discuss problems or opportunities and plan for change. A large-group intervention might involve 50 to 500 people and last several days. The idea is to include everyone who has a stake in the change, gather perspectives from all parts of the system, and enable people to create a collective future through sustained, guided conversation and dialogue.

Large-group interventions reflect a significant shift in the approach to organizational change from earlier OD concepts and approaches. Exhibit 8.7 lists the primary differences between the traditional OD model and the large-scale intervention model of organizational change.[79] In the newer approach, the focus is on the entire system, which takes into account the organization's interaction with its environment. The source of information for discussion is expanded to include customers, suppliers, community members, and competitors, and this information is shared widely so everyone has the same picture of the organization and its environment. The acceleration of change when the entire system is involved can be remarkable. In addition, learning occurs across all parts of the organization simultaneously, rather than in individuals, small groups, or business units. The result is that the large-group approach offers greater possibilities for fundamental, radical transformation of the entire culture, whereas the traditional approach creates incremental change in a few individuals or small groups at a time. General Electric's Work Out Program provides an excellent example of the large-group intervention approach.

---

team building

A type of OD intervention that enhances the cohesiveness of departments by helping members learn to function as a team.

survey feedback

A type of OD intervention in which questionnaires on organizational climate and other factors are distributed among employees and their results reported back to them by a change agent.

large-group intervention

An approach that brings together participants from all parts of the organization (and may include key outside stakeholders as well) to discuss problems or opportunities and plan for major change.

	Traditional Organizational Development Model	Large-Group Intervention Model
Focus for action	Specific problem or group	Entire system
Information Source Distribution	Organization Limited	Organization and environment Widely shared
Time frame	Gradual	Fast
Learning	Individual, small group	Whole organization

Change process	Incremental change	Rapid transformation

EXHIBIT 8.7

OD Approaches to Culture Change

SOURCE: Adapted from Barbara Benedict Bunker and Billie T. Alban, "Conclusion: What Makes Large Group Interventions Effective," *The Journal of Applied Behavioral Science* 28, no. 4 (December 1992), 579–591.

General Electric

GE's Work Out began in large-scale off-site meetings facilitated by a combination of top leaders, outside consultants, and human resources specialists. In each business unit, the basic pattern was the same. Hourly and salaried workers came together from many different parts of the organization in an informal three-day meeting to discuss and solve problems. Gradually, the Work Out events began to include external stakeholders such as suppliers and customers as well as employees. Today, Work Out is not an event but a process of how work is done and problems are solved at GE.

The format for Work Out includes seven steps:

1. Choose a work process or problem for discussion.

2. Select an appropriate cross-functional team, to include external stakeholders.

3. Assign a champion to follow through on recommendations.

4. Meet for several days and come up with recommendations to improve processes or solve problems.

5. Meet with leaders, who are asked to respond to recommendations on the spot.

6. Hold additional meetings as needed to implement the recommendations.

7. Start the process again with a new process or problem.

GE's Work Out process forces a rapid analysis of ideas, the creation of solutions, and the development of a plan for implementation. Over time, this large-group process creates an organizational culture where ideas are rapidly translated into action and positive business results.[80]

Large-group interventions represent a significant shift in the way leaders think about change and reflect an increasing awareness of the importance of dealing with the entire system, including external stakeholders, in any significant change effort.

OD Steps. OD experts acknowledge that changes in corporate culture and human behavior are tough to accomplish and require major effort. The theory underlying OD proposes three distinct stages for achieving behavioral and attitudinal change: (1) unfreezing, (2) changing, and (3) refreezing.[81]

The first stage, **unfreezing**, means that people throughout the organization are made aware of problems and the need for change. This stage creates the motivation for people to change their attitudes and behaviors. Unfreezing may begin when managers present information that shows discrepancies between desired behaviors or performance and the current state of affairs. In addition, as we discussed earlier in the chapter, managers

unfreezing

The stage of organization development in which participants are made aware of problems to increase their willingness to change their behavior.

change agent

An OD specialist who contracts with an organization to facilitate change.

changing

The intervention stage of organization development in which individuals experiment with new workplace behavior.

refreezing

The reinforcement stage of organization development in which individuals acquire a desired new skill or attitude and are rewarded for it by the organization.

need to establish a sense of urgency to unfreeze people and create an openness and willingness to change. The unfreezing stage is often associated with diagnosis, which uses an outside expert called a change agent. The **change agent** is an OD specialist who performs a systematic diagnosis of the organization and identifies work-related problems. He or she gathers and analyzes data through personal interviews, questionnaires, and observations of meetings. The diagnosis determines the extent of organizational problems and unfreezes managers by making them aware of problems in their behavior.

The second stage, **changing**, occurs when individuals experiment with new behavior and learn new skills to be used in the workplace. This is sometimes known as intervention, during which the change agent implements a specific plan for training managers and employees. The changing stage might involve a number of specific steps.[82] For example, managers put together a coalition of people with the will and power to guide the change, create a vision for change that everyone can believe in, and communicate the vision and plans for change throughout the company. In addition, successful change involves using emotion as well as logic to persuade people and empowering employees to act on the plan and accomplish the desired changes.

The third stage, **refreezing**, occurs when individuals acquire new attitudes or values and are rewarded for them by the organization. The impact of new behaviors is evaluated and reinforced. The change agent supplies new data that show positive changes in performance. Managers may provide updated data to employees that demonstrate positive changes in individual and organizational performance. Top executives celebrate successes and reward positive behavioral changes. This is the stage where changes are institutionalized in the organizational culture, so employees begin to view the changes as a normal, integral part of how the organization operates. Employees may also participate in refresher courses to maintain and reinforce the new behaviors.

Manager's Solution

Change is inevitable in organizations. This chapter discussed the techniques available for managing the change process. Managers should think of change as having four elements: the forces for change, the perceived need for change, the initiation of change, and the implementation of change. Forces for change can originate within or outside the firm, and managers are responsible for monitoring events that may require a planned organizational response. Techniques for initiating changes include designing the organization for creativity, encouraging change agents, establishing new-venture teams and idea incubators, and using open innovation. The final step is implementation. Managers should be prepared to encounter resistance to change. Some typical reasons for resistance include self-interest, lack of trust, uncertainty, and conflicting goals. Force-field analysis is one technique for diagnosing barriers, which often can be removed. Managers should draw on the implementation tactics of communication, participation, negotiation, coercion, or top management support.

This chapter discussed specific types of change. Technology changes are accomplished through a bottom-up approach that utilizes experts close to the technology. Successful new-product introduction requires horizontal linkage among marketing, research and development, manufacturing, and perhaps other departments, customers, partners, and suppliers. Structural changes tend to be initiated in a top-down fashion because upper managers are the administrative experts and champion these ideas for approval and implementation. Culture/people change pertains to the skills, behaviors, and attitudes of employees. Training and organization development are important approaches to change people's mindset and corporate culture. The OD process entails three steps: unfreezing (diagnosis of the problem), the actual change (intervention), and refreezing (reinforcement of new attitudes and behaviors). Popular OD techniques include team building, survey feedback, and large-group interventions.

As described in the beginning of the chapter, Aldo DiBelardino had many challenges ahead to pull the struggling X-It out of the gutter, to save his innovation of the ladder. As the new CEO, he realized he had to act quickly to bring necessary changes to the company. First, he straightened out the relationship with important customers, such as Hohman. To send more ladders to Hohman, DiBelardino needed cash to order them from China. And cash was nowhere in sight. He approached several investors and asked for small, short-term loans to get cash and to re-establish trust with the investors. By using negotiation and because of his concern for people, he had developed a positive relationship with a Chinese shipper, who extended credit to him, allowing transport of the ladders. He saw the performance gap between existing and desired performance levels and executed major cutbacks, reducing expenses from $25,000 per month to $9,000 by giving up the Manhattan office and the contract with an expensive PR firm that Ive had contracted. Ive's departure meant lower costs, as no salary to him was needed anymore. An old school friend rented DiBelardino a cheap warehouse near Chesapeake Bay where he set up an office with a $300 computer. Using other hometown relationships, he contracted cheap labor. In the meantime, the jury awarded X-It more than $17.4 million in compensatory damages, a ruling that X-It decided not to appeal, realizing the need to move on and the huge lawyers fees that could be incurred. DiBelardino learned a lot about himself and the company through the whole process and, as a result, company sales rose 23 percent in 2001, up to $320,000.[83]

Discussion Questions

1. A manager of an international chemical company said that very few new products in her company were successful. What would you advise the manager to do to help increase the company's success rate?

2. What are internal and external forces for change? Which force do you think is the major cause of organizational change?

3. Carefully planned change often is assumed to be effective. Do you think unplanned change can sometimes be beneficial to an organization? Discuss.

4. Why do organizations experience resistance to change? What techniques can managers use to overcome resistance?

5. Explain force-field analysis. Analyze the driving and restraining forces for a change with which you have been associated.

6. Define the roles associated with an idea champion. Why are idea champions so essential to the initiation of change?

7. To what extent would changes in technology affect products and vice versa? Compare the process for changing technology and that for product change.

8. Given that structural change is often made top down, should coercive implementation techniques be used?

9. Do the underlying values of organizational development differ from assumptions associated with other types of change? Discuss.

10. How do large-group interventions differ from OD techniques such as team building and survey feedback?

Manager's Workbook

Personal Change

Think of a situation where you wanted to (or had to) change and successfully executed the change. Then, think of another time when your attempt to change was unsuccessful. Referring to Exhibit 8.1 in the chapter, answer the following questions:

	When change was successful	When change was not successful
1. Describe the situation.		
2. What was the motive or need to change?		
3. How did you feel initially about the change?		
4. What were sources of resistance?		
5. How did you get beyond the resistance? What *worked* in the process of changing?		
6. What did you learn about yourself in the process of change?		
7. What have you learned about change? About motivating others to change?		

Manager's Workshop

An Ancient Tale

1. Read the introduction and case study and answer the questions.

2. In groups of three to four discuss your answers.

3. Groups report to the whole class and the instructor leads a discussion on the issues raised.

Introduction

To understand, analyze, and improve organizations, we must carefully think through the issue of who is responsible for what activities in different organizational settings. Often we hold responsible someone who has no control over the outcome, or we fail to teach or train someone who could make the vital difference.

To explore this issue, the following exercise could be conducted on either an individual or group basis. It provides an opportunity to see how different individuals assign responsibility for an event. It is also a good opportunity to discuss the concept of organizational boundaries (what is the organization, who is in or out, etc.).

Case Study

Read the short story and respond quickly to the first three questions. Then take a little more time on questions four through six. Then, discuss in groups the results, criteria, and implications.

Long ago in an ancient kingdom there lived a princess who was very young and very beautiful. The princess, recently married, lived in a large and luxurious castle with her husband, a powerful and wealthy lord. The young princess was not content, however, to sit and eat strawberries by herself while her husband took frequent and long journeys to neighboring kingdoms. She felt neglected and soon became quite unhappy. One day, while she was alone in the castle gardens, a handsome vagabond rode out of the forest bordering the castle. He spied the beautiful princess, quickly won her heart, and carried her away with him.

Following a day of dalliance, the young princess found herself ruthlessly abandoned by the vagabond. She then discovered that the only way back to the castle led through the bewitched forest of the wicked sorcerer. Fearing to venture into the forest alone, she sought out her kind and wise godfather. She explained her plight, begged the forgiveness of the godfather, and asked his assistance in returning home before her husband returned. The godfather, however, surprised and shocked at her behavior, refused forgiveness and denied her any assistance. Discouraged but still determined, the princess disguised her identity and sought the help of the most noble of all the kingdom's knights. After hearing the sad story, the knight pledged his unfailing aid—for a modest fee. But alas, the princess had no money and the knight rode away to save other damsels.

The beautiful princess had no one else from whom she might seek help, and decided to brave the great peril alone. She followed the safest path she knew, but when she was almost through the forest, the wicked sorcerer spied her and caused her to be devoured by the fire-breathing dragon.

1. Who was inside the organization and who was outside? Where were the boundaries?

2. Who is most responsible for the death of the beautiful princess?

3. Who is second most responsible? Least responsible?

4. What criteria did you employ to reach your decisions for problems 2 and 3?

5. What interventions would you suggest to prevent a recurrence?

6. What are the implications for *organizational development and change?*

Character	Most Responsible	Next Most Responsible	Least Responsible
Princess			
Husband			
Vagabond			
Godfather			
Knight			
Sorcerer			

Check one character in each column.

SOURCE: Adapted from J. B. Ritchie and Paul Thompson. Reprinted with permission from *Organization and People: Readings, Cases and Exercises in Organizational Behavior.* Copyright 1980 by West Publishing, pp. 68–70. All rights reserved, in Dorothy Marcic, *Organizational Behavior: Experiences and Cases,* 4/e, pp. 378–379.

Management in Practice: Ethical Dilemma

Research for Sale

Lucinda Jackson walked slowly back to R&D Laboratory 4 at Reed Pharmaceuticals. She was stunned. Top management was planning to sell her entire team project to Trichem Industries in an effort to raise the capital Reed needed to buy a small, competing drug company. Two years ago, when she was named project administrator for the cancer treatment program, Jackson was assured that the program was the highest priority at Reed. She was allowed to recruit the best and the brightest in the research center in their hunt for an effective drug to treat lung cancer. There had been press releases and personal appearances at stockholder meetings.

When she first approached a colleague, Len Rosen, to become head chemist on the project, he asked her if Reed was in cancer research for the long haul or if it was grabbing headlines. Based on what she had been told by the vice president in charge of R&D, Jackson assured him that their project was protected for as long as it took. Now, two years later, she learned that Reed was backing out, and the project was being sold as a package to an out-of-state firm. There were no jobs at Reed being offered as alternatives for the team. They were only guaranteed jobs if they moved with the project to Trichem.

Jackson felt betrayed, but she knew it was nothing compared to what the other team members would feel. Rosen was a 10-year veteran at Reed, and his wife and family had deep roots in the local community. A move would devastate them. Jackson had a few friends in top management, but she did not know if any would back her if she fought the planned sale.

What Would You Do?

1. Approach top management with the alternative of selling the project and sending the team temporarily to train staff at Trichem but allowing them to return to different projects at Reed after the transition. After all, Reed promised a commitment to the project.

2. Wait for the announcement of the sale of the project and then secure as much support as possible for the staff and families in their relocation: moving expense reimbursement, job placement for spouses, and so on.

3. Tell a few people, such as Rosen, and combine forces, and then threaten to quit if the project is sold. Make attempts to scuttle the sale to Trichem before it happens and perhaps leak the news to the press. Perhaps the threat of negative publicity will cause top management to reconsider.

SOURCE: Adapted from Doug Wallace, "Promises Made, Promises Broken," *What Would You Do? Business Ethics* 1 (March–April 1990): 16–18. Reprinted with permission from *Business Ethics*, P.O. Box 8439, Minneapolis, MN 55408, (612) 879-0695.

Case for Critical Analysis

Southern Discomfort

Jim Malesckowski remembers the call of two weeks ago as if he just put down the telephone receiver. "I just read your analysis and I want you to get down to Mexico right away," Jack Ripon, his boss and chief executive officer, had blurted in his ear. "You know we can't make the plant in Oconomo work anymore—the costs are just too high. So go down there, check out what our operational costs would be if we move, and report back to me in a week."

At that moment, Jim felt as if a shiv had been stuck in his side, just below the rib cage. As president of the Wisconsin Specialty Products Division of Lamprey, Inc., he knew quite well the challenge of dealing with high-cost labor in a third-generation, unionized U.S. manufacturing plant. And although he had done the analysis that led to his boss's knee-jerk response, the call still stunned him. There were 520 people who made a living at Lamprey's Oconomo facility, and if it closed, most of them wouldn't have a journeyman's prayer of finding another job in the town of 9,000 people.

Instead of the $16-per-hour average wage paid at the Oconomo plant, the wages paid to the Mexican workers—who lived in a town without sanitation and with an unbelievably toxic effluent from industrial pollution—would amount to about $1.60 an hour on average. That's a savings of nearly $15 million a year for Lamprey, to be offset in part by increased costs for training, transportation, and other matters.

After two days of talking with Mexican government representatives and managers of other companies in the town, Jim had enough information to develop a set of comparative figures of production and shipping costs. On the way home, he started to outline the report, knowing full well that unless some miracle occurred, he would be ushering in a blizzard of pink slips for people he had come to appreciate.

The plant in Oconomo had been in operation since 1921, making special apparel for persons suffering from injuries and other medical conditions. Jim had often talked with employees who would recount stories about their fathers or grandfathers working in the same Lamprey company plant—the last of the original manufacturing operations in town.

But friendship aside, competitors had already edged past Lamprey in terms of price and were dangerously close to overtaking it in product quality. Although both Jim and the plant manager had tried to convince the union to accept lower wages, union leaders resisted. In fact, on one occasion when Jim and the plant manager tried to discuss a cell-manufacturing approach, which would cross-train employees to perform up to three different jobs, local union leaders could barely restrain their anger. Yet probing beyond the fray, Jim sensed the fear that lurked under the gruff exterior of the union reps. He sensed their vulnerability, but could not break through the reactionary bark that protected it.

A week has passed and Jim just submitted his report to his boss. Although he didn't specifically bring up the point, it was apparent that Lamprey could put its investment dollars in a bank and receive a better return than what its Oconomo operation is currently producing.

Tomorrow, he'll discuss the report with the CEO. Jim doesn't want to be responsible for the plant's dismantling, an act he personally believes would be wrong as long as there's a chance its costs can be lowered. "But Ripon's right," he says to himself. "The costs are too high, the union's unwilling to cooperate, and the company needs to make a better return on its investment if it's to continue at all. It sounds right but feels wrong. What should I do?"

Questions

1. Assume you want to lead the change to save the Oconomo plant. How would you proceed, using the four stages of the change process described in the chapter—forces, need, initiation, and implementation?

2. What is the primary type of change needed—technology, product, structure, or people/culture? To what extent will the primary change have secondary effects on other types of change at the Oconomo factory?

3. What techniques would you use to overcome union resistance and implement change?

SOURCE: Doug Wallace, "What Would You Do?" *Business Ethics*, March/April 1996, pp. 52–53. Reprinted with permission.

CHAPTER

9

Human Resource Management and Diversity

CHAPTER OUTLINE

LEARNING OBJECTIVES

After studying this chapter, you should be able to do the following:

1 **Explain the role of human resource management in organizational strategic planning.**

2 **Describe federal legislation and societal trends that influence human resource management.**

3 **Explain what the changing social contract between organizations and employees means for workers and human resource managers.**

4 **Describe the tools managers use to recruit, select, train, and evaluate employees.**

5 **Explain how organizations maintain a workforce through the administration of wages and salaries, benefits, and terminations.**

6 **Explain the dimensions of employee diversity, as well as the changing workplace and how to manage a culturally diverse workforce.**

7 **Explain affirmative action and why factors such as the glass ceiling have kept it from being more successful.**

8 **Explain the importance of addressing sexual harassment in the workplace.**

Manager's Challenge

Every hour or so throughout the night, big brown trucks back into the bays at UPS's distribution center in Buffalo, New York, where part-time workers load, unload, and sort packages at a rate of 1,200 boxes an hour. A typical employee handles a box every three seconds. The packages do not stop until the shift is over, and there is little time for friendly banter and chit-chat even if you could hear over the din of the belts and ramps that carry packages through the cavernous 270,000-square-foot warehouse. It is not the easiest job in the world, and many people do not stick around for long. When Jennifer Shroeger arrived in Buffalo as the new district manager, the attrition rate of part-time workers, who account for half of Buffalo's workforce, was 50 percent a year. With people deserting at that rate, hiring and training costs were through the roof, not to mention the slow-down in operations caused by continually training new workers. Something had to be done to bring in the right employees and make them want to stay longer than a few weeks.[1]

If you were Jennifer Shroeger, how would you address this enormous human resources challenge? What changes in recruiting, hiring, training, and other human resource practices can help to solve Jennifer Shroeger's problem in Buffalo?

The situation at UPS's Buffalo distribution center provides a dramatic example of the challenges that managers face every day. The people who make up an organization give that organization its primary source of competitive advantage, and human resource management plays a key role in finding and developing the organization's people as human resources that contribute to and directly affect company success. The term **human resource management (HRM)** refers to the design and application of formal systems in an organization to ensure the effective and efficient use of human talent to accomplish organizational goals.[2] This includes activities undertaken to attract, develop, and maintain an effective workforce.

Managers at Electronic Arts, the world's largest maker of computer games, include a commitment to human resources as one of the company's four worldwide goals. They have to in a company where the creativity and mindpower of artists, designers, model makers, mathematicians, and filmmakers determine strategic success, and the war for talent is intense.[3] HRM is equally important for government and nonprofit organizations. For example, public schools in the United States are facing a severe teacher shortage, with HRM directors struggling to fill an estimated 2.2 million teacher vacancies over the next decade. Many are trying innovative programs such as recruiting in foreign countries, establishing relationships with leaders at top universities, and having their most motivated and enthusiastic teachers work with university students considering teaching careers.[4]

Over the past decade, HRM has shed its old "personnel" image and gained recognition as a vital player in corporate strategy.[5] Today's best HRM departments support the organization's strategic objective and actively pursue an ongoing, integrated plan for furthering the organization's performance.[6] Research has found that effective HRM has a positive impact on strategic performance, including higher employee productivity and stronger financial results.[7] Human resource (HR) personnel are considered key players on the management team. In addition, all managers need to be skilled in HRM basics. Today's flatter organizations often require that managers throughout the organization play an active role in recruiting and selecting the right personnel, developing effective training programs, or creating appropriate performance appraisal systems. HRM professionals act to guide and assist line managers in managing their human resources to achieve the organization's strategic goals.

The Strategic Role of Human Resource Management

The strategic approach to HRM recognizes three key elements. First, as we just discussed, all managers are HR managers. For example, at IBM every manager is expected to pay attention to the development and satisfaction of subordinates. Line managers use surveys, career planning, performance appraisal, and compensation to encourage commitment to IBM.[8] Second, employees are viewed as assets. Employees, not buildings and machinery, give a company a competitive advantage.

How a company manages its workforce may be the single most important factor in sustained competitive success.[9] Third, HRM is a matching process, integrating the organization's strategies and goals with the correct approach to managing the firm's human resources.[10] Current strategic issues of particular concern to managers include the following:

- Becoming more competitive on a global basis

- Improving quality, productivity, and customer service

- Managing mergers and acquisitions

- Applying new information technology (IT) for e-business

All of these strategic decisions determine a company's need for skills and employees.

This chapter examines the three primary goals of HRM as illustrated in Exhibit 9.1. HRM activities and goals do not take place inside a vacuum but within the context of

---

human resource management (HRM)
Activities undertaken to attract, develop, and maintain an effective workforce within an organization.

Take **ACTION**

Employees are an important asset of the company.

© DANIEL ACKER/BLOOMBERG NEWS/Landov

issues and factors affecting the entire organization, such as globalization, changing technology and the shift to knowledge work, rapid shifts in markets and the external environment, societal trends, government regulations, and changes in the organization's culture, structure, strategy, and goals.

The three broad HR activities outlined in Exhibit 9.1 are designed to attract an effective workforce to the organization, develop the workforce to its potential, and maintain the workforce over the long term.[11] Achieving these goals requires skills in planning, recruiting, training, performance appraisal, wage and salary administration, benefit programs, and even termination. Each of the activities in Exhibit 9.1 will be discussed in this chapter.

Environmental Influences on HRM

"Our strength is the quality of our people."
"Our people are our most important resource."

These often-repeated statements by executives emphasize the importance of HRM. HR managers must find, recruit, train, nurture, and retain the best people.[12] Without the right people, the brightest idea or management trend—whether virtual teams, e-business, or flexible compensation—is doomed to failure. In addition, when employees do not feel valued, usually they are not willing to give their best to the company and often leave to find a more supportive work environment. For these reasons, HR executives must be involved in competitive strategy. HR executives interpret federal legislation and respond to the changing nature of careers and work relationships.

Competitive Strategy

HRM contributes directly to the bottom line through its appreciation that it is the organization's human assets—its people—that meet or fail to meet strategic goals. To keep companies competitive, HRM is changing in three primary ways: focusing on building human capital; developing global HR strategies; and using IT.

Building Human Capital. More than ever, strategic decisions are related to HR considerations. In many companies, especially those that rely more on employee information, creativity, knowledge, and service rather than on production machinery,

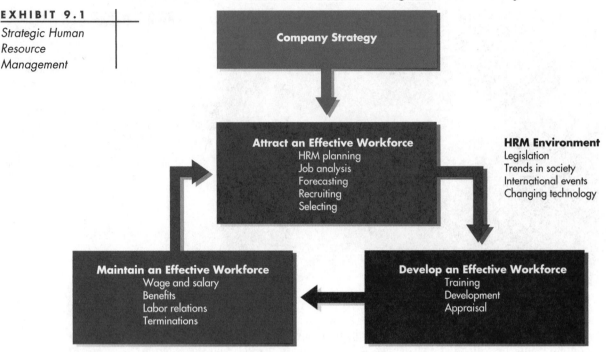

human capital

The economic value of the knowledge, experience, skills, and capabilities of employees.

success depends on the ability to manage human capital.[13] **Human capital** refers to the economic value of the combined knowledge, experience, skills, and capabilities of employees.[14] To build human capital, HRM develops strategies for finding the best talent, enhancing the talent's skills and knowledge with training programs and opportunities for personal and professional development, and providing compensation and benefits that enhance the sharing of knowledge and appropriately reward people for their contributions to the organization. HR managers create an environment that gives highly talented people compelling reasons to stay with the company. Judy Lyles of DET Distributing Company in Nashville, Tennessee, sees the HR department as the keeper of the rules and as the "keeper of workers' hearts, in other words, why they want to come to work every day."[15] A related concern for managers is social capital, which refers to the quality of interactions among employees and whether they share a common perspective.[16] In organizations with a high degree of social capital, for example, relationships are based on honesty, trust, and respect, and people cooperate smoothly to achieve shared goals and outcomes.

Take **ACTION**

Do not hire people just because they are available. Get the right person for your job.

Information Technology. Information technology (IT) is transforming HRM and meeting the challenges of today's global environment. A study of the transition from traditional HR to e-HR found that the Internet and IT has significantly affected every area of HRM, from recruiting and training to retention strategies.[17] A **human resource information system** is an integrated computer system designed to provide data and information used in HR planning and decision making. The most basic use is the automation of administrative duties such as handling pay, benefits, and retirement plans, which can lead to significant cost savings. At General Motors, automating just one task—how managers authorize subordinates' pay increases—saved an estimated $650,000 a year. Allowing employees to make changes to their personal information or benefits can save even more.[18]

human resource information system

An integrated computer system designed to provide data and information used in HR planning and decision making.

Federal Legislation

Over the past 40 years, a number of federal laws have been passed to ensure equal employment opportunity (EEO). Some of the most significant legislation and executive orders are summarized in Exhibit 9.2. The point of the laws is to stop discriminatory practices unfair to specific groups and to define enforcement agencies for these laws. EEO legislation attempts to balance the pay given to men and women; provide employment opportunities without regard to race, religion, national origin, and gender; ensure fair treatment for employees of all ages; and avoid discrimination against disabled individuals.

The Equal Employment Opportunity Commission (EEOC) created by the Civil Rights Act of 1964 initiates investigations in response to complaints concerning discrimination. The EEOC is the major agency involved with employment discrimination. **Discrimination** occurs when some applicants are hired or promoted based on criteria not relevant to the job. For example, refusing to hire a black applicant for a job he is qualified to fill, or paying a woman a lower wage than a man for the same work are discriminatory acts. When discrimination is found, remedies include providing back pay and taking affirmative action. Affirmative action requires that an employer take positive steps to guarantee EEOs for people within protected groups. An affirmative action plan is a formal document that can be reviewed by employees and enforcement agencies. The goal of organizational affirmative action is to reduce or eliminate internal inequities among affected employee groups.

discrimination
The hiring or promoting of applicants based on criteria that are not job relevant.

Failure to comply with EEO legislation can result in substantial fines and penalties for employers. Suits for discriminatory practices can cover a broad range of employee complaints. One issue of growing concern is sexual harassment, which is also a violation of Title VII of the Civil Rights Act. The EEOC guidelines specify that behavior such as unwelcome advances, requests for sexual favors, and other verbal or physical conduct of a sexual nature becomes sexual harassment when submission to the conduct is tied to continued employment or advancement, or when the behavior creates an intimidating, hostile, or offensive work environment.[19] Sexual harassment will be discussed later in the chapter.

Exhibit 9.2 lists the major federal laws related to compensation and benefits and health and safety issues. The scope of HR legislation is increasing at federal, state, and municipal levels. The working rights and conditions of women, minorities, older employees, and the disabled will likely receive increasing legislative attention in the future. Some companies, such as Young Electric Sign, have used outsourced software to comply with federal regulations, as described in the example below.

Young Electric Sign

When a Las Vegas company starts getting calls saying, "You know what we want. Give it to us now or else!" many people would start to think that thugs were making those calls. Not so. They were Utah state officials demanding information about employees of family-owned Young Electric Sign. As required by the Welfare Reform Act, bosses must file a New Hire Reporting form to the state within 20 days, so its bureaucrats in other states can see if a new employee owes any child support. Any worker who turns up as a "deadbeat" gets pay docked by the employer, who sends that sum to the state.

HRM chief Paul Bradley spent a lot of time filling out the appropriate paperwork for all the relevant 1,200 employees but often did not get documents filed on time. Spending 80 hours automating the reports, he was more frustrated when those reports kept bouncing back from Utah's state computer. That's when Bradley started getting those ugly calls from government officials.

Finally, in desperation Bradley contracted the work to HR outsourcing company Ceridian, Ltd, paying $90,000 for hardware and software, with a yearly fee of $39,000. Young Electric is not the only one. About 30 percent of HR directors use outside services for their new hire reports. Now able to get to his other work of helping the company meet customer needs, Bradley does not mind the cost of the program. "Well worth it," he says.[20]

EXHIBIT 9.2

Major Federal Laws Related to Human Resource Management

Federal Law	Year	Provisions
Equal Opportunity/ Discrimination Laws		
Civil Rights Act	1991	Provides for possible compensatory and punitive damages plus traditional back pay for cases of intentional discrimination brought under Title VII of the 1964 Civil Rights Act. Shifts the burden of proof to the employer.
Americans with Disabilities Act	1990	Prohibits discrimination against qualified individuals by employers on the basis of disability and demands that "reasonable accommodations" be provided for the disabled to allow performance of duties.
Vocational Rehabilitation Act	1973	Prohibits discrimination based on physical or mental disability and requires that employees be informed about affirmative action plans.
Age Discrimination in Employment Act (ADEA)	1967 (amended 1978, 1986)	Prohibits age discrimination and restricts mandatory retirement.
Civil Rights Act, Title VII	1964	Prohibits discrimination in employment on the basis of race, religion, color, sex, or national origin.
Compensation/Benefits Laws Health Insurance Portability and Accountability Act (HIPPA)	1996	Allows employees to switch health insurance plans when changing jobs and get the new coverage regardless of preexisting health conditions; prohibits group plans from dropping a sick employee.
Family and Medical Leave Act	1993	Requires employers to provide up to 12 weeks unpaid leave for childbirth, adoption, or family emergencies.
Equal Pay Act	1963	Prohibits sex differences in pay for substantially equal work.
Health/Safety Laws Consolidated Omnibus Budget Reconciliation Act (COBRA)	1985	Requires continued health insurance coverage (paid by employee) following termination.
Occupational Safety and Health Act (OSHA)	1970	Establishes mandatory safety and health standards in organizations.

The Changing Nature of Careers

Another current issue is the changing nature of careers. HRM can benefit employees and organizations by responding to recent changes in the relationship between employers and employees and new ways of working, such as telecommuting, job sharing, and virtual teams.

The Changing Social Contract

Take **ACTION**

Learn to be flexible and work with various people in different teams.

In the old social contract between organization and employee, the employee could contribute ability, education, loyalty, and commitment and expect, in return, that the company would provide wages and benefits, work, advancement, and training throughout the employee's working life. But volatile changes in the environment have disrupted this contract. Many organizations have been downsized, eliminating many employees. Employees who are left may feel little stability. In a fast-moving company, a person is hired and assigned to a project. The project changes over time, as do the person's tasks. Then the person is assigned to another project and then to still another. These new projects require working with different groups and leaders and schedules, and people may be working in a virtual environment, where they rarely see their colleagues face to face.[21] Careers no longer progress up a vertical hierarchy but move across jobs horizontally. In many of today's companies, everyone is expected to be a self-motivated worker who has excellent interpersonal relationships and is continuously acquiring new skills. Part of the phenomenon is the growth of self-employed, or contingent workers, some of whom form loose alliances, as described in the Focus on Collaboration box.

Exhibit 9.3 lists some elements of the new social contract. The new contract is based on the employability concept rather than lifetime employment. Individuals manage their own careers; the organization no longer takes care of them or guarantees employment. Companies agree to pay somewhat higher wages and invest in creative training and development opportunities so people will be more employable when the company no longer needs their services. Employees take more responsibility and control in their jobs, becoming partners in business improvement rather than cogs in a machine. In return, the organization provides challenging work assignments as well as information and resources to enable people to learn new skills. The new contract can provide many opportunities for employees to be more involved and express new aspects of themselves.

However, many employees are unprepared for new levels of cooperation or responsibility on the job. Employment insecurity is stressful for most employees, and it is harder than it was in the past to gain an employee's full commitment and enthusiasm.

FOCUS ON COLLABORATION

Home-based Businesses

As more educated women choose to stay home with their children, more than a few are dallying with eBay. What starts out as a hobby can turn into a real business. Kim Kincaid was a Dow Chemical engineer and started her eBay career selling a cookie jar for $75, with $68 of that profit. Now, she moves $100,000 of goods every month. These are women who realized as corporate employees, most of their salary was going to childcare. When they stay home, they still want to be earning money and are initially dumbfounded by the volume of goods sold on the site. But they are not the only ones working from home. There are now over 20 million self-employed workers.

Josh Ostroff has a ten-minute morning commute: from his bedroom downstairs to his computer, stopping on the way to brew coffee. After getting laid off from an advertising agency in the Boston area, he started his own media consulting firm. Instead of lost time in traffic, he is on the phone, Internet or e-mail, gathering data, talking to clients, and spending time with his family.

Jennifer Overholt, an admitted nightowl, does much of her work in the still of the night. With the streets dark and quiet, she pores over reports and information, helping clients form strategic and marketing analyses. Sometimes, she sends a middle-of-the-night e-mail to one of her five partners, some of whom are working at that time, too, all from their homes. California-based Indigo Partners is a loose confederation of solo consultants, who join together on projects, but who retain the autonomy of solo workers. There is no hierarchy or regular meetings, and individuals take on projects, forming a small team to do it. Any partner can take off as long as desired, for any reason. One took off a year to help with a start-up and another left for the summer to join her husband in London.

The downsides include lack of a steady paycheck; no one to bounce ideas off of; work coming in waves making scheduling difficult, especially around family needs. Overholt says all the Indigo partners have talked about someday going back to Corporate America. "The thing is, this is a great life. Why would I want to give it up?"

Exactly. That's why the eBay mompreneurs keep it up. Selling on eBay turns out to be a recession-proof option for these moms, particularly because it makes an advantage of the things which become impediments to women moving up a corporation hierarchy, for example, their detail-orientation, inclination to work harder and eat lunch at their desks. In this new e-business venture those disadvantages become virtues as they provide high-touch customer service, which is what buyers crave. Think of all the experience they are gaining that they can use when they go back to corporate work. But wait, who says they want to go back?

SOURCES: Michelle Conlin, "The Rise of the Mompreneurs," *BusinessWeek*, (June 7, 2004): 70–72; Marcelo Prince, "On Their Own: Freelance Workers," *The Wall Street Journal* (March 27, 2002): R14; Julie Bick, "Solo: The New Age of Self-employment," *Inc.* (Nov. 1, 2001): 86–91; John Grossman, "Meetings at 9, I'll Be the One in Slippers," *Inc.* (May 19, 1998): 47–48.

EXHIBIT 9.3

The Changing Social Contract

	New Contract	Old Contract
Employee	Employability, personal responsibility Partner in business improvement Learning	Job security A cog in the machine Knowing
Employer	Continuous learning, lateral career movement, incentive compensation Creative development opportunities Challenging assignments Information and resources	Traditional compensation package Standard training programs Routine jobs Limited information

SOURCES: Based on Louisa Wah, "The New Workplace Paradox," *Management Review*, January 1998, 7; and Douglas T. Hall and Jonathan E. Moss, "The New Protean Career Contract: Helping Organizations and Employees Adapt," *Organizational Dynamics* (Winter, 1998), 22–37.

In addition, one study found that though most workers today feel they are contributing to their companies' success, they are increasingly skeptical that their hard work is being fully recognized.[22] Some companies are finding it difficult to keep good workers because employee trust has been destroyed. An important challenge for HRM is revising performance evaluation, training, career development, compensation, and reward practices to address the changing way of working. In addition, smart organizations contribute to employees' long-term success by offering career information and assessment, combined with career coaching, to help people determine new career directions.[23] This helps to preserve trust and enhance the organization's social capital. Even when employees are let go or voluntarily leave, they often maintain feelings of goodwill toward the company.

HR Issues in the New Workplace

The rapid change and turbulence in today's business environment brings significant new challenges for HRM. As we have discussed, one important issue is responding to the increasing use of teams and project management. In addition, HRM must devise policies to address the needs of temporary employees and virtual workers, effectively manage downsizing, and acknowledge growing employee demands for work-life balance.

Teams and Projects.   The advent of teams and project management is a major trend in today's workplace. People who used to work alone on the shop floor, in the advertising department, or in middle management are now thrown into teams and succeed as part of a group. Each member of the team acts like a manager, becoming responsible for quality standards, scheduling, and hiring and firing other team members. With the emphasis on projects, the distinctions between job categories and descriptions are collapsing. Many of today's workers straddle functional and departmental boundaries and handle multiple tasks and responsibilities.[24]

Temporary Employees.   In the opening years of the twenty-first century, the largest employer in the United States was a temporary employment agency, Manpower Inc.[25] Temporary agencies such as Manpower grew rapidly during the 1990s, and by 2001, more than 3.3 million workers were in temporary firm placements. People in these temporary jobs do everything from data entry to becoming the interim CEO. In the past, most temporary workers were in clerical and manufacturing positions; in recent years, demand has grown for professionals, particularly financial analysts, IT specialists, accountants, product managers, and operations experts.[26] **Contingent workers** are people who work for an organization, but not on a permanent or full-time basis. This might include temporary placements, contracted professionals, leased employees, or part-time workers. One estimate is that contingent workers make up at least 25 percent of the U.S.

contingent workers

People who work for an organization but not on a permanent or full-time basis, including temporary placements, contracted professionals, or leased employees.

workforce.[27] The use of contingent workers means reduced payroll and benefit costs, as well as increased flexibility for employers and employees.

Technology.   Related trends are virtual teams and telecommuting. Some **virtual teams** are made up entirely of people who are hired on a project-by-project basis. Team members are geographically or organizationally dispersed and rarely meet, doing their work instead through advanced ITs and collaborative software. **Telecommuting** means using computers and telecommunications equipment to do work without going to an office. TeleService Resources has more than 25 telephone agents who work entirely from home, using state-of-the-art call-center technology that provides seamless interaction with TSR's Dallas-Fort Worth call center.[28] Millions of people in the United States and Europe telecommute on a regular or occasional basis.[29] Wireless Internet devices, laptops, cell phones, and fax machines make it possible for people to work just about anywhere. There's a growth of what is called extreme telecommuting, which means that people live and work in countries far away from the organization's physical location. For example, Paolo Concini works from his home in Bali, Indonesia, even though his company's offices are located in China and Europe.[30] Technology can sometimes be misused by employees, one reason for the increased monitoring of e-mail, as shown in the Focus on Skills box.

virtual teams

A team made up of members who are geographically or organizationally dispersed, rarely meet face to face, and do their work using advanced information technologies.

telecommuting

Using computers and telecommunications equipment to perform work from home or another remote location.

FOCUS ON SKILLS

Regulating E-mail in the Workplace

The CEO of Boeing was forced to resign after an e-mail he sent to his colleague/lover was intercepted and the affair became public. Top executives around the globe are discovering that casual e-mail messages can come back to haunt them in court. The American Management Association (AMA) surveyed 1,100 companies and found that 14 percent of them had been ordered to disclose e-mail messages. In 2005, it was estimated that 60% of companies use some version of software to monitor workers' e-mails. In 2002, eight brokerage firms were fined $8 million for not keeping and producing e-mail in accordance with SEC guidelines. Some companies have had to pay millions to settle sexual harassment lawsuits arising from inappropriate e-mail.

As with any powerful tool, e-mail has the potential to be hazardous, backfiring on the employee and on the organization as well. One study found that "potentially dangerous or nonproductive" messages account for fully 31 percent of all company e-mail. Experts say a formal written policy is the best way for companies to protect themselves, and they offer some tips for managers on developing effective policies governing the use of e-mail.

- *Clarify that all e-mail and its contents are the property of the company.* Many experts recommend warning employees that the company reserves the right to read any messages transmitted over its system. "Employees need to understand that a company can access employees' e-mail at any time without advance notice or consent," says lawyer Pam Reeves. This discourages frivolous e-mails or those that might be considered crude and offensive.

- *Tie the policy to the company's sexual harassment policy or other policies governing employee behavior on the job.* In almost all sexual harassment cases, judges have ruled that the use of e-mail was considered part of the workplace environment.

- *Establish clear guidelines on matters such as the use of e-mail for jokes and other non-work related communications, the sending of confidential messages, and how to handle junk e-mail.* At Prudential Insurance, for example, employees are prohibited from using company e-mail to share jokes, photographs, or any kind of nonbusiness information.

- *Establish guidelines for deleting or retaining messages.* Retention periods of 30 to 90 days for routine messages is typical. Most organizations set up a centralized archive for retaining essential e-mail messages.

- *Consider having policies pop up on users' screens when they log on.* It is especially important to remind employees that e-mail belongs to the employer and may be monitored.

Even deleted e-mails can usually be tracked down by a computer-forensics expert. An effective policy is the best step companies can take to manage the potential risks of e-mail abuse.

SOURCES: Pui-Wing Tam, Erin White, Nick Wingfield, and Kris Maher, "Snooping Email by Software is Now a Workplace Norm,' *The Wall Street Journal* (March 9, 2005): B1, B3; "E-mail: The DNA of Office Crimes," *Electric Perspectives 28:5* (September-October 2003): 4; Marcia Stepanek with Steve Hamm, "When the Devil Is in the E-mails," *BusinessWeek* (June 8, 1998): 72–74; Joseph McCafferty, "The Phantom Menace," *CFO* (June 1999): 89–91; and "Many Company Internet and Email Policies Are Worth Revising," *The Kiplinger Letter* (February 21, 2003): 1.

Work-Life Balance. Telecommuting is one way organizations are helping employees lead more balanced lives. By working part of the time from home, for example, parents can avoid some of the conflicts they often feel with coordinating their work and family responsibilities. Flexible scheduling for regular employees is also important in today's workplace. Approximately 27 percent of the workforce has flexible hours. When and where an employee does the job is becoming less important.[31] In addition, broad work-life balance initiatives have become a critical retention strategy. Managers are recognizing that people have personal needs that may require special attention. Some HR responses include benefits such as on-site gym facilities and childcare, assistance with arranging childcare and eldercare, and paid leaves or sabbaticals. In some industries, the war for talent is intense, and companies cannot afford to lose experienced and knowledgeable employees. Many European companies are miles ahead of U.S. firms in supporting work-life balance.

Downsizing. In some cases, organizations have more people than they need and have to let some employees go. **Downsizing** refers to an intentional, planned reduction in the size of a company's workforce. Some researchers have found that massive downsizing has often not achieved the intended benefits and, in some cases, has harmed the organization.[32] Unless HRM departments manage the downsizing process, layoffs can lead to decreased morale and performance. Managers can smooth the downsizing process by regularly communicating with employees and providing them with as much information as possible, providing assistance to workers who will lose their jobs, and using training and development to help address the emotional needs of remaining employees and enable them to cope with new or additional responsibilities.[33]

These issues present many challenges for organizations and HRM, such as new ways of recruiting and compensation that address the interests and needs of contingent and virtual workers, new training methods that help people work in a cross-functional way, or new ways to retain valuable employees. All of these concerns are taken into consideration as HR managers work toward the three primary HR goals described earlier: attracting, developing, and maintaining an effective workforce.

Attracting an Effective Workforce

The first goal of HRM is to attract individuals who show signs of becoming valued, productive, and satisfied employees. The first step in attracting an effective workforce involves HR planning, in which managers or HRM professionals predict the need for new employees based on the types of vacancies that exist, as illustrated in Exhibit 9.4. The second step is to use recruiting procedures to communicate with potential applicants. The third step is to select from the applicants those persons believed to be the best potential contributors to the organization. Finally, the new employee is welcomed into the organization.

Underlying the organization's effort to attract employees is a matching model. With the **matching model**, the organization and the individual attempt to match the needs, interests, and values they offer each other.[34] HRM professionals attempt to identify a correct match. For example, a small software developer might require long hours from creative, technically skilled employees. In return, it can offer freedom from bureaucracy, tolerance of idiosyncrasies, and potentially high pay. A large manufacturer can offer employment security and stability, but it might have more rules and regulations and require greater skills for "getting approval from the higher-ups." The individual who would thrive working for the software developer might feel stymied and unhappy working for a large manufacturer. The company and the employee are interested in finding a good match. A new approach, called job sculpting, attempts to match people to jobs that enable them to fulfill deeply embedded life interests.[35] This often requires that HR managers play detective to find out what makes a person happy. The idea is that people can fulfill deep-seated needs and interests on the job, which will induce them to stay with the organization.

Human Resource Planning

Human resource planning is the forecasting of human resource needs and the projected matching of individuals with expected vacancies. HR planning begins with several questions:

- What new technologies are emerging, and how will these affect the work system?

- What is the volume of the business likely to be in the next five to ten years?

- What is the turnover rate, and how much, if any, is avoidable?

The responses to these questions are used to formulate specific questions pertaining to HR activities, such as the following:

- How many senior managers will we need during this time period?

- What types of engineers will we need and how many?

- Are persons with adequate computer skills available for meeting our projected needs?

- How many administrative personnel—technicians, IT specialists—will we need to support the additional managers and engineers?

- Can we use temporary, contingent, or virtual workers to handle some tasks?[36]

Answers to these questions help define the direction for the organization's HRM strategy. For example, if forecasting suggests a strong need for more technically trained individuals, the organization can define the jobs and skills needed in some detail, hire and train recruiters to look for the specified skills, and provide new training for existing employees. By anticipating future HRM needs, the organization can prepare itself to meet competitive challenges more effectively than organizations that react to problems only as they arise.

Recruiting

Recruiting is defined as "activities or practices that define the characteristics of applicants to whom selection procedures are ultimately applied."[37] Though we frequently think of campus recruiting as a typical recruiting activity, many organizations use internal recruiting, or promote-from-within policies, to fill their high-level positions.[38] At Mellon Bank, for example, current employees are given preference when a position opens. Internal recruiting has several advantages: It is less costly than an external search, and it generates higher employee commitment, development, and satisfaction because it offers opportunities for career advancement to employees rather than outsiders.

Frequently, however, external recruiting—recruiting newcomers from outside the organization—is advantageous. Applicants are provided by various outside sources including advertising, state employment services, private employment agencies (headhunters), job fairs, and employee referrals.

Courtesy of Christine Burgin Gallery and Victoria Sambunaris

CONCEPT CONNECTION

This employee is working in the wiring room at Cobalt Boats, whose high-performance craft are widely admired as the Steinways of the runabout class. Cobalt builds its boats in Neodesha, Kansas, a town of 2,800 in the middle of the prairie, about as far from a lapping tide as one can get in America. But the location has a tremendous advantage—it enables Cobalt to **attract an effective workforce**, *mostly second- and third-generation farmers who can no longer make a living from farming alone. These farm-toughened employees have a can-do attitude and an owner's mindset that matches perfectly with Cobalt's emphasis on individual initiative, ingenuity, and responsibility. Cobalt truly values its employees as "the finest boat builders in the world."*

human resource planning

The forecasting of HR needs and the projected matching of individuals with expected vacancies.

recruiting

The activities or practices that define the desired characteristics of applicants for specific jobs.

Take *ACTION*

When recruiting, make sure you cast a wide net to get enough candidates from which to choose.

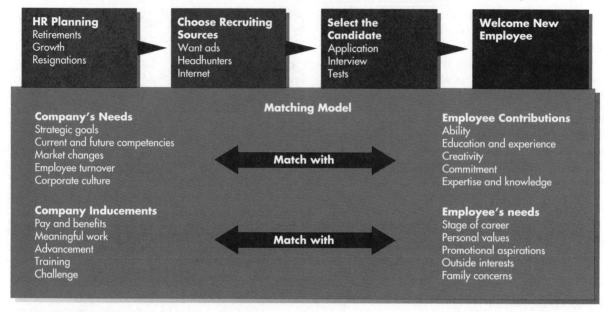

HR Planning	Choose Recruiting Sources	Select the Candidate	Welcome New Employee
Retirements Growth Resignations	Want ads Headhunters Internet	Application Interview Tests	

Matching Model

Company's Needs
Strategic goals
Current and future competencies
Market changes
Employee turnover
Corporate culture

Match with ←→

Employee Contributions
Ability
Education and experience
Creativity
Commitment
Expertise and knowledge

Company Inducements
Pay and benefits
Meaningful work
Advancement
Training
Challenge

Match with ←→

Employee's needs
Stage of career
Personal values
Promotional aspirations
Outside interests
Family concerns

EXHIBIT 9.4

Attracting an Effective Workforce

job analysis

The systematic process of gathering and interpreting information about the essential duties, tasks, and responsibilities of a job.

job description

A concise summary of the specific tasks and responsibilities of a particular job.

job specification

An outline of the knowledge, skills, education, and physical abilities needed to perform a job.

realistic job previews (RJPs)

A recruiting approach that gives applicants all pertinent and realistic information about the job and the organization.

Assessing Organizational Needs.   An important step in recruiting is to get a clear picture of what people the organization needs. Basic building blocks of HRM include job analysis, job descriptions, and job specifications. **Job analysis** is a systematic process of gathering and interpreting information about the essential duties, tasks, and responsibilities of a job, as well as about the context within which the job is performed.[39] To perform job analysis, managers or specialists ask about work activities and work flow, the degree of supervision given and received in the job, knowledge and skills needed, performance standards, working conditions, and so forth. The manager prepares a written **job description**, which is a clear and concise summary of the specific tasks, duties, and responsibilities, and **job specification**, which outlines the knowledge, skills, education, physical abilities, and other characteristics needed to perform the job.

Job analysis helps organizations recruit the right kind of people and match them to appropriate jobs. For example, to enhance internal recruiting, Sara Lee Corporation identified six functional areas and 24 significant skills that it wants its finance executives to develop, as illustrated in Exhibit 9.5. Managers are tracked on their development and moved into other positions to help them acquire the needed skills.[40]

Realistic Job Previews.   Job analysis helps enhance recruiting effectiveness by enabling the creation of **realistic job previews (RJPs)**. A realistic job preview gives applicants all pertinent and realistic information—positive and negative—about the job and the organization.[41] RJPs enhance employee satisfaction and reduce turnover because they facilitate matching individuals, jobs, and organizations. Individuals have a better basis on which to determine their suitability to the organization and "self-select" into or out of positions based on full information.

Legal Considerations.   Organizations must ensure their recruiting practices conform to the law. As discussed earlier in this chapter, EEO laws stipulate that recruiting and hiring decisions cannot discriminate on the basis of race, national origin, religion, or gender. The Americans with Disabilities Act (ADA) underscored the need for well-written job descriptions and specifications that accurately reflect the mental and physical dimensions of jobs. Affirmative action refers to the use of goals, timetables, or other methods in recruiting to promote the hiring, development, and retention of protected groups,

EXHIBIT 9.5

Sara Lee's Required Skills for Finance Executives

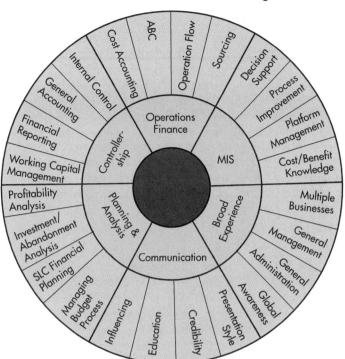

SOURCE: Adapted from Victoria Griffith, "When Only Internal Expertise Will Do," *CFO* (October 1998), 95–96, 102.

persons historically underrepresented in the workplace. For example, a city might establish a goal of recruiting one black firefighter for every white firefighter until the proportion of black firefighters is commensurate with the black population in the community.

Most large companies try to comply with affirmative action and EEO guidelines. Prudential Insurance Company's policy is presented in Exhibit 9.6. Prudential actively recruits employees and takes affirmative action steps to recruit individuals from all walks of life.

E-cruiting. One of the fastest-growing approaches to recruiting is use of the Internet, which dramatically extends an organization's recruiting reach.[42] Though traditional recruiting methods such as print advertisements and job fairs work well for many companies, e-cruiting, or recruiting job applicants online, offers access to a wider pool of applicants and can save time and money. In addition to posting job openings on company Web sites, many organizations use commercial recruiting sites such as

Take ACTION

Make sure you do a competent job analysis, as performance appraisal and accountability are based on it.

An Equal Opportunity Employer

Prudential recruits, hires, trains, promotes, and compensates individuals without regard to race, color, religion or creed, age, sex, marital status, national origin, ancestry, liability for service in the armed forces of the United States, status as a special disabled veteran or veteran of the Vietnam era, or physical or mental handicap.

This is official company policy because:
- we believe it is right
- it makes good business sense
- it is the law

We are also committed to an ongoing program of affirmative action in which members of underrepresented groups are actively sought out and employed for opportunities in all parts and at all levels of the company. In employing people from all walks of life, Prudential gains access to the full experience of our diverse society.

EXHIBIT 9.6

Prudential's Corporate Recruiting Policy

SOURCE: Prudential Insurance Company.

Monster.com, CareerBuilder.com, and hotjobs.com where job seekers can post their résumés and companies can search for qualified applicants. Forrester Research reports that approximately 2.5 million résumés are posted online, and the number is growing.[43] Companies as diverse as Prudential Insurance, Cisco Systems, and Atkinsson Congregational Church have used the Web for recruiting. Cisco, which gets about 66 percent of new hires from the Web, claims that e-cruiting has cut the time it takes to fill a job from 113 days down to 45 days.[44] Costs go down, too. The Employee Management Association estimates that the cost per hire using Internet recruiting is $377, versus $3,295 per hire using print media.[45] Organizations have not given up their traditional recruiting strategies, but the Internet has given HR managers new tools for searching the world to find the best available talent. The do-it-yourself retail giant B&Q combines e-cruiting with psychometric testing to eliminate unsuitable candidates and build a database of potential applicants.

B&Q

B&Q, the United Kingdom's version of The Home Depot, grew in eight years from 0 to 100 warehouse stores that employ about 250 staff members. In addition, the company has numerous supercenters that employ 40–60 staff members each. B&Q is creating about 1,000 new management positions and 5,000 staff and shopfloor jobs each year through the opening of new stores. With such rapid growth comes the problem of finding good people.

B&Q uses a unique recruiting tool: online pyschometric testing. The recruiting strategy has been used for all management applicants since July of 2002 and was later extended to applicants for any position. Applicants answer a series of questions that were developed over the course of seven years by Colin Gill, chief psychologist at Psychological Solutions. Much of Gill's research was done with B&Q staff, so executives believe the instrument is a good indicator of whether a person will succeed at the company. The test is immediately assessed by complex formulae that rate an applicant's suitability for the job. For some applicants, this serves as a self-selecting mechanism because the applicant sees that he or she will not be happy working in the B&Q culture.

Top executives like the unbiased nature of the online recruiting tool. Our image of candidates used to be founded on their [résumé]," says HR Director Mike Cutt. Now the initial screening is done blind, it is totally unbiased as to age, gender, and ethnic background. We think that's a big step forward in systematically avoiding the bias you would get in any recruitment drive."

By streamlining and eliminating bias during the initial stage of recruitment, the online recruiting system has helped B&Q dramatically improve the quality of its candidates. Cutt thinks it has helped the company spot employee talent and potential earlier and more carefully align training and career development activities.[46]

Other Recent Approaches to Recruiting. Organizations are finding other ways to enhance their recruiting success. One highly effective approach is getting referrals from current employees. A company's employees often know of someone who would be qualified for a position and fit in with the organization's culture. Many organizations offer cash awards to employees who submit names of people who subsequently accept employment because referral by current employees is one of the cheapest and most reliable methods of external recruiting.[47] The professional service firm Deloitte has shelled out more than $3.5 million in cash awards to employees who refer candidates through the "Refer Potential Movers and Shakers" program, the firm's single best source of high-talent hires.[48]

In addition, some companies turn to nontraditional sources to find dedicated employees, particularly when there is a tight labor market. Manufacturer Dee Zee, which makes aluminum truck accessories in a factory in Des Moines, Iowa, found a source of loyal, hard-working employees among refugees from Bosnia, Vietnam, and Kosovo.[49] Since

Take ACTION

When selecting an employee, make sure you have enough means of seeing all sides of the person's personality and qualifications. Do not just look at the superficial criteria.

1998, Bank of America has hired and trained more than 3,000 former welfare recipients in positions that offer the potential for promotions and long-term careers. Days Inn has experimented with hiring the homeless, offering them wages plus a room for a small fee. Recruiting on a global basis is on the rise, as well. Public schools are recruiting teachers from overseas. High-tech companies are looking for qualified workers in foreign countries because they cannot find people with the right skills in the United States.[50]

Selecting

The next step for managers is to select desired employees from the pool of recruited applicants. In the **selection** process, employers assess applicants' characteristics in an attempt to determine the "fit" between the job and applicant characteristics. Several selection devices are used for assessing applicant qualifications. The most frequently used are the application form, interview, employment test, and assessment center. HR professionals may use a combination of these devices to obtain a valid prediction of employee job performance. **Validity** refers to the relationship between one's score on a selection device and one's future job performance. A valid selection procedure will provide high scores that correspond to subsequent high job performance. One way to determine fit, as described in the Best Practices box, is to look at your customer base.

selection
The process of determining the skills, abilities, and other attributes a person needs to perform a particular job.

validity
The relationship between an applicant's score on a selection device and his or her future job performance.

Application Form. The **application form** is used to collect information about the applicant's education, previous job experience, and other background characteristics. Research in the life insurance industry shows that biographical information inventories can validly predict future job success.[51]

One pitfall to be avoided is the inclusion of questions irrelevant to job success. In line with affirmative action, the application form should not ask questions that will create an adverse impact on protected groups unless the questions are clearly related to the job.[52] For example, employers should not ask if the applicant rents or owns his

application form
A device for collecting information about an applicant's education, previous job experience, and other background characteristics.

BEST PRACTICES

Eastern Mountain Sports (EMS)

When Will Manzer bought sporting-goods chain Eastern Mountain Sports (EMS) last year, it had $200 million dollars in revenue. But careful analysis showed him that sales were starting to dip, as were profits, though overall profits in the apparel business were way up. Started in 1967 by a gritty mountain man, the company had gone more mainstream in recent years, moving away from technical gear like rock climbing shoes and kayaks to softer goods like fleece jackets and cotton sweaters. The company was now a tag-along in the industry. "EMS had become a Gap with climbing ropes," said Manzer. He knows he has to reshape the company to make it more competitive, that it has to bite the bullet to survive and grow again. He realized EMS had become too "safe" and was not differentiated to the outdoor athlete. "We have to become a brand. There's no way out." The wrong customers cost retailers a lot of money, so Manzer went after the passionate ones, as they are less work and bring more profits. Their ideal customer is the person living in primitive conditions, putting every last penny and off-work time into outdoor sports. Part of this process meant alienating the mainstream crowd, but Manzer knew it was necessary.

But in the process, Manzer saw he had to hire a new breed of worker. He started a system to identify key customers, whose lives revolved around their sport, and to offer them jobs. "Which is easier," asks an EMS executive, "teaching kids who can fold sweaters how to ice climb, or teaching ice climbers to fold sweaters?" The gearhead people know the business of sports, and their contacts in those sports are better than any expensive marketing campaign. To attract and keep those outdoor-enthusiast employees, EMS offers flexible hours with long sabbatical-like stretches of vacation time. Some of them go mountain climbing in the Himalayas or Thailand. After a year, any employee can take unpaid leave for 90 days. Manzer has learned that the best customers make the best employees.

SOURCE: Lucas Conley, "Climbing Back up the Mountain,' *Fast Company* (April 2005): 85–86.

or her own home because an applicant's response might adversely affect his or her chances at the job, minorities and women may be less likely to own a home, and home ownership is probably unrelated to job performance. By contrast, the CPA exam is relevant to job performance in a CPA firm; thus, it is appropriate to ask whether an applicant for employment has passed the CPA exam even if only one-half of all female or minority applicants have done so versus nine tenths of male applicants.

Interview.   The interview serves as a two-way communication channel that allows the organization and the applicant to collect information that would otherwise be difficult to obtain. This selection technique is used in almost every job category in nearly every organization. This is another area where the organization can get into legal trouble if the interviewer asks questions that violate EEO guidelines. Exhibit 9.7 lists some examples of appropriate and inappropriate interview questions.

Though widely used, the interview is not generally a valid predictor of job performance. Studies of interviewing have suggested that people tend to make snap judgments of others within the first few seconds of meeting them and only rarely change their opinions based on anything that occurs in the interview.[53] However, the interview as a selection tool has high face validity. That is, it seems valid to employers, and managers prefer to hire someone only after they have been through some form of interview, preferably face-to-face. The Focus on Skills box offers some tips for effective interviewing and provides a humorous look at some interview blunders. Today's organizations are trying

EXHIBIT 9.7

Employment Applications and Interviews: What Can You Ask?

Category	Okay to Ask	Inappropriate or Illegal to Ask
National origin	• The applicant's name • If applicant has ever worked under a different name	• The origin of applicant's name • Applicant's ancestry/ethnicity
Race	• Nothing	• Race or color of skin
Disabilities	• Whether applicant has any disabilities that might inhibit performance of job	• If applicant has any physical or menttal defects • If applicant has ever filed workers' compensation claim
Age	• If applicant is over 18	• Applicant's age • When applicant graduated from high school
Religion	• Nothing	• Applicant's religious affiliation • What religious holidays applicant observes
Criminal record	• If applicant has ever been convicted of a crime	• If applicant has ever been arrested
Marital/family status	• Nothing	• Marital status, number of children or planned children • Child care arrangements
Education and Experience	• Where applicant went to school • Prior work experience	• When applicant graduated • Hobbies
Citizenship	• If applicant has a legal right to work in the United States	• If applicant is a citizen of another country

SOURCE: Based on "Appropriate and Inappropriate Interview Questions," in George Bohlander, Scott Snell, and Arthur Sherman, *Managing Human Resources,* 12th ed. (Cincinnati, Ohio: South-Western College Publishing, 2001), 207; and "Guidelines to Lawful and Unlawful Preemployment Inquiries," Appendix E, in Robert L. Mathis and John H. Jackson, *Human Resource Management,* 2nd ed. (Cincinnati, Ohio: South-Western, 2002), 189–190.

different approaches to overcome the limitations of the interview. Some put candidates through a series of interviews, each one conducted by a different person and each one probing a different aspect of the candidate. Other companies, including Virginia Power and Philip Morris USA, use panel interviews, in which the candidate meets with several interviewers who take turns asking questions, to increase interview validity.[54] Microsoft and other high-tech companies often use puzzle questions, riddles, or other tricky queries to assess a candidate's creativity, problem-solving skills, and ability to think under pressure. Typical questions might include: "Why are manhole covers round rather than square?" or "How would you weigh a jet plane without using a scale?"[55] The idea is that people who can successfully handle these types of questions are more adept at solving the problems high-tech companies face in today's turbulent business environment.

Some organizations use computer-based interviews to complement traditional interviewing information. These typically require a candidate to answer a series of multiple-choice questions tailored to the specific job. The answers are compared to an ideal profile or to a profile developed on the basis of other candidates. Companies such as Pinkerton Security, Coopers & Lybrand, and Pic n' Pay Shoe Stores have found computer-based

FOCUS ON SKILLS

The Right Way to Interview a Job Applicant

A so-so interview usually nets a so-so employee. Many hiring mistakes can be prevented during the interview. The following techniques will ensure a successful interview:

1. *Know what you want.* Before the interview, prepare questions based on your knowledge of the job to be filled.

2. *Prepare a road map.* Develop questions that will reveal if the candidate has the correct background and qualifications. The questions should focus on previous experiences relevant to the current job.

3. *Use open-ended questions in which the right answer is not obvious.* Ask the applicant to give specific examples of previous work experiences. For example, do not ask, "Are you a hard worker?" or "Tell me about yourself." Instead ask, "Can you give me examples from your previous work history that reflect your level of motivation?" or "How did you go about getting your current job?"

4. *Do not ask questions irrelevant to the job.* This is particularly important when the irrelevant questions might adversely affect minorities or women.

5. *Listen; do not talk.* You should spend most of the interview listening. If you talk too much, the focus will shift to you, and you might miss important cues. One expert recommends stating all your questions right at the beginning of the interview. This forces you to sit back and listen and gives you a chance to watch a candidate's behavior and body language.

6. *Allow enough time so the interview will not be rushed.* Leave time for the candidate to ask questions about the job.

The types of questions the candidate asks can be an important clue to his or her interest in the job.

7. *Avoid reliance on your memory.* Request the applicant's permission to take notes; then do so unobtrusively during the interview or immediately after.

Even a well-planned interview may be disrupted by the unexpected. Here are some of the unusual things that have happened during job interviews, based on surveys of vice-presidents and human resource directors at major U.S. corporations:

- The applicant announced she had not had lunch and proceeded to eat a hamburger and french fries in the interviewer's office.

- When asked if he had any questions about the job, the candidate answered, "Can I get an advance on my paycheck?"

- The applicant chewed bubble gum and constantly blew bubbles.

- The job candidate said the main thing he was looking for in a job was a quiet place where no one would bother him.

- The job applicant challenged the interviewer to arm wrestle.

- The applicant dozed off and started snoring during the interview.

- When asked how she would handle a difficult situation, the candidate replied, "I'd let you do it."

SOURCES: James M. Jenks and Brian L. P. Zevnik, "ABCs of Job Interviewing," *Harvard Business Review* (July-August 1989): 38–42; Dr. Pierre Mornell, "Zero Defect Hiring," *Inc.* (March 1998): 75–83; Martha H. Peak, "What Color Is Your Bumbershoot?" *Management Review* (October 1989): 63; and Meridith Levinson, "How to Hire So You Don't Have to Fire," *CIO* (March 1, 2004): 72–80.

interviews to be valuable for searching out information regarding the applicant's honesty, work attitude, drug history, candor, dependability, and self-motivation.[56]

Employment Test. **Employment tests** may include intelligence tests, aptitude and ability tests, and personality inventories, particularly those shown to be valid predictors. Many companies are interested in personality inventories that measure such characteristics as openness to learning, initiative, responsibility, creativity, and emotional stability. Brian Kautz of Arnold Logistics has used a Web-based personality assessment called the Predictive Index (PI) to hire six people in Arnold's IT department since 2001, and all six still work at the company. The PI, originally developed in the 1950s, provides information about the working conditions that are most rewarding to an applicant and that make the person the most motivated and productive. The test is based on the notion that different types of jobs require different personality characteristics and behaviors.[57]

Assessment Center. First developed by psychologists at AT&T, assessment centers are used to select individuals with high potential for managerial careers by such organizations as IBM, General Electric (GE), and JCPenney.[58] **Assessment centers** present a series of managerial situations to groups of applicants over, say, a two-day or three-day period. One technique is the in-basket simulation, which requires the applicant to play the role of a manager who must decide how to respond to ten memos in his or her in-basket within a two-hour period. Panels of two or three trained judges observe the applicant's decisions and assess the extent to which they reflect interpersonal communication, and problem-solving skills.

Assessment centers have proven to be valid predictors of managerial success, and some organizations use them for hiring front-line workers as well. Mercury Communications, in England, uses an assessment center to select telecommunications customer assistants. Applicants participate in simulated exercises with customers and in various other exercises designed to assess their listening skills, customer sensitivity, and ability to cope under pressure.[59] Many organizations also work with consulting companies such as Development Dimensions International (DDI), which makes extensive use of assessments to help fill jobs—whether it be a supermarket checker or a CEO—with the right people. DDI works closely with clients to determine what skills and competencies are needed for the job and designs the assessment exercises to assess those specific areas.[60]

Developing an Effective Workforce

Following selection, the next goal of HRM is to develop employees into an effective workforce. Development includes training and development, and performance appraisal.

Training and Development

Training and development represent a planned effort by an organization to facilitate employees' learning of job-related skills and behaviors.[61] Organizations spend nearly $100 billion each year on training. Training may occur in various forms. The most common method is on-the-job training. In **on-the-job training (OJT)**, an experienced employee is asked to take a new employee "under his or her wing" and show the newcomer how to perform job duties. OJT has many advantages, such as few out-of-pocket costs for training facilities, materials, or instructor fees and easy transfer of learning back to the job. When implemented well, OJT is considered the fastest and most effective means of facilitating learning in the workplace.[62] One type of OJT involves moving people to various jobs within the organization, where they work with experienced

---

employment tests

A written or computer-based test designed to measure a particular attribute such as intelligence or aptitude.

assessment centers

A technique for selecting individuals with high managerial potential based on their performances on a series of simulated managerial tasks.

on-the-job training (OJT)

A type of training in which an experienced employee "adopts" a new employee to teach him or her how to perform job duties.

employees to learn different tasks. This cross-training may place an employee in a new position for as short a time as a few hours or for as long as a year, enabling the employee to develop new skills and giving the organization greater flexibility.

Another type of OJT is mentoring, which means a more experienced employee is paired with a newcomer or a less-experienced worker to provide guidance, support, and learning opportunities. An innovative program at GE has turned the mentoring relationship upside down, pairing older, senior executives with little or no computer knowledge and expertise with young, computer and Internet-savvy employees to help the old-timers learn about the world of e-business.[63]

Other frequently used training methods include the following:

- *Orientation training*, in which newcomers are introduced to the organization's culture, standards, and goals

- *Classroom training*, including lectures, films, audiovisual techniques, and simulations

- *Self-directed learning*, also called programmed instruction, which involves the use of books, manuals, or computers to provide subject matter in highly organized and logical sequences that require employees to answer a series of questions about the material

- *Computer-based training*, sometimes called e-training, including computer-assisted instruction, Web-based training, and teletraining. (As with self-directed learning, the employee works at his or her own pace and instruction is individualized, but the training program is interactive and more complex, nonstructured information can be communicated.)

Exhibit 9.8 shows the most frequently used types and methods of training in today's organizations.

Corporate Universities. A recent popular approach to training and development is the corporate university. A **corporate university** is an in-house training and education facility that offers broad-based learning opportunities for employees—and frequently for customers, suppliers, and strategic partners as well—throughout their careers.[64] The number of corporate universities ballooned during the 1990s, with more than 2,000 in operation by 2001. With the economic decline of the early 2000s, many companies cut budgets for training, but smart managers at places like Intel, Harley-Davidson, and Capital One kept pumping money into their corporate universities to keep building human capital.[65] Perhaps the most well-known example of a corporate university is Hamburger University, McDonald's worldwide training center, which has been in existence for more than 40 years. Tens of thousands of FedEx employees, from couriers to top executives, have attended training at FedEx's Leadership Institute located near Memphis, Tennessee. And the U.S. Department of Defense runs Defense Acquisition University to provide ongoing training to 129,000 military and civilian workers in acquisitions, technology, and logistics.[66] Though corporate universities have extended their reach with new technology that enables distance learning via videoconferencing and online education, most emphasize the importance of classroom interaction. Participants at a recent corporate university conference indicated they try to keep electronic forms of learning to about 25 percent of their course offerings.[67]

Promotion from Within. Another way to further employee development is through promotion from within, which can help companies retain valuable employees. This provides challenging assignments, prescribes new responsibilities, and helps employees grow by expanding and developing their abilities. The Peebles Hydro Hotel, in Scotland, is passionate about promoting from within as a way to retain good people and

corporate university

An in-house training and education facility that offers broad-based learning opportunities for employees.

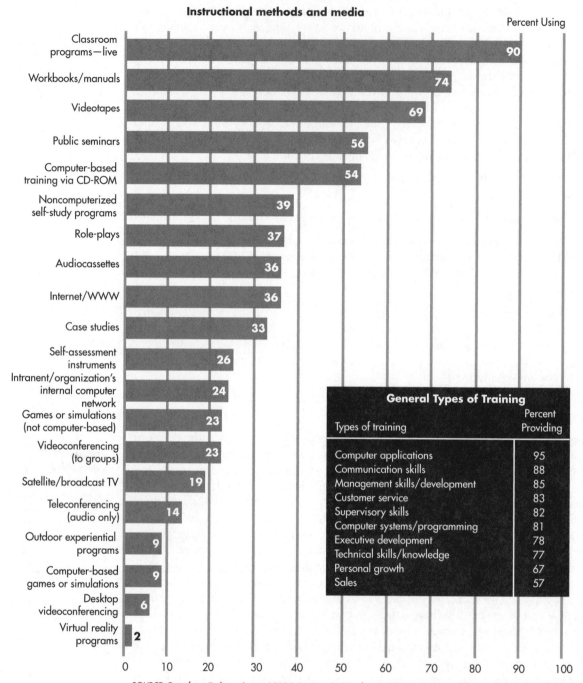

Instructional methods and media

Percent Using

Method	Percent
Classroom programs—live	90
Workbooks/manuals	74
Videotapes	69
Public seminars	56
Computer-based training via CD-ROM	54
Noncomputerized self-study programs	39
Role-plays	37
Audiocassettes	36
Internet/WWW	36
Case studies	33
Self-assessment instruments	26
Intranet/organization's internal computer network	24
Games or simulations (not computer-based)	23
Videoconferencing (to groups)	23
Satellite/broadcast TV	19
Teleconferencing (audio only)	14
Outdoor experiential programs	9
Computer-based games or simulations	9
Desktop videoconferencing	6
Virtual reality programs	2

0   10   20   30   40   50   60   70   80   90   100

General Types of Training

Types of training	Percent Providing
Computer applications	95
Communication skills	88
Management skills/development	85
Customer service	83
Supervisory skills	82
Computer systems/programming	81
Executive development	78
Technical skills/knowledge	77
Personal growth	67
Sales	57

SOURCE: Data from "Industry Report 1999," *Training 36* (October 1999), 54, 56. Reprinted with permission from the October 1999 issue of *Training* magazine. Copyright 1999, Bill Communications, Minneapolis, Minn. All rights reserved. Not for resale.

EXHIBIT 9.8

Types and Methods of Training

give them opportunities for growth. A maid can be promoted to head housekeeper, a wine waitress to restaurant head, and a student worker to deputy manager. The hotel provides constant training in all areas. These techniques, combined with a commitment to job flexibility, have helped the hotel retain high-quality workers at a time when others in the tourism and hospitality industry are suffering from a shortage of skilled labor. Isobelle Nairn started at Hydro 24 years ago as a receptionist and is still there, organizing 350 conferences a year as the hotel's conference coordinator. Staff members with 10, 15, or 20 years of service are common at Hydro.[68]

Performance Appraisal

Performance appraisal is another important technique for developing an effective workforce. **Performance appraisal** comprises the steps of observing and assessing employee performance, recording the assessment, and providing feedback to the employee. During performance appraisal, skillful managers give feedback and praise concerning the acceptable elements of the employee's performance. They describe performance areas that need improvement. Employees can use this information to change their job performance.

Performance appraisal can reward high performers with merit pay, recognition, and other rewards. However, the most recent thinking is that linking performance appraisal to rewards has unintended consequences. The idea is that performance appraisal should be ongoing, and not something done once a year as part of a consideration of raises.

Generally, HRM professionals concentrate on two things to make performance appraisal a positive force in their organizations: (1) the accurate assessment of performance through the development and application of assessment systems, such as rating scales and (2) training managers to use the performance appraisal interview, so managers can provide feedback that will reinforce good performance and motivate employee development.

Assessing Performance Accurately. To obtain an accurate performance rating, managers acknowledge that jobs are multidimensional and performance thus may be multidimensional as well. For example, a sports broadcaster may perform well on the job knowledge dimension; that is, she or he may be able to report facts and figures about the players and describe which rule applies when there is a questionable play on the field. But the same sports broadcaster may not perform as well on another dimension, such as communication. She or he may be unable to express the information in a colorful way that interests the audience or may interrupt the other broadcasters.

If performance is to be rated accurately, the performance appraisal system should require the rater to assess each relevant performance dimension. A multidimensional form increases the usefulness of the performance appraisal and facilitates employee growth and development.

A recent trend in performance appraisal is called **360-degree feedback**, a process that uses multiple raters, including self-rating, as a way to increase awareness of strengths and weaknesses and guide employee development. Members of the appraisal group may include supervisors, co-workers, and customers, as well as the individual, thus providing appraisal of the employee from various perspectives.[69] One study found that 26 percent of companies used some type of multirater performance appraisal in 2000, up from 11 percent in 1995.[70]

Other alternative performance evaluation methods have been gaining ground. One controversial method of evaluating managers, which is nevertheless growing in popularity, is the performance review ranking system.[71] As most commonly used, a manager evaluates his or her direct reports relative to one another and categorizes each on a scale, such as A = outstanding performance, B = high-middle performance, or C = in need of improvement. Most companies routinely fire those managers falling in the bottom 10 percent of the ranking. Capital One, Ford Motor Company, Cisco Systems, Intel, GE, Microsoft, and Sun Microsystems all use versions of the ranking system. Proponents say the technique provides an effective way to assess performance and offer guidance for employee development. Critics of these systems, sometimes called rank and yank, argue they are based on subjective judgments, produce skewed results, and

performance appraisal

The process of observing and evaluating an employee's performance, recording the assessment, and providing feedback to the employee.

Take *ACTION*

Frequent feedback to employees is more effective than the yearly evaluation.

360-degree feedback

A process that uses multiple raters, including self-rating, to appraise employee performance and guide development.

discriminate against employees who are "different" from the mainstream. A class-action lawsuit charges that Ford's ranking system discriminates against older managers. Use of the system has triggered employee lawsuits at Conoco and Microsoft, and employment lawyers warn that other suits will follow.[72] Nevertheless, appropriate use of performance ranking has been useful for many companies. A variation of the system is helping Applebee's retain quality workers in the high-turnover restaurant business.

Applebee's	Most people working in fast food and casual dining restaurants do not stay long. Turnover of hourly employees is a perpetual problem, averaging more than 200 percent a year in the casual dining sector for the past 30 years. Applebee's managers wanted to reduce their turnover rate and wanted to focus their retention efforts on the best people.

A key aspect of the new retention strategy was the Applebee's Performance Management system, called ApplePM. ApplePM took performance appraisal to the Web, making it easier for managers to complete the evaluations and—more importantly—put the results to good use. Twice a year each hourly employee conducts a self-evaluation that covers nine areas: appearance, reliability, fun (including the ability to tolerate frustration), ability, guest service, willingness to be a team player, initiative, stamina, and cooperation. The store manager does the same for each employee; then they meet, compare results, and discuss areas for improvement. But the feedback loop does not end there. With a few mouse clicks, the manager looks at how each employee ranks with respect to all others in the restaurant, separating employees into the top 20 percent, the middle 60 percent, and the bottom 20 percent.

The system is not the basis for firing low-ranking employees, but they usually leave soon enough anyway. Its value lies in helping managers focus their retention efforts on the top 20 percent, who have management potential, and provide training and development opportunities to the middle 60 percent, who have the potential to move up the ranking. Concentrating on certain employees is paying off for Applebee's. The turnover rate dropped almost 50 percentage points in fewer than two years.[73]

Performance Evaluation Errors.   Though we would like to believe that every manager assesses employees' performance in a careful and bias-free manner, researchers have identified several rating problems.[74] One of the most dangerous is **stereotyping**, which occurs when a rater places an employee into a class or category based on one or a few traits or characteristics, for example, stereotyping an older worker as slower and more difficult to train. Another rating error is the **halo effect**, in which a manager gives an employee the same rating on all dimensions even if his or her performance is good on some dimensions and poor on others.

One approach to overcome performance evaluation errors is to use a behavior-based rating technique, such as the behaviorally anchored rating scale. The **behaviorally anchored rating scale (BARS)** is developed from critical incidents pertaining to job performance. Each job performance scale is anchored with specific behavioral statements that describe varying degrees of performance. By relating employee performance to specific incidents, raters can more accurately evaluate an employee's performance.[75]

Exhibit 9.9 illustrates the BARS method for evaluating a production line supervisor. The production supervisor's job can be broken into several dimensions, such as equipment maintenance, employee training, or work scheduling. A BARS should be developed for each dimension. The dimension in Exhibit 9.9 is work scheduling. Good performance is represented by a 4 or 5 on the scale and unacceptable performance as a 1 or 2. If a production supervisor's job has eight dimensions, the total performance evaluation will be the sum of the scores for each of eight scales.

stereotyping

Placing an employee into a class or category based on one or a few traits or characteristics.

halo effect

A type of rating error that occurs when an employee receives the same rating on all dimensions regardless of his or her performance on individual ones.

behaviorally anchored rating scale (BARS)

A rating technique that relates an employee's performance to specific job-related incidents.

Job: Production Line Supervisor
Work Dimension: Work Scheduling

9 — Develop a comprehensive schedule, document it, obtain required approvals, and distribute it to all concerned.

Plan, communicate, and observe target dates and update the status of operations relative to plans, making schedule modifications as quickly as necessary. — 8

7 — Experience minor operational problems but still communicate effectively, laying out all parts of the job and schedules for each.

Usually satisfy time constraints, with time and cost overruns coming up infrequently. — 6

5 — Make a list of due dates and revise them but are frequently surprised by unforeseen events.

Have a sound plan but neglect to keep track of target dates or to report schedule slippages or other problems as they occur. — 4

3 — Plan poorly, with ill-defined, unrealistic time schedules.

Have no plan or schedule of work and no concept of realistic due dates. — 2

1 — Fail consistently to complete work on time because of no planning or to express any interest in how to improve.

SOURCES: Based on J. P. Campbell, M. D. Dunnette, R. D. Arvey, and L. V. Hellervik, "The Development and Evaluation of Behaviorally Based Rating Scales," *Journal of Applied Psychology 57* (1973), 15–22; and Francine Alexander, "Performance Appraisals," *Small Business Reports* (March 1989), 20–29.

EXHIBIT 9.9

Example of a Behaviorally Anchored Rating Scale

Maintaining an Effective Workforce

Now we turn to the topic of how managers and HRM professionals maintain a workforce that has been recruited and developed. Maintenance of the current workforce involves compensation, wage and salary systems, benefits, and occasional terminations.

Compensation

The term **compensation** refers to all monetary payments and all goods or commodities used in lieu of money to reward employees.[76] An organization's compensation structure includes wages and/or salaries and benefits such as health insurance, paid vacations, or employee fitness centers. Developing an effective compensation system is an important part of HRM because it attracts and retains talented workers. In addition, a company's compensation system has an impact on strategic performance.[77] HR managers design the pay and benefits systems to fit company strategy and to provide compensation equity.

Wage and Salary Systems. Ideally, management's strategy for the organization should be a critical determinant of the features and operations of the pay system.[78] For example, managers may have the goal of maintaining or improving profitability or market share by stimulating employee performance. Thus, they should design and use a merit pay system rather than a system based on other criteria such as seniority.

The most common approach to employee compensation is job-based pay, which means linking compensation to the specific tasks an employee performs. However, these systems present several problems. For one thing, job-based pay may fail to reward the type of learning behavior needed for the organization to adapt and survive

compensation

Monetary payments (wages, salaries) and nonmonetary goods/commodities (benefits, vacations) used to reward employees.

Take *ACTION*

As a manager, remember that low pay often means higher turnover, which costs you more money.

in today's environment. In addition, these systems reinforce an emphasis on organizational hierarchy and centralized decision making and control, which are inconsistent with the growing emphasis on employee participation and increased responsibility.[79]

Skill-based pay systems are becoming increasingly popular in large and small companies, including Sherwin-Williams, Au Bon Pain, and Quaker Oats. Employees with higher skill levels receive higher pay than those with lower skill levels. At Quaker Oats pet food plant in Topeka, Kansas, for example, employees start at $8.75 per hour but can reach a top hourly rate of $14.50 when they master a series of skills.[80] Also called competency-based pay, skill-based pay systems encourage employees to develop their skills and competencies, thus making them more valuable to the organization as well as more employable if they leave their current jobs.

Compensation Equity.   Whether the organization uses job-based pay or skill-based pay, good managers strive to maintain a sense of fairness and equity within the pay structure and, thereby, fortify employee morale. **Job evaluation** refers to the process of determining the value or worth of jobs within an organization through an examination of job content. Job evaluation techniques enable managers to compare similar and dissimilar jobs and to determine internally equitable pay rates, that is, pay rates that employees believe are fair compared with those for other jobs in the organization.

Organizations want to make sure their pay rates are fair compared to other companies. HRM managers may obtain **wage and salary surveys** that show what other organizations pay incumbents in jobs that match a sample of "key" jobs selected by the organization. These surveys are available from a number of sources, including the U.S. Bureau of Labor Statistics National Compensation Survey.

Pay for Performance.   Many of today's organizations develop compensation plans based on a pay-for-performance standard to raise productivity and cut labor costs in a competitive global environment. **Pay-for-performance**, also called incentive pay, means tying at least part of compensation to employee effort and performance, whether it be through merit-based pay, bonuses, team incentives, or various gainsharing or profit-sharing plans.

Benefits

The best HR managers know that a compensation package requires more than money. Though wage and salary is an important component, it is only a part. Equally important are the benefits offered by the organization. Benefits make up 40 percent of labor costs in the United States.[81]

Some benefits are required by law, such as Social Security, unemployment compensation, and workers' compensation. In addition, companies with 50 or more employees are required by the Family and Medical Leave Act to give up to twelve weeks of unpaid leave for such things as the birth or adoption of a child, the serious illness of a spouse or family member, or an employee's serious illness. Other types of benefits, such as health insurance, vacations, and on-site day care or fitness centers, are not required by law but are provided by organizations to maintain an effective workforce.

One reason that benefits make up such a large portion of the compensation package is that health care costs have been increasing so quickly. Many organizations are requiring that employees absorb a greater share of the cost of medical benefits, such as through higher co-payments and deductibles.

Computerization has cut the time and expense of administering benefits programs tremendously. At companies such as Wells Fargo and LG&E Energy, employees access their benefits package through an Intranet, creating a "self-service" benefits administration.[82] This enables employees to change their benefits selections easily. Today's organizations realize that the "one-size-fits-all" benefits package is no longer appropriate, so

---

job evaluation

The process of determining the value of jobs within an organization through an examination of job content.

wage and salary surveys

Surveys that show what other organizations pay incumbents in jobs that match a sample of "key" jobs selected by the organization.

pay-for-performance

Incentive pay that ties at least part of compensation to employee effort and performance.

they frequently offer cafeteria-plan benefits packages that allow employees to select the benefits of greatest value to them.[83] Other companies use surveys to determine which combination of fixed benefits is most desirable. The benefits packages provided by large companies attempt to meet the needs of all employees.

Termination

Despite the best efforts of line managers and HRM professionals, the organization will lose employees. Some will retire, others will depart voluntarily for other jobs, and still others will be forced out through mergers and cutbacks or for poor performance.

The value of termination for maintaining an effective workforce is twofold. First, employees who are poor performers can be dismissed. Productive employees often resent disruptive, low-performing employees who are allowed to stay with the company and receive pay and benefits comparable to theirs. Second, employers can use exit interviews as a valuable HR tool, regardless of whether the employee leaves voluntarily or is forced out. An **exit interview** is an interview conducted with departing employees to determine why they are leaving. The value of the exit interview is to provide an excellent and inexpensive way to learn about pockets of dissatisfaction within the organization and, hence, reduce future turnover.

When companies experience downsizing through mergers or because of global competition or a shifting economy, often a large number of managers and workers are terminated at the same time. In these cases, enlightened companies try to find a smooth transition for departing employees. For example, GE laid off employees in three gradual steps. It set up a reemployment center to assist employees in finding new jobs or in learning new skills. It provided counseling in how to write a résumé and conduct a job search. Additionally, GE placed an advertisement in local newspapers saying that these employees were available.[84] By showing genuine concern in helping laid-off employees, a company communicates the value of human resources and helps maintain a positive corporate culture. By showing genuine concern in helping place laid-off employees, a company communicates the value of human resources and helps maintain a positive corporate culture, as shown on the following page.

exit interview
An interview conducted with departing employees to determine the reasons for their termination.

© Elena Dorfman

CONCEPT CONNECTION

*Managers at Agilent Technologies, an $8.3 billion technology spin-off from Hewlett-Packard, have worked hard to gain employees' trust. When **downsizing** became necessary and managers had to terminate a large number of workers, they made the layoffs easier by showing empathy and respect for employees. As a result, after the workers at this Agilent plant in Newark, California, were told their plant was closing, they upped production higher than ever before—out of respect for their managers and concern for co-workers in other plants. Agilent's humane approach helped the company attain a spot on Fortune magazine's list of Best Companies to Work For even in the midst of downsizing and cost-cutting.*

| **Hunt Tractor** | Imagine you get layed off or downsized, and your employer hires a grief counselor to help you deal with the trauma. |

Then imagine a company that never lays off anyone. Construction equipment dealership Hunt Tractor's president, Frank Miske, Jr., says he does not even "fantasize" about axing workers. "We don't lay people off because we don't want to lose them. Besides that, it's not morally right to lay them off because loyal employees built this company," which has been profitable since it began in 1969.

Hunt Tractor belongs to a rare group of businesses that have never laid off anyone. During down times, chairman and WWII naval hero Roy Hunt keeps workers busy with painting, roofing, building renovation, training, machine repairs and tidying up. What does the company see as the benefits? High rates of retention of its highly skilled workers, increased productivity, lower recruiting costs, superior customers service due to extremely loyal and satisfied employees, and costs savings because of lower turnover and absenteeism. Not a bad deal.

Roy Hunt knows all too well the difficulties of layoffs and then rehiring later when business picks up. "Our people are not robots," he says. "You can't just take somebody from off the street and expect them to do the job." He gets tired of reading all the headlines about cold and uncaring companies which eliminate thousands of jobs at will. "Our business isn't run like that," he adds. "I'd like to dispel the notion that we're all only interested in the bottom line."[85]

Meeting the Challenge of Diversity

Many companies have faced difficulties with issues of diversity. In recent years, high-profile racial discrimination or harassment lawsuits have been filed against Texaco, Lockheed Martin, Coca-Cola, and Boeing. Mitsubishi is still reeling from the effects of a sexual harassment lawsuit charging that managers ignored complaints that women were regularly groped on the factory floor and made to endure crude jokes and lewd photographs.[86]

Diversity in the population, the workforce, and the marketplace is a fact of life no manager can afford to ignore. In addition, diversity issues have become more complex than they were 30 years ago. Among the groups now seeking full inclusion in the workforce, many are not considered back, including the disabled, the obese, and non-heterosexuals. Managing diversity today entails recruiting, training, valuing, and maximizing the potential of people who reflect the broad spectrum of society in all areas: gender, race, age, disability, ethnicity, religion, sexual orientation, education, and economic level.

Many companies, including IBM, Pfizer, Allstate Insurance, and Ford Motor Company, are finding innovative ways to integrate diversity initiatives into their business. These initiatives teach current employees to value differences, direct corporate recruiting efforts, influence supplier decisions, and provide development training for women and minorities. Smart managers value diversity and enforce the value in daily decision making. One company that strives to be on the cutting edge of diversity is MTV, as shown in the Focus on Innovation box.

Today's companies reflect the U.S. image as a melting pot, but with a difference. In the past, the United States was a place where people of different national origins, ethnicities, races, and religions came together and blended to resemble one another. Opportunities for advancement were limited to those workers who fit easily into the mainstream of the larger culture. Some immigrants chose desperate measures to fit in, such as abandoning their native languages, changing their last names, and sacrificing their own unique cultures. In essence, everyone in workplace organizations was encouraged to share similar beliefs, values, and lifestyles despite differences in gender, race, and ethnicity.[87]

FOCUS ON INNOVATION

MTV Desi

One of the newest stars on MTV is 28-year old Reshma Taufiq, who was the first to audition for the new MTV channel aimed at Desis, second generation immigrants from India. She lives in Queens, NY, is fluent in English and Hindi and she wears navel-baring bodices over tight-fitting jeans. She's a rising R&B singer who also conducts radio phone-in quizzes on Bollywood trivia, a frequent visitor on the desi party scene, a woman who thinks arranged marriages aren't as bad as Americans think, and a software engineer for Hewlett-Packard.

Another new host is the 29 year-old bearded comedian and lawyer Azhar Usman. Recruited by an MTV executive, who said: "We're going to redefine the identity of the MTV host. It doesn't have to be someone sexy and good-looking." His new MTV character: Vijay the V.J., who has a rather exaggerated and funny accent.

MTV is counting on a demographic ready for its own channel, like Sri-Lankan Tara Austin from Los Angeles. "I am just an American girl at the end of the day, but I have a strong South Asian background. I eat with my hands, you know? We're, like, so hungry for hearing our own culture."

Three new channels are set to air for MTV: Desi, Chi for Chinese-Americans and MTV K for Korean-Americans. Desi will be the prototype, with Bollywood videos, English-Gujarati hip-hop, electronic tabla music, funny skits relating to Asian-American generational conflicts, documentary clips of desis, bicultural artist interviews and live desi house parties. The Chinese channel will include Mandarin rock, Chinese-American rap and Canto pop, while the Korean version will feature South Korean hip-hop and the exciting Korean-American pop culture.

MTV is ahead of the curve in understanding that these transnational youths have different tastes than average American youth. "If you're a young Chinese-American or Indian-American, what channel do you tune into to see yourself, to see artists that reflect your lifestyle?" asked 44 year-old MTV manager of MTV World Nusrat Durrani, who has a missionary zeal about the new channels, being an immigrant himself from India. "This country has had the African-American experience, the Hispanic-American experience, and now it is the time for the third-largest group, the Asian-Americans."

SOURCE: *Deborah Sontag*, I Want My Hyphenated-Identity MTV, New York Times, Jun 19, 2005. pg. 2.1

Now organizations recognize that everyone is different, and the differences people bring to the workplace are valuable.[88] Rather than expecting all employees to adopt similar attitudes and values, managers are learning that these differences enable their companies to compete globally and to tap into rich sources of new talent. Though diversity in North America has been a reality for some time, genuine efforts to accept and manage diverse people began only in recent years. Exhibit 9.10 lists some interesting milestones in the history of corporate diversity.

This chapter introduces the topic of diversity, its causes and consequences. We will look at some of the challenges minorities face, ways managers deal with workforce diversity, and organizational responses to create an environment that welcomes and values diverse employees. This chapter will look at issues of sexual harassment, global diversity, and new approaches to managing diversity in today's workplace.

Valuing Diversity

Top managers say their companies value diversity for a number of reasons, such as to give the organization access to a broader range of opinions and viewpoints, to reflect an increasingly diverse customer base, to obtain the best talent in a competitive environment, and to demonstrate the company's commitment to "doing the right thing."[89] Moreover, a survey commissioned by *The New York Times* found that 91 percent of job seekers think diversity programs make a company a better place to work. Nearly all minority job seekers said they would prefer to work in a diverse workplace.[90]

However, many managers are ill-prepared to handle diversity issues. Many Americans grew up in racially unmixed neighborhoods and had little exposure to people substantially different from themselves.[91] The challenge is particularly great when

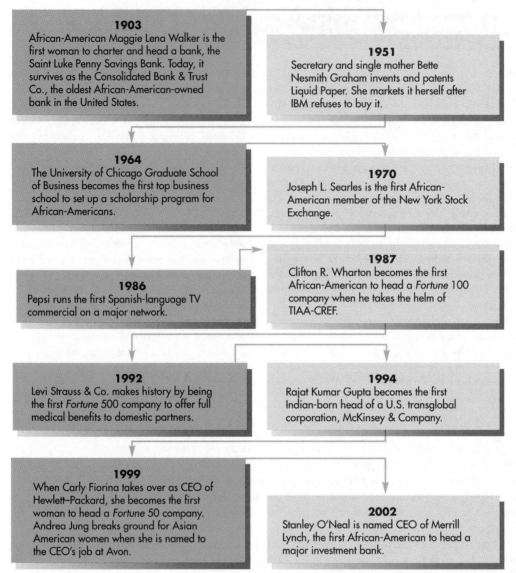

1903
African-American Maggie Lena Walker is the first woman to charter and head a bank, the Saint Luke Penny Savings Bank. Today, it survives as the Consolidated Bank & Trust Co., the oldest African-American-owned bank in the United States.

1951
Secretary and single mother Bette Nesmith Graham invents and patents Liquid Paper. She markets it herself after IBM refuses to buy it.

1964
The University of Chicago Graduate School of Business becomes the first top business school to set up a scholarship program for African-Americans.

1970
Joseph L. Searles is the first African-American member of the New York Stock Exchange.

1986
Pepsi runs the first Spanish-language TV commercial on a major network.

1987
Clifton R. Wharton becomes the first African-American to head a *Fortune* 100 company when he takes the helm of TIAA-CREF.

1992
Levi Strauss & Co. makes history by being the first *Fortune* 500 company to offer full medical benefits to domestic partners.

1994
Rajat Kumar Gupta becomes the first Indian-born head of a U.S. transglobal corporation, McKinsey & Company.

1999
When Carly Fiorina takes over as CEO of Hewlett–Packard, she becomes the first woman to head a *Fortune* 50 company. Andrea Jung breaks ground for Asian American women when she is named to the CEO's job at Avon.

2002
Stanley O'Neal is named CEO of Merrill Lynch, the first African-American to head a major investment bank.

SOURCE: "Spotlight on Diversity," special advertising section, *MBA Jungle* (March–April 2003), 58–61.

EXHIBIT 9.10

Some Milestones in the History of Corporate Diversity in the United States

working with people from other countries and cultures. For example, one recent challenge at IBM involved a new immigrant, a Muslim woman who was required to have a photo taken for a company identification badge. She protested that her religious beliefs required that, as a married woman, she wear a veil and not expose her face to men in public. A typical American manager, schooled in traditional management training, might insist that she have the photo taken or hit the door. Fortunately, IBM has a well-developed diversity program and managers worked out a satisfactory compromise.[92] Consider some other mistakes that American managers could easily make:[93]

- To reward a Vietnamese employee's high performance, her manager promoted her, placing her at the same level as her husband, who also worked at the factory. Rather than being pleased, the worker became upset and declined the promotion because Vietnamese husbands are expected to have a higher status than their wives.

- A manager, having learned that a friendly pat on the arm or back would make work-ers feel good, took every chance to touch his subordinates. His Asian employees hated being touched and, thus, started avoiding him, and several asked for transfers.

- A manager declined a gift offered by a new employee, an immigrant who wanted to show gratitude for her job. He was concerned about ethics and explained the company's policy about not accepting gifts. The employee was so insulted, she quit.

These issues related to cultural diversity are difficult and real. But before discussing how companies handle them, let us define diversity and explore people's attitudes toward it.

Attitudes toward Diversity

Valuing diversity by recognizing, welcoming, and cultivating differences among people so they can develop their unique talents and be effective organizational members is dif-ficult to achieve. **Ethnocentrism** is the belief that one's own group and subculture are inherently superior to other groups and cultures. Ethnocentrism makes it difficult to value diversity. Viewing one's own culture as the best culture is a natural tendency among most people. Moreover, the business world still tends to reflect the values, behaviors, and assumptions based on the experiences of a rather homogeneous, white, middle-class, male workforce.[94] Indeed, most theories of management presume that workers share similar values, beliefs, motivations, and attitudes about work and life in general. These theories presume one set of behaviors best helps an organization to be productive and effective and, therefore, should be adopted by all employees.[95]

ethnocentrism
The belief that one's own group and subculture are inherently superior to other groups and cultures.

Take a moment to complete the instrument below that pertains to your knowledge about diversity.

Diversity and Work Quiz

1. Women account for 47 percent on the total U.S. workforce.   T   F

2. By 2006, women will account for 50 percent of the total growth in the labor force. T   F

3. Of divorced women, 75 percent are in labor force, while 52 percent of married women work. T   F

4. The largest group occupational group for women is secretaries, while the sec-ond largest is cashiers. T   F

5. About 4 million women hold more than one job. T   F

6. Women's 1999 median earnings working full time, year-round was $28,324. T   F

7. In families with a working wife, the median income is $68,000; a family with-out a wife in the paid labor force is $40,000. T   F

8. Fourteen percent of women over the age of 65 live below the poverty line, but only 7 percent of men do. T   F

9. The number of working women has doubled since 1970, from 30 million to 60 million. T   F

10. Fifty-five percent of women with infants under the age of 1 are in the labor force. T   F

11. Women earn 80 cents on the dollar compared to men. T   F

12. Twenty-four percent of wives earn more than their husbands. T   F

13. The highest weekly earnings for women come from which group: lawyers, engineers, or physicians? _____

14. By the year 2050, what percentage of the total U.S. population will be Asians, Hispanics, blacks, or other non-whites? _____

15. Of the 43 million people in the United States with disabilities, how many are working age (16–64)? _____
How many are employed? _____
How many unemployed want to work? _____

16. What percentage of the total U.S. population speaks a language other than English at home? _____
What percentage of those speaks Spanish? _____

17. Of the 8.7 million immigrants who arrived in the United States between 1980–1990, what percentage has college degrees? _____
What percentage of U.S. natives has college degrees? _____
What percentage of male versus female? _____

18. According to a recent *Newsweek* poll, what percentage of Americans believes gays and lesbians should be given equal rights and opportunities in the workplace?

_____

19. What are the two most racially and ethnically diverse states in the United States? _____
The two least? _____

20. By 2020, what percentage of U.S. population will be 65 or older?

_____

Between 1998–2008, what will be the percentage increase of workers 55 and older?

_____

monoculture

A culture that accepts only one way of doing things and one set of values and beliefs, which can cause problems for minority employees.

Ethnocentric viewpoints and a standard set of cultural practices produce a **monoculture,** a culture that accepts only one way of doing things and one set of values and beliefs, which can cause problems for minority employees. People of color, women, gays, the disabled, the elderly, and other diverse employees may feel undue pressure to conform, may be victims of stereotyping attitudes, and may be presumed deficient because they are different. White, heterosexual men, many of whom themselves do not fit the notions of the "ideal" employee, may also feel uncomfortable with the monoculture and resent stereotypes that label white males as racists and sexists. Valuing diversity means ensuring that all people are given equal opportunities in the workplace.[96]

The goal for organizations seeking cultural diversity is pluralism rather than a monoculture and ethnorelativism rather than ethnocentrism. **Ethnorelativism** is the belief that groups and subcultures are inherently equal. **Pluralism** means that an organization accommodates several subcultures. Movement toward pluralism seeks to integrate into the organization the employees who otherwise would feel isolated and ignored. The Focus on Diversity box shows that dealing with a unique culture is the goal of Black Entertainment Television.

Most organizations must undertake conscious efforts to shift from a monoculture perspective to one of pluralism. For example, a recent report from the National Bureau of Economic Research, entitled *Are Greg and Emily More Employable than Lakisha and Jamal?*, shows that employers often unconsciously discriminate against job applicants based solely on the Afrocentric or black-sounding names on their résumé. In interviews prior to the research, most HR managers surveyed said they expected only a small gap and some expected to find a pattern of reverse discrimination. The results showed instead that white-sounding names got 50 percent more callbacks than black-sounding names, even when skills and experience were equal.[97]

This type of discrimination is often not intentional but is based on deep-seated personal biases and deep-rooted organizational assumptions. Employees in a monoculture may not be aware of their biases and the negative stereotypes they apply toward people who represent diverse groups. Through effective training, employees can be helped to accept different ways of thinking and behaving, the first step away from narrow, ethnocentric thinking. Ultimately, employees are able to integrate diverse cultures, which

ethnorelativism
The belief that groups and subcultures are inherently equal.

Pluralism
This means that an organization accommodates several subcultures.

Take **ACTION**
Remember that another culture's way of doing something may have validity; it is just different.

FOCUS ON DIVERSITY

Black Entertainment Television (BET)

Robert L. Johnson started the Black Entertainment Television (BET) network 22 years ago with little more than a good idea: a cable channel for black viewers. Today, BET is the leading African-American-owned and -operated media and entertainment company in the United States. The core BET network reaches into more than 65 million homes and is worth over $2 billion; 90 percent of African-American households with cable regularly tune in. Johnson has leveraged the brand to establish a successful book company for African-American titles, a film company that produces and markets African-American-themed films, documentaries, and made-for-television movies, and, most recently, a successful Web site.

As the premier multimedia company for African-Americans, it only made sense for BET to expand into the Internet world. Johnson worked out partnerships with Microsoft, Liberty Digital Media, News Corporation, and USA Networks to launch BET.com. Though dozens of community portals and sites target African-Americans, BET is rapidly emerging as the leading online destination. Part of that is thanks to BET's emphasis on building an online community for African-Americans who want to stay in touch with black music, lifestyle, and culture. Everything is tailored to the preferences and needs of the black community. For example, the news channel provides the latest news from around the world, with specific emphasis on how it

affects the African-American community. Other channels include Health, Music, Money, Relationships, and Style. The career center lists thousands of job postings and offers advice, resources, and networking opportunities for African-American professionals and entrepreneurs. Some of the most popular aspects of BET.com, however, are the message boards, chat rooms, and community sections, where members can participate with others in the GetFit Club, the Movie Club, a spirituality area, professional groups, or other areas of special interest.

This rich community life helped BET.com get voted "Best African-American Community Site 2001" by Yahoo! Internet Life magazine. Though blacks continue to lag behind whites in Internet access, the digital divide is narrowing. Today, African-Americans are going online at a rate twice that of the general population and will soon make up around 40 percent of the total U.S. Internet population. BET.com is ready, giving African-Americans a place where they can be part of a thriving online community, explore new areas of interest, take advantage of opportunities for economic advancement, and obtain information related to virtually any aspects of their lives.

SOURCES: http://www.BET.com, accessed on November 15, 2001; David Whitford, "BET's Johnson: On the Air and in the Air," *Fortune* (July 24, 2000): 50; T. J. DeGroat, "Blacks Make Most Out of Internet," *DiversityInc.com*; and Jason McKay, "African American Websites Are Hooking People Up in More Ways Than One," *Black Enterprise* (October 2000): accessed at http://www.blackenterprise.com.

means that judgments of appropriateness, goodness, badness, and morality are no longer applied to racial or cultural differences. These differences are experienced as essential, natural, and joyful, enabling an organization to enjoy true pluralism and take advantage of diverse human resources.[98]

One organization that is making a firm commitment to break out of monoculture thinking is Ford Motor Company. Ford sponsors ten different employee resource groups—one each for African-Americans, Latinos, Middle Easterners, gays, lesbians, bisexuals, Chinese, Asian-Indians, parents, and women, which come up with recommendations for how to make Ford a better place to work for diverse employees. A Minority Dealer Operations program is aimed at increasing minority ownership, sometimes financing up to 90 percent of the cost for opening a dealership. Members of ethnic minority groups now own about 350 Ford dealerships, and women own an additional three hundred.[99] Since September 11, 2001, Ford has made a strong effort to improve understanding between Arab-Americans and their colleagues. For example, at the Ford plant in Dearborn, Michigan, home of the nation's largest Arab-American community, Ford holds regular Islam 101 meetings and other programs to further understanding between Muslims and non-Muslims.[100]

> **Take ACTION**
> Remember that most discrimination is not overt, but rather unconscious; therefore, even if you do not realize you are discriminating, you might still be.

The Changing Workplace

Diversity is no longer just the right thing to do; it has become a business imperative. One reason is the dramatic change taking place in the workplace, in our society, and in the economic environment. These changes include globalization and the changing workforce and customer base.[101] Earlier chapters described the impact of global competition on business in North America. Competition is intense. At least 70 percent of all U.S. businesses are engaged directly in competition with companies overseas. Companies that succeed in this environment need to adopt radical new ways of doing business, with sensitivity toward the needs of different cultural practices. Consider the consulting firm McKinsey & Co. In the 1970s, most consultants were American, but by 1999, McKinsey's chief partner was a foreign national (Rajat Gupta from India), only 40 percent of consultants were American, and the firm's foreign-born consultants came from 40 different countries.[102] Companies that ignore diversity have a hard time competing in today's global marketplace.

The other dominant trend is the changing composition of the workforce and the customer base. The average worker is older now, and many more women, people of color, and immigrants are seeking job and advancement opportunities. The demographics of the U.S. population are shifting dramatically. According to the 2000 U.S. Census, Hispanics, African-Americans, and Asian Americans make up about 30 percent of the U.S. population. Non-white residents are the majority in 48 of the nation's 100 largest cities, as they are in New Mexico, Hawaii, the District of Columbia, and California, the largest consumer market in the country. Hispanics, African-Americans, and Asian Americans together represent $1.5 trillion in annual purchasing power.[103] Some smaller companies, such as Lopez Negrete Communications, described below, have capitalized on the difficulties of multiculturalism and are helping large companies to understand the issues.

> **Take ACTION**
> As a manager, always notice the changing landscape of your customer demographics.

Lopez Negrete Communications

"He quit his job? Oh boy," was Alex Lopez Negrete's mother's not-exactly-thrilled response when she heard her son quit his job as head of a successful advertising agency to start his own company. The 43-year-old Mexican immigrant always knew what he wanted to do. And when he came to America, he did as many new immigrants, he relished his own culture. And that is part of the secret of his success.

CONCEPT CONNECTION

*The Carol H. Williams Advertising agency reflects today's **changing workplace**. The staff is an intentional mix of conservative, funky, trendy, and Bohemian types who represent a cross-section of cultures: African, African-American, Caribbean, Asian, Italian, Hispanic, and various ethnic combinations. "They hail from Morehouse to Harvard," and are led by a black woman, Carol H. Williams (center). For clients such as General Motors, Procter & Gamble, Kmart, Coors, and Pacific Bell, the Williams mix of diversity, business savvy, and creative talent creates winning advertising campaigns, resulting in explosive growth for the agency.*

More than 90 percent of his advertising business is based on helping clients market more effectively to the growing Hispanic market. Finally, taking note of the tremendous buying power of African and Hispanic markets, his firm gets some of the top U.S. companies, such as Wal-Mart and Tyson Chicken. He has learned a lot from big and small clients, and he especially urges small business owners to adopt a multicultural strategy. "It's not just advertising," he says, but a whole way to thinking and doing business that becomes "in-language" and "in-culture." Here are some tips he has learned: (1) Do not use stereotyped portrayals of ethnic groups—all that will do is drive away your intended ethnic market; (2) Do not skimp on ads because it is an ethnic market, it will turn off potential customers, who may feel one-down; 3) If your Spanish is imperfect, hire someone else to do a voice-over of commercials.

Because Lopez Negrete has refused to sell his agency and feels that allows greater intimacy with the client's needs, his business has rapidly expanded to $45 million in revenues. It also shows how the marketplace has changed. As fellow entrepreneuer African-American Byron Lewis says, "Diversity represents an opportunity to increase profits for many advertisers."[104]

During the 1990s, the foreign-born population of the United States nearly doubled, and immigrants now make up more than 12 percent of the total U.S. workforce. By 2050, 85 percent of entrants into the workforce will likely be women and people of color. White males, the majority of workers in the past, represent less than half of the workforce.[105] So far, the ability of organizations to manage diversity has not kept pace with these demographic trends, thus creating a number of significant challenges for minority workers and managers.

The Digital, Inc. box describes a company with a goal of helping African-Americans achieve career success and stay connected to black culture and lifestyle.

Management Challenges

What does this mean for managers who are responsible for creating a workplace that offers fulfilling work, opportunities for professional development and career advancement, and respect for all individuals? Inappropriate behavior by employees lands squarely at the door of the organization's top executives. Managers can look at different areas of the organization to see how well they are doing in creating a workplace that values and supports all people. Exhibit 9.11 illustrates some of the key areas of management challenge for dealing with a diverse workforce. Managers focus on these

DIGITAL, INC.

Living on BlackPlanet.com

When Omar Wasow started BlackPlanet.com in 1999, industry skeptics dismissed the site as too racially specific and doomed to failure. It did not take long to prove them wrong. BlackPlanet is the most heavily trafficked African-American Web destination, with nearly 12 million registered members and 1.5 million different visitors in any given month. At just about any time of the day or night, more than 20,000 people are logged on. Not long ago, Media Metrix rated BlackPlanet.com as the eighth "stickiest" Web site, referring to how often people come back to the site and how long they stay.

In the past five years, African-Americans have embraced the Internet at about twice the rate of the general population. BlackPlanet.com was ready, giving African-Americans a place where they could be part of a thriving online community, investigate new areas of interest, explore job and education opportunities, examine paths to economic advancement, build social and romantic relationships, and obtain information related to almost any aspect of their lives.

The essence of BlackPlanet.com's success, according to Wasow, is building connections. "We focus on the conversation," he says. "What we've done is taken the grapevine in the black community and extended it to the Internet." Wasow believes African-Americans have always found ways to communicate within the black community and stay in touch with their history and culture. The Internet is just a new way for people to explore issues of common interest with others who understand their frustrations and share their experiences as African-Americans. Some of the most popular aspects are the message boards, chat rooms, and community sections, where members can interact with others.

The Internet is today's fastest highway to information, entertainment, and cultural connections, and BlackPlanet.com has tapped into a deep desire among African-Americans for a site that caters to their interests, preferences, and needs.

SOURCE: Ines Bebea, "Blacks and the Internet: Power Resides in Interconnectivity," *Network Journal* (October 31, 2003): 46; Lynda Richardson, "Enterpreneur Takes Black-Oriented Site Out of Red," *The New York Times* (November 27, 2002): B4 and *http://www.blackplanet.com*.

---

issues to see how well they are addressing the needs and concerns of diverse employees. One step is to ensure that their organizations' HR systems are designed to be bias-free, dropping the perception of the middle-aged white male as the ideal employee. Consider how the FBI has expanded its recruiting efforts, as shown below.

Federal Bureau of Investigation (FBI)	How does the FBI gain credibility and obtain the information it needs to investigate and solve crimes? One way is by looking and thinking like the people in the communities where it seeks information. Not so long ago, if you were a woman or member of a minority group, you did not stand a chance of becoming an FBI agent. Today, though, the agency's goal is to reflect the diversity of U.S. society. Each of the FBI's 56 field offices gets a report card on how well they have done in terms of making their offices reflective of the community. Each office is responsible for bringing minorities on board and providing them with advancement opportunities.

In addition, the FBI's national recruitment office was launched specifically to develop programs for recruiting women and minorities. One innovative initiative was the EdVenture Partners Collegiate Marketing Program, which worked with two historically black universities. The program gave students college credit and funding to devise and implement a local marketing plan for the FBI. As a result of the program, the agency received 360 minority applications. "In many cases, the students' perceptions about the FBI were totally changed," says Gwen Hubbard, acting chief of the national recruitment office. "Initially, we were not viewed as an employer of choice by the diverse student populations." The EdVenture Partners program is being expanded to eight colleges and universities. Another initiative is a minority summer intern program, which started with 21 full-time student interns and is being expanded to at least 40 interns.

These programs on the national level, along with emphasis in the field offices on reflecting the local communities, ensure that the FBI recruits diverse candidates. Today, the FBI has thousands of female and minority agents. Top leaders are focusing on ways to make sure those people have full opportunity to move up the ranks so that there is diversity at leadership levels as well.[106]

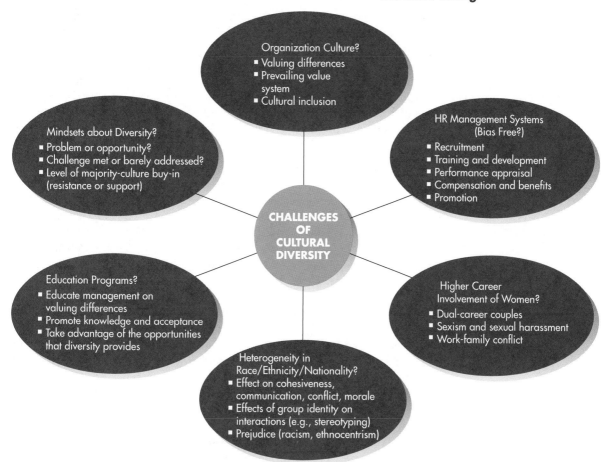

Organization Culture?
- Valuing differences
- Prevailing value system
- Cultural inclusion

Mindsets about Diversity?
- Problem or opportunity?
- Challenge met or barely addressed?
- Level of majority-culture buy-in (resistance or support)

HR Management Systems (Bias Free?)
- Recruitment
- Training and development
- Performance appraisal
- Compensation and benefits
- Promotion

CHALLENGES OF CULTURAL DIVERSITY

Education Programs?
- Educate management on valuing differences
- Promote knowledge and acceptance
- Take advantage of the opportunities that diversity provides

Higher Career Involvement of Women?
- Dual-career couples
- Sexism and sexual harassment
- Work-family conflict

Heterogeneity in Race/Ethnicity/Nationality?
- Effect on cohesiveness, communication, conflict, morale
- Effects of group identity on interactions (e.g., stereotyping)
- Prejudice (racism, ethnocentrism)

SOURCE: Taylor H. Cox and Stacy Blake, "Managing Cultural Diversity: Implications for Organizational Competitiveness," *Academy of Management Executive 5,* no. 3 (1991), 45–56.

EXHIBIT 9.11

Management Challenges for a Culturally Diverse Workforce

Current Debates about Affirmative Action

Affirmative action refers to government-mandated programs that focus on providing opportunities to women and members of minority groups who have previously been discriminated against. It is not the same thing as diversity, but affirmative action has facilitated greater recruitment, retention, and promotion of minorities and women. Affirmative action has made workplaces fairer and more equitable. However, recent research shows that full integration of women and racial minorities into organizations is still at least a decade away.[107] Despite affirmative action's successes, salaries and promotion opportunities for women and minorities continue to lag behind those of white males.

Affirmative action was developed in response to conditions 40 years ago. Adult white males dominated the workforce, and economic conditions were stable and improving. Because of widespread prejudice and discrimination, legal and social coercion were necessary to allow women, people of color, immigrants, and other minorities to become part of the economic system.[108]

affirmative action
Refers to government-mandated programs that focus on providing opportunities to women and members of minority groups who have previously been discriminated against.

The Glass Ceiling

The **glass ceiling** is an invisible barrier that separates women and minorities from top management positions. They can look up through the ceiling and see top management, but prevailing attitudes and stereotypes are invisible obstacles to their own advancement.

glass ceiling
An invisible barrier that separates women and minorities from top management positions.

In addition, women and minorities are often excluded from informal manager networks and often do not get access to the type of general and line management experience that is required for moving to the top.[109] Research has suggested the existence of glass walls that serve as invisible barriers to important lateral movement within the organization. Glass walls bar experience in areas such as line supervision or general management that would enable women and minorities to advance vertically.[110]

Women in a number of organizations are taking action against discrimination and the glass ceiling, as shown below.

| **Wal-Mart** | It started in July 2001, when seven women filed suit in a California court charging that Wal-Mart systematically denies women equal pay and opportunities for promotion. It could balloon into the largest gender discrimination lawsuit in U.S. history and cost the giant corporation hundreds of millions of dollars. The women have won a major battle when the courts required Wal-Mart to turn over workforce data from 3,400 U.S. stores, information that the company had previously closely guarded. Though Wal-Mart is vigorously denying discriminatory practices, one analysis of the data indicates that between the years of 1996 and 2001, women at Wal-Mart earned from 5 to 15 percent less than men performing the same job even though women typically received higher performance evaluations. Another study reports that women employees wait much longer than men for their first promotion at Wal-Mart. In 1999, Wal-Mart had a lower percentage of female managers than its retail counterparts had in 1975. Lawyers are arguing that the patterns reflect discriminatory attitudes embedded in the famous Wal-Mart culture that call for strict penalties and serious reform.

CEO Lee Scott has publicly vowed to work harder to equalize pay and promote more women to management positions. At the company's 2004 annual meeting, Scott announced that executives' bonuses will be cut 7.5 percent this year and 15 percent next year if Wal-Mart fails to meet its goals of promoting women and minorities in proportion to the number who apply for management positions. Scott has also set up a 140-person compliance office to ensure the new goals are met. The diversity issues at Wal-Mart will not be resolved easily. Top executives want to revise structures, policies, and processes so they are unequivocally fair without losing the culture that makes Wal-Mart special. Some believe, however, that massive culture change is the only way to solve the deep-rooted problems that led to the lawsuit. There are indications that top Wal-Mart managers have long been aware that some of the company's policies and practices might create barriers for women and minorities. It is likely that legal action will ultimately force the company to make big changes designed to create a more inclusive work environment.[111] |

The Opt-Out Trend

Many women are never hitting the glass ceiling because they choose to get off the fast track long before it comes into view. There is currently much discussion of something referred to as the opt-out trend. The opt-out proponents say that greater numbers of highly educated, professional women are deciding that corporate success is not worth the price in terms of reduced family and personal time, greater stress, and negative health effects.[112] Women do not want corporate power and status in the same way that men do, and clawing one's way up the corporate ladder has become less appealing. For example, Brenda Barnes was on the fast track right to the top of PepsiCo, but she stepped down when the toll of the job—rising at 3:30 a.m., consistent 14-hour work days, a grueling travel schedule—began to outweigh its rewards. "When you talk about those big jobs, those CEO jobs, you just have to give them your life," Barnes says.[113] For many women, today, it is just not worth it. Some are opting out to be stay-at-home moms; others want to continue working but just not in the kind of fast, competitive, aggressive environment that exists in most corporations. Most women, some who have studied the opt-out trend say, do not want to work as hard and competitively as most men want to or have to work.[114]

Critics, however, argue that is another way to blame women themselves for the dearth of female managers at higher levels.[115] Though many women are voluntarily leaving the fast track, many more genuinely want to move up the corporate ladder but find their paths blocked. Fifty-five percent of executive women surveyed by Catalyst said they aspire to senior leadership levels.[116] In addition, a recent survey of 103 women voluntarily leaving executive jobs in *Fortune* 1000 companies found that corporate culture was cited as the number one reason for leaving.[117] The greatest disadvantages of women leaders stem largely from prejudicial attitudes and a heavily male-oriented corporate culture.[118] Top-level corporate culture evolves around white, heterosexual, American males, who tend to hire and promote people who look, act, and think like them. Compatibility in thought and behavior plays an important role at higher levels of organizations. For example, in a survey of women who have managed to break through the glass ceiling, fully 96 percent said adapting to a predominantly white male culture was an important factor in their success.[119]

The Female Advantage

Some people think women might actually be better managers, partly because of a more collaborative, less hierarchical, relationship-oriented approach that is in tune with today's global and multicultural environment.[120] As attitudes and values change with changing generations, the qualities women naturally seem to possess may lead to a gradual role reversal in organizations. For example, there is a stunning gender reversal in U.S. education, with girls taking over almost every leadership role from kindergarten to graduate school. In addition, women of all races and ethnic groups are outpacing men in earning bachelor's and master's degrees. Among 25-year-olds to 29-year-olds, 32 percent of women have college degrees, compared to 27 percent of men. Women are rapidly closing the M.D. and Ph.D. gap and make up about half of all U.S. law students. They make up half of all undergraduate business majors and about 30 percent of MBA candidates. Overall, women's participation in the labor force and civic affairs has steadily increased since the mid-1950s, while men's participation has slowly but steadily declined.[121]

According to James Gabarino, an author and professor of human development at Cornell University, women are "better able to deliver in terms of what modern society requires of people—paying attention, abiding by rules, being verbally competent, and dealing with interpersonal relationships in offices."[122] His observation is supported by female managers being typically rated higher by subordinates on interpersonal skills as well as on factors such as task behavior, communication, ability to motivate others, and goal accomplishment.[123] Recent research found a correlation between balanced gender composition in companies (that is, roughly equal male and female representation) and higher organizational performance. Moreover, a study by Catalyst indicates that organizations with the highest percentage of women in top management financially outperform, by about 35 percent, those with the lowest percentage of women in higher-level jobs.[124] It seems that women should be marching right to the top of the corporate hierarchy, but prevailing attitudes, values, and perceptions in organizations create barriers and a glass ceiling.

CHAPTER 9

Defining New Relationships in Organizations

One outcome of diversity is an increased incidence of close personal relationships in the workplace, which can have positive and negative results for employees as well as the organization. Two issues of concern are emotional intimacy and sexual harassment.

Emotional Intimacy

Close emotional relationships, particularly between men and women, often have been discouraged in companies for fear that they would disrupt the balance of power and threaten organizational stability.[125] This opinion grew out of the assumption that organizations are designed for rationality and efficiency, which were best achieved in a nonemotional environment.

However, a recent study of friendships in organizations sheds interesting light on this issue.[126] Managers and workers responded to a survey about emotionally intimate relationships with male and female coworkers. Many men and women reported having close relationships with an opposite-sex coworker. Called non-romantic love relationships, the friendships resulted in trust, respect, constructive feedback, and support in achieving work goals. Intimate friendships did not necessarily become romantic, and they affected each person's job and career in a positive way. Rather than causing problems, non-romantic love relationships, according to the study, affected work teams in a positive manner because conflict was reduced. Indeed, men reported somewhat greater benefit than women from these relationships, perhaps because the men had fewer close relationships outside the workplace upon which to depend.

However, when such relationships do become romantic or sexual in nature, real problems can result. Romances that require the most attention from managers are those that arise between a supervisor and a subordinate. These relationships often lead to morale problems among other staff members, complaints of favoritism, and questions about the supervisor's intentions or judgment. Though few companies have written policies about workplace romance in general, 70 percent of companies surveyed have policies prohibiting romantic relationships between a superior and a subordinate.[127] Sometimes an office romance becomes public and messy, as shown in the Focus on Ethics box.

Take ACTION

As a managaer, be careful not to cross boundaries with employees at work because having too close a relationship with one employee can cause demotivation with others.

FOCUS ON ETHICS

The Cost of Love

It is one thing to have a fling, but when you are CEO, the costs can be high. For Harry Stonecipher, it was $38 million, losing a stock award when he was forced out of the company. In some companies, the CEO might keep his job, but he has lost the respect of the workforce because the perception is often (correctly) that the boss is unfairly favoring his lover. Boeing CEO Harry Stonecipher, age 68, sent his paramour a raunchy e-mail, which somehow fell into unintended hands. When confronted, Stonecipher immediately confessed to Chairman Lew Platt but denied that he used the affair to enhance the 48-year-old divorced woman's career and salary.

Still, it put the man who is the chief ethics enforcer in a bad light and he was asked to resign. Such behavior sends up red flags in the defense industry. Stonecipher had come out of retirement in 2003 to revive Boeing after a series of ethical scandals, including bribery and dirty tricks that sent two executives to jail, not to mention a still-unsettled sexual harassment class-action suit. Stonecipher came to clean up the place and he was improving the company's image, having won the support of Wall Street and the business community with his reforms. His own downfall was brought about by the system he put in place to prevent other ethical lapses. What is surprising is Stonecipher's lapse of judgment, sending such graphic e-mails in a monitored system that had been punished for e-mails about unethical actions. And a pity that a man with such an illustrious career would lose it all at the end for an eight-week relationship. A month later, his wife of 50 years filed for divorce.

SOURCE: Paul Tharp, "Costly Affair—Three Months of Reckless Passion = $38M," *New York Post* (March 11, 2005): 37; Lynn Lunsford, Andy Passtor and Joann S. Lublin, Boeings' "CEO Forced to Resign Over His Affair with Employee," *The Wall Street Journal* (March 8, 2005): A1, A8.

Sexual Harassment

Though psychological closeness between men and women in the workplace may be a positive experience, sexual harassment is not. Sexual harassment is illegal. As a form of sexual discrimination, sexual harassment in the workplace is a violation of Title VII of the 1964 Civil Rights Act. Sexual harassment in the classroom is a violation of Title VIII of the Education Amendment of 1972. The following categorize various forms of sexual harassment as defined by one university:

- *Generalized.* This form involves sexual remarks and actions unintended to lead to sexual activity but are directed toward a coworker based solely on gender and reflect on the entire group.

- *Inappropriate/offensive.* Though not sexually threatening, it causes discomfort in a coworker, whose reaction in avoiding the harasser may limit his or her freedom and ability to function in the workplace.

- *Solicitation with promise of reward.* This action treads a fine line as an attempt to "purchase" sex, with the potential for criminal prosecution.

- *Coercion with threat of punishment.* The harasser coerces a coworker into sexual activity by using the threat of power (through recommendations, grades, promotions, and so on) to jeopardize the victim's career, as shown below in the Business Blooper.

- *Sexual crimes and misdemeanors.* The highest level of sexual harassment, these acts would, if reported to the police, be considered felony crimes and misdemeanors.[128]

Statistics in Canada indicate that between 40 and 70 percent of women and about 5 percent of men have been sexually harassed at work.[129] The situation in the United States is just as dire. Between 1992 and 2002, the EEOC shows a 150 percent increase in the number of sexual harassment cases filed annually.[130] About 10 percent of those were filed by males. The Supreme Court has held that same-sex harassment as well as harassment of men by female coworkers is as illegal as the harassment of women by men. In the suit that prompted the Court's decision, a male oil-rig worker claimed he was singled out by other members of the all-male crew for crude sex play, unwanted touching, and threats of rape.[131] A growing number of men are urging recognition that sexual harassment is no longer a woman's problem.[132]

Because the corporate world is dominated by a male culture, however, sexual harassment affects women to a much greater extent. Companies such as Dow Chemical, Xerox, and *The New York Times* have been swift to fire employees for circulating pornographic images, surfing pornographic Web sites, or sending offensive e-mails.[133]

BUSINESS BLOOPER

Tasty Flavors Sno Biz

Giving new meaning to the fruits of your labors, a 19-year-old employee at Red Bank, Tennessee's Tasty Flavors Sno Biz forgot to put a banana in a smoothie drink, so her 57-year-old boss took her in the back room and spanked her behind 20 times. He repeated the same behavior when another young woman made a mistake. In a weird attempt to avoid prosecution, the boss evidently coerced the two teenagers to sign statements saying the spankings were fine with them: "I give Gene permission to bust my behind any way he sees fit." The allegedly religious boss was arrested anyway on sexual battery charges and had to post $2,000 bail. Too bad he did not attend that sexual harassment seminar a while back.

SOURCE: Bill Hoffman, "Slap-Happy Boss Busted," *The New York Post* (Nov. 11, 2004): 31.

Manager's Solution

This chapter described several important points about HRM in organizations. All managers are responsible for human resources, and most organizations have an HR department that works with line managers to ensure a productive workforce. HRM plays a key strategic role in today's organizations. HRM is changing in three ways to keep today's organizations competitive: focusing on human and social capital; globalizing HR systems, policies, and structures; and using IT to achieve strategic HR goals. The HR department must implement procedures to reflect federal and state legislation and respond to changes in working relationships and career directions. The old social contract of the employee being loyal to the company and the company taking care of the employee until retirement no longer holds. Employees are responsible for managing their own careers. Though many people still follow a traditional management career path, others look for new opportunities as contingent workers, telecommuters, project managers, and virtual employees. Other current issues of concern to HRM are downsizing and implementing work-life balance initiatives.

The HR department strives to achieve three goals for the organization. The first goal of the HR department is to attract an effective workforce through HR planning, recruiting, and employee selection. The second is to develop an effective workforce. Newcomers are introduced to the organization and to their jobs through orientation and training programs. Moreover, employees are evaluated through performance appraisal programs. The third goal is to maintain an effective workforce. HR managers retain employees with wage and salary systems, benefits packages, and termination procedures. In many organizations, IT is being used to meet all three of these important HR goals more effectively.

At UPS, described in the opening example, new district manager Jennifer Shroeger worked with the HRM department to solve the problem of high turnover at the Buffalo distribution center, dramatically cutting the attrition rate in the first quarter of 2002 to a low 6 percent. Managers realized that keeping more people had a lot to do with how those people were selected in the first place. Previously, UPS had basically been hiring the first applicant who walked in and was capable of handling heavy packages. Shroeger decided UPS needed to start asking what the applicant was looking for in the job. Many of those hired as part-timers were really looking for full-time jobs, which rarely opened up. After a few months, these people realized their chances of full-time work were slim, so they would move on. UPS started giving realistic job previews, emphasizing the hard, intimidating environment of the warehouse and that these were part-time jobs and short shifts that were never going to be anything else. The upside to this aspect of the job was that it was perfect for students, mothers, and other people who genuinely want to work only part time. But hiring those people meant UPS needed to build in flexibility. Students and mothers, for example, tend to need more occasional days off or frequent changes in their schedule. Instead of just saying "we can't do that," HRM started looking for ways the company could do it. Other changes involved improved training and mentoring for new employees, handled by part-time shift supervisors who understood the problems of the work environment. The supervisors got upgraded training in communication skills, motivation, and flexibility to meet the needs of diverse workers. A final, important aspect of the new strategy was to accept that most people they hired would not want to load and unload boxes for their entire careers. "Instead of worrying about them leaving, we should be taking an interest in their future," Shroeger says. "I'd like for all of those part-time workers to graduate from college and start their own businesses and become UPS customers."[134]

Discussion Questions

1. It is the year 2010. In your company, central planning has given way to frontline decision making, and bureaucracy has given way to teamwork. Shop floor workers use computers and robots. There is a labor shortage for many job openings, and the few applicants lack skills to work in teams, make decisions, or use sophisticated technology. As vice president of human resource management since 1990, what did you do to prepare for this problem?

2. If you were asked to advise a private company about its equal employment opportunity responsibilities, what two points would you emphasize as most important? Why?

3. How can the human resource activities of planning, recruiting, performance appraisal, and compensation be related to corporate strategy?

4. Recall your own job experience. What human resource management activities described in this chapter were performed for the job you filled? Which ones were absent?

5. How might the changing social contract affect the ways human resource departments recruit, develop, and retain workers?

6. If you were a senior manager at a company such as R. R. Donnelley, Allstate Insurance, or Texaco, how would you address the challenges faced by minority employees?

7. Do you think any organization can successfully resist diversity today? Discuss.

8. What is the glass ceiling, and why do you think it has proved to be such a barrier to women and minorities?

9. In preparing an organization to accept diversity, do you think it is more important to change the corporate culture or to change structures and policies? Explain.

10. Many single people meet and date people from the office because the organization provides a context within which to know and trust another person. How do you think this practice affects the potential for emotional intimacy? Sexual harassment?

Manager's Workbook

Want Ads

1. Find 10 want ads for jobs. Five should be from a local newspaper and five from a professional journal (there are many available in the university's library). Choose a selection of jobs from professional, technical, clerical, and manual labor.

2. Prepare a report, with ads attached, to turn in to your instructor answering the following questions:

   a. What differences do you notice in the way the ads are worded or designed between the journal and newspaper?

b. Write a short paragraph for each ad, indicating the strengths and weaknesses of the ad itself (not the job). Look at qualities such as: ability to gain interest of job seeker, adequate information, ease of contact to company, etc.

c. What type of ad grabbed your interest the most?

d. If you were hired as a consultant to the companies that placed those ads, what would you recommend to them in order to make their job advertisements more effective?

e. Write an advertisement for your dream job.

Manager's Workshop

Hiring and Evaluating Using Core Competencies

1. Form groups of four to seven members. Develop a list of "core competencies" for the job of student in this course. (Or alternately, you may choose a job in one of the group members' organizations.) List the core competencies below.

    1. _____   5. _____

    2. _____   6. _____

    3. _____   7. _____

    4. _____   8. _____

2. Which of the above are the most important four?

    1. _____   3. _____

    2. _____   4. _____

3. What questions would you ask a potential student to determine if that person could be successful in this class, based on the four most important core competencies as listed in problem 2? (interviewing process)

    1. _____

    2. _____

    3. _____

    4. _____

4. What learning experiences would you develop to enhance those core competencies? (training and development process)

    1. _____

    2. _____

    3. _____

    4. _____

5. How would you evaluate or measure the success of a student in this class, based on the four core competencies? (performance evaluation process)

    1. _____

    2. _____

    3. _____

    4. _____

Manager's Workshop

Women and Work Quiz

How well do you know the status of women in the workplace? Test yourself below:

_____ 1. Women account for 40 percent of the total U.S. workforce.   T   F

_____ 2. By 2006, women will account for 50 percent of the total growth in the labor force.   T   F

_____ 3. Of divorced women, 75 percent percent are in the labor force, while 52 percent of married women work.   T   F

_____ 4. The largest occupational group for women is secretaries, while the second largest is cashiers.   T   F

_____ 5. About 4 million women hold more than one job.   T   F

_____ 6. In families with a working wife, the median income is $68,000, while a family without a wife in the paid labor force is $40,000.   T   F

_____ 7. Over the age of 65, 14 percent of women live below the poverty line, while only 7 percent of men do.   T   F

_____ 8. The number of working women has doubled since 1970—from 30 million to 60 million.   T   F

_____ 9. Overall, women earn 80 cents on the dollar compared to men.   T   F

_____10. The highest weekly earnings for women come from which group: lawyers, engineers, or physicians?   T   F

Answers: 1. False, 46 percent; 2. False, 59 percent; 3. False, divorced 75 percent, married 63 percent; 4. True; 5. True; 6. False, working wife $60,000, other is $34,000; 7. True; 8. True; 9. False, 74 cents; 10. lawyers.

SOURCE: Adadpted from Department of Labor, *Facts on Working Women,* 1998.

Management in Practice: Ethical Dilemma

Promotion or Not?

You are the president of CrownCutters, Inc. You have worked closely with Bill Smith for several years now. In many situations, he has served as your de facto right-hand person.

Due to a retirement, you have an opening in the position of executive vice president. Bill is the natural choice—and this is obvious to the other mid- and senior-level managers at CrownCutters. Bill is popular with most of the managers in the company. Of course, he also has his share of detractors.

Prior to announcing the appointment of Bill Smith, you receive a memo from Jane Jones, your controller. Jane's memo indicates that she was subjected to sporadic sexual harassment by Bill starting 10 years ago when she first joined the company and was working for him. Her memo indicates that the harassment essentially stopped six years ago when she moved to a position in which Bill was no longer her superior. She requests that this information be kept totally confidential.

You have never heard of any allegations like this about Bill before.

What Do You Do?

1. Move ahead with the promotion because, even if true, this is an isolated incident that is a part of Bill's past and is not his current behavior.

2. Stop the promotion because Bill is not the type of person who should help lead the company and shape its values.

3. Put the promotion on hold until you can discuss the situation extensively with Bill and Jane, although this means the accusation probably will become public knowledge.

SOURCE: This case was provided by Professor David Scheffman, Owen Graduate School of Management, Vanderbilt University, Nashville, Tennessee.

Case for Critical Analysis

Draper Manufacturing

You have just been hired as a diversity consultant by Draper Manufacturing. Ralph Draper, chairman and CEO, and other top managers feel a need to resolve some racial issues that have been growing over the past several years at their plant in Nashville, Tennessee. Draper Manufacturing is a small, family-owned company that manufactures mattresses. It employs 90 people full time, including African Americans, Asians, and Hispanics, with 75 percent of the workforce being female. The company also occasionally hires part-time workers, most of whom are Hispanic women. Most of these part-timers are hired for periods of a few months at a time, when production is falling behind schedule.

To begin your orientation to the company, Draper has asked his production manager, Wallace Burns, to take you around the plant. As Burns points out the various areas responsible for each stage of the production process, you overhear several different languages being spoken. In the shipping and receiving department, you notice that most workers are black men. Burns confirms that 90 percent of the workers in shipping and receiving are African American and points out that the manager of that department, Adam Fox, is also African American.

Later in the afternoon you attend a regular meeting of top managers to meet everyone and get a feel for the organizational culture. Draper introduces you as a diversity consultant and notes that several of his managers have expressed concerns about festering racial tensions in the company. He notes that "Each of the minority groups sticks together. The blacks and Orientals rarely mix, and most of the Mexicans stick together and speak only in Spanish. It seems that some of our workers are just downright lazy sometimes. We keep falling behind in our production schedule and having to hire part-time workers, but then we generally have to fire two or three of those a month for goofing off on the job." He closes his introduction by saying that you have been hired to help the company solve their growing diversity problems.

Draper then turns toward the management committee's routine daily business. The others present are the general manager, human resources manager (the only woman), sales manager, quality control manager, plant manager (Wallace Burns), and shipping and receiving manager (Adam Fox, the only nonwhite manager). Soon an angry debate begins between Fox and the sales manager. The sales manager says that orders are not being shipped on time, and several complaints have been received about the quality of the product. Fox argues that he needs more workers in shipping and receiving to do the job right, and he adds that the quality of incoming supplies is lousy. While this debate continues, the other managers remain silent and seem quite uncomfortable. Finally, the quality control manager attempts to calm things down with a joke about his wife. Most of the men in the group laugh loudly, and the conversation shifts to other topics on the agenda.

Questions

1. What suggestions would you make to Draper's managers to help them move toward successfully managing diversity issues?

2. If you were the shipping and receiving or human resources manager, how do you think you would feel about working at Draper? What are some of the challenges you might face at this company?

SOURCE: Based on "Northern Industries," a case prepared by Rae Andre of Northeastern University.

Controlling

The point of a film project is to tell a story that feels so true that audiences flock to theaters and then emerge telling everyone they know that it is a must-see movie.

The director, as storyteller-in-chief, is held accountable for accomplishing this feat. Throughout the process, directors constantly review the work-in-progress and make mid-course corrections. Those corrections are based on their own perceptions about whether the film is living up to their artistic vision and are based on studio executives' dictates and test audience reactions.

It begins on the set when directors have actors perform a scene repeatedly until the directors' instincts and experience tell them they have enough usable takes. Then, at the end of the day, the director—often along with actors and others—view dailies, or the unedited film footage from a day's shooting; they check on everything from the quality of the performances to the photography.

However, the director's moment of truth comes during postproduction, the phase when the staff assembles all the various elements into a film. At some point during this process, the director sits down with a select few to view a preliminary edit. *Lord of the Ring's* director Peter Jackson observes, a little ruefully, that contrary to public opinion, even a fairly complete edit should not be confused with the final product. "It never ever is because at that point, you know, problems with the script start to show themselves." The director might shorten, expand, or even eliminate some scenes, depending on if the story is dragging in spots or moving too quickly.

Directors often tweak films by doing "pickups": they recall the actors, reassemble the crew, and re-shoot. For example, at the time Jackson originally filmed *Return of the King's* climactic coronation scene, he was under enormous pressure to wrap up filming by Christmas for budgetary reasons. The actors were exhausted, the filming rushed, and the results satisfied no one. Three years later, the cast (including extras) and crew all reconvened, took their time, and did the scene over.

King Arthur, released in 2004, is a case where director Antoine Fuqua made major changes he did not initiate in the film's style and substance. Originally, he envisioned making a gritty, realistic movie about the possible historical origins of the legendary King Arthur. Partway through production, however, word came from the studio that he should make the movie considerably less gritty and graphic since executives decided that appealing to families would improve the film's commercial prospects. Fuqua complied. Then after a test screening of a close-to-final edit, the studio concluded that audiences found Fuqua's original ending depicting Lancelot's cremation entirely too depressing. Fuqua responded by tacking on a cheerier ending where Arthur marries Guinivere and is crowned king.

As managers of the movie-making process, directors are constantly gathering information, measuring their work against their own aesthetic standards and the commercial expectations of financial backers, and making any necessary corrections. It is an ongoing process that ends only when the last DVD version hits the market.

CHAPTER

10

Productivity through Management and Quality Control Systems

CHAPTER OUTLINE

LEARNING OBJECTIVES

After studying this chapter, you should be able to do the following:

1   **Define organizational control and explain why it is a key management function.**

2   **Describe differences in control focus, including feedforward, concurrent, and feedback control.**

3   **Explain the four steps in the control process.**

4   **Contrast the bureaucratic and decentralized control approaches.**

5   **Discuss how to measure and manage productivity.**

6   **Describe the concept of total quality management and major TQM techniques.**

7   **Explain the value of open-book management and the balanced scorecard approaches to control in a turbulent environment.**

Ted and Norm Waitt co-founded Gateway Inc. in an Iowa farmhouse in 1985 and soon gained national acclaim with the company's quality computers and distinctive cow-spotted boxes. The company's management style reflected the founders' cattleman heritage. CEO Ted Waitt wore his long hair in a ponytail and built the company on plain talk, loose control, and fair dealing with employees and customers. He stayed closely involved with almost all of the company's decisions, from advertising spots to corporate partnerships, and worked closely with other managers in the daily operations. If managers were failing to perform as expected, they often got a friendly chat from Waitt in the hallway. Decisions at Gateway were often made cowboy style, and the "shoot from the hip" approach worked. Gateway was known for innovation, being the first PC company to offer systems with color monitors as standard, the first to offer a standard three-year warranty, and the first to explore commercial convergence between the PC and television. Over the years, Gateway evolved from a PC maker to a full-service technology provider. But as the technology industry grew more complex and competitive, the undisciplined ways were no longer working. Costs spiraled out of control. In 2001, Gateway posted a loss of $1 billion and sales fell 37 percent. The company is searching for its way back to profitability. Waitt knows he needs to improve efficiency or Gateway is doomed.[1]

If you were a consultant to Ted Waitt at Gateway, what advice would you give him about using control systems and strategies to improve cost efficiency and revive the organization? What is the first step you would recommend top managers take to gain better control over the company?

Control is a critical issue facing every manager in every organization. At Gateway, managers need to find new ways to cut costs, increase efficiency, and build sales, or the organization will not survive. Other organizations face similar challenges, such as improving product quality, minimizing the time needed to resupply merchandise in retail stores, decreasing the number of steps to process an online merchandise order, or improving the tracking procedures for overnight package delivery. Control, including quality control, involves office productivity, such as elimination of bottlenecks and reduction in paperwork mistakes. In addition, every organization needs basic systems for allocating financial resources, developing human resources, analyzing financial performance, and evaluating overall profitability.

This chapter introduces basic mechanisms for controlling the organization. It begins by summarizing the basic structure and objectives of the control process. Then it discusses controlling financial performance, including the use of budgets and financial statements. The next sections examine the changing philosophy of control, today's approach to total quality management (TQM), and recent trends such as ISO 9000 certification and economic value-added (EVA) systems. The chapter concludes with a look at control systems for a turbulent environment, including the use of open-book management and the balanced scorecard, and control problems in the new workplace.

The Meaning of Control

On a bright October day in 2003, storm clouds gathered over Wall Street. A just-issued Securities and Exchange Commission (SEC) report blasted the New York Stock Exchange (NYSE) for failing to monitor its elite floor-trading firms, track violations, and address blatant abuses in which investors were shortchanged by millions of dollars. The criticism of the exchange's regulatory and compliance procedures was a big blow to an institution reeling from months of difficulties, including the ouster of Chairman Dick Grasso. Poor control systems had gotten the venerable NYSE into a public relations and political nightmare. Interim Chairman John Reed has proposed major revisions in the exchange's control systems, including committing more personnel and resources to regulation.[2]

A lack of effective control can seriously damage an organization's health and threaten its future. Consider Enron, which was held up as a model of modern management in the late 1990s but came crashing down a couple of years later.[3] There are numerous reasons for Enron's shocking collapse—including unethical managers and an arrogant, free-wheeling culture—but it comes down to a lack of control. No one was keeping track to ensure managers stayed within acceptable ethical and financial boundaries. Though Chairman Kenneth Lay claimed he did not know the financial shenanigans were going on at the company, federal investigators disagreed and indicted him on criminal charges.[4] At a minimum, Lay along with other top managers neglected their responsibilities by failing to set up and maintain adequate controls on the giant corporation.

Organizational control refers to the systematic process of regulating organizational activities to make them consistent with the expectations established in plans, targets, and standards of performance. In a classic article on the control function, Douglas S. Sherwin summarizes this concept as follows: "The essence of control is action, which adjusts operations to predetermined standards, and its basis is information in the hands of managers."[5] Thus, controlling an organization requires information about performance and its standards as well as actions taken to correct any deviations from the standards.

CONCEPT CONNECTION

*A new philosophy about **organizational control** involves lower-level workers in management and control decisions. At the Honeywell Industrial Automation and Control facility in Phoenix, employees' quality-control decisions cut defect rates by 70 percent, inventory by 46 percent, and customer lead times by an average of 75 percent.*

Courtesy of Honeywell, Inc.

Managers need to decide what information is essential, how they will obtain that information (and share it with employees), and how they can and should respond to it. Having the correct data is essential. Managers have to decide which standards, measurements, and metrics are needed to monitor and control the organization and set up systems for obtaining that information. For example, an important metric for a pro football or basketball team might be the number of season tickets, which reduces the organization's dependence on more labor-intensive box-office sales.[6] One issue of current concern to many managers is how to track valuable metrics for e-commerce, as discussed in this chapter's Digital, Inc.

organizational control

The systematic process through which managers regulate organizational activities to make them consistent with expectations established in plans, targets, and standards of performance.

Organizational Control Focus

Control can focus on events before, during, or after a process. For example, a local automobile dealer can focus on activities before, during, or after sales of new cars. Careful inspection of new cars and cautious selection of sales employees are ways to ensure high quality or profitable sales, even before those sales take place. Monitoring how salespeople act with customers would be considered control during the sales task. Counting the number of new cars sold during the month or telephoning buyers about their satisfaction with sales transactions would constitute control after sales have occurred. These three types of control are formally called feedforward, concurrent, and feedback, and are illustrated in Exhibit 10.1.

Take **ACTION**

As a manager, always measure your goals and standards against the results.

DIGITAL, INC.

E-Commerce Metrics

How do organizations know how well their Web site is doing? It is not too difficult to find out how many people visit the site and how many pages they look at. But that is only the first step toward finding out how effective the site is in terms of achieving organizational goals. Managers have been struggling to identify metrics that will help them evaluate a company's performance and compare it to others. During the dot-com heydey, measures such as *eyeballs* and *stickiness* (measuring how much attention a site gets over time) were important. More sophisticated metrics have evolved. Though different companies will use different standards and measurements, some common e-commerce metrics have emerged:

- *Conversion rate.* Conversion means the moment a customer buys, signs up for a seminar, subscribes to a newsletter, and so on. *Cost per conversion* is a critical number to track because it tells managers how much money they are spending to get one person to buy. Companies track the *conversion rate*, which means the ratio of buyers to visitors, and the average order size.
- *Clickstream.* Clickstream analysis is more than a metric; it is a way to analyze customer behavior by looking at where people enter a site, where they typically convert from visitors to customers, and where the site typically loses visitors. Clickstream analysis helps companies track

their *customer drop-off rate*, which means how many customers start to purchase a product or sign up for a service but abandon it before completion.

- *Retention* or *customer loyalty.* Companies want people to buy repeatedly, so it is important to track customer retention. The online auction site eBay has a high retention rate because the same people keep coming back to the site to buy and sell merchandise.
- *Site performance.* How well the site performs, including raw performance data on such matters as how long it takes to load a page, how easy it is to find what you are looking for, how long it takes to place an order, and so forth, is one of the most important metrics for many sites, especially business-to-business (B2B) sites that sell to time-pressed business users.

E-commerce organizations track many other metrics. Numerous software programs are available to help managers better measure, analyze, guide, and control e-commerce operations. These new analytical tools enable managers to get a broader, clearer picture of Web site performance and customer activity so they can cut costs and maximize efficiency.

SOURCES: Susannah Patton, "Web Metrics That Matter," *CIO* (November 15, 2002): 84–88; Jim Sterne, "Making Metrics Count," *Business2.com* (April 3, 2001): 72; and Ramin Jaleshgari, "The End of the Hit Parade," *CIO* (May 15, 2000): 183–190.

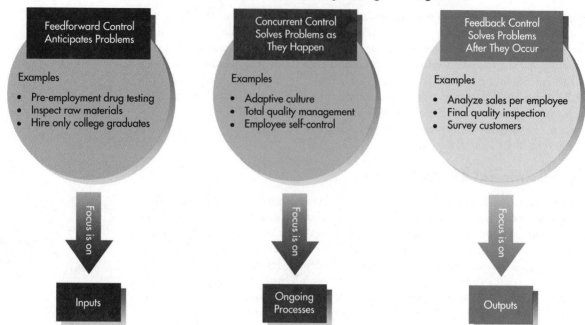

EXHIBIT 10.1

*Organizational
Control Focus*

Feedforward Control

Control that attempts to identify and prevent deviations before they occur is called **feedforward control**. Sometimes called preliminary or preventive control, it focuses on human, material, and financial resources that flow into the organization. Its purpose is to ensure that input quality is high enough to prevent problems when the organization performs its tasks. Tamara Mellon understands the importance of saying "no" at the right times, to avoid wasting company resources, as shown below.

**Jimmy Choo
Shoes**

When Tamara Mellon was a little girl she loved shoes, really loved them. On a trip with her convent school's kindergarten class, she begged a nun to buy her some cowboy boots. After college, she worked at British *Vogue,* and her boss soon realized Tamara had an obsession with extraordinarily stylish shoes. When she traveled to Nepal and needed to trek for miles, she was nearly neurotic about which boot was best to wear. Her attention to detail on shoes, fashion layouts, and photographs was quite unusual.

She needed to find the perfect Greek sandal for a layout and found London's East End cobbler, Jimmy Choo, who had such clients as Princess Diana. After Tamara was promoted to *Vogue*'s accessories editor, she and Jimmy Choo worked closely together. When she decided to go out on her own, she saw an opportunity that could be exploited: luxury shoes, which had no real competitor to Manolo Blahnik. Convincing her father to invest $250,000, she would run the company while Jimmy Choo and his fashion school-educated niece, Sandra Choi, would design and make the shoes. It was a typical start-up, working out of a basement, no computer. A larger problem surfaced. Though Jimmy Choo was a nice man and decent cobbler, he was incapable of designing a shoe line. Tamara and Choi had never done it either. But Tamara realized they had one thing Manolo Blahnik didn't have: a female CEO. So they made shoes that Tamara loved, because she was the model customer: young, good-looking, style-conscious, and rich.

Tamara and her father had visions of opening 35 stores, but Jimmy Choo was nervous. He was, after all, a working man, with a family to support, and these wild speculative investments scared him. When Equinox Luxury Holdings offered to buy a controlling interest in Jimmy Choo, they took the $100 million, allowing Jimmy Choo himself to bow out with $25 million. The business grew further and they expect to have 50 stores open worldwide within two years, as the Asian market develops.

A careful businesswoman and manager, Tamara doesn't let her success keep her from making sound decisions. When a group of fragrance-branders were trying to woo her and the company name, she pointedly asked them, "What went wrong with Patrick Cox?" (A shoe designer whose foray into fragrances was not successful.) That's the kind of thinking that has made her Britain's highest-profile female executive and her company into a $200-million brand. It's all about smart decision-making and high-heeled courage.[7]

Feedforward controls are evident in the selection and hiring of new employees. Organizations attempt to improve the likelihood that employees will perform up to standards by identifying the necessary skills, using tests and other screening devices to hire people who have those skills, and providing necessary training to upgrade important skills. Numerous nursing homes and assisted living centers have come under fire in recent years due to lax feedforward controls, such as failing to ensure workers have the appropriate skills or provide them with the training needed to care for residents. Brookside Gables, an assisted living center in the Panhandle region of Florida, closed after a resident died because caregivers did not have basic skills in first aid and emergency procedures.[8] Another type of feedforward control is forecasting trends in the environment and managing risk. In tough economic times, for example, consulting companies such as A.T. Kearney try to stay in close touch with clients to monitor how much business and money will be coming in. The fashion company Liz Claiborne gathers information about consumer fads to determine what supplies to purchase and inventory to stock. Banks typically require extensive documentation before approving major loans to identify and manage risks.[9]

feedforward control

Control that focuses on human, material, and financial resources flowing into the organization; also called preliminary or preventive control.

Concurrent Control

Control that monitors ongoing employee activities to ensure they are consistent with performance standards is called **concurrent control**. Concurrent control assesses current work activities, relies on performance standards, and includes rules and regulations for guiding employee tasks and behaviors. One way to control is to pay only for outcomes, as shown in the Focus on Skills box.

concurrent control

Control that consists of monitoring ongoing activities to ensure they are consistent with standards.

FOCUS ON SKILLS

PayPerClip and Unbundled Ads

Public relations firms are notorious for charging high fees and not doing much. So, when Angie Morgan and Courtney Lynch started their leadership consulting firm, LeadStar, they were shocked when they got PR bids for monthly retainers of $15,000, and no one would guarantee results. Luckily, they stumbled on to PR company PayPerClip, which only charges when it does a placement; for example $750 for an article in a smaller newspaper. PayPerClip soon got them on CNN and CNBC, plus others, for 8,000 dollars.

We have moved to an itemized economy, with a price on everything. Customers in many industries are insisting they buy what they want and no more. We can thank the Internet for much of this, as it has made us all into seasoned shoppers. And hats off, too, to Wal-Mart, which has brought out the

cheapskate in many people. A prime example of results-based unbundled ads is Google and Yahoo, which pay only when surfers click on their ads. And what a success. Before pricing per click, Googles ad revenues were $86 million in 2001. Now, they are $2.7 billion.

"Any product that can be digitized, can be taken apart," says Texas A&M prof Manjit Yadav. Rather than spending $481 for a one-year *New York Times* subscription, you can now buy one article online for $2.95.

Eventually, the unbundled strategy will not work for some companies. Angie Morgan and Courtney Lynch are doing so well, they are searching for a full-service PR firm. "When you look at PayPerClip," says Lynch, "it eventually gets expensive."

SOURCE: George Mannes, "The Urge to Unbundled," *Fast Company* (Feb. 2005): 23–24.

Many manufacturing operations include devices that measure whether the items being produced meet quality standards. Employees monitor the measurements; if they see that standards are not met in some area, they make the correction or signal the appropriate person that a problem is occurring. Technology advancements are adding to the possibilities for concurrent control in services as well. For example, retail stores such as Beall's, Sunglass Hut, and Saks use cash-register management software to monitor cashiers' activities in real time and help prevent employee theft. Trucking companies like Schneider National and Covenant use computers to track the position of their trucks and monitor the status of deliveries.[10]

Other concurrent controls involve the ways in which organizations influence employees. An organization's cultural norms and values influence employee behavior, as do the norms of an employee's peers or work group. Concurrent control includes self-control, through which individuals impose concurrent controls on their own behavior because of personal values and attitudes. Use of feedforward and concurrent methods is used by Tokyopop, as shown in the Focus on Collaboration box.

Feedback Control

feedback control

Control that focuses on the organization's outputs; also called postaction or output control.

Sometimes called postaction or output control, **feedback control** focuses on the organization's outputs, in particular, the quality of an end product or service. An example of feedback control in a manufacturing department is an intensive final inspection of a refrigerator at an assembly plant. In Kentucky, school administrators conduct feedback control by evaluating each school's performance every other year. They review reports of students' test scores as well as the school's dropout and attendance rates. The state rewards schools with rising scores and brings in consultants to work with schools whose scores have fallen.[11]

Besides producing high-quality products and services, businesses need to earn a profit. Even nonprofit organizations need to operate efficiently to carry out their missions. Therefore, many feedback controls focus on financial measurements. Budgeting, for example, is a form of feedback control because managers monitor whether they have

---

Take ACTION

Periodically review your own performance at school or on the job; that way you are using control mechanisms to improve your own performance.

FOCUS ON COLLABORATION

Tokyopop

The biggest marketer of *manga*—animated Japanese novels— is Los Angeles-based Tokyopop, the brainchild of Georgetown Law Grad Stuart Levy. Without any publishing experience, Levy turned *manga* into a $100-million industry. How did an American guy do such a great job selling an Asian product to Americans? After graduating, he went to Japan, largely because of his love for sushi. There, he saw the magnetism *manga* had on the population and believed the same would happen in North America. "I never liked comic books," he says, "but fell in love with *manga*. They are so visual and have such a broad subject range, they are more like TV or film." Though comics are mostly for teenage boys, *manga* appeals to both genders in a wider age range.

Levy saw how *anime* TV shows (cartoons of Japanese style) were catching on the late 1990s, so he used that info to pitch his ideas to mainstream booksellers, such as Barnes & Noble. To make it easier to sell, Levy designed the books so that each one would be a 5-inch by 7.5-inch paperback with a cost of

$10, simplifying the display problem. Getting story ideas to book has been systemized:

1. A committee in Japan comes up with basic stories they think Americans will like and they send it on to the Los Angeles office,
2. Employees who do not speak Japanese evaluate the story's appeal from a text summary and graphics,
3. The company quantifies reader interest through e-mails to its 100,000 fan base, as well as chat rooms and newsgroups,
4. An in-house translator adds American slang to the story.

While the story is in development, it is available on Tokyopop's Intranet to any U.S. or Tokyo employee, who can monitor its progress. Tokyopop has new visions: selling in Europe and taking some of the stories and finding customers back in Japan.

SOURCE: Julie Boornstin, "Small & Global: License for Adventure," *FSB* (June 2004): 38–39.

Wonder Bread

Ever wonder why Wonder Bread tastes, so, well, dull? Interstate Bakeries, which makes Wonder Bread and Twinkies filed for bankruptcy last year, blaming its demise on the low-carb mania. But word got out that that is not the way the bread was sliced, as they say. Turns out Interstate was trying to save money. So, instead of cooking its books, as some other companies have, it tinkered with its Wonder Bread recipe to lengthen shelf life and reduce waste. But consumers knew the difference. The bread they had loved now tasted stale and gummy, so they quit buying it, and the company had a net loss last year of $26 million. That is a lot of dough.

SOURCE: Adam Horowitz, Mark Athitakis, Mark Lasswell and Owen Thomas, "101 Dumbest Moments in Business," *Business 2.0* (Jan/Feb. 2005): 103–110.

operated within their budget targets and make adjustments accordingly. Wonder Bread managers didn't do enough feedback control when they changed the recipe for the popular bread.

Feedback Control Model

All well-designed control systems involve the use of feedback to determine whether performance meets established standards. In this section, we will examine the key steps in the feedback control model and look at how the model applies to organizational budgeting.

Steps of Feedback Control

Managers set up control systems that consist of the four key steps illustrated in Exhibit 10.2: establish standards, measure performance, compare performance to standards, and make corrections as necessary.

Establish Standards of Performance. Within the organization's overall strategic plan, managers define goals for organizational departments in specific, operational terms that include a standard of performance against which to compare organizational activities. A standard of performance could include "reducing the reject rate from 15 to 3 percent," "increasing the corporation's return on investment to 7 percent," or "reducing the number of accidents to one per each 100,000 hours of labor."

Managers should assess what they will measure and how they will define it. Tracking such matters as customer service, employee involvement, and turnover is an important supplement to traditional financial performance measurement, but many companies fail to identify and define nonfinancial measurements.[12] To evaluate and reward employees for the achievement of standards, managers need clear standards

EXHIBIT 10.2

Feedback Control Model

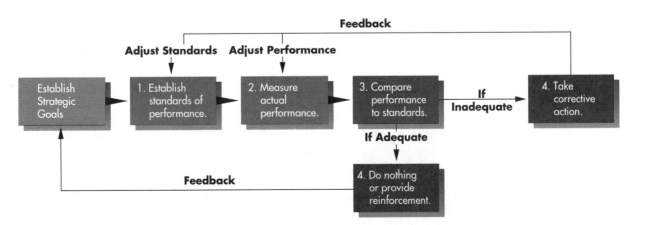

that reflect activities that contribute to the organization's overall strategy in a significant way. Standards should be defined clearly and precisely so employees know what they need to do and can determine whether their activities are on target.[13]

Measure Actual Performance. Most organizations prepare formal reports of quantitative performance measurements that managers review daily, weekly, or monthly. These measurements should be related to the standards set in the first step of the control process. For example, if sales growth is a target, the organization should have a means of gathering and reporting sales data. If the organization has identified appropriate measurements, regular review of these reports helps managers stay aware of whether the organization is doing what it should be doing.

In most companies, managers do not rely exclusively on quantitative measures. They get out into the organization to see how things are going, especially for such goals as increasing employee participation or improving customer satisfaction. Managers have to observe for themselves if employees are participating in decision making and have opportunities to add to and share their knowledge. Interaction with customers is necessary for managers to understand if activities are meeting customer needs. Richard Snyder made sure his employees participated in reengineering the plant as described below.

Latt-Green

Mention reengineering to employees and you are likely to elicit fear, anxiety, and lots of resistance to change. For good reason, because reengineering has been the reason often given for massive layoffs of workers. No wonder people are scared. Plus, reengineering has been seen as for big corporations only.

When Richard Snyder took over as controller of Latt-Green, an ailing knitting and converting operation of eight employees, he walked into a nest of problems: negative cash flow, a poor billing system that let some customers off scott-free, and a system so heavy with paper it was crushed under its own weight. But how do you get employee buy-in to make drastic changes and go for reengineering, when those employees had been doing the same things for years and were, in fact, heavily invested in the current process?

As he introduced financial software to get some order to the system, Snyder discovered that orders sometimes got lost in a paper file, the costs from vendors did not match the product, and shipping orders did not correlate to any specific products. Snyder knew everyone had to be included in decisions for change. Though he knew what needed to be done, Snyder realized the workers would add new perspective and ask important questions. After all, they knew the operation.

Through the process of changing the system, Snyder talked to as many people as he could, soliciting ideas. But a few employees were dead set against changing "the way we've always done it." He had to let them know the new system would be installed, and they needed to learn it. Gradually, everyone was on board with it.

To get the best system for Latt-Green, Snyder talked to everyone inside and outside the company who was involved in the process of converting yarn into a dyed and printed textile. He looked at every piece of paper involved with the process in the past month and involved as many employees as possible in identifying problems and solutions. So, by the time the new system was developed, the employees had ownership of it and the transition was relatively smooth.

The cost of the new system was $150,000, but Latt-Green has saved that many times over. No downsizing occurred. They have roughly the same number of staff, but now they know what comes in, what it is used for, where it goes, and all invoices are collected. Snyder attributes success of the change to three things: be open with employees about the change, involve as many of them in the change process, and know the new process thoroughly yourself, so you do not have to rely so much on consultants.[14]

Compare Performance to Standards. The third step in the control process is comparing activities to performance standards. When managers read computer reports or walk through the plant, they identify if actual performance meets, exceeds, or falls short of standards. Typically, performance reports simplify such comparisons by placing the performance standards for the reporting period alongside the performance for the same period and by computing the variance, that is, the difference between each amount and the associated standard. To correct the problems that most require attention, managers focus on variances.

When performance deviates from a standard, managers must interpret the deviation. They are expected to dig beneath the surface and find the cause of the problem. If the sales goal is to increase the number of sales calls by 10 percent and a salesperson achieved an increase of 8 percent, where did she fail to achieve her goal? Perhaps several businesses on her route closed, additional salespeople were assigned to her area by competitors, or she needs training in making cold sales calls more effectively. Managers should take an inquiring approach to deviations to gain a broad understanding of factors that influence performance. Effective management control involves subjective judgment and employee discussions, as well as objective analysis of performance data.

Take Corrective Action. Managers determine what changes, if any, are necessary. In a traditional top-down approach to control, managers exercise their formal authority to make necessary changes. Managers may encourage employees to work harder, redesign the production process, or fire employees. In contrast, managers using a participative control approach collaborate with employees to determine the corrective action necessary.

In some cases, managers may take corrective action to change performance standards. They may realize that standards are too high or too low if departments fail to meet or routinely exceed standards. If contingency factors that influence organizational performance change, performance standards may need to be altered to make them realistic and to provide continued motivation for employees. German fashion company Hugo Boss suffered losses from a poor decision and took action to fix the problem as described in the Focus on Skills box.

Managers may wish to provide positive reinforcement when performance meets or exceeds targets. They may reward a department that has exceeded its planned goals or congratulate employees for a job well done. Managers should not ignore high-performing departments at the expense of taking corrective actions elsewhere. The online auction company eBay provides a good illustration of the feedback control model.

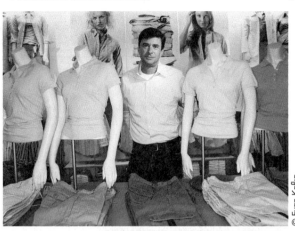

© Evan Kafka

CONCEPT CONNECTION

*When Paul Pressler became CEO of retailer Gap Inc. two years ago, he launched a makeover. By **comparing performance to standards**, Pressler could see that basic operations, marketing, and inventory were out of control. He took **corrective action** by tightening operations, increasing focus on the customer, and implementing inventory control measures that would prevent boatloads of unsold merchandise from sitting in warehouses and storerooms. To avoid panicky clearance sales, Pressler insisted that managers rely on new software that helps determine when and how much to mark down items. These control actions have resulted in increasing sales and six straight quarters of earnings growth.*

Take *ACTION*

As a manager, you must correct deficiencies; it is not enough just to measure.

eBay

Here is one of Meg Whitman's guiding rules: "If you can't measure it, you can't control it." As CEO of eBay, Whitman runs a company that is obsessed with performance measurement. She personally monitors a slew of performance metrics, including standard measurements such as site visitors, new users, and time spent on the site, as well as the ratio of eBay's revenues to the value of goods traded. She recently brought in a benchmarking consultant to measure eBay against peers to see how fast it adds features to the Web site. The results showed Whitman the company has some improvement to make in that area.

FOCUS ON SKILLS

Hugo Boss

"What drives us is not the love of fabric," said Hugo Boss production head Werner Lackas, "but a desire to move production through a distribution system." Surely, Gianni Versace would roll over in his grave to hear that from a fashion company.

After a few mistakes, German-based Hugo Boss has created a customer-driven, disciplined, and hype-resistant clothing firm, outperforming other flashier German companies, such as Jil Sander and Escada. One of its mistakes was moving the company's new female line to Milan about 10 years ago, hoping the proximity to other fashion houses would be beneficial. About $72 million later, it moved the unit back to Metzingen, Germany. It learned an important lesson in German business tradition: To be a global player, you should have parochial roots. During tight economic times, these firms relied on their hometown corporate cultures, workmanship

traditions, and financial discipline. As the economy is picking up, they are poised to take on more far-flung markets, such as China.

After the heavy losses from Boss Woman, the company has bounced back, with sales rising 11 percent in 2004 to 1.16 billion Euros, or $1.5 billion dollars, and profits increasing 7 percent. It has even redone the women's line. After it returned from Italy, control of Boss Woman was turned over to former Nivea executive Bruno Sälzer, who brought all the designers under one roof, retooled the line, and produced a 36 percent increase in sales last year. Another lesson learned: Just because you are good in men's fashions, it does not mean you will be successful with women's clothing. It is a learned skill. A skill that Sälzer must be learning well because he was made CEO of Hugo Boss.

SOURCE: Mark Landler, "A Small Town in Germany Fits Hugo Boss Nicely," *The New York Times* (April 12, 2005): C1, C4.

Managers and employees throughout the company monitor performance almost obsessively. Category managers, for example, have clear standards of performance for their auction categories (such as sports memorabilia, jewelry and watches, health and beauty, and fashion). They are constantly measuring, tweaking, and promoting their categories to meet or outperform the targets.

Whitman believes that getting a firm grip on performance measurement is essential for a company to know where to spend money, where to assign more personnel, and which projects to promote or abandon. But performance measurement is not just about numbers. At eBay, "it's all about the customer," and gauging customer (user) satisfaction requires a mix of methods, such as surveys, monitoring eBay's discussion boards, and personal contact. Whitman gets her chance to connect with users at the annual eBay Live conference. There, she wanders the convention hall floor talking with anyone and everyone about their eBay experiences.

By defining standards, using a combination of measurement approaches, and comparing performance to standards, eBay managers can identify trouble spots and move to correct when and where it is needed.[15]

Application to Budgeting

Budgetary control, one of the most commonly used methods of managerial control, is the process of setting targets for an organization's expenditures, monitoring results and comparing them to the budget, and making changes as needed. As a control device, budgets are reports that list planned and actual expenditures for cash, assets, raw materials, salaries, and other resources. In addition, budget reports usually list the variance between the budgeted and actual amounts for each item.

Take a moment to complete the experiential exercise below that pertains to budgetary control.

Is Your Budget in Control?

By the time you are in college, you are in charge of at least some of your own finances. How well you manage your personal budget may indicate how well you will manage your company's budget on the job. Respond to the following statements to evaluate your own budgeting habits. If the statement does not apply directly to you, respond the way you think you would behave in a similar situation.

1. I spend all my money as soon as I get it.
Yes No

2. At the beginning of each week (or month, or term), I write down all my fixed expenses.
Yes No

3. I never seem to have any money left over at the end of the week (or month).
Yes No

4. I pay all my expenses, but I never seem to have any money left over for fun.
Yes No

5. I am not putting any money away in savings right now; I will wait until after I graduate from college.
Yes No

6. I cannot pay all my bills.
Yes No

7. I have a credit card, but I pay the balance in full each month.
Yes No

8. I take cash advances on my credit card.
Yes No

9. I know how much I can spend on eating out, movies, and other entertainment each week.
Yes No

10. I pay cash for everything.
Yes No

11. When I buy something, I look for value and determine the best buy.
Yes No

12. I lend money to friends whenever they ask even if it leaves me short of cash.
Yes No

13. I never borrow money from friends.
Yes No

14. I am putting aside money each month to save for something that I need.
Yes No

Yes responses to statements 2, 9, 10, 13, and 14 point to the most disciplined budgeting habits; yes responses to 4, 5, 7, and 11 reveal adequate budgeting habits; yes responses to 1, 3, 6, 8, and 12 indicate the poorest budgeting habits. If you have answered honestly, chances are you will have a combination of all three. Look to see where you can improve your budgeting.

A budget is created for every division or department within an organization, no matter how small, so long as it performs a distinct project, program, or function. The fundamental unit of analysis for a budget control system is called a responsibility center. A **responsibility center** is defined as any organizational department or unit under the supervision of a single person who is responsible for its activity.[16] A three-person appliance sales office in Watertown, New York, is a responsibility center, as is a quality control department, a marketing department, and an entire refrigerator manufacturing plant. The manager of each unit has budget responsibility. Top managers use budgets for the company, and middle managers traditionally focus on the budget performance of their department or division. Budgets that managers typically use include expense budgets, revenue budgets, cash budgets, and capital budgets.

Budgeting is an important part of organizational planning and control. Many traditional companies use **top-down budgeting**, which means that the budgeted amounts for the coming year are imposed on middle-level and lower-level managers.[17] These managers set departmental budget targets in accordance with overall company revenues and expenditures specified by top executives. Though the top-down process has some advantages, the movement toward employee empowerment, participation, and learning means that many organizations are adopting **bottom-up budgeting**, a process in which lower-level managers anticipate their departments' resource needs and pass them up to top management for approval.[18] At MediHealth Outsourcing, top executives give department managers the financial information for the entire company and ask them to define their own departmental budget needs. Then, the budgets are reviewed and approved by top management.[19]

The Changing Philosophy of Control

Managers' approach to control is changing in many of today's organizations. In connection with the shift to employee participation and empowerment, many companies are adopting a decentralized rather than a bureaucratic control process. Bureaucratic control and decentralized control represent different philosophies of corporate culture, which was discussed in Chapter 2. Most organizations display some aspects of bureaucratic and decentralized control, but managers generally emphasize one or the other, depending on the organizational culture and their own beliefs about control.

Bureaucratic control involves monitoring and influencing employee behavior through extensive use of rules, policies, hierarchy of authority, written documentation, reward systems, and other formal mechanisms.[20] In contrast, decentralized control relies on cultural values, traditions, shared beliefs, and trust to foster compliance with organizational goals. Managers operate on the assumption that employees are trustworthy and willing to perform without extensive rules and close supervision.

Exhibit 10.3 contrasts the use of bureaucratic and decentralized methods of control. Bureaucratic methods define explicit rules, policies, and procedures for employee behavior. Control relies on centralized authority, the formal hierarchy, and close personal supervision. Responsibility for quality control rests with quality control inspectors and supervisors rather than with employees. Job descriptions generally are specific and task related, and managers define minimal standards for acceptable employee performance. In exchange for meeting the standards, individual employees are given extrinsic rewards such as wages, benefits, and possibly promotions up the hierarchy. Employees rarely participate in the control process, with any participation being formalized through mechanisms such as grievance procedures. With bureaucratic control, the organizational culture is somewhat rigid, and managers do not consider culture a useful means of controlling employees and the organization. Technology often is used to control the flow and pace of work or to monitor employees, such as by measuring how long employees spend on phone calls or how many keystrokes they make at the computer.

---

responsibility center

An organizational unit under the supervision of a single person who is responsible for its activity.

top-down budgeting

A budgeting process in which middle-level and lower-level managers set departmental budget targets in accordance with overall company revenues and expenditures specified by top management.

bottom-up budgeting

A budgeting process in which lower-level managers budget their departments' resource needs and pass them up to top management for approval.

bureaucratic control

The use of rules, policies, hierarchy of authority, reward systems, and other formal devices to influence employee behavior and assess performance.

Bureaucratic Control	Decentralized Control
Uses detailed rules and procedures; formal control systems	Limited use of rules; relies on values, group and self-control, selection and socialization
Top-down authority, formal hierarchy, position power, QC inspectors	Flexible authority, flat structure, expert power, everyone monitors quality
Task-related job descriptions; measurable standards define minimum performance	Results-based job descriptions; emphasis on goals to be achieved
Emphasis on extrinsic rewards (pay, benefits, status)	Extrinsic and intrinsic rewards (meaningful work, opportunities for growth)
Rewards given for meeting individual performance standards	Rewards individual and team; emphasis on equity across employees
Limited, formalized employee participation, e.g., grievance procedures	Broad employee participation, including quality control, system design, and organizational governance
Rigid organizational culture; distrust of cultural norms as means of control	Adaptive culture; culture recognized as means for uniting individual, team, and organizational goals for overall control

EXHIBIT 10.3

Bureaucratic and Decentralized Methods of Control

SOURCES: Based on Richard E. Walton, "From Control to Commitment in the Workplace," *Harvard Business Review* (March–April 1985), 76–84; and Don Hellriegel, Susan E. Jackson, and John W. Slocum, Jr., *Management*, 8th ed. (Cincinnati, Ohio: South-Western College Publishing, 1999), 663.

Bureaucratic control techniques can enhance organizational efficiency and effectiveness. Many employees appreciate a system that clarifies what is expected of them, and they may be motivated by challenging, but achievable, goals.[21] Though many managers use bureaucratic control, too much control can backfire. Employees resent being watched too closely, and they may sabotage the control system. One veteran truck driver expressed his unhappiness with electronic monitoring to a *Wall Street Journal* reporter investigating the use of devices that monitor truck locations. According to the driver, "It's getting worse and worse all the time. Pretty soon, they'll want to put a chip in the drivers' ears and make them robots." He added that he occasionally escapes the relentless monitoring by parking under an overpass to take a needed nap out of the range of the surveillance satellites.[22]

Decentralized control is based on values and assumptions almost opposite to those of bureaucratic control. Rules and procedures are used only when necessary. Managers rely instead on shared goals and values to control employee behavior. The organization places great emphasis on the selection and socialization of employees to ensure that workers have the appropriate values needed to influence behavior toward meeting company goals. No organization can control employees 100 percent of the time, and self-discipline and self-control are what keep workers performing their jobs up to standard. Empowerment of employees, effective socialization, and training can contribute to internal standards that provide self-control.

With decentralized control, power is more dispersed and is based on knowledge and experience as much as position. The organizational structure is flat and horizontal, as discussed in Chapter 7, with flexible authority and teams of workers solving problems and making improvements. Everyone is involved in quality control on an ongoing basis. Job descriptions generally are results-based, with an emphasis more on the outcomes to be achieved than on the specific tasks to be performed. Managers use extrinsic rewards such as pay and the intrinsic rewards of meaningful work and the opportunity to learn and grow. Technology is used to empower employees by giving them the information they need to make effective decisions, work together, and solve problems. People are rewarded for team and organizational success as well as their individual performance, with an emphasis on equity among employees. Employees participate in a wide range of areas, including setting goals, determining standards of performance, governing quality, and designing control systems.

decentralized control

The use of organizational culture, group norms, and a focus on goals, rather than rules and procedures, to foster compliance with organizational goals.

Take **ACTION**

As a manager, determine if you need organizational controls or if the values and goals can shape employee behavior.

With decentralized control, the culture is adaptive, and managers recognize the importance of organizational culture for uniting individual, team, and organizational goals for greater overall control. Ideally, with decentralized control, employees will pool their areas of expertise to arrive at procedures better than managers could come up with working alone.

Managing Productivity

Productivity is significant because it influences the well-being of the entire society as well as of individual companies. The only way to increase the output of goods and services to society is to increase organizational productivity.

Lean Manufacturing

Lean manufacturing was pioneered by Toyota and has spread around the world. Today's organizations are trying to become more efficient, and implementing the lean manufacturing philosophy is one popular approach to doing do. **Lean manufacturing** uses highly-trained employees at every stage of the production process who take a painstaking approach to details and problem solving to cut waste and improve quality and productivity.

The heart of lean manufacturing is not machines or technology but is employee involvement. Employees are trained to "think lean," and empowered to make changes to attack waste and strive for continuous improvement in all areas.[23] Toyota's system combines techniques such as just-in-time inventory, continuous-flow production, quick changeover of assembly lines, continuous improvement, and preventive maintenance with a management system that encourages employee involvement and problem solving. Any employee can stop the production line at any time to solve a problem. In addition, equipment is often designed to stop automatically so a defect can be fixed.[24]

Before the manufacturing process begins, a location for the plant must be found. New location scouting software is helping managers turn facilities location from guesswork into a science. These programs use sophisticated number crunching tools, for example, to help fast food chains like Arby's determine the best areas for expansion.

Measuring Productivity

Two important questions when considering productivity improvements are: What is productivity, and how do managers measure it? In simple terms, **productivity** is the organization's output of goods and services divided by its inputs. This means that productivity can be improved by increasing the amount of output using the same level of inputs or by reducing the number of inputs required to produce the output. Sometimes a company can do both. Ruggieri & Sons, for example, invested in mapping software to help it plan deliveries of heating fuel. The software plans the most efficient routes based on the locations of customers and fuel reloading terminals, as well as the amount of fuel each customer needs. When Ruggieri switched from planning routes by hand to using the software, its drivers began driving fewer miles but making 7 percent more stops each day; in others words, burning less fuel to sell more fuel.[25]

The accurate measure of productivity can be complex. Two approaches for measuring productivity are total factor productivity and partial productivity. **Total factor productivity** is the ratio of total outputs to the inputs from labor, capital, materials, and energy:

$$Total\ factor\ productivity = \frac{Output}{Labor + Capital + Materials + Energy}$$

Total factor productivity represents the best measure of how the organization is doing. Often, however, managers need to know about productivity with respect to certain inputs. **Partial productivity** is the ratio of total outputs to a major category of

---

lean manufacturing
Uses highly trained employees at every stage of the production process who take a painstaking approach to details and problem solving to cut waste and improve quality and productivity.

Take ACTION
As a manager, remember that productivity means you are adding value to the raw materials and making something economically valuable.

productivity
The organization's output of goods and services divided by its inputs.

total factor productivity
The ratio of total outputs to the inputs from labor, capital, materials, and energy.

partial productivity
The ratio of total outputs to a major category of inputs.

inputs. For example, many organizations are interested in labor productivity, which would be measured as follows:

$$Labor\ productivity = \frac{Output}{Labor\ dollars}$$

Calculating this formula for labor, capital, or materials provides information on if improvements in each element are occurring. However, managers often are criticized for relying too heavily on partial productivity measures, especially direct labor.[26] Measuring direct labor misses the valuable improvements in materials, work processes, and quality. Labor productivity is easily measured but may show an increase as a result of capital improvements. Thus, managers will misinterpret the reason for productivity increases.

Total Quality Management (TQM)

One popular approach based on a decentralized control philosophy is **total quality management (TQM)**, an organization-wide effort to infuse quality into every activity in a company through continuous improvement. TQM became attractive to U.S. managers in the 1980s because it had been successfully implemented by Japanese companies that were gaining market share and an international reputation for high quality. The Japanese system was based on the work of such U.S. researchers and consultants as Deming, Juran, and Feigenbaum, whose ideas attracted U.S. executives after the methods were tested overseas.[27]

The TQM philosophy focuses on teamwork, increasing customer satisfaction, and lowering costs. Organizations implement TQM by encouraging managers and employees to collaborate across functions and departments, as well as with customers and suppliers, to identify areas for improvement, no matter how small. Each quality improvement is a step toward perfection and meeting a goal of zero defects. Quality control becomes part of the employee's daily, rather than being assigned to specialized departments.

The implementation of TQM is similar to other decentralized control methods. Feedforward controls include training employees to think in terms of prevention, not detection, of problems and giving them the responsibility and power to correct errors, expose problems, and contribute to solutions. Concurrent controls include an organizational culture and employee commitment that favor total quality and employee participation. Feedback controls include targets for employee involvement and for zero defects.

TQM Techniques

TQM implementation involves the use of many techniques, including quality circles, benchmarking, Six Sigma principles, reduced cycle time, and continuous improvement.

Quality Circles.   One technique for implementing the decentralized approach of TQM is to use quality circles. A **quality circle** is a group of 6 to 12 volunteer employees who meet regularly to discuss and solve problems affecting the quality of their work.[28] At a set time during the workweek, the members of the quality circle meet, identify problems, and try to find solutions. Circle members are free to collect data and take surveys. Many companies train team members in team building, problem solving, and statistical quality control. The reason for using quality circles is to push decision making to an organization level at which recommendations can be made by the people who do the job and know it better than anyone else.

Benchmarking.   Introduced by Xerox in 1979, benchmarking is now a major TQM component. **Benchmarking** is defined as "the continuous process of measuring products,

total quality management (TQM)

An organization-wide commitment to infusing quality into every activity through continuous improvement.

quality circle

A group of six to 12 volunteer employees who meet regularly to discuss and solve problems affecting the quality of their work.

benchmarking

The continuous process of measuring products, services, and practices against major competitors or industry leaders.

services, and practices against the toughest competitors or those companies recognized as industry leaders."[29] The key to successful benchmarking lies in analysis. Starting with its own mission statement, a company should honestly analyze its current procedures and determine areas for improvement. As a second step, a company selects competitors worthy of copying. For example, Xerox studied the order fulfillment techniques of L. L. Bean and learned ways to reduce warehouse costs by 10 percent. Companies can emulate internal processes and procedures of competitors but must take care to select companies whose methods are compatible. Once a strong, compatible program is found and analyzed, the benchmarking company can then devise a strategy for implementing a new program.

Six Sigma.   Six Sigma quality principles were first introduced by Motorola in the 1980s and were later popularized by General Electric (GE), where former CEO Jack Welch praised Six Sigma for quality and efficiency gains that saved the company billions of dollars. Based on the Greek letter *sigma*, which statisticians use to measure how far something deviates from perfection, **Six Sigma** is a highly ambitious quality standard that specifies a goal of no more than 3.4 defects per million parts. That essentially means being defect-free 99.9997 percent of the time.[30] However, Six Sigma has deviated from its precise definition to become a generic term for a quality-control approach that takes nothing for granted and emphasizes a disciplined and relentless pursuit of higher quality and lower costs. The discipline is based on a five-step methodology referred to as Define, Measure, Analyze, Improve, and Control (DMAIC, pronounced "de-May-ick" for short), which provides a structured way for organizations to approach and solve problems.[31] GE bought a Hollywood studio and is trying to implement a form of Six Sigma, as shown in the Focus on Skills box.

Implementing Six Sigma requires a major commitment from top management because Six Sigma requires widespread change throughout the organization. Hundreds of organizations have adopted some form of Six Sigma program in recent years. Highly committed companies, including ITT Industries, Motorola, GE, Allied Signal, ABB Ltd., and DuPont & Co., send senior managers to weeks of training to become qualified as Six Sigma "black belts." These black belts lead projects aimed at improving targeted areas of the business.[32] Though originally applied to manufacturing, Six Sigma has evolved to a process used in all industries and affecting every aspect of company operations, from human resources to customer service. Exhibit 10.4 lists some statistics that illustrate why Six Sigma is important for manufacturing and service organizations.

Take *ACTION*

When starting a new venture or bringing change, go out and benchmark similar successful programs.

Six Sigma

A quality control approach that emphasizes a relentless pursuit of higher quality and lower costs.

FOCUS ON SKILLS

Universal Studios

Rigorous Six Sigma business methods with quantifiable results has not been the Hollywood Way. Now that $134 billion corporate giant GE—which makes everything from medical imaging equipment to jet engines—has bought Universal Studios, there are frequent trips to GE offices in New York. Both sides talk about quarterly budget reviews and strategic planning, topics which were discussed before but not with such intensity or results-orientation. Marketing people are teamed with counterparts at GE's network, NBC. Previously, the studio had not been partnered with a TV network. Agents and producers are being told by executives to hold the line on budgets.

Though GE has approved Universal's $800-million budget to make about 16 movies this year, they are coming down on cost-control and producers are feeling it. They have clamped down on smaller expenses. Films recently completed are the *Bridget Jones* sequel, *Dawn of the Dead*, and *Chronicles of Riddick*. Still, there is pressure to adopt a more GE approach. "They have a lot of meetings," says Universal President Ron Meyer. "They are very focused on results. They don't want surprises."

SOURCE: Laura M. Holson, "Six Sigma: A Hollywood Studio Learns the GE Way," *The New York Times* (Sept. 27, 2004): C1.

99 Percent Amounts to:	Six Sigma Amounts to:
117,000 pieces of lost first-class mail per hour	1 piece of lost first-class mail every two hours
800,000 mishandled personal checks each day	3 mishandled checks each day
23,087 defective computers shipped each month	8 defective computers shipped each month
7.2 hours per month without electricity	9 seconds per month without electricity

SOURCE: Based on data from *Statistical Abstract for the United States*, U.S. Postal Service, as reported in Tracy Mayor, "Six Sigma Comes to IT: Targeting Perfection," *CIO* (December 1, 2003), 62–70.

EXHIBIT 10.4

The Importance of Quality Improvement Programs

Reduced Cycle Time. Recall our discussion of fast cycle teams from Chapter 8. Cycle time has become a critical quality issue in today's fast-paced world. **Cycle time** refers to the steps taken to complete a company process, such as teaching a class, publishing a textbook, or designing a new car. The simplification of work cycles, including the dropping of barriers between work steps and among departments and the removal of worthless steps in the process, enables a TQM program to succeed. Even if an organization decides not to use quality circles or other techniques, substantial improvement is possible by focusing on improved responsiveness and acceleration of activities into a shorter time. Reduction in cycle time improves overall company performance as well as quality.[33]

cycle time
The steps taken to complete a company process.

L.L. Bean, Inc., the Freeport, Maine, mail-order firm, is a recognized leader in cycle time control. Workers used flowcharts to track their movements, pinpoint wasted motions, and redesign the order-fulfillment process. Today, a computerized system breaks down an order based on the geographic area of the warehouse in which items are stored. Items are placed on conveyor belts, where electronic sensors re-sort the items for individual orders. After orders are packed, they are sent to a FedEx facility on site. Improvements such as these have enabled L.L. Bean to process most orders within two hours after the order is received.[34]

Continuous Improvement. In North America, crash programs and designs have traditionally been the preferred method of innovation. Managers measure the expected benefits of a change and favor the ideas with the biggest payoffs. In contrast, Japanese companies have realized extraordinary success from making a series of mostly small improvements. This approach, called **continuous improvement**, or *kaizen*, is the implementation of a large number of small, incremental improvements in all areas of the organization on an ongoing basis. In a successful TQM program, all employees learn that they are expected to contribute by initiating changes in their own job activities. The basic philosophy is that improving things a little bit at a time, all the time, has the highest probability of success. Innovations can start simple, and employees can build on their success in this unending process. Chris Exline has learned through trial and error how to have a smoother business process as shown in the example below.

continuous improvement
The implementation of a large number of small, incremental improvements in all areas of the organization on an ongoing basis.

Home Essentials

For someone who had never left the United States until he was 32, Chris Exline does well abroad. In fact, he is rarely in North America anymore. Though his company is based in Dallas, you will more likely find him in Dubai, Kuala Lampur, Singapore, Hong Kong, or Baghdad.

It all started six years ago when he went to Singapore to visit some expatriate friends, who told him their employer had given them $5,000 to buy Singapore-compatible appliances. But they had to declare that $5,000 as income. Why not just rent, asked Exline, which would create a tax deduction. On the plane back home, Exline made up his business plan. Furniture rental hardly exists internationally, unlike the United States, where it is a $6-billion industry. Home Essentials customers are multinational corporations, like IBM and Ernst & Young, in addition to local landlords who rent to the corporations. Unlike the common—and six-week-long—practice of shipping employees furniture in containers, Exline rents them everything from couches to microwave ovens for a few hundred dollars a month.

In 1998, Exline invested $750,000 of his own money he had earned as a real estate agent and got the company into the black by 2001, with revenues now at $3.5 million. He knows that where there is an increasing expatriate community, there is a need for end tables and cubicles. To get into Iraq, he needed persistence and found some friends who gave him a ride from Jordan to Baghdad. After several visits with U.S. officials, they realized he was serious, and he was awarded a $90,000 contract from the Agency for International Development for dressers, beds, nightstands, and sofas to go in employee homes. But how to get the furniture there? After a lot of trial and error, he found out the quickest way was to ship containers to Dubai and then truck them in to Iraq. It takes about five weeks for furniture to be manufactured in Asia and move it to Baghdad, to a secure warehouse. But he knows what he is up against. "You can't expect to enter a market like this without factoring in certain disruptions," he says.

A good thing his company motto is: We furnish solutions![35]

TQM Success Factors

Despite its promise, TQM sometimes fails. A few firms have had disappointing results. In particular, Six Sigma principles might not be appropriate for all organizational problems, and some companies have expended tremendous energy and resources for little payoff.[36] Many contingency factors (quality program success factors, listed in Exhibit 10.5) can influence the success of a TQM program. For example, quality circles are most beneficial when employees have challenging jobs; participation in a quality circle can contribute to productivity because it enables employees to pool their knowledge and solve interesting problems. TQM tends to be most successful when it enriches jobs and improves employee motivation. In addition, when participating in the quality program improves workers' problem-solving skills, productivity is likely to increase. Finally, a quality program has the greatest chance of success in a corporate culture that values quality and stresses continuous improvement as a way of life. The best illustration of a successful quality program is still the Japanese car company, Toyota.

Toyota   At many of Toyota's manufacturing plants, workers can assemble as many as eight different models on the same line. Production has been streamlined to the point where workers can build a car in just 20 hours. But speed and flexibility are only part of Toyota's success. Quality is the primary goal. Toyota has a defect rate far below that of any other Japanese or U.S. automaker.

EXHIBIT 10.5

Quality Program Success Factors

Positive Factors	Negative Factors
• Tasks make high skill demands on employees.	• Management expectations are unrealistically high.
• TQM serves to enrich jobs and motivate employees.	• Middle managers are dissatisfied about loss of authority.
• Problem-solving skills are improved for all employees.	• Workers are dissatisfied with other aspects of organizational life.
• Participation and teamwork are used to tackle significant problems.	• Union leaders are left out of QC discussions.
• Continuous improvement is a way of life.	• Managers wait for big, dramatic innovations.

Toyota managers created the doctrine of *kaizen* or continuous improvement. Today, methodically studying problems and quickly solving them is second nature to people throughout the organization. Employees can receive cash awards for searching out glitches in production and coming up with solutions. No detail is too small. The impact of *kaizen* can be seen in the revamping of Toyota's 2004 Sienna minivan after the previous model got disappointing reviews. A lot of small changes amounted to a tremendous improvement. The engine of the Sienna is bigger and more powerful, but it gets better gas mileage. Turning diameter was reduced by 3.2 feet, making the new model nimbler and easier to handle. The third row seats fold flat rather than having to be removed to maximize cargo space. Although the new model is longer and wider and has more head and leg room, the cost of the 2004 Sienna minivan is $920 less than the previous model.

Toyota has kicked its *kaizen* process into overdrive in its quest to become the world's leading automaker (it overtook Ford to become Number 2 in 2004). Unfortunately, the rapid growth has strained Toyota's focus on quality. To stop the quality slide, Toyota is getting back to basics by launching special task forces to reinvigorate the *kaizen* concept. In the Kentucky factory, for example, a group of highly productive employees has been pulled off regular assembly to serve on a special *Kaizen* team. The team works in a barracks-like structure and spends all its time inventing ways to save time and money while maintaining standards of excellence.[37]

Toyota has a slogan emblazoned on a giant banner than hangs in its Takaoka assembly plant just outside Nagoya, Japan: "Yoi Kangae, Yoi Shina!" It means "Good thinking means good products," and the culture of Toyota supports the belief that everyone throughout the company should continuously be thinking of ways to make products better, faster, and cheaper. Though many U.S. and European automakers have implemented elements of TQM, no company has yet come close to Toyota in its execution.

Trends in Quality Control

Many companies are responding to changing economic realities and global competition by reassessing organizational management and processes, including control mechanisms. Some of the major trends in quality and financial control include international quality standards and economic value-added (EVA).

International Quality Standards

One impetus for TQM in the United States is the increasing significance of the global economy. Many countries have endorsed a universal framework for quality assurance called **ISO 9000**, a set of international standards for quality management systems established by the International Organization for Standardization (ISO) in 1987 and revised in late 2000.[38] Hundreds of thousands of organizations in 150 countries, including the United States, have been certified to demonstrate their commitment to quality. Europe continues to lead in the total number of certifications, but the greatest number of new certifications in recent years has been in the United States. One of the more interesting organizations to recently become ISO 9000 certified was the Phoenix, Arizona, Police Department's Records and Information Bureau. In today's environment, where the credibility of law enforcement agencies has been called into question, the Bureau wanted to make a clear statement about its commitment to quality and accuracy of information provided to law enforcement personnel and the public.[39] ISO 9000 has become the recognized standard for evaluating and comparing companies on a global basis, and more U.S. companies are feeling the pressure to participate to remain competitive in international markets. In addition, many countries and companies require ISO 9000 certification before they will do business with an organization.

ISO 9000

A set of international standards for quality management, setting uniform guidelines for processes to ensure that products conform to customer requirements.

economic value-added (EVA)

A control system that measures performance in terms of after-tax profits minus the cost of capital invested in tangible assets.

Economic Value-Added (EVA).   Hundreds of companies, including AT&T, Quaker Oats, the Coca-Cola Company, and Philips Petroleum Company, have set up **economic value-added (EVA)** measurement systems as a new way to gauge financial performance. EVA can be defined as a company's net (after-tax) operating profit minus the cost of capital invested in the company's tangible assets.[40] Measuring performance in terms of EVA is intended to capture all the things a company can do to add value from its activities, such as run the business more efficiently, satisfy customers, and reward shareholders. Each job, department, process, or project in the organization is measured by the value added. EVA can help managers make more cost-effective decisions. At Boise Cascade, the vice president of IT used EVA to measure the cost of replacing the company's existing storage devices against keeping the existing storage assets that had higher maintenance costs. Using EVA demonstrated that buying new storage devices would lower annual maintenance costs significantly and easily make up for the capital expenditure.[41]

Control Systems for Turbulent Times

As we have discussed throughout this text, globalization, increased competition, rapid change, and uncertainty have resulted in new organizational structures and management methods that emphasize information sharing, employee participation, learning, and teamwork. These shifts have, in turn, led to some new approaches to control. Two significant aspects of control in today's organizations are open-book management and the use of the balanced scorecard.

Open-Book Management

In an organizational environment that touts information sharing, teamwork, and the role of managers as facilitators, executives cannot hoard information and financial data. They must admit employees throughout the organization into the loop of financial control and responsibility to encourage active participation and commitment to goals. A growing number of managers are opting for full disclosure in the form of open-book management. **Open-book management** allows employees to see—through charts, computer printouts, meetings, and so forth—the financial condition of the company. Second, open-book management shows the individual employee how his or her job fits into the big picture and affects the financial future of the organization. Finally, open-book management ties employee rewards to the company's overall success. With training in interpreting the financial data, employees can see the interdependence and importance of each function. If they are rewarded according to performance, they become motivated to take responsibility for their entire team or function, rather than merely their individual jobs.[42] Cross-functional communication and cooperation are enhanced.

The goal of open-book management is to get every employee thinking and acting like a business owner. To get employees to think like owners, management provides them with the same information owners have: what money is coming in and where it is going. Open-book management helps employees appreciate why efficiency is important to the organization's—and their own—success. Open-book management turns traditional control on its head. This chapter's Best Practices box describes how Ricardo Semler runs a successful company by being an "anti-control freak" when it comes to financial data and information.

CONCEPT CONNECTION

The war in Iraq created a need for security contractors to perform many military functions outsourced by the stretched-thin Pentagon. Many of these firms are headed by former members of elite units, such as the ex-Navy SEALs in this photo, who are employees of Blackwater. Managers at these firms are typically very mission-oriented, but they may lack the management expertise to develop effective **control systems for turbulent times**. *They might know everything about securing a building or guarding a top officer, but nothing at all about business ideas such as* **open book management** *or new* **financial control systems**. *As these firms branched into more varied activities and events in Iraq grew more complex and volatile, the lack of business experience led to chaos for many contractors.*

In some countries, managers have more trouble running an open-book company because prevailing attitudes and standards encourage confidentiality and even secrecy concerning financial results. Many businesspeople in countries such as China, Russia, and South Korea are unaccustomed to disclosing financial details, which can present problems for multinational companies operating there.[43] Exhibit 10.6 lists a portion of a recent *Opacity Index*, developed by PricewaterhouseCoopers, which indicates the degree to which various countries are open regarding economic matters. The higher the rating, the more opaque, or hidden, the economy of that country. In the partial index in Exhibit 10.6, China has the highest opacity rating at 87, and Singapore the lowest at 29. The United States has an opacity rating of 36, which is fairly low. In countries with higher ratings, financial figures are typically closely guarded, and managers may be discouraged from sharing information with employees and the public. Globalization is beginning to have an impact on economic opacity in various countries by encouraging a convergence toward global accounting standards that support more accurate collection, recording, and reporting of financial information.

The Balanced Scorecard

Another recent innovation is to integrate the various dimensions of control, combining internal financial measurements and statistical reports with a concern for markets and customers as well as employees.[44] Whereas many managers once focused primarily on measuring and controlling financial performance, they are recognizing the need to measure other, intangible aspects of performance to assess the value-creating activities of the contemporary organization.[45] Many of today's companies compete primarily on the basis of ideas and

> **Take ACTION**
>
> As a manager, consider letting subordinates know what is going on and what is in the financial statements.

> **open-book management**
>
> Sharing financial information and results with all employees in the organization.

BEST PRACTICES

Semco's Open Book Policy

When Ricardo Semler took over from his father as head of the family business, Brazil's Semco, he decided to manage based on a philosophy of "giving up control" by having faith in people and respect for their ideas. At Semco, he designed a business model in which employees have no set work schedules, no dress codes, no strict rules and regulations, and no employee manuals. Workers choose their own training and nobody approves expense accounts. About 30 percent of employees even set their own pay, and everyone in the company knows everyone else's salary. All workers receive the company's financial statements and are taught how to read them through classes set up by the labor union. Two board seats are reserved for employees, and board meetings are open to all employees who want to attend. Self-managed teams have replaced the management hierarchy, and people have a chance to choose how they can best contribute to the company. Top managers are evaluated on a regular basis by employees with the outcomes posted for all to see.

The idea that ties all this together is Semler's belief in taking top management out of running the business, which led *Fortune* magazine to give him the title of "anti-control freak." Semler believes that if an organization gives people complete freedom and full information, they will act in their own, and consequently the company's, best interests. "It is only when you rein them in, when you tell them what to do and how to think, that they become inflexible, bureaucratic, and stagnant," says Semler. Semler dislikes the American organization model, which he sees as basically a military hierarchy. Despite all the freedom, organizational control at Semco is strong, based not on power and authority but on organizational vision and cultural values that emphasize self-initiative, self-discipline, and full disclosure of all types of information. Employees think like business owners because they can see how their jobs and actions fit in and contribute to the organization's—and their own—success or failure.

The decentralized approach must be working. In the past ten years, Semco has quadrupled its revenues and increased its workforce from 450 to 1,300 employees. Semler believes his company's success is a powerful reminder that it is possible to have an efficient business with shared norms, values, and self-discipline replacing strict rules and controls, guided by managers who lead rather than wield their power.

SOURCES: A. J. Vogl, "The Anti-CEO," *Across the Board*, (May/June 2004): 30–36; Geoffrey Colvin, "The Anti-Control Freak," *Fortune* (November 26, 2001): 60, 80; and Ricardo Semler, "How We Went Digital Without a Strategy," *Harvard Business Review* (September/October 2000): 51–58

EXHIBIT 10.6

International Opacity Index: Which countries have the most secretive economies?

Country	Opacity Rating
China	87
Russia	84
Indonesia	75
Turkey	74
South Korea	73
Romania	71
Poland	64
India	64
Argentina	61
Taiwan	61
Japan	60
Italy	48
Mexico	48
United Kingdom	38
United States	36
Singapore	29

SOURCE: The Opacity Index, http://www.opacity-index.com accessed on July 22, 2004.

The higher the opacity rating, the more secretive the national economy, meaning that prevailing attitudes and standards discourage openness regarding financial results and other data.

balanced scorecard

A comprehensive management control system that balances traditional financial measures with measures of customer service, internal business processes, and the organization's capacity for learning and growth.

Take *ACTION*

As a manager, try the balanced scorecard to get away from a strictly financial method of determining success.

relationships, which requires that managers find ways to measure intangible as well as tangible assets.

One fresh approach is the balanced scorecard. The **balanced scorecard** is a comprehensive management control system that balances traditional financial measures with operational measures relating to a company's critical success factors.[46] A balanced scorecard contains four major perspectives, as illustrated in Exhibit 10.7: financial performance, customer service, internal business processes, and the organization's capacity for learning and growth.[47] Within these four areas, managers identify key performance metrics the organization will track. The financial performance perspective reflects a concern that the organization's activities contribute to improving short-term and long-term financial performance. It includes traditional measures such as net income and return on investment. Customer service indicators measure such things as how customers view the organization, as well as customer retention and satisfaction. Business process indicators focus on production and operating statistics, such as order fulfillment or cost per order. The final component looks at the organization's potential for learning and growth, focusing on how well resources and human capital are being managed for the company's future. Metrics may include employee retention and the introduction of new products. The components of the scorecard are designed in an integrative manner as illustrated in Exhibit 10.7.

Managers record, analyze, and discuss these various metrics to determine how well the organization is achieving its strategic goals. At its best, the use of the scorecard cascades down from the top levels of the organization, so everyone becomes involved in thinking about and discussing strategy.[48] The scorecard has become the core management control system for many organizations today, including well-known organizations such as Bell Emergis (a division of Bell Canada), ExxonMobil, Cigna Insurance, British Airways, Hilton Hotels Corp., and even some units of the United States federal government.[49] British Airways clearly ties its use of the balanced scorecard to the feedback control model we discussed early in this chapter. Scorecards are used as the agenda for monthly management meetings. Managers focus on the various elements of the scorecard to set targets, evaluate performance, and guide discussion about what further actions are needed.[50] As with all management systems, the balanced scorecard is not right for every organization in every situation. The simplicity of the

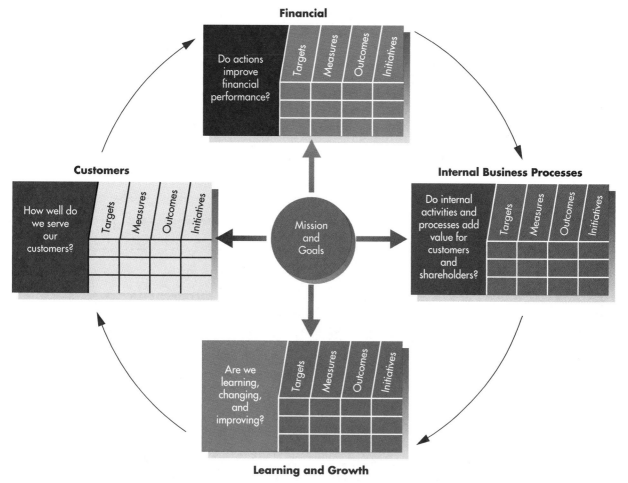

SOURCES: Based on Robert S. Kaplan and David P. Norton, "Using the Balanced Scorecard as a Strategic Management System," *Harvard Business Review* (January–February 1996), 75–85; and Chee W. Chow, Kamal M. Haddad, and James E. Williamson, "Applying the Balanced Scorecard to Small Companies," *Management Accounting 79*, no. 2 (August 1997), 21–27.

EXHIBIT 10.7

The Balanced Scorecard

system causes some managers to underestimate the time and commitment that is needed for the approach to become a useful management control system.

New Workplace Concerns

Managers in today's organizations face some difficult control issues. The matter of control has come to the forefront in light of the failure of top executives and corporate directors to provide oversight and control at companies such as Enron, HealthSouth, Adelphia, and WorldCom. Thus, there is a move toward increasing control in many organizations, particularly in terms of **corporate governance**, which refers to the system of governing an organization so the interests of corporate owners are protected. The financial reporting systems and the roles of boards of directors are being scrutinized in organizations around the world. At the same time, top leaders are keeping a closer eye on the activities of lower-level managers and employees. In a fast-moving environment, undercontrol can be a problem because managers cannot keep personal tabs on everything in a large, global organization. Consider, for example, that many of the CEOs who have been indicted in connection with financial misdeeds have claimed they were unaware the misconduct was going on. In some cases, this might be true, and it reflects a significant breakdown in control. Because managers cannot personally keep tabs on every employee and activity at all times, effective control systems are essential. Top managers are responsible for what goes on in the organization.

corporate governance

The system of governing an organization so the interests of corporate owners are protected.

However, overcontrol can be an equally touchy situation. Managers might feel justified in monitoring e-mail and Internet use, for example, to ensure employees are directing their behavior toward work rather than personal outcomes and alleviate concerns about potential racial or sexual harassment. Yet employees often resent and feel demeaned by close monitoring that limits their personal freedom and makes them feel as if they are constantly being watched. Excessive control of employees can lead to demotivation, low morale, lack of trust, and hostility among workers. Managers have to find an appropriate balance, as well as develop and communicate clear policies regarding workplace monitoring. Although oversight and control are important, good organizations depend on mutual trust and respect among managers and employees.

Manager's Solution

This chapter introduced a number of important concepts about organizational control. Organizational control is the systematic process through which managers regulate organizational activities to meet planned goals and standards of performance. The focus of the control system may include feedforward control to prevent problems, concurrent control to monitor ongoing activities, and feedback control to evaluate past performance. Well-designed control systems include four key steps: establish standards, measure performance, compare performance to standards, and make corrections as necessary.

Budgeting is one of the most commonly used forms of managerial control. Managers might use expense budgets, revenue budgets, cash budgets, and capital budgets, for example. Other financial controls include use of the balance sheet, income statement, and financial analysis of these documents.

The philosophy of controlling has shifted to reflect changes in leadership methods. Traditional bureaucratic controls emphasize establishing rules and procedures, then monitoring employee behavior to make sure the rules and procedures are followed. With decentralized control, employees assume responsibility for monitoring their own performance.

Besides monitoring financial results, organizations control the quality of their goods and services. They might do this by adopting TQM techniques such as quality circles, benchmarking, Six Sigma, reduced cycle time, and continuous improvement.

Recent trends in control include the use of international quality standards and EVA systems. Other important aspects of control in today's turbulent environment are open-book management and use of the balanced scorecard. In addition, concerns such as corporate governance and employee monitoring are significant issues for managers.

The story of Gateway, Inc., at the beginning of the chapter demonstrates the importance of control. The control system at Gateway, developed and based on the personal preferences of co-founder and CEO Ted Waitt, was too loose for the organization as it grew large and complex. The company's losses began piling up and market share was declining. Waitt shifted toward a system emphasizing rigorous measurement and discipline to get Gateway back on track. At the company's new Poway, California, headquarters, a 9-foot by 12-foot screen that is visible to all employees displays a running daily score comparing sales and costs with projected targets. Specific goals for all managers and departments are clearly defined, and their performance is regularly reviewed by Gateway's top human resources executive. This new approach to performance measurement has led to the departure of several managers who consistently failed to meet goals or did not agree with action plans for correction. After Gateway acquired eMachines, Waitt turned the CEO's job over to eMachines head Wayne Inouye, who takes a more disciplined approach to measurement and control than Waitt. In addition to monitoring costs, sales, and other financial metrics, the new system includes ways to measure customer service and satisfaction. Gateway is still struggling, and it is too soon to tell if the more disciplined control approach can save the company. However, focusing on specific targets has had a significant impact. For example, the first week Gateway began tracking customer service indicators, managers were hitting their performance targets only 60 percent of the time. Within a couple of weeks, the rate had increased to 98 percent. In the second quarter of 2004, Gateway announced a better-than-expected increase in sales, indicating that performance in that area is improving as well.[51]

Discussion Questions

1. Why is it important for managers to understand the process of organizational control?

2. How might a public school system use feedforward control to identify the best candidates for its teaching positions?

3. How might the manager of a family-style restaurant use concurrent controls to ensure that the restaurant is providing customers with the highest quality food and service? What feedback controls could be useful?

4. What standards of performance has your professor established for this class? How will your actual performance be measured? How will your performance be compared to the standards? Do you think the standards and methods of measurement are fair? Why or why not?

5. What is the difference between budgeting and financial analysis? Why is each type of control important to a company?

6. Imagine that you are going to be the manager of a new Wal-Mart being built in your area. What items might be listed in your capital budget? What items might be listed in your expense budget?

7. In what ways could a university benefit from bureaucratic control? In what ways might it benefit from decentralized control? Overall, which approach do you think would be best at your college or university? Why?

8. If you were managing a local video rental store, which company would you choose to benchmark one aspect of your store's performance against? Why?

9. Would you like to work for a company that uses open-book management? Would you like to be a manager in the company? Why or why not?

10. Why is it important for an organization's control system to be linked to its overall strategy?

Manager's Workbook

Are You Fast Enough to Succeed in Internet Time?

Is your company, or idea of a company, ready to handle the kind of productivity and speed required to make it on the Internet? Do YOU have what it takes to be a successful and productive Netprenuer? Take the quiz below and find out.

Does Your Business Have What It Takes to Move at Internet Speed?

What is an Internet year? It's the time in which an e-company needs to accomplish the kind of business goals that once took a year. Conventional wisdom puts an Internet year anywhere from 60 to 90 days. Regardless, few will argue that companies need to move faster now than ever imagined.

Can you afford the luxury of in-depth analysis, full due diligence, building consensus, test marketing—all the cornerstones of responsible corporate management? Does their value change when you weigh it against the cost to your company's scarcest commodity—time?

Kelsey Biggers, executive vice president of Micro Modeling Associates (MMA), offers the following scenarios to help determine whether you are capable of operating at Internet speed. Choose the best course of action from the choices given.

1. You have met a company that can be a potential strategic partner for marketing your service to a new industry online. The vibes are good and you want to map out the potential relationship, but in order to do so you need to share client and billing information. A nondisclosure agreement is necessary, and the company hands you their standard agreement. What do you do?

   a. Get a copy of your company's standard nondisclosure agreement and submit it to your potential partner as an alternative to their NDA.

   b. Fax the agreement to your lawyer and ask her to get back to you ASAP with any amendments so you can continue the conversation.

   c. Look over the agreement and sign it right away.

2. You're looking for a creative director for your Web site, and you know the position will be critical to your whole look and feel online. You hope to have three or four excellent candidates to choose from and have considered doing a retained search for the position. Out of nowhere your old college roommate, whom you respect enormously, refers you to an associate of his for the

position. Meeting the candidate for breakfast and reviewing his work, you are blown away. You have three choices:

a. Offer the candidate the job before the check arrives.

b. Give the candidate a strong "warm and fuzzy" that there is a job for him while you initiate a quick search for a couple alternate candidates.

c. Schedule a round of interviews with your senior colleagues back in the office to confirm your positive instincts, while also identifying one or two alternative candidates for comparison.

3. Your online strategy calls for targeting two vertical markets for your service in the next nine months. Your service can be tailored to meet the buying needs of companies in several industries, so it's a matter of picking the right industries to target. High-growth, dynamic industries are obviously preferred. Which approach would you select?

a. Hire an MBA with finance and marketing and ask her to create high-level screening criteria for target industries and identify the five best fits for your services.

b. Hire your neighbor, who happens to be a doctor and knows the health-care industry and can make several introductions into HMOs and pharmaceutical companies.

c. Ask an intern to research publicly available information from Gartner Group, Forrester Research, and other industry analyst organizations for online spending habits in different industries and make recommendations.

4. Your company has been looking to merge with a strategic partner for some time. You have identified three companies that would be good fits, but each has its advantages and disadvantages. Which would you choose?

a. Company A offers a service that is perfectly complementary to your own, and the price is right.

However, the company has indicated that it doesn't feel it has enough scale to do a merger now and would rather wait nine months until after the holiday selling season to complete the transaction.

b. Company B is smaller and dynamic, but has grown too fast and has a bad balance sheet. They could be picked up immediately, but your company would have to assume some unwanted debt along with the merger.

c. Company C has a great offline presence in their space, but has not yet executed their e-commerce plan. They feel the two companies would be a great fit once they had established their online presence by mid-summer.

5. Your e-commerce strategy requires a real-time fulfillment system that can process orders straight through and provide data on client buying patterns. You have looked outside your firm for technology support to help bring this capability online and have been presented with three alternative approaches from which you must choose one:

a. A senior programmer from your prior firm is now a freelance consultant. He can get started immediately and hire a dozen coders who promise to get a capability up and running in 60 days and grow out the functionality.

b. Your internal technology group can staff a team of a dozen people to build out the system in a year and will then have the ability to support and grow the service when it goes live.

c. An e-solutions consultancy can project, manage, and build the entire system, but would want to take 60 days to design the technical architecture before starting development. They insist this time is necessary to ensure a scaleable service.

Note to Student: See Appendix B to check your responses.

SOURCE: Adapted by Dorothy Marcic from "Are You Fast Enough to Succeed in Internet Time? Does Your Business Have What It Takes to Move at Internet Speed?" *Entrepreneur Magazine*, September 1999.

Manager's Workshop

Organizational Control Mechanisms

1. Divide into groups of five or six members.

2. Each group examines the following university request form for a complimentary parking pass and identifies flaws with the design of the form.

3. After identifying basic design flaws, groups then answer the following questions:

   a. *Is the control cost effective?* Are the costs associated with the control mechanism offset by the benefits derived?

   b. *Is the control acceptable?* Do the people affected believe it is necessary?

   c. *Is the control appropriate?* Are the steps involved commensurate with the activity?

   d. *Is the process strategic?* Is it a critical activity in the operation of the university?

   e. *Is the control reliable and effective?* Is it clear what criteria are necessary for the approval of the request and what will be construed as sufficient justification?

REQUEST FOR COMPLIMENTARY CAMPUS PARKING PERMITS

Requesting Department: _____

Person Requesting: _____

Phone: _____

Event: _____

Date(s): _____

Time(s): _____

Number of Persons for Event: _____

Number of Permits Requested: _____

Permits Mailed: _____

Justification for Waived Fee: _____

Dean Signature _____

Vice-President Signature _____

Approve: _____

Approve: _____

Disapprove: _____

Disapprove: _____

SOURCE: Adapted by Dorothy Marcic from H. Eugene Baker III and Kenneth M. Jennings, (1994). "An Out of Control Organizational Control Mechanism." *Journal of Management Education*, vol. 18 (3), pp. 380–384.

Management in Practice: Ethical Dilemma

Go Along to Get Along?

Rhonda Gilchrist became a nurse because she wanted to help people. As the home health-care industry began to take off, she was presented with what she thought was a terrific opportunity:

A startup home health-care agency offered her a position managing its staff of visiting nurses. She supported home health care because patients were treated in the relaxed, comfortable atmosphere of their homes; home visits gave patients and nurses more independence; and home visits were intended to be much cheaper than hospital stays or doctor's office visits. Therefore, Rhonda eagerly accepted the job.

Most of the patients treated by Gilchrist's nurses were elderly, with a variety of complaints ranging from diabetes to hip injuries. At first, Gilchrist encouraged her staff to make their visits efficient and productive so that patients could be weaned from care in a timely manner. She assumed this was what the head of the agency wanted. However, when she reported that one patient had recovered enough from a heart attack that he no longer needed three visits a week, the agency owner replied, "You should be looking for ways to increase the number of visits, not decrease them!" Gilchrist was shocked, but she soon understood that the only way to keep her job—and the jobs of her nurses—was to go along with her company's wishes. Those extra visits, paid for by Medicare, were paying her salary.

Meanwhile, Gilchrist did some research on her own. She learned that the average home-care patient now gets 80 visits per year (nearly four times the number of a decade ago), for which Medicare pays up to $90 per visit. In 1995, Medicare spent $16 billion on home care. Although lawmakers eagerly embraced the idea of home health care in the 1980s, believing that the shift would save insurance companies, Medicare, and even average citizens a huge sum, the savings haven't materialized. In fact, the opposite has happened. Rhonda knows home health care is extremely important to many patients, but she also realizes it is being abused by others, as well as by the agencies. As she learned in her research, people who want to start up home health agencies

don't even need any type of special training. One local doctor told her in confidence that the owner of her own agency, an engineer by training, simply wanted to open his own business, so he chose between retail clothing and home health care. The latter, with its guaranteed payments from Medicare, was a sure bet.

As she drove to the office, Rhonda considered her alternatives. She knew that some of her clients no longer needed care. But she also knew that she needed a job, and most patients were lonely and looked forward to the visits. She wondered if there was a better way to control costs and deliver the best care to her patients.

What Do You Do?

1. Go along with the status quo and forget about the abuses of the system—that's your boss's problem. Besides, Medicare has deep pockets.

2. Look for another job as soon as possible. You don't want to be associated with unethical, and potentially illegal, practices.

3. Approach the owner of the agency and suggest other ways the agency might make a profit and deliver high-quality care, such as innovative ways to attract new clients to replace those that leave the roster in better health.

SOURCE: Based on George Anders and Laurie McGinley, "Medical Morass: How Do You Tame a Wild U.S. Program?" *The Wall Street Journal,* March 6, 1997, pp. A1, A8.

Case for Critical Analysis

Lincoln Electric

Imagine having a management system that is so successful people refer to it with capital letters—the Lincoln Management System—and other businesses benchmark their own systems by it. That is the situation of Ohio-based Lincoln Electric. For a number of years, other companies have tried to figure out Lincoln Electric's secret—how management coaxes maximum

productivity and quality from its workers, even during difficult financial times.

Lincoln Electric is a leading manufacturer of welding products, welding equipment, and electric motors, with more than $1 billion in sales and 6,000 workers worldwide. The company's products are used for cutting, manufacturing, and repairing other metal products. Although it is now a publicly traded company, members of the Lincoln family still own more than 60 percent of the stock.

Lincoln uses a diverse control approach. Tasks are rigidly defined, and individual employees must meet strict measurable standards of performance. However, the Lincoln system succeeds largely because of an organizational culture based on openness and trust, shared control, and an egalitarian spirit. Although the line between managers and workers at Lincoln is firmly drawn, managers respect the expertise of production workers and value their contributions to many aspects of the business. The company has an open-door policy for all top executives, middle managers, and production workers, and regular face-to-face communication is encouraged. Workers are expected to challenge management if they believe practices or compensation rates are unfair. Most workers are hired right out of high school, then trained and cross-trained to perform different jobs. Some eventually are promoted to executive positions, because Lincoln believes in promoting from within. Many Lincoln workers stay with the company for life.

One of Lincoln's founders felt that organizations should be based on certain values, including honesty, trustworthiness, openness, self-management, loyalty, accountability, and cooperativeness. These values continue to form the core of Lincoln's culture, and management regularly rewards employees who manifest them. Because Lincoln so effectively socializes employees, they exercise a great degree of self-control on the job. Production workers are paid on a piece-rate system, plus merit pay based on performance. Employees also are eligible for annual bonuses that fluctuate according to the company's fortunes, and they participate in stock purchase plans. Bonuses are based on a number of factors, such as productivity, quality, dependability, and cooperation with others. Factory workers at Lincoln have been known to earn more than $100,000 a year, and the average compensation in 1996 was $62,000. However, there also are other, less tangible rewards. Pride of workmanship and feelings of involvement, contribution, and esprit de corps are intrinsic rewards that flourish at Lincoln Electric. Cross-functional teams, empowered to make decisions, take responsibility for product planning, development, and marketing. Information about the company's operations and financial performance is openly shared with workers throughout the company.

Lincoln places emphasis on anticipating and solving customer problems. Sales representatives are given the technical training they need to understand customer needs, help customers understand and use Lincoln's products, and solve problems. This customer focus is backed up by attention to the production process through the use of strict accountability standards and formal measurements for productivity, quality, and innovation for all employees. In addition, a software program called Rhythm is used to streamline the flow of goods and materials in the production process.

Lincoln's system has worked extremely well in the United States. The cultural values, open communication, and formal control and reward systems interact to align the goals of managers, workers, and the organization as well as encourage learning and growth. Now Lincoln is discovering whether its system can hold up overseas. Although most of Lincoln's profits come from domestic operations, and a foreign venture in the 1990s lost a lot of money for the company, top managers want to expand globally because foreign markets are growing much more rapidly than domestic markets. Thus far, Lincoln managers have not developed a strategic control plan for global operations, relying instead on duplicating the domestic Lincoln system.

Questions

1. What types of control—feedforward, concurrent, or feedback—are illustrated in this case? Explain.

2. Based on what you've just read, what do you think makes the Lincoln System so successful?

3. What changes might Lincoln managers have to make to adapt their management system to overseas operations?

SOURCE: Joseph Maciariello, "A Pattern of Success: Can This Company Be Duplicated?" *Drucker Management*, 1 (1) (Spring 1997), pp. 7–11.

PART

6

Leading

Someone once observed that a director must be artist and commander. As an artist, the director is a leader, a passionate and creative visionary inspiring all involved to make the best movie they can. When the director is wearing a commander's hat, he or she functions as an authoritative, tough-minded manager, one who makes countless decisions and solves various problems.

Communicating with cast and crew is the main means directors employ to exert their leadership role. Stephen Spielberg has observed that directing is 80 percent communication and only 20 percent know-how. What a director needs to communicate to members of the filmmaking team is how to make their contributions to the story they are all committed to telling. There is no one communication style that guarantees a project's success. As director and actress Jodie Foster puts it, "Any language is good language. Anything that gets through to the actor is fine."

Communicating with actors is a particularly fascinating and curious process because the director and the actor are trying to put themselves into the shoes of a third person who does not, strictly speaking, exist. Some directors are more open to two-way communication than others. When working with Alfred Hitchcock, an artist who never shied away from the commander role, actors usually found that communications was a one-way affair. The director did not feel in need of anyone else's creative input in part due to his uncanny ability to visualize a movie in great detail when he read the script. He knew what he wanted, and it was the actor's job to deliver. Still communication—often in shorthand form—took place. Though Jimmy Stewart, hero of *Rear Window* (1954) and other Hitchcock classics, could not recall the director ever discussing a scene with an actor, he did remember Hitchcock occasionally telling him at the end of a take, "Jim, the scene is tired." Stewart understood what he meant: the next time, he needed to work on his timing and pacing.

In contrast, most directors today welcome collaboration with cast members. For example, Spike Lee, director of 1998's *He Got Game*, believes it is his role to make the actors feel comfortable. "I just try to make them feel a part of the process and let them feel that they can contribute." Leonardo DiCaprio, who has worked with director Martin Scorsese in both *Gangs of New York* (2002) and *The Aviator* (2004), says that Scorsese "loves to have actors come to the table with an array of different information and different new ideas and challenging things." Unlike Hitchcock, most directors feel that having a firm grasp of where the film is heading and sharing that vision with cast and crew allow them to entertain suggestions; they can confidently sort out which ones make sense and which do not. Like all managers, then, directors spend most of their working days in purpose-driven communication with subordinates: listening to their ideas, closely observing their performance, and giving them feedback, all of which is designed to accomplish an articulated, shared goal.

CHAPTER

11

Foundations of Behavior in Organizations

LEARNING OBJECTIVES

After studying this chapter, you should be able to do the following:

1 **Define attitudes, including their major components, and explain their relationship to personality, perception, and behavior.**

2 **Discuss the importance of work-related attitudes.**

3 **Identify major personality traits and describe how personality can influence workplace attitudes and behaviors.**

4 **Define the four components of emotional intelligence and explain why they are important for today's managers.**

5 **Explain how people learn in general and in terms of individual learning styles.**

6 **Discuss the effects of stress and identify ways individuals and organizations can manage stress to improve employee health, satisfaction, and productivity.**

Vinita Gupta never expected running a company to be easy, but she was not prepared for this. Gupta had founded the networking equipment maker Quick Eagle Networks in 1985 under the name Digital Link, took it public 10 years later, and then stepped out for a couple of years. After sales plummeted, she returned as CEO to turn things around. Sales and profits improved, but employee morale kept getting worse. Employees were quitting in droves, with annual turnover hitting 30 percent. Spirits were so low that key executives were jumping ship, leaving profitable Quick Eagle to join profitless competitors. When Gupta tried to determine what was going on, she uncovered an unnerving possibility: Could her own personality and attitudes be part of the problem? Introverted, soft-spoken, and highly focused on work, Gupta had always depended on other managers to be the cheerleaders and coaches in the company. But now, she was hearing through the grapevine that people found her aloof and unapproachable, and that the stiff, serious atmosphere she created made Quick Eagle not a fun place to work. Gupta was accustomed to focusing on details of the business and making necessary changes to keep quality, sales, and profits high. But maybe boosting morale and stemming the tide of talented workers walking out the door meant she had to make some changes in herself.[1]

If you were Vinita Gupta, how would you gain a better understanding of yourself, your employees, and the changes you need to make to improve morale at Quick Eagle Networks? Do you believe the personality of a company's CEO affects organizational performance?

People differ in many ways. Some are quiet and shy, and others are gregarious; some are thoughtful and serious, and others are impulsive and fun-loving. Employees—and managers—bring their individual differences to work each day. Differences in attitudes, values, personality, and behavior influence how people interpret an assignment, whether they like to be told what to do, how they handle challenges, and how they interact with others. Managers' personalities and attitudes, as well as their ability to understand individual differences among employees, can profoundly affect the workplace and influence employee motivation, morale, and job performance. People are an organization's most valuable resource and the source of some of managers' most difficult problems. Three basic leadership skills are at the core of identifying and solving people problems: diagnosing or gaining insight into the situation a manager wants to influence; adapting individual behavior and resources to meet the needs of the situation; and communicating in a way that others can understand and accept. Thus, managers need insight about individual differences to understand what a behavioral situation is now and what it may be in the future.

To handle this responsibility, managers must understand the principles of organizational behavior, that is, the ways individuals and groups tend to act in organizations. By increasing their knowledge of individual differences in the areas of attitudes, personality, perception, learning, and stress management, managers can understand and lead employees and colleagues through many workplace challenges. This chapter introduces basic principles of organizational behavior in each of these areas.

Organizational Behavior

organizational behavior (OB)

An interdisciplinary field dedicated to the study of how individuals and groups tend to act in organizations.

Organizational behavior, commonly called OB, is an interdisciplinary field dedicated to the study of human attitudes, behavior, and performance in organizations. OB draws concepts from many disciplines, including psychology, sociology, cultural anthropology, industrial engineering, economics, ethics, and vocational counseling, as well as the discipline of management. The concepts and principles of OB are important to managers because in every organization human beings ultimately make the decisions that control how the organization will acquire and use resources. Those people may cooperate with, compete with, support, or undermine one another. Their beliefs and feelings about themselves, their coworkers, and the organization shape what they do and how well they do it. People can distract the organization from its strategy by engaging in conflict and misunderstandings, or they can pool their diverse talents and perspectives to accomplish much more as a group than they could ever do as individuals.

organizational citizenship

Work behavior that goes beyond job requirements and contributes as needed to the organization's success.

By understanding what causes people to behave as they do, managers can exercise leadership to achieve positive outcomes. They can foster behaviors such as **organizational citizenship,** that is, work behavior that goes beyond job requirements and contributes as needed to the organization's success. An employee demonstrates organizational citizenship by being helpful to coworkers and customers, doing extra work when necessary, and looking for ways to improve products and procedures. These behaviors enhance the organization's performance by helping to build social capital, as described in Chapter 9.[2] Organizational citizenship helps build positive relationships within the organization and with customers, leading to a high level of social capital and smooth organizational functioning. Managers can encourage organizational citizenship by applying their knowledge of human behavior, such as selecting people with positive attitudes and personalities, helping them see how they can contribute, and enabling them to learn from and cope with workplace challenges.

Take **ACTION**

No matter what job you have, strive to be a good corporate citizen, work hard, get along with others, and be the kind of colleague with whom others want to work.

Attitudes

Most students have probably heard the expression that someone "has an attitude problem," which means there is some consistent quality about the person that affects his or her behavior in a negative way. An employee with an attitude problem might be hard to get along with, might constantly gripe and cause problems, and might persistently resist new ideas. We all seem to know intuitively what an attitude is, but we do not consciously think about how strongly attitudes affect behavior. Defined formally, an **attitude** is an evaluation—positive or negative—that predisposes a person to act in a certain way. Understanding employee attitudes is important to managers because attitudes determine how people perceive the work environment, interact with others, and behave on the job. A person who has the attitude "I love my work; it's challenging and fun" probably will tackle work-related problems cheerfully; one who comes to work with the attitude "I hate my job" is not likely to show much enthusiasm or commitment to solving problems. Managers strive to develop and reinforce positive attitudes among employees.

Managers should recognize that negative attitudes can be the result of underlying problems in the workplace as well as a contributor to forthcoming problems.[3] For example, top executives at Federated Department Stores appointed a young, computer whiz-kid as chief operating officer for its e-commerce division. Older managers with years of experience in retailing had negative attitudes about this guy they considered still wet behind the ears, and the new COO had negative attitudes about older workers, whom he considered slow to accept new ideas or learn new methods. Soon, experienced managers started leaving the company. Federated's top leaders realized that the company needed to do a better job of handling generational diversity and help employees develop more positive attitudes.[4]

Components of Attitudes

One important step for managers is recognizing and understanding the components of attitudes, which is particularly important when attempting to change attitudes. Behavioral scientists consider attitudes to have three components: cognitions (thoughts), affect (feelings), and behavior.[5] The cognitive component of an attitude includes the beliefs, opinions, and information the person has about the object of the attitude, such as knowledge of what a job entails and opinions about personal abilities. The affective component is the person's emotions or feelings about the object of the attitude, such as enjoying or hating a job. The behavioral component of an attitude is the person's intention to behave toward the object of the attitude in a certain way. Exhibit 11.1 illustrates the three components of a positive attitude toward one's job. The cognitive element is the conscious thought that "my job is interesting and challenging." The affective element is the feeling that "I love this job." These, in turn, are related to the behavioral component: An employee might choose to arrive at work early because he or she is happy with the job.

Often, when we think about attitudes, we focus on the cognitive component. However, managers must remember the other components as well. When people feel strongly about something, the affective component may influence them to act in a certain way, no matter what someone does to change their opinions. Recall the discussion of idea champions in Chapter 8. When someone is passionate about a new idea, he or she may go to great lengths to implement it, even when colleagues and superiors say the idea is stupid. Another example is an employee who is furious about being asked to work overtime on his birthday. The supervisor might present clear, rational reasons for the need to work overtime, but the employee might still act based on his anger by failing to cooperate, lashing out at coworkers, or quitting. In cases such as these, effective leadership includes addressing the affect (emotions) associated with the attitude. Are employees so excited that their judgment may be clouded, or so discouraged that

attitude
A cognitive and affective evaluation that predisposes a person to act in a certain way.

Take ACTION

If you find yourself having a negative reaction toward someone, look within yourself and see what it is inside of you that might be causing that attitude.

EXHIBIT 11.1

*Components of an
Attitude*

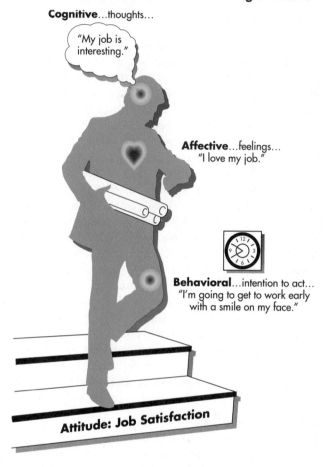

Cognitive...thoughts...

"My job is
interesting."

Affective...feelings...
"I love my job."

Behavioral...intention to act...
"I'm going to get to work early
with a smile on my face."

Attitude: Job Satisfaction

they have given up trying? If nothing else, the manager probably needs to be aware of situations that involve strong emotions and should give employees a chance to vent their feelings appropriately. Leaders, too, can allow emotions to cloud their judgment, as Umang Gupta did when he started his company. He paid dearly for his over-rated self-assessment, as described below.

Keynote Systems

Ever since Umang Gupta moved from India to the United States in 1980, he wanted to start his own computer company. Realizing Silicon Valley was a good place for training, he first worked at IBM and then moved to the start-up Oracle, helping to write its business plan.

His dream persisted, and in 1984, he launched Gupta Corp., sparsely financed from fees of early customers, such as Lotus Corp. This is a riskier strategy than venture capital financing because it demands a lengthy technological lead to withstand competition from later and better financed rivals. But the strategy worked for a while anyway. Gupta's vision of creating software to manage databases brought in enough revenue to peak at $400 million, allowing Gupta to have a net worth of $100 million "for a few days." He had a mission to change the world, and so far, it had worked. Because of the power of his mission, he was cramming as many meetings as he could each day.

Then the bottom fell out. Powerful new well-financed competitors piled into the market and Gupta Corp. suffered through seven quarters of losses. Stock prices plummeted. Gupta resigned as CEO and the company changed its name to Centura Software. He now realizes he made a number of mistakes. First, he was undercapitalized and could not withstand later competition. Then, he rode the company on one techncology only, making it too vulnerable. But the root of these problems, he says, was his own ego, or the "hubris danger zone." He felt so certain of his own ideas that he did not listen to others enough. One result of that was he did not anticipate the importance of the Internet. "The company wasn't a company but a cause. We were going to change the world." That attitude can motivate young employees, but it can blind leaders and employees to market realities. In his current position as CEO of Keynote Systems, which measures performance of commercial Web sites, he is careful to construct the business around several technologies and technological services. Plus, he delegates strategic information-gathering to a number of employees, who keep their minds and eyes open to new developments outside. Some of those developments include the acquisition of other companies. Rather than cramming meetings together like pieces of bread on a peanut butter sandwich, he now blocks out time to roam the halls and brainstorm with employees. And he regularly attends venture capital conferences. "I'm making sure my peripheral vision remains intact so I'm not blindsided again," he says.[6]

As a general rule, changing just one component—cognitions, affect, or behavior—can contribute to an overall change in attitude. Suppose a manager concludes that some employees have the attitude that the manager should make all the decisions affecting the department, but the manager prefers that employees assume more decision-making responsibility. To change the underlying attitude, the manager would consider whether to educate employees about the areas in which they can make good decisions (changing the cognitive component), build enthusiasm with pep talks about the satisfaction of employee empowerment (changing the affective component), or insist that employees make their own decisions (behavioral component) with the expectation that, once they experience the advantages of decision-making authority, they will begin to like it.

High-Performance Work Attitudes

The attitudes of most interest to managers are those related to work, especially attitudes that influence how well employees perform. To lead employees effectively, managers logically seek to cultivate the kinds of attitudes associated with high performance. Two attitudes that might relate to high performance are satisfaction with one's job and commitment to the organization.

Job Satisfaction. A positive attitude toward one's job is called **job satisfaction**. In general, people experience this attitude when their work matches their needs and interests, when working conditions and rewards (such as pay) are satisfactory, when they like their coworkers, and when they have positive relationships with supervisors. You can take the quiz in Exhibit 11.2 to understand some of the factors that contribute to job satisfaction.

Many managers believe job satisfaction is important because they think satisfied employees will do better work. In fact, research shows that the link between satisfaction and performance is generally small and is affected by other factors.[7] The importance of satisfaction varies according to the amount of control the employee has; an employee doing routine tasks may produce about the same output no matter how he or she feels about the job. However, an internal study at Sears found a clear link between employee satisfaction, customer satisfaction, and revenue. In particular, employees' attitudes about whether their workloads were manageable and well-organized ranked among the top 10 indicators of company performance.[8]

Managers of today's knowledge workers often rely on job satisfaction to keep motivation and enthusiasm for the organization high. Organizations do not want to lose talented, highly skilled workers. In addition, most managers care about their employees and want them to feel good about their work, and almost everyone prefers being

job satisfaction
A positive attitude toward one's job.

Take **ACTION**
As a manager, make sure your employees have a reasonable workload and that they get enough help to organize their jobs.

EXHIBIT 11.2

*Rate Your Job
Satisfaction*

Think of a job—a current or previous job—that was important to you, and then answer the questions below with respect to how satisfied you were with that job. Please answer the six questions below with a number 1–5 that reflects the extent of your satisfaction.

1 = Very dissatisfied	3 = Neutral 5 = Very satisfied
2 = Dissatisfied	4 = Satisfied

1. Overall, how satisfied are you with your job?	1	2	3	4	5
2. How satisfied are you with the opportunities to learn new things?	1	2	3	4	5
3. How satisfied are you with your boss?	1	2	3	4	5
4. How satisfied are you with the people in your work group?	1	2	3	4	5
5. How satisfied are you with the amount of pay you receive?	1	2	3	4	5
6. How satisfied are you with the advancement you are making in the organization?	1	2	3	4	5

Scoring and Interpretation: Add your responses to the six questions to obtain your total score: _____. The questions represent various aspects of satisfaction that an employee may experience on a job. If your score is 24 or above, you probably feel satisfied with the job. If your score is 12 or below, you probably do not feel satisfied. What is your level of performance in your job, and is your performance related to your level of satisfaction?

SOURCES: These questions were adapted from Daniel R. Denison, *Corporate Culture and Organizational Effectiveness* (New York, John Wiley, 1990; and John D. Cook, Susan J. Hepworth, Toby D. Wall, and Peter B. Warr, *The Experience of Work: A Compendium and Review of 249 Measures and their Use* (San Diego, Calif. Academic Press, 1981).

around people who have positive attitudes. However, a survey by International Survey Research found that Generation X employees, those who are carrying the weight of much of today's knowledge work, are the least satisfied of all demographic groups.[9] Managers play an important role in whether employees have positive or negative attitudes toward their jobs.[10] The CEO of General Mills recognizes that managers have to pay attention to their own attitudes and behaviors to influence the attitudes and performance of employees.

General Mills

Steve Sanger, CEO of General Mills, recently told his coworkers that he was working on being a better leader by developing his coaching skills. Sanger had been reviewing his 360-degree feedback, in which people told him he needed to do a better job of coaching his direct reports. Rather than becoming defensive, Sanger adopted the attitude that he needed to improve himself to help others grow and improve.

When the top leader of a company displays arrogance and tells everyone else how they need to improve, that attitude and behavior filters down to every level of management. An "us-versus-them" mindset often develops between employees and managers and job satisfaction, motivation, and performance decline.

Steve Sanger, though, had an insight. By being open with people and admitting his own weaknesses and efforts to improve, he set an example for others to do the same. Sanger is noted for his enlightened attitudes about how to help employees be successful at work and in their personal lives. The first step, he knows, is for a leader to be aware of how his attitudes and behaviors influence others and create a positive or a negative organizational environment.[11]

By creating a positive environment, leaders like Steve Sanger contribute to higher job satisfaction for employees. A related attitude is organizational commitment.

Organizational Commitment. Organizational commitment refers to an employee's loyalty to and engagement with the organization. An employee with a high degree of organizational commitment is likely to say *we* when talking about the company. Such a person likes being a part of the organization and tries to contribute to its success. This attitude is illustrated by an incident at the A. W. Chesterton Company, a Massachusetts company that produces mechanical seals and pumps. When two Chesterton pumps that supply water on Navy ship *USS John F. Kennedy* failed on a Saturday night just before the ship's scheduled departure, Todd Robinson, the leader of the team that produces the seals, swung into action. He and his fiancèe, who also works for Chesterton, worked through the night to make new seals and deliver them to be installed before the ship left port.[12]

Most managers want to enjoy the benefits of loyal, committed employees, including low turnover and willingness to do more than the job's basic requirements. In addition, results of a recent survey of more than 650,000 employees in global organizations suggest that companies with committed employees perform better. The study found that companies with highly committed employees outperformed the industry average over a 12-month period by 6 percent, while those with low levels of commitment underperformed the average by 9 percent.[13] Alarmingly, levels of commitment in the United States are significantly lower than those in half of the world's other large economies, as illustrated in Exhibit 11.3. U.S. employees are less committed than those in Brazil, Spain, Germany, Canada, and Italy. This low level of organizational commitment puts U.S. firms at a serious disadvantage in the global marketplace.[14]

The high motivation and engagement that comes with organizational commitment is essential to the success of knowledge-based organizations that depend on employees' ideas and creativity. Trust in management's decisions and integrity is an important component of organizational commitment.[15] Unfortunately, in recent years, many employees have lost that trust, resulting in a decline in commitment.

Managers can take action to promote organizational commitment by keeping employees informed, giving them a say in decisions, providing the necessary training and other resources that enable them to succeed, treating them fairly, and offering rewards they value. For example, recent studies suggest that employee commitment in today's workplace is correlated with initiatives and benefits that help people balance

organizational commitment

Loyalty to and heavy involvement in one's organization.

Take **ACTION**

As a manager, if you want committed employees, make sure you are acting in a trustworthy fashion.

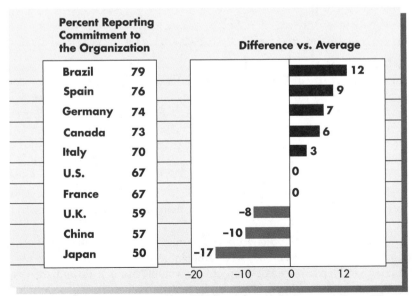

Shaded difference bar denotes a statistically significant difference

EXHIBIT 11.3

Variations in Organizational Commitment: The World's Ten Largest Economies

SOURCE: "Employee Commitment—U.S.: Leader or Follower?" International Survey Research, *http://www.isrsurveys.com* 1-800-300-0750.

FOCUS ON INNOVATION

The Rokenbok Magic

Paul Eichen wondered what a company would look like if its only aim was to promote a balanced, healthy, soulful life. Work was everything to Eichen, who had helped start a successful technology company and grow it to sales of $100 million. However, work was eating him alive, so he walked away from his lucrative, successful job and began pursuing the answer to his question.

As a boy, Eichen had loved LEGOs, model kits, and machines, a love that would prove to be his salvation for a better life. "I think people tend to know what they need to do in their lives, and they can either ignore it or get on with it," Eichen says. He knew what he needed to do: start a toy company. More importantly, he wanted to create a new kind of business, one in which every company-defining decision was based on the way it would make work feel for the people who worked there. When Eichen opened the doors to Rokenbok Toy Co., it was not in an industrial park but in a village by the beach, in an old, rehabilitated warehouse a short walk from the sand, with ethnic restaurants and sundries emporiums, coffee shops, and used bookstores as neighbors. Having the real world surround Rokenbok held a kind of magic for Eichen and his employees, who realized that where a company is located determines the commute and the richness of life outside the office.

The pattern of work at Rokenbok was different from many companies. As long as employees did their work, they were encouraged to set their own hours, dress as they liked, tend to their health, and put their families first. One Rokenbok engineer describes playing on the living room floor with his child and company toys, piecing together problems, working as he played, playing as he worked. For most company employees, work became a source of reconnection with family, friends, and neighbors. "We're trying to make something classic, not disposable. Values that are important personally—quality, constructive fun, learning, design sophistication—are things we're trying to design right into the product, and that feels great."

Rokenbok's employees have accomplished something noteworthy: They have created an independent American toy company, establishing a product that has won toy industry accolades and climbed from sales of $2.6 million in 1997 to $10 million in 1999. And though Eichen believes that during the dot-com heyday every one of his managers was recruited and promised "instant millions," none of them left. "Our executives have chosen quality of life over the seductiveness of E-wealth," says Eichen.

Eichen does not kid himself that even the most balanced workplaces can prevent life from getting a little messy, but the Rokenbok work style allows employees to have the energy and flexibility to pay attention to health, friends, family, and dreams, as well as their work "Look," Eichen says, "at a company like Rokenbok you still get to keep the good parts [of work]: intellectual stimulation, social activity, the fun of competing to win." Plus, you get to have a personal life, too. It's a winning combination.

SOURCE: Michael Hopkins, "The Pursuit of Happiness," *Inc.* (August 2000): 72–89.

---

their work and personal lives.[16] The Focus on Innovation box describes one organization that was built on the concept of fostering a good life for the people who work there.

Conflicts among Attitudes

Sometimes a person may discover that his or her attitudes conflict with one another or are not reflected in behavior. For example, a person's high level of organizational commitment might conflict with a commitment to family members. If employees routinely work evenings and weekends, their long hours and dedication to the job might conflict with their belief that family ties are important. This can create a state of **cognitive dissonance**, a psychological discomfort that occurs when individuals recognize inconsistencies in their own attitudes and behaviors.[17] The theory of cognitive dissonance, developed by social psychologist Leon Festinger in the 1950s, says that people want to behave in accordance with their attitudes and usually will take corrective action to alleviate the dissonance and achieve balance.

In the case of working overtime, people who can control their hours might restructure responsibilities so they have time for work and family. In contrast, those who are unable to restructure workloads might develop an unfavorable attitude toward the employer, reducing their organizational commitment. They might resolve their dissonance by saying

cognitive dissonance

A condition in which two attitudes or a behavior and an attitude conflict.

they would like to spend more time with their kids, but their unreasonable employer demands that they work too many hours.

Perception

Another critical aspect of understanding behavior is perception. **Perception** is the cognitive process people use to make sense out of the environment by selecting, organizing, and interpreting information from the environment. Attitudes affect perceptions, and vice versa. For example, a person might have developed the attitude that managers are insensitive and arrogant based on a pattern of perceiving arrogant and insensitive behavior from managers over a period of time. If the person moves to a new job, this attitude will continue to affect the way he or she perceives superiors in the new environment even though managers in the new workplace might take great pains to understand and respond to employees' needs.

Because of individual differences in attitudes, personality, values, interests, and so forth, people often "see" the same thing in different ways. A class that is boring to one student might be fascinating to another. One student might perceive an assignment to be challenging and stimulating, whereas another might find it a waste of time. Referring back to the topic of diversity discussed in Chapter 9, many African-Americans perceive that blacks are regularly discriminated against, whereas many white employees perceive that blacks are given special opportunities in the workplace.[18]

We can think of perception as a step-by-step process, as shown in Exhibit 11.4. First, we observe information (sensory data) from the environment through our senses: taste, smell, hearing, sight, and touch. Next, our mind screens the data and will select only the items we will process further. Third, we organize the selected data into meaningful patterns for interpretation and response. Most differences in perception among people at work are related to how they select and organize sensory data.

Perceptual Selectivity

We are aware of our environment, but not everything in it is equally important to our perception of it. We tune in to some data (e.g., a familiar voice off in the distance) and tune out other data (e.g., paper shuffling next to us). People are bombarded by so much sensory data that they cannot process it all. The brain's solution is to run the data through a perceptual filter that retains some parts (selective attention) and eliminates others. **Perceptual selectivity** is the process by which individuals screen and select the various objects and stimuli that vie for their attention. Certain stimuli catch their attention, and others do not.

People typically focus on stimuli that satisfy their needs and are consistent with their attitudes, values, and personality. For example, employees who need positive feedback to feel good about themselves might pick up on positive statements made by a supervisor but tune out most negative comments. A supervisor could use this understanding to tailor his feedback in a positive way to help the employee improve his or her work. The influence of needs on perception has been studied in laboratory experiments and found to have a strong impact on what people perceive.[19]

perception

The cognitive process people use to make sense out of the environment by selecting, organizing, and interpreting information.

Take *ACTION*

Remember that your reactions to some incident will not necessarily be the same as others'.

perceptual selectivity

The process by which individuals screen and select the various stimuli that vie for their attention.

Take *ACTION*

Remember that other people will not always hear everything you say, especially if it is difficult information.

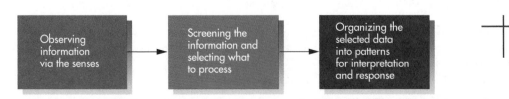

EXHIBIT 11.4

The Perception Process

Characteristics of the stimuli affect perceptual selectivity. People tend to notice stimuli that stand out against other stimuli or that are more intense than surrounding stimuli. Examples would be a loud noise in a quiet room or a bright red dress at a party where most women are wearing black. People tend to notice things familiar to them, such as a familiar voice in a crowd, as well as things that are new or different from their previous experiences. In addition, primacy and recency are important to perceptual selectivity. People pay relatively greater attention to sensory data that occur toward the beginning of an event or toward the end. Primacy supports the old truism that first impressions do count, whether it be on a job interview, meeting a date's parents, or participating in a new social group. Recency reflects the reality that the last impression might be a lasting impression. For example, Malaysian Airlines has discovered its value in building customer loyalty. A woman traveling with a 9-month-old might find the flight itself an exhausting blur, but one such traveler enthusiastically told people for years how Malaysian Airlines flight attendants helped her with baggage collection and ground transportation.[20]

As these examples show, perceptual selectivity is a complex filtering process. Managers can use an understanding of perceptual selectivity to obtain clues about why one person sees things differently from others, and they can apply the principles to their own communications and actions, especially when they want to attract or focus attention.

Perceptual Distortions

Once people have selected the sensory data to be perceived, they begin grouping the data into recognizable patterns. Perceptual organization is the process by which people organize or categorize stimuli according to their own frame of reference. Of particular concern in the work environment are **perceptual distortions**, which are errors in perceptual judgment that arise from inaccuracies in any part of the perceptual process.

Some types of errors are so common that managers should become familiar with them. These include stereotyping, the halo effect, projection, and perceptual defense. Managers who recognize these perceptual distortions can better adjust their perceptions to more closely match objective reality.

Stereotyping is the tendency to assign an individual to a group or broad category (e.g., female, black, elderly, male, white, or disabled) and then to attribute widely held generalizations about the group to the individual. Thus, someone meets a new colleague, sees he is in a wheelchair, assigns him to the category "physically disabled," and attributes to this colleague generalizations she believes about people with disabilities, which may include a belief that he is less able than other coworkers. However, the person's inability to walk should not be seen as indicative of lesser abilities in other areas. Indeed, the assumption of limitations may offend him or her and may prevent the person making the stereotypical judgment from benefiting from the many ways in which this person can contribute. Stereotyping prevents people from knowing those they classify in this way. In addition, negative stereotypes prevent talented people from advancing in an organization and contributing their talents to the organization's success. Dr. Bill Thomas is creating a new kind of nursing home. Seeking to overcome stereotypes toward the elderly, he sees these perceptions contributing to poor living conditions in the homes, as described in the Focus on Collaboration box.

perceptual distortions

Errors in perceptual judgment that arise from inaccuracies in any part of the perceptual process.

stereotyping

The tendency to assign an individual to a group or broad category and then attribute generalizations about the group to the individual.

BUSINESS BLOOPER

John Chambers' Perception Distortions

Cisco CEO John Chambers had his own problems with perceptual distortions. The day before he spent $89 million to buy router maker Procket, he proudly announced, "I'm not going to buy another router company for a router. I could not be more comfortable with our router strategy."

SOURCE: Adam Horowitx, et al, "101 dumbest moments in Business," *Business 2.0*, (Jan/Feb. 2005): 106.

Eden Alternative

"**D**oes anyone want to leave his home and live in a nursing home?" asks physician-actor-novelist and Harvard graduate Dr. Bill Thomas, referring to his new nursing home venture, Eden Alternative. "That's why we're turning the industry upside-down." Believing humans are not meant to live in cold, impersonal institutions, but rather in an eden-type garden designed for growth, Thomas wrote about nurturing nursing homes that respect "elders," then took his one-man show on the road a few years ago. Seeing that nursing home patients suffer from the three plagues of boredom, helplessness, and loneliness, Thomas and his wife Jude decided to put those ideas into practical action.

The next step was turning his farm into a non-profit organization that so far has 300 nursing homes edenized: turned into warm and nurturing environments, which create more satisfied patients and a better bottom line. Eden encourages input from the residents and staff on how to make a better facility. Such behaviors are difficult for more traditional administrators to swallow.

Thomas found edenizing works better in certain environments. "Warm" cultures are more open to change because residents and employees have trust and generosity for one another, but "cold" cultures are characterized by cynicism and pessimism. Eden surveys new nursing homes for their "temperature" and then proceeds to "warm the soil" by having administrators hold potlucks where no work is discussed. Plus, employees start doing good deeds for one another. "You open people's minds by opening their hearts," Thomas says.

Moving on, Eden has a new venture, Green Houses in Tupelo, Mississippi, where 40 people moved into four single-story homes, each with their own bedrooms and bath, unheard of in like facilities. So far, the residents seem healthier and happier than in traditional homes. Green Houses are cheaper to build and the same to maintain, so Thomas believes the time for such an alternative is ripe.

When not in his office, Thomas is out spreading the word on nursing home changes, realizing it will take a long time. Trying to be a realist, he is still the optimist, as his business card says, "It can be different."

SOURCE: Chuck Salter, "Health Alternative," *Fast Company* (March 2005): 22.; Chuck Salter, "(Not) the Same Old Story," *Fast Company* (Feb. 2002): 78–84.

The **halo effect** occurs when the perceiver develops an overall impression of a person or situation based on one characteristic, favorable or unfavorable. In other words, a halo blinds the perceiver to other characteristics that should be used in generating a more complete assessment. The halo effect can play a significant role in performance appraisal, as we discussed in Chapter 9. For example, a person with an outstanding attendance record may be assessed as responsible, industrious, and highly productive; another person with less-than-average attendance may be assessed as a poor performer. Either assessment may be true, but it is the manager's job to ensure the assessment is based on complete information about all job-related characteristics and not just his or her preferences for good attendance.

Projection is the tendency of perceivers to see their own personal traits in other people; that is, they project their own needs, feelings, values, and attitudes into their judgment of others. An achievement-oriented manager might assume that subordinates are as well. This might cause the manager to restructure jobs to be less routine and more challenging, without regard for employees' actual satisfaction. The best guards against errors based on projection are self-awareness and empathy.

Perceptual defense is the tendency of perceivers to protect themselves against threatening ideas, objects, or people. People perceive satisfying and pleasant things but tend to disregard disturbing and unpleasant things. In essence, people develop blind spots in the perceptual process so negative sensory data do not hurt them. For example, the director of a nonprofit educational organization in Tennessee hated dealing with conflict because he had grown up with parents who constantly argued and often put him in the middle of their arguments. The director consistently overlooked discord among staff members until things would reach a boiling point. When the blow-up occurred, the director would be shocked and dismayed because he had truly perceived that everything was going smoothly among the staff. Recognizing perceptual blind spots can help people develop a clearer picture of reality.

halo effect

An overall impression of a person or situation based on one characteristic, favorable or unfavorable.

Take *ACTION*

As a manager, avoid having some employees become your favorites, or wear the proverbial halo; guard against this kind of favoritism, as it causes other workers to withdraw emotionally from their work.

projection

The tendency to see one's own personal traits in other people.

perceptual defense

The tendency of perceivers to protect themselves by disregarding ideas, objects, or people that are threatening to them.

Attributions

As people organize what they perceive, they often draw conclusions, such as about an object or a person. For example, stereotyping involves assigning a number of traits to a person. Among the judgments people make as part of the perceptual process are attributions. **Attributions** are judgments about what caused a person's behavior, i.e., something about the person or something about the situation. An internal attribution says characteristics of the person led to the behavior. ("My boss yelled at me because he's impatient and doesn't listen.") An external attribution says something about the situation caused the person's behavior. ("My boss yelled at me because I missed the deadline and the customer is upset.") Attributions are important because they help people decide how to handle a situation. In the case of the boss yelling, a person who blames the yelling on the boss's personality will view the boss as the problem and might cope by avoiding the boss. In contrast, someone who blames the yelling on the situation might try to help prevent such situations in the future.

Social scientists have studied the attributions people make and identified three factors that influence whether an attribution will be external or internal.[21] These three factors are illustrated in Exhibit 11.5.

1. *Distinctiveness.* Whether the behavior is unusual for that person (in contrast to a person displaying the same kind of behavior in many situations). If the behavior is distinctive, the perceiver probably will make an external attribution.

2. *Consistency.* Whether the person being observed has a history of behaving in the same way. People generally make internal attributions about consistent behavior.

3. *Consensus.* Whether other people tend to respond to similar situations in the same way. A person who has observed others handle similar situations in the same way will likely make an external attribution; that is, it will seem that the situation produces the type of behavior observed.

attributions

Judgments about what caused a person's behavior, either characteristics of the person or of the situation.

EXHIBIT 11.5

Factors Influencing Whether Attributions Are Internal or External

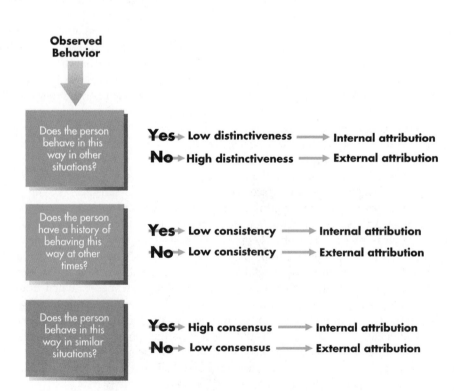

In addition to these general rules, people tend to have biases they apply when making attributions. When evaluating others, we tend to underestimate the influence of external factors and overestimate the influence of internal factors. This tendency is called the **fundamental attribution error**. Consider the case of someone being promoted to CEO. Employees, outsiders, and the media generally focus on the characteristics of the person that allowed him or her to achieve the promotion. In reality, however, the selection of that person might have been heavily influenced by external factors, such as business conditions creating a need for someone with a strong financial or marketing background at that particular time.

Another bias that distorts attributions involves attributions we make about our own behavior. People tend to overestimate the contribution of internal factors to their successes and overestimate the contribution of external factors to their failures. This tendency, called the **self-serving bias**, means people give themselves too much credit for what they do well and give external forces too much blame when they fail. Thus, if your manager says you do not communicate well enough, and you think your manager does not listen well enough, the truth may lie somewhere in between.

Personality and Behavior

Another area of particular interest to OB is personality. In the workplace, we find people whose behavior is consistently pleasant, aggressive, or stubborn in various situations.

An individual's **personality** is the set of characteristics that underlie a relatively stable pattern of behavior in response to ideas, objects, or people in the environment. Understanding personality can help managers predict how that person might act in a particular situation. Managers who appreciate the ways their employees' personalities differ have insight into what kinds of leadership behavior will be most influential.

Personality Traits

In common usage, people think of personality in terms of traits, or relatively stable characteristics of a person. Researchers have investigated if any traits stand up to scientific scrutiny. Though investigators have examined thousands of traits over the years, their findings have been distilled into five general dimensions that describe personality. These are often called the "Big Five" personality factors.[22] Each factor may contain a wide range of specific traits. The **Big Five personality factors** describe an individual's extroversion, agreeableness, conscientiousness, emotional stability, and openness to experience:

1. *Extroversion.* The degree to which a person is sociable, talkative, assertive, and comfortable with interpersonal relationships.

2. *Agreeableness.* The degree to which a person is able to get along with others by being good-natured, cooperative, forgiving, understanding, and trusting.

3. *Conscientiousness.* The degree to which a person is focused on a few goals, thus behaving in ways that are responsible, dependable, persistent, and achievement oriented.

4. *Emotional stability.* The degree to which a person is calm, enthusiastic, and secure, rather than tense, nervous, depressed, moody, or insecure.

5. *Openness to experience.* The degree to which a person has a broad range of interests and is imaginative, creative, artistically sensitive, and willing to consider new ideas.

These factors represent a continuum. That is, a person may have a low, moderate, or high degree of each quality.

fundamental attribution error

The tendency to underestimate the influence of external factors on another's behavior and to overestimate the influence of internal factors.

self-serving bias

The tendency to overestimate the contribution of internal factors to one's successes and the contribution of external factors to one's failures.

personality

The set of characteristics that underlie a relatively stable pattern of behavior in response to ideas, objects, or people in the environment.

Big Five personality factors

Dimensions that describe an individual's extroversion, agreeableness, conscientiousness, emotional stability, and openness to experience.

Take a moment to complete the instrument below to see where you fall on the Big Five scale for each of the factors.

The Big Five Personality Traits

Each individual's collection of personality traits is different; it is what makes us unique. Though each collection of traits varies, we share many common traits. The following phrases describe various traits and behaviors. Rate how accurately each statement describes you, based on a scale of 1 to 5, with 1 being inaccurate and 5 accurate. Describe yourself as you are now, not as you wish to be. There are no right or wrong answers.

	1	2	3	4	5
	Very Inaccurate			Very Accurate	

Extroversion

I am usually the life of the party.	1	2	3	4	5
I feel comfortable around people.	1	2	3	4	5
I am talkative.	1	2	3	4	5

Agreeableness

I am kind and sympathetic.	1	2	3	4	5
I have a good word for everyone.	1	2	3	4	5
I never insult people.	1	2	3	4	5

Conscientiousness

I am systematic and efficient.	1	2	3	4	5
I pay attention to details.	1	2	3	4	5
I am always prepared for class.	1	2	3	4	5

Neuroticism (Low Emotional Stability)

I often feel critical of myself.	1	2	3	4	5
I often envy others.	1	2	3	4	5
I am temperamental.	1	2	3	4	5

Openness to New Experiences

I am imaginative.	1	2	3	4	5
I prefer to vote for liberal political candidates.	1	2	3	4	5
I really like art.	1	2	3	4	5

Which are your most prominent traits? For fun and discussion, compare your responses with those of classmates.

SOURCE: These questions were adapted from a variety of sources.

A person who has a high degree of agreeableness would likely be described as warm, friendly, and good natured, but one at the opposite extreme might be described as cold, rude, or hard to get along with. In general, having a moderate-to-high degree of each of the personality factors is considered desirable for a wide range of employees. In addition, certain factors may be particularly important for specific kinds of work. For example, Nancy Naatz works for Aramark, a company that caters big events and runs cafeterias for universities and corporate clients. Naatz, a district manager, needs a high degree of extroversion and agreeableness to build the relationships critical to her success working with clients such as Sears. These traits might be less important for an employee who has little need to interact with others.

Many companies, including JCPenney, Toys "R" Us, and the Union Pacific Railroad, use personality testing to hire, evaluate, or promote employees. American MultiCinema (AMC), one of the largest theater chains in the United States, looks for front-line workers with high conscientiousness and high emotional stability.[23] Marriott Hotels looks for people who score high on conscientiousness and agreeableness because it believes these individuals will provide better service to guests.[24] Companies use personality testing for managers. Hewlett-Packard, Dell Computers, and General Electric put candidates for top positions through testing, interviews with psychologists, or both to see if they have the "right stuff" for the job.[25] The Digital, Inc. box describes how a young Harvard Business School graduate found Internet success with a company built around personality testing.

Despite growing use, there is little evidence that personality tests are a valid predictor of job success. In addition, the Big Five dimensions have been criticized because they are difficult to measure precisely. Because each dimension is made up of a number of specific traits, a person might score high on some traits but low on others. For example, considering the dimension of conscientiousness, a person might score high on a trait such as dependability but score low on achievement orientation. Furthermore, research on the Big Five has mostly been limited to the United States, so there are dangers in applying the theory cross-culturally.

> Take **ACTION**
>
> Remember that the way you do things is not necessarily the only way; people with varying personality types may choose another way of operating.

DIGITAL, INC.

Tickle Lets You Get To Know All About You

When James Currier took the Myers-Briggs Type Inventory (MBTI) at Harvard Business School, he learned his personality type and saw his future. Currier was looking for an Internet business idea, and the interest and excitement the Myers-Briggs test generated among his classmates told him there was potential in bringing personality testing online.

Currier's company, originally called eMode.com and renamed Tickle, managed to survive the dot-com collapse and is growing and profitable today. Tickle offers a range of online tests on personality, careers, and relationships. The site makes these tests highly personal with customized results and gives people a chance to share them with each other. Some of the tests are based on standard measurements like MBTI, and others are for fun. For example, there are quizzes to tell you what breed of dog you are or what the theme song of your life is. The dog test attracted a million users within two weeks of its introduction.

Currier's goal is to keep a good balance among science, entertainment, and commercialism. "Everyone says you can't be scientific and fun, but we think you can," he says. Test results are always phrased in a positive way. For example, someone might be told, "You are more optimistic than 15 percent of the other people who took this quiz." (The reverse side, of course, is that the person scored exceedingly high on being a pessimistic Gloomy Gus.)

To grow, Currier has added a dating service as well as a social network to help people find friends based on their compatible personality types. He is thinking about getting into the market for job placements and classifieds. The links to career and personality testing could give Tickle an advantage over other job sites, for example. And Currier thinks used car buyers just might like the idea of buying from someone who scores high on honesty and integrity.

SOURCE: Saul Hansell, "Getting to Know Me, Getting to Know All About Me: Web Personality Tests," *The New York Times* (March 8, 2004): http://www.nytimes.com.

Emotional Intelligence

In recent years, new insights into personality have been gained through research in the area of emotional intelligence. Emotional intelligence (or emotional quotient, EQ) includes four basic components:[26]

1. *Self-awareness.* The basis for all the other components; being aware of what you are feeling. People who are in touch with their feelings are able to guide their own lives and actions better. A high degree of self-awareness means you can assess your own strengths and limitations and have a healthy sense of self-confidence.

2. *Self-management.* The ability to control disruptive or harmful emotions and balance one's moods so worry, anxiety, fear, or anger do not cloud thinking and get in the way of what needs to be done. People who are skilled at self-management remain optimistic and hopeful despite setbacks and obstacles. This ability is crucial for pursuing long-term goals. For example, MetLife found that applicants who failed the regular sales aptitude test but scored high on optimism made 21 percent more sales in their first year and 57 percent more in their second year than those who passed the sales test but scored high on pessimism.[27]

3. *Social awareness.* The ability to understand others and practice empathy, which means putting yourself in someone else's shoes, and to recognize what others are feeling without them needing to tell you. People with social awareness are capable of understanding divergent points of view and interacting effectively with many different types of people. Director Paul Weitz succeeds because of his continual improvement of his social awareness skills, as shown in the Best Practices box.

4. *Relationship awareness.* The ability to connect to others, build positive relationships, respond to the emotions of others, and influence others. People with relationship awareness know how to listen and communicate, and they treat others with compassion and respect.

Studies have found a positive relationship between job performance and high degrees of emotional intelligence in a variety of jobs. Numerous organizations, including the U.S. Air Force and Canada Life, have used EQ tests to measure such things as self-awareness, ability to empathize, and capacity to build positive relationships.[28] EQ seems to be important for jobs that require a high degree of social interaction, which includes managers, who are responsible for influencing others and building positive

---

BEST PRACTICES

Paul Weitz, Writer and Director

For Paul Weitz, being a leader is one of the few cases where he can impact what kind of workday people will have. If he is organized, the shoot is organized. If he is polite to people, everyone else is polite. He loves being able to set the tone for how the cast and crew will work together. Before the first day of shooting, he gets the crew list (usually about 75 names) and memorizes them. Sometimes he messes up, but people still know he is trying and that he cares and wants to treat them with respect. They are surprised that he would want to learn everyone's name and that gives him a lot of latitude with the crew.

Weitz was a screenwriter for ten years and operated mostly out of his head. He did not know how much he would like managing people until he started having to deal with a couple hundred people on a daily basis. Directing forces him to make a lot of decisions every hour. What color should this bottle be: brown or green? Should his collar be buttoned or unbuttoned? "At some point," he says, "You realize it's more important to make a decision than to worry about making the right decision."

SOURCE: Paul Weitz, "Directing the Workday," *Fast Company* (March 2005): 42.

attitudes and relationships in the organization. Managers with low EQ can harm the organization. Consider Peter Angelos, who bought the Baltimore Orioles in 1993. Angelos' domineering approach to leadership drove away some of the team's most experienced managers and executives, leaving the Orioles weakened and demoralized.[29]

At times of great change or crisis, managers need a higher EQ level to help employees cope with the anxiety and stress they may be experiencing. In the United States, fears of terrorism, anxiety and sorrow over the war in Iraq, and continuing economic hardships for many people have made meeting the psychological and emotional needs of employees a new role for managers. The Focus on Skills box outlines some EQ elements important in times of crisis and turmoil. Remember that EQ is not an in-born personality characteristic but something that can be learned and developed throughout one's lifetime.[30]

© Marc Austin/CORBIS

*Harvard Law School's Program on Negotiation offers seminars that help small-business owners develop their **emotional intelligence** and be more effective leaders. "People [wrongly] assume that you check your feelings at the door when you go to work," says Sheila Heen, a Harvard Law School lecturer. The program offers training in topics such as Improving Your Listening Skills, Managing Anger at Work, Managing Your Feelings, and Getting Straight on Purposes. In the photo, participants practice expressing their emotions without becoming "emotional."*

Attitudes and Behaviors Influenced by Personality

An individual's personality influences many work-related attitudes and behaviors. Among those that are of particular interest to managers are locus of control, authoritarianism, Machiavellianism, and problem-solving styles.

Locus of Control. People differ in terms of what they tend to attribute as the cause of their success or failure. Their **locus of control** defines if they place the primary responsibility within themselves or on outside forces.[31] Some people believe that their actions can influence what happens to them. They feel in control of their own fate. These individuals have a high internal locus of control. Other people believe that events in their lives occur because of chance, luck, or outside people and events. They feel more like pawns of their fate. These individuals have a high external locus of control. Many top leaders of e-commerce and high-tech organizations possess a high internal locus of control. These managers have to cope with rapid change and uncertainty associated with Internet business. They must believe that they and their employees can counter the negative impact of outside forces and events. John Chambers, CEO of Cisco Systems, is a good example. Despite a tough economy and a drastically diminished stock price, Chambers maintained his belief that Cisco can defeat any challenge thrown its way.[32] A person with a high external locus of control would likely feel overwhelmed making the rapid decisions and changes needed to keep pace with the industry, particularly in the current environment of uncertainty.

Research on locus of control has shown real differences in behavior across a wide range of settings. People with an internal locus of control are easier to motivate because they believe the rewards are the result of their behavior. They are better able to handle complex information and problem solving, are more achievement oriented, and are more independent and, therefore, more difficult to lead. By contrast, people with an external locus of control are harder to motivate, less involved in their jobs, more likely to blame others when faced with a poor performance evaluation, but more compliant and conforming and, therefore, easier to lead.[33]

Do you believe luck plays an important role in your life, or do you feel that you control your own fate? To find out more about your locus of control, read the instructions and complete the questionnaire in Exhibit 11.6.

locus of control
The tendency to place the primary responsibility for one's success or failure within oneself (internally) or on outside forces (externally).

Take **ACTION**
Take responsibility for your actions rather than blaming others or the situation (external locus).

What's Your Crisis EQ?

Threats of terrorist attacks. Downsizing. The SARS virus. Company failures. Anthrax in the mail. Stock market crashes. Rapid technological changes. Information overload. The turbulence of today's world has left lingering psychological and emotional damage in workplaces all across the United States, as well as in the rest of the world. Even when a minor crisis hits an organization, uncertainty and fear are high. Today's managers need the skills to help people deal with their emotions and return to a more normal work routine. Though managers cannot take the place of professional counselors, they can use patience, flexibility, and understanding to assist people through a crisis. Here are some important elements of crisis EQ for managers:

- Be visible and provide as much current, accurate information as possible about what is going on in the company and the industry. Rumor control is critical.
- Find simple ways to get employees together. Order pizza for the entire staff. Invite telecommuters to come in to the office so they can connect with others and have a chance to share their emotions.
- Give employees room to be human. People naturally feel anger and other strong emotions, so allow those feelings to

be expressed as long as they are not directed at other employees.
- Publicize the company's charitable endeavors and make employees aware of the various opportunities within and outside the organization to volunteer and donate to charity.
- Thank employees in person and with handwritten notes when they go above and beyond the call of duty during a difficult time.
- Recognize that routine, structured work can help people heal. Postpone major, long-term projects and decisions to the extent possible and break work into shorter, more manageable tasks. Listen to employees and determine what they need to help them return to a normal work life.
- Provide professional counseling services for people who need it. Those with a history of alcohol abuse, trouble at home, or previous mental or emotional problems are especially at risk, but anyone who has trouble gradually returning to his or her previous level of work may need outside counseling.

SOURCES: Based on Matthew Boyle, "Nothing Really Matters," *Fortune* (October 15, 2001): 261–264; and Sue Shellenbarger, "Readers Face Dilemma Over How Far to Alter Post-Attack Workplace," *The Wall Street Journal* (October 31, 2001): Work & Family column, B1.

authoritarianism
The belief that power and status differences should exist within the organization.

Authoritarianism.   Authoritarianism is the belief that power and status differences should exist within the organization.[34] Individuals high in authoritarianism tend to be concerned with power and toughness, obey recognized authority above them, stick to conventional values, critically judge others, and oppose the use of subjective feelings. The degree to which managers possess authoritarianism will influence how they wield and share power. The degree to which employees possess authoritarianism will influence how they react to their managers. If a manager and employees differ in their degree of authoritarianism, the manager may have difficulty leading them. The trend toward empowerment and shifts in expectations among younger employees for more equitable relationships have contributed to a decline in strict authoritarianism in many organizations. The shift can be seen in the National Football League (NFL), where a rising number of coaches put more emphasis on communication and building relationships than on ruling with an iron hand. Coaches Steve Mariucci (San Francisco 49ers), Tony Dungy (Indianapolis Colts), and Jeff Fisher (Tennessee Titans) are aware that today's players have different expectations than those of previous generations. "This is not old Rome with gladiators," says San Francisco's Mariucci. "This is modern-day football.... If you cannot relate to today's player, you are through as a coach."[35]

Machiavellianism
The tendency to direct much of one's behavior toward the acquisition of power and the manipulation of other people for personal gain.

Machiavellianism.   Another personality dimension that helps in understanding work behavior is **Machiavellianism**, which is characterized by the acquisition of power and the manipulation of other people for purely personal gain. Machiavellianism is named after Niccolo Machiavelli, a sixteenth-century author who wrote *The Prince*, a book for noblemen of the day on how to acquire and use power.[36] Psychologists have

EXHIBIT 11.6

Measuring Locus of Control

The questionnaire below is designed to measure locus-of-control beliefs. Researchers using this questionnaire in a study of college students found a mean of 51.8 for men and 52.2 for woman, with a standard deviation of 6 for each. The higher your score on this questionnaire, the more you tend to believe you are generally responsible for what happens to you; in other words, higher scores are associated with internal locus of control. Low scores are associated with external locus of control. Scoring low indicates you tend to believe that forces beyond your control, such as powerful other people, fate, or chance, are responsible for what happens to you.

For each of these ten statements, indicate the extent to which you agree or disagree using the following scale:

1 = strongly disagree   5 = slightly agree
2 = disagree   6 = agree
3 = slightly disagree   7 = strongly agree
4 = neither disagree nor agree

_____ 1. When I get what I want, it is usally because I worked hard for it.

_____ 2. When I make plans, I am almost certain to make them work.

_____ 3. I prefer games involving some luck over games requiring pure skill.

_____ 4. I can learn almost anything if I set my mind to it.

_____ 5. My major accomplishments are entirely due to my hard work and ability.

_____ 6. I usally do not set goals because I have a hard time following through on them.

_____ 7. Competition discourages excellence.

_____ 8. Often people get ahead just by being lucky.

_____ 9. On any sort of exam or competition, I like to know how well I do relative to everyone else.

_____ 10. It is pointless to keep working on something that is too difficult for me.

To determine your score, reverse the values you selected for statements 3, 6, 7, 8, and 10 (1 = 7, 2 = 6, 3 = 5, 4 = 4, 5 = 3, 6 = 2, 7 = 1). For example, if you strongly disagree with statement 3, you would have given it a value of 1. Change this value to 7. Reverse the scores in a similar manner for statements 6, 7, 8, and 10. Now add the point values from all 10 statements together.

Your score: _____

SOURCE: Adapted from J. M. Burger, *Personality: Theory and Research* (Belmont, Calif.: Wadsworth, 1986), 400–401, cited in D. Hellriegel, J. W. Slocum, Jr., and R. W. Woodman, *Organizational Behavior*, 6th ed. (St. Paul, Minn.: West, 1992), 97–100. Original Source: "Sphere-Specific Measures of Perceived Control," by D. L. Paulhus, *Journal of Personality and Social Psychology*, 44, 1253–1265.

developed instruments to measure a person's Machiavellianism (Mach) orientation.[37] Research shows that high Machs are predisposed to being pragmatic, capable of lying to achieve personal goals, more likely to win in win-lose situations, and more likely to persuade than be persuaded.[38]

Different situations may require people who demonstrate one or the other type of behavior. In loosely structured situations, high Machs actively take control, but low Machs accept the direction given by others. Low Machs thrive in highly structured situations, but high Machs perform in a detached, disinterested way. High Machs are particularly good in jobs that require bargaining skills or that involve substantial rewards for winning.[39]

Problem-Solving Styles and the Myers-Briggs Type Indicator (MBTI).
Managers need to understand that individuals differ in the way they solve problems and make decisions. One approach to understanding problem-solving styles grew out of the work of psychologist Carl Jung. Jung believed differences resulted from our preferences in how we go about gathering and evaluating information.[40] According to Jung, gathering information and evaluating information are separate activities. People gather information by sensation or intuition but not by both simultaneously. Sensation-type people would rather work with known facts and hard data and prefer routine and order in gathering information. Intuitive-type people would rather look for possibilities than work with facts and prefer solving new problems and using abstract concepts.

Evaluating information involves making judgments about the information a person has gathered. People evaluate information by thinking or feeling. These represent the extremes in orientation. Thinking-type individuals base their judgments on impersonal analysis, using reason and logic rather than personal values or emotional aspects of the situation. Feeling-type individuals base their judgments more on personal feelings such as harmony and tend to make decisions that result in approval from others.

According to Jung, only one of the four functions—sensation, intuition, thinking, or feeling—is dominant in an individual. However, the dominant function usually is backed up by one of the functions from the other set of paired opposites. Exhibit 11.7 shows the four problem-solving styles that result from these matchups, as well as occupations that people with each style tend to prefer.

Two additional sets of paired opposites not directly related to problem solving are introversion-extroversion and judging-perceiving. Introverts gain energy by focusing on personal thoughts and feelings; extroverts gain energy from being around others and interacting with others. On the judging versus perceiving dimension, people with a judging preference like certainty and closure and tend to make decisions quickly based on available data. Perceiving people, on the other hand, enjoy ambiguity, dislike deadlines, and may change their minds several times as they gather large amounts of data and information to make decisions.

A widely used personality test that measures how people differ on all four of Jung's sets of paired opposites is the **Myers-Briggs Type Indicator (MBTI)**. The MBTI measures a person's preferences for introversion versus extroversion, sensation versus intuition, thinking versus feeling, and judging versus perceiving. The various combinations of these four preferences result in 16 unique personality types.

Myers-Briggs Type Indicator (MBTI)

Personality test that measures a person's preference for introversion vs. extroversion, sensation vs. intuition, thinking vs. feeling, and judging vs. perceiving.

EXHIBIT 11.7

Four Problem-Solving Styles

Personal Style	Action Tendencies	Likely Occupations
Sensation–thinking	• Emphasizes details, facts, certainty • Is a decisive, applied thinker • Focuses on short-term, realistic goals • Develops rules and regulations for judging performance	• Accounting • Production • Computer programming • Market research • Engineering
Intuitive–thinking	• Prefers dealing with theoretical or technical problems • Is a creative, progressive, perceptive thinker • Focuses on possibilities using impersonal analysis • Can consider a number of options and problems simultaneously	• Systems design • Systems analysis • Law • Middle/top management • Teaching business, economics
Sensation–feeling	• Shows concern for current, real-life human problems • Is pragmatic, analytical, methodical, and conscientious • Emphasizes detailed facts about people rather than tasks • Focuses on structuring organizations for the benefit of people	• Directing supervisor • Counseling • Negotiating • Selling • Interviewing
Intuitive–feeling	• Avoids specifics • Is charismatic, participative, people oriented, and helpful • Focuses on general views, broad themes, and feelings • Decentralizes decision making, develops few rules and regulations	• Public relations • Advertising • Human Resources • Politics • Customer service

Each of the 16 different personality types can have positive and negative consequences for behavior. Based on the limited research, the two preferences that seem to be most strongly associated with effective management in various organizations and industries are thinking and judging.[41] However, people with other preferences can also be good managers. One advantage of understanding your natural preferences is to maximize your innate strengths and abilities. Dow Chemical manager Kurt Swogger believes the MBTI can help put people in the right jobs where they will be happiest and make the strongest contribution to the organization.

| | **Dow Chemical** |

When Kurt Swogger arrived at Dow Chemical's plastics business in 1991, it took anywhere from 6 to 15 years to launch a new product, and the unit had not launched a single one for three years. Today, a new product launch takes two to four years, and Swogger's R&D team has launched 13 product hits over the past decade.

How did Swogger lead such an amazing transformation? By making sure people were doing the jobs they were best suited for. The simple fact, Swogger says, "is that some [people] do development better than others. The biggest obstacle to launching great new products was not having the right people in the right jobs." Swogger began reassigning people based on his intuition and insight, distinguishing pure inventors from those who could add value later in the game and others who were best at marketing the new products. Swogger says he was right-on about 60 percent of the time. If someone didn't work out after six months, he'd put them in another assignment.

Seeking a better way to determine people's strengths, Swogger turned to a former Dow employee, Greg Stevens, who now owns a consulting firm. Stevens and Swogger used the MBTI, predicting which types would be best suited to each stage of the product development and launch cycles. After administering the test to current and former Dow plastics employees, they found some startling results. In 1991, when Swogger came on board, the match between the right personality type and the right role was only 29 percent. By 2001, thanks to Swogger's great instincts, the rate had jumped to 93 percent.

Swogger's next step is to administer the MBTI to new hires, so the job match is right to begin with. He believes the MBTI can help him assign people to jobs that match their natural abilities and interests, leading to happier employees and higher organizational performance.[42]

Matching the right people to the right jobs is an important responsibility for managers, whether they do it based on intuition and experience or by using personality tests such as the MBTI. Managers strive to create a good fit between the person and the job he or she is asked to do.

Person-Job Fit

Given the wide variation among personalities and among jobs, an important responsibility of managers is to match employee and job characteristics so work is done by people who are well suited to do it. This requires that managers be clear about what they expect employees to do and have a sense of the kinds of people who would succeed at various types of assignments. The extent to which a person's ability and personality match the requirements of a job is called **person-job fit**. When managers achieve person-job fit, employees are more likely to contribute and have higher levels of job satisfaction and commitment.[43] The importance of person-job fit became apparent during the dot-com heyday of the late 1990s. People who had rushed to Internet companies in hopes of finding a new challenge—or making a quick buck—found themselves floundering in jobs for which they were unsuited. One manager recruited by a leading executive

person-job fit
The extent to which a person's ability and personality match the requirements of a job.

CONCEPT CONNECTION

*Andrew Field, who owns a $10.3 million printing services company, PrintingForLess.com., uses dogs to help him create the **person–environment fit** when hiring new employees. Every day for five years, Jessie (far left), Field's Border collie and black Labrador mix, has accompanied him to work. The idea caught on and as many as eight dogs frequent the company offices. With rules such as owner accountability, a dog review board, and a dog-approval process, employees find that the dogs are a great release for stress. Field says that the dog policy helps him make good hires; candidates who respond favorably to the canine rule are likely to fit in with the office culture.*

Take **ACTION**

Look for the kind of job that uses your strengths rather than weaknesses. Look for the type of work that you really love.

search firm lasted less than two hours at his new job. The search firm, a division of Russell Reynolds Associates, later developed a "Web Factor" diagnostic to help determine whether people have the right personality for the Internet, including such things as a tolerance for risk and uncertainty, an obsession with learning, and a willingness to do whatever needs doing, regardless of job title.[44]

A related concern is person-environment fit, which looks at if the person and job are suited to one another and at how well the individual will fit in the overall organizational environment. An employee who is, by nature, authoritarian, for example, would have a hard time in an organization such as W.L. Gore and Associates, where there are few rules, no hierarchy, no fixed or assigned authority, and no bosses. Many of today's organizations pay attention to person-environment fit from the beginning of the recruitment process. Texas Instruments' Web page includes an area called Fit Check that evaluates personality types anonymously and gives prospective job candidates a chance to evaluate for themselves if they would be a good match with the company.[45]

Learning

Years of schooling have conditioned many of us to think that learning is something students do in response to teachers in a classroom. With this view, in the managerial world of time deadlines and concrete action, learning seems remote and irrelevant. However, today's successful managers need specific knowledge and skills as well as the ability to adapt to changes in the world around them. Managers have to learn.

learning

A change in behavior or performance that occurs as the result of experience.

Learning is a change in behavior or performance that occurs as the result of experience. Experience may take the form of observing others, reading or listening to sources of information, or experiencing the consequences of one's own behavior. This important way of adapting to events is linked to individual differences in attitudes, perception, and personality.

Two individuals who undergo similar experiences—for example, a business transfer to a foreign country—probably will differ in how they adapt their behaviors to (that is, learn from) the experience. In other words, each person learns in a different way.

The Learning Process

One model of the learning process, shown in Exhibit 11.8, depicts learning as a four-stage cycle.[46] First, a person encounters a concrete experience. This is followed by thinking and reflective observation, which lead to abstract conceptualization and, in

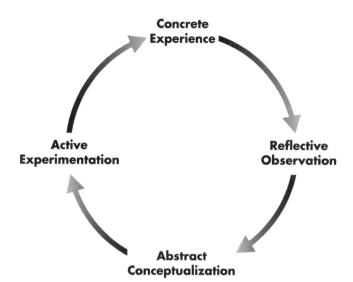

EXHIBIT 11.8
Experiential Learning Cycle

turn, to active experimentation. The results of the experimentation generate new experiences, and the cycle repeats.

The Best Buy chain of consumer electronics superstores owes its birth to the learning process of its founder, Richard M. Schulze. In the 1960s, Schulze built a stereo store called Sound of Music into a chain of nine stores in and near St. Paul, Minnesota. However, a tornado destroyed his largest and most profitable store, so he held a massive clearance sale in the parking lot. So many shoppers descended on the lot that they caused traffic to back up for 2 miles. Reflecting on this experience, Schulze decided there was great demand for a store featuring large selection and low prices, backed by heavy advertising. He tested his idea by launching his first Best Buy superstore. Today, more than 700 Best Buy retail outlets exist as well as a thriving online division, and the chain's profits are in the billions of dollars.[47]

The arrows in the model of the learning process in Exhibit 11.8 indicate that this process is a recurring cycle. People continually test their conceptualizations and adopt them as a result of their personal reflections and observations about their experiences.

Learning Styles

Individuals develop personal learning styles that vary in terms of how much they emphasize each stage of the learning cycle. These differences occur because the learning process is directed by individual needs and goals. For example, an engineer might place greater emphasis on abstract concepts, but a salesperson might emphasize concrete experiences. Because of these preferences, personal learning styles typically have strong and weak points.

Questionnaires can assess a person's strong and weak points as a learner by measuring the relative emphasis the person places on each of the four learning stages shown in Exhibit 11.8: concrete experience, reflective observation, abstract conceptualization, and active experimentation. Some people have a tendency to overemphasize one stage of the learning process or to avoid some aspects of learning. Not many people have totally balanced profiles, but the key to effective learning is competence in each of the four stages when it is needed.

Researchers have identified four fundamental learning styles that combine elements of the four stages of the learning cycle.[48] Exhibit 11.9 summarizes the characteristics and dominant learning abilities of these four styles, labeled Diverger, Assimilator, Converger,

EXHIBIT 11.9

Learning Style Types

Learning Style Type	Dominant Learning Abilities	Learning Characteristics	Likely Occupations
Diverger	• Concrete experience • Reflective observation	• Is good at generating ideas, seeing a situation from multiple perspectives, and being aware of meaning and value • Tends to be interested in people, culture, and the arts	• Human resource management • Counseling • Organization development specialist
Assimilator	• Abstract conceptualization • Reflective observation	• Is good at inductive reasoning, creating theoretical models, and combining disparate observations into an integrated explanation • Tends to be less concerned with people than ideas and abstract concepts	• Research • Strategic planning
Converger	• Abstract conceptualization • Active experimentation	• Is good at decisiveness, practical application of ideas, and hypothetical deductive reasoning • Prefers dealing with technical tasks rather than interpersonal issues	• Engineering • Production
Accommodator	• Concrete experience • Active experimentation	• Is good at implementing decisions, carrying out plans, and getting involved in new experiences • Tends to be at ease with people but may be seen as impatient or pushy	• Marketing • Sales

and Accommodator. The exhibit lists occupations that frequently attract individuals with each of the learning styles. For example, people whose dominant style is Accommodator are often drawn to sales and marketing. A good example is Gertrude Boyle, who took over Columbia Sportswear after the death of her husband. She and her son, Tim, propelled the company from sales of $13 million to $358 million over a 13-year period by observing what competitors were doing and actively experimenting to find a novel sales approach. The 74-year-old Gert Boyle decided to star in her own "Tough Mother" ads as a way to distinguish the company from competitors who advertised their products worn by fit, young models. Boyle believes in constantly pushing herself and her company, questioning everything, and trying new ideas.[49] Exhibit 11.9 lists other likely occupations for Divergers, Assimilators, Convergers, and Accommodators.

Through awareness of their learning styles, managers can understand how they approach problems and issues, their learning strengths and weaknesses, and how they react to employees or coworkers who have different learning styles.

Continuous Learning

To thrive in today's turbulent business climate, individuals and organizations must be continuous learners. For individuals, continuous learning entails looking for opportunities to learn from classes, reading, and talking to others, as well as looking for the lessons in life's experiences. One manager who embodies the spirit of continuous learning is Larry Ricciardi, senior vice president and corporate counsel at IBM. Ricciardi is an avid traveler and voracious reader who likes to study art, literature, and history. In addition, Ricciardi likes to add supermarket tabloids to his daily fare of *The Wall Street*

Journal. On business trips, he scouts out side trips to exotic or interesting sites, so he can learn something new.[50] Ricciardi never knows when he might be able to apply a new idea or understanding to improve his life, his job, or his organization.

For organizations, continuous learning involves the processes and systems through which the organization enables its people to learn, share their growing knowledge, and apply it to their work. In an organization in which continuous learning is taking place, employees actively apply comments from customers, news about competitors, training programs, and more to increase their knowledge and improve the organization's practices. For example, at the Mayo Clinic, doctors are expected to consult with doctors in other departments, with the patient, and with anyone else inside or outside the clinic who might help with any aspect of the patient's problem.[51] The emphasis on teamwork, openness, and collaboration keeps learning strong at Mayo.

Managers can foster continuous learning by consciously stopping from time to time and asking, "What can we learn from this experience?" They can allow employees time to attend training and reflect on their experiences. Recognizing that experience can be the best teacher, managers should focus on how they and their employees can learn from mistakes, rather than fostering a climate in which employees hide mistakes because they fear being punished for them. Managers encourage organizational learning by establishing information systems that enable people to share knowledge and learn in new ways. Information technology was discussed in detail in Chapter 6. As individuals, managers can help themselves and set an example for their employees by being continuous learners, listening to others, reading widely, and reflecting on what they observe. Can leaders learn and change their own behavior? Marshall Goldsmith shows they can. He helps managers listen to feedback and self-reflect, causing real behavior changes as shown below.

Marshall Goldsmith

The more obnoxious the better. That is what Marshall Goldsmith is after with clients he coaches to become better managers. Often brilliant, honest, and hard-working, these people have low EQ and usually treat others with no respect. One man was a complete jerk at work and considered a hopeless case by his colleagues. Goldsmith changed him by asking how he treated his family members. "Oh, I'm totally different at home," he replied. Picking up the phone right then, Goldsmith asked the wife, who said, "He's a jerk." Kids said, "Jerk."

Goldsmith will not take on a client unless that person does desire change, which allows the person to hear feedback and make adjustments in behavior. He most often works with high performers who need to hone their people skills. First, Goldsmith asks colleagues for comprehensive information on the leaders' strengths and weaknesses and confronts them with data on what everybody thinks. Then he makes them apologize and ask for help on how to improve, focusing on future rather than past behaviors. Not allowed to explain or defend themselves in any way, the leaders must act humbly and ask for forgiveness. Such behavior breaks down their egos and allows self-reflection and examination.

Goldsmith advises clients to be happy and not wait until they get that promotion or raise or the new house; learn to see the self as an obstacle to corporate and spiritual innovation. (Habits, mind views, smugness, and past memories all can get in the way.) It is easier to change your behavior than understand how you got that way, so why not change the behavior? Goldsmith credits his own quality family life with applying his own principles at home. "How can I be a better dad?" he asks his children.

His work is the logical extension of encounter groups, which have the same purpose: The shocking revelations of how others see you jolts you into becoming humbler person. But instead of recreation, Goldsmith's 360-degree feedbacks are used for organizational effectiveness. Self-knowledge, humility, and sensitivity are seen as business assets.

"I've heard every excuse in the history of the world," he says of people who blame mom, dad and their CEO. He tells them, "Quit whining. Let it go."[52]

Stress and Stress Management

stress

A physiological and emotional response to stimuli that place physical or psychological demands on an individual.

Just as organizations can support or discourage learning, organizational characteristics interact with individual differences to influence other behaviors in the organization. In every organization, these characteristics include sources of stress. Formally defined, **stress** is an individual's physiological and emotional response to external stimuli that place physical or psychological demands on the individual and create uncertainty and lack of personal control when important outcomes are at stake.[53] These stimuli, called stressors, produce some combination of frustration (the inability to achieve a goal, such as the inability to meet a deadline because of inadequate resources), and anxiety (such as the fear of being disciplined for not meeting deadlines).

People's responses to stressors vary according to their personalities, the resources available to help them cope, and the context in which the stress occurs. Thus, a looming deadline will feel different depending on the degree to which the individual enjoys a challenge, the willingness of coworkers to team up and help each other succeed, and family members' understanding of an employee's need to work extra hours, among other factors.

When the level of stress is low relative to a person's coping resources, stress can be a positive force, stimulating desirable change and achievement. However, too much stress is associated with many negative consequences, including sleep disturbances, drug and alcohol abuse, headaches, ulcers, high blood pressure, and heart disease. People who are experiencing the ill effects of too much stress may become irritable or withdraw from interactions with their coworkers, take excess time off, and have more health problems. For example, a recent study of manufacturing workers in Bangladesh found a significant connection between job stress and absenteeism. Another study of 46,000 workers in the United States found that health-care costs are 147 percent higher for individuals who are stressed or depressed.[54] People suffering from stress are less productive and may leave the organization. Clearly, too much stress is harmful to employees as well as to companies.

Type A and Type B Behaviors

Type A behavior

Behavior pattern characterized by extreme competitiveness, impatience, aggressiveness, and devotion to work.

Type B behavior

Behavior pattern that lacks Type A characteristics and includes a more balanced, relaxed lifestyle.

Researchers have observed that some people seem to be more vulnerable than others to the ill effects of stress. From studies of stress-related heart disease, they have categorized people as having behavior patterns called Type A and Type B.[55] The **Type A behavior** pattern includes extreme competitiveness, impatience, aggressiveness, and devotion to work. In contrast, people with a **Type B behavior** pattern exhibit less of these behaviors. They consequently experience less conflict with other people and a more balanced, relaxed lifestyle. Type A people tend to experience more stress-related illness than Type B people.

Most Type A individuals are high-energy people and may seek positions of power and responsibility. One example is John Haughom, senior vice president for health-care improvement at PeaceHealth, a network of private hospitals in the Pacific Northwest. When Haughom was in charge of establishing an information network of community-wide medical records to support patient care, he typically began his day at 6 A.M. and worked until 11 P.M. His days were a blur of conference calls, meetings, and e-mail exchanges. "I could move mountains if I put my mind to it," he says. "That's what good executives do."[56]

By pacing themselves and learning control and intelligent use of their natural high-energy tendencies, Type A individuals can be powerful forces for innovation and leadership within their organizations as John Haughom has been at PeaceHealth. However, many Type A personalities cause stress-related problems for themselves and, sometimes, for those around them. Haughom reached burnout. He could not sleep, he began

Take **ACTION**

If you are a Type A person with a high stress job, take a relaxing vacation; if you are a Type B with a low-key job, then you can do the seven-countries-in-five-days kind of trip.

snapping at colleagues, and he finally took a sabbatical and learned to lead a more balanced life.[57] Type B individuals typically live with less stress unless they are in high-stress situations. There are a number of factors that can cause stress in the workplace, even for people who are not naturally prone to high stress.

Causes of Work Stress

Workplace stress is skyrocketing. The percentage of working Americans reporting that stress is a major problem in their lives more than doubled between 1992 and 2002. The number of people calling in sick due to stress tripled over a four-year period. And the United States is not alone. In 2002, the European Committee officially cited stress as the second biggest occupational health problem facing the European Union.[58]

Most people have a general idea of what a stressful job is like: difficult, uncomfortable, exhausting, and even frightening. Managers can cope with their own stress better and establish ways for the organization to help employees cope if they define the conditions that tend to produce work stress. One way to identify work stressors is to place them in four categories: demands associated with job tasks, physical conditions, roles (sets of expected behaviors), and interpersonal pressures and conflicts.

©Evan Sklar

CONCEPT CONNECTION

Sylvia Weinstock is founder of Sylvia Weinstock Cakes in New York City, known for celebrity wedding cakes, including those for Catherine Zeta-Jones and Donald Trump. With annual revenues of nearly $2 million, and 16 employees, including eight who are devoted solely to making "botanically correct" sugar flowers by hand, Weinstock loves her job, but feels the work stress of **task demands**. *"This is an obsessive business because of the intensity and personal value that everyone places on their occasion," she says. "And I honor that. I fret. I worry. And unless I heard that the cake arrived happy, I'm checking that phone all the time."*

- *Task demands* are stressors arising from the tasks required of a person holding a particular job. Some kinds of decisions are inherently stressful: those made under time pressure, those that have serious consequences, and those that must be made with incomplete information. For example, emergency room doctors are under tremendous stress as a result of the task demands of their jobs. They regularly have to make quick decisions, based on limited information, that may determine if a patient lives or dies. Almost all jobs, especially those of managers, have some level of stress associated with task demands.

- *Physical demands* are stressors associated with the setting in which an individual works. Some people must work in a poorly designed setting, such as an office with inadequate lighting or little privacy. Some employees must maneuver in a cramped workspace; some have too little or too much heat for comfort. Some workplaces even present safety and health hazards, from greasy floors to polluted air.

- *Role demands* are challenges associated with a role, that is, the set of behaviors expected of a person because of that person's position in the group. Some people encounter **role ambiguity**, meaning they are uncertain about what behaviors are expected of them. **Role conflict** occurs when an individual perceives incompatible demands from others. Managers often feel role conflict because the demands of their superiors conflict with those of the employees in their department. They may be expected to support employees and provide them with opportunities to experiment and be creative; at the same time, top executives are demanding a consistent level of output that leaves little time for creativity and experimentation. Filmmaker Doug Liman was hired because of his fresh creativity but then confined at every turn with rules and structure of the big studio, causing conflict and high stress, which led to difficulties in working together.

role ambiguity
Uncertainty about what behaviors are expected of a person in a particular role.

role conflict
Incompatible demands of different roles.

Colossal battles on script and shooting locations, plus a continually delayed release date, plagued the production of Universal Pictures $60 million *The Bourne Identity*, starring Matt Damon. Why all the drama? Most people point to inexperienced and idiosyncratic director Doug Liman, a self-proclaimed "paranoid" who stunned the film world with the low-budget $250,000 "Swingers."

The Bourne Identity

With so many knock-offs or boring adaptation flicks, moviegoers have turned hostile, causing studios to hire new directors with fresh voices to supply creativity. Unfortunately, inexperienced and imaginative directors are not accustomed to the complexity of a big-budget studio production. Independent films have smaller crews and can make changes more easily. With a major-studio movie, changes can mean rewriting, destroying or building sets, or delays that typically cost millions, because the final product ends up at millions per movie-minute.

It all started when Universal tried to save money and film the Paris scenes in Montreal. With shooting in seven countries, cutting costs in any location would make a big difference. Liman protested, now admitting he was flippant and difficult. "What are they talking about?" he said. "Because they speak French in Montreal, it's going to look like Paris? Nothing looks like Paris." He won that argument and then decided to hire a crew that only spoke French, so he could practice his collegiate French. That was only the beginning of the problems. When Matt Damon arrived, he did not like recent changes to the script, so Liman tore apart the schedule.

"We wanted to wanted to be daring, to take risks," says Universal Chairman Stacey Snider. "But you can't just say 'Let's be bold and daring' without any parameters. Then it becomes reckless."

So the studio and Liman continued to bicker, about locations, about the final action scene. "Doug came from a world where he had a lot more independence," says Snider. Because of all the conflicts, the film went $8 million over budget and took two weeks longer to shoot. Liman admits he had difficulty delegating tasks and managing the mammoth project, saying the experience was a "nightmare." If they asked him, would he do another major studio movie? "I'd love to," he says.

And then there was the well-received sequel, *The Bourne Supremacy*. Despite his own riches from that movie as well as *Ocean's 12*, star Matt Damon poo-pooed Hollywood sequels, saying, "Often they're really crap and try to fleece the moviegoer because they have goodwill towards the movie."[59]

- *Interpersonal demands* are stressors associated with relationships in the organization. In some cases interpersonal relationships can alleviate stress, but they can be a source of stress when the group puts pressure on an individual or when there are conflicts between individuals. Managers can resolve many conflicts using techniques that will be discussed in Chapter 15. A particularly challenging stressor is the personality clash. A personality clash occurs when two people cannot get along and do not see eye-to-eye on any issue. This type of conflict can be exceedingly difficult to resolve, and many managers have found that it is best to separate the two people so they do not have to interact with one another.

Almost everyone experiences some degree of job stress associated with these various factors. For example, consider the stress caused by task demands on Verizon's call center representatives.

Verizon Communications

Roland G. Collins Jr. loves his job as a call center representative for Verizon Communications. He enjoys connecting with customers; he makes good money, and has good benefits. But he admits that the job is not for everyone. About a third of the 100 or so calls a representative handles each day are stressful. Besides dealing with irate customers and handling calls regarding billing or other problems, representatives have to be able to rattle off Verizon's string of products and services, including terms and rates, and sell them to each and every call. It does not matter how angry or rude the customer on the other end of the line; pushing new services is a key requirement of the job.

What makes matters worse is that representatives often have to do all this under observation. Managers routinely sit next to a representative or listen in on a call to check whether the rep has hit on nearly 80 different points required in every customer contact. Call center reps must meet precise performance specifications, and managers defend the observation practice as a way to ensure consistency and better customer service. However, employees almost always find the experience adds to their stress level. For some employees, particularly inexperienced ones, an observation can create a panic situation, causing heart pounding and profuse sweating, which, in turn, creates even more stress.[60]

Can you think of task, physical, role, or interpersonal demands associated with your job? Take the quick quiz in Exhibit 11.10 to assess your level of stress in your work or student life.

Stress Management

Organizations that want to challenge their employees and stay competitive in a fast-changing environment will never be stress-free. But because many consequences of stress are negative, managers need to make stress management a priority. In Britain, lawmakers have implemented a new requirement that employers meet certain conditions that help to manage workplace stress, such as ensuring that employees are not exposed to a poor physical work environment, have the necessary skills and training to meet their job requirements, and are given a chance to offer input into the way their work is done.[61]

Individual Stress Management. Various techniques help individuals manage stress. Among the most basic strategies are those that help people stay healthy: exercising regularly, getting plenty of rest, and eating a healthful diet.

In addition, most people cope with stress more effectively if they lead balanced lives and are part of a network of people who support and encourage them. Family, relationships,

---

EXHIBIT 11.10

How Stressed Are You?

SOURCE: This quiz appeared in Cora Daniels, "The Last Taboo," *Fortune* (October 28, 2002), 137–144, and was adapted from a stress test created by workplace research firm Marlin Company and the American Institute of Stress.

Respond to the following on a 1-to-5 scale, with 1 meaning Never and 5 meaning Often. The higher the score, the higher your stress level. If you have a high score, what will you do to cope with stress at school or work?

	1 Never	2	3	4	5 Often
1. Conditions at work are unpleasant and sometimes unsafe.	1	2	3	4	5
2. I feel that my job is making me physically and emotionally sick.	1	2	3	4	5
3. I have too much work or too many unreasonable deadlines.	1	2	3	4	5
4. I cannot express my opinions or feelings about my job to my boss.	1	2	3	4	5
5. My work interferes with my family or personal life.	1	2	3	4	5
6. I have no control over my life at work.	1	2	3	4	5
7. My good performance goes unrecognized and unrewarded.	1	2	3	4	5
8. My talents are underutilized at work.	1	2	3	4	5

Add up the numbers for your Total Score   **Total Score:** _____

Scoring and Interpretation

15 or lower: Low stress level.
16 to 20: Fairly low stress. Coping should be easy, but you probably have a tough day now and then.
21 to 25: Moderate stress. You are suffering about the same amount of pressure as most people cope with today.
26 to 30: Severe stress. You may be coping, but you could probably benefit from stress counseling or stress management techniques.
31 to 40: Potentially dangerous stress. Seek professional help.

friendships, and memberships in non-work groups such as community or religious organizations are helpful for stress management, as well as for other benefits. People who do not take care of themselves physically and emotionally are more susceptible to stress in their personal as well as professional lives. Managers and employees in today's hectic, competitive work environment may sometimes think of leisure activities as luxuries. The study of OB, however, offers a reminder that employees are human resources with human needs.

New Workplace Responses to Stress Management. Though individuals can pursue stress management strategies on their own, today's enlightened companies support healthy habits to help employees manage stress and be more productive. Stress costs U.S. businesses billions of dollars a year in absenteeism, lower productivity, staff turnover, accidents, and higher health insurance and workers' compensation costs.[62] In the new workplace, taking care of employees has become a business as well as ethical priority.

Supporting employees can be as simple as encouraging people to take regular breaks and vacations. BellSouth, First Union, and Tribble Creative Group are among the companies that have designated areas as quiet rooms or meditation centers where employees can take short, calming breaks at any time they feel the need.[63] The time off is a valuable investment when it allows employees to approach their work with renewed energy and a fresh perspective. Companies have developed other programs aimed at helping employees reduce stress and lead healthier, more balanced lives. Some have wellness programs that provide access to nutrition counseling and exercise facilities. A worldwide study of wellness programs conducted by the Canadian government found that for each dollar spent, the company gets from $1.95 to $3.75 return payback from benefits.[64] Other organizations create broad work-life balance initiatives that may include flexible work options such as telecommuting and flexible hours, as well as benefits such as onsite daycare, fitness centers, and personal services such as pick-up and delivery of dry cleaning. Daily flextime is considered by many employees to be the most effective work-life practice, which means giving employees the freedom to vary their hours as needed, such as leaving early to take an elderly parent shopping or taking time off to attend a child's school play.[65]

By acknowledging the personal aspects of employees' lives, work-life practices communicate that managers and the organization care about employees as human beings. In addition, managers' attitudes make a difference in whether employees are stressed out and unhappy or relaxed, energetic, and productive.

Manager's Solution

The principles of OB describe how people as individuals and groups behave and affect the performance of the organization as a whole. Desirable work-related attitudes include job satisfaction and organizational commitment. Attitudes affect people's perceptions and vice versa. Individuals often "see" things in different ways. The perceptual process includes perceptual selectivity and perceptual organization. Perceptual distortions such as stereotyping, the halo effect, projection, and perceptual defense are errors in judgment that can arise from

inaccuracies in the perception process. Attributions are judgments that individuals make about whether a person's behavior was caused by internal or external factors.

Another area of interest is personality, the set of characteristics that underlie a relatively stable pattern of behavior. One way to think about personality is the Big Five personality traits of extroversion, agreeableness, conscientiousness, emotional stability, and openness to experience. Some important work-related attitudes and behaviors influenced by personality are locus of control, authoritarianism, Machiavellianism, and problem-solving styles. A widely used personality test is the MBTI. Managers want to find a good person–job fit by ensuring that a person's personality, attitudes, skills, abilities, and problem-solving styles match the requirements of the job and the organizational environment.

New insight into personality has been gained through research in the area of EQ. EQ includes the components of self-awareness, self-management, social awareness, and relationship management. EQ is not an in-born personality characteristic but can be learned and developed. Vinita Gupta, described at the beginning of this chapter, needed to strengthen her emotional intelligence, particularly in the areas of self-awareness and relationship management. Gupta hired a corporate coach to help her learn more about herself and manage the personality characteristics and behaviors that could be contributing to decreased performance and higher turnover at Quick Eagle. Gupta worked on a series of exercises to help develop greater empathy and improve her social skills, including coaching employees, being more open and less defensive, and using humor to create a lighter atmosphere. She now makes a point of greeting people upon arrival, introducing herself to employees she has never met, and having lunch with colleagues. Gupta has learned that she cannot change some of her personality characteristics: For example, she will never score high on extroversion. However, she has learned to manage her attitudes and behaviors to make Quick Eagle a more pleasant, comfortable place to work. Employees have noticed that the atmosphere is lighter, and people are no longer afraid to speak up in meetings or if they have a concern. Turnover has decreased by 20 percent from a year earlier.[66]

Though people's personalities may be relatively stable, individuals, like Vinita Gupta, can learn new behaviors. Learning refers to a change in behavior or performance that occurs as a result of experience. The learning process goes through a four-stage cycle, and individual learning styles differ. Four learning styles are Diverger, Assimilator, Converger, and Accommodator. Rapid changes in today's marketplace create a need for ongoing learning. They may create greater stress for many of today's workers. The causes of work stress include task demands, physical demands, role demands, and interpersonal demands. Individuals and organizations can alleviate the negative effects of stress by engaging in a variety of techniques for stress management.

Discussion Questions

1. What are the three basic leadership skills that lie at the core of identifying and solving people problems? Why is it important for managers to develop these skills?

2. In what ways might the cognitive and affective components of attitude influence the behavior of employees who are faced with learning an entirely new set of computer-related skills in order to retain their jobs at a manufacturing facility?

3. What steps might managers at a company (about to be merged with another company) take to promote organizational commitment among employees?

4. Think about an important event in your life. Do you believe that the success or failure of the event was your responsibility (internal locus of control) or the responsibility of outside forces or people (external locus of control)? Has your belief changed since the event took place? How does your locus of control affect the way you now view the event?

5. In the Big Five personality factors, extroversion is considered a "good" quality to have. Why might introversion be an equally positive quality?

6. Which type of problem-solving style do you prefer: sensation–thinking, intuitive–thinking, sensation–feeling, or intuitive–feeling? Describe briefly a decision you have made using this style.

7. Why is it important for managers to achieve person–job fit when they are hiring employees?

8. How might a design manager use a combination of novelty, familiarity, and repetition in the presentation of a new product idea to the company's financial managers?

9. What characteristics of perceivers might influence the attendees of a human resources seminar on employee benefits (such as retirement planning, health-care insurance, vacation, and the like)?

10. Describe a situation in which you learned how to do something—use a computer or ride a snowboard. In your description, identify the four stages of the learning cycle.

11. Do you think that a Type A person or a Type B person would be better suited to managing a health-care facility? Why?

Manager's Workbook

Your personality is what you are. You have similarities and differences from other people. The differences measured here are not better or worse, merely different. Complete and score the inventory below to find out your personality type.

Personality Inventory

For each item, circle either *a* or *b*. If you feel both *a* and *b* are true, decide which one is more like you, even if it is only slightly more true.

1. When making a decision, the most important considerations are
   a. rational thoughts, ideas, and data.
   b. people's feelings and values.

2. When discussing a problem with colleagues, it is easy for me
   a. to see "the big picture."
   b. to grasp the specifics of the situation.

3. When I am working on an assignment, I tend to
   a. work steadily and consistently.
   b. work in bursts of energy with "down time" in between.

4. When I listen to someone talk on a subject, I usually try to
   a. relate it to my own experience and see if it fits.
   b. assess and analyze the message.

5. In work, I prefer spending a great deal of time on issues of
   a. ideas.
   b. people.

6. In meetings I am most often annoyed with people who
   a. come up with many sketchy ideas.
   b. lengthen meetings with many practical details.

7. I would rather work for an organization where
   a. my job was intellectually stimulating.
   b. I was committed to its goals and mission.

8. I would rather work for a boss who is
   a. full of new ideas.
   b. practical.

In the following, choose the word in each pair that appeals to you more:

9. a. social
   b. theoretical

10. a. ingenuity
    b. practicality

Scoring Key

Count one point for each item listed below that you circled in the inventory.

Score for S	Score for N
2b	2a
3a	3b
6a	6b
8b	8a
10b	10a

Total

Circle the one with more points: S or N

Score for T	Score for F
1a	1b
4b	4a
5a	5b
7a	7b
9b	9a

Total

Circle the one with more points: T or F

Your score is:
S or N _____   **T or F** _____

Manager's Workshop

Apply what you know about perceptual biases and rater errors.

Scully and Mulder have to speak with a number of informants about a UFO sighting that occurred in Flatbush, Kansas. The informants are all poor, middle-aged farmers who have little education and strong rural accents. It appears that they don't bathe very often, and they also happen to have poor dental hygiene (many in fact are missing their teeth). Listed below are a number of perceptual biases and rater errors and examples of how Scully and Mulder may be susceptible to each of them when interacting with these people or evaluating the quality of their stories. Match each of the biases with the example that best reflects that error.

	Primacy effect	Recency effect
Implicit personality theory	Projection	Stereotyping
Contrast effects	Leniency (too easy on some things)	Harshness (intensity)
Central tendency (seeing all things at same level)	Halo effect	Similar-to-me effect (familiarity)

1. At the beginning of her first interview, Scully discovers that the informant can't read and has very slow, drawn out speech, which leads her to conclude that the person is probably mentally disabled. She conducts the rest of her interview based on that assumption.

2. Scully is a Christian, and her religion is very important to her. As a result, she is very skeptical about the whole UFO phenomenon and thinks that others are as well. Her interview questions are often phrased to reflect her skepticism: "Do you think the light you saw might have been an airplane?" and "You don't really believe that what you saw were visitors from another planet, do you?"

3. Because Scully thinks that there is no such thing as UFOs, she has a tendency to invalidate the stories of all the farmers by finding flaws and inconsistencies in them.

4. Mulder has interviewed three people, all of whom fit the general description of the residents of this area. The fourth person who arrives is clean, well dressed, and very articulate. The difference is amazing and leads Mulder to put more weight on what this individual has to tell him.

5. On their way into town, Scully and Mulder nearly get into an accident with one of the local farmers. An argument ensues, and Mulder is tempted to arrest the man for obstruction of justice. When they meet later during one of the interview sessions, Mulder can't shake his negative impression of the guy and finds himself being very harsh.

6. At the conclusion of an interview that was going very well, an informant suddenly bursts into a medley of Broadway show tunes. Mulder is stunned by how nutty this person appears to be and forgets all the apparently rational things the individual has told him.

7. Because Mulder believes that UFOs are very real, he has a tendency to accept all of the stories of the farmers as being highly accurate and valid.

8. The sheriff helped Mulder and Scully conduct the interviews. When it came time to evaluate them, however, he had a hard time distinguishing the good stories from the bad, so he classified them all as somewhat believable but flawed.

9. Scully thinks personal hygiene is extremely important; therefore, she concludes that if these people aren't very good at taking care of themselves, they are probably not very reliable as witnesses due to a lack of attention to detail.

10. One person whom Scully interviews is also a devout Christian, and she articulates many of the same concerns and skepticism that Scully has. Because of their

obvious similarities, Scully is predisposed to like this woman and to believe her version of events.

11. Mulder thinks of farmers as having a strong work ethic and being very honest and forthright. Therefore, he is predisposed to believe everything that the informants tell him, even though the sheriff has told him that one of the farmers is a known liar and a convicted criminal.

12. Mulder thinks that people who are hard-working and make a lot of sacrifices are also generally honest. He therefore tends to believe the stories of the farmers who seem to be very hard-working and self-sacrificing.

SOURCE: Courtney Hunt, Northern Illinois University. Used with permission.

Management in Practice: Ethical Dilemma

Should I Fudge the Numbers?

Sara MacIntosh recently joined MicroPhone, a large telecommunications company with headquarters in Denver, to take over the implementation of a massive customer service training project. The program was created by Kristin Cole, head of human resources and Sara's new boss. According to the grapevine, Kristin was hoping this project alone would give her the "star quality" she needed to earn a promotion she'd been longing for. Industry competition was heating up, and MicroPhone's strategy called for being the very best at customer service. That meant having the most highly trained people in the industry, especially those who would work directly with customers. Kristin had put together a crash team to develop the new training program, which called for an average of one full week of intense customer service training for each of 3,000 people and had a price tag in the neighborhood of $40 million. Kristin's team, made up of several staffers who already felt overwhelmed with their day-to-day workload, rushed to put the proposal together. It was scheduled to go to the board of directors next month.

Kristin knew she needed someone well qualified and dedicated to manage and implement the project, and Sara, with eight years of experience, a long list of accomplishments, and advanced degrees in finance and organizational behavior, was perfect for the job. When Sara agreed to come aboard, Kristin expressed great relief and confidence in Sara's ability to make the program work. However, during a thorough review of the proposal, Sara discovered some assumptions built into the formulas of the proposal that raised red flags. She approached Dan Sotal, the team's coordinator, about her concerns, but the more Dan tried to explain how the financial projections were derived, the more Sara realized that Kristin's proposal was seriously flawed. No matter how she tried to work them out, the most that could be squeezed out of the $40 million budget was 20 hours of training a week, not the 40 hours everyone expected for such a high price tag.

Sara knew that although the proposal had been largely developed before she came on board, it would bear her signature. As she carefully described the problems with the proposal to Kristin and outlined the potentially devastating consequences, Kristin impatiently tapped her pencil on the marble tabletop. Finally, she stood up, leaned forward, and interrupted Sara, quietly saying, "Sara, make the numbers work so that it adds up to forty hours and stays within the $40 million budget." Sara glanced up and replied, "I don't think it can be done unless we either change the number of employees who are to be trained or the cost figure. . . ." Kristin's smile froze on her face and her eyes began to snap as she again interrupted. "I don't think you understand what I'm saying. We have too much at stake here. Make the previous numbers work." Stunned, Sara belatedly began to realize that Kristin was ordering her to fudge the numbers. She felt an anxiety attack coming on as she wondered what she should do.

What Do You Do?

1. Make the previous numbers work. Kristin and the entire team have put massive amounts of time into the project and they all expect you to be a team player. You don't want to let them down. Besides, this is a great opportunity for you in a highly visible position.

2. Stick to your ethical principles and refuse to fudge the numbers. Tell Kristin you will work overtime to help develop an alternate proposal that stays within the budget by providing more training to employees who work directly with customers and fewer training hours for those who don't have direct customer contact.

3. Go to the team and tell them what you've been asked to do. If they refuse to support you, threaten to reveal the true numbers to the CEO and board members.

SOURCE: Adapted from Doug Wallace, "Fudge the Numbers or Leave," *Business Ethics*, May–June, 1996, pp. 58–59. Adapted with permission.

Case for Critical Analysis

Volkswagen's Ferdinand Piëch

While many of today's organizations are shifting toward more democratic, participative types of management, one is not: Volkswagen. In fact, Volkswagen's chief executive, Ferdinand Piëch, rules his realm with an iron hand. After a long executive career at such prestigious automakers as Audi and Porsche (Piëch's maternal grandfather was Ferdinand Porsche), Piëch took over as Volkswagen's CEO in 1993. He immediately centralized power in the organization, firing managers who questioned his ideas or who didn't follow his lead. He dove into engineering projects himself, proposing new projects, tinkering with designs. He presided over meetings with the demeanor of an autocrat. "Critical questions aren't asked, because people know things can rapidly get uncomfortable," notes one former executive.

Piëch had—and still has—a reason for ruling supreme over his company. He isn't satisfied that VW is Europe's leading mass-market auto manufacturer; he wants to turn it into the most powerful, most respected carmaker in the world. He won't settle for less. "We're trying to redefine the status game," explains Jens Neumann, a member of Volkswagen's management board and supporter of Piëch. After creating successes at both Porsche and Audi, such as the Quattro all-wheel drive, Piëch is intent on doing even more at VW. "He is the most brilliant and forward-looking CEO in the business today," claims an analyst for a major VW investor. Indeed, in the first five years at the wheel, Piëch turned around several languishing auto models, increased the company's lead in Europe, and created a comeback in the U.S. market. His most famous project perhaps is his reintroduction of the beloved VW Beetle. Despite warnings by market experts, Piëch pushed the bug ahead—redesigned so it's a little larger than its predecessor and with all the necessary technological bells and whistles—to a warm welcome from U.S. customers.

Perhaps one reason Piëch is so successful in his method of management is his extensive knowledge of and passion for the cars themselves. From his days as an automotive engineering student at Zurich's Swiss Federal Institute of Technology, through his stint at Porsche, where he helped create world-class race cars, to his development of Audi's Quattro and now the launch of the VW Beetle, Piëch has been found under the hood, tinkering. Thus, he knows his product and his customers and how to fit them together better than anyone else in the industry.

Critics charge that Piëch has too tight a hold over his company. "At VW, nothing happens without Piëch," notes a former colleague. One-person rule can result in massive mistakes. For instance, several years ago, Piëch pushed for the purchase of Rolls-Royce Motors from its parent, Vickers PLC. But in a botched deal, he lost the rights to the Rolls-Royce brand name, which actually belongs to Rolls-Royce PLC, the aerospace manufacturer. Critics also point out that Piëch's fanatical grip on VW has more to do with his personal insecurity than a philosophy of management. "He wants to prove that he has been underestimated for years," muses one former VW executive. But with Piëch in the lead, VW now is reporting more than $2 billion a year in earnings, more than 100 percent more than before he took the driver's seat.

Questions

1. What personality traits do you think Ferdinand Piëch exhibits? Do you think these contribute to a good person–job fit? Why or why not?

2. Hardly anyone would argue that Piëch is an authoritarian executive. Do you sense that he is machiavellian as well? Do you think these characteristics have a positive or negative impact on the way Volkswagen is run? Explain your answer.

3. Imagine that you are a manager at Volkswagen, and you are experiencing some cognitive dissonance about being asked to work long hours on one of Piëch's pet projects—a new car model whose success you have doubts about. How might you resolve your dissonance?

SOURCE: David Woodruff and Keith Naughton, "Hard-Driving Boss," *Business Week,* October 5, 1998, pp. 82–87.

CHAPTER

12

Leadership in Organizations

LEARNING OBJECTIVES

After studying this chapter, you should be able to do the following:

1 **Define leadership and explain its importance for organizations.**

2 **Identify personal characteristics associated with effective leaders.**

3 **Describe the leader behaviors of initiating structure and consideration and when they should be used.**

4 **Describe Hersey and Blanchard's situational theory and its application to subordinate participation.**

5 **Explain the path–goal model of leadership.**

6 **Discuss how leadership fits the organizational situation and how organizational characteristics can substitute for leadership behaviors.**

7 **Describe transformational leadership and when it should be used.**

8 **Identify the five sources of leader power and how each causes different subordinate behavior.**

9 **Explain innovative approaches to leadership in a turbulent environment.**

Building a motivated, satisfied, and committed workforce for low-skill, low-wage jobs like food service, hospital cleaning, and lawn mowing can be a nightmare. Aramark Corp. is involved in all those businesses and more as a leader in managed services for corporations, universities, hospitals, parks and resorts, and other organizations. Roy Pelaez loves working for Aramark, and he takes great pride in his new job as head of a service operation that cleans airplanes for Delta and Southwest in several northeastern cities. Yet, he had no idea how hard it would be to keep 400 mostly non-English-speaking immigrants motivated and inspired to give their best to a $6-an-hour job. Morale is dismal, and turnover exceeds 100 percent a year. Employees do not seem to take any pride in their work. Moreover, wallets or other valuables that passengers leave on planes have a funny way of disappearing. Pelaez is determined to turn the operation around by creating an environment where employees feel committed to the company and their fellow workers. But how is he to do it? He has always believed that managers should not get involved in their subordinates' personal problems, but Pelaez thinks he might need a different approach to tap into the energy and enthusiasm of his employees.[1]

If you were in Roy Pelaez's position, what leadership approach would you take? Do you think it is possible to improve job satisfaction and organizational commitment for low-skilled, low-paid employees such as those Pelaez is supervising?

In the previous chapter, we explored differences in attitudes and personality that affect behavior. The attitudes and behaviors of leaders play an important role in shaping employee attitudes, such as their job satisfaction and organizational commitment. Different leaders behave in different ways, depending on their individual differences as well as their followers' needs and the organizational situation. Different styles of leadership can be effective. For example, contrast the styles of two leaders of software companies. Tom Siebel, CEO of Siebel Systems, is known as a disciplined and dispassionate manager who likes to maintain control over every aspect of the business. He enforces a dress code, sets tough goals and standards, and holds people strictly accountable. "We go to work to realize our professional ambitions, not to have a good time," Siebel says. Contrast Siebel's style with that of David A. Duffield, founder, chairman, and former CEO of PeopleSoft. As CEO, Duffield was known for hugging his employees, letting people bring their pets to work, providing free snacks, and signing his e-mails D.A.D.[2] Siebel and Duffield have been successful as leaders although their styles are different.

This chapter explores one of the most widely discussed and researched topics in management: leadership. Here we will define leadership and explore the differences between leadership and management. We will examine trait, behavioral, and contingency theories of leadership effectiveness, discuss charismatic and transformational leadership, and consider how leaders use power and influence to get things done. The final section of the chapter looks at new leadership approaches for today's turbulent environment. Chapters 13 through 15 will look in detail at many of the functions of leadership, including employee motivation, communication, and encouraging teamwork.

The Nature of Leadership

There is probably no topic more important to business success today than leadership. The concept of leadership continues to evolve as the needs of organizations change. Among all the ideas and writings about leadership, three aspects stand out: people, influence, and goals. Leadership occurs among people, involves the use of influence, and is used to attain goals.[3] Influence means that the relationship among people is active. Moreover, influence is designed to achieve some end or goal. Thus, **leadership** as defined here is the ability to influence people toward the attainment of goals. This definition captures the idea that leaders are involved with other people in the achievement of goals.

Leadership is reciprocal, occurring among people.[4] Leadership is a "people" activity, distinct from administrative paper shuffling or problem-solving activities. Leadership is dynamic and involves the use of power to get things done.

leadership
The ability to influence people toward the attainment of organizational goals.

Leadership versus Management

Much has been written in recent years about the leadership role of managers. Management and leadership are important to organizations. Effective managers have to be leaders, too, because distinctive qualities are associated with management and leadership that provide different strengths for the organization, as illustrated in Exhibit 12.1. As shown in the exhibit, management and leadership reflect two sets of qualities and skills that frequently overlap within a single individual. A person might have more of one set of qualities than the other, but ideally a manager develops a balance of manager and leader qualities.

A primary distinction between management and leadership is that management promotes stability, order and problem solving within the existing organizational structure and systems. Leadership promotes vision, creativity, and change. In other words, "a manager takes care of where you are; a leader take you to a new place."[5] Leadership means questioning the status quo so that outdated, unproductive, or socially irresponsible norms can be replaced to meet new challenges. Leadership cannot replace management; it should be in addition to management. Good management is needed to help

Leader Qualities

Manager Qualities

SOUL
Visionary
Passionate
Creative
Flexible
Inspiring
Innovative
Courageous
Imaginative
Experimental
Initiates change
Personal power

MIND
Rational
Consulting
Persistent
Problem solving
Tough-minded
Analytical
Structured
Deliberate
Authoritative
Stabilizing
Position power

EXHIBIT 12.1

Leader and Manager Qualities

SOURCE: Based on Genevieve Capowski, "Anatomy of a Leader: Where Are the Leaders of Tomorrow?" *Management Review*, March 1994, 12.

the organization meet current commitments, and good leadership is needed to move the organization into the future.[6]

Leadership Traits

Early efforts to understand leadership success focused on the leader's personal characteristics or traits. **Traits** are the distinguishing personal characteristics of a leader, such as intelligence, values, self-confidence, and appearance. The early research focused on leaders who had achieved a level of greatness and, hence, was referred to as the *Great Man* approach. The idea was relatively simple: Find out what made these people great, and select future leaders who exhibited the same traits or could be trained to develop them. Generally, early research found a weak relationship between personal traits and leader success.[7]

In recent years, there has been a resurgence of interest in examining leadership traits. In addition to personality traits, physical, social, and work-related characteristics of leaders have been studied.[8] Exhibit 12.2 summarizes the physical, social, and personal leadership characteristics that have received the greatest research support. However, these characteristics do not stand alone. The appropriateness of a trait or set of traits depends on the leadership situation. The same traits do not apply to every organization or situation. Consider the personal traits that are helping Ralph Szygenda transform General Motors into the first totally wired car company, as described in the Digital, Inc. box.

Further studies have expanded the understanding of leadership beyond the personal traits of the individual to focus on the dynamics of the relationship between leaders and followers.

Behavioral Approaches

The inability to define effective leadership based solely on traits led to an interest in looking at the behavior of leaders and how it might contribute to leadership success or failure. Perhaps any leader can adopt the correct behavior with appropriate training.

traits

Distinguishing personal characteristics, such as intelligence, values, and appearance.

Take **ACTION**

To be a good manager, you must organize resources; to be a good leader, you must help others to follow the vision.

EXHIBIT 12.2

Personal Characteristics of Leaders

SOURCE: Based on Bernard M. Bass, *Bass & Stogdill's Handbook of Leadership: Theory, Research, and Managerial Applications,* 3rd ed. (New York: Free Press, 1990), 80–81; and S. A. Kirkpatrick and E. A. Locke, "Leadership: Do Traits Matter?" *Academy of Management Executive 5,* no. 2 (1991), 48–60.

Physical characteristics
Energy
Physical stamina

Intelligence and ability
Intelligence, cognitive ability
Knowledge
Judgment, decisiveness

Personality
Self-confidence
Honesty and integrity
Enthusiasm
Desire to lead
Independence

Social characteristics
Sociability, interpersonal skills
Cooperativeness
Ability to enlist cooperation
Tact, diplomatic

Work-related characteristics
Achievement drive, desire to excel
Conscientiousness in pursuit of goals
Persistence against obstacles, tenacity

Social Background
Education
Mobility

Two basic leadership behaviors that have been identified as important for leadership are task-oriented behavior and people-oriented behavior. These two metacategories, or broadly defined behavior categories, have been found to be applicable to effective leadership in various situations and time periods.[9] Though these are not the only important leadership behaviors, concern for tasks and for people must be shown at some reasonable level. Thus, many approaches to understanding leadership use these metacategories as a basis for study and comparison. Important research programs on

DIGITAL, INC.

An E-Commerce Revolution at General Motors

When Ralph Szygenda first arrived at General Motors, the company's information technology (IT) systems were so outdated, inflexible, and poorly integrated that they were practically useless. As GM's first chief information officer (CIO), Szygenda has brought GM into the Internet Age. According to vice chairman Harry Pearce, prodding GM out of its inertia "was as tough a challenge as there was in corporate America."

Fortunately, Szygenda has always loved a challenge. "In my career, I've always tried to take on impossible jobs," he says. After nearly a decade on the job, the CIO has taken GM a long way toward his goal of creating the first totally wired car company. GM buys more IT products and services than any other company in the world. Today, employees around the globe can communicate and collaborate on projects. Before, the company's systems were so walled off from one another that the Cadillac division could not access marketing data assembled by Buick, and project engineers at headquarters in Michigan had no easy way to collaborate with their overseas colleagues. In addition, GM's site for consumers, GMBuyPower, is one of the most powerful on the Internet, offering more configuration and comparison options than Ford's or DaimlerChrysler's, as well as the ability to find out whether the car is in dealers' stock and where. The company's GMPowerSupply site lets suppliers tap directly into GM factories to access production schedules, inventories, and so forth.

The next step for Szygenda is to tie everything together into a seamless "sense and respond" system that would make GM a superefficient information link between customers and suppliers. This integration would allow GM to build at least half of its cars to order, cut delivery times of custom vehicles from months to weeks, and slash inventory in half. In other words, Szygenda wants to do for cars what Michael Dell has done for computers. It is a tremendous undertaking, but Szygenda thrives on such monumental tasks. He is known as an overachiever who loves the sense of accomplishment that comes from completing seemingly impossible jobs. His high energy level enables him to work 70-hour weeks and take home massive amounts of work on the weekends. He is a tough boss who sets high standards and expects everyone to be as focused on meeting them as he is. However, Szygenda does not insist on "his way or the highway." To build his executive team, he deliberately picked strong-willed people he knew would challenge him and each other. He likes to have a lot of people looking at and debating a problem. Szygenda also is known as a consummate diplomat and a skillful negotiator, who can get things accomplished through tact and compromise. His executive team members typically see him as a demanding but supportive boss with a good sense of humor.

Szygenda believes persistence and determination are his best qualities. He will do whatever it takes to get the job done, and he has the confidence to see it through to the end. "My job," he says, "is to make sure this all comes together."

SOURCES: Alex Taylor III, "Ralph's Agenda," *eCompany* (July 2000): 96–101; Robin Gareiss, "Chief of the Year: Ralph Szygenda," *Information Week* (December 2, 2002): 34–40; and Craig Zarley, "Ralph Szygenda," *CRN* (December 15, 2003): 60.

leadership behavior were conducted at The Ohio State University, the University of Michigan, and the University of Texas.

Ohio State Studies

Researchers at The Ohio State University surveyed leaders to study hundreds of dimensions of leader behavior.[10] They identified two major behaviors, called consideration and initiating structure.

Consideration falls in the category of people-oriented behavior and is the extent to which the leader is mindful of subordinates, respects their ideas and feelings, and establishes mutual trust. Considerate leaders are friendly, provide open communication, develop teamwork, and are oriented toward their subordinates' welfare.

Initiating structure is the degree of task behavior, that is, the extent to which the leader is task oriented and directs subordinate work activities toward goal attainment. Leaders with this style typically give instructions, spend time planning, emphasize deadlines, and provide explicit schedules of work activities.

Consideration and initiating structure are independent of each other, which means that a leader with a high degree of consideration may be high or low on initiating structure. A leader may have any of four styles: high initiating structure–low consideration, high initiating structure–high consideration, low initiating structure–low consideration, or low initiating structure–high consideration. The Ohio State research found that the high consideration–high initiating structure style achieved better performance and greater satisfaction than the other leader styles. The value of the high-high style is illustrated by some of today's successful pro football coaches, such as Brian Billick of the Baltimore Ravens and Herman Edwards of the New York Jets.[11] Coaches have to keep players focused on winning football games by scheduling structured practices, emphasizing careful planning, and so forth. However, today's best coaches are those who genuinely care about and show concern for their players. The Focus on Collaboration box profiles Bob Ladouceur, the coach of an extraordinary high school football team, who personifies the high-high leadership style.

However, new research has found that the high-high style is not necessarily the best. These studies indicate that effective leaders may be high on consideration and low on initiating structure or low on consideration and high on initiating structure, depending on the situation.[12]

Michigan Studies

Studies at the University of Michigan at about the same time took a different approach by comparing the behavior of effective and ineffective supervisors.[13] The most effective supervisors were those who focused on the subordinates' human needs to "build effective work groups with high performance goals." The Michigan researchers used the term "employee-centered leaders" for leaders who established high performance goals and displayed supportive behavior toward subordinates. The less-effective leaders were called job-centered leaders; these tended to be less concerned with goal achievement and human needs in favor of meeting schedules, keeping costs low, and achieving production efficiency.

The Leadership Grid

Blake and Mouton of the University of Texas proposed a two-dimensional leadership theory called the **leadership grid** that builds on the work of The Ohio State and Michigan studies.[14] The two-dimensional model and five of its seven major management styles are depicted in Exhibit 12.3. Each axis on the grid is a nine-point scale, with 1 meaning low concern and 9 high concern.

consideration
The type of behavior that describes the extent to which the leader is sensitive to subordinates, respects their ideas and feelings, and establishes mutual trust.

initiating structure
A type of leader behavior that describes the extent to which the leader is task oriented and directs subordinate work activities toward goal attainment.

Take *ACTION*
As a manager, work to have consideration and structure to achieve a balance.

leadership grid
A two-dimensional leadership theory that measures the leader's concern for people and for production.

FOCUS ON COLLABORATION

The De La Salle Spartans Win with Soul

The last time the De La Salle Spartans lost a football game was December 7, 1991. Since then, coach Bob LaDouceur has led his team of players, many of whom are derided as "undersized" and "untalented," to one victory after another, year after year. Despite competing against bigger schools and tougher players, the De La Salle Spartans keep on winning.

De La Salle is a small, private parochial school in Concord, California. Years ago, LaDouceur sized up his team of a few, small demoralized players and made a decision. He was going to teach these guys what it takes to win, and then make it a day-to-day process. LaDouceur directs close attention to the tasks needed to accomplish the goal of winning. He keeps his players on a year-round strength and conditioning program. Each practice is methodical, and LaDouceur constantly tells his players to leave every practice a little bit better than they were when it started. He teaches players to make up for what they lack in size and talent with intelligence and wit.

However, the coach has not just institutionalized the process of drills, workouts, and practices. He has also institutionalized a process of building bonds and intimacy among his players.

"If a team has no soul," LaDouceur says, "you're just wasting your time." Tasks are important, but for LaDouceur, people always come first. "It's not about how we're getting better physically, it's about how we're getting better as people," he says. During the off-season, players go camping and rafting together and volunteer for community service. When the season starts, the team attends chapel together for readings and songs. After every practice, there is a dinner at a player's home.

Then comes what LaDouceur's considers his central task and his main goal for the team. As tensions build during the season, players are encouraged to speak their hearts, to confess their fears and shortcomings, and to talk about their commitments and expectations of themselves for the next game. On Thursday night before Friday games, LaDouceur does not give a typical locker room speech. He talks about the "L word." "Love. Why is that word so hard to say?" he asks his players. And then he waits—as long as it takes—until a few players overcome their embarrassment enough to say it.

SOURCE: Don Wallace, "The Soul of a Sports Machine," *Fast Company* (October 2003): 100–102.

Team management (9,9) often is considered the most effective style and is recommended for managers because organization members work together to accomplish tasks. Country club management (1,9) occurs when primary emphasis is given to people rather than to work outputs. Authority compliance management (9,1) occurs when efficiency in operations is the dominant orientation. Middle-of-the-road management (5,5) reflects a moderate amount of concern for people and production. Impoverished management (1,1) means the absence of a management philosophy; managers exert little effort toward interpersonal relationships or work accomplishment. Consider these examples:

TrueServ and Tires Plus

When Pamela Forbes Lieberman learned that her subordinates called her The Dragon Lady, she embraced the moniker and hung a watercolor of a dragon in her office. Lieberman makes no apologies for her hard-driving leadership style. Her emphasis on ambitious goals, tough standards, and bottom-line results has brought renewed health and vitality to hardware cooperative TruServ, which supplies inventory to True Value hardware stores. As soon as Lieberman became CEO, she began slashing costs and setting tough performance targets. "If [people] succeed, they will be rewarded, but if they don't, then we're going to have to look for new people sitting in their chairs," Lieberman says.

Compare Lieberman's hard-nosed approach to that of Tom Gegax, who calls himself the head coach of Tires Plus, a fast-growing chain of retail tire stores. Gegax believes that you cannot manage people like you manage fixed assets. His emphasis is on treating employees as well as they are expected to treat their customers. Gegax personally leads classes at Tires Plus University, where employees learn about changing tires and about how to make their whole lives better. Gegax makes sure stores are clean, bright, and airy, so employees have a pleasant work environment. He believes all this translates into better service. Employees, as well as customers, like the approach. "The last thing the world

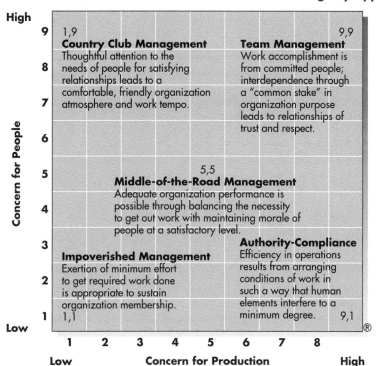

EXHIBIT 12.3

The Leadership Grid® Figure

SOURCE: "The Leadership Grid®" figure, by Robert R. Blake and Anne Adams McCanse (formerly the Managerial Grid figure by Robert R. Blake and Jane S. Mouton), from *Leadership Dilemmas—Grid Solutions*, copyright © 1991 Grid International, Inc., Austin, Texas.

needs is another chain of stores," Gegax says. "What it does need is a company with a new business model—one that embraces customers and employees as whole people."[15]

The leadership style of Pamela Lieberman is characterized by high concern for tasks and production (task-oriented behavior) and low-to-moderate concern for people (people-oriented behavior). Tom Gegax, in contrast, is high on concern for people and moderate on concern for production. Both leaders are successful though they display different leadership styles because of their different situations. The next group of theories builds on the leader-follower relationship of behavioral approaches to explore how organizational situations affect the leader's approach.

Contingency Approaches

There are several models of leadership that explain the relationship between leadership styles and specific situations. These are termed **contingency approaches** and include the leadership model developed by Fiedler and his associates, the situational theory of Hersey and Blanchard, the path-goal theory presented by Evans and House, and the substitutes-for-leadership concept.

Fiedler's Contingency Theory

An early, extensive effort to combine leadership style and organizational situation into a comprehensive theory of leadership was made by Fiedler and his associates.[16] The basic idea is simple: Match the leader's style with the situation most favorable for his or her success. By diagnosing leadership style and the organizational situation, the correct fit can be arranged.

Leadership Style. The cornerstone of Fiedler's contingency theory is the extent to which the leader's style is relationship oriented or task oriented. A relationship-oriented

contingency approaches
A model of leadership that describes the relationship between leadership styles and specific organizational situations.

Take **ACTION**
As a leader, find the right kind of style for each situation.

leader is concerned with people, similar to the consideration style described earlier. A task-oriented leader is primarily motivated by task accomplishment, which is similar to the initiating structure style described earlier.

Take a moment and complete the personality inventory below that measures your leadership style according to Fiedler's model.

The Least Preferred Co-worker (LPC) scale

least preferred co-worker (LPC) scale

A questionnaire designed to measure relationship-oriented versus task-oriented leadership style according to the leader's choice of adjectives for describing the least preferred co-worker.

Leadership style was measured with a questionnaire known as the **least preferred co-worker (LPC) scale.** The LPC scale has a set of 16 bipolar adjectives along an 8-point scale.

Think of another student you have worked with that you have trouble liking, the one person you hope is not on your team again. Circle a number on each scale below, with your circle showing how close to which word you would describe this person.

open	1	2	3	4	5	6	7	8	guarded
quarrelsome	8	7	6	5	4	3	2	1	harmonious
efficient	1	2	3	4	5	6	7	8	inefficient
self-assured	1	2	3	4	5	6	7	8	hesitant
gloomy	8	7	6	5	4	3	2	1	cheerful

Total in Each column ___ ___ ___ ___ ___ ___ ___ ___

Add the totals from each column. The total number will be between 5 and 40. Place the Grand Total here:

Interpretation: If you describe the LPC using positive concepts (and your grand total is between 5 and 20), you are considered relationship oriented, that is, a leader who cares about and is sensitive to other people's feelings. Conversely, if you use negative concepts to describe the LPC (and your grand total is 21–40, you are considered task oriented—that is, a leader who places greater value on task activities than on people. The lower your score, the more relationship oriented you are and the greater your score, the more task-oriented you are.

Situation. Leadership situations can be analyzed in terms of three elements: the qual-

---

ity of leader-member relationships, task structure, and position power.[17] Each of these elements can be described as favorable or unfavorable for the leader.

1. *Leader-member relations* refers to group atmosphere and members' attitude toward and acceptance of the leader. When subordinates trust, respect, and have confidence in the leader, leader-member relations are considered good. When subordinates distrust, do not respect, and have little confidence in the leader, leader-member relations are poor.

2. *Task structure* refers to the extent to which tasks performed by the group are defined, involve specific procedures, and have clear, explicit goals. Routine, well-defined tasks, such as those of assembly-line workers, have a high degree of structure. Creative, ill-defined tasks, such as research and development or strategic planning, have a low degree of task structure. When task structure is high, the situation is considered

favorable to the leader; when low, the situation is less favorable.

3. *Position power* is the extent to which the leader has formal authority over subordinates. Position power is high when the leader has the power to plan and direct the work of subordinates, evaluate it, and reward or punish them. Position power is low when the leader has little authority over subordinates and cannot evaluate their work or reward them. When position power is high, the situation is considered favorable for the leader. When low, the situation is unfavorable.

©Ken Hawkins

At Earnest Partners, an asset management firm in Atlanta, Georgia, the quality of **leader-member relationships** *is high. CEO Paul Viera has gained the respect and trust of colleagues and followers because he has proven that he has the integrity, skills, and commitment to keep the company thriving. In 2004, Earnest had $8.2 billion in assets under management. Viera can be characterized as a* **task-oriented leader** *because he is focused, prepared, and competitive, and he expects others to be as well. According to Fiedler's contingency theory, Viera's style succeeds at Earnest because of positive leader-member relations, strong leader position power, and jobs that contain some degree of task structure.*

Combining the three situational characteristics yields a list of eight leadership situations, which are illustrated in Exhibit 12.4. Situation I is most favorable to the leader because leader-member relations are good, task structure is high, and leader position power is strong. Situation VIII is most unfavorable to the leader because leader-member relations are poor, task structure is low, and leader position power is weak. All other octants represent intermediate degrees of favorableness for the leader.

Contingency Theory. When Fiedler examined the relationships among leadership style, situational favorability, and group task performance, he found the pattern shown in Exhibit 12.4. Task-oriented leaders are more effective when the situation is highly favorable or unfavorable. Relationship-oriented leaders are more effective in situations of moderate favorability.

The task-oriented leader excels in the favorable situation because everyone gets along, the task is clear, and the leader has power; all that is needed is for someone to take charge and provide direction. Similarly, if the situation is highly unfavorable to the leader, a great deal of structure and task direction is needed. A strong leader defines task structure and can establish authority over subordinates. Because leader-member relations are poor anyway, a strong task orientation will make no difference in the leader's popularity.

The relationship-oriented leader performs better in situations of intermediate favorability because human relations skills are important in achieving high group performance. In these situations, the leader may be moderately well liked, have some power, and supervise jobs that contain some ambiguity. A leader with good interpersonal skills can create a positive group atmosphere that will improve relationships, clarify task structure, and establish position power.

A leader, then, needs to know two things to use Fiedler's contingency theory. First, the leader should know if he or she has a relationship-oriented or task-oriented style. Second, the leader should diagnose the situation and determine if leader-member relations, task structure, and position power are favorable or unfavorable.

Consider how Stanley O'Neal's style fits his current situation as CEO of Merrill Lynch.

Merrill Lynch

A lot of people inside Merrill Lynch just do not like Stan O'Neal, who took over the CEO's job at the lowest point in the firm's history. They grumble that he is cold, aloof, and ruthless. O'Neal does not care. "People say all these things about me," O'Neal acknowledges. "But...I can't do anything about it. I have a job to do, and it has nothing to do with worrying about what people call me."

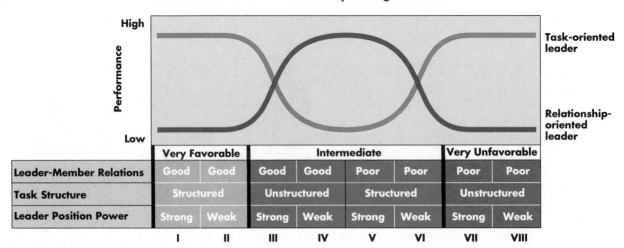

	Very Favorable		Intermediate				Very Unfavorable	
Leader-Member Relations	Good	Good	Good	Good	Poor	Poor	Poor	Poor
Task Structure	Structured		Unstructured		Structured		Unstructured	
Leader Position Power	Strong	Weak	Strong	Weak	Strong	Weak	Strong	Weak
	I	II	III	IV	V	VI	VII	VIII

EXHIBIT 12.4

How Leader Style Fits the Situation

SOURCE: Based on Fred E. Fiedler, "The Effects of Leadership Training and Experience: A Contingency Model Interpretation," *Administrative Science Quarterly* 17 (1972), 455.

The job to do is saving Merrill Lynch, which only a few years ago was sliding toward irrelevance. Few believed the firm could survive its massive problems, and rumors were that it would be swallowed up by a big bank. Merrill's financial results were dismal and costs were out of control. In addition, Merrill and nine other large securities firms were forced to pay a whopping $1.4 billion in penalties to settle government charges of investor abuses. The loss of public trust, combined with a declining stock market and general economic uncertainty, was a heavy blow to the struggling firm.

From the beginning, O'Neal took a tough approach to cutting costs. He froze everyone's pay, cut bonuses, and did away with the free gourmet meals provided for top managers. He met with every one of his direct reports and told them they were personally accountable for the company's profitability and performance. He set brutally ambitious targets for cost-cutting and profit margins and weeded out anyone who would not commit to meeting them.

By early 2004, O'Neal had slashed 24,000 jobs, closed more than 300 field offices, and demoted or fired dozens of veteran managers. He had also achieved one of the most remarkable turnarounds in recent corporate history, perhaps saving Merrill Lynch from extinction. "Stan was made CEO at the ultimate moment of truth," said the head of Merrill's retail brokerage unit. "Our world was imploding, and he had the courage to make difficult decisions."[18]

Stan O'Neal might be characterized as using a task-oriented style in an unfavorable situation. The recent environment has been as challenging as any the company has ever faced. Task structure is low, and leader-member relations are poor. Many employees oppose O'Neal's massive changes and do not like his aloof personality. When O'Neal was first promoted, his personal power with managers was low. Many did not believe he should have gotten the top job and did not agree with his plans for the company. Overall, the situation can be considered unfavorable to the leader, suggesting that O'Neal's strong task-oriented style might be the best approach. Even O'Neal's critics have grudgingly admitted that he is what Merrill Lynch needed. The company has become the leanest and most profitable on Wall Street under O'Neal's leadership. A leader using a relationship-oriented style might not be able to impose the structure and discipline needed for the organization to succeed in this difficult situation. "Ruthless," O'Neal once said, "isn't always that bad."[19]

An important contribution of Fiedler's research is that it goes beyond the notion of leadership styles to show how styles fit the situation to improve organizational effectiveness. Fitting leader style to the situation can yield big dividends in profits and efficiency.[20] On the other hand, the model has been criticized.[21] Using the LPC score as a measure of relationship-oriented or task-oriented behavior seems simplistic, and how the model works over time is unclear. For example, if a task-oriented leader is matched with an unfavorable situation and is successful, the organizational situation is likely to improve and become more favorable to the leader. Thus, the leader might have to adjust his or her style or go to a new situation. For example, employees at Merrill Lynch are feeling a great sense of relief and pride that the company is thriving again. As the situation continues to become more favorable, Stan O'Neal's strong task-oriented style will be less effective.

©AP/Wide World Photos

CONCEPT CONNECTION

The labor, technology, and infrastructure required to get a box of bananas from the plantations of Latin America to supermarkets in the United States is truly astounding. United Fruit Company, owner of the Chiquita brand of bananas, was responsible for building many roads and train tracks, and entire villages with homes, schools, medical facilities, and factories. Consistent with the **situational theory of leadership**, leaders used a telling style to direct the activities of low-skilled workers. However, as the company's power in the region grew, critics charged that leaders sought total control of workers—as well as attempting to control the leaders of the republics where the company did business. These alleged abuses of power led to devastating results. Over the past decade, the company has lost $700 million and watched its stock price plunge from a high of $50 to a low of 48 cents.

Hersey and Blanchard's Situational Theory

The **situational theory** of leadership is an interesting extension of the behavioral theories described earlier and summarized in the leadership grid (Exhibit 12.3). More than previous theories, Hersey and Blanchard's approach focuses a great deal of attention on the characteristics of employees in determining appropriate leadership behavior. The point of Hersey and Blanchard is that subordinates vary in readiness level. People low in task readiness, because of little ability or training, or insecurity, need a different leadership style than those who are high in readiness and have good ability, skills, confidence, and willingness to work.[22]

According to the situational theory, a leader can adopt one of four leadership styles, based on a combination of relationship (concern for people) and task (concern for production) behavior. These four styles are illustrated in Exhibit 12.5. The telling style reflects a high concern for tasks and a low concern for people and relationships. This is a directive style. It involves giving explicit directions about how tasks should be accomplished. The selling style is based on a high concern for people and tasks. With this approach, the leader explains decisions and gives subordinates a chance to ask questions and gain clarity and understanding about work tasks. The next leader behavior style, the participating style, is based on a combination of high concern for people and relationships and low concern for production tasks. The leader shares ideas with subordinates, gives them a chance to participate, and facilitates decision making. The fourth style, the delegating style, reflects a low concern for relationships and tasks. This leader style provides little direction and support because the leader turns over responsibility for decisions and their implementation to subordinates.

situational theory

A contingency approach to leadership that links the leader's behavioral style with the task readiness of subordinates.

The essence of Hersey and Blanchard's situational theory is to select a leader style that is appropriate for the readiness level of subordinates and their degree of education and skills, experience, self-confidence, and work attitudes. Followers may be at low, moderate, high, or very high levels of readiness.

Low Readiness Level. A telling style is appropriate when followers are at a low readiness level because of poor ability and skills, little experience, insecurity, or unwillingness to take responsibility for their own task behavior. When one or more subordinates exhibit very low levels of readiness, the leader is specific, telling followers exactly what to do, how to do it, and when.

EXHIBIT 12.5

Hersey and Blanchard's Situational Theory of Leadership

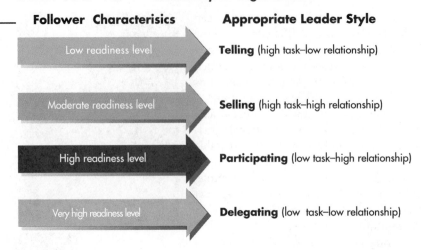

Follower Characterisics | **Appropriate Leader Style**

Low readiness level → **Telling** (high task–low relationship)

Moderate readiness level → **Selling** (high task–high relationship)

High readiness level → **Participating** (low task–high relationship)

Very high readiness level → **Delegating** (low task–low relationship)

Moderate Readiness Level. A selling style works best for followers with moderate levels of readiness. These subordinates, for example, might lack some education and experience for the job, but they demonstrate high confidence, ability, interest, and willingness to learn. The selling style involves giving direction, but it includes seeking input from others and clarifying tasks rather than instructing they be performed.

High Readiness Level. When subordinates demonstrate a high readiness level, a participating style is effective. These subordinates might have the necessary education, experience, and skills but might be insecure in their abilities and need some guidance from the leader. The participating style enables the leader to guide followers' development and act as a resource for advice and assistance.

Very High Readiness Level. When followers have very high levels of education, experience, and readiness to accept responsibility for their own task behavior, the delegating style can effectively be used. Because of the high readiness level of followers, the leader can delegate responsibility for decisions and their implementation to subordinates, who have the skills, abilities, and positive attitudes to follow through. The leader provides a general goal and sufficient authority to do the task as followers see fit.

In summary, the telling style is best suited for subordinates who demonstrate very low levels of readiness to take responsibility for their own task behavior, the selling and participating styles work for subordinates with moderate-to-high readiness, and the delegating style is appropriate for employees with very high readiness. This contingency model is easier to understand than Fiedler's model, but it incorporates only the characteristics of followers and not those of the situation. The leader diagnoses the readiness level of followers and adopts whichever style is necessary: telling, selling, participating, or delegating. For example, Phil Hagans, who owns two McDonald's franchises in northeast Houston, uses different styles as employees grow in their readiness level. Hagans gives many young employees their first job, and he tells them every step to take during their first days, instructing them on everything from how to dress to how to clean the grill. As they grow in ability and confidence, he shifts to a selling or participating style. Hagans has had great success by guiding young workers through each level of readiness.[23] A fast food franchise leader would probably need to take a different approach with a part-time worker who was retired after 40 years in the business world.

Path-Goal Theory

Another contingency approach to leadership is called the path-goal theory.[24] According to the **path-goal theory**, the leader's responsibility is to increase subordinates' motivation

---

Take ACTION

As a leader, only use the delegating style if the group has enough training, education and experience; otherwise, it can be a disaster.

---

path-goal theory

A contingency approach to leadership specifying that the leader's responsibility is to increase subordinates' motivation by clarifying the behaviors necessary for task accomplishment and rewards.

to attain personal and organizational goals. As illustrated in Exhibit 12.6, the leader increases subordinates' motivation by clarifying the subordinates' path to the available rewards or by increasing the rewards that the subordinates value and desire. Path clarification means that the leader works with subordinates to help them identify and learn the behaviors that will lead to successful task accomplishment and organizational rewards. Increasing rewards means that the leader talks with subordinates to learn which rewards are important to them, that is, whether they desire intrinsic rewards from the work itself or extrinsic rewards such as raises or promotions. The leader's job is to increase personal payoffs to subordinates for goal attainment and to make the paths to these payoffs clear and easy to travel.[25]

This model is called a contingency theory because it consists of three sets of contingencies: leader behavior and style, situational contingencies, and the use of rewards to meet subordinates' needs.[26] Whereas in the Fiedler theory described earlier the assumption would be to switch leaders as situations change, in the path-goal theory, leaders switch their behaviors to match the situation.

Leader Behavior. The path-goal theory suggests a fourfold classification of leader behaviors.[27] These classifications are the types of leader behavior the leader can adopt and include supportive, directive, achievement-oriented, and participative styles.

Supportive leadership involves leader behavior that shows concern for subordinates' well-being and personal needs. Leadership behavior is open, friendly, and approachable, and the leader creates a team climate and treats subordinates as equals. Supportive leadership is similar to the consideration, employee-centered, or relationship-oriented leadership described earlier.

Directive leadership occurs when the leader tells subordinates what they are supposed to do. Leader behavior includes planning, making schedules, setting performance goals and behavior standards, and stressing adherence to rules and regulations. Directive leadership behavior is similar to the initiating-structure, job-centered, or task-oriented leadership style described earlier.

EXHIBIT 12.6

Leader Roles in the Path–Goal Model

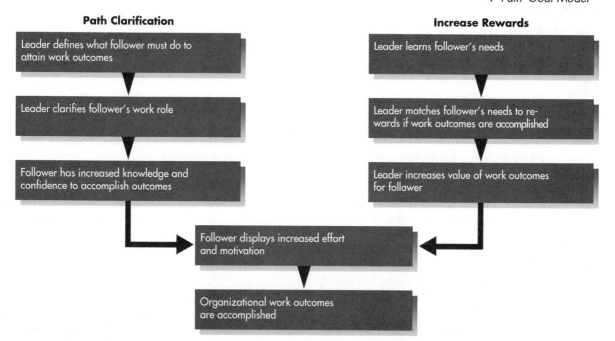

SOURCE: Based on Bernard M. Bass, "Leadership: Good, Better, Best," *Organizational Dynamics* 13 (Winter 1985), 26–40.

Participative leadership means the leader consults with his or her subordinates about decisions. Leader behavior includes asking for opinions and suggestions, encouraging participation in decision making, and meeting with subordinates in their workplaces. The participative leader encourages group discussion and written suggestions. The Focus on Collaboration box show how the Hunterdon High School used participative leadership to achieve some important goals.

Achievement-oriented leadership occurs when the leader sets clear and challenging goals for subordinates. Leader behavior stresses high-quality performance and improvement over current performance. Achievement-oriented leaders show confidence in subordinates and assist them in learning how to achieve high goals.

The four types of leader behavior are not considered ingrained personality traits as in the Fiedler theory; rather, they reflect types of behavior that every leader is able to adopt, depending on the situation.

Situational Contingencies.   The two important situational contingencies in the path-goal theory are the personal characteristics of group members and the work environment. Personal characteristics of subordinates include such factors as ability, skills, needs, and motivations. For example, if employees have low ability or skill, the leader may need to provide additional training or coaching for workers to improve performance. If subordinates are self-centered, the leader must use rewards to motivate them. Subordinates who want clear direction and authority require a directive leader who will tell them what to do. Craftworkers and professionals, however, may want more freedom and autonomy and work best under a participative leadership style. Considering individual needs of players is important for high school coaches, as described in the Focus on Ethics box.

The work environment contingencies include the degree of task structure, the nature of the formal authority system, and the work group itself. The task structure is

---

FOCUS ON COLLABORATION

Hunterdon High School

According to Ray Farley, "Once you put people in charge of their own destiny and say, 'Here's where you need to go if you want to be ready for the future,' the rest just happens." Farley has turned some of the traditional power of a school superintendent over to teams of students, teachers, and parents. Now, they decide what gets taught, who gets hired, and what the school calendar looks like. It was the school counselor, for example, who suggested running a grief program because so many students were self-medicating with drugs as a result of deep loss of loved ones.

One of the most important outcomes of this participative leadership has been a technological revolution at Hunterdon High School. The school's team found a way to equip the school with PCs, video facilities, ISDN lines, fiber-optic cables—the works—for $40,000 per classroom. Hunterdon has a student-run FM radio station, a television studio, a telephone in every classroom, and a state-of-the-art instructional media center. Each classroom is linked to the school library, to the Internet,

and to a host of other databases. The technology has led to a sort of virtual busing that links suburban, mostly white Hunterdon to four inner-city, mostly black New Jersey schools. Students at Hunterdon collaborate, for example, with their counterparts at Asbury Park to produce a poetry magazine in real time. With a mouse-click, a teacher can drop in and participate in the teamwork going on. Now, Asbury Park is increasing its technological edge as well. According to Dan Murphy, Asbury Park's principal, "One year ago, we had two computers hooked up to the Internet. Right now, technicians are setting up 200 computers, providing them all with access.... And all of this is just the tip of the iceberg. It's unbelievable."

"Kids today live in a nanosecond world," Farley says. "You have to make available all the technology you can get your hands on. And then you have to do one more thing: You have to trust them."

SOURCES: Margo Nash, "The High School Where Grieving is Part of the Curriculum," *The New York Times* (Oct 22, 2000): 3; Nicholas Morgan, "Fast Times at Hunterdon High," *Fast Company* (February/March 1998): 42, 44.

FOCUS ON ETHICS

High School Coaches

Is it leadership, or is it abuse? That's the controversy now in high school sports. Some years ago, everyone expected coaches to yell at players, criticize their mistakes, raising their voices and their hands. "It used to be that sports was the last bastion for emotionally confrontational treatment, and usually players years later look back at it as something they valued, a badge of honor," says high school basketball coach Dennis King. Now those same coaches are seen as politically incorrect, needing sensitivity training and anger management. Coach King sees it as a "trend that is seen in all aspects of society."

A new breed of parent is complaining. Philip George has two daughters in Smyrna High School soccer and he thinks that what some call negative reinforcement crosses the line. "No one at our school deserves to be abused," he says. He believes continued and unrelenting verbal abuse to diminish a kid is no way to treat kids. Soccer coach Pete Dakis agrees

and resigned after several complaints from parents. Other coaches have been fired or resigned in recent years for similar reasons.

Tennessee high school sports administrator Chris Madewell is only 31 and not too many years away from his days as a high school athlete. But he sees changes. "Something as simple as grabbing a kid by the helmet and just talking to him, something like that was pretty normal when I was in school. And now you are kind of wary of it," because of negative ramifications.

There are parents, though, who feel that coaches raising their voice and calling them names is teaching them important life lessons. Shelbyville girls basketball coach Rick Insell knows he has to treat every player differently. Some can handle rougher treatment; in fact, they need it. Others need a more gentle approach. It is contingency leadership for athletes.

SOURCE: Jessica Hopp, "Tough Line to Draw for Coaches," *Tennessean*, (March 6, 2005): 19A–20A.

---

similar to the same concept described in Fiedler's contingency theory; it includes the extent to which tasks are defined and have explicit job descriptions and work procedures. The formal authority system includes the amount of legitimate power used by managers and the extent to which policies and rules constrain employees' behavior. Work group characteristics are the educational level of subordinates and the quality of relationships among them.

Use of Rewards. Recall that the leader's responsibility is to clarify the path to rewards for subordinates or to increase the value of rewards to enhance satisfaction and job performance. In some situations, the leader works with subordinates to help them acquire the skills and confidence needed to perform tasks and achieve available rewards. In others, the leader may develop new rewards to meet the specific needs of a subordinate.

Exhibit 12.7 illustrates four examples of how leadership behavior is tailored to the situation. In the first situation, the subordinate lacks confidence; thus, the supportive leadership style provides the social support with which to encourage the subordinate to undertake the behavior needed to do the work and receive the rewards. In the second situation, the job is ambiguous, and the employee is performing ineffectively. Directive leadership behavior is used to give instructions and clarify the task so the follower will know how to accomplish it and receive rewards. In the third situation, the subordinate is unchallenged by the task; thus, an achievement-oriented behavior is used to set higher goals. This clarifies the path to rewards for the employee. In the fourth situation, an incorrect reward is given to a subordinate, and the participative leadership style is used to change this. By discussing the subordinate's needs, the leader is able to identify the correct reward for task accomplishment. In all four cases, the outcome of fitting the leadership behavior to the situation produces greater employee effort by clarifying how subordinates can receive rewards or by changing the rewards to fit their needs.

> **Take ACTION**
>
> As a leader, get to know your people and their needs; do not treat everyone the same, but be careful not to show favorites.

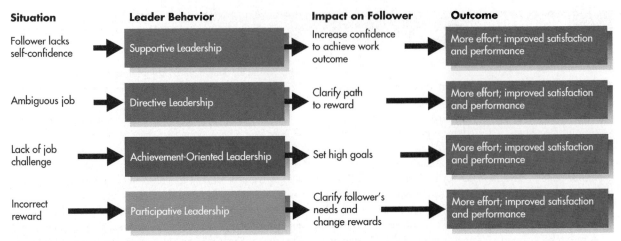

EXHIBIT 12.7

Path–Goal Situations and Preferred Leader Behaviors

SOURCE: Adapted from Gary A. Yukl, *Leadership in Organizations* (Englewood Cliffs, N.J.: Prentice-Hall, 1981), 146–152.

Pat Kelly, founder and CEO of PSS World Medical, a specialty marketer and distributor of medical products, hires people who exhibit a desire to win and then keeps them motivated with his achievement-oriented leadership.

PSS World Medical

Pat Kelly strives to hire enterprising, hard-working professionals who thrive on challenge, responsibility, and recognition. He keeps them performing at high levels by establishing ambitious goals and making sure people have the skills and resources to reach them. Kelly realizes that what gets people's juices flowing is not just reaching a new financial target but the idea of winning. So Kelly makes sure employees have what they need to win and receive high rewards for their performance. PSS spends about 5 percent of its payroll budget each year on training, so employees have the knowledge and skills they need to succeed. The company emphasizes promotion from within. Moving people around to different divisions and different roles gives them opportunities for learning and advancement. If an employee does not do well in one position, PSS will help the person find another avenue to success.

Open communication plays an important role in Kelly's leadership. To meet high goals, employees have to know how they contribute and where they stand. Open book management is a cornerstone of corporate culture because Kelly believes people can succeed only when everyone knows the numbers and how they fit in. By setting high goals, providing people with the knowledge and skills to succeed, and running an open company, Kelly has created an organization full of people who think and act like CEOs. In fact, all delivery drivers have business cards with their names and "CEO" printed on them. As Kelly puts it, "When you're standing in front of the customer, you are the CEO."[28]

Kelly's achievement-oriented leadership is successful because it keeps talented, ambitious professionals challenged and motivated. Path-goal theorizing can be complex, but much of the research on it has been encouraging.[29] Using the model to specify precise relationships and make exact predictions about employee outcomes may be difficult, but the four types of leader behavior and the ideas for fitting them to situational contingencies provide a useful way for leaders to think about motivating subordinates.

Substitutes for Leadership

The contingency leadership approaches considered so far have focused on the leaders' style, the subordinates' nature, and the situation's characteristics. The final contingency approach suggests that situational variables can be so powerful that they substitute for or neutralize the need for leadership.[30] This approach outlines those organizational settings in which a leadership style is unimportant or unnecessary.

Exhibit 12.8 shows the situational variables that tend to substitute for or neutralize leadership characteristics. A **substitute** for leadership makes the leadership style unnecessary or redundant. For example, highly professional subordinates who know how to do their tasks do not need a leader who initiates structure for them and tells them what to do. A **neutralizer** counteracts the leadership style and prevents the leader from displaying certain behaviors. For example, if a leader has no position power or is physically removed from subordinates, the leader's ability to give directions to subordinates is greatly reduced.

Situational variables in Exhibit 12.8 include characteristics of the group, the task, and the organization itself. For example, when subordinates are highly professional and experienced, both leadership styles are less important. The employees do not need much direction or consideration. With respect to task characteristics, highly structured tasks substitute for a task-oriented style, and a satisfying task substitutes for a people-oriented style. With respect to the organization, group cohesiveness substitutes for both leader styles. Formalized rules and procedures substitute for leader task orientation. Physical separation of leader and subordinate neutralizes both leadership styles.

The value of the situations described in Exhibit 12.8 is that they help leaders avoid leadership overkill. Leaders should adopt a style with which to complement the organizational situation. Consider the work situation for bank tellers. A bank teller performs highly structured tasks, follows clearly written rules and procedures, and has little flexibility in terms of how to do the work. The head teller should not adopt a task-oriented style because the organization provides structure and direction. The head teller should concentrate on a people-oriented style. In other organizations, if group cohesiveness or previous training meets employees' social needs, the leader is free to concentrate on task-oriented behaviors. The leader can adopt a style complementary to the organizational situation to ensure that task and people needs of the work group will be met.

substitute

A situational variable that makes a leadership style unnecessary or redundant.

neutralizer

A situational variable that counteracts a leadership style and prevents the leader from displaying certain behaviors.

Take **ACTION**

As a leader, be only as much of a leader as the situation demands.

Leading Change

In Chapter 1, we defined management to include the functions of leading, planning, organizing, and controlling. But recent work on leadership has begun to distinguish leadership as something more: a quality that inspires and motivates people beyond their normal levels of performance. Leadership is particularly important in companies meeting the challenges of a turbulent environment. Leaders in many organizations

Variable		Task-Oriented Leadership	People-Oriented Leadership
Organizational variables:	Group cohesiveness	Substitutes for	Substitutes for
	Formalization	Substitutes for	No effect on
	Inflexibility	Neutralizes	No effect on
	Low positional power	Neutralizes	Neutralizes
	Physical separation	Neutralizes	Neutralizes
Task characteristics:	Highly structured task	Substitutes for	No effect on
	Automatic feedback	Substitutes for	No effect on
	Intrinsic satisfaction	No effect on	Substitutes for
Group characteristics:	Professionalism	Substitutes for	Substitutes for
	Training/experience	Substitutes for	No effect on

EXHIBIT 12.8

Substitutes and Neutralizers for Leadership

have had to reconceptualize almost every aspect of how they do business to meet the needs of increasingly demanding customers, keep employees motivated and satisfied, and remain competitive in a rapidly changing global environment.

Research has found that some leadership approaches are more effective than others for bringing about change in organizations. Two types of leadership that can have a substantial impact are charismatic and transformational. These types of leadership are best understood in comparison to transactional leadership.[31] **Transactional leaders** clarify the role and task requirements of subordinates, initiate structure, provide appropriate rewards, and try to be considerate to and meet the social needs of subordinates. The transactional leader's ability to satisfy subordinates may improve productivity. Transactional leaders excel at management functions. They are hardworking, tolerant, and fair minded. They take pride in keeping things running smoothly and efficiently. Transactional leaders often stress the impersonal aspects of performance, such as plans, schedules, and budgets. They have a sense of commitment to the organization and conform to organizational norms and values. Transactional leadership is important to all organizations, but leading change requires a different approach.

Charismatic and Visionary Leadership

Charismatic leadership goes beyond transactional leadership techniques. Charisma has been referred to as "a fire that ignites followers' energy and commitment, producing results above and beyond the call of duty."[32] The **charismatic leader** has the ability to inspire and motivate people to do more than they would normally do despite obstacles and personal sacrifice. Followers transcend their own self-interests for the sake of the department or organization. The impact of charismatic leaders is normally from stating a lofty vision of an imagined future that employees identify with, shaping a corporate value system for which everyone stands, and trusting subordinates and earning their complete trust in return.[33] Charismatic leaders tend to be less predictable than transactional leaders. They create an atmosphere of change, and they may be obsessed by visionary ideas that excite, stimulate, and drive other people to work hard.

Charismatic leaders are often skilled in the art of visionary leadership. Visionary leaders speak to the hearts of employees, letting them be part of something bigger than themselves. They see beyond current realities and help followers believe in a brighter future as well. A **vision** is an attractive, ideal future that is credible yet not readily attainable. In an examination of leadership lessons from one of history's most famous and most successful leaders, Alexander the Great, no factor emerges more clearly than his capacity for visionary leadership. Alexander the Great knew what he wanted to accomplish, and he was able to communicate a vision that spoke to the collective imagination of his followers.[34] His vision enabled Alexander within a period of 12 years to conquer for the Greek kingdom almost the entire known world of the time. Vision is as powerful for less legendary leaders. Consider Michael Dell, who had a vision of conquering the personal computer (PC) market with a new build-to-order model for making and selling PCs. Twenty years ago, no one thought Dell stood a chance, but the company quickly rose to number one in PC sales. Dell's vision continues to grow and change. Today, his vision is to double sales by 2007, with half of that coming from non-PC businesses like corporate computing and services.[35]

Vision is an important component of charismatic and transformational leadership. Charismatic leaders typically have a strong vision for the future, almost an obsession, and they can motivate others to help realize it.[36] These leaders have an emotional impact on subordinates because they strongly believe in the vision and can communicate it to others in a way that makes the vision real, personal, and meaningful to others. the Focus on Skills box provides a short quiz to help you determine if you have the potential to be a charismatic leader.

---

transactional leaders

Leaders who clarify subordinates' role and task requirements, initiates structure, provides rewards, and displays consideration for subordinates.

charismatic leader

A leader who has the ability to motivate subordinates to transcend their expected performance.

vision

An attractive, ideal future that is credible yet not readily attainable.

Take **ACTION**

As a leader, create a compelling vision and bring others along to follow the vision.

Are You a Charismatic Leader?

If you were the head of a major department in a corporation, how important would each of the following activities be to you? Answer yes or no to indicate if you would strive to perform each activity.

1. Help subordinates clarify goals and how to reach them.

2. Give people a sense of mission and overall purpose.

3. Help get jobs out on time.

4. Look for the new product or service opportunities.

5. Use policies and procedures as guides for problem solving.

6. Promote unconventional beliefs and values.

7. Give monetary rewards in exchange for high performance from subordinates.

8. Command respect from everyone in the department.

9. Work alone to accomplish important tasks.

10. Suggest new and unique ways of doing things.

11. Give credit to people who do their jobs well.

12. Inspire loyalty to yourself and to the organization.

13. Establish procedures to help the department operate smoothly.

14. Use ideas to motivate others.

15. Set reasonable limits on new approaches.

16. Demonstrate social nonconformity.

The even-numbered items represent behaviors and activities of charismatic leaders. Charismatic leaders are personally involved in shaping ideas, goals, and direction of change. They use an intuitive approach to develop fresh ideas for old problems and seek new directions for the department or organization. The odd-numbered items are considered more traditional management activities, or what would be called transactional leadership. Managers respond to organizational problems in an impersonal way, make rational decisions, and coordinate and facilitate the work of others. If you answered yes to more even-numbered than odd-numbered items, you may be a potentially charismatic leader.

SOURCES: Based on "Have You Got It?" a quiz that appeared in Patricia Sellers, "What Exactly Is Charisma?" *Fortune* (January 15, 1996): 68–75; Bernard M. Bass, *Leadership and Performance Beyond Expectations* (New York: Free Press, 1985); and Lawton R. Burns and Selwyn W. Becker, "Leadership and Managership," in *Health Care Management*, eds. S. Shortell and A. Kaluzny (New York: Wiley, 1986).

Charismatic leaders include Mother Teresa, Adolf Hitler, Sam Walton, Ronald Reagan, David Koresh, Martin Luther King Jr., and Osama bin Laden. Charisma can be used for positive outcomes that benefit the group, but it can be used for self-serving purposes that lead to deception, manipulation, and exploitation. When charismatic leaders respond to organizational problems in terms of the needs of the entire group rather than their own emotional needs, they can have a powerful, positive influence on organizational performance.[37] Visionary leaders who do not develop enough infrastructure, or who spread themselves too thin, can run into serious problems, as shown below.

George Clooney

Actor and director George Clooney knows he is not curing cancer or feeding the starving masses. "Anyone who thinks this stuff lasts and is permanent, to me, is an idiot." Still, he's putting his heart and soul into *Section Eight*, a movie production company he started with Stephen Soderbergh, who won Academy Awards for *Traffic* and *Erin Brockovich*. Section Eight aspires to a more maverick goal, to be more innovative, like Francis Ford Coppola and Stanley Kubrick. Section Eight's philosophy is simple: Provide a wide berth for directors and protect them from the inevitable studio meddling. They want to give new directors a place and a voice in an increasingly hostile studio system that only wants worldwide block busters. Yet Clooney and Soderbergh themselves are being crushed under the weight of correspondence, studio meetings, and project development.

Clooney and Soderbergh are known for finding and developing some of Hollywood's most creative minds, such as *Memento* director Chris Nolan, who directed *Insomnia*, for the company. But their approach has not always been successful. Their movie, *Rumor Has It*, was a disaster, with fired directors and cinematographers plus escalated budgets. Partly it has been due to Clooney and Soderbergh being distracted with *Ocean's Twelve* and other Section Eight business. "If you dragged me into court for paying too little attention, I'd be in jail," says Soderbergh. "It's a huge, huge learning curve with a lot of human wreckage left behind."[38]

Transformational Leaders

transformational leaders

Leaders distinguished by a special ability to bring about innovation and change.

Transformational leaders are similar to charismatic leaders but are distinguished by their special ability to bring about innovation and change by recognizing followers' needs and concerns, helping them look at old problems in new ways, and encouraging them to question the status quo. Transformational leaders inspire followers to believe in the leader personally and to believe in their own potential to imagine and create a better future for the organization. Transformational leaders create significant change in followers and the organization.[39] They have the ability to lead changes in the organization's mission, strategy, structure, and culture, as well as to promote innovation in products and technologies. Transformational leaders do not rely solely on tangible rules and incentives to control specific transactions with followers. They focus on intangible qualities such as vision, shared values, and ideas to build relationships, give larger meaning to diverse activities, and find common ground to enlist followers in the change process.[40]

A recent study confirmed that transformational leadership has a positive impact on follower development and performance. Moreover, transformational leadership skills can be learned and are not ingrained personality characteristics.[41] However, some personality traits may make it easier for a leader to display transformational leadership behaviors. For example, a study of transformational leadership and the Big Five model of personality discussed in the previous chapter found that the traits of extroversion and agreeableness are associated with transformational leaders.[42] This is unsurprising considering that these leaders accomplish change by building networks of positive relationships.

Take ACTION

To be a transformational leader, work at building networks of positive relationships.

A good example of a transformational leader is Richard Kovacevich, who steered mid-sized Norwest Corp. (now Wells Fargo & Co.) through numerous acquisitions to make it one of the largest and most powerful banking companies in the United States.

Wells Fargo & Company

A community banker listening to Wells Fargo's Richard Kovacevich discuss the secrets of his success might think, "There is nothing his bank does that we cannot do." That might be true, but Kovacevich seems to do it better than anyone. Why? It comes down to his leadership style, a style that puts accountability for success in the hands of each and every employee.

Kovacevich has inspired his followers with a vision of becoming the Wal-Mart of financial services, and the company is well on its way. The average customer buys four financial products (such as checking accounts, credit cards, home equity loans, and certificates of deposit), compared to the industry average of two. To motivate employees, Kovacevich leads with slogans such as, "Mind share plus heart share equals market share." Though some people might think it sounds hokey, Kovacevich and his employees do not care. It is the substance behind the slogans that matters. Kovacevich believes it is not what employees know that is important, but whether they care. Employees are rewarded for putting their hearts and minds into their work. Kovacevich spends a lot of time out in the field, meeting employees, patting backs, and giving pep talks. He likes to personally remind people on the front lines that they are the heart and soul of Wells Fargo, and that only through their efforts can the company succeed.

At the beginning of his speech accepting American Banker's 2003 Banker of the Year Award, Kovacevich stressed that the award was won not by him but by the 140,000 Wells Fargo employees spread throughout the nation.[43]

© John Sommers/Reuters/Landov

Using Power and Influence

Recall our definition of leadership, which is the ability to influence people to achieve goals. Particularly for leaders involved in major change initiatives, the effective and appropriate use of power is crucial. Some leaders can overuse their power, not seeing reality accurately, as shown in the Business Blooper. One way to understand power and influence is to look at the source of power and the level of compliance and commitment it engenders within followers.

Power is the potential ability to influence the behavior of others.[44] Sometimes the terms power and influence are used synonymously, but the two are distinct. Basically, **influence** is the effect a person's actions have on the attitudes, values, beliefs, or behavior of others. Whereas power is the capacity to cause a change in a person, influence may be thought of as the degree of actual change.

Power results from an interaction of leader and followers. Some power comes from an individual's position in the organization. Power may come from personal sources that are not as invested in the organization, such as a leader's personal interests, goals, and values. A good example of personal power is Josh Raskin, a middle school teacher in upper Manhattan who became a mission-critical leader in the hours and days following the destruction of the World Trade Center in September 2001. Though he did not have a formal position of authority, Raskin found himself in charge of coordinating a massive psych-clergy effort for crisis counseling, as well as guiding hundreds of other volunteers, based on his personal power. As he assigned a volunteer to guard a medical supply room, for example, Raskin infused the mundane chore with a higher vision and purpose by telling the young man everyone was counting on him to make sure no one stole drugs that would be desperately needed for the injured.[45]

power

The potential ability to influence others' behavior.

influence

The effect a person's actions have on the attitudes, values, beliefs, or behavior of others.

BUSINESS BLOOPER

Donald Trump's Debt and Bankruptcy: No Big Deal

Despite $1.8 billion debt and filing for bankruptcy protection for Trump Hotels & Casino Resorts in November 2004, real estate developer and *Apprentice* star Donald Trump thought it was no big deal. He commented that it was "something that worked better than other alternatives. It's really just a technical thing."

SOURCE: Adam Horowitz, et al 101 Dumbest Moments in Business, *Business 2.0*, Jan/Feb 2005, p. 106.

Within organizations, there are typically five sources of power: legitimate, reward, coercive, expert, and referent.[46]

Position Power

The traditional manager's power comes from the organization. The manager's position gives him or her the power to reward or punish subordinates to influence their behavior. Legitimate power, reward power, and coercive power are all forms of position power used by managers to change employee behavior.

Legitimate Power.   Power coming from a formal management position in an organization and the authority granted to it is called **legitimate power**. For example, once a person has been selected as a supervisor, most workers understand that they are obligated to follow his or her direction with respect to work activities. Subordinates accept this source of power as legitimate, which is why they comply.

Reward Power.   Another kind of power, **reward power**, stems from the authority to bestow rewards on other people. Managers may have access to formal rewards, such as pay increases or promotions. They have at their disposal such rewards as praise, attention, and recognition. Managers can use rewards to influence subordinates' behavior.

Coercive Power.   The opposite of reward power is **coercive power**: It refers to the authority to punish or recommend punishment. Managers have coercive power when they have the right to fire or demote employees, criticize, or withdraw pay increases. For example, if Sanjay, a salesman, does not perform as expected, his supervisor has the coercive power to criticize him, reprimand him, put a negative letter in his file, and hurt his chance for a raise.

Different types of position power elicit different responses in followers.[47] Legitimate power and reward power are most likely to generate follower compliance. Compliance means that workers will obey orders and carry out instructions though they may personally disagree with them and might not be enthusiastic. Coercive power most often generates resistance. Resistance means that workers will deliberately avoid carrying out instructions or will attempt to disobey orders.

Personal Power

In contrast to the external sources of position power, personal power most often comes from internal sources, such as a person's special knowledge or personal characteristics. Personal power is the leader's primary tool. Subordinates follow a leader because of the respect, admiration, or caring they feel for the individual and his or her ideas. Personal power is becoming increasingly important as more businesses are run by teams of workers who are less tolerant of authoritarian management.[48] Two types of personal power are expert power and referent power.

Expert Power.   Power resulting from a leader's special knowledge or skill regarding the tasks performed by followers is referred to as **expert power**. When the leader is a true expert, subordinates go along with recommendations because of his or her superior knowledge. Leaders at supervisory levels often have experience in the production process that gains them promotion. At top management levels, however, leaders may lack expert power because subordinates know more about technical details than they do. One top manager who benefits from expert power is Hector de Jesus Ruiz, president and COO of Advanced Micro Devices (AMD). Ruiz has a B.S. in electrical engineering and nearly 30 years of experience in all facets of the semiconductor industry, from top to bottom. Employees respect Ruiz's technical knowledge and operational expertise as a valuable strength as AMD battles Intel in the microprocessor wars. They appreciate having someone in top management who understands the nitty gritty technical and production details that lower-level employees deal with every day.[49]

---

legitimate power

Power that stems from a formal management position in an organization and the authority granted to it.

reward power

Power that results from the authority to bestow rewards on other people.

coercive power

Power that stems from the authority to punish or recommend punishment.

Take *ACTION*

As a leader, use coercive power rarely; if you use it too much, you will create a culture of fear.

---

expert power

Power that stems from special knowledge of or skill in the tasks performed by subordinates.

Referent Power. The last kind of power, **referent power**, comes from a leader's personal characteristics that command followers' identification, respect, and admiration so they wish to emulate the leader. When workers admire a supervisor because of the way he or she deals with them, the influence is based on referent power. Referent power does not depend on a formal title or position. Referent power is most visible in the area of charismatic leadership. In social and religious movements, for example, we often see charismatic leaders who emerge and gain a tremendous following based solely on their personal power.

An example of referent power in the business world is Mary Cadigan, who was called upon to lead a project to move Fannie Mae's computer data center from Washington, D.C., to a new location 25 miles away in Reston, Virginia. The job required employees to do their "day jobs" all week and then throw themselves into the massive and complicated computer center relocation over 13 consecutive weekends. Cadigan used humor, caring, and food to keep people psyched and create a sense of community and fun. Every Friday at 5 P.M., things would kick off with a meal. Snacks were served at midnight, and a full breakfast was brought out at 8 A.M. on Saturday morning. Cadigan made herself highly visible and constantly available throughout the project. She made sure the company provided whatever people needed to get the job done with as little stress and hardship as possible, such as offering hotel rooms to anyone who was too tired to drive home. In the end, she convinced Fannie Mae to give everyone on the team a bonus. By relying on referent power, Cadigan inspired 550 employees to accomplish an extraordinary feat, transferring the data center without a single interruption to Fannie Mae's business.[50]

The follower reaction most often generated by expert power and referent power is commitment. Commitment means that workers will share the leader's point of view and enthusiastically carry out instructions. Needless to say, commitment is preferred to compliance or resistance. It is particularly important when change is the desired outcome of a leader's instructions, because change carries risk or uncertainty. Commitment assists the follower in overcoming fear of change.

Leaders can increase their referent power when they share power and authority with followers. A significant recent trend in corporate America is for top executives to empower lower employees. Empowering employees works because total power in the organization seems to increase. Everyone has more say and, hence, contributes more to organizational goals. The goal of senior executives in many corporations today is not to wield power but to give it away to people who can get jobs done.[51]

Post-Heroic Leadership for Turbulent Times

The concept of leadership continues to grow and change. A significant influence on leadership styles in recent times is the turbulence and uncertainty of the environment in which most organizations are operating. Ethical and economic difficulties, corporate governance concerns, globalization, changes in technology, new ways of working, shifting employee expectations, and significant social transitions have all contributed to a shift in how we think about and practice leadership.

Of particular interest for leadership during these turbulent times is a post-heroic approach that focuses on the subtle, unseen, and often unrewarded acts that good leaders perform every day, rather than on the grand accomplishments of celebrated business heroes.[52] During the 1980s and 1990s, leadership became equated with larger-than-life personalities, strong egos, and personal ambitions. In contrast, the post-heroic leader's major characteristic is humility. **Humility** means being unpretentious and modest rather than arrogant and prideful. Humble leaders do not have to be in the center of things. They quietly build a strong, enduring company by developing and supporting others rather than touting their own abilities and accomplishments.[53] Five approaches that are in tune with post-heroic leadership for turbulent times are servant leadership, Level 5 leadership, interactive leadership, e-leadership, and moral leadership.

referent power

Power that results from characteristics that command subordinates' identification with respect and admiration for and desire to emulate the leader.

humility

Being unpretentious and modest rather than arrogant and prideful.

Servant Leadership

There have always been leaders who operate from the assumption that work exists for the development of the worker as much as the worker exists to do the work.[54] For example, a young David Packard, who co-founded Hewlett-Packard, made a spectacle of himself in 1949 by standing up in a roomful of business leaders and arguing that companies had a responsibility to recognize the dignity and worth of their employees and share the wealth with those who helped to create it.[55]

The concept of servant leadership, first described by Robert Greenleaf, is leadership upside-down because leaders transcend self-interest to serve others and the organization.[56] **Servant leaders** operate on two levels: for the fulfillment of their subordinates' goals and needs and for the realization of the larger purpose or mission of their organization. Servant leaders give things away: power, ideas, information, recognition, credit for accomplishments, and money. Harry Stine, founder of Stine Seed Company in Adel, Iowa, casually announced to his employees at the company's annual post-harvest luncheon that they would each receive $1,000 for each year they had worked at the company. For some loyal workers, that amounted to a $20,000 bonus.[57] Servant leaders value other people. They are trustworthy, and they trust others. They encourage participation, share power, enhance others' self-worth, and unleash people's creativity, full commitment, and natural impulse to learn and contribute. Servant leaders can bring their followers' higher motives to the work and connect their hearts to the organizational mission and goals.

Servant leaders often work in the nonprofit world because it offers a natural way to apply their leadership drive and skills to serve others. Consider the example of Susie Scott Krabacher, a former Playboy Playmate, who sold a thriving restaurant business and mortgaged her house to set up a network of schools and orphanages in Haiti.[58] But servant leaders can succeed in the business world. George Merck believed the purpose of a corporation was to do something useful. At Merck & Co., he insisted that people always come before profits. By insisting on serving people rather than profits, Merck shaped a company that averaged 15 percent earnings growth for an amazing 75 years.[59]

Level 5 Leadership

A recent five-year study conducted by Jim Collins and his research associates identified the critical importance of what Collins calls *Level 5 leadership* in transforming companies from merely good to truly great organizations.[60] As described in his book *Good to Great: Why Some Companies Make the Leap... and Others Don't*, Level 5 leadership refers to the highest level in a hierarchy of manager capabilities, as illustrated in Exhibit 12.9. A key characteristic of Level 5 leaders is an almost complete lack of ego. In contrast to the view of great leaders as larger-than-life personalities with strong egos and big ambitions, Level 5 leaders often seem shy and unpretentious. Though they accept full responsibility for mistakes, poor results, or failures, Level 5 leaders give credit for successes to other people. For example, Joseph F. Cullman III, former CEO of Philip Morris, staunchly refused to accept credit for the company's long-term success, citing his great colleagues, successors, and predecessors as the reason for the accomplishments.

Yet, despite their personal humility, Level 5 leaders have a fierce determination to do whatever it takes to produce great and lasting results for their organizations. They are ambitious for their companies rather than for themselves. This becomes most evident in the area of succession planning. Level 5 leaders develop a solid corps of leaders throughout the organization, so when they leave the company it can continue to thrive

---

servant leaders

Leaders who work to fulfill subordinates' needs and goals as well as to achieve the organization's larger mission.

Take **ACTION**

As a leader, see yourself as serving your employees; you are there to meet their needs.

Level 5: The Level 5 Leader
Builds an enduring great organization through a combination of personal humility and professional resolve.

Level 4: The Effective Executive
Builds widespread commitment to a clear and compelling vision; stimulates people to high performance.

Level 3: Competent Manager
Sets plans and organizes people for the efficient and effective pursuit of objectives.

Level 2: Contributing Team Member
Contributes to the achievement of team goals; works effectively with others in a group.

Level 1: Highly Capable Individual
Productive contributor; offers talent, knowledge, skills, and good work habits as an individual employee.

SOURCE: "The Level 5 Leadership Hierarchy" from *Good to Great: Why Some Companies Make the Leap... and Others Don't*, by Jim Collins. Copyright © 2001 by Jim Collins. Reprinted by permission of HarperCollins Publishers, Inc.

EXHIBIT 12.9

The Level 5 Leadership Hierarchy

and grow even stronger. Egocentric leaders, by contrast often set their successors up for failure because it will be a testament to their own greatness if the company does not perform well without them. Rather than an organization built around "a genius with a thousand helpers," Level 5 leaders build an organization with many strong leaders who can step forward and continue the company's success. These leaders want everyone in the organization to develop to their fullest potential. A good example of Level 5 leadership is Meg Whitman, described in this chapter's Best Practices box.

BEST PRACTICES

Meg Whitman at eBay

It came out of nowhere and one of the few sweet spots in the otherwise dim dot.com revolution. And a dream company it was, a venture that added economic value, remained attractive to vendors and customers, and one where most of the work was done by the users. The company became one of the fastest growing in history, and it changed the economy by reallocating forgotten inventories and made 100 million people into sellers.

Meg Whitman is CEO of eBay, but she is not brash or outspoken like so many other corporate top dogs. She is soft-spoken, refuses most TV interviews and often takes colleagues to lunch at the nearby outdoor smoothie shop. Accustomed as we are to the Masters of the Universe, Whitman is the polar opposite (and likely will not be sent to prison for corruption either).

In the nine years since she has been CEO, eBay's revenues have jumped from $5.7 million to $3.3 billion. If you think it is easy running a high-tech company that is user-friendly, you are naïve. Whitman and her team are building, tinkering and tuning an enterprise with minimum employees and maximum profitability. And

because Whitman is not the forceful command-and-control leader, it took her longer to gain power. She did it a simple, but too-often forgotten way: by establishing credibility, doing what she said she would do. Not that she shies away from risks. In 2000, when revenues were $431 million, she announced they would reach $3 billion and everyone—her board included—thought she was crazy. What a surprise to everyone else that she reached the $3 billion goal a year early. The growth came also from her ability to know when to do nothing. When everyone else told her to chase growth, to buy up other companies, to become like Amazon, she resisted, instead building up the collectibles that eBays most passionate users love to sell.

One of Whitman's favorite words is enable. She enables employees rather than directs them; uses carrots, not sticks. She wears the same clothing as eBay employees, Navy polo shirt and khakis. "It's egalitarian," she says. That is so Meg.

SOURCES: Michael S. Malone, "Meet Meg Whitman," *The Wall Street Journal* (March 16, 2005): A24; Patricia Sellers, "eBay's Secret," *Fortune* (October 18, 2004): 161–178.

Interactive Leadership

The focus on minimizing personal ambition and developing others is a hallmark of interactive leadership, which has been found to be common among female leaders. Recent research indicates that women's style of leadership is particularly suited to today's organizations.[61] Using data from actual performance evaluations, one study found that when rated by peers, subordinates, and bosses, female managers score significantly higher than men on abilities such as motivating others, fostering communication, and listening.[62] Women's leadership skills are often different than men's, as shown in the Focus on Skills box.

interactive leadership

A leadership style characterized by values such as inclusion, collaboration, relationship building, and caring.

Interactive leadership means that the leader favors a consensual and collaborative process, and influence derives from relationships rather than position power and formal authority.[63] For example, Nancy Hawthorne, former chief financial officer at Continental Cablevision Inc., felt that her role as a leader was to delegate tasks and authority to others and to help them be more effective. "I was being traffic cop and coach and facilitator," Hawthorne says. "I was always into building a department that hummed."[64] Men can be interactive leaders as well. The characteristics associated with interactive leadership are emerging as valuable qualities for male and female leaders in today's workplace Values associated with interactive leadership include personal humility, inclusion, relationship building, and caring. D. Michael Abrashoff illustrates characteristics of both interactive and servant leadership, as well as the potential to become a Level 5 leader, showing that a leader can become more effective as described on the following page.

FOCUS ON SKILLS

Leading Women

Women started pouring into the workplace more than 30 years ago and found too many glass ceilings. The solution often was to act more like men: talk sports, wear power suits, do not show too many emotions. Recent studies are giving the topic a new light and suggest that men ought to be the ones doing the imitating. Their conclusions suggest that if you want a quality executive, hire a woman.

A wide range of studies of leaders in everything from consumer products to high-tech show that when bosses, colleagues, and underlings are questioned, they mostly give higher scores to females on many skills, such as goal setting, to mentoring to producing high-quality work. Though researchers were not originally looking at gender issues, they discovered that women were rated higher on almost every index, in 42 of 52 skills measured. Women are more collaborative, think through issues more clearly, and are less personally glory-seeking, says head of IBM's Global Services Doug Elix. Management guru Rosabeth Moss Kanter says "Women get high ratings on exactly those skills needed to succeed in the global Information Age, where teamwork and partnering are so important." In England, small businesses run by women outperform those run by men.

If women are so great, why are they not running the world? Well, they are, almost, at the middle level where they make up 45 percent of managers. At CEO level, though, there are only a handful. It is a pipeline problem, as the large cohort of women work their way up, though they suffer from lack of mentorship and being kept outside the inner communication circle. Also, too many women get stuck in HR or PR, career tracks that do not go anywhere. Because women's unique skills were unappreciated, they were not noticed until recently. In fact, people skills were often seen as lower order than so-called business skills. These dynamics have frustrated millions of capable women, who sometimes bail out of the corporate world and start their own companies: Nine million companies are female owned, a 100 percent increase in 12 years. Another reason women have not gotten ahead is that they are more team focused, rather than looking what makes them individually look better. "You should be looking out for yourself, not your people," one woman was told. Women have been good at getting the job done, but men are better at promoting their own images and their overconfidence propels them in to positions that a woman would feel underqualified for.

What makes these results compelling is that they come directly from bosses and coworkers in the corporations, and not from a simulated study situation in the research laboratory. Still, the investigators were not prepared for what they learned. Researcher Janet Irwin said, "We were startled by the results."

SOURCE: Kim Thomas, "Hidden Barriers that Stall Women Leaders," *The Guardian* (March 31, 2005): 4; Rochelle Sharp, "As Leaders, Women Rule," *Business Week* (Nov. 20, 2001): 74–84.

Keeping good employees is tough for businesses; for the U.S. Navy, it has been a nightmare in recent years. Forty percent of recruits wash out before their first four-year term is up. Considering it costs $35,000 to recruit one sailor and put him or her through nine weeks of boot camp, that is an expensive problem. In addition, only 30 percent of people who make it through their first tour re-enlist for a second. When D. Michael Abrashoff took command of the destroyer *USS Benfold*, he came face to face with the biggest leadership challenge of his Navy career. Though the *Benfold* was a technological marvel, most of its sailors could not wait to leave. People were so deeply unhappy and demoralized that walking aboard ship felt like entering a deep well of despair. Abrashoff knew that he needed to be a different kind of leader to turn things around and tap into the energy, enthusiasm, and creativity of his sailors.

To do so meant casting aside the long Navy tradition of relying on formal position power and authority. Abrashoff led with vision and values instead of command and control. Rather than issuing orders from the top, he started listening to ideas from below. He made an effort to get to know each and every sailor as an individual. When the *Benfold*'s sailors saw that Abrashoff was sincere, they responded with energy, enthusiasm, and commitment. Good ideas that came from the bottom up were implemented immediately, and many of them have now become standard throughout the U.S. Navy. Abrashoff began handing over responsibility so that people could learn and grow. "If all you do is give orders, then all you get are order takers," he says. One important lesson he learned was the need to relinquish control. "The more control you give up, the more power you gain," argues Abrashoff. "And really, you can't order great performance." Abrashoff wanted to develop strong leaders at all levels and help people understand that they were the ones who made the ship successful. Under Abrashoff's leadership, the *Benfold* set all-time records for performance and retention. However, Abrashoff nor the crew are worried about what will happen when the captain moves on. "This crew... [knows] what results they get when they play an active role," Abrashoff says. "And they now have the courage to raise their hands and get heard. That's almost irreversible."[65]

E-Leadership

In today's workplace, many people may work from home or other remote locations, connected to the office and one another through IT. People from all over the world participate in virtual teams and rarely or never meet face to face. Leaders sometimes lead a complete project from a distance, interacting with followers solely online. This new way of working brings new challenges for leadership.[66] In a virtual environment, leaders face a constant tension in balancing structure and accountability with flexibility.[67] They have to provide enough structure and direction so people have a clear understanding of what is required of them, but they have to trust virtual workers will perform their duties responsibly without close control and supervision. Effective e-leaders set clear goals and timelines and are explicit about how people will communicate and coordinate their work. However, the details of daily activities are left up to employees. This does not mean, however, that virtual workers are left on their own. Leaders take extra care to keep people informed and involved with one another and with the organization.[68]

People who excel at e-leadership tend to be open-minded and flexible, exhibit positive attitudes that focus on solutions rather than problems, and have superb communication, coaching, and relationship-building skills.[69] Good e-leaders never forget that work is accomplished through people and not technology. Though they must understand how to select and use technology appropriately, e-leaders emphasize human interactions as the key to success. Building trust, maintaining open lines of communication, caring about people, and being open to subtle cues from others are crucial leadership qualities in a virtual environment.[70]

USS Benfold

Moral Leadership

Since leadership can be used for good or evil, to help or harm others, all leadership has a moral component. Leaders carry a tremendous responsibility to use their power wisely and ethically. Sadly, in recent years, too many have chosen to act from self-interest and greed rather than behaving in ways that serve and uplift others. The disheartening ethical climate in American business has led to a renewed interest in moral leadership. **Moral leadership** is about distinguishing right from wrong and choosing to do right. It means seeking the just, the honest, the good, and the decent behavior in the practice of leadership.[71] Moral leaders remember that business is about values, not just economic performance.

Distinguishing the right thing to do can be difficult and doing it is sometimes even harder. Leaders are often faced with right-versus-right decisions, in which several responsibilities conflict with one another.[72] Commitments to superiors, for example, may mean a leader feels the need to hide unpleasant news about pending layoffs from followers. Moral leaders strive to find the moral answer or compromise rather than taking the easy way out. Consider Katherine Graham, the long-time leader of *The Washington Post*, when she was confronted with a decision in 1971 about what to do with the Pentagon Papers, a leaked Defense Department study that showed Nixon administration deceptions about the Vietnam War. Graham admitted she was terrified. She knew she was risking the whole company on the decision, possibly inviting prosecution under the Espionage Act and jeopardizing thousands of employees' jobs. She decided to go ahead with the story, and reporters Bob Woodward and Carl Bernstein made Watergate—and *The Washington Post*—a household name.[73]

Clearly, moral leadership requires **courage**, the ability to step forward through fear and act on one's values and conscience. Leaders often behave unethically because they lack courage. Most people want to be liked, and it is easy to do the wrong thing to fit in or impress others. One example might be a leader who holds his tongue to "fit in with the guys" when colleagues are telling sexually or racially offensive jokes. Moral leaders summon the fortitude to do the right thing even if it is unpopular. Standing up for what is right is the primary way in which leaders create an environment of honesty, trust, and integrity in the organization.

moral leadership

Distinguishing right from wrong and choosing to do right in the practice of leadership.

Take *ACTION*

When in a moral dilemma, think of what is the right thing to do, rather than only the most financially beneficial.

courage

The ability to step forward through fear and act on one's values and conscience.

Manager's Solution

This chapter covered several important ideas about leadership. The early research on leadership focused on personal traits such as intelligence, energy, and appearance. Later, research attention shifted to leadership behaviors appropriate to the organizational situation. Behavioral approaches dominated the early work in this area; task-oriented behavior and people-oriented behavior were suggested as essential behaviors that lead work groups toward high performance. The Ohio State and Michigan approaches and the managerial grid are in this category. Contingency approaches include Fiedler's theory, Hersey and Blanchard's situational theory, the path-goal model, and the substitutes-for-leadership concept.

Leadership concepts have evolved from the transactional approach to charismatic and transformational leadership behaviors. Charismatic leadership is the ability to articulate a vision and motivate followers to make it a reality. Transformational leadership extends charismatic qualities to guide and foster dramatic organizational change. Leadership involves the use of power to influence others. Five types of power are legitimate, reward, coercive, expert, and referent. Leaders rely more on personal power than position power.

The concept and practice of leadership continues to grow and change. Of particular interest in today's turbulent times is a post-heroic leadership approach. Five significant leadership concepts in line with the post-heroic approach are servant leadership, Level 5 leadership, interactive leadership, e-leadership, and moral leadership. Servant leaders facilitate the growth, goals, and development of others to liberate their best qualities in pursuing the organization's mission. Level 5 leaders are characterized by personal humility combined with ambition to build a great organization that will thrive beyond the leader's direct influence. Interactive leadership emphasizes relationships and helping others develop to their highest potential, and may be particularly well-suited to today's workplace. E-leadership requires flexibility and open-mindedness, as well as the ability to build trusting, positive relationships. Moral leadership means seeking to do the honest and decent thing in the practice of leadership.

Returning to our opening example, Roy Pelaez wanted to create an organization where people cared about each other and about the customer and willingly gave their best. To do so meant breaking some "unwritten management rules" about not getting involved with followers' personal problems. Pelaez quickly realized that his subordinates (many of whom were immigrants) had low levels of skill, ability, and confidence, along with tremendous personal needs that consumed much of their attention and motivation. In terms of the theories discussed in the chapter, Pelaez combined a telling leadership style, as indicated by the Hersey and Blanchard theory for followers at a low readiness level, with a supportive leadership approach, as defined by the path-goal theory. Pelaez had to use a telling style because if he did not, many of his workers would not know what to do. However, he knew he needed to be supportive to help build the pride and confidence of employees.

In addition, Pelaez acted as a servant leader by being deeply committed to helping his followers grow and improve in their personal as well as their work lives, such as setting up classes for anyone interested in improving his or her English language skills. He instituted an Employee of the Month recognition program, which provided a reward beyond a weekly paycheck. Anyone who had perfect attendance over a six-week period or who turned in a purse or wallet with cash and credit cards got a day off without pay. Members of the "Top Crew of the Month" were rewarded with free movie passes, calling cards, or "burger bucks." These forms of recognition and reward were a real boost to workers who had received little attention and appreciation in their lives. The outcome of Pelaez's leadership was a drop in the turnover rate from 100 percent a year to 12 percent a year and an increase in revenue from $5 million to $14 million. Employees began turning in large amounts of money found on planes, returning some 250 wallets with more than $50,000 in cash to passengers who had left them on board. By genuinely caring about and giving to his employees, Pelaez increased his personal power and built a community of highly satisfied and committed employees. According to one observer, Pelaez "created a group of people who will do anything in the world for him."[74]

Discussion Questions

1. Rob Martin became manager of a forklift assembly plant and believed in participative management, even when one supervisor used Rob's delegation to replace two competent line managers with his own friends. What would you say to Rob about his leadership style in this situation?

2. Suggest some personal traits that you believe would be useful to a leader. Are these traits more valuable in some situations than in others?

3. What is the difference between trait theories and behavioral theories of leadership?

4. Suggest the sources of power that would be available to a leader of a student government organization. To be effective, should student leaders keep power to themselves or delegate power to other students?

5. Would you prefer working for a leader who has a consideration or an initiating-structure leadership style? Discuss the reasons for your answer.

6. Consider Fiedler's theory. How often do very favorable, intermediate, or very unfavorable situations occur in real life? Discuss.

7. What is transformational leadership? Differentiate between transformational leadership and transactional leadership. Give an example of each.

8. Some experts believe that leadership is more important than ever in a learning organization. Do you agree? Explain.

9. What is meant by "servant leadership"? Have you ever known a servant leader? Discuss.

10. Do you think leadership style is fixed and unchangeable for a leader or flexible and adaptable? Discuss.

11. Consider the leadership position of a senior partner in a law firm. What task, subordinate, and organizational factors might serve as substitutes for leadership in this situation?

Manager's Workbook

T–P Leadership Questionnaire: An Assessment of Style
Some leaders deal with general directions, leaving details to subordinates. Other leaders focus on specific details with the expectation that subordinates will carry out orders. Depending on the situation, both approaches may be effective. The important issue is the ability to identify relevant dimensions of the situation and behave accordingly. Through this questionnaire, you can identify your relative emphasis on two dimensions of leadership: task orientation (T) and people orientation (P). These are not opposite approaches, and an individual can rate high or low on either or both.

Directions: The following items describe aspects of leadership behavior. Respond to each item according to the way you would most likely act if you were the leader of a work group. Circle whether you would most likely behave in the described way: always (A), frequently (F), occasionally (O), seldom (S), or never (N).

1. I would most likely act as the spokesperson of the group. A F O S N

2. I would encourage overtime work. A F O S N

3. I would allow members complete freedom in their work. A F O S N

4. I would encourage the use of uniform procedures. A F O S N

5. I would permit members to use their own judgment in solving problems. A F O S N

6. I would stress being ahead of competing groups. A F O S N

7. I would speak as a representative of the group. A F O S N

8. I would needle members for greater effort. A F O S N

9. I would try out my ideas in the group. A F O S N

10. I would let members do their work the way they think best. A F O S N

11. I would work hard for a promotion. A F O S N

12. I would tolerate postponement and uncertainty. A F O S N

13. I would speak for the group if there were visitors present. A F O S N

14. I would keep the work moving at a rapid pace. A F O S N

15. I would turn the members loose on a job and let them go to it. A F O S N

16. I would settle conflicts when they occur in the group. A F O S N

17. I would get swamped by details. A F O S N

18. I would represent the group at outside meetings. A F O S N

19. I would be reluctant to allow the members any freedom of action. A F O S N

20. I would decide what should be done and how it should be done. A F O S N

21. I would push for increased production. A F O S N

22. I would let some members have authority, which I could keep. A F O S N

23. Things would usually turn out as I had predicted. A F O S N

24. I would allow the group a high degree of initiative. A F O S N

25. I would assign group members to particular tasks. A F O S N

26. I would be willing to make changes. A F O S N

27. I would ask members to work harder. A F O S N

28. I would trust the group members to exercise good judgment. A F O S N

29. I would schedule the work to be done. A F O S N

30. I would refuse to explain my actions. A F O S N

31. I would persuade others that my ideas are to their advantage. A F O S N

32. I would permit the group to set its own pace. A F O S N

33. I would urge the group to beat its previous record. A F O S N

34. I would act without consulting the group. A F O S N

35. I would ask that group members follow standard rules and regulations. A F O S N

T _____ P_____

The T–P Leadership Questionnaire is scored as follows:

a. Circle the item number for items 8, 12, 17, 18, 19, 30, 34, and 35.

b. Write the number 1 in front of a circled item number if you responded S (seldom) or N (never) to that item.

c. Also write a number 1 in front of item numbers not circled if you responded A (always) or F (frequently).

d. Circle the number 1's that you have written in front of the following items: 3, 5, 8, 10, 15, 18, 19, 22, 24, 26, 28, 30, 32, 34, and 35.

e. Count the circled number 1's. This is your score for concern for people. Record the score in the blank following the letter P at the end of the questionnaire.

f. Count uncircled number 1's. This is your score for concern for task. Record this number in the blank following the letter T.

SOURCE: The T–P Leadership Questionnaire was adapted by J. B. Ritchie and P. Thompson in *Organization and People* (New York: West, 1984). Copyright 1969 by the American Educational Research Association. Adapted by permission of the publisher.

Manager's Workshop

Developing Meeting Leadership Roles

1. Divide the class into groups of six to eight students. Each group develops a list of desirable ("Do") and undesirable ("Do Not") behavioral roles for leading a meeting.

To run an effective meeting a leader must:

Do the following	Do not do the following

2. Each group develops a plan of action for a convenience store that is continually plagued by random cash drawer shortages.

   A participant from each group is selected to serve as the group meeting leader for each group during the decision-making process to develop the action plans.

Plan of Action:

a.

b.

c.

d.

e.

f.

3. After 10 minutes, the group leader describes what it was like to serve as group leader. The group then provides feedback to the group leader, using the previously developed list of "Do" and "Do Not" group leadership roles.

4. Next, a new leader is selected to continue the development of the action plan. After 5 minutes, the steps described in step 3 are repeated for the new leader. This process continues until each group participant has had an opportunity to serve as group leader.

Discussion Questions

1. What is the difference between listing a desirable behavior and exhibiting it?

2. How can leaders learn to be more effective?

SOURCE: Adapted by Dorothy Marcic from Gerald Klein, Meeting Leadership. *Journal of Management Education*, Vol. 18 (3), 1994, pp. 375–379.

Management in Practice: Ethical Dilemma

Does Wage Reform Start at the Top?

Paula Smith has just been offered the opportunity of a lifetime. The chairman of the board of Resitronic Corporation has just called to ask her to take the job as director of the troubled audio equipment manufacturing subsidiary. The first question Smith asked was, "Will the board give me the autonomy to turn this company around?" The answer was yes. Resitronic's problems were so severe that the board was desperate for change and ready to give Smith whatever it took to save the company.

Smith knows that cost cutting is the first place she needs to focus. Labor expenses are too high, and product quality and production times are below industry standards. She sees that labor and management at Resitronic are two armed camps, but she needs cooperation at all levels to achieve a turnaround. Smith is energized. She knows she finally has the autonomy to try out her theories about an empowered workforce. Smith knows she must ask managers and workers to take a serious pay cut, with the promise of incentives to share in any improvements they might make. She also knows that everyone will be looking at her own salary as an indication of whether she walks her talk.

Smith is torn. She realizes she faces a year or two of complete hell, with long hours, little time for her family or outside interests, bitter resistance in subordinates, and no guarantees of success. Even if she comes in at the current director's salary, she will be taking a cut in pay. But if she takes a bigger cut coming in, with the promise of bonuses and stock options tied to her own performance, she sends a strong message to the entire subsidiary that they rise or fall together. She wonders what might happen if she fails. Many influences on the audio equipment subsidiary are beyond her control. Resitronic itself is in trouble. From her current vantage point, Smith believes she can turn things around, but what will she discover when she gets inside? What if the board undercuts her? Doesn't she owe it to herself and her family to be compensated at the highest possible level for the stress and risk they will be enduring? Can she afford to risk her own security to send a message of commitment to the plan she is asking others to follow?

What Do You Do?

1. Take the same salary as the current director for one year. Circulate the information that although you are taking a cut to come to Resitronic, you are confident that you can make a difference. Build in pay incentive bonuses for the following years if the subsidiary succeeds.

2. Take a bigger cut in pay with generous incentive bonuses. Ask the board and the entire workforce to do the same. Open the books and let the whole company know exactly where they stand.

3. Ask for the same salary you are making now. You know you are going to be worth it, and you don't want to ask your family to suffer monetarily as well as in their quality of life during this transition.

Case for Critical Analysis

DGL International

When DGL International, a manufacturer of refinery equipment, brought in John Terrill to manage its Technical Services division, company executives informed him of the urgent situation. Technical Services, with 20 engineers, was the highest-paid, best-educated, and least-productive division in the company. The instructions to Terrill: Turn it around. Terrill called a meeting of the engineers. He showed great concern for their personal welfare and asked point blank: "What's the problem? Why can't we produce? Why does this division have such turnover?"

Without hesitation, employees launched a hail of complaints. "I was hired as an engineer, not a pencil pusher." "We spend over half our time writing asinine reports in triplicate for top management, and no one reads the reports."

After a two-hour discussion, Terrill concluded he had to get top management off the backs of the engineers. He promised the engineers, "My job is to stay out of your way so you can do your work, and I'll try to keep top management off your backs, too." He called for the day's reports and issued an order effective immediately that the originals be turned in daily to his office rather than mailed to headquarters. For three weeks, technical reports piled up on his desk. By month's end, the stack was nearly three feet high. During that time no one called for the reports. When other managers entered his office and saw the stack, they usually asked, "What's all this?" Terrill answered, "Technical reports." No one asked to read them.

Finally, at month's end, a secretary from finance called and asked for the monthly travel and expense report. Terrill responded, "Meet me in the president's office tomorrow morning."

The next morning the engineers cheered as Terrill walked through the department pushing a cart loaded with the enormous stack of reports. They knew the showdown had come.

Terrill entered the president's office and placed the stack of reports on his desk. The president and the other senior executives looked bewildered.

"This," Terrill announced, "is the reason for the lack of productivity in the Technical Services division. These are the reports you people require every month. The fact that they sat on my desk all month shows that no one reads this material. I suggest that the engineers' time could be used in a more productive manner, and that one brief monthly report from my office will satisfy the needs of other departments."

Questions

1. What leadership style did John Terrill use? What do you think was his primary source of power?

2. Based on the Hersey-Blanchard theory, should Terrill have been less participative? Should he have initiated more task structure for the engineers? Explain.

3. What leadership approach would you have taken in this situation?

CHAPTER

13

Motivation in Organizations

CHAPTER OUTLINE

LEARNING OBJECTIVES

After studying this chapter, you should be able to do the following:

1 **Define motivation and explain the difference between current approaches and traditional approaches to motivation.**

2 **Identify and describe content theories of motivation based on employee needs.**

3 **Identify and explain process theories of motivation.**

4 **Describe reinforcement theory and how it can be used to motivate employees.**

5 **Discuss major approaches to job design and how job design influences motivation.**

6 **Explain how empowerment heightens employee motivation.**

7 **Describe ways that managers can create a sense of meaning and importance for employees at work.**

Manager's Challenge

After graduating from pharmacy school, Sadie Christianson was looking forward to a challenging career. Instead, her job in Minneapolis turned out to be routine and boring. Most of her day was spent on an elevated counter, counting pills one by one, as well as checking over her assistant's work for accuracy. "It was like you got into the pharmacy world and stepped back 25 years," she said. Most pharmacies are housed in larger drug stores, and when customers cannot find a harried salesperson, they ask the pharmacist which aisle the shampoo is in. Anyone with a prescription waits a slow 20 minutes before one simple antibiotic is placed into a bag. With an aging populat[ion] more people buying prescription drugs, having unenthusiastic employees is bad for business.

If you were the pharmacy decision-maker, what would you do to ensure that pharmacists not only use their eduction, but are also motivated to do the best job possible?

A similar problem occurred at drug-manufacturer Pfizer. After nearly 30 years as a global sales representative for Pfizer, a leading pharmaceuticals company, James Shumsky has lost his spark. He knows he is not the only one. For several years, Shumsky had noticed that the veteran sales reps were growing increasingly frustrated and alienated. The rapid growth of Pfizer over the years had brought many opportunities, but it also brought a lot of new, young, and ambitious staffers who fought hard for promotions. Now, most of the senior sales reps reported to younger, less experienced district managers and were surrounded by young go-getters who often treated their older colleagues like dinosaurs. "Well," thought Shumsky, "might as well act like one." He knew he and his senior colleagues had a lot to contribute to the company, but their motivation was in the toilet. As a consequence, Pfizer's most experienced people in the field were regularly underperforming the sales force. Many of Shumsky's colleagues were just putting in time, waiting for retirement.[1]

Top managers realized these senior employees no longer felt like an important part of the organization. Their first step was to create a program originally called "The Second Wind," which set up self-reinforcing peer groups of four to seven senior sales reps, who kept in close touch via phone, e-mail, and personal contact. The teams compete with one another and with the rest of the sales force to meet specific sales goals. The most important part of the program was asking the veteran sales reps to give talks to groups of new management trainees and to speak and lead sessions at district manager conferences, helping to fulfill higher-level esteem and self-actualization needs. The older reps were assigned mentoring relationships with younger staffers. Soon, some amazing things started happening. The sales of the older sales representatives took off like a rocket. Many times, these employees far exceeded their sales quotas and were recognized as leading the nation in the sales of certain drugs. Rick Burch, senior vice president, saw the program as a way to engage the older employees by recognizing and helping them to see their value to the company, thus allowing them to reap intrinsic as well as extrinsic rewards. He renamed the program the Master's Group, after the famous golf tournament. The 700 or so nationwide participants meet annually, most of them wearing company-provided green jackets that resemble those awarded at the prestigious Master's Tournament. "It was like recharging a battery," said veteran rep James Shumsky. "A lot of energy and enthusiasm came out. What makes it go is...that senior people are now respected for what they bring to meetings, and their mentoring is invaluable."[2]

The problem for Pfizer was that experienced employees had lost their drive and were not achieving the sales targets they are capable of reaching. This can be a problem even for the most successful and admired of organizations, when experienced, valuable employees lose the motivation and commitment they once felt, causing a decline in their performance. One secret for success in organizations is motivated and enthusiastic employees. The challenge for Pfizer and other companies is to keep employee motivation consistent with organizational goals. Motivation is a challenge for managers because motivation arises from within employees and typically differs for each person. For example, Janice Rennie makes $350,000 a year selling residential real estate in Toronto; she attributes her success to her enjoyment in listening carefully to clients and finding houses to meet their needs. Greg Storey is a skilled machinist who is challenged by writing programs for numerically controlled machines. After dropping out of college, he swept floors in a machine shop and was motivated to learn to run the machines. Frances Blais sells educational books and software. She is a top salesperson, but she does not care about the $50,000-plus commissions: "I'm not even thinking money when I'm selling. I'm really on a crusade to help children read well." In stark contrast, Rob Michaels gets sick to his stomach before he goes to work. Rob is a telephone salesperson who spends all day getting people to buy products they do not need, and the rejections are painful. His motivation is money; he earned $120,000 in the past year and cannot make nearly that much doing anything else.[3]

Rob is motivated by money, Janice by her love of listening and problem solving, Frances by the desire to help children read, and Greg by the challenge of mastering numerically controlled machinery. Each person is motivated to perform, yet each has different reasons for performing. With such diverse motivations, it is a challenge for managers to motivate employees toward common organizational goals.

This chapter reviews theories and models of employee motivation. First, we will review several perspectives on motivation and cover models that describe the employee needs and processes associated with motivation. We will discuss the reinforcement perspective on motivation and examine how job design—changing the structure of the work itself—can affect employee satisfaction and productivity. Finally, we will discuss the trend of empowerment, where authority and decision making are delegated to subordinates to increase employee motivation, and will look at how managers can imbue work with a sense of meaning to inspire and motivate employees to higher performance.

The Concept of Motivation

Most of us get up in the morning, go to school or work, and behave in ways that are predictably our own. We respond to our environment and the people in it with little thought as to why we work hard, enjoy certain classes, or find some recreational activities so much fun. Yet all these behaviors are motivated by something. **Motivation** refers to the forces within or external to a person that arouse enthusiasm and persistence to pursue a certain course of action. Employee motivation affects productivity, and part of a manager's job is to channel motivation toward the accomplishment of organizational goals.[4] The study of motivation helps managers understand what prompts people to initiate action, what influences their choice of action, and why they persist in that action over time.

A simple model of human motivation is illustrated in Exhibit 13.1. People have basic needs, such as for food, achievement, or monetary gain, which translate into an internal tension that motivates specific behaviors with which to fulfill the need. To the extent that the behavior is successful, the person is rewarded in the sense that the need is satisfied. The reward informs the person the behavior was appropriate and can be used again in the future.

Rewards are intrinsic or extrinsic. **Intrinsic rewards** are the satisfactions a person receives in the process of performing a particular action. The completion of a complex task may bestow a pleasant feeling of accomplishment, or solving a problem that benefits others may fulfill a personal mission. For example, Frances Blais sells educational materials for the intrinsic reward of helping children read well. **Extrinsic rewards** are given by another person, typically a manager, and include promotions and pay increases. They originate externally, as a result of pleasing others. Rob Michaels, who hates his sales job, nevertheless is motivated by the extrinsic reward of high pay. Though extrinsic rewards are important, good managers strive to help people achieve intrinsic rewards as well. Today's managers are finding that the most talented and

Take *ACTION*

As a manager, always learn what motivates each individual who works for you, remembering that different people have different motivators.

motivation
The arousal, direction, and persistence of behavior.

intrinsic rewards
The satisfaction received in the process of performing an action.

extrinsic rewards
A reward given by another person.

EXHIBIT 13.1
A Simple Model of Motivation

NEED Creates desire to fulfill needs (food, friendship, recognition, achievement) → BEHAVIOR Results in actions to fulfill needs → REWARDS Satisfy needs; intrinsic or extrinsic rewards

FEEDBACK Reward informs person whether behavior was appropriate and should be used again.

innovative employees are rarely motivated exclusively by rewards such as money and benefits, or even praise and recognition. Instead, they seek satisfaction from the work.[5]

The importance of motivation as illustrated in Exhibit 13.1 is that it can lead to behaviors that reflect high performance within organizations. Studies have found that high employee motivation goes hand-in-hand with high organizational performance and profits.[6] Managers can use motivation theory to help satisfy employees' needs and simultaneously encourage high work performance. With recent massive layoffs in many U.S. organizations and a decline in trust of corporate leadership, managers are struggling to keep employees focused and motivated. Finding and keeping talented workers may be a significant challenge because of weakened trust and commitment. Managers have to find the right combination of motivational techniques and rewards to keep workers satisfied and productive in various organizational situations.

Foundations of Motivation

A manager's assumptions about employee motivation and use of rewards depend on his or her perspective on motivation. Four distinct perspectives on employee motivation have evolved: the traditional approach, the human relations approach, the human resource approach, and the contemporary approach.[7]

Traditional Approach

The study of employee motivation really began with the work of Frederick W. Taylor on scientific management. Recall from Chapter 1 that scientific management pertains to the systematic analysis of an employee's job for the purpose of increasing efficiency. Economic rewards are provided to employees for high performance. The emphasis on pay evolved into the notion of the economic man: people would work harder for higher pay. This approach led to the development of incentive pay systems in which people were paid for the quantity and quality of their work outputs.

Human Relations Approach

The economic man was gradually replaced by a more sociable employee in managers' minds. Beginning with the landmark Hawthorne studies at a Western Electric plant, as described in Chapter 1, noneconomic rewards, such as congenial work groups that met social needs, seemed more important than money as a motivator of work behavior.[8] For the first time, workers were studied as people, and the concept of the social man was born. This idea is alive in a number of companies, including Harbor Sweets.

Harbor Sweets

Benneville Strohecker created Harbor Sweets candy company in his Salem, Massachusetts, basement in 1973. Today, it is a $3 million business, and Strohecker is proud to have built a company that ignores convention. Increasingly, most of the workforce is part time, with flexible hours, and is composed of a diverse group of teenagers, old-agers, the handicapped, and immigrants from Laos to the Dominican Republic.

Strohecker paid his 150 employees similarly to a McDonald's with no benefits except paid vacation, but they are part of a company profit-sharing plan and receive discounted candy. In a seasonal business centered around holidays, summer layoffs are common.

If you think these workers feel like exploited stepchildren, think again. Harbor Sweets attracts smart, dedicated people who stay around. Strohecker sums up the key to the company's success and the essence of his management style: "Trust still remains the most important ingredient in our recipes. But I believe it is not just being nice. Relying on trust is good business." He believed in those ideas so much that when he was ready to let go of some responsibility and sell part of the business, he chose a former part-time worker, Phyllis LeBlanc, who had earned an MBA and moved up to marketing manager, Chief Operating Officer, and ultimately CEO when Strohecker recently retired. He is not fully retired, as he is often asked for advice.

Trust. A lofty sentiment, and Strohecker means it. In an age of background checks and integrity profiles, he "hired by gut." Trust extended to allowing employees to fill out their own time cards. Only recently, at the request of employees, were time clocks installed at Harbor Sweets.

On occasion, Strohecker deviated from reliance on trust. He once brought in a consultant group to increase plant efficiency. What at first seemed prudent and reasonable turned out to be self-defeating, and the system was discarded. "The very fact that we were measuring is not the culture of Harbor Sweets," said Strohecker. Instead, he told his employees to work as hard as they could; they responded with many suggestions of their own, and the former sense of freedom was restored. A similar scenario evolved when a financial consultant wanted to present Strohecker some benefit options, but the boss suggested going directly to the employees. The astonished consultant was certain Strohecker had lost his mind and the employees would plunder him. He was wrong on both counts. They decided on a package probably more conservative than even Strohecker would have chosen.

LeBlanc made some mistakes early on, investing in an expensive machine that was supposed to replace handmade candies. The machine made a mess and the candies are once again done by hand. These mistakes resulted in poor profits, so LeBlanc brought in another efficiency effort and now shift managers have production goals. Some of the workers whispered "factory" under their breath as an accusation.

Even though the world is changing, LeBlanc is holding on to Harbor's culture and its quality products. When another machine failed to wrap a candy properly, a meeting was called to get ideas from workers, and the new CEO told them comfortingly, "We've had an awful lot of changes this year. And although we are trying to produce more candy and be more efficient, we don't want to ruin our best product!"[9]

Human Resource Approach

The human resource approach carries the concepts of economic man and social man further to introduce the concept of the whole person. Human resource theory suggests that employees are complex and motivated by many factors. For example, the work by McGregor on Theories X and Y, described in Chapter 1, argued that people want to do a good job and that work is as natural and healthy as play. Proponents of the human resource approach believed that earlier approaches had tried to manipulate employees through economic or social rewards. By assuming employees are competent and able to make major contributions, managers can enhance organizational performance. The human resource approach laid the groundwork for contemporary perspectives on employee motivation.

Contemporary Approach

The contemporary approach to employee motivation is dominated by three types of theories: content theories, process theories, and reinforcement theories. Each will be discussed in the following sections. Content theories stress the analysis of underlying human needs, provide insight into the needs of people in organizations, and help managers understand how needs can be satisfied in the workplace. Process theories concern the thought processes that influence behavior. They focus on how employees seek rewards in work circumstances. Reinforcement theories focus on employee learning of desired work behaviors. In Exhibit 13.1, content theories focus on the concepts in the first box, process theories on those in the second, and reinforcement theories on those in the third.

Content Perspectives on Motivation

content theories

A group of theories that emphasize the needs that motivate people.

Content theories emphasize the needs that motivate people. At any point in time, people have basic needs such as those for food, achievement, or monetary reward. These needs translate into an internal drive that motivates specific behaviors in an attempt to fulfill the needs. An individual's needs are like a hidden catalog of the things he or she wants and will work to get. To the extent that managers understand worker needs, the organization's reward systems can be designed to meet them and reinforce employees for directing energies and priorities toward attainment of organizational goals.

Hierarchy of Needs Theory

hierarchy of needs theory

A content theory that proposes that people are motivated by five categories of needs—physiological, safety, belongingness, esteem, and self-actualization—that exist in a hierarchical order.

Probably the most famous content theory was developed by Abraham Maslow.[10] Maslow's **hierarchy of needs theory** proposes that humans are motivated by multiple needs, and these needs exist in a hierarchical order as illustrated in Exhibit 13.2. Maslow identified five general types of motivating needs in order of ascendance:

1. Physiological needs. These are the most basic human physical needs, including food, water, and oxygen. In the organizational setting, these are reflected in the needs for adequate heat, air, and base salary to ensure survival.

2. Safety needs. These are the needs for a safe and secure physical and emotional environment and freedom from threats, that is, for freedom from violence and for an orderly society. In an organizational workplace, safety needs reflect the needs for safe jobs, fringe benefits, and job security.

3. Belongingness needs. These needs reflect the desire to be accepted by one's peers, have friendships, be part of a group, and be loved. In the organization, these needs influence the desire for good relationships with coworkers, participation in a work group, and a positive relationship with supervisors.

4. Esteem needs. These needs relate to the desire for a positive self-image and to receive attention, recognition, and appreciation from others. Within organizations, esteem needs reflect a motivation for recognition, an increase in responsibility, high status, and credit for contributions to the organization.

5. Self-actualization needs. These represent the needs for self-fulfillment, which are the highest needs category. They concern developing one's full potential, increasing

EXHIBIT 13.2

Maslow's Hierarchy of Needs

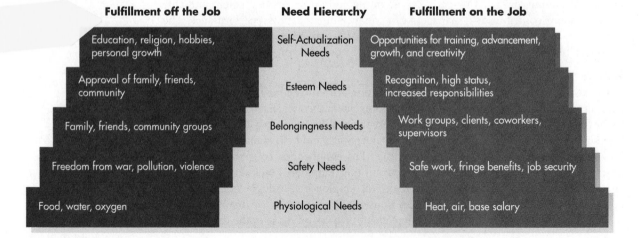

Fulfillment off the Job	Need Hierarchy	Fulfillment on the Job
Education, religion, hobbies, personal growth	Self-Actualization Needs	Opportunities for training, advancement, growth, and creativity
Approval of family, friends, community	Esteem Needs	Recognition, high status, increased responsibilities
Family, friends, community groups	Belongingness Needs	Work groups, clients, coworkers, supervisors
Freedom from war, pollution, violence	Safety Needs	Safe work, fringe benefits, job security
Food, water, oxygen	Physiological Needs	Heat, air, base salary

one's competence, and becoming a better person. Self-actualization needs can be met in the organization by providing people with opportunities to grow, be creative, and acquire training for challenging assignments and advancement.

According to Maslow's theory, lower-level needs take priority; they must be satisfied before higher-level needs are activated. The needs are satisfied in sequence: Physiological needs come before safety needs, safety needs before social needs, and so on. A person desiring physical safety will devote his or her efforts to securing a safer environment and will not be concerned with esteem needs or self-actualization needs. Once a need is satisfied, it declines in importance and the next higher need is activated.

At All Metro Health Care in Lynbrook, New York, CEO Irving Edwards set up a special "employee service" department for his home health aides to help meet their basic needs, such as applying for food stamps and finding transportation and child care. Three employees are available solely to help workers with these issues. Once these lower-level needs are met, employees desire to have higher-level needs met in the workplace, so Irving developed programs such as an award for caregiver of the year, essay contests with prizes, and special recognition for high scoring on quarterly training exercises.[11]

ERG Theory

Clayton Alderfer proposed a modification of Maslow's theory in an effort to simplify it and respond to criticisms of its lack of empirical verification.[12] His **ERG theory** identified three categories of needs:

1. Existence needs. These are the needs for physical well-being.

2. Relatedness needs. These pertain to the needs for satisfactory relationships with others.

3. Growth needs. These focus on the development of human potential and the desire for personal growth and increased competence.

The ERG model and Maslow's need hierarchy are similar because both are in hierarchical form and presume that individuals move up the hierarchy one step at a time. However, Alderfer reduced the number of need categories to three and proposed that movement up the hierarchy is more complex, reflecting a **frustration-regression principle**, namely, that failure to meet a higher-order need may trigger a regression to an already fulfilled lower-order need. Thus, a worker who cannot fulfill a need for personal growth may revert to a lower-order need and redirect his or her efforts toward making a lot of money. The ERG model, therefore, is less rigid than Maslow's need hierarchy, suggesting that individuals may move down as well as up the hierarchy, depending on their ability to satisfy needs.

Needs hierarchy theory explains why organizations want to recognize employees, encourage their participation in decision making, and give them opportunities to make significant contributions to the organization and society. J. M. Smucker, the 105-year-old company best known for jams and jellies, offers employees paid time off for volunteer activities, which helps people meet higher-level needs and, thus, contributes to high employee satisfaction and motivation.[13] Sterling Bank, with headquarters in Houston, Texas, no longer uses bank tellers. These positions are now front-line managers who are expected to make decisions and contribute ideas for improving the business.[14] A recent survey found that employees who contribute ideas at work are more

ERG theory

A modification of the needs hierarchy theory that proposes three categories of needs: existence, relatedness, and grov⁙

frustration-regression principle

The idea that failure to meet a high-order need may cause a regression to an already satisfied lower-order need.

likely to feel valued, committed, and motivated. In addition, when employees' ideas are implemented and recognized, there tends to be a motivational ripple effect throughout the workforce.[15] Half-Price Books values its employees so much that it has helped them become enormously successful.

Half-Price Books	When customers come to Half-Price Books, they are not ordering lattes—they have come for great deals on books. Sharon Wright, daughter of the founder of Dallas's Half-Price Books, is following in her late mother's footsteps by keeping costs low to make the business flourish. "I still shop at garage sales," she says, "and I pick up a used newspaper at the airport. People laugh at me." When is the last time you heard of the CEO of a $100 million company driving a 1986 Volkswagen and earning only $50,000 per year?

Everything in the first store in 1972 was homemade or second-hand, and employees were hired for their eccentricities as well as love of books, meaning they were educated and often had gifts in display and promotion. Pat Anderson—Wright's mother—had a knack for pricing books low enough so that they flew off the shelves at a profit.

Half-Price Books has a number of unusual practices. The one that defies common business practice most is its stubborn refusal to grow intentionally through a systematic plan or analysis of optimum market conditions. Instead, the company opened new stores mostly to reward valuable employees who wanted to be managers. When Dallas became saturated with Half-Price stores, expansion took place in cities where employees had a desire to relocate. By 2002, Half-Price Books had 74 stores in ten states. But she recognized that a business must create benefits that emanate outward to society. This is manifested by encouraging all 1,400 employees to be involved in some philanthropic pursuit. Wright believes there must be an organizing principal—simpler is better—to the firm. Hers? Providing a livelihood and career growth to friends and family. Finally, though this seems contradictory to her rejection of systematic plans, she understood it is better to track information than it is to control people, who, when allowed to be playful, make a more successful business.

After Pat Anderson died in 1995, many employees assumed Wright would sell off the business and start to live the good life. But Wright never thought of that. "Why would I want to sell?" she asks. "My family and friends all work here!"[16]

Many companies are finding that creating a humane work environment that allows people to achieve a balance between work and personal life is a great higher-level motivator. Flexibility in the workplace, including options such as telecommuting, flexible hours, and job sharing, is highly valued by today's employees because it enables them to manage their work and personal responsibilities. Flexibility is good for organizations, too. Employees who have control over their work schedules are significantly less likely to suffer job burnout and are more highly committed to their employers, as shown in Exhibit 13.3. This idea was supported by a survey conducted at Deloitte, which found that client service professionals cited workplace flexibility as a strong reason for wanting to stay with the firm. Another study at Prudential Insurance found that work-life satisfaction and work flexibility directly correlated to job satisfaction, organizational commitment, and employee retention.[17]

Making work fun plays a role in creating this balance as well. One psychologist has recently updated Maslow's hierarchy of needs for a new generation, and he includes the need to have fun as a substantial motivator for employees.[18] Having fun at work relieves stress and enables people to feel more "whole," rather than feeling that their personal lives are totally separate from their work lives. A manager does not have to be like Herb Kelleher, the retired CEO of Southwest Airlines, who called himself the "High Priest of Ha Ha" and dressed up like the Easter Bunny and Elvis Presley to amuse employees.

Commitment Score | Burnout Score

8.7 | 7.3 | 1.7 | 4.0

☐ Employees who have control over their work schedules
☐ Employees who lack control over their work schedules

EXHIBIT 13.3

The Motivational Benefits of Job Flexibility

SOURCE: WFD Consulting data, as reported in Karol Rose, "Work-Life Effectiveness," special advertising supplement, *Fortune* (September 29, 2003), S1–S17.

Something as simple as a choice of language can create a lighter, more fun environment. Research suggests the use of phrases such as "Play around with this.... Explore the possibility of.... Have fun with.... Do not worry about little mistakes.... View this as a game...." can effectively build elements of fun and playfulness into a workplace.[19]

Two-Factor Theory

Frederick Herzberg developed another popular theory of motivation called the two-factor theory.[20] Herzberg interviewed hundreds of workers about times when they were highly motivated to work and other times when they were dissatisfied and unmotivated at work. His findings suggested that the work characteristics associated with dissatisfaction were different from those pertaining to satisfaction, which prompted the notion that two factors influence work motivation.

The two-factor theory is illustrated in Exhibit 13.4. The center of the scale is neutral, meaning that workers are neither satisfied nor dissatisfied. Herzberg believed that two separate dimensions contribute to an employee's behavior at work. The first, called **hygiene factors**, involves the presence or absence of job dissatisfiers, such as working conditions, pay, company policies, and interpersonal relationships. When hygiene factors are poor, work is dissatisfying. However, good hygiene factors remove the dissatisfaction; they do not cause people to become highly satisfied and motivated in their work.

The second set of factors influences job satisfaction. **Motivators** focus on higher-level needs and include achievement, recognition, responsibility, and opportunity for growth. Herzberg believed that when motivators are absent, workers are neutral toward work; when motivators are present, workers are highly motivated and satisfied. Thus, hygiene factors and motivators represent two distinct factors that influence motivation. Hygiene factors work only in the area of dissatisfaction. Unsafe working conditions or a noisy work environment will cause people to be dissatisfied, but their correction will not lead to a high level of motivation and satisfaction. Motivators such as challenge, responsibility, and recognition must be in place before employees will be highly motivated to excel at their work, as workers do in Finland's SOL Cleaning Service, described in the Focus on Skills box.

A few companies today still use Theory X management, but many are trying Theory Y techniques. One organization that taps into the full potential of every worker by operating from Theory Y assumptions is Finland's SOL Cleaning Service.

Take ACTION

As a manager, remember that some people are motivated by money and others by interesting work and recognition.

hygiene factors

Factors that involve the presence or absence of job dissatisfiers, including working conditions, pay, company policies, and interpersonal relationships.

motivators

Factors that influence job satisfaction based on fulfillment of high-level needs such as achievement, recognition, responsibility, and opportunity for growth.

EXHIBIT 13.4

Herzberg's Two-Factor Theory

Highly Satisfied

Area of Satisfaction

Motivators

Achievement
Recognition
Responsibility
Work
Personal growth

Motivators influence level of satisfaction

Neither Satisfied nor Dissatisfied

Area of Dissatisfaction

Hygiene Factors

Working conditions
Pay and security
Company policies
Supervisors
Interpersonal relationships

Hygiene factors influence level of dissatisfaction

Highly Dissatisfied

The implication of the two-factor theory for managers is clear. On one hand, providing hygiene factors will eliminate employee dissatisfaction but will not motivate workers to high achievement levels. On the other hand, recognition, challenge, and opportunities for

FOCUS ON SKILLS

SOL Cleaning Service

They work in one of the world's least glamorous industries, but employees at SOL love their jobs. The industrial cleaning business is characterized by back-breaking labor, low wages, high turnover, and lousy service. SOL, however, presents a picture of a fast-paced, high-energy, knowledge-driven company with happy employees and superior customer service. Each SOL supervisor leads a team of up to 50 cleaners who cheerfully fan out across Finland each morning wearing bright red and yellow jumpsuits. The company headquarters in Helsinki explodes with color and creativity. Employees wander the halls talking on bright yellow cordless phones and meet in rooms that look more like playgrounds than offices. In Finland, and increasingly across Europe, SOL is known as an icon of what it takes to win in today's tough business environment.

Part of SOL's success is its management approach based on Theory Y assumptions. There are no job titles, executive perks, or assigned parking spaces and other status symbols at SOL. Everyone is considered equal, and each employee's contribution

is valued. In addition, SOL has no individual offices and no set working hours. All work is performed by self-directed teams that create their own budgets, do their own hiring, set their own performance goals, and negotiate their own arrangements with customers. Employees actively and enthusiastically strive toward meeting goals and solving customer problems. If a team builds up enough business, it can set up its own satellite office and run it like a minibusiness. SOL has a training program that would be the envy of any high-tech corporation, providing training in topics such as time management, budgeting, relationship skills, and customer service.

By operating from Theory Y principles, SOL has turned cleaners into entrepreneurs and changed the perception of the industrial cleaning industry in Finland. Few people grow up dreaming of becoming an industrial cleaner, but at SOL employees are motivated and fulfilled, committed to doing their best for the team, the company, and the customer.

SOURCE: Gina Imperato, "Dirty Business, Bright Ideas," *Fast Company* (February-March 1997): 89–93.

personal growth are powerful motivators and will promote high satisfaction and performance. The manager's role is to remove dissatisfiers—to provide hygiene factors sufficient to meet basic needs—and then use motivators to meet higher-level needs and propel employees toward greater achievement and satisfaction. Consider how Vision Service Plan (VSP), the nation's largest provider of eyecare benefits, uses hygiene factors and motivators.

Based in Sacramento, California, VSP has seen its workforce nearly triple over the past decade. Despite the challenges of rapid growth, employee satisfaction levels have continued to climb, reaching a high of 98 percent.

VSP does not offer outrageous salaries and stock options, but it does make sure people are paid fairly and provided with the benefits they need to live comfortably. For example, the company offers a full benefits package to all domestic partners, gives parental leave and adoption assistance, and allows employees to "gift" their accrued sick leave to fellow employees with long-term illnesses. Flexible scheduling enables employees to work when they are most productive and balance their home and work commitments.

But what contributes most to high motivation and satisfaction at VSP is making employees feel valued and important. The process starts the minute someone is hired. Managers use a New Employee Checklist of things that should be ready and waiting for the new hire upon arrival. Having such basics as a computer, voice mail and e-mail accounts, a nameplate, and business cards helps the newcomer feel like a member of the team. Supervisors give each new employee a picture frame with a note from the company CEO encouraging them to use it to display the important people in their lives. A formal career development program gives employees opportunities to examine their personal priorities, develop their skills, and discuss their career objectives. If someone wants a new job in the company that he or she is not qualified for, VSP sets up an individualized training program to help bridge the gaps.

Open communication is another higher-level motivator. Issues are raised, debated, and dealt with openly, and people have all the information they need to do their best work. CEO Roger Levine personally answers e-mails from any employee, randomly sits with employees in the company cafeteria, and holds biannual employee meetings where

Vision Service Plan (VSP)

© Peter Yang

CONCEPT CONNECTION

Guerra DeBerry Coody, a full-service marketing firm based in San Antonio, reflects a high level of positive **hygiene factors,** *provided in part by its on-site child-care facility. According to partner Tess Coody, "We were always family focused, and we wanted to create a work environment that championed that ethic." Video writer and producer Michelle Brown, who checks on her son Noah each afternoon during naptime, has had other offers but can't imagine leaving her job. "What we have here is really special. There is a quality of life here that no other place can offer."*

BUSINESS BLOOPER

AOL/Time Warner Merger

Not wanting to be controlled is the flip side of need for power (n Power), as Time Warner employees showed after the AOL/Time Warner merger. AOL CEO Steve Case hailed the joining of the two companies, saying they would "fundamentally change the way people get information, communicate with others, buy products, and are entertained." A portent of things going downhill was the refusal of Time Warner employees to use AOL as their e-mail provider. The company is now worth one-fifth of its previous combined worth and is still recovering from the hangover of Time Warner's bigwigs, who "got silly and drank the convergence Kool-Aid."

SOURCE: Alex Markels, "10 Big Business Blunders," *U.S. News & World Report* (Nov. 8, 2004): EE2–EE8.

he shares all company information and allows employees to ask any questions on the spot. This openness is intrinsically motivating to employees, who appreciate the higher level of responsibility and the trust it implies.[21]

By incorporating hygiene factors and motivators, managers at VSP have created an environment where employees are highly motivated and want to stay. The company regularly shows up on *Fortune* magazine's list of the 100 Best Companies to Work For.

Acquired Needs Theory

The final content theory was developed by David McClelland. The acquired needs theory proposes that certain types of needs are acquired during the individual's lifetime. In other words, people are not born with these needs but may learn them through their life experiences.[22] The three needs most frequently studied are these:

1. Need for achievement (n Ach). The desire to accomplish something difficult, attain a high standard of success, master complex tasks, and surpass others.

2. Need for affiliation (n Aff). The desire to form close personal relationships, avoid conflict, and establish warm friendships.

3. Need for power (n Power). The desire to influence or control others, be responsible for others, and have authority over others.

Early life experiences determine if people acquire these three needs. If children are encouraged to do things for themselves and receive reinforcement, they will acquire a need to achieve. If they are reinforced for forming warm human relationships, they will develop a need for affiliation. If they get satisfaction from controlling others, they will acquire a need for power. For example, Jack Welch, former CEO of General Electric, has credited his mother for his ambition and achievement drive. Welch's mother was determined that he be successful, so she constantly encouraged and pushed him to do better in school.[23]

Take a moment to complete the following instrument.

Motivation

Manifest needs
Circle one letter for each item, depending on how you are most of the time.

1. At work or in class, I would rather work
   a. alone
   b. in a group

2. When working on a project, I usually
   a. spend a great deal of time to make it excellent
   b. try to just make it acceptable

3. In a group,
   a. I try to be a leader
   b. I let others take the lead

4. With a project, I prefer
   a. to do it my way
   b. to see how others have done it or want it done

5. My goals at work or school are usually to
   a. be good enough, to get by
   b. to outperform others

6. When there is a disagreement, I usually
   a. refrain from saying much if people I like are arguing against my opinion
   b. speak my mind

7. In a group,
   a. I let the ideas or recommendations develop naturally
   b. I try to influence those in the group to my opinion

8. At work, I pretty much
   a. keep to myself and get the work done
   b. enjoy chatting with other people

9. At work or school, I usually
   a. avoid risks
   b. stick my neck out and take moderate risks to get ahead

10. Regarding rules and regulations, I generally
    a. follow them unless there is a compelling reason not to
    b. disregard them if they get in the way of freedom

11. When involved in sports or other games, I usually play
    a. to have a good time
    b. to win or at least to do better than I have previously

12. When working on a project, I like to
    a. have a lot of say in the outcome
    b. be an accepted "team player"

13. In my work life, I often
    a. make certain I give adequate time to my personal life (family, friends, etc.)
    b. get so over-scheduled I have less time for my personal life

14. When I am working with other people, I usually want to
    a. do better than they do
    b. organize and direct the activities of the others

(continued)

Scoring: Score one point in the following categories if you marked the appropriate letter.

n Aut		n Power		n Ach		n Aff	
1a	_____	3a	_____	2a	_____	1b	_____
4a	_____	5b	_____	9b	_____	6a	_____
6b	_____	7b	_____	11b	_____	8b	_____
8a	_____	12a	_____	13b	_____	12b	_____
10b	_____	14b	_____	14a	_____	13a	_____

Totals _____   _____   _____   _____

In the 1930s, Henry Murray developed a theory on motivation and personality, which was further developed by David McClelland. Four needs were identified: the need for autonomy (n Aut); the need for power (n Pow), the need for achievement (n Ach), and the need for affiliation (n Aff). The four needs co-exist in each person at varying levels. N Aut determines the requirement to do things alone, with a minimum of outside supervision. N Pow relates to the desire to be in charge, to be in control, to give orders. N Ach describes the desire to excel, to accomplish goals, to do better than others. Finally, n Aff is someone's need to be part of a group to be accepted and liked. The maximum in each category is five, so whichever you score the most in, that is your greatest tendency. There are no "right" or "wrong" answers. Each combination of strengths works best in some situations.

For more than 20 years, McClelland studied human needs and their implications for management. People with a high need for achievement are frequently entrepreneurs. They like to do something better than competitors and take sensible business risks. On the other hand, people who have a high need for affiliation are successful integrators, whose job is to coordinate the work of several departments in an organization.[24] Integrators include brand managers and project managers who must have excellent people skills. People high in need for affiliation can establish positive working relationships with others.

A high need for power often is associated with successful attainment of top levels in the organizational hierarchy. For example, McClelland studied managers at AT&T for 16 years and found that those with a high need for power were more likely to follow a path of continued promotion over time. More than half of the employees at the top levels had a high need for power. In contrast, managers with a high need for achievement but a low need for power tended to peak earlier in their careers and at a lower level. The reason is that achievement needs can be met through the task, but power needs can be met only by ascending to a level at which a person has power over others.

In summary, content theories focus on people's underlying needs and label those particular needs that motivate behavior. The hierarchy of needs theory, the ERG theory, the two-factor theory, and the acquired needs theory all help managers understand what motivates people. In this way, managers can design work to meet needs and, hence, elicit appropriate and successful work behaviors.

Process Perspectives on Motivation

Process theories explain how workers select behavioral actions to meet their needs and determine if their choices were successful. There are two basic process theories: equity theory and expectancy theory.

Equity Theory

Equity theory focuses on individuals' perceptions of how fairly they are treated compared with others. Developed by J. Stacy Adams, equity theory proposes that people are motivated to seek social equity in the rewards they expect for performance.[25]

According to equity theory, if people perceive their compensation as equal to what others receive for similar contributions, they will believe their treatment has been fair and equitable. People evaluate equity by a ratio of inputs to outcomes. Inputs to a job include education, experience, effort, and ability. Outcomes from a job include pay, recognition, benefits, and promotions. The input-to-outcome ratio may be compared to another person in the workgroup or to a perceived group average. A state of **equity** exists whenever the ratio of one person's outcomes to inputs equals the ratio of another's outcomes to inputs. Equity theory partly explains the success of a new motivational program at Google, as described in the Digital, Inc. box.

Inequity occurs when the input/outcome ratios are out of balance, such as when a person with a high level of education or experience receives the same salary as a new, less-educated employee. Perceived inequity occurs in the other direction. Thus, if an employee discovers she is making more money than other people who contribute the same inputs to the company, she may feel the need to correct the inequity by working harder, getting more education, or considering lower pay. Studies of the brain have shown that people get less satisfaction from money they receive without having to earn

process theories

A group of theories that explain how employees select behaviors with which to meet their needs and determine if their choices were successful.

equity theory

A process theory that focuses on individuals' perceptions of how fairly they are treated relative to others.

equity

A situation that exists when the ratio of one person's outcomes to inputs equals that of another's.

Take **ACTION**

As a manger, treat employees with fairness and equity and do not demotivate them.

DIGITAL, INC.

Simplicity Is the Key to Motivation at Google

Just as simplicity is the cornerstone of success for Google's search engine, it is also the key to powerful motivation.

Larry Page and Sergey Brin, co-founders of Google, wrote a software program that automatically e-mails engineers every week asking them what they have been working on for the week, their accomplishments, and their problems. Then, the program puts all the answers together into a document that everyone can read. Anyone who does not respond gets put at the top of the list so everyone will know he or she did not answer.

The simple idea turned out to have an unexpectedly strong impact on engineers' motivation. For one thing, it gives people a chance to share with others what they are doing and talk about their successes and challenges. Engineers at Google are permitted to spend 20 percent of their time on projects of their own choosing, so this is a way to promote their own projects. Another motivator is that engineers want to perform as well as or better than their colleagues. When everyone reads about what everyone else is doing, it encourages people to make sure

they are pulling their fair share of the workload. In line with equity theory, people do not want to be seen as a goof-off or to feel like a loafer when they compare their activities to those of their colleagues.

Google's flexible work hours and excellent benefits are powerful motivational tools. The company spends a lot of money on taking care of employees. Free lunches feature organic foods, vegetarian dishes, and a sandwich and salad bar. On-site laundry and dry cleaning facilities, a fitness center, and a staff masseuse are other perks. There is no dress code, dogs are allowed in the offices, and people have the flexibility to work when and how they feel most productive.

All these things go into creating a highly motivating environment at Google. However, the simple, specific technique of having people report on their activities via e-mail every week acts as a regular reminder for people to always do their best.

SOURCE: Larry Page, "Motivate Your Staff," segment of "How to Succeed in 2004," *Business 2.0*, http://www.business2.com and Steven Levy with Brad Stone, "All Eyes on Google," *Newsweek* (April 12, 2004): 40.

it than they do from money they work to receive.[26] Perceived inequity creates tensions within individuals that motivate them to bring equity into balance.[27]

The most common methods for reducing a perceived inequity are these:

- *Change inputs.* A person may choose to increase or decrease his or her inputs to the organization. For example, underpaid individuals may reduce their level of effort or increase their absenteeism. Overpaid people may increase effort on the job.

- *Change outcomes.* A person may change his or her outcomes. An underpaid person may request a salary increase or a bigger office. A union may want to improve wages and working conditions to be consistent with a comparable union whose members make more money.

- *Distort perceptions.* Research suggests that people may distort perceptions of equity if they cannot change inputs or outcomes. They may artificially increase the status attached to their jobs or distort others' perceived rewards to bring equity into balance.

- *Leave the job.* People who feel inequitably treated may decide to leave their jobs rather than suffer the inequity of being underpaid or overpaid. In their new jobs, they expect to find a more favorable balance of rewards.

The implication of equity theory for managers is that employees indeed compare the perceived equity of their rewards. An increase in salary or a promotion will have no motivational effect if it is perceived as inequitable relative to that of other employees. A good example of equity theory comes from the J. Peterman Company, the trendy catalog company that slid into bankruptcy before being acquired by another firm. John Peterman had created a comfortable, creative culture where employees were highly motivated to work together toward common goals. However, when the company began to grow, Peterman found himself having to hire people quickly, and he often had to offer them higher salaries than those of his current employees to match what they were making elsewhere. When making important decisions, leaders tended to pay more attention to the ideas and thoughts of the new staff than they did the "old-timers." Long-time employees felt slighted, and motivation declined significantly. Many employees began putting less energy and effort into their jobs. They were no longer willing to go the extra mile because of a perceived state of inequity.[28] Inequitable pay puts pressure on employees that is sometimes almost too great to bear. They attempt to change their work habits, change the system, or leave the job.[29]

Smart managers keep feelings of equity in balance to keep their workforces motivated.

Expectancy Theory

expectancy theory

A process theory that proposes that motivation depends on individuals' expectations about their ability to perform tasks and receive desired rewards.

Expectancy theory suggests that motivation depends on people's expectations about their ability to perform tasks and receive desired rewards. Expectancy theory is associated with the work of Victor Vroom, though a number of scholars have made contributions in this area.[30] Expectancy theory is concerned not with identifying types of needs but with the thinking process that individuals use to achieve rewards. Consider Amy Huang, a university student with a strong desire for a B in her accounting course. Amy has a C+ average and one more exam to take. Amy's motivation to study for that last exam will be influenced by the expectation that hard study will lead to an A on the exam and the expectation that an A on the exam will result in a B for the course. If Amy believes she cannot get an A on the exam or that receiving an A will not lead to a B for the course, she will not be motivated to study exceptionally hard.

Elements of Expectancy Theory. Expectancy theory is based on the relationship among the individual's effort, the individual's performance, and the desirability of outcomes associated with high performance. These elements and the relationships among them are illustrated in Exhibit 13.5. The keys to expectancy theory are the expectancies for the relationships among effort, performance, and outcomes with the value of the outcomes to the individual.

E → P expectancy involves whether putting effort into a task will lead to high performance. For this expectancy to be high, the individual must have the ability, previous experience, and necessary machinery, tools, and opportunity to perform. For Amy Huang to get a B in the accounting course, the E → P expectancy is high if Amy truly believes that with hard work, she can get an A on the final exam. If Amy believes she has neither the ability nor the opportunity to achieve high performance, the expectancy and her motivation will be low.

P → O expectancy involves whether successful performance will lead to the desired outcome. In the case of a person who is motivated to win a job-related award, this expectancy concerns the belief that high performance will lead to the award. If the P → O expectancy is high, the individual will be more highly motivated. If the expectancy is that high performance will not produce the desired outcome, motivation will be lower. If an A on the final exam is likely to produce a B in the accounting course, Amy Huang's P → O expectancy will be high. Amy might talk to the professor to see if an A will be sufficient to earn her a B in the course. If not, she will be less motivated to study hard for the final exam.

Valence is the value of outcomes, or attraction to outcomes, for the individual. If the outcomes available from high effort and good performance are not valued by employees, motivation will be low. Likewise, if outcomes have a high value, motivation will be higher.

Expectancy theory attempts not to define specific types of needs or rewards but only to establish they exist and may be different for every individual. One employee might want to be promoted to a position of increased responsibility, and another might have high valence for good relationships with peers. Consequently, the first person will be motivated to work hard for a promotion and the second for the opportunity for a team position that will keep him or her associated with a group.

© Rick Friedman/CORBIS

CONCEPT CONNECTION

Circuit City managers are using **expectancy theory** *principles to help meet employee's needs while attaining organizational goals. By creating an incentive program that is a commission-based plan designed to provide the highest compensation to sales counselors who are committed to serving every customer, Circuit City achieves its volume and profitability objectives. The incentive program is also used in other areas such as distribution, where employees are recognized for accomplishment in safety, productivity, and attendance.*

E → P expectancy
Expectancy that putting effort into a given task will lead to high performance.

P → O expectancy
Expectancy that successful performance of a task will lead to the desired outcome.

EXHIBIT 13.5

Major Elements of Expectancy Theory

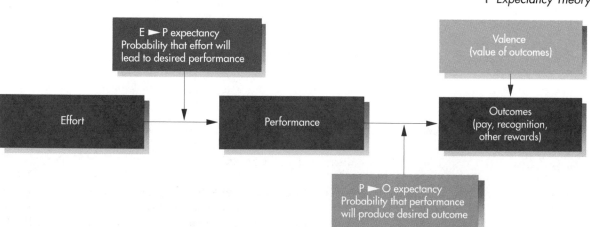

Take **ACTION**

Remember, if you believe that hard work will help you achieve your goals, you will be more likely to work hard.

valence

The value or attraction an individual has for an outcome.

A simple sales department example will explain how the expectancy model in Exhibit 13.5 works. If Carlos, a salesperson at the Diamond Gift Shop, believes that increased selling effort will lead to higher personal sales, we can say that he has a high E → P expectancy. Moreover, if Carlos believes that higher personal sales will lead to a promotion or pay raise, we can say that he has a high P → O expectancy. Finally, if Carlos places a high value on the promotion or pay raise, valence is high and he will have a high motivational force. On the other hand, if the E → P or P → O expectancy is low, or if the money or promotion has low valence for Carlos, the overall motivational force will be low. For an employee to be highly motivated, all three factors in the expectancy model must be high.[31]

Implications for Managers.   The expectancy theory of motivation is similar to the path-goal theory of leadership described in Chapter 12. Both theories are personalized to subordinates' needs and goals. Managers' responsibility is to help subordinates meet their needs and at the same time attain organizational goals. Managers must find a match between a subordinate's skills and abilities and the job demands. To increase motivation, managers can clarify an individual's needs, define the outcomes available from the organization, and ensure that each individual has the ability and support (namely, time and equipment) needed to attain outcomes.

Some companies use expectancy theory principles by designing incentive systems that identify desired organizational outcomes and give everyone the same shot at getting the rewards. The trick is to design a system that fits with employees' abilities and needs.

Goal-Setting Theory

Recall from Chapter 5 our discussion of the importance and purposes of goals. Numerous studies have shown that people are more motivated when they have specific targets or objectives to work toward.[32] You have probably noticed in your own life that you are more motivated when you have a specific goal, such as making an A on a final exam, losing 10 pounds before spring break, or earning enough money during the summer to buy a used car.

goal-setting theory

A motivation theory in which specific, challenging goals increase motivation and performance when the goals are accepted by subordinates and these subordinates receive feedback to indicate their progress toward goal achievement.

Goal-setting theory, described by Edwin Locke and Gary Latham, proposes that specific, challenging goals increase motivation and performance when the goals are accepted by subordinates and these subordinates receive feedback to indicate their progress toward goal achievement.[33] There are four key components of goal-setting theory:

1. Goal specificity refers to the degree to which goals are concrete and clear. As we discussed in Chapter 5, specific goals such as "Visit one new customer each day," or "Sell $1,000 worth of merchandise a week" are more motivating than vague goals such as "Keep in touch with new customers" or "Increase merchandise sales."

2. In terms of goal difficulty, hard goals are more motivating than easy ones. Easy goals provide little challenge for employees and do not require them to increase their output. Highly ambitious but achievable goals ask people to stretch their abilities.

Take **ACTION**

As a manager, give regular and meaningful feedback to employees.

3. Goal acceptance means that employees have to "buy into" the goals and be committed to them. Managers often find that having people participate in setting goals is a good way to increase acceptance and commitment.

4. Finally, the component of feedback means that people get information about how well they are doing in progressing toward goal achievement. Managers must provide performance feedback on a regular, ongoing basis. However, self-feedback,

where people can monitor their own progress toward a goal, has been found to be an even stronger motivator than external feedback.[34]

Why does goal setting increase motivation? For one thing, it enables people to focus their energies in the right direction. People know what to work toward, so they can direct their efforts toward the most important activities to accomplish the goals. Goals energize behavior because people feel compelled to develop plans and strategies to accomplish the objective. Specific, difficult goals provide a challenge and encourage people to put forth high levels of effort. When goal setting is not used, results can be disastrous, as shown in the Focus on Collaboration box.

Steve and Diane Warren, owners of Katzinger's Delicatessen in Columbus, Ohio, used elements of goal-setting theory to motivate employees and dramatically reduce food costs. The Katzingers had asked their employees to find ways to cut costs and offered to share any savings with them. But nothing happened because the goal was too vague to serve as a motivator. So, the deli owners proposed an explicit, ambitious goal: to reduce food costs to below 35 percent of sales without sacrificing food quality or service. With this goal as a motivator, employees focused their efforts and met the goal. By the end of the year, food quality and service had improved, and food costs were cut to below 35 percent of sales, saving the Katzinger's $30,000. As a reward, half of that amount was distributed to employees for helping to meet the goal.[35]

FOCUS ON COLLABORATION

Guns N' Roses

Back before Guns N' Roses were multi-platinum superstars, producer Tom Zutaut signed them to Geffen Records. By 2001, he had left the label but was coaxed back to work with Axl Rose, the only original remaining member of the band, to nudge him to finish the much-waited, "Chinese Democracy." Rose had started the album in 1994, but got waylaid by personal demons. Gossip had him focused on plastic surgery and past-life regression therapy, not to mention lawsuits. Axl Rose is not the only musician to drag his feet. But the irony is that the musician who cast himself as the "master of predatory Hollywood" in his 1991 hit song, "Welcome to the Jungle," is now seen as the master of the music industry's largest white elephant. As time wore on, a horrible truth emerged: The more record companies rely on musicians like Rose, the less they can be controlled.

By 1994, the band had dispersed, victim to drug abuse, onstage tantrums, and lyric controversies. But they reconvened for the new album, and Rose made himself leader, albeit more of a dictator. Not much got done. Because the band was still selling lots of old albums, no one seemed to mind. Leadership changed at Geffen, and it was bought by Seagram. When the original band dispersed again, Geffen records sent CDs to Rose, asking him to listen for people he might want to work with. Rose ran over the CDs with his car. One day Geffen talent agent Todd Sullivan gently encouraged Rose to pull together a lot of recorded riffs and song fragments into complete compositions. The next day the Geffen CEO pulled Sullivan off the project.

The record company kept paying Rose a million here, a million there, to keep on with the project, but he had built so many walls around himself he became isolated. Rose requested a specialized piece of equipment that cost about $150,000 to rent for two years and only used it 30 days. His pattern for years had been some flurried activity, creative chaos, and finally isolation. Label executives believed that if they brought in the right producer, the album would get done. But Rose's work (or lack of it) has outlasted scores of label managers, producers, even the corporate structure that first hired him. In fact, the entire music recording industry has consolidated and is more bottom-line driven than ever. So despite millions of dollars over budget, "Chinese Democracy," is not even on the release schedule anymore. Record executives have learned it is better to invest in reliable musicians, those who have a proven track record and are known to meet deadlines. A gifted musician, a moody man often unable to follow through, is seen as an unmanageable variable in anybody's business plan.

SOURCE: Jeff Leeds, "The Most Expensive Album Never Made," *The New York Times* (March 6, 2005): AR1, 28, 32.

Reinforcement Perspective on Motivation

The reinforcement approach to employee motivation sidesteps the issues of employee needs and thinking processes described in the content and process theories. **Reinforcement theory** looks at the relationship between behavior and its consequences. It focuses on changing or modifying the employees' job behavior through the appropriate use of immediate rewards and punishments.

reinforcement theory

A motivation theory based on the relationship between a given behavior and its consequences.

Reinforcement Tools

Behavior modification is the name given to the set of techniques by which reinforcement theory is used to modify human behavior.[36] The basic assumption underlying behavior modification is the **law of effect**, which states that positively reinforced behavior tends to be repeated, and nonreinforced behavior tends not to be repeated. **Reinforcement** is defined as anything that causes a certain behavior to be repeated or inhibited. The four reinforcement tools are positive reinforcement, avoidance learning, punishment, and extinction. Each type of reinforcement is a consequence of a pleasant or unpleasant event being applied or withdrawn following a person's behavior. The four types of reinforcement are summarized in Exhibit 13.6.

behavior modification

The set of techniques by which reinforcement theory is used to modify human behavior.

Positive Reinforcement.   Positive reinforcement is the administration of a pleasant and rewarding consequence following a desired behavior. A good example of positive reinforcement is immediate praise for an employee who arrives on time or does a little extra work. The pleasant consequence will increase the likelihood of the excellent work behavior occurring again. As another example, Frances Flood, CEO of Gentner Communications, a manufacturer of high-end audioconferencing equipment based in Salt Lake City, Utah, offered engineers a stake in the company's profits if they met targets for getting new products to market faster. Within two years, product development time had been slashed by 30 percent.[37] Studies have shown that positive reinforcement does improve performance. In addition, nonfinancial reinforcements such as positive feedback, social recognition, and attention are as effective as financial incentives.[38]

Take **ACTION**

As a leader, give positive feedback and other rewards for behaviors you want to be repeated.

EXHIBIT 13.6

Changing Behavior with Reinforcement

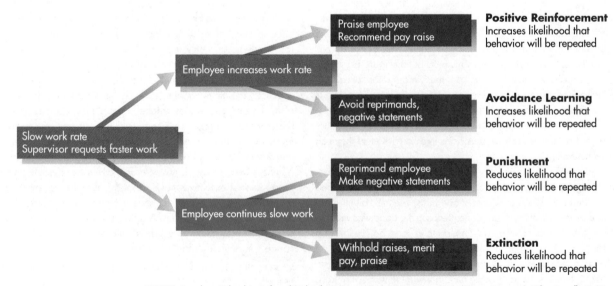

SOURCE: Based on Richard L. Daft and Richard M. Steers, *Organizations: A Micro/Macro Approach* (Glenview, Ill.: Scott, Foresman, 1986), 109.

Avoidance Learning. Avoidance learning is the removal of an unpleasant consequence following a desired behavior. Avoidance learning is sometimes called negative reinforcement. Employees learn to do the right thing by avoiding unpleasant situations. Avoidance learning occurs when a supervisor stops criticizing or reprimanding an employee once the incorrect behavior has stopped.

Punishment. Punishment is the imposition of unpleasant outcomes on an employee. Punishment typically occurs following undesirable behavior. For example, a supervisor may berate an employee for performing a task incorrectly. The supervisor expects that the negative outcome will serve as a punishment and reduce the likelihood of the behavior recurring. The use of punishment in organizations is controversial and often criticized because it fails to indicate the correct behavior. However, almost all managers report finding it occasionally necessary to impose forms of punishment ranging from verbal reprimands to employee suspensions or firings.[39]

Extinction. Extinction is the withdrawal of a positive reward. Whereas with punishment, the supervisor imposes an unpleasant outcome such as a reprimand, extinction involves withholding pay raises, praise, and other positive outcomes. The idea is that behavior that is negatively reinforced will be less likely to occur in the future. For example, if a perpetually tardy employee fails to receive praise and pay raises, he or she will begin to realize the behavior is not producing desired outcomes. The behavior will disappear if it is continually nonreinforced.

Some executives use reinforcement theory effectively to shape employees' behavior. Arunas Chesonis, CEO of PaeTec Communications, is a master motivator, relying primarily on positive reinforcement to encourage employee behavior that has enabled PaeTec to keep growing during the worst downturn in the history of the telecommunications industry. The example below further describes this leader's approach to motivation.

> PaeTec CEO Arunas Chesonis expects employees to put customers first. In the Network Operations Center, or NOC, irate customers reach a live human voice after the first ring. Employees in the NOC handle 4,000 problem calls a month, but they solve them so well and so cheerfully that the company has maintained a monthly customer retention rate of 99.5 percent since it was founded in 1998.
>
> To get his people to put customers first, Chesonis puts employees first. He is known for writing short notes to employees all over the company to praise them or thank them. He sends e-mails, makes phone calls, and personally visits people in their offices to tell them how much he appreciates their efforts and accomplishments. Though the company gives financial awards for some types of exceptional service, the smaller forms of recognition seem to have the most pervasive impact. The vice president of engineering recalls Chesonis asking who had worked the hardest recently. After he got his answer, Chesonis showed up in the employee's office with a flower arrangement as tall as the employee was and said, "Marion told me how hard you worked this week."
>
> Chesonis has incorporated other motivational ideas as well. For one thing, at PaeTec, everyone is considered equal, and everyone is a potential expert. There are no perks for anyone, from the CEO on down, and everyone gets stock options and bonuses based on the company's performance. People are expected to share knowledge and help each other instinctively. On any given day, the expert in the problem at hand might be a customer service representative, the CEO, an engineer, or a file clerk. "One thing that endeared this place to me from the start, you could have a good idea and that good idea can become company policy," says Jason Ellston, the manager of the NOC. At PaeTec, managers automatically assume that employees on the front lines know what needs to be done better than anyone else.

law of effect
The assumption that positively reinforced behavior tends to be repeated and unreinforced or negatively reinforced behavior tends to be inhibited.

reinforcement
Anything that causes a given behavior to be repeated or inhibited.

PaeTec Communications

People respond to this kind of respect, and they pass it on to their own subordinates and to PaeTec's customers. Some employees have taken a pay cut to come to work at PaeTec. Chesonis believes it only makes business sense to put people first and reap the rewards of having a team of motivated, committed, even devoted employees. Jason Ellston encapsulates the company's motivation philosophy in talking about a newly hired employee who was worried about being fired when he had to take excess time off work early in his career at PaeTec. Ellston told him to take all the time he needed, and his job would be there when he got back. "Just thinking like a human being, why would you not want to extend yourself for an employee?" Ellston asks. "That guy will run through a wall for me."[40]

Schedules of Reinforcement

A great deal of research into reinforcement theory suggests that the timing of reinforcement has an impact on the speed of employee learning. **Schedules of reinforcement** pertain to a) the frequency with which and b) intervals over which reinforcement occurs. A reinforcement schedule can be selected to have maximum impact on employees' job behavior. There are five basic types of reinforcement schedules, which include continuous reinforcement and four types of partial reinforcement.

schedule of reinforcement

The frequency with which, and intervals over which, reinforcement occurs.

continuous reinforcement schedule

A schedule in which every occurrence of the desired behavior is reinforced.

partial reinforcement schedule

A schedule in which only some occurrences of the desired behavior are reinforced.

Continuous Reinforcement. With a **continuous reinforcement schedule**, every occurrence of the desired behavior is reinforced. This schedule can be very effective in the early stages of learning new types of behavior, because every attempt has a pleasant consequence.

Partial Reinforcement. However, in the real world of organizations, reinforcing every correct behavior is often impossible. With a **partial reinforcement schedule**, the reinforcement is administered only after some occurrences of the correct behavior. There are four types of partial reinforcement schedules: fixed-interval, fixed-ratio, variable-interval, and variable-ratio.

1. Fixed-interval schedule. The fixed-interval schedule rewards employees at specified time intervals. If an employee displays the correct behavior each day, reinforcement may occur every week. Regular paychecks or quarterly bonuses are examples of a fixed-interval reinforcement. At Leone Ackerly's Mini Maid franchise in Marietta, Georgia, workers are rewarded with an attendance bonus each pay period if they have gone to work every day on time and in uniform.[41]

2. Fixed-ratio schedule. With a fixed-ratio schedule, reinforcement occurs after a specified number of desired responses, say, after every fifth. For example, paying a field hand $1.50 for picking 10 pounds of peppers is a fixed-ratio schedule. Most piece-rate pay systems are considered fixed-ratio schedules.

3. Variable-interval schedule. With a variable-interval schedule, reinforcement is administered at random times that cannot be predicted by the employee. An example would be a random inspection by the manufacturing superintendent of the production floor, at which time he or she commends employees on their good behavior.

4. Variable-ratio schedule. The variable-ratio schedule is based on a random number of desired behaviors rather than on variable time periods. Reinforcement may occur sometimes after 5, 10, 15, or 20 displays of behavior. One example is random monitoring of telemarketers, who may be rewarded after a certain number of calls in which they perform the appropriate behaviors and meet call performance specifications. Employees know they may be monitored but are never sure when checks will occur and when rewards may be given.

The schedules of reinforcement available to managers are illustrated in Exhibit 13.7. Continuous reinforcement is most effective for establishing new learning, but behavior is

Schedule of Reinforcement	Nature of Reinforcement	Effect on Behavior When Applied	Effect on Behavior When Withdrawn	Example
Continuous	Reward given after each desired behavior	Leads to fast learning of new behavior	Rapid extinction	Praise
Fixed-interval	Reward given at fixed time intervals	Leads to average and irregular performance	Rapid extinction	Weekly paycheck
Fixed-ratio	Reward given at fixed amounts of output	Quickly leads to high and stable performance	Rapid extinction	Piece-rate pay system
Variable-interval	Reward given at variable times	Leads to moderately high and stable performance	Slow extinction	Performance appraisal and awards given at random times each month
Variable-ratio	Reward given at variable amounts of output	Leads to high performance	Slow extinction	Sales bonus tied to number of sales calls, with random checks

EXHIBIT 13.7

Schedules of Reinforcement

vulnerable to extinction. Partial reinforcement schedules are more effective for maintaining behavior over extended time periods. The most powerful is the variable-ratio schedule because employee behavior will persist due to the administration of reinforcement only after a long interval.[42]

One example of a small business that successfully uses reinforcement theory is Emerald Packaging in Union City, California.

Emerald Packaging

Emerald Packaging is a family-owned business that prints plastic bags for prepackaged salads and other vegetables. The company employs about 100 people and is the tenth largest manufacturer in Union City, California, located about 30 miles southeast of San Francisco.

Kevin Kelly, CEO of Emerald, was looking for a way to reduce accidents and improve the company's safety record. Despite all efforts, employees continued to practice unsafe work habits, leading to accidents that caused workers' compensation costs to skyrocket. Kelly decided to try a positive reinforcement scheme that would reward employees for meeting safety goals.

Kelly set a goal of no more than 12 accidents for the year—half the total of the previous year—with none causing lost time. To motivate employees to achieve the goal, Kelly told employees that if they racked up no more than three injuries a quarter, he would buy them lunch, hand out company T-shirts, and raffle off $1,000. If they made it though the entire year with 12 or fewer minor accidents, the company would distribute a significant monetary reward among all employees.

The reinforcement plan worked. By the end of the year, Emerald had logged only 11 accidents, none causing lost-time injuries. Not a single employee missed work at Emerald because of injury for a full 1,252 days. Employees began policing one another, such as reprimanding one worker who was repeatedly injured while cleaning machines without his safety glasses.

In 2003, Emerald handed out a total of $50,000 to its 100 employees for their contribution to keeping injury and workers' comp costs low and giving the company one of the best safety records in the industry.[43]

This type of reinforcement worked so well at Emerald that Kelly later developed reinforcement programs for quality and waste reduction. Reinforcement works at organizations such as Campbell Soup Co., Emery Air Freight, Michigan Bell, and PSS World Medical because managers reward appropriate behavior. They tell employees what they can do to receive reinforcement, tell them what they are doing wrong, distribute rewards equitably, tailor rewards to behaviors, and keep in mind that failure to reward deserving behavior has an equally powerful impact on employees.

Reward and punishment motivational practices dominate organizations, with as many as 94 percent of companies in the United States reporting that they use practices that reward performance or merit with pay.[44] In addition, a recent report by human resources consulting firm Towers Perrin indicates that incentive systems that reward employees with bonuses or other rewards for meeting certain goals are becoming increasingly popular. However, less than one third of the companies reported seeing any noticeable impact of incentive pay on business results.[45] Despite the testimonies of numerous organizations that enjoy successful incentive programs, there is growing criticism of these carrot-and-stick methods, as discussed in the Focus on Skills box.

FOCUS ON SKILLS

The Carrot-and-Stick Controversy

Everybody thought Rob Rodin was crazy when he decided to wipe out all individual incentives for his sales force at Marshall Industries, a large distributor of electronic components based in El Monte, California. He did away with all bonuses, commissions, vacations, and other awards and rewards. All salespeople would receive a base salary plus the opportunity for profit sharing, which would be the same percent of salary for everyone, based on the entire company's performance. Six years later, Rodin says productivity per person has tripled at the company, but still he gets questions and criticism about his decision.

Rodin is standing right in the middle of a big controversy in modern management. Do financial and other rewards motivate the kind of behavior organizations want and need? A growing number of critics say no, arguing that carrot-and-stick approaches are a holdover from the Industrial Age and are inappropriate and ineffective. Today's workplace demands innovation and creativity from everyone, behaviors that rarely are inspired by money or other financial incentives. Three criticisms of carrot-and-stick approaches include the following:

1. *Extrinsic rewards diminish intrinsic rewards.* When people are motivated to seek an extrinsic reward, whether bonus, award, or supervisor approval, they generally focus on the reward rather than on the work they do to achieve it. Thus, the intrinsic satisfaction people receive from performing their jobs declines. When people lack intrinsic rewards in their work, their performance stays at an adequate level to achieve the reward offered. In the worst case, employees may cover up mistakes or cheat to achieve the reward. One study found that teachers who were rewarded for increasing test scores frequently used various forms of cheating.

2. *Extrinsic rewards are temporary.* Offering outside incentives may ensure short-term success but not long-term high performance. When employees are focused only on the

reward, they lose interest in their work. Without personal interest, the potential for exploration, creativity, and innovation disappears. Though employees may meet the current deadline or goal, better ways of working and serving customers will not be discovered and the company's long-term success will be affected.

3. *Extrinsic rewards assume people are driven by lower-level needs.* Rewards such as bonuses, pay increases, and praise presume that the primary reason people initiate and persist in behavior is to satisfy lower-level needs. However, behavior is based on yearnings for self-expression and on feelings of self-esteem and self-worth. Typical individual incentive programs do not reflect and encourage the myriad behaviors motivated by people's need to express themselves and realize their higher needs for growth and fulfillment.

As Rob Rodin discovered at Marshall Industries, organizations need employees who are motivated to think, experiment, and continuously search for ways to solve new problems. Alfie Kohn, one of the most vocal critics of carrot-and-stick approaches, offers the following advice to managers regarding how to pay employees: "Pay well, pay fairly, and then do everything you can to get money off people's minds." Indeed, some evidence shows that money is not primarily what people work for. Managers should understand the limits of extrinsic motivators and work to satisfy employees' higher, as well as lower, needs. To be motivated, employees need jobs that offer self-satisfaction in addition to a yearly pay raise.

SOURCES: Alfie Kohn, "Incentives Can Be Bad for Business," *Inc.* (January 1998): 93–94; A.J. Vogl, "Carrots, Sticks, and Self-Deception" (an interview with Alfie Kohn), *Across the Board* (January 1994): 39–44; Geoffrey Colvin, "What Money Makes You Do," *Fortune* (August 17, 1998): 213–214; and Jeffrey Pfeffer, "Sins of Commission," *Business 2.0* (May 2004): 56.

Job Design for Motivation

A job in an organization is a unit of work that a single employee is responsible for performing. A job could include writing tickets for parking violators in New York City or doing long-range planning for the Discovery cable television channel. Jobs are important because performance of their components may provide rewards that meet employees' needs. An assembly-line worker may install the same bolt repeatedly, and an emergency room physician may provide each trauma victim with a unique treatment package. Managers need to know what aspects of a job provide motivation as well as how to compensate for routine tasks that have little inherent satisfaction. **Job design** is the application of motivational theories to the structure of work for improving productivity and satisfaction. Approaches to job design are generally classified as job simplification, job rotation, job enlargement, and job enrichment.

Job Simplification

Job simplification pursues task efficiency by reducing the number of tasks one person must do. Job simplification is based on principles drawn from scientific management and industrial engineering. Tasks are designed to be simple, repetitive, and standardized. As complexity is stripped from a job, the worker has more time to concentrate on doing more of the same routine task. Workers with low skill levels can perform the job, and the organization achieves a high level of efficiency. Indeed, workers are interchangeable, because they need little training or skill and exercise little judgment. As a motivational technique, however, job simplification has failed. People dislike routine and boring jobs and react in a number of negative ways, including sabotage, absenteeism, and unionization. Job simplification is compared with job rotation and job enlargement in Exhibit 13.8. Job simplification is sometimes required by the employee or entrepreneur, as shown in the Best Practices box.

Job Rotation

Job rotation systematically moves employees from one job to another, thereby increasing the number of different tasks an employee performs without increasing the complexity of any one job. For example, an autoworker might install windshields one week and front bumpers the next. Job rotation takes advantage of engineering efficiencies, but it provides variety and stimulation for employees. Though employees might find the new job interesting at first, the novelty wears off as the repetitive work is mastered.

Companies such as Home Depot, Motorola, 1-800-Flowers, and Dayton Hudson have built on the notion of job rotation to train a flexible workforce. As companies break away from ossified job categories, workers can perform several jobs, thereby reducing labor costs and giving employees opportunities to develop new skills. At Home Depot, for example, workers scattered throughout the company's vast chain of stores can get a taste of the corporate climate by working at in-store support centers,

Take ACTION
As a leader, think about how you can design jobs more effectively to keep your employees more motivated.

job design
The application of motivational theories to the structure of work for improving productivity and satisfaction.

job simplification
A job design whose purpose is to improve task efficiency by reducing the number of tasks a single person must do.

job rotation
A job design that systematically moves employees from one job to another to provide them with variety and stimulation.

EXHIBIT 13.8
Types of Job Design

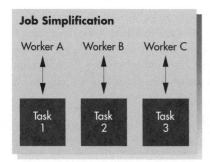
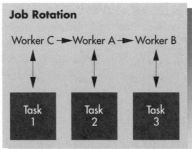
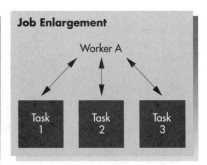

Just Ask a Woman

Mary Lou Quinlan dreamt she had broken her legs and then woke up, disappointed it was not true, that she could not stay in bed. That is when she knew things had to change. But what could she complain about? She had a wonderful marriage, a great job, and lots of friends. But the wear and tear from 23 years of nonstop work was taking its toll. Yet how could she take time off? "Women have to give themselves permission to rest," she said. Giving herself that permission in 1998, the 51-year-old CEO quit her high-pressure job and nine months later founded "Just Ask a Woman," a firm that helps companies understand the needs of distaff customers. With four employees she will not hire more, has refused to franchise her concept, and is unwilling to travel the globe for her clients. "I simply will not get into another situation where the price of success is giving up my life," she said.

She knows the pitfalls well. Employees give up $21 billion of unredeemed vacation time every year; dual earners with children work a total of 91 hours a week, up from 81 hours in 1977; overwork-related accidents, mistakes, and illnesses cost companies more than $300 billion per year. Add into the equation that Blackberries, cell phones, and the Internet make it harder to get away from work, fueling work addiction.

Not everyone can up and quit, but she does have suggestions to repair overwhelmed lives: 1) Recognize signs of your own burnout: If you wake up at 3 AM and must answer e-mail, gradually reduce nights you answer e-mail at home; 2) Start a buddy system with another colleague who is overworked, and cover for each other and encourage lunch breaks; 3) Make a list of what you love and hate to do and compare it with your average day: If you have too many disliked tasks, start sending out résumés; 4) Schedule time off and take those needed vacations: Realize you need rejuvenation, time with kids, two hours at the spa, time to write those stories. Ask yourself what will happen if you do not take time off. What price will you pay?

Quinlan's wake-up call came in 1998 on a vacation with her husband and with a cell phone tied to her ear. Her husband blew up at her. Two months later, she took a five-week leave and quit right after she returned. Her income is less now than as a CEO. But she has no regrets. "Finally, I am doing something I can picture doing for a long, long time."

SOURCE; Claudia H. Deutsch, "She Didn't Stop the World, but She Slowed It Down," *The New York Times* (Feb. 13, 2005): B6.

and associate managers can dirty their hands out on the sales floor.[46] Job rotation gives companies greater flexibility. One production worker might shift among the jobs of drill operator, punch operator, and assembler, depending on the company's need at the moment. Some unions have resisted the idea, but many now go along, realizing it helps the company be more competitive.[47]

Job Enlargement

job enlargement

A job design that combines a series of tasks into one new, broader job to give employees variety and challenge.

Job enlargement combines a series of tasks into one new, broader job. This is a response to the dissatisfaction of employees with oversimplified jobs. Instead of one job, an employee may be responsible for three or four and will have more time to do them. Job enlargement provides job variety and a greater challenge for employees. At Maytag, jobs were enlarged when work was redesigned such that workers assembled an entire water pump rather than doing each part as it reached them on the assembly line. Similarly, rather than just changing the oil at a Precision Tune location, a mechanic changes the oil, greases the car, airs the tires, checks fluid levels, battery, air filter, and so forth. Then, the same employee is responsible for consulting with the customer about routine maintenance or any problems he or she sees with the vehicle.

Job Enrichment

job enrichment

A job design that incorporates achievement, recognition, and other high-level motivators into the work.

Recall the discussion of Maslow's need hierarchy and Herzberg's two-factor theory. Rather than changing the number and frequency of tasks a worker performs, **job enrichment** incorporates high-level motivators into the work, including job responsibility, recognition, and opportunities for growth, learning, and achievement. In an enriched job, employees have control over the resources necessary for performing it, make decisions on how to do the work, experience personal growth, and set their own pace.

Many companies have undertaken job enrichment programs to increase employees' motivation and job satisfaction. At Ralcorp's cereal manufacturing plant in Sparks, Nevada, for example, managers enriched jobs by combining several packing positions into a single job and cross-training employees to operate all of the packing line's equipment. In addition, assembly line employees screen, interview, and train all new hires. They are responsible for managing the production flow to and from their upstream and downstream partners, making daily decisions that affect their work, managing quality, and contributing to continuous improvement. Enriched jobs have improved employee motivation and satisfaction, and the company has benefited from higher long-term productivity, reduced costs, and happier, more motivated employees.[48] Plum Pictures learned that by using job enrichment they could run pictures on a lower budget.

© Barbara Laing

CONCEPT CONNECTION

*At the Frito-Lay plant in Lubbock, Texas, Julia Garcia used to just pack bags of chips into cardboard cartons. Today, she's interviewing new hires, refusing products that don't meet quality standards, and sending home excess workers if machines shut down. Hourly workers have been enjoying the benefits of **job enlargement** and **job enrichment** since Frito-Lay introduced work teams six years ago. Garcia's 11-member potato chip team is responsible for everything from potato processing to equipment maintenance.*

Plum Pictures

After Graduating from Oxford University in England, Celine Rattray got a job at McKinsey & Co. doing strategic projects for entertainment companies; she later worked for HBO, but always wanted to get into films. Two years ago, she and two of her friends co-founded Plum Pictures, their own production company. While Rattray is good with business processes, the other two partners have strengths in the creative and production areas.

A small film company has almost no leverage. Since no one likes to work for low pay, their challenge is to motivate people in other ways. With low-budget films, they will assign the make-up person to be the lead make-up artist. Rather than paying $10,000 for a script, the writer gets work and credit as a producer, and he helps hire the director and cast.

One of the films—*Lonesome Jim*—made it into Sundance, but it required a lot of persistence and some luck. They really wanted Steve Buscemi for director and were thrilled—and surprised—when he agreed. Rejection is more the norm, whether an actor, director, or investor, they often get from 10 to 100 rejections per day. When things go right, you sell a pitch, make it in to Sundance, and get a movie funded, Rattray knows those are the moments to savor. It is a hard day's night getting there.[49]

Job Characteristics Model

One significant approach to job design is the job characteristics model developed by Richard Hackman and Greg Oldham.[50] Hackman and Oldham's research concerned **work redesign**, which is defined as altering jobs to increase the quality of employees' work experience and their productivity. Hackman and Oldham's research into the design of hundreds of jobs yielded the **job characteristics model**, which is illustrated in Exhibit 13.9. The model consists of three major parts: core job dimensions, critical psychological states, and employee growth-need strength.

work redesign

The altering of jobs to increase both the quality of employees' work experience and their productivity.

**job characteristics
model**

A model of job design that
comprises core job dimen-
sions, critical psychological
states, and employee
growth-need strength.

Core Job Dimensions.　Hackman and Oldham identified five dimensions that determine a job's motivational potential:

1. *Skill variety.* The number of diverse activities that compose a job and the number of
   skills used to perform it. A routine, repetitious, assembly line job is low in variety,
   but an applied research position that entails working on new problems every day
   is high in variety.

2. *Task identity.* The degree to which an employee performs a total job with a recognizable beginning and ending. A chef who prepares an entire meal has more task
   identity than a worker on a cafeteria line who ladles mashed potatoes.

3. *Task significance.* The degree to which the job is perceived as important and
   having impact on the company or consumers. People who distribute penicillin
   and other medical supplies during times of emergencies would feel they have
   significant jobs.

4. *Autonomy.* The degree to which the worker has freedom, discretion, and self-
   determination in planning and carrying out tasks. A house painter can determine how to paint the house; a paint sprayer on an assembly line has little
   autonomy.

5. *Feedback.* The extent to which doing the job provides information back to the
   employee about his or her performance. Jobs vary in their ability to let workers see
   the outcomes of their efforts. A football coach knows whether the team won or lost,
   but a basic research scientist may have to wait years to learn whether a research
   project was successful.

The job characteristics model says that the more these five core characteristics can
be designed into the job, the more the employees will be motivated and the higher will
be performance, quality, and satisfaction.

Critical Psychological States.　The model posits that core job dimensions are more
rewarding when individuals experience three psychological states in response to job
design. In Exhibit 13.9, skill variety, task identity, and task significance tend to influence

EXHIBIT 13.9

*The Job
Characteristics
Model*

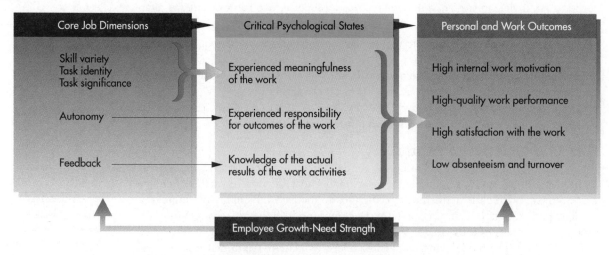

SOURCE: Adapted from J. Richard Hackman and G. R. Oldham, "Motivation through the Design of Work: Test of a Theory,"
Organizational Behavior and Human Performance 16 (1976), 256.

the employee's psychological state of experienced meaningfulness of work. The work itself is satisfying and provides intrinsic rewards for the worker. The job characteristic of autonomy influences the worker's experienced responsibility. The job characteristic of feedback provides the worker with knowledge of actual results. The employee thus knows how he or she is doing and can change work performance to increase desired outcomes.

Personal and Work Outcomes. The impact of the five job characteristics on the psychological states of experienced meaningfulness, responsibility, and knowledge of actual results leads to the personal and work outcomes of high work motivation, work performance, satisfaction, and low absenteeism and turnover.

Employee Growth-Need Strength. The final component of the job characteristics model is called employee growth-need strength, which means that people have different needs for growth and development. If a person wants to satisfy lower-level needs, such as safety and belongingness, the job characteristics model has less effect. When a person has a high need for growth and development, including the desire for personal challenge, achievement, and challenging work, the model is especially effective. People with a high need to grow and expand their abilities respond favorably to the application of the model and to improvements in core job dimensions.

One interesting finding is that there are cross-cultural differences in the impact of job characteristics. Intrinsic factors such as autonomy, challenge, achievement, and recognition can be highly motivating in countries such as the United States. However, they may contribute little to motivation and satisfaction in a country such as Nigeria and might even lead to demotivation. A recent study indicates that the link between intrinsic characteristics and job motivation and satisfaction is weaker in economically disadvantaged countries with poor governmental social welfare systems, and in high power distance countries, as defined in Chapter 3.[51] Thus, the job characteristics model would be expected to be less effective in these countries.

Motivational Ideas for Turbulent Times

Despite the controversy over carrot-and-stick motivational practices discussed in the Focus on Skills box earlier in this chapter, organizations are increasingly using various types of incentive compensation as a way to motivate employees to higher levels of performance. Exhibit 13.10 summarizes several methods of incentive pay.

Variable compensation and forms of "at risk" pay are key motivational tools and are becoming more common than fixed salaries at many companies. These programs can be effective if they are used appropriately and combined with motivational ideas that provide employees with intrinsic rewards and meet higher-level needs. Effective organizations do not use incentive plans as the sole basis of motivation.

In addition, many organizations give employees a voice in how pay and incentive systems are designed, which increases motivation by increasing employees' sense of involvement and control.[52] At Premium Standard Farms' pork processing plant, for example, managers hired a consultant to help slaughterhouse workers design and implement an incentive program. Annual payouts to employees in one recent year were around $1,000 per employee. More important, though, is that workers feel a greater sense of dignity and purpose in their jobs, which has helped to reduce turnover. As one employee put it, "Now I have the feeling that this is my company, too."[53] The most

EXHIBIT 13.10

New Motivational Compensation Programs

Program	Purpose
Pay for performance	Rewards individual employees in proportion to their performance contributions. Also called *merit pay*.
Gain sharing	Rewards all employees and managers within a business unit when predetermined performance targets are met. Encourages teamwork.
Employee Stock Ownership Plan (ESOP)	Gives employees part ownership of the organization, enabling them to share in improved profit performance.
Lump-sum bonuses	Rewards employees with a one-time cash payment based on performance.
Pay for knowledge	Links employee salary with the number of task skills acquired. Workers are motivated to learn the skills for many jobs, thus increasing company flexibility and efficiency.
Flexible work schedule	*Flextime* allows workers to set their own hours. *Job sharing* allows two or more part-time workers to jointly cover one job. *Telecommuting*, sometimes called *flex-place*, allows employees to work from home or an alternative workplace.
Team-based compensation	Rewards employees for behavior and activities that benefit the team, such as cooperation, listening, and empowering others.
Lifestyle awards	Rewards employees for meeting ambitious goals with luxury items, such as high-definition televisions, tickets to big-name sporting events, and exotic travel.

effective motivational programs typically involve much more than money or other external rewards. Two recent motivational trends are empowering employees and framing work to have greater meaning.

Empowering People to Meet Higher Needs

One significant way managers can meet higher motivational needs is to shift power down from the top of the organization and share it with subordinates to enable them to achieve goals. **Empowerment** is power sharing, the delegation of power or authority to subordinates in an organization.[54] Increasing employee power heightens motivation for task accomplishment because people improve their own effectiveness, choosing how to do a task and using their creativity.[55] Most people come into an organization with the desire to do a good job, and empowerment releases the motivation that exists. Research indicates that most people have a need for self-efficacy, which is the capacity to produce results or outcomes, to feel they are effective.[56] By meeting higher-level needs, empowerment can provide powerful motivation.

Empowering employees involves giving them four elements that enable them to act more freely to accomplish their jobs: information, knowledge, power, and rewards.[57]

1. *Employees receive information about company performance.* In companies where employees are fully empowered, such as Semco, a Brazilian manufacturing company, all employees have access to all financial and operational information.

2. *Employees have knowledge and skills to contribute to company goals.* Companies use training programs to help employees acquire the knowledge and skills they need to contribute to organizational performance. For example, when DMC, which makes pet supplies, gave employee teams the authority and responsibility for assembly-line shutdowns, it provided extensive training on how to diagnose and interpret

Take ACTION

As a leader, remember most people want to do well, to improve, so give them chances to learn and become more proficient.

line malfunctions, as well as the costs related to shut down and start up its machines. Employees worked through several case studies to practice decision making related to line shut-downs.[58]

3. *Employees have the power to make substantive decisions.* Workers have the direct authority to influence work procedures and organizational performance, often through quality circles or self-directed work teams. Semco pushes empowerment to the limits by allowing its employees to choose what they do, how they do it, and even how they get compensated for it. Employees set their own pay by choosing from a list of 11 different pay options, such as set salary or a combination of salary and incentives.[59]

4. *Employees are rewarded based on company performance.* Organizations that empower workers often reward them based on the results shown in the company's bottom line. For example, at Semco, in addition to employee-determined compensation, a company profit sharing plan gives each employee an even share of 23 percent of his or her department's profits each quarter.[60] Organizations may also use other motivational compensation programs described in Exhibit 13.10 to tie employee efforts to company performance.

Many of today's organizations are implementing empowerment programs, but they are empowering workers to varying degrees. At some companies, empowerment means encouraging workers' ideas while managers retain final authority for decisions; at others it means giving employees almost complete freedom and power to make decisions and exercise initiative and imagination.[61] Current methods of empowerment fall along a continuum, as illustrated in Exhibit 13.11. The continuum runs from a situation in which front-line workers have almost no discretion, such as on a traditional assembly line, to full empowerment, where workers participate in formulating organizational strategy. Studies indicate that higher-level empowerment programs are still relatively rare.[62] One U.S. company that has developed a high-level empowerment program is Delta Air Lines.

Delta Air Lines

Delta, like all the major airlines, has experienced tremendous uncertainty and turmoil since the events of September 11, 2001, caused the airline industry to change forever. Every big airline has suffered a dramatic drop in passenger traffic and revenue and has been forced to reduce capacity and cut costs. The difference at Delta from the other major carriers is that employees throughout the company have had a big voice in how the airline responded to current challenges.

Delta Air Lines has developed one of the most advanced and comprehensive empowerment programs in the country, ensuring that employees share in information, decision making, risks, and rewards. One element is the Delta Board Council (DBC), made up of seven peer-selected employees representing the seven major employee divisions. The DBC serves as the "eyes, ears, and voice of Delta people from the boardroom to the breakroom." These seven employees serve full time for two years and provide employee input at the top executive and board of directors level on the entire range of business issues. The DBC was actively involved in selecting Delta's current CEO, Leo Mullin, for instance, and worked with top managers to ensure employees' concerns and suggestions were addressed in a recent compensation review.

Other elements of Delta's empowerment program include division-level employee councils, continuous improvement teams, and local-level employee councils. At each level, employees are provided with the information they need to fully contribute to decision making.[63]

SOURCES: Based on Robert C. Ford and Myron D. Fottler, "Empowerment: A Matter of Degree," *Academy of Management Executive* 9, no. 3 (1995), 21–31; Lawrence Holpp, "Applied Empowerment" *Training* (February 1994), 39–44; and David P. McCaffrey, Sue R. Faerman, and David W. Hart, "The Appeal and Difficulties of Participative Systems," *Organization Science* 6, no. 6 (November–December 1995), 603–627.

EXHIBIT 13.11

A Continuum of Empowerment

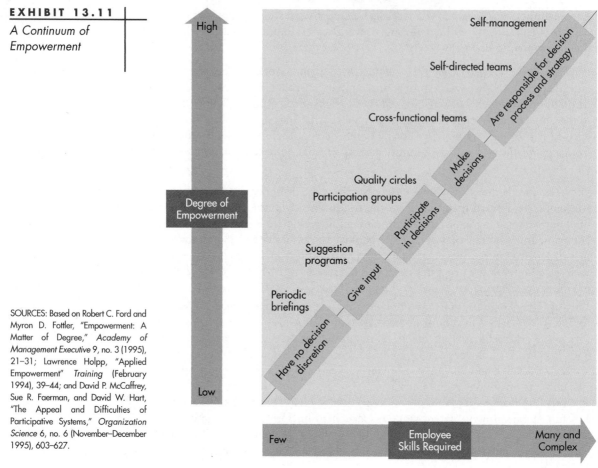

This example touches on a few of the elements of Delta's empowerment program, which operates on various levels throughout the organization. Taken together, these elements ensure employees have input and decision making power related to everyday operational issues and higher-level strategic decisions.

Giving Meaning to Work

Another way to meet higher-level motivational needs and help people get intrinsic rewards from their work is to instill a sense of importance and meaningfulness. Consider that people who work for a social cause or mission are often more highly motivated. David Maxwell understood this when he was brought in to save the troubled mortgage lender, the Federal National Mortgage Association, (Fannie Mae or FNMA) in the early 1980s. At the time, Fannie Mae was losing $1 million a day. Maxwell began a transformation by instilling employees with a sense of importance for the job he was asking them to do. Maxwell helped employees understand that if Fannie Mae did its job well, people who had traditionally been excluded from home ownership, such as immigrants and minorities, could more easily claim their piece of the American dream. Many employees poured their hearts and souls into saving the organization because they looked at it as a way to strengthen America's social fabric.[64]

Another example is Les Schwab, founder of Les Schwab Tire Centers. Schwab has created an organization where employees feel like partners united toward a goal of making people's lives easier. Stores fix flats free, and some have been known to install tires hours before opening time for an emergency trip. Employees frequently stop to help stranded motorists. Schwab rewards people with a generous profit-sharing plan for everyone and promotes store managers solely from within. However, these external rewards only supplement, not create, the high motivation Schwab's employees feel.[65]

Smart managers know that the way to create engaged, motivated employees and high performance has less to do with extrinsic rewards such as pay and more to do with fostering an environment in which people feel that they are making a genuine contribution. In addition, there is a growing recognition that the behavior of managers makes the biggest difference in employee motivation and whether people flourish in the workplace. A Gallup Organization study conducted over 25 years found that the single most important variable in whether employees feel good about their work is the relationship between employees and their direct supervisors.[66]

The role of today's manager is not to control others but to organize the workplace in such a way that each person can learn, contribute, and grow. Good managers channel employee motivation toward the accomplishment of organizational goals by tapping into each individual's unique set of talents, skills, interests, attitudes, and needs. Judy George, CEO of Domain Home Fashions learned to do this the hard way: She was fired from her last job because she did not engage her employees. "I treated everybody like they were all Judy Georges running around," she says now. "After I was fired, I began to realize not everybody operated the same way I did." George made a conscious decision when she founded Domain to hire people with different personalities, skills, and interests, and then listen to what they needed to help them be their best.[67] By treating each employee as an individual, managers can put people in the right jobs and provide intrinsic rewards to every employee every day. Then, managers make sure people have what they need to perform, clearly define the desired outcomes, and get out of the way.

One way to evaluate how a manager or a company is doing in meeting higher-level needs is a metric developed by the Gallup researchers called the Q12. When a majority of employees can answer these 12 questions positively, the organization enjoys a highly motivated and productive workforce:

1. Do I know what is expected of me at work?

2. Do I have the materials and equipment that I need to do my work right?

3. At work, do I have the opportunity to do what I do best every day?

4. In the past seven days, have I received recognition or praise for doing good work?

5. Does my supervisor, or someone at work, seem to care about me as a person?

6. Is there someone at work who encourages my development?

7. At work, do my opinions seem to count?

8. Does the mission or purpose of my company make me feel that my job is important?

9. Are my coworkers committed to doing quality work?

10. Do I have a best friend at work?

11. In the past six months, has someone at work talked to me about my progress?

12. This past year, have I had opportunities to learn and grow?[68]

Results of the Gallup study show that organizations where employees give high marks on the Q12 have less turnover, are more productive and profitable, and enjoy greater employee and customer loyalty.[69] When employees are more engaged and motivated, they—and their organizations—thrive.

Manager's Solution

This chapter introduced a number of important ideas about the motivation of people in organizations. Rewards are of two types: intrinsic rewards that result from the satisfaction a person receives in the process of performing a job, and extrinsic rewards such as promotions that are given by another person. Managers work to help employees receive intrinsic and extrinsic rewards from their jobs. The content theories of motivation focus on the nature of underlying employee needs. Maslow's hierarchy of needs, Alderfer's ERG theory, Herzberg's two-factor theory, and McClelland's acquired needs theory all suggest that people are motivated to meet a range of needs. Process theories examine how people go about selecting rewards with which to meet needs. Equity theory says that people compare their contributions and outcomes with others' and are motivated to maintain a feeling of equity. Expectancy theory suggests that people calculate the probability of achieving certain outcomes. Managers can increase motivation by treating employees fairly and by clarifying employee paths toward meeting their needs. Goal-setting theory indicates that employees are more motivated if they have clear, specific goals and receive regular feedback concerning their progress toward meeting goals. Another motivational approach is reinforcement theory, which says that employees learn to behave in certain ways based on the use of reinforcements.

The application of motivational ideas is illustrated in job design and other motivational programs. Job design approaches include job simplification, job rotation, job enlargement, job enrichment, and the job characteristics model. Managers can change the structure of work to meet employees' higher-level needs. The recent trend toward empowerment motivates by giving employees more information and authority to make decisions in their work while connecting compensation to the results. Managers can instill employees with a sense of importance and meaningfulness to help them reap intrinsic rewards and meet higher level needs for esteem and self-fulfillment. Managers create the environment that determines employee motivation. One way to measure the factors that determine whether people have high levels of engagement and motivation is the Q12, a list of 12 questions about the daily realities of a person's job.

Sadie Christianson got a chance to be motivated at her new job with the Minneapolis-based startup PrairieStone Pharmacy. All the drudgery is gone, as she has at her fingertips automated devices that dispense the most commonly requested drugs, along with an elaborate bar-coded system that helps her track her assistant's accuracy. Rather than being spaced out on horizontally long shelves, the drugs are placed in a high-tech vertically high (going into the ceiling) storage unit, which means she never has to move more than a few steps from her customers, who now get 100 percent more of her attention. The system is designed to turn around prescription requests more quickly and free workers from the mind-numbing parts of the job and let them focus on customers. With a dozen locations and 20 more in the works, PrairieStone is headed to become "the Starbucks of pharmacies." It has been so successful that Betsy Buy is talking to them to find a way to bring extra services to time-strapped female customers. PrairieStone is not resting on its laurels. Two new innovations are coming soon: an ATM-like device to refill prescriptions and a kiosk for new prescriptions, linked by TV to a real pharmacist. Their ultimate goal is to automate all manual procedures, so the pharmacist becomes an "absolute consultant." Now is that high motivation?[70]

Discussion Questions

1. Low-paid service workers represent a motivational problem for many companies. Consider the ill-trained and poorly motivated X-ray machine operators trying to detect weapons in airports. How might these people be motivated to reduce boredom and increase their vigilance?

2. One small company recognizes an employee of the month, who is given a parking spot next to the president's space near the front door. What theories would explain the positive motivation associated with this policy?

3. One executive argues that managers have too much stability because of benefit and retirement plans. He rewards his managers for taking risks and has removed many guaranteed benefits. Would this approach motivate managers? Why?

4. Would you rather work for a supervisor high in need for achievement, need for affiliation, or need for power? Why? What are the advantages and disadvantages of each?

5. A survey of teachers found that two of the most important rewards were the belief that their work was important and a feeling of accomplishment. Is this consistent with Hackman and Oldham's job characteristics model?

6. Many organizations use sales contests and motivational speakers to energize salespeople to overcome frequent rejections and turndowns. How would these devices help motivate salespeople?

7. What characteristics of individuals determine the extent to which work redesign will have a positive impact on work satisfaction and work effectiveness?

Manager's Workbook

What Motivates You?

You are to indicate how important each characteristic is to you. Answer according to your feelings about the most recent job you had or about the job you currently hold. Circle the number on the scale that represents your feeling—1 (very unimportant) to 7 (very important).

When you have completed the questionnaire, score it as follows:

Rating for question 5 = _____, then divide by 1 _____ = security.

Rating for questions 9 and 13 = _____, then divide by 2 = _____ social.

Rating for questions 1, 3, and 7 = _____. Divide by 3 = _____ esteem.

Rating for questions 4, 10, 11, and 12 = _____. Divide by 4 = _____ autonomy.

Rating for questions 2, 6, and 8 = _____. Divide by 3 = _____ self-actualization.

The instructor has national norm scores for presidents, vice presidents, and upper middle-level, lower middle-level, and lower-level managers with which you can compare your mean importance scores. How do your scores compare with the scores of managers working in organizations?

1. The feeling of self-esteem a person gets from being in that job
   1 2 3 4 5 6 7

2. The opportunity for personal growth and development in that job
   1 2 3 4 5 6 7

3. The prestige of the job inside the company (that is, regard received from others in the company)
   1 2 3 4 5 6 7

4. The opportunity for independent thought and action in that job
   1 2 3 4 5 6 7

5. The feeling of security in that job
   1 2 3 4 5 6 7

6. The feeling of self-fulfillment a person gets from being in that position (that is, the feeling of being able to use one's own unique capabilities, realizing one's potential)
   1 2 3 4 5 6 7

7. The prestige of the job outside the company (that is, the regard received from others not in the company)
   1 2 3 4 5 6 7

8. The feeling of worthwhile accomplishment in that job
   1 2 3 4 5 6 7

9. The opportunity in that job to give help to other people
   1 2 3 4 5 6 7

10. The opportunity in that job for participation in the setting of goals
    1 2 3 4 5 6 7

11. The opportunity in that job for participation in the determination of methods and procedures
    1 2 3 4 5 6 7

12. The authority connected with the job
    1 2 3 4 5 6 7

13. The opportunity to develop close friendships in the job
    1 2 3 4 5 6 7

SOURCE: Lyman W. Porter, *Organizational Patterns of Managerial Job Attitudes* (New York: American Foundation for Management Research, 1964), pp. 17, 19.

Manager's Workshop

Hey, That's Not Fair!

These six vignettes depict situations in which the Brady kids have perceived an unfair situation. For each vignette, identify the equity theory method (change inputs, change outcomes, distort perceptions, or leave the situation) that you feel the Brady kids should employ. Then, in groups of four to six discuss which method is most relevant for each situation.

1. Greg just found out that Tommy has been picked by the coach to be the new quarterback for the football team because his dad and the coach are old high school buddies. He is really bummed because that is the position he has been hoping to play ever since junior high.

2. Marcia was upset about being turned down for the job of emcee for the school talent show, but she was even more bothered by the fact that the director of the show made her wait for half an hour and was rude and inconsiderate when giving her feedback about her tryout performance. To top it off, she found out later the person chosen as emcee was the homecoming queen.

3. Jan studied about five hours for her geometry final, but her friend Sue only spent about 30 minutes cramming at the last minute. They just got back their test results today—much to Jan's surprise, she only got a B−, but Sue got an A!

4. Peter has been working really hard at the malt shop for the last six months, doing extra chores and helping out other employees when they needed it. The manager of the store just told him that he was going to give him a raise, but Peter is frustrated by the fact that it's only an extra 15¢ an hour. He thought he deserved more. Then

yesterday he found out that the new guy hired just two months ago got the same raise.

5. Bobby and his friend Dennis just finished doing a bunch of yard work for Mr. Wilson. Bobby worked nonstop, rarely taking a break, but Dennis kept goofing off and playing around. In the end Mr. Wilson gave them both the same amount of money, which Bobby didn't think was right.

6. Cindy is upset because her science teacher selected three other people to compete in the upcoming science fair without first asking if anybody wanted to volunteer to participate in it.

SOURCE: Courtney Hunt, Northern Illinois University, "Must See TV: The Timelessness of Television as a Teaching Tool," presented at Academy of Management, August 2000. Used with permission.

Management in Practice: Ethical Dilemma

Compensation Showdown

When Suzanne Lebeau, human resources manager, received a call from Bert Wilkes, comptroller of Farley Glass Works, she anticipated hearing good news to share with the Wage and Bonus Committee. She had already seen numbers to indicate that the year-end bonus plan, which was instituted by her committee in lieu of the traditional guaranteed raises of the past, was going to exceed expectations. It was a real relief to her, because the plan, devised by a committee representing all levels of the workforce, had taken eleven months to complete. It had also been a real boost to morale at a low point in the company's history. Workers at the glass shower production plant were bringing new effort and energy to their jobs, and Lebeau wanted to see them rewarded.

She was shocked to see Wilkes's face so grim when she arrived for her meeting. "We have a serious problem, Suzanne," Wilkes said to open the meeting. "We ran the numbers from third quarter to project our end-of-the-year figures and discovered that the executive bonus objectives, which are based on net operating profit, would not be met if we paid out the employee bonuses first. The executive bonuses are a major source of their income. We can't ask them to do without their salary to ensure a bonus for the workers."

Lebeau felt her temper rising. After all their hard work, she was not going to sit by and watch the employees be

disappointed because the accounting department had not structured the employee bonus plan to work with the executive plan. She was afraid they would undo all the good that the bonus plan had done in motivating the plant workers. They had kept their end of the bargain, and the company's high profits were common knowledge in the plant.

What Do You Do?

1. Ask to appear before the executive committee to argue that the year-end bonus plan for workers be honored. Executives could defer their bonuses until the problem in the structure of the compensation plan is resolved.

2. Go along with the comptroller. It isn't fair for the executives to lose so much money. Begin to prepare the workers to not expect much this first year of the plan.

3. Go to the board of directors and ask for a compromise plan that splits the bonuses between the executives and the workers.

SOURCE: Based on Doug Wallace, "Promises to Keep," *What Would You Do?* (reprinted from *Business Ethics*), vol. II (July–August 1993), pp. 11–12. Reprinted with permission from *Business Ethics Magazine*, P.O. Box 8439, Minneapolis, MN 55408, (612) 879-0695.

Case for Critical Analysis

Bloomingdale's

Bloomingdale's is at the forefront of a quiet revolution sweeping department store retailing. Thousands of hourly sales employees are being converted to commission pay. Bloomingdale's hopes to use commissions to motivate employees to work harder, to attract better salespeople, and to enable them to earn more money. For example, under the old plan, a Bloomingdale's salesclerk in women's wear would earn about $16,000 a year, based on $7 per hour and 0.5 percent commission on $500,000 sales. Under the new plan, the annual pay would be $25,000 based on 5 percent commission on $500,000 sales.

John Palmerio, who works in the men's shoe salon, is enthusiastic about the changeover. His pay has increased an average of $175 per week. But in women's lingerie, employees are less enthusiastic. A target of $1,600 in sales per week is difficult to achieve but is necessary for salespeople to earn their previous salary and even to keep their jobs. In previous years, the practice of commission pay was limited to big-ticket items such as furniture, appliances, and men's suits, where extra sales skill pays off. The move into small-item purchases may not work as well, but Bloomingdale's and other stores are trying anyway.

One question is whether Bloomingdale's can create more customer-oriented salespeople when they work on commission. They may be reluctant to handle complaints, make returns, and clean shelves, preferring instead to chase customers. Moreover, it cost Bloomingdale's about $1 million per store to install the commission system because of training programs, computer changes, and increased pay in many departments. If the overall impact on service is negative, the increased efficiency may not seem worthwhile.

Questions

1. What theories about motivation underlie the switch from salary to commission pay?

2. Are high-level needs met under the commission system?

3. As a customer, would you prefer to shop where employees are motivated to make commissions?

SOURCES: Based on Francine Schwadel, "Chain Finds Incentives a Hard Sell," *The Wall Street Journal*, July 5, 1990, p. B4; and Amy Dunkin, "Now Salespeople Really Must Sell for Their Supper," *Business Week*, July 31, 1989, pp. 50–52.

CHAPTER

14

Communicating in Organizations

LEARNING OBJECTIVES

After studying this chapter, you should be able to do the following:

1. **Explain why communication is essential for effective management and describe how nonverbal behavior and listening affect communication among people.**

2. **Explain how managers use communication to persuade and influence others.**

3. **Describe the concept of channel richness, and explain how communication channels influence the quality of communication.**

4. **Explain the difference between formal and informal organizational communications and the importance of each for organization management.**

5. **Identify how structure influences team communication outcomes.**

6. **Explain why open communication, dialogue, and feedback are essential approaches to communication in a turbulent environment.**

7. **Identify the skills managers need for communicating during a crisis situation.**

8. **Describe barriers to organizational communication, and suggest ways to avoid or overcome them.**

Bill Ernstrom was like a lot of other CEOs in technology companies. He could not get his engineers at the Colorado-based Voyant Technologies to listen to the marketing department. It got worse after a costly mistake, resulting from his chief engineer mentioning that some customers wanted streaming media built into their flagship product, RediVoice. It seemed like a good idea, so Ernstrom gave the go-ahead. Four months later and $200,000 poorer, the CEO discovered his customers did not care about streaming anything.

Realizing this was not an uncommon problem did not help Ernstrom, who could not see any solution to the Grand Canyon-sized gulf between computer geeks and the suits. Ernstrom had seen it repeatedly happen. In early stages of a project, engineers have the control. So, they end up designing and manufacturing elegant products no one wants to buy. Remember Apple's Newton or the G4 or Atari's Falcon? Ernstrom realized he needed to solve this problem if his company was going to remain profitable. He hired more business people, redesigned floor plans to change office arrangements, and changed the compensation package. Finally, he hit on what he thought was a solution—he hired four managers to head up each of the four product lines, thinking they would bring balance between engineering and marketing. But the engineers did not trust the new product managers, considering them interlopers who had little knowledge about the company's culture or technology. Ernstrom was at his wits end. Nothing was working.[1]

If you were Bill Ernstrom, what would you do to help engineering listen more to marketing and the other business associates?

Consider another high-pressure communication situation. Patrick Charmel faced one of the most difficult decisions of his career as president and CEO of Griffin Hospital, located in Derby, Connecticut. It started when a 94-year-old patient checked into the hospital complaining of flu-like symptoms—no one was particularly alarmed. After all, elderly people get sick a lot, and it had been a bad year for flu. Within a short time, though, doctors advised Charmel that they suspected the patient, Ollie Lundgren, was suffering from anthrax poisoning. Quick as a blink, word was put out to the state health department, the governor, the FBI, the Centers for Disease Control and Prevention, and other state and federal agencies involved in fighting America's new war against terrorism. The governor and the FBI asked Charmel to keep quiet—even to his own employees—and pretend that this was a normal case of flu until a final analysis confirmed the diagnosis and federal agencies could plan a news conference. They argued that putting out the news would start a panic and do no one any good.[2]

Charmel had to communicate effectively in this crisis. His primary concern was for the safety of his employees and of the larger community. He immediately scheduled informational meetings with employees throughout the hospital to let them know about the possible case of anthrax and to review guidelines and procedures for handling such a crisis. Prior to making the information public, Charmel gathered as much information and data as he could and sought the counsel of trusted advisors. Ultimately, he decided honesty was the best policy. Rather than shunning publicity, Charmel welcomed reporters. Along with members of his management team and several physicians, Charmel told the media and the public what was happening with the case throughout the night and into the next day, when the diagnosis of anthrax poisoning was confirmed and Mrs. Lundgren died. Most news stories related to anthrax poisonings in organizations such as the U.S. Postal Service, newsrooms, and the U.S. Congress focused on the failure of these organizations to deal with the crisis adequately. The news stories of Griffin Hospital, instead, looked to the hope and strength that comes from putting people first and meeting challenges with honesty and openness. "Our concern," said Charmel, "was for the patient, the employees who work here, and the health of our community."[3]

Charmel believes in open communication, but he had some advisors telling him to keep quiet. This dilemma could confront any manager in today's turbulent environment, where crisis communication is at the top of everyone's needed skills list. Derby, Connecticut, is a place where no one would ever expect an anthrax scare, and Charmel never expected to find himself in such a fix.

Effective communication, within the organization and without, is a major challenge and responsibility for managers. In today's uncertain and intensely competitive environment, managers at many companies are improving their communications knowledge and skills. To break down communication barriers at Guidant Corporation, owned by pharmaceutical giant Eli Lilly, CEO Ginger Graham assigned each top manager a coach from within lower levels of the organization. The coaches were trained to ask questions and gather information from people throughout the company about the manager's openness and communication skills. With the support of top management, this reverse mentoring program closed a communication gap at Guidant.[4] Michael J. Critelli, chairman and CEO of Pitney Bowes, has more than 150 one-hour "skip-level" meetings a year, where he meets with managers from lower levels of the company to learn what is going on from their point of view. In addition, Critelli takes advantage of opportunities during lunch in the cafeteria or while visiting field offices for impromptu conversations with employees.[5]

To stay connected with employees and customers and shape company direction, managers must excel at interpersonal communication. Nonmanagers are often amazed at how much energy successful executives put into communication. Consider this comment about Robert Strauss, former chairman of the Democratic National Committee and former ambassador to Russia:

> *One of his friends says, "His network is everywhere. It ranges from bookies to bank presidents...."*
>
> *He seems to find time to make innumerable phone calls to "keep in touch"; he cultivates secretaries as well as senators; he will befriend a middle-level White House aide whom other important officials will not bother with. Every few months, he sends candy to the White House switchboard operators.*[6]

This chapter explains why executives such as Robert Strauss, Michael Critelli, and Ginger Graham are effective communicators. First, we will see how managers' jobs require communication and describe a model of the communication process. Next, we will consider the interpersonal aspects of communication, including communication channels, persuasion, listening skills, and nonverbal communication, all which affect managers' ability to communicate. Then, we will look at the organization as a whole and consider formal upward, downward, and horizontal communications as well as personal networks and informal communications. We will discuss the importance of keeping multiple channels of communication open and examine how managers can effectively communicate during times of turbulence, uncertainty, and crisis. Finally, we will examine barriers to communication and how managers can overcome them.

> **Take ACTION**
>
> As a manager, keep in touch with all your employees, find out what is going on, and learn to listen.

Communication and the Manager's Job

How important is communication? Consider this: Managers spend at least 80 percent of every working day in direct communication with others. In other words, 48 minutes of every hour is spent in meetings, on the telephone, communicating online, or talking informally while walking around. The other 20 percent of a typical manager's time is spent doing desk work, most of which is communication in the form of reading and writing.[7]

Exhibit 14.1 illustrates the crucial role of managers as communication champions (and information nerve center). Managers gather important information from inside and outside the organization and then distribute appropriate information to others who need it.

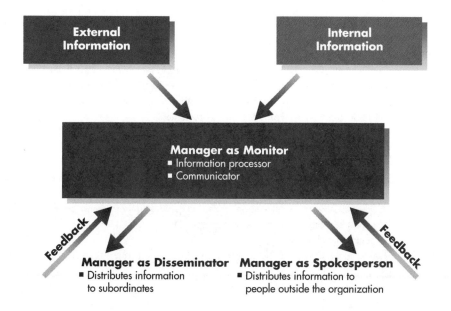

EXHIBIT 14.1

The Manager as Information Nerve Center

SOURCE: Adapted from Henry Mintzberg, *The Nature of Managerial Work* (New York: Harper & Row, 1973), 72.

strategic conversation

Dialogue across boundaries and hierarchical levels about the team's or organization's vision, critical strategic themes, and the values that help achieve important goals.

Managers' communication is purpose-directed in that it directs everyone's attention toward the vision, values, and desired goals of the team or organization and influences people to act in a way to achieve these goals. Managers facilitate strategic conversations by using open communication, actively listening to others, applying the practice of dialogue, and using feedback for learning and change. **Strategic conversation** refers to people talking across boundaries and hierarchical levels about the team's or organization's vision, critical strategic themes, and the values that help achieve important goals.[8] For example, at Royal Philips Electronics, president Gerald Kleisterlee defined four strategic technology themes that he believes should define Philips' future in the industry: display, storage, connectivity, and digital video processing. These themes intentionally cross technology boundaries, which requires that people communicate and collaborate across departments and divisions to accomplish goals.[9] Effective managers use many communication methods, including selecting "rich" channels of communication, facilitating upward, downward, and horizontal communication, understanding and using nonverbal communication, and building informal communication networks that cross organization boundaries.

One good example of a manager as communication champion is David Neeleman, CEO of the fast-growing, low-fare airline, JetBlue. Neeleman demonstrates a genuine commitment to communication by regularly going on flights to talk with customers and employees, as described in the Focus on Leadership box.

Communication permeates every management function described in Chapter 1.[10] For example, when managers plan, they gather information, write letters, memos, and reports, and meet with other managers to formulate the plan. When managers lead, they communicate to share a vision of what the organization can be and motivate employees to achieve it. When managers organize, they gather information about the state of the organization and communicate a new structure to others. Communication skills are a fundamental part of every managerial activity.

Take ACTION

As a manager, make it a point to talk to people who are outside your group, finding out what is happening in other departments and how they see the situation; do not stay in your own clique.

FOCUS ON LEADERSHIP

JetBlue CEO Walks His Talk—Up and Down the Airplane Aisles

On a recent flight from New York to California, passengers on JetBlue had an unusual experience: being served by the company's CEO, Dave Neeleman. Neeleman cheerfully joined other flight attendants in passing out snacks even though it took him hours to get through the plane because he stopped to chat with anyone who wanted to talk.

As it turns out, this was common. Neeleman tries to come on flights and talk to customers at least once a month. He says it is where he gets his best ideas for JetBlue. As JetBlue grows, Neeleman is making a conscious effort to ensure he does not lose contact with the people who made the company a success. As he slowly makes his way through the plane, Neeleman listens to complaints, answers questions, and helps passengers network with other people on the plane who share their interests.

Serving as a flight attendant strengthens communication with employees, who say they bump into Neeleman all the time

in their jobs. His actions serve as a symbolic, nonverbal communication to employees of the importance of customer service. People see him going out of his way to help customers and they feel inspired to do the same. They see him putting in overtime when he could easily stay in his office and go home at the end of the day, and they think of him as one of the team. As a result, a high level of trust, respect, and goodwill exists between employees and managers at JetBlue, as well as between the company and its customers.

Another advantage of Neeleman's efforts is that it facilitates and improves upward communication. Not only do employees like the chance to talk with Neeleman informally, the CEO also gets to see first hand what employees go through and how management's actions affect them. Employees feel that Neeleman understands what is happening on the front lines because he has been there.

SOURCE: Norm Brodsky, "Learning From JetBlue" *Inc.* (March 2004): 59–60.

What Is Communication?

A professor at Harvard once asked a class to define communication by drawing pictures. Most students drew a manager typing on a computer keyboard or speaking. Some placed "speech balloons" next to their characters; others showed pages flying from a laser printer. "No," the professor told the class, "none of you has captured the essence of communication." He went on to explain that communication means "to share" and not "to speak" or "to write."

Communication can be defined as the process by which information is exchanged and understood by two or more people, usually with the intent to motivate or influence behavior. Communication is not just sending information. Honoring this distinction between sharing and proclaiming is crucial for successful management. A manager who does not listen is like a used-car salesperson who claims, "I sold a car. They just did not buy it." Management communication is a two-way street that includes listening and other forms of feedback. Effective communication, in the words of one expert, is as follows:

> *When two people interact, they put themselves into each other's shoes, try to perceive the world as the other person perceives it, try to predict how the other will respond. Interaction involves reciprocal role-taking, the mutual employment of empathetic skills. The goal of interaction is the merger of self and other, a complete ability to anticipate, predict, and behave in accordance with the joint needs of self and other.*[11]

The desire to share understanding motivates executives to visit employees on the shop floor, hold small, informal meetings, or eat with employees in the company cafeteria. The knowledge managers get from direct communication with employees shape their understanding of the organization.

The Communication Process

Many people think communication is simple. After all, we communicate every day without thinking about it. However, communication is usually complex, and the opportunities for sending or receiving the wrong messages are innumerable. No doubt, you have heard someone say, "But that is not what I meant." Have you ever received directions you thought were clear, yet still got lost? How often have you wasted time on misunderstood instructions?

To better understand the complexity of the communication process, note the key elements outlined in Exhibit 14.2. Two common elements in every communication situation are the sender and the receiver. The sender is anyone who wishes to convey an idea or concept to others, to seek information, or to express a thought or emotion. The receiver is the person to whom the message is sent. The sender **encodes** the idea by selecting symbols with which to compose a message. The **message** is the tangible formulation of the idea that is sent to the receiver. The message is sent through a **channel**, which is the communication carrier. The channel can be a formal report, telephone call, e-mail message, or face-to-face meeting. The receiver **decodes** the symbols to interpret the meaning of the message. Encoding and decoding are potential sources for communication errors because knowledge, attitudes, and context act as filters and create noise when translating from symbols to meaning. Finally, **feedback** occurs when the receiver responds to the sender's communication with a return message. Without feedback, the communication is one-way; with feedback, it is two-way. Feedback is a powerful aid to communication effectiveness because it enables the sender to determine whether the receiver correctly interpreted the message. Bruce Woolpert of Granite Rock Company used two-way communication to improve his company's profitability as described next.

communication
The process by which information is exchanged and understood by two or more people, usually with the intent to motivate or influence behavior.

encodes
To select symbols with which to compose a message.

message
The tangible formulation of an idea to be sent to a receiver.

channel
The carrier of a communication.

decodes
To translate the symbols used in a message for the purpose of interpreting its meaning.

feedback
A response by the receiver to the sender's communication.

EXHIBIT 14.2

*A Model of the
Communication
Process*

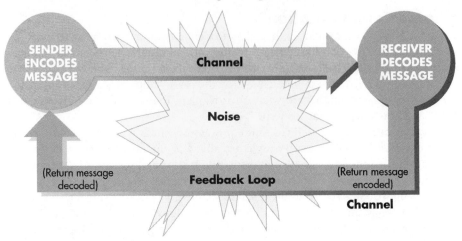

Granite Rock Company

Granite Rock Co. of Watsonville, California, has been owned and operated by the Wilson/Woolpert family for over 100 years but was hit with big changes 15 years ago. The threat of absorption into a conglomerate was added to California's tightening industrial regulations, and customers were clamoring for high-quality materials and more responsive service. However, computer technology to automate quarry work was new and expensive. Granite Rock would have to find new ways of doing business amidst a host of changes and well-financed predators.

Bruce Woolpert, a joint CEO with brother Steve, and an eight-year veteran of Hewlett-Packard (HP), wanted to be as efficient and customer-oriented as HP. First, he got maximum information flowing throughout the company—instead of the industry standard of a dozen internal process controls, Granite Rock kept track of one hundred. Then, Bruce started asking customers to rate the company against competitors on "report cards."

Bruce went out and benchmarked within the company, identifying best practices by visiting cement plants and the quarry. Asking workers what they liked and disliked about their jobs and the company, he set up a model for two-way communication up and down the entire organization. He organized 100 highly-focused "quality" teams of managers and hourly workers to analyze problems. Both groups attended many seminars together. Merging the two groups together increased input and united the company's 736 employees.

Technology and training have made Granite Rock the regions' low-cost producer of crushed rock with annual sales of more than $110 million. Quality and service levels are high enough to allow charging a 6 percent premium and still increase market share. To keep high quality levels, the company offers "short pay," like a restaurant. If you do not like it, you do not pay for it.

The company has embraced many changes, including women truck drivers, something unheard of not long ago. One of them started driving trucks, "because my dad said I couldn't." Granite Rock inspires fierce loyalty among workers. As a result, *Fortune* has listed in among its Top 100 places to work in the past few years, with its ranking moving up to #16 in 2001. Former CEO Betsy Wilson Woolpert, Bruce's mother and daughter of founder Arthur Wilson, says, "Most Granite Rock people remain with us for their entire career. We like that and hope it can be maintained."[12]

Managers who are effective communicators understand and use the circular nature of communication. Consider Nortel Networks' *Virtual Leadership Academy*, a monthly televised program hosted by Dan Hunt, president of Nortel's Caribbean and Latin American operations, and Emma Carrasco, vice president of marketing and communications. Hunt and Carrasco use a talk-show format to get people talking. Employees from about 40 different countries watch the show from their regional offices and call in their questions and comments. "We're always looking for ways to break down barriers," says Carrasco. "People watch talk shows in every country, and they've learned that it's okay to say what's on their minds."[13] The television program is the channel through which Hunt and Carrasco send their encoded message. Employees decode and interpret the message and encode their feedback, which is sent through the channel of the telephone hookup. The communications circuit is complete.

Communicating among People

The communication model in Exhibit 14.2 illustrates the components that must be mastered for effective communication. Communication can break down if the sender and receiver do not encode or decode language in the same way.[14] We all know how difficult it is to communicate with someone who does not speak our language, and managers in U.S. organizations often communicate with people who speak many different native languages and have limited English skills. However, communication breakdowns can occur between people who speak the same language.

Many factors can lead to a communication breakdown. For example, the selection of the communication channel can determine whether the message is distorted by noise and interference. The listening skills of both parties and attention to nonverbal behavior can determine whether a message is shared. Thus, for managers to be effective communicators, they must understand how factors such as communication channels, nonverbal behavior, and listening work to enhance or detract from communication.

Communication Channels

Managers have a choice of many channels through which to communicate to other managers or employees. A manager may discuss a problem face-to-face, make a telephone call, use instant messaging (IM), send an e-mail, write a memo or letter, or put an item in a newsletter, depending on the nature of the message. Research has attempted to explain how managers select communication channels to enhance communication effectiveness.[15] The research has found that channels differ in their capacity to convey information. Just as a pipeline's physical characteristics limit the kind and amount of liquid that can be pumped through it, a communication channel's physical characteristics limit the kind and amount of information that can be conveyed among managers. The channels available to managers can be classified into a hierarchy based on information richness. **Channel richness** is the amount of information that can be transmitted during a communication episode. The hierarchy (or pyramid) of channel richness is illustrated in Exhibit 14.3.

The capacity of an information channel is influenced by three characteristics: the ability to handle multiple cues simultaneously; the ability to facilitate rapid, two-way feedback; and the ability to establish a personal focus for the communication. Face-to-face discussion is the richest medium because it permits direct experience, multiple information cues, immediate feedback, and personal focus. Face-to-face discussions facilitate the assimilation of broad cues and deep, emotional understanding of the situation. Telephone conversations are next in the richness hierarchy.

channel richness
The amount of information that can be transmitted during a communication episode.

© Deborah Mesa-Pelly

CONCEPT CONNECTION

*Equipped with laptops, pagers, and cell phones, Intel employees can now communicate and collaborate on group projects from anywhere in the world. These forms of communication lack the **channel richness** found in face-to-face discussions. However, new technology such as instant messaging, groupware, and wireless Internet applications enable these devices to facilitate rapid feedback, thus increasing their value for organizational communication.*

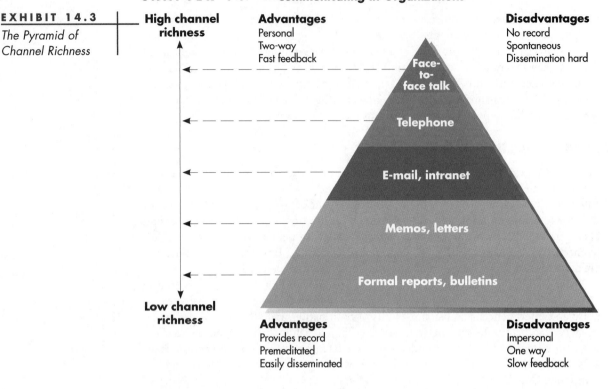

EXHIBIT 14.3

The Pyramid of Channel Richness

High channel richness

Advantages
Personal
Two-way
Fast feedback

Disadvantages
No record
Spontaneous
Dissemination hard

Face-to-face talk

Telephone

E-mail, intranet

Memos, letters

Formal reports, bulletins

Low channel richness

Advantages
Provides record
Premeditated
Easily disseminated

Disadvantages
Impersonal
One way
Slow feedback

Though eye contact, posture, and other body language cues are missing, the human voice can carry a tremendous amount of emotional information. Diddy has learned that face-to-face and direct communication is necessary for business success.

| Sean John | "There will be only three 'Sean John' T-shirts in the coming collection," Sean John Combs said to his designers at his $400 million company, Sean John. Some of the designers were not happy, because clothing bearing "Sean John" makes up a large part of the company's revenues. "I'm putting you on rations," he laughed. "From now on, I want people to read the name without seeing the name. You get me?" Though most of the sales now are from baggy-to-the-crotch pants, noticeably branded shirts, and hooded sweatshirts, Diddy, wants to expand beyond the so-called urban market.

Other hip-hop artists have ventured into the fashion field. Among them is Beyonce and Snoop Dogg, but analysts say Combs has the greatest chance of success, partly because he had learned a lot about management and strategy and partly because he keeps control of his own company by being engaged in day-to-day operations. Unlike many other companies, Sean John makes 70 percent of its own clothing. Combs has learned the hard way: with clothing sales flat as the urban look has peaked, and from being distracted running an empire that includes restaurants and music publishing. In order to address these issues, he fired long-time business associate and friend, Jeffrey Tweedy, putting in his stead former Joseph Aboud Apparel CEO Robert J. Wichser. Combs vowed at the recent meeting with his closely-directed designers that he would focus more on the clothing line.

After a two-year lull, clothing sales are up again, but the future depends on the new women's line Combs is launching. Because of his celebrity status, he's able to gain more attention in the marketplace than many other brands. But this "personality muscle" doesn't help much in HR or the boardroom. "You have to invest in executive talent in order to one day own or be part of a *Fortune* 500 company," he said, thinking, "I'm more mature now. I understand. It's all right to need people."[16]

Electronic messaging, such as e-mail and IM, is increasingly being used for messages that were once handled via the telephone. A survey by researchers at The Ohio State University found that about half the respondents reported making fewer telephone calls since they began using e-mail. However, respondents said they preferred the telephone or face-to-face conversation for communicating difficult news, giving advice, or expressing affection.[17] Because e-mail messages lack visual and verbal cues and do not allow for interaction and feedback, messages can sometimes be misunderstood. Using e-mail to discuss disputes, for example, can lead to an escalation rather than a resolution of conflict.[18] This chapter's Focus on Skills box offers some tips for using electronic mail.

Instant messaging (IM) alleviates the problem of miscommunication to some extent by allowing for immediate feedback. **Instant messaging (IM)** allows users to see who is connected to a network and share short-hand messages or documents with them instantly. A growing number of managers and organizations are using IM, indicating that it helps people get responses faster and collaborate more smoothly.[19] In March 2003, 84 percent of companies surveyed in North America reported using IM, and one market research firm predicts 300 million business users worldwide by the end of 2005.[20] Organizations are using interactive meetings over the Internet, sometimes adding video capabilities to provide visual cues and greater channel richness.

One psychiatrist argues that the growing use of technology for communicating has created hidden problems for individuals and organizations by depriving people of the "human moments" needed to energize people, inspire creativity, and support emotional well-being.[21] People need to interact with others in physical space to build the connections that create great organizations. However, some research indicates that electronic messaging can enable reasonably rich communication if the technology is used appropriately.[22]

instant messaging (IM)
Electronic communication that allows users to see who is connected to a network and share information instantly.

Take *ACTION*

Do not use e-mail when you need to send an emotionally charged or complicated message; instead have a face-to-face interaction.

FOCUS ON SKILLS

Make Your E-Mails Count

Electronic communication has many advantages, but the quick and easy nature of e-mail increases the potential for communication errors. Managers can learn to benefit from the tremendous efficiencies of e-mail while preventing its unintended problems. Here are some Dos and Don'ts for using e-mail.

Do

- Keep e-mail messages short and to the point. Use the subject line to convey key, precise information. Bullet points make messages easier to read.
- Remember your manners. Use salutations and proper forms of closing. Turn on your grammar and spell-checker.
- Use e-mail to set up meetings, recap spoken conversations, or follow up on information discussed.
- Use the "out of office" feature to let people know when you are traveling.
- Respond to e-mail messages as quickly as possible, preferably by the end of the same day.
- Slow down and take the time to read your message a couple of times before hitting the Send button.

Don't

- Use e-mail to mock the boss or lambaste a colleague.
- Treat e-mail casually. Never write anything in an e-mail you would not want to see published in a newspaper or broadcast on *60 Minutes*.
- Hire and fire via e-mail. Important, personal, and difficult messages should be conveyed in person or at least by telephone.
- Use profanity. It always looks bad in print, and you can get your point across in other ways.
- Copy to the world. Smart managers use group mail sparingly.
- Use e-mail to start or perpetuate a feud. E-mail should never be used to convey feelings of anger. Take the old-fashioned approach and chew people out in person.

SOURCES: Based on Andrea C. Poe, "Don't Touch That 'Send' Button," *HR Magazine* (July 2001): 74-80; Michael Goldberg, "The Essentials of E-Mail," *CIO* (June 1, 2003): 24; and Jared Sandberg, "Workplace E-Mail Can Turn Radioactive in Clumsy Hands," *The Wall Street Journal* (February 12, 2003): B1.

Lower on the hierarchy of channel richness are written letters and memos. These can be personally focused, but they convey only the cues written on paper and are slow to provide feedback. Impersonal written media, including fliers, bulletins, and standard computer reports, are the lowest in richness. These channels are not focused on a single receiver, use limited information cues, and do not permit feedback.

It is important for managers to understand that each communication channel has advantages and disadvantages, and that each can be an effective means of communication in the appropriate circumstances.[23] Channel selection depends on whether the message is routine or nonroutine. Nonroutine messages typically are ambiguous, concern novel events, and impose great potential for misunderstanding. They are often characterized by time pressure and surprise. Managers can communicate nonroutine messages effectively only by selecting rich channels. Routine messages are simple and straightforward. They convey data or statistics or put into words what managers have agreed on and understand. Routine messages can be efficiently communicated through a channel lower in richness. Written communications should be used when the audience is widely dispersed or when the communication is official and a permanent record is required.[24] E-mail is used so commonly that people often forget to use correct grammar when sending a message for a business reason, as described in the Focus on Collaboration box.

Consider law enforcement personnel working out a press release concerning the sniper shootings in the Washington, D.C., area in the fall of 2002. An immediate response was critical. This type of nonroutine communication forces a rich information exchange. The group should meet face-to-face, brainstorm ideas, and provide rapid feedback to resolve disagreement and convey the correct information. If, in contrast, an agency director is preparing a press release about a routine matter such as a policy change or new K9 training, less information capacity is needed. The director and public relations people might begin developing the press release with an exchange of memos, telephone calls, and e-mail messages.

The key is to select a channel to fit the message. During a major acquisition, one firm decided to send top executives to all major work sites of the acquired company,

---

FOCUS ON COLLABORATION

E-mail Grammar

"I need help," started the unpunctuated e-mail to a business writing professor. "i am writing essay on writing i work for this company and my boss want me to help improve the workers writing skills can yall help me with some information thank you." Dr. Craig Hogan gets hundreds of messages a month like this as people are required to do more and more writing on the job and are messing up. "E-mail is a party to which English teachers have not been invited. It has companies tearing their hair out."

Corporations report that one-third of employees in top companies are poor writers, costing $3.1 billion per year on remedial training. These employers are not asking for Tolstoy; they just want clear, understandable writing.

Dr. Hogan started his online writing course a decade ago and says that use of multiple exclamation points (!!) are all right for personal e-mails, but not for business use. HR departments are having to reteach people how to write professionally.

"E-mail has erupted like a weed, and instead of considering what to say when they write, people now just let their thoughts drool out onto the screen," says Hogan.

SOURCE: Sam Dillon, What Corporate American Can't Build: a Sentence, *The New York Times* (Dec. 7, 2004): 23.

where 75 percent of the workers met the managers in person, heard about their plans for the company, and had a chance to ask questions. The results were well worth the time and expense of the personal meetings because the acquired workforce saw their new managers as understanding, open, and willing to listen.[25] Communicating their nonroutine message about the acquisition in person prevented damaging rumors and misunderstandings. The choice of a communication channel can convey a symbolic meaning to the receiver; in a sense, the medium becomes the message. The firm's decision to communicate face-to-face with the acquired workforce signaled to employees that managers cared about them as individuals.

Communicating to Persuade and Influence Others

Communication is not just for conveying information, but can persuade and influence people as well. Though communication skills have always been important to managers, the ability to persuade and influence others has become more critical. Businesses are run largely by cross-functional teams who are actively involved in making decisions. Issuing directives is no longer an appropriate or effective way to get things done.[26]

To persuade and influence, managers have to communicate frequently and easily with others. Yet some people find interpersonal communication experiences unrewarding or difficult and, thus, tend to avoid situations where communication is required. Many people have a great fear of speaking in front of others, as described in the Focus on Skills box.

The term **communication apprehension** describes this avoidance behavior, and is defined as "an individual's level of fear or anxiety associated with real or anticipated communication." With training and practice, managers can overcome their communication apprehension and become more effective communicators.

communication apprehension

An individual's level of fear or anxiety associated with interpersonal communications.

FOCUS ON SKILLS

Speaking of...Fear

Racing heart, dry mouth, voice a-quiver. You know it. The most common fear: public speaking. What can you do to avoid those times when you are up there, staring at the floor, mumbling and saying mostly "umm"? Here are five tips:

1. Forget childhood. We all have irrational fears that came from childhood, and you can overcome them by changing your beliefs. If you think that doing a bad job means people will not like you, it might paralyze you when you are doing that talk. Work on changing that belief, because it affects how you act.

2. Expose—yourself. Look for the scariest public speaking gig you can find, then confront it face-to-face. Then repeat. The best way to overcome a fear is to face it head on. If you avoid what you fear, those fears become greater over time.

3. Try the basics. If you are oratory-challenged, join an organization like Toastmasters International, whose goal is

to have members speak to one another, overcome their fears, and become fearsome speakers. And it's fun!

4. Do not worry about mistakes. It is how you learn. Some people keep raising the standards for themselves and then anything less sends them into a panic. Take Barbra Streisand. She kept putting more and more pressure on herself until she descended into total stage fright.

5. Medicate yourself. If you tend towards anxiety attacks or racing heart, see a doctor and see if you might need a prescription for a mild dose of beta blocker, which slows the heart a bit. Some people get so worked up, their fight-or-flight response gets out of control.

Do not let an overwhelming fear of speaking before crowds derail your career path. Take charge of your life—and your presentations.

SOURCE: Ryan Underwood, "Speak Easy," *Fast Company* (March 2005): 30.

Take a moment to complete the experiential exercise that pertains to your level of communication apprehension.

Personal Assessment of Communication Apprehension

The questions below are about your feelings toward communication with other people. Indicate the degree to which each statement applies to you by marking (5) Strongly agree, (4) Agree, (3) Are undecided, (2) Disagree, or (1) Strongly disagree. There are no right or wrong answers. Many of the statements are similar to other statements. Do not be concerned about this. Work quickly and record your first impressions.

Strongly disagree   Strongly agree
    1   2   3   4   5

1. When talking in a small group of acquaintances, I am tense and nervous.
    1 2 3 4 5

2. When presenting a talk to a group of strangers, I am tense and nervous.
    1 2 3 4 5

3. When conversing with a friend or colleague, I am calm and relaxed.
    1 2 3 4 5

4. When talking in a large meeting of acquaintances, I am calm and relaxed.
    1 2 3 4 5

5. When presenting a talk to a group of friends or colleagues, I am tense and nervous.
    1 2 3 4 5

6. When conversing with an acquaintance or colleague, I am calm and relaxed.
    1 2 3 4 5

7. When talking in a large meeting of strangers, I am tense and nervous.
    1 2 3 4 5

8. When talking in a small group of strangers, I am tense and nervous.
    1 2 3 4 5

9. When talking in a small group of friends or colleagues, I am calm and relaxed.
    1 2 3 4 5

10. When presenting a talk to a group of acquaintances, I am calm and relaxed.
    1 2 3 4 5

11. When I am conversing with a stranger, I am calm and relaxed.
    1 2 3 4 5

12. When talking in a large meeting of friends, I am tense and nervous.
    1 2 3 4 5

13. When presenting a talk to a group of strangers, I am calm and relaxed.
    1 2 3 4 5

14. When conversing with a friend or colleague, I am tense and nervous.
1 2 3 4 5

15. When talking in a large meeting of acquaintances, I am tense and nervous.
1 2 3 4 5

16. When talking in a small group of acquaintances, I am calm and relaxed.
1 2 3 4 5

17. When talking in a small group of strangers, I am calm and relaxed.
1 2 3 4 5

18. When presenting a talk to a group of friends, I am calm and relaxed.
1 2 3 4 5

19. When conversing with an acquaintance or colleague, I am tense and nervous.
1 2 3 4 5

20. When talking in a large meeting of strangers, I am calm and relaxed.
1 2 3 4 5

21. When presenting a talk to a group of acquaintances, I am tense and nervous.
1 2 3 4 5

22. When conversing with a stranger, I am tense and nervous.
1 2 3 4 5

23. When talking in a large meeting of friends or colleagues, I am calm and relaxed.
1 2 3 4 5

24. When talking in a small group of friends or colleagues, I am tense and nervous.
1 2 3 4 5

Scoring:

This questionnaire permits computation of four subscores and one total score. Subscores relate to communication apprehension in four common situations: public speaking, meetings, group discussions, and interpersonal conversations. To compute your scores, add or subtract your scores for each item as indicated next.

Subscore/Scoring Formula

For each subscore, start with 18 points. Then add the scores for the plus (+) items and subtract the scores for the negative (–) items.

Public Speaking

18 + scores for items 2, 5, and 21; – scores for items 10, 13, and 18.

Score = ＿＿＿＿＿＿＿＿

Meetings

18 + scores for items 7, 12, and 15; – scores for items 4, 20, and 23.

Score = ＿＿＿＿＿＿＿＿

Group Discussions

18 + scores for items 1, 8, and 24; – scores for items 9, 16, and 17.

Score = ＿＿＿＿＿＿＿＿

(continued)

Interpersonal Conversations
18 + scores for items 14, 19, and 22; – scores for items 3, 6, and 11.
Score = _____

Total Score
Sum the four scores above for the Total Score _____

Interpretation:

This personal assessment provides an indication of how much apprehension (fear or anxiety) you feel in various communication settings. Total scores may range from 24 to 120. Scores above 72 indicate you are more apprehensive about communication than the average person. Scores above 85 indicate a high level of communication apprehension. Scores below 59 indicate a low level of apprehension. These extreme scores (below 59 and above 85) are generally outside the norm. They suggest the degree of apprehension you may experience in any given situation may not be associated with a realistic response to that communication situation.

Scores on the subscales can range from a low of 6 to a high of 30. Any score above 18 indicates some degree of apprehension. For example, if you score above 18 for the public speaking context, you are like the overwhelming majority of people.

To be a communication champion, you should work to overcome communication anxiety. The interpersonal conversations create the least apprehension for most people, followed by group discussions, larger meetings, and then public speaking. Compare your scores with another student. What aspect of communication creates the most apprehension for you? How do you plan to improve it?

SOURCES: J. C. McCroskey, "Measures of Communication-Bound Anxiety," *Speech Monographs 37* (1970): 269–277; J. C. McCroskey and V. P. Richmond, "Validity of the PRCA as an Index of Oral Communication Apprehension," *Communication Monographs 45* (1978): 192–203; J. C. McCroskey and V. P. Richmond, "The Impact of Communication Apprehension on Individuals in Organizations," *Communication Quarterly 27* (1979): 55–61; J. C. McCroskey, *An Introduction to Rhetorical Communication* (Englewood Cliffs, NJ: Prentice Hall, 1982).

One important way managers influence others is by using symbols, metaphors, and stories to deliver their messages. Stories tap into people's imaginations and emotions, helping managers make sense of a changing environment in ways people can understand and share. When Hubertus von Grünberg was CEO of Germany's Continental AG, he used storytelling to set the company on a path toward transformation. Von Grünberg knew Continental AG, the world's fourth-largest tire company, could never compete as a global player without building alliances and partnerships with other companies, a strategy that went against Continental AG's self-reliant culture. Rather than using facts and figures to persuade others of the need for new partnership strategies, von Grünberg told a story illustrating Continental's shrinking place in a rapidly changing industry. It worked. Managers throughout the company were inspired to begin discussing how Continental AG could increase its global power by sharing its innovation and expertise and in turn learning from others.[27]

Take *ACTION*

When persuading someone, use a compelling story rather than merely facts and information.

If we think of our early school years, we may remember that the most effective lessons often were couched in stories. Presenting hard facts and figures rarely has the same power. Evidence of the compatibility of stories with human thinking was demonstrated by a study at Stanford Business School.[28] The point was to convince MBA students that a company practiced a policy of avoiding layoffs. For some students, only a story was used. For others, statistical data were provided that showed little turnover compared to competitors. For other students, statistics and stories were combined, and yet other students were shown the company's official policy statements. Of all these approaches, the students presented with a vivid story alone were most convinced the company practiced a policy of avoiding layoffs. Managers can learn to use elements of storytelling to enhance their communication.[29] Stories need not be long, complex, or carefully constructed. A story can be a joke, an analogy, or a verbal snapshot of something from the manager's own past experiences.[30]

Nonverbal Communication

Managers use symbols to communicate what is important. Managers are watched, and their behavior, appearance, actions, and attitudes are symbolic of what they value and expect of others.

Most of us have heard the saying that "actions speak louder than words." Indeed, we communicate without words all the time, whether we realize it or not. **Nonverbal communication** refers to messages sent through human actions and behaviors rather than through words.[31] Most managers are astonished to learn that words carry little meaning. Major parts of the shared understanding from communication come from the nonverbal messages of facial expression, voice, mannerisms, posture, and dress.

Nonverbal communication occurs mostly face-to-face. One researcher found three sources of communication cues during face-to-face communication: the verbal source, which is the actual spoken words; the vocal source, which includes the pitch, tone, and timbre of a person's voice; and facial expressions. According to this study, the relative weights of these three factors in message interpretation are as follows: verbal impact, 7 percent; vocal impact, 38 percent; and facial impact, 55 percent.[32] To some extent, we are all natural face readers. Managers can hone this skill by consciously reading facial expressions and, therefore, will improve their ability to connect with and influence followers.[33]

This research implies that "it is not what you say but how you say it." Nonverbal messages and body language often convey our real thoughts and feelings with greater force than do our most carefully selected words. Thus, while the conscious mind may be formulating vocal messages such as "I am happy," or "Congratulations on your promotion," body language may be signaling true feelings through blushing, perspiring, glancing, crying, or avoiding eye contact. When the verbal and nonverbal messages are contradictory, the receiver will usually give more weight to behavioral actions than to verbal messages.[34]

A manager's office sends powerful nonverbal cues. For example, what do the following seating arrangements mean? (1) The supervisor stays behind her desk, and you sit in a straight chair on the opposite side. (2) The two of you sit in straight chairs away from her desk, perhaps at a table. (3) The two of you sit in a seating arrangement consisting of a sofa and easy chair. To most people, the first arrangement indicates, "I am the boss here," or "I am in authority." The second arrangement indicates, "This is serious business." The third indicates a more casual and friendly, "Let us get to know each other."[35] Nonverbal messages can be a powerful asset to communication if they complement and support verbal messages. Managers should pay close attention to nonverbal behavior when communicating. They can learn to coordinate their verbal and nonverbal messages and at the same time be sensitive to what their peers, subordinates, and supervisors are saying nonverbally. How close you get to someone is culturally determined, and it can signal an invasion of someone's body space.

nonverbal communication

A communication transmitted through actions and behaviors rather than through words.

Take **ACTION**

Always remember how important nonverbals are: If you smirk while giving a positive comment, the comment gets lost.

Desk Surfers

Carol Kromminga knows her body space. Three feet on all sides. And you better not get closer unless you are a doctor or family member. She does not like it when colleagues at work saunter around to her side of the desk, eye papers on her desk, or glance at her computer screen. When a desk surfer crashes her space, she always responds the same way: swivels around to face them, puts her elbows on desk documents, and looks straight at them to "control those roaming eyes." But the computer screen is the hardest to protect. She has clicked off one embarrassing site (where she was ordering cosmetics), only to find another embarrassing site. What she does now is click on the start button, which brings up a big pop-up menu.

Office privacy may be a contradiction in terms as the evidence of snoopers suggest. Some coworkers foolishly think they are subtle about it, making this delusion on par with people who believe they have great leadership skills or are great interpersonally. One equity trader gets knots in his stomach when the person he calls the "chief surfing officer" visits. She pretends to be interested in his son, and as she leans forward to grab the picture, she scans the contents of his three flat-panel screens.

Some victims mostly do not like the clandestine quality of snooping. "If you ask me, I will probably give you to the key to the castle," says a worker whose colleague tries to glean information in a sneaky fashion. "On principle now, I do not want to share anything with her: what I had for breakfast, how I spent my weekend, or what Web site I am visiting."[36]

Listening

listening

The skill of receiving messages to accurately grasp facts and feelings to interpret the genuine meaning.

Take **ACTION**

When someone is talking to you, force yourself to listen to their words and the underlying meaning rather than thinking about what you want to say next.

One of the most important tools of manager communication is listening to employees and customers. Most managers have recognized that important information flows from the bottom up and not the top down, and managers had better be tuned in.[37] In the communication model in Exhibit 14.2, the listener is responsible for message reception, which is a vital link in the communication process. **Listening** involves the skill of grasping facts and feelings to interpret a message's genuine meaning. Only then can the manager provide the appropriate response. Listening requires attention, energy, and skill. Though about 75 percent of effective communication is listening, most people spend only 30 to 40 percent of their time listening, which leads to many communication errors.[38] One of the secrets of successful salespeople is they spend 60 to 70 percent of a sales call letting the customer talk.[39] However, listening involves much more than being silent. Many people do not know how to listen. They concentrate on formulating what they are going to say next rather than on what is being said to them. Our listening efficiency, as measured by the amount of material understood and remembered by subjects 48 hours after listening to a ten-minute message, is, on average, no better than 25 percent.[40]

What constitutes good listening? Exhibit 14.4 gives ten keys to effective listening and illustrates a number of ways to distinguish a bad from a good listener. A good listener finds areas of interest, is flexible, works hard at listening, and uses thought speed to summarize, weigh, and anticipate what the speaker says. Good listening means shifting from thinking about self to empathizing with the other person and, thus, requires

EXHIBIT 14.4

Ten Keys to Effective Listening

Keys	Poor Listener	Good Listener
1. Listen actively	Is passive, laid back	Asks questions, paraphrases what is said
2. Find areas of interest	Tunes out dry subjects	Looks for opportunities, new learning
3. Resist distractions	Is easily distracted	Fights or avoids distractions, tolerates bad habits, knows how to concentrate
4. Capitalize on the fact that thought is faster than speech	Tends to daydream with slow speakers	Challenges, anticipates, mentally summarizes, weighs the evidence, listens between the lines to tone of voice
5. Be responsive	Is minimally involved	Nods, shows interest, give and take, positive feedback
6. Judge content, not delivery	Tunes out if delivery is poor	Judges content, skips over delivery errors
7. Hold one's fire	Has preconceptions, starts to argue	Does not judge until comprehension is complete
8. Listen for ideas	Listens for facts	Listens to central themes
9. Work at listening	Shows no energy output, faked attention	Works hard, exhibits active body state, eye contact
10. Exercise one's mind	Resists difficult material in favor of light, recreational material	Uses heavier material as exercise for the mind

SOURCE: Adapted from Sherman K. Okum, "How to Be a Better Listener," *Nation's Business* (August 1975), 62; and Philip Morgan and Kent Baker, "Building a Professional Image: Improving Listening Behavior," *Supervisory Management* (November 1985), 34–38.

a high degree of emotional intelligence, as described in Chapter 11. Dr. Robert Buckman, a cancer specialist who teaches other doctors, as well as businesspeople, how to break bad news, emphasizes the importance of listening: "The trust that you build just by letting someone say what they feel is incredible."[41] Few things are as maddening to people as not being listened to.

Some organizations have created a culture that emphasizes active manager listening. Listening may be one of the most important skills a leader has. Several CEOs note how important it is to a company's long-term success, as described in the Focus on Skills box.

Organizational Communication

Another aspect of management communication concerns the organization as a whole. Organization-wide communications typically flow in three directions: downward, upward, and horizontally. Managers are responsible for establishing and maintaining formal channels of communication in these three directions. Managers use informal channels, which means they get out of their offices and mingle with employees.

Formal Communication Channels

Formal communication channels are those that flow within the chain of command or task responsibility defined by the organization. The three formal channels and the types of information conveyed in each are illustrated in Exhibit 14.5.[42] Downward and upward communication are the primary forms of communication used in most traditional, vertically organized companies. However, many organizations emphasize horizontal communication, with people continuously sharing information across departments and levels.

formal communication channels

A communication channel that flows within the chain of command or task responsibility defined by the organization.

FOCUS ON SKILLS

CEOtalk

CEO Jeffrey Skilling's defense when asked over and over about Enron's improper financial transactions? "I didn't know." According to many experts, that is a death call: for the top leader to not have a clue what is going on. Add Bernie Ebbers of WorldCom/MCI to that list of executives who claim they did not know what the company was doing.

Other CEO's do not necessarily follow suit if they want their company to succeed. Take John Much of San Diego's HNC Software, who says his best source of information is informal conversations with employees. "As a leader, you need a network of people from the highest to the lowest levels who can be your trusted advisers, and who know you are open to hearing any message, bad as well as good, they may send you," he says. One way he stimulates this network is to hold weekly "Java with John" session for the first 20 who sign up, and he asks them to talk about their problems. Much acts as a moral compass for his company in meetings, challenging proposed actions. "Maybe if a deal is at risk, we may think about a better pricing, but there are lines we don't cross—such as negotiating barter deals. We don't do that, and it's my job to remind people of our standards," he notes.

One CEO who sees his responsibility as knowing what is going on is UK-based Shire Pharmeceutical's Rolf Stahel, who is bombarded with mountains of data and resports. How does he know what is the most important to focus on? "It takes an enormous amount of energy and time to filter out what is critical and focus on essentials," he says. Using a traffic light system, he has learned to discriminate areas that need immediate attention versus those that need little oversight.

The former CEO of Honeywell, Michael Bonsignore, would spend half his time visiting various company sites around the world. "We encouraged straight talk and bad news," he says, so they could find and solve problems before they erupted into crises. When going to a new location, he talked to executives and to employees at the lowest levels. "There's no substitute for skipping down management layers and finding out what lower level employees think."

Even so, there are times when the CEO won't know everthing. But that top leader certainly better try. "You have to delegate authority," says Bonsignore, "But at the end of the day, you are accountable for everything that happens."

SOURCE: Steve Maich, "Prosecuting a Culture," *McLean's* (March 21, 2005): 44; Carol Hymowitz, " How CEOs Can Keep Informed Even as Work Stretches Across Globe," *The Wall Street Journal* (March 12, 2002): B1.

EXHIBIT 14.5

Downward, Upward, and Horizontal Communication in Organizations

SOURCE: Adapted from Richard L. Daft and Richard M. Steers, *Organizations: A Micro-Macro Approach*, 538. Copyright © 1986 by Scott, Foresman and Company. Used by permission.

Upward Communication
- Problems and exceptions
- Suggestions for improvement
- Performance reports
- Grievances and disputes
- Financial and accounting information

Downward Communication
- Implementation of goals, strategies
- Job instructions and rationale
- Procedures and practices
- Performance feedback
- Indoctrination

Horizontal Communication
- Intradepartmental problem solving
- Interdepartmental coordination
- Change initiatives and improvements

Coordinate

Interpret

Influence

Electronic communication, such as e-mail and IM, have made information flow easier in all directions. For example, the U.S. Army is using technology to transmit communications about weather conditions and the latest intelligence on the enemy rapidly to lieutenants on the battlefield. Similarly, the Navy uses IM to communicate within ships, across Navy divisions, and back to the Pentagon in Washington, DC. "Instant messaging has allowed us to keep our crew members on the same page at the same time," says Lt. Cmdr. Mike Houston, who oversees the Navy's communications program. "Lives are at stake in real time, and we're seeing a new level of communication and readiness."[43]

downward communication

Messages sent from top management down to subordinates.

Downward Communication. The most familiar and obvious flow of formal communication, **downward communication**, refers to the messages and information sent from top management to subordinates in a downward direction.

Managers can communicate downward to employees in many ways. Some of the most common are through speeches, messages in company newsletters, e-mail, information leaflets tucked into pay envelopes, material on bulletin boards, and policy and procedures manuals. Managers sometimes use creative approaches to downward communication to make sure employees get the message. Mike Olson, plant manager at Ryerson Midwest Coil Processing, noticed that workers were dropping expensive power tools, so he hung price tags on the tools to show the replacement cost. Employees solved the problem by finding a way to hook up the tools so they would not drop them. Olson's symbolic communication created a climate of working together for solutions.[44]

Managers have to decide what to communicate about. Managers cannot communicate with employees about everything that goes on in the organization, so they have to make choices about the important information to communicate.[45] Recall our discussion of purpose-directed communication from early in this chapter. Downward communication usually encompasses these five topics:

1. *Implementation of goals and strategies.* Communicating new strategies and goals provides information about specific targets and expected behaviors. It gives direction for lower levels of the organization, as in this example: "The new quality campaign is for real. We must improve product quality if we are to survive." Movie directors need to communicate their visions to the location scouts.

Wal-Mart

Wal-Mart prides itself in giving books at steep discounts and it screens books and movies for appropriate content suitable for families. What a surprise when Wal-Mart started selling *How Wal-Mart is Destroying America and the World and What You Can Do about It,* for $3.40 off the list price, or for only $7.55. The policy for suitable material must not have been communicated down clearly to the censors. That is, until links to the product page started turning up on many blogs. Finally, Wal-Mart removed the book from its inventory.

SOURCE: Adam Horowitz, Mark Athitakis, Mark Lasswell and Owen Thomas, "101 Dumbest Moments in Business," *Business 2.0* (Jan/Feb. 2005): 103–110.

Location Scouting

If the director does not communicate his vision of the movie and its various locales to the location scout, the scout will not be able to implement that vision. Christian McWilliams worked on Oliver Stone's *Alexander*, helping find the right locations. Stone had worked for 14 years on *Alexander*, so he knew what he wanted and was able to relay that information to McWilliams. Stone wanted nothing modern, but close enough to hotels to commute each day.

In finding the right landscape, McWilliams searched for possibilities in nine countries, all places Alexander had marched to, from Ancient Greece to India. He began looking in Morocco. But everywhere he found the right kinds of hills, there were some modern villas nearby. One of his local scouts suggested looking near Essaouira by the Atlantic Ocean, and it was perfect. Beautiful scenery and no mobile towers, no villas, no satellite dishes. It was Stone's dream: olive trees, unspoiled landscape and gorgeous views of the sea.[46]

2. *Job instructions and rationale.* These directives specify how to do a task and how the job relates to other organizational activities, as in this example: "Purchasing should order the bricks now so the work crew can begin construction of the building in two weeks."

3. *Procedures and practices.* These messages define the organization's policies, rules, regulations, benefits, and structural arrangements, as in this example: "After your first 90 days of employment, you are eligible to enroll in our company-sponsored savings plan."

4. *Performance feedback.* These messages appraise how well individuals and departments are doing their jobs, as in this example: "Joe, your work on the computer network has greatly improved the efficiency of our ordering process."

5. *Indoctrination.* These messages motivate employees to adopt the company's mission and cultural values and to participate in special ceremonies, such as picnics and United Way campaigns, as in this example: "The company thinks of its employees as family and would like to invite everyone to attend the annual picnic and fair on March 3rd." Cinnamon Girl feels so strongly about communicating its vision and values to employees that it limits its growth, as shown in the Best Practices box.

The major problem with downward communication is drop-off, which is the distortion or loss of message content. Though formal communications are a powerful way to reach all employees, much information gets lost—25 percent or so each time a message is passed from one person to the next. In addition, the message can be distorted if it travels a great distance from its originating source to the ultimate receiver. A tragic example is the following historical example:

A reporter was present at a hamlet burned down by the U.S. Army 1st Air Cavalry Division in 1967. Investigations showed that the order from the Division headquarters to the brigade was: "On no occasion must hamlets be burned down."

BEST PRACTICES

Cinnamon Girl

Having a vision is one thing, but it is another challenge to communicate it to employees. That is one of the main reasons the Hawaii-based women's apparel chain Cinnamon Girl has resisted opening stores too quickly, or letting anyone else franchise its label. It is easy to understand how an ultra-feminine line of dresses and skirts, etc., in island colors—at reasonable prices—have become a success in the bland homogenized world of Gap, Express, or Abercrombie & Fitch. Founders/owners husband and wife Ried and Jonelle Fugita are besieged with requests from mall owners all over the country. Not only is it one of the few unique clothing concepts, but Cinnamon Girl brings in $1,000 per store square foot, compared to the average $400.

The Fujitas want to hold on to their ideals, so they do not want to grow too quickly or lose control. "We want everything to be correct for the customer," they say, and they find it intolerable for a customer to arrive at one of their stores and be greeted by a distracted employee. Everyone who enters Cinnamon Girl needs to interact with a friendly salesperson, smell the spicy potpourri, and see sundresses carefully placed right next to the pine armoires. "That means our people have to really understand Cinnamon Girl values, and that takes time," says Reid.

Communicating with customers is important, too. Next to each cash register is a delicate pink lockbox, with pencil and paper beside it, encouraging customers to write suggestions. "We call it 'Tea Leaves,'" says Jonelle, "and we get all kinds of feedback from our customers and employees that way. If it comes up a lot—the dress is too short or too long, or that style would be better with a ruffle—we really try to listen to our customers and see what they want. At our meetings, we go over every suggestion, every complaint." No wonder they are so successful.

SOURCES: Ellyn Spragine and Verne Harnish, Size Doesn't Matter, Profits Do," *FSB* (March 2004) 37–42; *Ronna Bolante, "Spice It Up," Hawaii Business* (Dec. 1, 2002): S4.

The brigade radioed the battalion: "Do not burn down any hamlets unless you are absolutely convinced that the Viet Cong are in them."

The battalion radioed the infantry company at the scene: "If you think there are any Viet Cong in the hamlet, burn it down."

The company commander ordered his troops: "Burn down that hamlet."[47]

Information drop-off cannot be completely avoided, but the techniques described in the previous sections can reduce it substantially. Using the right communication channel, consistency between verbal and nonverbal messages, and active listening can maintain communication accuracy as it moves down the organization.

Upward Communication. Many organizations make a great effort to facilitate upward communication. Mechanisms include suggestion boxes, employee surveys, open-door policies, management information system reports, and face-to-face conversations between workers and executives. Consider how one entrepreneur keeps the upward communication flowing.

Pat Croce, Entrepreneur

Pat Croce is currently involved in the development of Pirate Soul, "the ultimate pirate museum," in Key West. But he has several other businesses going, too. Like many entrepreneurs, Croce spends a lot of time on the road, traveling from his home office in Philadelphia all across the country.

To make sure he stays in touch with what is going on in his various businesses, Croce implemented a key communication tool he calls the Five-Fifteen. Each Friday, all employees and managers take 15 minutes to write brief progress reports and forward them to their immediate supervisors. Within a few days, all the information trickles up to

Croce in a sort of "corporate Cliff Notes" version. The idea is that the reports take Croce only five minutes to read (hence the name Five-Fifteen). Croce says the Five-Fifteens have enabled him to keep in touch with the little details that make a big difference in the success of his businesses.

Employees typically look at the Five-Fifteens as a chance to be heard, and Croce looks at them as a way to keep his finger on the pulse of each business. In addition, the reports give him a chance to compliment and thank people for their accomplishments and offer questions or suggestions in areas that need improvement.[48]

Another company that took upward communication to heart is Wild Oats.

Wild Oats Market

From its beginnings, Wild Oats Market was offbeat, serving up health foods in a tiny market in Boulder, Colorado. Owners Libby Cook, Michael Gilliland, and Randy Clapp rang up sales and stocked the shelves themselves. It was easy back then to stay in touch with employees and customers. After four years, though, their success had exacted a price. With 11 stores scattered across three states, they found themselves managing a corporation rather than a tiny market. Employee training and performance reviews had deteriorated. Back when they worked side by side with shelf stockers and produce clerks, they could gauge employee morale, which was important information for them. As Cook said, "In our business, we need to keep our staff happy because they are the first line of defense when customers come into the store." But now they could not work alongside them and could not even visit them all. The three owners knew they had to devise some means of knowing what was happening in each store, to get feedback from each worker, so they could prevent potential problems before customers shopped elsewhere.

Because Wild Oats staffers were known for their free spirited attitudes, Cook, Gilliland, and Clapp developed a questionnaire to evaluate employee morale and satisfaction using potential measures of "awful," "remarkably bad," to "wonderful," and "terrific." Their "Happiness Index" rated respondents sentiments from "giddy" to "suicidal." Gilliland discovered that store managers were taking negative criticisms hard even if they had a lot of "terrifics." To prevent this, he began reviewing the questionnaires to remove gratuitous or nonconstructive, carping comments before going over them personally with each manager. The feedback has given a clear idea of work force morale and has resulted in employee solutions to specific problems, such as employee participation in a stock option program and a $200/worker wellness program allowance. Since the program began, turnover has dramatically decreased.

Communication and management practices at Wild Oats continue to be successful, for the company now operates 115 stores nationwide and is up to yearly revenues of over $1.1 billion.[49]

In today's fast-paced world, many managers find it hard to maintain constant communication: Ideas such as the Five-Fifteen help keep information flowing upward so managers get feedback from lower levels. This chapter's Digital, Inc. box describes an idea that Amazon.com uses to find out what is on employees' minds.

Despite these efforts, however, barriers to accurate upward communication exist. Managers may resist hearing about employee problems, or employees might not trust managers sufficiently to push information upward.[50] Innovative companies search for ways to ensure that information gets to top managers without distortion. One creative approach is found at Golden Corral, a restaurant chain with headquarters in Raleigh, North Carolina. Top managers spend at least one weekend a year in the trenches, cutting steaks, rolling silverware, setting tables, and taking out the trash. By understanding the daily routines and challenges of waiters, chefs, and other employees at their restaurants, Golden Corral executives increase their awareness of how management actions affect others.[51]

DIGITAL, INC.

Amazon.com Keeps Track of Employees' "Pulse Rate"

How do managers at Amazon.com keep in touch with employees' opinions and feelings about company decisions? By taking the organization's collective pulse twice a week.

Amazon works with eePulse, an Ann Arbor, Michigan-based applications service provider, to poll employees biweekly on their opinions and attitudes about various company developments. The electronic survey and communications tool uses a question format and asks employees to rate their "pulse," or energy level. Responses range from "not doing much, not having fun" to "overwhelmed by work and need help." Employees have an opportunity for open comments about their work environment. These quick e-mail surveys, which take about two minutes to complete, provide feedback on a regular basis, enabling managers to collect information and assess how things are going in real time. "Changes happen very quickly here," says one manager. "By polling people this way, by e-mail, it's consistent and fast and

provides the data we need." Employees are encouraged to talk to their managers about any specific concerns, and managers are trained to use the eePulse and follow up on potential problems, such as low pulse rates or an employee whose pulse is about to go through the roof from overwork.

Whereas managers loved the new communications tool from the beginning, employees took a little longer to warm up to it. With typical management surveys, employees rarely see changes after results are compiled and publicized, and Amazon's workers expected this was another useless poll. However, after numerous months in which Amazon's managers consistently reported back results to the employees and made sincere efforts to address concerns, attitudes toward eePulse have changed. Some people enjoy regularly keeping tabs on the survey results and finding out what their co-workers are saying about their jobs and the company.

Source: Teresa Welbourne, "New ASP Takes Workforce's 'Pulse,'" *The New Corporate University Review* (July-August 2000): 20–21.

---

horizontal communication

The lateral or diagonal exchange of messages among peers or co-workers.

Horizontal Communication.   Horizontal communication is the lateral or diagonal exchange of messages among peers or coworkers. It may occur within or across departments. The purpose of horizontal communication is to inform and to request support and coordinate activities. Horizontal communication falls into one of three categories:

1. *Intradepartmental problem solving.* These messages take place among members of the same department and concern task accomplishment, as in this example: "Kelly, can you help us figure out how to complete this medical expense report form?"

2. *Interdepartmental coordination.* Interdepartmental messages facilitate the accomplishment of joint projects or tasks, as in this example: "Bob, please contact marketing and production and arrange a meeting to discuss the specifications for the new subassembly. It looks like we might not be able to meet their requirements."

3. *Change initiatives and improvements.* These messages are designed to share information among teams and departments that can help the organization change, grow, and improve, as in this example: "We are streamlining the company travel procedures and would like to discuss them with your department."

Horizontal communication is particularly important in learning organizations, where teams of workers are continuously solving problems and searching for new ways of doing things. Recall from Chapter 7 that many organizations build in horizontal communications in the form of task forces, committees, or a matrix structure to encourage coordination.

Team Communication Channels

A special type of horizontal communication is communicating in teams. Teams are the basic building block of many organizations. Team members work together to accomplish tasks, and the team's communication structure influences team performance and employee satisfaction.

Research into team communication has focused on two characteristics: the extent to which team communications are centralized and the nature of the team's task.[52] The relationship between these characteristics is illustrated in Exhibit 14.6. In a **centralized network**, team members must communicate through one individual to solve problems or make decisions. In a **decentralized network**, individuals can communicate freely with other team members. Members process information equally among themselves until all agree on a decision.[53]

In laboratory experiments, centralized communication networks achieved faster solutions for simple problems. Members could pass relevant information to a central person for a decision. Decentralized communications were slower for simple problems because information was passed among individuals until someone finally put the pieces together and solved the problem. However, for more complex problems, the decentralized communication network was faster. Because all necessary information was not restricted to one person, a pooling of information through widespread communications provided greater input into the decision. Similarly, the accuracy of problem solving was related to problem complexity. The centralized networks made fewer errors on simple problems but more errors on complex ones. Decentralized networks were less accurate for simple problems but more accurate for complex ones.[54]

The implication for organizations is as follows: In a highly competitive global environment, organizations typically use teams to deal with complex problems. When team activities are complex and difficult, all members should share information in a decentralized structure to solve problems. Teams need a free flow of communication in all directions.[55] At start-up Alteon Web Systems (now owned by Nortel Networks), teams learned to make important decisions in a single meeting. Each person would collect as much information as possible to support his or her proposed ideas or solutions and then share it with the team. Constructive conflict was encouraged, with one team member acting as a referee to help the team arrive at the best decision based on the information available.[56] Teams that perform routine tasks spend less time processing information, and communications can be centralized. Data can be channeled to a supervisor for decisions, freeing workers to spend a greater percentage of time on task activities.

Personal Communication Channels

Personal communication channels exist outside the formally authorized channels. These are informal communications that coexist with formal channels but may skip hierarchical levels, cutting across vertical chains of command to connect almost anyone

---

centralized network

A team communication structure in which team members communicate through a single individual to solve problems or make decisions.

decentralized network

A team communication structure in which team members freely communicate with one another and arrive at decisions together.

Take **ACTION**

If you have a complex task, make sure members of the team can all communicate easily with one another.

---

personal communication channels

Communication channels that exist outside the formally authorized channels and do not adhere to the organization's hierarchy of authority.

	Slower and less accurate	Faster and more accurate
Simple Tasks	⬠ ⬠	Y ⊢
Complex Tasks	Y ⊢	⬠ ⬠

Centralized = Y   Wheel

Decentralized = Circle   All channel

EXHIBIT 14.6

Effectiveness of Team Communication Network

SOURCES: Adapted from A. Bavelas and D. Barrett, "An Experimental Approach to Organization Communication," *Personnel* 27 (1951), 366–371; M. E. Shaw, *Group Dynamics: The Psychology of Small Group Behavior* (New York: McGraw–Hill, 1976); and E. M. Rogers and R. A. Rogers, *Communication in Organizations* (New York: Free Press, 1976).

in the organization. In most organizations, these informal channels are the primary way information spreads and work gets accomplished. Three important types of personal communication channels are personal networks, management by wandering around, and the grapevine.

personal networking

The acquisition and cultivation of personal relationships that cross departmental, hierarchical, and organizational boundaries.

Developing Personal Communication Networks. **Personal networking** refers to the acquisition and cultivation of personal relationships that cross departmental, hierarchical, and organizational boundaries.[57] Smart managers consciously develop personal communication networks and encourage others to do so. In a communication network, people share information across boundaries and reach out to anyone who can further the goals of the team and organization. Exhibit 14.7 illustrates a communication network. Some people are central to the network, yet others play only a peripheral role. The key is that relationships are built across functional and hierarchical boundaries.

The value of personal networks for managers is that people who have more contacts have a greater influence in the organization and get more accomplished. For example, in Exhibit 14.7, Sharon has a well-developed personal communication network, sharing information and assistance with many people across the marketing, manufacturing, and engineering departments. Contrast Sharon's contacts with those of Mike's or Jasmine's. Who do you think is likely to have greater access to resources and more influence in the organization? Here are a few tips from one expert networker for building a personal communication network:[58]

1. *Build it before you need it.* Smart managers do not wait until they need something to start building a network of personal relationships because by then, it is too late. Instead, they show genuine interest in others and develop honest connections.

Take ACTION

Use your lunches and breaktime to develop closer relationships and communications with colleagues.

2. *Never eat lunch alone.* People who excel at networking make an effort to be visible and connect with as many people as possible. Master networkers keep their social as well as business conference and event calendars full.

3. *Make it win–win.* Successful networking is not just about getting what you want; it is about ensuring other people in the network get what they want.

4. *Focus on diversity.* The broader your base of contacts, the broader your range of influence. Build connections with people from as many different areas of interest as possible (within and outside of the organization).

EXHIBIT 14.7

An Organizational Communication Network

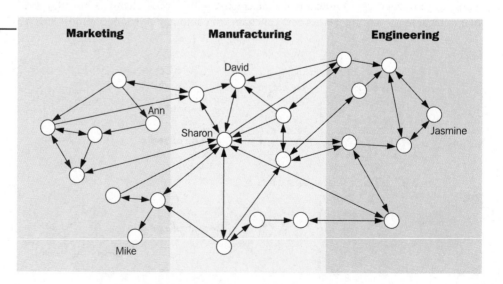

Most of us know from personal experience that who you know sometimes counts for more than what you know. By cultivating a broad network of contacts, managers can significantly extend their influence and accomplish greater results.

Management by Wandering Around.   The communication technique known as **management by wandering around (MBWA)** was made famous by the books *In Search of Excellence* and *A Passion for Excellence*.[59] These books describe executives who talk directly with employees to learn what is going on. MBWA works for managers at all levels. They mingle and develop positive relationships with employees and learn directly from them about their department, division, or organization. For example, the president of ARCO had a habit of visiting a district field office. Rather than schedule a big strategic meeting with the district supervisor, he would come in unannounced and chat with the lowest-level employees. In any organization, MBWA enhances upward and downward communications. Managers have a chance to describe key ideas and values to employees and, in turn, learn about the problems and issues confronting employees.

When managers fail to take advantage of MBWA, they become aloof and isolated from employees. For example, Peter Anderson, president of Ztel, Inc., a maker of television switching systems, preferred not to communicate with employees personally. He managed at arm's length. As one manager said, "I don't know how many times I asked Peter to come to the lab, but he stayed in his office. He wasn't that visible to the troops." This formal, impersonal management style contributed to Ztel's troubles and eventual bankruptcy.[60]

The Grapevine.   One type of informal, person-to-person communication network of employees that is not officially sanctioned by the organization is referred to as the **grapevine**.[61] The grapevine links employees in all directions, ranging from the CEO through middle management, support staff, and line employees. The grapevine will always exist in an organization, but it can become a dominant force when formal channels are closed. In such cases, the grapevine is a service because the information it provides helps makes sense of an unclear or uncertain situation. Employees use grapevine rumors to fill in information gaps and clarify management decisions. One estimate is that as much as 70 percent of all communication in a firm is carried out through its grapevine.[62] The grapevine tends to be more active during periods of change, excitement, anxiety, and sagging economic conditions. For example, a recent survey by professional employment services firm Randstad found that about half of all employees reported first hearing of major company changes through the grapevine.[63] Consider what happened at Jel, Inc., an auto supply firm that was under great pressure from Ford and GM to increase quality. Management changes to improve quality—learning statistical process control, introducing a new compensation system, buying a fancy new screw machine from Germany—started out as rumors, circulating days ahead of the actual announcements, and were generally accurate.[64]

Surprising aspects of the grapevine are its accuracy and its relevance to the organization. About 80 percent of grapevine communications pertain to business-related topics rather than personal, vicious gossip. Moreover, from 70 to 90 percent of the details passed through a grapevine are accurate.[65] Many managers would like the grapevine to be destroyed because they consider its rumors to be untrue, malicious, and harmful. Typically, this is not the case; however, managers should be aware that almost five of every six important messages are carried to some extent by the grapevine rather than through official channels. In a survey of 22,000 shift workers in varied industries, 55 percent said they get most of their information via the grapevine.[66] Smart managers understand the company's grapevine. They recognize who is connected to whom and

management by wandering around (MBWA)

A communication technique in which managers interact directly with workers to exchange information.

grapevine

An informal, person-to-person communication network of employees not officially sanctioned by the organization.

which employees are key players in the informal spread of information. In all cases, and particularly in times of crisis, executives need to manage communications so the grapevine is not the only source of information.[67]

Communicating during Turbulent Times

During turbulent times, communication becomes more important. To build trust and promote learning and problem solving, managers incorporate ideas such as open communication, dialogue, feedback, and learning. In addition, they develop their crisis communication skills for communicating with employees and the public in exceptionally challenging or frightening circumstances.

Open Communication

A recent trend that reflects managers' increased emphasis on empowering employees, building trust and commitment, and enhancing collaboration is open communication. **Open communication** means sharing all types of information throughout the company, across functional and hierarchical levels. Many companies, such as Springfield Remanufacturing Corporation, AmeriSteel, and Whole Foods Markets, are opening the financial books to workers at all levels and training employees to understand how and why the company operates as it does. At Wabash National Corporation, one of the nation's leading truck-trailer manufacturers, employees complete several hours of business training and attend regular meetings on the shop floor to review the company's financial performance.[68]

Open communication runs counter to the traditional flow of selective information downward from supervisors to subordinates. By breaking down conventional hierarchical barriers to communication, the organization can gain the benefit of all employees' ideas. The same ideas batted back and forth among a few managers do not lead to effective learning or to a network of relationships that keep companies thriving. New voices and conversations, involving a broad spectrum of people, revitalize and enhance organizational communication.[69] Open communication builds trust and a commitment to common goals, which is essential in organizations that depend on collaboration and knowledge sharing to accomplish their purpose. Fifty percent of executives surveyed report that open communication is a key to building trust in the organization.[70]

Dialogue

Another popular means of fostering trust and collaboration in organizations is through dialogue. The "roots of dialogue" are *dia* and *logos*, which can be thought of as *stream of meaning*. **Dialogue** is a group communication process in which people together create a stream of shared meaning that enables them to understand each other and share a view of the world.[71] People may start out at polar opposites, but by talking openly, they discover common ground, common issues, and shared goals on which they can build a better future.

A useful way to describe dialogue is to contrast it with discussion (see Exhibit 14.8). The intent of discussion, generally, is to deliver one's point of view and persuade others to adopt it. A discussion is often resolved by logic or "beating down" opponents. Dialogue, by contrast, asks that participants suspend their attachments to a particular viewpoint so a deeper level of listening, synthesis, and meaning can evolve from the group. A dialogue's focus is to reveal feelings and build common ground. Both forms of communication—dialogue and discussion—can result in change. However, the result of discussion is limited to the topic being deliberated, whereas the result of dialogue is characterized by group unity, shared meaning, and transformed mindsets. As new and deeper solutions are developed, a trusting relationship is built among team members.[72]

---

open communication

Sharing all types of information throughout the company, across functional and hierarchical levels.

Take *ACTION*

As a manager, remember that organizational secrets do not often remain that way; therefore, tell the truth and be open from the beginning.

---

dialogue

A group communication process aimed at creating a culture based on collaboration, fluidity, trust, and commitment to shared goals.

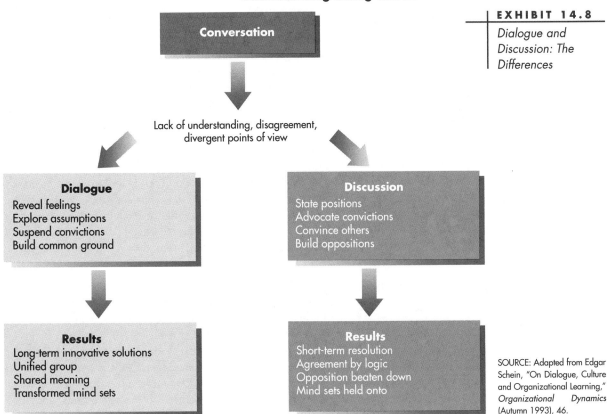

EXHIBIT 14.8

Dialogue and Discussion: The Differences

SOURCE: Adapted from Edgar Schein, "On Dialogue, Culture and Organizational Learning," *Organizational Dynamics* (Autumn 1993), 46.

Crisis Communication

Over the past few years, the sheer number and scope of crises has made communication a more demanding job for managers. Organizations face small crises every day, such as charges of racial discrimination, a factory fire, or a flu epidemic. Moreover, acts of intentional evil, such as bombings or kidnappings, continue to increase, causing serious repercussions for people and organizations.[73] Managers can develop four primary skills for communicating in a crisis:[74]

- *Maintain your focus.* Good crisis communicators do not allow themselves to be overwhelmed by the situation. Calmness and listening become more important than ever. Managers learn to tailor their communications to reflect hope and optimism as they acknowledge the current difficulties.

- *Be visible.* Many managers underestimate how important their presence is during a crisis.[75] As we discussed in Chapter 1, people need to feel that someone is in control. A manager's job is to step out immediately to reassure employees and respond to public concerns. Face-to-face communication with employees is crucial for letting people know that managers care about them and what they are going through.

- *Get the awful truth out.*[76] Effective managers gather as much information as they can, do their best to determine the facts, and tell the truth to employees and the public as soon as possible. Getting the truth out quickly prevents rumors and misunderstandings.

- *Communicate a vision for the future.* People need to feel that they have something to work for and look forward to. Moments of crisis present opportunities for managers to communicate a vision of a better future and unite people toward common goals.

Feedback and Learning

Feedback occurs when managers use evaluation and communication to help individuals and the organization learn and improve. It enables managers to determine if they have been successful in communicating with others. Recall from Exhibit 14.2 that feedback is an important part of the communication process. However, despite its importance, feedback is often neglected. Giving and receiving feedback is typically difficult for managers and employees. Yet, by avoiding feedback, people miss a valuable opportunity to help one another learn, develop, and improve.[77] At General Electric, managers are evaluated partly on their ability to give and receive effective feedback.[78]

Successful managers focus their feedback to develop the capacities of subordinates and to teach the organization how to reach its goals better. Feedback is an important means by which individuals and organizations learn from their mistakes and improve their work. When managers enlist the whole organization in reviewing the outcomes of activities, they can quickly learn what works, what does not, and use that information to improve the organization. Consider how the U.S. Army's feedback system promotes whole-system learning.

> **Take ACTION**
>
> When people give you negative feedback, rather than defending yourself and proving them wrong, listen quietly and say, "thank you for the information" and nothing more.

U.S. Army

At the National Training Center just south of Death Valley, U.S. Army troops engage in a simulated battle: The "enemy" has sent unmanned aerial vehicles (UAVs) to gather targeting data. When the troops fire on the UAVs, they reveal their location to attack helicopters hovering behind a nearby ridge. After the exercise, unit members and their superiors hold an after-action review to review battle plans, discuss what worked and what did not, and talk about how to do things better. General William Hertzog suggests that inexpensive decoy UAVs might be just the thing to make a distracted enemy reveal its location. The observation became a "lesson learned" for the entire army, and UAVs became an important part of battle operations in Iraq.

Many researchers attribute the transformation of the U.S. Army from a demoralized, dysfunctional organization following the Vietnam War into an elite force capable of accomplishing Operation Iraqi Freedom to this unique feedback and learning system. In the U.S. Army, after-action reviews take 15 minutes, and they occur after every identifiable event, large or small and simulated or real. The review involves asking four simple questions: What was supposed to happen? What happened? What accounts for any difference? What can we learn? It is a process of identifying mistakes, of innovating, and of continually learning from experience.

The lessons are based on simulated battles and on real-life experiences of soldiers in the field. The Center for Army Lessons Learned (CALL) sends experts into the field to observe after-action reviews, interview soldiers, and compile intelligence reports. Leaders in all army divisions are currently engaged in a detailed analysis of lessons learned during Operation Iraqi Freedom and Operation Enduring Freedom. The lessons will be used to train soldiers and develop action plans for resolving problems in future conflicts. For example, many of the problems and issues from a similar process following Operation Desert Storm had been resolved by the time of Operation Iraqi Freedom. A primary focus for current leaders is to improve training regarding the difficult shift from offensive operations to humanitarian and relief efforts.[79]

In this example, the organization is learning by communicating feedback about the consequences of field operations and simulated battles. Compiling what is learned and using communication feedback create an improved organization. After-action reviews are used in corporate America. Steelcase Inc., an office furniture manufacturer, and BP are among the companies adapting the army's system to create a process of continuous learning and improvement. BP credits the feedback system for $700 million in cost savings and other gains.[80] Negative feedback is difficult to hear but invaluable for greater performance as shown on the following page.

Two weeks before Carly Fiorina was fired from Hewlett-Packard, she was describing to the press how "excellent" her relationship was with the board. Admitting weakness does not come easily to most CEO's, whose ego is usually large. When problems arise, there is always someone or something to blame.

But fessing up can have positive outcomes. Consider Anne Mulcahy, discussed in Chapter 2. When she was named CEO, she announced that Xerox's business model was unsustainable and the company needed restructuring. Within hours, the stock fell 60 percent. She visited various company sites and told employees that what they were about to do would be the most stressful thing they had experienced, and if they did not have the stomach for it, to get out. She did turn the company around, largely because she faced reality and was willing to tell people like it is.

Not all managers can face reality. Some are sensitive and do not want bad news or suggestions from employees, not matter how much they might say they do. This is particularly true for entrepreneurs. The same self-confidence that launches a company, despite warnings on all sides, is not open to lots of suggestions for improvement. (We "are doing great," thinks the boss, "so why is this person being such a bother?") But this nonlistening quality can be disastrous as things will fall apart without listening to competent warnings. Being unaware has a business cost.

Experts suggest that business owners listen to feedback and work on not getting defensive. They think through what the person is saying, rather than dismissing the idea quickly. It is also a good idea to ask for negative feedback periodically. At Home Depot, they call it "Stupid Hour," when the employees tell the bosses what they do that is stupid. It is one reason Home Depot has grown so consistently. The employees know the value of positive and negative feedback.[81]

Managing Organizational Communication

Many of the ideas described in this chapter pertain to barriers to communication and how to overcome them. Exhibit 14.9 lists some of the major barriers to communication, along with some techniques for overcoming them.

Barriers to Communication

Barriers can be categorized as those that exist at the individual level and those that exist at the organizational level.

Barriers	How to Overcome
Individual	
Interpersonal dynamics	Active listening
Channels and media	Selection of appropriate channel
Defense mechanisms	Question underlying assumptions
Semantics	Knowledge of other's perspective
Inconsistent cues	MBWA
Organizational	
Status and power differences	Climate of trust, dialogue
Departmental needs and goals	Development and use of formal channels
Lack of formal channels	Encouragement of multiple channels, formal and informal
Communication network unsuited to task	Changing organization or group structure to fit communication needs
Poor coordination	Feedback and learning

EXHIBIT 14.9

Communication Barriers and Ways to Overcome Them

© AP/Wide World Photos

Individual Barriers. First, interpersonal barriers include problems with emotions and perceptions held by employees. For example, rigid perceptual labeling or stereotyping prevents people from modifying or altering their opinions. If a person's mind is made up before the communication starts, communication will fail. Moreover, people with different backgrounds or knowledge may interpret a communication in different ways.

Second, selecting the wrong channel or medium for sending a communication can be a problem. For example, when a message is emotional, it is better to transmit it face to face rather than in writing. E-mail can be particularly risky for discussing difficult issues. On the other hand, e-mail is efficient for routine messages but lacks the capacity for rapid feedback and multiple cues needed for difficult messages.

semantics

The meaning of words and the way they are used.

Third, semantics often causes communication problems. **Semantics** pertains to the meaning of words and the way they are used. A word such as *effectiveness* may mean achieving high production to a factory superintendent and employee satisfaction to a human resources staff specialist. Many common words have an average of 28 definitions; thus, communicators must take care to select the words that will accurately encode ideas.[82] Language differences can be a barrier in today's organizations. At Semifreddi's, an artisan bread bakery in Emeryville, California, CEO Tom Frainier had to hire translators to help him communicate with his employees, most of whom came from Mexico, Laos, China, Peru, Cambodia, Yemen, and Vietnam.[83]

Fourth, sending inconsistent cues between verbal and nonverbal communications will confuse the receiver. If one's facial expression does not reflect one's words, the communication will contain noise and uncertainty. The tone of voice and body language should be consistent with the words, and actions should not contradict words.

Organizational Barriers. Organizational barriers pertain to factors for the organization as a whole. First is the problem of status and power differences. Low-power people may be reluctant to pass bad news up the hierarchy, thus giving the wrong impression to upper levels.[84] High-power people may not pay attention or may think that low-status people have little to contribute.

Take **ACTION**

As a manager, energetically solicit bad information from below so you can avoid problems erupting.

Second, differences across departments in terms of needs and goals interfere with communications. Each department perceives problems in its own terms. The production department is concerned with production efficiency whereas the marketing department's goal is to get the product to the customer in a hurry.

Third, the absence of formal channels reduces communication effectiveness. Organizations must provide adequate upward, downward, and horizontal communication in the form of employee surveys, open-door policies, newsletters, memos, task forces, and liaison personnel. Without these formal channels, the organization cannot communicate as a whole.

Fourth, the communication flow may not fit the team's or organization's task. If a centralized communication structure is used for nonroutine tasks, not enough information will circulate to solve problems. The organization, department, or team is most efficient when the amount of communication flowing among employees fits the task.

A final problem is poor coordination, so different parts of the organization are working in isolation without knowing and understanding what other parts are doing. Top executives are out of touch with lower levels, or departments and divisions are poorly coordinated so people do not understand how the system works together as a whole.

Overcoming Communication Barriers

Managers can design the organization to encourage positive, effective communication. Designing involves individual skills and organizational actions.

Individual Skills.   Perhaps the most important individual skill is active listening. Active listening means asking questions, showing interest, and occasionally paraphrasing what the speaker has said to ensure that one is interpreting accurately. Active listening means providing feedback to the sender to complete the communication loop.

Second, individuals should select the appropriate channel for the message. A complicated message should be sent through a rich channel, such as a face-to-face discussion or telephone. Routine messages and data can be sent through memos, letters, or e-mail because there is little chance of misunderstanding.

Third, senders and receivers should make a special effort to understand each other's perspective. Managers can sensitize themselves to the information receiver so they will be able to target the message, detect bias, and clarify missed interpretations. By communicators understanding others' perspectives, semantics can be clarified, perceptions understood, and objectivity maintained.

The fourth individual skill is MBWA. Managers must be willing to get out of the office and check communications with others. Glenn Tilton, the CEO of United Airlines, takes every opportunity to introduce himself to employees and customers and find out what is on their minds. He logs more airplane time than many of his company's pilots, visits passenger lounges, and chats with employees on concourses, galleys, and airport terminals.[85] Through direct observation and face-to-face meetings, managers develop an understanding of the organization and can communicate important ideas and values directly to others.

Organizational Actions.   Perhaps the most important thing managers can do for the organization is to create a climate of trust and openness. Open communication and dialogue can encourage people to communicate honestly with one another. Subordinates will feel free to transmit negative as well as positive messages without fear of retribution. Efforts to develop interpersonal skills among employees can foster openness, honesty, and trust.

Second, managers should develop and use formal information channels in all directions. Scandinavian Design uses two newsletters to reach employees. GM's Packard Electric plant is designed to share all pertinent information—financial, future plans, quality,

CONCEPT CONNECTION

The scoreboard at Colonial Mills, Inc., a $7 million specialty-rug manufacturer in Pawtucket, Rhode Island, overcomes **communication barriers** *by helping all employees get involved in business targets and results. The board stretches 30 feet and covers most of the lunchroom wall. A big gold rocket ship in the middle shows the year-to-date company profit. Columns for winding, braiding, and other production departments show monthly output—cans filled, square feet braided, etc.—all compared with the company's plan. The Colonial Mills scoreboard is a unique* **communication channel** *that encourages upward, downward, and horizontal communication. "Our targets aren't the powers-that-be coming down and saying 'This shall be the number,'" says Colonial Mills CEO Don Scarlata. "They're numbers everybody has discussed and signed off on."*

Take **ACTION**

As a manager, you can develop a climate of trust by becoming more trustworthy yourself.

performance—with employees. Dana Corporation has developed innovative programs such as the "Here's a Thought" board—called a HAT rack—to get ideas and feedback from workers. Other techniques include direct mail, bulletin boards, and employee surveys.

Third, managers should encourage the use of multiple channels, including formal and informal communications. Multiple communication channels include written directives, face-to-face discussions, MBWA, and the grapevine. For example, managers at GM's Packard Electric plant use multimedia, including a monthly newspaper, frequent meetings of employee teams, and an electronic news display in the cafeteria. Sending messages through multiple channels increases the likelihood they will be properly received.

Fourth, the structure should fit communication needs. An organization can be designed to use teams, task forces, project managers, or a matrix structure as needed to facilitate the horizontal flow of information for coordination and problem solving. Structure should reflect information needs. When team or department tasks are difficult, a decentralized structure should be implemented to encourage discussion and participation.

A system of organizational feedback and learning can help to overcome problems of poor coordination. Harrah's created a *Communication Team* as part of its structure at the Casino/Holiday Inn in Las Vegas. The team includes one member from each department. This cross-functional team deals with urgent company problems and helps people think beyond the scope of their own departments to communicate with anyone and everyone to solve those problems.

Manager's Solution

This chapter described several important points about communicating in organizations. Communication takes up at least 80 percent of a manager's time. Managers' communication is purpose-directed, in that it unites people around a shared vision and goals and directs attention to the values and behaviors that achieve goals. Communication is a process of encoding an idea into a message, which is sent through a channel and decoded by a receiver. Communication among people can be affected by communication channels, nonverbal communication, and listening skills. An important aspect of management communication is persuasion. The ability to persuade others to behave in ways that help accomplish the vision and goals is crucial to good management. Managers frequently use symbols, stories, and metaphors to persuade and influence others.

At the organizational level, managers are concerned with managing formal communications in a downward, upward, and horizontal direction. Informal communications are important, especially with MBWA, developing personal networks, and the grapevine. Moreover, research shows that communication structures in teams and departments should reflect the underlying tasks. Open communication, dialogue, feedback, and learning are important communication mechanisms during times of turbulence and uncertainty. In addition, managers have to develop effective crisis

communication skills. Four important skills for communicating in a crisis are to remain calm and focused, be visible, get the awful truth out, and communicate a vision for a brighter future.

At Voyant, described in the opening challenge, Bill Ernstrom could not get the engineers to listen to the marketing department, having tried many various options. After his other ideas failed, Ernstrom found one that worked. Because the product managers did not have experience in the field, it was difficult for them to talk to the technology people who had worked at the company for years. Ernstrom created the position of chief product officer and hired John Guillame, with years of telecom experience, who was able to chat with the engineers as well as make sense to the businesspeople. Not one to let things be, Guillame had some radical ideas about how to unsettle Voyant's balkanized culture. "If I'd known what he was going to do up front, I would've been worried," says Ernstrom. First off, Guillame gave higher profile to the product managers by giving them more visible tasks, such as presenting market research and writing definitions for products. Next, he asked two of Voyant's top engineers to head up the product group, which would give credibility to the product teams and allow the two groups to work together. As part of the whole restructuring, the executive team reconfigured seating arrangements, breaking up clumps of engineers and mixing with their product management teams. Finally, Guillame developed some systemic process for new ideas or changes to existing products. When people have an idea, they put it on the Intranet, where engineers, accountants, marketing people all look at it and assess its financial potential and impact. It is nearly like an internal venture capital process. And it works. Since instituting the changes, Voyant has kept all its engineers and increased sales by 25 percent, improved time to market by 40 percent, added three products to the line, and reduced research and development costs by 20 percent. All from figuring out new ways to communicate.[86]

The final part of this chapter described several individual and organizational barriers to communication. These barriers can be overcome by active listening, selecting appropriate channels, engaging in MBWA, using dialogue, developing a climate of trust, using formal channels, designing the correct structure to fit communication needs, and using feedback for learning.

Discussion Questions

1. ATI Medical, Inc., has a "no-memo" policy. The 300 employees must interact directly for all communications. What impact do you think this policy would have on the organization?

2. Describe the elements of the communication process. Give an example of each part of the model as it exists in the classroom during communication between teacher and students.

3. Why do you think stories are more effective than hard facts and figures in persuading others?

4. Should the grapevine be eliminated? How might managers control information that is processed through the grapevine?

5. What do you think are the major barriers to upward communication in organizations? Discuss.

6. What is the relationship between group communication and group task? For example, how should communications differ in a strategic planning group and a group of employees who stock shelves in a grocery store?

7. Some senior managers believe they should rely on written information and computer reports because these yield more accurate data than do face-to-face communications. Do you agree?

8. Why is management by wandering around considered effective communication? Consider channel richness and nonverbal communications in formulating your answer.

9. Is speaking accurately or listening actively the more important communication skill for managers? Discuss.

10. Assume that you have been asked to design a training program to help managers become better communicators. What would you include in the program?

Manager's Workbook

Listening Self-Assessment

Instructions: Choose one response for each of the items below. Base your choice on what you usually do, not on what you think a person should do.

1. When you are going to lunch with a friend, you:
   a. Focus your attention on the menu and then on the service provided
   b. Ask about events in your friend's life and pay attention to what's said
   c. Exchange summaries of what is happening to each of you while focusing attention on the meal

2. When someone talks nonstop, you:
   a. Ask questions at an appropriate time in an attempt to help the person focus on the issue

   b. Make an excuse to end the conversation
   c. Try to be patient and understand what you are being told

3. If a group member complains about a fellow employee who, you believe, is disrupting the group, you:
   a. Pay attention and withhold your opinions
   b. Share your own experiences and feelings about that employee
   c. Acknowledge the group member's feelings and ask the group member what options he or she has

4. If someone is critical of you, you:
   a. Try not to react or get upset
   b. Automatically become curious and attempt to learn more
   c. Listen attentively and then back up your position

5. You are having a very busy day and someone tells you to change the way you are completing a task. You believe the person is wrong, so you:
   a. Thank her or him for the input and keep doing what you were doing
   b. Try to find out why she or he thinks you should change
   c. Acknowledge that the other may be right, tell her or him you are very busy, and agree to follow up later

6. When you are ready to respond to someone else, you:
   a. Sometimes will interrupt the person if you believe it is necessary
   b. Almost always speak before the other is completely finished talking
   c. Rarely offer your response until you believe the other has finished

7. After a big argument with someone you have to work with every day, you:
   a. Settle yourself and then try to understand the other's point of view before stating your side again
   b. Just try to go forward and let bygones be bygones
   c. Continue to press your position

8. A colleague calls to tell you that he is upset about getting assigned to a new job. You decide to:
   a. Ask him if he can think of options to help him deal with the situation
   b. Assure him that he is good at what he does and that these things have a way of working out for the best
   c. Let him know you have heard how badly he feels

9. If a friend always complains about her problems but never asks about yours, you:
   a. Try to identify areas of common interest
   b. Remain understanding and attentive, even if it becomes tedious
   c. Support her complaints and mention your own complaints

10. The best way to remain calm in an argument is to:
    a. Continue to repeat your position in a firm but even manner
    b. Repeat what you believe is the other person's position
    c. Tell the other person that you are willing to discuss the matter again when you are both calmer

Score Each Item of Your Listening Self-Assessment

	(a)	(b)	(c)
1.	0	10	5
2.	10	0	5
3.	5	0	5
4.	5	10	0
5.	0	10	5
6.	5	0	10
7.	10	5	0
8.	5	5	10
9.	0	10	5
10.	0	10	5

Add Up Your Total Score

80–100: You are an active, excellent listener. You achieve a good balance between listening and asking questions, and you strive to understand others.

50–75: You are an adequate-to-good listener. You listen well, although you may sometimes react too quickly to others before they are finished speaking.

25–45: You have some listening skills but need to improve them. You may often become impatient when trying to listen to others, hoping they will finish talking so you can talk.

0–20: You listen to others very infrequently. You may prefer to do all of the talking and experience extreme frustration while waiting for others to make their point.

SOURCE: Richard G. Weaver and John D. Farrell, *Managers As Facilitators: A Practical Guide to Getting Work Done in a Changing Workplace* (San Francisco: Berrett-Koehler Publishers, 1997), pp. 134–136. Used with permission.

Manager's Workshop

Evaluate This!

1. Form groups of five to eight members. The instructor will assign role of either Pat or Chris to each group. In other words, some groups will be "Pat" groups and some will be "Chris" groups. Only read the role you are assigned. *Do not* read the other role.

2. Fill in the box after each role, answering the questions. Role-play the next meeting between Pat and Chris. Be prepared to do your role-play in front of the class.

3. The instructor will call certain people to the front for the role-play.

4. The instructor will pick a Chris from one of the Chris groups and a Pat from a Pat group and bring them up to role-play. After 5 to 10 minutes, the role-play will stop and the class will be asked to comment on what happened. Then the instructor will choose another Chris and Pat and perform a second role-play, followed by class discussion.

5. Class discussion on communication in organizations.

Role for Pat to Read

It's time for annual performance evaluations at the Topflight Music Publishing Company. Pat, the new manager of the marketing department, has one employee, Bob, who is not cutting it. Pat has convinced his/her boss, Chris, the vice president of marketing, to reassign Bob to a less client-oriented position. It was difficult for Chris to accept the fact that Bob was a nuisance in the department. After all, Bob's wife, Veronica, executive vice president at Oldies Records, is an old friend and mentor of Chris's and helped Chris get the job with Topflight.

Bob has been very erratic in his behavior for the past two months. He comes in late to work three out of five days a week. He has become disruptive in the workplace and has thrown papers and files at coworkers. No one can explain his unpredictable behavior.

Pat meets with Bob on Thursday afternoon. Pat reviews Bob's past performance for the entire year with him. Near the end of the evaluation Pat explains to Bob that there is going to be a bit of a change in his workday. Pat demotes Bob. Bob is devastated. Suddenly he jumps up and begins yelling obscenities. He says to Pat, "With everything else going wrong in my life, I thought I could count on you for friendship and understanding. I'm going to talk to your boss Chris and I'll take you on later." He leaves Pat's office.

Thirty minutes later, Pat's phone rings. It's Chris saying, "I think we ought to give Bob another chance. I've told Bob that we want to meet with him tomorrow to discuss your meeting with him today."

What concepts or principles are important in this interaction relevant to each player? What communication principles are important here?	What should have been done differently?	What should happen at the next meeting between Pat and Chris? What will you say?
Chris		
Pat		
Bob		

Role for Chris to Read

It's time for annual performance evaluations at the Topflight Music Publishing Company. Pat, the new manager of the marketing department, has one employee, Bob, who is not cutting it. Pat has convinced his/her boss, Chris, the vice president of marketing, to reassign Bob to a less client-oriented position. It was difficult for Chris to accept the fact that Bob was a nuisance in the department. After all, Bob's wife, Veronica, executive vice president at Oldies Records, is an old friend and mentor of Chris's and helped Chris get the job with Topflight.

Bob has been very erratic in his behavior for the past two months. He comes in late to work three out of five days a week. He has become disruptive in the workplace and has thrown papers and files at coworkers. No one can explain his unpredictable behavior.

Pat has just met with Bob to tell him that he is fired, after reviewing his performance for the year. Right after the meeting, Bob storms into Chris's office and sputters at Chris, as Bob leans menacingly over Chris's desk, "You better watch out. If you two fire me, I'll, why, well, my wife has friends in high places, at record companies and in the media, some who know where the bones are buried—if you get my drift." His eyes were wide and bulging as he came around the desk and poked his finger into Chris's face. "You better not mess with me, not if you want to… ." And then Bob stood staring hatefully at Chris, turned and stalked out of the office.

After a few minutes, Chris realized there could be a big mess if Bob was not appeased, so Chris telephoned Bob. Then Chris called Pat and said, "I think we ought to give Bob another chance. I've told Bob that we want to meet with him tomorrow to discuss your meeting with him today."

What concepts or principles are important in this interaction relevant to each player? What communication principles are important here?	What should have been done differently?	What should happen at the next meeting between Pat and Chris? What will you say?
Chris		
Pat		
Bob		

SOURCE: Adapted by Dorothy Marcic from Lee Bolman's case. Used with permission.

Management in Practice: Ethical Dilemma

The Voice of Authority

When Gehan Rasinghe was hired as an account assistant at Werner and Thompson, a business and financial management firm, he was very relieved. He was overqualified for the job with his degree in accounting, but the combination of his accented English and his quiet manner had prevented him from securing any other position. Beatrice Werner, one of the managing partners of the firm, was impressed by his educational credentials and his courtly manner. She assured him he had advancement potential with the firm, but the account assistant position was the only one available. After months of rejections in his job hunt, Rasinghe accepted the position. He was committed to making his new job work at all costs.

Account Manager Cathy Putnam was Rasinghe's immediate superior. Putnam spoke with a heavy Boston accent, speaking at a lightning pace to match her enormous workload. She indicated to Rasinghe that he would need to get up to speed as quickly as possible to succeed in working with her. It was soon apparent that Putnam and Rasinghe were at odds. She resented having to repeat directions more than once to teach him his responsibilities. He also seemed resistant to making the many phone calls asking for copies of invoices, disputing charges on credit cards, and following up with a client's staff to get the information necessary to do his job. His accounting work was impeccable, but the public contact part of his job was in bad shape. Even his quiet answer of "No problem" to all her requests was starting to wear thin on Putnam. Before giving Rasinghe his three-month review, Putnam appealed to Beatrice Werner for help. Putnam was frustrated at their communication problems and didn't know what to do.

Werner had seen the problem coming. Although she had found Rasinghe's bank reconciliations and financial report preparations to be first-rate, she knew that phone work and client contact were a big part of any job in the firm. But as the daughter of German immigrants, Werner also knew that language and cultural barriers could be overcome with persistence and patience. Diversity was one of her ideals for her company, and it was not always easy to achieve. She felt sure that Rasinghe could become an asset to the firm in time. She worried that the time it would take was more than they could afford to give him.

What Do You Do?

1. Give Rasinghe his notice, with the understanding that a job that is primarily paperwork would be a better fit for him. Make the break now rather than later.

2. Place him with an account manager who has more time to help him develop his assertiveness and telephone skills and appreciates his knowledge of accounting.

3. Create a new position for him, where he could do the reports and reconciliations for several account managers, while their assistants concentrated on the public contact work. He would have little chance of future promotion, however.

Case for Critical Analysis

Inter-City Manufacturing, Inc.

The president of Inter-City Manufacturing Inc., Rich Langston, wanted to facilitate upward communication. He believed an open-door policy was a good place to start. He announced that his own door was open to all employees and encouraged senior managers to do the same. He felt this would give him a way to get early warning signals that would not be filtered or redirected through the formal chain of command. Langston found that many employees who used the open-door policy had been with the company for years and were comfortable talking to the president. Sometimes messages came through about inadequate policies and procedures. Langston would raise these issues and explain any changes at the next meeting of senior managers.

The most difficult complaints to handle were those from people who were not getting along with their bosses. One employee, Leroy, complained bitterly that his manager had overcommitted the department and put everyone under too much pressure. Leroy argued that long hours and low morale were major problems. But he would not allow Rich Langston to bring the manager into the discussion nor to seek out other employees to confirm the complaint. Although Langston suspected that Leroy might be right, he could not let the matter sit and blurted out, "Have you considered leaving the company?" This made Leroy realize that a meeting with his immediate boss was unavoidable.

Before the three-party meeting, Langston contacted Leroy's manager and explained what was going on. He insisted that the manager come to the meeting willing to listen and without hostility toward Leroy. During the meeting, Leroy's manager listened actively and displayed no ill will. He learned the problem from Leroy's perspective and realized he was over his head in his new job. After the meeting, the manager said he was relieved. He had been promoted into the job from a technical position just a few months earlier and had no management or planning experience. He welcomed Rich Langston's offer to help him do a better job of planning.

Questions

1. What techniques increased Rich Langston's communication effectiveness? Discuss.

2. Do you think that an open-door policy was the right way to improve upward communications? What other techniques would you suggest?

3. What problems do you think an open-door policy creates? Do you think many employees are reluctant to use it? Why?

SOURCE: Based on Everett T. Suters, "Hazards of an Open-Door Policy," *Inc.*, January 1987, pp. 99–102.

CHAPTER

15

Teamwork in Organizations

LEARNING OBJECTIVES

After studying this chapter, you should be able to do the following:

1   Identify the types of teams in organizations.

2   Discuss new applications of teams to facilitate employee involvement.

3   Identify roles within teams and the type of role you could play to help a team be effective.

4   Explain the general stages of team development.

5   Identify ways in which team size and diversity of membership affects team performance.

6   Explain the concepts of team cohesiveness and team norms and their relationship to team performance.

7   Understand the causes of conflict within and among teams and how to reduce conflict.

8   Discuss the assets and liabilities of organizational teams.

Manager's Challenge

Nestled in the foothills of the Appalachian Mountains, the Rowe Furniture Company of Salem, Virginia, has been producing sofas, loveseats, and easy chairs for more than 40 years. When Charlene Pedrolie arrived as the plant's new manufacturing chief, she found 500 people who came to work, punched their time cards, turned off their brains, and did what they were told to do. The pay was good by local standards, but workers were bored and apathetic. The traditional assembly line, which required that workers repeat the same tasks—one person cutting, another sewing, another gluing, and so forth—had worked well for Rowe in the past, but the marketplace was undergoing a revolution. Furniture shoppers used to be content to buy what was on the showroom floor or else wait months for a custom-made product. But not any longer, because customers were demanding custom pieces, but they balked at the idea of waiting the standard three to six months for delivery. Managers wanted to increase sales by installing a network of showroom computers, which would allow customers to choose fabrics and furniture designs to their individual taste and zap the order directly to the Rowe plant. And, they wanted to promise delivery within a month. Plant workers snorted at the preposterous idea. How on earth were they supposed to do it? Pedrolie knew the factory needed a more efficient assembly process and a management system that tapped into the minds and energy of every single worker.[1]

If you were Charlene Pedrolie, how would you meet this challenge? Can the formation of teams help solve the problem?

The problems facing Rowe Furniture confront other companies. How can they be more flexible and responsive in an increasingly competitive, changing environment? One solution is the formation of teams. A quiet revolution has been taking place in organizations across the country and around the world. From the assembly line to the executive office, from large corporations such as Ford Motor Company and 3M to small businesses such as Growing Green, a St. Louis plantscaping firm, and Radius, a Boston restaurant, teams are becoming the basic building block of organizations.

Over the past two decades, the use of teams has increased dramatically in response to new competitive pressures, the need for greater flexibility and speed, and a desire to give people more opportunities for involvement. Hecla Mining Company uses teams for company goal setting; a major telecommunications company uses teams of salespeople to deal with big customers with complex purchasing requirements; and Lassiter Middle School in Jefferson County, Kentucky, uses teams of teachers to prepare daily schedules and handle student discipline problems. Some companies use virtual teams composed of managers and employees working in different countries.[2] Many organizations have had great success with teams, including increased productivity, quality improvements, greater innovation, and higher employee satisfaction. Federal Express (FedEx), for example, cut service problems such as incorrect bills and lost packages by 13 percent by using teams. At Xerox, production plants using teams reported a 30 percent increase in productivity.[3] A study of team-based organizations in Australia supports the idea that teams provide benefits to employees and organizations.[4]

This chapter focuses on teams and their applications within organizations. We will define various types of teams, explore their stages of development, and examine such characteristics as size, cohesiveness, diversity, and norms. We will discuss how individuals can make contributions to teams and review the benefits and costs associated with teamwork. Teams are an important aspect of organizational life, and the ability to manage them is an important component of manager and organization success.

Teams at Work

In this section, we will define teams and then discuss a model of team effectiveness that summarizes the important concepts.

What Is a Team?

team
A unit of two or more people who interact and coordinate their work to accomplish a specific goal.

A **team** is a unit of two or more people who interact and coordinate their work to accomplish a specific goal.[5] This definition has three components. First, two or more people are required. Teams can be large, though most have fewer than 15 people. Second, people in a team have regular interaction. People who do not interact, such as when standing in line at a lunch counter or riding in an elevator, do not compose a team. Third, people in a team share a performance goal, whether it be to design a new hand-held computer, build a car, or write a textbook. Students are often assigned to teams to do classwork assignments, in which case the purpose is to perform the assignment and receive an acceptable grade.

Take **ACTION**
Remember that it takes work to turn a group of people into a team.

Though a team is a group of people, the two terms are not interchangeable. An employer, a teacher, or a coach can put together a group of people and never build a team. The team concept implies a sense of shared mission and collective responsibility. Exhibit 15.1 lists the primary differences between groups and teams. One example of a true team comes from the military, where U.S. Navy surgeons, nurses, anesthesiologists, and technicians make up eight-person forward surgical teams that operated for the first time in combat during Operation Iraqi Freedom. These teams were scattered over Iraq and were able to move to new locations in four trucks and be set up within

EXHIBIT 15.1

Differences between Groups and Teams

Group	Team
• Has a designated strong leader	• Shares or rotates leadership roles
• Individual accountability	• Individual and mutual accountability (accountable to each other)
• Identical purpose for group and organization	• Specific team vision or purpose
• Individual work products	• Collective work products
• Runs efficient meetings	• Meetings encourage open-ended discussion and problem solving
• Effectiveness measured indirectly by influence on business (such as financial performance)	• Effectiveness measured directly by assessing collective work
• Discusses, decides, delegates work to individuals	• Discusses, decides, shares work

SOURCE: Adapted from Jon R. Katzenbach and Douglas K. Smith, "The Discipline of Teams," *Harvard Business Review* (March–April 1995), 111–120.

an hour. With a goal of saving the 15 to 20 percent of wounded soldiers and civilians who would die unless they received critical care within 24 hours, members of these teams coordinate their activities to accomplish a critical shared mission.[6] The sports world provides many examples of the importance of teamwork. One manager learned valuable lessons about team building by participating in the ten-month BT Global Challenge around-the-world race, as described below.

BT Global Challenge

Much of what Doug Webb knows about teamwork he learned during his ten months as a crew member on the yacht Logica, participating in the BT Global Challenge, an around-the-world race for amateurs, many of whom had never sailed before. Competitors put to sea in identical boats, and crews are selected by race organizers to be as equal as possible. What makes the difference is the ability to turn a group of diverse individuals into a high-performance team.

One key, Webb discovered, is to ensure everyone feels equal and to help each individual contribute to his or her full potential. In business, the tendency is to identify the least dependable or weakest members of a team and replace them, but during the BT Global Challenge, that was not possible. Therefore, it was important to identify and understand every person's motivations, interests, and capabilities and use these to benefit the common good. With effective coaching, individuals who at first seemed less competent became key team members, with the leader enabling them to fill roles where they could make a maximum contribution and avoid areas where they were likely to fail. Success breeds confidence, and as people grew in their roles, their contributions expanded. Another important aspect of building a team is communication. The Logica crew met long before the race to get to know one another and set ground rules for how they would communicate, learning to accept positive and negative feedback. The emphasis was on the ability to have open and frank conversations without crew members feeling hurt or insecure about their performance.

During the race, everyone engaged in evaluating and learning from mistakes, as well as celebrating each accomplishment. Conflicts were discussed openly instead of being allowed to fester and grow. The Logica team finished fourth out of a group of 12 racing teams. But the most important win for Webb was that as he returned to his job as CFO of Logica, a leading information technology company with more than 11,000 employees in 28 countries, he took with him the lessons of teamwork he learned at sea.[7]

Model of Work Team Effectiveness

Some of the factors associated with team effectiveness are illustrated in Exhibit 15.2. Work team effectiveness is based on two outcomes: productive output and personal satisfaction.[8]

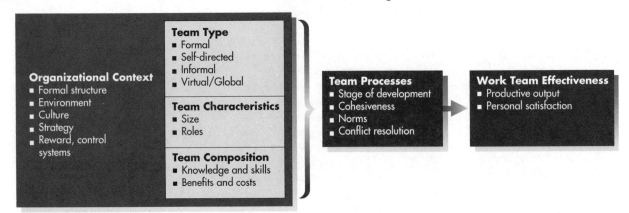

EXHIBIT 15.2

*Work Team
Effectiveness Model*

Productive output pertains to the quality and quantity of task outputs as defined by team goals. Personal satisfaction pertains to the team's ability to meet the personal needs of its members and hence maintain their membership and commitment.

The factors that influence team effectiveness begin with the organizational context.[9] The organizational context in which the team operates is described in other chapters and includes such factors as structure, strategy, environment, culture, and reward systems. Within that context, managers define teams. Important team characteristics are the type of team, the team structure, and team composition. Managers must decide when to create permanent teams within the formal structure and when to use a temporary task team. Factors such as team diversity in terms of gender and race, as well as knowledge, skills, and attitudes, can have a tremendous impact on team processes and effectiveness.[10] Team size and roles are important. Managers must consider if a team is the best way to do a task. If costs outweigh benefits, managers may wish to assign an individual employee to the task.

These team characteristics influence processes internal to the team, which, in turn, affect output and satisfaction. Good team leaders understand and manage stages of team development, cohesiveness, norms, and conflict to establish an effective team. These processes are influenced by team and organizational characteristics and by the ability of members and leaders to direct these processes in a positive manner.

The model of team performance in Exhibit 15.2 is the basis for this chapter. In the following sections, we will examine types of organizational teams, team structure, internal processes, and team benefits and costs.

Types of Teams

Many types of teams can exist within organizations. The easiest way to classify teams is in terms of those created as part of the organization's formal structure and those created to increase employee participation.

Formal Teams

formal teams

A team created by the organization as part of the formal organization structure.

Formal teams are created by the organization as part of the formal organization structure. Two common types of formal teams are vertical and horizontal, which typically represent vertical and horizontal structural relationships, as described in Chapter 7. These two types of teams are illustrated in Exhibit 15.3. A third type of formal team is the special-purpose team.

vertical team

A formal team composed of a manager and his or her subordinates in the organization's formal chain of command.

Vertical Team. A vertical team is composed of a manager and his or her subordinates in the formal chain of command. Sometimes called a functional team or a command team, the vertical team may in some cases include three or four levels of hierarchy within a functional department. Typically, the vertical team includes a single

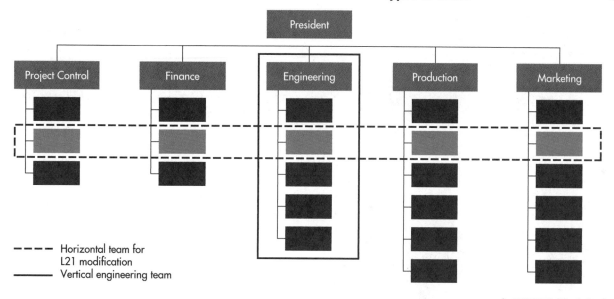

- - - - Horizontal team for
        L21 modification
———— Vertical engineering team

EXHIBIT 15.3

Horizontal and Vertical Teams in an Organization

department in an organization. The third-shift nursing team on the second floor of St. Luke's Hospital is a vertical team that includes nurses and a supervisor. A financial analysis department, a quality control department, an accounting department, and a human resource department are all command teams. Each is created by the organization to attain specific goals through members' joint activities and interactions.

Horizontal Team. A **horizontal team** is composed of employees from about the same hierarchical level but from different areas of expertise.[11] A horizontal team is drawn from several departments, is given a specific task, and may be disbanded after the task is completed. The two most common types of horizontal teams are cross-functional teams and committees.

As described in Chapter 7, a cross-functional team is a group of employees from different departments formed to deal with a specific activity and existing only until the task is completed. Sometimes called a task force, the team might be used to create a new product in a manufacturing organization or a new history curriculum in a university. Several departments are involved, and many views have to be considered, so these tasks are best served with a horizontal, cross-functional team.

A **committee** generally is long-lived and may be a permanent part of the organization's structure. Membership on a committee usually is decided by a person's title or position rather than by personal expertise. A committee often needs official representation, compared with selection for a cross-functional team, which is based on personal qualifications for solving a problem. Committees typically are formed to deal with recurring tasks. For example, a grievance committee handles employee grievances, an advisory committee makes recommendations in the areas of employee compensation and work practices, and a worker-management committee may be concerned with work rules, job design changes, and suggestions for work improvement.[12]

As part of the horizontal structure of the organization, cross-functional teams and committees offer several advantages: They allow organization members to exchange information, they generate suggestions for coordinating the organizational units that are represented, they develop new ideas and solutions for existing organizational problems, and they assist in the development of new organizational practices and policies.

Special-Purpose Team. Special-purpose teams, sometimes called project teams, are created outside the formal organization structure to undertake a project of special

horizontal team

A formal team composed of employees from about the same hierarchical level but from different areas of expertise.

Take *ACTION*

As a manager, ensure you periodically form cross-functional teams, so you have new people in the conversations; otherwise, with the same people you will likely have the same outcome.

committee

A long-lasting, sometimes permanent team in the organization structure created to deal with tasks that recur regularly.

© Bern Auers

*James Frankel, James McLurkin, and Jennifer Smith serve on the SwarmBot team, a **special-purpose team** at iRobot in Burlington, Massachusetts, that is researching how SwarmBots can benefit mankind. SwarmBots are small robots in the form of cubes with rechargeable batteries that can potentially collaborate like a colony of ants to accomplish difficult tasks, such as disposing of land mines or taking over buildings held by bad guys. The team is perfecting software that can work with as few as 10 robots or as many as 10,000, and asking the critical question: "If you could make small robots cheaply, what would you use them for?"*

special-purpose teams

A team created outside the formal organization to undertake a project of special importance or creativity.

problem-solving teams

Typically, 5 to 12 hourly employees from the same department who meet to discuss ways of improving quality, efficiency, and the work environment.

importance or creativity. Special-purpose teams focus on a specific purpose and expect to disband once the specific project is completed.[13] Examples include the team that developed the first IBM ThinkPad and the project team for the Chrysler PT Cruiser. A special-purpose team is part of the formal organization and has its own reporting structure, but members perceive themselves as a separate entity.[14] Many of today's companies are using special-purpose teams to accelerate development of a special product or execute a highly important project. These fast-cycle teams, set up to work on projects that top management deems important, are provided the freedom and resources to complete projects quickly.[15] Special purpose teams bring former foes together to work on creating a better environment as described in the Focus on Collaboration box.

Self-Directed Teams

Employee involvement through teams is designed to increase the participation of low-level workers in decision making and the conduct of their jobs, with the goal of improving performance. Employee involvement began with techniques such as information sharing with employees or asking employees for suggestions about work improvement. Gradually, companies moved toward greater autonomy for employees, which led first to problem-solving teams and then to self-directed teams.[16]

Problem-solving teams typically consist of 5 to 12 hourly employees from the same department who voluntarily meet to discuss ways of improving quality, efficiency, and the work environment. Recommendations are proposed to management for approval. Problem-solving teams usually are the first step in a company's move toward greater employee participation. The most widely known application is quality circles, first used by Japanese companies, in which employees focus on ways to improve quality in the production process. USX adopted this approach in several of its steel mills, recognizing that quality takes a team effort. Under the title All Product Excellence Program (APEX), USX set up APEX teams of up to 12 employees who met several times a month to solve quality problems.[17]

As a company matures, problem-solving teams can gradually evolve into self-directed teams, which represent a fundamental change in how employee work is organized. Self-directed teams enable employees to feel challenged, find their work meaningful, and develop a strong sense of identity with the company.[18] **Self-directed teams** typically consist of 5 to 20 multiskilled workers who rotate jobs to produce an entire product or service or at least one complete aspect or portion of a product or service (e.g., engine assembly, insurance claim processing). The central idea is that the teams, rather than managers or supervisors, take responsibility for their work, make decisions, monitor their own performance, and alter their work behavior as needed to solve problems, meet goals, and adapt to changing conditions.[19] Self-directed teams are permanent teams that can include the following elements:

- The team includes employees with several skills and functions, and the combined skills are sufficient to perform a major organizational task. A team may include members from the foundry, machining, grinding, fabrication, and sales departments,

FOCUS ON COLLABORATION

Sustainable Northwest and others

A few years ago, third-generation lumberjack Mike McMahon considered enviromentalists his enemy. He, after all, was cutting down the forests they were trying to sustain. These days, you might find him using a shredding machine to reduce thick shrubbery to pulp, leaving more breathing room for the tall Douglas firs in the Wallowa County area. With severe logger layoffs in recent years, economics brought new cooperation.

Thanks to the nonprofit Sustainable Northwest, McMahon and other loggers are working on the same goals as the environmentalists. With help from federal grants, the organization tries to pump up local economies with eco-friendly projects, creating more than 100 Green jobs in the process. Their goal is for people to see that environmental health and economic well-being "are partners, not predators."

The Arizonan Sonoran Institute leads cattle ranchers away from the soil-eroding grazing and into hosting eco-tours, while San Francisco Sustainable Conservation (SC) helped struggling strawberry farmers find work helping to control steep slope soil runoff. "To make these projects work," says SC's executive director, Ashley Boren, "It has to benefit both sides."

Wallowa County's greening is one of the more visible successes in the sustainability movement. Unlike some confrontation-only environmentalists, this compromise-minded faction turns foes into allies by offering jobs and incentives. Unemployed loggers are lining up to help. McMahon, a 43-year-old burly lumberjack found himself in a new world. "This is sure a lot different from what I used to do," he says. "But at least it keeps me in the woods."

SOURCE: Jonathan Nicholas, "Book 'em, Dano This Time, Mike Powell's Serious," *The Oregonian* (Jan. 14, 2005): p. C1; Jim Carlton, "A Quiet Truce in the Green Wars," *The Wall Street Journal* (Nov. 15, 2001): B1–B4.

---

with members cross-trained to perform one another's jobs. The team eliminates barriers among departments, enabling excellent coordination to produce a product or service.

- The team is given access to resources such as information, equipment, machinery, and supplies needed to perform the complete task.

- The team is empowered with decision-making authority, which means that members have the freedom to select new members, solve problems, spend money, monitor results, and plan for the future.[20]

In a self-directed team, team members take over managerial duties such as scheduling or ordering materials. They work with minimum supervision, perhaps electing one of their own as supervisor, who may change each year. The most effective self-directed teams are those that are fully empowered, as described in the discussion of empowerment in Chapter 13. In addition to having increased responsibility and discretion, empowered teams have a strong belief in their capabilities, find value and meaning in their work, and recognize the impact the team's work has on customers, other stakeholders, and organizational success.[21] Managers create the conditions that determine if self-directed teams are empowered by giving teams true power and decision-making authority, complete information, knowledge and skills, and appropriate rewards. The manager to whom the team and team leaders report, sometimes referred to as the external leader, has a tremendous impact on the team's success. In addition to creating conditions for empowerment, effective external leaders serve as an active link between the team and the organization, building constructive relationships and getting the team what it needs to do its best work.[22] An interesting example of the use of self-directed teams is the Orpheus Orchestra of New York City.

Most orchestras are strongly hierarchical and structured around a conductor who wields almost complete power and control. Not Orpheus, a world-renowned chamber orchestra established in the 1970s by a small group of musicians committed to democratic power sharing.

Orpheus operates completely without a conductor. Teams of musicians determine the repertoire, schedule concerts, select new musicians, interpret musical works, and handle all the other artistic and performance duties a conductor usually controls. The

self-directed team

A team consisting of 5 to 20 multiskilled workers who rotate jobs to produce an entire product or service, often supervised by an elected member.

Take **ACTION**

As a manager, make sure you allow self-directed teams to be self-directed but with enough management support to achieve their goals.

Orpheus Orchestra

instrument sections constitute natural, specialized self-directed teams. Leadership rotates among different members who are elected by their teammates.

The actual structure of teams at Orpheus is complex and is designed to facilitate participative leadership, avoid hierarchical control, and allow everyone to participate in decision making.[23]

The Orpheus Orchestra has found that using self-directed teams provides a number of advantages. The greater information flow and diverse artistic input contributes to a superb performance. In addition, members feel a high degree of commitment, and turnover is quite low. One business organization that succeeds with teamwork is Consolidated Diesel's engine factory in Whitakers, North Carolina. In its 20 or so years of operation as a team-based organization, the plant has had higher revenues, lower turnover, and lower injury rates than the industry average. In addition, while most plants average 1 supervisor for every 25 workers, Consolidated Diesel has 1 for every 100 employees because the plant workers handle many supervisory duties. The difference yields a savings of about $1 million a year.[24]

Teams in the New Workplace

Some exciting new approaches to teamwork have resulted from advances in information technology, shifting employee expectations, and the globalization of business. Two types of teams that are increasingly being used are virtual teams and global teams.

virtual team

A team that uses advanced information and telecommunications technologies so geographically distant members can collaborate on projects and reach common goals.

Virtual Teams.   A **virtual team** is made up of geographically or organizationally dispersed members who are linked primarily through advanced information and telecommunications technologies.[25] Though some virtual teams consist only of organizational members, virtual teams can include contingent workers, members of partner organizations, customers, suppliers, consultants, or other outsiders. Team members use e-mail, voice mail, videoconferencing, Internet and Intranet technologies, and collaboration software to perform their work, though they might meet face to face. Many virtual teams are cross-functional teams that emphasize solving customer problems or completing specific projects. Others are permanent self-directed teams. A new and radical kind of virtual team predicts certain outcomes, as shown in the Focus on Collaboration box.

FOCUS ON COLLABORATION

Wisdom of Crowds

Ever wonder why the best lifeline on *Who Wants to be a Millionaire?* is the audience (with a 91 percent rate of correct answers)? It is because of something called "The Wisdom of Crowds," first discovered by social scientist James Surowiecki and it concerns collective intelligence, the reason the average/mean answer is the most correct for how many jellybeans are in the jar. The stock market is based on collective wisdom. No one person knows everything about the companies they invest in, but collectively there is some competence most of the time (except in bubbles, when crowd fever takes over).

In 1995, Paul Johnson started using the Academy Awards in to test this theory. He gave hundreds of people ballots before the event and asked who would win in 12 categories. The average person was correct only 4.8 times out of 12. But the group average

got 11 of 12 correct. Another example is the Iowa Electronic Markets (IEM), which allows people to buy and sell their shares based on which candidate they think will gain the most votes in elections. The IEM has outperformed 600 polls in the last six elections. The Hollywood Stock Exchange, similar to IEM, has stock traders getting 35 of 40 categories correct for Academy Awards.

This works because collective electronic decisions are smart at taking the best and smartest information. It is data-mining at its finest because people are only rewarded for being correct, with no incentive to hide or distort information. Want to try? See http://www.hsx.com/.

SOURCES: Joseph Nocera, "The Oscar Experiment," *Fortune* (March 22, 2004): 52–53; James Surowiecki, "Decision, Decisions," *The New Yorker* (March 27, 2003): 33.

With virtual teams, team leadership is shared or rotated, depending on the area of expertise needed at each stage of the project.[26] In addition, team membership in virtual teams may change quickly, depending on the tasks to be performed. One of the primary advantages of virtual teams is the ability to assemble the most appropriate group of people to complete a complex project, solve a particular problem, or exploit a specific strategic opportunity. Virtual teams present unique challenges. Managers as team leaders should consider these critical issues when building virtual teams:[27]

- *Select the right team members.* The first step is creating a team of people who have the right mix of technical and interpersonal skills, task knowledge, and personalities to work in a virtual environment. Interviews with virtual team members and leaders find that the ability to communicate and a desire to work as a team are the most important personal qualities for virtual team members.[28]

- *Manage socialization.* People need to get to know one another and understand the appropriate behaviors and attitudes. Smart team leaders establish team norms and ground rules for interaction early in the team's formation.

- *Foster trust.* Trust might be the most important ingredient in a virtual team. Teams that exhibit high trust levels tend to have clear roles and expectations of one another, get to know one another as individuals, and maintain positive action-oriented attitudes.

- *Manage communications.* Frequent communication is essential. Team leaders need to understand when and how to use various forms of communication to their best advantage. Some experts suggest regular face-to-face meetings, and others believe virtual teams can be successful even if they always interact electronically. One time when face-to-face communication might be essential is when misunderstandings, frustrations, or conflicts threaten the team's work.[29]

> **Take ACTION**
> Getting the right people to do the job is important; do not put someone on the team only because he or she asks for it and is available.

Global Teams.   Virtual teams are also sometimes global teams. **Global teams** are cross-border work teams made up of members of different nationalities whose activities span multiple countries.[30] Global teams generally fall into two categories: intercultural teams, whose members come from different countries or cultures and meet face to face, and virtual global teams, whose members remain in separate locations around the world and conduct their work electronically.[31] For example, the research department at BT Labs has 660 researchers spread across the United Kingdom and several other countries. The researchers work in global virtual teams that investigate virtual reality, artificial intelligence, and other advanced information technologies.[32] The following example describes the use of virtual teams at STMicroelectronics.

> **global teams**
> A work team made up of members of different nationalities whose activities span multiple countries; may operate as a virtual team or meet face to face.

STMicroelectronics

If you worked at STMicroelectronics (STMicro), formed from the 1987 merger of two ailing European semiconductor companies—one French and one Italian—you might work side by side with people from London and New Dehli, Singapore and Sicily, and Geneva and Madrid. STMicro is a global corporation and teams include people from various countries. STMicro has grown to become one of the world's largest computer chip makers and continues to win new business all over the world.

But managers faced a problem when the company won a coveted order for microchips to power the brains for a navigational mapping system to be installed in new Fiats and Peugeots. Getting the order was a major coup, but filling it was going to be hard. STMicro executives knew a chip project of this magnitude required collaboration among a wide range of disciplines, including chip design, engineering, fabrication, systems integration, quality control, packaging, marketing, and sales. Moreover, the people with the expertise to complete the project lived in five different countries, spanned 14 time zones, and spoke six different native languages.

The car makers needed the chips in a big hurry. If they could not get the navigational systems installed for the new models, they would lose sales. The time constraints on the project, as well as personal and cost factors, made it impossible to get everyone together in one location, so a virtual global team was formed to collaborate on the project using electronic communication systems and collaborative software.

Thanks to training and excellent leadership, STMicro's first major virtual team project was a success. One reason is that team leaders united everyone around a common purpose of designing and developing the new chips in time to meet the customers' needs. Members were willing to sublimate their individual goals, viewpoints, and egos for the sake of achieving this ambitious goal. As the team's work progressed, members began to care about each other as well as the project, though many of them had never met face-to-face. At the project's end, one of the team members said, "This was the best experience of my life. I learned so much."

As STMicro continues to build business and open customer support and design centers in different areas of the world, the use of virtual global teams will be an important way to accomplish organizational goals. Virtual teams enable the company to tap into knowledge around the globe to develop creative solutions to customers' problems.[33]

Global teams can present enormous challenges for team leaders, who have to bridge gaps of time, distance, and culture. In some cases, members speak different languages, use different technologies, and have different beliefs about authority, time orientation, decision making, and teamwork. For example, multinational organizations have found that many team phenomena are culture-specific. The acceptance and effectiveness of team-based systems can vary across different cultures, which makes implementing and evaluating teams complex.[34] Organizations using global teams invest the time and resources to educate employees. They have to make sure all team members appreciate and understand cultural differences, are focused on goals, and understand their responsibilities to the team. For an effective global team, all team members must be willing to deviate somewhat from their own values and norms and establish new norms for the team.[35] As with virtual teams, selecting team members, building trust, and sharing information are critical to success.

Team Characteristics

The next issue of concern to managers is designing the team for greatest effectiveness. One factor is team characteristics, which can affect team dynamics and performance. Characteristics of particular concern are team size, diversity, and member roles.

Size

The ideal size of work teams often is thought to be 7, though variations from 5 to 12 typically are associated with good team performance. These teams are large enough to take advantage of diverse skills, enable members to express good and bad feelings, and solve problems. They also are small enough to permit members to feel an intimate part of the group. A recent Gallup poll in the United States found that 82 percent of employees surveyed believe small teams are more productive.[36] In general, as a team increases in size, it becomes harder for each member to interact with and influence the others. Ray Oglethorpe, president of AOL Technologies, which makes extensive use of teams, believes keeping teams small is the key to success. "If you have more than 15 or 20 people, you're dead," he says. "The connections between team members are too hard to make."[37]

Take **ACTION**

Smaller teams are more nimble and tend to function more effectively.

A summary of research on group size suggests the following:[38]

1. Small teams (two to four members) show more agreement, ask more questions, and exchange more opinions. Members want to get along with one another. Small teams report more satisfaction and enter into more personal discussions. They tend to be informal and make few demands on team leaders. W.L. Gore keeps its teams small to keep the company, vibrant as shown in the Best Practices box.

2. Large teams (12 or more) tend to have more disagreements and differences of opinion. Subgroups often form, and conflicts among them occur, ranging from protection of "turf" to trivial matters, such as "What kind of coffee is brewing in the pot?" Demands on leaders are greater because there is more centralized decision making and less member participation. Large teams also tend to be less friendly. Turnover and absenteeism are higher in a large team, especially for blue-collar workers. Because less satisfaction is associated with specialized tasks and poor communication, team members have fewer opportunities to participate and feel like an important part of the group.

As a general rule, large teams make needs satisfaction for individuals more difficult; thus, people have less of a reason to remain committed to their goals. Teams of from five to 12 seem to work best. If a team grows larger than 20, managers should divide it into subgroups, each with its own members and goals.

Diversity

Since teams require various skills, knowledge, and experience, it seems likely that heterogeneous teams would be more effective than homogeneous ones. In general, research supports this idea, showing that diverse teams produce more innovative solutions to problems.[39] Diversity in terms of functional area and skills, thinking styles, and personal characteristics is often a source of creativity. In addition, diversity may contribute to a healthy conflict level that leads to better decision making.

Recent research studies have confirmed that functional diversity and gender diversity can have a positive impact on work team performance.[40] Racial, national, and ethnic diversity can be good for teams, but in the short term these differences might hinder team interaction and performance. Teams made up of racially and culturally diverse members tend to have more difficulty learning to work well together; with effective leadership, the problems fade over time.[41]

BEST PRACTICES

W.L. Gore

Gore-Tex manufacturer W.L. Gore is arguably the most innovative company in the United States. One of its secrets is its lack of stultifying structure, becoming a place of open communications and strong teamwork. It does have rules, though, on how to design the way people interact and how teams are patterned.

1. Teams are kept small, to increase familiarity and a sense of community. The company even limits plant size to 200 workers.
2. No chain-of-command rules. Anyone can talk to anyone. Written memos are frowned upon, with a preference for face-to-face interactions.
3. No ranks or job descriptions. Everyone is supposed to be like an amoeba, and morph into what is needed for the job at hand.
4. The long view is the norm, taking sometimes years for a product to get to market.
5. Failure is celebrated. When a team decides an idea is not worthy of further pursuit, it kills the venture and celebrates with food or drink. This lets everyone know that part of risk-taking is that some ideas will not work. When failure is feared and punished, innovation suffers.

SOURCE: Alan Deutschman, "The Fabric of Creativity," *Fast Company* (Dec. 2004): 54; Alan Deutschman, "Gore's Text for Innovation," *Fast Company* (Dec. 2004): 59.

CONCEPT CONNECTION

This landscaping team from Christy Webber & Company is working on the Millennium Park in Chicago, which opened in 2004. Christy Webber, who owns the firm head-quartered on Chicago's West Side, appreci-ates the value of **team diversity***. Her 100 employees are formed into teams that include both union and nonunion members and represent a mix of ethnic groups, gen-ders, and skills. Yet, diversity can occasion-ally be a challenge. "Sometimes there is friction between the groups," Webber says. "It's really hard to get them to mix." Webber's excellent people skills enable her to help people work well together and gain the benefits of diverse opinions and skills.*

© Doug Fogelson/DRFP

task specialist role

A role in which the individ-ual devotes personal time and energy to helping the team accomplish its task.

Take *ACTION*

When assigning team members, have each role represented; you need task and socioe-motional roles filled.

socioemotional role

A role in which the individ-ual provides support for team members' emotional needs and social unity.

Member Roles

For a team to be successful over the long run, it must be structured so it can maintain its members' social well-being and accomplish its task. In successful teams, the require-ments for task performance and social satisfaction are met by the emergence of two types of roles: task specialist role and socioemotional role.[42]

People who play the **task specialist role** spend time and energy helping the team reach its goal.

They often display the following behaviors:

- *Initiate ideas.* Propose new solutions to team problems.

- *Give opinions.* Offer opinions on task solutions; give candid feedback on others' suggestions.

- *Seek information.* Ask for task-relevant facts.

- *Summarize.* Relate various ideas to the problem at hand; pull ideas together into a summary perspective.

- *Energize.* Stimulate the team into action when interest drops.[43]

People who adopt a **socioemotional role** support team members' emotional needs and help strengthen the social entity. They display the following behaviors:

- *Encourage.* Are warm and receptive to others' ideas; praise and encourage others to draw forth their contributions.

- *Harmonize.* Reconcile group conflicts; help disagreeing parties reach agreement.

- *Reduce tension.* Tell jokes or in other ways draw off emotions when group atmosphere is tense.

- *Follow.* Go along with the team; agree to other team members' ideas.

- *Compromise.* Will shift own opinions to maintain team harmony.[44]

Exhibit 15.4 illustrates task specialist and socioemotional roles in teams. When most indi-viduals in a team play a social role, the team is socially oriented. Members do not criticize or disagree with one another and do not forcefully offer opinions or accomplish team tasks

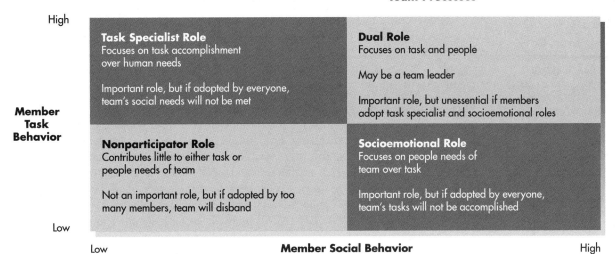

High

Task Specialist Role
Focuses on task accomplishment
over human needs

Important role, but if adopted by everyone,
team's social needs will not be met

Dual Role
Focuses on task and people

May be a team leader

Important role, but unessential if members
adopt task specialist and socioemotional roles

Nonparticipator Role
Contributes little to either task or
people needs of team

Not an important role, but if adopted by too
many members, team will disband

Socioemotional Role
Focuses on people needs of
team over task

Important role, but if adopted by everyone,
team's tasks will not be accomplished

Low

**Member
Task
Behavior**

Low   **Member Social Behavior**   High

EXHIBIT 15.4
Team Member Roles

because their primary interest is to keep the team happy. Teams with mostly socioemotional roles can be satisfying, but they can be unproductive. At the other extreme, a team primarily made up of task specialists will tend to have a singular concern for task accomplishment. This team will be effective for a short period of time but will be dissatisfying for members over the long run. Task specialists convey little emotional concern for one another, are unsupportive, and ignore team members' social and emotional needs. The task-oriented team can be humorless and unsatisfying.

As Exhibit 15.4 illustrates, some team members may play a **dual role**. People with dual roles contribute to the task and meet members' emotional needs. Such people often become team leaders. A study of new product development teams in high-technology firms found that the most effective teams were headed by leaders who balanced the technical needs of the project with human interaction issues, thus meeting task and socioemotional needs.[45] Exhibit 15.4 shows the final type of role, called the **nonparticipator role**, in which people contribute little to the task or the social needs of team members. Nonparticipators are typically held in low esteem by the team.

The important thing for managers to remember is that effective teams must have people in task specialist and socioemotional roles. Humor and social concern are as important to team effectiveness as are facts and problem solving. Managers should remember that some people perform better in one type of role; some are inclined toward social concerns and others toward task concerns. A well-balanced team will do best over the long term because it will be personally satisfying for team members and permit the accomplishment of team tasks.

dual roles

A role in which the individual contributes to the team's task and supports members' emotional needs.

nonparticipator role

A role in which the individual contributes little to the task or members' socioemotional needs.

Team Processes

Now we turn our attention to internal team processes. Team processes pertain to those dynamics that change over time and can be influenced by team leaders. In this section, we will discuss the team processes of stages of team development, cohesiveness, and norms. The fourth type of team process, conflict, will be covered in the next section.

Stages of Team Development

After a team has been created, it develops through distinct stages.[46] New teams are different from mature teams. Recall a time when you were a member of a new team, such as a fraternity or sorority pledge class, a committee, or a small team formed to do a class assignment. Over time, the team changed. In the beginning, team members had to get to know one another, establish roles and norms, divide the labor, and clarify the team's task. In this way, each member became part of a smoothly operating team.

Take *ACTION*

When you are on a team that is having conflicts in the early stages, that is a normal part of the developmental process.

forming

The stage of team development characterized by orientation and acquaintance.

EXHIBIT 15.5

Five Stages of Team Development

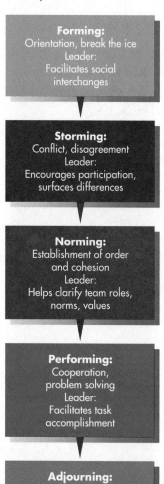

Forming:
Orientation, break the ice
Leader:
Facilitates social interchanges

Storming:
Conflict, disagreement
Leader:
Encourages participation, surfaces differences

Norming:
Establishment of order and cohesion
Leader:
Helps clarify team roles, norms, values

Performing:
Cooperation, problem solving
Leader:
Facilitates task accomplishment

Adjourning:
Task completion
Leader:
Brings closure, signifies completion

The challenge for leaders is to understand the stages of team development and take action that will improve the group's ability. Research findings suggest that team development is not random but evolves over definitive stages. One useful model for describing these stages is shown in Exhibit 15.5. Each stage confronts team leaders and members with unique problems and challenges.[47]

Forming. The forming stage of development is a period of orientation and getting acquainted. Members break the ice and test one another for friendship possibilities and task orientation. Team members find which behaviors are acceptable to others. Uncertainty is high during this stage, and members usually accept whatever power or authority is offered by formal or informal leaders. Members are dependent on the team until they find out what the ground rules are and what is expected of them. During this initial stage, members are concerned about such things as, "What is expected of me?" "What is acceptable?" "Will I fit in?" During the forming stage, the team leader should provide time for members to get acquainted with one another and encourage them to engage in informal social discussions.

Storming. During the **storming** stage, individual personalities emerge. People become more assertive in clarifying their roles and what is expected of them. This stage is marked by conflict and disagreement. People may disagree over their perceptions of the team's mission. Members may jockey for position, and coalitions or subgroups based on common interests may form. One subgroup may disagree with another over the total team's goals or how to achieve them. Unless teams can move beyond this stage, they may get bogged down and never achieve high performance. During the storming stage, the team leader should encourage participation by each team member. Members should propose ideas, disagree with one another, and work through the uncertainties and conflicting perceptions about team tasks and goals.

Norming. During the **norming** stage, conflict is resolved, and team harmony and unity emerge. Consensus develops on who has the power, who are the leaders, and members' roles. Members come to accept and understand one another. Differences are resolved, and members develop a sense of team cohesion. This stage typically is of short duration. During the norming stage, the team leader should emphasize unity within the team and help clarify team norms and values.

Performing. During the **performing** stage, the major emphasis is on problem solving and accomplishing the assigned task. Members are committed to the team's mission. They are coordinated with one another and handle disagreements in a mature way. They confront and resolve problems in the interest of task accomplishment. They interact frequently and direct their discussions and influence toward achieving team goals. During this stage, the leader should concentrate on managing high task performance. Socioemotional and task specialists should contribute.

Adjourning. The **adjourning** stage occurs in committees and teams that have a limited task to perform and are disbanded afterward. During this stage, the emphasis is on wrapping up and gearing down. Task performance is no longer a top priority. Members may feel heightened emotionality, strong cohesiveness, and depression or even regret over the team's disbandment. They may feel happy about mission accomplishment and sad about the loss of friendship and associations. At this point, the leader may wish to signify the team's disbanding with a ritual or ceremony, perhaps giving out plaques and awards to signify closure and completeness.

© AP/Wide World Photos

CONCEPT CONNECTION

To accomplish their goals—whether in the business world or on the basketball court—teams have to successfully advance to the **performing stage of team development**. The WNBA's Phoenix Mercury teammates shown here blend their talents and energies so effortlessly that they play the game not like separate people but like a coordinated piece of a whole. Phoenix recently began using psychological testing as part of the appraisal of new coaches and potential draft picks. Managers think testing gives them another tool for building a high-performance team. As part-owner Anne Mariucci puts it, "If a person isn't dotting the I's and crossing the T's, we know why, and we can surround that person with people who complement that. . . ."

The five stages of team development typically occur in sequence. In teams that have a time pressure or will exist for a short period of time, the stages may occur rapidly. The stages may be accelerated for virtual teams. For example, bringing people together for a couple of days of team building can help virtual teams move rapidly through the forming and storming stages. McDevitt Street Bovis, one of the country's largest construction management firms, uses an understanding of the stages of team development to put teams on a solid foundation.

storming

The stage of team development in which individual personalities and roles, and resulting conflicts, emerge.

McDevitt Street Bovis

The team-building process at McDevitt Street Bovis is designed to take teams to the performing stage as quickly as possible by giving everyone an opportunity to get to know one another; explore the ground rules; and clarify roles, responsibilities, and expectations. The company credits this process for effectively unifying teams, circumventing damaging and time-consuming conflicts, and preventing lawsuits related to major construction projects.

Rather than the typical construction project characterized by conflicts, frantic scheduling, and poor communications, Bovis wants its collection of contractors, designers, suppliers, and other partners to function like a true team by putting the success of the project ahead of their own individual interests. The team is first divided into separate groups that may have competing objectives—such as the clients in one group, suppliers in another, engineers and architects in a third—and is asked to come up with a list of their goals for the project. Though interests sometimes vary in purely accounting terms, common themes usually emerge. By talking about conflicting goals and interests, as well as what all the groups share, facilitators help the team gradually come together around a common purpose and begin to develop shared values to guide the project. After jointly writing a team mission statement, each party says what it expects from the others, so that roles and responsibilities are clarified. The intensive team-building session takes members through the forming and storming development stages. "We prevent conflicts from happening," says facilitator Monica Bennett. Leaders at McDevitt Street Bovis believe building better teams builds better buildings.[48]

norming

The stage of team development in which conflicts developed during the storming stage are resolved and team harmony and unity emerge.

performing

The stage of team development in which members focus on problem solving and accomplishing the team's assigned task.

adjourning

The stage of team development in which members prepare for the team's disbandment.

team cohesiveness

The extent to which team members are attracted to the team and motivated to remain in it.

Team Cohesiveness

Another important aspect of the team process is cohesiveness. **Team cohesiveness** is defined as the extent to which members are attracted to the team and motivated to remain in it.[49] Members of highly cohesive teams are committed to team activities, attend meetings, and are happy when the team succeeds. Members of less cohesive teams are less concerned about the team's welfare. High cohesiveness is normally considered an attractive feature of teams.

Determinants of Team Cohesiveness. Characteristics of team structure and context influence cohesiveness. The first characteristic is team interaction. The greater the contact among team members and the more time spent together, the more cohesive the team. Through frequent interactions, members get to know one another and become more devoted to the team.[50] Second is the concept of shared goals. If team members agree on goals, they will be more cohesive. Agreeing on purpose and direction binds the team together. Third is personal attraction to the team, meaning that members have similar attitudes and values and enjoy being together.

Take a moment to complete the experiential exercise below that pertains to evaluating team cohesiveness.

Is Your Group a Cohesive Team?

Think about a student group with which you have worked. Rate the statements below as they pertain to the functioning of that group.

Disagree Strongly			Agree Strongly	
1	2	3	4	5

1. Group meetings were held regularly and everyone attended.
    1   2   3   4   5

2. We talked about and shared the same goals for group work and grade.
    1   2   3   4   5

3. We spent most of our meeting time talking business, but discussions were open-ended and active.
    1   2   3   4   5

4. We talked through any conflicts and disagreements until they were resolved.
    1   2   3   4   5

5. Group members listened to one another.
    1   2   3   4   5

6. We trusted each other, speaking personally about what we felt.
    1   2   3   4   5

7. Leadership roles were rotated and shared, with people taking initiative at appropriate times for the good of the group.
    1   2   3   4   5

8. Each member found a way to contribute to the final work product.

1   2   3   4   5

9. I was satisfied being a member of the group.

1   2   3   4   5

10. We gave each other credit for jobs well done.

1   2   3   4   5

11. Group members gave and received feedback to help the group do better.

1   2   3   4   5

12. We held each other accountable; each member was accountable to the group.

1   2   3   4   5

13. Group members liked and respected each other.

1   2   3   4   5

Scoring and Interpretation

The questions here are about team cohesion. Add your scores for all 13 statements to obtain your total score: _____. If you scored 52 or greater, your group experienced authentic teamwork. Congratulations. If you scored between 39 and 51, a positive group identity might have been developed even further. If you scored between 26 and 38, group identity was weak and probably unsatisfying. If you scored below 26, it was hardly a group at all, resembling a loose collection of individuals.

Remember, teamwork does not happen by itself. Individuals like you have to understand what a team is and then work to make it happen. What can you do to make a student group more like a team? Do you have the courage to take the initiative?

Two factors in the team's context influence group cohesiveness. The first is the presence of competition. When a team is in moderate competition with other teams, its cohesiveness increases as it strives to win. Finally, team success and the favorable evaluation of the team by outsiders add to cohesiveness. When a team succeeds in its task and others in the organization recognize the success, members feel good, and their commitment to the team will be high.

Consequences of Team Cohesiveness.   The outcome of team cohesiveness can fall into two categories: morale and productivity. As a general rule, morale is higher in cohesive teams because of increased communication among members, a friendly team climate, maintenance of membership because of commitment to the team, loyalty, and member participation in team decisions and activities. High cohesiveness has almost uniformly good effects on the satisfaction and morale of team members.[51]

With respect to team performance, research findings are mixed, but cohesiveness may have several effects.[52] First, in a cohesive team, members' productivity tends to be more uniform. Productivity differences among members are small because the team exerts pressure toward conformity. Noncohesive teams do not have this control over member behavior and, therefore, tend to have wider variation in member productivity.

With respect to the productivity of the team as a whole, research findings suggest that cohesive teams have the potential to be productive, but the degree of productivity depends on the relationship between management and the working team. Thus, team cohesiveness does not necessarily lead to higher team productivity. One study surveyed more than 200 work teams and correlated job performance with their cohesiveness.[53]

Take **ACTION**

As a manager, give adequate support to your teams so productivity will be high.

Highly cohesive teams were more productive when team members felt management support and were less productive when they sensed management hostility and negativism. Management hostility led to team norms and goals of low performance, and the highly cohesive teams performed poorly in accordance with their norms and goals.

The relationship between performance outcomes and cohesiveness is illustrated in Exhibit 15.6. The highest productivity occurs when the team is cohesive and has a high performance norm, which is a result of its positive relationship with management. Moderate productivity occurs when cohesiveness is low, because team members are less committed to performance norms. The lowest productivity occurs when cohesiveness is high and the team's performance norm is low. Thus, cohesive teams are able to attain their goals and enforce their norms, which can lead to high or low productivity.

A good example of team cohesiveness combined with high performance norms occurred at the Ralston Foods plant in Sparks, Nevada.

Ralston Foods.

When the Ralston Foods plant in Sparks, Nevada, was being retrofitted from an operation that produced pet foods to one producing cereals, plant manager Daniel Kibbe wanted to transform it into a team-based organization.

After gaining the support of divisional and top executives, Kibbe's first task was to put together the right management team. He put in place a small group of leaders who believed in and supported the idea of participative management. Next, before the plant made a pound of cereal, it spent millions of dollars training people how to work in teams and make the kinds of decisions once made by managers. Managers received training that helped them create an environment of empowerment, trust, and credibility.

The plant's 150 or so workers were divided into six operating work groups, which were, in turn, divided into small teams of around ten people. Managers wanted to keep teams small so people could get to know one another, develop bonds of trust and commitment, and manage themselves more easily. Some teams function entirely without designated leaders and handle all issues and problems that arise in their areas, including hiring and firing, scheduling, budgeting, quality, and disciplinary problems. Other teams have leaders assigned by management. Yet, in all cases, the teams function independently and have developed strong bonds that motivate them to perform well for the sake of the team. The teams that have progressed to total self-direction outperform teams with assigned leaders.[54]

At Ralston Foods, a combination of team cohesiveness and management support that created high performance norms from the beginning has led to record-breaking production output levels and generated significant cost savings.

Team Norms

A **team norm** is a standard of conduct shared by team members and guides their behavior.[55] Norms are informal. They are not written down as are rules and procedures. Norms are valuable because they define boundaries of acceptable behavior. They make life easier

EXHIBIT 15.6

Relationship Among Team Cohesiveness, Performance Norms, and Productivity

Team Performance Norms	Low Cohesiveness	High Cohesiveness
High	**Moderate Productivity** Weak norms in alignment with organization goals	**High Productivity** Strong norms in alignment with organization goals
Low	**Low/Moderate Productivity** Weak norms in opposition to organization goals	**Low Productivity** Strong norms in opposition to organization goals

Low   **Team Cohesiveness**   High

for team members by providing a frame of reference for what is right and wrong. Norms identify key values, clarify role expectations, and facilitate team survival. For example, union members may develop a norm of not cooperating with management because they do not trust management's motives. In this way, norms protect the group and express key values.

Norms begin to develop in the first interactions among members of a new team.[56] Thus, leaders, especially of virtual teams, must shape early interactions that will lead to norms that help the team succeed. Norms that apply to daily behavior and to employee output and performance gradually evolve, letting members know what is acceptable and directing their actions toward acceptable performance. Four common ways in which norms develop for controlling and directing behavior are illustrated in Exhibit 15.7.[57]

Critical Events.   Often, critical events in a team's history establish an important precedent. One example occurred when an employee at a forest products plant was seriously injured while standing too close to a machine being operated by a teammate. This led to a norm that team members regularly monitor one another to make sure all safety rules are observed. Any critical event can lead to the creation of a norm.

Primacy.   Primacy means that the first behaviors that occur in a team often set a precedent for later team expectations. For example, at one company a team leader began his first meeting by raising an issue and then "leading" team members until he got the solution he wanted. The pattern became ingrained so quickly into an unproductive team norm that team members dubbed meetings the "Guess What I Think" game.[58]

Carryover Behaviors.   Carryover behaviors bring norms into the team from outside. One current example is the strong norm against smoking in many management teams. Some team members sneak around, gargling with mouthwash, and fear expulsion because the team culture believes everyone should kick the habit. Carryover behavior influences small teams of college students assigned by instructors to do class work. Norms brought into the team from outside suggest that students should participate equally and help members get a reasonable grade.

team norm
A standard of conduct that is shared by team members and guides their behavior.

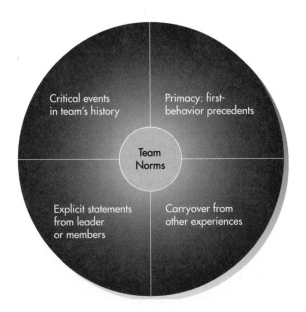

| **EXHIBIT 15.7**
Four Ways Team Norms Develop

Critical events in team's history

Primacy: first-behavior precedents

Team Norms

Explicit statements from leader or members

Carryover from other experiences

Explicit Statements.   With explicit statements, leaders or team members can initiate norms by articulating them to the team. Explicit statements symbolize what counts and have considerable impact. Making explicit statements can be an effective way for leaders to influence or change team norms. At Warner Brothers Television, Greg Berlanti (described in Chapter 7), who is the head writer and "show runner" for the WB Network's popular *Everwood*, clarifies that his team of writers should "leave on a successful note." Berlanti believes people are more creative when they feel upbeat; whenever the team has been struggling and reaches a breakthrough, he ends the meeting so they can pick up at a high point the next day. Though the writers' rooms can be nerve-wracking with deadlines approaching, Berlanti's explicit statements about starting from a positive place establish norms of taking needed breaks and down time.[59] Sometimes norms can develop that are not productive and need an explicit intervention to bring change as shown in the Digital, Inc. box.

Take ACTION

As a manager, consider developing a list of values and norms and sharing those with the group and new members as they join the group.

Managing Team Conflict

The final characteristic of team process is conflict. Of all the skills required for effective team management, none is more important than handling the conflicts that inevitably arise among members. Whenever people work together in teams, some conflict is inevitable. Conflict can arise among members within a team or between one team and another. **Conflict** refers to antagonistic interaction in which one party attempts to block the intentions or goals of another.[60] Competition, which is rivalry among individuals or teams, can have a healthy impact because it energizes people toward higher performance.[61]

conflict

Antagonistic interaction in which one party attempts to thwart the intentions and/or goals of another.

DIGITAL, INC.

Eze Castle Software

Sean McLaughlin realized it was time to take action when an employee approved paying $100 a month for a contractor to water Eze Castle Software's office plants. CEO McLaughlin's company had lost its entrepreneurial edge. When starting out in the securities trading software business six years ago, everyone took responsibility. If a package went FedEx, they knew what that cost the firm. Now, employees were acting with big-company sloppiness. One big bill was from overloaded access on the company's T1 line because workers were downloading MP3 files. The entrepreneur was frustrated because employees did not take responsibility for costs that negatively impacted the bottom line.

When both administrative assistants quit, McLaughlin saw a chance for change. A shock to lose the mail sorters and supply room stockers. The refrigerator had no milk, and the store room was penless. While visiting his daughter's kindergarten, McLaughlin saw the teacher divided classroom chores among children with a chore wheel. It seemed the thing to institute corporate responsibility.

COO Tom Gavin posts the eight tasks and who is responsible on the company Intranet. Tasks rotate weekly and include maintaining supply closet, stocking kitchen with food, washing dishes,

assigning tasks, etc. At first, employees balked. They were already putting in 12-hour days. "I have to do all this stuff plus the dishes?" asked one. To reduce resistance, McLaughlin did dishes the first week and Gavin took the closet. McLaughlin announced that of the $100,000 saved in salary and benefits by not replacing the two employees, $20,000 would go to the employees and the rest to activities for workers. As the new system began to work, people started talking to each other more about tasks, assignments and improvements, and they got a greater sense of responsibility. Eze's electrical bill went from the astronomical $4,000 per month to $1,000 as workers became more conscious of turning off lights and computers.

Another problem was how little employees knew one another. So, McLaughlin instituted another kindergarten tradition: milk and cookie breaks. "I wanted to build relationships among the employees to make them feel more company morale," says the CEO. Every day at 2:30 p.m. people leave their cubicles for the kitchen after turning out their lights.

SOURCE: Ilan Mochari, "It's All in the Details," *Inc. Magazine* (March 2002): 120–122.

Balancing Conflict and Cooperation

Some conflict can be beneficial to teams.[62] A healthy level of conflict helps to prevent **groupthink**, in which people are so committed to a cohesive team that they are reluctant to express contrary opinions. Author and scholar Jerry Harvey tells a story of how members of his extended family in Texas decided to drive 40 miles to Abilene on a hot day when the car's air conditioning did not work. Everyone was miserable. Later, each person admitted he or she had not wanted to go but went along to please the others. Harvey used the term *Abilene Paradox* to describe this tendency to go along with others for the sake of avoiding conflict.[63] Similarly, when people in work teams go along simply for the sake of harmony, problems typically result. Thus, a degree of conflict leads to better decision making because multiple viewpoints are expressed. Among top management teams, for example, low levels of conflict have been found to be associated with poor decision making.[64]

However, conflict that is too strong, that is focused on personal rather than work issues, or that is not managed appropriately can damage the team's morale and productivity. Too much conflict can be destructive, tear relationships apart, and interfere with the healthy exchange of ideas and information.[65] Team leaders have to find the right balance between conflict and cooperation, as illustrated in Exhibit 15.8. Too little conflict can decrease team performance because the team does not benefit from a mix of opinions and ideas—even disagreements—that might lead to better solutions or prevent the team from making mistakes. At the other end of the spectrum, too much conflict outweighs the team's cooperative efforts and leads to a decrease in employee satisfaction and commitment, hurting team performance. A moderate amount of conflict that is managed appropriately can result in the highest levels of team performance.

groupthink
The tendency for people to be so committed to a cohesive team that they are reluctant to express contrary opinions.

Take **ACTION**
As a manager, keep the right balance between conflict and cooperation: Too much conflict is harmful, but too little squelches ideas and creativity.

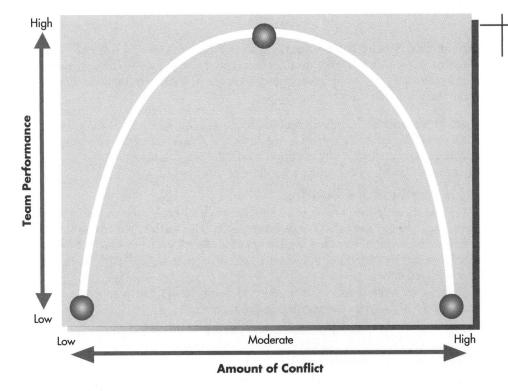

EXHIBIT 15.8
Balancing Conflict and Cooperation

Causes of Conflict

Six factors can cause people to engage in conflict: scarce resources, jurisdictional ambiguities, communication breakdown, personality clashes, power and status differences, and goal differences.[66]

Scarce Resources. Resources include money, information, and supplies. Whenever individuals or teams must compete for scarce or declining resources, conflict is almost inevitable. The introduction of fast-cycle teams, as described earlier, for example, frequently leads to conflict because it creates a new competition for resources.[67] Some projects may be delayed because managers reallocate resources to fast-cycle projects, leading to conflicts.

Jurisdictional Ambiguities. Conflicts emerge when job boundaries and responsibilities are unclear. When task responsibilities are well defined and predictable, people know where they stand. When responsibilities are unclear, people may disagree about who has responsibility for specific tasks or who has a claim on resources. Virtual teams are particularly susceptible to this area of conflict because the lack of regular interaction and on-site monitoring sometimes leads to uncertainty and disagreement regarding areas of task responsibility.

Communication Breakdown. The potential for communication breakdown is greater with virtual teams and global teams, but faulty communication can occur in any team. Poor communication results in misperceptions and misunderstandings of other people and teams. In some cases, information is intentionally withheld, which can jeopardize trust among teams and lead to long-lasting conflict.

Personality Clashes. A personality clash occurs when people do not get along or agree on any issue. Personality clashes are caused by basic differences in personality, values, and attitudes. In one study, personality conflicts were the number one reported cause preventing front-line management teams from working together effectively.[68] Some personality differences can be overcome. However, severe personality clashes are difficult to resolve. Often, you should separate the parties so they do not have to interact with one another.

Power and Status Differences. Power and status differences occur when one party has disputable influence over another. Low-prestige individuals or departments might resist their low status. People might engage in conflict to increase their power and influence in the team or organization.

Goal Differences. Conflict often occurs because people are pursuing conflicting goals. Goal differences are natural in organizations. Individual salespeople's targets may put them in conflict with one another or with the sales manager. Moreover, the sales department's goals might conflict with those of manufacturing.

Styles to Handle Conflict

Teams, as well as individuals, develop specific styles for dealing with conflict based on the desire to satisfy their own concern versus the other party's concern. A model that describes five styles of handling conflict is in Exhibit 15.9. The two major dimensions are the extent to which an individual is assertive versus cooperative in his or her approach to conflict.

Effective team members vary their style of handling conflict to fit a specific situation. Each of these five styles is appropriate in certain cases.[69]

1. The competing style reflects assertiveness to get one's own way, and should be used when quick, decisive action is vital on important issues or unpopular actions, such as during emergencies or urgent cost cutting.

Take *ACTION*

As a manager, ensure team members know each other's responsibilities; this can be done through written roles and plenty of conversations among members to discuss assumptions.

EXHIBIT 15.9
A Model of Styles to Handle Conflict

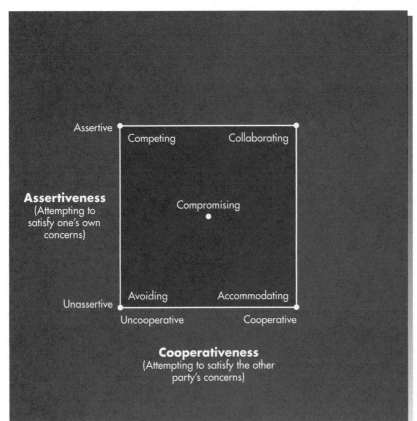

SOURCE: Adapted from Kenneth Thomas, "Conflict and Conflict Management," in *Handbook of Industrial and Organizational Behavior*, ed. M. D. Dunnette (New York: John Wiley, 1976), 900.

2. The avoiding style reflects neither assertiveness nor cooperativeness. It is appropriate when an issue is trivial, when there is no chance of winning, when a delay to gather more information is needed, or when a disruption would be costly.

3. The compromising style reflects a moderate amount of assertiveness and cooperativeness. It is appropriate when the goals on both sides are equally important, when opponents have equal power and both sides want to split the difference, or when people need to arrive at temporary or expedient solutions under time pressure.

4. The accommodating style reflects a high degree of cooperativeness, which works best when people realize they are wrong, when an issue is more important to others than to oneself, when building social credits for use in later discussions, and when maintaining harmony is especially important.

5. The collaborating style reflects a high degree of assertiveness and cooperativeness. The collaborating style enables both parties to win, though it may require substantial bargaining and negotiation. The collaborating style is important when both sets of concerns are too important to be compromised, when insights from different people need to be merged into an overall solution, and when the commitment of both sides is needed for a consensus.

The various styles of handling conflict are effective when an individual disagrees with others. But what does a manager or team leader do when a conflict erupts among others within a team or among teams for which the manager is responsible? Research suggests that several techniques can be used as strategies for resolving conflicts among people or departments. These techniques might be used when conflict is formalized, such as between a union and management.

Superordinate Goals.   The larger objective that cannot be attained by a single party is identified as a **superordinate goal**.[70] This is similar to the concept of vision. A powerful vision of where the organization wants to be in the future often compels people to overcome conflicts and cooperate for the greater good. Similarly, a superordinate goal requires the cooperation of conflicting team members for achievement. People must pull together. To the extent that employees can be focused on team or organization goals, the conflict will decrease because they see the big picture and realize they must work together to achieve it.

superordinate goal
A goal that cannot be reached by a single party.

Bargaining/Negotiation.   Bargaining and negotiation mean the parties engage one another in an attempt to systematically reach a solution. They attempt logical problem solving to identify and correct the conflict. This approach works well if the individuals can set aside personal animosities and deal with the conflict in a businesslike way. Books, software, newsletters, and training seminars on negotiating have proliferated in recent years. Most emphasize that the key to effectiveness is to see negotiation not as a zero-sum game but as a process for reaching a creative solution that benefits everyone.[71]

mediation
The process of using a third party to settle a dispute.

Mediation.   Using a third party to settle a dispute involves **mediation**. A mediator could be a supervisor, higher-level manager, or someone from the human resource department. The mediator can discuss the conflict with each party and work toward a solution. If both sides cannot reach a satisfactory solution, the parties might be willing to turn the conflict over to the mediator and abide by his or her solution.

Facilitating Communication.   Managers can facilitate communication to ensure that conflicting parties hold accurate perceptions. Providing opportunities for the disputants to get together and exchange information reduces conflict. As they learn more about one another, suspicions diminish and improved teamwork becomes possible.

Four guidelines can help managers facilitate communication and keep teams focused on substantive issues rather than interpersonal conflicts.[72]

1. *Focus on facts.* Keep team discussions focused on issues, not personalities. Working with more data and information rather than less can keep team members focused on facts and prevent meetings from degenerating into pointless debates over opinions. At Star Electronics, the top management team meets daily, weekly, and monthly to examine many operating measures. Looking at the details helps team members debate critical issues and avoid useless arguments.

2. *Develop multiple alternatives.* Teams that deliberately develop many alternatives, sometimes considering four or five options at once, have a lower incidence of interpersonal conflict. Having a multitude of options to consider concentrates team members' energy on solving problems. In addition, the process of generating multiple choices is fun and creative, which sets a positive tone for the meeting and reduces the chance for conflict.

3. *Maintain a balance of power.* Managers and team leaders should accept the team's decision as fair even if they do not agree with it. Fairness requires a balance of power within the team.

4. *Never force a consensus.* There will naturally be conflict over some issues, which managers find a way to resolve without forcing a consensus. When there are persistent differences of opinion, the team leader sometimes has to make a decision

guided by input from other team members. At Andromeda Processing, the CEO insisted on consensus from his top management team, causing a debate to rage for months. Conflict and frustration mounted to the point where some top managers left the company. The group achieved consensus only at the price of losing several key managers.

Teamwork in a Turbulent World

Ninety-one percent of companies responding to a survey by the Society for Human Resource Management believe that team diversity initiatives help maintain a competitive advantage. Some specific benefits include improving employee morale, decreasing interpersonal conflict, facilitating progress into new markets, and increasing the organization's creativity.[73] In addition to the ideas we have discussed, two new approaches to diversity management—multicultural teams and employee network groups—have arisen in response to the rapid change and complexity of organizations in today's global environment.

Multicultural Teams

Companies have long known that putting together teams made up of members from different functional areas results in better problem solving and decision making. Now, they are recognizing that **multicultural teams**—teams made up of members from diverse national, racial, ethnic, and cultural backgrounds—provide greater potential for enhanced creativity, innovation, and value in today's global marketplace.[74] Research has found that diverse teams generate more and better alternatives to problems and produce more creative solutions than homogeneous teams.[75] A team made up of people with different perspectives, backgrounds, and cultural values creates a healthy mix of ideas and leads to greater creativity and better decisions.

Some organizations, such as RhonePoulenc Rorer (RPR), based in Collegeville, Pennsylvania, are committed to mixing people from diverse countries and cultures, from the top to the bottom of the organization. There are 15 nationalities represented in RPR's top management teams, including a French CEO, an Austrian head of operations, an American general counsel, an Egyptian head of human resources, and an Italian director of corporate communications.[76] The technology start-up Obongo has teams made up of people from 12 countries and 18 different cultures.[77]

Multicultural teams are becoming common in U.S. and Canadian organizations. One consultant notes that the workforce of many Canadian organizations is often jokingly referred to as the *United Nations* because companies have so many different nationalities working together on project teams.[78] New skills must often be learned with multicultural and international groups, as described in the Focus on Skills box.

Despite their many advantages,[79] multicultural teams are more difficult to manage because of the increased potential for miscommunication and misunderstanding. Multicultural teams typically have more difficulty learning to communicate and work well together, but with effective cross-cultural training and good management, the problems seem to dissipate over time.[80] One management team videotaped its meetings so members could see how their body language reflects cultural differences. An American manager remarked, "I couldn't believe how even my physical movements dominated the table, while Ron (a Filipino America)... actually worked his way off-camera within the first five minutes."[81]

Employee Network Groups

Employee network groups are based on social identity, such as gender or race, and are organized by employees to focus on concerns of employees from that group.[82] For example, when Marita Golden was teaching at George Mason University, she often

multicultural teams
Teams made up of members from diverse national, racial, ethnic, and cultural backgrounds.

employee network groups
Groups based on social identity, such as gender or race, and organized by employees to focus on concerns of employees from that group.

FOCUS ON SKILLS

A Guide for Expatriate Managers in America

Though each person is different, individuals from a specific country typically share certain values and attitudes. Managers who are planning to work in a foreign country can learn about these broad value patterns to help them adjust to working and living in a foreign country. The following characteristics are some that are often used to help foreign managers understand what Americans are like.

1. Americans are informal. They tend to treat everyone alike even when there are significant differences in age or social status.

2. Americans are direct. They do not beat around the bush, which means they do not talk around things but get right to the point. To some foreigners, this may seem abrupt or rude.

3. Americans are competitive. Some foreigners might think they are aggressive or overbearing.

4. Americans are achievers. They like to keep score, whether at work or play. They emphasize accomplishments.

5. Americans are independent and individualistic. They place a high value on freedom and believe that people can control their own destinies.

6. Americans are questioners. They ask a lot of questions even of someone they have just met. Some of these questions may seem pointless ("How ya' doin'?") or personal ("What kind of work do you do?")

7. Americans dislike silence. They would rather talk about the weather than deal with silence in a conversation.

8. Americans value punctuality. They keep appointment calendars and live according to schedules and clocks.

9. Americans value cleanliness. They may seem obsessed with bathing, eliminating body odors, and wearing clean clothes.

How many of these statements do you agree with? Discuss them with your friends and classmates, including people from different countries and members of different subcultural groups from the United States.

SOURCES: "What Are Americans Like?," Exhibit 4-6 in Stephen P. Robbins and Mary Coulter, *Management*, 8th ed. (Upper Saddle River, NJ: Pearson Prentice Hall, 2005), as adapted from M. Ernest, ed., *Predeparture Orientation Handbook: For Foreign Students and Scholars Planning to Study in the United States* (Washington, D.C.:)

---

heard other African-American women at the university talk about how they felt isolated and needed to get together. So, Golden started a networking group that has grown and expanded, incorporating women from other local colleges and universities as well, who get together and share their research interests, talk about career and personal development issues, and explore positive and negative experiences of their work lives.[83] At Visteon Corp., a global automotive systems producer, the women's network group develops the leadership and technical skills of female employees, designs strategies for how members can contribute to Visteon's business and diversity goals, and works to keep top managers informed of members' contributions, concerns, and needs.[84] Whereas multicultural teams help bind diverse people together for the accomplishment of shared goals, network groups provide people with comfort and support in a crazy world. The idea behind network groups is that minority employees can join together across traditional organizational boundaries for mutual support and to extend member influence in the organization.

Network groups pursue various activities, such as meetings to educate top managers, mentoring programs, networking events, training sessions and skills seminars, minority intern programs, and community volunteer activities. Network groups give people a chance to meet, interact with, and develop social and professional ties to others throughout the organization, which may include key decision makers. Network groups are a powerful way to reduce social isolation for women and minorities, help these employees be more effective, and enable members to achieve greater career advancement. A recent study confirms that network groups can be an important tool for helping organizations retain managerial-level minority employees.[85]

An important characteristic of network groups is that they are created informally by employees, not the organization, and membership is voluntary. However, successful

Take **ACTION**

As a manager, encourage employee network groups so marginalized group members can feel more included and valuable.

organizations support and encourage network groups. Even managers who once thought of minority networks as "gripe groups" now see them as essential to organizational success because they help to retain minority employees, enhance diversity efforts, and spark new ideas that can benefit the organization.[86] At first glance, the proliferation of employee network groups seems to be in direct opposition to the trend toward multicultural teams, but the two mechanisms work well together. At Kraft Foods, networks are considered critical to the success of multicultural teams because they build awareness and acceptance of cultural differences and help people feel more comfortable working together.[87]

Employee networks for minorities have grown and include those who have faced barriers to advancement in organizations: African-Americans, Hispanics, American Indians, Asian Americans, women, gays and lesbians, and disabled employees. In general, female and minority employees who participate in a network group feel more pride about their work and are more optimistic about their careers than those who do not have network support.[88]

Benefits and Costs of Teams

In deciding whether to use teams to perform specific tasks, managers must consider benefits and costs. Teams may have a positive impact on the output productivity and satisfaction of members. On the other hand, teams may create a situation in which motivation and performance decline.

Potential Benefits of Teams

Teams come closest to achieving their full potential when they enhance individual productivity through increased member effort, members' personal satisfaction, integration of diverse abilities and skills, and increased organizational flexibility.

Level of Effort. Employee teams often unleash enormous energy and creativity from workers who like the idea of using their brains as well as their bodies to accomplish an important goal. Teams are an important part of the move to the learning organization and more horizontal forms of organizing, as described in Chapters 1 and 7. To facilitate learning and problem solving, managers are breaking down barriers, empowering workers, and encouraging employees to use their minds and creativity. Research has found that working in a team often increases an individual's motivation and performance. **Social facilitation** refers to the tendency for the presence of others to enhance one's motivation and performance. Being in the presence of other people has an energizing effect.[89] Eileen Fisher runs her company in a way that facilitates people working together and having fun, with the idea that they will be happier people and more productive workers, as the Focus on Collaboration box describes.

Satisfaction of Members. As described in Chapter 13, employees have needs for belongingness and affiliation. Working in teams can help meet these needs. Participative teams reduce boredom and often increase employees' feeling of dignity and self-worth because the whole person is employed. For example, at Radius, a Boston restaurant, two-person kitchen teams have full responsibility for their part of a meal, which gives them a greater sense of accomplishment and importance.[90] People who have a satisfying team environment cope better with stress, enjoy their jobs, and have a higher level of organizational commitment. Movie actors can find teamwork satisfying, as described in the Focus on Skills box.

Expanded Job Knowledge and Skills. The third major benefit of using teams is the empowerment of employees to bring greater knowledge and ability to the task. For one thing, multiskilled employees learn all of the jobs that the team performs.

social facilitation

The tendency for the presence of others to influence an individual's motivation and performance.

Take **ACTION**

As a manager, use participative teams whenever practical, to increase productivity and reduce boredom.

FOCUS ON COLLABORATION

Eileen Fisher, Inc.

When Eileen Fisher was in college, one assignment was designing a house. She told a few friends about her vision and before long she had 40 people in her dorm room, wanting to contribute their ideas. She has taken this same vision-building and has inspired teams in her like-named women's apparel company, which was featured in Chapter 2. It all started in 1984 with her investment of $350 dollars, sewing some clothes and taking them to a trade show. Now her company does $143 million yearly.

Great pains are taken to ensure teamwork flourishes, while simultaneously encouraging individual empowerment. Her 400 employees see her as a down-to-earth boss, one who promotes from within, and who knows everybody by name. To encourage teamwork and create justice, Fisher practices profit-sharing, giving 10 percent of the profits in year-end bonuses, which sometimes equal eight weeks pay.

To develop a sense of belonging in the community, or one might say team spirit, Fisher encourages all employees to volunteer on company time. Service includes assisting firefighters, redecorating the abused women's shelter, or working at the local Chamber of Commerce.

As CEO, Fisher is the head of the company's design team, but she says she spends most of her time keeping the staff happy and productive. Her management philosophy is based on values and human connection, whether through communication or teamwork. She encourages open and honest communication, to create a joyful and fun work environment, and to keep it simple.

Keeping it simple—and natural—describes her clothing, which is made for women who want to put on their clothes easily in the morning and then not have to think about them again. With smooth and sleek lines, the focus is not on the clothes. As she says, "I want people to notice the woman, not the clothes."

Fisher believes women are highly qualified to develop the kind of bonds that make an effective team. "Women have a unique way of approaching the world," she says. "The way we listen, the value we place on relationships, and our instinct to connect enhances our capacity to make a difference every day, whether we are running a company or running a home (or both)."

SOURCES: "Go for the Green," *PR Newswire* (Feb. 11, 2005): 1; Ellyn Spragins, "The Best Bosses," FSB (*April* 2003): 44.; Claudia Z. Carlin, "Eileen Fisher Simplifies," *Westchester Magazine* (May 2002): 44–45+.

Teams gain the intellectual resources of several members who can suggest shortcuts and offer alternative points of view for team decisions. Teams at Radius work for six weeks at one station and then rotate to another. This makes the work experience fun, exciting, and educational and enables employees to learn a broad range of skills.

Organizational Responsiveness. Employee teams enhance flexibility because workers can be reorganized and employees reassigned as needed. People work closely together, learn various skills, and can exchange jobs as needed to accomplish the team's task. In addition, teams can break down traditional organizational boundaries so that people collaborate across functional and hierarchical lines, which enables the organization to respond to changing customer needs.

Potential Costs of Teams

Managers must assess certain costs or liabilities associated with teamwork. When teams do not work well, the major reasons usually are power realignment, free riding, coordination costs, or system revisions.

FOCUS ON SKILLS

Bigger than the Sky

Actor John Corbett is getting tired of the business. He gets "crabby and grumpy" on movie sets, waiting for someone to knock on his trailer so he can say his lines. Because he is on location so often shooting and then traveling around giving too many interviews, he has no time for his personal life. At 43, he is not married, has no children.

But his recent movie, *Bigger than the Sky*, changed all that. Suddenly, he found himself having fun again. As a movie about community theater folks performing *Cyrano de Bergerac*, it is covered under Hollywood unions' Schedule F, which means they can get away with paying cast and crew minimal salaries. When he was asked to be in the movie, the producer wanted to know the least they could pay him. Corbett jumped at the chance to be part of a real team. When he played opposite Kate Hudson in *Raising Helen*, he got $100,000 and she got $5 million. That kind of inequity felt wrong to many on the set.

He has decided not to do any more TV shows because of the intense pressure. His goal: to find some more small scripts with film companies that will not pay much. Then it becomes fun again to be a team member, standing around waiting to say his lines.

SOURCE: Chris Hewitt, "Corbett Puts Art above Money for New Film," *Sunday Gazette-Mail* (March 13, 2005): 2F.

Power Realignment. When companies form front-line employees into teams, the major losers are low-level and middle-level managers. These managers are sometimes reluctant to give up power. Indeed, when teams are successful, fewer supervisors are needed. This is especially true for self-directed teams because workers take over supervisory responsibility. The adjustment is difficult for managers who fear the loss of status or even their jobs and who have to learn new, people-oriented and team leadership skills to survive.[91]

> **Take ACTION**
>
> As a manager, let go of some responsibility when a team takes on those tasks.

Free Riding. The term **free rider** refers to a team member who attains benefits from team membership but does not do a proportionate share of the work.[92] Free riding sometimes is called social loafing because members do not exert equal effort. One study of global virtual teams found a greater propensity among members for shirking their duties or giving less than their full effort.[93] In large teams, some people are likely to work less. For example, research found that the pull exerted on a rope was greater by individuals working alone than by individuals in a group. Similarly, people who were asked to clap and make noise made more noise on a per person basis when working alone or in small groups than they did in a large group.[94] The problem of free riding has been experienced by people who have participated in student project groups. Some students put more effort into the group project than others do but often it seems that no members work as hard for the group as they do for their individual grades. Another kind of free riding was attempted by former HealthSouth CEO Richard Scrushy, who wanted the rest of the team to suffer as much as he did, as shown in the Business Blooper box.

> **free rider**
>
> A person who benefits from team membership but does not make a proportionate contribution to the team's work.

BUSINESS BLOOPER

HealthSouth's Richard Scrushy

"We all go down," is how Birmingham-based HealthSouth CEO Richard Scrushy described two years ago what would happen if his company's financial statements went public. Former CEO Scrushy believes in teams, evidently, but only to make a group target. Now under indictment for allegedly defrauding stockholders, his defense team has been working overtime to tarnish the reputations of former employees who will be testifying against him. One former executive has been accused of being a hard-drinking philanderer. At the same time, Scrushy wants to untarnish his own reputation

and has become a regular attendee and contributor to one of Birmingham, Alabama's best known African-American congregations. With Birmingham's population being 70 percent black, some accuse Scrushy of disingenuously ingratiating himself to that population. Former associates say that before his indictment, Scrushy was not particularly religious and he did not seem to care much about African-Americans as it was hard to find any employees of color. The strategy may backfire for Scrushy as juries dislike being manipulated.

SOURCES: Simon Romero, "Will the Real Richard Scrushy Please Step Forward?" *The New York Times* (Feb. 17, 2005): C1; "Notebook," *Time Magazine* (Feb. 21, 2005): 39.

---

coordination costs

The time and energy to coordinate the activities of a team to enable it to perform its task.

Coordination Costs.   The time and energy required to coordinate the activities of a group to enable it to perform its task are called **coordination costs**. Groups must spend time getting ready to do work and lose productive time in deciding who is to do what and when.[95] Once again, student project groups illustrate coordination costs. Members must meet after class to decide when they can meet to perform the task. Schedules must be checked, telephone calls made, and meeting times arranged in order to get down to business. Hours may be devoted to the administration and coordination of the group. Students often feel they could do the same project by themselves in less time. Teams typically have frequent meetings throughout a project, so leaders have to know how to keep meetings focused and productive. The Focus on Skills box offers some tips for running a great meeting.

Take ACTION

As a leader, try to create more value in the product or service than went in to the production of it.

Revising Systems.   Implementing teams requires changes in other parts of the organization. In particular, performance appraisal and reward systems have to be revised to reflect the new team approach; otherwise, teamwork will fail. Managers should be aware that a shift to teams requires that time and resources be invested to develop new systems that support and reinforce collaboration, sharing of information, and empowerment rather than pitting team members against one another.

How to Run a Great Meeting

Many managers think meetings are a waste of time. Busy executives may spend up to 70 percent of their time in meetings where participants doodle, drink coffee, tap away on their laptops, and think about what they could be doing back in their offices.

However, effective meetings help people process important information and solve problems. Good meetings do not just happen; they are designed through careful thought and planning. The success of a meeting depends on what is done in advance of, during, and after it.

Prepare in Advance

Advance preparation is the single most important tool for running an efficient, productive meeting. Advance preparation should include the following:

- *Define the purpose.* The leader should be explicit in setting goals and communicating them clearly and meaningfully. If a meeting is unessential, do not have it.
- *Prepare an agenda.* The agenda is a list of the topics to be discussed. The agenda lets people know what to expect and keeps the meeting on track.
- *Issue invitations selectively.* If the group gets too big, the meeting will not be productive. However, ensure every department with a stake in the topic is represented.
- *Set a time limit.* The ending time for the meeting should be announced in advance, and the agenda should require things to move along at a reasonable pace.

During the Meeting

If the leader is prepared in advance, the meeting will go smoothly. Moreover, certain techniques will bring out the best in people and make the meeting even more productive:

- *Start on time.* Though this sounds obvious, many meetings get started 10 or 15 minutes late. Starting on time has symbolic value because it tells people the topic is important and that the leader values their time.
- *Outlaw cell phones and laptops.* Having the flow of discussion interrupted by the ringing of a cell phone can throw the meeting completely off-track. Unless they will be used for the purposes of the meetings, laptops should be prohibited.
- *State the purpose and review the agenda.* The leader should start the meeting by stating the explicit purpose and clarifying what should be accomplished by the time the meeting is over.

- *Encourage participation.* Good meetings contain lots of discussion. If the leader wants to present one-way information to members, he or she should send a memo. A few subtle techniques go a long way toward increasing participation:
  - *Draw out the silent.* This means saying, "Bob, what do you think of Nancy's idea?"
  - *Control the talkative.* Some people overdo it and dominate the discussion. The chairperson's job is to redirect the discussion toward other people. One organization has a rule called NOSTUESO (No one speaks twice until everyone speaks once).
  - *Encourage the clash of ideas.* A good meeting is not a series of dialogues but a crosscurrent of discussion and debate. The leader listens, guides, mediates, stimulates, and summarizes this discussion.
- *Stick to the purpose.* Encouraging a free flow of ideas does not mean allowing participants to sidetrack the meeting into discussions of issues not on the agenda. This can waste time and prevent the group from reaching its goals.

After the Meeting

The actions following the meeting are designed to summarize and implement agreed-upon points.

- *End with a call to action.* The last item of the meeting's agenda is to summarize the main points and ensure everyone understands his or her assignments.
- *Follow up.* Send minutes of the meeting to all participants. Use this memorandum also to summarize the key accomplishments of the meeting and suggest schedules for agreed-upon activities.

SOURCES: Based on Jeff Siegel, "Mending Your Meetings," *Southwest Airlines Spirit* (March 2004): 46–49; Edward Michaels, "Business Meetings," *Small Business Reports* (February 1989): 82–88; Daniel Stoffman, "Waking Up to Great Meetings," *Canadian Business* (November 1986): 75–79; Antoney Jay, "How to Run a Meeting," *Harvard Business Review* (March-April 1976): 120–134; Jana Kemp, "Avoiding Agenda Overstack," *Corporate University Review* (May-June 1997), 42–43; and Jeffrey L. Seglin, "We've Got to Start Meeting Like This," *CIO* (March 1, 2001): 168–170.

Manager's Solution

Several important concepts about teams were described in this chapter. Organizations use teams to achieve coordination as part of the formal structure and to encourage employee involvement. Formal teams include vertical teams along the chain of command and horizontal teams such as cross-functional teams and committees. Special-purpose teams are used for special, large-scale, creative projects. Employee involvement via teams is designed to bring lower-level employees into decision processes to improve quality, efficiency, and job satisfaction. Companies typically start with problem-solving teams, which may evolve into self-directed teams that take on responsibility for management activities. New approaches to teamwork include virtual teams and global teams. These teams may include contingent workers, customers, suppliers, and other outsiders. Though team members sometimes meet in person, they use advanced information and telecommunications technology to accomplish much of their work.

Most teams go through systematic stages of development: forming, storming, norming, performing, and adjourning. Team characteristics that can influence organizational effectiveness are size, diversity, cohesiveness, norms, and members' roles. All teams experience some conflict because of scarce resources, ambiguous responsibilities, communication breakdown, personality clashes, power and status differences, and goal conflicts. Some conflict is beneficial, but too much can hurt the team and the organization. Techniques for managing and resolving conflicts include superordinate goals, bargaining, mediation, and communication. Techniques for facilitating team communication to minimize conflict are to focus on facts, develop multiple

alternatives, maintain a balance of power, and never force a consensus. Advantages of using teams include increased motivation, diverse knowledge and skills, team member satisfaction, and organizational responsiveness. Potential costs of using teams are power realignment, free riding, coordination costs, and system revision.

Returning to the opening example of Rowe Furniture, Charlene Pedrolie believed teamwork could be the answer for helping Rowe meet the challenges of a fast, competitive environment. She eliminated most supervisory positions, cross-trained employees to perform the different tasks required to build a piece of furniture, and then asked frontline workers to form horizontal clusters, or cells, to design the new production system. Each group selected its own members from the various functional areas and then created the processes, schedules, and routines for a particular product line. The assembly line was a thing of the past. Five hundred workers who had been accustomed to standing in one place and having the furniture come to them worked in teams, wandering from one partially assembled piece to another, performing various tasks. Every team had instant access to current information about order flows, output, productivity, and quality. The sense of personal control and responsibility led to a dramatic change in workers, who began holding impromptu meetings to discuss problems, check each other's progress, or talk about new ideas and better ways of doing things. Productivity and quality shot through the roof. Before long, the factory was delivering custom-made pieces within a month. Only a few months later, that lead time had decreased to 10 days.[96]

Discussion Questions

1. Volvo went to self-directed teams to assemble cars because of the need to attract and keep workers in Sweden, where pay raises are not a motivator (high taxes) and many other jobs are available. Is this a good reason for using a team approach? Discuss.

2. During your own work experience, have you been part of a formal vertical team? A task force? A committee? An employee involvement team? How did your work experience differ in each type of team?

3. What are the five stages of team development? What happens during each stage?

4. How would you explain the emergence of problem-solving and self-directed teams in companies throughout North America? Do you think implementation of the team concept is difficult in these companies? Discuss.

5. Do you think a moderate level of conflict might be healthy for an organization? Discuss.

6. When you are a member of a team, do you adopt a task specialist or socioemotional role? Which role is more important for a team's effectiveness? Discuss.

7. What is the relationship between team cohesiveness and team performance?

8. Describe the advantages and disadvantages of teams. In what situations might the disadvantages outweigh the advantages?

9. What is a team norm? What norms have developed in teams to which you have belonged?

10. One company had 40 percent of its workers and 20 percent of its managers resign during the first year after reorganizing into teams. What might account for this dramatic turnover? How might managers ensure a smooth transition to teams?

Manager's Workbook

Is Your Group a Cohesive Team?

Think about a student group with which you have worked. Answer the questions below as they pertain to the functioning of that group.

	Disagree Strongly				Agree Strongly
1. Group meetings were held regularly and everyone attended.	1	2	3	4	5
2. We talked about and shared the same goals for group work and grade.	1	2	3	4	5
3. We spent most of our meeting time talking business, but discussions were open-ended and active.	1	2	3	4	5
4. We talked through any conflicts and disagreements until they were resolved.	1	2	3	4	5
5. Group members listened carefully to one another.	1	2	3	4	5
6. We really trusted each other, speaking personally about what we really felt.	1	2	3	4	5
7. Leadership roles were rotated and shared, with people taking initiative at appropriate times for the good of the group.	1	2	3	4	5
8. Each member found a way to contribute to the final work product.	1	2	3	4	5
9. I was really satisfied being a member of the group.	1	2	3	4	5
10. We freely gave each other credit for jobs well done.	1	2	3	4	5
11. Group members gave and received feedback to help the group do even better.	1	2	3	4	5
12. We held each other accountable; each member was accountable to the group.	1	2	3	4	5
13. Group members really liked and respected each other.	1	2	3	4	5

Total Score

The questions here are about team cohesion. If you scored 52 or greater, your group experienced authentic teamwork. Congratulations. If you scored between 39 and 51, there was a positive group identity that might have been developed even further. If you scored between 26 and 38, group identity was weak and probably not very satisfying. If you scored below 26, it was hardly a group at all, resembling a loose collection of individuals.

Remember, teamwork doesn't happen by itself. Individuals like you have to understand what a team is and then work to make it happen. What can you do to make a student group more like a team? Do you have the courage to take the initiative?

Manager's Workshop

Team-Based Decision Processes

As organizations shift from traditional hierarchical designs to learning organizations, the reliance on team-based decision processes increases. During this transition, a shift occurs in problem solving. It is from

* *adaptive thinking,* where individuals follow established norms, "My way is the only way," to

* *generative thinking,* where teams examine the underlying structure of problems to determine cause and effect. Teams can increase their ability to use generative thinking by practice with looking at events or decisions and discussing what would be the impact of those events or decisions.

The purpose of this exercise is to help you to better understand this concept of generative thinking in teams.

1. Each student independently completes the immediate and long-term impact/effect for the events or situations described in the box below. Optionally, think of two

other events or situations with their impacts. Or you may think of a situation where you made an important decision and look at the possible impacts of that decision.

2. Divide into groups of four to six. The group discusses the three or four events/situations, coming to a consensus on the immediate and long-term impacts for each situation. If you have time, think of one or two other situations, events or decisions and discuss impacts of those.

3. The entire class shares impacts discussed in small groups and answers the following questions:

   a. How is adaptive thinking different from generative?

   b. What are some examples of adaptive and generative thinking you have seen or experienced?

   c. Why does understanding impacts help develop more generative thinking?

Situation	Immediate Impact/Effect	Long-Term Impact/Effect
(Example) Passed driving test	Could drive independently	Increased self-esteem, greater self-reliance, responsible for safety of other drivers, began part-time employment to pay for auto, job expanded social circle outside of homogeneous surroundings
Admission to graduate school		
Employed as research analyst with newly created e-commerce business		
Eight percent of the workforce in your company is retiring in three years		
Other		

SOURCE: Adapted by Dorothy Marcic from Marcia Salner, (1999). "The Learning Organization," *Journal of Management Education,* vol. 23 (5), pp. 489–508.

Management in Practice: Ethical Dilemma

Consumer Safety or Team Commitment?

Nancy was part of a pharmaceutical team developing a product called loperamide, a liquid treatment for diarrhea for people unable to take solid medicine, namely infants, children, and the elderly. Loperamide contained 44 times the amount of saccharin allowed by the FDA in a 12-ounce soft drink, but there were no regulations governing saccharin content in medication.

Nancy was the only medical member of the seven-person project team. The team made a unanimous decision to reduce the saccharin content before marketing loperamide, so the team initiated a three-month effort for reformulation. In the meantime, management was pressuring the team to allow human testing with the original formula until the new formula became available. After a heated team debate, all the team members except Nancy voted to begin testing with the current formula.

Nancy believed it was unethical to test on old people and children a drug she considered potentially dangerous. As the only medical member of the team, she had to sign the forms allowing testing. She refused and was told that unless she signed, she would be removed from the project, demoted, and seen as a poor team player, nonpromotable, lacking in judgment, and unable to work with marketing people. Nancy was aware that no proof existed that high saccharin would be directly harmful to potential users of loperamide.

What Do You Do?

1. Refuse to sign. As a medical doctor, Nancy must stand up for what she believes is right.

2. Resign. There is no reason to stay in this company and be punished for ethically correct behavior. Testing the drug will become someone else's responsibility.

3. Sign the form. The judgment of other team members cannot be all wrong. The loperamide testing is not illegal and will move ahead anyway, so it would preserve team unity and company effectiveness to sign.

SOURCE: Based on Tom L. Beauchamp, *Ethical Theory and Business*, 2d ed. (Englewood Cliffs, N.J.: Prentice-Hall, 1983).

Case for Critical Analysis

Acme Minerals Extraction Company

Several years ago, Acme Minerals Extraction Company introduced teams in an effort to solve morale and productivity problems at its Wichita plant. Acme used highly sophisticated technology, employing geologists, geophysicists, and engineers on what was referred to as the "brains" side of the business, as well as skilled and semiskilled labor on the "brawn" side to run the company's underground extracting operations. The two sides regularly clashed, and when some engineers locked several operations workers out of the office in 100-degree heat, the local press had a field day. Suzanne Howard was hired to develop a program that would improve productivity and morale at the Wichita plant, with the idea that it would then be implemented at other Acme sites.

Howard had a stroke of luck in the form of Donald Peterson, a long-time Acme employee who was highly respected at the Wichita plant and was looking for one final, challenging project before he retired. Peterson had served in just about every possible line and staff position at Acme over his 39-year career, and he understood the problems workers faced on both the "brains" and the "brawn" sides of the business. Howard was pleased when Peterson agreed to serve as leader for the Wichita pilot project. There were three functional groups at the Wichita plant: operations, made up primarily of hourly workers who operated and maintained the extracting equipment; the "belowground" group, consisting of engineers, geologists, and geophysicists who determined where and how to drill; and the "aboveground" group of engineers in charge of cursory refinement and transportation of the minerals. Howard and Peterson decided the first step was to get these different groups talking to one another and sharing ideas. They instituted a monthly "problem chat," an optional meeting to which all employees were invited to discuss unresolved problems. At the first meeting, Howard and Peterson were the only two people who showed up. However, people gradually began to attend the meetings, and after about six months they had become lively problem-solving discussions that led to many improvements.

Next, Howard and Peterson introduced teams to "select a problem and implement a tailored solution," or SPITS. These were ad hoc groups made up of members from each of the three functional areas. They were formed to work on a specific problem identified in a chat meeting and were disbanded when the problem was solved. SPITS teams were given the authority to address problems without seeking management approval. There were some rocky moments, as engineers resented working with operations personnel and vice versa. However, over time, and with the strong leadership of Peterson, the groups began to come together and focus on the issues rather than spending most of their time arguing. Eventually, workers in Wichita were organized into permanent cross-functional teams that were empowered to make their own decisions and elect their own leaders. After a year and a half, things were really humming. The different groups weren't just working together; they had also started socializing together. At one of the problem chats, an operations worker jokingly suggested that the brains and the brawn should duke it out once a week to get rid of the tensions so they could focus all their energy on the job to be done. Several others joined in the joking, and eventually, the group decided to square off in a weekly softball game. Peterson had T-shirts printed up that said BRAINS and BRAWN. The softball games were well attended, and both sides usually ended up having a few beers together at a local bar afterward. Productivity and morale soared at the Wichita plant, and costs continued to decline.

Top executives believed the lessons learned at Wichita should make implementing the program at other sites less costly and time-consuming. However, when Howard and her team attempted to implement the program at the Lubbock plant, things didn't go well. They felt under immense pressure from top management to get the team-based productivity project running smoothly at Lubbock. Because people weren't showing up for the problem chat meetings, attendance was made mandatory. However, the meetings still produced few valuable ideas or suggestions. Although a few of the SPITS teams solved important problems, none of them showed the kind of commitment and enthusiasm Howard had seen in Wichita. In addition, the Lubbock workers refused to participate in the softball games and other team-building exercises that Howard's team developed for them. Howard finally convinced some workers to join in the softball games by bribing them with free food and beer. "If I just had a Donald Peterson in Lubbock, things would go a lot more smoothly," Howard thought. "These workers don't trust us the way workers in Wichita trusted him." It seemed that no matter how hard Howard and her team tried to make the project work in Lubbock, morale continued to decline and conflicts between the different groups of workers actually seemed to increase.

Questions

1. What types of teams described in the chapter are represented in this case?

2. Why do you think the team project succeeded at Wichita but isn't working in Lubbock?

3. What advice would you give Suzanne Howard and her team for improving the employee involvement climate at the Lubbock plant?

SOURCE: Based on Michael C. Beers, "The Strategy That Wouldn't Travel," *Harvard Business Review*, November–December 1996, pp. 18–31.

Part One: Ford Motor Company Makes History

THE HISTORY OF FORD MOTOR COMPANY EMBODIES THE history of American management itself. When Henry Ford began a manufacturing revolution with his company's mass production of automobiles, much of the country was still bouncing along in horse-drawn carriages. A hundred years later, despite many ups and downs, Ford Motor Company is firmly established as the world's largest pickup-truck manufacturer and the number-two maker of cars (behind General Motors). Ford has progressed from an offering of one color—black—to a wide range of makes, models, and hues from which consumers may choose, depending on their budget, lifestyle, and mood. In addition to the autos it produces under its own name, Ford's brands now include Jaguar, Lincoln, Mercury, and Volvo, a 33 percent stake in Mazda, BMW's Land Rover SUV, along with the Hertz rental agency. Ford has had hugely successful models, such as the Taurus, as well as duds that it would rather forget, such as the Pinto. In recent years, the company has been mired in a public-relations disaster surrounding its popular SUV, the Explorer, and the vehicle's standard tires, which were manufactured by Firestone/Bridgestone. Still, the company has managed to survive by making changes in leadership, improving efficiency and effectiveness of its management and manufacturing operations, and embracing new management competencies. As you study your course of management this semester, you'll follow the rises, dips, and turns of one of America's most well-known and enduring organizations.

Fast-forward from that original assembly line spewing out those black Model Ts and Model As to the end of the twentieth century, when a whirlwind known as Jacques (Jac) Nasser took over as CEO of Ford Motor Company and immediately began to change management practices that previously had included a complex bureaucracy bogged down by centralized decision making and an unwillingness to budge from the status quo.

Although Nasser didn't explicitly use the term *learning organization*, he set out to turn his company into one. He hired a group of skilled managers from different automakers around the world (including Volkswagen and BMW), lured a number of marketers and salespeople from consumer-goods manufacturers, and pushed the entire Ford workforce to get as close to customers as possible to find out what people really wanted in their automobiles. He encouraged information sharing with such initiatives as a venture with MSN's CarPoint Web site that would provide data from online purchases. Ford marketers and designers would learn which models, colors, and features certain buyers preferred. And he let managers know in no uncertain terms that Ford Motor Company was now on the move—with their help as empowered workers who were accountable for their own (and their employees') performance. "You've got to earn [a promotion,]" Nasser supposedly thundered in one meeting. "The days of entitlement at Ford Motor Company are gone forever." To that end, he instituted a forced-ranking system, under which a certain number of employees would be considered underperformers and laid off each year. The system, which worked something like a grading curve, drew much criticism and was eventually abandoned.

On a grand scale, Nasser announced an organizational shakeup that meant decentralizing authority and decision-making powers, and transferring them to semiautonomous business units around the world. "Jac learned to make decisions without a lot of bureaucratic oversight from [Ford headquarters at] Dearborn," recalled Robert Lutz, Nasser's former boss. Now Nasser was promoting this kind of independent decision making with a new generation of Ford managers.

All of these actions were part of Nasser's strategy to transform a century-old industrial giant into a nimble, flexible company that could rapidly meet consumers' wants and needs. Designers, engineers, and marketers were required to attend seminars at a Consumer Insight Center to learn how to listen to customers and engage them in conversations designed to reveal what products and features they would most likely buy. Then they were sent in small teams out into the field for eight weeks of "customer immersion." Nasser wasn't kidding. He wanted all managers at all levels to understand their customers, inside and out.

Nasser made some radical changes at Ford Motor Company, an organization that has long been a symbol of American business and ingenuity. The company has been around so long that it has passed through several historical phases of management, from scientific management to today's learning organization. In 1913, one of the first moving assembly lines was installed in the company's Highland Park plant, reducing production time by 50 percent. With this new system, a Ford Model T came off the assembly line every ten seconds. Today, Ford managers rely on teams, empowerment, the Internet, and high-speed technology to produce thousands of cars a day. Ford's ability to change when the environment demands it may be the single most important factor in its long-term survival.

Questions

1. How have the necessary skills for a successful manager changed at Ford over the decades?
2. Why was it important for Ford to become a learning organization?
3. Do you think that Jacques Nasser was an effective manager? Why or why not?

SOURCES: "Ford Motor Company," Hoover's Capsule, Hoover's Online (November 16, 2001), http://www.hoovers.com; "Profile—Ford Motor Company," Yahoo! Finance; Julie Cantwell, "Exec Changes Help Ford with Basics," *Automotive News* (November 12, 2001), http://www.autonews. com; Geoffrey Colvin, "We Can't All Be Above Average," *Fortune*, August 13, 2001, http://www.fortune.com; Kathleen Kerwin and Keith Naughton, "Remaking Ford," *Businessweek Online* (October 11, 1999), http://www.businessweek.com.

Part Two: Ford Operates in a Complex Environment

HENRY FORD WAS AN ENTREPRENEUR WHOSE COMPANY became an American icon over the course of a century. He never could have guessed that by late 2001, CEO Jacques Nasser, the aggressive, embattled Australian businessman who had been in Ford's driver's seat for only three years, would be standing by the side of the road, briefcase in hand. Nasser had shaken up Ford's stodgy, bureaucratic corporate culture and attempted to lead the organization through the worst crisis of its history—the Firestone tire debacle—but the company had suffered too many blows during his reign. During this period, Ford and its managers faced enormous challenges involving ethics, social responsibility, a change in culture, and a competitive, constantly changing environment both in the United States and abroad. Ultimately, Nasser was asked to step aside.

In August 2000, Ford's world blew apart as it became apparent that some of its standard tires, those manufactured by Bridgestone/Firestone and installed in Ford's top-selling Explorer SUV, were doing exactly that: the treads were separating from the tire's core, leading to injurious and fatal crashes. Although Nasser chose to endure public scrutiny and Bridgestone/Firestone's Japanese leaders remained in relative seclusion, neither company immediately took responsibility. Instead, they engaged in finger pointing, damaging a relationship that had gone back as far as Henry Ford and Harvey Firestone. Firestone recalled the 6 million tires it believed were faulty, but meanwhile accused Ford of poor automobile design. Ford announced that it would replace all 13 million of the Wilderness AT tires that were on its Explorers, even those that were presumed safe. Then Firestone severed its relationship with Ford. The recall program took so long that consumers and dealers became frustrated and fearful of the consequences—and increasingly distrustful of both companies. Ford and Firestone officials were called to testify before Congress. Meanwhile, as more accidents were investigated and analyzed, the death toll associated with the faulty tires rose to more than two hundred. Who was right, Ford or Firestone? Did Ford handle the situation ethically? Much has been written about the debacle, and the answers most likely will not be resolved for many years.

Meanwhile, Ford's general and task environments were continually changing. General Motors revamped its truck lineup, and Toyota opened up the throttle on its SUVs with its new Highlander and Sequoia models. Ford's quality was suffering, increasing the cost of its warranties and decreasing consumers' confidence in its products. Also, Ford had purchased several European brands, including Volvo and BMW Land Rover, and the economic downturn in Europe was of concern. Ford, along with other car manufacturers, tried to attract new buyers with innovative features and design. "It is a reflection of the market softening generally," explained Ford Europe's chairman and chief executive, David Thursfield. "We have to bring out more new innovative products to give the market a boost. That is what we are certainly doing at Ford." And the slowdown of the American economy, along with the $3 billion price tag attached to the tire recall, forced Ford to offer early retirement packages to nearly 5,000 managers in order to cut costs. Finally, relationships with dealers and suppliers, who continued to struggle

with the tire recall, needed to be repaired. In this midst of all the turmoil, Ford's board of directors announced that Jacques Nasser would be leaving the company and that Bill Ford, Jr., would be taking over. Ford, in his mid-forties, was the first Ford family member to be CEO of the company since Henry Ford II resigned in 1979.

Bill Ford, known for his commitment to environmental issues, immediately pledged to make Ford Motor Company a leader in environmental protection as part of a company turnaround plan. A visit to the company's Web site reveals a whole host of environmentally friendly initiatives—not all introduced by Bill Ford, but indicative of the company's push toward social responsibility. For instance, Ford has teamed up with Environmental Defense to "provide automotive shoppers with comprehensive information about the environmental impact of automobiles sold in North America." Environmental Defense is a group that sponsors "For My World," a Web site that allows visitors to learn about the "Green Score" of particular vehicles. In addition, Ford is experimenting with water-based paints for its vehicles and working on ways to tackle pollution-producing manufacturing processes as well as traffic congestion.

Of course, these measures deal with only one facet of the overall environment in which Ford conducts its business. Bill Ford and his team of managers need to deal with quality issues, resolve the Firestone tire situation, and get new, more exciting autos into the pipeline. As he took the wheel of his family's company, Ford was closemouthed about his strategy for guiding the company into the future. "Everything is up for review—every asset, every piece of geography," he said. "We continue to review our mix of businesses." In November 2001, Ford announced that its Australian subsidiary would begin designing and manufacturing a new vehicle for the local Australian market, creating as many as 10,000 jobs there. Code-named Raptor, the new model would be poised to take on new cars introduced in Australia by General Motors. Despite the many roadblocks, Ford was showing signs of rolling forward again.

Questions
1. Add to your knowledge of the Firestone tire debacle by researching it on the Internet or at the library. Then prepare for a class discussion or written summary on whether or not you believe Ford acted ethically throughout the crisis and why.
2. Visit the Ford Web site and click on several of the company's pages dealing with socially responsible initiatives—the environment, education, and so forth. Then discuss the role you think these initiatives play in Ford's overall corporate culture.
3. Ford Motor Company was founded by an entrepreneur and was once a small business. Name three ways in which you think Ford has contributed to the American economy and culture over the last century.

SOURCES: Ford Motor Company Web site, http://www.ford.com, accessed January 8, 2002; Tim Burt, "Thursfield Champions Ford of Europe," *Financial Times*, November 28, 2001, http://news.ft.com; Virginia Marsh, "Ford Launch Could Create 10,000 Jobs in Australia," *Financial Times*, November 15, 2001, http://news.ft.com; Kathleen Kerwin and Joann Muller, "Bill Ford Takes the Wheel,"

BusinessWeek Online, November 1, 2001, http://www.businesseek. com; Charles Child and Mary Connelly, "Nasser Out; Bill Ford Takes Over," *Automotive News*, October 29, 2001, http://www.autonews.com; "Ford Concern on Europe Downturn," *BBC News*, September 10, 2001, http://news.bbc.co.uk; Jamie

Butters, "Job Cuts at Ford Likely to Increase," Auto.com, August 10, 2001, http://www.auto.com; "Tire Trouble: The Ford-Firestone Blowout," *Forbes*, June 20, 2001, http://www.forbes.com.

Part Three: A Tale of Two Strategies

THE STORY OF BILL FORD AND JACQUES NASSER IS NOT ONLY the story of two leaders but also the story of two strategies marked by differing management styles, differing goals, and perhaps even differing views of the company's mission. When Nasser came to the top position at Ford, he had already worked for the company for thirty years. No one would argue that his sometimes harsh, autocratic decision-making style made him less than popular among Ford workers, managers, and media members. But Nasser arrived at the top in the late 1990s with bold plans to turn an aging, stumbling company into a streamlined, flexible contender in the auto industry. Ford's ventures into the financial services and defense industries in the 1980s had turned out to be disastrous. Nasser pledged that his new mission for the company, "to be the world's leading consumer company for automotive services and products," would be backed by solid strategic planning. "It's a world going through tremendous change," said Nasser early in his reign, "not just through economic events, but largely through technology. We're trying not to be left behind." So Nasser set a goal of hiring 20 percent new managers while also developing leaders from within the company. He also emphasized team building. He began to acquire other brands, in the United States and abroad, including Land Rover, Jaguar, and a chain of British auto-service centers called Kwik-Fit. He vowed to turn Ford's less profitable car lines around (the company was much stronger in the truck and SUV business): "In the past, we tried to do too much in the car business and dispersed our resources. Now we're simplifying the product line. And we're separating the models that remain and giving them better brand identities." He planned to jump into e-business with all four wheels. "Technology and networks in particular determine the shape of everything else," Nasser remarked. He began with a joint venture with Microsoft's CarPoint, which allowed consumers to build cars to order online (the site also provided Ford with data about car buyers).

How did Nasser's planning work out? Within a couple of years, Wall Street named Ford the most profitable and best-managed automaker of the Big Three (the other two are General Motors and DaimlerChrysler). Then came the Firestone tire recall, quality problems that began to surface, a sluggish economy, and other woes. Nasser's grand Internet plans didn't work out as he had hoped—the information technology department simply wasn't ready. In the summer of 2001, Ford's board of directors voted to give company chairman Bill Ford "a greater strategic role" in the company. In other words, Ford and Nasser would share power and responsibilities that would "focus on policy, strategy, key issues affecting the future direction of the company and other major business issues." For several months, the two men remained diplomatic in public, but there was no mistaking their differing management styles, visions for the

company, or proposed strategies. Eventually, Nasser was voted out. Bill Ford had a huge task ahead of him.

First, Bill Ford created a triumvirate—a team of three top executives—to formulate a new vision and strategies for the company. He named Carl E. Reichardt vice-chairman and Nick Scheele chief operating officer. Scheele came from Ford's Jaguar division and Reichardt, former head of a bank, from the board of directors. "I expect the three of us will have an easygoing relationship," noted Ford. Scheele began his term with a "back to basics" slogan that indicated the company's new strategy would focus on its core business: making and selling cars and trucks. Then came the massive restructuring plan, whose goal was to cut $3 billion to $5 billion in costs. Most experts believe that Nasser would have favored downsizing in order to meet Ford's shrinking share in the marketplace, but Bill Ford would likely favor other strategies. Still, he warned in an early press release that the company would have to take "tough action" to reverse its losses. "It is not going to surprise anyone that there will be some pretty dramatic changes," noted Greg Melich of Morgan Stanley Dean Witter. "The one area where you can do more quickly is in the managerial and administrative areas, whereas restructuring the manufacturing side is much more difficult." However, it was clear that there was surplus manufacturing capacity in North America that needed to be addressed. And before Nasser's departure, the company was considering laying off as much as 20 percent of its U.S. white-collar staff, or more than 8,000 salaried workers, as part of a strategic overhaul. Also, the company proposed delaying the release of certain new auto models, including the Ford Ranger. Another part of the plan involved using more shared parts to cut manufacturing costs, even in Ford's premium car lines such as Volvo and Jaguar. A "strategy board" was developed specifically to formulate plans for the Premier Automotive Group (PAG), which would open the door for more than shared parts—perhaps shared engineering, sales, and purchasing teams—while maintaining the individual identities of the brands. "We have developed a structure which will allow us to more effectively support all our PAG brands," announced Wolfgang Reitzle, chairman of the PAG. "Individually, the companies do not have the critical mass to compete on equal terms."

Finally, Bill Ford began to push for a reconciliation between his company and Firestone/Bridgestone; after all, there are Fords and Firestones in both families. Mending the relationship might indicate a return to normalcy on the road "back to the basics." What are Ford's basics? "It's not the Internet, junkyards, or auto parts," quips David E. Cole, director of the Center for Automotive Research in Ann Arbor, Michigan. "It's building cars and trucks." Now there's a plan.

Questions

1. Based on what you've read, formulate a brief mission statement for the "new" Ford Motor Company.
2. Imagine that you are part of Bill Ford's management team. Set a stretch goal either for the company as a whole or for the Premier group strategy board that you think would realistically help the company turn around. Explain why you chose this goal.
3. Describe the differences between Jacques Nasser and Bill Ford as decision makers.

SOURCES: John Griffiths and Tim Burt, "Moving to Drive the Premier Growth Machine Faster," *Financial Times*, November 23, 2001, http://news.ft.com; Tim Burt and Nikki Tait, "Ford May Axe 20 percent of U.S. White Collar Staff," *Financial Times*, November 6, 2001, http://news.ft.com; Kathleen Kerwin and Joann Muller, "Bill Ford Takes the Wheel," *BusinessWeek Online*, November 1, 2001, http://www.businessweek.com; David Ibison, "New Ford Chief Edges Closer to Truce with Bridgestone," *Financial Times*, November 1, 2001, http://news.ft.com; Tim Burt, "Nasser Signals Further Cuts in Ford's U.S. Production," *Financial Times*, October 25, 2001, http://news.ft.com; Tim Burt, "Nasser Says Ford Has the Strategy to Confound Critics," *Financial Times*, September 13, 2001, http://news.ft.com; Jerry Flint, "Ford: A Distracted Driver," *Forbes.com*, September 6, 2001, http://www.forbes.com; Tim Burt and Nikki Tait, "Getting Ford Around the Corner," *Financial Times*, July 30, 2001, http://news.ft.com; Jeff Moad, "Ford Rebuilds IT Engine," ZDNet News, January 28, 2001, http://www.zdnet.com; Amey Stone and Kathleen Kerwin, "Can Nasser Get Ford's Stock onto a Smoother Road?" *BusinessWeek Online*, October 11, 1999, http://www.businessweek.com; "Jac Nasser: In the Past, We Tried to Do Too Much," *BusinessWeek Online*, October 11, 1999, http://www.businessweek.com.

Part Four: Managing Organizational Changes at Ford

MOST OF US RESIST CHANGE: IT IS HUMAN NATURE TO WANT things to stay the same, even if the conditions of our lives are less than ideal. Changes within organizations are just as difficult for managers to implement and employees to accept. Whether it is learning a new technology, increasing or decreasing staff, expanding or downsizing manufacturing capabilities, adding or deleting products to the line, change can be stressful for everyone in the organization. Conceiving of and announcing the change may fall to upper-level executives, but implementing the change is usually the responsibility of managers, including human resource managers. When the restructuring plan put together by Bill Ford's new executive team began to unfold in late 2001 and early 2002, all of Ford Motor Company was on edge.

After announcing a series of management changes, including the retirement of the chief financial officer, the elevation of Nick Scheele to chief operating officer, and the appointment of three new group vice presidents, the team focused on massive restructuring of Ford's U.S. operations. In January 2002, the team announced that Ford would be closing key manufacturing plants in New Jersey, Missouri, Ohio, Michigan, and Ontario, citing too much capacity at those plants. In other words, the company was overproducing and did not need to build as many cars in a weak economy. In addition, Ford took several well-known but slow-selling models out of production—the Ford Escort, the Mercury Villager (a minivan), the Mercury Cougar, and the Lincoln Continental. Saying that former CEO Jacques Nasser had diversified the organization too much, the new group declared that Ford was now focusing on its core business of building cars and trucks. Overall, 35,000 Ford workers (10 percent of the total global workforce) would probably lose their jobs, at least temporarily. Although this sounds grim, managers and other experts believed that these massive changes would ultimately help Ford survive a weak economy and the costs incurred by the Firestone tire debacle and ultimately lead to its growth.

A company such as Ford naturally has a huge, diverse workforce to manage. Although diversity challenges most often relate to ensuring that a variety of people have equal job opportunity, rarely do we think of older, white male employees as needing protection by the law. But that is exactly what happened at Ford, when a class-action lawsuit was filed against the company for reverse discrimination. The suit alleged that the company's performance appraisal system was targeting those workers for dismissal or early retirement. How could this happen? Under a system instituted by former CEO Nasser, called the Performance Management Process, workers were given performance grades of A, B, or C. Those who received a C could lose their bonuses and raises; those who received two C grades in a row could be fired. If that sounds fair, here's the catch: Under the original plan, a quota of at least 10 percent of Ford employees were to receive C grades; later, the percentage was lowered to 5 percent. Many liken the ranking system, currently being used by a number of leading companies, to a grading curve because regardless of actual performance, a certain number of employees received high scores and a certain number received low ones. As it turned out at Ford, many of the C grades were handed out to older white males. Ford's system was eventually changed to one designating top achievers, achievers, and those requiring improvement. But within a year and a half, Ford agreed to abandon the system, which affected about 18,000 managers. As Bill Ford took over the CEO spot in late 2001, negotiations in the lawsuits continued. However, it seemed clear that both sides wanted the cases settled as amicably as possible.

Compensating nearly half a million employees in different countries is another huge challenge for human resource managers at Ford. In the fall of 2001, the combination of sluggish car sales and the Firestone recall forced the human resource department to circulate a memo announcing that about 6,000 managers would not be receiving their typical yearly bonuses. The company simply did not have the pool of cash—about $440 million—it had had in the past to pay out the bonuses. Nasser's retirement package was also tied to the company's overall financial performance, but he still received a bonus worth more than $5 million.

It is doubtful that anyone would dispute that Ford's management team has had an extremely rocky ride during the past few years. Managers at every level have faced constant challenges as their organization has struggled with massive changes. However, Ford's is taking clear steps to survive and ultimately come out on top with its focus on producing new car models and perhaps even a retooled organization model.

Questions

1. What factors in the environment do you believe have affected Ford's structure in the past? What environmental factors do you believe will affect its structure in the future?
2. What internal forces for change has Ford faced in the last five years?
3. From a human resource management perspective, why do you think Jacques Nasser's performance appraisal system failed?

SOURCES: Ed Garsten, "Tentative Terms in Ford Bias Cases," Associated Press, (November 16, 2001), http://www.ford.com; "Ford Moving Closer to Settling Suits— WSJ," Reuters Limited (November 16, 2001); Ed Garsten, "Ford Announces Management Shuffle," Associated Press (November 15, 2001), http://dailynews.yahoo.com; August Cole, "Ford Shuffles Another Round of Execs," CBS MarketWatch.com (November 15, 2001), http://www.marketwatch.com; "Nasser's Retirement Package Tied to Ford's Performance," Auto.co (November 15, 2001), http://www.auto.com; "Exec Changes Help Ford with Basics," Automotive News (November 12, 2001), http://www.autonews.com; Nikki Tait, "Lincoln Bears Brunt of Ford Restructuring," Financial Times (November 11, 2001), http://news.ft.com; Tim Burt and Nikki Tait, "Ford May Axe 20 Percent of White Collar Staff," Financial Times (November 6, 2001), http://news.ft.com; John Gallagher, "No Bonuses This Year for Ford's Top Bosses," Detroit Free Press (August 29, 2001), http://www.freep.com; Tim Burt and Nikki Tait, "Ford Refines Chain of Command in U.S," Financial Times (July 16, 2001), http://news.ft.com; Tim Burt, "Ford's White Knight Summoned to Aid of U.S. in Distress," Financial Times (July 15, 2001), http://news.ft.com.

Part Five: At Ford, Quality Is Job 1—Again

A FEW YEARS AGO, FORD RAN AN ADVERTISING CAMPAIGN whose motto was "At Ford, Quality, Is Job 1." The company boasted top quality not only in the manufacture of its trucks and cars, but also in its service. In the summer of 2000, the old slogan came back to haunt the company, as it became evident that literally millions of tires—made by Firestone—on Ford's popular SUVs, including the Explorer, were separating and shredding, causing serious and even fatal accidents. Even though Ford didn't manufacture the tires, those tires were installed on Ford vehicles; and the press, general public, and even Congress had a hard time distinguishing between the two. The situation was exacerbated as Bridgestone/Firestone accused Ford of building inferior vehicles. Finger pointing between the two organizations, centered on quality issues, continued for months as the tires were recalled and replaced. A year later, the National Highway Traffic Safety Administration reported that the defective tires, not the Ford vehicles, were to blame for the crashes; but the damage was already done in the public's eyes. "I think as long as this battle is going on in the press nobody is going to win," noted Anne Sceia Klein, a public-relations expert in Philadelphia. "The general public will walk away from [the Ford Explorer] if they can't sort it out."

Maintaining the quality of goods and services is a major part of the controlling function in an organization. Unfortunately, even if a quality problem is only a perceived one—or is exaggerated by publicity—damage to the organization's reputation can occur, and ultimately sales can drop. Ford faced both real and perceived quality issues in its struggle with the tire/SUV problem. Former CEO Jacques Nasser disputed Firestone's charges that the Explorer was at least partially to blame for the rollover crashes. "If you happen to be in a vehicle that had a tread separation, and that vehicle happens to be a compact SUV, you'd be much safer in an Explorer," argued Nasser. "If those Firestone tires were on other SUVs, the rollover instance would be much worse."

Some experts believe that the right information technology, which would have allowed greater knowledge sharing between Bridgestone/Firestone and Ford, and better designed production systems could have prevented the mismatch of tires and vehicles. In fact, Ford already had in place its own Best Practices Replication Process, which was designed to improve the efficiency of various parts of the manufacturing process. In 1995, Dale McKeehan, then vice president of manufacturing, called together his vehicle operations people, including the heads of body construction, painting, and final assembly and said, "Figure out a way to share best practices." Stan Kwiecien, then head of a group working on plant productivity recalls, "So we figured it out. We're engineers." Around the same time, McKeehan met with another manager, Dar Wolford, who was using early information technology to improve efficiency at Ford plants. McKeehan introduced Wolford to Kwiecien, and Ford's Best Practices Replication Process was born. Within four years, more than 2,800 proven superior practices had been shared among Ford's widespread manufacturing facilities, at a total documented value of $850 million. But knowledge sharing did not extend outside the company, so Ford and Firestone never communicated with each other about potential problems with the pairing of their two products.

Around the time of the tire recall, Ford began training managers in a program called Six Sigma, which is a system for continuous improvement in quality and efficiency to help the organization avoid manufacturing mistakes. Six Sigma uses statistical analysis to find the root of a problem that other methods can't seem to locate. For instance, the company's new Lincoln LS sedan had trouble starting on the first try. Using Six Sigma, an engineering team traced the problem to a screw that wasn't properly tightened. How did so many of these screws come off the assembly line loose? Because workers were using the wrong power tool to tighten them. Ford managers claim that Six Sigma saved the company $52 million in errors the first year, with another $300 million projected for the following year.

Feedback is a vital component of control, and recently Ford faced a hard feedback fact: although customers who participated in marketing surveys consistently said they wanted more environmentally responsible vehicles, they are unwilling to pay a higher sticker price for them. Meanwhile, Ford received feedback from the Insurance Institute for Highway Safety in the form of poor results from low-speed crash tests designed to test bumper damage. Still, the Ford Explorer remains the most popular sport utility vehicle on the market, accounting for 20 percent of Ford Motor Company's sales. And Bill Ford remains firm in his commitment to improve the overall quality of his company's vehicles, including reducing their impact on the environment. As for his competitors, Ford notes, "If we didn't provide [the SUV], someone else would, and they wouldn't provide it as responsibly as we do." Already, Ford Motor Company voluntarily builds its SUVs to emit less tailpipe pollution than allowed by law. If Bill Ford has his way, quality will indeed be job 1 at the century-old company for the next one hundred years.

Questions

1. Do you think that Ford Motor Company would benefit from open-book management? Why or why not?
2. In what ways might Ford Motor Company further use information technology to manage knowledge and create a competitive strategy?

3. Which stage of operations strategy would you say is illustrated by Ford Motor Company in this case? Why?

SOURCES: Nedra Pickler, "Explorer Fender Benders Costly," Auto.com, November 30, 2002, http://www.auto.com; "Jacques Knifed," The Economist, November 3, 2001, http://www.economist.com; Alex Taylor III, "What's Behind Ford's Fall?" Fortune, October 29, 2001, http://www.fortune.com; Joann Muller, "Ford: Why It's Worse Than You Think," BusinessWeek Online, June 25, 2001, http://www.businessweek.com; "Ford Goes on Offensive to Explain Massive Tire Replacement Plan," Fox News, May 24, 2001, http://www.foxnews.com; Thomas A. Stewart, "Knowledge Worth $1.25 Billion," Fortune, November 27, 2001, http://www.fortune.com; Keith Bradsher, "Ford Is Conceding S.U.V. Drawbacks," The New York Times, May 12, 2000, http://www.serv.com.

Part Six: Ford Enters a New Era of Leadership

LEADERS COME IN ALL SHAPES AND SIZES. THEY MAY COME FROM different countries and cultures. They exhibit different personality traits. They practice different leadership styles. They may be team players or loners. They may have legitimate power, like Jacques Nasser and Bill Ford. They may practice coercive power, as Nasser did with his controversial performance appraisal system. They often have personal power, as demonstrated by Bill Ford in his commitment to good relationships with union workers. They may possess different visions for the same company, but they all want to motivate their managers and employees toward that vision. And they look for ways to communicate their goals.

Jacques Nasser's entire tenure as CEO of Ford Motor Company was driven by his goal for the company to become "the world's leading consumer company for automotive services and products." He began by slashing costs and reducing payrolls, earning the nickname "Jac the Knife." Then he diversified Ford's business activities around the world, to the dismay of critics who believed he was carrying the company too far afield from its core business of building and selling cars and trucks. (Some thought he invested too much time and money on the Internet prematurely.) He professed to be a believer in teams and open communication, stating in one interview, "You let your teams have room to work and give them air cover. I'm not a believer in telling people [exactly] what to do. If you start giving people a cookbook, you start to get very narrow solutions." Despite cutting a number of jobs, Nasser claimed to be looking for the best people within the company, to motivate them and move them up. "We are spending more time and effort developing leaders from inside the company," he said. "We're trying to strengthen the team. Like any sports team, if you stop recruiting, over time, you'd lose your competitiveness. If you look at the team we've got today, there's a tremendous mix of different backgrounds, even among the people who came up through Ford Motor Co." But Nasser also had a reputation for being an intimidating leader who kept tight controls on his managers—he had sixteen senior managers reporting directly to him instead of creating a team of top executives with the authority to make decisions.

Bill Ford is a completely different type of leader, one who actually sees himself on par with the rank and file workers instead of heir to a family dynasty. His personal power is partly expert—he not only grew up in the business (as did Nasser) but prepared to take over the chairmanship by heading up the company's finance committee—and partly referent. People at all levels of the organization genuinely like him. "You can't get mad at Bill Ford," says Lincoln-Mercury dealer Martin J. McInerney. "He's just too nice a guy." He truly believes that Ford Motor Co. can—and should—have a positive relationship with all its workers and associated unions. And he is passionate about the environment. He sees no reason why the company can't set an example as an environmentally friendly auto manufacturer. "I've staked much of my personal reputation on the environment," he says. "Sometimes I wake up wondering whether I'm taking the company on a diversionary course that won't pay off . . . but on other nights I wake up thinking we're not doing enough." Since taking over as CEO, Ford has redrawn the lines of communication within the company, establishing an executive team that he believes will work well together. "I expect the three of us [Ford, Nick Scheele, and Carl Reichardt] will have an easygoing relationship," predicts Ford.

Ford had already tried to share the leadership role when he took over the chairmanship position while Jacques Nasser was still CEO. The company's board of directors urged the two men to hammer out an arrangement to share power to benefit the company. "You guys need each other," the directors said to each man in separate meetings. So the two tried to establish their roles. "We wanted to ensure that there was clear accountability and clarity with the roles so that we didn't confuse the organization," said Nasser at the time. The result was an arrangement that continued Nasser's primary responsibility for running the company's day-to-day operations and tied Ford more closely to management, but it only lasted for a few short months.

By November 2001, Nasser was out. Some reports say he resigned; others say he was fired. Chances are, both are true. Although Bill Ford certainly had a hand in Nasser's departure, he also takes responsibility for perhaps waiting too long to replace Nasser as the company was stumbling. "I'll always accept my share of the blame," he concedes. Although skeptics are waiting to see whether Bill Ford is tough enough to be the transformational leader that they believe the company now needs, he does have a vision for the company's role not only as a high-quality auto manufacturer, but also as an agent of change. "I'm in this for my children and my grandchildren," he explains. "I want them to inherit a legacy they're proud of. I don't want anybody, whether it's my grandchildren or any of our employees' grandchildren, to have to apologize for working for Ford Motor Co. In fact, I want the opposite. I want them to look and say, 'What a difference we made!'"

Questions

1. Using Exhibit 12.2, make a chart showing what you believe are the personal characteristics of leaders that Bill Ford and Jacques Nasser possess.
2. Do you think Bill Ford and Jacques Nasser are effective communicators? Explain your answer for each.
3. In what ways might Bill Ford use problem-solving teams to benefit his organization? Give one example describing a problem-solving team that might be effective at Ford Motor Co.

SOURCES: Alex Taylor, "Car Jacqued!" *Fortune,* November 26, 2001, *http://www.fortune.com;* David Booth, "FoMoCo on Firmer Ground with Family Back at Helm," *Financial Times,* November 16, 2001, *http://globalarchive.ft.com;* "Bill Ford Takes the Wheel," *BusinessWeek Online,* November 1, 2001, *http://www.businessweek.com;* Doron Levin, "Bill Ford Jr. Got His Wish, and Has Much to Prove," *Bloomberg.com,* October 31, 2001, *http://quote.bloomberg.com;* "Getting Ford Round the Corner," *Financial Times,* July 30, 2001, *http://news.ft.com;* Mary Connelly, "Where Jacques Nasser Went Wrong," *Automotive News,* October 15, 2001, *www.autonews.com;* Jeffrey E. Garten, "The Mind of the C.E.O.," *BusinessWeek Online,* February 5, 2001, *http://www.businessweek.com;* Keith H. Hammonds, "Grassroots Leadership—Ford Motor Company," *Fast Company,* April 2000, *http://www.fastcompany.com;* Alex Taylor, "The Fight at Ford," *Fortune,* April 3, 2000, *www.fortune.com;* Betsy Morris, "Idealist on Board," *Fortune,* April 3, 2000, *www.fortune.com.*

Answers to Manager's Workbook Exercises

Answers to Chapter 3

1. China (1.3 b)
   India (982 m)
   US (256 m)
   Indonesia (206 m)
   Brazil (166)
   Russia (147 m)

2. 1. Pakistan (148 m)   11. Italy (58)
   2. Japan (126 m)   12. United Kingdom (58)
   3. Bangladesh (124 m)   13. France (59)
   4. Nigeria (106 m)   14. Thailand (60)
   5. Mexico (88 m)   15. Egypt (66)
   6. Germany (82 m)   16. Ethiopia (60)
   7. Vietnam (69)   17. Ukraine (51)
   8. Phillippines (73)   18. South Korea (44)
   9. Iran (66)   19. Myanmar (Burma) (44)
   10. Turkey (64)

3. 1. Mandarin (885)   6. Arabic (202)
   2. English (450)   7. Bengali (187)
   3. Hindi (367)   8. Portugese (174)
   4. Spanish (353)   9. Malay-Portuguese (145)
   5. Russian (294)   10. Japanese (126)

4. c. 223
5. b. 188
6. Japan
7. United States
8. e. increased substantially (by about 35 percent, although since then changes have been more erratic due to a number of political, economic, and climatic factors)
9. c. increased (from 5 to 15 percent, and has continued to increase since 1985)
10. c. 6,000
11. c. $17 trillion
12. c. 2/3
13. 1/10
14. b. 20 percent
15. 35 percent

Answers to Chapter 4

Compare your answers with other Americans who were surveyed.

1. 34 percent said personal e-mail on company computers is wrong
2. 37 percent said using office equipment for schoolwork is wrong
3. 49 percent said playing computer games at work is wrong
4. 54 percent said Internet shopping at work is wrong
5. 61 percent said it's unethical to blame your error on technology
6. 87 percent said it's unethical to visit pornographic sites at work

7. 33 percent said $25 is the amount at which a gift from a supplier or client becomes troubling, while 33 percent said $50, and 33 percent said $100
8. 35 percent said a $50 gift to the boss is unacceptable
9. 12 percent said a $50 gift from the boss is unacceptable
10. 70 percent said it's unacceptable to take the $200 football tickets
11. 70 percent said it's unacceptable to take the $120 theater tickets
12. 35 percent said it's unacceptable to take the $100 food basket
13. 45 percent said it's unacceptable to take the $25 gift certificate
14. 40 percent said it's unacceptable to take the $75 raffle prize
15. 11 percent reported they lie about sick days
16. 4 percent reported they take credit for the work or ideas of others

Answers to Chapter 10

Answers: (each correct answer is worth one point)

1. c. The objective is to make a decision quickly and to move the process forward without a great deal of red tape and delay. The legal process can often slow decision making—whether by three weeks or three months—and time is of the essence in the online world. Moreover, when was the last time an NDA about client information materially impacted your business? Better to spend your time building trust than protecting against an unlikely downside.

2. a. Give the candidate a job while waiting for the check. If he has been vouched for by someone you trust and you love his work, grab him while he's available and put him to work. If you think he's a great hire, chances are so will your competitors.

3. b. Hire your neighbor. Any list of dynamic industries you put together is bound to include health care, and your biggest challenge is to find a credible person with industry know-how and contacts who can take you into the industry. Your neighbor can do that. Now start looking for the other industries you want to focus on.

4. b. Buy Company B. Company B has proven itself to be fast moving and dynamic, and their balance sheet issues make them open to a favorable price. Company A and C are both tying their success to future events—a strong holiday selling season or a successful online launch—either of which may not happen and are in the distant Internet future.

5. c. The one area a company cannot afford to get wrong is its technical architecture. It must scale and be reliable, or its whole business will be at risk. Programmers without a blueprint cannot ensure a successful online environment, and staffing internally is time-consuming and uncertain. Better to outsource the project immediately while building an internal team to take it over after its launch.

360-degree feedback A process that uses multiple raters, including self-rating, to appraise employee performance and guide development.

accountability That the people with authority and responsibility are subject to reporting and justifying task outcomes to those above them in the chain of command.

achievement culture A results-oriented culture that values competitiveness, personal initiative, and achievement.

adaptability culture A culture characterized by values that support the company's ability to interpret and translate signals from the environment into new behavior responses.

adjourning The stage of team development in which members prepare for the team's disbandment.

administrative model A decision-making model that describes how managers make decisions in situations characterized by nonprogrammed decisions, uncertainty, and ambiguity.

affirmative action Refers to government-mandated programs that focus on providing opportunities to women and members of minority groups who have previously been discriminated against.

ambiguity The goals to be achieved or the problem to be solved is unclear, alternatives are difficult to define, and information about outcomes is unavailable.

application form A device for collecting information about an applicant's education, previous job experience, and other background characteristics.

assessment centers A technique for selecting individuals with high managerial potential based on their performances on a series of simulated managerial tasks.

attitude A cognitive and affective evaluation that predisposes a person to act in a certain way.

attributions Judgments about what caused a person's behavior, either characteristics of the person or of the situation.

authoritarianism The belief that power and status differences should exist within the organization.

authority The formal and legitimate right of a manager to make decisions, issue orders, and allocate resources to achieve organizationally desired outcomes.

balanced scorecard A comprehensive management control system that balances traditional financial measures with measures of customer service, internal business processes, and the organization's capacity for learning and growth.

behavior modification The set of techniques by which reinforcement theory is used to modify human behavior.

behaviorally anchored rating scale (BARS) A rating technique that relates an employee's performance to specific job-related incidents.

benchmarking The continuous process of measuring products, services, and practices against major competitors or industry leaders.

Big Five personality factors Dimensions that describe an individual's extroversion, agreeableness, conscientiousness, emotional stability, and openness to experience.

blog A running Web log that allows an individual to post opinions and ideas on anything from products to management.

bottom-up budgeting A budgeting process in which lower-level managers budget their departments' resource needs and pass them up to top management for approval.

bounded rationality The concept that people have the time and cognitive ability to process a limited amount of information on which to base decisions.

brainstorming A technique that uses a face-to-face group to suggest a broad range of alternatives spontaneously for decision making.

bureaucratic control The use of rules, policies, hierarchy of authority, reward systems, and other formal devices to influence employee behavior and assess performance.

centralization The location of decision authority near top organizational levels.

centralized network A team communication structure in which team members communicate through a single individual to solve problems or make decisions.

ceremony A planned activity that makes up a special event and is conducted for the benefit of an audience.

certainty All the information the decision maker needs is fully available.

chain of command An unbroken line of authority that links all individuals in the organization and specifies who reports to whom.

change agent An OD specialist who contracts with an organization to facilitate change.

changing The intervention stage of organization development in which individuals experiment with new workplace behavior.

channel richness The amount of information that can be transmitted during a communication episode.

channel The carrier of a communication.

charismatic leader A leader who has the ability to motivate subordinates to transcend their expected performance.

chief ethics officer A company executive who oversees ethics and legal compliance.

classical model A decision-making model based on the assumption that managers should make logical decisions that will be in the organization's best economic interests.

coalition An informal alliance among managers who support a specific goal.

code of ethics A formal statement of the organization's values regarding ethics and social issues.

coercive power Power that stems from the authority to punish or recommend punishment.

cognitive dissonance A condition in which two attitudes or a behavior and an attitude conflict.

G-1

collectivism A preference for a tightly knit social framework in which individuals look after one another and organizations protect their members' interests.

committee A long-lasting, sometimes permanent team in the organization structure created to deal with tasks that recur regularly.

communication The process by which information is exchanged and understood by two or more people, usually with the intent to motivate or influence behavior.

communication apprehension An individual's level of fear or anxiety associated with interpersonal communications.

compensation Monetary payments (wages, salaries) and nonmonetary goods/commodities (benefits, vacations) used to reward employees.

compensatory justice The concept that individuals should be compensated for the cost of their injuries by the responsible party and that individuals should not be held responsible for matters over which they have no control.

competitive advantage What sets the organization apart from others and provides it with a distinctive edge for meeting customer needs in the marketplace.

competitors Other organizations in the same industry or business that provide goods or services to the same set of customers.

concurrent control Control that consists of monitoring ongoing activities to ensure they are consistent with standards.

conflict Antagonistic interaction in which one party attempts to thwart the intentions and/or goals of another.

consideration The type of behavior that describes the extent to which the leader is sensitive to subordinates, respects their ideas and feelings, and establishes mutual trust.

consistency culture A culture that values and rewards a methodical, rational, orderly way of doing things.

content theories A group of theories that emphasizes the needs that motivate people.

contingency This means that one thing depends on other things, and for organizations to be effective, there must

be a "goodness of fit" between their structure and the conditions in their external environment.

contingency approaches A model of leadership that describes the relationship between leadership styles and specific organizational situations.

contingency plans Plans that define company responses to specific situations, such as emergencies, setbacks, or unexpected conditions.

contingent workers People who work for an organization but not on a permanent or full-time basis, including temporary placements, contracted professionals, or leased employees.

continuous improvement The implementation of a large number of small, incremental improvements in all areas of the organization on an ongoing basis.

continuous process production A type of technology involving mechanization of the entire work flow and nonstop production.

continuous reinforcement schedule A schedule in which every occurrence of the desired behavior is reinforced.

coordination The quality of collaboration across departments.

coordination costs The time and energy to coordinate the activities of a team to enable it to perform its task.

core competence Something the organization does especially well in comparison to its competitors. A core competence represents a competitive advantage because the company acquires expertise that competitors do not have.

corporate university An in-house training and education facility that offers broad-based learning opportunities for employees.

corporate governance The system of governing an organization so the interests of corporate owners are protected.

cost leadership strategy Aggressively seeks efficient facilities, pursues cost reductions, and uses tight cost controls to produce products more efficiently than competitors.

courage The ability to step forward through fear and act on one's values and conscience.

creativity The generation of novel ideas that might meet perceived needs or offer opportunities for the organization.

cross-functional teams A group of employees from various functional departments that meet as a team to resolve mutual problems.

cultural leader A manager who uses signals and symbols to influence corporate culture.

culture The set of key values, beliefs, understandings, and norms that members of an organization share.

culture shock Feelings of confusion, disorientation, and anxiety that result from being immersed in a foreign culture.

culture/people change A change in employees' values, norms, attitudes, beliefs, and behavior.

customer relationship management (CRM) This system helps companies track customers' interactions with the firm and allows employees to call up a customer's past sales and service records, outstanding orders, or unresolved problems.

customers People and organizations in the environment who acquire goods or services from the organization.

cycle time The steps taken to complete a company process.

data Raw facts and figures that by themselves may be useless.

decentralization The location of decision authority near lower organizational levels.

decentralized control The use of organizational culture, group norms, and a focus on goals, rather than rules and procedures, to foster compliance with organizational goals.

decentralized network A team communication structure in which team members freely communicate with one another and arrive at decisions together.

decision A choice made from available alternatives.

decision making The process of identifying problems and opportunities and then resolving them.

decision styles Differences among people with respect to how they perceive problems and make decisions.

decodes To translate the symbols used in a message for the purpose of interpreting its meaning.

delegation The process managers use to transfer authority and responsibility to positions below them in the hierarchy.

departmentalization The basis on which individuals are grouped into departments and departments into the total organization.

descriptive An approach that describes how managers make decisions rather than how they should.

devil's advocate A decision-making technique in which an individual is assigned the role of challenging the assumptions and assertions made by the group to prevent premature consensus.

diagnosis The step in the decision-making process in which managers analyze underlying causal factors associated with the decision situation.

dialogue A group communication process aimed at creating a culture based on collaboration, fluidity, trust, and commitment to shared goals.

differentiation An attempt to distinguish the firm's products or services from others in the industry. The organization may use advertising, distinctive product features, exceptional service, or new technology to achieve a product perceived as unique.

digital technology Technology characterized by use of the Internet and other digital processes to conduct or support business operations.

discretionary responsibility Organizational responsibility that is voluntary and guided by the organization's desire to make social contributions not mandated by economics, law, or ethics.

discrimination The hiring or promoting of applicants based on criteria that are not job relevant.

distributive justice The concept that different treatment of people should not be based on arbitrary characteristics. In the case of substantive differences, people should be treated differently in proportion to the differences among them.

downsizing Intentional, planned reduction in the size of a company's workforce.

downward communication Messages sent from top management down to subordinates.

dual roles A role in which the individual contributes to the team's task and supports members' emotional needs.

E → P expectancy Expectancy that putting effort into a given task will lead to high performance.

e-business Refers to the work an organization does by using electronic linkages (including the Internet) with customers, partners, suppliers, employees, or other key constituents.

e-commerce Specifically refers to business exchanges or transactions that occur electronically. E-commerce replaces or enhances the exchange of money and products with the exchange of data and information from one computer to another.

economic dimension The dimension of the general environment representing the overall economic health of the country or region in which the organization operates.

economic forces Pertain to the availability, production, and distribution of resources in a society.

economic value-added (EVA) A control system that measures performance in terms of after-tax profits minus the cost of capital invested in tangible assets.

electronic brainstorming Bringing people together in an interactive group over a computer network to suggest alternatives; sometimes called brainwriting.

electronic data interchange (EDI) These networks link the computer systems of buyers and sellers to allow the transmission of structured data primarily for ordering, distribution, and payables and receivables.

employee network groups Groups based on social identity, such as gender or race, and organized by employees to focus on concerns of employees from that group.

employment tests A written or computer-based test designed to measure a particular attribute such as intelligence or aptitude.

empowerment The delegation of power or authority to subordinates.

encodes To select symbols with which to compose a message.

equity A situation that exists when the ratio of one person's outcomes to inputs equals that of another's.

equity theory A process theory that focuses on individuals' perceptions of how fairly they are treated relative to others.

ERG theory A modification of the needs hierarchy theory that proposes three categories of needs: existence, relatedness, and growth.

escalating commitment Continuing to invest time and resources in a failing decision.

ethical dilemma A situation that arises when all alternative choices or behaviors have been deemed undesirable because of potentially negative consequences, making it difficult to distinguish right from wrong.

ethics The code of moral principles and values that govern the behaviors of a person or group with respect to what is right or wrong.

ethics committee A group of executives assigned to oversee the organization's ethics by ruling on questionable issues and disciplining violators.

ethics training Training programs to help employees deal with ethical questions and values.

ethnocentrism A cultural attitude marked by the tendency to regard one's own culture as superior to others.

ethnorelativism The belief that groups and subcultures are inherently equal.

euro A single European currency that replaced the currencies of 12 European nations.

event-driven planning This is a continuous, sequential process rather than a staid planning document. It is evolutionary and interactive, taking advantage of unforeseen events to shift the company as needed to improve performance.

exit interview An interview conducted with departing employees to determine the reasons for their termination.

expectancy theory A process theory that proposes that motivation depends on individuals' expectations about their ability to perform tasks and receive desired rewards.

expert power Power that stems from special knowledge of, or skill, in the tasks performed by subordinates.

extranet This is an external communications system that uses the Internet and is shared by two or more organizations.

extrinsic rewards A reward given by another person.

feedback control Control that focuses on the organization's outputs; also called postaction or output control.

feedback A response by the receiver to the sender's communication.

feedforward control Control that focuses on human, material, and financial resources flowing into the organization; also called preliminary or preventive control.

femininity A cultural preference for relationships, cooperation, group decision making, and quality of life.

flat structure A management structure characterized by an overall broad span of control and relatively few hierarchical levels.

focus strategy Concentrating on a specific regional market or buyer group. The company will use a differentiation or low-cost approach, but only for a narrow target market.

force-field analysis The process of determining which forces drive and which resist a proposed change.

formal communication channels A communication channel that flows within the chain of command or task responsibility defined by the organization.

formal teams A team created by the organization as part of the formal organization structure.

forming The stage of team development characterized by orientation and acquaintance.

free rider A person who benefits from team membership but does not make a proportionate contribution to the team's work.

frustration-regression principle The idea that failure to meet a high-order need may cause a regression to an already satisfied lower-order need.

fundamental attribution error The tendency to underestimate the influence of external factors on another's behavior and to overestimate the influence of internal factors.

general environment The layer of the external environment that affects the organization indirectly.

glass ceiling An invisible barrier that separates women and minorities from top management positions.

global outsourcing Engaging in the international division of labor so as to obtain the cheapest sources of labor and supplies regardless of country; also called global sourcing.

global teams A work team made up of members of different nationalities whose activities span multiple countries; may operate as a virtual team or meet face to face.

goal A desired future state that the organization attempts to realize.

goal-setting theory A motivation theory in which specific, challenging goals increase motivation and performance when the goals are accepted by subordinates and these subordinates receive feedback to indicate their progress toward goal achievement.

grapevine An informal, person-to-person communication network of employees not officially sanctioned by the organization.

groupthink The tendency for people to be so committed to a cohesive team that they are reluctant to express contrary opinions.

halo effect A type of rating error that occurs when an employee receives the same rating on all dimensions regardless of his or her performance on individual ones. An overall impression of a person or situation based on one characteristic, favorable or unfavorable.

hero A figure who exemplifies the deeds, character, and attributes of a strong corporate culture.

hierarchy of needs theory A content theory that proposes that people are motivated by five categories of needs—physiological, safety, belongingness, esteem, and self-actualization—that exist in a hierarchical order.

horizontal communication The lateral or diagonal exchange of messages among peers or co-workers.

horizontal team A formal team composed of employees from about the same hierarchical level but from different areas of expertise.

human capital The economic value of the knowledge, experience, skills, and capabilities of employees.

human resource information system An integrated computer system designed to provide data and information used in HR planning and decision making.

human resource management (HRM) Activities undertaken to attract, develop, and maintain an effective workforce within an organization.

human resource planning The forecasting of HR needs and the projected matching of individuals with expected vacancies.

humility Being unpretentious and modest rather than arrogant and prideful.

hygiene factors Factors that involve the presence or absence of job dissatisfiers, including working conditions, pay, company policies, and interpersonal relationships.

idea champion A person who sees the need for and champions productive change within the organization.

idea incubator An in-house program that provides a safe harbor where ideas from employees throughout the organization can be developed without interference from company bureaucracy or politics.

implementation The step in the decision-making process that involves using managerial, administrative, and persuasive abilities to translate the chosen alternative into action.

individualism A preference for a loosely knit social framework in which individuals are expected to take care of themselves.

individualism approach The ethical concept that acts are moral when they promote the individual's best long-term interests, which ultimately leads to the greater good.

influence The effect a person's actions have on the attitudes, values, beliefs, or behavior of others.

information Data converted into a meaningful and useful context for specific users.

information technology (IT) Consists of the hardware, software, telecommunications, database management, and other technologies it uses to store data and make them available in the form of information for organizational decision making.

infrastructure A country's physical facilities that support economic activities.

initiating structure A type of leader behavior that describes the extent to which the leader is task oriented and directs subordinate work activities toward goal attainment.

instant messaging (IM) Electronic communication that allows users to see who is connected to a network and share information instantly.

interactive leadership A leadership style characterized by values such as inclusion, collaboration, relationship building, and caring.

internal environment The environment that includes the elements within the organization's boundaries.

international dimension The portion of the external environment that represents events originating in foreign countries as well as opportunities for U.S. companies in other countries.

international management The management of business operations conducted in more than one country.

Internet A global collection of computer networks linked together for the exchange of data and information.

Intranet An internal communications system that uses the technology and standards of the Internet but is accessible only to people within the company.

intrinsic rewards The satisfaction received in the process of performing an action.

intuition The immediate comprehension of a decision situation based on past experience but without conscious thought.

involvement culture A culture that places high value on meeting the needs of employees and values cooperation and equality.

ISO 9000 A set of international standards for quality management, setting uniform guidelines for processes to ensure that products conform to customer requirements.

job analysis The systematic process of gathering and interpreting information about the essential duties, tasks, and responsibilities of a job.

job characteristics model A model of job design that comprises core job dimensions, critical psychological states, and employee growth-need strength.

job description A concise summary of the specific tasks and responsibilities of a particular job.

job design The application of motivational theories to the structure of work for improving productivity and satisfaction.

job enlargement A job design that combines a series of tasks into one new, broader job to give employees variety and challenge.

job enrichment A job design that incorporates achievement, recognition, and other high-level motivators into the work.

job evaluation The process of determining the value of jobs within an organization through an examination of job content.

job rotation A job design that systematically moves employees from one job to another to provide them with variety and stimulation.

job satisfaction A positive attitude toward one's job.

job simplification A job design whose purpose is to improve task efficiency by reducing the number of tasks a single person must do.

job specification An outline of the knowledge, skills, education, and physical abilities needed to perform a job.

justice approach The ethical concept that moral decisions must be based on standards of equity, fairness, and impartiality.

knowledge management Refers to the systematic efforts to find, organize, and make available a company's intellectual capital and to foster a culture of continuous learning and knowledge sharing so a company's activities build on what is known.

labor market The people available for hire by the organization.

large-group intervention An approach that brings together participants from all parts of the organization (and may include key outside stakeholders as well) to discuss problems or opportunities and plan for major change.

law of effect The assumption that positively reinforced behavior tends to be repeated and unreinforced or negatively reinforced behavior tends to be inhibited.

leadership grid A two-dimensional leadership theory that measures the leader's concern for people and for production.

leadership The ability to influence people toward the attainment of organizational goals.

lean manufacturing Uses highly trained employees at every stage of the production process who take a painstaking approach to details and problem solving to cut waste and improve quality and productivity.

learning organization Can be defined as one in which everyone is engaged in identifying and solving problems, enabling the organization to experiment, change, and improve continuously, thus increasing its capacity to grow, learn, and achieve its purpose.

learning A change in behavior or performance that occurs as the result of experience.

least preferred co-worker (LPC) scale A questionnaire designed to measure relationship-oriented versus task-oriented leadership style according to the leader's choice of adjectives for describing the least preferred co-worker.

legal-political dimension The dimension of the general environment that includes federal, state, and local government regulations and political activities designed to influence company behavior.

legitimate power Power that stems from a formal management position in an organization and the authority granted to it.

line authority A form of authority in which individuals in management positions have the formal power to direct and control immediate subordinates.

listening The skill of receiving messages to accurately grasp facts and feelings to interpret the genuine meaning.

locus of control The tendency to place the primary responsibility for one's success or failure within oneself (internally) or on outside forces (externally).

long-term orientation A greater concern for the future and high value on thrift and perseverance.

Machiavellianism The tendency to direct much of one's behavior toward the acquisition of power and the manipulation of other people for personal gain.

management The effective and efficient attainment of organizational goals through planning, organizing, leading, and controlling organizational resources.

management by objectives (MBO) A method of management whereby managers and employees define goals for every department, project, and person and use them to monitor subsequent performance.

management by wandering around (MBWA) A communication technique in which managers interact directly with workers to exchange information.

management information system (MIS) This is a computer-based system that provides information and support for effective managerial decision making.

market entry strategies An organizational strategy for entering a foreign market.

masculinity A cultural preference for achievement, heroism, assertiveness, work centrality, and material success.

mass production A type of technology characterized by the production of a large volume of products with the same specifications.

matching model An employee selection approach in which the organization and the applicant attempt to match each other's needs, interests, and values.

mediation The process of using a third party to settle a dispute.

message The tangible formulation of an idea to be sent to a receiver.

mission The organization's reason for existence.

mission statement A broadly stated definition of the organization's basic business scope and operations that distinguishes it from similar types of organizations.

modular approach A manufacturing company uses outside suppliers to provide large components of the product, which are then assembled into a final product by a few workers.

monoculture A culture that accepts only one way of doing things and one set of values and beliefs, which can cause problems for minority employees.

moral leadership Distinguishing right from wrong and choosing to do right in the practice of leadership.

moral rights approach The ethical concept that moral decisions are those that best maintain the rights of those people affected by them.

most favored nation clause A term describing a GATT clause that calls for member countries to grant other member countries the most favorable treatment they accord any country concerning imports and exports.

motivation The arousal, direction, and persistence of behavior.

motivators Factors that influence job satisfaction based on fulfillment of high-level needs such as achievement, recognition, responsibility, and opportunity for growth.

multicultural teams Teams made up of members from diverse national, racial, ethnic, and cultural backgrounds.

Myers-Briggs Type Indicator (MBTI) Personality test that measures a person's preference for introversion vs. extroversion, sensation vs. intuition, thinking vs. feeling, and judging vs. perceiving.

neutralizer A situational variable that counteracts a leadership style and prevents the leader from displaying certain behaviors.

new-venture fund A fund providing resources from which individuals and groups can draw to develop new ideas, products, or businesses.

new-venture team A unit separate from the mainstream of the organization that is responsible for developing and initiating innovations.

nonparticipator role A role in which the individual contributes little to the task or members' socioemotional needs.

nonprogrammed decisions Decisions made in response to a unique situation, are poorly defined and largely unstructured, and have important consequences for the organization.

nonverbal communication A communication transmitted through actions and behaviors rather than through words.

normative An approach that defines how a decision maker should make decisions and provides guidelines for reaching an ideal outcome for the organization.

norming The stage of team development in which conflicts developed during the storming stage are resolved and team harmony and unity emerge.

office automation systems These combine modern hardware and software such as word processors, desktop publishers, e-mail, and teleconferencing to handle the tasks of publishing and distributing information.

on-the-job training (OJT) A type of training in which an experienced employee "adopts" a new employee to teach him or her how to perform job duties.

open communication Sharing all types of information throughout the company, across functional and hierarchical levels.

open innovation Extending the search for and commercialization of new ideas beyond the organization's boundaries and perhaps beyond the industry's boundaries.

open-book management Sharing financial information and results with all employees in the organization.

operational goals Specific, measurable results expected from departments, work groups, and individuals within the organization.

operational plans Plans developed at the organization's lower levels that specify action steps toward achieving operational goals and that support tactical planning activities.

operations information sytems These support information-processing needs of a business's daily operations and low-level operations management functions.

opportunity A situation in which managers see potential organizational accomplishments that exceed current goals.

organization A goal-directed and deliberately structured social entity.

organization chart The visual representation of an organization's structure.

organization development (OD) The application of behavioral science techniques to improve an organization's health and effectiveness through its ability to cope with environmental changes, improve internal relationships, and increase learning and problem-solving capabilities.

organization structure The framework in which the organization defines how tasks are divided, resources are deployed, and departments are coordinated.

organizational behavior (OB) An interdisciplinary field dedicated to the study of how individuals and groups tend to act in organizations.

organizational change The adoption of a new idea or behavior by an organization.

organizational citizenship Work behavior that goes beyond job requirements and contributes as needed to the organization's success.

organizational commitment Loyalty to and heavy involvement in one's organization.

organizational control The systematic process through which managers regulate organizational activities to make them consistent with expectations established in plans, targets, and standards of performance.

organizational effectiveness The degree to which the organization achieves a stated goal.

organizational efficiency Refers to the amount of resources used to achieve an organizational goal. Efficiency is the use of minimal resources—raw materials, money, and people—to produce a desired volume of output.

organizational environment All elements existing outside the organization's boundaries that have the potential to affect the organization.

organizing The deployment of organizational resources to achieve strategic goals.

P → O expectancy Expectancy that successful performance of a task will lead to the desired outcome.

partial productivity The ratio of total outputs to a major category of inputs.

partial reinforcement schedule A schedule in which only some occurrences of the desired behavior are reinforced.

path-goal theory A contingency approach to leadership specifying that the leader's responsibility is to increase subordinates' motivation by clarifying the behaviors necessary for task accomplishment and rewards.

pay-for-performance Incentive pay that ties at least part of compensation to employee effort and performance.

peer-to-peer (P2P) file sharing This allows personal computers (PCs) to communicate directly with one another over the Internet, bypassing central databases, servers, control points, and Web pages.

perception The cognitive process people use to make sense out of the environment by selecting, organizing, and interpreting information.

perceptual defense The tendency of perceivers to protect themselves by disregarding ideas, objects, or people that are threatening to them.

perceptual distortions Errors in perceptual judgment that arise from inaccuracies in any part of the perceptual process.

perceptual selectivity The process by which individuals screen and select the various stimuli that vie for their attention.

performance The attainment of organizational goals by efficiently and effectively using resources.

performance appraisal The process of observing and evaluating an employee's performance, recording the assessment, and providing feedback to the employee.

performance gap A disparity between existing and desired performance levels.

performing The stage of team development in which members focus on problem solving and accomplishing the team's assigned task.

permanent teams A group of participants from several functions who are permanently assigned to solve ongoing problems of common interest.

person-job fit The extent to which a person's ability and personality match the requirements of a job.

personal communication channels Communication channels that exist outside the formally authorized channels and do not adhere to the organization's hierarchy of authority.

personal networking The acquisition and cultivation of personal relationships that cross departmental, hierarchical, and organizational boundaries.

personality The set of characteristics that underlie a relatively stable pattern of behavior in response to ideas, objects, or people in the environment.

plan A blueprint specifying the resource allocations, schedules, and other actions necessary for attaining goals.

planning The act of determining the organization's goals and the means for achieving them.

planning task force A group of managers and employees who develop a strategic plan.

pluralism This means that an organization accommodates several subcultures.

point-counterpoint A decision-making technique in which people are assigned to express competing points of view.

political forces Refer to the influence of political and legal institutions on people and organizations. Political forces include basic assumptions underlying the political system, such as the desirability of self-government, property rights, contract rights, the definition of justice, and the determination of innocence or guilt of a crime.

political risk A company's risk of loss of assets, earning power, or managerial control due to politically based events or actions by host governments.

power distance The degree to which people accept inequality in power among institutions, organizations, and people.

power The potential ability to influence others' behavior.

pressure group An interest group that works within the legal-political framework to influence companies to behave in socially responsible ways.

problem-solving teams Typically, 5 to 12 hourly employees from the same department who meet to discuss ways of improving quality, efficiency, and the work environment.

problem A situation in which organizational accomplishments have failed to meet established goals.

procedural justice The concept that rules should be clearly stated and consistently and impartially enforced.

process control systems These special sensing devices monitor and record physical phenomena such as temperature or pressure changes.

process theories A group of theories that explain how employees select behaviors with which to meet their needs and determine if their choices were successful.

process An organized group of related tasks and activities that work together to transform inputs into outputs and create value.

product change A change in the organization's product or service output.

productivity The organization's output of goods and services divided by its inputs.

programmed decisions Decisions made in response to a situation that has occurred often enough to enable decision rules to be developed and applied in the future.

project manager A person responsible for coordinating the activities of several departments on a full-time basis for the completion of a specific project.

projection The tendency to see one's own personal traits in other people.

quality circle A group of 6 to 12 volunteer employees who meet regularly to discuss and solve problems affecting the quality of their work.

realistic job previews (RJPs) A recruiting approach that gives applicants all pertinent and realistic information about the job and the organization.

recruiting The activities or practices that define the desired characteristics of applicants for specific jobs.

reengineering The radical redesign of business processes to achieve dramatic improvements in cost, quality, service, and speed.

referent power Power that results from characteristics that command subordinates' identification with respect and admiration for and desire to emulate the leader.

refreezing The reinforcement stage of organization development in which individuals acquire a desired new skill or attitude and are rewarded for it by the organization.

reinforcement Anything that causes a given behavior to be repeated or inhibited.

reinforcement theory A motivation theory based on the relationship between a given behavior and its consequences.

responsibility center An organizational unit under the supervision of a single person who is responsible for its activity.

responsibility The duty to perform the task or activity an employee has been assigned.

reward power Power that results from the authority to bestow rewards on other people.

risk A decision has clear goals and good information is available, but the future outcomes associated with each alternative are subject to chance.

risk propensity The willingness to undertake risk with the opportunity of gaining an increased payoff.

role A set of expectations for a manager's behavior.

role ambiguity Uncertainty about what behaviors are expected of a person in a particular role.

role conflict Incompatible demands of different roles.

satisficing To choose the first solution alternative that satisfies minimal decision criteria regardless of whether better solutions are presumed to exist.

scenario building Looking at trends and discontinuities and imagining possible alternative futures to build a framework within which unexpected future events can be managed.

schedule of reinforcement The frequency with which, and intervals over which, reinforcement occurs.

scientific management Postulates that decisions about organizations and job design should be based on precise, scientific study of individual situations.

search The process of learning about current developments inside or outside the organization that can be used to meet a perceived need for change.

selection The process of determining the skills, abilities, and other attributes a person needs to perform a particular job.

self-directed team A team consisting of 5 to 20 multiskilled workers who rotate jobs to produce an entire product or service, often supervised by an elected member.

self-serving bias The tendency to overestimate the contribution of internal factors to one's successes and the contribution of external factors to one's failures.

semantics The meaning of words and the way they are used.

servant leaders Leaders who work to fulfill subordinates' needs and goals as well as to achieve the organization's larger mission.

service technology Technology characterized by intangible outputs and direct contact between employees and customers.

short-term orientation A concern with the past and present and a high value on meeting social obligations.

single-use plans Plans developed to achieve a set of goals unlikely to be repeated in the future.

situation analysis Typically includes a search for strengths, weaknesses, opportunities, and threats (SWOT) that affect organizational performance.

situational theory A contingency approach to leadership that links the leader's behavioral style with the task readiness of subordinates.

Six Sigma A quality control approach that emphasizes a relentless pursuit of higher quality and lower costs.

skunkworks A separate, small, informal, highly autonomous, and often secretive group that focuses on breakthrough ideas for the business.

slogan A phrase or sentence that succinctly expresses a key corporate value.

small-batch production A type of technology that involves the production of goods in batches of one or a few products designed to customer specification.

social entrepreneur Entrepreneurial leaders who are committed to good business and changing the world for the better.

social facilitation The tendency for the presence of others to influence an individual's motivation and performance.

social forces Refer to those aspects of a culture that guide and influence relationships among people. What do people value? What do people need? What are people's behavior standards?

social responsibility The obligation of organization management to make decisions and take actions that will enhance the welfare and interests of society as well as the organization.

sociocultural dimension The dimension of the general environment representing the demographic characteristics, norms, customs, and values of the population within which the organization operates.

socioemotional role A role in which the individual provides support for team members' emotional needs and social unity.

span of management The number of employees reporting to a supervisor; also called span of control.

special-purpose teams A team created outside the formal organization to undertake a project of special importance or creativity.

staff authority A form of authority granted to staff specialists in their area of expertise.

stakeholder Any person or group within or outside the organization that has a stake in the organization's performance.

standing plans Ongoing plans used to provide guidance for tasks performed repeatedly within the organization.

stereotyping Placing an employee into a class or category based on one or a few traits or characteristics. The tendency to assign an individual to a group or broad category and then attribute generalizations about the group to the individual.

storming The stage of team development in which individual personalities and roles, and resulting conflicts, emerge.

story A narrative based on true events that is repeated frequently and shared among organizational employees.

strategic conversation Dialogue across boundaries and hierarchical levels about the team's or organization's vision, critical strategic themes, and the values that help achieve important goals.

strategic goals Broad statements of where the organization wants to be in the future; pertaining to the organization as a whole rather than to specific divisions or departments.

strategic management The set of decisions and actions used to formulate and implement strategies that will provide a competitively superior fit between the organization and its environment so as to achieve organizational goals.

strategic plans The action steps by which an organization intends to attain strategic goals.

strategy The plan of action that describes resource allocation and activities for dealing with the environment, achieving a competitive advantage, and attaining the organization's goals.

strategy formulation May include assessing the external environment and internal problems and integrating the results into goals and strategy.

strategy implementation The use of managerial and organizational tools to direct resources toward accomplishing strategic results.

stress A physiological and emotional response to stimuli that place physical or psychological demands on an individual.

structural changes Any change in the way in which the organization is designed and managed.

substitute A situational variable that makes a leadership style unnecessary or redundant.

superordinate goal A goal that cannot be reached by a single party.

suppliers People and organizations who provide the raw materials the organization uses to produce its output.

survey feedback A type of OD intervention in which questionnaires on organizational climate and other factors are distributed among employees and their results reported back to them by a change agent.

sustainability Economic development that meets the needs of the current population while preserving the environment for the needs of future generations.

symbol An object, act, or event that conveys meaning to others.

synergy When organizational parts interact to produce a joint effect that is greater than the sum of the parts acting alone.

tactical goals Goals that define the outcomes that major divisions and departments must achieve for the organization to reach its overall goals.

tactical plans Plans designed to help execute major strategic plans and to accomplish a specific part of the company's strategy.

tall structure A management structure characterized by an overall narrow span of management and a relatively large number of hierarchical levels.

task environment The layer of the external environment that directly influences the organization's operations and performance.

task force A temporary team or committee formed to solve a specific short-term problem involving several departments.

task specialist role A role in which the individual devotes personal time and energy to helping the team accomplish its task.

team A unit of two or more people who interact and coordinate their work to accomplish a specific goal.

team building A type of OD intervention that enhances the cohesiveness of departments by helping members learn to function as a team.

team cohesiveness The extent to which team members are attracted to the team and motivated to remain in it.

team norm A standard of conduct that is shared by team members and guides their behavior.

team-based structure Structure in which the entire organization is made up of horizontal teams that coordinate their activities and work directly with customers to accomplish the organization's goals.

technical complexity The degree to which complex machinery is involved in the production process to the exclusion of people.

technological dimension The dimension of the general environment that includes scientific and technological advancements in the industry and society at large.

technology change A change that pertains to the organization's production process.

telecommuting Using computers and telecommunications equipment to perform work from home or another remote location.

top-down budgeting A budgeting process in which middle-level and lower-level managers set departmental budget targets in accordance with overall company revenues and expenditures specified by top management.

total factor productivity The ratio of total outputs to the inputs from labor, capital, materials, and energy.

total quality management (TQM) A concept that focuses on managing the total organization to deliver quality to customers. Four significant elements of TQM are employee involvement, focus on the customer, benchmarking, and continuous improvement. An organization-wide commitment to infusing quality into every activity through continuous improvement.

traits Distinguishing personal characteristics, such as intelligence, values, and appearance.

transaction processing system (TPS) Records and processes data resulting from business operations.

transactional leaders Leaders who clarify subordinates' role and task requirements, initiate structure, provide rewards, and display consideration for subordinates.

transformational leaders Leaders distinguished by a special ability to bring about innovation and change.

Type A behavior Behavior pattern characterized by extreme competitiveness, impatience, aggressiveness, and devotion to work.

Type B behavior Behavior pattern that lacks Type A characteristics and includes a more balanced, relaxed lifestyle.

uncertainty Managers know which goals they wish to achieve, but information about alternatives and future events is incomplete.

uncertainty avoidance A value characterized by people's intolerance for uncertainty and ambiguity and resulting support for beliefs that promise certainty and conformity.

unfreezing The stage of organization development in which participants are made aware of problems to increase their willingness to change their behavior.

utilitarian approach The ethical concept that moral behaviors produce the greatest good for the greatest number.

valence The value or attraction an individual has for an outcome.

validity The relationship between an applicant's score on a selection device and his or her future job performance.

vertical team A formal team composed of a manager and his or her subordinates in the organization's formal chain of command.

virtual network structure An organization structure that disaggregates major functions to separate companies that are brokered by a small headquarters organization.

virtual teams A team made up of members who are geographically or organizationally dispersed, rarely meet face to face, and do their work using advanced information technologies.

vision An attractive, ideal future that is credible yet not readily attainable.

Vroom-Jago model A model designed to help managers gauge the amount of subordinate participation in decision making.

wage and salary surveys Surveys that show what other organizations pay incumbents in jobs that match a sample of "key" jobs selected by the organization.

whistle-blowing The disclosure by an employee of illegal, immoral, or illegitimate practices by the organization.

work redesign The altering of jobs to increase both the quality of employees' work experience and their productivity.

work specialization The degree to which organizational tasks are subdivided into individual jobs; also called division of labor.

World Wide Web (WWW or Web) A set of central servers for accessing information on the Internet.

End Notes

Chapter 1

The Changing Paradigm of Management & Foundations of Learning Organizations

1. Andrew Park and Peter Burrows, "What You Don't Know About Dell," *Business Week* (Nov. 3, 2003): 74–84; Kevin P. Hopkins, "Value Opportunity One," *Business Week Online* (Feb. 6, 2005).
2. Daniel Roth, "Catch Us If You Can," *Fortune* (February 9, 2003): 64–74; Ian Austen, "Downloading Again," *The New York Times* (May 3, 2004): C12; Christie Eliezer, "Kazaa Case Grinds on in Australia," *Billboard* (April 17, 2004): 60; and Steve Knopper, "Tower in Trouble," *Rolling Stone* (March 18, 2004): 26.
3. Ian Mitroff and Murat C. Alpaslan, "Preparing for Evil," *Harvard Business Review* (April 2003): 109–115.
4. Keith H. Hammonds, "The Monroe Doctrine," *Fast Company* (October 1999): 230–236; and David Beardsley, "This Company Doesn't Brake for (Sacred) Cows," *Fast Company* (August 1998): 66–68.
5. Elvis Presley Enterprises Web Site, "EPE History and Structure," *http://www.elvis.com/corporate/elvis_epe.asp*, accessed on February 6, 2003.
6. James A. F. Stoner and R. Edward Freeman, *Management*, 4th ed. (Englewood Cliffs, N.J.: Prentice Hall, 1989).
7. Peter F. Drucker, *Management Tasks, Responsibilities, Practices* (New York: Harper & Row, 1974).
8. Louis Uchitelle, "Ready for an Upturn. Not Ready to Spend," *The New York Times* (June 23, 2002): Section 3, 1, 13.
9. Martha Brannigan and Eleena De Lisser, "Cost Cutting at Delta Raises the Stock Price But Lowers the Service," *The Wall Street Journal* (June 20, 1996): A1.
10. Robert L. Katz, "Skills of an Effective Administrator," *Harvard Business Review 52* (September–October 1974): 90–102.
11. Dom Amore, "Perked up Joe," *Hartford Courant* (Nov. 28, 2004): E4; Joe Torre with Henry Dreher, *Joe Torre's Ground Rules for Winners: 12 Keys to Managing Team Players, Tough Bosses, Setbacks, and Success* (New York: Hyperion, 1999); Jerry Useem, "A Manager for All Seasons," *Fortune* (April 30, 2001): 66–72; and Malcolm Moran, "Conflict Resolution, the Joe Torre way," *The New York Times* (July 14, 1997): C5.
12. Heath Row, "Force Play" (Company of Friends column), *Fast Company* (March 2001): 46.
13. Charles Fishman, "Sweet Company," *Fast Company* (February 2001): 136–145.
14. Based on Sydney Finkelstein, "7 Habits of Spectacularly Unsuccessful Executives," *Fast Company* (July 2003): 84–89; Bam Charan and Jerry Useem, "Why Companies Fail"; and John W. Slocum Jr., Cass Ragan, and Albert Casey, "On Death and Dying: The Corporate Leadership Capacity of CEOs," *Organizational Dynamics 30:3* (Spring 2002): 269–281.
15. Matthew Rose and Laurie P. Cohen, "Man in the News: Amid Turmoil, Top Editors Resign at New York Times," *The Wall Street Journal* (June 6, 2003): A1, A6.
16. Dan Tynan, "Jungletalk with Google's Minnie Ingersoll," MBA Jungle (October – November 2003), 24–25.
17. Jennifer Couzin, "Tick, Tick, Tick," *The Industry Standard* (April 16, 2001): 62–67.
18. Henry Mintzberg, "Managerial Work: Analysis from Observation," *Management Science 18* (1971): B97–B110.
19. Based on Carol Saunders and Jack William Jones, "Temporal Sequences in Information Acquisition for Decision Making: A Focus on Source and Medium," *Academy of Management Review 15* (1990): 29–46; Kotter, "What Effective General Managers Really Do"; and Mintzberg, "Managerial Work."
20. Mintzberg, "Managerial Work."
21. Anita Lienert, "A Day in the Life: Airport Manager Extraordinaire," *Management Review* (January 1995): 57–61.
22. Lance B. Kurke and Howard E. Aldrich, "Mintzberg Was Right!: A Replication and Extension of The Nature of Managerial Work," *Management Science 29* (1983): 975–984; Cynthia M. Pavett and Alan W. Lau, "Managerial Work: The Influence of Hierarchical Level and Functional Specialty," *Academy of Management Journal 26* (1983): 170–177; and Colin P. Hales, "What Do Managers Do? A Critical Review of the Evidence," *Journal of Management Studies 23* (1986): 88–115.
23. Mintzberg, "Rounding out the Manager's Job," Sloan Management Review, (Fall 1994), 11–26.
24. Edward O. Welles, "There Are No Simple Businesses Anymore," *The State of Small Business* (1995): 66–79.
25. This section is based largely on Peter F. Drucker, *Managing the Non-Profit Organization: Principles and Practices* (New York: HarperBusiness, 1992); and Thomas Wolf, *Managing a Nonprofit Organization* (New York: Fireside/Simon & Schuster, 1990).
26. Christine W. Letts, William P. Ryan, and Allen Grossman, *High Performance Nonprofit Organizations* (New York: John Wiley & Sons, 1999).
27. Harry G. Barkema, Joel A. C. Baum, and Elizabeth A. Mannix, "Management Challenges in a New Time," *Academy of Management Journal 45:5* (2002): 916–930. The following section is based on Barkema, Baum, and Mannix, "Management Challenges," Michael Harvey and M. Ronald Buckley, "Assessing the 'Conventional Wisdoms' of Management for the 21st Century Organization," *Organizational Dynamics 30:4* (2002): 368–378; and Toby J. Tetenbaum, "Shifting Paradigms: From Newton to Chaos," *Organizational Dynamics* (Spring 1998): 21–32.
28. Caroline Ellis, "The Flattening Corporation," *MIT Sloan Management Review* (Summer 2003): 5.
29. Carla Joinson, "Managing Virtual Teams," *HR Magazine* (June 2002): 69–73.
30. Barkema, Baum, and Mannix, "Management Challenges in a New Time."
31. Laura M. Holson, "Halo" for Hollywood? New York Times, June 10, 2005, pp. C1 & C8.
32. Keith H. Hammonds, "Smart, Determined, Ambitious, Cheap: The New Face of Global Competition," *Fast Company* (February 2003): 91–97.
33. Tetenbaum, "Shifting Paradigms: From Newton to Chaos."
34. Jon Pareles, "David Bowie, 21st Century entrepreneur," *The New York Times* (June 9, 2002): Section 2, 1, 30; "MusicNow Empowers Artists to Reach Fans Directly and Partners with UltraStar entertainment," *PR Newswire* (May 12, 2004): 1.
35. Scott Kirsner, "Every Day, It's a New Place," *Fast Company* (April–May 1998): 130–134; Peter Coy, "The Creative Economy," *BusinessWeek* (August 28, 2000): 76–82; and Jeremy Main, "The Shape of the New Corporation," *Working Woman* (October 1998): 60–63.
36. This section is based on Loretta Ucelli, "The CEO's 'How To' Guide to Crisis Communications," *Strategy & Leadership 30:2* (2002): 21–24; Eric Beaudan, "Leading in Turbulent Times," *Ivey Business Journal* (May–June 2002): 22–26; Christine Pearson, "A Blueprint for Crisis Management," *Ivey Business Journal* (January–February 2002): 68–73; Leslie Wayne and Leslie Kaufman, "Leadership, Put to a New Test," *The New York Times* (September 16, 2001): Section 3, 1, 4; Jerry Useem, "What It Takes," *Fortune* (November 12, 2001): 126–132; and Andy Bowen, "Crisis Procedures that Stand the Test of Time," *Public Relations Tactics* (August 2001): 16.
37. Beaudan, "Leading in Turbulent Times."
38. Paul Argenti, "Crisis Communication: Lessons from 9/11," *Harvard Business Review* (December 2002): 103–109.
39. Ronald A. Heifetz and Donald L. Laurie, "The Leader as Teacher: Creating the Learning Organization," *Ivey Business Journal* (January–February 2003): 1–9.
40. Peter Senge, *The Fifth Discipline: The Art and Practice of Learning Organizations* (New York: Doubleday/Currency, 1990).
41. Khoo Hsien Hui and Tan Kay Chuan, "Nine Approaches to Organizational Excellence," *Journal of Organizational Excellence* (Winter 2002): 53–65; Leon Martel, "The Principles of High Performance—And How to Apply Them," *Journal of Organizational Excellence* (Autumn 2002): 49–59; and Jeffrey Pfeffer, "Producing Sustainable Competitive Advantage through the Effective Management of People," *Academy of Management Executive 9:1* (1995): 55–69.

42. Alex Markels, "The Wisdom of Chairman Ko," *Fast Company* (November 1999): 258–276.
43. Edward O. Welles, "Mind Gains," *Inc.* (December 1999): 112–124.
44. Kevin Kelly, *New Rules for the New Economy: 10 Radical Strategies for a Connected World* (New York: Viking Penguin, 1998).
45. Nick Wingfield, "In the Beginning...," *The Wall Street Journal* (May 21, 2001): R18.
46. Andy Reinhardt,"From Gearhead to Grand High Pooh-Bah," *BusinessWeek* (August 28, 2000): 129–130.
47. Julia Angwin, "Used Car Auctioneers, Dealers Meet Online," *The Wall Street Journal* (November 20, 2003): B1, B13; William J. Holstein and Edward Robinson, "The Re-Education of Jacques Nasser," *Business2.Com* (May 29, 2001): 60–73.
48. Bernard Wysocki, Jr., "Corporate Caveat: Dell or Be Delled," *The Wall Street Journal* (May 10, 1999): A1.
49. Reinhardt, "From Gearhead to Grand High Pooh-Bah."
50. Robert D. Hof, "The eBay Economy: The Company is Not Just a Wildly Successful Startup. It Has Invented a Whole New Business World," *BusinessWeek,* (August 25, 2003): 124.
51. Amber Chung, "Music Retailers Face Tough Times as File-Sharing Grows," *Taipei Times* (February 10, 2004): 11; *http://www.taipeitimes.com* accessed on February 10, 2004.
52. Quoted in Colvin, "Managing in the Info Era," Furtune (March 6, 2000), F-5 – F-9.
53. Jeffrey Zygmont, "The Ties That Bind," *Inc. Tech 3* (1998): 70–84; and Nancy Ferris, "ERP: Sizzling or Stumbling?" *Government Executive* (July 1999): 99–102.
54. Ann Harrington, "The Big Ideas," *Fortune* (November 22, 1999), 152–154; Peter Drucker, *Post-Capitalist Society*, (Oxford, UK: Butterworth Heinemann, 1993).
55. Based on Andrew Mayo, "Memory Bankers," *People Management* (January 22, 1998): 34–38; William Miller, "Building the Ultimate Resource," *Management Review* (January 1999): 42–45; and Todd Datz, "How to Speak Geek," *CIO Enterprise* (April 15, 1999): Section 2, 46–52.
56. Louisa Wah, "Behind the Buzz," *Management Review* (April 1999): 17–26.
57. Daniel A. Wren, *The Evolution of Management Thought*, 2nd ed. (New York: Wiley, 1979). Much of the discussion of these forces comes from Arthur M. Schlesinger, *Political and Social History of the United States, 1829–1925* (New York: Macmillan, 1925); and Homer C. Hockett, *Political and Social History of the United States, 1492–1828* (New York: Macmillan, 1925).
58. The discussion of trends is based on Cam Marston, "Managing Gen X and Gen Y," *http://www.programresources.com/ professional_speakers_tips/marston_managing_gen_X* accessed on February 6, 2004; and Marnie E. Green, "Beware and Prepare: The Government Workforce of the Future," *Public Personnel Management* (Winter 2000): 435+.
59. Green, "Beware and Prepare: The Government Workforce of the Future."
60. Robin Wright and Doyle McManus, *Flashpoints: Promise and Peril in a New World* (New York: Alfred A. Knopf, 1991).
61. This section is based on Thomas Petzinger, Jr., "So Long Supply and Demand," *The Wall Street Journal* (January 1, 2000): R31.
62. Petzinger, "So Long Supply and Demand."
63. Darrell Rigby, "Management Tools Survey 2003: Usage Up as Companies Strive to Make Headway in Tough Times," *Strategy & Leadership* 31:5 (2003): 4–11.
64. Daniel James Rowley, "Resource Reviews," *Academy of Management Learning and Education* 2:3 (2003): 313–321; Jane Whitney Gibson, Dana V. Tesone, and Charles W. Blackwell, "Management Fads: Here Yesterday, Gone Today?" *SAM Advanced Management Journal* (Autumn 2003): 12–17; David Collins, *Management Fads and Buzzwords: Critical-Practices Perspective*, (London, UK: Routledge, 2000); Timothy Clark, "Management Research on Fashion: A Review and Evaluation," *Human Relations* 54:12 (2001): 1650–1661; Brad Jackson, *Management Gurus and Management Fashions* (London, UK: Routledge, 2001); Patrick Thomas, *Fashions in Management Research: An Empirical Analysis* (Aldershot, UK: Ashgate, 1999).
65. Daniel A. Wren, "Management History: Issues and Ideas for Teaching and Research," *Journal of Management* 13 (1987), 339–350.
66. Business historian Alfred D. Chandler, Jr., quoted in Jerry Useem, "Entrepreneur of the Century," *Inc.* (20th Anniversary Issue, 1999), 159–174.
67. Useem, "Entrepreneur of the Century."
68. Ann Harrington, "The Big Ideas"; Robert Kanigel, *The One Best Way: Frederick Winslow Taylor and the Enigma of Efficiency* (New York: Viking, 1997); and Alan Farnham, "The Man Who Changed Work Forever," *Fortune* (July 21, 1997): 114. For a discussion of the impact of scientific management on American industry, government, and nonprofit organizations, see Mauro F. Guillén, "Scientific Management's Lost Aesthetic: Architecture, Organization, and the Taylorized Beauty of the Mechanical," *Administrative Science Quarterly* 42 (1997): 682–715.
69. Douglas McGregor, *The Human Side of Enterprise* (New York: McGraw-Hill, 1960), 16–18.
70. Douglas McGregor, *The Human Side of Enterprise* (New York: McGraw-Hill, 1960): 33–48.
71. Amanda Bennett, *The Death of the Organization Man* (New York: William Morrow, 1990).
72. Johannes M. Pennings, "Structural Contingency Theory: A Reappraisal," *Research in Organizational Behavior 14* (1992): 267–309.
73. Samuel Greengard, "25 Visionaries Who Shaped Today's Workplace," *Workforce* (January 1997): 50–59; and Harrington, "The Big Ideas."
74. Mauro F. Guillen, "The Age of Eclecticism: Current Organizational Trends and the Evolution of Managerial Models," *Sloan Management Review* (Fall 1994): 75–86.
75. Jeremy Main, "How to Steal the Best Ideas Around," *Fortune* (October 19, 1992): 102–106.
76. Andrew Park and Peter Burrows, "What You Don't Know About Dell," *BusinessWeek* (Nov. 3, 2003): 74–84; Kevin P. Hopkins, "Value Opportunity One," *BusinessWeek Online* (Feb. 6, 2005), A1.

Chapter 2
The Environment and Corporate Culture

1. Quoted in Mark Litwak, *Reel Power: The Struggle for Influence and Success in the New Hollywood* (New York: William Morrow and Company, Inc., 1986): 101.
2. Accessed at *http://www.wired.com/wired/archive/5.02/fflucas.html Wired Magazine* (Feb 1997): Issue 5.02.
3. Nicole Gull, "Entrepreneurs we love: Kathleen Wehner," *Inc. Magazine* (April 2004): 138.
4. Ann Carns, "Point Taken: Hit Hard by Imports, American Pencil Icon Tries to Get a Grip," *The Wall Street Journal* (November 24, 1999): A1, A6; Lucette Lagnado, "Strained Peace: Gerber Baby Food, Grilled by Greenpeace, Plans Swift Overhaul," *The Wall Street Journal* (July 30, 1999): A1, A6; and "Group Sows Seeds of Revolt Against Genetically Altered Foods in U.S.," *The Wall Street Journal* (October 12, 1999): B1, B4.
5. Christopher Joyce, reporter, transcript of "Analysis: International Panel Says U.S. Department of Agriculture Should Take Further Steps to Protect the U.S. From Mad Cow Disease," *NPR: All Things Considered* (February 5, 2004): 1; Sue Kirchhoff, "Natural Beef Industry Might See Boost from Mad Cow Fears," *USA Today* (January 12, 2004): *http://www. usatoday.com/money/industries/ food/2004-01-12-organic_x.htm*; June Kronholz, "Kindergarten Crisis: By Federal Order, Snail Races Are Over," *The Wall Street Journal* (February 11, 2004): A1.
6. This section is based on Richard L. Daft, *Organization Theory and Design*, 8th ed. (Cincinnati, Ohio: South-Western, 2004).
7. L.J. Bourgeois, "Strategy and Environment: A Conceptual Integration," *Academy of Management Review 5* (1980): 25–39.
8. Jim Milliott, "Leapfrog IPO Looks to Raise $150 million," *Publisher's Weekly* (May 6, 2002): 13; Miguel Helft, "Leapfrogging the Competition," *The Industry Standard* (April 9, 2001): 68–75; Edward C. Baig, "Will Pen Be Mightier than Other Toys?"*USA Today* (Jan 18, 2005):. B.3.
9. "Toyota Shoots for No. 1," *Ward's Auto World* (December 1, 2003).
10. Paola Hjelt, "The World's Most Admired Companies," *Fortune* (March 3, 2003): 81; David Pringle, Jesse Drucker, and Evan Ramstad, "World Circuit: Cellphone Makers Pay a Heavy Toll for Missing Fads," *The Wall Street Journal* (October 30, 2003): A1.
11. Jim Rose and Salim Teja, "The Americans Are Coming!" *Business 2.0* (May 2000): 215.
12. Robert Rosen, with Patricia Digh, Marshall Singer, and Carl Phillips, *Global Literacies: Lessons on Business Leadership and National Cultures*, (New York: Simon and Schuster, 2000).
13. Richard I. Kirkland, Jr., "Entering a New Age of Boundless Competition," *Fortune* (March 14, 1988): 40–48; and Kenichi Ohmae, "Managing in a Borderless World," *Harvard Business Review* (May–June 1989): 152–161.

14. James Myring, "Mobile Saturation Leads to Higher Churn," *New Media Age* (October 2, 2003): 15; and Pringle, et al., "World Circuit: Cellphone Makers Pay a Heavy Toll for Missing Fads."

15. Ian Mount, The Great Persuader, *Inc. Magazine* (March 2005): 93.

16. Gene Bylinsky, "Mutant Materials," *Fortune* (October 13, 1997): 140–147;

17. John Teresko, "The Next Material World," *Industry Week* (April 2003): 41–47.

18. Suzanne Vranica and Charles Goldsmith, "Nielsen Adapts its Methods as TV Evolves," *The Wall Street Journal* (Sept. 29, 2003), B1; "Massive Incorporated and Nielsen Entertainment Team to Deliver Household Measurement Reports for Video Game Advertising," *PR Newswire* (Dec. 15, 2004): 1.

19. William B. Johnston, "Global Work Force 2000: The New World Labor Market," *Harvard Business Review* (March–April 1991): 115–127.

20. U.S. Census Bureau statistics reported in "Minorities Should Be Very Close to Majority by 2050, Census Projection Says," AP Story in *Johnson City Press* (March 18, 2004): 5A; and Peter Coy, "The Creative Economy," *BusinessWeek* (August 28, 2000): 76–82.

21. U.S. Census, *http://www.census.gov/*.

22. Michelle Conlin, "UnMarried America," *BusinessWeek* (October 20, 2003): 106–116.

23. Julie Dunn, "Restaurant Chains, Too, Watch Their Carbs," *The New York Times* (January 4, 2004): Section 3; and Brian Grow with Gerry Khermouch, "The Low-Carb Food Fight Ahead," *BusinessWeek* (December 22, 2003): 48.

24. Marc Gunter, "God & Business," *Fortune* (July 9, 2001): 58–80.

25. Anne Marie Squeo and Joe Flint, "FCC Tells Cable Industry to Clean Up Content—Or Else," *The Wall Street Journal* (February 11, 2004): B1; Damien Cave, "Fighting for Free Speech," *Rolling Stone* (May 27, 2004): 13.

26. Samuel Loewenberg, "Europe Gets Tougher on U.S. Companies," *The New York Times* (April 20, 2003): Section 3, 6.

27. Linda Himelstein and Laura Zinn, with Maria Mallory, John Carey, Richard S. Dunham, and Joan O'C. Hamilton, "Tobacco: Does It Have a Future?" *BusinessWeek* (July 4, 1994): 24–29; Bob Ortega, "Aging Activists Turn, Turn, Turn Attention to Wal-Mart Protests," *The Wall Street Journal* (October 11, 1994): A1, A8;

28. Chistopher Palmeri, "Mattel's New Toy Story," *BusinessWeek* (November 18, 2002): 72–74; Queena Sook Kim and Merissa Marr, "Holy Bat-Ray! New Batman Toys Get Signals from Your TV," *The Wall Street Journal* (February 11, 2004): B1.

29. John Simons, "Stop Moaning About Gripe Sites and Log On," *Fortune* (April 2, 2001): 181–182.

30. Rick Brooks, "Home Depot Turns Copycat in Its Efforts to Stoke New Growth," *The Wall Street Journal* (November 21, 2000): A1; Dan Sewell, "Home Depot, Lowe's Building Up Competition," *Lexington Herald-Leader*: Business Profile supplement (December 8, 1997): 3.

31. Julia Angwin and Motoko Rich, "Inn Fighting: Big Hotel Chains Are Striking Back Against Web Sites," *The Wall Street Journal* (March 14, 2003): A1.

32. Chana R. Schoenberger, "Bull's Eye," *Forbes* (September 2, 2002): 76.

33. Paul Glader, "Steel-Price Rise Crimps Profits, Adds Uncertainty," *The Wall Street Journal* (February 23, 2004): A1.

34. Bernard Simon, "A Bright New Day for the Telecom Industry, If the Public Will Go Along," *The New York Times* (January 12, 2004): C3; Mark Heinzl, "Nortel's Profit of $499 Million Exceeds Forecast," *The Wall Street Journal* (January 30, 2004): B4; Joseph Weber with Andy Reinhardt and Peter Burrows, "Racing Ahead at Nortel," *BusinessWeek* (November 8, 1999): 93–99; Ian Austen, "Hooked on the Net," *Canadian Business* (June 26–July 10, 1998): 95–103; "Nortel's Waffling Continues; First Job Cuts, Then Product Lines, and Now the CEO. What's Next?" *Telephony* (May 21, 2001): 12.

35. Robert B. Duncan, "Characteristics of Organizational Environment and Perceived Environmental Uncertainty," *Administrative Science Quarterly* 17 (1972): 313–327; and Daft, *Organization Theory and Design*.

36. Sarah Moore, "On Your Markets," *Working Woman* (February 2001): 26; and John Simons, "Stop Moaning about Gripe Sites and Log On," *Fortune* (April 2, 2001): 181–182.

37. Edwin M. Epstein, "How to Learn from the Environment about the Environment—A Prerequisite for Organizational Well-Being," *Journal of General Management* 29:1 (Autumn 2003): 68–80.

38. Mark McNeilly, "Gathering Information for Strategic Decisions, Routinely," *Strategy & Leadership* 30:5 (2002): 29–34.

39. Stephan M. Wagner and Roman Boutellier, "Capabilities for Managing a Portfolio of Supplier Relationships," *Business Horizons* (November-December 2002): 79–88; Peter Smith Ring and Andrew H. Van de Ven, "Developmental Processes of Corporate Interorganizational Relationships," *Academy of Management Review* 19 (1994): 90–118; Myron Magnet, "The New Golden Rule of Business," *Fortune* (February 21, 1994): 60–64; and Peter Grittner, "Four Elements of Successful Sourcing Strategies," *Management Review* (October 1996): 41–45.

40. Yoash Wiener, "Forms of Value Systems: A Focus on Organizational Effectiveness and Culture Change and Maintenance," *Academy of Management Review* 13 (1988): 534–545; V. Lynne Meek, "Organizational Culture: Origins and Weaknesses," *Organization Studies* 9 (1988): 453–473; John J. Sherwood, "Creating Work Cultures with Competitive Advantage," *Organizational Dynamics* (Winter 1988): 5–27; and Andrew D. Brown and Ken Starkey, "The Effect of Organizational Culture on Communication and Information," *Journal of Management Studies* 31:6 (November 1994): 807–828.

41. Joanne Martin, *Organizational Culture: Mapping the Terrain* (Thousand Oaks, Calif.: Sage Publications, 2002); Ralph H. Kilmann, Mary J. Saxton, and Roy Serpa, "Issues in Understanding and Changing Culture," *California Management Review* 28 (Winter 1986): 87–94; and Linda Smircich, "Concepts of Culture and Organizational Analysis," *Administrative Science Quarterly* 28 (1983): 339–358.

42. Based on Edgar H. Schein, *Organizational Culture and Leadership*, 2d ed. (San Francisco: Jossey-Bass, 1992).

43. Betsy Morris, "The Accidental CEO," *Fortune* (June 23, 2003): 58–67; Pamela L. Moore, "She's Here to Fix the Xerox," *BusinessWeek* (August 6, 2001): 47–48; and Claudia H. Deutsch, "Carl Fiorina? He'd Probably Be Out of Work, Too," *The New York Times* (Feb. 13, 2005): 5.

44. Michael G. Pratt and Anat Rafaeli, "Symbols as a Language of Organizational Relationships," *Research in Organizational Behavior*, 23 (2001): 93–132.

45. Christine Canabou, "Here's the Drill," *Fast Company* (February 2001): 58.

46. Emily Barker, "Cheap Executive Officer," *Inc. Magazine*(April 1, 2002); Rusty Cawley, "Rick Sapio Banks on 1-800-MUTUALS Concept," *Dallas Business* (Oct 22, 1999): 22–23l; "MUTUALS.com Vice Fund Ranked in Top 1% for 2004," *Business Wire* (Jan 11, 2005): 1.

47. James M. Higgins and Craig McAllaster, "Want Innovation? Then Use Cultural Artifacts That Support It," *Organizational Dynamics* 31:1 (2002), 74–84.

48. Patrick M. Lencioni, "Make Your Values Mean Something," *Harvard Business Review* (July 2002): 113–117.

49. Robert E. Quinn and Gretchen M. Spreitzer, "The Road to Empowerment: Seven Questions Every Leader Should Consider," *Organizational Dynamics* (Autumn 1997): 37–49.

50. Martin, *Organizational Culture: Mapping the Terrain*.

51. Terrence E. Deal and Allan A. Kennedy, *Corporate Cultures: The Rites and Rituals of Corporate Life* (Reading, Mass.: AddisonWesley, 1982).

52. Patricia Jones and Larry Kahaner, *Say It and Live It: 50 Corporate Mission Statements That Hit the Mark* (New York: Currency Doubleday, 1995).

53. Harrison M. Trice and Janice M. Beyer, "Studying Organizational Cultures through Rites and Ceremonials," *Academy of Management Review* 9 (1984): 653–669.

54. Alan Farnham, "Mary Kay's Lessons in Leadership," *Fortune* (September 20, 1993): 68–77.

55. Jennifer A. Chatman and Karen A. Jehn, "Assessing the Relationship Between Industry Characteristics and Organizational Culture: How Different Can You Be?" *Academy of Management Journal* 37:3 (1994): 522–553.

56. John P. Kotter and James L. Heskett, *Corporate Culture and Performance* (New York: The Free Press, 1992).

57. Norm Brodsky, "Street SmartsL Learning from JetBlue," *Inc. Magazine* (March 2004): 59–60.

58. This discussion is based on Paul McDonald and Jeffrey Gandz, "Getting Value from Shared Values," *Organizational Dynamics* 21:3 (Winter 1992): 64–76; Daniel R. Denison and Aneil K. Mishra, "Toward a Theory of Organizational Culture and Effectiveness," *Organization Science* 6:2 (March–April 1995): 204–223; and Richard L. Daft, *The Leadership Experience* 3rd ed. (Cincinnati, OH: South-Western, 2005).

59. Ian Wylie, "Calling for a Renewable Future," *Fast Company* (May 2003): 46–48; Paul Kaihla, "Nokia's Hit Factory," *Business 2.0* (August 2002): 66–70; and David Pringle, "Wrong Number: How Nokia Chased Top End of Market, Got Hit in Middle," *The Wall Street Journal* (June 1, 2004): A1, A11.

60. Robert Hooijberg and Frank Petrock, "On Cultural Change: Using the Competing Values Framework to Help Leaders Execute a Transformational Strategy," *Human Resource Management* 32:1 (1993): 29–50.

61. Lencioni, "Make Your Values Mean Something"; and Melanie Warner, "Confessions of a Control Freak," *Fortune* (September 4, 2000): 130–140.

62. Julia Boorstin, "Secret Recipe: J. M. Smucker," *Fortune* (January 12, 2004): 58–59.

63. Patricia Jones and Larry Kahaner, *Say It and Live It: 50 Corporate Mission Statements That Hit the Mark* (New York: Currency Doubleday, 1995).

64. Charles Fishman, "Sanity Inc.," *Fast Company* (January 1999): 85–96; Sharon Overton, "And to All a Goodnight," *Sky* (October 1996): 37–40; Tricia Bisoux, Corporate Counter Culture, *BizEd* (Nov./Dec. 2004): 16–19.

65. Rekha Balu, "Pacific Edge Projects Itself," *Fast Company* (October 2000): 371–381.

66. Jeffrey Pfeffer, *The Human Equation: Building Profits by Putting People First* (Boston, MA: Harvard Business School Press, 1998).

67. Jeremy Kahn, "What Makes a Company Great?" *Fortune* (October 26, 1998): 218; James C. Collins and Jerry I. Porras, *Built to Last: Successful Habits of Visionary Companies* (New York: HarperCollins, 1994); and James C. Collins, "Change is Good—But First Know What Should Never Change," *Fortune* (May 29, 1995): 141.

68. Jennifer A. Chatman and Sandra Eunyoung Cha, "Leading by Leveraging Culture," *California Management Review* 45:4 (Summer 2003): 20–34.

69. This section is based on Jeff Rosenthal and Mary Ann Masarech, "High Peformance Cultures: How Values Can Drive Business Results," *Journal of Organizational Excellence* (Spring 2003): 3–18.

70. Rosenthal and Masarech, "High-Performance Cultures: How Values Can Drive Business Results."

71. Katherine Mieszkowski, "Community Standards," *Fast Company* (September 2000): 368; Rosabeth Moss Kanter, "A More Perfect Union," *Inc.* (February 2001): 92–98; Raizel Robin, "Net Gains" segment of "E-Biz That Works," *Canadian Business* (October 14–October 26, 2003): 107.

72. Rosenthal and Masarech, "High-Performance Cultures: How Values Can Drive Business Results."

73. Chatman and Cha, "Leading by Leveraging Culture."

74. John P. Kotter and James L. Heskett, *Corporate Culture and Performance* (New York: The Free Press, 1992); Jim Collins, *Good to Great: Why Some Companies Make the Leap...and Others Don't* (New York: HarperBusiness, 2001); James C. Collins and Jerry I. Porras, *Built to Last: Successful Habits of Visionary Companies* (New York: HarperBusiness, 1994); and James C. Collins, "Change Is Good—But First Know What Should Never Change," *Fortune* (May 29, 1995): 141. Also see J. M. Kouzes and B. Z. Posner, *The Leadership Challenge: How to Keep Getting Extraordinary Things Done in Organizations*, 3d ed. (San Francisco: Jossey-Bass, 2002).

75. Micah R. Kee, "Corporate Culture Makes a Fiscal Difference," *Industrial Management* (November–December 2003): 16–20.

76. Rosenthal and Masarech, "High-Performance Cultures: How Values Can Drive Business Results;" Lencioni, "Make Your Values Mean Something;" and Thomas J. Peters and Robert H. Waterman, Jr., *In Search of Excellence* (New York: Warner, 1988).

77. Jenny C. McCune, "Exporting Corporate Culture," *Management Review* (December 1999): 52–56.

78. Lencioni, "Make Your Values Mean Something."

79. Evan Perez, "Lennar Corp. Thrives as Residential Builder with Oddball Culture," *The Wall Street Journal* (July 27, 2001): A1, A4; "Zacks Return on Equity Strategy Highlights: D.R. Horton, Lennar Corporation, and Rayovac Corporation," *Business Wire* (Feb. 2, 2005): 1

80. Lencioni, "Make Your Values Mean Something."

81. Rosenthal and Masarech, "High-Performance Cultures: How Values Can Drive Business Results."

82. Jill Rosenfeld, "MTW Puts People First," *Fast Company* (December 1999): 86–88.

83. Excerpt from Peter B. Grazier, "Before It's Too Late: Employee Involvement...An Idea Whose Time Has Come," *Pete's Corner* by Peter B. Grazier, *http://www. teambuilding.com*.

84. Robert Levering and Milton Moskowitz, "The 100 Best Companies to Work For," *Fortune* (January 20, 2003): 127–152.

85. Nicole Gull, "Entrepreneurs We Love: Kathleen Wehner," *Inc. Magazine* (April 2004): 138.

Chapter 3

Managing in a Global Environment

1. Richard Ernsberger Jr., "Wal-Mart World; Can the Arkansas Giant Export Its Price-Cutting Culture Around the World?" *Newsweek* (May 20, 2002): 50; Isabelle de Pommereau, "Wal-Mart Lesson: Smiling Service Won't Win Germans; The Retailer Closed Two Stores in Germany," *The Christian Science Monitor* (October 17, 2002): 7; Ann Zimmerman and Martin Fackler, "Pacific Aisles; Wal-Mart's Foray Into Japan Spurs A Retail Upheaval," *The Wall Street Journal* (September 19, 2003): A1; and *http://www.walmartstores.com* accessed on February 13, 2004.

2. David Kirkpatrick, "One World—For Better or Worse," *Fortune* (November 26, 2001): 74–75.

3. Nilly Ostro-Landau and Hugh D. Menzies, "The New World Economic Order," in *International Business 97/98, Annual Editions*, Fred Maidment, ed. (Guilford, Conn.: Dushkin Publishing Group, 1997); and Murray Weidenbaum, "American Isolationism versus the Global Economy," in *International Business 97/98, Annual Editions*, Fred Maidment, ed. (Guilford Conn.: Dushkin Publishing Group, 1997).

4. Jason Dean, "Upgrade Plan: Long a Low-Tech Player, China Sets Its Sights on Chip Making," *The Wall Street Journal* (February 17, 2004): A1.

5. Joseph B. White, "There Are No German or U.S. Companies, Only Successful Ones," *The Wall Street Journal* (May 7, 1998): A1.

6. Jane L. Levere, "A Small Company, A Global Approach," *The New York Times* (January 1, 2004): accessed at *http://www.nytimes.com/2004*.

7. Raju Narisetti and Jonathan Friedland, "Diaper Wars of P&G and Kimberly-Clark Now Heat Up in Brazil," *The Wall Street Journal* (June 4, 1997); and Stephen Baker, "The Bridges Steel is Building," *BusinessWeek* (June 2, 1997): 39.

8. Figures provided by CXO Media, reported in Steve Ulfelder, "All the Web's a Stage," *CIO* (October 1, 2000): 133–142.

9. Howard LaFranchi, "Women Have Their Cake (and E-commerce, Too)," *Christian Science Monitor* (Jun. 13, 2000): 1; "UN: Opportunities rising for women in e-commerce, but glass ceiling remains to be broken," *M2 Presswire* (Nov. 19, 2002): 1.

10. Christopher Bartlett, *Managing Across Borders*, 2d ed. (Boston, MA: Harvard Business School Press, 1998); Eric Matson, "How to Globalize Yourself," *Fast Company* (April–May 1997): 133–139; and Gunnar Beeth, "Multicultural Managers Wanted," *Management Review* (May 1997): 17–21.

11. Holstein et al., "The Stateless Corporation"; Carol Matlack, "Nestlé Is Starting to Slim Down at Last," *BusinessWeek* (October 27, 2003): 56; Carla Rapoport, "Nestlé's Brand Building Machine," *Fortune* (September 19, 1994): 147–156; and Karl Moore, "Great Global Managers," *Across the Board* (May–June 2003): 40–43.

12. Cited in Gary Ferraro, *Cultural Anthropology: An Applied Perspective*, 3d ed. (Belmont, Calif.: West/Wadsworth, 1998).

13. Jim Holt, "Gone Global?" *Management Review* (March 2000): 13.

14. Ibid.

15. "Slogans Often Lose Something in Translation," *The New Mexican* (July 3, 1994): F1, F2.

16. Louis S. Richman, "Global Growth is on a Tear," in *International Business 97/98, Annual Editions*, Fred Maidment, ed., (Guilford, Conn.: Dushkin Publishing Group, 1997).

17. International Data Corporation, reported in Ian Katz and Elisabeth Malkin, "Battle for the Latin American Net," *BusinessWeek* (November 1, 1999): 194–200.

18. Katz and Malkin, "Battle for the Latin American Net"; Pamela Drukerman and Nick Wingfield, "Lost in Translation: AOL's Big Assault on Latin America Hits Snags in Brazil," *The Wall Street Journal*, (July 11, 2000): A1.

19. Amal Kumar Jaj, "United Technologies Looks Far from Home for Growth," *The Wall Street Journal* (May 26, 1994): B4.

20. Marcelo Jelen, "Latin America: Cell Phones—From Status Symbol to Everyman's Tool," *Global Information Network* (December 10, 2003): 1.

21. Catherine Yang, "Sharing Knowledge Globally," *BusinessWeek* (Sept. 18, 2000): 102; "Finalists Named in Global Competition for Contribution of Information Technology to Development," *PR Newswire* (June 8, 2004): 1.

22. Kathleen Deveny, "McWorld?" *BusinessWeek* (October 13, 1986): 78–86; and Andrew E. Serwer, "McDonald's Conquers the World," *Fortune* (October 17, 1994): 103–116.
23. David W. Conklin, "Analyzing and Managing Country Risks," *Ivey Business Journal* (January–February 2002): 37–41.
24. Bruce Kogut, "Designing Global Strategies: Profiting from Operational Flexibility," *Sloan Management Review* 27 (Fall 1985): 27–38.
25. Mark Fitzpatrick, "The Definition and Assessment of Political Risk in International Business: A Review of the Literature," *Academy of Management Review* 8 (1983): 249–254.
26. Kevin Sullivan, "Kidnapping Is Growth Industry in Mexico; Businessmen Targeted in Climate of Routine Ransoms, Police Corruption," *The Washington Post* (September 17, 2002): A1.
27. Brian O'Keefe, "Global Brands," *Fortune* (November 26, 2001): 102–110.
28. Conklin, "Analyzing and Managing Country Risks;" Nicolas Checa, John Maguire, and Jonathan Barney, "The New World Disorder," *Harvard Business Review* (August 2003): 71–79.
29. Conklin, "Analyzing and Managing Country Risks."
30. Susan E. Reed, "Helping the Poor, Phone by Phone," *The New York Times* (May 26, 2002) 2; "Telenor to Increase Its Ownership Stake in GrameenPhone to 55.5 Percent, PR Newswire (Oct. 27, 2004): 1.
31. Mei Fong, "For a Muslim woman from two cultures, swimsuits are tricky—Born in Pakistan, raised in US, Neelam Nourani nervously dips into beauty pageants," *The Wall Street Journal* (March 22, 2002): A1, A6; "Miss Earth Winner," *BusinessWorld* (Oct. 26, 2004): 1.
32. Geert Hofstede, "The Interaction between National and Organizational Value Systems," *Journal of Management Studies* 22 (1985): 347–357; and Geert Hofstede, "The Cultural Relativity of the Quality of Life Concept," *Academy of Management Review* 9 (1984): 389–398.
33. Geert Hofstede, "Cultural Constraints in Management Theory," *Academy of Management Executive* 7 (1993): 81–94; and G. Hofstede and M. H. Bond, "The Confucian Connection: From Cultural Roots to Economic Growth," *Organizational Dynamics* 16 (1988): 4–21.
34. "Retrospective: *Culture's Consequences*," a collection of articles focusing on Hofstede's work, appeared in *The Academy of Management Executive* 18:1 (February 2004): 72–93. See also Michele J. Gelfand, D. P. S. Bhawuk, Lisa H. Nishii, and David J. Bechtold, "Individualism and Collectivism," in R. J. House, et al., eds., *Culture, Leadership and Organizations: The Globe Study of 62 Societies* (Thousand Oaks, CA: Sage, 2004).
35. This discussion is based on Mansour Javidan and Robert J. House, "Cultural Acumen for the Global Manager: Lessons from Project GLOBE," *Organizational Dynamics* 29:4 (2001): 289–305; and R. J. House, M. Javidan, Paul Hanges, and Peter Dorfman, "Understanding Cultures and Implicit Leadership Theories Across the Globe: An Introduction to Project GLOBE," *Journal of World Business* 37 (2002): 3–10.
36. Chantell E. Nicholls, Henry W. Lane, and Mauricio Brehm Brechu, "Taking Self-Managed Teams to Mexico," *Academy of Management Executive* 13:2 (1999): 15–27; Carl F. Fey and Daniel R. Denison, "Organizational Culture and Effectiveness: Can American Theory Be Applied in Russia?" *Organization Science* 14:6 (November–December 2003): 686–706; Ellen F. Jackofsky, John W. Slocum, Jr., and Sara J. McQuaid, "Cultural Values and the CEO: Alluring Companions?" *Academy of Management Executive* 2 (1988): 39–49.
37. Terence Jackson, "The Management of People Across Cultures: Valuing People Differently," *Human Resource Management* 41:4 (Winter 2002): 455–475.
38. Carol Hymowitz, "Companies Go Global, But Many Managers Just Don't Travel Well," *The Wall Street Journal* (August 15, 2000): Lead column, B1.
39. Orla Sheehan, "Managing a Multinational Corporation: Tomorrow's Decision Makers Speak Out," *Fortune* (August 24, 1992): 233; Jonathan Friedland and Louise Lee, "The Wal-Mart Way Sometimes Gets Lost in Translation Overseas," *The Wall Street Journal* (October 8, 1997): A1, A12.
40. Carol Matlack with Pallave Gogoi, "What's This? The French Love McDonald's?" *Business Week* (January 13, 2003): 50; and Shirley Leung, "'McHaute Cuisine' Armchairs, TVs, and Expresso—Is It McDonald's?" *The Wall Street Journal* (August 30, 2002): A1, A6.
41. Michael R. Czinkota, Ilkka A. Ronkainen, Michael H. Moffett, and Eugene O. Moynihan, *Global Business* (Fort Worth, Tex.: The Dryden Press, 1995); and Robert D. Gatewood, Robert R. Taylor, and O. C. Ferrell, *Management* (Burr Ridge, Ill.: Irwin, 1995): 131–132.
42. This discussion of WTO is based on William J. Kehoe, "GATT and WTO Facilitating Global Trade," *Journal of Global Business* (Spring 1998): 67–76.
43. "The History of the European Union," *http://www.europa.eu.int/abc/history/index_en.htm*, accessed on February 16, 2004.
44. Justin Fox, "Introducing the Euro," *Fortune* (December 19, 2001): 229–236.
45. Barbara Rudolph, "Megamarket," *Time* (August 10, 1992): 43–44.
46. Tapan Munroe, "NAFTA Still a Work in Progress," *Knight Ridder/Tribune News Service* (January 9, 2004): accessed at *http://www.contracostatimes.com*; and J. S. McClenahan, "NAFTA Works," *IW* (January 10, 2000): 5–6.
47. Eric Alterman, "A Spectacular Success?" *The Nation* (February 2, 2004): 10; Jeff Faux, "NAFTA at 10: Where Do We Go From Here?" *The Nation* (February 2, 2004): 11; Geri Smith and Cristina Lindblad, "Mexico: Was NAFTA Worth It? A Tale of What Free Trade Can and Cannot Do," *BusinessWeek* (December 22, 2003) 66; Jeffrey Sparshott, "NAFTA Gets Mixed Reviews," *The Washington Times* (December 18, 2003): C10; and Munroe, "NAFTA Is Still Work in Progress."
48. Munroe, "NAFTA Is Still Work In Progress;" Jeffrey Sparshott, "NAFTA Gets Mixed Reviews," *The Washington Times* (December 18, 2003): C10; Amy Borrus, "A Free-Trade Milestone, with Many More Miles to Go," *BusinessWeek* (August 24, 1992): 30–31.
49. This review is based on Jyoti Thottam, "Is Your Job Going Abroad?" *Time* (March 1, 2004): 26–36; and Pete Engardio, Aaron Bernstein, and Manjeet Kripalani, "Is Your Job Next?" *BusinessWeek* (February 3, 2003): 50–60.
50. Reported in "IBM Data Give Rare Look at Sensitive 'Offshoring' Plans," *CNNMoney* (January 19, 2004), accessed at *http://www.money.cnn.com* on January 19, 2004.
51. Thottam, "Is Your Job Going Abroad?"
52. Jerry Useem, "There's Something Happening Here," *Fortune* (May 15, 2000); Paul Magnusson, "Meet Free Traders' Worst Nightmare," *BusinessWeek* (March 20, 2000): 113–118; Elisabeth Malkin, "Backlash," *BusinessWeek* (April 24, 2000): 38–44.
53. See, for example, Alan Greenspan, "International Trade: Globalization vs. Protectionism," address printed in *Vital Speeches of the Day* (April 15, 2001) 386–388.
54. Michael Schroeder and Timothy Aeppel, "Skilled Workers Sway Politicians with Fervor Against Free Trade," *The Wall Street Journal* (December 10, 2003): A1, A11.
55. Joanne Lee-Young and Megan Barnett, "Furiously fast fashions," *The Industry Standard*, June 11, 2001, 72–79; Li & Fung, "USA Expands Cannon Team; Former Calvin Klein Home Executive to Oversee Design Direction," *Business Wire* (Jan. 17, 2005): 1.
56. Jean Kerr, "Export Strategies," *Small Business Reports* (May 1989): 20–25.
57. Company sales figures are from data reported in "The Global Giants," *The Wall Street Journal* (October 14, 2002): R10, R11. GNI data are from the World Development Indicators database, World Bank, August 2002, accessed at *http://www.worldbank.org/data/* on November 15, 2002.
58. Morgan W. McCall Jr. and George P. Hollenbeck, "Global Fatalities: When International Executives Derail," *Ivey Business Journal* (May–June 2002): 75–78.
59. Karl Moore, "Great Global Managers," *Across the Board* (May–June 2003): 40–43.
60. James L. Gibson, John M. Ivancevich, and James H. Donnelly, Jr., *Organizations*, 8th ed. (Burr Ridge, Ill.: Irwin, 1994).
61. McCall and Hollenbeck, "Global Fatalities."
62. Joann S. Lublin, "Younger Managers Learn Global Skills," *The Wall Street Journal* (March 31, 1992): B1.
63. Richard E. Nisbett, *The Geography of Thought: How Asians and Westerners Think Differently...and Why* (New York: The Free Press, 2003); reported in Sharon Begley, "East Vs. West: One Sees the Big Picture, The Other is Focused," *The Wall Street Journal* (March 28, 2003): Science Journal column, B1.
64. Robert T. Moran and John R. Riesenberger, *The Global Challenge* (London: McGraw-Hill, 1994): 251–262.
65. Patricia M. Carey, "Culture Club," *Working Woman* (July/August 1999): 71–72.
66. Valerie Frazee, "Keeping Up on Chinese Culture," *Global Workforce* (October 1996): 16–17; and Jack Scarborough, "Comparing Chinese and Western Cultural Roots: Why 'East Is East and . . .'" *Business Horizons* (November/December 1998): 15–24.

67. Fons Trompenaars, *Riding the Waves of Culture: Understanding Diversity in Global Business* (Burr Ridge, IL: Irwin, 1994).

68. Mansour Javidan and Ali Dastmalchian, "Culture and Leadership In Iran: The Land of Individual Achievers, Strong Family Ties, and Powerful Elite," *Academy of Management Executive* 17:4 (2003): 127–142.

69. Randall S. Schuler, Susan E. Jackson, Ellen Jackofsky, and John W. Slocum, Jr., "Managing Human Resources in Mexico: A Cultural Understanding," *Business Horizons* (May–June 1996): 55–61.

70. Xu Huang and Evert Van De Vliert, "Where Intrinsic Job Satisfaction Fails to Work: National Moderators of Intrinsic Motivation," *Journal of Organizational Behavior* 24 (2003): 159–179.

71. Shari Caudron, "Lessons from HR Overseas," *Personnel Journal* (February 1995): 88.

72. Reported in Begley, "East Vs. West."

73. Ken Belson, "Wal-Mart Hopes It Won't Be Lost in Translation," *The New York Times* (December 14, 2003): 1; Ann Zimmerman and Martin Fackler, "Pacific Aisles: Wal-Mart's Foray Into Japan Spurs a Retail Upheaval," *The Wall Street Journal* (September 19, 2003): A1, A6.

74. By Dr. Mai Van Trang. Reasons for living and hoping: The Spiritual and Psychosocial needs of Southeast Asian refugee children and youth resettled in the United States. Washington, D.C.: Educational Resource Information Center, October 16, 1988, p64.

Chapter 4

Managerial Ethics and Corporate Social Responsibility

1. Christopher Marquis, "Doing Well and Doing Good," *The New York Times* (July 3, 2003): Section 3, 2; and Joseph Pereira, "Career Journal: Doing Good and Doing Well at Timberland," *The Wall Street Journal* (September 9, 2003): B1.

2. Bethany McLean, "Why Enron Went Bust," *Fortune* (December 24, 2001): 58–68; survey results reported in Patricia Wallington, "Honestly?!" *CIO* (March 15, 2003): 41–42.

3. Data from KPMG, reported in Muel Kaptein, "The Diamond of Managerial Integrity," *European Management Journal* 21:1 (2003): 99–108.

4. Jon Gertner, "Newman's Own: Two Friends and a Canoe Paddle," *The New York Times* (November 16, 2003): BU4; Michelle Conlin and Jessi Hempel, with Joshua Tanzer and David Polek, "Philanthropy 2003: The Corporate Donors," *BusinessWeek* (December 1, 2003): 92–96.

5. Gordon F. Shea, *Practical Ethics* (New York: American Management Association, 1988); and Linda K. Treviño, "Ethical Decision Making in Organizations; A Person-Situation Interactionist Model," *Academy of Management Review* 11 (1986): 601–617.

6. Thomas M. Jones, "Ethical Decision Making by Individuals in Organizations: An Issue-Contingent Model," *Academy of Management Review* 16 (1991): 366–395.

7. John R. Emshwiller and Alexei Barrionuevo, "U.S. Prosecutors File Indictment Against Skilling," *The Wall Street Journal* (February 20, 2004): A1, A13.

8. See Clinton W. McLemore, *Street-Smart Ethics: Succeeding in Business Without Selling Your Soul* (Louisville, KY: Westminster John Knox Press, 2003) for a cogent discussion of some ethical and legal issues associated with Enron's collapse.

9. Rushworth M. Kidder, "The Three Great Domains of Human Action," *Christian Science Monitor* (January 30, 1990): 13

10. Jeanne Anne Naujeck, "RCA labels cut ties with promoters," *The Tennessean* (Jan. 6, 2005): E1; Ralph Blumenthal, "Charges of payola over radio music," *New York Times* (May 25, 2002): 7; Craig Havignurt, "Labels say radio needs 'new set of rules,'" *The Tennessean* (June 3, 2002): E1.

11. Linda K. Treviño and Katherine A. Nelson, *Managing Business Ethics: Straight Talk About How to Do It Right* (New York: John Wiley & Sons, Inc. 1995): 4.

12. Jones, "Ethical Decision Making by Individuals in Organizations: An Issue-Contingent Model."

13. Based on information in Constance E. Bagley, "The Ethical Leader's Decision Tree," *Harvard Business Review* (February 2003): 18–19.

14. Based on information in Vadim Liberman, "Scoring on the Job," *Across the Board* (November–December 2003): 46–50.

15. "Baseball Whiffs," *Chicago Tribune* (March 19, 2005): 28; Dave Anderson, "Putting the Con Back in Confession," *The New York Times* (Feb. 11, 2005) C15, C17; Alan Schwarz, "Scoring Hits, Runs and Asterisks," *The New York Times* (June 9, 2002): Section 4, 1, 5; Amy Shipley, "Baseball Payers Says Steroid Use Is Heavy," *The Washington Post* (May 29, 2002).

16. This discussion is based on Gerald F. Cavanagh, Dennis J. Moberg, and Manuel Velasquez, "The Ethics of Organizational Politics," *Academy of Management Review* 6 (1981): 363–374; Justin G. Longenecker, Joseph A. McKinney, and Carlos W. Moore, "Egoism and Independence: Entrepreneurial Ethics," *Organizational Dynamics* (Winter 1988): 64–72; Carolyn Wiley, "The ABCs of Business Ethics: Definitions, Philosophies, and Implementation," *IM* (February 1995): 22–27; and Mark Mallinger, "Decisive Decision Making: An Exercise Using Ethical Frameworks," *Journal of Management Education* (August 1997): 411–417.

17. Michael J. McCarthy, "Now the Boss Knows Where You're Clicking," and "Virtual Morality: A New Workplace Quandary," *The Wall Street Journal* (October 21, 1999): B1, B4; and Jeffrey L. Seglin, "Who's Snooping on You?" *Business 2.0* (August 8, 2000): 202–203.

18. Ron Winslow, "Rationing Care," *The Wall Street Journal* (November 13, 1989): R24.

19. Alan Wong and Eugene Beckman, "An Applied Ethical Analysis System in Business," *Journal of Business Ethics* 11 (1992): 173–178.

20. John Kekes, "Self-Direction: The Core of Ethical Individualism," *Organizations and Ethical Individualism*, ed. Konstanian Kolenda (New York: Praeger, 1988): 1–18.

21. Tad Tulega, *Beyond the Bottom Line* (New York: Penguin Books, 1987).

22. Lynn Sharp Paine, "Managing for Organizational Integrity," *Harvard Business Review* (March–April 1994): 106–117.

23. This discussion is based on Treviño, "Ethical Decision Making in Organizations; A Person-Situation Interactionist Model."

24. L. Kohlberg, "Moral Stages and Moralization: The Cognitive-Developmental Approach," in *Moral Development and Behavior: Theory, Research, and Social Issues*, T. Lickona, Ed. (New York: Holt, Rinehart & Winston, 1976); L. Kohlberg, "Stage and Sequence: The Cognitive-Developmental Approach to Socialization," in *Handbook of Socialization Theory and Research*, D. A. Goslin, Ed. (Chicago: Rand McNally, 1969); and Jill W. Graham, "Leadership, Moral Development, and Citizenship Behavior," *Business Ethics Quarterly* 5:1 (January 1995): 43–54.

25. Carol Gilligan, *In a Different Voice: Psychological Theory and Women's Development* (Cambridge, MA: Harvard University Press, 1982).

26. Thomas Donaldson and Thomas W. Dunfee, "When Ethics Travel: The Promise and Peril of Global Business Ethics," *California Management Review* 41:4 (Summer 1999): 45–63.

27. Transparency International, "Transparency International Releases New Bribe Payers Index," accessed at http://www.transparency.org on February 24, 2004.

28. Susan Pulliam, "Over the Line: A Staffer Ordered to Commit Fraud Balked, Then Caved," *The Wall Street Journal* (June 23, 2003): A1.

29. Duane M. Covrig, "The Organizational Context of Moral Dilemmas: The Role of Moral Leadership in Administration in Making and Breaking Dilemmas," *The Journal of Leadership Studies* 7:1 (2000): 40–59; and James Weber, "Influences Upon Organizational Ethical Subclimates: A Multi-Departmental Analysis of a Single Firm," *Organizational Science* 6:5 (September–October 1995): 509–523.

30. Linda Klebe Treviño, "A Cultural Perspective on Changing and Developing Organizational Ethics," in *Research and Organizational Change and Development*, R. Woodman and W. Pasmore, Eds. (Greenwich, CT: JAI Press, 1990).

31. *Ibid*; John B. Cullen, Bart Victor, and Carroll Stephens, "An Ethical Weather Report: Assessing the Organization's Ethical Climate," *Organizational Dynamics* (Autumn 1989): 50–62; and Bart Victor and John B. Cullen, "The Organizational Bases of Ethical Work Climates," *Administrative Science Quarterly* 33 (1988): 101–125.

32. Eugene W. Szwajkowski, "The Myths and Realities of Research on Organizational Misconduct," in *Research in Corporate Social Performance and Policy*, James E. Post, Ed. (Greenwich, CT: JAI Press, 1986); and Keith Davis, William C. Frederick, and Robert L. Blostrom, *Business and Society: Concepts and Policy Issues* (New York: McGraw-Hill, 1979).

33. Douglas S. Sherwin, "The Ethical Roots of the Business System," *Harvard Business Review 61* (November–December 1983): 183–192.

34. Nancy C. Roberts and Paula J. King, "The Stakeholder Audit Goes Public," *Organizational Dynamics* (Winter 1989): 63–79; Thomas Donaldson and Lee E. Preston, "The Stakeholder Theory of

the Corporation: Concepts, Evidence, and Implications," *Academy of Management Review* 20:1 (1995): 65–91; and Jeffrey S. Harrison and Caron H. St. John, "Managing and Partnering with External Stakeholders," *Academy of Management Executive* 10:2 (1996): 46–60.

35. Charles Fishman, "The Wal-Mart You Don't Know—Why Low Prices Have a High Cost," *Fast Company* (December 2003): 68–80.

36. David Wheeler, Barry Colbert, and R. Edward Freeman, "Focusing on Value: Reconciling Corporate Social Responsibility, Sustainability, and a Stakeholder Approach in a Networked World," *Journal of General Management* 28:3 (Spring 2003): 1–28; and James E. Post, Lee E. Preston, and Sybille Sachs, "Managing the Extended Enterprise: The New Stakeholder View," *California Management Review* 45:1 (Fall 2002): 6–28.

37. Max B. E. Clarkson, "A Stakeholder Framework for Analyzing and Evaluating Corporate Social Performance," *Academy of Management Review* 20:1 (1995): 92–117.

38. "The World We Serve," *Bristol-Myers Squibb 2002 Annual Report*, Bristol-Myers Squibb Company.

39. Mark A. Cohen, "Management and the Environment," *The Owen Manager* 15:1 (1993): 2–6.

40. R. E. Freeman, J. Pierce, and R. Dodd, *Shades of Green: Business Ethics and the Environment* (New York: Oxford University Press, 1995).

41. Greg Toppo, "Company Agrees to Pay Record Pollution Fine," Associated Press, *Johnson City Press* (July 21, 2000): 9.

42. Andrew C. Revkin, "7 Companies Agree to Cut Gas Emissions," *The New York Times* (October 18, 2000): C1, C6.

43. This definition is based on Marc J. Epstein and Marie-Josée Roy, "Improving Sustainability Performance: Specifying, Implementing and Measuring Key Principles," *Journal of General Management* 29:1 (Autumn 2003): 15–31, World Commission on Economic Development, *Our Common Future* (Oxford: Oxford University Press, 1987): and Marc Gunther, "Tree Huggers, Soy Lovers, and Profits," *Fortune* (June 23, 2003): 98–104.

44. Gunther, "Tree Huggers, Soy Lovers, and Profits."

45. *Operating in Unison: UPS 2002 Corporate Sustainability Report*, UPS Corporate, Atlanta, Georgia.

46. Brian Deagon, "New Technology Could Boost Efficiency and Green Image for UPS," *Investor's Business Daily* (December 10, 2003); and Charles Haddad with Christine Tierney, "FedEx and Brown Are Going Green," *BusinessWeek* (August 11, 2003): 60.

47. Gunther, "Tree Huggers, Soy Lovers, and Profits."

48. The discussion of ISO 14001 is based on Pratima Bansal, "The Corporate Challenges of Sustainable Development," *Academy of Management Executive* 16:2 (2002): 122–131.

49. Karina Funk, "Sustainability and Performance," *MIT Sloan Management Review* (Winter 2003): 65–70; and "The Fast 50: Trendsetters," *Fast Company* (March 2002): 95.

50. Mark S. Schwartz and Archie B. Carroll, "Corporate Social Responsibility: A Three-Domain Approach," *Business Ethics Quarterly* 13:4 (2003): 503–530; and Archie B. Carroll, "A Three-Dimensional Conceptual Model of Corporate Performance," *Academy of Management Review* 4 (1979): 497–505. For a discussion of various models for evaluating corporate social performance, also see Diane L. Swanson, "Addressing a Theoretical Problem by Reorienting the Corporate Social Performance Model," *Academy of Management Review* 20:1 (1995): 43–64.

51. N. Craig Smith, "Corporate Social Responsibility: Whether or How?" *California Management Review* 45:4 (Summer 2003): 52–76.

52. Milton Friedman, *Capitalism and Freedom* (Chicago: University of Chicago Press, 1962); and Milton Friedman and Rose Friedman, *Free to Choose* (New York: Harcourt Brace Jovanovich, 1979).

53. Eugene W. Szwajkowski, "Organizational Illegality: Theoretical Integration and Illustrative Application," *Academy of Management Review* 10 (1985): 558–567.

54. Kurt Eichenwald, "U.S. Awards Tenet Whistle-Blowers $8.1 Million," *The New York Times* (January 8, 2004): accessed at http://www.nytimes.com.

55. David J. Fritzsche and Helmut Becker, "Linking Management Behavior to Ethical Philosophy—An Empirical Investigation," *Academy of Management Journal* 27 (1984): 165–175.

56. Sydney Finkelstein, "Jayson Blair, Meet Nicholas Leeson," (Manager's Journal column), *The Wall Street Journal* (May 20, 2003): B2; Matthew Rose and Laurie P. Cohen, "Man in the News: Amid Turmoil, Top Editors Resign at *New York Times*," *The Wall Street Journal* (June 6, 2003): A1.

57. Conlin, et al., "Philanthropy 2003: The Corporate Donors."

58. Saul W. Gellerman, "Managing Ethics from the Top Down," *Sloan Management Review* (Winter 1989): 73–79.

59. This discussion is based on Linda Klebe Treviño, Laura Pincus Hartman, and Michael Brown, "Moral Person and Moral Manager: How Executives Develop a Reputation for Ethical Leadership," *California Management Review* 42:4 (Summer 2000): 128–142.

60. Muel Kaptein, "The Diamond of Managerial Integrity," *European Management Journal* 21:1 (2003): 99–108.

61. Business Roundtable Institute for Corporate Ethics, accessed at http://www.corporate-ethics.org; and "Corporate Ethics: A Prime Business Asset," *The Business Roundtable*, 200 Park Avenue, Suite 2222, New York, NY, 10166, February 1988.

62. Michael Barrier, "Doing the Right Thing," *Nation's Business* (March 1998): 33–38; Joseph L. Badaracco, Jr., and Allen P. Webb, "Business Ethics: A View from the Trenches," *California Management Review* 37:2 (Winter 1995): 8–28.

63. Linda Klebe Treviño, Gary R. Weaver, David G. Gibson, and Barbara Ley Toffler, "Managing Ethics and Legal Compliance: What Works and What Hurts?" *California Management Review* 41:2 (Winter 1999): 131–151.

64. Linda Klebe Treviño and Katherine A. Nelson, *Managing Business Ethics: Straight Talk About How to Do It Right*, 2nd ed. (New York: John Wiley & Sons, 1999): 274–283.

65. Treviño, Hartman, and Brown, "Moral Person and Moral Manager."

66. "Corporate Ethics: A Prime Business Asset."

67. Ibid.

68. Treviño et al., "Managing Ethics and Legal Compliance: What Works and What Hurts?"

69. Carolyn Wiley, "The ABC's of Business Ethics: Definitions, Philosophies, and Implementation," *IM* (January–February 1995): 22–27; Badaracco and Webb, "Business Ethics: a View from the Trenches"; and Ronald B. Morgan, "Self- and Co-Worker Perceptions of Ethics and Their Relationships to Leadership and Salary," *Academy of Management Journal* 36:1 (February 1993): 200–214.

70. Journal Communications—Code of Ethics, from Codes of Ethics Online, The Center for the Study of Ethics in the Professions, Illinois Institute of Technology, accessed at http://www.iit.edu/departments/csep/ PublicWWW/codes/index.html

71. Alan Yuspeh, "Do the Right Thing," *CIO* (August 1, 2000): 56–58.

72. The Ethics Officers Association, accessed at http://www.eoa.org on February 25, 2004.

73. Beverly Geber, "The Right and Wrong of Ethics Offices," *Training* (October 1995): 102–118.

74. Amy Zipkin, "Getting Religion on Corporate Ethics," *The New York Times* (October 18, 2000): C1.

75. Marcia Parmarlee Miceli and Janet P. Near, "The Relationship among Beliefs, Organizational Positions, and Whistle-Blowing Status: A Discriminant Analysis," *Academy of Management Journal* 27 (1984): 687–705.

76. Carrick Mollenkamp, "Missed Signal: Accountant Tried in Vain to Expose HealthSouth Fraud," *The Wall Street Journal* (May 20, 2003): A1.

77. Eugene Garaventa, "*An Enemy of the People* by Henrik Ibsen: The Politics of Whistle-Blowing," *Journal of Management Inquiry* 3:4 (December 1994): 369–374; Marcia P. Miceli and Janet P. Near, "Whistleblowing: Reaping the Benefits," *Academy of Management Executive* 8:3 (1994): 65–74.

78. Steven L. Schooner, "Badge of Courage," *Government Executive* (August 2002): 65.

79. Jay Rath, "Love At First Site; So Many Choices: The Internet Abounds With Services That Promise Help Finding A Match," *Wisconsin State Journal* (March 5, 2005): C1; Warren St. John, "Young, Single and Dating at Hyperspeed," *The New York Times* (April 21, 2002): 9–10.

80. Jerry G. Kreuze, Zahida Luqmani,, and Mushtaq Luqmani, "Shades of Gray," *Internal Auditor* (April 2001): 48.

81. Sandra A. Waddock, Charles Bodwell, and Samuel B. Graves, "Responsibility: The New Business Imperative," *Academy of Management Executive* 16:2 (2002): 132–148.

82. The Global Compact Web site, accessed at http://www.unglobalcompact.org on July 18, 2001; and Zipkin, "Getting Religion on Corporate Ethics."

83. Kate Kelly, Ethan Smith, and Peter Wonacott, "Movie, Music Giants Try New Weapon Against Pirates: Price," *The Wall Street Journal* (March 7, 2005): B1, B3.

84. Homer H. Johnson, "Does It Pay to Be Good? Social Responsibility and Financial Performance," *Business Horizons* (November–December 2003): 34–40; Jennifer J. Griffin and John F. Mahon, "The Corporate Social Performance and Corporate Financial Performance Debate: Twenty-Five Years of Incomparable

Research," *Business and Society* 36:1 (March 1997): 5–31; Bernadette M. Ruf, Krishnamurty Muralidar, Robert M. Brown, Jay J. Janney, and Karen Paul, "An Empirical Investigation of the Relationship between Change in Corporate Social Performance and Financial Performance: A Stakeholder Theory Perspective," *Journal of Business Ethics* 32:2 (July 2001): 143; Philip L. Cochran and Robert A. Wood, "Corporate Social Responsibility and Financial Performance," *Academy of Management Journal* 27 (1984): 42–56.

85. Curtis C. Verschoor and Elizabeth A. Murphy, "The Financial Performance of Large U. S. Firms and Those with Global Prominence: How Do the Best Corporate Citizens Rate?" *Business and Society Review* 107:3 (Fall 2002): 371–381; Johnson, "Does It Pay to Be Good?"; Dale Kurschner, "5 Ways Ethical Business Creates Fatter Profits," *Business Ethics* (March–April 1996): 20–23. Also see studies reported in Lori Ioannou, "Corporate America's Social Conscience," *Fortune* (May 26, 2003): S1–S10.

86. Verschoor and Murphy, "The Financial Performance of Large U.S. Firms and Those with Global Prominence: How Do the Best Corporate Citizens Rate?"

87. Gretchen Morgenson, "Shares of Corporate Nice Guys Can Finish First," *The New York Times* (April 27, 2003): Section 3, 1.

88. Jean B. McGuire, Alison Sundgren, and Thomas Schneeweis, "Corporate Social Responsibility and Firm Financial Performance," *Academy of Management Journal* 31 (1988): 854–872; and Louisa Wah, "Treading the Sacred Ground," *Management Review* (July–August 1998): 18–22.

89. Daniel W. Greening and Daniel B. Turban, "Corporate Social Performance as a Competitive Advantage in Attracting a Quality Workforce," *Business and Society* 39:3 (September 2000): 254.

90. "The Socially Correct Corporate Business," segment in Leslie Holstrom and Simon Brady, "The Changing Face of Global Business,"*Fortune* (July 24, 2000): Special advertising section, S1–S38.

91. Based on survey results from PriceWaterhouseCoopers, *2002 Sustainability Survey Report*, reported in Ioannou, "Corporate America's Social Conscience."

92. Cheryl Dahle, "Social Capitalists: The Top 20 Groups That Are Changing the World," *Fast Company* (January 2004): 45–57.

93. Tricia Tunstall, "Giving Beyond Their Means," *FSB* (December 2003–January 2004): 109–112.

94. Albert R. Hunt, "Social Entrepreneurs: Compassionate and Tough-Minded," *The Wall Street Journal* (July 13, 2000): A27; David Puttnam, "Hearts Before Pockets," *The New Statesman* (February 9, 2004): 26.

95. David Bornstein, *How to Change the World: Social Entrepreneurs and the Power of New Ideas* (Oxford and New York: Oxford University Press, 2004).

96. Brian Dumaine, "See Me, Hear Me," segment in "Two Ways to Help the Third World," *Fortune* (October 27, 2003): 187–196.

97. Marquis, "Doing Well and Doing Good," and Pereira, "Career Journal: Doing Good and Doing Well at Timberland."

Chapter 5

Organizational Goal Setting and Planning

1. Geoff Keighley, "Is Nintendo Playing the Wrong Game?" *Business 2.0* (August 2003): 111–115; Mike Musgrove, "Not-So-Super Mario: Stodgy Nintendo Is Falling Behind in the Game Wars," *The Washington Post* (December 25, 2003): E1.

2. Quoted in Oren Harari, "Good/Bad News about Strategy," *Management Review* (July 1995): 29–31.

3. Amitai Etzioni, *Modern Organizations* (Englewood Cliffs, N.J.: Prentice-Hall, 1984): 6.

4. Ibid.

5. Max D. Richards, *Setting Strategic Goals and Objectives*, 2d ed. (St. Paul, MN: West, 1986).

6. Sandra I. Erwin, "Experimental Battle-Planning Software Rushed to Iraq," *National Defense* (October 2003), 22.

7. C. Chet Miller and Laura B. Cardinal, "Strategic Planning and Firm Performance: A Synthesis of More than Two Decades of Research," *Academy of Management Journal* 37:6 (1994): 1649–1685.

8. This discussion is based on Richard L. Daft and Richard M. Steers, *Organizations: A Micro/Macro Approach* (Glenview, IL: Scott, Foresman, 1986); Herbert A. Simon, "On the Concept of Organizational Goals," *Administrative Science Quarterly* 9 (1964): 1–22; and Charles B. Saunders and Francis D. Tuggel, "Corporate Goals," *Journal of General Management* 5 (1980): 3–13.

9. See "2004 Special Report: The 100 Best Companies to Work For," *Fortune* (January 12, 2004): 56–80; and Kevin E. Joyce, "Lessons for Employers from *Fortune's* 100 Best," *Business Horizons* (March-April 2003): 77–84.

10. David Whitford, "A Human Place to Work," *Fortune* (January 8, 2001): 108–121.

11. Ji Baek, "Minority Rule: Ji Baek," *FSB*, Jan. 2004, p. 81.

12. J. Lynn Lunsford, "Lean Times: With Airbus on Its Tail, Boeing Is Rethinking How It Builds Planes," *The Wall Street Journal* (September 5, 2001): A1, A16.

13. Marc Gunther, "Tree Huggers, Soy Lovers, and Profits," *Fortune* (June 23, 2003): 98–104; Gary Fields and John R. Wilke, "The Ex-Files: FBI's New Focus Places Big Burden on Local Police," *The Wall Street Journal* (June 30, 2003): A1, A12.

14. David Pearson, "Breaking Away," *CIO,* (May 1, 1998): Section 1, 34–46.

15. Lee Hawkins Jr., "GM Seeks Chevrolet Revival: 'Restocked' Showroom Will Feature 10 New Models," *The Wall Street Journal* (December 19, 2003): B4; Ellen Piligian, "Chevrolet Greets the New Year with an Ambitious Campaign to Introduce 10 Vehicles in 20 Months," *The New York Times* (December 19, 2003): C6; and Dave Guilford and K.C. Crain, "Chevy Dealers Get Incentives to Sell 3 Million," *Automotive News* (February 9, 2004): 63.

16. Mary Klemm, Stuart Sanderson, and George Luffman, "Mission Statements: Selling Corporate Values to Employees," *Long-Range Planning* 24:3 (1991): 73–78; John A. Pearce II and Fred David, "Corporate Mission Statements: The Bottom Line," *Academy of Management Executive* (1987): 109–116; Jerome H. Want, "Corporate Mission: The Intangible Contributor to Performance," *Management Review* (August 1986): 46–50; and Forest R. David and Fred R. David, "It's Time to Redraft Your Mission Statement," *Journal of Business Strategy* (January-February 2003): 11–14.

17. "Tennessee News and Notes from State Farm," State Farm Mutual Automobile Insurance Company, 2004.

18. Charles A. O'Reilly III and Jeffrey Pfeffer, "Star Makers," (book excerpt from *From Hidden Value: How Great Companies Achieve Extraordinary Results with Ordinary People* (Boston, MA: Harvard University Press, 2000): in *CIO* (September 15, 2000): 226–246.

19. "Strategic Planning: Part 2," *Small Business Report* (March 1983): 28–32.

20. Paul Meising and Joseph Wolfe, "The Art and Science of Planning at the Business Unit Level," *Management Science* 31 (1985): 773–781.

21. Based in part on information about 1-800-Flowers in Jenny C. McCune, "On the Train Gang," *Management Review* (October 1994): 57–60.

22. "Study: IRS Employees Often Steer Taxpayers Wrong on Law Questions," Associated Press story in *Johnson City Press* (September 4, 2003): 4A.

23. Mark Fischetti, "Team Doctors, Report to ER!" *Fast Company* (February/March 1998): 170–177.

24. John O. Alexander, "Toward Real Performance: The Circuit-Breaker Technique," *Supervisory Management* (April 1989): 5–12.

25. Mark J. Fritsch, "Balanced Scorecard Helps Northern States Power's Quality Academy Achieve Extraordinary Performance," *Corporate University Review* (September-October 1997): 22.

26. Joy Riggs, "Empowering Workers by Setting Goals," *Nation's Business* (January 1995): 6.

27. Joel Hoekstra, "3M's Global Grip," *WorldTraveler* (May 2000): 31–34; and Thomas A. Stewart, "3M Fights Back," *Fortune* (February 5, 1996): 94–99.

28. Edwin A. Locke, Gary P. Latham, and Miriam Erez, "The Determinants of Goal Commitment," *Academy of Management Review* 13 (1988): 23–39.

29. George S. Odiorne, "MBO: A Backward Glance," *Business Horizons* 21 (October 1978): 14–24.

30. Jan P. Muczyk and Bernard C. Reimann, "MBO as a Complement to Effective Leadership," *The Academy of Management Executive* 3 (1989): 131–138; and W. Giegold, *Objective Setting and the MBO Process*, v. 2 (New York: McGraw-Hill, 1978).

31. John Ivancevich, J. Timothy McMahon, J. William Streidl, and Andrew D. Szilagyi, "Goal Setting: The Tenneco Approach to Personnel Development and Management Effectiveness," *Organizational Dynamics* (Winter 1978): 48–80.

32. Brigitte W. Schay, Mary Ellen Beach, Jacqueline A. Caldwell, and Christelle LaPolice, "Using Standardized Outcome Measures in the Federal Government," *Human Resource Management* 41:3 (Fall 2002): 355–368.

33. Eileen M. Van Aken and Garry D. Coleman, "Building Better Measurement," *Industrial Management* (July-August 2002): 28–33.

34. Curtis W. Roney, "Planning for Strategic Contingencies," *Business Horizons* (March-April 2003): 35–42; and "Corporate Planning: Drafting a Blueprint for Success," *Small Business Report* (August 1987): 40–44.

35. Bernard Wysocki Jr., "Soft Landing or Hard? Firm Tests Strategy on 3 Views of Future," *The Wall Street Journal* (July 7, 2000): A1, A6.

36. Saul Hansell and Joseph B. Treaster, "The Job of Imagining the Unimaginable, and Bracing For It," *The New York Times* (October 20, 2001): C1.

37. Syed H. Akhter, "Strategic Planning, Hypercompetition, and Knowledge Management," *Business Horizons* (January-February 2003): 19–24; and Steven Schnaars and Paschalina Ziamou, "The Essentials of Scenario Writing," *Business Horizons* (July-August 2001): 25–31.

38. Schnaars and Ziamou, "The Essentials of Scenario Writing."

39. Ian Wylie, "There Is No Alternative To . . . ," *Fast Company* (July 2002): 106–110.

40. Ian Mitroff with Gus Anagnos, *Managing Crises Before They Happen* (New York: AMACOM, 2001).

41. Ian Mitroff and Murat C. Alpaslan, "Preparing for Evil," *Harvard Business Review* (April 2003): 109–115.

42. This discussion is based largely on W. Timothy Coombs, *Ongoing Crisis Communication: Planning, Managing, and Responding* (Thousand Oaks, CA: Sage Publications, 1999).

43. Ian Wylie, "He's Belfast's Security Blanket," *Fast Company* (December 2001): 54–58.

44. Ibid.

45. Ibid., 28–29.

46. Ian I. Mitroff, "Crisis Leadership," *Executive Excellence* (August 2001): 19; Andy Bowen, "Crisis Procedures that Stand the Test of Time," *Public Relations Tactics* (August 2001): 16.

47. Mitroff and Alpaslan, "Preparing for Evil."

48. Kirstin Downey Grimsley, "Many Firms Lack Plans for Disaster," *The Washington Post* (October 3, 2001): E1.

49. Christine Pearson, "A Blueprint for Crisis Management," *Ivey Business Journal* (January-February 2002): 69–73.

50. See Mitroff and Alpaslan, "Preparing for Evil," for a discussion of the "wheel of crises" outlining the many different kinds of crises organizations may face.

51. Grimsley, "Many Firms Lack Plans for Disaster"; "Girding Against New Risks: Global Executives Are Working to Better Protect Their Employees and Businesses from Calamity," *Time* (October 8, 2001): B8+.

52. Mitroff, "Crisis Leadership." Also see Loretta Ucelli, "The CEO's 'How To' Guide to Crisis Communications," *Strategy & Leadership* 30:2 (2002): 21–24; and Paul Argenti, "Crisis Communication: Lessons from 9/11," *Harvard Business Review* (December 2002): 103–109 for tips on crisis communication.

53. Allison Fass, "Duking It Out," *Forbes* (June 9, 2003): 74–76.

54. See "Girding Against New Risks: Global Executives Are Working to Better Protect Their Employees and Businesses from Calamity."

55. Jay Finegan, "Everything According to Plan," *Inc.* (March 1995): 78–85; Art Kleiner, "Jack Stack's Story is an Open Book," *Strategy & Business* (Third Quarter 2001): 76–85; Jack Stack and Bo Burlingham, *A Stake in the Outcome: Building a Culture of Ownership for the Long-Term Success of Your Business* (New York: Currency, 2002); and Bo Burlingham, "Jack Stack: We Love Him for Going Naked," *Inc.* (April 2004): 134+.

56. This discussion of the importance of vision and mission is based on Khoo Hsien Hui and Tan Kay Chuan, "Nine Approaches to Organizational Excellence," *Journal of Organizational Excellence* (Winter 2002): 53–65; Gerald E. Ledford, Jr., Jon R. Wendenhof, and James T. Strahley, "Realizing a Corporate Philosophy," *Organizational Dynamics* (Winter 1995): 5–18; James C. Collins, "Building Companies to Last," *The State of Small Business* (1995): 83–86; James C. Collins and Jerry I. Porras, "Building a Visionary Company," *California Management Review* 37:2 (Winter 1995): 80–100; and James C. Collins and Jerry I. Porras, "The Ultimate Vision," *Across the Board* (January 1995): 19–23.

57. See Kenneth R. Thompson, Wayne A. Hockwarter, and Nicholas J. Mathys, "Stretch Targets: What Makes Them Effective?" *Academy of Management Executive* 11:3 (August 1997): 48.

58. Leon Martel, "The Principles of High Performance—and How to Apply Them," *Journal of Organizational Excellence* (Autumn 2002): 49–59.

59. Gary Hamel, "Avoiding the Guillotine," *Fortune* (April 2, 2001): 139–144.

60. This discussion is based on Chuck Martin, "How to Plan for the Short Term," Book excerpt from Chuck Martin, *Managing for the Short Term* (New York: Doubleday, 2002): in *CIO* (September 15, 2002): 90–97.

61. Martin, "How to Plan for the Short Term."

62. Jeffrey A. Schmidt, "Corporate Excellence in the New Millennium," *Journal of Business Strategy* (November-December 1999): 39–43.

63. Polly LaBarre, "The Company Without Limits," *Fast Company* (September 1999): 160–186.

64. Keith H. Hammonds, "Michael Porter's Big Ideas," *Fast Company* (March 2001): 150–156.

65. John E. Prescott, "Environments as Moderators of the Relationship between Strategy and Performance," *Academy of Management Journal* 29 (1986): 329–346; John A. Pearce II and Richard B. Robinson, Jr., *Strategic Management: Strategy, Formulation, and Implementation*, 2d ed. (Homewood, IL: Irwin, 1985); and David J. Teece, "Economic Analysis and Strategic Management," *California Management Review* 26 (Spring 1984): 87–110.

66. Markides, "Strategic Innovation."

67. Michael E. Porter, "What is Strategy?" *Harvard Business Review* (November–December 1996): 61–78.

68. Arthur A. Thompson, Jr., and A. J. Strickland III, *Strategic Management: Concepts and Cases*, 6th ed. (Homewood, IL: Irwin, 1992); and Briance Mascarenhas, Alok Baveja, and Mamnoon Jamil, "Dynamics of Core Competencies in Leading Multinational Companies," *California Management Review* 40:4 (Summer 1998): 117–132.

69. Ronald B. Lieber, "Smart Science," *Fortune* (June 23, 1997): 73.

70. Paul Roberts, "Live! From Your Office! It's..." *Fast Company* (October 1999): 151–170.

71. Kathryn Jones, "The Dell Way," *Business 2.0* (February 2003): 61–66; Betsy Morris, "Can Michael Dell Escape The Box?" *Fortune* (October 16, 2000): 93–110; and Stewart Deck, "Fine Line," *CIO* (February 1, 2000): 88–92.

72. Michael Goold and Andrew Campbell, "Desperately Seeking Synergy," *Harvard Business Review* (September-October 1998): 131–143.

73. Chris Woodyard, "FedEx Ponies Up $2.4B for Kinko's," *USA Today* (December 30, 2003): accessed at *http://www.usatoday.com/money/industries/2003-12-30-fdx-kinkos_x.htm* on January 2, 2004; and Claudia H. Deutsch, "FedEx Moves to Expand with Purchase of Kinko's," *The New York Times* (December 31, 2003): C1.

74. Cathy Olofson, "No Place Like Home," *Fast Company* (July 2000): 328–329.

75. Linda Tischler, "How Pottery Barn Wins with Style," *Fast Company* (June 2003): 106.

76. Milton Leontiades, "The Confusing Words of Business Policy," *Academy of Management Review* 7 (1982): 45–48.

77. Lawrence G. Hrebiniak and William F. Joyce, *Implementing Strategy* (New York: Macmillan, 1984).

78. John Sterling, "Strategy Development for the Real World," *Strategy & Leadership* 30:1 (2002): 10– 17.

79. Pallavi Gogoi, "The Heat in Kraft's Kitchen; Cheap Rivals and Demands for Leaner Fare Close In," *BusinessWeek* (August 4, 2003): 82; and Shelly Branch, "Critical Curds; At Kraft, Making Cheese 'Fun' Is Serious Business," *The Wall Street Journal* (May 31, 2002): A1, A6.

80. Michael E. Porter, *Competitive Strategy* (New York: Free Press, 1980); Danny Miller, "Relating Porter's Business Strategies to Environment and Structure: Analysis and Performance Implementations," *Academy of Management Journal* 31 (1988): 280–308; and Michael E. Porter, "From Competitive Advantage to Corporate Strategy," *Harvard Business Review* (May–June 1987): 43–59.

81. Michael E. Porter, "Strategy and the Internet," *Harvard Business Review* (March 2001): 63–78.

82. Symonds, "Can Gillette Regain Its Edge?"

83. Jim Kerstetter and Spencer E. Ante, "IBM vs. Oracle: It Could Get Bloody," *BusinessWeek* (May 28, 2001): 65–66.

84. Joseph T. Hallinan, "Service Charge: As Banks Elbow for Consumers, Washington Mutual Thrives," *The Wall Street Journal* (November 6, 2003): A1.

85. Erik Sherman, "Happy in Harleysville," *CIO* (October 15, 2000), 84–86.

86. Thomas L. Wheelen and J. David Hunger, *Strategic Management and Business Policy* (Reading, MA: Addison-Wesley, 1989).

87. Andrew Park and Peter Burrows, "Dell, the Conqueror," *BusinessWeek* (September 24, 2001): 92–102; and Thompson, Jr., and Strickland, "Strategic Management; Concepts and Cases."

88. "We Weren't Just Airborne Yesterday; A Brief History of Southwest Airlines," accessed at *http://www.southwest.com/about_swa/airborne.html* on March 29, 2004; Micheline Maynard, "Are Peanuts No Longer Enough?" *The New York Times* (March 7, 2004): Section 3, 1; and Wendy Zellner with Michael Arndt, "Holding Steady," *BusinessWeek* (February 3, 2003): 66–68.

89. Richard Teitelbaum, "The Wal-Mart of Wall Street," *Fortune* (October 13, 1997): 128–130.

90. Joshua Rosenbaum, "Guitar Maker Looks for a New Key," *The Wall Street Journal* (February 11, 1998): B1, B5.

91. Nitin Nohria, William Joyce, and Bruce Roberson, "What Really Works," *Harvard Business Review* (July 2003): 43–52.

92. Porter, "Strategy and the Internet"; Hammonds, "Michael Porter's Big Ideas"; and G. T. Lumpkin, Scott B. Droege, and Gregory G. Dess, "E-Commerce Strategies: Achieving Sustainable Competitive Advantage and Avoiding Pitfalls," *Organizational Dynamics 30:4* (2002): 325–340.

93. Lumpkin, et al., "E-Commerce Strategies: Achieving Sustainable Competitive Advantage and Avoiding Pitfalls."

94. Based on John Burton, "Composite Strategy: The Combination of Collaboration and Competition," *Journal of General Management 21:1* (Autumn 1995): 1–23; and Roberta Maynard, "Striking the Right Match," *Nation's Business* (May 1996): 18–28.

95. Joe Flint, "Disney-Time Warner Cable Dispute Turns Many TV Screens Black," *The Wall Street Journal* (May 2, 2000): B1, B4; and Bruce Orwall, Joe Flint, and Martin Peers, "Sparring Partners—Moral of Disney's War Against Time Warner: Don't Dis Distribution," *The Wall Street Journal* (May 3, 2000): A1, A12.

96. Don Tapscott, "Rethinking Strategy in a Networked World," *Strategy & Business 24* (Third Quarter 2001): 34–41.

97. Nick Wingfield, "New Chapter; A Web Giant Tries to Boost Profits by Taking on Tenants," *The Wall Street Journal* (September 24, 2003): A1, A10.

98. Julia Angwin and Motoka Rich, "Inn Fighting; Big Hotel Chains Are Striking Back Against Web Sites," *The Wall Street Journal* (March 14, 2003): A1, A7.

99. David Lei, "Strategies for Global Competition," *Long-Range Planning 22* (1989) 102–109.

100. Keith H. Hammonds, "Motorola Bets on Its Chips," *Fast Company* (March 2003): 42–44.

101. Burton, "Composite Strategy: The Combination of Collaboration and Competition."

102. L. J. Bourgeois III and David R. Brodwin, "Strategic Implementation: Five Approaches to an Elusive Phenomenon," *Strategic Management Journal 5* (1984): 241–264; Anil K. Gupta and V. Govindarajan, "Business Unit Strategy, Managerial Characteristics, and Business Unit Effectiveness at Strategy Implementation," *Academy of Management Journal* (1984): 25–41; and Jeffrey G. Covin, Dennis P. Slevin, and Randall L. Schultz, "Implementing Strategic Missions: Effective Strategic, Structural, and Tactical Choices," *Journal of Management Studies 31:4* (1994): 481–505.

103. Rainer Feurer and Kazem Chaharbaghi, "Dynamic Strategy Formulation and Alignment," *Journal of General Management 20:3* (Spring 1995): 76–90; and Henry Mintzberg, *The Rise and Fall of Strategic Planning* (Toronto: Maxwell Macmillan Canada, 1994).

104. Jay R. Galbraith and Robert K. Kazanjian, *Strategy Implementation: Structure, Systems and Process,* 2d ed. (St. Paul, MN: West, 1986); and Paul C. Nutt, "Selecting Tactics to Implement Strategic Plans," *Strategic Management Journal 10* (1989): 145–161.

105. Spencer E. Ante, "The New Blue," *BusinessWeek* (March 17, 2003): 80–88.

106. James E. Skivington and Richard L. Daft, "A Study of Organizational 'Framework' and 'Process' Modalities for the Implementation of Business-Level Strategies" (unpublished manuscript, Texas A&M University, 1987).

107. Thomas M. Begley and David P. Boyd, "The Need for a Corporate Global Mind-Set," *MIT Sloan Management Review* (Winter 2003): 25–32.

108. Abby Ghobadian and Nicholas O'Regan, "The Link Between Culture, Strategy, and Performance in Manufacturing SMEs," *Journal of General Management 28:1* (Autumn 2002): 16–34.

109. Melvyn P. Stark, "Five Years of Insight Into the World's Most Admired Companies," *Journal of Organizational Excellence* (Winter 2002): 3–12.

110. Nitin Nohria, William Joyce, and Bruce Roberson, "What Really Works," *Harvard Business Review* (July 2003): 43–52; and Jeff Rosenthal and Mary Ann Masarech, "High Performance Cultures: How Values Can Drive Business Results," *Journal of Organizational Excellence* (Spring 2003): 3–18.

111. Stanley H. Holmes, "Boeing: What Really Happened?" *BusinessWeek* (December 15, 2003): 33–38; and; Jerry Useem, "Boeing to Pieces," *Fortune* (December 29, 2003): 41.

112. Lumpkin, et al. "E-Commerce Strategies: Achieving Sustainable Competitive Advantage and Avoiding Pitfalls."

113. Chana R. Schoenberger, "Bull's Eye," *Forbes* (September 2, 2002): 76.

114. Keighley, "Is Nintendo Playing the Wrong Game?"; Musgrove, "Not-So-Super Mario: Stodgy Nintendo Is Falling Behind in the Game Wars"; and Laurie J. Flynn, "Deep Price Cuts Help Nintendo Climb to No. 2 in Game Sales," *The New York Times* (January 26, 2004): C2.

Chapter 6

Managerial Decision Making and Information Technology

1. Bob Parks, "Let's Remake a Dealership," *Business 2.0* (June 2004): 65–67; Warren Brown, "Savvy Buyers Might Appreciate the Smart Approach," *The Washington Post* (April 18, 2004): G2; and Jaclyn Olsen, "Mazda to Unveil New Prototype in Bountiful," *The Enterprise* (May 13, 2002): 5.

2. Rick Brooks, "Sealing Their Fate: A Deal with Target Put Lid on Revival at Tupperware," *The Wall Street Journal* (February 18, 2004): A1, A9.

3. Brooks, "Sealing Their Fate: A Deal with Target Put Lid on Revival at Tupperware."

4. Linda Yates and Peter Skarzynski, "How Do Companies Get to the Future First?" *Management Review* (January 1999): 16–22.

5. Michael V. Copeland and Owen Thomas, "Hits (& Misses)," *Business 2.0* (January–February 2004): 126.

6. Stanley Holmes, "Boeing: What Really Happened?" *BusinessWeek* (December 15, 2003): 33–38; Adam Horowitz, Mark Athitakis, Mark Lasswell, and Owen Thomas, "101 Dumbest Moments in Business," *Business 2.0* (January–February 2004):72–81.

7. Herbert A. Simon, *The New Science of Management Decision* (Englewood Cliffs, NJ: Prentice-Hall, 1977).

8. Marc Gunther, "Jeff Zucker Faces Life Without *Friends*," *Fortune* (May 12, 2003): 94–98.

9. Gregory L. White, "Why GM Rewound Its Product Strategy, Delaying New Cavalier," *The Wall Street Journal* (July 30, 1999): A1, A6.

10. Samuel Eilon, "Structuring Unstructured Decisions," *Omega 13* (1985): 369–377; and Max H. Bazerman, *Judgment in Managerial Decision Making* (New York: Wiley, 1986).

11. James G. March and Zur Shapira, "Managerial Perspectives on Risk and Risk Taking," *Management Science 33* (1987): 1404–1418; and Inga Skromme Baird and Howard Thomas, "Toward a Contingency Model of Strategic Risk Taking," *Academy of Management Review 10* (1985): 230–243.

12. Hugh Courtney, "Decision-Driven Scenarios for Assessing Four Levels of Uncertainty," *Strategy & Leadership 31:1* (2003): 14–22.

13. Stanley Holmes, "GE: Little Engines that Could," *BusinessWeek* (January 20, 2003): 62–63.

14. Susanne Craig, Mitchell Pacelle, and Kate Kelly, "NYSE Will Delay Governance Report," *The Wall Street Journal* (September 23, 2003).

15. Markham Johnson, "Business for Dummies," Feb. 2005, pp. 51-52.

16. Michael Masuch and Perry LaPotin, "Beyond Garbage Cans: An AI Model of Organizational Choice," *Administrative Science Quarterly 34* (1989): 38–67; and Richard L. Daft and Robert H. Lengel, "Organizational Information Requirements, Media Richness and Structural Design," *Management Science 32* (1986): 554–571.

17. David M. Schweiger, William R. Sandberg, and James W. Ragan, "Group Approaches for Improving Strategic Decision Making: A Comparative Analysis of Dialectical Inquiry, Devil's Advocacy, and Consensus," *Academy of Management Journal 29* (1986): 51–71; and Richard O. Mason and Ian I. Mitroff, *Challenging Strategic Planning Assumptions* (New York: Wiley Interscience, 1981).

18. Michael Pacanowsky, "Team Tools for Wicked Problems," *Organizational Dynamics 23:3* (Winter 1995): 36–51.

19. Boris Blai, Jr., "Eight Steps to Successful Problem Solving," *Supervisory Management* (January 1986): 7–9; and Earnest R. Archer, "How to Make a Business Decision: An Analysis of Theory and Practice," *Management Review 69* (February 1980): 54–61.

20. Bernard Wysocki Jr., "The Rules: At One Hospital, A Stark Solution for Allocating Care," *The Wall Street Journal* (September 23, 2003): A1, A21.

21. Stacie McCullough, "On the Front Lines," *CIO* (October 15, 1999): Section 1, 78–81.

22. Srinivas Bollapragada, Prasanthi Ganti, Mark Osborn, James Quaile, and Kannan Ramanathan, "GE's Energy Rentals Business Automates Its Credit Assessment Process," *Interfaces* 33:5 (September-October 2003): 45–56; Julie Schlosser, "Markdown Lowdown," *Fortune* (January 12, 2004): 40.

23. Srinivas Bollapragada, Hong Cheng, Mary Phillips, Marc Garbinas, Michael Scholes, Tim Gibbs, and Mark Humphreville, "NBC's Optimization Systems Increase Revenues and Productivity," *Interfaces* 32:1 (January-February 2002): 47–60.

24. Herbert A. Simon, *The New Science of Management Decision* (New York: Harper & Row, 1960); and Amitai Etzioni, "Humble Decision Making," *Harvard Business Review* (July-August 1989): 122–126.

25. James G. March and Herbert A. Simon, *Organizations* (New York: Wiley, 1958).

26. Herbert A. Simon, *Models of Man* (New York: Wiley, 1957); and Herbert A. Simon, *Administrative Behavior*, 2d ed. (New York: Free Press, 1957).

27. John Taylor, "Project Fantasy: A Behind-the-Scenes Account of Disney's Desperate Battle against the Raiders," *Manhattan* (November 1984).

28. George T. Doran and Jack Gunn, "Decision Making in High-Tech Firms: Perspectives of Three Executives," *Business Horizons* (November-December 2002): 7–16.

29. Weston H. Agor, "The Logic of Intuition: How Top Executives Make Important Decisions," *Organizational Dynamics* 14 (Winter 1986): 5–18; and Herbert A. Simon, "Making Management Decisions: The Role of Intuition and Emotion," *Academy of Management Executive* 1 (1987): 57–64.

30. Lisa A. Burke and Monica K. Miller, "Taking the Mystery Out of Intuitive Decision Making," *Academy of Management Executive* 13:4 (1999): 91–99.

31. Reported in Bill Breen, "What's Your Intuition?" *Fast Company* (September 2000): 290–300.

32. Sharon Begley, "Follow Your Intuition: The Unconscious You May Be the Wiser Half," *The Wall Street Journal* (August 30, 2002): B1.

33. Geraldine Fabrikant, "The Paramount Team Puts Profit Over Splash," *The New York Times* (June 30, 2002): Section 3.1; Chris Smith, "Chao, Baby," *New York* (October 18, 1993): 66–75; and "Chao in Charge," *Cablevision* (November 29, 1999): 24.

34. William B. Stevenson, Jon L. Pierce, and Lyman W. Porter, "The Concept of 'Coalition' in Organization Theory and Research," *Academy of Management Review* 10 (1985): 256–268.

35. Jonathan Harris, "Why Speedy Got Stuck in Reverse," *Canadian Business* (September 26, 1997): 87–88.

36. Merissa Mahr and Joe Flint, "DVDs are finally Paramount," *Wall Street Journal*, Feb. 23, 2005, B2.

37. James W. Fredrickson, "Effects of Decision Motive and Organizational Performance Level on Strategic Decision Processes," *Academy of Management Journal* 28 (1985): 821–843; James W. Fredrickson, "The Comprehensiveness of Strategic Decision Processes: Extension, Observations, Future Directions," *Academy of Management Journal* 27 (1984): 445–466; James W. Dean, Jr., and Mark P. Sharfman, "Procedural Rationality in the Strategic Decision-Making Process," *Journal of Management Studies* 30:4 (July 1993): 587–610; Nandini Rajagopalan, Abdul M. A. Rasheed, and Deepak K. Datta, "Strategic Decision Processes: Critical Review and Future Directions," *Journal of Management* 19:2 (1993): 349–384; and Paul J. H. Schoemaker, "Strategic Decisions in Organizations: Rational and Behavioral Views," *Journal of Management Studies* 30:1 (January 1993): 107–129.

38. Marjorie A. Lyles and Howard Thomas, "Strategic Problem Formulation: Biases and Assumptions Embedded in Alternative Decision-Making Models," *Journal of Management Studies* 25 (1988): 131–145; and Susan E. Jackson and Jane E. Dutton, "Discerning Threats and Opportunities," *Administrative Science Quarterly* 33 (1988): 370–387.

39. Anita Lienert, "Can Liz Wetzel's Baby Save Buick?" *Working Woman* (May 2001): 33–36, 78.

40. Richard L. Daft, Juhani Sormunen, and Don Parks, "Chief Executive Scanning, Environmental Characteristics, and Company Performance: An Empirical Study" (unpublished manuscript, Texas A&M University, 1988).

41. C. Kepner and B. Tregoe, *The Rational Manager* (New York: McGraw-Hill, 1965).

42. Pallavi Gogoi and Michael Arndt, "Hamburger Hell," *BusinessWeek* (March 3, 2003): 104–108.

43. Paul C. Nutt, "Surprising But True: Half the Decisions in Organizations Fail," *Academy of Management Executive* 13:4 (1999): 75–90.

44. Gogoi and Arndt, "Hamburger Hell."

45. Peter Mayer, "A Surprisingly Simple Way to Make Better Decisions," *Executive Female* (March-April 1995): 13–14; and Ralph L. Keeney, "Creativity in Decision-Making with Value-Focused Thinking," *Sloan Management Review* (Summer 1994): 33–41.

46. Robert Levering and Milton Moskowitz, "The 100 Best Companies to Work For: The Best in the Worst of Times," *Fortune* (February 4, 2002): 60

47. Mark McNeilly, "Gathering Information for Strategic Decisions, Routinely," *Strategy & Leadership* 30:5 (2002): 29–34.

48. Ibid.

49. Danny Hakim, "GM Executive Preaches: Sweat the Smallest Details," *The New York Times* (January 5, 2004): Section C, 1.

50. Jenny C. McCune, "Making Lemonade," *Management Review*, (June 1997): 49–53, 51.

51. Based on A. J. Rowe, J. D. Boulgaides, and M. R. McGrath, *Managerial Decision Making* (Chicago, IL: Science Research Associates, 1984); and Alan J. Rowe and Richard O. Mason, *Managing with Style: A Guide to Understanding, Assessing, and Improving Your Decision Making* (San Francisco, CA: Jossey-Bass, 1987).

52. Gunther, "Jeff Zucker Faces Life Without *Friends*."

53. V. H. Vroom and Arthur G. Jago, *The New Leadership: Managing Participation in Organizations* (Englewood Cliffs, NJ: Prentice-Hall, 1988).

54. Victor H. Vroom, "Leadership and the Decision-Making Process," *Organizational Dynamics* 28:4 (Spring 2000): 82–94.

55. R.H.G. Field, "A Test of the Vroom-Yetton Normative Model of Leadership," *Journal of Applied Psychology* (October 1982): 523–532; and R.H.G. Field, "A Critique of the Vroom-Yetton Contingency Model of Leadership Behavior," *Academy of Management Review* 4 (1979): 249–257.

56. Vroom, "Leadership and the Decision-Making Process"; Jennifer T. Ettling and Arthur G. Jago, "Participation Under Conditions of Conflict: More on the Validity of the Vroom-Yetton Model," *Journal of Management Studies* 25 (1988): 73–83; Madeline E. Heilman, Harvey A. Hornstein, Jack H. Cage, and Judith K. Herschlag, "Reactions to Prescribed Leader Behavior as a Function of Role Perspective: The Case of the Vroom-Yetton Model," *Journal of Applied Psychology* (February 1984): 50–60; and Arthur G. Jago and Victor H. Vroom, "Some Differences in the Incidence and Evaluation of Participative Leader Behavior," *Journal of Applied Psychology* (December 1982): 776–783.

57. Based on a decision problem presented in Victor H. Vroom, "Leadership and the Decision-Making Process," *Organizational Dynamics* 28:4 (Spring, 2000): 82–94.

58. Nathaniel Foote, Eric Matson, Leigh Weiss, and Etienne Wenger, "Leveraging Group Knowledge for High-Performance Decision-Making," *Organizational Dynamics* 31:3 (2002): 280–295.

59. Kathleen M. Eisenhardt, "Strategy as Strategic Decision Making," *Sloan Management Review* (Spring, 1999): 65–72.

60. John Case, "The Power of Listening,"*Inc.* (March 2003): 77–85.

61. See Katharine Mieskowski, "Digital Competition," *Fast Company* (December 1999): 155–162; Thomas A. Stewart, "Three Rules for Managing in the Real-Time Economy," *Fortune* (May 1, 2000): 333–334; and Geoffrey Colvin, "How to Be a Great eCEO," *Fortune* (May 24, 1999): 104–110.

62. R. B. Gallupe, W. H. Cooper, M. L. Grise, and L. M. Bastianutti, "Blocking Electronic Brainstorms," *Journal of Applied Psychology* 79 (1994): 77–86; R.B. Gallupe and W.H. Cooper, "Brainstorming Electronically," *Sloan Management Review* (Fall 1993): 27–36; and Alison Stein Wellner, "A Perfect Brainstorm," *Inc.* (October 2003): 31–35.

63. Wellner, "A Perfect Brainstorm"; Gallupe and Cooker, "Brainstorming Electronically."

64. Michael V. Copeland, "Mistakes Happen," *Red Herring* (May 2000): 346–354.

65. Ibid.

66. Joshua Klayman, Richard P. Larrick, and Chip Heath, "Organizational Repairs," *Across the Board* (February 2000): 26–31.

67. Michael A. Roberto, "Making Difficult Decisions in Turbulent Times," *Ivey Business Journal* (May-June 2003): 1–7.
68. Eisenhardt, "Strategy as Strategic Decision Making"; and David A. Garvin and Michael A. Roberto, "What You Don't Know About Making Decisions," *Harvard Business Review* (September 2001): 108–116.
69. Roberto, "Making Difficult Decisions in Turbulent Times."
70. David M. Schweiger and William R. Sandberg, "The Utilization of Individual Capabilities in Group Approaches to Strategic Decision-Making," *Strategic Management Journal 10* (1989): 31–43; and "The Devil's Advocate," *Small Business Report* (December 1987): 38–41.
71. Doran and Gunn, "Decision Making in High-Tech Firms: Perspectives of Three Executives."
72. Eisenhardt, "Strategy as Strategic Decision Making."
73. Garvin and Roberto, "What You Don't Know About Making Decisions."
74. Christopher Palmeri, "Believe in Yourself, Believe in the Merchandise," *Continental* (December 1997): 49–51; Timothy J. Mullaney with Heather Green, Michael Arndt, Robert D. Hof, and Linda Himelstein, "The E-Biz Surprise," *Business Week*, (May 12, 2003): 60–68.
75. Timothy J. Mullaney, "E-Biz Strikes Again," *BusinessWeek* (May 10, 2004): 80–82; and Mullaney et al., "The E-Biz Surprise."
76. Mullaney, et al., "The E-Biz Surprise."
77. Derek Slater, "Chain Commanders," *CIO Enterprise* (August 15, 1998): 29–30+.
78. Jane Linder and Drew Phelps, "Call to Action," *CIO* (April 1, 2000): 166–174.
79. James A. O'Brien, *Introduction to Information Systems*, 8th ed. (Burr Ridge, IL.: Irwin, 1997); and Nathaniel Foote, Eric Matson, Leigh Weiss, and Etienne Wenger, "Leveraging Group Knowledge for High-Performance Decision Making," *Organizational Dynamics 31:3* (2002): 280–295.
80. John P. Mello Jr., "Fly Me To the Web," *CFO* (March 2000): 79–84.
81. Heather Harreld, "Pick-Up Artists," *CIO* (November 1, 2000): 148–154.
82. Roger Fillion, "No receptionist necessary," *Inc. Technology* 2001, No. 2, p. 23.
83. Jim Turcotte, Bob Silveri, and Tom Jobson, "Are You Ready for the E-Supply Chain?" *APICS–The Performance Advantage* (August 1998): 56–59.
84. Steve Hamm with David Welch, Wendy Zellner, Faith Keenan, and Peter Engardio, "E-Biz: Down but Hardly Out," *BusinessWeek* (March 26, 2001): 126–130.
85. David Drickhamer, "EDI Is Dead! Long Live EDI!," *Industry Week* (April 2003): 31–38; Ian Mount, "Why EDI Won't Die," *Business 2.0* (August 2003): 68–69; and Marie-Claude Boudreau, Karen D. Loch, Daniel Robey, and Detmar Straud, "Going Global: Using Information Technology to Advance the Competitiveness of the Virtual Transnational Organization," *Academy of Management Executive 12:4* (1998) 120–128.
86. This discussion is based on Long W. Lam and L. Jean Harrison-Walker, "Toward an Objective-Based Typology of E-Business Models," *Business Horizons* (November–December 2003): 17–26; and Detmar Straub and Richard Klein, "E-Competitive Transformations," *Business Horizons* (May-June 2001): 3–12.
87. Straub and Klein, "E-Competitive Transformations."
88. Megan Santosus, "How REI Scaled E-Commerce Mountain," *CIO* (May 15, 2004): 52–54.
89. Brian Caulfield, "Facing Up to CRM," *Business 2.0* (August-September 2001): 149–150; and "Customer Relationship Management: The Good. The Bad. The Future." *BusinessWeek* (April 28, 2003): special advertising section, 53–64.
90. Alix Nyberg, "Buyer Be Aware," *CFO* (July 2003): 69–72.
91. Reported in Eric Seubert, Y. Balaji, and Mahesh Makhija, "The Knowledge Imperative," *CIO Advertising Supplement* (March 15, 2001): S1–S4.
92. Ryan K. Lahti and Michael M. Beyerlein, "Knowledge Transfer and Management Consulting: A Look at 'The Firm,'" *Business Horizons* (January-February 2000): 65–74.
93. "Mandate 2003: Be Agile and Efficient," *Microsoft Executive Circle* (Spring 2003): 46–48.
94. Anthony Scaturro, "All in the Family," *Inc. Technology 1* (1998): 25–26.
95. Liz Thach and Richard W. Woodman, "Organizational Change and Information Technology: Managing on the Edge of Cyberspace," *Organizational Dynamics* (Summer 1994): 30–46; and Elizabeth Horwitt, "Going Deep: Empowering Employees," *Microsoft Executive Circle* (Summer 2003): 24–26.
96. Greg Jaffe, "Tug of War: In the New Military, Technology May Alter Chain of Command," *The Wall Street Journal* (March 30, 2001): A3, A6.
97. Tonya Vinas, "Surviving Information Overload," *Industry Week* (April 2003): 24–29.
98. Joseph McCafferty, "Coping with Infoglut," *CFO* (September 1998): 101–102.
99. Leonard M. Fuld, "The Danger of Data Slam," *CIO Enterprise* (September 15, 1998): Section 2, 28–33.
100. Janine Adams, "Want a New Pet? Check the Web," *The Christian Science Monitor* (April 28, 2004): 11.
101. Based on Faith Keenan and Spencer E. Ante, "The New Teamwork," *BusinessWeek e.biz* (February 18, 2002): EB12–EB16; Dave Guilford, "As Clay Fades, GM Relies on Digital Imagery," *Automotive News* (April 12, 2004): 4; and Paul McDougall, "EDS Can't Afford To Be Tech Agnostic," *Information Week* (February 23, 2004): 25.
102. Michael A. Fontaine, Salvatore Parise, and David Miller, "Collaborative Environments: An Effective Tool for Transforming Business Processes," *Ivey Business Journal* (May-June 2004).
103. Ibid.
104. Matthew Boyle, "The Really Really Messy Wi-Fi Revolution," *Fortune* (May 12, 2003): 86–92.
105. Ibid.
106. Susannah Patton, "The Wisdom of Starting Small," *CIO* (March 15, 2001): 80–86.
107. Spencer E. Ante, et al., "In Search of the Net's Next Big Thing," *BusinessWeek* (March 26, 2001): 140–141; Amy Cortese, "Peer to Peer: P2P Taps the Power of Distant Computers in a Way that Could Transform Whole Industries," *The BusinessWeek 50*, *BusinessWeek* (Spring 2001): Supplement, 194–196.
108. Mark Roberti, "Peer-to-Peer Isn't Dead," *The Industry Standard* (April 23, 2001): 58–59.
109. This discussion is based on Jena McGregor, "It's a Blog World After All," *Fast Company* (April 2004): 84–86.
110. Tony Kontzer, "Kitchen Sink: Many Collaborative Options," *Information Week* (May 5, 2003): 35; sidebar in Kontzer, "Learning to Share."
111. Parks, "Let's Remake a Dealership"; Brown, "Savvy Buyers Might Appreciate the Smart Approach"; and Olsen, "Mazda to Unveil New Prototype in Bountiful."

Chapter 7

Structure and Fundamentals of Organizing

1. Emily Nelson, "Think You've Got a Tricky Staff? Try Herding Writers," *The Wall Street Journal* (May 16, 2003): A1.
2. Karen Chan, "From Top to Bottom," *The Wall Street Journal* (May 21, 2001); R12.
3. Peter Burrows, "The Radical," *BusinessWeek* (February 19, 2001): 70–80.
4. John Child, *Organization: A Guide to Problems and Practice*, 2d ed. (London, UK: Harper & Row, 1984).
5. Adam Smith, *The Wealth of Nations* (New York: Modern Library, 1937).
6. This discussion is based on Richard L. Daft, *Organization Theory and Design*, 4th ed. (St. Paul, MN.: West, 1992).
7. C. I. Barnard, *The Functions of the Executive* (Cambridge, MA: Harvard University Press, 1938).
8. Thomas A. Stewart, "CEOs See Clout Shifting," *Fortune* (November 6, 1989): 66.
9. Michael G. O'Loughlin, "What Is Bureaucratic Accountabilities and How Can We Measure It?" *Administration & Society 22:3* (November 1990): 275–302; and Brian Dive, "When Is An Organization Too Flat?" *Across the Board* (July–August 2003): 20–23.
10. Carrie R. Leana, "Predictors and Consequences of Delegation," *Academy of Management Journal 29* (1986): 754–774.
11. Robert A. Guth, "Midlife Correction: Inside Microsoft, Financial Managers Win New Clout," *The Wall Street Journal* (July 23, 2003): A1, A6.
12. Curtis Sittenfeld, "Powered By the People," *Fast Company* (July–August 1999): 178–189.
13. Barbara Davison, "Management Span of Control: How Wide Is Too Wide?" *Journal of Business Strategy 24:4* (2003): 22–29; Paul D. Collins and Frank Hull, "Technology and Span of Control: Woodward

Revisited," *Journal of Management Studies* 23 (March 1986): 143–164; David D. Van Fleet and Arthur G. Bedeian, "A History of the Span of Management," *Academy of Management Review* 2 (1977): 356–372; and C. W. Barkdull, "Span of Control—A Method of Evaluation," *Michigan Business Review* 15 (May 1963): 25–32.

14. Barbara Davison, "Management Span of Control"; Brian Dive, "When Is an Organization Too Flat?"; and Brian Dumaine, "What the Leaders of Tomorrow See," *Fortune* (July 3, 1989): 48–62.

15. Raghuram G. Rajan and Julie Wulf, "The Flattening Firm: Evidence From Panel Data on the Changing Nature of Corporate Hierarchies," working paper, reported in Caroline Ellis, "The Flattening Corporation," *MIT Sloan Management Review* (Summer 2003): 5.

16. Charles Haddad, "How UPS Delivered through the Disaster," *BusinessWeek* (October 1, 2001): 66.

17. Brian O'Reilly, "J&J Is on a Roll," *Fortune* (December 26, 1994): 178–191; and Joseph Weber, "A Big Company That Works," *BusinessWeek* (May 4, 1992): 124–132.

18. Clay Chandler and Paul Ingrassia, "Just as U.S. Firms Try Japanese Management, Honda Is Centralizing," *The Wall Street Journal* (April 11, 1991): A1, A10.

19. The following discussion of structural alternatives draws heavily from Jay R. Galbraith, *Designing Complex Organizations* (Reading, Mass.: Addison-Wesley, 1973); Jay R. Galbraith, *Organization Design* (Reading, Mass.: Addison-Wesley, 1977); Jay R. Galbraith, *Designing Dynamic Organizations* (New York: AMACOM, 2002); Robert Duncan, "What Is the Right Organization Structure?" *Organizational Dynamics* (Winter 1979): 59–80; and J. McCann and Jay R. Galbraith, "Interdepartmental Relations," in *Handbook of Organizational Design*, ed. P. Nystrom and W. Starbuck (New York: Oxford University Press, 1981).

20. Susan Carey, "US Air 'Peon' Team Pilots Start-Up of Low-Fare Airline," *The Wall Street Journal* (March 24, 1998): B1.

21. Charles Fishman, "Total Teamwork: Imagination Ltd.," *Fast Company* (April 2000): 156–168.

22. Melissa A. Schilling and H. Kevin Steensma, "The Use of Modular Organizational Forms: An Industry-Level Analysis," *Academy of Management Journal*, 44, no. 6 (December 2001): 1149–1169.

23. Susan G. Cohen and Don Mankin, "Complex Collaborations for the New Global Economy," *Organizational Dynamics* 31:2 (2002): 117–133; David Lei and John W. Slocum Jr., "Organizational Designs to Renew Competitive Advantage," *Organizational Dynamics* 31:1 (2002): 1–18.

24. Raymond E. Miles and Charles C. Snow, "The New Network Firm: A Spherical Structure Built on a Human Investment Philosophy," *Organizational Dynamics* (Spring 1995): 5–18; and Raymond E. Miles, Charles C. Snow, John A. Matthews, Grant Miles, and Henry J. Coleman, Jr., "Organizing in the Knowledge Age: Anticipating the Cellular Form," *Academy of Management Executive* 11:4 (1997): 7–24.

25. Raymond E. Miles and Charles C. Snow, "Organizations: New Concepts for New Forms," *California Management Review* 28 (Spring 1986): 62–73; and "Now, The Post-Industrial Corporation," *BusinessWeek* (March 3, 1986): 64–74.

26. N. Anand, "Modular, Virtual, and Hollow Forms of Organization Design," Working paper, London Business School, 2000; Don Tapscott, "Rethinking Strategy in a Networked World," *Strategy & Business* 24 (Third Quarter 2001): 34–41.

27. Malcolm Wheatley, "Cycle Company with a Virtual Spin," *MT* (September 2003): 78–81.

28. Gregory G. Dess, Abdul M. A. Rasheed, Kevin J. McLaughlin, and Richard L. Priem, "The New Corporate Architecture," *Academy of Management Executive* 9:3 (1995): 7–20.

29. Philip Siekman, "The Snap-Together Business Jet," *Fortune* (January 21, 2002): 104[A]–104[H].

30. Kathleen Kerwin, "GM: Modular Plants Won't Be a Snap," *BusinessWeek* (November 9, 1998): 168, 172.

31. Raymond E. Miles, "Adapting to Technology and Competition: A New Industrial Relations System for the Twenty-First Century," *California Management Review* (Winter 1989): 9–28; and Miles and Snow, "The New Network Firm: A Spherical Structure Built on a Human Investment Philosophy."

32. Dess et al., "The New Corporate Architecture"; Henry W. Chesbrough and David J. Teece, "Organizing for Innovation: When Is Virtual Virtuous?" *The Innovative Entrepreneur* (August 2002): 127–134; N. Anand, "Modular, Virtual, and Hollow Forms"; and M. Lynne Markus, Brook Manville, and Carole E. Agres, "What Makes a Virtual Organization Work?" *Sloan Management Review* (Fall 2000): 13–26.

33. Laurie P. O'Leary, "Curing the Monday Blues: A U.S. Navy Guide for Structuring Cross-Functional Teams," *National Productivity*

Review (Spring 1996): 43-51; and Alan Hurwitz, "Organizational Structures for the 'New World Order,'" *Business Horizons* (May–June 1996): 5–14.

34. Jay Galbraith, Diane Downey, and Amy Kates, *Designing Dynamic Organizations*, Chapter 4: Processes and Lateral Capability (New York: AMACOM, 2002).

35. Lee Iacocca with William Novak, *Iacocca: An Autobiography* (New York: Phantom Books, 1984).

36. Miriam Jordan and Jonathan Karp, "Machines for the Masses," *The Wall Street Journal* (December 9, 2003): A1, A20.

37. William J. Altier, "Task Forces: An Effective Management Tool," *Management Review* (February 1987): 52–57.

38. "Task Forces Tackle Consolidation of Employment Services," *Shawmut News*, Shawmut National Corp. (May 3, 1989): 2.

39. Henry Mintzberg, *The Structure of Organizations* (Englewood Cliffs, NJ: Prentice Hall, 1979).

40. Paul R. Lawrence and Jay W. Lorsch, "New Managerial Job: The Integrator," *Harvard Business Review* (November–December 1967): 142–151.

41. Ronald N. Ashkenas and Suzanne C. Francis, "Integration Managers: Special Leaders for Special Times," *Harvard Business Review* (November–December 2000): 108–116.

42. Jeffrey A. Tannenbaum, "Why Are Companies Paying Close Attention to This Toilet Maker?," *The Wall Street Journal* (August 20, 1999): (The Front Lines column) B1.

43. This discussion is based on Michael Hammer and Steven Stanton, "How Process Enterprises *Really* Work," *Harvard Business Review* (November–December 1999): 108–118; Richard L. Daft, *Organization Theory and Design*, 5th ed. (Minneapolis, MN.: West Publishing Company, 1995); Raymond L. Manganelli and Mark M. Klein, "A Framework for Reengineering," *Management Review* (June 1994): 9–16; and Barbara Ettorre, "Reengineering Tales from the Front," *Management Review* (January 1995): 13–18.

44. Hammer and Stanton, "How Process Enterprises *Really* Work."

45. Michael Hammer, definition quoted in "The Process Starts Here," *CIO* (March 1, 2000): 144–156; and David A. Garvin, "The Processes of Organization and Management," *Sloan Management Review* (Summer 1998): 33–50.

46. Frank Ostroff, *The Horizontal Organization: What the Organization of the Future Looks Like and How It Delivers Value to Customers* (New York: Oxford University Press, 1999).

47. Hammer and Stanton, "How Process Enterprises *Really* Work."

48. Richard Koonce, "Reengineering the Travel Game," *Government Executive* (May 1995): 28–34, 69–70.

49. John A. Byrne, "The Horizontal Corporation," *BusinessWeek* (December 20, 1993): 76–81.

50. Erik Brynjolfsson, Amy Austin Renshaw, and Marshall Van Alstyne, "The Matrix of Change," *Sloan Management Review* (Winter 1997): 37–54.

51. For a discussion of the benefits and problems of hierarchies, see Harold J. Leavitt, "Why Hierarchies Thrive," *Harvard Business Review* (March 2003): 96–102.

52. Michael E. Porter, *Competitive Strategy* (New York: Free Press, 1980): 36–46.

53. Marc Gunther, "MTV's passage to India," *Fortune* (Aug. 9, 2004): 117–125; Kerry Capell, "MTV's World," *BusinessWeek* (Feb. 18, 2002): 81–84.

54. Pam Black, "Finally, Human Rights for Motorists," *BusinessWeek* (May 1, 1995): 45.

55. Paul R. Lawrence and Jay W. Lorsch, *Organization and Environment* (Homewood, IL: Irwin, 1969).

56. William J. Holstein, "Innovation, Leadership and Still No Satisfaction," *The New York Times* (Dec. 1, 2004): 3, 11; Robert A. Watson and Ben Brown, *The Most Effective Organization in the US: Leadership Secrets of the Salvation Army* (New York: Crown Business, 2001).

57. Robert B. Duncan, "Characteristics of Organizational Environments and Perceived Environmental Uncertainty," *Administrative Science Quarterly* 17 (1972): 313–327; W. Alan Randolph and Gregory G. Dess, "The Congruence Perspective of Organization Design: A Conceptual Model and Multivariate Research Approach," *Academy of Management Review* 9 (1984): 114–127; and Masoud Yasai-Ardekani, "Structural Adaptations to Environments," *Academy of Management Review* 11 (1986): 9–21.

58. Joshua Hyatt, "Chocolate Bores," *FSB* (Feb. 2005): 130.

59. Tom Burns and G. M. Stalker, *The Management of Innovation* (London: Tavistock, 1961).

60. John A. Coutright, Gail T. Fairhurst, and L. Edna Rogers, "Interaction Patterns in Organic and Mechanistic Systems," *Academy of Management Journal* 32 (1989): 773–802.

61. Robert Pool, "In the Zero Luck Zone," *Forbes ASAP* (November 27, 2000): 85+.

62. Ibid.

63. Denise M. Rousseau and Robert A. Cooke, "Technology and Structure: The Concrete, Abstract, and Activity Systems of Organizations," *Journal of Management* 10 (1984), 345–361; Charles Perrow, "A Framework for the Comparative Analysis of Organizations," *American Sociological Review* 32 (1967): 194–208; and Denise M. Rousseau, "Assessment of Technology in Organizations: Closed versus Open Systems Approaches," *Academy of Management Review* 4 (1979): 531–542.

64. Joan Woodward, *Industrial Organizations: Theory and Practice* (London, UK: Oxford University Press, 1965); and Joan Woodward, *Management and Technology* (London, UK: Her Majesty's Stationery Office, 1958).

65. Woodward, *Industrial Organizations: Theory and Practices*.

66. Peter K. Mills and Thomas Kurk, "A Preliminary Investigation into the Influence of Customer-Firm Interface on Information Processing and Task Activity in Service Organizations," *Journal of Management* 12 (1986): 91–104; Peter K. Mills and Dennis J. Moberg, "Perspectives on the Technology of Service Operations," *Academy of Management Review* 7 (1982): 467–478; and Roger W. Schmenner, "How Can Service Businesses Survive and Prosper?" *Sloan Management Review* 27 (Spring 1986), 21–32.

67. Richard B. Chase and David A. Tansik, "The Customer Contact Model for Organization Design," *Management Science* 29 (1983): 1037–1050; and Gregory B. Northcraft and Richard B. Chase, "Managing Service Demand at the Point of Delivery," *Academy of Management Review* 10 (1985): 66–75.

68. Michael Hammer in "The Process Starts Here"; and Emelie Rutherford, "End Game," (an interview with David Weinberger, coauthor of *The Cluetrain Manifesto*), CIO (April 1, 2000): 98–104.

69. Thomas A. Stewart, "Three Rules for Managing in the Real-Time Economy," *Fortune* (May 1, 2000): 333–334.

70. Emily Nelson, "Think You've Got a Tricky Staff? Try Herding Writers," *The Wall Street Journal* (May 16, 2003): A1.

Chapter 8
Innovation and Change

1. "Winning Square and Fair Against a Business Goliath," *Virginian-Pilot* (Oct. 23, 2002): B8; Ilan Mochari, "Climbing Back Up," *Inc Magazine* (March 1, 2002): 92–100; "Ladder Inventors Win Design Case," *The New York Times* (August 19, 2001): 1.

2. Keith Bracsher, "Newest Export Out of China: Inflation Fears," *The New York Times* (April 16, 2004): http://www.nytimes.com.

3. Scott Kirsner, "5 Technologies That Will Change the World," *Fast Company* (September 2003): 93–98; Stuart F. Brown, "The Automaker's Big-Time Bet on Fuel Cells," *Fortune* (March 30, 1998): 122(B)–122(D).

4. Kirsner, "5 Technologies that Will Change the World."

5. Richard L. Daft, "Bureaucratic vs. Nonbureaucratic Structure in the Process of Innovation and Change," in *Perspectives in Organizational Sociology: Theory and Research*, ed. Samuel B. Bacharach (Greenwich, CT: JAI Press, 1982).

6. Tom Broersma, "In Search of the Future," *Training and Development* (January 1995): 38–43.

7. Andre L. Delbecq and Peter K. Mills, "Managerial Practices that Enhance Innovation," *Organizational Dynamics* 14 (Summer 1985): 24–34.

8. Interview with Art Collins in Ellen Florian, "CEO Voices: 'I Have a Cast-Iron Stomach,'" Special Insert: CEOs on Innovation, *Fortune* (March 8, 2004).

9. Chuck Salter, "On the Road Again," *Fast Company* (January 2002): 50–58.

10. Interview with A. G. Lafley in Ellen Florian, "CEO Voices"; and Patricia Sellers, "Teaching an Old Dog New Tricks," *Fortune* (May 31, 2004): 166–180.

11. Carol Hymowitz, "Managing in a Crisis Can Bring Better Ways to Conduct Business," *The Wall Street Journal* (October 23, 2001): Lead column, B1.

12. John P. Kotter, *Leading Change* (Boston, MA: Harvard University Press, 1996); and "Leading Change: Why Transformation Efforts Fail," *Harvard Business Review* (March–April, 1995): 59–67.

13. Almar Latour, "Trial by Fire: A Blaze in Albuquerque Sets Off Major Crisis for Cell-Phone Giants," *The Wall Street Journal* (January 29, 2001): A1, A8.

14. Attributed to Gregory Bateson in Andrew H. Van de Ven, "Central Problems in the Management of Innovation," *Management Science* 32 (1986): 595.

15. Teresa M. Amabile, "Motivating Creativity in Organizations: On Doing What You Love and Loving What You Do," *California Management Review* 40:1 (Fall 1997): 39–58; Brian Leavy, "Creativity: The New Imperative," *Journal of General Management* 28:1 (Autumn 2002): 70–85; and Timothy A. Matherly and Ronald E. Goldsmith, "The Two Faces of Creativity," *Business Horizons* (September/October 1985): 8.

16. Gordon Vessels, "The Creative Process: An Open-Systems Conceptualization," *Journal of Creative Behavior* 16 (1982): 185–196.

17. Robert J. Sternberg, Linda A. O'Hara, and Todd I. Lubart, "Creativity as Investment," *California Management Review* 40:1 (Fall 1997): 8–21; Teresa M. Amabile, "Motivating Creativity in Organizations: On Doing What You Love and Loving What You Do"; Leavy, "Creativity: The New Imperative"; and Ken Lizotte, "A Creative State of Mind," *Management Review* (May 1998): 15–17.

18. James Brian Quinn, "Managing Innovation: Controlled Chaos," *Harvard Business Review* 63 (May–June 1985): 73–84; Howard H. Stevenson and David E. Gumpert, "The Heart of Entrepreneurship," *Harvard Business Review* 63 (March–April 1985): 85–94; and Marsha Sinetar, "Entrepreneurs, Chaos, and Creativity—Can Creative People Really Survive Large Company Structure?" *Sloan Management Review* 6 (Winter 1985): 57–62.

19. Cynthia Browne, "Jest for Success," *Moonbeams* (August 1989): 3–5; and Rosabeth Moss Kanter, *The Change Masters* (New York: Simon and Schuster, 1983).

20. S. Thomke and A. Nimgade, "IDEO Product Development", Case #9-600-143, Harvard Business School, 2000, reported in Leavy, "Creativity: The New Imperative"; Daniel H. Pink, "Out of the Box," *Fast Company* (October 2003): 104–106.

21. Ian Wylie, "Calling for a Renewable Future," *Fast Company* (May 2003): 46–48.

22. Ann Harrington, "Who's Afraid of a New Product?" *Fortune* (November 10, 2003): 189–192.

23. Harold J. Leavitt, "Why Hierarchies Thrive," *Harvard Business Review* (March 2003): 96–102.

24. "Hands On: A Manager's Notebook," *Inc.* (January 1989): 106.

25. Katy Koontz, "How to Stand Out from the Crowd," *Working Woman* (January 1988): 74–76.

26. George Anders, "Hard Cell," *Fast Company* (May 2001): 108–122.

27. Harold L. Angle and Andrew H. Van de Ven, "Suggestions for Managing the Innovation Journey," in *Research in the Management of Innovation: The Minnesota Studies*, ed. A. H. Van de Ven, H. L. Angle, and Marshall Scott Poole (Cambridge, MA: Ballinger/Harper & Row, 1989).

28. Robert I. Sutton, "The Weird Rules of Creativity," *Harvard Business Review* (September 2001): 94–103.

29. C. K. Bart, "New Venture Units: Use Them Wisely to Manage Innovation," *Sloan Management Review* (Summer 1988): 35–43; Michael Tushman and David Nadler, "Organizing for Innovation," *California Management Review* 28 (Spring 1986), 74–92; Peter F. Drucker, *Innovation and Entrepreneurship* (New York: Harper & Row, 1985); and Henry W. Chesbrough, "Making Sense of Corporate Venture Capital," *Harvard Business Review* (March 2002): http://www.hbsp.harvard.edu.

30. Christine Canabou, "Fast Ideas for Slow Times," *Fast Company* (May 2002): 52.

31. Christopher Hoenig, "Skunk Works Secrets," *CIO* (July 1, 2000): 74–76; and Tom Peters and Nancy Austin, *A Passion for Excellence: The Leadership Difference* (New York: Random House, 1985).

32. Hoenig, "Skunk Works Secrets."

33. Sutton, "The Weird Rules of Creativity."

34. Interview with Craig Barrett in Ellen Florian, "CEO Voices: 'I Have a Cast-Iron Stomach,'" Special Insert: CEOs on Innovation, *Fortune* (March 8, 2004); and Sherry Eng, "Hatching Schemes," *The Industry Standard* (November 27–December 4, 2000): 174–175.

35. Ibid.

36. Ibid.

37. Henry Chesbrough, "The Logic of Open Innovation: Managing Intellectual Property," *Califoenia Management Review* 45:3 (Spring 2003): 33–58.

38. This discussion is based on Henry Chesbrough, "The Era of Open Innovation," *MIT Sloan Management Review* (Spring 2003): 35–41; and Amy Muller and Liisa Välikangas, "Extending the Boundary of Corporate Innovation," *Strategy & Leadership 30:3* (2002): 4–9.
39. Chesbrough, "The Era of Open Innovation"; Robert Berner, "Why P&G's Smile Is So Bright," *BusinessWeek* (August 12, 2002): 58–60; Interview with A. G. Lafley in Ellen Florian, "CEO Voices: 'I Have a Cast Iron Stomach'"; and Sellers, "P&G: Teaching an Old Dog New Tricks."
40. Muller and Välikangas, "Extending the Boundary of Corporate Innovation."
41. C. K. Prahalad and Venkatram Ramaswamy, "The New Frontier of Experience Innovation,"*MIT Sloan Management Review* (Summer 2003): 12–18.
42. J. P. Kotter and L. A. Schlesinger, "Choosing Strategies for Change," *Harvard Business Review 57* (March–April 1979): 106–114.
43. Interview with Fred Smith in Ellen Florian, "CEO Voices."
44. G. Zaltman and Robert B. Duncan, *Strategies for Planned Change* (New York: Wiley Interscience, 1977).
45. Leonard M. Apcar, "Middle Managers and Supervisors Resist Moves to More Participatory Management," *The Wall Street Journal* (September 16, 1985): 25.
46. Dorothy Leonard-Barton and Isabelle Deschamps, "Managerial Influence in the Implementation of New Technology," *Management Science 34* (1988): 1252– 1265.
47. Kurt Lewin, *Field Theory in Social Science: Selected Theoretical Papers* (New York: Harper & Brothers, 1951).
48. Paul C. Nutt, "Tactics of Implementation," *Academy of Management Journal 29* (1986): 230–261; Kotter and Schlesinger, "Choosing Strategies"; R. L. Daft and S. Becker, *Innovation in Organizations: Innovation Adoption in School Organizations* (New York: Elsevier, 1978); and R. Beckhard, *Organization Development: Strategies and Models* (Reading, MA: Addison-Wesley, 1969).
49. Rob Muller, "Training for Change," *Canadian Business Review* (Spring 1995): 16–19.
50. Gerard H. Seijts and Grace O'Farrell, "Engage the Heart: Appealing to the Emotions Facilitates Change," *Ivey Business Journal* (January-February 2003): 1–5; John P. Kottter and Dan S. Cohen, *The Heart of Change: Real-Life Stories of How People Change Their Organizations* (Boston, MA: Harvard Business School Press, 2002); and Shaul Fox and Yair Amichai-Hamburger, "The Power of Emotional Appeals in Promoting Organizational Change Programs," *Academy of Management Executive 15:4* (2001): 84–95.
51. Taggart F. Frost, "Creating a Teamwork-Based Culture Within a Manufacturing Setting," *IM* (May-June 1994): 17–20.
52. Dean Foust with Gerry Khermouch, "Repairing the Coke Machine," *BusinessWeek* (March 19, 2001): 86–88.
53. Joy Persaud, "Strongest Links," *People Management* (May 29, 2003): 40–41.
54. Jerry Harkavy, "Footwear Maker Stays Step Ahead to Keep 'Made-in-USA' on Shoes," Associated Press story in *Johnson City Press* (March 3, 2002): 27; and accessed *http://www.newbalance.com* on April 15, 2004.
55. Richard Teitelbaum, "How to Harness Gray Matter," *Fortune* (June 9, 1997): 168.
56. R.L. Daft, *Organization Theory and Design*, 8th ed. (Cincinnati, OH: South-Western, 2004, Chapter 11; and Tom Burns and G. M. Stalker, *The Management of Innovation* (London, UK: Tavistock Publications, 1961).
57. Richard L. Daft, "A Dual-Core Model of Organizational Innovation," *Academy of Management Journal 21* (1978): 193–210; and Kanter, *The Change Masters*.
58. Stuart K. Brown, "A Sweet Triumph," *FSB* (April 2002): 49–54.
59. Michael L. Tushman and Charles A. O'Reilly III, "Building Ambidextrous Organizations: Forming Your Own 'Skunk Works,'" *Health Forum Journal 42:2* (March-April 1999): 20–23.
60. James B. Treece, "Improving the Soul of an Old Machine," *BusinessWeek* (October 25, 1993): 134–136.
61. Harold J. Leavitt, "Applied Organizational Change in Industry: Structural, Technical, and Human Approaches," in *New Perspectives in Organization Research*, ed. W. W. Cooper, H. J. Leavitt, and M. W. Shelly II (New York: Wiley, 1964).
62. Glenn Rifkin, "Competing through Innovation: The Case of Broderbund," *Strategy & Business 11* (Second Quarter, 1998): 48–58; and Deborah Dougherty and Cynthia Hardy, "Sustained Product Innovation in Large, Mature Organizations: Overcoming Innovation-to-Organization Problems," *Academy of Management Journal 39:5* (1996): 1120–1153.

63. Cliff Edwards, "Many Products Have Gone the Way of the Edsel," *Johnson City Press* (May 23, 1999): 28; Robert McMath, *What Were They Thinking? Marketing Lessons I've Learned from Over 80,000 New Product Innovations and Idiocies* (New York: Times Business, 1998); and Paul Lukas, "The Ghastliest Product Launches," *Fortune* (March 16, 1998): 44.
64. Melissa A. Schilling and Charles W. L. Hill, "Managing the New Product Development Process," *Academy of Management Executive 12:3* (1998): 67–81.
65. Andrew H. Van de Ven, "Central Problems in the Management of Innovation," *Management Science 32* (1986): 590–607; Daft, *Organization Theory*; and Science Policy Research Unit, University of Sussex, *Success and Failure in Industrial Innovation* (London, UK: Centre for the Study of Industrial Innovation, 1972).
66. William L. Shanklin and John K. Ryans, Jr., "Organizing for High-Tech Marketing," *Harvard Business Review 62* (November-December 1984): 164–171; and Arnold O. Putnam, "A Redesign for Engineering," *Harvard Business Review 63* (May-June 1985): 139–144.
67. Fariborz Damanpour, "The Adoption of Technological, Administrative, and Ancillary Innovations: Impact of Organizational Factors," *Journal of Management 13* (1987): 675–688.
68. Greg Jaffe, "New Formation: A Maverick's Plan to Revamp Army Is Taking Shape," *The Wall Street Journal* (December 12, 2003): A1.
69. Eliza Newlin Carney, "Calm in the Storm," *Government Executive* (October 2003): 57–63.
70. Avan R. Jassawalla and Hemant C. Sashittal, "Building Collaborative New Product Processes: Why Instituting Teams Is Not Enough," *SAM Advanced Management Journal* (Winter 2002): 27–36.
71. E. H. Schein, "Organizational Culture," *American Psychologist 45* (February 1990): 109–119; Eliza Newlin Carey, "Calm in the Storm," *Government Executive* (October 2003): 57-63.
72. Michelle Conlin, "Tough Love for Techie Souls," *BusinessWeek* (November 29, 1999): 164–170.
73. Michael A. Prospero, "Full of Mullarkey," *Fast Company* (March 2005): 33.
74. M. Sashkin and W. W. Burke, "Organization Development in the 1980s," *General Management 13* (1987): 393–417; and Richard Beckhard, "What Is Organization Development?" in *Organization Development and Transformation: Managing Effective Change*, Wendell L. French, Cecil H. Bell, Jr., and Robert A. Zawacki, eds., (Burr Ridge, Ill.: Irwin McGraw Hill, 2000): 16–19.
75. Wendell L. French and Cecil H. Bell, Jr., "A History of Organization Development," in French, Bell, and Zawacki, *Organization Development and Transformation,* 20–42; and Christopher G. Worley and Ann E. Feyerherm, "Reflections on the Future of Organization Development," *The Journal of Applied Behavioral Science 39:1* (March 2003): 97–115.
76. Paul F. Buller, "For Successful Strategic Change: Blend OD Practices with Strategic Management," *Organizational Dynamics* (Winter 1988): 42–55; Robert M. Fulmer and Roderick Gilkey, "Blending Corporate Families: Management and Organization Development in a Postmerger Environment," *The Academy of Management Executive 2* (1988): 275–283; and Worley and Feyerherm, "Reflections on the Future of Organization Development."
77. W. Warner Burke, "The New Agenda for Organization Development," *Organizational Dynamics* (Summer 1997): 7–19.
78. This discussion is based on Kathleen D. Dannemiller and Robert W. Jacobs, "Changing the Way Organizations Change: A Revolution of Common Sense," *The Journal of Applied Behavioral Science 28:4* (December 1992): 480–498; and Barbara Benedict Bunker and Billie T. Alban, "Conclusion: What Makes Large Group Interventions Effective?" *The Journal of Applied Behavioral Science 28:4* (December 1992): 570–591.
79. Bunker and Alban, "Conclusion: What Makes Large Group Interventions Effective?"
80. Dave Ulrich, Steve Kerr, and Ron Ashkenas, with Debbie Burke and Patrice Murphy, *The GE Work-Out: How to Implement GE's Revolutionary Method for Busting Bureaucracy and Attacking Organizational Problems—Fast!* (New York: McGraw-Hill, 2002); J. Quinn, "What a Work-Out!" *Performance* (November 1994): 58–63; and B. B. Bunker and B. T. Alban, "Conclusion: What Makes Large Group Interventions Effective?" *The Journal of Applied Behavioral Science 28:4* (December 1992): 572–591.
81. Kurt Lewin, "Frontiers in Group Dynamics: Concepts, Method, and Reality in Social Science," *Human Relations 1* (1947): 5–41; and E. F. Huse and T. G. Cummings, *Organization Development and Change*, 3rd ed. (St. Paul, MN: West, 1985).

82. Based on John Kotter's eight-step model of planned change, which is described in John Kotter, *Leading Change* (Boston, MA: Harvard Business School Press, 1996): 20–25, and "Leading Change: Why Transformation Efforts Fail," *Harvard Business Review* (March–April, 1995): 59–67.

83. "Winning Fair and Square Against a Business Goliath," *Virginian-Pilot* (Oct. 23, 2002): B8; Ilan Mochari, "Climbing Back Up," *Inc Magazine* (March 1, 2002): 92–100; "Ladder Inventors Win Design Case," *The New York Times* (Aug. 19, 2001): 1; Ilan Mochari, "Climbing Back Up," *Inc Magazine* (March 1, 2002): 92–100.

Chapter 9

Human Resource Management and Diversity

1. Keith H. Hammonds, "Handle with Care," *Fast Company* (August 2002): 103–107.

2. Robert L. Mathis and John H. Jackson, *Human Resource Management: Essential Perspectives*, 2nd ed. (Cincinnati, Ohio: South-Western Publishing, 2002).

3. Joy Persaud, "Game On," *People Management* (September 25, 2003): 40–41.

4. Jonathan Poet, "Schools Looking Overseas for Teachers," *Johnson City Press* (April 20, 2001): 6; and Jill Rosenfeld, "How's This for a Tough Assignment?" *Fast Company* (November 1999): 104–106.

5. See Jonathan Tompkins, "Strategic Human Resources Management in Government: Unresolved Issues," *Public Personnel Management* (Spring 2002): 95–110; Noel M. Tichy, Charles J. Fombrun, and Mary Anne Devanna, "Strategic Human Resource Management," *Sloan Management Review* 23 (Winter 1982): 47–61; Cynthia A. Lengnick-Hall and Mark L. Lengnick-Hall, "Strategic Human Resources Management: A Review of the Literature and a Proposed Typology," *Academy of Management Review* 13 (July 1988): 454–470; Eugene B. McGregor, *Strategic Management of Human Knowledge, Skills, and Abilities*, (San Francisco: Jossey-Bass, 1991).

6. Tompkins, "Strategic Human Resource Management in Government: Unresolved Issues."

7. Mark A. Huselid, Susan E. Jackson, and Randall S. Schuler, "Technical and Strategic Human Resource Management Effectiveness as Determinants of Firm Performance," *Academy of Management Journal* 40:1 (1997): 171–188; and John T. Delaney and Mark A. Huselid, "The Impact of Human Resource Management Practices on Perceptions of Organizational Performance," *Academy of Management Journal* 39:4 (1996): 949–969.

8. D. Kneale, "Working at IBM: Intense Loyalty in a Rigid Culture," *The Wall Street Journal* (April 7, 1986): 17.

9. Jeffrey Pfeffer, "Producing Sustainable Competitive Advantage through the Effective Management of People," *Academy of Management Executive* 9:1 (1995): 55–72; and Harry Scarbrough, "Recipe for Success," *People Management* (January 23, 2003): 32–25.

10. James N. Baron and David M. Kreps, "Consistent Human Resource Practices," *California Management Review* 41:3 (Spring 1999): 29–53.

11. Cynthia D. Fisher, "Current and Recurrent Challenges in HRM," *Journal of Management* 15 (1989): 157–180.

12. Dave Ulrich, "A New Mandate for Human Resources," *Harvard Business Review* (January-February 1998): 124–134; Philip H. Mirvis, "Human Resource Management: Leaders, Laggards, and Followers," *Academy of Management Executive* 11:2 (1997): 43–56; Richard McBain, "Attracting, Retaining, and Motivating Capable People," *Manager Update* (Winter 1999): 25–36; and Oren Harari, "Attracting the Best Minds," *Management Review* (April 1998): 23–26.

13. Floyd Kemske, "HR 2008: A Forecast Based on Our Exclusive Study," *Workforce* (January 1998): 46–60.

14. This definition and discussion is based on George Bollander, Scott Snell, and Arthur Sherman, *Managing Human Resources* 12th ed. (Cincinnati, OH: South-Western, 2001); and Scarbrough, "Recipe for Success."

15. Jennifer J. Laabs, "It's OK to Focus on Heart and Soul," *Workforce* (January 1997): 60–69.

16. Mark C. Bolino, William H. Turnley, and James M. Bloodgood, "Citizenship Behavior and the Creation of Social Capital in Organizations," *Academy of Management Review* 27:5 (2002): 505–522.

17. Ellen A. Ensher, Troy R. Nielson, and Elisa Grant-Vallone, "Tales from the Hiring Line: Effects of the Internet and Technology on HR Processes," *Organizational Dynamics* 31:3 (2002): 224–244.

18. Peter Krass, "Precious Resources?" *CFO-IT* (Summer 2003): 38–45.

19. Section 1604.1 of the EEOC Guidelines based on the Civil Rights Act of 1964, Title VII.

20. "YESCO Signs up with Arizona MEP for Quality Improvement," *PR Newswire* (March 11, 2005): 1; Brigid McMenamin, "Payroll Paternalism," *Fortune* (April 16, 2001): 114–120.

21. Charles F. Falk and Kathleen A. Carlson, "Newer Patterns in Management for the Post–Social Contract Era," *Midwest Management Society Proceedings* (1995): 45–52.

22. Richard Pascale, "The False Security of 'Employability,'" *Fast Company* (April-May 1996): 62, 64; and Louisa Wah, "The New Workplace Paradox," *Management Review* (January 1998): 7.

23. Douglas T. Hall and Jonathan E. Moss, "The New Protean Career Contract: Helping Organizations and Employees Adapt," *Organizational Dynamics* (Winter 1998): 22–37.

24. Sean Donahue, "New Jobs for the New Economy," *Business 2.0* (July 1999): 102–109.

25. The discussion of temporary employment agencies is based on David Wessel, "Capital: Temp Workers Have a Lasting Effect," *The Wall Street Journal* (February 1, 2001): A1.

26. Brenda Paik Sunoo, "Temp Firms Turn Up the Heat on Hiring," *Workforce* (April 1999): 50–54.

27. Jaclyn Fierman, "The Contingency Workforce," *Fortune* (January 24, 1994): 30–31.

28. Nancy B. Kurland and Diane E. Bailey, "Telework: The Advantages and Challenges of Working Here, There, Anywhere, Anytime," *Organizational Dynamics* (Autumn 1999): 53–68.

29. Kevin Voigt, "For 'Extreme Telecommuters,' Remote Work Means Really Remote," *The Wall Street Journal* (January 31, 2001): B1.

30. Ibid.

31. John Challenger, "There Is No Future for the Workplace," *Public Management* (February 1999): 20–23.

32. James R. Morris, Wayne F. Cascio, and Clifford Young, "Downsizing After All These Years: Questions and Answers About Who Did It, How Many Did It, and Who Benefited From It," *Organizational Dynamics* (Winter 1999): 78–86; William McKinley, Carol M. Sanchez, and Allen G. Schick, "Organizational Downsizing: Constraining, Cloning, Learning," *Academy of Management Executive* 9:3 (1995): 32–42; and Brett C. Luthans and Steven M. Sommer, "The Impact of Downsizing on Workplace Attitudes," *Group and Organization Management* 2:1 (1999): 46–70.

33. Effective downsizing techniques are discussed in detail in Bob Nelson, "The Care of the Un-Downsized," *Training and Development* (April 1997): 40–43; Shari Caudron, "Teaching Downsizing Survivors How to Thrive," *Personnel Journal* (January 1996): 38; Joel Brockner, "Managing the Effects of Layoffs on Survivors," *California Management Review* (Winter 1992): 9–28; and Kim S. Cameron, "Strategies for Successful Organizational Downsizing," *Human Resource Management* 33:2 (Summer 1994): 189–211.

34. James G. March and Herbert A. Simon, *Organizations* (New York: Wiley, 1958).

35. Richard McBain, "Attracting, Retaining, and Motivating Capable People: A Key to Competitive Advantage," *Manager Update* (Winter 1999): 25–36.

36. Dennis J. Kravetz, *The Human Resources Revolution* (San Francisco, CA: Jossey-Bass, 1989).

37. J. W. Boudreau and S. L. Rynes, "Role of Recruitment in Staffing Utility Analysis," *Journal of Applied Psychology* 70 (1985): 354–366.

38. Brian Dumaine, "The New Art of Hiring Smart," *Fortune* (August 17, 1987): 78–81.

39. This discussion is based on Mathis and Jackson, *Human Resource Management*, Chapter 4, 49–60.

40. Victoria Griffith, "When Only Internal Expertise Will Do," *CFO* (October 1998): 95–96, 102.

41. J. P. Wanous, *Organizational Entry* (Reading, MA: Addison-Wesley, 1980).

42. Samuel Greengard, "Technology Finally Advances HR," *Workforce* (January 2000): 38–41; and Scott Hays, "Hiring on the Web," *Workforce* (August 1999): 77–84.

43. Marlene Piturro, "The Power of E-Cruiting," *Management Review* (January 2000): 33–37.

44. Jerry Useem, "For Sale Online: You," *Fortune* (July 5, 1999): 67–78.

45. George Bohlander, Scott Snell, and Arthur Sherman, *Managing Human Resources*, 12th ed. (Cincinnati, OH: South-Western College Publishing, 2001).

46. Elizabeth Davidson, "You Can Do It..." *People Management* (February 20, 2003): 42–43.

47. Kathryn Tyler, "Employees Can Help Recruit New Talent," *HR Magazine* (September 1996): 57–60.

48. Carol Leonetti Dannhauser, "Putting the Ooh in Recruiting," *Working Woman* (March 2000): 32–34.

49. Ann Harrington, "Anybody Here Want a Job?" *Fortune* (May 15, 2000): 489–498.

50. "Bank of America to Hire 850 Ex-Welfare Recipients," *Johnson City Press* (January 14, 2001): 29; E. Blacharczyk, "Recruiters Challenged by Economy, Shortages, Unskilled," *HR News* (February 1990): B1; Victoria Rivkin, "Visa Relief," *Working Woman* (January 2001): 15.

51. P. W. Thayer, "Somethings Old, Somethings New," *Personnel Psychology 30* (1977): 513–524.

52. J. Ledvinka, *Federal Regulation of Personnel and Human Resource Management* (Boston, MA: Kent, 1982); and Civil Rights Act, Title VII, 42 U.S.C. Section 2000e et seq. (1964).

53. Studies reported in William Poundstone, "Impossible Questions," *Across the Board* (September–October 2003): 44–48.

54. Bohlander, Snell, and Sherman, *Managing Human Resources.*

55. Poundstone, "Impossible Questions." Also see *How Would You Move Mount Fuji? Microsoft's Cult of the Puzzle—How the World's Smartest Companies Select the Most Creative Thinkers* (New York: Little Brown 2003).

56. Bohlander, Snell, and Sherman, *Managing Human Resources.*

57. Meridith Levinson, "How to Hire So You Don't Have to Fire," *CIO* (March 1, 2004): 72–80.

58. "Assessment Centers: Identifying Leadership through Testing," *Small Business Report* (June 1987): 22–24; and W. C. Byham, "Assessment Centers for Spotting Future Managers," *Harvard Business Review* (July–August 1970): 150–167.

59. Mike Thatcher, "'Front-line' Staff Selected by Assessment Center," *Personnel Management* (November 1993): 83.

60. Adam Hanft, "Smarter Hiring, the DDI Way," *Inc.* (March 2003): 92–98.

61. Bernard Keys and Joseph Wolfe, "Management Education and Development: Current Issues and Emerging Trends," *Journal of Management 14* (1988): 205–229.

62. William J. Rothwell and H. C. Kazanas, *Improving On-The-Job Training: How to Establish and Operate a Comprehensive OJT Program* (San Francisco, CA: Jossey-Bass, 1994).

63. Matt Murray, "GE Mentoring Program Turns Underlings into Teachers of the Web," *The Wall Street Journal* (February 15, 2000): B1, B16.

64. Jeanne C. Meister, "The Brave New World of Corporate Education," *The Chronicle of Higher Education* (February 9, 2001): B10; and Meryl Davids Landau, "Corporate Universities Crack Open Their Doors," *The Journal of Business Strategy* (May-June 2000): 18–23.

65. Meister, "The Brave New World of Corporate Education,"; and Edward E. Gordon, "Bridging the Gap," *Training* (September 2003): 30.

66. John Byrne, "The Search for the Young and Gifted," *BusinessWeek* (October 4, 1999): 108–116; and Joel Schettler, "Defense Acquisition University: Weapons of Mass Instruction," *Training* (February 2003): 20–27.

67. Gordon, "Bridging the Gap."

68. Jim Dow, "Spa Attraction," *People Management* (May 29, 2003): 34–35.

69. Walter W. Tornow, "Editor's Note: Introduction to Special Issue on 360-Degree Feedback," *Human Resource Management 32:2/3* (Summer/Fall 1993): 211–219; and Brian O'Reilly, "360 Feedback Can Change Your Life," *Fortune* (October 17, 1994): 93–100.

70. Kris Frieswick, "Truth & Consequences," *CFO* (June 2001): 56–63.

71. This discussion is based on Dick Grote, "Forced Ranking: Behind the Scenes," *Across the Board,* (November–December 2002): 40–45; Matthew Boyle, "Performance Reviews: Perilous Curves Ahead," *Fortune* (May 28, 2001): 187–188; Carol Hymowitz, "Ranking Systems Gain Popularity But Have Many Staffers Riled," (In the Lead column), *The Wall Street Journal* (May 15, 2001): B1; and Frieswick, "Truth & Consequences."

72. Hymowitz, "Ranking Systems Gain Popularity," and Boyle, "Performance Reviews."

73. Lou Kaucic, "Finding Your Stars," *Microsoft Executive Circle* (Summer 2003): 14.

74. V. R. Buzzotta, "Improve Your Performance Appraisals," *Management Review* (August 1988): 40–43; and H. J. Bernardin and R. W. Beatty, *Performance Appraisal: Assessing Human Behavior at Work* (Boston, MA: Kent, 1984).

75. Ibid.

76. Richard I. Henderson, *Compensation Management: Rewarding Performance*, 4th ed. (Reston, VA: Reston, 1985).

77. L. R. Gomez-Mejia, "Structure and Process Diversification, Compensation Strategy, and Firm Performance," *Strategic Management Journal 13* (1992): 381–397; and E. Montemayor, "Congruence Between Pay Policy and Competitive Strategy in High-Performing Firms," *Journal of Management 22:6* (1996): 889–908.

78. Renée F. Broderick and George T. Milkovich, "Pay Planning, Organization Strategy, Structure and 'Fit': A Prescriptive Model of Pay" (paper presented at the 45th Annual Meeting of the Academy of Management, San Diego, CA, August 1985).

79. E. F. Lawler, III, *Strategic Pay: Aligning Organizational Strategies and Pay Systems* (San Francisco, CA: Jossey-Bass, 1990); and R. J. Greene, "Person-Focused Pay: Should It Replace Job-Based Pay?" *Compensation and Benefits Management 9:4* (1993): 46–55.

80. L. Wiener, "No New Skills? No Raise," *U.S. News and World Report* (October 26, 1992): 78.

81. Employee Benefits (Washington, DC: U. S. Chamber of Commerce, 1997): 7.

82. Frank E. Kuzmits, "Communicating Benefits: A Double-Click Away," *Compensation and Benefits Review 30:5* (September-October 1998): 60–64; and Lynn Asinof, "Click and Shift: Workers Control Their Benefits Online," *The Wall Street Journal* (November 27, 1997): C1.

83. Robert S. Catapano-Friedman, "Cafeteria Plans: New Menu for the '90s," *Management Review* (November 1991): 25–29.

84. Yvette Debow, "GE: Easing the Pain of Layoffs," *Management Review* (September 1997): 15–18.

85. "In contact," *Naval History,* (Oct. 2001): 8; Greg Jaffe, "After the Ax Falls, a Plant's Workers Find Good News in the Bad," *The Wall Street Journal* (November 30, 1999): A1, A6.

86. Kenneth Labich, "No More Crude at Texaco," *Fortune* (September 6, 1999): 205–212; and Aaron Bernstein with Michael Arndt, "Racism in the Workplace," *BusinessWeek* (July 30, 2001); Reed Abelson, "Can Respect Be Mandated? Maybe Not Here," *The New York Times* (September 10, 2000): BU1.

87. M. Fine, F. Johnson, and M. S. Ryan, "Cultural Diversity in the Workforce," *Public Personnel Management 19* (1990): 305–319.

88. Taylor H. Cox, "Managing Cultural Diversity: Implications for Organizational Competitiveness," *Academy of Management Executive 5:3* (1991): 45–56; and Faye Rice, "How to Make Diversity Pay," *Fortune* (August 8, 1994): 78–86.

89. Roy Harris, "The Illusion of Inclusion," *CFO* (May 2001): 42–50.

90. Survey results reported in "Diversity Initiatives Shown to Be Critical to Job Seekers," *The New York Times Magazine* (September 14, 2003): 100, part of a special advertisement, "Diversity Works."

91. Lennie Copeland "Valuing Diversity, Part I: Making the Most of Cultural Differences at the Workplace," *Personnel* (June 1988): 52–60.

92. Lee Smith, "The Business Case for Diversity" in "The Diversity Factor," Special Advertising Section, *Fortune* (October 13, 2003): S1–S12.

93. Lennie Copeland, "Learning to Manage a Multi-cultural Workforce," *Training* (May 25, 1988): 48–56; and D. Farid Elashmawi, "Culture Clashes: Barriers to Business," *Managing Diversity 2:11* (August 1993): 1–3.

94. N. Songer, "Workforce Diversity," *B&E Review* (April-June 1991): 3–6.

95. Robert Doktor, Rosalie Tung, and Mary Ann von Glinow, "Future Directions for Management Theory Development," *Academy of Management Review 16* (1991), 362–365; and Mary Munter, "Cross-Cultural Communication for Managers," *Business Horizons* (May-June 1993): 69–78.

96. Renee Blank and Sandra Slipp, "The White Male: An Endangered Species?" *Management Review* (September 1994): 27–32; Michael S. Kimmel, "What Do Men Want?" *Harvard Business Review* (November-December 1993): 50–63; and Sharon Nelton, "Nurturing Diversity," *Nation's Business* (June 1995): 25–27.

97. Marianne Bertrand and Sendhil Mullainathan, *Are Emily and Greg More Employable than Lakisha and Jamal?* National Bureau of Economic Research report, as reported in L. A. Johnson, "What's in a Name: When Emily Gets the Job Over Lakisha," *The Tennessean* (January 4, 2004): 14A.

98. M. Bennett, "A Developmental Approach to Training for Intercultural Sensitivity," *International Journal of Intercultural Relations 10* (1986): 179–196.

99. Reported in "The Diversity Factor," *Fortune* (October 13, 2003): S1–S12.

100. Judy C. Nixon and Judy F. West, "Growing Importance: America Addresses Work Force Diversity," *Business Forum* 25:1-2 (Winter-Spring, 2000): 4–9.
101. Jason Forsythe, "Winning with Diversity," *The New York Times Magazine* (March 28, 2004): special advertising supplement, 65–72; Amy Aronson, "Getting Results: Corporate Diversity, Integration, and Market Penetration," *BusinessWeek* (October 20, 2003): special advertising section, 140–144; and Nixon and West, "America Addresses Work Force Diversity."
102. G. Pascal Zachary, "Mighty is the Mongrel," *Fast Company* (July 2000): 270–284.
103. Elizabeth Wasserman, "A Race for Profits," *MBA Jungle* (March–April 2003): 40–41; Amy Aronson, "Getting Results."
104. Mary Sit-Duvall, "Houston Advertising Guru Helps US Companies Appeal to Hispanic Market," *Knight Ridder Tribune Business News* (May 19, 2002): 1; Chris Sandlund, "There's a New Face to America," *Success* (April 1999): 38–45.
105. Steven Greenhouse, N.Y. Times News Service, "Influx of Immigrants Having Profound Impact on Economy," *Johnson City Press* (September 4, 2000): 9; Richard W. Judy and Carol D'Amico, *Workforce 2020: Work and Workers in the 21st Century* (Indianapolis, IN: Hudson Institute, 1997); statistics reported in Jason Forsythe, "Diversity Works," special advertising supplement to *The New York Times Magazine* (September 14, 2003): 75–100.
106. "Diversity in the Federal Government," report of a roundtable discussion on "Addressing Diversity Issues in the Government," July 10, 2003, moderated by Omar Wasow, executive director of BlackPlanet.com, reported in *The New York Times Magazine* (September 14, 2003): 95–99.
107. Fred L. Fry and Jennifer R. D. Burgess, "The End of the Need for Affirmative Action: Are We There Yet?" *Business Horizons* (November-December 2003): 7–16.
108. Roosevelt Thomas, Jr., "From Affirmative Action to Affirming Diversity," *Harvard Business Review* (March–April 1990): 107–117; Nicholas Lemann, "Taking Affirmative Action Apart," *The New York Times Magazine* (July 11, 1995): 36–43; and Terry H. Anderson, *The Pursuit of Fairness: A History of Affirmative Action* (New York: Oxford University Press, 2004).
109. Sheila Wellington, Marcia Brumit Kropf, and Paulette R. Gerkovich, "What's Holding Women Back?" *Harvard Business Review* (June 2003): 18–19.
110. Julie Amparano Lopez, "Study Says Women Face Glass Walls as Well as Ceilings," *The Wall Street Journal* (March 3, 1992): B1, B2; Ida L. Castro, "Q: Should Women Be Worried About the Glass Ceiling in the Workplace?" *Insight* (February 10, 1997): 24–27; Debra E. Meyerson and Joyce K. Fletcher, "A Modest Manifesto for Shattering the Glass Ceiling," *Harvard Business Review* (January–February 2000): 127–136; and Wellington, Brumit Bropf, and Gerkovich, "What's Holding Women Back?" ; Finnegan, "Different Strokes."
111. Wendy Zellner, "No Way to Treat a Lady," *BusinessWeek* (March 3, 2003): 63, 66; Ann Zimmerman, "Judge to Weigh Wal-Mart Suit for Class Action," *The Wall Street Journal* (September 23, 2003): B1; and Douglas P. Shuit, "People Problems on Every Aisle, Part 1 of 2," *Workforce Management* (February 1, 2004): 26+.
112. Belkin, "The Opt-Out Revolution."
113. Linda Tischler, "Where Are the Women?" *Fast Company* (February 2004): 52–60.
114. John Byrne, "The Price of Balance," *Fast Company* (February 2004); Tischler, "Where Are the Women?" *Fast Company* (February 2004): 52–60; Patricia Sellers, "Power: Do Women Really Want It?" *Fortune* (October 13, 2003): 80–100.
115. C. J. Prince, "Media Myths: The Truth About the Opt- Out Hype," *NAFE Magazine* (Second Quarter, 2004): 14–18; Sellers, "Power: Do Women Really Want It?"
116. Welllington et al., "What's Holding Women Back?"
117. The Leader's Edge/Executive Women Research 2002 survey, reported in "Why Women Leave," *Executive Female* (Summer 2003): 4.
118. Alice H. Eagly and Linda L. Carli, "The Female Leadership Advantage: An Evaluation of the Evidence," *The Leadership Quarterly* 14 (2003): 807–834.
119. C. Soloman, "Careers under Glass," *Personnel Journal* 69:4 (1990): 96–105; and Belle Rose Ragins, Bickley Townsend, and Mary Mattis, "Gender Gap in the Executive Suite: CEOs and Female Executives Report on Breaking the Glass Ceiling," *Academy of Management Executive* 12:1 (1998): 28–42.
120. Eagly and Carli, "The Female Leadership Advantage: An Evaluation of the Evidence"; Sally Helgesen, *The Female Advantage: Women's Ways of Leadership* (New York: Doubleday Currency, 1990); Rochelle Sharpe, "As Leaders, Women Rule: New Studies Find that Female Managers Outshine Their Male Counterparts in Almost Every Measure," *BusinessWeek* (November 20, 2000): 5+; and Del Jones, "2003: Year of the Woman Among the Fortune 500?" (December 30, 2003): 1B
121. Michelle Conlin, "The New Gender Gap," *BusinessWeek* (May 26, 2003): 74–82; and "A Better Education Equals Higher Pay."
122. Quoted in Conlin, "The New Gender Gap."
123. Kathryn M. Bartol, David C. Martin, and Julie A. Kromkowski, "Leadership and the Glass Ceiling: Gender and Ethnic Group Influences on Leader Behaviors at Middle and Executive Managerial Levels," *The Journal of Leadership and Organizational Studies* 9:3 (2003): 8–19; Bernard M. Bass and Bruce J. Avolio, "Shatter the Glass Ceiling: Women May Make Better Managers," *Human Resource Management* 33:4 (Winter 1994): 549–560; and Rochelle Sharpe, "As Leaders, Women Rule," *BusinessWeek* (November 20, 2002): 75–84.
124. Dwight D. Frink, Robert K. Robinson, Brian Reithel, Michelle M. Arthur, Anthony P. Ammeter, Gerald R. Ferris, David M. Kaplan, and Hubert S. Morrisette, "Gender Demography and Organization Performance: A Two-Study Investigation with Convergence," *Group & Organization Management* 28:1 (March 2003): 127–147; Catalyst research project cited in Jason Forsythe, "Winning with Diversity." Also see Jones, "2003: Year of the Woman Among the Fortune 500?"
125. E. G. Collins, "Managers and Lovers," *Harvard Business Review* 61 (1983): 142–153.
126. Sharon A. Lobel, Robert E. Quinn, Lynda St. Clair, and Andrea Warfield, "Love without Sex: The Impact of Psychological Intimacy between Men and Women at Work," *Organizational Dynamics* (Summer 1994): 5–16.
127. William C. Symonds with Steve Hamm and Gail DeGeorge, "Sex on the Job," *BusinessWeek* (February 16, 1998): 30–31.
128. "Sexual Harassment: Vanderbilt University Policy" (Nashville, TN: Vanderbilt University, 1993).
129. Rachel Thompson, "Sexual Harassment: It Doesn't Go with the Territory," *Herizons* 15:3 (Winter 2002): 22–26.
130. Statistics reported in Jim Mulligan and Norman Foy, "Not in My Company: Preventing Sexual Harassment," *Industrial Management* (September/October 2003): 26–29; Also see *EEOC Charge Complaints* at http://www.eeoc.gov.
131. Jack Corcoran, "Of Nice and Men," *Success* (June 1998): 65–67.
132. Barbara Carton, "At Jenny Craig, Men Are Ones Who Claim Sex Discrimination," *The Wall Street Journal* (November 29, 1994): A1, A11.
133. Thompson, "Sexual Harassment: It Doesn't Go with the Territory."
134. Hammonds, "Handle with Care."

Chapter 10

Productivity through Management and Quality Control Systems

1. Gary McWilliams, "Gateway Adopts Tough New Style as Sales Tumble," *The Wall Street Journal* (May 28, 2002): B1, B4; Mike Musgrove, "Gateway's Changes Yield Little Reward," *The Washington Post* (January 11, 2003): E1; and http://www.gateway.com.
2. Deborah Solomon and Susanne Craig, "Taking Stock: SEC Blasts Big Board Oversight of 'Specialist' Trading Firms," *The Wall Street Journal* (November 3, 2003): A1, A6.
3. John A. Byrne with Mike France and Wendy Zellner, "The Environment Was Ripe for Abuse," *BusinessWeek* (February 25, 2002): 118–120.
4. Susan Pulliam, "The 'It Wasn't Me' Defense; CEOs from Enron to Sotheby's Blame Scandals on Underlings; Too Busy for All The Details?" *The Wall Street Journal* (July 9, 2004): B1.
5. Douglas S. Sherwin, "The Meaning of Control," *Dunn's Business Review* (January 1956).
6. Russ Banham, "Nothin' But Net Gain," *eCFO* (Fall 2001): 32–33.
7. Evgenia Peretz, "The Lady and the Heel," *Vanity Fair*, Aug. 2005, pp. 134–136 and 172–175.
8. Kevin McCoy and Julie Appleby, "Problems with Staffing, Training Can Cost Lives," *USA Today* (May 26, 2004): accessed at http://www.usatoday.com.
9. Carol Hymowitz, "As Economy Slows, Executives Learn Ways to Make Predictions," *The Wall Street Journal* (August 21, 2001): Lead column, B1.

10. Jennifer S. Lee, "Tracking Sales and the Cashiers," *The New York Times* (July 11, 2001): C1, C6; Anna Wilde Mathews, "New Gadgets Track Truckers' Every Move," *The Wall Street Journal* (July 14, 1997): B1, B10.
11. Steve Stecklow, "Kentucky's Teachers Get Bonuses, but Some Are Caught Cheating," *The Wall Street Journal* (September 2, 1997): A1, A5.
12. Richard E. Crandall, "Keys to Better Performance Measurement," *Industrial Management* (January–February 2002): 19–24; Christopher D. Ittner and David F. Larcker, "Coming Up Short on Nonfinancial Performance Measurement," *Harvard Business Review* (November 2003): 88–95.
13. Crandall, "Keys to Better Performance Measurement."
14. Richard H. Snyder, "How I Engineered a Small Business," *Strategic Finance* (May 1999).
15. Adam Lashinsky, "Meg and the Machine," *Fortune* (September 1, 2003): 68–78.
16. Sumantra Ghoshal, *Strategic Control* (St. Paul, Minnesota: West, 1986); and Robert N. Anthony, John Dearden, and Norton M. Bedford, *Management Control Systems*, 5th ed. (Homewood, IL: Irwin, 1984).
17. Anthony, Dearden, and Bedford, *Management Control Systems*.
18. Participation in budget setting is described in a number of studies, including Neil C. Churchill, "Budget Choice: Planning versus Control," *Harvard Business Review* (July-August 1984): 150–164; Peter Brownell, "Leadership Style, Budgetary Participation, and Managerial Behavior," *Accounting Organizations and Society 8* (1983): 307–321; and Paul J. Carruth and Thurrell O. McClandon, "How Supervisors React to 'Meeting the Budget' Pressure," *Management Accounting 66* (November 1984): 50–54.
19. Donna Fenn, "Personnel Best," *Inc.* (February 2000): 75–83.
20. William G. Ouchi, "Markets, Bureaucracies, and Clans," *Administrative Science Quarterly 25* (1980): 129–141; and B. R. Baligia and Alfred M. Jaeger, "Multinational Corporations: Control Systems and Delegation Issues," *Journal of International Business Studies* (Fall 1984): 25–40.
21. Sherwin, "The Meaning of Control."
22. Mathews, "New Gadgets Track Truckers' Every Move," B10.
23. Fara Warner, "Think Lean," *Fast Company* (February 2002): 40, 42.
24. Peter Strozniak, "Toyota Alters Face of Production," *Industry Week* (August 13, 2001): 46–48.
25. Emily Esterson, "First-Class Delivery," *Inc. Technology* (September 15, 1998): 89.
26. W. Bouce Chew, "No-Nonsense Guide to Measuring Productivity," *Harvard Business Review* (January-February 1988): 110–118.
27. V. Feigenbaum, *Total Quality Control: Engineering and Management* (New York: McGraw-Hill, 1961); John Lorinc, "Dr. Deming's Traveling Quality Show," *Canadian Business* (September 1990): 38–42; Mary Walton, *The Deming Management Method* (New York: Dodd-Meade & Co., 1986); and J. M. Juran and Frank M. Gryna, eds., *Juran's Quality Control Handbook*, 4th ed. (New York: McGraw-Hill, 1988).
28. Edward E. Lawler III and Susan A. Mohrman, "Quality Circles after the Fad," *Harvard Business Review* (January-February 1985): 65–71; and Philip C. Thompson, *Quality Circles: How to Make Them Work in America* (New York: AMACOM, 1982).
29. Howard Rothman, "You Need Not Be Big to Benchmark," *Nation's Business* (December 1992): 64–65.
30. Tracy Mayor, "Six Sigma Comes to IT: Targeting Perfection," *CIO* (December 1, 2003): 62–70; Hal Plotkin, "Six Sigma: What It Is and How to Use It," *Harvard Management Update* (June 1999): 3–4; Tom Rancour and Mike McCracken, "Applying 6 Sigma Methods for Breakthrough Safety Performance," *Professional Safety 45:10* (October 2000): 29–32; G. Hasek, "Merger Marries Quality Efforts," *Industry Week* (August 21, 2000): 89–92; and Lee Clifford, "Why You Can Safely Ignore Six Sigma," *Fortune* (January 22, 2001): 140.
31. Dick Smith and Jerry Blakeslee "The New Strategic Six Sigma," *Training & Development* (September 2002): 45–52; Michael Hammer and Jeff Goding, "Putting Six Sigma in Perspective," *Quality* (October 2001): 58–62; and Mayor, "Six Sigma Comes to IT."
32. Plotkin, "Six Sigma: What It Is"; Timothy Aeppel, "Nicknamed 'Nag,' She's Just Doing Her Job," *The Wall Street Journal* (May 14, 2002): B1, B12; John S. McClenahen, "ITT's Value Champion," *IndustryWeek* (May 2002): 44–49.
33. Philip R. Thomas, Larry J. Gallace, and Kenneth R. Martin, *Quality Alone Is Not Enough* (AMA Management Briefing), (New York: American Management Association, August 1992).
34. Kate Kane, "L. L. Bean Delivers the Goods," *Fast Company* (August/September 1997): 104–113.
35. Julie Sloane, "Small & Global: Following the Action," *FSB* (June 2004): 39-40.
36. Clifford, "Why You Can Safely Ignore Six Sigma"; and Hammer and Goding, "Putting Six Sigma in Perspective."
37. Brian Bremmer and Chester Dawson, "Can Anything Stop Toyota?" *BusinessWeek* (November 17, 2003): 114–122; and Norihiko Shirouzu and Sebastian Moffett, "Bumpy Road: As Toyota Closes In on GM, It Develops a Big Three Problem," *The Wall Street Journal* (August 4, 2004): A1.
38. Syed Hasan Jaffrey, "ISO 9001 Made Easy," *Quality Progress 37:5* (May 2004): 104; Frank C. Barnes, "ISO 9000 Myth and Reality: A Reasonable Approach to ISO 9000," *SAM Advanced Management Journal* (Spring 1998): 23–30; and Thomas H. Stevenson and Frank C. Barnes, "Fourteen Years of ISO 9000: Impact, Criticisms, Costs, and Benefits," *Business Horizons* (May-June 2001): 45–51.
39. David Amari, Don James, and Cathy Marley, "ISO 9001 Takes On a New Role—Crime Fighter," *Quality Progress 37:5* (May 2004): 57+.
40. Don L. Bohl, Fred Luthans, John W. Slocum Jr., and Richard M. Hodgetts, "Ideas That Will Shape the Future of Management Practice," *Organizational Dynamics* (Summer 1996): 7–14.
41. John Berry, "How To Apply EVA to I.T.," *CIO* (January 15, 2003): 94–98.
42. Perry Pascarella, "Open the Books to Unleash Your People," *Management Review* (May 1998): 58–60.
43. Mel Mandell, "Accounting Challenges Overseas," *World Trade* (December 1, 2001).
44. This discussion is based on a review of the balanced scorecard in Richard L. Daft, *Organization Theory and Design*, 7th ed. (Cincinnati, OH: South-Western, 2001): 300–301.
45. "On Balance," a *CFO* Interview with Robert Kaplan and David Norton, *CFO* (February 2001): 73–78; and Bill Birchard, "Intangible Assets + Hard Numbers = Soft Finance," *Fast Company* (October 1999): 316–336.
46. Robert Kaplan and David Norton, "The Balanced Scorecard: Measures that Drive Performance," *Harvard Business Review* (January-February 1992): 71–79; and Chee W. Chow, Kamal M. Haddad, and James E. Williamson, "Applying the Balanced Scorecard to Small Companies," *Management Accounting 79:2* (August 1997): 21–27.
47. Based on Kaplan and Norton, "The Balanced Scorecard"; Chow, Haddad, and Williamson, "Applying the Balanced Scorecard"; and Cathy Lazere, "All Together Now," *CFO* (February 1998): 28–36.
48. Nils-Göran Olve, Carl-Johan Petri, Jan Roy, and Sofie Roy, "Twelve Years Later: Understanding and Realizing the Value of Balanced Scorecards," *Ivey Business Journal* (May-June 2004); Eric M. Olson and Stanley F. Slater, "The Balanced Scorecard, Competitive Strategy, and Performance," *Business Horizons* (May-June 2002): 11–16; and Eric Berkman, "How to Use the Balanced Scorecard," *CIO* (May 15, 2002): 93–100.
49. Ibid.; and Brigitte W. Schay, Mary Ellen Beach, Jacqueline A. Caldwell, and Christelle LaPolice, "Using Standardized Outcome Measures in the Federal Government," *Human Resource Management 41:3* (Fall 2002): 355–368.
50. Olve et al., "Twelve Years Later: Understanding and Realizing the Value of Balanced Scorecards."
51. McWilliams, "Gateway Adopts Tough New Style as Sales Tumble;" Jeffrey Burt and Shelley Solheim, "Users Back Moves; PC Maker's Store Closings, New Retail Direction Supported," *eWeek* (April 12, 2004): 53; and "Gateway Inc.: Narrower Operating Loss Seen for 2nd Period as Sales Grow," *The Wall Street Journal* (June 16, 2004): A1.

Chapter 11

Foundations of Behavior in Organizations

1. Julia Lawlor, "Personality 2.0," *Red Herring* (April 1, 2001): 98–103.
2. See Mark C. Bolino, William H. Turnley, and James M. Bloodgood, "Citizenship Behaviors and the Creation of Social Capital in Organizations," *Academy of Management Review 27:4* (2002): 505–522.
3. John W. Newstrom and Keith Davis, *Organizational Behavior: Human Behavior at Work*, 11th ed. (Burr Ridge, IL: McGraw-Hill Irwin, 2002).
4. Feuerstein, "E-marketing Firm Lands Hotshot CEO," *San Francisco Business Times* (January 17, 2000): 1–2; and J. Kaufman, "What Happens When a 20-Something Whiz Is Suddenly the Boss," *The Wall Street Journal* (October 8, 1999): A1, A10.
5. S. J. Breckler, "Empirical Validation of Affect, Behavior, and Cognition as Distinct Components of Attitude," *Journal of Personality and Social Psychology* (May 1984): 1191–1205; and J. M. Olson and M. P. Zanna, "Attitudes and Attitude Change," *Annual Review of Psychology 44* (1993): 117–154.

6. Mayank Chhaya, "Umang Gupta of Keynote Systems," *News India-Times* (Jan. 7, 2005): 22; Bob Brown, "Q&A: Gupta Touts Network Services," *Network World* (April 8, 2002): 31–32; Hal Lancaster, "A Founder's Lesson: Market Reality Matters More than a Mission," *The Wall Street Journal* (Nov. 2, 1999): B1.

7. M. T. Iaffaldano and P. M. Muchinsky, "Job Satisfaction and Job Performance: A Meta-Analysis," *Psychological Bulletin* (March 1985): 251–273; C. Ostroff, "The Relationship between Satisfaction, Attitudes, and Performance: An Organizational Level Analysis," *Journal of Applied Psychology* (December 1992): 963–974; and M. M. Petty, G. W. McGee, and J. W. Cavender, "A Meta-Analysis of the Relationship between Individual Job Satisfaction and Individual Performance," *Academy of Management Review* (October 1984): 712–721.

8. Sue Shellenbarger, "Companies Are Finding Real Payoffs in Aiding Employee Satisfaction," *The Wall Street Journal* (October 11, 2000): Work and Family column, B1.

9. "Worried at Work: Generation Gap in Workplace Woes," International Survey Research, *http://www.isrsurveys.com* accessed on May 19, 2004.

10. Tony Schwartz, "The Greatest Sources of Satisfaction in the Workplace Are Internal and Emotional," *Fast Company* (November 2000): 398–402.

11. Marshall Goldsmith, "To Help Others Develop, Start with Yourself," *Fast Company* (March, 2004): 100; and Bonnie Miller Rubin and Sharman Stein, "Think Outside the [Cereal] Box," *Working Mother* (October 2002): 60.

12. William C. Symonds, "Where Paternalism Equals Good Business," *BusinessWeek* (July 20, 1998): 16E4, 16E6.

13. "The People Factor: Global Survey Shows That an Engaged Workforce Measurably Improves the Bottom Line—and How," International Survey Research, *http://www.isrsurveys.com* accessed on May 19, 2004.

14. "Employee Commitment; U.S.: Leader or Follower?" International Survey Research, *http://www.isrsurveys.com* accessed on May 19, 2004.

15. W. Chan Kin and Renée Mauborgne, "Fair Process: Managing in the Knowledge Economy," *Harvard Business Review* (January 2003): 127–136.

16. Jennifer Laabs, "They Want More Support—Inside and Outside of Work," *Workforce* (November 1998): 54–56.

17. For a discussion of cognitive dissonance theory, see Leon A. Festinger, *Theory of Cognitive Dissonance* (Stanford, CA: Stanford University Press, 1957).

18. D. A. Kravitz and S. L. Klineberg, "Reactions to Two Versions of Affirmative Action Among Whites, Blacks, and Hispanics," *Journal of Applied Psychology 85* (2000): 597–611; and Robert J. Grossman, "Race in the Workplace," *HR Magazine* (March 2000): 41–45.

19. J. A. Deutsch, W. G. Young, and T. J. Kalogeris, "The Stomach Signals Satiety," *Science* (April 1978): 22–33.

20. Richard B. Chase and Sriram Dasu, "Want to Perfect Your Company's Service? Use Behavioral Science," *Harvard Business Review* (June 2001): 79–84.

21. H. H. Kelley, "Attribution in Social Interaction," in E. Jones et al. (eds.), *Attribution: Perceiving the Causes of Behavior* (Morristown, NJ: General Learning Press, 1972).

22. See J. M. Digman, "Personality Structure: Emergence of the Five-Factor Model," *Annual Review of Psychology 41* (1990): 417–440; M. R. Barrick and M. K. Mount, "Autonomy as a Moderator of the Relationships Between the Big Five Personality Dimensions and Job Performance," *Journal of Applied Psychology* (February 1993): 111–118; and J. S. Wiggins and A. L. Pincus, "Personality: Structure and Assessment," *Annual Review of Psychology 43* (1992): 473–504.

23. Michelle Leder, "Is That Your Final Answer?" *Working Woman* (December–January 2001): 18; "Can You Pass the Job Test?" *Newsweek* (May 5, 1986): 46–51.

24. Alan Farnham, "Are You Smart Enough to Keep Your Job?" *Fortune* (January 15, 1996): 34–47.

25. Cora Daniels, "Does This Man Need a Shrink?" *Fortune* (February 5, 2001): 205–208.

26. Daniel Goleman, "Leadership That Gets Results," *Harvard Business Review* (March–April 2000): 79–90; Richard E. Boyatzis and Daniel Goleman, *The Emotional Competence Inventory–University Edition* (The Hay Group, 2001); and Daniel Goleman, *Emotional Intelligence: Why It Can Matter More than IQ* (New York: Bantam Books, 1995).

27. Farnham, "Are You Smart Enough to Keep Your Job?"

28. Hendrie Weisinger, *Emotional Intelligence at Work* (San Francisco, Calif.: Jossey–Bass, 2000); D. C. McClelland, "Identifying Competencies with Behavioral-Event Interviews," *Psychological Science* (Spring 1999): 331–339; Daniel Goleman, "Leadership That Gets Results," *Harvard Business Review* (March–April 2000): 78–90; D. Goleman, *Working with Emotional Intelligence* (New York: Bantam Books, 1999); and Lorie Parch, "Testing... 1, 2, 3," *Working Woman* (October 1997): 74–78.

29. "Dumb and Dumberer—Hall of Infamy," *MBA Jungle* (October–November 2003): 49.

30. Goleman, "Leadership That Gets Results."

31. J. B. Rotter, "Generalized Expectancies for Internal versus External Control of Reinforcement," *Psychological Monographs 80:609* (1966).

32. Andy Serwer, "There's Something about Cisco," *Fortune* (May 15, 2000): Stephanie N. Mehta, "Cisco Fractures Its Own Fairy Tale," *Fortune* (May 14, 2001): 104–112.

33. P. E. Spector, "Behavior in Organizations as a Function of Employee's Locus of Control," *Psychological Bulletin* (May 1982): 482–497.

34. T. W. Adorno, E. Frenkel-Brunswick, D. J. Levinson, and R. N. Sanford, *The Authoritarian Personality* (New York: Harper & Row, 1950).

35. Mike Freeman, "A New Breed of Coaches Relates Better to Players," *The New York Times* (August 19, 2001): Y36.

36. Niccolo Machiavelli, *The Prince*, trans. George Bull (Middlesex, UK: Penguin, 1961).

37. Richard Christie and Florence Geis, *Studies in Machiavellianism* (New York: Academic Press, 1970).

38. R. G. Vleeming, "Machiavellianism: A Preliminary Review," *Psychological Reports* (February 1979): 295–310.

39. Christie and Geis, *Studies in Machiavellianism*.

40. Carl Jung, *Psychological Types* (London, UK: Routledge and Kegan Paul, 1923).

41. Mary H. McCaulley, "Research on the MBTI and Leadership: Taking the Critical First Step," Keynote Address, The Myers-Briggs Type Indicator and Leadership: An International Research Conference, January 12–14, 1994.

42. Alison Overhold, "Are You a Polyolefin Optimizer? Take This Quiz!" *Fast Company* (April 2004): 37.

43. Charles A. O'Reilly III, Jennifer Chatman, and David F. Caldwell, "People and Organizational Culture: A Profile Comparison Approach to Assessing Person-Organization Fit," *Academy of Management Journal 34:3* (1991): 487–516.

44. Anna Muoio, "Should I Go .Com?" *Fast Company* (July 2000): 164–172.

45. Leder, "Is That Your Final Answer?"

46. David A. Kolb, "Management and the Learning Process," *California Management Review 18:3* (Spring 1976): 21–31.

47. De' Ann Weimer, "The Houdini of Consumer Electronics," *BusinessWeek* (June 22, 1998): 88, 92; and *http://www.bestbuy.com* accessed on May 19, 2004.

48. David. A. Kolb, I. M. Rubin, and J. M. McIntyre, *Organizational Psychology: An Experimental Approach*, 3rd ed. (Englewood Cliffs, NJ: Prentice-Hall, 1984): 27–54.

49. Stephanie Gruner, "Our Company, Ourselves," *Inc.* (April 1998): 127–128.

50. Ira Sager, "Big Blue's Blunt Bohemian," *BusinessWeek* (June 14, 1999): 107–112.

51. Paul Roberts, "The Best Interest of the Patient Is the Only Interest to be Considered," *Fast Company* (April 1999): 149–162.

52. Jim Bohman, "Coaches Helping Bosses Improve,' *Dayton Daily News* (Sept. 19, 2004): D1; Larissa MacFarquhar, "The Better Boss," *The New Yorker* (April 22, 2002): 114–136.

53. T. A. Beehr and R. S. Bhagat, *Human Stress and Cognition in Organizations: An Integrated Perspective* (New York: Wiley, 1985); and Bruce Cryer, Rollin McCraty, and Doc Childre, "Pull the Plug on Stress," *Harvard Business Review* (July 2003): 102–107.

54. Ekramul Hoque and Mayenul Islam, "Contribution of Some Behavioural Factors to Absenteeism of Manufacturing Workers in Bangladesh," *Pakistan Journal of Psychological Research 18:3-4* (Winter 2003): 81–96; U.S. research study conducted by HERO, a not-for-profit coalition of organizations with common interests in health promotion, disease management, and health-related productivity research, and reported in Bruce Cryer, Rollin McCraty, and Doc Childre, "Pull the Plug on Stress," *Harvard Business Review* (July 2003): 102–107.

55. M. Friedman and R. Rosenman, *Type A Behavior and Your Heart* (New York: Knopf, 1974).

56. John L. Haughom, "How to Pass the Stress Test," *CIO* (May 1, 2003): 50–52; Quote from Cora Daniels, "The Last Taboo," *Fortune* (October 28, 2002): 137–144.
57. Haughom, "How to Pass the Stress Test."
58. U.S. research study results by the National Institute for Occupational Safety and Health, reported in Daniels, "The Last Taboo."
59. "Wicked Whisper," *London Daily Mail* (March 29. 2005): 24; Tom King, "'Bourne' to Be Wild," *The Wall Street Journal* (May 3, 2002): W1, W7.
60. Kris Maher, "At Verizon Call Center, Stress Is Seldom On Hold," *The Wall Street Journal* (January 16, 2001): B1, B12.
61. Donalee Moulton, "Buckling Under the Pressure," *OH & S Canada* 19:8 (December 2003): 36.
62. Claire Sykes, "Say Yes to Less Stress,"*Office Solutions* (July–August 2003): 26; and Andrea Higbie, "Quick Lessons in the Fine Old Art of Unwinding," *The New York Times* (February 25, 2001): BU–10.
63. Leslie Gross Klass, "Quiet Time at Work Helps Employee Stress," *Johnson City Press* (January 28, 2001): 30.
64. Moulton, "Buckling Under the Pressure."
65. David T. Gordon, "Balancing Act," *CIO* (October 15, 2001): 58–62.
66. Lawlor, "Personality 2.0."

Chapter 12

Leadership in Organizations

1. John A. Bryne, "How to Lead Now: Getting Extraordinary Performance When You Can't Pay For It," *Fast Company* (August 2003): 62–70.
2. Melanie Warner, "Confessions of a Control Freak," *Fortune* (September 4, 2000): 130–140; Ian Mount, "Underlings: That's Mister Conway to You. And I Am Not a People Person," *Business 2.0* (February 2002): 53–58.
3. Gary Yukl, "Managerial Leadership: A Review of Theory and Research," *Journal of Management 15* (1989): 251–289.
4. James M. Kouzes and Barry Z. Posner, "The Credibility Factor: What Followers Expect from Their Leaders," *Management Review* (January 1990): 29–33.
5. James E. Colvard, "Managers Vs. Leaders," *Government Executive 35:9* (July 2003): 82–84.
6. Richard L. Daft, *The Leadership Experience*, 3rd ed. (Cincinnati, OH: South-Western, 2005).
7. G. A. Yukl, *Leadership in Organizations* (Englewood Cliffs, NJ: Prentice-Hall, 1981); and S. C. Kohs and K. W. Irle, "Prophesying Army Promotion," *Journal of Applied Psychology 4* (1920): 73–87.
8. R. Albanese and D. D. Van Fleet, *Organizational Behavior: A Managerial Viewpoint* (Hinsdale, IL: The Dryden Press, 1983).
9. Gary Yukl, Angela Gordon, and Tom Taber, "A Hierarchical Taxonomy of Leadership Behavior: Integrating a Half Century of Behavior Research," *Journal of Leadership and Organizational Studies 9:1* (2002): 13–32.
10. C. A. Schriesheim and B. J. Bird, "Contributions of the Ohio State Studies to the Field of Leadership," *Journal of Management 5* (1979): 135–145; and C. L. Shartle, "Early Years of the Ohio State University Leadership Studies," *Journal of Management 5* (1979): 126–134.
11. Patrick J. Sauer, "Are You Ready for Some Football Clichés?" *Inc.* (October 2003): 96–99.
12. P. C. Nystrom, "Managers and the High-High Leader Myth," *Academy of Management Journal 21* (1978): 325–331; and L. L. Larson, J. G. Hunt, and Richard N. Osborn, "The Great High-High Leader Behavior Myth: A Lesson from Occam's Razor," *Academy of Management Journal 19* (1976): 628–641.
13. R. Likert, "From Production- and Employee-Centeredness to Systems 1–4," *Journal of Management 5* (1979): 147–156.
14. Robert R. Blake and Jane S. Mouton, *The Managerial Grid III* (Houston, TX: Gulf, 1985).
15. Jo Napolitano, "No, She Doesn't Breathe Fire," *The New York Times* (September 1, 2002): Section 3, 2; Katharine Mieszkowski, "Changing Tires, Changing the World," *Fast Company* (October 1999): 58–60.
16. Fred E. Fiedler, "Assumed Similarity Measures as Predictors of Team Effectiveness," *Journal of Abnormal and Social Psychology 49* (1954): 381–388; F. E. Fiedler, *Leader Attitudes and Group Effectiveness* (Urbana, IL: University of Illinois Press, 1958); and F. E. Fiedler, *A Theory of Leadership Effectiveness* (New York: McGraw-Hill, 1967).
17. Fred E. Fiedler and M. M. Chemers, *Leadership and Effective Management* (Glenview, IL: Scott, Foresman, 1974).
18. David Rynecki, "Putting the Muscle Back in the Bull," *Fortune* (April 5, 2004): 162–170; and David Rynecki, "Can Stan O'Neal Save Merrill?" *Fortune* (September 20, 2002): 76–88.
19. Rynecki, "Putting the Muscle Back in the Bull."
20. Fred E. Fiedler, "Engineer the Job to Fit the Manager," *Harvard Business Review 43* (1965): 115–122; and F. E. Fiedler, M. M. Chemers, and L. Mahar, *Improving Leadership Effectiveness: The Leader Match Concept* (New York: Wiley, 1976).
21. R. Singh, "Leadership Style and Reward Allocation: Does Least Preferred Coworker Scale Measure Tasks and Relation Orientation?" *Organizational Behavior and Human Performance 27* (1983): 178–197; and D. Hosking, "A Critical Evaluation of Fiedler's Contingency Hypotheses," *Progress in Applied Psychology 1* (1981): 103–154.
22. Paul Hersey and Kenneth H. Blanchard, *Management of Organizational Behavior: Utilizing Human Resources*, 4th ed. (Englewood Cliffs, N.J.: Prentice-Hall, 1982).
23. Jonathan Kaufman, "A McDonald's Owner Becomes a Role Model for Black Teenagers," *The Wall Street Journal* (August 23, 1995): A1, A6.
24. M. G. Evans, "The Effects of Supervisory Behavior on the Path-Goal Relationship," *Organizational Behavior and Human Performance 5* (1970): 277–298; M. G. Evans, "Leadership and Motivation: A Core Concept," *Academy of Management Journal 13* (1970): 91–102; and B. S. Georgopoulos, G. M. Mahoney, and N. W. Jones, "A Path-Goal Approach to Productivity," *Journal of Applied Psychology 41* (1957): 345–353.
25. Robert J. House, "A Path-Goal Theory of Leader Effectiveness," *Administrative Science Quarterly 16* (1971): 321–338.
26. M. G. Evans, "Leadership," in *Organizational Behavior*, ed. S. Kerr (Columbus, OH: Grid, 1974).
27. Robert J. House and Terrence R. Mitchell, "Path-Goal Theory of Leadership," *Journal of Contemporary Business* (Autumn 1974): 81–97.
28. Charles A. O'Reilly III and Jeffrey Pfeffer, "Star Makers," book excerpt from *From Hidden Value: How Great Companies Achieve Extraordinary Results with Ordinary People* (Cambridge, MA: Harvard Business School Press, 2000) published in *CIO* (September 15, 2000): 226–246.
29. Charles Greene, "Questions of Causation in the Path-Goal Theory of Leadership," *Academy of Management Journal 22* (March 1979): 22–41; and C. A. Schriesheim and Mary Ann von Glinow, "The Path-Goal Theory of Leadership: A Theoretical and Empirical Analysis," *Academy of Management Journal 20* (1977): 398–405.
30. S. Kerr and J. M. Jermier, "Substitutes for Leadership: Their Meaning and Measurement," *Organizational Behavior and Human Performance 22* (1978): 375–403; and Jon P. Howell and Peter W. Dorfman, "Leadership and Substitutes for Leadership among Professional and Nonprofessional Workers," *Journal of Applied Behavioral Science 22* (1986): 29–46.
31. The terms *transactional* and *transformational* come from James M. Burns, *Leadership* (New York: Harper & Row, 1978); and Bernard M. Bass, "Leadership: Good, Better, Best," *Organizational Dynamics 13* (Winter 1985): 26–40.
32. Katherine J. Klein and Robert J. House, "On Fire: Charismatic Leadership and Levels of Analysis," *Leadership Quarterly 6:2* (1995): 183–198.
33. Jay A. Conger and Rabindra N. Kanungo, "Toward a Behavioral Theory of Charismatic Leadership in Organizational Settings," *Academy of Management Review 12* (1987): 637–647; Walter Kiechel III, "A Hard Look at Executive Vision," *Fortune* (October 23, 1989): 207–211; and William L. Gardner and Bruce J. Avolio, "The Charismatic Relationship: A Dramaturgical Perspective," *Academy of Management Review 23:1* (1998): 32–58.
34. Manfred Kets de Vries, "'Doing an Alexander': Lessons on Leadership by a Master Conqueror," *European Management Journal 21:3* (2003): 370–375.
35. Steve Lohr, "On a Roll, Dell Enters Uncharted Territory," *The New York Times* (August 25, 2002): Section 3, 1; and Andrew Park with Faith Keenan and Cliff Edwards, "Whose Lunch Will Dell Eat Next?" *BusinessWeek* (August 12, 2002): 66–67.
36. Robert J. House, "Research Contrasting the Behavior and Effects of Reputed Charismatic vs. Reputed Non-Charismatic Leaders" (paper presented as part of a symposium, "Charismatic Leadership: Theory and Evidence," Academy of Management, San Diego, CA, 1985).
37. Robert J. House and Jane M. Howell, "Personality and Charismatic Leadership," *Leadership Quarterly 3:2* (1992): 81–108; and Jennifer O'Connor, Michael D. Mumford, Timothy C. Clifton, Theodore L. Gessner, and Mary Shane Connelly, "Charismatic Leaders and Destructiveness: A Historiometric Study," *Leadership Quarterly 6:4* (1995): 529–555.
38. Laura M. Holson, "Confessions of a Perplexed Mind," *The New York Times* (Jan. 17, 2005): C1.

39. Bernard M. Bass, "Theory of Transformational Leadership Redux," *Leadership Quarterly* 6:4 (1995): 463–478; Noel M. Tichy and Mary Anne Devanna, *The Transformational Leader* (New York: John Wiley & Sons, 1986); and Badrinarayan Shankar Pawar and Kenneth K. Eastman, "The Nature and Implications of Contextual Influences on Transformational Leadership: A Conceptual Examination," *Academy of Management Review* 22:1 (1997): 80–109.

40. Richard L. Daft and Robert H. Lengel, *Fusion Leadership: Unlocking the Subtle Forces that Change People and Organizations* (San Francisco, CA: Berrett-Koehler, 1998).

41. Taly Dvir, Dov Eden, Bruce J. Avolio, and Boas Shamir, "Impact of Transformational Leadership on Follower Development and Performance: A Field Experiment," *Academy of Management Journal* 45:4 (2002): 735–744.

42. Timothy A. Judge and Joyce E. Bono, "Five-Factor Model of Personality and Transformational Leadership," *Journal of Applied Psychology* 85:5 (October 2000): 751+.

43. Paul Nadler, "The Litttle Things That Help Make Wells a Giant," *American Banker* (December 10, 2003): 4; John R. Enger, "Cross-Sell Campaign," *Banking Strategies* 77:6 (November–December 2001): 34; Bethany McLean, "Is This Guy the Best Banker in America?" *Fortune* (July 6, 1998): 126–128; and Jacqueline S. Gold, "Bank to the Future," *Institutional Investor* (September 2001): 54–63.

44. Henry Mintzberg, *Power In and Around Organizations* (Englewood Cliffs, NJ: Prentice-Hall, 1983); and Jeffrey Pfeffer, *Power in Organizations* (Marshfield, MA: Pitman, 1981).

45. Andy Raskin, "The Accidental Leader," *Business 2.0* (November 2001): 32.

46. J. R. P. French, Jr., and B. Raven, "The Bases of Social Power," in *Group Dynamics*, ed. D. Cartwright and Alvin F. Zander (Evanston, IL: Row, Peterson, 1960).

47. G. A. Yukl and T. Taber, "The Effective Use of Managerial Power," *Personnel* (March-April 1983): 37–44.

48. Jay A. Conger, "The Necessary Art of Persuasion," *Harvard Business Review* (May-June 1998): 84–95.

49. Andy Reinhardt, "Meet AMD's Rags-to-Riches Heir Apparent," *BusinessWeek* (October 2, 2000): 112–117.

50. John A. Byrne, "How to Lead Now," *Fast Company* (August 2003): 62–70.

51. Thomas A. Stewart, "New Ways to Exercise Power," *Fortune* (November 6, 1989): 52–64; and Thomas A. Stewart, "CEOs See Clout Shifting," *Fortune* (November 6, 1989): 66.

52. Joseph L. Badaracco, Jr. "A Lesson for the Times: Learning From Quiet Leaders," *Ivey Business Journal* (January-February 2003): 1–6; and Matthew Gwyther, "Back to the Wall," *Management Today* (February 2003): 58–61.

53. See James C. Collins, *From Good to Great: Why Some Companies Make the Leap... And Others Don't* (New York: HarperCollins 2001); Charles A. O'Reilly III and Jeffrey Pfeffer, *Hidden Value: How Great Companies Achieve Extraordinary Results with Ordinary People* (Boston, MA: Harvard Business School Press, 2000); Rakesh Khurana, "The Curse of the Superstar CEO," *Harvard Business Review* (September 2002): 60–66, excerpted from his book, *Searching for a Corporate Savior: The Irrational Quest for Charismatic CEOs* (Princeton, NJ: Princeton University Press, 2002); and Joseph Badaracco, *Leading Quietly* (Boston, MA: Harvard Business School Press, 2002).

54. Daft and Lengel, *Fusion Leadership*.

55. Jim Collins, "The 10 Greatest CEOs of All Time," *Fortune* (July 21, 2003): 54–68.

56. Robert K. Greenleaf, *Servant Leadership: A Journey into the Nature of Legitimate Power and Greatness* (Mahwah, NJ: Paulist Press, 1977).

57. Anne Fitzgerald, "Christmas Bonus Stuns Employees," *The Des Moines Register* (December 20, 2003): http://www.desmoinesregister.com.

58. José de Córdoba, "Why Susie Krabacher Sold the Sushi Bar to Buy an Orphanage," *The Wall Street Journal* (March 1, 2004): A1.

59. Collins, "The 10 Greatest CEOs of All Time."

60. Jim Collins, "Level 5 Leadership: The Triumph of Humility and Fierce Resolve," *Harvard Business Review* (January 2001): 67–76; Collins, "Good to Great," *Fast Company* (October 2001): 90–104; A.J. Vogl, "Onward and Upward" (an interview with Jim Collins) *Across the Board* (September–October 2001): 29–34; and Jerry Useem, "Conquering Vertical Limits," *Fortune* (February 19, 2001): 84–96.

61. Alice H. Eagly and Linda L. Carli, "The Female Leadership Advantage: An Evaluation of the Evidence," *The Leadership Quarterly* 14 (2003): 807–834; Judy B. Rosener, *America's Competitive Secret: Utilizing Women as a Management Strategy* (New York: Oxford University Press, 1995); Rosener, "Ways Women Lead," *Harvard Business Review* (November-December 1990): 119–125; Sally Helgesen, *The Female Advantage: Women's Ways of Leadership* (New York: Currency/ Doubleday, 1990); and Bernard M. Bass and Bruce J. Avolio, "Shatter the Glass Ceiling: Women May Make Better Managers," *Human Resource Management* 33:4 (Winter 1994): 549–560.

62. Rochelle Sharpe, "As Leaders, Women Rule," *BusinessWeek* (November 20, 2000): 75–84.

63. Rosener, *America's Competitive Secret*. 129–135.

64. Sharpe, "As Leaders, Women Rule."

65. Sharda Prashad, "Leaders on Land and Sea," *Toronto Star*, (September 27, 2003): 27; D. Michael Abrashoff, "Retention Through Redemption," *Harvard Business Review* (February 2001): 136–141; and Polly LaBarre, "The Most Important Thing a Captain Can Do Is to See the Ship from the Eyes of the Crew," *Fast Company* (April 1999): 115–126.

66. For an overview of issues and challenges of virtual leadership, see Bruce J. Avolio and Surinder S. Kahai, "Adding the 'E' to E-Leadership: How It May Impact Your Leadership," *Organizational Dynamics* 31:4 (2003): 325–338.

67. Deborah L. Duarte and Nancy Tennant Snyder, *Mastering Virtual Teams: Strategies, Tools, and Techniques That Succeed*, (San Francisco, CA: Jossey-Bass, 1999).

68. Avolio and Kahai, "Adding the 'E' to E-Leadership."

69. This discussion is based on Wayne F. Cascio, "Managing a Virtual Workplace," *Academy of Management Executive* 14:3 (August 2000): 81–90; and Charlene Marmer Solomon, "Managing Virtual Teams," *Workforce* (June 2001): 60–65.

70. Nancy Chase, "Learning to Lead a Virtual Team," *Quality* (August 1999): 76.

71. Richard L. Daft *The Leadership Experience*, 3rd ed. Chapter 6: Courage and Moral Leadership, (Cincinnati, OH: South-Western, 2005).

72. Badaracco, "A Lesson for the Times: Learning From Quiet Leaders."

73. Jim Collins, The 10 Greatest CEOs of All Time."

74. Byrne, "How to Lead Now."

Chapter 13
Motivation in Organizations

1. Jena McGregor, "The Starbucks of Pharmacies," *Fast Company* (April 2005): 62–63.

2. John A. Byrne, "How to Lead Now: Getting Extraordinary Performance When You Can't Pay For It," *Fast Company* (August 2003): 62–70.

3. David Silburt, "Secrets of the Super Sellers," *Canadian Business* (January 1987), 54–59; "Meet the Savvy Supersalesmen," *Fortune* (February 4, 1985): 56–62; Michael Brody, "Meet Today's Young American Worker," *Fortune* (November 11, 1985): 90–98; and Tom Richman, "Meet the Masters. They Could Sell You Anything...," *Inc.* (March 1985): 79–86.

4. Richard M. Steers and Lyman W. Porter, eds., *Motivation and Work Behavior*, 3d ed. (New York: McGraw-Hill, 1983); Don Hellriegel, John W. Slocum, Jr., and Richard W. Woodman, *Organizational Behavior*, 7th ed. (St. Paul, MN: West, 1995); and Jerry L. Gray and Frederick A. Starke, *Organizational Behavior: Concepts and Applications*, 4th ed. (New York: Macmillan, 1988): 104–105.

5. Carol Hymowitz, "Readers Tell Tales of Success and Failure Using Rating Systems," *The Wall Street Journal* (May 29, 2001): Lead column, B1.

6. Linda Grant, "Happy Workers, High Returns," *Fortune* (January 12, 1998): 81; Elizabeth J. Hawk and Garrett J. Sheridan, "The Right Stuff," *Management Review* (June 1999): 43–48; Michael West and Malcolm Patterson, "Profitable Personnel," *People Management* (January 8, 1998): 28–31; Anne Fisher, "Why Passion Pays," *FSB* (September 2002): 58; and Curt Coffman and Gabriel Gonzalez-Molina, *Follow This Path: How the World's Great Organizations Drive Growth By Unleashing Human Potential* (New York: Warner Books, 2002).

7. Steers and Porter, *Motivation and Work Behavior*.

8. J. F. Rothlisberger and W. J. Dickson, *Management and the Worker* (Cambridge, MA: Harvard University Press, 1939).

9. Bella English, "He Found the Sweet Spot, twice," *Boston Globe* (Oct. 12, 2003): 13; Martha E. Mangelsdorf , "Managing the New Workforce," *Inc.com* (April 24, 2002); Ben Strohehecker, "A Business Built on Trust," *Guideposts* (August 1996) 6–9; and Martha Mangelsdorf, "Managing the New Work Force," *Inc* (January): 78–83.

10. Abraham F. Maslow, "A Theory of Human Motivation," *Psychological Review 50* (1943): 370–396.
11. Roberta Maynard, "How to Motivate Low-Wage Workers," *Nation's Business* (May 1997): 35–39.
12. Clayton Alderfer, *Existence, Relatedness and Growth* (New York: Free Press, 1972).
13. Robert Levering and Milton Moskowitz, "100 Best Companies to Work For," *Fortune* (January 20, 2003): 127–152.
14. Robert Levering and Milton Moskowitz, "2004 Special Report: The 100 Best Companies To Work For," *Fortune* (January 12, 2004): 56–78.
15. Jeff Barbian, "C'mon, Get Happy," *Training* (January 2001): 92–96.
16. Ellyn Spragins and Verne Harnish, "Size Doesn't Matter—Profits Do," *FSB* (March 2004): 37–42; Jason Lynch and Gabrielle Cosgroff, "Shelf Help," *People Weekly* (May 20, 2002): 127–128; Thomas Petzinger, Jr., "In Search of the New World (of Work)," *Fast Company* (April 1999): 219–226.
17. Karol Rose, "Work-Life Effectiveness," *Fortune* (September 29, 2003): Special advertisement supplement, S1–S17.
18. W. Glaser, *The Control Theory Manager* (New York: HarperBusiness, 1994); and John W. Newstrom, "Making Work Fun: An Important Role for Managers," *SAM Advanced Management Journal* (Winter 2002): 4–8, 21.
19. Newstrom, "Making Work Fun: An Important Role for Managers."
20. Frederick Herzberg, "One More Time: How Do You Motivate Employees?" *Harvard Business Review* (January 2003): Best of HBR, 87–96.
21. Elaine Leuchars, Shauna Harrington, and Carrie Erickson, "Putting People First: How VSP Achieves High Employee Satisfaction Year After Year," *Journal of Organizational Excellence* (Spring 2003): 33–41; Levering and Moskowitz, "The 100 Best Companies to Work For 2004."
22. David C. McClelland, *Human Motivation* (Glenview, IL: Scott, Foresman, 1985).
23. Carol Hymowitz, "For Many Executives, Leadership Lessons Started with Mom," *The Wall Street Journal* (May 16, 2000): Lead column, B1.
24. David C. McClelland, "The Two Faces of Power," in *Organizational Psychology,* ed. D.A. Colb, I.M. Rubin, and J.M. McIntyre (Englewood Cliffs, NJ: Prentice-Hall, 1971).
25. J. Stacy Adams, "Injustice in Social Exchange," in *Advances in Experimental Social Psychology,* 2d ed., ed. L. Berkowitz (New York: Academic Press, 1965); and J. Stacy Adams, "Toward an Understanding of Inequity," *Journal of Abnormal and Social Psychology* (November 1963): 422–436.
26. "Study: The Brain Prefers Working Over Getting Money For Nothing," *TheJournalNews.com* (May 14, 2004): *http://www.thejournalnews.com/newsroom/051404/d01a/4moneyfornothing.html.*
27. Ray V. Montagno, "The Effects of Comparison to Others and Primary Experience on Responses to Task Design," *Academy of Management Journal 28* (1985): 491–498; and Robert P. Vecchio, "Predicting Worker Performance in Inequitable Settings," *Academy of Management Review 7* (1982): 103–110.
28. John Peterman, "The Rise and Fall of the J. Peterman Company," *Harvard Business Review* (September-October 1999): 59–66.
29. James E. Martin and Melanie M. Peterson, "Two-Tier Wage Structures: Implications for Equity Theory," *Academy of Management Journal 30* (1987): 297–315.
30. Victor H. Vroom, *Work and Motivation* (New York: Wiley, 1964); B. S. Gorgopoulos, G. M. Mahoney, and N. Jones, "A Path-Goal Approach to Productivity," *Journal of Applied Psychology 41* (1957): 345–353; and E. E. Lawler III, *Pay and Organizational Effectiveness: A Psychological View* (New York: McGraw-Hill, 1981).
31. Richard L. Daft and Richard M. Steers, *Organizations: A Micro/Macro Approach* (Glenview, IL: Scott, Foresman, 1986).
32. See Edwin A. Locke and Gary P. Latham, "Building a Practically Useful Theory of Goal Setting and Task Motivation: A 35-Year Odyssey", *The American Psychologist 57:9* (September 2002): 705+; Gary P. Latham and Edwin A. Locke, "Self-Regulation Through Goal Setting", *Organizational Behavior and Human Decision Processes 50:2* (1991): 212+; G. P. Latham and G. H. Seijts, "The Effects of Proximal and Distal Goals on Performance of a Moderately Complex Task," *Journal of Organizational Behavior 20:4* (1999): 421+; P. C. Early, T. Connolly, and G. Ekegren, "Goals, Strategy Development, and Task Performance: Some Limits on the Efficacy of Goal Setting," *Journal of Applied Psychology 74* (1989): 24–33; E. A. Locke, "Toward a Theory of Task Motivation and Incentives," *Organizational Behavior and Human Performance 3* (1968): 157-189; Gerard H. Seijts, Ree M. Meertens, and Gerjo Kok, "The Effects of Task Importance and Publicness on the Relation Between Goal Difficulty and Performance," *Canadian Journal of Behavioural Science 29:1* (1997): 54+.
33. Locke and Latham, "Building a Practically Useful Theory of Goal Setting and Task Motivation."
34. J. M. Ivanecevich and J. T. McMahon, "The Effects of Goal Setting, External Feedback, and Self-Generated Feedback on Outcome Variables: A Field Experiment," *Academy of Management Journal* (June 1982): 359+; G. P. Latham and E. A. Locke, "Self-Regulation Through Goal Setting," *Organizational Behavior and Human Decision Processes 50:2* (1991): 212+.
35. Mike Hofman, "Everyone's a Cost Cutter," *Inc.* (July 1998): 117; and Abby Livingston, "Gain-Sharing Encourages Productivity," *Nation's Business* (January 1998): 21–22.
36. Alexander D. Stajkovic and Fred Luthans, "A Meta-Analysis of the Effects of Organizational Behavior Modification on Task Performance, 1975–95," *Academy of Management Journal* (October 1997): 1122–1149; H. Richlin, *Modern Behaviorism* (San Francisco, CA: Freeman, 1970); and B. F. Skinner, *Science and Human Behavior* (New York: Macmillan, 1953).
37. Lea Goldman, "Over the Top," *Forbes* (October 29, 2001): 146–147.
38. Stajkovic and Luthans, "A Meta-Analysis of the Effects of Organizational Behavior Modification on Task Performance, 1975–95"; and Fred Luthans and Alexander D. Stajkovic, "Reinforce for Performance: The Need to Go Beyond Pay and Even Rewards," *Academy of Management Executive 13:2* (1999): 49–57.
39. Kenneth D. Butterfield and Linda Klebe Treviño, "Punishment from the Manager's Perspective: A Grounded Investigation and Inductive Model," *Academy of Management Journal 39:6* (December 1996): 1479–1512; and Andrea Casey, "Voices from the Firing Line: Managers Discuss Punishment in the Workplace," *Academy of Management Executive 11:3* (1997): 93–94.
40. David Dorsey, "Happiness Pays," *Inc.* (February 2004): 88–94.
41. Roberta Maynard, "How to Motivate Low-Wage Workers."
42. L. M. Sarri and G. P. Latham, "Employee Reaction to Continuous and Variable Ratio Reinforcement Schedules Involving a Monetary Incentive," *Journal of Applied Psychology 67* (1982): 506–508; and R. D. Pritchard, J. Hollenback, and P. J. DeLeo, "The Effects of Continuous and Partial Schedules of Reinforcement on Effort, Performance, and Satisfaction," *Organizational Behavior and Human Performance 25* (1980): 336–353.
43. Kevin Kelly, "Getting What You Pay For," *FSB* (March 2003): 24.
44. J. Vogl, "Carrots, Sticks, and Self-Deception" (an interview with Alfie Kohn), *Across the Board* (January 1994): 39–44.
45. Hilary Rosenberg, "Building a Better Carrot," *CFO* (June 2001): 64–70.
46. Barbian, "C'mon, Get Happy."
47. Norm Alster, "What Flexible Workers Can Do," *Fortune* (February 13, 1989): 62–66.
48. Glenn L. Dalton, "The Collective Stretch," *Management Review* (December 1998): 54–59.
49. Celine Rattray, "A Plum Partnership," *Fast Company* (March 2005): 39.
50. J. Richard Hackman and Greg R. Oldham, *Work Redesign* (Reading, Mass.: Addison-Wesley, 1980); and J. Richard Hackman and Greg Oldham, "Motivation through the Design of Work: Test of a Theory," *Organizational Behavior and Human Performance 16* (1976): 250–279.
51. Xu Huang and Evert Van de Vliert, "Where Intrinsic Job Satisfaction Fails to Work: National Moderators of Intrinsic Motivation," *Journal of Organizational Behavior 24* (2003): 157–179.
52. Ann Podolske, "Giving Employees a Voice in Pay Structures," *Business Ethics* (March-April 1998): 12.
53. Rekha Balu, "Bonuses Aren't Just For the Bosses," *Fast Company* (December 2000): 74–76.
54. Edwin P. Hollander and Lynn R. Offermann, "Power and Leadership in Organizations," *American Psychologist 45* (February 1990): 179–189.
55. Jay A. Conger and Rabindra N. Kanungo, "The Empowerment Process: Integrating Theory and Practice," *Academy of Management Review 13* (1988): 471–482.
56. Ibid.
57. David E. Bowen and Edward E. Lawler III, "The Empowerment of Service Workers: What, Why, How, and When," *Sloan Management Review* (Spring 1992): 31–39; and Ray W. Coye and James A. Belohav, "An Exploratory Analysis of Employee Participation," *Group and Organization Management 20:1,* (March 1995): 4–17.

58. Russ Forrester, "Empowerment: Rejuvenating a Potent Idea," *Academy of Management Executive* 14:3 (2000): 67–80.

59. Ricardo Semler, "How We Went Digital Without a Strategy," *Harvard Business Review* (September-October 2000): 51–58.

60. Podolske, "Giving Employees a Voice in Pay Structures."

61. This discussion is based on Robert C. Ford and Myron D. Fottler, "Empowerment: A Matter of Degree," *Academy of Management Executive* 9:3 (1995): 21–31.

62. Bruce E. Kaufman, "High-Level Employee Involvement at Delta Air Lines," *Human Resource Management* 42:2 (Summer 2003): 175–190.

63. Ibid.

64. Jim Collins, "The 10 Greatest CEOs of All Time," *Fortune* (July 21, 2003): 54–68.

65. Cheryl Dahle, "Four Tires, Free Beef," *Fast Company* (September 2003): 36.

66. This discussion is based on Tony Schwartz, "The Greatest Sources of Satisfaction in the Workplace are Internal and Emotional," *Fast Company* (November 2000): 398–402; and Marcus Buckingham and Curt Coffman, *First, Break All the Rules: What the World's Greatest Managers Do Differently* (New York: Simon and Schuster, 1999).

67. Margaret Littman, "Best Bosses Tell All," *Working Woman* (October 2000): 48–56.

68. The Gallup Organization, Princeton, NJ. All rights reserved. Used with permission.

69. Curt Coffman and Gabriel Gonzalez-Molina, *Follow This Path: How the World's Greatest Organizations Drive Growth by Unleashing Human Potential* (New York: Warner Books, 2002), as reported in Anne Fisher, "Why Passion Pays," *FSB* (September 2002): 58.

70. Jena McGregor, "The Starbucks of Pharmacies," *Fast Company* (April 2005): 62–63.

Chapter 14

Communicating in Organizations

1. Stephanie Clifford, "How to Get the Geeks and the Suits to Play Nice," *Business 2.0* (May 2002): 92–93.

2. Chris Serv, "Straight Talk," *Hospitals and Health Networks* (September 2002): 26+.

3. Chris Serb, "Straight Talk."

4. Ginger Graham, "If You Want Honesty, Break Some Rules," *Harvard Business Review* (April 2002): 42–47.

5. Michael J. Critelli, "How to Subvert Hierarchy: CEOs Must 'Skip Levels' To Manage More Effectively," *Chief Executive* (January-February 2004): 12.

6. Elizabeth B. Drew, "Profile: Robert Strauss," *The New Yorker* (May 7, 1979): 55–70.

7. Henry Mintzberg, *The Nature of Managerial Work* (New York: Harper & Row, 1973).

8. Phillip G. Clampitt, Laurey Berk, and M. Lee Williams, "Leaders as Strategic Communicators," *Ivey Business Journal* (May-June 2002): 51–55.

9. Ian Wylie, "Can Philips Learn to Walk the Talk?" *Fast Company* (January 2003): 44–45.

10. Fred Luthans and Janet K. Larsen, "How Managers Really Communicate," *Human Relations* 39 (1986): 161–178; and Larry E. Penley and Brian Hawkins, "Studying Interpersonal Communication in Organizations: A Leadership Application," *Academy of Management Journal* 28 (1985): 309–326.

11. D. K. Berlo, *The Process of Communication* (New York: Holt, Rinehart and Winston, 1960): 24.

12. Adapted from: Robert Levering and Milton Moskowitz, "100 Best Companies to Work For: The Best in the Worst of Times," *Fortune* (Feb. 2002): 60–61; Nancy Austin, "Rock Through the Ages, " *Inc.* (May 16, 2000): 68–76.

13. Paul Roberts, "Live! From Your Office! It's...," *Fast Company* (October 1999): 150–170.

14. Bruce K. Blaylock, "Cognitive Style and the Usefulness of Information," *Decision Sciences* 15 (Winter 1984): 74–91.

15. Robert H. Lengel and Richard L. Daft, "The Selection of Communication Media as an Executive Skill," *Academy of Management Executive* 2 (August 1988): 225–232; Richard L. Daft and Robert H. Lengel, "Organizational Information Requirements, Media Richness and Structural Design," *Managerial Science* 32 (May 1986): 554–572; and Jane Webster and Linda Klebe Treviño, "Rational and Social Theories as Complementary Explanations of Communication Media Choices: Two Policy-Capturing Studies," *Academy of Management Journal* 38:6 (1995): 1544–1572.

16. Patricia Hurtado, "The rap on Puffy," *New York Times*, (July 24, 2005) A 1 &3.

17. Research reported in "E-mail Can't Mimic Phone Calls," *Johnson City Press* (September 17, 2000): 31.

18. Raymond E. Friedman and Steven C. Currall, "E-Mail Escalation: Dispute Exacerbating Elements of Electronic Communication," *http://www.mba.vanderbilt.edu/ray.friedman/pdf/emailescalation.pdf*; and Lauren Keller Johnson, "Does E-Mail Escalate Conflict?" *MIT Sloan Management Review* (Fall 2002): 14–15.

19. Scott Kirsner, "IM Is Here. RU Prepared?" *Darwin Magazine* (February 2002): 22–24.

20. Daniel Nasaw, "Instant Messages Are Popping Up All Over," *The Wall Street Journal* (June 12, 2003): B4; William H. Bulkeley, "Instant Message Goes Corporate; 'You Can't Hide,'" *The Wall Street Journal* (September 4, 2002): B1.

21. Edward M. Hallowell, "The Human Moment at Work," *Harvard Business Review* (January-February 1999): 58–66.

22. John R. Carlson and Robert W. Smud, "Channel Expansion Theory and the Experiential Nature of Media Richness Perceptions," *Academy of Management Journal* 42:2 (1999): 153–170; R. Rice and G. Love, "Electronic Emotion," *Communication Research* 14 (1987): 85–108.

23. Ronald E. Rice, "Task Analyzability, Use of New Media, and Effectiveness: A Multi-Site Exploration of Media Richness," *Organizational Science* 3:4 (November 1992): 475–500; and M. Lynne Markus, "Electronic Mail as the Medium of Managerial Choice," *Organizational Science* 5:4 (November 1994): 502–527.

24. Richard L. Daft, Robert H. Lengel, and Linda Klebe Treviño, "Message Equivocality, Media Selection and Manager Performance: Implication for Information Systems," *MIS Quarterly 11* (1987): 355–368.

25. Mary Young and James E. Post, "Managing to Communicate, Communicating to Manage: How Leading Companies Communicate with Employees," *Organizational Dynamics* (Summer 1993): 31–43.

26. Jay A. Conger, "The Necessary Art of Persuasion," *Harvard Business Review* (May–June 1998): 84–95.

27. Douglas A. Ready, "How Storytelling Builds Next-Generation Leaders," *MIT Sloan Management Review* (Summer 2002): 63–69.

28. J. Martin and M. Powers, "Organizational Stories: More Vivid and Persuasive than Quantitative Data," in B. M. Staw, ed., *Psychological Foundations of Organizational Behavior* (Glenview, IL: Scott Foresman, 1982).

29. Bronwyn Fryer, "Storytelling that Moves People: A Conversation with Screenwriting Coach Robert McKee," *Harvard Business Review* (June 2003): 51–55.

30. Bill Birchard, "Once Upon a Time," *Strategy & Business* Issue 27 (Second Quarter, 2002): 99–104; and Laura Shin, "You Can Be a Great Storyteller," *USA Weekend* (January 16–18, 2004): 14.

31. Thomas Sheppard, "Silent Signals," *Supervisory Management* (March 1986): 31–33.

32. Albert Mehrabian, *Silent Messages* (Belmont, CA: Wadsworth, 1971); and Albert Mehrabian, "Communicating without Words," *Psychology Today* (September 1968): 53–55.

33. Mac Fulfer, "Nonverbal Communication: How To Read What's Plain as the Nose...Or Eyelid...Or Chin...On Their Faces," *Journal of Organizational Excellence* (Spring 2001): 19–27.

34. Sheppard, "Silent Signals."

35. Arthur H. Bell, *The Complete Manager's Guide to Interviewing* (Homewood, IL: Richard D. Irwin, 1989).

36. Jared Sandberg, "Desk Surfers Abound, but Some People Find Ways to Outwit Them," *The Wall Street Journal* (March 9, 2005): B1.

37. C. Glenn Pearce, "Doing Something about Your Listening Ability," *Supervisory Management* (March 1989): 29–34; and Tom Peters, "Learning to Listen," *Hyatt Magazine* (Spring 1988): 16–21.

38. M. P. Nichols, *The Lost Art of Listening* (New York: Guilford Publishing, 1995).

39. "Benchmarking the Sales Function," a report based on a study of 100 salespeople from small, medium, and large businesses, conducted by Ron Volper Group Inc. Sales Consulting and Training, White Plains, NY (1996): as reported in "Nine Habits of Highly Successful Salespeople," *Inc. Small Business Success* insert.

40. Gerald M. Goldhaber, *Organizational Communication*, 4th ed. (Dubuque, IA: Wm. C. Brown, 1980).

41. Curtis Sittenfeld, "Good Ways To Deliver Bad News," *Fast Company* (April 1999): 58, 60.

42. Richard L. Daft and Richard M. Steers, *Organizations: A Micro/Macro Approach* (New York: Harper Collins, 1986); and Daniel Katz and Robert Kahn, *The Social Psychology of Organizations*, 2d ed. (New York: Wiley, 1978).

43. Greg Jaffe, "Tug of War: In the New Military, Technology May Alter Chain of Command," *The Wall Street Journal* (March 30, 2001): A3; and Aaron Pressman, "Business Gets the Message," *The Industry Standard* (February 26, 2001): 58–59.

44. Roberta Maynard, "It Can Pay to Show Employees the Big Picture," *Nation's Business* (December 1994): 10.

45. Phillip G. Clampitt, Robert J. DeKoch, and Thomas Cashman, "A Strategy for Communicating about Uncertainty," *Academy of Management Executive* 14:4 (2000): 41–57.

46. Christian McWilliams, "The Importance of Being Local," *Fast Company* (March 2005): 43.

47. J. G. Miller, "Living Systems: The Organization," *Behavioral Science* 17 (1972): 69.

48. Pat Croce, "Catching the 5:15: A Simple Reporting System Can Help You Keep Tabs on Your Business," *FSB* (March 2004): 34.

49. Alexander Coolidge, "On the Market," *Cincinnati Post* (March 25, 2005): B7; Joann S. Lublin, "Ex-Chief of Ben & Jerry's to Join Wild Oats," *The Wall Street Journal* (March 7, 2001): B6; "Wild Oats Markets to Buy 13 Stores from Competitors," *The Los Angeles Times* (Nov. 1, 1999): 3.

50. Mary P. Rowe and Michael Baker, "Are You Hearing Enough Employee Concerns?" *Harvard Business Review* 62 (May-June 1984): 127–135; W. H. Read, "Upward Communication in Industrial Hierarchies," *Human Relations* 15 (February 1962): 3–15; and Daft and Steers, *Organizations*.

51. Barbara Ettorre, "The Unvarnished Truth," *Management Review* (June 1997): 54–57; and Roberta Maynard, "Back to Basics, From the Top," *Nation's Business* (December 1996): 38–39.

52. E. M. Rogers and R. A. Rogers, *Communication in Organizations* (New York: Free Press, 1976); and A. Bavelas and D. Barrett, "An Experimental Approach to Organization Communication," *Personnel* 27 (1951): 366–371.

53. This discussion is based on Daft and Steers, *Organizations*.

54. Bavelas and Barrett, "An Experimental Approach"; and M. E. Shaw, *Group Dynamics: The Psychology of Small Group Behavior* (New York: McGraw-Hill, 1976).

55. Richard L. Daft and Norman B. Macintosh, "A Tentative Exploration into the Amount and Equivocality of Information Processing in Organizational Work Units," *Administrative Science Quarterly* 26 (1981): 207–224.

56. Cathy Olofson, "So Many Decisions, So Little Time," *Fast Company* (October 1999): 62.

57. This discussion of informal networks is based on Rob Cross, Nitin Nohria, and Andrew Parker, "Six Myths About Informal Networks," *MIT Sloan Management Review* (Spring 2002): 67–75; and Rob Cross and Laurence Prusak, "The People Who Make Organizations Go—or Stop," *Harvard Business Review* (June 2002): 105–112.

58. Keith Ferrazi and Tahl Raz, *Never Eat Alone: And Other Secrets to Success, One Relationship at a Time,* (New York: Currency, 2005).

59. Thomas J. Peters and Robert H. Waterman Jr., *In Search of Excellence* (New York: Harper & Row, 1982); and Tom Peters and Nancy Austin, *A Passion for Excellence: The Leadership Difference* (New York: Random House, 1985).

60. Lois Therrien, "How Ztel Went from Riches to Rags," *Business Week* (June 17, 1985): 97–100.

61. Keith Davis and John W. Newstrom, *Human Behavior at Work: Organizational Behavior,* 7th ed. (New York: McGraw-Hill, 1985).

62. Suzanne M. Crampton, John W. Hodge, and Jitendra M. Mishra, "The Informal Communication Network: Factors Influencing Grapevine Activity," *Public Personnel Management* 27:4 (Winter, 1998): 569–584.

63. Survey results reported in Jared Sandberg, "Ruthless Rumors and the Managers Who Enable Them," *The Wall Street Journal* (October 29, 2003): B1

64. Joshua Hyatt, "The Last Shift," *Inc.* (February 1989): 74–80.

65. Donald B. Simmons, "The Nature of the Organizational Grapevine," *Supervisory Management* (November 1985): 39–42; and Davis and Newstrom, *Human Behavior*.

66. Barbara Ettorre, "Hellooo. Anybody Listening?" *Management Review* (November 1997): 9.

67. Lisa A. Burke and Jessica Morris Wise, "The Effective Care, Handling, and Pruning of the Office Grapevine," *Business Horizons* (May-June 2003): 71–74; "They Hear It Through the Grapevine," in Michael Warshaw, "The Good Guy's Guide to Office Politics," *Fast Company* (April-May 1998): 157–178 (page 160); and Carol Hildebrand, "Mapping the Invisible Workplace," *CIO Enterprise* (July 15, 1998): Section 2, 18–20.

68. John Case, "Opening the Books," *Harvard Business Review,* (March-April 1997): 118–127.

69. Gary Hamel, "Killer Strategies That Make Shareholders Rich," *Fortune* (June 23, 1997): 70–84.

70. "What Is Trust?" results of a survey by Manchester Consulting, reported in Jenny C. McCune, "That Elusive Thing Called Trust," *Management Review* (July-August 1998): 10–16.

71. David Bohm, *On Dialogue* (Ojai, CA: David Bohm Seminars, 1989).

72. This discussion is based on Glenna Gerard and Linda Teurfs, "Dialogue and Organizational Transformation," in *Community Building: Renewing Spirit and Learning in Business,* ed. Kazinierz Gozdz (New Leaders Press: San Francisco, 1995); and Edgar H. Schein, "On Dialogue, Culture, and Organizational Learning," *Organizational Dynamics* (Autumn 1993): 40–51.

73. Ian I. Mitroff and Murat C. Alpaslan, "Preparing for Evil," *Harvard Business Review* (April 2003): 109–115.

74. This section is based on Leslie Wayne and Leslie Kaufman, "Leadership, Put To a New Test," *The New York Times* (September 16, 2001): Section 3, 1, 4; Ian I. Mitroff, "Crisis Leadership," *Executive Excellence* (August 2001): 19; Jerry Useem, "What It Takes," *Fortune* (November 12, 2001): 126–132; Andy Bowen, "Crisis Procedures That Stand the Test of Time," *Public Relations Tactics* (August 2001): 16; and Matthew Boyle, "Nothing Really Matters," *Fortune* (October 15, 2001): 261–264.

75. Stephen Bernhut, "Leadership, with Michael Useem" (Leader's Edge Interview), *Ivey Business Journal* (January-February 2002): 42–43.

76. Mitroff, "Crisis Leadership."

77. Jay M. Jackman and Myra H. Strober, "Fear of Feedback," *Harvard Business Review* (April 2003): 101–108.

78. Carol Hymowitz, "How to Tell Employees All the Things They Don't Want to hear," *The Wall Street Journal* (August 22, 2000): Lead column, B1.

79. Thomas E. Ricks, "Army Devises System to Decide What Does, and Does Not, Work," *The Wall Street Journal* (May 23, 1997): A1, A10; Stephanie Watts Sussman, "CALL: A Model for Effective Organizational Learning," *Strategy* (Summer 1999): 14–15; John O'Shea, "Army: The Leader as Learner-in-Chief," *The Officer* (June 2003): 31; Michael D. Maples, "Fires First in Combat—Train the Way We Fight," *Field Artillery* (July–August 2003): 1; Thomas E. Ricks, "Intelligence Problems in Iraq Are Detailed," *The Washington Post* (October 25, 2003): A1; and Richard W. Koenig, "Forging Our Future: Using Operation Iraqi Freedom Phase IV Lessons Learned," *Engineer* (January-March 2004): 21–22.

80. Thomas A. Stewart, "Listen Up, Maggots! You Will Deploy a More Humane and Effective Managerial Style!" *Ecompany* (July 2001): 95.

81. Carol Hymowitz, "Should CEO's Tell Truth about Being in Trouble or Is that Foolhardy?" *The Wall Street Journal* (Feb. 5, 2005): B1; Alison Stein Wellner, "Everyone's a Critic," *Inc. Magazine* (July, 2004): 38–39.

82. James A. F. Stoner and R. Edward Freeman, *Management,* 4th ed. (Englewood Cliffs, NJ: Prentice-Hall, 1989).

83. Mike Hofman, "Lost in the Translation," *Inc.* (May 2000): 161–162.

84. Janet Fulk and Sirish Mani, "Distortion of Communication in Hierarchical Relationships," in *Communication Yearbook,* vol. 9, ed. M. L. McLaughlin (Beverly Hills, CA: Sage, 1986).

85. "CEO Stopping Descent of Airline That's In Trouble," Associated Press story, *Johnson City Press* (June 20, 2004): 7D.

86. Stephanie Clifford, "How to Get the Geeks and the Suits to Play Nice," *Business 2.0* (May 2002): 92–93.

Chapter 15

Teamwork in Organizations

1. Thomas Petzinger, Jr., *The New Pioneers: The Men and Women Who Are Transforming the Workplace and Marketplace* (New York: Simon & Schuster, 1999).

2. "Team Goal-Setting," *Small Business Report* (January 1988): 76–77; Frank V. Cespedes, Stephen X. Dole, and Robert J. Freedman, "Teamwork for Today's Selling," *Harvard Business Review* (March-April 1989): 44–55; Victoria J. Marsick, Ernie Turner, and Lars Cederholm, "International Managers as Team Leaders," *Management Review* (March 1989): 46–49; and Terry Adler, Janice A. Black, and John P. Loveland, "Complex Systems: Boundary-Spanning Training Techniques," *Journal of European Industrial Training* 27: 2–4 (2002): 111+.

3. J. D. Osburn, L. Moran, E. Musselwhite, and J. H. Zenger, *Self-Directed Work Teams: The New American Challenge* (Homewood, IL: Business One Irwin, 1990).

4. Linda I. Glassop, "The Organizational Benefits of Teams," *Human Relations* 55:2 (2002): 225–249.

5. Carl E. Larson and Frank M. J. LaFasto, *TeamWork* (Newbury Park, CA: Sage, 1989).

6. "'Golden Hour' Crucial Time for Surgeons on Front Line," *Associated Press* report in *Johnson City Press* (April 1, 2003): 9.

7. Doug Webb, "Rhyme of the Ancient Manager: A High-Tech Exec Takes a New Tack," *Forbes* (September 10, 2001): 76–79.

8. Eric Sundstrom, Kenneth P. DeMeuse, and David Futrell, "Work Teams," *American Psychologist* 45 (February 1990): 120–133.

9. Deborah L. Gladstein, "Groups in Context: A Model of Task Group Effectiveness," *Administrative Science Quarterly* 29 (1984): 499–517.

10. Dora C. Lau and J. Keith Murnighan, "Demographic Diversity and Faultlines: The Compositional Dynamics of Organizational Groups," *Academy of Management Review* 23:2 (1998): 325–340.

11. Thomas Owens, "Business Teams," *Small Business Report* (January 1989): 50–58.

12. "Participation Teams," *Small Business Report* (September 1987): 38–41.

13. Susanne G. Scott and Walter O. Einstein, "Strategic Performance Appraisal in Team-Based Organizations: One Size Does Not Fit All," *Academy of Management Executive* 15:2 (2001): 107–116.

14. Larson and LaFasto, *TeamWork*.

15. V. K. Narayanan, Frank L. Douglas, Brock Guernsey, and John Charnes, "How Top Management Steers Fast Cycle Teams to Success," *Strategy & Leadership* 30:3 (2002): 19–27.

16. James H. Shonk, *Team-Based Organizations* (Homewood, IL: Business One Irwin, 1992); and John Hoerr, "The Payoff from Teamwork," *BusinessWeek* (July 10, 1989): 56–62.

17. Gregory L. Miles, "Suddenly, USX Is Playing Mr. Nice Guy," *BusinessWeek* (June 26, 1989): 151–152.

18. Jeanne M. Wilson, Jill George, and Richard S. Wellings, with William C. Byham, *Leadership Trapeze: Strategies for Leadership in Team-Based Organizations* (San Francisco, CA: Jossey-Bass, 1994).

19. Ruth Wageman, "Critical Success Factors for Creating Superb Self-Managing Teams," *Organizational Dynamics* (Summer 1997): 49–61.

20. Thomas Owens, "The Self-Managing Work Team," *Small Business Report* (February 1991): 53–65.

21. Bradley L. Kirkman and Benson Rosen, "Powering Up Teams," *Organizational Dynamics* (Winter 2000): 48–66.

22. Vanessa Urch Druskat and Jane V. Wheeler, "Managing from the Boundary: The Effective Leadership of Self-Managing Work Teams," *Academy of Management Journal* 46:4 (2003): 435–457.

23. Donald Vredenburgh and Irene Yunxia He, "Leadership Lessons From a Conductorless Orchestra," *Business Horizons* (September-October 2003): 19–24.

24. Curtis Sittenfeld, "Powered by the People," *Fast Company* (July/August 1999): 178–189.

25. The discussion of virtual teams is based on Wayne F. Cascio and Stan Shurygailo, "E-Leadership and Virtual Teams," *Organizational Dynamics* 31:4 (2002): 362–376; Anthony M. Townsend, Samuel M. DeMarie, and Anthony R. Hendrickson, "Virtual Teams: Technology and the Workplace of the Future," *Academy of Management Executive* 12:3 (August 1998): 17–29; and Deborah L. Duarte and Nancy Tennant Snyder, *Mastering Virtual Teams* (San Francisco, CA: Jossey-Bass, 1999).

26. Jessica Lipnack and Jeffrey Stamps, "Virtual Teams: The New Way to Work," *Strategy & Leadership* (January/February 1999): 14–19.

27. Based on Bradley L. Kirkman, Benson Rosen, Cristina B. Gibson, Paul E. Tesluk, and Simon O. McPherson, "Five Challenges to Virtual Team Success: Lessons From Sabre, Inc.," *Academy of Management Executive* 16:3 (2002): 67–79; Wayne F. Cascio and Stan Shurygailo, "E-Leadership and Virtual Teams," *Organizational Dynamics* 31:4 (2002): 362–376; Ilze Zigurs, "Leadership in Virtual Teams: Oxymoron or Opportunity?" *Organizational Dynamics* 31:4 (2002): 339–351; and Manju K. Ahuja and John E. Galvin, "Socialization in Virtual Groups," unpublished manuscript.

28. Kirkman et al., "Five Challenges to Virtual Team Success."

29. Terri L. Griffith and Margaret A. Neale, "Information Processing in Traditional, Hybrid, and Virtual Teams: From Nascent Knowledge to Transactive Memory," *Research in Organizational Behavior* 23 (2001): 379–421.

30. Vijay Govindarajan and Anil K. Gupta, "Building an Effective Global Business Team," *MIT Sloan Management Review* 42:4 (Summer 2001): 63–71.

31. Charlene Marmer Solomon, "Building Teams Across Borders," *Global Workforce* (November 1998): 12–17.

32. Jane Pickard, "Control Freaks Need Not Apply," *People Management* (February 5, 1998): 49.

33. Based on Jon Katzenbach and Douglas Smith, "Virtual Teaming," *Forbes* (May 21, 2001): 48–51; and Cassell Bryan-Low, "Can STMicro's Run Continue?" *The Wall Street Journal* (July 21, 2004): B8.

34. Cristina B. Gibson, Mary E. Zellmer-Bruhn, and Donald P. Schwab, "Team Effectiveness in Multinational Organizations: Evaluation Across Contexts," *Group and Organizational Management* 28:4 (December 2003): 444–474.

35. Sylvia Odenwald, "Global Work Teams," *Training and Development* (February 1996): 54–57; and Debby Young, "Team Heat," *CIO*, Section 1 (September 1, 1998): 43–51.

36. Reported in "Vive La Difference," box in Julie Connelly, "All Together Now," *Gallup Management Journal* (Spring 2002): 13–18.

37. Ray Oglethorpe in Regina Fazio Maruca, ed., "What Makes Teams Work," *Fast Company* (November 2000), Unit of One column, 109–140.

38. For research findings on group size, see M. E. Shaw, *Group Dynamics*, 3d ed. (New York: McGraw-Hill, 1981); and G. Manners, "Another Look at Group Size, Group Problem-Solving and Member Consensus," *Academy of Management Journal* 18 (1975): 715–724.

39. Warren E. Watson, Kamalesh Kumar, and Larry K. Michaelsen, "Cultural Diversity's Impact on Interaction Process and Performance: Comparing Homogeneous and Diverse Task Groups," *Academy of Management Journal* 36 (1993): 590–602; Gail Robinson and Kathleen Dechant, "Building a Business Case for Diversity," *Academy of Management Executive* 11:3 (1997): 21–31; and David A. Thomas and Robin J. Ely, "Making Differences Matter: A New Paradigm for Managing Diversity," *Harvard Business Review* (September-October 1996): 79–90.

40. J. Stuart Bunderson and Kathleen M. Sutcliffe, "Comparing Alternative Conceptualizations of Functional Diversity in Management Teams: Process and Performance Effects," *Academy of Management Journal* 45:5 (2002): 875–893; and Marc Orlitzky and John D. Benjamin, "The Effects of Sex Composition on Small Group Performance in a Business School Case Competition," *Academy of Management Learning and Education* 2:2 (2003): 128–138.

41. Watson et al., "Cultural Diversity's Impact on Interaction Process and Performance."

42. George Prince, "Recognizing Genuine Teamwork," *Supervisory Management* (April 1989): 25–36; K. D. Benne and P. Sheats, "Functional Roles of Group Members," *Journal of Social Issues* 4 (1948): 41–49; and R. F. Bales, *SYMLOG* Case Study Kit (New York: Free Press, 1980).

43. Robert A. Baron, *Behavior in Organizations*, 2d ed. (Boston: Allyn & Bacon, 1986).

44. Ibid.

45. Avan R. Jassawalla and Hemant C. Sashittal, "Strategies of Effective New Product Team Leaders," *California Management Review* 42:2 (Winter 2000): 34–51.

46. Kenneth G. Koehler, "Effective Team Management," *Small Business Report* (July 19, 1989): 14–16; and Connie J. G. Gersick, "Time and Transition in Work Teams: Toward a New Model of Group Development," *Academy of Management Journal* 31 (1988): 9–41.

47. Bruce W. Tuckman and Mary Ann C. Jensen, "Stages of Small-Group Development Revisited," *Group and Organizational Studies* 2 (1977): 419–427; and Bruce W. Tuckman, "Developmental Sequences in

Small Groups," *Psychological Bulletin* 63 (1965): 384–399. See also Linda N. Jewell and H. Joseph Reitz, *Group Effectiveness in Organizations* (Glenview, Ill.: Scott, Foresman, 1981).

48. Thomas Petzinger Jr., "Bovis Team Helps Builders Construct a Solid Foundation," *The Wall Street Journal* (March 21, 1997), The Front Lines column, B1.

49. Shaw, *Group Dynamics.*

50. Daniel C. Feldman and Hugh J. Arnold, *Managing Individual and Group Behavior in Organizations* (New York: McGraw-Hill, 1983).

51. Dorwin Cartwright and Alvin Zander, *Group Dynamics: Research and Theory*, 3d ed. (New York: Harper & Row, 1968); and Elliot Aronson, *The Social Animal* (San Francisco, CA: W. H. Freeman, 1976).

52. Peter E. Mudrack, "Group Cohesiveness and Productivity: A Closer Look," *Human Relations* 42 (1989): 771–785. Also see Miriam Erez and Anit Somech, "Is Group Productivity Loss the Rule or the Exception? Effects of Culture and Group-Based Motivation," *Academy of Management Journal* 39:6 (1996): 1513–1537.

53. Stanley E. Seashore, *Group Cohesiveness in the Industrial Work Group* (Ann Arbor, MI: Institute for Social Research, 1954).

54. Daniel R. Kibbe and Jill Casner-Lotto, "Ralston Foods: From Greenfield to Maturity in a Team-Based Plant," *Journal of Organizational Excellence* (Summer 2002): 57–67.

55. J. Richard Hackman, "Group Influences on Individuals," in *Handbook of Industrial and Organizational Psychology*, ed. M. Dunnette (Chicago, IL: Rand McNally, 1976).

56. Kenneth Bettenhausen and J. Keith Murnighan, "The Emergence of Norms in Competitive Decision-Making Groups," *Administrative Science Quarterly* 30 (1985): 350–372.

57. The following discussion is based on Daniel C. Feldman, "The Development and Enforcement of Group Norms," *Academy of Management Review* 9 (1984): 47–53.

58. Wilson, et al., *Leadership Trapeze*, 12.

59. Emily Nelson, "TV Guide: Think You've Got a Tricky Staff? Try Herding Writers," *The Wall Street Journal* (May 16, 2003): A1.

60. Stephen P. Robbins, *Managing Organizational Conflict: A Nontraditional Approach* (Englewood Cliffs, NJ: Prentice-Hall, 1974).

61. Daniel Robey, Dana L. Farrow, and Charles R. Franz, "Group Process and Conflict in System Development," *Management Science* 35 (1989): 1172–1191.

62. Dean Tjosvold, Chun Hui, Daniel Z. Ding, and Junchen Hu, "Conflict Values and Team Relationships: Conflict's Contribution to Team Effectiveness and Citizenship in China," *Journal of Organizational Behavior* 24 (2003): 69–88; C. De Dreu and E. Van de Vliert, *Using Conflict in Organizations* (Beverly Hills, CA: Sage, 1997); and Kathleen M. Eisenhardt, Jean L. Kahwajy, and L. J. Bourgeois III, "Conflict and Strategic Choice: How Top Management Teams Disagree," *California Management Review* 39:2 (Winter 1997): 42–62.

63. Jerry B. Harvey, "The Abilene Paradox: The Management of Agreement," *Organizational Dynamics* (Summer 1988): 17–43.

64. Eisenhardt et al., "Conflict and Strategic Choice."

65. Koehler, "Effective Team Management"; and Dean Tjosvold, "Making Conflict Productive," *Personnel Administrator* 29 (June 1984): 121.

66. This discussion is based in part on Richard L. Daft, *Organization Theory and Design* (St. Paul, MN: West, 1992); and Paul M. Terry, "Conflict Management," *The Journal of Leadership Studies* 3:2 (1996): 3–21.

67. Narayanan et al. "How Top Management Steers Fast Cycle Teams to Success."

68. Clinton O. Longenecker and Mitchell Neubert, "Barriers and Gateways to Management Cooperation and Teamwork," *Business Horizons* (September-October 2000): 37–44.

69. This discussion is based on K. W. Thomas, "Towards Multidimensional Values in Teaching: The Example of Conflict Behaviors," *Academy of Management Review* 2 (1977): 487.

70. Robbins, *Managing Organizational Conflict.*

71. Rob Walker, "Take It Or Leave It: The Only Guide to Negotiating You Will Ever Need," *Inc.*, (August 2003): 75–82.

72. Based on Kathleen M. Eisenhardt, Jean L. Kahwajy, and L. J. Bourgeois III, "How Management Teams Can Have a Good Fight," *Harvard Business Review* (July-August 1997): 77–85.

73. "Impact of Diversity Initiatives on the Bottom Line: A SHRM Survey of the Fortune 1000," S12–S14, in *Fortune*, special advertising section; "Keeping Your Edge: Managing a Diverse Corporate Culture," produced in association with the Society for Human Resource Management, (June 3, 2001): accessed at *http://www.fortune.com/sections.*

74. Joseph J. Distefano and Martha L. Maznevski, "Creating Value with Diverse Teams in Global Management," *Organizational Dynamics* 29:1 (Summer 2000): 45–63; and Finnigan, "Different Strokes."

75. W. E. Watson, K. Kumar, and L. K. Michaelsen, "Cultural Diversity's Impact on Interaction Process and Performance: Comparing Homogeneous and Diverse Task Groups," *Academy of Management Journal* 36 (1993): 590–602; G. Robinson and K. Dechant, "Building a Business Case for Diversity," *Academy of Management Executive* 11:3 (1997): 21–31; and D. A. Thomas and R. J. Ely, "Making Differences Matter: A New Paradigm for Managing Diversity," *Harvard Business Review* (September-October 1996): 79–90.

76. Marc Hequet, Chris Lee, Michele Picard, and David Stamps, "Teams Get Global," *Training* (December 1996): 16–17.

77. Chiori Santiago, "Culture Club," *Working Woman* (April 2001): 46–47, 78.

78. Lionel Laroche, "Teaming Up," *CMA Management* (April 2001): 22–25.

79. See Distefano and Maznevski, "Creating Value with Diverse Teams" for a discussion of the advantages of multicultural teams.

80. Watson, Kumar, and Michaelsen, "Cultural Diversity's Impact on Interaction Process and Performance."

81. Distefano and Maznevski, "Creating Value with Diverse Teams."

82. This definition and discussion is based on Raymond A. Friedman, "Employee Network Groups: Self-Help Strategy for Women and Minorities," *Performance Improvement Quarterly* 12:1 (1999): 148–163.

83. Ann C. Logue, "Girl Gangs: They Got It Goin' On," *Training & Development* (January 2001): 24–28.

84. "Leveraging Diversity: Opportunities in the New Market," Part III of "Diversity: The Bottom Line," *Forbes* (November 13, 2000) special advertising section.

85. Raymond A. Friedman and Brooks Holtom, "The Effects of Network Groups on Minority Employee Turnover Intentions," *Human Resource Management* 41:4 (Winter 2002): 405–421.

86. Wasserman, "A Race for Profits."

87. Finnigan, "Different Strokes."

88. Raymond A. Friedman, Melinda Kane, and Daniel B. Cornfield, "Social Support and Career Optimism: Examining the Effectiveness of Network Groups Among Black Managers," *Human Relations* 51:9 (1998): 1155–1177; "Diversity in the New Millennium," *Working Woman* (March 2000): special advertising supplement.

89. R. B. Zajonc, "Social Facilitation," *Science* 149 (1965): 269–274; and Erez and Somech, "Is Group Productivity Loss the Rule or the Exception?"

90. Gina Imperato, "Their Specialty? Teamwork," *Fast Company* (January-February 2000): 54–56.

91. Aaron Bernstein, "Detroit vs. the UAW: At Odds over Teamwork," *BusinessWeek* (August 24, 1987): 54–55.

92. Robert Albanese and David D. Van Fleet, "Rational Behavior in Groups: The Free-Riding Tendency," *Academy of Management Review* 10 (1985): 244–255.

93. Debra L. Shapiro, Stacie A. Furst, Gretchen M. Spreitzer, and Mary Ann Von Glinow, "Transnational Teams in the Electronic Age: Are Team Identity and High Performance at Risk?" *Journal of Organizational Behavior* 23 (2002): 455–467.

94. Baron, *Behavior in Organizations.*

95. Harvey J. Brightman, *Group Problem Solving: An Improved Managerial Approach* (Atlanta, GA: Georgia State University, 1988).

96. Petzinger, *The New Pioneers*, 27–32.

Company Index

Subject Index